Wörterbuch für das Bank- und Börsenwesen

Deutsch – Englisch

Dictionary of Banking and Stock Trading

German – English

Hans E. Zahn

Wörterbuch für das Bank- und Börsenwesen

Dictionary of Banking and Stock Trading

Teil 1 / Part 1:

Deutsch – Englisch
German – English

6., überarbeitete und erweiterte Auflage
updated and much enlarged
6th edition

Fritz Knapp Verlag · Frankfurt am Main

Besuchen Sie uns auch im Internet unter
www.knapp-verlag.de

ISBN 978-3-8314-2040-7

Satz: DASACOM, Dirk Schüler, Hofheim/Ts.
Druck- und Bindearbeiten: A. Hellendoorn KG, Bad Bentheim

Printed in Germany

Vorwort zur sechsten Auflage

Bedingt durch die zahlreichen Veränderungsprozesse im Privat- und Firmenkundengeschäft der Kreditinstitute und der durch die Finanzkrise ausgelösten Flut neuer aufsichtlicher Regelungen wurden in der sechsten Auflage des Wörterbuches für das Bank- und Börsenwesen umfangreiche Aktualisierungen und textliche Veränderungen vorgenommen. Dabei wurde nahezu die Hälfte des in den Vorgängerauflagen erfassten Wortschatzes durch aktuellere Termini ersetzt.

Berücksichtigt wurden primär Begriffe aus den folgenden Bereichen des Banken- und Finanzdienstleistungssektors: Retail, Corporate und Investment Banking, Kreditgeschäft, Wertpapier- und Derivategeschäft, Abwicklungs- und Zahlungsverkehrssysteme, Börsenhandel und Börsenorganisation. Spezielle Beachtung fanden ferner Begriffe aus den für das Bank- und Finanzdienstleistungsgeschäft relevanten Bereichen des Handels- und Unternehmensrechts, im besonderen des Sicherungs- und Insolvenzrechts, sowie der Anlegerschutz- und Wertpapiergesetzgebung.

Weitere Schwerpunkte der Terminologierecherche und -erfassung: a) Begriffe in Verbindung mit den neuen gesetzlichen Regelungen des Banken- und Finanzdienstleistungssektors in Deutschland und der EU; b) die Terminologie der im Rahmen von Basel III vorgesehenen neuen Eigenkapital- und Liquiditätsstandards; c) die Terminologie der Rechnungslegung und Abschlusserstellung nach den International Financial Reporting Standards und dem Bilanzrechts-Modernisierungsgesetz.

Besonderer Wert wurde schließlich auf einen Ausbau der fremdsprachlichen Begriffserläuterungen gelegt. Ungeachtet der umfassenden Neuausrichtung wurde jedoch die bewährte Grundkonzeption aus Fachterminologie und Allgemeinsprache mit Satzbeispielen aus dem Bank- und Börsenalltag beibehalten.

Die Erstellung eines Wörterbuches ist ein komplexes und zeitintensives Unterfangen. So gilt besonderer Dank meiner Frau für Unterstützung und Verständnis.

Frankfurt/Main, Oktober 2011 *Hans E. Zahn*

Hinweise zur Benutzung

Alle Stichworteintragungen sind streng alphabetisch geordnet. Folgen auf ein nach links ausgerücktes Stichwort Anwendungsbeispiele, Wortverbindungen oder Komposita, wird das Stichwort durch eine Tilde ersetzt. Unterschiedliche Bedeutungen oder verschiedene Anwendungsmöglichkeiten eines Stichwortes werden durch die arabischen Ziffern 1, 2, 3, etc. gekennzeichnet. Eine weitere, wenn auch seltene, Bedeutungsdifferenzierung innerhalb einer arabischen Ziffer erfolgt durch die Buchstaben a, b, c. Stichwörter und Verbindungen erscheinen in halbfetter Schrift, ihre englischen Übersetzungen in der Grundschrift.

Klammern werden zu unterschiedlichen Zwecken verwendet. Schließen sie deutsche Wörter oder Sätze ein, so sind diese grundsätzlich kursiv gesetzt und zeigen entweder eine Bedeutungserläuterung, ein Anwendungsbeispiel zu der folgenden englischen Übersetzung oder eine Ableitung zu einem Kompositum an. Bei den der englischen Übersetzung in Klammern nachgestellten Wörtern handelt es sich entweder um Synonyme oder um einen ergänzenden, aber nicht unbedingt erforderlichen Bestandteil der englischen Übersetzung. Der englischen Übersetzung in Klammern vorangestellte Wörter haben immer rein ergänzenden Charakter.

Adjektive und Verben werden unter ihren jeweiligen Anfangsbuchstaben und nicht als substantivische Erweiterungen eingeordnet. Nur wenn sie einen untrennbaren Bestandteil eines bestimmten Substantivs bilden, werden sie zusammen mit diesem verzeichnet. Adverbien werden nur angeführt, wenn sie von der üblichen Bildung mit -ly abweichen bzw. diese ergänzen. Partizipien der Vergangenheit stehen bei ihren Verben, es sei denn, ihre häufige Verwendung ließ einen getrennten Eintrag angebracht erscheinen. Verbalsubstantive werden nur aufgenommen, wenn sich neben den Formen auf -ing weitere Übersetzungsmöglichkeiten anbieten. Ergeben die Pluralformen von Substantiven ergänzende oder weitere Übersetzungsmöglichkeiten, so werden diese unmittelbar unter dem Singular als eigenständige Stichwörter angeführt. Rechtschreibung und Silbentrennung der englischen Wörter basieren auf Webster's Third New International Dictionary.

Abkürzungen und Zeichen

adj.	Adjektiv
adv.	Adverb
AE	amerikanisches Englisch
BE	britisches Englisch
e.g.	exempli gratia/zum Beispiel
i.e.	id est/das heißt
i.S.	im Sinne von
i.e.S.	im engeren Sinn
i.w.S.	im weiteren Sinn
jmd.	jemand
jur.	Recht
o.s.	(oneself) sich
pl	Plural
s. o.	(someone) jemand
s. th.	(something) etwas
~	ersetzt das Stichwort innerhalb eines Wortartikels
/	trennt (a) das Stichwort von den folgenden Wortverbindungen oder Komposita; (b) zwei in ihrer Bedeutung verwandte oder entgegengesetzte Adjektive, Substantive oder Verben innerhalb von Stichwortableitungen
□	zeigt eine Erklärung zur englischen Übersetzung an
→	verweist (a) auf ein Stichwort mit gleicher oder gegensätzlicher Bedeutung; (b) auf ein ergänzendes Stichwort bzw. eine weiterführende Erklärung; (c) auf die vollständige Bezeichnung einer Institution, Organisation oder Verordnung aus dem Bank- und Börsenbereich, deren Abkürzung als Stichwort erscheint.

Preface to the sixth edition

In the light of the manifold changes in banks' corporate and retail banking operations and the plethora of new prudential regulations for the financial services sector, the update of the sixth edition of thc Dictionary of Banking and Stock Trading required extensive changes and supplements. As a result, nearly half of the vocabulary compiled in the previous editions has been replaced by more recent terminology.

When selecting the new terminology, particular emphasis has been given to the following sectors of the banking and financial services industry: Retail, Corporate and Investment Banking, Lending Operations, Securities and Derivatives Trading, Settlement and Funds Transfer Systems. Terminology research also centered on legal terms relevant to the business of banks, securities firms and investment funds.

Moreover, special focus has been laid in this new edition on i) terms relating to the new rules and regulations put in place for the banking and financial services sectors in Germany and in the European Community, ii) terms relevant to the new global capital and liquidity standards that will have to be met by financial institutions under the new Basel III Accord, iii) terms commonly used in business accounting and financial reporting according to IFRS and the German HGB-based Accounting Law Modernisation Act.

Particular attention has also been given to the update of explanatory notes. Despite the substantial revision in form and content, the well-proven concept of this dictionary, based on the combination of market terminology and everyday language in banking and stock trading, has been maintained.

To compile a dictionary is a time-consuming and protracted enterprise. I am, therefore, grateful to my wife for her unwavering support and encouragement.

Frankfurt/Main, October 2011 *Hans E. Zahn*

Notes to the user of the dictionary

All headword entries follow one another in alphabetical order. If a headword entry is followed by derivative or compound entries, the headword is replaced by a tilde. Where an entry has more than one meaning or varying levels of usage, the relevant translations are preceded by Arabic numerals (1, 2, 3, etc.). The letters a, b, c, serve to indicate a further, albeit rare, differentiation of meaning within an Arabic numeral. A boldface print has been chosen for headworks, derivative and compound entries; a plain print for the translations.

Brackets have been used for different purposes. Generally, bracketed German words and phrases are italicised and indicate either an explanation or an illustrative phrase. Bracketed words following an English translation represent either synonyms or a complementary, but not essential, part of the translation. Words preceding the translation are always of a complementary nature.

Adjectives and verbs are usually entered in their proper alphabetical order and not as subdivisions of nouns. They are listed together with nouns only in cases where they form an inseparable component of the latter. Adverbs are only entered when, in addition to the usual translation with the suffix -ly, other translations are possible. Past participles are usually listed together with their relevant verbs except in cases where their frequent use justified a separate alphabetical listing. Verbal nouns are only listed when some other form, in addition to the usual -ing, may be used in a translation. Plural forms of nouns, implying a meaning additional or complementary to the singular, are listed immediately below the singular as a separate headword. Spelling and syllabication are based on Webster's Third New International Dictionary.

Abbreviations and symbols

adj.	adjective
adv.	adverb
AE	American English
BE	British English
e.g.	exempli gratia/for example
i.e.	id est/that is
i.S.	(im Sinne von) in the sense of
i.e.S.	(im engeren Sinn) in a narrower sense
i.w.S.	(im weiteren Sinn) in a broader sense
jmd.	(jemand) someone
jur.	jurisprudence
o.s.	oneself (sich)
pl	Plural
s. o.	someone (jemand)
s. th.	something (etwas)
~	replaces a headword
/	separates (a) the headword from the following derivative or compound entries; (b) within a derivative entry, two adjectives, nouns or verbs with similar or opposite meanings
□	points to a note complementary to, or explanatory of, an English translation
→	is used for cross references to (a) an entry with the same or an opposite meaning; (b) to a complementary entry or relevant explanatory note; (c) to the full name of an agency, organisation, Act or stock trading instrument, the abbreviation of which has been listed as a separate entry in its correct alphabetical order.

A

ab *(Zinszahlungen ~ 1. Juli)* interest payments as from (beginning, starting) July 1

abandonnieren *(im Optionsgeschäft)* to abandon an option, to allow an option to expire (to lapse) unexercised

Abbau **1.** reduction, *(~ der liquiden Mittel)* rundown in (downsizing) liquid assets, *(~ von Personal)* staff retrenchment, job cuts, headcount reduction, *(~ von Verbindlichkeiten)* debt reduction, deleveraging
2. *(stufenweiser ~)* gradual removal, phasing out
3. *(~ der Spannungen an den Finanzmärkten)* easing tension in the financial markets

abbauen **1.** to reduce, to lower, to cut back (down), to run down, to downsize **2.** to remove gradually, to phase out **3.** to ease, to relieve

abbilden **1.** to map, to reflect, *(das Ausfallrisiko angemessen ~)* to adequately map the default (credit) risk, *(im Zinsergebnis abgebildet werden)* to be reflected in net interest income
2. *(einen Index ~)* to track (to replicate) an index
3. *(bilanziell ~)* to state (to report) in the financial statements, *(im Periodenerfolg ~)* to recognise in profit and loss

Abbildung **1.** mapping **2.** index tracking (replication) **3.** stating, recognition, reporting

Abbildungsverhältnis replication rate

abbrechen *(die Geschäftsbeziehung ~)* to sever (to discontinue) the business relationship, *(die Kreditverhandlungen ~)* to break off (to call off) the loan negotiations

abbremsen **1.** *(den Kursanstieg ~)* to slow down (to decelerate) the price rise **2.** *(den Zinsauftrieb ~)* to dampen (to moderate, to check) the upsurge in interest rates

abbröckeln **1.** *(nachgeben)* to crumble, to ease, to slip, to drift easier (lower) **2.** *(schrumpfen)* to wither, to dwindle away

Abbruch **1.** discontinuance, breaking (calling) off, severance **2.** *(~ tun)* to be detrimental to, to impair

abbuchen **1.** *(belasten)* to debit **2.** *(im Abbuchungsverfahren)* to debit (to charge) directly **3.** *(einen Verlust ~)* to write (to charge) off a loss

Abbuchung **1.** debit **2.** *(im Abbuchungsverfahren)* pre-authorised debit **3.** *(Ausbuchung)* writing off, charge-off

Abbuchungs / ~auftrag pre-authorised debit (payment) instruction; **~auftragslastschrift** pre-authorised debit; **~auftragslastschriftverfahren** pre-authorised debit system, pre-authorised payment scheme; **~ermächtigung** pre-authorised debit mandate, charge authority; **~verfahren** pre-authorised debit system

abdeckbar coverable, insurable, *(~es Währungsrisiko)* hedgeable (coverable) currency risk

abdecken **1.** *(Risiken ~)* to hedge (to cover, to lay off) risks, to provide cover for risks
2. *(einlösen, erfüllen)* to meet, to honour
3. to settle, *(einen Kredit ~)* to repay (to pay down) a loan, *(aus Umsatzerlösen ~)* to repay from (out of) sales revenue

Abdeckung 1. hedging, providing cover for, *(~ des Haftungsrisikos)* liability coverage, *(~ von Positionsrisiken)* covering (laying off) position risks, *(~ des Verlustrisikos)* hedging (covering) the exposure to loss, exposure hedging, *(~ des Währungsrisikos)* hedging the exchange risk (currency exposure), currency hedge
2. *(~ der Schuldendienstverpflichtungen)* meeting debt service obligations
3. repayment, paying down, *(~ des Sollsaldos)* settlement of the debit balance

Abdeckungsgrad degree of coverage

abdingbar *(~e gesetzliche Regelungen)* legal provisions modifiable by mutual consent

Abdingbarkeit modifiability by mutual consent

abdiskontieren to discount, *(abdiskontierte Papiere)* discount paper, discounted securities

Abdiskontierung *(~ zum Marktzinssatz)* discounting at the current market rate

abdisponierbar withdrawable, freely available, *(~es Guthaben eines Kreditkarteninhabers)* available credit, open-to-buy

abdisponieren 1. *(abheben)* to withdraw **2.** *(veräußern)* to sell, to dispose of **3.** *(auf ein anderes Konto übertragen)* to transfer (to branch off) to another account

Abdisponierung/Abdisposition 1. withdrawal of funds **2.** sale (e. g. of securities) **3.** transfer to another account

Abend-Kassenbestände overnight cash holdings

abfallend *(~es Dreieck)* descending triangle, *(~er Trendkanal)* descending trend channel, *(~e Trendlinie)* descending trendline

abfassen 1. to formulate, to word **2.** *(das Protokoll ~)* to draw up the minutes, *(einen Vertrag ~)* to draft (to draw up, to prepare) an agreement

Abfassung 1. formulation, wording **2.** drawing up, drafting, preparation

abfedern *(gegen Verluste/Konjunkturschwankungen ~)* to cushion against losses/cyclical fluctuations, *(die Erschütterung des Marktes ~)* to soften the blow to the market

abfinanzieren to repay (by instalments), *(über einen Zeitraum von zehn Jahren ~)* to repay over a period of ten years

Abfinanzierung debt repayment, repayment by instalments

abfinden 1. *(entschädigen)* to indemnify, to compensate, to pay a compensation
2. *(eine Abfindungszahlung leisten)* to pay a severance compensation, to make a redundancy payment
3. *(einen Gesellschafter/Minderheitsaktionär ~)* to buy out a partner/minority shareholder
4. *(sich ~ mit)* to reconcile o. s. to, to put up with

Abfindung 1. indemnification, compensation, *(~ in bar)* cash compensation (indemnity), *(~ in Sachwerten)* indemnification in kind **2.** severance compensation, redundancy payment, → Abfindungszahlung **3.** partner buyout **4.** financial settlement, *(~ der Gläubiger)* settlement (composition) with the creditors

Abfindungs / ~angebot 1. compensation offer **2.** *(~ an die Aktionäre)* offer to shareholders, tender offer **3.** *(an einen Mitarbeiter)* severance offer; **~anspruch 1.** claim (entitlement) to compensation, indemnification claim **2.** entitlement to severance (redundancy) compensation

Abfindungs / ~betrag amount of the severance (redundancy) payment, severance amount; **~höhe** level of severance payments, → Abfindungsbetrag; **~paket** severance package; **~regelung** severance arrangement, *(gesetzliche~)* statutory redundancy arrangement, → Abfindungsvereinbarung

Abfindungs / ~summe, → Abfindungsbetrag; **~vereinbarung/~vertrag 1.** *(mit einem Mitarbeiter)* severance agreement, compromise agreement, redundancy agreement **2.** *(mit einem Gesellschafter)* buy-out agreement; **~vergütung** →Abfindungspaket, Abfindungszahlung

Abfindungs / ~werte *(Wertpapiere von Übernahmekandidaten)* take-over (bid) candidates; **~zahlung 1.** compensation (compensatory) payment **2.** *(an Mitarbeiter)* severance payment (compensation), redundancy payment, *(größere Zahlung an Führungskräfte)* severance package, golden handshake (parachute)

abflachen to flatten (out), to level off, to slow down

Abflachung *(~ des Kursanstiegs)* slowing down of the price rise, *(~ der Renditekurve)* flattening (flattening out) of the yield curve

abflauen to drop, to slacken, to slow down, to abate, to flag, to wane

Abflauen *(~ der Geschäftstätigkeit)* slowing down of business, drop in market activity, *(~ der Haussestimmung)* abatement (flagging, waning) of the bullish sentiment

abfließen *(von Geldern)* to flow off

Abfluss outflow, efflux, drain, *(~ von Spareinlagen)* savings outflow, drain on savings deposits

Abflussrate *(von Einlagen)* deposit runoff rate, deposit withdrawal rate

abfordern 1. to claim **2.** to request payment (delivery)

Abforderung 1. claim **2.** payment (delivery) request

Abfrage inquiry, query, *(~ des Kontostandes)* (account) balance inquiry

abfragen to inquire, to query, *(Informationen ~)* to call (to retrieve) information

abführen to transfer, *(an die Finanzbehörde ~)* to pay over to the tax office, *(an die Muttergesellschaft ~)* to upstream (to transfer) to the parent

Abführung transfer, payment

Abgabe 1. *(Einreichung, Übergabe)* filing, submission, delivery, *(~einer Erklärung)* delivering (making) a statement, issue of a statement, *(~ einer Steuererklärung)* filing a tax return, *(~ eines Gutachtens)* giving (rendering) an expert opinion
2. *(Gebühr, Steuer)* tax, levy, charge
3. *(Abgaben an der Börse)* sales, selling
4. *(soziale Abgaben)* social security contributions
5. *(~ von Stimmen)* casting of votes

Abgabe / ~druck *(an der Börse)* selling pressure; **~frist** filing period, term for filing (delivery)

Abgaben / ~ befreiung exemption from charges; **~bescheid** assessment notice; **~ordnung** German Fiscal Code; **~saldo** net selling; **~sätze 1.** levies, tax rates **2.** offering prices, selling rates **3.** contribution rates

Abgang 1. disposal, sale, *(~ von Finanzanlagen/Gegenständen des Anlagevermögens)* asset retirement, disposal of investment securities/fixed assets **2.** deduction, *(~ der Bezugsrechte/Dividende)* deduction of rights/dividend, markdown ex rights/ex dividend, *(~ der Kupons)* detachment of the coupons **3.** *(Auslieferung von Papieren, z. B. aus einem Depot)* outward delivery, withdrawal **4.** *(Verlassen, Ausscheiden)* departure, withdrawal

Abgangs / ~entschädigung severance payment; **~ergebnis** net result on disposal, → Abgangsgewinne; **~erlös** disposal (sales) proceeds; **~gewinne(~verluste)** gains (losses) on disposal, net realised gains (losses); **~kosten** disposal cost(s)

abgeben 1. to deliver, to file, *(ein Angebot/Gebot ~)* to submit an offer, to tender, to bid, *(eine Erklärung ~)* to issue (to make, to deliver) a statement **2.** *(ein einheitliches Bild ~)* to exhibit a uniform pattern **3.** *(an eine andere*

A

Instanz ~) to refer (to remit) to another court
4. *(die Kontrolle über ein Unternehmen ~)* to cede control over a company **5.** *(an den Markt ~)* to sell in the market, *(den gesetzlichen Rahmen ~)* to provide the legal framework, *(ein günstiges Umfeld ~)* to provide a favourable background **6.** *(seine Stimme ~)* to vote, to cast one's vote

abgehen 1. *(abweichen)* to deviate (to depart) from **2.** *(reduziert werden)* to be deducted

Abgehen *(~ von Dividenden/Bezugsrechten)* deduction of dividends/subscription rights, *(~ vom straffen geldpolitischen Kurs)* deviation (departure) from the tight course in monetary policy

Abgeld discount

abgelten 1. *(Ansprüche)* to settle, to satisfy, *(alle Ansprüche sind als abgegolten anzusehen)* all claims shall be deemed satisfied **2.** *(Verpflichtungen)* to discharge, to clear

Abgeltung 1. settlement, satisfaction **2.** discharge

Abgeltungssteuer flat rate withholding tax

Abgleich 1. *(~ der Kontounterlagen)* reconciliation of the account records **2.** *(~ von Bestätigungen/Nachrichten)* confirmation matching/matching of messages

abgleichen to reconcile, to match

abgleiten *(in die roten Zahlen ~)* to slide into the red, *(in eine Rezession ~)* to plunge into a recession

abgrenzen 1. to delimit, to define, to mark out (off), to separate, to make a distinction, *(abgegrenzte Einheiten)* separate (special) units, *(genau abgegrenzte Kompetenzen)* clearly defined (delineated) powers
2. *(im Rechnungswesen)* to defer, to accrue, →aktive/passive Rechnungsabgrenzungsposten, *(Zinsen auf den Buchwert ~)* to accrue interest on the carrying amount, *(Zinserträge periodengerecht ~)* to recognise interest income on an accrual basis
(abgegrenzte Erträge) deferred income (revenue), unearned income □ payments received for goods/services delivered in a subsequent accounting period, *(abgegrenzte Umrechnungsgewinne)* deferred currency translation gains, *(abgegrenzte Schulden)* accruals □ payment obligations for goods or services that have been received but have not been invoiced, *(abgegrenzte Zinsen)* accrual interest, *(in voller Höhe abgegrenzt werden)* to be fully accrued/deferred

Abgrenzung 1. delimitation, delineation, *(~ zwischen Handelsbuch und Anlagebuch)* distinction between trading book and banking book, *(steuerliche ~)* fiscal distinction, *(~ der Geldmenge)* definition of the money stock **2.** deferral, accrual, → abgrenzen (2), abgegrenzt

Abgrenzungs / ~posten *(Aktivseite)* prepaid expenses, prepayments, *(Passivseite)* deferrals, deferred items, → abgrenzen, abgegrenzte Erträge/Schulden, → aktive/passive Rechnungsabgrenzungsposten; **~risiko** deferral risk □ risk of failure to allocate deferrals to the envisaged accounting period

abhalten *(eine Hauptversammlung ~)* to hold a general meeting

abhanden kommen 1. to get lost **2.** to be lost (missing), *(abhanden gekommene Schecks/Wechsel)* lost or stolen cheques/bills

abhängen to depend on, *(von der Bereitstellung neuer Mittel ~)* to hinge upon (to be contingent on) the provision of fresh funds, *(stark von Fremdmitteln ~)* to be heavily dependent on external funds, *(von der Zustimmung des Kreditausschusses ~)* to be subject to approval by the loan committee (loan sanctioning committee)

abhängig *(~ Beschäftigte)* wage and salary earners, persons in dependent employment, *(~es Unternehmen)* dependent (controlled) company

abhängig machen *(die Kreditgewährung von zusätzlichen Sicherheiten ~)* to make the loan accommodation conditional upon the provision of further collateral, *(von der Zustimmung der Gläubiger ~)* to make contingent upon the creditors' approval

Abhängigkeit **1.** *(~ von Fremdmitteln)* dependence (reliance) on external funds **2.** *(die gegenseitige ~ der internationalen Finanzmärkte)* the interdependence (interrelationship) of international financial markets

abheben to withdraw, to draw money at the bank, *(Geld bis zu einer bestimmten Höhe ~)* to draw cash up to a prearranged limit

Abhebung *(~en an Geldautomaten)* cash withdrawals at ATMs, *(~en an fremden Automaten)* → Fremdabhebung, *(~en gegen Vorlage eines Identitätsnachweises)* cash withdrawals against presentation (on production) of an identity card

abhelfen to redress, to remedy, to set right, to remove the causes of a grievance

Abkaufsverpflichtung **1.** obligation to purchase **2.** debt purchase undertaking

Abkehr **1.** break with, abandonment **2.** shift, *(~ von Aktien hin zu Renten)* shift away from shares to bonds, *(~ von der Finanzierung über Bankkredite)* shift away from bank finance, disintermediation

abklären to clarify, to check (back) with, to make sure

abklingen to wane, to ease (to fall) off, *(~de Anlegerängste)* waning (fading) investor fears

Abkommen **1.** agreement, accord, arrangement **2.** settlement

abkoppeln to decouple, to uncouple, to untie

Abkoppelung *(~ von der internationalen Kursentwicklung)* decoupling from the international price trend

abkühlen *(die überhitzte Konjunktur ~)* to cool the overheated economy

Abkühlung *(~ des Handelsgeschehens)* cooling off in trading

abkürzen **1.** to abbreviate, to abridge **2.** *(Laufzeit)* to shorten, to curtail

Abkürzung **1.** abbreviation **2.** shortening, curtailment

Ablader consignor, shipper

Abladerindossament shipper's endorsement

Ablauf **1.** expiration, expiry, lapse, *(nach ~ der Aufbewahrungsfrist)* once the period of preservation has elapsed, *(~ der Festlegungsfrist)* expiration of the blocking period (of the fixed rate period), *(vor ~ der Zeichnungsfrist)* before the end (expiry) of the subscription (application) period **2.** *(Arbeitsablauf)* workflow, process **3.** *(Beendigung)* termination, completion **4.** *(Fälligkeit)* maturity, due date **5.** *(Verlauf)* course

ablaufen **1.** to expire, to run out, to lapse, to elapse **2.** to fall (to become) due, to mature

Ablauf / ~beschreibung workflow description; **~diagramm** flow (process) chart

Ablauffonds withdrawal fund □ arrangement that provides for the investment of a fixed amount in a fund and subsequent periodic withdrawals by the investor over a predetermined period of time

Ablauf / ~hemmung suspension of the limitation period; **~leistungen** maturity benefits, amounts paid upon expiration of the policy term; **~normierung** standardisation of workflows; **~ organisation** workflow (process) organisation; **~plan** flow chart, sequence of operations

A

ablehnen 1. *(einen Antrag/ein Angebot ~)* to reject (to turn down, to rebuff, to decline) an application/an offer, *(eine Erbschaft ~)* to disclaim an estate, to refuse to accept an estate, *(die Haftung ~)* to disclaim any liability, to assume no responsibility **2.** *(missbilligen)* to disapprove

Ablehnung 1. rejection, turning down, refusal, disclaiming, disclaimer **2.** disapproval, denying approval

Ablehnungsrecht right to disclaim

ableiten *(einen Anspruch ~)* to derive a claim from, *(Schlussfolgerungen ~)* to draw conclusions from, *(einen Trend ~)* to deduce a trend from, *(abgeleitete Bonitätsbeurteilung)* inferred credit assessment (rating)

Ablöseentschädigung *(bei einer vorzeitigen Darlehensrückzahlung)* early repayment fee

ablösen 1. to repay, to redeem, *(eine Anleihe ~)* to redeem (to retire, to call in) a bond, *(ein Darlehen ~) (a)* to repay (to pay off, to clear) a loan, *(b)* to take over a loan commitment (an exposure), *(eine Hypothek ~)* to pay off (to discharge) a mortgage

2. to supersede, *(durch ein neues Darlehensprogramm abgelöst werden)* to be superseded (replaced) by a new loan scheme

3. *(durch Umschuldung)* to refund, *(eine Schuld zinsgünstig ~)* to refund (to refinance) a debt at a favourable rate of interest

Ablösung 1. repayment, redemption, discharge, *(~ aus einbehaltenen Gewinnen)* repayment out of retained earnings, *(~ eines Kredites)* loan repayment (clearance), *(~ eines Pfandrechtes)* lien discharge, *(~ von Schuldtiteln)* redemption (retirement) of debt securities

2. superseding, *(~ eines Kredites durch eine neue Fazilität)* replacing an existing loan commitment with a new facility

3. *(durch Umschuldung)* refunding, refinancing, *(~ einer Anleihe durch eine Neuemission)* bond refunding, replacement of an outstanding bond issue by the issuance of another debt instrument

Ablösungs / ~finanzierung 1. *(Umschuldung)* refunding, refinancing, take-out (consolidation) financing **2.** raising equity to repay borrowed funds; **~fonds** redemption (sinking) fund

Ablösungs / ~recht 1. right of redemption **2.** *(vorzeitiges ~ des Anleiheschuldners)* call privilege, right to call in a bond **3.** *(des Kreditnehmers)* right to repay a loan;~ **summe** redemption (repayment) amount; **~verpflichtungen** redemption (repayment) commitments

abmahnen 1. *(einen Mitarbeiter ~)* to give an employee a written warning **2.** to serve a cease-and-desist letter

Abmahnung warning letter (notice), written warning, reminder of legal consequences, cease-and-desist letter

Abnahme 1. *(Entgegennahme)* acceptance **2.** *(Rückgang)* decline, decrease, reduction, fall, shrinkage, dwindling **3.** *(im Wertpapier- und Börsentermingeschäft)* taking delivery, acceptance of the underlying instrument **4.** *(techn.)* acceptance

Abnahme / ~anspruch claim to acceptance (e.g. of the underlying instrument); **~frist** *(bei Kreditverträgen)* loan acceptance period, *(für eine Lieferung)* period for taking delivery

Abnahme / ~pflicht → Abnahmeverpflichtung; **~protokoll** acceptance certificate, certification of completion; **~risiko** acceptance risk, risk that a party fails to take delivery

Abnahmeverpflichtung 1. purchase commitment, (statutory) acceptance requirement **2.** *(bei Börsen-Termingeschäften)* duty to take delivery, obligation to accept the underlying instrument **3.** *(des Kreditnehmers)* obligation to avail o.s. of the loan granted, → Nichtabnahmeentschädigung

Abnahme / ~**verweigerung** failure (refusal) to take delivery, refusal of acceptance; ~**verzug** default in taking delivery

abnehmen 1. *(entgegennehmen)* to accept, *(den Basiswert ~)* to take delivery of the underlying instrument 2. *(einen Eid ~)* to administer an oath 3. *(nachlassen, sich verringern)* to decline, to decrease, to drop, to fall, to diminish, to wane

Abnehmer 1. recipient 2. buyer, purchaser, customer 3. *(im Factoring)* account debtor, debtor company

Abnehmerzins buyer interest, interest to be paid by the debtor (customer)

Abneigung *(~ der Anleger)* investors' dislike of, investors' reluctance (aversion) to

abnutzbar subject to wear and tear, *(~es Anlagevermögen)* depreciable fixed assets, *(~e Wirtschaftsgüter)* wasting assets

Abnutzung wear and tear, *(~ der Markenloyalität)* brand attrition, *(~ der Werbebotschaft)* advertising wear-out

Abnutzungseffekt wear-out (decay) effect

abrechnen 1. *(regulieren)* to settle, to square, *(Kreditnehmern abgerechnete eigene Ziehungen)* own drawings discounted and credited to borrowers, *(abrechnende Bank)* → Abrechnungsbank
2. *(belasten, in Rechnung stellen)* to charge, to invoice, to bill, *(Zinsen werden zum Quartalsende abgerechnet)* interest will be computed and debited (or credited) at the end of each quarter
3. *(verrechnen)* to clear
4. *(in Abzug bringen)* to deduct, to subtract

Abrechnung 1. *(Aufstellung)* statement 2. *(Wertpapierabrechnung)* contract (settlement) note
3. *(Belastung, Inrechnungstellung)* charging, invoicing, billing
4. *(Regulierung) (~ von Aktiengeschäften)* settlement of equity trades, *(~ der zum Diskont eingereichten Wechsel)* settlement of bills presented for discount, discounting bills, *(~ der Kauf- und Verkaufsaufträge am gleichen Tag)* same-day settlement of buy and sell orders, *(~ zu Nettokursen)* net settlement, → Nettogeschäft

Abrechnungs / ~**bank** 1. settlement bank 2. *(im Kreditkartengeschäft: mit den Vertragsunternehmen abrechnende Bank)* acquirer, acquiring bank; ~**beleg** 1. settlement (clearing) voucher 2. *(bei einer Kreditkartenzahlung)* sales slip, sales draft, charge slip, ticket, hard copy

Abrechnungs / ~**kurs** settlement price (rate); ~**mitglieder** clearing house members; ~**papiere** clearing instruments, clearings; ~**periode** 1. settlement period 2. *(Rechnungsperiode)* accounting period; ~**preis** settlement price; ~**regelung** settlement (clearing) arrangement

Abrechnungs / ~**salden** clearing balances; ~**spitzen** settlement fractions; ~**stelle** 1. clearinghouse, clearing agency (office) 2. *(diskontierende Bank)* discounting banker; ~**tag** settlement date, day of settlement; ~**teilnehmer** clearing member (participant)

Abrechnungs / ~**unterlagen** settlement (clearing) records; ~**valuta** 1. *(Währung)* settlement currency 2. *(Termin)* settlement date; ~**verbindlichkeiten** 1. settlement obligations 2. payables; ~**verfahren** settlement (clearing) procedure

Abrechnungs / ~**verkehr** clearing transactions (operations); ~**wert** settlement asset; ~**zeitraum** settlement (accounting) period; ~**zyklus** billing (settlement) cycle

Abrede agreement, understanding, *(vertragliche ~)* contractual arrangement, covenant

abrücken *(von der Rückzahlungszusage ~)* to back away from the repayment undertaking

Abruf 1. *(von Geldern)* calling funds, call for funds, withdrawal, *(zahlbar bei ~)* payable on demand, *(Lieferung der Stücke auf ~)* delivery of physical securities (certificates) upon request
2. *(Inanspruchnahme)* drawing, *(~ der zweiten Kredittranche)* drawing on the second loan tranche
3. *(von Informationen)* information retrieval
4. *(Handelsregister)* copy dd…
5. *(Rückruf)* recall

abrufbar callable, accessible, *(~ im Internet)* available on the Internet, *(~e Zahlungsverpflichtungen)* payment obligations due and callable

abrufen 1. to call, to request, *(die Lieferung der Stücke ~)* to call for delivery of the securities
2. *(den nicht in Anspruch genommenen Teil des Darlehens ~)* to draw on the uncalled portion of the loan
3. *(Kontoinformationen ~)* to retrieve information on the account

Abrufkredit call facility

Abrufrisiko 1. withdrawal risk, call risk, risk of an unexpected withdrawal of deposits **2.** drawing risk, risk of unexpected drawings on a credit line

abrunden 1. *(einen Betrag ~)* to round down (off) an amount **2.** *(seine Beteiligungen in der Kreditwirtschaft ~)* to round off (out) its finance interests

Abrundung rounding, *(~ der Produktlinie)* product line filling

abrutschen to slide, to slip, *(in die roten Zahlen ~)* to slide into the red, *(umsatzmäßig auf den dritten Platz ~)* to slip (to move) down to third place in terms of volume

Absage 1. calling off, cancellation **2.** refusal, rejection

absagen 1. *(ein Treffen ~)* to call off (to cancel) a meeting **2.** to refuse, to reject

ABS-Anleihe ABS bond □ bond backed by assets consisting of receivables such as credit card receivables

Absatz 1. *(Abschnitt)* paragraph, subsection **2.** *(Umsatz)* sales, turnover **3.** *(Verkauf)* sale, selling **4.** *(Vertrieb)* distribution, marketing

Absatz / ~belebung recovery of (in) sales, market recovery (revival), upturn in business; **~dichte** sales density; **~erwartungen** sales (market) prospects; **~finanzierung** sales financing; **~flaute** slackness in sales, market stagnation

Absatz / ~kredit sales credit; **~leasing** vendor leasing; **~menge** total sales, sales volume; **~netz** sales (distribution) network; **~organisation** sales (marketing) organisation; **~prognose** sales forecast (predictions)

Absatz / ~rückgang slump in sales, decline of (in) sales, downturn in business; **~schwund** shrinkage in sales; **~steigerung** increase (rise) in sales, sales increase, upturn in business; **~stufe** level of distribution

Absatz / ~vereinbarung sales (marketing) agreement; **~wege** sales channels, channels of distribution; **~wirtschaft** distributive trades

abschaffen *(ein Gesetz/eine Verordnung ~)* to abolish (to rescind, to repeal) an Act/a regulation

Abschaffung abolition, rescission, repeal

abschätzen 1. to assess, *(die Folgen ~)* to gauge (to measure) the impact (consequences), *(den Schaden ~)* to assess the damage, *(den Wert ~)* to evaluate, to appraise the value, *(die weitere Zinsentwicklung ~)* to assess the further trend in interest rates
2. *(den Kapitalaufwand ~)* to estimate the capital outlay required

abschirmen *(gegen Marktrisiken ~)* to protect (to shield, to shelter) from market risks, → absichern

Abschlag 1. *(Abzug, Diskont)* deduction, discount, *(~ vom Ausgabekurs)* offering discount, discount from the offering price, *(~ vom Kassakurs)* discount from the spot rate, *(mit einem ~ auf den Nennwert handeln)* to trade at a discount from (to) face value, *(~ vom Rücknahmepreis) (bei Fondsanteilen)* repurchase discount, *(~ auf den Substanzwert)* discount to the net asset value
2. *(Dividendenabschlag)* deduction of dividend, quotation ex dividend
3. *(Kursabschlag) (~ nach kräftigen Verkäufen)* price markdown following heavy selling, → Minusankündigung
4. *(vom Sicherheitenwert)* haircut, *(10%iger ~ auf den Marktwert der Sicherheit)* 10 % haircut on the collateral's market value

abschlagen to refuse, to decline, to turn down

abschlägig *(~e Antwort)* negative reply (answer), *(einen Kreditantrag ~ bescheiden)* to turn down a loan request

Abschlags / ~dividende interim dividend, dividend on account, **~tag** *(bei Dividendenausschüttungen/Bezugsrechtsabschlägen)* ex dividend/ex rights date, first day of dealing ex dividend/ex rights

Abschlags / ~verteilung interim distribution; **~zahlung** 1. payment on account, instalment, part payment, *(regelmäßige monatliche ~en)* budget billing 2. *(Fortschrittszahlung)* progress payment

abschließen 1. *(beenden)* to conclude, to terminate, to finish, to close, *(das Geschäftsjahr ~)* to end the business year, to close the accounts, *(mit einem Gewinn/Verlust ~)* to close at a profit/loss, *(abgeschlossenes Verfahren)* settled case
2. *(ein Börsengeschäft/eine Transaktion ~)* to trade, to deal, to strike a deal (bargain), to conclude a stock trade, to conclude a transaction
3. *(ein Konto ~) (i. S. von löschen)* to close (to close out) an account, *(jeweils zum Quartalsende ~)* to balance an account at the end of each quarter
4. *(eine Versicherung ~)* to take out an insurance
5. *(einen Vertrag ~)* to conclude a contract, to enter into an agreement

abschließend 1. *adj.* concluding, *(endgültig)* final, definitive, *(~e Bemerkungen zur Bonität des Kunden)* concluding remarks on the customer's creditworthiness
2. *adv.* in conclusion, *(~ klären)* to settle conclusively (authoritatively)

Abschluss 1. *(Beendigung)* conclusion, completion, end, close, closing, *(~ eines Vertrages)* conclusion of contract, entering into an agreement
2. *(an der Börse)* trade, transaction, bargain, deal, *(~ eines Devisen-Termingeschäftes (a)* forward exchange deal (transaction) *(b)* entering into a forward exchange contract
3. *(Kontoabschluss)* account balancing, *(~ der Kundenkonten jeweils zum Quartalsende)* quarterly balancing of customer accounts at the end of each quarter
4. *(Geschäftsergebnis)* annual performance, results for the year, *(~ des Unternehmens zum Jahresende) (a)* company's annual financial statements *(b)* annual (yearly) closing of the company's books
5. *(Regulierung)* settlement

Abschlüsse *(~ per Kasse)* spot dealings, dealings for cash, *(~ erfolgen zum Kassakurs)* trades are settled at the spot rate (at the cash price), *(~ bei Kurzläufern/Langläufern)* dealings in shorts/longs *(~ auf neue Rechnung)* dealings (transactions) for new account, *(~ am Sekundärmarkt)* secondary market dealings (transactions), *(~ per Termin)* forward dealings, dealings (transactions) for future delivery

Abschluss / ~agent originating agent, policy-writing agent; **~arbeiten** end-of-year accounting work; **~aufrechnung** trade (contract) netting;

A

~ **aufwendungen** acquisition cost, → Abschlusskosten

Abschluss / ~bereitschaft 1. *(von Darlehensinteressenten)* propensity to borrow (to take out a loan) **2.** *(der Anleger)* propensity to invest; ~**bestätigung** trade confirmation, confirmation of a transaction; ~**bilanz 1.** closing accounts (balance sheet) **2.** *(i. S. von Jahresabschluss)* annual accounts, annual financial statements

Abschluss / ~buchung 1. *(bei Kontoschließung)* closing entry **2.** *(bei der Viertel- oder Halbjahresabrechnung eines Kontos)* balancing entry, entry covering interest and charges; ~ **darstellung** presentation of the financial statements (annual accounts); ~ **daten** trade (transaction) data; ~ **erfassung** trade capture

Abschluss / ~erläuterungen notes to the financial statements; ~**erstellung** drawing up the accounts, preparation of the accounts; ~**freiheit** freedom of contract, freedom to enter into a contract

Abschlussgebühr 1. acquisition (transaction) fee, initial sales charge(s) **2.** *(bei Kreditverträgen bzw. Finanztransaktionen)* arrangement fee, upfront fee, origination fee, contract fee **3.** *(beim Erwerb von Fondsanteilen)* sales charge, load **4.** *(bei einem Kaufvertrag)* contract fee

Abschlusskosten 1. transaction cost (charges), → Abschlussgebühr **2.** *(bei Kontoschließung)* closing charges **3.** *(bei der Viertel- oder Halbjahresabrechnung eines Kontos)* balancing charges, interest and charges **4.** *(bei einem Versicherungsabschluss)* acquisition cost (fee), initial expenses

Abschluss / ~kurs contract (settlement) price; ~**pflicht** duty to contract; ~**posten** interest and charges, → Abschlussrechnung; ~**prämie** upfront premium; ~**preis** → Abschlusskurs

Abschluss / ~provision selling commission, → Abschlussgebühr; ~**prüfer** auditor; ~ **prüferhonorar** auditor's fee; ~**prüferrichtlinie** Statutory Audit Directive; ~**prüfung** audit of the annual accounts

Abschluss / ~rechnung 1. *(bei Kontoschließung)* closing statement **2.** *(Viertel- oder Halbjahresabrechnung eines Kontos)* statement of interest and charges **3.** *(Wertpapierabrechnung)* contract (settlement) note; ~**saldo** closing (final) balance

Abschluss / ~stichtag 1. date of accounts, balance sheet day, accounting date, balancing (closing) date, reporting date **2.** closing deadline; ~**tag 1.** settlement day **2.** *(bei Börsengeschäften)* trade date, dealing day (date), transaction date, → Abschlussstichtag

Abschluss / ~vermittler contract broker (intermediary); ~**vermittlung** contract brokerage (broking), purchase and/or sale for third-party account; ~**veröffentlichung** publication of the annual accounts

Abschluss / ~vollmacht power (authority) to contract, contractual power, authority to bind the principal; ~**volumen 1.** trading (business) volume **2.** *(Kontraktwert)* contract value

Abschluss / ~zahlen balance sheet figures, *(~ für das Geschäftsjahr 2012)* figures for fiscal 2012; ~**zahlung** final payment (instalment); ~**zeitpunkt** → Abschlusstag

abschmelzen *(die Rücklagen ~ lassen)* to allow the reserves to shrink (to melt away)

Abschmelzen *(~ des Einlagenbestandes)* shrinkage of the deposit portfolio, *(~ des Zeitwertes)* time value decay

abschneiden 1. to perform, to fare, to score, *(ausgezeichnet ~)* to put on an excellent performance, *(gut/schlecht ~)* to perform well/poorly
2. to cut off, to truncate, *(die Liquiditätszufuhr ~)* to cut off the supply of liquidity, *(bis auf 4 Dezimalstellen ~)* to truncate to 4 decimal digits

Abschneiden 1. performance, *(über-/unterdurchschnittliches ~)* outperformance/underperformance 2. truncation

Abschnitt 1. *(eines Wertpapiers)* tranche 2. *(Gesetzesabschnitt)* section 3. *(Kapitel)* chapter 4. *(Kontrollabschnitt)* counterfoil, stub 5. *(Periode, Phase)* period, phase, stage 6. *(Stückelung)* denomination 7. *(Wechsel)* bill 8. *(Zinsschein)* coupon

Abschnittsbesteuerung period taxation

abschöpfen *(den Liquiditätsüberhang im Bankensystem ~)* to skim off (to siphon off) surplus liquidity from banks, *(überschüssige Kaufkraft ~)* to absorb (to mop up, to soak up) excessive purchasing power

Abschöpfung 1. skimming (siphoning) off, absorption, mopping up 2. *(Abgabe)* levy

Abschöpfungsmaßnahmen measures designed to skim off (e. g. excess liquidity)

abschrecken *(Anleger ~)* to put off (to deter) investors, to discourage (to scare away) investors

abschreibbar depreciable, amortisable, *(~e Aktiva)* depreciable assets

abschreiben 1. *(materielle Anlagewerte)* to depreciate, to write down, *(degressiv/linear/progressiv ~)* to depreciate on diminishing values/on a straight line basis/on a rising scale
(die Beteiligung auf den Börsenwert ~) to write down the investment to the stock market value, *(in gleichen Raten während der geschätzten Nutzungsdauer ~)* to write down in equal instalments over the estimated working life
(immaterielle Anlagewerte über die Gewinn- und Verlustrechnung ~) to amortise intangible assets to the profit and loss account, *(planmäßig ~)* to depreciate (to amortise) on a scheduled basis, *(auf den geschätzten Restwert ~)* to write down to the estimated scrap (residual) value
2. *(immaterielle Anlagewerte)* to amortise
3. *(Forderungen)* to write off, *(ein Kreditengagement ~)* to write off (to charge off) a loan (loan exposure), *(abgeschriebene Kreditforderungen)* loan write-offs, loans charged off, *(als Verlust ~)* to write off as a loss (as uncollectible)

Abschreibung 1. depreciation, write-down, impairment 2. *(immaterieller Anlagewerte)* amortisation
3. *(~ von Kreditforderungen)* write-off (charge-off) of loan assets, *(~ gegen vorhandene Rücklagen)* write-off against available reserves, *(~ über die Gewinn- und Verlustrechnung)* write-off through profit and loss

Abschreibungen auf *(~ Beteiligungen/Finanzanlagen)* impairments on investments/financial assets, *(~ Immobilien)* real estate impairments, *(~ Immobilienkredite)* property loan write-offs (charge-offs), *(~ notleidende Kredite)* writedowns on non-performing loans, bad loan writedowns
(~ den Rentenbestand) bond write-offs, write-offs (writedowns) on fixed income securities, *(~ Sachanlagen)* depreciation on (of) fixed assets, *(~ die Wiederbeschaffungskosten)* writedowns to replacement cost

Abschreibungs / ~aufwand depreciation charge (expense), impairment charge; **~bedarf** write-off (write-down) requirements; **~beginn** commencement of depreciation; **~betrag** 1. depreciation amount, *(jährlicher ~)* annual depreciation allowance 2. amount written off; **~dauer** → Abschreibungszeitraum

abschreibungsfähig *(~ nach dem gegenwärtigen Steuerrecht)* eligible for depreciation under current tax laws, *(~er Betrag)* depreciable amount

Abschreibungs / ~gesellschaft tax loss company; **~methode** method of depreciation, amortisation method;

A

~**plan** depreciation schedule; ~**quote** depreciation (amortisation) rate

Abschreibungs / ~**richtlinien** depreciation (charge-off) policy; ~**umfang**/~**volumen** total depreciation (write-offs); ~**vergünstigungen** special depreciation allowances

Abschreibungs / ~**wahlrecht** depreciation option; ~**wert** depreciable value; ~**zeitraum** depreciation period (age), depreciable (amortisable) life, recovery period

abschütteln *(Marktängste ~)* to shrug off market worries (fears)

abschwächen 1. *(sich abschwächen)* to weaken, to turn (to drift) lower, to slacken, to sag, *(sich gegen Ende der Börsensitzung ~)* to skid late in the session
2. *(Aussage ~)* to modify (to qualify) a statement
3. *(Auswirkungen ~)* to mitigate (to soften) the impact

Abschwächung 1. *(~ der Aktienkurse)* weakening (easing) of stock prices, *(~ der Konjunktur)* slowdown in economic activity, *(~ des Umsatzes)* decrease in sales, slackening (sagging) of sales
2. modification, qualification
3. mitigation, softening

Abschwächungstendenz downward trend, downturn tendency

Abschwung downswing, downturn, decline

absehbar *(~e Zinserhöhung)* foreseeable rise in interest rates, *(~e Folgen der Zinssenkung)* conceivable (predictable) impact of the cut in interest rates

absehen 1. to foresee, to predict **2.** *(~ von)* to refrain from

absenden to forward, to send, to dispatch, to consign

Absender *(auf Verschiffungsdokumenten)* consignor

absenken *(das Risikovorsorgeniveau ~)* to lower the level of risk provisions

absetzbar 1. saleable, marketable
2. *(von der Steuer ~)* tax deductible, allowable against (for) tax, *(~e Schuldzinsen)* debt interest deductible from taxable income, *(in voller Höhe von der Einkommensteuer ~)* to be fully deductible for income tax purposes

Absetzbarkeit 1. marketability **2.** deductibility, *(steuerliche ~ von Hypothekenzinsen)* tax deductibility of mortgage interest

absetzen 1. *(von der Steuer ~)* to deduct from taxable income, to set off against income for tax purposes
2. *(Wertpapiere am Markt ~)* to sell (to place) securities in the market
3. *(von der Tagesordnung ~)* to remove from the agenda

Absetzen/Absetzung 1. deduction from taxable income **2.** sale, placement **3.** removal **4.** *(Absetzung für Abnutzung)* depreciation for wear and tear

absicherbar *(~e Transaktion)* insurable (hedgeable) transaction

absichern 1. to hedge, to protect from (against), to cover, *(über die Terminmärkte ~)* to hedge through the forward or futures markets, *(Währungsrisiken durch Devisentermingeschäfte ~)* to hedge (to cover) currency exposure through forward exchange transactions, *(sich gegen einen Kursrückgang ~)* to hedge against a downward movement in stock prices, to protect o. s. on the downside
2. to collateralise, to guarantee, *(erstrangig grundpfandrechtlich ~)* to secure by a first charge over real property, *(gegen Zahlungsverzug ~)* to provide security against default, to cover the risk of default

Absicherung 1. hedge, protection, cover, *(~ eines Aktiendepots)* stock portfolio hedge, hedging a share (stock) portfolio, hedging a long stock position, *(~ durch Derivate)* hedging through derivatives, *(~ der Fälligkeitsstruktur)* maturity hedging, *(~ von*

Forderungen) receivables hedge, hedging accounts receivable *(~ gegen Kursrückgänge)* (stock) price hedge, downside protection, *(~ gegen inflationsbedingte Verluste)* inflation-proofing, *(~ von Zahlungsströmen)* cash flow hedge, *(~ von Zinsrisiken)* interest rate hedge (protection), hedging interest rate exposure, *(~ des beizulegenden Zeitwerts)* fair value hedge **2.** collateralisation, *(~ durch eine Hypothek)* security (collateralisation) by way of a mortgage (mortgage charge), *(~ eines Kreditengagements)* loan collateralisation, providing security for a loan exposure

Absicherungs / ~bedarf hedging demand (requirements); **~ergebnis** hedging gain/loss, hedging performance; **~fazilität** backup facility, support (standby) facility

Absicherungs / ~gewinn hedging gain, hedge profit; **~instrumente** hedging instruments (tools); **~kapital** guarantee (hedge) capital; **~käufer** protection buyer; **~kosten** hedging cost(s)

Absicherungs / ~limit 1. coverage (cover) limit **2.** *(im Factoring)* purchase limit, factoring facility limit; **~möglichkeiten** hedging opportunities (options, facilities); **~quote** hedge ratio, *(im Kreditgeschäft)* provisioning ratio; **~strategie** hedging strategy

Absicherungs / ~techniken hedging techniques; **~verkäufer** protection seller; **~verlust** hedging (hedge) loss; **~zeitraum 1.** hedge (protection) period **2.** contract period

Absicht intention, intent, purpose, *(in betrügerischer ~)* with intent to defraud

absichtlich intentional, *(~e Schädigung)* deliberate tort

Absichtserklärung letter (statement) of intent, memorandum of understanding

absinken to fall, to decline, to drop

Absinken *(~ des Index)* index decline

absolut *(~es Recht)* absolute (perfect) title, *(~e Rendite)* absolute return, *(~er Tiefstand)* all-time low, lowest-ever level, rock-bottom

absondern 1. to set aside (apart), to segregate **2.** *(im Insolvenzverfahren)* to settle (to satisfy) separately, *(abgesonderte Befriedigung)* separate satisfaction

Absonderung 1. setting aside (apart), segregation **2.** *(im Insolvenzverfahren)* separation of assets, separate satisfaction (settlement), → Aussonderung

Absonderungs / ~anspruch claim to separate satisfaction; **~berechtigung** entitlement to separate satisfaction; **~gläubiger** *(absonderungsberechtigter Gläubiger)* creditor entitled to separate satisfaction; **~recht** right to separate satisfaction; **~ verfahren** procedure for separate satisfaction

Absorption absorption, → Abschöpfung

abspalten to split (to spin, to hive) off

Abspaltung split-off, spin-off

abspecken to make leaner, *(abgespeckte Organisation)* lean (slimmed down) organisation

Absprache 1. consultation, agreement, arrangement, *(in enger ~ getroffene Maßnahmen)* measures undertaken in close consultation with... **2.** *(betrügerische, wettbewerbswidrige ~)* collusion

absprechen 1. to agree, to arrange **2.** *(sich ~)* to consult among themselves, *(in betrügerischer Absicht)* to collude, to conspire **3.** *(jmd. ein Recht ~)* to deny s. o. (to deprive s. o. of) a right

Abstand 1. distance, gap **2.** interval **3.** difference

absteigend *(~es Dreieck) (in der Chart-Analyse)* descending triangle □ bearish chart trend, indicates the continuation of a bearish trend or a breakout

A

to lower prices, *(in ~er Reihenfolge)* in descending order

abstellen 1. *(ausrichten auf)* to gear to, to tailor to, to direct towards, to orientate at, *(neue Produkte auf Kundenwünsche ~)* to tailor new products to customer requirements, *(die Zinssätze auf die gegenwärtige Marktsituation ~)* to gear interest rates to the present state of the market
2. *(beenden)* to put an end to, to terminate
3. *(beheben)* to remedy, to redress, to set right
4. *(konzentrieren auf)* to focus on, to concentrate on
5. *(Mitarbeiter ~)* to delegate (to second, to assign, to transfer) staff

Abstellung 1. gearing, tailoring, orientation 2. focussing, concentration 3. delegation, secondment, assignment, transfer

abstimmen 1. to reconcile, to match, to harmonise, *(Ein- und Ausgänge aufeinander ~)* to match payments and receipts, *(zeitlich)* to synchronise inflows and outflows
(die Konten ~) to reconcile (to collate) the accounts, to bring the accounts into line, *(die Einzelheiten des Abschlusses mit dem Kontrahenten ~)* to verify trade details with the counterparty
2. to coordinate, to agree, *(abgestimmte Aktion)* concerted action, *(eine Anlagestrategie ~)* to agree upon (to fine tune) an investment strategy
3. to vote, to cast a vote, *(über einen Vorschlag ~lassen)* to put a proposal to the vote
4. *(~ auf)* to tailor to, *(auf den erwarteten Cashflow abgestimmt)* tailored to the expected cash flow, *(auf den Kunden abgestimmte Lösungen)* solutions tailored to the customer's individual needs

Abstimmung 1. reconciliation, *(~ von Kontounterlagen)* reconciliation (matching) of account documents
2. coordination, harmonisation, bringing into line (into agreement), gearing to, *(in enger ~ mit dem Kunden)* in close consultation with the customer
3. voting, *(~ durch einen Bevollmächtigten)* voting by proxy, *(~ über eine Entschließung)* vote (voting) on a resolution, *(~ in mehreren Wahlgängen)* vote in several ballots

Abstimmungs / ~berechtigung voting power (right), *(abstimmungsberechtigt)* entitled to vote; **~ergebnis** result of the vote, poll result; **~vorschläge** voting recommendations; **~zwecke** reconciliation purposes

abstoßen 1. *(Anlagen, Beteiligungen)* to divest, to sell off, to shed 2. *(Wertpapiere)* to sell, to unload, to liquidate

abstrakt non-accessory, not bound to an underlying transaction, *(~e Garantie)* non-accessory guarantee, *(~es Schuldversprechen/~e Zahlungsverpflichtung)* non-accessory payment undertaking

Abstraktheit non-accessoriness, *(~ der Grundschuld)* non-accessory nature of the land charge

Abstrich cut, curtailment, reduction, *(~e bei den Dividendenzahlungen)* dividend cuts, cuts (cutbacks) in dividend payments, *(~e machen)* to make concessions, to accept cuts

abstufen to grade, to graduate, *(abgestufter Ausgleich)* tiered settlement, *(abgestufte Einführung)* phased introduction

Abstufung 1. *(~en im Rating)* rating gradations 2. *(Bonitätsstufe)* grade

Absturz plunge, sharp fall, nosedive

abstürzen to plunge, to plummet, to fall sharply, *(vom diesjährigen Jahreshöchststand ~)* to collapse from this year's high, *(auf den niedrigsten Stand der Börsensitzung ~)* to tumble to the session's low

abstützen to prop, to support, to reinforce, to underpin, *(Rücklagen ~)* to bolster (to boost) reserves

abteilbar separable, *(teilbar)* divisible

Abteilung 1. *(größere)* department, division **2.** *(kleinere)* unit, section, desk **3.** *(im Grundbuch)* section

Abteilungsleiter Department (Section) Head

abtragen *(eine Hypothek/Schuld ~)* to repay (to pay off, to clear, to discharge) a mortgage/debt

abträglich *(der Bonität des Kreditnehmers ~ sein)* to be detrimental (harmful) to the borrower's financial standing

Abtragung repayment, paying off (down), clearing, discharge

abtrennbar *(~e Zinsscheine)* detachable coupons

abtrennen 1. to separate, to segregate **2.** *(Kupons ~)* to detach (to clip, to cut off) coupons **3.** *(ein Verfahren ~)* to sever (to divide) a lawsuit

Abtrennung 1. separation, segregation, partitioning **2.** detachment, clipping, stripping **3.** severing (a case from ...)

abtretbar assignable, transferable

Abtretbarkeit assignability, transferability

abtreten to assign, to transfer, to cede, *(als Sicherheit für einen Kredit ~)* to assign as collateral for a loan

Abtretender assignor, transferor

Abtretung assignment, transfer, *(~ von Forderungen)* assignment of receivables, *(~ in notarieller Form)* assignment under a notarised deed

Abtretungs / ~anerkenntnis acknowledgement of assignment; **~anzeige** notice (notification) of assignment; **~ausschluss** precluding the right to assign, non-assignability

Abtretungs / ~beschränkungen restrictions on assignment; **~empfänger** assignee, transferee; **~erklärung** declaration (letter, memorandum) of assignment

abtretungsfähig assignable, capable of being assigned

Abtretungs / ~gegenstand subject matter of the assignment; **~gläubiger** assignment creditor; **~offenlegung** disclosure of an assignment; **~urkunde** deed of assignment

Abtretungs / ~verbot non-assignability, prohibition to assign; **~verbotsklausel** non-assignability clause; **~ vermerk** notice of assignment; **~vertrag** deed (contract) of assignment, transfer deed; **~zweck** purpose of assignment

Abverfügung *(~ der Kreditmittel)* drawdown on the loan funds

Abverkauf *(~ von Risiken)* selldown of risks

abwägen 1. to weigh (up), to consider, to assess, *(das Kreditrisiko ~)* to assess (to weigh up) the credit risk, *(die Optionen ~)* to weigh the options

Abwägung consideration, *(~ des Währungsrisikos)* assessment of the currency risk, *(nach ~)* after duly considering

abwälzen to pass on (along), *(höhere Refinanzierungskosten auf die Kunden ~)* to pass on higher funding costs to customers

abwandern to drift (to move) away, to be transferred, to flow off, *(in Aktien ~de Gelder)* funds shifted (transferred) to equities, funds finding their way into the stock markets, *(in neue Märkte ~)* to migrate to new markets

Abwanderung drift, shift, migration, *(~ vom Inlandsmarkt)* drifting away from the domestic market, *(~ von Liquidität)* liquidity drain, outflow of liquidity, *(~ von Einlagen in höherverzinsliche Anlagen)* shift (switch, migration) from deposits into higher-yielding investments

abwartend *(die Anleger verhalten sich ~)* investors remain (stay) on the sidelines, investors are biding their time

Abwärts / ~ausbruch downward break-out; **~bewegung** downward move (movement), downward trend

A

(path); ~**dynamik** downward momentum; ~-**Gap** down gap; ~**kanal** downtrend channel, descending (declining) channel, downward sloping channel

Abwärts / ~**keil** *(Chart-Analyse)* falling wedge □ signals in a downtrend the reversal from a bearish to a bullish trend and in an uptrend the continuation of the bullish trend; ~**korrektur** downward revision, downward correction in the market; ~**migration** *(~ des Portfolios)* downward migration of the portfolio

Abwärts / ~**sog/strudel** downhill slide; ~**trend** *(die Zinssätze befinden sich in einem ~)* interest rates are on a downward path, interest rates are caught in a downward trend

Abwärts / ~**verschmelzung** downstream merger, reverse meger □ parent company absorbed by its subsidiary; ~**wimpel** *(Chart-Analyse)* falling pennant, downmarket pennant □ continuation pattern, i.e. it confirms the underlying trend to lower prices

abwechseln *(sich ~)* to take turns (e. g. in the lead management), to alternate

Abwehr warding off, rejection, *(~ einer Übernahme)* frustration of a takeover bid

abwehren 1. to ward off, to fight off, *(einen feindlichen Übernahmeversuch ~)* to fend off a hostile takeover bid **2.** *(zurückweisen)* to rebuff, to reject, to repeal

abweichen 1. to deviate from, to diverge from, *(von* den *Vereinbarungen ~)* to deviate (to depart) from the agreements reached
2. *(sich unterscheiden)* to differ from, *(deutlich voneinander ~)* to vary significantly (widely), *(vom ursprünglichen Preis um mehr als 10 % ~)* to vary by more than 10 % from the original price

abweichend deviating, *(stark voneinander ~e Bewertungen)* widely divergent valuations, *(~e Regelungen)* differing regulations, *(~es Urteil)* dissenting (divergent) opinion, *(~ wirtschaftlich berechtigte Partei)* different economic beneficiary

Abweichung 1. deviation, departure, *(bei Akkreditivdokumenten)* discrepancy, *(~ von den Bestimmungen)* departure from the regulations
2. *(in der Statistik)* variance, variation
3. *(Unterschied)* difference, divergence
4. *(~ vom Referenzwert/Benchmark)* tracking error

Abweichungs / analyse variance analysis; ~**indikator** divergence indicator; ~**schwelle** divergence threshold

abweisen 1. *(einen Antrag/Vorschlag ~)* to reject (to decline) an application/a proposal **2.** *(eine Klage ~)* to dismiss a suit

Abweisen/Abweisung 1. rejection, refusal (to accept), *(~ eines Kreditantrages)* rejection of (turning down) a loan request **2.** *(~ einer Klage)* dismissal of a suit

Abwesenheitsrate absenteeism rate

abwenden to avert, *(die Insolvenz ~)* to ward off (to stave off, to fend off, to forestall) insolvency proceedings, *(eine finanzielle Krise ~)* to head off a financial crisis, *(die Zwangsvollstreckung ~)* to avert enforcement

Abwendung averting, heading off, *(~ der Zahlungsunfähigkeit des Kreditnehmers)* warding off the borrower's insolvency, averting default on a loan

abwerben 1. *(Kunden ~)* to woo customers away **2.** *(Mitarbeiter ~)* to poach staff, to headhunt

abwerfen to yield, to generate, to bring in, to provide, *(eine attraktive/geringe Rendite ~)* to yield (to provide) an attractive/poor (bad) return, *(eine garantierte Rendite ~)* to generate a guaranteed yield, *(eine hohe Verzinsung ~)* to bear a high rate of interest

abwerten to devalue

Abwertung 1. devaluation **2.** *(Wertminderung)* decrease in value, impairment

Abwertungs / ~druck devaluation pressure; **~satz** devaluation rate

abwertungsverdächtig *(~e Währung)* devaluation-prone currency

Abwertungsverlust impairment loss

abwesend *(entschuldigt ~)* absent with valid excuse

Abwesenheitsprotest noting a bill in absence of the drawee

abwickeln 1. to settle, to execute, to handle, to process, *(eine Börsenorder ~)* to execute a buy or sell order, to settle a stock trade, *(über die Börse ~)* to settle (to clear) through the stock exchange, to execute via the stock exchange
2. *(auflösen)* to wind up, to liquidate, to run down

Abwickler liquidator, liquidating agent

Abwicklung 1. settlement, handling, servicing, *(~ eines Aktien-/Wertpapiergeschäftes)* settlement, trade processing, *(~ einen Tag nach Ausführung)* settlement T+1 (transaction date plus one day), *(~ eines Kreditengagements)* loan processing (servicing)
(~ eines notleidenden Engagements) loan workout, *(~ eines Nachlasses)* settlement of an estate, *(~ der Zahlungen über die AB Bank)* settling (routing) payments through AB bank
2. *(Abteilung) (a)* back office *(b)* clearing unit
3. *(Unternehmensauflösung)* liquidation, winding-up, dissolution

Abwicklungsabteilung 1. back office, settlement department **2.** workout unit, → Abwicklungsanstalt

Abwicklungsanstalt workout agency (entity), winding-up agency, Bad Bank □ established under Germany's → Finanzmarktstabilisierungs-Fortentwicklungsgesetz (Bad Bank Act)

Abwicklungsbank 1. → Abwicklungsanstalt **2.** *(im Dokumentengeschäft)* settling (settlement) bank

Abwicklungs / ~bestätigung trade (settlement) confirmation; **~einheit 1.** settlement unit **2** workout unit, → Abwicklungsanstalt; **~entgelt** settlement fee (charge); **~ erfolg** income from liquidation

Abwicklungsergebnis 1. gain (loss) on liquidation **2.** *(im Versicherungsgeschäft) (positives/negatives ~)* positive/negative run-off result □ difference between a provision made at the beginning of the year and the aggregated payments made during the year with respect to that provision

Abwicklungs / ~eröffnungsbilanz opening liquidation accounts; **~fazilität** settlement facility; **~frist** settlement period, execution time; **~gebühr** transaction (processing, servicing) fee

Abwicklungs / ~geschäft *(eines Kreditinstitutes)* back office operations; **~geschwindigkeit** settlement speed; **~gesellschaft 1.** liquidating company **2.** clearinghouse

Abwicklungs / ~institut 1. settlement institution, clearinghouse **2.** → Abwicklungsanstalt; **~instrumente** settlement devices (tools); **~kette** *(finanzielle)* financial settlement chain; **~konto** settlement (clearing) account; **~kosten** settlement cost (fee), processing fee; **~kredit** workout loan

Abwicklungs / ~management workout management; **~modalitäten** terms of settlement; **~organisation** clearing organisation; **~periode** settlement (clearing) period; **~pflicht** settlement obligation (duty)

Abwicklungs / ~risiko settlement risk □ risk of loss due to the inability or unwillingness of a counterparty to effect agreed payments; **~risikoposition** settlement risk exposure

Abwicklungs / ~schlussbilanz closing liquidation accounts; **~stelle 1.** settlement (processing) agent **2.** clearinghouse; **~system für Wertpapiergeschäfte** securities settlement system

A

Abwicklungs / ~termin settlement date, date (day) of settlement; **~usancen** settlement conventions (practice); **~valuta** settlement currency; **~verfahren 1.** settlement proceedings, clearing procedure **2.** liquidation (winding-up) proceedings

Abwicklungs / ~vereinbarung/~vertrag 1. settlement (clearing) agreement **2.** servicing agreement **3.** *(i. S. von Aufhebungsvertrag)* severance (termination) agreement; **~verzug** failure to settle; **~vollstreckung** *(im Nachlassrecht)* settlement and partition of the estate

Abwicklungs / ~währung settlement currency; **~wert** liquidation (breakup) value; **~zeitraum** settlement (clearing) period, time required for settling the payment (transmitting the funds)

abwürgen 1. *(den Aufwärtstrend ~)* to stall the upward trend **2.** *(die Kreditnachfrage ~)* to choke off the demand for credit

abzahlen 1. to repay, to pay off **2.** *(in Raten)* to pay by instal(l)ments

Abzahlung 1. paying off, repayment **2.** payment by instal(l)ments

Abzahlungs / ~geschäfte instalment sales, instalment credit transactions; **~hypothek** instalment mortgage, mortgage repayable by fixed annual instalments; **~kauf** buying by instalments, buying on hire purchase; **~vertrag** instalment credit agreement

abzeichnen 1. *(genehmigen)* to approve **2.** *(paraphieren)* to initial **3.** *(sich ~)* to loom (ahead), to be on the horizon, to become evident, *(ein sich ~der Gewinneinbruch)* a looming plunge in profits

abziehen 1. to deduct, to subtract **2.** *(einbehalten)* to retain, to withhold **3.** *(Gelder ~)* to withdraw funds **4.** *(Liquidität ~)* to drain off liquidity

abzielen to aim at, *(auf institutionelle Anleger ~)* to be targeted at (to be directed at, to focus on) institutional investors

abzinsen to discount, *(abgezinster Cashflow)* discounted cash flow, *(auf abgezinster Basis emittieren)* to issue on a discount basis, *(abgezinst mit dem Dreimonats-Euribor-Satz)* discounted at the three months Euribor rate, *(abgezinste Forderungen)* discounted receivables, *(stark abgezinste Anleihen)* deep discount bonds

Abzinsung discounting, *(~ latenter Steueransprüche)* discounting of deferred tax assets, *(~ von Rücklagen)* reserve discounting

Abzinsungs / ~betrag discount, amount deducted from face value, *(~ zum Emissionszeitpunkt)* original issue discount; **~darlehen** discount loan □ loan facility where interest and charges are deducted from the face amount upon disbursement to the borrower; the borrower must repay the original face amount upon maturity.

Abzinsungs / ~faktor discount factor; **~gebot** discounting requirement; **~papier** discount (discounted) security, original issue discount security, security issued at a discount and redeemed at maturity for full face value

Abzinsungs / ~satz discounting rate; **~typ** type of discounted savings bond, → Abzinsungspapier; **~verfahren** discount method; **~zeitraum** discount period

Abzug 1. deduction, *(nach ~ von)* after deducting, after deduction of, after allowing for, net of, *(nach ~ aller Kosten)* all expenses deducted, *(nach ~ der Risikovorsorge)* net of allowances for loan losses, *(nach ~ der Tilgungen)* net of repayments (redemptions), *(nach ~ der Steuern)* after tax, net of tax
2. *(Einbehaltung)* retention, withholding
3. *(~ von Einlagen)* withdrawal of deposits, drain on deposits
4. *(Nachlass, Rabatt)* discount, rebate

Abzüge *(~ vom harten Kernkapital)* deductions from common equity,

(~ vom Kernkapital und Ergänzungskapital) Tier 1 and Tier 2 capital deductions, → Kapitalabzüge

Abzugsbeteiligungen equity investments to be deducted from own funds

abzugsfähig deductible, *(steuerlich ~)* tax deductible, allowable against tax, *(~e Ausgaben)* deductible expenses, *(~er Betrag)* allowable deduction

Abzugs / ~fähigkeit *(~ von Zinszahlungen)* deductibility (allowability) of interest payments; **~kredite** *(nach dem KWG)* loans and advances to related parties □ to be deducted from equity; **~posten** → Abzüge; **~verbot** non-deductibility requirement (rule)

abzweigen *(einen Kredit ~)* to branch off a loan

Abzweiglimit sub-limit, allocation line

achtfach *(~e Steigerung)* eightfold increase

achtprozentig *(ein ~er Zuwachs gegenüber dem Vorjahresergebnis)* an eight percent increase over last year's performance

addieren to add, *(sich auf 3 Mrd. € ~)* to add up to (to total) € 3bn, *(addiertes Geschäftsvolumen/Kreditvolumen)* aggregate business volume/loan portfolio

Ad-hoc Publizitätspflicht obligation to provide ad hoc publicity □ issuers are obligated to publish immediately any company information of relevance to the share price

Adresse 1. *(Emittent)* issuer, name 2. *(Kreditnehmer)* borrower, name 3. *(Kontrahent)* counterparty, contracting party 4. *(Kunde)* customer, client 5. *(Markt-/Börsenteilnehmer)* trader, operator 6. *(Wechselbezogener)* drawee

Adressenausfallrisiko credit risk, risk of counterparty default, *(Adressenausfallrisiken aus Handelsgeschäften/des Anlagebuchs)* credit risks from trading operations/credit risks on the banking book

Adressen / ~bestand address database; **~bewertung** counterparty credit rating; **~eingabe** address input; **~feld** address field;**~gewichtung** *(bei Bilanzaktiva, Termin- und außerbilanziellen Geschäften)* counterparty risk weighting; **~grenze** counterparty limit, borrower-specific lending limit

Adressen / ~konzentration counterparty concentration; **~management** list management; **~obligo** counterparty exposure; **~pflege** address maintenance; **~risiko** credit risk, *(adressenrisikobehaftet)* subject to credit risk

Adressen / ~verifizierung *(im Kreditkartengeschäft)* address verification, verifying the cardholder's address; **~ vermittler** list broker; **~vermittlung** list (address) brokerage; **~verwaltung** list (address) management

A-E Konten income and expenditure accounts

AfA → Absetzung für Abnutzung

Affidavit affidavit, sworn statement in writing

AfS-Finanzanlagen *(zur Veräußerung verfügbare finanzielle Vermögenswerte)* available-for-sale investments

AfS-Rücklage available-for-sale reserve

AGB-Gesetz Standard Contract Terms Act

AGB-Pfandrecht lien under the bank's General Business Conditions

Agent/Agent-Bank agent, agent bank

Agenturvereinbarung agency agreement

Aggregate *(monetäre ~)* monetary aggregates, monetary measures, *(aggregierte Bilanzsumme)* aggregated total assets

Agio premium; **~anleihe** premium bond, bond issued at a price above par; **~erträge/~gewinne** premiums received; **~notierung** premium quotation; **~papiere** premium securities, securities repayable at a premium

A

(redeemable above par); ~**rücklage** share premium account

Agrar / ~**derivate** agricultural derivatives; ~**finanzierung** farm financing; ~**kredit** farm credit, agricultural credit (loan); ~**kreditgeschäft** farm credit operations, agricultural lending; ~**kreditinstitut** farm credit bank, agricultural credit bank

AIDA-Modell → Anstalt-in-der-Anstalt-Modell

AKA → Ausfuhrkreditgesellschaft

akkreditieren 1. to open a documentary credit 2. *(akkreditierte elektronische Signatur)* accredited electronic signature

Akkreditierter beneficiary under a documentary credit, accreditee

Akkreditiv documentary credit, *(Kurzform)* credit, *(~ mit aufgeschobenem Zahlungsziel)* deferred payment credit

Akkreditiv / ~**ablauf** expiry of a documentary credit; ~**abteilung** documentary credits department; ~**abwicklung** handling of (processing) a documentary credit; ~**änderung** amendment to a documentary credit

Akkreditiv / ~**ansprüche** rights (claims) under a documentary credit; ~**anzeige** notification of credit; ~**auftrag** credit application, instructions to open a documentary credit; ~**auftraggeber** applicant for the credit; ~**auskehrung** payment of the credit

Akkreditiv / ~**ausnutzung** drawing on a documentary credit; ~**auszahlungsanspruch** right to payment under a credit; ~**avisierung** advising a credit, notification of credit

Akkreditiv / ~**bank** issuing (opening) bank, bank opening a documentary credit; ~**bedienung** payment under a documentary credit; ~**bedingungen** terms and conditions of a documentary credit, credit terms; ~**begünstigter** beneficiary under a documentary credit, accreditee

Akkreditiv / ~**bestätigung** credit confirmation; ~**betrag** amount of the credit; ~**bevorschussung** packing (anticipatory) credit, red clause credit; ~**brief** letter of credit

Akkreditiv / ~**deckung** credit cover, cover for a documentary credit; ~**deckungskonto** credit cover account; ~**dokumente** credit documents, documents called for in a documentary credit (presented under a documentary credit)

Akkreditiv / ~**einlösungsverpflichtung** obligation (liability) to honour the credit; ~**erlös** credit proceeds; ~**ermächtigung** letter of authority

Akkreditiv / ~**eröffnung** credit opening, opening of a documentary credit, *(akkreditiveröffnende Bank)* issuing (opening) bank; ~**eröffnungsauftrag** credit application

akkreditivgemäß/-gerecht *(~e Dokumente)* complying documents, documents in accordance with the terms and conditions of the credit

Akkreditiv / ~**geschäft** documentary credit transaction(s); ~**gültigkeit** validity of a credit; ~**haftungsübernahme** taking on the liability under the credit; ~**hinauslegung** credit accommodation (opening)

Akkreditiv / ~**inanspruchnahme** drawing on a credit, credit availment; ~**institut** → Akkreditivbank; ~**klausel** documentary credit clause, clause stipulating payment by documentary credit

Akkreditiv / ~**kreditrahmen** general documentary credit facility; ~**leistung** payment under a credit, effecting (making) payment under a credit

Akkreditivmäßigkeit *(die ~ der Dokumente prüfen)* to check whether the documents are in accordance with the terms and conditions of the documentary credit, *(akkreditivmäßig absichern)* to secure by way of a documentary credit

Akkreditiv / ~**partei** party to a documentary credit; ~**sicherheit** security of payment under a documentary credit; ~**steller** applicant for the credit; ~**stellung** issuance (opening) of a documentary credit

Akkreditiv / ~**übertragung** transferring a documentary credit, transfer of a credit; ~**verkehr** documentary credit operations; ~**verlängerung** extending the term (life) of a documentary credit; ~**versprechen** documentary credit undertaking; ~**vorausavisierung** pre-advising a documentary credit

Akkreditiv / ~**währung** credit currency; ~**zahlstelle** paying bank; ~**ziehung** drawing under a documentary credit

akkumulieren to accumulate, *(akkumulierter Gewinn)* accumulated (retained) earnings, *(akkumuliertes Haftungslimit)* aggregate liability limit

Akkumulierungsfonds capital growth fund, cumulative fund

akquirieren 1. *(Neugeschäfte)* to solicit (to develop, to acquire, to source) new business 2. *(Kunden)* to win (to seek out) new customers

Akquirierung/Akquisition 1. soliciting (acquiring, sourcing) new business, new business development, prospecting, acquisition
2. *(Unternehmensakquisition)* buying (taking over) a company, company takeover

Akquisitions / ~**analyse** acquisition analysis (review); ~**aufwand** → Akquisitionskosten; ~**bemühungen** efforts to win new customers, efforts to solicit business, acquisition drive; ~**darlehen** acquisition loan; ~**finanzierung** acquisition finance (financing), financing corporate takeovers

Akquisitions / ~**kosten** order generation costs, business development cost, cost of soliciting business; ~**kunde** prospect; ~**potenzial** acquisition potential; ~**strategie** soliciting (sourcing) strategy

Akte file, record, *(zu den Akten nehmen)* to file, to put (to place) on file

Akteur *(~e am Aktienmarkt)* stock market operators, players in the stock market

Aktie share, stock, equity

Aktien / ~**abschlag** share (stock) discount, discount on shares (stock); ~**agio** share premium

aktienähnlich similar in nature to equities, *(~e Rechte)* stock equivalents, equity-like rights, *(~e Wertpapiere)* equity-like (share-like) securities, quasi-equity securities

Aktien / ~**analyse** share (stock) analysis, analysis of the equity (stock) market, equity research; ~**analyst** equity research analyst; ~**andienungsanleihe** → Aktienanleihe

Aktien / ~**anlage** investment in equities (shares, stocks), share (stock) investment; ~**anlageplan** share investment plan; ~**anlagerisiko** risk inherent in equity (stock) investments; ~**anleger** equity (stock) investor, stock market investor

Aktienanleihe reverse convertible bond, equity-like bond □ entitles its issuer to tender upon the bond's maturity a specific number of shares instead of repaying the bond's nominal amount

Aktienanteil *(an einem Portefeuille)* equity allocation, weighting given to equities (stocks) in a portfolio, *(Portefeuille mit einem hohen ~)* portfolio with a high equity exposure

Aktienarbitrage equity arbitrage □ trying to profit from the expected different share price performance of two different but related companies by purchasing company A stock and shorting company B stock

Aktien / ~**aufgeld** stock surplus, share premium; ~**aufkauf** buying up shares (stock); ~**aufschlag** → Aktienaufgeld;

~**ausgabe** → Aktienemission; ~**austausch** exchange of shares, stock swap; ~**auswahl** stockpicking, choice (selection) of stocks

Aktien / ~**baisse** slump in the stock market, sharp drop in equity prices, bear equity market; ~**barometer** stock price indicator

aktienbasiert *(~es Handelsgeschäft)* equities-related trading activities, *(~e Vergütungstransaktion)* share-based payment transaction

Aktien / ~**besitz** share ownership, stock (equity) ownership, shareholding, shares (stock) held; ~**besitzer** share-owner, shareholder, stockholder; ~**bestand** holding of shares, shareholding, stockholding, equity holdings, stock portfolio

Aktien / ~**beteiligung** 1. equity holding (interest), shareholding 2. *(von Mitarbeitern)* employee shareholding; ~ **beteiligungsprogramm** employee share ownership plan; ~**betreuung** sponsoring; ~**bewertung** 1. valuation of equities (stocks), stock pricing 2. *(bonitätsmäßige)* rating of a share, stock rating; ~**bewertungsmodell** stock pricing model

aktienbezogen *(~e Sicherungsderivate)* equity-related hedging derivatives

Aktienbezug 1. share (stock) purchase 2. subscription to shares

Aktienbezugsangebot share (stock) offering

Aktienbezugsrecht 1. *(allgemein)* warrant, warrant to subscribe for shares, option warrant 2. *(in Verbindung mit einer Kapitalerhöhung)* stock (share) subscription right, stock right 3. *(für leitende Angestellte)* stock option (granted to management and key officers)

Aktienbezugsrechts / ~**plan** stock (share) option scheme; ~**schein** stock (share) warrant, share purchase warrant

Aktien / ~**börse** stock exchange; ~**buch** 1. *(Register)* share (stock) ledger, stockholders' ledger, stock record book 2. *(Gesamtportfolio)* equity exposure book

Aktien-CFD → Aktiendifferenzkontrakt

Aktiendarlehen share loan

Aktiendepot equities (stock) portfolio, *(wenn kleiner)* securities account

Aktienderivate equity derivatives, equity-linked structured products; ~**markt** equity derivatives market, → Aktien-Option/Futures, → Aktiendifferenzkontrakte, → Aktienindexderivate, → Aktienkorbderivate

Aktiendifferenzkontrakte share CDFs, share (equity) contracts for difference □ the seller of the contract will pay the buyer the difference in price if the value of the underlying share has increased after a specific period of time (if the price has dropped then the buyer pays instead to the seller)

Aktien / ~**disagio** share discount; ~**eindeckungen** 1. *(zur Erfüllung von Leerverkaufsverpflichtungen)* short covering, stock buy-in 2. *(in Erwartung einer Kurssteigerung)* buying in expectation of higher prices; ~**einziehung** stock retirement (redemption, liquidation), calling in shares

Aktien / ~**emission** share (stock) issue, share (equity) offering, stock market flotation, → Börsengang; ~**emissionsagio** share (stock) issue premium, premium on an equity offering

Aktien / ~**empfehlungen** recommended stocks, stock recommendations; ~**engagement** 1. *(Einzelkauf)* purchase of stock (equities) 2. *(Gesamtposition)* exposure in equities, equity exposure

Aktien / ~**finanzierung** equity financing, financing through the issue of shares, raising funds by issuing stocks; ~**flaute** stalemate in the equity (stock) market; ~**fonds** equities (stock) fund, equity unit trust

Aktien-Futures *(Futures auf Einzelaktien)* single stock futures □ undertaking to buy or sell a specific stock at a specified future date; like most futures contracts, SSFs are cash-settled, → Barausgleich

Aktiengattung class of shares (stock), stock category

aktiengebundene Anleihe equity-linked bond

Aktien / ~geschäft 1. *(einzelnes Aktiengeschäft)* stock (equity) trade, *(Abwicklung von ~en)* equity transaction settlement **2.** *(Gesamtheit)* equity business, stock market operations; **~gesellschaft** stock corporation

Aktien / ~gesetz German Stock Corporation Act, German Companies Act; **~gewichtung** share (stock) weighting, *(~ im Portefeuille)* weighting given to stocks in the portfolio; **~gewinn** equity gain

Aktien / ~handel share (equity, stock) trading, share dealings; **~handelsplatz** equity trading venue; **~händler** stock dealer (trader), equity dealer; **~hausse** upsurge (steep rise) in share prices, bull market in equities, rocketing (soaring) equity prices

Aktien / ~hochfrequenzhandel high-frequency equity trading; **~ im Handelsbestand** equities in the trading book

Aktienindex share price index, stock price average, stock index, equity market index (average); → DAX, →TecDAX, → CDAX, → HDAX, → MDAX, → Midcap Market Index, → SDAX

Aktienindex-Derivate equity index derivatives, derivative equity index products ***(Aktienindex-Future)*** equity index future, stock market index future □ cash-settled futures contract based on the performance of a particular stock market index, ***(Aktienindex-Option)*** equity index option, ***(Aktienindex-Swap)*** equity index swap, exchange of one index return for another, → Index-Swap, ***(Aktienindex-Zertifikat)*** equity index certificate

Aktien / ~inhaber shareowner, stockowner, shareholder, stockholder; **~kapital** share (stock) capital, equity; **~kapitalverzinsung** return on stockholders' equity; **~kassahandel** cash equity trading; **~kassamarkt** cash stock market

Aktien / ~kategorie class of shares, stock category; **~kauf** stock purchase, purchase of shares (equities), buying shares; **~kaufoption** equity call option

Aktienkorb equity basket, stock basket

Aktienkorb-Derivate equity basket derivatives □ futures, options and similar instruments based on the performance of an underlying basket of shares

Aktien / ~kredit loan to finance a stock purchase; **~kultur** shareholding culture, equity culture, *(i.w.S.)* investor relations

Aktienkurs share (stock) price, equity price, *(aktienkursbezogene Risikoposition)* equity price related risk exposure

Aktienkurs / ~gewinne share price gains; **~index** → Aktienindex; **~risiken** share price risks, equity exposure; **~sicherung** stock price hedge (hedging), *(Festschreibung eines erzielten Gewinns)* locking in a price gain; **~verluste** share price losses

Aktien / ~leihe stock lending, stock lending and borrowing, equity lending; **~ leihevertrag** stock lending agreement; **~mantel** share (stock) certificate; **~markt** stock market, equity market; **~mehrheit** majority of shares, majority shareholding

Aktien / ~nettoposition net equities position; **~neuemissionen** new issuance of equities; **~notierung 1.** *(Kurs)* share (stock) price, quotation **2.** *(an der Börse)* listing of a share on the stock exchange

A

Aktienoption 1. *(Option auf den Kauf oder Verkauf einer Aktie)* equity option, stock option, → Aktienkaufoption, Aktienverkaufsoption **2.** *(bei einer Optionsanleihe)* warrant

Aktienoptions / ~handel equity (stock) options trading; **~programm** stock option scheme; **~schein** share (stock, equity) warrant

Aktien / ~order instructions to buy or sell shares, stock buy or sell order; **~paket** share block, block of shares, large parcel of shares; **~pakethandel** block trading in shares; **~platzierung** share (stock) placing, equity (stock) placement, stock flotation

Aktien / ~portefeuille stock (equity) portfolio, portfolio of shares; **~position** equity (stock) position, *(Aktienpositionen im Handelsbestand)* equities in the trading book; **~positionsrisiko** equity position risk

Aktien / ~promesse scrip certificate; **~quote** *(in einem Portefeuille)* equity allocation, stock allocation, share allocation ratio, *(40%ige Aktienquote)* 40 % allocation to equity investments

Aktien / ~recht Stock Corporation Law, *(aktienrechtliche Organhaftung)* management liability under corporate law; **~register** shareholders' ledger; **~rendite** stock yield

Aktien / ~risiko equity risk, risk inherent in stocks; **~risikopositionen** equity risk positions; **~rückkauf** share buyback, stock buyback (repurchase)

Aktien / ~sparen saving through equities, equity saving, equities as a form of savings, investment in shares; **~sparer** equity (stock) investor; **~sparplan** share investment plan, equity plan, stock accumulation plan

Aktien / ~spekulant stock market player, trader; **~spekulation** speculative trading in equities, speculative buying and selling of stock, playing the equity market; **~spitze** fraction

Aktiensplit share (stock) split, *(Aufteilung in eine höhere Zahl von Aktien)* split-up, splitting one share into a larger number of shares, *(Aufteilung in eine kleinere Zahl von Aktien, umgekehrter Split)* split-down, reverse split, combining a number of shares to form a smaller number of shares

Aktien / ~stimmrecht share (stock) voting right: **~streubesitz** freely floating stock, free float of stock; **~streuung 1.** diversification of equity investments **2.** selling (offering) shares to the general public; **~stückelung 1.** share (stock) denomination **2.** share (stock) unit

Aktientausch share exchange, share (stock) swap, equity switching, exchange of shares; **~angebot** share exchange offering, stock swap offering

Aktientermingeschäft 1. equity forward contract □ contract that calls for the purchase or sale of a specified number of equities at a fixed price and at specified date in the future
2. → Aktien-Futures

Aktienterminhandel 1. equity forward trading **2.** equity futures trading

Aktienübereignung stock assignment, assignment of shares, assigning (transferring) the ownership of stock

Aktienübernahme 1. share deal, acquisition (takeover) of the company's stock **2.** *(~ im Emissionsgeschäft)* stock underwriting

Aktienübernahme / ~angebot share bid, stock tender offer, *(~ gegen Barzahlung)* share cash bid; **~ konsortium** share (stock) underwriting group; **~verpflichtung** share (stock) underwriting commitment

Aktien / ~übertragung share (stock) transfer; **~umlauf** total shares outstanding; **~umsätze** stock market turnover, level of activity in the equity market; **~umtausch** exchange of shares, stock swap; **~urkunde** share (stock) certificate; **~verflechtungen** cross shareholdings

Aktienverkauf share (stock) sale, selling shares

Aktienverkaufs / ~angebot share (stock) offering; **~option** equity (stock) put option; **~prospekt** share offering prospectus

Aktien / ~verpfändung pledging of shares (e. g. as collateral); **~verwahrung** safe custody of shares; **~verwaltung 1.** share portfolio administration **2.** share registration services

Aktien / ~werte equities, equity securities, *(~ des Anlagevermögens)* equity securities held for investment, *(Verringerung des Engagements in ~n)* reducing the exposure to equities (stocks); **~wertentwicklung** stock performance; **~wertzuwachs** equity (stock) appreciation

Aktien / ~zeichner share applicant, subscriber to shares; **~zeichnung** share application, subscription to (for) shares; **~zeichnungsbetrag** share application money; **~zertifikat** share (stock) certificate

Aktien / ~zusammenlegung stock consolidation, consolidation of shares; **~zuteilung** share allotment, allotment of shares (stocks)

Aktionär shareholder, stockholder

Aktionärs / ~banken shareholding banks; **~beschluss** shareholders' resolution; **~brief** newsletter to shareholders; **~gruppe** class of shareholders, stockholder group; **~haftung** shareholder liability

Aktionärs / ~klage 1. *(Einzelklage)* shareholder action (suit), **2.** *(Gruppenklage)* stockholders' representative action, class action; **~kreis 1.** shareholder (stockholder) group **2.** → Aktionärsstruktur

Aktionärs / ~pflege investor relations; **~pflichten** shareholder rights (duties)

Aktionärs / ~rechte shareholder rights; **~rechterichtlinie** (EU) Shareholder Rights Directive; **~register** shareholder register, stock register, stock record book; **~risiko** shareholder risk, risk to the shareholder

Aktionärs / ~schutz protection of shareholder rights; **~struktur** shareholder structure, setup of stockholders, stockholder pattern, membership

Aktionärs / ~vereinigung shareholder association; **~versammlung** shareholders' (stockholders') meeting; **~vertreter** spokesman for the shareholders (stockholders), shareholders' representative; **~vollmachten** shareholder's powers

Aktionsplan *(Aktionsplan für Finanzdienstleistungen)* (EU) Financial Services Action Plan (FSAP) □ designed to integrate Europe's financial markets; introduced The Markets in Financial Instruments Directive (MiFID), → Finanzmarktrichtlinie

Aktionsradius range of action, → Spielraum

aktiv 1. *adj.* *(~e Anlagedispositionen)* active portfolio management, *(~er Gesellschafter)* managing partner, partner active in the conduct of the business, *(~er Konsolidierungsausgleichsposten)* positive consolidation difference, *(~e latente Steuern)* deferred tax assets, *(~e Leistungsbilanz)* current account surplus *(~e Rechnungsabgrenzungsposten)* prepaid expenses, prepayments, cost for services/materials not yet received, but for which payment has been made, → abgrenzen, *(~e Rückversicherung)* → Rückdeckung, *(~er Unterschiedsbetrag)* → aktivischer Unterschiedsbetrag, *(~er Verrechnungssaldo)* positive clearing balance, clearing surplus **2.** *adv.* *(~ fördern)* to promote actively, *(~ gemanagter Fonds)* actively managed fund

Aktiva assets, *(~ des Handelsbuches)* trading book assets

Aktiva Stufe 1 Level 1 assets □ Part of the stock of unencumbered high-quality liquid assets (erstklassige liquide Aktiva) to be held by banks under the → Basel III liquidity standards. Level 1 assets comprise cash, central bank

A

reserves, marketable securities representing claims on sovereigns, central banks, international financial institutions, → Mindestliquiditätsquote

Aktiva Stufe 2 Level 2 assets □ limited to 40% of the stock of high-quality liquid assets; comprise marketable securities, corporate and covered bonds that meet specific criteria

Aktiv / ~devisenposition long currency position; **~engpass** shortage of assets; **~fälligkeit** asset maturity, loan maturity; **~finanzierung** *(aus Bankensicht)* provision of finance (to other economic entities), → Passivfinanzierung

Aktiv / ~geschäft *(einer Bank)* lending business (operations), asset side, asset operations; **~grenze** upper lending limit; **~hypotheken** mortgage lendings

aktivieren 1. to capitalise, to carry (to report) as assets, to recognise as an asset, *(mit ... € aktiviert sein)* to be capitalised at € . ., *(aktivierte Abschlusskosten)* deferred acquisition cost, *(aktivierte Eigenleistungen)* company-produced additions to assets, capitalised own work
2. *(intensivieren)* to intensify, to reinforce, to stimulate, to push
3. *(vorantreiben)* to activate, to spur into action

Aktivierung 1. capitalisation, carrying as assets, *(~ von Fremdkapitalzinsen)* capitalising interest on borrowed funds (on outside capital), interest capitalisation **2.** intensification, stimulation

aktivierungsfähig capitalisable, *(~e Aufwendungen)* capitalisable expenditure, expenses recognisable as an addition to assets, expenses of a capital nature

Aktivierungsgebot/-pflicht obligation to capitalise, capitalisation requirement, mandatory capitalisation

Aktivierungsverbot non-capitalisation rule

Aktivierungswahlrecht optional capitalisation (asset recognition), option to capitalise

aktivisch 1. *adj. (~e Bestände)* long positions, *(~e Bestandskonten)* asset accounts, *(~e Festzinslücke)* asset-related fixed rate gap, *(~e Festzinsposition)* fixed rate position on the asset side, *(~e Posten)* asset items, *(~e Rechnungsabgrenzungsposten)* → aktive Rechnungsabgrenzungsposten, *(~es Terminrisiko)* asset-related time risk □ loss to the bank resulting from non-compliance with debt servicing dates
(~er Unterschiedsbetrag) surplus, positive difference, balancing item on the asset side, *(~er Unterschiedsbetrag aus Kapitalkonsolidierung)* positive goodwill
2. *adv. (~ ausweisen)* to state (to report) on the asset side

Aktivitätenportfolio (portfolio of) operations

Aktiv / ~kennziffer asset ratio; **~klage 1.** action as plaintiff **2.** *(im Insolvenzrecht)* action brought by the insolvency administrator; **~konditionen** lending terms (rates); **~konto** asset account, creditor account; **~kundschaft** borrowing customers, borrowers

Aktiv / ~marge lending spread; **~mehrungen 1.** asset additions, increase in assets **2.** increase in lendings; **~minderungen 1.** asset cuts, decrease in assets **2.** decrease in lendings

Aktiv-Passiv-Management asset-liabilities mangement

Aktiv / ~position 1. asset item **2.** *(i. S. von Bestands-/Kaufposition)* long position; **~posten** asset, asset item; **~prozess** litigation as plaintiff, *(Aufnahme von ~ en)* joinder of pending actions as plaintiff, → Aktivklage

Aktiv / ~saldo credit (favourable) balance, surplus; **~seite** *(der Bilanz)* asset side (asset section) of the balance sheet

Aktiv / ~steuerung asset management; **~swap** asset swap, exchange of one asset for another; **~tausch** → Aktiv-Swap; **~tilgungen** loan repayments, redemptions on lendings

Aktivüberhang 1. net surplus, net asset position, surplus of assets **2.** *(im Devisenhandel, Terminhandel)* net long position **3.** *(im Geldhandel)* net selling (lending) position, net lending position in interbank dealings **4.** *(Zinsbindungsbilanz)* net fixed rate position

Aktivum 1. asset **2.** positive aspect, positive (favourable) feature

Aktiv / ~vorlauf *(im Kreditgeschäft)* lendings without matching fundings; **~wechsel** bills receivable; **~ zins 1.** loan interest rate, lending rate **2.** interest receivable; **~ zinsüberschuss** net interest income from lendings

aktualisieren to update, to bring up to date, *(aktualisierte Bewertung)* updated valuation

Aktualisierung bringing up to date, (continuous) updating, *(~ der Zahlen des Vorjahres)* update of last year's figures

Aktualität topical significance (interest), relevance, *(die ~ der Finanzkennzahlen)* the up-to-dateness of the financial ratios

aktuell/aktuell *(Zinsberechnungsmethode)* actual/actual □ day count convention based on the actual number of calendar days elapsed in a given interest period (numerator) and the actual number of calendar days in the year (denominator)

aktuell/360 actual/360 □ day count convention based on the actual number of calendar days elapsed in a given interest period, assuming a 360 day year

aktuell *(~es Ausfallrisiko)* current exposure, *(von ~em Interesse sein)* to be of topical (special) interest, *(~er Kassakurs)* current spot rate, *(~e Konditionen)* currently valid terms, *(~er Kreditbedarf)* current (immediate) borrowing requirements, *(zum ~en Kurs)* at the currently available price *(~er Marktkurs)* prevailing (going) market rate, *(~e Notierung)* current quote (quotation), *(~es Obligo)* current exposure, *(~er Wiederbeschaffungswert)* current replacement cost, *(~es Zahlenmaterial zur Finanzlage)* up-to-date (recent) figures on the financial situation

akut 1. pressing, urgent, *(~er Mittelbedarf)* pressing need for (fresh) funds **2.** critical, *(in ein ~es Stadium eintreten)* to enter a critical (crucial) stage **3.** *(bevorstehend)* imminent, *(~es Verzugsrisiko)* imminent risk of default

AKV → Allgemeine Kreditvereinbarungen

Akzent 1. *(Betonung)* emphasis, focus, *(~e setzen)* to focus on, to emphasise, to put the emphasis on, to leave one's mark **2.** *(Merkmal)* feature, factor

Akzept acceptance

Akzeptakkreditiv documentary acceptance credit □ payment will be made against presentation of the documents and a bill drawn on the issuing bank

Akzeptant 1. acceptor **2.** → Akzeptanzstelle

Akzeptanz 1. acceptance **2.** acceptability, acceptableness; **~analyse** acceptance analysis; **~messung** acceptance measurement; **~rate** rate of acceptance

Akzeptanz / ~stelle merchant, merchant location, card acceptor; **~stellenvertrag** merchant agreement, agreement between the merchant and the card processing bank

Akzept / ~austausch interbank exchange of own acceptances; **~einholung** presentation for acceptance, obtaining acceptance; **~ermächtigung** authorisation to accept; **~forderungen** due from acceptances, acceptances outstanding

akzeptgebende Bank accepting bank

akzeptieren 1. *(einen Wechsel/einen Vorschlag ~)* to accept a bill/a proposal 2. *(ein höheres Marktrisiko ~)* to put up with a higher market risk

Akzeptierung acceptance

Akzeptierungsakkreditiv acceptance credit

Akzept / ~kredit acceptance credit; **~kreditnehmer** customer (borrower) taking out an acceptance credit; **~leistung** acceptance, effecting acceptance, writing the acceptance on a bill

Akzept / ~linie acceptance credit line, acceptance facility; **~meldung** notification (advice) of acceptance; **~provision** acceptance commission; **~retoure** returned acceptances; **~umlauf** acceptances outstanding

Akzept / ~verbindlichkeiten acceptance liabilities; **~verweigerung** non-acceptance, refusing acceptance, failure to accept; **~vorlage** presentation (presentment) for acceptance; **~zusage** undertaking (commitment) to accept, acceptance commitment

Akzessorietät accessoriness, *(~ einer Sicherheit)* accessory (accessorial) nature of a security

akzessorisch *(~e Sicherheit)* accessory security □ i.e. accessory to a specific debt, → Bürgschaft, → Hypothek

Algo-Händler algorithmic trader

algorithmischer Handel algorithmic trading, algo trading, flash trading

allein *adj.*sole, single, exclusive, *adv.* solely, exclusively, to the exclusion of all others, *(~ haften)* to be solely liable (e. g. for the debts of a business)

Allein / ~aktionär sole shareholder; **~auftrag/~beauftragung** sole (exclusive) agency; **~bürge** sole guarantor

Allein / ~eigentum 1. sole (single, exclusive) ownership 2. separate ownership; **~eigentümer** sole (single, exclusive) owner; **~entscheidungsrecht** sole decision-making power; **~erbe** sole (universal) heir; **~gesellschafter** sole shareholder

alleinig *(~e Führungsbank)* sole lead manager, *(~es Nutzungsrecht)* right to exclusive use, *(~es Platzierungsinstitut)* sole placing agent, sole dealer, *(~er Rechtsnachfolger)* sole (universal) successor

Allein / ~kompetenz sole (decision-making) authority, **~makler** exclusive agent; **~stellungsmerkmal** unique selling position

Alleinverfügungsberechtigung sole authorisation (e.g. to draw on the account or to represent the company), *(allein verfügungsberechtigte Person)* sole authorised signatory, sole person holding discretionary powers

Allein / ~verkaufsauftrag exclusive agency (mandate) to sell; **~verkaufsrecht** exclusive right to sell, exclusive distributorship; **~vertreter** sole representative (agent, distributor)

Allein / ~vertretung 1. exclusive agency, exclusive distributorship 2. sole representation, *(alleinvertretungsberechtigt sein)* to hold sole power of representation; **~vertretungsrecht** sole power of representation

Allein / ~vertrieb exclusive (sole) distribution; **~vertriebsrechte** sole distributorship rights; **~zeichnungsberechtigte/r** sole authorised signatory

allererste Adresse top-grade (top-quality, blue-chip) borrower/issuer

Allfinanz integrated financial services, wide-scale financial services under one roof, one-stop financial services, bancassurance

Allfinanzaufsicht 1. integrated financial supervision 2. *(Behörde)* integrated financial supervisory agency

Allfinanz / ~geschäft → Allfinanz; **~konzept** integrated (one-stop) financial services concept; **~konzern** all-round financial services provider; **~palette** all-inclusive range of financial services; **~prinzip** principle of offering financial services under one roof

Allgefahrendeckung all risks insurance, block (all-risks) coverage

allgemein 1. *adj.* general, common, *(~ es Korrelationsrisiko)* general wrong-way risk → Korrelationsrisiko, *(~ e Vertretungsvollmacht)* general power of attorney, general proxy, *(~e Verwaltungsaufwendungen)* general administrative expenses, *(nach ~en Regeln ermitteln)* to determine according to generally valid rules
2. *adv.* generally, *(~ anerkannte Grundsätze der Rechnungslegung)* generally accepted accounting principles, *(~ erwartet)* widely expected, *(im ~en schwächer bei geringen Umsätzen)* generally lower in slow trading

Allgemein / ~gültigkeit *(ohne die ~ der vorstehenden Ausführungen zu beeinträchtigen)* without limiting the generality of the foregoing; **~verfügung** administrative ordinance

Allheilmittel *(~ für Liquiditätsprobleme)* panacea for liquidity problems

Allokation allocation, allotment, *(alloziertes Kapital)* allocated capital, capital allocated to a specific segment

Allonge allonge □ *(a)* slip of paper attached to a bill of exchange to accommodate additional endorsements *(b)* document attached to a contract

Alphawert Alpha performance, *(positiver/negativer ~)* positive/negative Alpha □ denoting an outperformance/underperformance of the benchmark/index

alt *(ehemalig)* previous, old, *(auf ~e Rechnung)* for previous account, *(unter ~er Wertstellung)* under good value, *(~e Wertpapierpensionen)* maturing repurchase agreements

Alt-Aktionäre existing (current) shareholders

Alt-Bestand 1. existing positions (holdings), claims already existing **2.** loans extended in previous years, *(~ an Realkrediten)* existing portfolio of mortgage loans

alteingeführt *(~e Emissionsadresse)* seasoned (well-established) issuer, *(~es Unternehmen)* old-established company

Alt-Emission secondary market issue, seasoned issue

Alternativ-Anlagen alternative investments □ investments other than the traditional products, e.g. private equity, futures, structured products, hedge funds, *(Richtlinie über die Verwalter alternativer Investmentfonds)* (EU) Alternative Investment Fund Managers (AIFM) Directive

Alternative Handelssysteme alternative trading systems, off-board and screen-based trading platforms

Alternativer Risikotransfer alternative risk transfer, transferring risks to the capital and derivatives markets, → Katastrophen-Anleihe, Katastrophen-Option

Alternativer Standardansatz *(Basel II)* alternative standardised approach □ use of alternative indicators in the standardised approach to measure operational risk

Alternative Streitbeilegung alternative dispute resolution (ADR); arbitration, mediation, conciliation

Altersversorgungsplan *(des Arbeitgebers)* retirement benefits scheme, *(kapitalgedeckter ~)* fully funded retirement (pension) benefits scheme

Altersversorgungsverpflichtungen retirement benefit obligations

Altersvorsorge old age provision, retirement provision, *(private ~)* privately funded old age provision, individual retirement arrangement

Altersvorsorge / ~produkte retirement products, old age provision instruments; **~sondervermögen** old age provision fund; **~sparplan** retirement savings scheme

Alt / ~geschäfte already concluded contracts, previous contracts, *(Berücksichtigung von ~n)* backloading;

A

~**investments** existing investments; ~**kunde** existing customer; ~ **last** **1.** existing debt (indebtedness) **2.** contaminated site; ~**veräußerungen** old sales transactions, transactions concluded prior to …; ~**verbindlichkeiten** existing debt load, → Altgeschäfte

ambitionierter Messansatz *(Basel II)* advanced measurement approach

amerikanische Option American option, American-style option □ option that may be exercised into its underlying instrument at any time prior to maturity

amerikanisches Zuteilungsverfahren US-style rate tender, → Zinstender *(amerikanisches Zuteilungsverfahren)*

am Geld at-the-money □ a call or put option is at-the-money when the market price of the underlying instrument equals, or nearly equals the strike price

Amortisation redemption, amortisation, repayment

Amortisations / ~anleihe redemption bond; ~**anteil** *(des monatlichen Schuldendienstes)* share of principal repaid; ~**dauer 1.** period (term) of redemption, repayment period **2.** *(Kapitalrückflussdauer)* payback (payoff) period; ~**fonds** sinking fund; ~**hypothek** amortising (instalment) mortgage, redemption mortgage, direct reduction mortgage

Amortisations / ~plan repayment schedule; ~**prämie** redemption premium; ~**satz** redemption rate; ~**swap** amortising swap □ swap in which the notional amount decreases according to a preset schedule

amortisieren to amortise, to redeem, to repay

Ampelkennzeichnung traffic light labelling

Ampellogik traffic light system (method), traffic light system used to pinpoint major changes

Amt office, *(Mitglied von ~s wegen)* ex-officio member

amtierend *(~e Geschäftsführung)* incumbent management, *(~er Vorsitzender) (a)* incumbent chairman *(b) (vorübergehend, stellvertretend)* acting chairman

amtlich 1. *adj.* *(~er Einheitskurs)* official cash market quotation, *(~er Handel)* official trading (dealing), official market, first trading segment, *(~er Kurs)* official price (rate), *(~es Kursblatt)* Official List, Official Stock Exchange Price List, *(~e Kursfeststellung/Kursfestsetzung)* official price fixing, fixing the official price (quotation) *(~er Markt) (Börsensegment)* official market, first trading segment □ superseded by → Regulierter Markt on November 1, 2007, *(~e Notierung)* official quotation, official listing, *(~er Vergleich)* court settlement, *(~es Vergleichsverfahren)* court-supervised composition, *(~er Wechselkurs)* official exchange rate
2. *adv.* *(~ bekanntgeben)* to gazette, *(~ bestellter Vertreter)* court-appointed representative, *(~ notierte Wertpapiere)* securities officially quoted (listed) on the stock exchange, listed securities

Amts / ~blatt Official Journal (Gazette); ~**dauer** → Amtszeit; ~**führung** execution of office; ~ **gericht** Local Court, *(in England – for minor civil cases:* County Court; *for minor criminal offences:* Magistrates Court)

Amts / ~gewalt official powers; ~**haftungsklage** action brought against a public official (an agency); ~**inhaber** office holder (bearer), holder of an office; ~**missbrauch** abuse of official powers

Amts / ~nachfolger successor in office; ~**notar** civil servant/public official acting as notary; ~**pfleger** legal curator; ~**richter** Local Court Judge, Magistrate; ~**vergehen** malfeasance in office, abuse of office

Amts / ~vorgänger predecessor in office; **~vormund** statutory guardian, guardian appointed by the court; **~wechsel** change in office; **~zeit** term (tenure, period) of office

Analyse analysis, research, *(~ der technischen/wirtschaftlichen Realisierbarkeit)* feasibility study

anberaumen to fix (to set) a date, to schedule, *(eine außerordentliche Hauptversammlung für Oktober ~)* to call (to summon) an extraordinary general meeting for October

anbieten to offer, to proffer, *(Anteile zum Rückkauf ~)* to offer (to tender) shares for repurchase, *(im Weg der Daueremission ~)* to offer by way of tap issues, *(im Tenderverfahren ~)* to offer for sale by tender, *(finanzielle Unterstützung ~)* to offer (to proffer) financial assistance, *(zum Verkauf ~)* to offer (to put up) for sale

Anbieter provider (e.g. of financial services)

Anbietungs / ~pflicht duty to tender; **~zeitraum** tender period

anbinden 1. to peg to, to tie to, *(an den US Dollar ~)* to peg (to tie) to the US dollar **2.** to index to, to link to, *(an die Schatzwechselrendite ~)* to index to the Treasury bill yield

Anbindung 1. pegging to, tying to **2.** indexing to, indexation

An-Bord-Konnossement shipped on board bill of lading

An-Bord-Vermerk on board notation

anbringen 1. *(Änderungen ~)* to make changes (amendments) **2.** *(ein Siegel ~)* to affix a seal **3.** *(eine Unterschrift ~)* to append a signature

andauern to persist, to continue, *(~de Bemühungen um eine Sanierung des Unternehmens)* persistent (continued, sustained) efforts to put the company on a sound footing, *(solange der Inflationsdruck andauert)* as long as the inflationary pressure persists, *(die Untersuchungen dauern noch an)* investigations are still in progress

Anderdepot securities escrow account

Anderkonto 1. *(Treuhandkonto)* escrow (trust) account **2.** *(Notar-Anderkonto)* client account

ändern to change, to modify, to alter, to amend

Änderung change, modification, alteration, amendment

Änderungs / ~gesetz Amendment Act; **~kreditvertrag** modified loan agreement; **~kündigung** *(betriebsbedingte~)* redundancy notice with the option to be reemployed on new terms; **~vorbehalt** modification option, reservation of the right to amend

andeuten to indicate, to suggest, to signal, to intimate, *(Zinserhöhungen ~)* to hint at a rise in interest rates

Andeutung hint, indication, suggestion

andienen 1. *(Dokumente ~)* to tender documents **2.** *(zum Verkauf ~)* to offer for sale **3.** *(bei Börsentermingeschäften)* to deliver, to make delivery

Andienung delivery, making delivery, tender, tendering, offering, *(Anspruch auf ~ des Geschäftsgegenstandes/Basiswerts)* right to deliver the underlying instrument, *(~ zur Einsichtnahme)* tendering (submittal, submission) for inspection, *(~ durch Erfüllung)* settlement by delivery

Andienungsabsicht *(Anzeige der ~)* notice of intention to deliver

andienungsfähig eligible for delivery, *(~er Terminkontrakt)* deliverable futures contract

Andienungs / ~gebot → Andienungspflicht; **~monat** delivery (contract) month; **~ort** place of delivery; **~periode** delivery period; **~pflicht** obligation to deliver, duty to tender; **~preis** delivery price

Andienungsrecht 1. right to tender (to offer) **2.** *(bei Börsentermingeschäften)* right to make delivery **3.** *(des Anleihe-*

A

inhabers) put option **4.** *(~ des Leasinggebers)* lessor's put option

Andienungs / ~verfahren delivery process; **~verpflichtung** → Andienungspflicht; **~versprechen** undertaking to deliver (to tender, to sell); **~zeitraum** delivery period

androhen *(die Verwertung einer Sicherheit ~)* to threaten to enforce a security

Androhung *(~ der Verwertung)* warning of enforcement

Aneignung *jur.* taking possession of, appropriation

Aneignungsermächtigung 1. authority to take possession of **2.** *(im Depotgeschäft)* title acquisition authority

aneinanderbinden *(Märkte enger ~)* to tie markets more closely together

anerkannt recognised, *(~e Usance)* established (accepted) practice

anerkennen 1. to recognise, to acknowledge, *(als Eigenkapital ~)* to recognise as equity
2. *(eine Forderung/einen Anspruch ~)* to admit (to allow) a claim
3. *(nicht ~)* to fail to recognise, to refuse to acknowledge, to reject as invalid

Anerkenntnis acknowledgement (of debt), confirmation (of balance)

Anerkenntnisurteil consent judgment

Anerkennung recognition, *(~ finden)* to gain widespread acceptance, *(~ einer Forderung)* acknowledgement (admission, allowance) of a claim, *(~ als Kernkapital)* recognition as core (Tier 1) capital

anerkennungsfähig *(~e liquide Aktiva)* qualifying liquid assets, → erstklassige liquide Aktiva, *(~ als Kernkapital)* eligible for inclusion in Tier 1 Capital, → Kernkapital, *(~e Sicherheiten)* eligible collateral (assets), *(~ als gebundenes Vermögen)* eligible as restricted assets

Anerkennungskriterien eligibility criteria

Anfall → Anfallen

Anfallberechtigter remainderman, party entitled to receive benefits/assets at some point in the future

anfallen 1. *(von Kosten/Zinsen)* to accrue, to accumulate, *(angefallene Stückzinsen)* interest accrued **2.** *(eintreten)* to arise, to occur **3.** *(fällig werden)* to mature, to fall due

Anfallen 1. accrual, accumulation **2.** occurrence **3.** maturing, falling due, *(Zinsen bei ~ vereinnahmen)* to recognise interest in the income statement as it accrues

anfällig vulnerable, *(~ gegenüber Konjunkturschwankungen)* vulnerable (prone, susceptible) to the vagaries of the economy, *(~ gegenüber Zinsbewegungen)* sensitive to interest rate movements

Anfälligkeit vulnerability, susceptibility

anfänglich *(~er Jahreszins)* initial annual percentage rate of interest, *(~e Unmöglichkeit der Leistungserfüllung)* → ursprüngliche Unmöglichkeit

Anfangs / ~belastung initial debt service, initial interest and redemption payments; **~bestand 1.** initial (opening) balance **2.** initial holdings, initial (opening) inventory; **~einschuss** initial margin

Anfangs / ~gewinne *(an der Börse)* early gains, gains on early trading; **~investition** initial capital outlay; **~kapital** initial (starting) capital; **~kurs** opening price; **~laufzeit** initial (original) maturity, *(~ einer Hypothek)* early years of a mortgage

Anfangs / ~stadium initial phase (stage), *(sich noch weitgehend im ~ befinden)* to be still largely in its infancy (in a nascent stage); **~tilgungssatz** initial redemption rate

Anfangs / ~verluste start-up losses, *(Börse)* losses in early trading, early losses; **~verzinsung** initial return, *(einer Anleihe)* initial coupon, **~zahlung**

upfront (initial) payment; ~**zins** initial interest rate, start rate

anfechtbar contestable, disputable, defeasible, *(~er Beschluss)* voidable resolution

Anfechtbarkeit contestability, voidability, defeasibility

anfechten 1. to contest, to challenge, *(einen Beschluss ~)* to contest (to dispute, to question the validity of) a resolution **2.** *(Berufung einlegen)* to appeal against

Anfechtung 1. contestation, challenging, refutation, questioning the validity, → Anfechtungsklage **2.** *(~ von Transaktionen im Insolvenzverfahren)* transaction avoidance in insolvency, insolvency transaction avoidance

Anfechtungs / ~fall transaction avoidance case; ~**frist** time limit for bringing an avoidance action, time limit for challenging the validity

Anfechtungs /~gegner *(im Insolvenzverfahren)* defendant in an avoidance action; ~**gesetz** German Avoidance in Insolvency Act; ~**gründe** grounds for avoidance (contestation)

Anfechtungs / ~klage 1. opposition action (complaint), *(gegen Hauptversammlungs-Beschlüsse)* action for annulment (for avoidance) of decisions taken in a general meeting **2.** *(im Insolvenzverfahren)* avoidance action; ~**kläger** plaintiff filing an avoidance action

Anfechtungs / ~klausel avoidance clause; ~**recht 1.** right of avoidance, right to challenge, *(pl)* avoidance powers **2.** avoidance rules; ~**verfahren** avoidance proceedings; ~**vorschriften** *(der Insolvenzordnung)* (insolvency transaction) avoidance rules

anfordern 1. to demand, to request, to require, to call (for) **2.** *(bestellen)* to order

Anfordern *(auf einfaches ~)* on simple demand

Anforderung 1. demand, request, call, *(neue ~en an die Banken stellen)* to make new demands on (of) the banks, *(die Bank durch einfache ~ des Begünstigten in Anspruch nehmen)* to call upon the bank to pay up under its guarantee upon the beneficiary's simple demand, *(Zahlung auf erste ~ leisten)* to make payment upon first demand (first call), to pay upon the first call (request)
2. *(Erfordernis)* requirement, *(~en an die Bonität des Darlehensnehmers)* requirements with regard to the borrower's financial standing, *(~en an die Eigenkapitalausstattung/zur Eigenkapitalunterlegung)* capital (adequacy) requirements

Anforderungs / ~analyse requirements analysis; ~**datei** request file; ~**katalog** requirements specification; ~**management** requirements management (engineering); ~**profil** requirements profile

Anfrage inquiry, query, *(auf ~ verfügbar)* to be available (up)on request

anfragen to inquire, *(anfragende Bank)* inquiring (calling) bank

anführen 1. to lead, *(die Rangliste ~)* to head the league table, *(das Konsortium ~)* to lead the syndicate **2.** to state, to quote, to refer to

Angabe 1. indication, stating, *(ohne ~ von Gründen beenden)* to terminate without giving reasons **2.** *(Angaben)* information, data, *(nähere ~n)* details, particulars **3.** *(Ausführung/Erklärung)* statement, declaration, representation **4.** *(eines Kurses/Preises)* quotation, indication

Angabepflicht disclosure duty (requirement, obligation), *(angabepflichtig)* required to be disclosed

angeben 1. to indicate, to state, to mention **2.** *(benennen)* to name **3.** *(festlegen)* to fix, to specify **4.** *(einen Kurs/Preis ~)* to quote a rate/price

Angebot 1. offer, offering, quotation, proposal, making an offer **2.** *(i. S. von*

Gebot) bid, tender **3.** *(Marktangebot)* supply **4.** *(Vorschlag)* proposal, proposition

Angebots / ~anfrage request for quotation (tender, proposal); **~bedingungen** terms of the offer, offering terms; **~befristung** *(bei einem Kreditangebot)* (setting a) deadline for acceptance of the loan offer

Angebots / ~bindung *(der Bank)* commitment period, validity period of the bank's offer; **~druck** *(Börse)* selling pressure; **~frist 1.** bidding (tender) period **2.** *(bei einer Emission)* offering period; **~garantie** bid bond, tender guarantee (bond)

angebotsgetrieben *(~e/von Anbietern initiierte Transaktionen)* supply-driven transactions

Angebots / ~kurve supply curve; **~orientierung** supply orientation, *(angebotsorientierte Wirtschaftspolitik)* supply-side economic policy

Angebots / ~palette range of products (services) offered; **~preis** offering price; **~satz** offered quotation, offering rate; **~schwankungen** fluctuations in the supply of …; **~seite** *(auf der ~)* on the supply side

Angebots / ~überhang/~überschüsse 1. *(Börse)* surplus of offers (of offerings, of sell orders) **2.** surplus supply; **~unterlagen** tender documents, specifications; **~verknappung** scarcity of offers; **~wert** contract value; **~zinssatz** interest rate offered

angehen *(die finanziellen Probleme ~)* to address the financial problems

angehören *(einem Konzern ~)* to belong to (to be part of, to be a member of) a group

Angeklagte/r defendant

Angeld earnest money

angemessen *(~e Eigenmittelausstattung)* adequate level of equity funds, *(innerhalb einer ~en Frist)* within a reasonable period of time, *(~er Gegenwert)* fair consideration, *(~e Konditionen)* reasonable terms, *(~e Reaktion)* measured response, *(~e Risikovorsorge treffen)* to provide adequately against lending risks, *(dem Zinsrisiko ~e Absicherungskosten)* hedging cost commensurate with the interest rate risk

Angemessenheit adequacy, appropriateness, reasonableness, *(~ des Eigenkapitals)* capital adequacy

Angemessenheitstest *(i. S. der MiFID)* test of appropriateness, reasonableness (suitability) test

angeschlagen *(~e Gruppe)* floundering group, *(finanziell ~es Unternehmen)* company in poor financial health, financially troubled company, *(stark ~es Unternehmen)* crippled (embattled) company

angesehen *(~er Kunde)* esteemed (respected) customer, customer of good standing

angesichts *(~ des derzeitigen wirtschaftlichen Umfelds)* given the present economic environment, *(~ des gestiegenen Wettbewerbs)* in the face (light) of increased competition

angespannt *(~e Beziehung)* tense relationship, *(~er Geldmarkt)* tight money market, *(~e Liquiditätslage)* strained (tight) liquidity position

Angestellte/r employee, staff

angleichen 1. to harmonise, to align, to bring into line **2.** *(anpassen)* to adjust, to adapt

Angleichung 1. harmonisation, alignment, *(~ der Eigenmittelrichtlinien)* harmonisation (convergence) of capital rules, *(~ der Geldpolitik)* alignment of monetary policies, *(~ an die nationale Gesetzgebung)* bringing into line with domestic laws, *(~ der Zinssätze)* alignment of interest rate levels
2. *(Anpassung)* adjustment, adaptation

angliedern 1. to affiliate, to annex, to incorporate **2.** *(übernehmen)* to take over

Angliederung 1. affiliation, incorporation **2.** take-over

Angliederungsfinanzierung take-over financing

angreifen 1. to attack **2.** *(Rücklagen ~)* to tap the reserves, to dip into (to draw on) the reserves **3.** *(beeinträchtigen, schaden)* to impair, to undermine

Angriff 1. attack **2.** *(die finanziellen Probleme in ~ nehmen)* to tackle (to attend to) the financial problems

Angst / ~indossament liability-free endorsement, endorsement without recourse; **~klausel** escape clause, nonliability clause; **~kurse** panic prices; **~verkäufe** panic selling

anhalten 1. to stop **2.** *(andauern)* to last, to continue, *(ein seit drei Monaten ~der Trend)* a trend which has lasted for three months

anhaltend persistent, *(~ hohes Zinsniveau)* persistently high interest rate level, *(~ lebhafte Nachfrage)* sustained buoyant demand, *(~er Zahlungsverzug)* protracted default in payment

Anhaltspunkt *(~ hinsichtlich der weiteren Zinsentwicklung)* clue with regard to the future trend in interest rates

Anhang 1. annex, enclosure, *(Anhänge und Beilagen)* annexes and supplements **2.** *(zu einem Gesetzentwurf)* rider **3.** *(zu einem Testament)* codicil **4.** *(zu einer Urkunde)* appendix, addendum, rider

Anhangangaben disclosures in the notes to the financial statements

anhängen *(Börse) (Verbot des Anhängens)* ban on after-running, → Vorlaufen

Anhänger *(einer Strategie)* proponent (supporter) of a specific strategy

anhängig *(rechtsanhängig)* pending at law

Anhängigkeit *(~ eines Rechtsstreites)* pendency of a suit

anhäufen to accumulate

anheben 1. *(die Dividende/den Diskontsatz ~)* to increase (to raise, to lift) the dividend **2.** *(Kurse ~)* to mark up prices

Anhebung 1. increase, rise, lifting **2.** marking up

anheimfallen to devolve upon

anheizen *(die Spekulation ~)* to fuel (to fan) speculation, *(die Inflation ~)* to stoke inflation

Anhörung hearing

Ankauf 1. purchase, acquisition, *(~ von Forderungen)* purchase of receivables, forfaiting **2.** *(~ von Dokumenten/dokumentärer Tratten)* negotiation of documents/documentary drafts

ankaufen 1. to purchase, to acquire, *(rediskontfähiges Wechselmaterial ~)* to buy bills eligible for rediscount **2.** *(Dokumente ~)* to negotiate, *(~de Bank)* acquiring (negotiating) bank

Ankaufsermächtigung *(im Dokumentengeschäft)* authority to purchase (to negotiate)

ankaufsfähig *(~e Akzepte)* acceptances eligible for purchase (for rediscount), *(~e Dokumente)* negotiable documents

Ankaufs / ~fähigkeit eligibility for purchase (negotiation); **~fazilität** purchase facility; **~garantie** → Ankaufszusage; **~gesellschaft** acquiring entity; **~kurs 1.** buying price **2.** *(für Devisen)* buying rate

Ankaufsmethode *(bei Übernahmen)* purchase method of accounting □ recognising the difference between the cost of acquisition and the fair value of the net assets as goodwill

Ankaufs / ~satz *(für rediskontfähiges Wechselmaterial, Sorten)* buying rate; **~vereinbarung** purchase agreement; **~verpflichtung** purchase commitment; **~zusage 1.** purchase guarantee, undertaking to buy (to negotiate) **2.** rediscount undertaking

Anker / ~produkt anchor product; **~währung** anchor currency

anknüpfen 1. *(Geschäftsbeziehungen ~)* to establish (to enter into) business relations, *(Verhandlungen ~)* to enter into (to open) negotiations **2.** *(~ an)* to continue, to pick up

Anknüpfung 1. establishment, entering into, opening **2.** continuation

ankommen *(die Emission ist schlecht beim Anlagepublikum angekommen)* the issue has gone down badly with the general investing public

ankoppeln to link to, to tie to, → anbinden

ankreuzen *(bitte das zutreffende Kästchen ~)* please tick the appropriate box

ankündigen 1. to announce, *(öffentlich ~)* to advertise, *(eine Dividende ~)* to announce (to declare) a dividend, *(die Tilgung ~)* to give notice of redemption **2.** *(anzeigen, signalisieren)* to signal, to presage, *(eine Trendwende ~)* to signal the reversal of a trend, *(eine weitere Zinserhöhung ~)* to herald a further rise in interest rates, *(mit Plus ~)* to mark up sharply, → Plus-Ankündigung **3.** *(vorankündigen)* to give (prior) notice

Ankündigung announcement, advertisement, notice

Ankündigungs / ~frist notice period; **~tag** notice day

ankurbeln *(die Konjunktur ~)* to stimulate (to boost) economic activity

Ankurbelungspaket economic stimulus package

Anlage 1. *(zu einem Schreiben)* enclosure **2.** *(im Geldhandel)* placing funds (money)
3. *(~ in Aktien)* equity investment, investment in shares, stock market investment, *(~ im kurz-/langfristigen Laufzeitenbereich)* investment at the short/long end, *(~ überschüssiger Gelder)* investing surplus funds

Anlage / ~art type of investment, investment vehicle; **~ausschuss** investment policy committee; **~auswahl** investment choice, selection of investments; **~bedarf** investment requirements (needs), funds available for investment

Anlageberater investment advisor (counsellor)

Anlageberatung investment advice (counselling), providing investment advice

Anlageberatungs / ~dienstleistungen investment advisory services; **~protokoll** investment advisory (consultation) record; **~vertrag** investment advisory agreement

Anlage / ~bereitschaft propensity (willingness) to invest; **~beschränkungen** investment restrictions; **~betrag** amount invested, amount available for investment

Anlagebewertung 1. *(des Anlagevermögens)* asset valuation **2.** *(von Vermögensanlagen)* valuation of investments **3.** *(bonitätsmäßige Bewertung)* investment rating (appraisal)

Anlagebuch *(eines Kreditinstitutes)* banking book, non-trading book □ a bank's traditional lending activities, *(im ~ gehaltene Derivate)* derivatives held in the banking book, *(Bewertungsverluste im ~)* impairment losses in the banking book, *(Umwidmung von Positionen des Handelsbuches in das ~)* reclassification of exposures from trading into the banking book, *(Zinsänderungsrisiko im ~)* interest rate risk in the banking book, *(Zuordnung zum ~)* allocation to the banking book

Anlagebuch / ~beteiligungen investments held in the banking book; **~gesamtposition** aggregate banking book exposure; **~geschäft** banking book transactions

Anlagebuch / ~großkredit large banking book exposure; **~positionen** *(Absicherung von ~)* hedging banking book positions (exposure); **~risiken** banking book exposures (risks)

Anlage / ~dauer investment period, duration (life) of an investment, holding period, ~**depot** investment portfolio; ~**dispositionen 1.** investing, investment arrangements **2.** (making) investment decisions **3.** *(i.w.S.)* portfolio management

Anlage / ~**empfehlungen** investment recommendations, securities recommended for investment; ~**entscheidungen** investment decisions; ~**erfolg** investment performance; ~**erfolgsprämie** performance fee

Anlage / ~**ergebnis** investment performance (result); ~**erträge** investment income; ~**form 1.** type (form) of investment, investment vehicle **2.** asset class; ~**frist** investment period (term), life of an investment; ~**gesichtspunkte** investment criteria (considerations), *(unter ~n)* from an investment standpoint; ~**grenzprüfung** investment compliance control, monitoring the compliance with investment limits

Anlage / ~**höchstbetrag** maximum investment; ~**horizont** investment horizon; ~**interesse** investors' interest; ~**investitionen** fixed asset investments, fixed capital expenditure, capital equipment spending

Anlage / ~**kapital 1.** funds (capital) available for investment, investment capital **2.** fixed capital, → Anlagevermögen; ~**käufe** long-term investment buying, portfolio buying; ~**klasse** asset class; ~**klima** investment conditions (climate); ~**kontrolle** investment control, monitoring investments; ~**konzept** investment concept (blueprint)

Anlage / ~**mandat** investment mandate; ~**medien** investment vehicles (media); ~**mischung** investment (asset) mix; ~**mittel** funds available for investment; ~**möglichkeiten** investment opportunities, outlet for funds

Anlagen 1. *(Anlagevermögen)* fixed assets, *(Anlagen im Bau)* construction in progress, *(Anlagen, Betriebs-und Geschäftsausstattung)* plant and equipment **2.** *(Vermögensanlagen)* investments, *(mit hohen Kursschwankungen)* high-volatility investments

Anlagen / ~**abgänge** fixed asset sales, asset disposals; ~**abschreibung** depreciation of fixed assets; ~**deckung** ratio of fixed to net assets; ~**erneuerung** asset replacement

Anlagen / ~**finanzierung** asset financing, financing investments in fixed assets; ~**gitter** fixed assets movement schedule; ~**intensität** ratio of fixed assets to total assets; ~**kredit** capital investment loan

Anlagen / ~**-Leasing** plant leasing; ~**rechnung** fixed asset accounting; ~**verwaltung** investment (asset) management; ~**wirtschaft** asset management; ~**zugänge** fixed asset additions

Anlage / ~**nutzung** investment yield; ~**opportunitätskosten** investment opportunity cost(s); ~**palette** range (spectrum) of investment vehicles; ~**papiere** portfolio securities, securities suitable for long-term investments, investment (portfolio) securities

Anlage / ~**plan** formula plan, contractual investment plan, periodic payment plan; ~**politik** investment policy, *(anlagepolitische Überlegungen)* investment policy considerations; ~**produkte** investment products; ~**publikum** investing public

Anlage / ~**rendite** investment return (yield), return on an investment; ~**resultat** investment performance; ~**risiko** investment risk, investment exposure, risk associated with an investment, risk involved in a financial investment

Anlage / ~**schwerpunkt** investment focus, principal investment objective; ~**segment** asset class; ~**sicherheit** investment security; ~**spektrum 1.** range of investments **2.** range of investment products; ~**spiegel** fixed asset movements schedule, statement of changes in fixed assets; ~**spielraum**

scope for investments, investment leeway

Anlage / ~**stock** investment portfolio; ~**streuung** investment spread (diversification), diversification of assets, allocation of assets to various investment vehicles; ~**studie** investment analysis (study)

anlagesuchend *(~es Kapital)* money (capital, funds) seeking investment

Anlage / ~**transparenz** investment transparency; ~**universum** investment universe; ~**verhalten** investment (investing) behaviour, attitudes toward(s) investment; ~**vermittler** investment broker (intermediary); ~**vermittlung** investment intermediation, investment brokerage (broking)

Anlagevermögen 1. fixed assets, long-term assets, non-current assets, *(nicht in Grundbesitz bestehendes Anlagevermögen)* fixed assets other than real estate
2. investment capital, funds (capital) available for investment
3. *(eines Investmentfonds)* fund's assets

Anlage / ~**verordnung für Versicherungen** Investment Regulation for Insurance Undertakings; ~**verzinsung** investment return, return on an investment; ~**vorschlag** investment proposition, proposed investment; ~**vorschriften** investment rules (regulations), investment policy rules

Anlage / ~**wahl** choice (selection) of investments, *(freie ~)* freedom of investment choice; ~**währung** investment currency; ~**werte 1.** *(im Rechnungswesen)* assets **2.** *(Wertpapiere)* investment (portfolio) securities, → Anlagepapiere

Anlage / ~**wertminderung** capital depreciation; ~**wertpapiere 1.** → Anlagepapiere **2.** *(in der Bilanz)* investment securities; ~**wertsteigerung** capital appreciation

Anlage / ~**zeitraum** investment horizon; ~**ziel** investment objective (goal); ~**zielfonds** strategy fund; ~**zinssatz** interest rate on deposits

Anlass cause, reason, motive

Anlaufdividende start-up dividend

anlaufen to start, to begin, *(die Zusammenarbeit ist jetzt angelaufen)* the co-operation is now under way

Anlauf / ~**jahr** first year, *(tilgungsfreie Anlaufjahre)* repayment-free initial years; ~**kosten** start-up expenditure; ~**verluste** start-up losses

anlegen to invest, to commit funds to, *(kurz-/langfristig angelegte Gelder)* funds invested for the short/long term

Anleger investor(s), investing public

Anleger / ~**ängste** investor fears (concerns, anxieties); ~**beratung** investment counselling (advisory); ~**bereitschaft** investors' willingness

Anlegerentschädigung investor compensation

Anlegerentschädigungseinrichtung investor compensation scheme, investor indemnification fund

Anlegerentschädigungsgesetz → Einlagensicherungs- und Anlegerentschädigungsgesetz

Anlegerentschädigungsrichtlinie (EU) Investor Compensation Schemes Directive

anlegergerecht *(~e Beratung)* counselling (advice) fair to the investor, investor-tailored investment advice

Anleger / ~ **gesetz** → Einlagensicherungs- und Anlegerentschädigungsgesetz; ~**richtlinie** (EU) Investor Compensation Schemes Directive; ~**gruppe** group (class) of investors

Anleger / ~**informationen** (key) investor information; ~**interesse** buying (investment) interest, investor interest (appetite), retail interest; ~**kapital** investors' equity (capital)

Anleger / ~**mentalität** investor mentality; ~**nachfrage** demand from investors; ~**publikum** investing public, investors; ~**reaktion** investor response;

~**risiko** risk for investors, investors' risk (exposure)

Anlegerschutz investor protection (safeguards)

Anlegerschutz- und Funktionsverbesserungsgesetz *(Gesetz zur Stärkung des Anlegerschutzes und der Funktionsfähigkeit des Kapitalmarktes)* Investor Protection and Capital Market Improvement Act *(Act to strengthen investor protection and to improve the efficiency of the capital market)*

Anlegerschutzverbesserungsgesetz Investor Protection Improvement Act II, → Anlegerschutz- und Funktionsverbesserungsgesetz

Anlegerschutzvorschriften investor protection rules

Anlegervertrauen investor confidence

Anleihe bond, debenture, *(~ der öffentlichen Hand)* public sector bond, public authority issue, *(~ mit Kapitalschutz)* principal protected note, guarantee-linked note, *(~ mit unbefristeter Laufzeit)* undated bond, *(~ mit/ohne Optionsscheine)* bond cum/without warrants, *(~ mit fester Verzinsung)* fixed income bond, *(~ mit variabler Verzinsung)* floater, floating rate bond

Anleihe / ~**ablösung** bond redemption, repayment of a bond; ~**abschlag** bond discount; ~**abschnitt** tranche of a bond issue; ~**agio** bond premium

anleiheähnlich *(~e Papiere)* bond-like securities, securities similar in nature to bonds

Anleihe / ~**angebot** bond offering; ~**anlagen** bond market investments; ~**anleger** bond market investor; ~**aufschlag** bond premium; ~**ausstattung** bond features, bond terms, terms of a bond issue

Anleihe / ~**bedarf** bond borrowing requirements; ~**bedienung** servicing a bond issue, bond servicing; ~**bedingungen** bond terms (features); ~**begebung** bond issuance, issuing (launching) a bond, bond launch

Anleihe / ~**besicherung** 1. bond collateralisation, providing security for a bond issue 2. *(Sicherheit in Form einer Anleihe)* bond collateral; ~**bestand** bond holdings (inventory); ~**betrag** bond principal, face amount of the bond; ~**bewertung** bond rating, rating a bond issue

Anleihe / ~**depot** bond portfolio; ~**dienst** bond debt service, redemption and coupon service, servicing a bond; ~**disagio** bond discount

Anleihe / ~**emission** bond issue; ~**emissionskurs** bond issuing price; ~**emissionsverfahren** bond issuing procedure; ~**erlös** bond proceeds, funds raised from a bond issue

Anleihe / ~**fälligkeit** bond maturity, maturity (due date) of a bond issue, *(~en)* bonds falling due for repayment; ~**finanzierung** bond financing, financing (fund-raising) through the issue of bonds, raising capital by issuing bonds

Anleihe / ~**forderungen** bonds receivable; ~**führung** lead management of a bond issue; ~**-Future** bond future (e.g. Bund-Future, T-Bond Future)

Anleihe / ~**geschäft** bond underwriting operations; ~**gläubiger** bond creditor, obligee; ~**handel** bond trading; ~**händler** bond trader (dealer)

Anleihe / ~**indexfonds** bond index fund, fixed income exchange-traded fund; ~**inhaber** bondholder, noteholder

Anleihe / ~**kapital** debt capital (raised through the issuance of secured bonds and notes), debenture capital (raised through the sale of unsecured bonds); ~**kassamarkt** bond cash market; ~**käufer** bond buyer, bond market investor

Anleihe / ~**konditionen** bond features (terms); ~**konsolidierung** bond consolidation; ~**konsortium** bond issuing syndicate; ~**konversion**/~**konvertierung** bond

A

conversion; ~**kosten** bond issuing cost(s)

Anleihe / ~**kündigung** calling in a bond, call for redemption, bond redemption notice; ~**kündigungsrecht** *(des Emittenten)* bond call privilege, option (right) to call a bond, *(des Anleiheinhabers)* put option; ~**kurs** bond price (quotation), price quoted for a bond

Anleihe / ~**laufzeit** life (term) of a bond, bond life (maturity); ~**leerstücke** stripped bonds, → Stripping; ~-**Leihe** bond lending, bond lending facility

Anleihe / ~**mantel** corpus; ~**markt** bond market, long-term debt market; ~**modalitäten** bond features (terms), terms of a bond issue

Anleihe / ~**nennwert** bond principal, face amount of a bond; ~**notierungen** bond prices (quotations); ~**option** bond option □ entitles its holder to buy or sell a bond at a particular time and at a specified price (e.g. Bund-Option); ~**optionsschein** bond warrant

Anleihe / ~**platzierung** bond placement, placing (placement of) a bond issue; ~**politik** bond issuing policy; ~**portefeuille** bond portfolio; ~**position** *(~ am Kassamarkt)* bond position in the cash market

Anleihe / ~**registrierung** bond registration, registering a bond issue; ~**rendite** bond yield; ~**rückzahlung** bond redemption (repayment, retirement)

Anleihe / ~**schein** bond certificate; ~**schuld** bond debt, → Anleiheverschuldung; ~**schuldner** bond (loan) debtor, borrower, obligor; ~**sicherheit** bond collateral (security), → Anleihebesicherung

Anleihe-Spread bond spread □ interest rate difference between two bonds reflecting the risk of the two bonds being compared (e.g. government and corporate bonds)

Anleihe / ~**stopp** bond issuing ban (freeze); ~**stripping** bond stripping, → Stripping; ~**stücke** bonds, bond certificates; ~**stückelung** bond denomination; ~**syndizierung** bond syndication, syndication of a bond issue; ~**tender** bond tender

Anleihetilgung bond (loan) redemption, redeeming (paying off) a bond

Anleihetilgungs / ~**fonds** sinking fund, bond amortisation fund; ~**kurs** bond redemption price; ~**leistungen** principal repayments on bonds

Anleihe / ~**treuhänder** bond trustee, trustee of a bond issue; ~**übernahme** bond underwriting, underwriting a bond issue; ~**übernahmevertrag** bond underwriting (purchase) agreement

Anleihe / ~**umlauf** bonds outstanding; ~**umschuldung** refunding a bond issue; ~**unterbringung** bond placement, placing a bond issue

Anleihe / ~**valutierung** start of (the bond's) interest period; ~**verbindlichkeiten** bonds payable; ~**verschuldung** bond indebtedness, total indebtedness represented by outstanding bonds and notes

Anleihe / ~**versicherer** bond insurance company, monoline insurance company, monoline insurer, credit wrap provider, *(pl)* monolines; ~**versicherung** monoline insurance, bond insurance, credit wrap, wrap for a bond issue □ insurance/guarantee that enhances the credit of the issuer

Anleihe / ~**vertrag** bond indenture, bond contract, deed of trust; ~**verzinsung** **1.** bond coupon **2.** paying interest on a bond issue; ~**vorhaben** planned bond issue; ~**wandlung** bond conversion

Anleihe / ~**zeichner** bond subscriber; ~**zeichnungskurs** bond subscription price; ~**zertifikat** bond certificate; ~**zins**/~**zinssatz** coupon, bond interest rate; ~**zinsen** bond interest

anmahnen to demand (to request) payment, *(die fälligen Tilgungsleistungen ~)* to remind the borrower of payments due, to send a reminder note, → mahnen

Anmahnung payment request, reminder, → Mahnung

anmeldbar *(~e Insolvenzforderung)* provable debt

Anmeldefrist declaration period, filing period

anmelden 1. to file, to submit, *(Insolvenz ~)* to file a petition in insolvency, *(eine Insolvenzforderung ~)* to lodge a proof, to file a proof of claim, to prove 2. *(einen Anspruch ~)* to assert (to set up, to establish, to bring forward) a claim 3. *(Interesse ~)* to express interest 4. *(Vorbehalte ~)* to make reservations 5. *(sich ~)* to register, to enrol, to enter one's name

Anmeldung 1. *(Einreichung)* filing, submission, *(~ eines Anspruches)* lodgement (filing, establishment) of a claim, bringing (putting) forward a claim, *(~ der Insolvenz)* filing an insolvency petition, *(~ einer Insolvenzforderung)* lodgement (submission) of a proof, proof in insolvency 2. *(Eintragung)* registration, enrolment

anmerken 1. to note, to annotate 2. to observe, to remark

Anmerkung 1. note, annotation 2. remark, observation

annähern 1. to reconcile, to approximate, to harmonise, *(~ an die internationale Praxis)* to bring into line with international practice 2. *(sich ~)* to come closer to a settlement 3. *(konvergieren)* to converge

annähernd approximate, *(~e Schätzung)* rough estimate

Annäherungs / ~kurs approximate price; **~wert** approximate value

Annahme 1. acceptance, *(~ der Lieferung)* taking delivery, *(~ an Erfüllungs Statt)* acceptance in settlement (discharge) of, *(~ unter Vorbehalt)* conditional (qualified) acceptance 2. *(Billigung)* approval, agreement 3. *(Verabschiedung)* passing, carrying, adoption 4. *(zugrundeliegende Annahmen)* underlying assumptions

Annahme / ~bedingungen terms of acceptance; **~erklärung** acceptance statement, undertaking to accept; **~frist** term for acceptance, → Annahmeschluss; **~gebot** acceptance requirement, duty to accept, mandatory acceptance

Annahme / ~pflicht 1. → Annahmegebot 2. (für → SEPA-Lastschriften) reachability; **~schluss** *(für die Annahme von Buchungs-/Zahlungsaufträgen)* cut-off time, acceptance (submission) deadline; **~stelle** *(bei Emissionen, Umtausch von Optionsscheinen)* receiving agent

Annahme / ~vermerk acceptance, notice of acceptance; **~verweigerung** 1. non-acceptance, refusal to accept 2. failure to take (to accept) delivery 3. *(bei Wechseln)* (dishonouring a bill by) non-acceptance; **~verzug** default in acceptance; **~widerruf** *(gelieferter Waren)* revocation of acceptance; **~zeit** acceptance time (period), → Annahmeschluss

annehmbar acceptable, reasonable, fair, *(für die Bank ~e Sicherheit)* collateral (security) acceptable to the bank, *(zu ~en Konditionen)* on acceptable terms

annehmen 1. *(akzeptieren/einlösen)* to accept, to honour, to meet 2. *(billigen)* to approve 3. *(eine Lieferung im Börsenterminhandel)* to take delivery 4. *(verabschieden)* to pass, to carry, to adopt 6. *(vermuten)* to assume, *(angenommene Ausschüttung)* deemed distribution, *(angenommene Nutzungsdauer)* imputed (expected) useful life, *(angenommene Zinsen)* imputed interest

Annuität annuity, annual interest and redemption payments, annual debt service

Annuitäten / ~anleihe annuity bond, bond repayable in regular (annual)

instalments comprising interest and redeemed capital; ~**darlehen** annuity loan, → Annuitätenhypothek; ~**hypothek** annuity mortgage, mortgage repayable by equal periodic payments of interest and capital

Annuitäten / ~**methode** annuity method; ~**tilgung** redemption by annuities, redemption by equal periodic payments of interest and capital, level debt service; ~**zuschüsse** interest and redemption subsidies

annullierbar cancellable, *(~er Rechtstitel)* defeasible (voidable) title, *(~e Vereinbarung)* rescindable agreement

annullieren 1. to annul, to cancel, to rescind **2.** *(absagen)* to call off **3.** *(für ungültig erklären)* to invalidate, to void, to declare null and void, to nullify **4.** *(widerrufen)* to revoke, to render inoperative

Annullierung 1. annulment, cancellation, rescission **2.** calling off **3.** invalidation, voidance, declaring null and void, nullification **4.** revocation

Annullierungsgebühr cancellation charge (fee)

anordnen 1. *(anweisen)* to order, to instruct, to direct **2.** *(arrangieren)* to arrange

Anordnung 1. order, instruction, directive **2.** arrangement **3.** *(richterliche)* court order (ruling)

anpassen 1. to adjust, to realign, to adapt, to match, *(den Marktgegebenheiten ~)* to realign to market conditions, *(internationalen Standards ~)* to bring into line with international standards
2. *(an den Marktwert ~)* to mark to the market
3. *(sich ~)* to adapt (to adjust) o. s. to, to move into line with

Anpassung 1. adjustment, realignment, adaptation, *(~ des Aktivgeschäfts an neue Eigenkapitalregelungen)* bringing lending operations into line with new capital adequacy requirements, *(~ der Kreditbewertung)* credit value adjustment (CVA), *(~ der Leitkurse)* realignment of central rates, *(~ an Marktgegebenheiten)* adjustment to the prevailing market conditions, *(~ an Marktzinsen)* adjusting (repricing) to market rates
2. *(von Finanzpositionen)* marking financial positions to the market, adjusting the value of financial positions or portfolios to reflect current market values
3. *(~ der Darlehenskonditionen)* adjusting the terms of the loan agreement, renegotiation of the loan terms, recasting the loan agreement, *(~ des Kreditzinssatzes an veränderte Geldmarktbedingungen)* adjusting the loan interest rate to changed conditions in the money market, *(angepasste Tilgungszahlung)* adjusted redemption payment
4. *(Anpassungen)* → Kapitalabzüge

Anpassungs / ~**buchung 1.** adjustment entry (posting) **2.** *(~en zwischen Bilanz und Gewinn-und Verlustrechnung)* reclassification adjustments; ~**darlehen** renegotiated loan; ~**druck** pressure to adjust; ~**fähigkeit** adaptability, *(~ an veränderte Marktbedingungen)* ability to adjust to changed market conditions; ~**geschäft** renegotiated lendings

Anpassungs / ~**klausel** adjustment clause □ clause authorising the lender to adjust the interest rate to a reference rate or to the prevailing market rate; ~**kredit** *(des IWF)* adjustment facility; ~**termin** → Zinsanpassungstermin

anpeilen to aim at, to target

anrechenbar 1. eligible, recognisable, includable, *(~e Eigenmittel)* eligible own funds, *(~ auf die Eigenkapitalbasis)* eligible for inclusion in the capital base, *(als Tier 1 Kapital ~e Kapitalinstrumente)* capital instruments qualifying (recognisable) as Tier 1 capital *(in voller Höhe auf das Limit ~)* fully applicable against the limit, *(für die Ermittlung der Eigenkapitalquote ~e*

Rücklagen) reserves eligible for determination of the capital ratio, *(in voller Höhe als Zahlungsmittel ~)* to be fully eligible as liquid assets, *(~ bis zu 80 %)* recognisable up to 80 %
2. deductible, offsettable, *(auf die Mindestreserve ~e Kassenbestände)* cash in hand deductible from minimum reserve requirements, *(~e Quellensteuer)* offsettable withholding tax, → Fondseingangs-/ausgangsquellensteuer, *(~ auf die Steuerschuld)* deductible from tax payable, offsettable against tax payable, eligible for setting off against the tax bill
3. chargeable, *(~es Einkommen)* taxable income, *(~e Kapitalertragssteuer)* chargeable capital gains tax
4. creditable, *(~e Vorsteuer)* creditable input VAT

Anrechenbarkeit 1. eligibility for inclusion in (e.g. equity), recognisability, *(~ auf das Eigenkapital)* equity eligibility, *(~ von Eigenmitteln)* eligibility of own funds, *(Kriterien für die ~ als Eigenmittel)* own funds eligibility criteria
2. deductibility, option (right) to set off, *(~ auf die Mindestreserveverpflichtung)* eligibility for deduction from reserve requirements, *(steuerliche ~)* eligibility for deduction from taxable income

anrechnen 1. to count (towards), to include, to apply, *(auf die Eigenkapitalbasis ~)* to count towards the capital base, *(Garantien auf die Kreditlinie ~)* to apply guarantees against the credit line, *(auf Grundsatz I ~)* to count towards Principle I of the German Banking Act
2. *(verrechnen)* to set off, to net against, *(auf den ausstehenden Betrag ~)* to set off against the amount outstanding
3. *(in Abzug bringen, gutschreiben)* to deduct, to credit, *(steuerlich ~)* to deduct from the tax load, to set off against tax payable, *(auf die Einkommensteuer ~)* to credit against income tax
4. *(in Rechnung stellen)* to charge, to debit, *(auf die Produktionskosten ~)* to charge against the cost of production

Anrechnung 1. counting towards, applying against, inclusion, *(vollständige ~ auf die gewährte Fazilität)* applying in full against the facility granted, full deduction from the facility amount, *(~ auf die Großkreditgrenze)* counting towards the large exposure limit, *(doppelte ~ von Risiken)* double counting of risks, *(~ auf die Risikoposition)* inclusion in the risk position
2. setting off (netting) against, *(~ auf die geschuldete Einkommensteuer)* setting off against income tax payable, *(~ der im Ausland gezahlten Steuer)* allowing foreign tax as a credit against (setting off foreign tax against) the domestic income tax charge, double taxation relief
3. *(~ auf die Mindestreservepflicht)* deduction from the minimum reserve requirement

Anrechnungsanspruch *(steuerlicher ~)* entitlement to a tax credit

Anrechnungsbetrag 1. capital charge, → Anrechnungssatz, *(~ für Marktrisikopositionen)* capital charge for market risk exposure, *(~ für das operationelle Risiko)* capital charge for operational risk, *(~ für die Rohwarenposition/Währungsgesamtposition)* capital charge for the commodity exposure/aggregate currency exposure
2. eligible amount, → anrechenbar (1)
3. deductible amount, → anrechenbar (2)
4. chargeable/creditable amount, → anrechenbar (3/4)

Anrechnungsentlastung/-erleichterung reduction in capital requirements, reduction in the required capital charge

anrechnungsfähig → anrechenbar

Anrechnungs / ~fähigkeit → Anrechenbarkeit; **~faktor** → Anrechnungssatz; **~grenze 1.** eligibility limit 2. deduction threshold; **~kriterien** eligibility criteria, criteria for

A

inclusion in (for classification as), e.g. →zusätzliches Kernkapital, → Ergänzungskapital

Anrechnungs / ~minderung 1. reduction of the recognisable amount **2.** reduction of the capital charge, *(anrechnungsmindernde Sicherheit)* collateral that reduces the required capital charge; **~pflicht 1.** requirement to include (to recognise) in ..., obligatory inclusion in ... **2.** mandatory capital charge

anrechnungspflichtig 1. subject to inclusion in ... **2.** *(~e Positionen)* positions (exposure) subject to a capital charge

Anrechnungssatz 1. capital charge, → Anrechnungsbetrag **2.** weight, weighting (applied e.g. to risk assets), weighting factor, *(der ~ bei Finanz-Swaps)* the weighting given (assigned) to financial swaps

Anrechnungsverfahren *(steuerliches ~)* imputation system

Anrechnungswert 1. → Anrechnungsbetrag **2.** current value

Anrecht 1. right, title, *(~ auf Gewinnbeteiligung)* entitlement to a share in the profits
2. *(Anspruch)* claim, award, *(seine ~e bei Beendigung des Beschäftigungsverhältnisses behalten)* to retain past service entitlements upon termination of employment

Anrechtsschein 1. *(Zwischenschein)* temporary (provisional, scrip) certificate **2.** *(Bezugsrechtsschein)* warrant

Anrede salutation

anregen 1. to stimulate, *(das Interesse der Anleger ~)* to stimulate investor interest, to whet the appetite of investors **2.** *(vorschlagen)* to suggest, to propose

Anregung 1. stimulation **2.** suggestion, proposal, *(auf ~ von)* at the suggestion of

anreichern to enrich, to amplify, *(die Geldmenge/die Liquidität ~)* to enrich the money stock/the liquidity

Anreicherung enrichment, amplification

Anreicherungsfonds growth fund

Anreiz incentive, stimulus, inducement, *(~ für die Investitionstätigkeit)* investment incentive, *(~ für die Konjunktur)* stimulus to economic activity

anrufen to call, to call upon (in), to appeal to, *(einen Vermittler ~)* to call upon (to have recourse to) a mediator

ansammeln 1. to accumulate, to amass, to gather, *(beträchtliche Gelder ~)* to accumulate (to amass) sizeable funds, *(Rücklagen ~)* to build up reserves **2.** to mount up, *(Kosten haben sich angesammelt)* costs have mounted up **3.** *(horten)* to hoard

Ansammlung accumulation, building up, mounting up

Ansässige *(~ innerhalb/außerhalb des Euro-Währungsgebietes)* euro area residents/non-euro area residents

Ansatz 1. *(in der Bilanz) (a)* recognition *(b)* amount stated (reported), carrying value, *(~ und Bewertung von Finanzinstrumenten)* recognition and measurement of financial instruments, *(~ zum Erfüllungswert)* recognition at the settlement value, *(~ von Krediten)* loan recognition, *(~ von Wertminderungen)* recognition of impairments
2. *(Etatansatz)* budget appropriation, amount budgeted, budget estimate **3.** *(Vorgehensweise)* approach, strategy, *(~ zur Berechnung der Eigenkapitalerfordernisse)* approach for calculating capital requirements

Ansatz / ~inkongruenz/~inkonsistenz accounting mismatch, inconsistency in presentation of the accounts; **~kriterien** recognition criteria; **~pflicht** mandatory recognition

Ansatz / ~stetigkeit consistency of presentation; **~vorschriften** recognition (accounting) rules, reporting (recognition) requirements, → handelsrechtliche Ansatz- und Bewertungsvorschriften; **~wahlrecht** recognition option

anschaffen 1. *(erwerben)* to purchase, to acquire 2. *(liefern) (Wertpapiere ~)* to deliver securities 3. *(überweisen)* to remit, *(Deckung ~)* to provide cover, to remit cover funds

Anschaffung 1. purchase, acquisition 2. delivery, *(~ der effektiven Stücke)* physical delivery, delivery of the actual securities, *(~ im Ausland/im Inland)* delivery abroad/in Germany 3. remittance, *(~ des fehlenden Betrages)* remittance of the amount not yet transferred, *(~ der Deckung)* provision of cover, remitting cover funds, *(~ des Dokumentengegenwertes)* remittance of the proceeds of the documents

Anschaffungs / ~adresse beneficiary, name (party) to which the relevant amount is to be remitted; **~darlehen** personal loan, personal instalment credit; **~geschäfte** *(bei Wertpapieren)* securities transactions for third-party account

Anschaffungskosten cost of acquisition, historical cost, *(bei Wertpapieren)* cost (purchase) price, *(zu den ~ ausgewiesene Beteiligungen)* investments stated at cost, *(zu den ~ abzüglich der kumulierten Abschreibung ausweisen)* to state at cost less accumulated depreciation (impairments)

Anschaffungs / ~kostenprinzip historical cost principle; **~nebenkosten** incidental acquisition cost; **~risiko** risk of non-delivery

Anschaffungs / ~verpflichtung delivery obligation, commitment to deliver; **~vertrag** delivery agreement; **~wert** acquisition value, *(zum ~)* at cost

Anscheins / ~beweis prima facie evidence; **~vollmacht** apparent authority

Anschleichen *(an ein börsennotiertes Unternehmen)* silent stakebuilding

anschließen 1. to link up (to), to connect to (with), *(angeschlossene Marktteilnehmer)* market operators linked to a system 2. *(sich ~)* to join, to follow, *(sich einer Risikoeinschätzung/einem Vorschlag ~)* to concur with a risk appraisal/a proposal, *(sich der Vorgehensweise der anderen Banken ~)* to fall into line with the approach adopted by the other banks

Anschluss 1. connection, linkup, *(~ an den Marktführer finden)* to catch up with the market leader, *(~ an das Zahlungsverkehrssystem)* connectivity to the funds transfer system 2. *(~ an eine Unternehmensgruppe)* affiliation (association) with a group 3. *(im ~ an unser Schreiben vom)* further to (with reference to, referring back to) our letter dd., *(im ~ an die Zinssenkung)* in the wake of (following) the cut in interest rates

Anschluss / ~aufträge *(Börse)* follow-through support, follow-up orders; **~finanzierung** ongoing (follow-up, follow-on) financing; **~finanzierungsrisiko** funding liquidity risk; **~geschäfte** 1. follow-up transactions 2. rollovers

Anschluss / ~insolvenz insolvency proceedings following the failure of composition proceedings; **~kredit** ongoing (follow-up) loan; **~kunde** factoring client, seller of accounts receivable

Anschluss / ~pfändung collateral attachment □ an attachment superadded to an attachment already enforced in respect of the same asset; **~risiko** 1. transformation risk 2. rollover risk □ risk of not being able to roll over an investment or to borrow funds at identical terms upon maturity

Anschluss / ~vertrag follow-on agreement; **~zession** follow-on assignment □ allows the sale of goods pledged as collateral against assignment of the sales proceeds

anschneiden *(ein Thema ~)* to bring up (to raise) an issue

Anschreiben accompanying (covering) letter

Anschwellen *(~der Investitionstätigkeit)* surge of investment activity,

A

(~des Mittelzuflusses) swell in the inflow of funds

ansehen to regard, to view, to consider, *(als negativ für den Aktienmarkt ~)* to perceive as negative for the equity market, *(als sichere Anlage angesehen werden)* to be viewed as a safe haven investment

Ansehen 1. standing, reputation, repute **2.** financial respectability (credit)

ansetzen 1. to state, to report, *(in der Bilanz ~)* to state (to recognise, to report) in the balance sheet, *(im Etat ~)* to budget for, to appropriate, *(nach dem Niederstwertprinzip ~)* to state at the lower of cost or market
2. to value, to estimate at, *(zu hoch ~)* to overstate, to overvalue, *(zu niedrig ~)* to understate, to undervalue, *(den Unternehmenswert mit 5 Mio € ~)* to value the company at € 5m, *(den möglichen Verlust mit ungefähr 1 Mio € ~)* to put the potential loss at about € 1m

AnsFuG → Anlegerschutz- und Funktionsverbesserungsgesetz

Ansinnen *(das ~ des Kunden zurückweisen)* to reject the customer's request (demands)

anspannen to strain, to tighten, *(angespannte Finanzlage)* strained financial situation (position)

Anspannung 1. strain, tension, tightness, *(~ an den Devisenmärkten)* tension in the currency markets, *(~ am Geldmarkt)* constraints (tightness) in the money market, *(~ der Liquiditätslage)* liquidity squeeze, drain on liquidity **2.** tension

Anspannungskoeffizient debt/equity ratio

ansparen 1. to save, to save up **2.** to make regular deposits under a savings scheme

Anspar / ~betrag contractually agreed savings, → Ansparleistung; **~guthaben** amount saved; **~leistung 1.** savings available **2.** *(bei einem* → Bausparvertrag) minimum savings required to qualify for a home loan

Anspar / ~phase saving phase; **~prozess** accumulation of savings; **~plan** savings scheme; **~zeit/~zeitraum** deposit accumulation period, time available for making the required deposits

Ansporn stimulus, incentive, *(~ für den Aktienmarkt)* stimulus to (fillip for) the equity market

Ansprache address, speech, *(eine ~ halten)* to address, to deliver an address

ansprechen 1. *(kontaktieren)* to contact, to approach, *(einen bestimmten Kundenkreis ~)* to appeal to a specific customer segment, to target (to direct) marketing efforts at a specific group of customers
2. *(auf die Stabilisierungsbemühungen ~)* to respond to the stabilisation efforts

Anspruch 1. *(Rechtsanspruch)* claim, right, title, *(einen ~ geltend machen)* to set up (to put in) a claim, *(einen wirtschaftlichen ~ besitzen)* to hold a beneficial interest **2.** *(Berechtigung)* entitlement **3.** *(Erfordernis)* requirement, demand

Anspruch auf *(~ Absonderung im Insolvenzverfahren)* right to separate satisfaction in insolvency proceedings, *(~ vorzugsweise Befriedigung)* right to preference in payment, *(~ Besitzeinräumung)* claim to possession
(~ Eigentumsumschreibung) claim to transfer of title, *(~ Lieferung)* claim to delivery, *(~ Lieferung oder Abnahme von Wertpapieren/des Basiswertes)* right to deliver or take securities/the underlying instrument
(~ Rückgewähr) (a) claim to retransfer (of property) *(b)* claim to refund (of payments made), *(~ Schadenersatz)* claim for compensatory damages, *(~ einen Steuernachlass)* claim to a tax relief, qualifying for a tax relief, *(~ Zahlung des Akkreditivbetrages)* claim to payment of the amount of the credit

Anspruch, in ~ nehmen *(die Bank aus ihrer Garantie ~)* to call upon the bank

under its guarantee, to hold the bank liable under its guarantee, *(den Kapitalmarkt ~)* to tap the capital market, to call on (to access) the capital market *(eine Kreditfazilität ~)* to draw on a credit facility (line), to avail o. s. of a credit facility, *(nicht in Anspruch genommene Fazilität)* undrawn (unused) facility, *(die Fazilität wurde bisher nicht in Anspruch genommen)* the facility has not yet been taken up, *(nicht in Anspruch genommene Rücklagen)* untapped reserves
(voll ~) to borrow to the limit, to make full use of the facility, *(bis zur vereinbarten Höhe ~)* to draw up to the agreed limit, *(erneut ~)* to redraw on the facility, *(in einer Summe ~)* to draw down in one amount, *(Mittel in unterschiedlichen Währungen ~)* to draw down funds in different currencies

Ansprüche 1. claims, entitlements, *(~ Dritter)* third party claims, *(~ gegenüber Dritten)* claims on third parties, *(~ aus einem Kontokorrentverhältnis)* claims from a current account relationship, *(~ aus dem Kreditvertrag)* claims under (rights arising from) the loan agreement, *(~ aus ungerechtfertigter Bereicherung)* claims based on unjust enrichment, *(wirtschaftliche ~)* beneficial interests, *(für alle bestehenden und künftigen ~ der Bank)* for and in consideration of all existing and future claims of the bank 2. requirements, demands, aspirations

Anspruchs / **~abtretung** assignment of a claim; **~ausgleich** claims settlement; **~befriedigung** satisfaction of a claim; **~befristung** setting a time-limit for claims; **~begründung** substantiation of a claim, *(anspruchsbegründende Umstände)* circumstances substantiating the claim

anspruchsberechtigt to be entitled (e. g. to benefits), to qualify, to be eligible for, *(~er Gläubiger)* qualifying creditor

Anspruchs / **~berechtigter** 1. rightful claimant, person entitled to, person qualifying for 2. beneficiary, party to whom the benefits will accrue; **~berechtigung** entitlement to, eligibility for; **~besicherung** providing security for a claim, collateralisation of a claim

Anspruchs / **~entstehung** origination (creation) of a claim, **~erlöschungsklausel** defeasance clause; **~fälligkeit** claim falling due, maturity of a claim, **~gruppe** stakeholders

anspruchshemmend *(~e Einrede)* dilatory plea

Anspruchs / **~konkurrenz** conflicting claims, collision of claims; **~nachweis** proof of a claim; **~sicherung** securing a claim; **~übergang** transfer of rights/of a claim; **~verwirkung** forfeiture of a right; **~verzicht** relinquishment of a claim (right), waiving a claim

anspruchsvoll demanding, *(~e Finanzdienstleistungen)* state-of-the-art (sophisticated) financial services, *(~er Kunde)* discerning client

Anspruchsvoraussetzungen claim requirements

Anstalt agency, corporation, organisation, institution, establishment; ~ **des öffentlichen Rechts** public law entity, agency (corporation) incorporated under public law

Anstalt-in-der-Anstalt Modell institution within the institution model □ allows the transfer of risk positions and non-strategic business lines to public entities, → Finanzmarktstabilisierungs-Fortentwicklungsgesetz

Anstaltshaushalt institutional household

Anstaltslast maintenance obligation □ liability assumed by the public sector owner (government authority or municipality) for the economic viability of a corporation incorporated under public law

anstehen to be (to come) up for, *(~de Entscheidung)* imminent (pending) decision, *(~de Verlängerung des Kre-*

A

ditengagements) upcoming renewal of the loan facility

ansteigen to rise, to increase, to advance, *(~der Trendkanal)* ascending trend channel

Anstellung employment, job, appointment, position, post

Anstellungs / ~bedingungen terms of employment; **~schreiben/~vertrag** letter/contract of employment

ansteuern *(einen Rekordgewinn ~)* to head (to be heading) for a bumper profit

Anstieg increase, rise, advance, *(~ der Aktienkurse auf breiter Front)* advance in equity (stock) prices across the board, *(~ der Zinssätze)* interest rate increase (hike), rise in interest rates

anstreben *(eine deutliche Umsatzsteigerung ~)* to strive for (to aim at) a noticeable increase in sales

anstrengen 1. *(sich ~)* to endeavour **2.** *(eine Klage ~)* to bring an action against, to sue, to file a lawsuit (an action), to institute legal proceedings

Anstrengung 1. effort, drive, *(~en unternehmen)* to put in efforts, *(große ~en unternehmen)* to go to great lengths, to go a long way towards **2.** *(~ einer Klage)* bringing an action against

AnSVG → Anlegerschutzverbesserungsgesetz

Anteil 1. share, portion **2.** *(Beteiligung)* interest, stake, shareholding, participating interest **3.** *(Fondsanteil)* unit, share

Anteile *(~ im Betriebsvermögen)* shares held as business assets, *(~ im Fremdbesitz)* minority interests, *(~ an geschlossenen Fonds)* interests in closed-end funds, *(~ an verbundenen Unternehmen)* investments in affiliated companies, investments (shares) in group undertakings

anteilig *(~er Gewinn/Verlust)* pro rata share of income/loss, *(~er Jahreskupon)* pro rata annual coupon, *(~e Zahlung)* proportional (pro rata) payment, *(~er Zins)* pro rata interest, *(~er Zinsanspruch)* pro rata entitlement to interest, pro rata interest income

Anteils / ~aufbau stakebuilding, → Anschleichen; **~ausgabe** unit (share) offering, offering (issue) of units; **~ausgabekurs** unit (share) offering price

Anteilsbesitz 1. *(von Beteiligungen)* shareholdings, investments (interests) held **2.** *(von Fondsanteilen)* units (shares) held, unitholding, shareholding, *(~ im Handelsbuch)* equity holdings in the trading book

Anteils / ~bestand unitholding, shareholding; **~bewertung 1.** *(~ zu Anschaffungskosten)* valuation of shareholdings (investments) at cost **2.** valuation of units; **~bruchteile** fractional units (shares)

Anteilschein share certificate

Anteilseigner 1. owner, shareholder **2.** *(Gesellschafter)* partner; **~kontrolle** shareholder control; **~risiko** shareholder risk; **~vertreter** shareholder representative

Anteils / ~einheiten *(Zahlungen in ~)* payments in investment fund units; **~finanzierung** private equity finance (loan); **~fungibilität** fungibility of shares (units); **~inhaber** unitholder, shareholder, stakeholder; **~klasse** share class; **~klassenfonds** multi-class fund

anteilsmäßig 1. *adj. (~er Besitz)* proportionate share of ownership, *(~er Besitz am Gesellschaftskapital)* proportionate holding of the company's capital, *(~er Betrag)* pro rata (proportional, proportionate) amount, *(~es Bezugsrecht)* pro rata subscription right, *(~e Gewinnbeteiligung)* proportional share in profits, *(~e Zuteilung)* allotment on a pro rata basis
2. *adv. (~ zu den gehaltenen Aktien ausschütten)* to distribute in proportion to the number of shares held, to pay out pro rata to the number of shares held, *(~ zum bestehenden Be-*

stand) in proportion to existing holdings, *(~ zu dem gezeichneten Betrag)* proportionate to the amount subscribed, *(~ konsolidieren)* to consolidate proportionately

Anteils / **~mehrheit** majority of shares; **~notierung** unit (share) quotation, quotation of unit prices; **~papiere** shares, equities, equity securities; **~platzierung** unit placing, placement of units (shares)

Anteils / **~preis** unit (share) price; **~preisberechnung** establishment (determination) of the unit price; **~recht** **1.** ownership interest **2.** profit participation right; **~register** unit (share) register; **~rückgaben** unit (share) redemptions, units (shares) redeemed

Anteils / **~stückelung** unit (share) denomination; **~übernahme** acquiring an interest (holding, stake); **~umlauf** units (shares) outstanding; **~verkauf** sale of an interest (a shareholding); **~vertrieb** placement of shares

Anteils / **~wertermittlung** valuation of fund shares, → Anteilsbewertung; **~zeichner** subscriber to (for) units, share applicant; **~zeichnung** subscription to (application for) units; **~zertifikat** unit, share certificate

antizipativ *(~e Bewertungseinheiten)* anticipatory valuation units, *(~es Sicherungsgeschäft)* anticipatory hedge

antizyklisches Anlageverhalten countercyclical (anticyclic) investment behaviour, buying and selling against the market trend

antizyklische Investitionen investments against the cyclical trend

antizyklisches Polster *(Basel III)* countercyclical buffer □ will be imposed by national supervisory authorities in the event of excessive credit growth and must be met with common equity (→ hartes Kernkapital) or other fully absorbing form of capital; → Basel III

Antrag **1.** application, request, *(~ auf Börseneinführung)* application for listing, *(~ auf Einberufung einer Hauptversammlung)* application (requisition) to convene a general meeting, *(~ auf Eröffnung des Insolvenzverfahrens)* application for the opening of insolvency proceedings, *(~ auf Eröffnung eines Liquidationsverfahrens)* application for winding-up, *(~ auf Steuerrückerstattung)* refund claim
2. motion, petition, *(~ auf Erlass einer einstweiligen Verfügung)* motion for an interlocutory injunction, *(vor Gericht den ~ stellen)* to petition the Court for the (e.g. winding up of the company)
3. *(Versicherungsantrag)* proposal

Antrags / **~bearbeitung** processing the (loan) application, → Antragsverfahren; ~ **begründung** substantiation of the application, rationale behind the application; ~ **berechtigung** application eligibility, entitlement; **~bewilligung** application acceptance, allowing an application (request)

Antrags / **~entscheidung** decision on the application; **~formular** application form; **~frist** filing term, period for filing an application; **~gegner** opposing (adverse) party, opponent; **~prüfung** application review, examining an application

Antrag / **~steller** **1.** applicant **2.** *(jur.)* claimant, petitioner, requisitionist **3.** *(einer Versicherung)* proposer; **~stellung** filing an application (e. g. for a loan), *(Frist für die ~)* application period

Antrags / **~verfahren** application process; **~voraussetzungen** application requirements

antreten **1.** *(ein Amt ~)* to enter (to take) office **2.** *(den Beweis ~)* to offer in evidence **3.** *(eine Erbschaft ~)* to enter upon (to come into) an inheritance

Antriebskräfte impellent (stimulating, driving) forces

Antritt **1.** assumption of office **2.** production of evidence **3.** accession to an estate, coming into (taking up) an inheritance

anvertrauen to entrust (to commit) to s. o.'s care (custody), *(der Bank Wertgegenstände ~)* to entrust valuables to the bank

anwachsen to accumulate, to build up, to roll up, *(dem Gesellschafter ~)* to accrue to the shareholder, *(angewachsene Pensionsansprüche)* accrued pension rights

Anwachsen accumulation, accrual, buildup, rollup, (~ *des Schuldenberges*) increase in the debt pile, buildup of debt, *(~ von Vermögenswerten)* accretion (accumulation) of assets, *(~ von Zinsen)* accrual of interest

Anwalt lawyer, attorney, counsel, *(~ des Beklagten)* counsel for the defense, attorney for the defendant, defendant's attorney (counsel), *(~ des Klägers)* attorney (counsel) for the plaintiff, plaintiff's attorney (counsel)

Anwalts / ~büro solicitor's office, lawyer's (attorney's) office, law office; **~gebühren/~kosten** attorney's (lawyer's) fees, solicitor's costs; **~zwang** mandatory representation by counsel, requirement to be represented by counsel, compulsory legal representation

Anwartschaft 1. rights accrued, expectancy, contingent right(s), accrued entitlements, *(eine unverfallbare ~ besitzen)* to be fully vested, → Anwartschaftsrecht **2.** *(auf spätere Leistungen)* deferred benefits **3.** *(Rückfallanspruch)* reversionary interest

Anwartschafts / ~-Barwertverfahren projected-unit-credit method; **~frist** vesting period; **~phase** accumulation phase, → Anwartsschaftszeit

Anwartschaftsrecht expectant right, expectancy, right to the future enjoyment of property, *(~ der Bank)* bank's reversionary interest, *(~ auf den Eigentumserwerb)* right to the future acquisition of title, reversionary interest in title

Anwartschaftszeit qualifying period, waiting period

anweisen 1. *(anordnen)* to order, to direct, *(wie durch den Kunden angewiesen)* as instructed by the client **2.** *(überweisen)* to remit (to transfer) funds

Anweisende/r remitter, originator

Anweisung 1. order, instruction, directive **2.** *(Überweisung)* remittance, transfer **3.** *(Zahlungsanweisung)* money order

Anweisungsempfänger remittee, beneficiary

anwendbar *(~es Recht)* applicable (governing) law

anwenden 1. to use, to employ, to make use of **2.** to implement **3.** *(~ auf)* to apply to

Anwender 1. user **2.** factoring client

Anwendung use, employment, implementation, application

Anwendungs / ~anforderungen application (user) requirements; **~bereich** field (scope) of application; **~datum** effective date; **~erlass** implementing rules, *(~ zur Abgabenordnung)* German Fiscal Code Regulations

Anwendungs / ~gebiet field (area) of application; **~komfort** ease of use, user convenience; **~nutzen** user benefits; **~optionen** application (user) options; **~verfahren** method of application, application process

anwesend present, *(persönlich ~e oder vertretene Aktionäre)* shareholders present in person or represented by proxy

Anwesenheit 1. presence **2.** *(Teilnahme)* attendance

Anwesenheitsprotokoll attendance list (sheet), record of attendance

Antwort / ~bestätigung response acknowledgment; **~nachricht** response message; **~zeit** response time

Anzahl 1. number, *(eine große ~)* a large number, a host of, a great many **2.** *(Menge)* quantity

anzahlen to pay on account, to make a deposit

Anzahlung downpayment, payment on account, advance payment, initial instalment, making a deposit

Anzahlungs / ~aval → Anzahlungsgarantie, **~betrag** downpayment, deposit; **~finanzierung** pre-delivery financing; **~garantie** advance payment guarantee, downpayment guarantee

anzapfen *(den Kapitalmarkt ~)* to tap the capital market

Anzeichen indication, indicator, *(~ für eine wirtschaftliche Erholung)* signs of (indications for) an economic recovery, *(erste ~ sprechen für)* early indications point to

Anzeige 1. advertisement, announcement
2. notification, advice, reporting to, *(~ der Andienungsabsicht)* notice of intention to deliver, *(~ der Forderungsabtretung)* notification of assignment, debtor notification, *(~ an den Kreditnehmer)* notification to the borrower, *(jederzeit mit* einer *schriftlichen ~ widerrufen)* to revoke at any time by delivering written notice, *(~ von Verdachtsfällen, i. S. der* → Marktmissbrauchsrichtlinie) suspicious transactions reporting
3. *(von Kursen)* display
4. *(eines Versicherungsfalles)* loss advice

Anzeigegerät display unit

anzeigen 1. to advertise, to announce
2. to notify, to give notice of, to advise of, *(anzeigendes Institut)* reporting institution, *(die Nichteinlösung ~)* to give notice of non-payment (of dishonour), *(einen Protest ~)* to give notice of protest, *(dem Schuldner die Abtretung ~)* to disclose the assignment to the debtor
3. *(Kursinformationen in Euro und USD anzeigen)* to display prices in Euros and in USD

Anzeigenverordnung Reports Regulation, Notification Directive

Anzeigepflicht notification duty, disclosure obligation, reporting requirement, *(~ für Großkredite)* duty to report large loan exposures (to the Financial Supervisory Authority)

anzeigepflichtig *(~e Kreditgeber)* lenders subject to reporting requirements, *(~e Transaktion)* reportable transaction, transaction subject to notification requirements, *(~e Übernahme)* acquisition subject to notification

Anzeige / ~tafel *(Börse)* quotations board; **~verfahren** notification procedure; **~vorschriften** reporting rules, notification rules (provisions)

anziehen 1. to attract, *(Anleger ~)* to attract (to appeal to) investors
2. to firm, to move up (ahead), to advance, *(gegenüber dem Dollar ~)* to firm against the dollar, *(auf breiter Front ~)* to harden across the board, *(gegen Schluss der Börsensitzung ~)* to pick up at the close of trading
3. to tighten, *(die Kreditschraube ~)* to tighten the credit screw

Anziehen *(~ der Aktienkurse)* hardening of (advance in) prices, *(~ der Kreditbremsen/Zinsschraube)* tightening of the credit reins/interest screw

Anziehungskraft *(~ des Dollar)* appeal of the dollar, *(~ einer Anlage)* attraction of an investment

AO → Abgabenordnung

arbeiten to operate, to function, *(mit Gewinn/Verlust ~)* to operate profitably/at a loss, *(mit guten Resultaten ~)* to perform well, *(an einer eigenen Strategie ~)* to work on one's own strategy

Arbeitgeber employer, **~anteil/beitrag** employer's contribution; **~darlehen** employer's loan

Arbeitnehmer employee, *(Plural)* wage and salary earners; **~ansprüche** employee entitlements; **~anteil/beitrag** employee's contribution; **~vertreter** *(im Aufsichtsrat)* staff representative(s)

A

Arbeits / ~ablauf workflow; **~ablaufplan** process chart; **~anweisungen** procedure manual; **~beschaffung** job creation; **~bewertung** job evaluation (rating); **~direktor** employee relations director; **~einkommen** earned income; **~gemeinschaft** group, consortium, association

Arbeits / ~leistung job performance; **~liquidität** operating liquidity; **~marktlage** employment situation, situation in (on) the labour market; **~mobilität** job (labour) mobility; **~papier** position (working) paper

Arbeitsplatz job, position, employment; **~beschreibung** job description; **~profil** job profile; **~verluste** job losses; **~wechsel** change of employment, job change, *(intern, i. S. einer Rotation)* job rotation

Arbeits / ~tageregelung business day convention;**~teilung 1.** division of labour **2.** division of responsibilities; **~vertrag** contract of employment (service); **~wertanalyse** earned value analysis ; **~zeit** working hours; **~zufriedenheit** job satisfaction

Arbitrage 1. *(an den Finanzmärkten)* arbitrage **2.** *(Schiedsverfahren)* arbitration

Arbitrage / ~geschäfte arbitrage transactions, *(~ zwischen Kassa- und Terminmärkten)* arbitraging between spot and forward markets; **~gewinn** arbitrage profit; **~instrumente** arbitrage tools; **~klausel** arbitration clause; **~möglichkeiten** arbitrage opportunities

Arbitrageur arbitrageur, arbitrager

Arbitrage / ~verkäufe arbitrage (arbitrage-induced) selling; **~werte** arbitrage stocks

arbitrierbar usable (eligible) for an arbitrage transaction

Archiv 1. archives **2.** *(Räume)* archives, record office, filing room (cabinet)

archivieren to file, to archive

arglistig *(~e Täuschung)* fraudulent misrepresentation, *(~ handeln)* to act maliciously

Argument 1. argument, reason, criterion **2.** argument, dispute, controversy

Argumentation (line of) reasoning

argumentieren to reason

Arrangeur *(bei Kreditsyndizierungen, Emissionen)* arranger, arranging bank

arrangieren to arrange, to put together, to package

Arrangierung arrangement, putting together, packaging

Arrangierungsprovision arrangement fee (commission)

Arrest distraint, attachment, freezing, seizing property as security

Arrest / ~anordnung freezing (attachment) order, distraint order; **~antrag** petition for a freezing order; **~aufhebung** lifting a distraint; **~beklagter** defendant against whom a freezing order is sought; **~beschluss** freezing order, → Arrestanordnung

Arrest / ~hypothek compulsory mortgage, mortgage entered to secure satisfaction of a claim; **~verfahren** freezing order proceedings, *(steuerliches ~)* distraining (seizure of) property to enforce payment of taxes; **~vollziehung** distraint proceedings

arrondieren to round off (out)

Arrondierungskäufe rounding off buying

Arrosierung coupon increase, raising the coupon of outstanding bonds

Art 1. *(Beschaffenheit)* nature, character **2.** *(Gattung)* type, class, category **3.** *(Methode)* method, manner, mode

Artikel 1. *(bei Gesetzen)* paragraph, section **2.** *(bei Verträgen)* article

Artvollmacht → Gattungsvollmacht

ARUG → Aktionärsrichtlinie

AS-Fonds → Altersvorsorge-Sondervermögen

Assekuranztitel insurance stock

Assistenz support staff

AstG → Außensteuergesetz

Asymmetrie *(~ im Fälligkeitsprofil)* maturity mismatch

asymmetrisch *(~es Risiko)* asymmetric risk exposure □ wide gap between gains and losses, e.g. when gains from uptrends are significantly different from losses in downtrends, *(~e Verschlüsselungsverfahren)* asymmetric cryptography □ using two different keys (public and private keys), *(~e Volatiltät)* asymmetric volatility □ when volatility is higher in upmarkets than in downmarkets

Atempause *(der Aktienmarkt legte eine ~ ein)* the stock market took a breather

Attentismus *(~ am Kapitalmarkt)* wait-and-see attitude in the capital market

attrahieren *(Kapital aus dem Ausland ~)* to attract foreign capital

attraktiv attractive, alluring, appealing, *(für den Kreditnehmer ~e Konditionen)* terms attractive to the borrower

Attraktivität attractiveness, attraction, allure, appeal, *(~ für Anleger)* attractiveness (attraction) to investors, *(an ~ gewinnen/verlieren)* to gain/to lose allure (appeal)

Attraktivitätssteigerung increasing the attractiveness, enhancing the appeal (e. g. of stock)

atypische stille Gesellschaft non-typical silent partnership □ partnership in which the dormant partner takes a co-entrepreneurial role

Auditierung auditing

Auf *(das ~ und Ab am Aktienmarkt)* ups and downs in the equity market, roller-coaster on the stock market

aufaddieren *(Positionen ~)* to add up positions

Aufbau 1. construction **2.** *(Wiederaufbau)* reconstruction **3.** *(~ von Positionen)* opening (initiating) positions, entering into positions **4.** *(Struktur)* structure, setup **5.** *(~ enger Kundenbeziehungen)* building strong customer relationships, relationship building

Aufbaudarlehen reconstruction (redevelopment) loan

aufbauen 1. to construct, to build **2.** *(eine Fremdwährungsposition ~)* to enter into (to open) a currency position, *(eine Kauf-/Verkaufsposition ~)* to enter into a long/short position, to go long/short **4.** *(~ auf)* to build on

Aufbau / ~finanzierung development (reconstruction) financing; **~programm** development (reconstruction) scheme

aufbereiten 1. *(Daten ~)* to prepare (to edit) data **2.** to process

Aufbereitung preparation, editing, processing

aufbessern 1. to improve, to enhance, to increase **2.** *(i. S. von schönen)* to patch up

Aufbesserung improvement, enhancement, increase, *(~ der Portefeuillerendite)* enhancement of the portfolio yield

aufbewahren 1. to preserve, to retain, *(die Unterlagen für zwei Jahre ~)* to preserve the records for two years **2.** *(hinterlegen)* to deposit, to place in safe custody **3.** *(verwahren)* to hold in safe custody (in safekeeping)

Aufbewahrung 1. preservation, retention, *(~ der Kontounterlagen für einen Zeitraum von drei Jahren)* preservation of the account records for a period of three years, *(~ von Kundendaten)* storage of customer data (files) **2.** holding in safe custody, *(~ der Kreditkarte)* safekeeping of the credit card, *(~ des Sicherungsgegenstandes bei der Bank)* depositing the collateral with the bank

Aufbewahrungs / ~frist 1. retention (preservation) period **2.** safekeeping period; **~gegenstand** item in safe custody; **~kosten** custodian (safe custody) fees

A

Aufbewahrungs / ~ort 1. custody (safekeeping) location **2.** depository; **~pflicht** compulsory safe custody; **~vertrag** safe custody (safekeeping) agreement

aufbieten to muster, to summon, to gather, *(seine gesamte Finanzkraft ~)* to muster all its financial power (strength)

aufblähen to inflate, *(aufgeblähte Bilanz)* inflated (bloated) balance sheet

Aufblähung inflation, bubble, *(~ der Geldbestände)* inflation of money stock, *(~ der Lagerbestände)* bloating of stock levels, *(spekulative ~ der Immobilienpreise)* speculative bubble in property prices

aufblühen to prosper, to thrive, to flourish

aufbrauchen *(die verfügbaren Rücklagen ~)* to exhaust (to use up, to consume) the available reserves

aufbringen to raise, to obtain, to generate, to procure, *(die erforderlichen Finanzierungsmittel ~)* to raise the necessary finance

Aufbringung raising, obtaining, generation, procurement, *(~ des Kapitaldienstes)* meeting debt service requirements, raising (procuring) the funds required to service the debt

aufdecken 1. *(Unregelmäßigkeiten ~)* to uncover irregularities, *(Verluste ~)* to reveal losses **2.** *(offenlegen)* to disclose, *(aufgedeckte stille Reserven)* disclosed (hidden) reserves

Aufdeckung uncovering, revelation, *(~ stiller Reserven)* disclosure (release) of hidden reserves, asset step-up

aufeinanderfolgend consecutive, successive, *(Rückzahlung in zwölf ~en Raten)* repayment in twelve successive instalments

auferlegen to impose, to dictate, to prescribe, *(Abgaben/Steuern ~)* to impose (to levy) duties/taxes, *(die Verfahrenskosten ~)* to order to pay the costs of the proceedings, to sentence to the cost

Auferlegung *(~ einer gesetzlichen Obergrenze)* imposition (enforcement) of a statutory limit

auffächern *(die Refinanzierungsbasis ~)* to spread (to diversify) the funding base

Auffächerung spreading, diversification

auffangen 1. *(Kursverluste ~)* to cushion (to absorb) price losses **2.** *(ein Unternehmen vor dem Zusammenbruch retten)* to rescue (to bail out) a company

Auffangen rescue, bailout

Auffang / ~gesellschaft rescue company, receiving company; **~kredit** rescue (bail-out) facility; **~linie 1.** *(Deckungslinie in Verbindung mit der Emission von Schuldtiteln)* support facility, backup facility (line) **2.** → Auffangkredit

Auffassung 1. *(Ansicht)* view, opinion **2.** *(Auslegung)* interpretation, construction **3.** *(Konzeption)* conception **4.** *(Verständnis)* understanding, comprehension

aufflackern *(~de Währungsspekulation)* flaring-up currency speculation

auffordern 1. to call, to request, to ask, *(zu zusätzlichen Einlagen ~)* to call for further contributions, to call upon the shareholders (partners) to pay additional funds, *(den Garantiegeber zur Zahlung ~)* to call upon the guarantor to pay up under his/her guarantee, *(die Konsortialbanken zur Übernahme von Titeln ~)* to call on the underwriting banks to take up securities
2. *(im Rahmen einer Ausschreibung)* to invite tenders for
3. *(jur.)* to summon

Aufforderung 1. request, call, *(~ zur Abgabe von Zinsgeboten)* call to submit interest quotes (bids), *(~ zur Einzahlung auf Aktien)* call on shareholders, call for funds, *(~ an den Kreditnehmer*

zur Stellung zusätzlicher Sicherheiten) call on (requesting) the borrower to furnish additional collateral, *(~ zur Stellungnahme)* invitation to comment, *(~ zur Zahlung)* payment request, *(gerichtliche ~)* summons to pay, *(~ zur Zeichnung)* invitation to subscribe
2. *(im Rahmen einer Ausschreibung)* invitation for tenders, invitation to tender **3.** *(jur.)* summoning, summons

auffrisieren *(die Bilanz ~)* to patch up (to embellish) the balance sheet

auffüllen to replenish, *(Lagerbestände ~)* to restock, to replenish the inventory, *(den Rücklagenfonds ~)* to replenish (to pour fresh funds into) the reserve fund

Auffüllkredit replenishment loan

Auffüllung replenishment, restocking

Aufgabe 1. *(Beleg)* advice, voucher, ticket
2. *(Benennung der Gegenpartei)* naming the counterparty (contracting) party, advising as to the identity of the counterparty, → Aufgabegeschäft
3. *(Funktion, Tätigkeit)* task, function, responsibility, duty, assignment
4. *(Verzicht)* abandonment, relinquishment, renunciation, waiver, surrender, *(~ eines Amtes)* resignation from office, *(~ eines Anspruchs)* relinquishment of a right, renunciation (abandonment) of a claim, surrender of (dropping) a claim, *(~ eines Rechtstitels)* surrender (waiver) of title, *(~ eines Sicherungsrechtes)* relinquishment of a security interest

Aufgabegeschäfte name-to-follow deals (transactions) □ transactions where the designation of the counterparty is deferred for a specified period

Aufgabemakler unofficial broker dealing for own account □ name and address of his counterparty must be released within the following 24 hours

Aufgaben / ~analyse job analysis; **~bereich/~gebiet** province, range (scope) of duties, area of responsibility, scope of duties, field of activities, remit; **~bereicherung** job enrichment; **~erweiterung** expansion of responsibilities, job enlargement; **~folge** activity sequence

Aufgaben / ~ stellung 1. job description, remit, performance requirement **2.** objective; **~teilung/~trennung** division of responsibilities, segregation of duties □ e.g. of front and back office duties; **~verteilung** allocation of duties (responsibilities); **~zuordnung** task allocation, assignment of responsibilities (jobs)

Aufgabeschließung closing a name-to-follow deal

Aufgabetag ticket day

aufgeben 1. to surrender, *(einen Anspruch ~)* to abandon (to relinquish, to waive, to give up, to drop) a claim, *(die Kontrolle über ein Unternehmen ~)* to relinquish control over a company, *(die vertraglichen Rechte ~)* to surrender the contractual rights
2. to resign, *(ein Amt ~)* to resign from office, *(ein Geschäft ~)* to retire from business, *(aufgegebene Geschäftsbereiche)* discontinued operations
3. *(die Fälligkeit ~)* to notify of the maturity, *(dem Kunden die Einzelheiten des Abschlusses ~)* to notify the customer of the details of the trade
4. *(die Gegenpartei benennen)* to name the counterparty

Aufgebot public notice (notification), public notice to present claims within a specified time period

Aufgebotsverfahren *(zur Kraftloserklärung von vernichteten oder abhanden gekommenen Wertpapieren)* public notification procedure, invalidation procedure for securities lost or stolen

aufgehen 1. *(stimmen)* to tally **2.** to merge, *(in der übernehmenden Gesellschaft ~)* to be absorbed by (to be merged with) the transferee company **3.** *(die Spekulation geht auf)* the gamble (speculation) is paying off **4.** *(voll-*

ständig in der Konsolidierung ~) to be fully eliminated in consolidation

Aufgeld 1. premium, markup, surcharge, *(~ auf das ausgegebene Kapital)* premium on capital stock issued, *(~ aus der Kapitalerhöhung)* premium from the capital increase, *(~ auf den Kassakurs)* premium over spot, *(~ für vorzeitige Tilgung)* premium on early redemption
2. *(auf einen Zinssatz)* spread, margin

aufgeschlossen *(sich gegenüber Wünschen des Kreditnehmers ~ zeigen)* to prove accommodating to the borrower's requests

aufgliedern to break down, to classify, to subdivide, to categorise

Aufgliederung 1. breakdown, classification, categorisation, *(~ nach Einkommensgruppen/nach Regionen)* breakdown according to income brackets/by regions, *(~ der Konten)* classification of accounts, *(~ der Kosten)* breakdown of costs
2. division, disaggregation, split, splitting

aufgreifen *(die Frage einer Kreditverlängerung ~)* to take up the matter of extending the loan, → anschneiden

aufhalten to hold up, to halt, *(den Liquiditätsabfluss ~)* to halt (to stop, to check) the liquidity drain, *(den Rückgang ~)* to stem the decline, *(eine Übereinkunft ~)* to hold up an agreement

aufheben 1. *(annullieren)* to annul, to cancel, to rescind, to void, *(ein Gesetz ~)* to abolish (to repeal) a law, *(ein Schuldverhältnis ~)* to extinguish an obligation, *(einen Vertrag ~)* to rescind (to repudiate) a contract
2. *(beenden) (das Arbeitsverhältnis ~)* to terminate the contract of employment, *(das Insolvenzverfahren ~)* to close insolvency proceedings
3. *(freigeben)* to release, to lift, to remove, *(die Schecksperre ~)* to lift the stop payment order on a cheque
4. *(umstoßen/widerrufen)* to overturn, to quash, *(ein Urteil ~)* to overrule (to supersede, to reverse, to set aside) a judgement, *(in der Berufung ~)* to reverse on appeal, *(eine Ermächtigung ~)* to revoke an authority
5. *(sich gegenseitig ~)* to cancel each other out, to net out

Aufhebung 1. annulment, cancellation, rescission, repeal, abolishment, *(~ des Vertragsverhältnisses)* repudiation of contract
2. *(~ des Arbeitsverhältnisses)* termination of employment, *(~ des Insolvenzverfahrens)* closure of insolvency proceedings
3. release, removal, lifting, *(~ eines Pfandrechtes)* discharge of lien, removal of a lien, *(~ der Positionsbegrenzung)* lifting the position limit
4. *(~ der Entscheidung der unteren Instanz)* quashing the lower court ruling, revocation, *(~ des Schriftformerfordernisses)* revocation of the written form requirement, *(~ der Vollmacht)* revocation of the power of attorney (authority)
5. *(~ der Preisbindung)* decontrol of prices

Aufhebungs / ~anspruch entitlement to rescission; **~antrag 1.** request for annulment **2.** claim for rescission of contract; **~beschluss** *(bezüglich eines Insolvenzverfahrens)* closure order

Aufhebungs / ~grund cause for annulment (rescission), reason for termination; **~klage** rescissory action, action for rescission, action seeking the rescission of the contract of sale; **~klausel** cancellation (rescinding, termination) clause; **~recht** right of (entitlement to) rescission

Aufhebungs / ~urteil order of annulment; **~vereinbarung/~vertrag 1.** rescission agreement **2.** *(zur Beendigung eines Arbeitsverhältnisses)* severance (termination) agreement; **~verfahren** rescission proceedings, proceedings for annulment; **~zahlung 1.** break fee **2.** → Abfindungszahlung

aufhellen *(die Stimmung am Aktienmarkt beginnt sich aufzuhellen)* the mood is brightening in the equity market, the picture for equities is brightening

aufholen *(gegenüber den anderen Finanzplätzen ~)* to catch up with the other financial centres, *(die Umsatzverluste ~)* to make up for lost turnover

Aufkauf acquisition, take-over, buying up, *(Aufkäufe am Markt)* buying in the market

aufkaufen *(Aktien an der Börse ~)* to buy up shares on the stock exchange, *(ein Unternehmen ~)* to acquire (to take over) a company

Aufkäufer *(an der Börse)* buyer, speculative buyer (operator), raider

aufkeimen *(~de Zinshoffnungen)* sprouting hopes for a cut in interest rates

aufklären **1.** *(eine Angelegenheit ~)* to clarify (to clear up) a matter **2.** *(informieren, offenlegen)* to inform, to explain, to disclose

Aufklärung **1.** clarification, clearing up **2.** information, explanation, *(~ hinsichtlich der Anlagerisiken)* risk disclosure

Aufklärungspflicht **1.** duty to explain (to disclose) **2.** information (disclosure) requirements

aufkommen **1.** to pay, to meet, *(für die Kosten ~)* to pay (to bear, to meet) the cost **2.** to assume, *(für einen Verlust ~)* to assume the liability for a loss, to be responsible for (to answer for) a loss, *(nicht für den Verlust ~)* to assume no liability (to disclaim any responsibility) for the loss
3. *(am Markt ~de Innovationen)* innovations springing up (appearing, coming into fashion) in the market

Aufkommen **1.** paying, meeting **2.** assuming, assumption of **3.** *(Einnahmen)* revenue, amount raised

aufkommensneutral *(~e Änderungen)* revenue-neutral changes (e.g. in the tax system)

Aufkommensneutralität revenue neutrality

aufkündigen to terminate, to give notice of termination, to cancel, to repudiate, to call in, to discontinue

Aufkündigung termination, cancellation, calling in, discontinuance, repudiation, *(~ der Kontoverbindung)* termination of the account (business) relationship, *(~ einer Kreditlinie)* calling in (discontinuance of) a credit line, *(~ eines Vertrages)* repudiation (termination) of contract

aufladbar *(~e Karte)* (re)loadable card

Auflagen **1.** requirements, covenants, *(Genehmigung mit ~)* authorisation with strings attached, *(~ für den Darlehens-/Kreditnehmer)* loan covenants, borrowing covenants, restrictive loan provisions, *(Kreditverträge mit leicht einzuhaltenden ~)* covenant-light (co-lite) loan agreements, *(einen Kreditvertrag mit ~ versehen)* to put conditions on a credit accord, to stipulate loan covenants, *(mit hohen ~ versehen sein)* to be burdened with onerous clauses
2. restrictions, *(~ bei Gewinnausschüttungen)* restrictions (constraints) on earnings distributions

auflassen *(Grundbesitz ~)* to convey real property

Auflassung **1.** (notarised) property conveyance, deed of transfer □ agreement on the transfer of title (on the change in ownership)
2. *(~ über USD 3 Mrd. für den Internationalen Währungsfonds)* central bank governors' agreement to a USD 3bn loan for the International Monetary Fund

Auflassungsvormerkung priority notice □ entry of the conveyance agreement in the land register; designed to secure the claim to transfer of title; prevents the seller from mortgaging or selling the property to another person

auflaufen 1. to accrue, *(Rückzahlung des Kapitals zusammen mit den aufgelaufenen Zinsen)* repayment of capital together with interest accrued
2. to accumulate, *(aufgelaufener Gewinn)* accumulated profit, *(zusätzlich aller aufgelaufenen Erträge)* plus all accumulated income, *(Dividenden ~ lassen)* to allow dividends to accumulate

Auflaufen accrual, accumulation

aufleben *(Zinshoffnungen ~ lassen)* to revive hopes for an interest rate cut

auflegen to launch, to float, to set up, *(eine Anleihe ~)* to launch a bond issue, *(ein CP-Programm ~)* to arrange a commercial paper programme, *(einen Investmentfonds ~)* to launch (to set up, to establish) a unit trust, *(im Wege der Privatplatzierung ~)* to float as private placement, *(zur Zeichnung ~)* to offer for subscription, to invite subscriptions for

aufliegen *(zur Einsichtnahme ~)* to be available (open) for inspection, *(zur Zeichnung ~de Titel)* bonds available (offered) for subscription

auflisten to specify, to detail, to itemise, to enumerate

auflockern *(den Inlandsgeldmarkt/die Kreditkonditionen ~)* to ease (to relax) the conditions in the domestic money market/the loan terms

auflösen 1. to cancel, to annul, *(einen Vertrag ~)* to terminate (to rescind) an agreement
2. to write back, to reverse, *(zu Gunsten der Gewinn- und Verlustrechnung ~)* to release and credit to income, to reverse to the profit and loss account, *(Rückstellungen ~)* to write back (to reverse, to release) provisions, *(Wertberichtigungen ~)* to reverse loss allowances, *(zeitanteilig ~)* to write back on a pro rata basis
3. to liquidate, *(einen Handelsbestand ~)* to liquidate (to unwind) a trading portfolio, to liquidate an inventory, *(eine Position ~)* to liquidate (to square, to close) a position
4. dissolve, *(eine Gesellschaft ~)* to dissolve (to wind up) a company, *(eine Unternehmenseinheit ~)* to dissolve (to disband) a corporate unit
5. *(sich ~)* to dissolve, to disintegrate

auflösend *(~e Bestimmung)* resolutory condition, *(~ bedingte Forderungen)* claims subject to a resolutory condition

Auflösung 1. cancellation, annulment, *(~ des Vertragsverhältnisses)* rescission (repudiation) of contract
2. release, reversal, writing back, *(~ temporärer Differenzen)* reversal of temporary differences, *(~ von Rückstellungen im Kreditgeschäft/der Risikovorsorge)* release of loan loss provisions, *(~ der Neubewertungsrücklage)* release of the revaluation reserve, *(~ von aktivierten Vorteilen)* writing back capitalised advantages, *(~ von Wertberichtigungen)* reversal of loss allowances (of value adjustments)
3. liquidation, *(~ von Positionen)* liquidating positions, position closeouts, *(~ von Positionen zum Monatsende)* end-of-month position squaring, *(~ einer Swap-Position)* unwinding a swap position, swap unwinding, *(~von Wertpapierleihegeschäften)* winding up (reversal) of securities lending deals
4. dissolution, *(~ eines Unternehmens durch die Gesellschafter)* dissolution (liquidation, winding up) of a company by the partners (shareholders)
5. *(~ eines Marktes)* disintegration of a market
6. *(~ von Kostenabgrenzungen)* amortising deferred charges

Auflösungs / ~antrag 1. petition for dissolution (winding-up) **2.** request to repudiate a contract, rescission request;**~beschluss** winding-up resolution; **~bilanz** liquidation (winding-up) accounts

Auflösungs / ~klage rescission action, action to enforce rescission (repudiation) of contract; ~**klausel** rescission clause; ~**vertrag** → Aufhebungsvertrag; ~**vorbehalt** reservation of the right to rescind (to repudiate)

aufmerksam *adj. (zuvorkommend)* attentive, *(wachsam)* heedful, watchful, *adv.* attentively, *(~ beobachten)* to watch closely, to keep a close watch on

Aufmerksamkeit 1. attentiveness **2.** attention, heed, *(besondere ~ beimessen)* to pay special attention to, to focus attention on, *(die ~ der Anleger gewinnen)* to capture the attention of investors, *(Marktentwicklungen wenig ~ schenken)* to pay little heed to market developments

Aufnahme 1. *(Akzeptanz)* acceptance, *(~ einer Emission am Markt)* market acceptance of an issue, reception of an issue in the market
2. *(Beginn, Eröffnung)* beginning, starting, opening, *(~ eines Verfahrens) (a)* opening of proceedings *(b)* implementation of a process, *(~ von Verhandlungen)* entering into (opening of) negotiations
3. *(Bestandsaufnahme) (~ von Währungs-/Wertpapierbeständem)* position-taking, *(~ von Lagerbeständen)* taking stock, inventory taking
4. *(Einbeziehung, Eintrag)* inclusion, incorporation, *(~ in das Handelsbuch)* inclusion in the trading book, *(~ einer Klausel)* inclusion of a clause, *(~ in ein Register)* enrolment (recording) in a register, *(~ in die Tagesordnung)* inclusion in (putting on) the agenda
5. *(~ akkreditivkonformer Dokumente)* taking up documents that are in accordance with the terms and conditions of the documentary credit
6. *(~ eines Darlehens)* raising a loan, taking out a loan, *(~ einer Hypothek)* taking out a mortgage, mortgage borrowing, *(~ von Kreditmitteln am Markt)* raising loan funds in the market, borrowings in the market, *(~ zusätzlicher Mittel)* raising fresh capital (additional funds), fresh cash call, additional call on shareholders, *(~ von Tagesgeld)* overnight borrowing, buying (borrowing) overnight money
7. *(~ von Liquiditätsüberschüssen)* absorption of excess liquidity
8. *(~ in den amtlichen Handel)* admission to official trading

Aufnahmebedingungen terms of admission (of entry), membership terms

aufnahmebereit *(~ gegenüber neuen Ideen)* receptive to new ideas, *(~e Anleger)* investors willing to take up securities

Aufnahmebereitschaft receptiveness

aufnahmefähig *(~e Dokumente)* acceptable documents, *(~er Markt)* receptive (ready) market

Aufnahme / ~**fähigkeit** receptivity, *(~ des Marktes)* absorptive (absorbing) capacity of the market; ~**gebühr** membership fee; ~**land** host country, recipient state; ~**saldo** *(bei Wertpapieren)* net buying

Aufnahme / ~**staat** *(Aufsichtsbehörde des ~es)* host country supervisory authority; ~**verpflichtung** obligation to take up the documents (the underlying instrument); ~**verweigerung** *(~ der Dokumente)* refusal to take up the documents; ~**zusage** *(im Dokumentengeschäft)* undertaking to take up documents

aufnehmen 1. to receive, to accept, *(positiv am Kapitalmarkt aufgenommen werden)* to be well received in the capital market, *(aufnehmendes Konto)* receiving account
2. to open, to start (to begin) with, *(Geschäftsbeziehungen ~)* to open (to enter into, to establish) business relations
3. to include, *(in den Vertrag ~)* to incorporate into (to include in) the agreement
4. to take up, *(die eingereichten Dokumente ~)* to take up the documents presented under the documentary credit, *(nicht platzierte Titel ~)* to take up unplaced securities
5. to honour, *(Dispositionen ~)* to honour drawings, *(einen Wechsel bei Fälligkeit ~)* to honour (to meet) a bill

A

upon maturity
6. to borrow, *(bei Banken ~)* to raise (to borrow) from banks, *(eine Hypothek auf ein Haus ~)* to raise a mortgage on a house, to mortgage a house, *(Kapital über die Börse ~)* to raise capital through the stock market
(am Kapitalmarkt ~) to raise (to borrow) in the capital market, to tap the capital market, to call on the capital market, *(zu günstigen Konditionen ~)* to raise on attractive terms
(einen Kredit ~) to raise (to contract) a loan, to borrow, to take out a loan, *(Mittel durch Wertpapieremissionen ~)* to raise capital by way of securities offerings, *(über ein öffentliches Zeichnungsangebot am Aktienmarkt ~)* to raise through a public share offering
7. to absorb, to acquire, *(überschüssige Liquidität ~)* to absorb excess liquidity, *(aufnehmendes Unternehmen)* acquiring (receiving) company, transferee
8. to record, to register, *(das Protokoll ~)* to draw up the minutes
9. *(~ in)* to admit to

aufrechenbar offsettable, eligible for offsets (for netting against)

aufrechnen 1. to set off, to net, to offset, *(gegen Forderungen der Bank ~)* to set off against claims asserted by the bank, *(Guthaben- und Schuldzinsen ~)* to net (to set off) interest income against interest payable, *(Verbindlichkeiten gegen Forderungen ~)* to net payables against receivables
2. *(Börsenaufträge)* to pair off, *(Kaufaufträge gegen Verkaufsaufträge ~)* to pair off buy orders with (against) sell orders, to cross buy and sell orders

Aufrechnung 1. setting off, netting, offset, *(~ von Abschlüssen)* trade (contract) netting, offsetting individual trades (contracts, deals) into a net amount, *(~ des Eigenkapitals im Konzernabschluss)* equity consolidation, *(~ von Positionen)* position netting
(~ gegenseitiger Verpflichtungen) offsetting reciprocal obligations, *(~ von Zahlungsverpflichtungen)* netting of payment obligations, *(~ von Liefer- und Zahlungsverpflichtungen aus einer Transaktion)* settlement netting
2. pairing off, crossing

Aufrechnungseinrede objection of setoff

aufrechnungsfähig *(~e Guthaben)* balances eligible for setoff

Aufrechnungs / ~gebot netting requirement; **~position** netting position; **~recht** netting option (privilege), *(~ der Bank)* banker's right of setoff, banker's right to offset payables against receivables

Aufrechnungs / ~system netting system; **~verbot** non-netting requirement, ban on netting arrangements; **~vereinbarung** netting agreement (arrangement); **~verzicht** waiver of right to set off

aufrechterhalten 1. to maintain, to keep up
2. *(festhalten an, z. B. einer Geschäftsstrategie)* to adhere to, to uphold, *(wir halten unser Kreditangebot aufrecht bis …)* our loan offer will hold firm until …, our loan offer will be held open until

Aufrechterhaltung maintenance, upkeep, upholding, *(~ einer Anwartschaft)* maintenance of rights accrued, *(~ einer Kreditfazilität)* upkeep of a loan facility, *(~ der bestehenden Risikovorsorge)* maintaining the current provisioning level, *(~ des Schwungs)* keeping up the momentum

aufrücken to move ahead, to be promoted

Aufruf 1. appeal, call, request **2.** public notice **3.** call, *(~ zur Tilgung)* redemption call, calling in for redemption

aufrufbar accessible, *(~ unter www…)* available at www…, *(diese Anzeige ist nicht mehr ~)* this display can no longer be activated

aufrufen 1. to appeal, to call for, to request

2. *(öffentlich anzeigen)* to give public notice
3. *(Banknoten ~)* to call in (to retire) bank notes, to withdraw bank notes from circulation, *(zur Tilgung ~)* to call in (up) for redemption, to give notice of redemption
4. *(eine Anzeige ~)* to activate a display

Aufrufphase *(Börsenparkett)* outcry phase

aufrunden to revise upward(s), to round up, *(nach oben aufgerundete Prognose)* upward-revised forecast

aufschieben 1. to defer, to postpone, to put off, *(aufschiebende Bedingung)* suspensive condition, *(aufschiebende Einrede)* dilatory plea, *(aufschiebende Wirkung)* suspensive effect, *(aufgeschobene Zahlung)* deferred payment, *(aufgeschobener Zahlungsausgleich)* deferred net settlement
2. *(bei Zahlungen ferner)* to extend the maturity
3. *(vertagen)* to adjourn

Aufschlag 1. *(Aufgeld, Kursaufschlag)* premium, *(~ auf den Ausgabekurs)* offering premium, premium over the issue price, *(~ auf Dreimonats-Termindollar)* premium on three months forward dollar, *(~ auf den Kassakurs)* premium over spot, premium on (to) the spot rate
2. *(Aufpreis)* additional (extra) charge
3. *(Gewinnaufschlag)* markup
4. contango, → Report
5. *(auf einen Referenz-Zinssatz)* spread, margin, *(~ von 1 % auf Sechsmonats-Libor)* spread (margin) of 1 % over six-month Libor
6. *(Risikoaufschlag)* risk premium, *(~ für das Ausfallrisiko)* default risk charge, *(~ für das spezifische Risiko)* specific risk charge, *(~ für künftige Verpflichtungen)* add-on for future obligations

aufschlagen to add, to increase, to mark up, *(10 % ~)* to add 10 % to the price, to charge an extra 10 %

aufschlüsseln to classify, to break down, *(einzeln ~)* to itemise

Aufschlüsselung classification, breakdown

Aufschrift *(eines Grundbuchblattes)* title

Aufschub 1. deferment, postponement, putting off **2.** *(Zahlungsaufschub)* extension of the time for payment, payment deferral **3.** *(Vertagung)* adjournment

aufschwänzen to corner

Aufschwung upturn, upswing, uplift, *(sich in einem ~ befinden)* to be on the upturn, to thrive, to prosper, to flourish, to boom

Aufschwungphase upward phase

aufsetzen *(entwerfen)* to draw up, to draft

Aufsicht supervision, control, inspection, monitoring, surveillance

aufsichtlich *(~e Beurteilung)* supervisory assessment, *(~e Eigenkapitalanforderungen)* prudential (regulatory) capital requirements, *(~e Eigenmittelrechnung)* regulatory equity calculation, *(~er Formelansatz)* supervisory formula approach
(~e Gewichtungsfaktoren) regulatory weighting factors, *(~e Kennzahlen)* prudential ratios, *(~ vorgegebene Forderungsklassen)* supervisory asset classes, *(~es Retailportfolio)* supervisory retail portfolio, *(~e Verlustquote)* supervisory loss given default (LGD), *(~es Überprüfungsverfahren)* supervisory review process

Aufsichtsbefugnisse supervisory powers, powers of supervision

Aufsichtsbehörde supervisory authority, *(Aufsichtsbehörde mit Regulierungsvollmachten)* regulatory authority (agency), *(umgangssprachlich)* market watchdog, *(Genehmigung durch die zuständige ~)* regulatory approval

aufsichtsbehördlich *(~es Meldewesen)* supervisory reporting

A

Aufsichts / ~funktion supervisory (regulatory) role; **~haftung** supervisory responsibility; **~harmonisierung** harmonisation of banking supervision; **~instanz** supervisory body; **~instrumentarium** supervisory tools (instruments)

Aufsichts / ~kollegium college of supervisors; **~kompetenzen** supervisory powers; **~organ** supervisory body, control institution; **~pflichten** supervisory duties (responsibilities)

Aufsichtsrat 1. supervisory board **2.** → Aufsichtsratsmitglied

Aufsichtsrats / ~beschluss supervisory board resolution; **~mandat/~sitz** seat on the supervisory board, non-executive directorship (BE); **~mitglied** supervisory board member, non-executive director (BE)

aufsichtsratspflichtig *(~e Themen)* issues requiring the approval of the supervisory board

Aufsichtsrats / ~sitzung supervisory board meeting; **~vorsitzender** chairman of the supervisory board

Aufsichtsrecht 1. right of supervision (of control) **2.** prudential regulations

aufsichtsrechtlich *(~e Anforderungen)* regulatory (prudential) requirements, *(~e Behandlung von Marktrisiken)* regulatory treatment of market risks, *(~es Berichtswesen)* regulatory reporting, *(~e Eigenkapitalquote)* regulatory capital ratio
(~e Filter) prudential filters, *(~ es Kernkapital)* regulatory core capital (common equity) → Basel III, → Kernkapital, *(~e Meldevorschriften)* regulatory (prudential) reporting requirements, *(~es Mindesteigenkapital)* regulatory minimum capital, *(~e Rahmenbedingungen)* regulatory framework

Aufsichts / ~richtlinie Supervision Directive; **~stärkungsgesetz** → Gesetz zur Stärkumg der Finanzmarkt- und Versicherungsaufsicht; **~wesen** supervisory (regulatory) system

aufspalten to split (to divide) up, to break up

Aufspaltung split, tiering, *(~ eines Konzerns)* demerger, breakup of a group

aufsplitten to split up

Aufsplittung splitting up, split-up, fragmentation

aufspüren *(neue Märkte ~)* to track down new markets

aufsteigen to rise, to move ahead, to be promoted

aufsteigend *(~es Dreieck) (Chart-Analyse)* ascending triangle □ bullish chart trend that indicates the continuation of an uptrend or a breakout to higher prices, *(in ~er Reihenfolge)* in ascending order

aufstellen 1. *(festlegen)* to fix, to lay down **2.** *(nominieren)* to nominate, to put up (forward) as candidate **3.** *(Etat, Bilanz, Programm)* to draw, to prepare

Aufstellung 1. fixing, laying down **2.** nomination **3.** drawing up **4.** *(Verzeichnis)* statement, list, schedule

Aufstellungspflicht duty to prepare (financial accounts)

Aufstieg 1. rise, ascent **2.** career, (professional) advancement

Aufstiegsmöglichkeiten career prospects, opportunities for advancement

aufstocken to increase, to raise, to augment, *(die Risikovorsorge ~)* to top up risk provisioning

Aufstockung increase, rise, *(~ der Eigenkapitalbasis)* increase in the capital base, boosting the capital base, *(~ des Kapitals)* capital increase, *(kräftige ~ der Rücklagen)* sizeable buildup of reserves, *(~ der Kreditwertberichtigungen)* increase in (addition to) loan loss allowances in the current period

Aufstockungstender topping-up auction

aufstreben 1. to rise **2.** to aspire, *(~des Unternehmen)* aspiring company, *(~de Volkswirtschaften)* emerging economies

auftauchen *(in der Bilanz ~)* to show up in the balance sheet

aufteilen 1. to divide, to split (up), to break up, to partition, *(den Markt unter mehreren Unternehmen ~)* to carve (to split) up the market between several companies, *(in mehrere Tranchen ~)* to split into several tranches
2. to share (to parcel) out, to partition, *(unter den Gläubigern ~)* to distribute amongst the creditors
3. to allocate, to apportion

Aufteilung 1. division, split, carving (splitting) up, *(~ unter den Aktionären)* dividing (splitting) among the shareholders, *(~ nach Branchen)* division along sector lines, *(~ einer Emission in zwei gleiche Tranchen)* splitting an issue into two equal tranches, *(~ des Gewinns nach Sparten)* divisional profits breakdown, *(~ von Grundbesitz)* partitioning real estate
2. sharing (out), *(~des Liquidationserlöses)* distribution of the liquidation proceeds
3. allocation, *(~ der Kosten unter den Parteien)* cost apportionment among the parties, *(~ von Vermögenswerten auf verschiedene Anlagemedien)* asset allocation

Auftrag 1. order, instruction(s), *(im ~ von)* by order of, on behalf of, *(eine Untersuchung in ~ geben)* to commission an investigation into, *(den ~ haben)* to be given the order, to be commissioned
2.*(Aufgabe)* assignment, task
3. *(Mandat)* mandate, brief, engagement
4. *(~ zur Akkreditiveröffnung)* documentary credit application

Auftraggeber 1. customer, client, ordering customer (party), principal, originator **2.** *(auftraggebende Bank)* principal bank, originating bank, bank placing the order **3.** *(eines Akkreditivs)* applicant for the credit
4. *(einer Garantie)* principal
5. *(öffentlicher ~)* contracting authority
6. *(einer Überweisung)* remitter, originator, payer, transferor

Auftraggeber / ~bank originator bank; **~konto** remitter's (originator's) account, originating account

Auftragnehmer contractor, supplier, manufacturer, company

Auftrags / ~abwicklung 1. order processing **2.** transaction settlement; **~abwicklungskosten** order filling (processing) cost; **~abwicklungssystem** order processing (routing) system

Auftrags / ~annullierung cancellation of an order; **~ausführung** execution of (filling) an order, order execution, → Ausführungsgrundsätze; **~ausführungsbestätigung** notice of execution, → Auftragsbestätigung

Auftrags / ~bearbeitung order processing; **~bedingungen** terms of contract; **~belebung** upturn in business (in the intake of orders); **~bestand** orders in (on) hand, backlog of orders, order level

Auftrags / ~bestätigung 1. confirmation of order **2.** *(eines Börsenauftrages)* trade confirmation, confirmation slip, notice of execution; **~buch** *(eines Börsenhändlers)* order book

Auftrags / ~durchleitung order routing; **~einbruch** slump in order intake; **~eingang** incoming orders, orders received, inflow of orders, order intake; **~entwicklung** trend of (in) incoming orders

Auftrags / ~erfüllungsbürgschaft contract bond, performance bond, completion guarantee; **~erteilung** placing an order, placement of an order, *(telefonische Auftragserteilung)* placing an order by phone, *(bei ~)* at the time of order placement

Auftrags / ~flaute stagnation in the inflow of orders, slowdown in order intake; **~fonds** private label fund; **~formular** order form (blank), *(Börse)* order ticket

A

auftragsgelenkt *(~er Markt)* order-driven market

auftragsgemäß according to (as per) order, in line with the instructions given

Auftrags / ~geschäft agency (commission) business; **~lage** order book; **~mangel** shortage of orders; **~papiere 1.** order documents **2.** documents accepted for collection; **~polster** backlog of orders in hand; **~rückgang** fall in orders (in order intake)

Auftrags / ~schreiben (bei einer Mandatserteilung) letter of engagement; **~sprung** leap in order intake; **~stimmrecht** proxy voting right; **~stornierung** cancellation of an order; **~summe** → Auftragswert; **~vergabe** placing of orders, contract award; **~verhältnis** agency relationship; **~weiterleitungssystem** order routing system; **~wert** contract value, transaction value; **~zufluss** inflow (influx) of orders

auftreten 1. *(fungieren)* to act as, *(am Geldmarkt ~)* to operate in the money market **2.** to occur, to arise, to appear, *(Interessenkonflikte traten auf)* conflicts of interest surfaced

Auftrieb 1. impetus, boost, *(dem Aktienmarkt ~ verleihen)* to spur (to boost, to give stimulus) to the equity market, *(die Finanzmärkte erhielten weiteren ~)* financial markets have been given further impetus **2.** *(Anstieg)* upsurge, rally, rise

Auftriebs / ~faktoren 1. stimulating factors **2.** *(bei einem Zinsanstieg)* factors driving (forcing) up interest rates; **~kräfte** stimulating (expansionary) forces

Aufwand expenditure, expense(s), charge(s), *(~ für die Risikovorsorge)* charge for risk provisioning, *(nach ~ berechnen)* to charge according to outlay, to bill as per outlay, *(als ~ verbuchen)* to expense

Aufwand/Ertrag Relation cost/income ratio

Aufwands / ~abgrenzung recognition of expenses on an accrual basis; **~buchung** expense posting; **~entschädigung** expense (representation) allowance; **~erfassung** recognition of expenditure; **~konsolidierung** consolidation of expenses; **~konto** expense (expenditure) account

Aufwands / ~posten expenditure (expense) item; **~quote** cost/income ratio; **~rentabilität** cost to income ratio, partial operating results as a percentage of operating expenditure;**~risiko** expense risk

Aufwands / ~rückstellungen expense provisions, provisions for operating expenses; **~saldo** expense balance; **~schätzung** cost estimate; **~seite** expense (expenditure) side; **~überhang** net expense, expenditure surplus

aufwandswirksam *(~ verbuchen)* to charge (to report) to expenditure, to record as a charge to the income statement, *(~e Zuführungen zur Wertberichtigung)* provisions charged to expense

Aufwandszinsen interest paid

Aufwärts / ~bewegung upward movement, uptrend, *(starke ~ am Aktienmarkt)* strong rally in the stock market, big move up in stock prices; **~dynamik** upward momentum; **~kanal** *(Chart-Analyse)* uptrend channel, ascending (upward sloping) channnel

Aufwärts / ~keil *(Chart-Analyse)* rising wedge □ indicates in a downtrend the continuation of a bearish trend; signals in an uptrend the reversal from a bullish to a bearish trend; **~korrektur** upward correction; **~lücke** up-gap; **~phase** upward phase

Aufwärts / ~trend uptrend, *(die Zinssätze befinden sich in einem ~)* interest rates are on an upward trend; **~trendlinie** ascending trend line, uptrend line; **~ verschmelzung** upstream merger □ merger of the subsidiary into the parent, → Abwärtsverschmelzung; **~wimpel** *(Chart-Analyse)* rising pennant □ continuation pattern; confirms the underlying trend to higher prices

aufweichen to water down, *(die Stärke einer Währung ~)* to undermine the strength of a currency

aufweisen *(einen Saldo von . . € ~)* to show a balance of € . .

aufwenden to use, to employ, to spend

Aufwendung expenditure, expense, disbursement

Aufwendungen *(~ und Abschreibungen aus dem Leasinggeschäft)* expenditure and depreciation from leasing operations, *(~ für Kapitalanlagen)* investment expenses, *(~ für den Schuldendienst)* debt service charge, charge for interest and redemption payments, *(~ aus Verlustübernahmen)* losses incurred under profit and loss transfer agreements, charges for losses assumed

Aufwendungs / **~darlehen** subsidised home-building loan; **~ersatz** reimbursement of expenses; **~ersatzanspruch** **1.** claim to reimbursement of expenses **2.** compensation claim, claim for indemnification; **~zuschüsse** home-building subsidies

aufwerten **1.** *(eine Position ~)* to upgrade a position **2.** *(eine Währung ~)* to revalue a currency

Aufwertung **1.** upgrading **2.** revaluation

Aufwertungs / **~druck** upward exchange rate pressure, revaluation pressure; ~ **gewinn** revaluation surplus; **~satz** revaluation rate

aufwertungsverdächtig *(~e Währung)* revaluation-prone currency

Aufwertungsverlust loss on revaluation

Auf-Widerruf-Auftrag *(Börse)* good till cancel order, GTC order

aufwiegen *(die inhärenten Risiken ~)* to offset (to make up for, to counterbalance) the inherent risks

aufzählen to enumerate, to list, to specify

Aufzählung enumeration, list, listing

aufzehren to deplete, to erode, to consume, *(die Barmittel ~)* to deplete cash resources, *(die Gewinne wurden durch neue Wertberichtigungen aufgezehrt)* profits were eroded by fresh bad debt charges, *(die Spanne ~)* to eat up the margin, *(die Tagesgewinne ~)* to wipe out the day's gains

Aufzehrung depletion, erosion

Aufzeichnung **1.** registration, recording **2.** *(~en)* notes, records

Aufzeichnungspflichten record-keeping obligations, recording requirements

aufzeigen to show, to indicate, to point out, to pinpoint, *(die Finanzierungsmöglichkeiten ~)* to show (to indicate, to outline) the funding options, *(die Indexentwicklung ~)* to track the index development

aufzinsen to add on interest, to roll up accruing interest, *(aufgezinste Gesamtsumme)* total with accruing interest added, *(aufgezinste Wertpapiere)* securities marked up for interest accruing

Aufzinsung adding interest (e.g. to the principal of the loan), rolling up interest accrued, interest rollup

Aufzinsungsanleihe / **~papier** accrual bond, accrual-type (appreciation-type) security □ A type of bond that pays no interest during its holding period. It is issued at par and redeemed at a substantially higher price above par. The difference represents the interest accumulated.

Auge *(das Risiko im ~ behalten)* to monitor (to keep a close watch on) the exposure, *(ins ~ fassen)* to contemplate, to envisage

Augenschein / **~beweis** evidence by inspection; **~nahme** *(in ~ durch das Gericht)* inspection by the Court

A

Auktion 1. auction, public sale 2. *(Schatzwechsel-Auktion)* treasury bill tender

Auktions / ~börse public auction market, **~handel** order-driven trading; **~prinzip** auction principle, *(Börsenhandel nach dem ~)* order-driven market

aus dem Geld out-of-the money □ an option is out-of-the money when the market price of the underlying instrument is lower (for calls) or higher (for puts) than the strike price of the option

ausarbeiten *(eine Strategie ~)* to formulate (to work out, to devise) a strategy, *(eine Vergleichsvereinbarung ~)* to prepare (to draw up) a composition agreement

Ausarbeitung 1. formulation, preparation, draft 2. (strategy) paper

Ausbau 1. development, extension, *(~ der Dienstleistungspalette)* enlargement of the range of services offered 2. intensification, strengthening, *(~von Positionen)* stepping (building) up positions

ausbauen 1. to develop, to enlarge 2. to intensify, to strengthen, *(Kundenbeziehungen ~)* to solidify and extend customer relationships

ausbedingen *(sich sofortige Barzahlung ~)* to stipulate immediate cash payment

Ausbietungsgarantie bidding guarantee

Ausbildung training, instruction, *(innerbetriebliche ~)* inhouse training

Ausbildungskosten cost of training, learning and development costs

ausbleiben to fail to materialise, to be omitted, *(~de Zahlung)* missing (overdue) payment

Ausbleiben failure to materialise, omission, *(~ der Dividendenzahlungen)* omission of dividend payments, *(~ der Zinszahlungen)* non-accrual of interest

ausbringen to produce, to generate, to yield

Ausbringung output, production

Ausbruch *(Chart-Analyse)* breakout □ point at which the market price moves out of the trend channel, *(~ nach oben)* upside (upward) breakout, breakout up, bullish breakout, *(~ nach unten)* downside (downward) breakout, breakout down, bearish breakout

Ausbruchs / ~bestätigung breakout confirmation; **~bewegung** breakout movement; **~lücke** breakaway gap; **~muster** breakout pattern; **~potenzial** breakout potential; **~punkt** breakout point, → Ausbruch; **~ziel** breakout target

ausbuchen 1. to derecognise, to delete (to eliminate) from the account(s), to take off the books, *(einen Vermögenswert vollständig ~)* to derecognise an asset in its entirety, *(~ mit dem Ziel der Bilanzentlastung)* to remove from the balance sheet
2. *(Darlehensverluste ~)* to write off (to charge off) loan losses, *(zu Lasten der Rücklagen ~)* to write off against reserves, *(als Totalverlust ~)* to write off as a total loss, *(zu Lasten der bestehenden Wertberichtigung ~)* to charge off against the existing allowance for loan losses

Ausbuchung 1. derecognition, deletion (elimination) from the accounts, taking off the books, *(~ einer Garantie)* deleting a guarantee from the accounts, charging off a guarantee, removal from the balance sheet, *(~ aus der Sammelverwahrung)* deletion from collective custody
2. write-off, charge-off, *(~ uneinbringlicher Forderungen aus dem Kreditgeschäft)* writing off irrecoverable claims from lending transactions, loan write-offs (charge-offs)

Ausbuchungs / ~bedarf write-off (charge-off) requirements; **~kompetenz** write-off powers, powers to charge off

ausbügeln to iron out

ausdehnen 1. to expand, to extend,to enlarge **2.** *(sich ~)* to branch out into

Ausdehnung *(~ der Geldmenge)* expansion of the money stock

Ausdruck 1. expression, *(wachsenden Befürchtungen ~ verleihen)* to give vent to growing fears, *(Unterstützung zum ~ bringen)* to voice (to express) support (e.g. for the troubled company)

ausdrücken to express, *(ausgedrückt in Basispunkten)* expressed in (translated into) basis points

ausdrücklich 1. *adj.* express, explicit, *(~e Bestimmung)* explicit (express) condition, *(~e Vereinbarung der Vertragsparteien)* express agreement of the parties to the contract, *(~e Zusage/Zusicherungen)* express undertaking/warranties
2. *adv.* expressly, explicitly, *(~ anweisen)* to instruct expressly, *(sich ~ verpflichten)* to bind o.s. in express terms, *(~ den Aktionären vorbehalten)* specifically reserved to shareholders, *(~ in dem Vertrag vorgesehen)* expressly (explicitly) provided in the agreement, expressly stipulated by contract

ausdünnen *(das Filialnetz ~)* to thin out the branch network

auseinanderdriften to drift apart

Auseinanderdriften *(~ von Leit- und Kapitalzinsen)* widening of the gap between key lending and capital market rates

auseinanderklaffen to be wide apart, to diverge largely (widely)

Auseinanderklaffen 1. *(~ von Angebot und Nachfrage)* wide gap between supply and demand **2.** *(~ der Prognosen zur weiteren Zinsentwicklung)* sharp divergence of forecasts over the future trend in interest rates

Auseinanderlaufen *(~ der Zinssätze)* divergence of interest rates

auseinandersetzen *(sich ~)* to deal with, to discuss in depth

Auseinandersetzung 1. dispute, conflict, controversy, *(streitige ~)* settlement of a dispute by litigation **2.** *(bei Unternehmensauflösung oder Ausscheiden eines Gesellschafters)* dissociation **3.** *(~ des Gesamtgutes)* partition (distribution) of the joint property

Auseinandersetzungs / ~bilanz dissociation (partition) accounts; **~guthaben** dissociation balance, partition proceeds; **~vereinbarung 1.** *(der Gesellschafter)* dissociation agreement, settlement between the partners **2.** *(der Erben)* deed of partition, settlement between the heirs; **~versteigerung** → Teilungsversteigerung

Ausfall 1. loss, *(Betrag des höchstmöglichen ~s)* worst case loss, credit value at risk
2. default, *(~ des Vertragspartners)* counterparty default, default (insolvency) of the contracting partner, *(bei einem Swapgeschäft)* counterparty default, *(ausstehende Forderungen zum Zeitpunkt des ~s)* exposure (outstanding claims) at (the time of) default
3. non-payment, failure to pay, *(~ der Dividendenzahlungen)* non-payment of dividends, passing (omitting) the dividend
4. *(Fehlbetrag)* shortage, deficit
5. *(Scheitern)* failure, breakdown, disruption

Ausfallanalyse 1. default analysis **2.** systems failure analysis

ausfallbedingt *(~e Verluste)* default-induced losses

ausfallbedroht threatened by default, *(~e Anleihe)* defaultable bond, → ausfallgefährdet

Ausfall / ~bürge indemnitor, indemnifier; **~bürgschaft** deficiency guarantee, indemnity bond, certificate (letter, deed) of indemnity; **~deckung** cover against default, default coverage; **~dichte** default density

Ausfälle *(~ im Auftragseingang)* shortfalls (losses) in order intake, *(~ im Kreditgeschäft)* loan losses, loan charge-offs

ausfallen 1. *(~ lassen)* to call off, to cancel, to omit, *(die Dividende ~ lassen)* to omit (to pass) the dividend
2. to default, *(ausgefallene Engagements)* defaulted exposures/assets, *(ausgefallener Kreditnehmer/Schuldner)* defaulted borrower/obligor, *(ausgefallene Retailforderungen)* retail exposures in default, non-performing retail loans
3. *(ergebnismäßig)* to turn out, *(niedriger als erwartet ~)* to turn out (to be) lower than expected, *(sehr unterschiedlich ~)* to show considerable divergence
4. to fail, to break down

Ausfall / ~entwicklung default history; **~erfahrungswerte** *(im Kreditgeschäft)* loan loss experience; **~ereignis** event of default, credit event

ausfallgefährdet vulnerable to default, *(~e Forderungen)* distressed debt, *(~e Kredite)* problem loans (exposure), impaired loans, subperforming loans, *(~er Kreditnehmer)* default-prone borrower, *(als weniger ~ gelten)* to be considered less likely to default

Ausfall / ~gefährdung vulnerability to default; **~gewichtung** default weighting, *(ausfallgewichtete durchschnittliche Verlustquote)* default-weighted average loss rate; **~haftung** liability in the event of default; **~häufigkeit** default frequency

Ausfall / ~klasse default category; **~korrelationen** default correlations; **~kosten 1.** disruption cost **2.** bad debt cost; **~prognose** default forecast

Ausfallquote/Ausfallrate default rate, *(~ im Kreditgeschäft)* loan loss rate (experience), loss rate in lending operations, charge-off rate, delinquency rate, *(~ aus der Vergangenheit)* past loan loss experience

Ausfallrisiko 1. *(Verzugs-/Kreditausfallrisiko)* risk of default, default risk, loan loss risk, *(~ von Handelsbuchpositionen)* default risks of trading book positions, *(~ des Kreditnehmers)* risk of borrower default
2. *(Nichtzahlungsrisiko)* risk of non-payment, non-payment risk, risk of dishonour
3. *(Verlustrisiko)* risk of loss
4. *(eines Staates/staatlicher Organe)* sovereign risk

Ausfallrisiko / ~aufschlag default risk surcharge; **~berechnung** determination of default risk; **~prämie** default risk premium, credit spread; **~ steuerung** default risk control; **~überwachung** monitoring default risk

Ausfall / ~schutz protection against default (against credit losses), loss protection, default coverage; **~schwelle** default threshold (point); **~sicherheit** default protection (security), *(ausfallsichere Anleihe)* default-proof bond

Ausfall / ~status default status, *(~ von mehr als 90 Tagen)* being more than 90 days past due; **~strukturkurve** credit default curve; **~urteil** deficiency (default) judgment; **~ versicherung** insurance against default, default insurance coverage; **~wagnis** risk of default

Ausfallwahrscheinlichkeit probability (likelihood) of default, *(geschätzte/prognostizierte ~)* estimated/forecast probability of default, *(Messung der ~)* measuring default probability

Ausfall / ~zahlung deficiency payment; **~zeit** downtime

ausfertigen 1. *(einen Scheck/Wechsel ~)* to issue (to make out) a cheque/bill **2.** *(eine Urkunde ~)* to execute a deed, *(einen Vollstreckungsbefehl ~)* to issue a writ of execution **3.** *(einen Vertrag ~)* to draw up a contract

Ausfertigung 1. drawing up, execution, issue, issuance **2.** *(Exemplar)* copy, *(in zwei-/drei-/vierfacher ~)* in duplicate/triplicate/quadruplicate **3.** *(Wech-*

selausfertigung) first, second or third of exchange

ausfinanzieren to fund externally, to outsource the funding

Ausfolgungsprotest protest for non-surrender of a bill

Ausfuhr / ~**bürgschaft** export guarantee; ~**deckung** provision of cover for exports, export credit insurance

ausführen 1. to execute, to carry out, to transact, *(die ~de Bank)* the bank executing (filling) the order, *(eine Kauf- oder Verkaufsorder ~)* to execute a buy or sell order, *(nicht ausgeführte Aufträge gegen eingehende Aufträge ~)* to match non-executed (unfilled) orders against incoming orders, *(zum angegebenen Kurs ~)* to execute at the price specified
2. *(durchführen)* to implement, to carry into effect
3. *(darlegen)* to explain
4. *(regulieren)* to settle

Ausfuhr / ~**finanzierung** export financing; ~**garantie**/~**gewährleistung** export credit guarantee; ~**kreditdeckung** export loan guarantee; ~**kreditgesellschaft** (German) export credit company; ~**kreditversicherung** export credit insurance

ausführlich 1. *adj. (~e Anlageberatung)* in-depth investment counselling **2.** *adv. (~ angeben)* to specify in detail

Ausfuhr / ~**-Pauschalgewährleistung** whole turnover policy, comprehensive risks policy; ~**risikodeckung** export risk coverage; ~**sammelbürgschaft** comprehensive export credit insurance

Ausführung 1. execution, carrying out, *(sofortige ~ zum bestmöglichen Kurs)* immediate execution at the best available price, *(bei ~ Ihrer Zahlungsanweisungen)* in carrying out your payment instructions **2.** implementation, carrying into effect **3.** settlement **4.** *(~en)* comments, remarks, explanations

Ausführungs / ~**anzeige** advice of deal, trade confirmation; ~**befugnis** authority to execute a trade, right to transact business; ~**bestätigung** execution confirmation; ~**bestimmungen** regulations for implementation; ~**börse** trading exchange

Ausführungs / ~**bürgschaft** contract bond, performance bond; ~**frist** transaction (execution) period; ~**geschäft** purchase and/or sale, *(reines Ausführungsgeschäft)* execution only; ~**gesetz** Implementation Act

Ausführungs / ~**grundsätze** execution policy (e.g for securities transactions), principles of order execution; ~**kosten 1.** implementation cost (expenses) **2.** transaction cost; ~**kurs** execution price; ~**platz** *(eines Wertpapiergeschäftes)* execution venue, place of execution (transaction)

Ausführungs / ~**system** execution facility; ~**tag** trade date, transaction (settlement) date; ~**verordnung** implementing order; ~**verpflichtung** obligation to execute (payments); ~**wahrscheinlichkeit** probability of execution

ausfüllen 1. *(ein Formular ~)* to complete (to fill in) a form **2.** *(eine Marktlücke ~)* to fill a market gap

Ausfüllen completion, filling

Ausfüllhilfe completion note

Ausgabe issue, issuing, issuance, offering, *(~ von Gratisaktien)* capitalisation issue, scrip issue, *(~ von jungen Aktien)* issue of new shares

Ausgabe / ~**abschlag** offering discount; ~**aufgeld** *(Emission)* offering premium; ~**aufschlag** *(Fondsanteile)* entry load, loading charge, front-end load, selling markup, subscription fee; ~**bedingungen** terms of issue, offering (issuing) terms; ~**genehmigung** issuing approval; ~**kurs** issuing (offering) price

Ausgaben expenditure, expense(s), charges, outlay

Ausgaben / ~**ansatz** expenditure appropriations; ~**bewilligung** expendi-

A

ture authorisation; ~**deckung** covering (meeting) the expenses; ~**kürzung** expenditure (spending) cut

Ausgabenlimit (~**obergrenze**/~**plafond**) **1.** expenditure ceiling (limit), spending (disbursement) limit **2.** *(eines Kreditkarteninhabers)* cardholder's credit line

Ausgaben / ~**spielraum** scope for spending (for further expenditure); ~**struktur** expenditure (cost) pattern; ~**subventionen** expenditure subsidies; ~**subventionierung** subsidising expenditure

Ausgaben / ~**überschuss** **1.** net expenditure **2.** financial deficit; ~**verteilung** expenditure spread

ausgabenwirksam *(~e Aufwendungen)* expenditure recognised in the profit and loss account

Ausgabe / ~**preis** *(bei Fondsanteilen)* unit offering price, selling (offer) price; ~**stelle** issuing agency; ~**tag** issuing date, date of issue

Ausgang *(Ergebnis)* outcome, result

Ausgangs / ~**basis** departure point; ~**bescheid** original ruling, initial decision; ~**kapital** initial (starting) capital; ~**option** *(bei einer Option auf eine Option)* front (underlying) option, back option; ~**punkt** starting point, point of departure, launchpad, *(~ der Besteuerung)* tax base

Ausgangs / ~**rechnung** sales invoice; ~**seite** **1.** distribution side, → Fondsausgangsseite **2.** expense side **3.** sell side; ~**volatilität** starting volatility; ~**wert** initial value; ~**zeitraum** reference period

ausgeben **1.** *(Aktien, Anleihen)* to issue **2.** *(Banknoten)* to issue, to emit **3.** *(Geld)* to spend

ausgefeilt *(~e Marketing-Strategie)* sophisticated (well-devised) marketing strategy

ausgeglichen **1.** *adj.* balanced, settled, even, *(~es Ergebnis)* break-even result, balanced result (performance), *(~e Positionen) (a)* balanced (settled, squared) positions *(b) (durch entsprechende Gegenpositionen)* matched positions
2. *adv.* *(~ abschließen)* to break even

ausgehen **1.** *(annehmen)* to proceed on the assumption, to assume, *(bei unserer Kreditzusage gehen wir davon aus, dass)* in making our loan commitment, it is understood that, *(ausgehend von einem Kontoumsatz von ...)* given an account turnover of ...
2. *(herrühren von)* to originate (to emanate) from, to be triggered by
3. *(zur Neige gehen)* to run out, to run short of, *(die Aktionäre gingen leer aus)* the shareholders went empty-handed

ausgehend *(~e Wertpapiere)* securities to be delivered, outgoing securities

ausgeprägt *(~es Interesse)* keen demand, *(~er Rückgang)* marked (pronounced) decline

ausgereift *(~es Produkt)* mature (fully developed) product, *(~e Strategie)* seasoned strategy

ausgereizt *(~ sein) (im Kurs)* to have no further upside potential

ausgeschlossen *(~e Risiken)* risks excluded, *(falls nicht ausdrücklich ~)* unless expressly ruled out

ausgestalten to structure, to shape, to frame, *(die vertragliche Vereinbarung ~)* to formulate the contractual agreement, *(individuell ausgestaltete Finanzinstrumente)* individually structured financial instruments, instruments tailored to the customer's requirements, *(unterschiedlich ausgestaltet sein)* to take different forms

Ausgestaltung formulation, design, *(~ der Fazilität als Festsatzkredit)* structuring the facility as fixed rate loan, *(~ der Vertragsbedingungen)* formulation of the contract terms, *(~ der Wertpapiere)* terms and conditions of the securities, *(~ der Zinspolitik)* shaping interest rate policy

ausgesucht/ausgewählt *(~e Anlagemöglichkeiten)* prime (choice, select) investment opportunities

ausgewogen *(~es Budget/Portefeuille)* balanced budget/portfolio

Ausgleich 1. *(Entschädigung)* compensation, indemnity, *(als ~ für den erlittenen Verlust)* in compensation for (to compensate for) the loss sustained, *(~ für die Wertminderung der Sicherheit)* compensation for the collateral's decline in value 2. *(Nivellierung) (~von Kursunterschieden)* evening out (levelling off) price differences 3. *(Regulierung)* settlement, payment, *(~ von Ansprüchen)* settlement of claims, *(zum ~ Ihrer Rechnung)* in settlement of your invoice, *(~ zum Tagesende)* end-of-day settlement 4. *(Saldierung)* balancing, *(~ inkongruenter Positionen)* redressing mismatched positions 5. *(Verrechnung mit)* setting off, netting out, *(~ des Sollsaldos mit einem Guthaben)* setting off (repaying) the debit balance against a credit

ausgleichen 1. to indemnify, to compensate, to make up for, *(einen Verlust ~)* to compensate for (to cover, to meet) a loss 2. *(glätten, nivellieren)* to even out, to level (off), to equalise, to equilibrate, to redress an imbalance 3. *(regulieren)* to settle, to square 4. *(verrechnen mit)* to set off, to net out

Ausgleichs / ~anspruch indemnification claim, right to indemnification (compensation); **~betrag** compensation amount; **~buchung** offsetting entry, balancing (adjustment) entry; **~finanzierung** compensatory financing

Ausgleichs / ~fonds equalisation fund, *(Ausgleichsfonds Währungsumstellung)* Currency Conversion Equalisation Fund; **~forderungen** equalisation (recovery) claims, compensations receivable

Ausgleichs / ~leistung → Ausgleichszahlung; **~obergrenze** indemnification limit, compensation cap; **~operationen** *(der Zentralbank am Geldmarkt)* compensatory (assistance) measures in the money market

Ausgleichs / ~posten 1. adjustment (reconciling) item 2. offsetting (balancing) item, *(~ für Anteile im Fremdbesitz)* minority interests; **~verfahren** netting procedure; **~zahlung** 1. compensation (compensatory) payment, indemnity 2. payment in settlement of ... 3. cash settlement, → Barausgleich

Ausgleichszoll countervailing duty

ausgliedern 1. *(einen Unternehmensbereich ~)* to spin (to hive) off a division (operations) 2. *(getrennt ausweisen)* to report (to state) separately

Ausgliederung 1. spin-off, hive-down 2. *(bilanzmäßige)* separate reporting, reporting separately

ausgründen to spin out, to carve out

Ausgründung spin-out, carve-out

Aushaftung liability (guarantee) beyond the expiry date

Aushaftungszeitraum additional liability (guarantee) period

aushandeln *(eine Vereinbarung ~)* to negotiate an agreement

aushändigen to deliver, to hand over, to surrender

Aushändigung delivery, handing over, surrender, *(~ zu getreuen Händen)* delivery in trust, *(~ des Hypothekenbriefes)* delivery of the mortgage deed, *(~ der Verschiffungsdokumente)* delivery of the shipping documents

auskehren to pay, to clear, *(einen Nachlass ~)* to pay out an estate, *(Rücklagen ~)* to write back reserves, *(Überschüsse ~)* to distribute the surplus

Auskehrung payment, distribution

ausklagen *(ausgeklagte Forderung)* litigated debt presumed irrecoverable

ausklammern to exclude, to leave out

Auskunft 1. information 2. *(über einen Bankkunden)* status report (information), credit position report

Auskunftei credit reporting agency, mercantile agency

Auskunfts / **~anfrage** status enquiry; **~einholung** making a status enquiry (on a customer), obtaining information on; **~ersuchen** status enquiry, request for information

Auskunfts / **~pflicht** **1.** duty to furnish the information requested **2.** obligation to disclose, disclosure requirement; **~recht** *(des Kunden)* customer's right to information

auslagern **1.** *(Aufgaben an einen externen Anbieter vergeben)* to outsource, to contract out, *(Versorgungsverpflichtungen ~)* to outsource the funding of pension liabilities **2.** *(Kreditrisiken ~)* to offload loan risks

Auslagerung **1.** outsourcing, contracting out, *(~ der Finanzierung)* external funding, *(~ auf außerbilanzielle Einheiten)* transfer to off-balance sheet units **2.** *(~ von Problemkrediten)* offloading (unloading) problem loans

Auslagerungs / **~unternehmen** external service provider; **~vertrag** outsourcing agreement

Ausland *(im ~ ruhende Werte)* assets held abroad

Ausländer / **~depot** non-resident securities account; **~konto** non-resident account; **~konvertibilität** non-resident convertibility

Auslands / **~abgaben** foreign selling, selling by foreign investors; **~aktiva** external assets; **~anleihe** external bond (floated by a foreign issuer in Germany); **~auftragsgeschäft** foreign agency (commission) business; **~ausfälle im Kreditgeschäft** foreign loan losses; **~aval** foreign aval

Auslands / **~beteiligungen** foreign shareholdings (interests), trade investments abroad; **~bond** foreign currency bond (floated by a German issuer abroad); **~einlagen** non-resident deposits

Auslands / **~engagements** **1.** *(im Kreditgeschäft)* foreign lendings (commitments), lendings to foreign customers, international exposure **2.** *(an der Börse)* foreign buying; **~forderungen** **1.** foreign accounts receivable **2.** *(einer Bank)* claims on foreign customers, foreign lendings

Auslands / **~gelder** foreign funds; **~geschäfte** *(einer Bank)* international business (operations), international banking; **~guthaben** assets (deposits) held abroad

Auslands / **~interesse** *(Börse)* foreign buying interest; **~investitionen** foreign investments, investments abroad; **~investmentgesetz** (German) Foreign Investment Act □ law governing the activities of foreign investment companies/the sale of foreign mutual fund shares in Germany

Auslands / **~kapital** foreign capital, *(Zuflüsse an ~)* inflow of foreign capital; **~käufe** *(Börse)* foreign (overseas) buying; **~korrespondent** *(Bankverbindung)* correspondent abroad

Auslandskredit **1.** *(an einen ausländischen Kreditnehmer)* foreign loan (lending) **2.** *(Kreditaufnahme im Ausland)* foreign borrowing, borrowing abroad

Auslandskredit / **~geschäft** international lending business (operations); **~portefeuille** foreign loan portfolio, foreign lending book, external lending volume; **~risiko** foreign (international) lending exposure; **~volumen** → Auslandskreditportefeuille

Auslands / **~kundenbetreuer** relationship manager (international business); **~netz** network of foreign branches; **~niederlassung** foreign branch; **~obligo** **1.** external liabilities, foreign (international) exposure **2.** foreign lendings (commitments), exposure from lendings to foreign customers; **~objektgesellschaft** foreign property company

Auslands / **~passiva** foreign liabilities; **~repräsentanz** representative office abroad; **~saldo** net external position; **~status** statement of foreign borrowings and lendings; **~stücke** (German)

securities held abroad; ~tranche foreign tranche, tranche placed abroad

Auslands / ~**überweisung** foreign credit transfer, → Auslandszahlungen; ~**valuta** 1. foreign currency (exchange) 2. property (assets) held abroad; ~**verschuldung** external debt (indebtedness), external debt position

Auslands / ~**vertretung** representative (branch) office abroad; ~**verwahrung** safe custody (safekeeping) abroad; ~**währung** foreign currency; ~**wechsel** foreign currency bill; ~**werte** foreign stocks (securities, issues)

Auslands / ~**zahlungen** 1. *(Eingänge)* foreign payments (remittances) received 2. *(Ausgänge)* international payments, credit transfers abroad; ~**zahlungsverkehr** international (foreign) payments, cross-border payments

auslassen 1. *(eine Dividendenzahlung ~)* to skip (to omit, to pass over) a dividend payment 2. *(wichtige Informationen ~)* to leave out important information

auslasten to utilise, *(eine zu 70 % ausgelastete Betriebsanlage)* plant working at 70 % of capacity

Auslastung utilisation, workload

Auslastungsgrad utilisation rate, load factor, usage ratio, degree of utilisation

Auslauf *(eines Kredites)* → Beleihungsauslauf

auslaufen 1. to expire, to end, to lapse, to terminate by lapse of time, *(~de Kreditvereinbarung)* loan agreement expiring shortly, *(~de Optionen)* expiring options
2. *(fällig werden)* to mature, *(~de Pensionsgeschäfte)* maturing (expiring) sale and repurchase agreements, *(~de Wechselfinanzierungen)* maturing bill finance arrangements
3. *(zu Ende gehen)* to taper off, to peter out, *(schrittweise ~ lassen, z. B. ein Kreditprogramm)* to phase out a loan scheme, *(~de Aufwärtsbewegung am Aktienmarkt)* ebbing rally in the stock market, bull period running out of steam

Auslaufen 1. expiry, expiration, lapse 2. maturity 3. petering out, tapering off, phasing out

Auslaufperiode phase-out period

auslegen 1. *(interpretieren)* to interpret, to construe 2. *(zur öffentlichen Einsichtnahme ~)* to display for public scrutiny, *(am Schalter ~)* to display at the bank's counters

Auslegung interpretation, construing

ausleihbar loanable, lendable

Ausleihe → Ausleihung

ausleihen 1. to lend, to loan, *(Gelder ~)* to lend (to lend out, to loan) money, *(ausgeliehene Gelder)* loaned money, *(Wertpapiere ~) (im Rahmen einer Wertpapierleihe)* to lend securities 2. *(borgen)* to borrow

Ausleih / ~**frist** lending period (term), life of a loan; ~**gebühr** lending fee; ~**geschäft** lending transaction, *(~ in Aktienwerten)* stock lending; ~**quote** lending ratio, ratio of lendings to total assets plus endorsement liabilities

Ausleihung *(~ von Wertpapieren)* securities lending, lending out securities

Ausleihungen *(Kredite)* lendings, loans, *(~ an Banken/Versicherer)* lendings to banks/insurance companies, *(~ an freie Berufe)* lendings to self-employed, *(~ an die Firmenkundschaft)* lendings to corporate customers, business lendings (loans), lendings to the corporate sector
(~ an die Privatkundschaft) retail loans, lendings to private customers, lendings to the personal sector, *(~ an Problemländer)* problem country lendings, problem country exposure, *(~ an staatliche Kreditnehmer)* sovereign lending, *(~ unter eigenem Risiko)* lendings at own risk, *(~ an verbundene Unternehmen)* loans to affiliated companies

A

Ausleihungs / ~struktur lending structure (pattern); **~volumen** total lendings, lending (loan) portfolio

ausliefern to deliver

Auslieferung (outward) delivery, *(~ effektiver Stücke)* physical delivery

Auslieferungsanspruch claim to delivery

ausliegen *(an unseren Schaltern ~)* to be available at our counters

auslosbar drawable, redeemable by drawings

auslöschen *(einen Gewinn ~)* to wipe out a profit

auslosen 1. *(Wertpapiere zu Tilgungszwecken)* to draw, to draw by lot
2. *(durch einen Zufallsgenerator den Optionsverkäufer bestimmen, der den Basiswert liefern bzw.entgegennehmen muss)* to assign on a random basis, *(ausgeloste Verkaufspositionen)* assigned short positions
3. *(Zuteilungen im Rahmen einer Neuemission ~)* to allot newly issued securities by way of a ballot

auslösen 1. to spark (off), to trigger, to cause, to provoke, *(neue Abgaben ~)* to prompt a fresh wave of selling, *(durch eine Verkaufsempfehlung ausgelöste Abgaben)* selling triggered (touched off) by a sell recommendation, *(das Inkrafttreten einer Klausel ~)* to trigger a clause
(eine Kurserholung am Rentenmarkt ~) to spark a rally in bond prices, *(eine positive Reaktion an der Börse ~)* to prompt a positive reaction in the stock market, *(einen Zinsrückgang ~)* to touch off a decline in interest rates
2. to originate, *(vom Kunden ausgelöste Transaktionen)* customer-originated transactions
3. *(tilgen, zurückkaufen)* to redeem, *(ein Pfand ~)* to redeem a pawn

Auslöser triggering event (factor), *(~ für eine vorzeitige Tilgung)* early amortisation trigger

Auslosung 1. drawing, drawing lots, *(~ zum Nennwert)* drawing at par, *(regelmäßig durch ~ zurückzahlen)* to redeem by drawings at regular intervals, *(Tilgung durch ~)* redemption by drawing lots
2. assignment, → auslosen (2)

Auslösung 1. triggering, sparking (touching) off, *(~ hektischer Käufe)* unleashing frenetic buying activity, *(~ der vorzeitigen Rückzahlung)* triggering early redemption
2. *(~ eines Pfandes)* redemption (release) of a pawn
3. allowance

Auslosungs / ~anleihe bond (loan) redeemable by drawings; **~anzeige 1.** notice of drawing, → auslosen (1) **2.** notice of assignment, → auslosen (2); **~kurs** drawing price

Auslosungs / ~liste list of drawings, list of bonds drawn; **~nummern** numbers drawn; **~risiko** risk of a premature drawing; **~termin** drawing date

Auslösungsrecht right of redemption, right of the borrower to redeem collateral furnished

ausloten *(Finanzierungsmöglichkeiten ~)* to explore (to sound out) funding options

ausmachen 1. to account for, to make up, *(gerade 10 % des Bruttosozialproduktes ~)* to equate to just 10 % of the gross national product, *(ein Drittel des gesamten Neuemissionsvolumens ~)* to account for one third of the total volume of new issues
2. *(betragen)* to amount to, to total, to equate

ausmachender Betrag 1. actual amount **2.** *(bei einem Kauf)* total purchase price, *(bei einem Verkauf)* net proceeds **3.** market value plus interest accrued

Ausmaß extent, scale, scope

Ausnahme 1. exception **2.** *(Freistellung)* exemption, *(~ von der Mindestreserveregelung)* exemption from minimum reserve requirements

Ausnahme / ~bestimmung exceptional provision, *(Vorbehaltsklausel)* saving clause; **~genehmigung** special permission, exemption; **~konditionen** preferential (concessional) rates; **~regelung** exceptional (special) regulation

ausnehmen to exempt, to except, to exclude, to bar, *(von einer Bestimmung ~)* to exempt from a rule

ausnutzbar utilisable, usable, *(die Fazilität ist als Euro-, Diskont- und Avalkredit ~)* drawings against the facility may take the form of a Euroloan, a discount or a guarantee credit

Ausnutzbarkeit *(~ des Kredites für Akkreditive)* availability (usability) of the loan for documentary credits

ausnutzen 1. to use, to make use of, to utilise, to exploit, *(das eingeräumte Limit voll ~)* to fully use up the limit
2. *(Kursunterschiede ~, arbitrieren)* to benefit from (to profit from, to take advantage of) price differences, to arbitrate
3. to draw, *(eine Fazilität zu mehr als 60 % ~)* to borrow more than 60 % under a facility, *(eine Kreditlinie ~)* to draw on (to make use of, to utilise, to avail o. s. of) a credit line

Ausnutzen/Ausnutzung 1. utilisation, making use of **2.** *(~ von Preisungleichgewichten)* capitalising on (taking advantage of, benefiting from) price anomalies **3.** *(~ einer Kreditlinie)* drawing on a credit line

Ausnutzungsgrad degree of utilisation, availment rate (ratio), *(eines Kreditrahmens)* drawing limit (availability)

ausplatzieren to place in the market *(ausplatzierte Ausleihungen)* outplaced lendings

Ausplatzierung *(~ von Hypothekendarlehen)* outplacement of mortgage loans, *(~ der mit den Kreditforderungen verbundenen Risiken)* outplacement of the risks inherent in lending operations, placing credit risks in the market

ausreichen 1. to be sufficient, to suffice **2.** *(einen Kredit ~)* to lend, to extend a loan **3.** *(eine Garantie ~)* to grant (to furnish) a guarantee

ausreichend 1. *adj.* sufficient, adequate, *(~e Besicherung)* adequate collateralisation, *(keine ~e Deckung aufweisen)* to be without sufficient cover, *(~er Nachweis)* satisfactory proof
2. *adv.* *(~ qualifiziert sein)* to be sufficiently qualified

Ausreichung 1. *(~ eines Darlehens)* loan extension (accommodation, origination), extending a loan **2.** *(~ einer Garantie)* granting (furnishing) a guarantee

Ausreißer-Gap runaway gap

ausrichten 1. to arrange, to organise **2.** *(~ auf)* to target at, to direct at, to gear to, to orientate, *(der Bezugsrechtskurs richtet sich am Marktkurs aus)* the subscription price takes its bearings from the current market price, *(das Geschäft auf Privatanleger ~)* to target business at retail investors

Ausrichtung 1. arrangement, organisation
2. orientation, direction, focus, *(mittelfristige ~)* medium-term orientation (projection), *(starke ~ auf Bankaktien)* heavy leaning in favour of bank shares, *(Gesellschaft mit globaler ~)* company with a global footprint, *(strategische ~)* strategic orientation, *(defensive ~ eines Portfolios)* defensive posture of a portfolio
3. targeting, *(~ der Anlagen auf Inlandswerte)* focus(s)ing investments on domestic equities

ausrollen *(einen Fonds ~)* to launch (to roll out) a fund

ausrufen 1. to declare, to proclaim **2.** to call out, e. g. the specific details of a buy or sell order

Ausrüstungsinvestitionen equipment spending, investments in machinery and equipment

Aussage 1. statement, declaration 2. *(jur.)* testimony, *(eine ~ erzwingen/verweigern)* to enforce/to refuse testimony

Aussagekraft informative value

aussagen 1. to state, to declare 2. to give evidence (e.g. to a committee), to testify, *(unter Eid ~)* to declare under oath, to depose, to make a deposition

ausschalten *(Kreditrisiken ~)* to eliminate (to lay off) credit risks, *(Wettbewerb ~)* to eliminate (to stifle) competition, *(alle Zweifel hinsichtlich der Kundenbonität ~)* to dismiss all doubt with regard to the customer's credit standing, *(das innewohnende Währungsrisiko ~)* to neutralise the inherent currency exposure

Ausschaltung 1. elimination 2. *(nach ~ der Saisoneinflüsse)* after adjustment for seasonal influences

ausscheiden to retire, to withdraw, *(aus einem Amt ~)* to leave (to resign from) office, *(als Gesellschafter ~)* to retire as a partner, *(aus einem Projekt ~)* to withdraw from a project, *(aus einem Rennen ~)* to drop out of a race, *(turnusmäßig ~)* to retire in rotation

Ausscheiden 1. retirement, resignation 2. withdrawal, departure

Ausschläge *(~ an den Aktienmärkten)* sharp swings (erratic fluctuations) in the stock markets

ausschlagen 1. to decline, to refuse, to turn down 2. *(verzichten auf)* to relinquish

ausschlaggebend *(~ sein)* to be decisive, to decide, to turn the scale, to be at the centre of, *(~e Faktoren für die weitere Entwicklung am Aktienmarkt)* determining (decisive) factors for the further trend in stock market prices, price determinants, *(~e Stimme)* casting (tie-breaking) vote

ausschließbar *(~e Haftung)* excludable liability

ausschließen 1. to exclude, to preclude, to rule out, *(sich gegenseitig ~)* to be mutually exclusive, *(von der Deckung ~)* to exclude from coverage, *(eine vorzeitige Rückzahlung des Kredites ~)* to preclude early repayment of the loan, *(eine Zinssenkung ~)* to rule out a cut in interest rates, *(andere Bestimmungen ~)* to override other provisions
2. *(aussperren)* to lock out, to shut out 3. *(einen Gesellschafter ~)* to disqualify a shareholder 4. *(von der Insolvenz ~)* to separate from the insolvency estate

ausschließlich 1. *(alleinig)* exclusive, *(~er Gerichtsstand)* exclusive jurisdiction, *(~es Recht)* exclusive (sole) right, *(im Geldhandel: ausschießlich Geber)* net sellers (lenders), *(im Geldhandel: ausschließlich Nehmer)* net buyers (borrowers)
2. *(außer, nicht mitgerechnet)* excluding, not included

Ausschließlichkeit exclusiveness

Ausschließlichkeitserklärung *(eines Kreditnehmers)* exclusive banking undertaking □ borrower's commitment to route all banking transactions through the lending bank

Ausschließungsklage → Ausschlussklage

Ausschluss 1. exclusion, preclusion, *(unter ~ der gesamtschuldnerischen Haftung)* excluding (to the exclusion) of joint and several liability, *(~ der Leistungspflicht)* exclusion of the right to specific performance, *(unter ~ der vorzeitigen Tilgung)* excluding the possibility of a premature redemption 2. *(Aussperrung)* lock-out 3. *(eines Gesellschafters)* disqualification 4. *(Rechtsverwirkung)* foreclosure

Ausschluss / ~bestimmung exclusory clause, preclusion clause; **~frist** preclusion (preclusive) period; **~gründe** *(bei einem Gesellschafterausschluss)* grounds for disqualification (foreclosure)

Ausschluss / ~klage 1. *(mit dem Ziel des Ausscheidens eines Gesellschafters)* application for a disqualification order **2.** foreclosure action; **~klausel** exclusory clause, preclusion clause, disclaimer

Ausschluss / ~prinzip exclusion principle; **~recht** right of exclusion; **~urteil 1.** disqualification order **2.** foreclosure order; **~verfahren** foreclosure (exclusion) proceedings

Ausschnittsfactoring sector factoring

ausschöpfen 1. to use, to exhaust, *(alle Rechtsmittel gegen den Schuldner ~)* to exhaust all remedies against the debtor, *(die vorhandenen Refinanzierungsquellen voll ~)* to make full use of available funding sources, *(ein Wahlrecht ~)* to take up an option **2.** to draw (fully), *(den Beleihungswert mit 60 % ~)* to borrow up to 60 % of the lending value, *(eine Kreditlinie ~)* to draw fully on a credit line, *(voll ausgeschöpfte Kreditlinie)* credit line fully drawn upon, credit line utilised in full **3.** *(sein Potenzial ~)* to live up to one's potential

Ausschöpfung exhaustion, full use, *(vollständige ~ einer Kreditlinie)* drawing fully upon (making full use of) a credit line

ausschreiben 1. to invite tenders for, to offer by tender, *(~des Unternehmen)* tenderee company **2.** *(ausgeschriebene Position)* advertised position **3.** *(Ziffern ~)* to write numbers in full

Ausschreibung tender, invitation for tenders (to tender), call for tenders, contract tender, *(im Wege der ~ anbieten)* to offer by tender

Ausschreibungs / ~bedingungen tender terms; **~formular** contract tender form; **~garantie** tender guarantee; **~schluss** tender closing date; **~teilnehmer** tenderer, tendering party; **~unterlagen** tender documents; **~verfahren** tender procedure

Ausschuss committee, commission, panel, (*Ausschuss der europäischen Aufsichtsbehörden für das Versicherungswesen und die betriebliche Altersversorgung)* Committee of European and Occupational Pension Supervisors □ replaced on 1 January 2011 by the European Insurance and Occupational Pensions Authority (EIOPA) *(Ausschuss der Europäischen Bankenaufseher)* Committee of European Banking Supervisors (CEBS) □ replaced on 1 January 2011 by the European Banking Authority *(Ausschuss der Europäischen Wertpapierregulierungsbehörden)* Committee of European Securities Regulators □ replaced on 1 January 2011 by the European Securities and Markets Authority (ESMA)

Ausschuss / ~bericht committee (panel) report; **~einsetzung** appointment (setting up) of a committee; **~entscheidung** committee ruling, decisions taken by the committee; **~mitglied** committee (panel) member

Ausschuss / ~sitzung committee meeting; **~sitzungsprotokoll** minutes of the committee meeting, committee record; **~untersuchungen** committee hearings (investigations); **~vorsitz/~vorsitzender** committee chairmanship/committee chairman

ausschüttbar *(~er Gewinn)* profit available for distribution, distributable profit, profit attributable to shareholders, *(~e Vermögenswerte)* distributable assets

ausschütten to distribute, to pay a dividend, *(nicht ausgeschütteter Jahresgewinn)* profit retained for the year, *(ausschüttender Fonds)* income fund, distributive fund, *(~de Gesellschaft)* distributing corporation

Ausschüttung distribution, payout, amount distributed, *(~ in bar)* cash payout, *(~ an die Aktionäre)* dividend payment to shareholders, *(~ aus dem Bilanzgewinn)* payout (payment) from the distributable profit; *(~ an die Gläubiger)* distribution to the creditors
(~ realisierter Kursgewinne) capital gains distribution, *(~ des Nettoge-*

A

winnes) distribution (apportionment) of the net profit, net profit allocation, *(~ in Form von Sachwerten)* distribution in kind, non-cash payout

Ausschüttungsanspruch claim (entitlement) to distribution, dividend claim (right), *(mit ~ ab ...)* carrying dividend rights as of (from) ...

Ausschüttungs / ~bedarf dividend requirements; **~belastung** tax burden on dividend payments, tax (charges) levied on distributions

ausschüttungsberechtigt *(~e Aktionäre)* shareholders entitled to dividend payments (to distributions), *(~e Titel)* securities ranking for dividend payments (distributions)

Ausschüttungs / ~betrag distribution amount, amount (to be) distributed; **~erlös** *(bei einem Insolvenzverfahren)* dividend in insolvency

ausschüttungsfähig → ausschüttbar

Ausschüttungsgarantie dividend (payout) guarantee, guaranteed payout (distribution)

ausschüttungsgleich *(~er Betrag)* dividend equivalent amount, *(Besteuerung ~er Erträge)* taxation of deemed distributions

Ausschüttungs / ~rendite distribution (payout) yield; **~satz** rate of distribution, dividend rate; **~sperre** payout freeze, ban on distributions; **~summe 1.** amount distributed **2.** amount available for distribution

Außenbeitrag current account surplus

Außenfinanzierung external financing

Außenfinanzierungsbedarf external funding needs, *(~ der Unternehmen)* corporate demand for external resources

Außenhaftung external liability

Außenhandels / ~finanzierung foreign trade financing; **~geschäfte** foreign trade; **~überschuss** foreign (external) trade surplus

Außen / ~prüfung field audit(ing); **~stände** receivables, accounts receivable, claims outstanding

außenstehende Dritte non-affiliated third parties

Außensteuer / ~gesetz International Transactions Tax Act; **~recht** Law Governing External Tax Relations

Außenumsatz external sales, total sales less intragroup sales

Außenverhältnis *(im ~)* in relations with third parties, *(Haftung im ~)* liability towards third parties, *(Vertretung der Gesellschaft im ~)* representation of the company in its dealings with third parties, external representation of the company

Außenwert *(einer Währung)* external value of a currency

Außenwirtschaft foreign trade and payments, foreign trade sector

Außenwirtschafts / ~gesetz Foreign Trade and Payments Act; **~verordnung** Foreign Trade and Payments Ordinance

außerbilanziell *(~e Geschäfte)* off-balance sheet transactions (activities), *(~e Positionen)* off-balance sheet positions, OBS exposure, *(~e Risiken)* off-balance sheet risks, *(~e Verpflichtungen)* off-balance sheet commitments, *(~e Verschuldung)* off-balance sheet leverage, *(~e Zinsgeschäfte)* interest-related operations not reflected in the balance sheet

außerbörslich 1. *adj. (~er Handel)* off-board (off-floor) trading, *(~er Handel in derivativen Produkten)* OTC derivatives trading, off-exchange derivatives trading, *(~e Notierung)* off-board price, quotation off the exchange, off-the-market quotation (price), free market price, *(~e Option)* OTC (over-the-counter) option, *(~es Termingeschäft)* OTC forward deal **2.** *adv. (~ handeln)* to trade off the floor (off the board)

Außerdeckungsgeschäft non-cover transactions

außergerichtlich *(~e Sanierung)* out-of-court restructuring, *(~e Streitbeilegung)* alternative dispute resolution, *(~es Verfahren)* non-judicial (out-of-court) proceedings, *(~er Vergleich)* out-of-court settlement (composition), private settlement

Außerkompetenzkredite loans exceeding the approval powers (of the relevant officer or branch establishment)

Außerkraftsetzung repeal, annulment, abrogation

Außerkurssetzung 1. withdrawal from circulation **2.** *(von Wertpapieren)* invalidation of securities

außerordentlich *(~e Abgänge des Anlagevermögens)* extraordinary retirements, *(~e Abschreibung)* exceptional write-down, → außerplanmäßige Abschreibung, *(~e Aufwendungen)* extraordinary (non-recurrent) expenses, *(~e Belastungen)* extraordinary charges (e. g. write-offs or loan losses), *(~e Einkünfte)* extraordinary capital income, *(~e Erträge)* extraordinary earnings, *(~e Hauptversammlung)* extraordinary general meeting, *(~e Rechnung)* extraordinary account(s)

außerplanmäßig *(~e Abschreibung)* unscheduled writedowns, impairment loss, *(~e Ausgaben)* unbudgeted (non-budgeted, extra-budgetary) expenditure, *(~e Tilgung) (a) (bei einer Anleihe)* unscheduled redemption *(b) (bei einem Kredit)* special (unscheduled) repayment, *(~e Wertminderung)* exceptional impairment

äußerst *(~e Konditionen)* lowest (minimum) terms, most keenly priced terms

außervertraglich *(~es Schuldverhältnis)* non-contractual obligation

aussetzen 1. to suspend, to halt, *(die Notierung einer Aktie vorübergehend ~)* to suspend temporarily the quotation of a share, *(die Vollziehung ~)* to suspend enforcement, *(das Verfahren ~)* to suspend (to stay, to defer) the proceedings
2. *(Zins- und Währungsrisiken ~)* to expose to interest and currency risks

Aussetzung 1. suspension, deferment, *(~ der Börsennotierung)* suspension of listing, *(~ des Handels)* trading halt, temporary stoppage of trading, *(~ der Tilgungszahlungen)* suspension of principal payments, halting debt repayments, redemption break, *(~ eines Vertrages)* suspension of contract performance
2. exposing, exposure
3. *(~ der (Hypotheken-)Zwangsvollstreckung)* deferment of enforcement action, stay of mortgage foreclosure proceedings

Aussetzungs / ~bescheid notice of suspension; **~vertrag** suspension agreement; **~zinsen** interest accruing to the Tax Office during the temporary suspension of the assessment notice

Aussicht outlook, *(~en für eine konjunkturelle Erholung)* prospects for an economic recovery, *(ohne ~ auf eine Kurserholung)* with no price rally in sight

aussitzen *(die Baisse ~)* to ride out the bear cycle

aussonderbar *(~e Vermögenswerte) (im Insolvenzververfahren)* assets eligible for segregation

aussondern 1. to set aside, to separate (out)
2. *(im Insolvenzverfahren)* to segregate (from the insolvency estate)
3. *(in der Konzernbilanz)* to eliminate from consolidation

Aussonderung 1. setting aside (apart)
2. *(im Insolvenzverfahren)* segregation, *(~ von Vermögenswerten)* segregation of assets from the debtor's estate, release from the insolvency estate
3. elimination from consolidation

Aussonderungsberechtigte/r *(aussonderungsberechtigter Gläubiger)* party entitled to demand segregation of an asset, creditor entitled to segregation

Aussonderungsrecht right (entitlement) to segregation

aussperren to lock out, to shut out

aussprechen 1. to express, to state, to declare **2.** *(die Kündigung ~)* to give notice of termination **3.** *(sich gegen eine Strategie ~)* to oppose a strategy

ausstatten to endow with, to provide with, *(mit einem marktgerechten Zinssatz ~)* to pay the going market rate, *(mit einer Reihe von Vorrechten ~)* to endow with a number of prerogatives (preferential rights), *(ausgestattet mit Dividendenansprüchen)* bearing dividends, carrying dividend rights *(ausgestattet mit einer Laufzeit von zehn Jahren)* with a life of ten years, running for ten years, *(ausgestattet mit einer Restlaufzeit von zwei Jahren)* having two years to run to maturity, *(besser ausgestattet sein)* to be better resourced, *(finanziell gut ausgestattetes Unternehmen)* company operating on a sound financial basis

Ausstattung 1. endowment, *(~ mit Eigenmitteln)* available equity, available capital resources, provision with capital resources, *(~ mit zusätzlichem Kapital)* endowment with additional capital, provision of fresh funds, *(~ mit einer attraktiven Verzinsung)* carrying an attractive coupon
2. *(~ einer Anleihe) (a)* bond coupon (yield) *(b)* bond terms
3. *(betriebliche)* fixtures and fittings

Ausstattungsmerkmale bond features

ausstehen 1. to be outstanding **2.** *(die Entscheidung steht noch aus)* the decision has yet to come (is still pending)

ausstehend 1. outstanding, *(~e Einlagen auf das Grundkapital)* unpaid contributions to subscribed capital, unpaid share capital, *(~e Forderungen)* outstanding receivables, *(~er Kreditbetrag)* outstanding amount of the loan, unpaid principal balance, *(~er Betrag bei Schuldnerausfall)* exposure at default
2. *(~e Kontrakte)* open contracts, open interest
3. *(überfällig) (~e Zinszahlungen)* overdue interest payments

aussteigen 1. to withdraw (from an agreement) **2.** to liquidate, to sell, *(aus dem Aktienmarkt ~)* to switch (to move) out of equity investments

ausstellen 1. exhibit, to display **2.** *(Schecks/Wechsel ~)* to issue (to make out, to draw, to write) cheques/bills of exchange, *(ausgestellt auf den Begünstigten)* made out to the beneficiary

Aussteller 1. exhibitor **2.** issuer, drawer, writer

Aussteller / ~bonität issuer's (drawer's) credit standing; **~datei** issuer file; **~haftung/ ~obligo** drawer's liability (exposure)

Ausstellung 1. exhibition **2.** issue, drawing

Ausstellungstermin 1. date of issue **2.** date of drawing

Ausstieg 1. exit, sale, *(~ aus einer Beteiligung/einem Investment)* investment exit, selling an interest **2.** *(~ aus einer Vereinbarung)* withdrawal from an agreement

Ausstiegsklausel exit clause, walk-away clause, opt-out clause

Ausstiegsmöglichkeit exit route (channel, opportunity)

ausstrahlen *(positiv auf das Börsengeschehen ~)* to have a positive impact on the stock market

Austausch 1. exchange, swap, *(~ von Forderungen/Vermögenswerten)* asset swap, *(~ von Verpflichtungen)* liabilities swap **2.** *(~ der Geschäftsleitung)* management shakeout

austauschbar exchangeable, interchangeable, *(fungibel)* fungible

Austauschbarkeit fungibility, substitutability

austauschen to exchange, to swap

Austrocknen *(~ eines Marktes)* drying up of a market

ausüben 1. to exercise, *(Bezugsrechte/Optionen ~)* to exercise (to take up) subscription rights/options **2.** *(Druck/Einfluss ~)* to exert (to wield) pressure/influence **3.** to pursue (to carry out) an activity **4.** *(ein Amt ~)* to hold an office

Ausübung 1. exercise, *(~ von Bezugsrechten)* exercise of subscription rights, taking up subscription (stock) rights, taking up one's entitlement (rights) in a capital issue, *(bei ~ seines/ihres Ermessens)* in the exercise of his/her reasonable discretion, *(bei ~ der Option)* upon (at the time of) exercise of the option **2.** exertion **3.** pursuance, carrying out

Ausübungs / ~anzeige *(im Optionsgeschäft)* notice of an exercise assignment; **~berechtigung** right of exercise, *(ausübungsberechtigt)* entitled to exercise; **~erklärung** exercise notice

Ausübungs / ~frist exercise period; **~limit** exercise limit (cap) ; **~preis** *(im Optionsgeschäft)* strike (striking) price, exercise price □ price at which the buyer has the right to buy (call option) or to sell (put option) the underlying instrument

Ausübungs / ~risiko execution risk; **~wahrscheinlichkeit** likelihood of the exercise; **~zeitraum** exercise period

Ausverkauf 1. clearance sale **2.** *(an der Börse)* sell-out **3.** *(wegen Geschäftsaufgabe)* winding-up sale

Auswahl choice, selection

auswählen to choose, to select

Auswahl / ~factoring selective factoring; **~fehler** selection (sampling) error; **~kriterien** selection (eligibility, choice) criteria

auswechseln to exchange, to replace

Auswechselung exchange, *(~ der Unternehmensführung)* replacing the current management, management shakeout

Ausweg *(~ aus der Finanzkrise)* way out of the financial crisis

ausweichen *(einer klaren Entscheidung ~)* to evade (to avoid) a clear-cut decision

Ausweich / ~bestimmungen fall-back provisions; **~klausel** escape clause

Ausweis 1. identity card
2. reporting, disclosure, *(~ zu den Gestehungskosten)* statement at cost, *(~ in der Handelsbilanz)* recognition in the commercial balance sheet, reporting for financial statement purposes, *(~ von Pensionsgeschäften)* accounting treatment of repo transactions, *(~ in der Steuerbilanz)* recognition in the tax accounts, reporting for tax purposes, *(~ der Zinserträge)* reporting interest income
3. *(Bankausweis)* return, statement

ausweisen 1. to show, *(sich ~)* to prove one's identity
2. to state, *(als Aufwand ~)* to report as net expense, *(getrennt in der Bilanz ~)* to show (to report) separately in the accounts, to separate out in the accounts, *(in der laufenden G+V ~)* to recognise in current period earnings, *(unmittelbar in der G+V ~)* to record directly in the income statement, *(zum Kurswert ~)* to report at market value
(unter Sonderaufwendungen ~) to record through special expenditure, *(unter dem Strich ~)* to show (to report) below the line, *(unter dem Umlaufvermögen ~)* to classify in the accounts as current assets, to carry as a current asset, to reflect under the section current assets
3. *(der nach Abzug der Wertberichtigungen ausgewiesene Betrag)* the amount reported net of allowances, *(in der Bilanz ausgewiesene Ausleihungen)* lendings reported (reflected) in the balance sheet, *(ausgewiesener Nettoaufwand)* net charge stated, *(ausgewiesene Rücklagen)* disclosed reserves

Ausweis / ~pflicht 1. obligation (duty) to report in the accounts, reporting requirement, disclosure duty, *(ausweispflichtig)* subject to reporting (recognition) in the accounts, subject to reporting requirements **2.** identification requirement; ~**wahlrecht** disclosure (recognition) option

Ausweitung expansion, enlargement, widening, *(~ im kurzfristigen Kreditbereich)* increase in short-term lendings, *(~ des Kreditvolumens)* expansion of the loan portfolio, *(~ der Zinsspanne)* widening of the interest margin

Auswertung analysis, evaluation, interpretation

auswirken *(sich belastend/günstig ~)* to have a detrimental/favourable effect, *(sich negativ auf das Ergebnis ~)* to have a negative (adverse) effect on earnings (on the performance), to take a heavy toll on profits

Auswirkung consequence, effect, fallout, *(~ auf die Kreditnachfrage)* impact (bearing, repercussions) on the demand for credit, *(~ auf die Marktposition der Bank)* implications for the bank's market position (standing)

Auswirkungs / ~**prinzip** effects doctrine; ~**studie** impact study

auszahlen 1. to pay, *(ein Darlehen ~)* to disburse (to pay out) a loan, *(ausgezahlter Darlehensbetrag)* loan proceeds, loan amount disbursed, *(am Schalter ~)* to pay out over the counter, *(gegen Vorlage der Dokumente ~)* to pay against presentation of the documents
2. *(einen Gesellschafter ~)* to pay off (to buy out) a partner
3. *(sich ~)* to pay off, to prove its worth, to prove successful, *(die Strategie wird sich längerfristig ~)* the strategy will pay off (will bear fruit) in the longer term

auszählen to count

Auszahl / ~**plan** withdrawal plan; ~**rate 1.** withdrawal rate, amount(s) withdrawn **2.** *(bei Krediten)* disbursement rate; ~**turnus** disbursement interval

Auszahlung payment, disbursement, *(~ der Anleihezinsen)* coupon payment, bond interest payment (distribution), *(~ des Darlehens an den Kreditnehmer)* disbursement of the loan to the borrower, crediting the borrower's account with the loan proceeds, *(~ in einer Summe)* paying out in one lump sum, *(mit 95 % ~)* loan proceeds being paid at a 5 % discount, *(mit 100 % ~)* loan proceeds being paid in full

Auszahlungen *(~ auf bereits zugesagte Darlehen)* disbursements on loans already committed, *(~ für den Erwerb von Finanzanlagen)* payments for the purchase of financial assets, *(~ aus dem Kredit)* disbursements under the loan agreement

Auszahlungs / ~**anspruch 1.** right to payment (disbursement) **2.** entitlement to the proceeds; ~**anweisung** disbursement (payment) instruction, payment order; ~**automat** cash dispenser, dispensing machine, → Geldautomat, → Einzahlungsautomat

Auszahlungs / ~**bedingungen** → Auszahlungsvoraussetzungen; ~**betrag** *(von Krediten)* net loan proceeds, net facility amount, disbursement amount, amount paid out; ~**bewilligung** authorisation of payment (disbursement), placing the loan principal at the borrower's disposal

Auszahlungs / ~**disagio** discount deducted from the loan principal; ~**ereignis** payout event; ~**ermächtigung** *(im Akkreditivgeschäft)* authority to pay; ~**frist** disbursement period; ~**funktionen** disbursement functions; ~**garantie** payment guarantee

Auszahlungs / ~**kurs** disbursement rate (i.e. loan principal less discount); ~**mechanismus** dispensing mechanism; ~**mittel** loan funds, funds required for disbursement; ~**modalitäten** terms of disbursement; ~**plan 1.** payment schedule **2.** *(für einen angesparten Betrag)* withdrawal plan

Auszahlungs / ~platz place of payment; **~pflicht** duty to disburse, mandatory disbursement; **~profil** *(~ bei Fälligkeit)* payoff profile at maturity (upon expiration); **~sperre** payment stop, *(Scheck)* countermand of payment; **~stelle** paying (disbursing) agency

Auszahlungs / ~überhang net lendings, lending surplus; **~überschuss** net disbursements; **~verlangen** payment request, request for disbursement; **~verlust** *(Disagio)* discount deducted from the loan principal

Auszahlungs / ~verpflichtungen disbursement (lending) commitments; **~voraussetzungen** disbursement requirements, conditions of (prerequisites for) disbursement, *(bei Großkrediten)* conditions precedent

Auszahlungs / ~wert net loan proceeds; **~zusage 1.** payment (disbursement) undertaking, undertaking to pay **2.** *(Kredit)* loan undertaking

Auszubildende/r vocational trainee

Auszug 1. *(Depotauszug)* statement of securities **2.** *(Kontoauszug)* statement of account **3.** *(~ aus einem Register)* extract from a register

Authentifizierung authentication, verifying a person's identity/the genuineness of a credit card

automatisch *(~er Abgleich)* automatic matching (reconciliation), *(~es Bietungssystem)* automatic bidding system, *(~e Ausführung/Ausübung)* automatic exercise, *(~e Stornierung)* automatic cancellation (reversal), *(~e Währungsumrechnung)* automatic currency conversion, → dynamische Währungsumrechnung, *(~e Wiederanlage der Ausschüttungen)* automatic reinvestment of distributions, *(~e Zusammenführung von Kauf- und Verkaufsaufträgen)* automatic matching of buy and sell orders

automatisiert *(~es Abrechnungssystem)* automated settlement system, *(~e Bankkundenbedienung)* automated servicing of bank customers, *(~er Handel)* automated trading, → algorithmischer Handel, *(~es Liegenschaftsbuch)* automated property register, *(~e Wertpapierleihe)* automated securities lending

Automobilaktien motors, automobile shares (stocks)

autorisieren *(autorisierte Zahlung)* authorised payment

Autorisierung *(~eines Kreditantrages)* approval of a loan request, *(~ einer Kreditkartenzahlung)* authorisation of a credit card payment

Autorisierungs / ~anforderung authorisation inquiry; **~anfrage** authorisation request; **~antwort** authorisation response; **~code** authorisation code; **~gebühr** authorisation fee (charge); **~nachricht** authorisation message; **~terminal** authorisation terminal; **~zentrale** authorisation centre

Aval (bill of exchange) guarantee, endorsement, *(speziell bei Forfaitierungen)* aval; **per ~** pour aval

Aval / ~akzept guarantee acceptance; **~auftrag** guarantee request, request to furnish a guarantee; **~ausreichung** → Avalhinauslegung

Aval / ~bank guarantor bank, bank providing a guarantee, → Avalist; **~bestandsvolumen** guarantee portfolio; **~forderungen** claims from guarantees furnished

Aval / ~geber guarantor; **~gemeinschaftskredit** syndicated (joint) guarantee credit; **~hinauslegung** provision of a guarantee, extending a guarantee credit (line), guarantee accommodation; **~inanspruchnahme 1.** drawing against a guarantee credit (line) **2.** calling on a guarantee

avalieren/avalisieren to guarantee, to avalise, to add the bank's name to a bill of exchange or promissory note, to provide one's aval, *(avalisiert durch die Bank des Importeurs)* guaranteed (avalised) by the importer's bank, *(avalierter Betrag)* guaranteed amount

Avalisierung avalisation, provision of an aval, guarantee undertaking given by a bank

Avalist guarantor, avalisor, party (bank) adding its name to a bill, guarantor bank, bank standing surety for the obligation of the drawee

Avalkonto guarantee account

Avalkredit guarantee credit, surety credit, credit by way of guarantee, guarantee line (facility); ~**geber** guarantor, *(avalkreditgebendes Institut)* guarantor bank, → Avalist; ~**linie** guarantee facility (line); ~**nehmer** guarantee; ~**vertrag** guarantee facility agreement

Aval / ~**laufzeit** life (term) of a guarantee; ~**linie** guarantee line; ~**nutzen** guarantee commission; ~**obligo** guarantee commitments, liability on payments guaranteed; ~**provision** guarantee commission; ~**provisionseinnahmen** guarantee commission income

Aval / ~**rahmen** guarantee line; ~**rahmenvertrag** guarantee facility agreement; ~**sicherheit** collateral for a guarantee furnished; ~**stellung**/~**übernahme** → Avalhinauslegung; ~**unterlegung** → Avalsicherheit

Aval / ~**urkunde** guarantee deed; ~**vermerk** guarantee undertaking; ~**verpflichtung** commitment (undertaking) to guarantee, undertaking to stand surety, *(pl)* commitments (obligations) under guarantees furnished

avisieren to advise, to notify, *(avisierende Bank)* advising (notifying) bank, *(dem Exporteur die Akkreditiveröffnung ~)* to advise the exporter of the opening of the credit, to notify the exporter that the credit is available

Avisierung advising, advice, notifying, *(~ eines Akkreditivs)* advising (notification of) a documentary credit, *(~ einer Remboursermächtigung)* notification of a reimbursement authority

Avisierungs / ~**gebühr** notification fee; ~**pflicht** notification requirement (duty); ~**provision** advising (notification) commission

AWG → Außenwirtschaftsgesetz

AWV → Außenwirtschaftsverordnung

AZV → Auslandszahlungsverkehr

B

b → bezahlt

B → Brief; – **B** → gestrichen, Brief

Backtesting backtesting □ testing a model, strategy or exposure on the basis of historical market conditions or past performances

Bad-Bank-Gesetz Bad Bank Act, → Finanzmarktstabilisierungs-Fortentwicklungsgesetz, → AIDA Modell

BaFin → Bundesanstalt für Finanzdienstleistungsaufsicht

Bagatell / ~betrag negligible (trifling, trifle) amount; **~grenzen** de minimis thresholds; **~marktklausel** de minimis exemption for small markets

Baisse sharp drop (fall), downhill slide, nosedive of stock (and/or bond) prices

Baisse / ~eindeckungen bear coverings, short coverings; **~engagement** bear commitment, bear (short) position; **~formation** *(Chart-Analyse)* bear (bearish) pattern

Baisse / ~manöver bear raid; **~markt** bear (depressed, slumping) market ; **~muster** bearish pattern (formation); **~phase** bear run; **~position** bear account (position), short position

Baisse / ~spekulant bear, short seller; **~-Spread** bear spread, *(mit Kaufoptionen)* bear call spread, *(mit Verkaufsoptionen)* bear put spread; **~stimmung** bearish mood (sentiment), bearishness; **~verkauf** bear sale; **~verkäufer** bear, short seller

Baissier bear, bearish player (market operator)

Balken / ~chart bar chart; **~code** bar code

Bandbreite 1. (fluctuation) band, variation range **2.** *(Spanne)* spread

Bandbreiten-Optionsschein range warrant

Bandposition time band position

Bank bank, banking organisation

Bankadresse *(am Kapitalmarkt)* bank name

bankähnlich *(~e Dienstleistungen)* banking-type services (facilities), near-banking services

Bank / ~aktien banks, bank shares (stocks); **~aktivitäten** banking operations; **~akzept** bank (banker's) acceptance; **~-an-Bank-Kredit** interbank lending (loan); **~-an-Bank-Sammelzahlung** interbank batch payment order; **~-an-Bank-Zahlung** interbank payment; **~angestellter** bank official, bank employee

Bank / ~anleihen bank bonds; **~arbeitstag** bank business day, *(bankarbeitstäglich ermitteln)* to determine on each banking day; **~aufsicht** → Bankenaufsicht

bankaufsichtlich *(~e Berichtspflichten)* supervisory reporting requirements, *(~e Erfassung)* capture (recording) under bank supervisory rules, *(~e Kontrolle)* prudential supervision, *(~e Liquiditätsvorschriften)* liquidity rules set by bank supervisory authorities, prudential liquidity rules, *(~e Regelungen/~es Regelwerk)* prudential regulations for banks, *(~er Überprüfungs- und Evaluierungsprozess)* supervisory review and evaluation process

bankaufsichtsrechtlich *(~ gewichtete Aktiva)* assets weighted for bank regulatory purposes, *(~es Eigenkapital)* regulatory capital, *(~e Erfordernisse)* bank regulatory requirements, *(~e Normen)* regulatory standards

B

Bank / ~auskunft banker's reference (opinion), status report, banking information; **~ausweis** bank return; **~auszug** bank statement, statement of account; **~automation** automation in banking; **~aval** bank guarantee, *(bankavalierter Solawechsel)* bank-guaranteed promissory note

Bank / ~beteiligungen banking interests, bank holdings; **~betrieb 1.** *(Tätigkeit)* banking, banking business (operations) **2.** *(Unternehmen)* bank, banking organisation; **~betriebskosten** bank's operating cost

Bank / ~bilanz bank balance sheet; **~bilanzierungsrichtlinie** (EU) Bank Accounts Directive; **~bürgschaft** banker's bond, bank surety bond

Bank / ~darlehen bank loan; **~darlehensforderungen** bank loan receivables; **~dienstleistung** banking service (facility, product); **~dienstleistungsautomat** automated teller machine; **~eigenmittel** bank's equity (own funds)

Bankeinlagen bank deposits

Bankeinlagen / ~schutz bank deposit protection; **~sicherung** bank deposit insurance; **~sicherungsfonds** bank deposit insurance fund

Bankeinzugsermächtigung → Einzugsermächtigung

Bankenabgabe bank levy □ comprises annual and special contributions to the restructuring fund (→ Restrukturierungsfonds); is imposed on all private, public and cooperative banks, as defined by Section 1 of the German Banking Act (KWG). → Restrukturierungsgesetz

Banken / ~abrechnungskurs settlement rate for banks; **~abrechnungsstelle** bankers' clearing house; **~apparat** banking system, banks

Bankenaufsicht banking (bank) supervision, supervising (monitoring) the banking industry, *(Genehmigung durch die ~)* regulatory approval, *(Kontrollbefugnisse der ~)* supervisory (regulatory) powers, *(Normen der ~)* supervisory (prudential) standards

Bankenaufsichtsbehörde bank supervisory authority, banking supervisor

Banken / ~bereich 1. banking industry (sector) **2.** *(Banktitel)* banks, bank shares (stocks); **~beschäftigungskartei** register of (a bank's) correspondents

Banken / ~bonifikation *(bei einer Emission)* selling commission, allowance; **~clearing** interbank clearing; **~debitoren** due from banks; **~-Direkthandel** direct interbank trading

Banken / ~einlagen deposits by banks; **~forderungen 1.** claims asserted by banks **2.** *(im Interbankgeschäft)* due from banks, claims on banks, lendings to banks; **~gelder** interbank money

Banken / ~gesetzgebung legislation on banks, bank (banking) regulation, regulation of the banking industry; **~gruppe 1.** group of banks, banking group **2.** *(i. S. von Institutsgruppe)* group of financial institutions

Banken / ~kartei correspondent file; **~konsortium** banking consortium (syndicate), consortium of banks; **~kreditoren** due to banks; **~liquidität** bank liquidity, liquidity of the banking system

Banken / ~marge 1. *(im Kreditgeschäft)* spread, margin **2.** *(im Emissionsgeschäft)* arrangement (management) fee; **~markt 1.** *(Interbanken-Markt)* interbank market **2.** *(Banktitel)* bank shares (stocks)

Banken / ~pfandrecht banker's lien; **~position** net interbank position, *(Überhang der Verbindlichkeiten)* net interbank borrowing position, *(Überhang der Forderungen)* net interbank lending position; **~publikum** *(Börse)* bank traders

Banken / ~rechtsharmonisierung harmonisation of banking laws; **~restrukturierungsgesetz** Bank Restructuring Act, → Kreditinstitute-Reorganisationsgesetz; ~**rettungsfonds** bank rescue fund

Banken / ~**sektor** → Bankenbereich; ~**selbstbehalt** bank's franchise; ~**spiegel** loan movement schedule □ list of lenders and borrowing commitments; ~**status** *(~ besitzen)* to be authorised to conduct banking operations

Banken / ~**stimmrecht** authority of the bank to vote customer shares (held under its custody); ~**stresstests** bank stress tests □ assess each institution's finances and its ability to withstand major adverse developments; ~**system** banking system

Banken / ~-**Telefonhandel** interbank off-board trading; ~**vertreter** representative of a bank (of the banking industry)

Bankentgelte bank charges (fees)

bankfähig bankable, negotiable, *(~er Wechsel)* bankable bill

Bank / ~**feiertag** bank holiday; ~**finanzierung** financing through a bank, bank financing, bank borrowing; ~**garantie** bank guarantee, banker's bond, bank letter of credit; ~**gebühren** bank charges

Bank / ~**geheimhaltungspflicht** banker's duty of secrecy; ~**geheimnis** banking (bank) secrecy, bank privacy, *(die Bank von der Wahrung des ~ses befreien)* to release the bank from its duty to maintain professional secrecy

Bank / ~**geld** bank (deposit) money; ~**gepflogenheiten** banking customs (practice); ~**geschäft 1.** banking business (operations) **2.** *(einzelnes)* banking transaction, *(im üblichen bankgeschäftlichen Verkehr)* in the course of ordinary banking operations

Bank / ~**gewerbe 1.** banking industry, banks **2.** banking profession (business); ~**giro 1.** bank giro **2.** bank endorsement; ~**girokonto** current (chequing, checking) account

Bank / ~**gläubiger** bank creditor; ~**guthaben 1.** money in the bank **2.** *(Bilanzposten)* cash in banks; ~**haus** bank, banking organisation; ~-**Identifizierungs-Code** Bank Identifier Code (BIC), → Bankleitzahl; ~**institut** banking institution (organisation)

bankintern *(~es Rating)* internal bank rating

Bank / ~**karte** bank card; ~**kauffrau**/~**kaufmann** bank officer, banker, banking professional, fully trained bank officer, *(Ausbildung zur/zum ~)* bank officer training

Bank / ~**konditionen** banking terms, bank's terms of business (business conditions); ~**konto** bank account; ~**kosten** bank charges

Bankkredit bank loan (credit), bank advance (accommodation), bank facility, *(~ mit festem/variablem Zinssatz)* fixed rate (floating rate) bank loan

Bankkredite *(durch ~ finanzieren)* to finance through bank borrowings; *(~ an den privaten Sektor)* bank lendings to the private sector (to private customers), *(~ an Unternehmen)* bank lendings to the corporate sector, *(~ an den Wohnungsbau)* bank lendings to the housing sector, residential lending by banks

Bank / ~**kreditkosten** cost of bank borrowing, cost of bank debt; ~**kreise** banking community; ~**lehre** bank officer training, student apprenticeship in banking, *(eine Banklehre absolvieren)* to undergo bank officer training

Bank / ~**leistungen** bank (banking) services, bank products, banking facilities; ~**leitzahl** bank code, *(international standardisierte Bankleitzahl)* bank identifier code (BIC), *(in den Vereinigten Staaten)* ABA routing number, transit routing number

bankmäßig *(im ~en Geschäftsverkehr)* in banking operations, *(~e Kreditbesicherung)* providing (putting up) bankable security for a loan, *(~e Seite der Transaktion)* banking side of the transaction, *(~e Sicherheit)* bankable

B

security, collateral acceptable to the bank, collateral (security) in form and substance satisfactory to the bank, *(~e Zahlung)* payment through a bank

Bank / **~nebenleistungen** incidental banking services, bank-related services; **~notenprivileg** note-issuing privilege; **~notenumlauf** bank notes in circulation, note circulation

Bank / **~obligation** bank bond (debenture); **~praxis** banking practice; **~produkt** banking product; **~prokurist** Assistant Vice President, authorised signatory, → Prokurist

Bank / **~provision** banking commission; **~prüfung** bank audit; **~publizität** disclosure requirements to be observed by banks; **~referenz** banker's reference; **~regel** → goldene Bankregel; **~rembours** bank documentary credit; **~schalter** bank counter(s); **~schalterhalle** banking hall; **~schalterstunden** banking (office) hours

Bank / **~scheck** bank cheque, banker's cheque, *(im internationalen Zahlungsverkehr)* banker's draft, international draft; **~schließfach** safe deposit box; **~schuldverschreibung** bank bond (note)

Bank / **~sicherheit** bank security, bank collateral; **~-Solawechsel** bank promissory note; **~sparen** bank saving; **~sparte** banking segment; **~spesen** bank charges; **~stellendichte** banking density; **~stellennetz** banking network

banktypisch *(~e Leistungen)* mainstream banking

Banküberweisung bank credit transfer, payment through a bank

banküblich *(~e Gebühren)* fees charged in line with banking practice, *(~e Sicherheit)* security in line with customary banking requirements (customary in banking operations), *(~e Sorgfalt)* care customary in banking, care stipulated by sound banking practice, *(~er Zinssatz)* going interest rate

Bank / **~usancen** banking customs; **~valoren** bank valuables; **~verbindlichkeiten** due to banks, bank debt; **~verbindung** banking (bank) relationship, banking connection; **~verkehr 1.** banking operations (activities) **2.** *(zwischen den Banken)* interbank dealings

bankverwandt *(~e Dienstleistungen)* near-banking services

Bank / **~vollmacht** bank power of attorney, power to operate a bank account, banking authorisation (authority); **~vollmachtsformular** power of attorney form; **~vorausdarlehen/~kredit** advance funding, prefinance facility, *(i. S. von Überbrückungskredit)* bridge-over facility (loan)

Bank / **~wechsel** bank bill (draft); **~werte** banks, bank shares (stocks); **~wesen** banking industry, banking; **~woche** bank return week; **~wochenstichtag** weekly bank return date

Bank / **~ziehung** bank (banker's) draft; **~zinsen** *(allgemein)* bank interest, *(Einlagensatz)* bank deposit rate, *(Kreditzins)* bank lending rate

bar *(~ abrechnen)* to settle for cash, *(~ angekaufte Kupons)* coupons purchased for cash, *(~ gegen Dokumente)* cash against documents

Bar / **~abfindung** cash compensation (settlement), compensation (indemnification) in cash; **~abfindungsangebot** *(an die Aktionäre)* cash bid (tender); **~abgänge** cash outflows; **~abgeltung** cash payment, → Barausgleich; **~abhebung 1.** cash drawing **2.** drawing money at a bank

Bar / **~abschluss** cash deal (transaction); **~akkreditiv** cash documentary credit; **~anschaffung** remittance in cash; **~aufwendungen** cash outlay

Bar / **~ausgleich** *(bei Börsentermingeschäften)* cash settlement □ cash payment for the difference between the opening and closing/exercise price of a contract, *(im Wege eines ~s regulieren)* to settle by cash; **~ausgleichsbe-**

trag cash settlement amount; ~**ausleihungen** cash lendings (advances)

Bar / ~**ausschüttung** cash distribution (payout); ~**ausstattung 1.** cash in (on) hand, available cash **2.** endowment with cash funds, cash endowment, cash allocation; ~**auszahlung** payment in cash, cash disbursement

Bar / ~**besicherung** cash collateralisation, → Barsicherheit; ~**bestand 1.** cash holdings, cash in (at) hand **2.** *(Kassenbestand)* cash in tills; ~**betrag** cash amount, amount in cash

Bar / ~**darlehen** cash loan (advance); ~**debitoren** cash lendings (advances); ~**deckung** cash cover, cash security; ~**depot** cash deposit, cash deposited as collateral; ~**dividende** cash dividend

Bar / ~**einforderung** cash call, calling in cash funds; ~**eingänge** cash receipts, cash takings; ~**einlage** cash contribution, contribution in cash; ~**einlageverpflichtung** cash contribution obligation; ~**einsatz** cash outlay

Bar / ~**einschuss 1.** cash injection, putting up cash resources (cash assets) **2.** *(Sicherheitsleistung bei Börsentermingeschäften, Effektenkrediten)* cash margin, margin deposited in cash; ~**einschusspflichten** cash margin requirements; ~**einzahlung** cash deposit (payment)

Bären / ~**divergenz** bearish divergence; ~**falle** bear trap, predicament facing short sellers when a sharply declining market reverses its trend; ~**flagge** *(Chart-Analyse)* bear flag

Bären / ~**formation** bearish pattern (formation); ~**markt** bear market, period of falling stock prices; ~**wimpel** bear pennant

Bar / ~**entnahme** cash drawing (withdrawal); ~**gebot** cash bid

bargedeckt *(~es Aval)* cash-supported guarantee

Bargeld cash, ready cash (money), notes and coin(s); ~**ausgabeautomat** cash dispenser; ~**bestand** cash in (on) hand, cash holdings

bargeldlos cashless, *(~es Zahlen an der Verkaufsstelle)* electronic funds transfer at the point of sale, *(~e Zahlung)* cashless payment, bank credit transfer, *(~er Zahlungsverkehr)* cashless payments, cashless money transmission

Bargeld / ~**sendung** cash remittance, remittance of notes and coins; ~**sicherheit** cash collateral (security); ~**umlauf** notes and coins in circulation, currency in circulation

Bar / ~**gut** cash commodity; ~**guthaben** cash in (on) hand, cash balance, cash assets; ~**inanspruchnahme** cash drawdown (drawing), drawdown (availment) in cash, *(~ in laufender Rechnung)* cash drawdown under current account

bärisch *(~e Ausbruchslücke)* bearish breakaway gap, *(~e Chartformation)* bearish chart formation, *(~es Dreieck)* bearish (descending) triangle, symmetrical triangle in a downtrend, *(~es Fortsetzungsmuster)* bearish continuation pattern, *(~es Umkehrmuster)* bearish reversal pattern

Bar / ~**kapital** cash capital, cash equity; ~**kapitalerhöhung** capital increase for cash, *(~ bei Einräumung eines Bezugsrechtes im Verhältnis 10:1)* cash capital increase on the basis of a one for ten rights issue; ~**kaution** cash security deposit, cash bail bond

Barkredit cash advance (loan), *(~ mit Zinsbegrenzung)* capped cash loan; ~**inanspruchnahme** drawing on a cash loan, cash drawing; ~**linie**/~**rahmen** cash line, cash credit line, cash drawing facility

Barleistungen 1. cash payments **2.** cash benefits

Barliquidität 1. liquid cash resources, cash liquidity **2.** *(Kennziffer)* tier 1 liquidity, cash ratio

Barmittel cash (liquid) funds, available cash, *(erhaltene/gezahlte ~)* cash received/cash disbursed; ~**abfluss**

B

cash outflow, outflow of cash funds; ~**rücklage** cash reserve, cash resources; ~**zufluss** cash inflow, inflow of cash funds

Barometer *(~ für das Anlegervertrauen)* barometer of investor confidence, *(~ für die Börsenstimmung)* indicator of stock market sentiment

Barregulierung cash settlement

Barren bar; ~**gold** gold bullion

Barreserve cash reserve assets □ cash in hand, central bank balances, public debt instruments and bills eligible for rediscount with central banks

Barrier-Option barrier option, trigger option □ option that is either activated or terminated if the cash price of the underlying asset reaches, exceeds or falls to a specified level (barrier)

Bar / ~**risiken** cash risks; ~**scheck** cash (open) cheque; ~**sicherheit** cash collateral, security (collateral) in the form of cash ; ~**sicherungsfonds** cash collateral account

Bar / ~**überschuss** cash surplus; ~**unterlegung** *(~ der hinausgelegten Garantien)* cash collateralisation of (provision of cash collateral for) the guarantees furnished; ~**verbriefung** cash securitisation; ~**verfügung** cash drawing, drawing in cash, cash withdrawal

Bar / ~**vergütung** **1.** cash remuneration, remuneration in cash **2.** cash bonus; ~**verlust** **1.** cash loss **2.** net loss; ~**vermögen** cash (liquid) assets; ~**vorschuss** cash advance, short-term cash facility

Barwert **1.** cash value, market value **2.** *(~ der erwarteten zukünftigen Cashflows)* net present value of expected future cash flows **3.** *(eines Wechsels)* discounting proceeds, face value less discount

Barwert / ~**methode** net present value concept, present valuing; ~**risiko** net present value risk

Barzahlung cash payment, payment in cash, *(~ bei Auftragserteilung)* cash with order, *(~ bei Lieferung/Verschiffung)* cash on delivery/on shipment, *(~ gegen Dokumente)* cash against documents

Barzahlungs / ~**bedingungen** cash terms; ~**rabatt** cash discount; ~**verkehr** cash transactions

Barzeichner cash subscriber

Basel I first international bank accord that came into force in 1992

Basel II Guidelines on minimum capital requiremets, supervisory review and market discipline set out in the International Convergence of Capital Measurement and Capital Standards (Internationale Konvergenz der Eigenkapitalmessung und Eigenkapitalanforderungen) published by the Basel Committee on Banking Supervision in 2005

Basel 2,5 amendments and enhancements to the → Basel II framework

Basel III Based on Basel II, the revised accord aims at building a safer financial system by strengthening and overhauling capital and liquidity standards. The new capital framework has three pillars: the minimum common equity requirement (→ hartes Kernkapital), the capital conservation buffer (→ Kapitalerhaltungspolster) and the countercyclical buffer (→ antizyklisches Polster). Other important features of Basel III are the new liquidity standards, → Mindestliquiditätsquote, → strukturelle Liquiditätsquote. The new standards will be phased in from January 2013 onwards and fully implemented by the end of 2017.

Baseler Ausschuss für Bankenaufsicht Basel Committee on Banking Supervision (BCBS) □ consists of representatives of bank supervisory authorities and central banks

Basis **1.** basis, base, *(Handel auf besicherter ~)* collateralised trading
2. basis □ difference between the cash

price of a financial instrument and the futures price for a particular month

Basis / ~**ansatz** *(Basel II)* foundation approach; ~**ausfallrate** basic default rate; ~**eigenmittel** core capital; ~**geschäft** underlying transaction; ~**gesellschaft** holding company operating abroad

Basis / ~**handel** basis trade, trading the spread between the futures market and the underlying cash market; ~**indikatoransatz** *(zur Bemessung des operationellen Risikos)* basic indicator approach □ links the capital charge for operational risk to the gross income; ~**instrument** host instrument

Basis / ~**konvergenz** basis convergence; ~**lastschrift** → SEPA-Basislastschrift; ~**metallderivate** derivatives on base metals; ~**option** → Ausgangsoption

Basispreis *(im Optionsgeschäft)* exercise price, strike (striking) price □ price at which the holder of an option may buy or sell the underlying asset; ~**schritte** strike price intervals

Basisprospekt base prospectus

Basispunkt basis point □ one basis point = 0.01 %; ~**wert** basis point value

Basisrisiko basis risk □ risk that the price development of a financial instrument or commodity in the futures market is not exactly correlated with the development of its price in the underlying cash market

Basisrisikogewicht base risk weight

Basissatz strike rate, basis rate □ specified interest rate at which the holder of an interest rate option may exercise his right

Basis-Swap basis swap □ subset of an interest rate swap, i.e. floating rate interest payments calculated on one basis are swapped for floating rate interest payments calculated on another basis

Basis / ~**titel** underlying security; ~**trend** basic trend; ~**vertrag** *(in Verbindung mit einem eingebetteten Derivat)* host contract; ~**währung** reference (base) currency; ~**wert** underlying instrument, underlying interest

Basis / ~**zeitraum** base period; ~**zins/zinssatz** 1. base rate, basic interest rate 2. *(Referenz-Zinssatz)* reference rate 3. *(bei Zinsbegrenzungsvereinbarungen)* → Basissatz

Bassin / ~**übereignung** assignment of goods to a trustee; ~**vertrag** deed of multiple assignment □ goods assigned under this deed to a trustee serve as collateral for several lendings

Bau / ~**aktien** building shares (stocks), buildings, constructions; ~**antrag** building application; ~**darlehen** building loan, construction loan; ~**darlehensgeber** construction lender

Baufinanzierung 1. *(a)* construction (building) finance *(b)* mortgage lending 2. *(im gewerblichen Bereich)* *(a)* commercial property financing *(b)* commercial mortgage lending 3. *(Wohnungsbaufinanzierung)* *(a)* housing finance *(b)* residential mortgage lending

Baufinanzierungs / ~**geschäft** building finance operations; ~**konditionen** building loan terms; ~**kredit** building (construction) loan, housing loan; ~**mittel** building (housing) finance

Bau / ~**genehmigung** building permit; ~**gelder** building finance; ~**geldkredit** interim building loan, bridging loan; ~**gesetzbuch** German Building Code; ~**gewerbe** building industry

Bau / ~**grundstück** building plot; ~**handwerkerbürgschaft** builder's guarantee; ~**herrenmodell** builder-owner model; ~**kastenprinzip** building block approach; ~**kosten** construction (building) cost; ~**kostenzuschüsse** building cost subsidies

Bau / ~**kredit** building loan; ~**kreditzinsen** building loan rates; ~**lastenverzeichnis** register of easements and servitudes; ~**leistungsdeckung** structural works cover

B

baulich *(~e Grundstücksbestandteile)* tangible appurtenances

Bau / **~nebenwerte** building-related stocks; **~nutzungsverordnung** Land Use Regulation; **~sicherungshypothek** builder's lien

Bauspar / **~antrag** application for a Bauspar contract, → Bausparvertrag; **~bedingungen** Standard Terms and Conditions for Savings and Loan Contracts; **~beiträge** → Bausparleistungen

Bauspar / **~darlehen** building society loan, loan taken out with a building and loan association; **~einlagen** building society deposits, deposits with building and loan associations

Bausparen saving with building societies, investment in building society savings schemes

Bausparer building society customer

Bauspar / **~finanzierung** → Bausparkassenfinanzierung; **~förderung** encouraging savings with building societies; **~gelder** building society funds (finance), funds provided by a building and loan association; **~guthaben** amount saved under a savings and loan contract

Bausparkasse building society, building and loan association, savings and loan association

Bausparkassen / **~-Einlagensicherungsfonds** Deposit Protection Fund of German Building and Loan Associations; **~finanzierung** financing through a building and loan association (with building society funds); **~gesetz** German Building and Loan Associations Act

Bausparkassen / **~konditionen** terms and conditions for building society accounts; **~konto** building society account, account with a building and loan association; **~mittel** → Bauspargelder; **~verordnung** Regulation on Building and Loan Associations

Bauspar / **~leistungen** payments under a (building society's) savings and loan contract; **~summe** principal (face value) of a savings and loan contract, contractually agreed Bauspar amount; **~tarif** building society tariff (rates)

Bauspar / **~vertrag** (building society's) savings and loan contract, Bauspar contract, *(Zuteilung eines ~es)* allocation of a savings and loan contract, allocating a Bauspar contract for disbursement □ i.e. repayment of the amount saved and disbursement of the home loan; **~zinsen** building society interest rates, deposit/loan rates offered by building and loan associations

Bausteinprinzip building block approach

Bauträger developer, property development company; **~finanzierungen** property development finance, lendings to property development companies; **~kredit** property development loan

Bau / **~vorschriften** building code; **~wechsel** building bill; **~wert** building value; **~werte** building shares (stocks), buildings, constructions

Bauzinsen 1. building loan rates **2.** interest paid to shareholders until commencement of the company's operations

Bauzwischenfinanzierung/~zwischenkredit bridge-over facility, interim building loan

b.a.w. / **~-Konditionen** terms (rates) valid until further notice; **~-Kredit** loan repayable on demand; **~-Zusage** loan facility valid until further notice

bB → bezahlt Brief

BDSG → Bundesdatenschutzgesetz

beabsichtigen to intend, to plan, to envisage

beachten 1. to pay attention to, *(Anlagerisiken ~)* to heed (to observe, to be mindful of) investment risks, *(nicht ~)* to pay no heed to **2.** *(berücksichtigen)* to consider, to take into account (consideration) 3. *(einhalten)* to observe, to comply with

Beachtung 1. attention, heed 2. consideration, taking into account 3. observance, compliance with

beanspruchbar *(~e Kreditlinie)* usable (available) credit line, line of credit that can be drawn upon

beanspruchen 1. to claim, to lay claim to, to demand 2. *(für sich in Anspruch nehmen)* to claim credit for 3. *(nutzen)* to make use of, to take recourse to, to avail o. s. of 4. *(eine Kreditlinie ~)* to draw on a credit line, → Anspruch, in ~ nehmen

Beanspruchung 1. claim, claiming, demand 2. making use of, availment, taking (having) recourse to 3. drawing 4. *(Druck)* pressure, strain, → Inanspruchnahme

beanstanden to object to, to complain about, to query

beantragen 1. to request, to demand, to apply for, *(einen Zahlungsaufschub ~)* to request a deferral in repayment
2. to file (to put in) a claim, *(die Insolvenzeröffnung ~)* to file a petition in insolvency
3. to sue, *(eine einstweilige Verfügung ~)* to sue for (to seek) an interlocutory injunction

Beantragung request, demand, application

bearbeiten to handle, to process, to deal with

Bearbeitung handling, processing, dealing with, *(die für die ~ des Kredites in Rechnung gestellten Gebühren)* fees charged for processing the loan

Bearbeitungs / ~dauer *(für einen Kreditantrag)* processing time, turnaround time; **~entgelt/~gebühr** processing fee, service charge, handling charge (fee); **~provision** handling commission

beaufsichtigen to supervise, to control, to monitor, to oversee

Beaufsichtigung supervision, control, monitoring, surveillance, *(~ auf konsolidierter Basis)* supervision on a consolidated basis

beauftragen 1. to instruct, to commission, to direct, to order, to charge with, to assign, *(der von der Bank beauftragte Berater)* the consultant retained by the bank, *(die Bank mit der Eröffnung des Akkreditivs ~)* to instruct the bank to open (to issue) the documentary credit
2. *(mit dem Inkasso ~)* to entrust with the collection of, to instruct to collect

Beauftragte/r 1. *(beauftragte Bank)* bank instructed to …, mandated bank 2. *(Bevollmächtigter)* proxy, mandatary 3. *(Vertreter)* representative, agent

Beauftragung commissioning, assignment, mandate

Bebauung *(~ für gewerbliche Nutzung)* development for commercial use

Bebauungsplan land use plan, zoning ordinance

Bedarf demand, requirement(s), need(s), *(~ an langfristigem Fremdkapital)* need for external long-term capital, *(~ an zusätzlichen Krediten)* additional borrowing requirements, *(bei ~ aufnehmen)* to raise as and when required

Bedarfs / ~analyse requirements analysis; **~dichte** demand density

bedarfsgerecht *(~ platzieren)* to place in line with market requirements, *(~e Kreditvergabe)* customised lending

bedarfsorientiert *(~e Beratung)* needs-oriented counselling (consultation)

Bedarfs / ~spanne 1. operating margin □ operating expenditure less net commission income 2. *(je Engagement)* cost requirement margin; **~spitzen** peak borrowing requirements

Bedauern regret, *(zu unserem ~)* much to our regret

bedecken 1. to cover 2. to account for, *(Kundeneinlagen ~ die Bilanzsumme*

B

mit 40 %) customer deposits account for 40 % of total assets

Bedeckung *(~ der Solvabilitätsspanne)* solvency margin cover

Bedeckungssatz solvency coverage ratio

bedenken *(beim Kauf und Verkauf von Wertpapieren ~)* to take into account (to bear in mind) when buying or selling securities

Bedenken *(~ gegen eine Verlängerung der Kreditfazilität)* objections to (reservations about) a renewal of the loan facility

Bedenkfrist *(im Wechselrecht)* grace period

bedeuten to mean, to represent, stand for, to signify

bedeutende Gegenpartei *(Basel III)* significant counterparty □ single counterparty or group of connected counterparties that account for more than 1% of a bank's total assets

Bedeutung 1. importance, significance, *(von großer ~ für die weitere Kursentwicklung sein)* to have a significant bearing on the future stock market trend, *(von großer ~ für den Käufer sein)* to be of great importance to the buyer, to be high on the buyer's agenda **2.** *(Sinn)* meaning **3.** *(Tragweite/Auswirkungen)* bearing, consequences, implications, repercussions

bedeutungslos 1. insignificant **2.** meaningless, *(die Garantie ~ werden lassen)* to render the guarantee meaningless

bedienen 1. *(eine Anleihe ~)* to service a bond, *(die Forderungen der Kreditgeber ~)* to service the claims of the lenders, *(ordnungsgemäß bediente Hypothek)* properly serviced mortgage, *(nicht bediente Hypothek)* defaulted (non-performing) mortgage
2. *(ein Akkreditiv ~)* to pay under a documentary credit, *(die Aktionäre ~)* to distribute (to pay) a dividend to shareholders, *(das Kapital ~)* to pay a dividend on the capital stock
3. *(die Käufererwartungen ~)* to cater to buyer expectations
4. *(die Rücklagen ~)* to transfer (to allocate) to reserves

Bedienung 1. service, debt repayment (payment of interest and principal) according to an agreed schedule, *(~ einer Anleihe)* bond servicing, servicing a bond issue, *(~ von Hypothekenkrediten)* mortgage servicing, servicing mortgage loans
2. *(~ der Rücklagen)* transfer to the reserves, reserve appropriation

Bedienungs / ~aufwand debt servicing charge (cost); **~quote 1.** servicing ratio **2.** *(bei Geboten)* allocation ratio; **~rechnung** debt service calculation, calculation of interest and principal payments due; **~rechte** servicing rights

bedingen 1. *(erfordern)* to necessitate, to call for, to require **2.** *(festlegen)* to stipulate, to condition, to lay down **3.** *(verursachen)* to cause

bedingt 1. conditional, contingent, *(~e Annahme)* qualified acceptance, *(~er Anspruch)* conditional claim, claim subject to a condition subsequent, *(~es Indossament)* conditional endorsement, *(~es Kapital)* contingent capital, conditionally authorised capital, *(~e Kapitalerhöhung)* contingent capital increase □ capital increase depending on the exercise of conversion rights, *(~es Recht)* contingent right, *(~e Übertragung)* conditional (qualified) transfer
2. *(spekulativ ~)* of a speculative nature, speculation-induced

Bedingung 1. *(Bestimmung)* provision, stipulation
2. *(Erfordernis, Voraussetzung)* requirement, precondition, prerequisite
3. *(pl)* terms, conditions, *(Bedingungen für den Überweisungsverkehr)* Conditions for Credit Transfers, *(Bedingungen für Festsatzkredite)* terms governing fixed rate loans

Bedingungs / **~anpassung** *(bei Krediten)* adjustment of the loan terms; **~eintritt** fulfillment of condition, occurrence of the event specified, *(Anzeige des ~s)* notice of fulfillment of condition

bedingungslos *(~e Entlassung aus der Haftung)* unconditional (unqualified) discharge from liability

bedrängen *(die finanziellen Probleme, die das Unternehmen ~)* the financial problems besetting (harassing) the company, *(bedrängter Schuldner)* hardpressed debtor

Bedrängnis *(in finanzieller ~)* in financial difficulties (straits, distress)

bedrohen *(die Gesundung des Unternehmens ~)* to endanger (to be a threat to, to imperil) the revitalisation of the company

bedürfnisgeleitet *(~e Kunden)* need-directed customers

Bedürfnis / **~hierarchie** need hierarchy; **~lückenanalyse** need-gap analysis

bedürfnisorientiert *(~er Ansatz)* need-satisfaction approach, *(~e Verkaufstechnik)* need-satisfaction selling

beeindruckend *(~e Kursgewinne)* impressive price gains

beeinflussen to influence, to affect, *(stark ~)* to impact significantly, *(sich ~ lassen)* to be influenced in one's own judgement

beeinträchtigen **1.** to impair, to mar, *(die Bonität des Kreditnehmers ~)* to be detrimental to the borrower's credit standing, to impair (to dent) the borrower's credit-worthiness, *(die Gewinnmargen ~)* to dent profit margins, *(durch ungünstige Wechselkursbewegungen beeinträchtigte Gewinne)* profits marred by adverse currency movements, *(durch Marktentwicklungen beeinträchtigt werden)* to be adversely affected by market movements **2.** *(stören)* to hamper, to interfere with, to restrict, *(den Handel stark ~)* to hamper trading activities severely **3.** *(verletzen) (ein Recht ~)* to infringe a right

B

Beeinträchtigung **1.** impairment, prejudice, adverse (negative) effect, *(~ der Glaubwürdigkeit)* damage done to (impairment of) creditibility, *(ohne ~ unserer Rechte)* without prejudice to our rights, *(~ des Sicherungsgutes)* impairment of the collateral
2. hampering, interference, restriction, *(~ der ordnungsgemäßen Vertragserfüllung)* hindering proper performance of the contract

beenden **1.** to terminate, to finish, to conclude, to end, to close **2.** *(fertigstellen)* to complete

Beendigung **1.** termination, end, *(~ des Kreditverhältnisses)* termination of the loan relationship (of the lending agreement), calling in the loan, *(~ des Vertragsverhältnisses)* termination (repudiation) of contract, discontinuance of the agreement
2. *(Ablauf)* expiration, expiry
3. *(Fertigstellung)* completion

Befähigung **1.** qualification, aptitude, ability **2.** *jur.* capacity

Befähigungsnachweis qualifying certificate, certificate of aptitude

befestigen *(sich ~)* to stiffen, to harden, to firm up, to pick up, to strengthen, to edge higher

Befestigung strengthening, *(~ der Kurse am Aktienmarkt)* firming up of prices in the equity market

beflügeln **1.** *(den Aktienmarkt ~)* to boost (to propel) the stock market **2.** *(die Börsenphantasie ~)* to capture investors' imagination, to fuel speculative trading

befolgen *(Grundsatz I des KWG ~)* to comply with (to observe, to ahere to) Principle I of the Banking Act

Befolgungskosten cost of compliance

befördern **1.** to promote **2.** *(transportieren)* to carry, to forward, to ship

B

Beförderung 1. promotion, advancement **2.** carriage, forwarding, shipment

Beförderungsbedingungen conditions of carriage

Befrachter shipper

befragen 1. to consult **2.** to interview, to survey, to question, to take a poll, *(60 % der befragten Kunden)* 60 % of the customers questioned, *(befragte Person)* interviewee, respondent

Befragung 1. consultation **2.** interview, inquiry, poll

Befragungsergebnisse findings of a survey

befreien 1. *(entbinden)* to release, to relieve, to discharge
2. *(freistellen)* to exempt, to exonerate, to grant exemption, *(befreite Parteien)* exempted (excluded) parties

befreiend *(~er Konzernabschluss)* exempting consolidated financial statements, *(~e Muttergesellschaft)* higher parent company, *(~e Schuldübernahme)* assumption of debt with full discharge of the original (previous) debtor, *(~e Schuldübernahme durch die Muttergesellschaft)* debt push-up, *(~e Wirkung besitzen)* to be operative as a discharge, to have a debt-discharging effect

Befreiung 1. release, relief, discharge, *(~ von der Bürgschaft)* release from the guarantee, *(~ von der Haftung)* release (discharge) from liability, *(~ des Schuldners)* discharge of the debtor, *(~ von Verbindlichkeiten)* debt discharge, release of obligations
2. exemption, exoneration, *(~ von der Leistungspflicht)* exemption from contributions, *(~ von der Prospektpflicht)* exemption from prospectus requirements

Befreiungs / ~anspruch 1. right to claim exemption **2.** *(eines Bürgen)* right to discharge; **~antrag** application for exemption (e.g. from payment); **~grenze** exemption limit; **~klausel** exemption clause; **~verordnung** exemption ordinance; **~vorschriften** exemption rules

befriedigen to satisfy, *(Ansprüche voll ~)* to satisfy (to meet) claims in their entirety, *(die Bank ist befugt, sich jederzeit aus den hinterlegten Wertpapieren zu ~)* the bank shall be entitled to use at any time the securities deposited to satisfy its claims, *(eine Forderung durch Verwertung des Sicherungsgegenstandes ~)* to satisfy (to recover) a debt by realising the collateral, *(die Gläubiger ~)* to satisfy (to pay off) the creditors, *(eine starke Kreditnachfrage ~)* to meet a strong loan demand

Befriedigung *(~ der Ansprüche gegenüber dem Kreditnehmer)* satisfaction of claims against the borrower, *(~ der Gläubiger nach der Rangfolge ihrer Rechte)* satisfaction of creditors on the basis of the priority of their rights, *(~ aus dem Grundstück suchen)* to seek satisfaction from the property, *(~ der Investorennachfrage)* meeting investors' demands

Befriedigung *(~ aus Pfand- oder anderen Sicherungsrechten)* satisfaction of claims by realising liens or other security interests, *(~ aus dem Verwertungserlös)* satisfaction out of the realisation proceeds, *(~ im Wege der Zwangsvollstreckung)* satisfaction of a claim by way of a compulsory enforcement, satisfaction by way of a forced sale

Befriedigungsrecht right to (of) satisfaction, *(Recht auf vollständige Befriedigung)* right to be paid in full

Befriedigungsvorrecht *(~ der Bank)* the bank's senior right of satisfaction (preferential right to satisfaction)

befristen to set (to fix) a time limit, to set an expiration date, to limit in time, *(die Laufzeit des Kredites ist bis zum … befristet)* the life of the loan is due to expire on …, the loan will expire on …

befristet *(~e Ansprüche)* claims limited in time, term claims, *(~e Einlagen)* term (time) deposits, *(~e Forderungen an ausländische Banken)* term lendings to foreign banks, *(~er Kredit)* term (time) loan, *(~e Mittel)* term money (funds), *(~es Tagesgeld)* term call money

befristete Transaktionen **1.** transactions limited in time, term transactions, transactions with fixed maturity dates
2. *(im ESZB)* reverse transactions □ open market transaction whereby the ECB or the National Central Banks buy or sell assets under repurchase agreements or grant loans against collateral

befristet *(~e Verbindlichkeiten)* term (time) liabilities, *(~er Vertrag)* contract of limited duration, time-limited contract, contract for a specified period of time

Befristung **1.** setting a time limit, agreeing on a fixed period, limitation in time, *(~ der Inanspruchnahmen)* setting a time limit for drawings, *(mit einer ~ von zwölf Monaten)* running for twelve months
2. duration, maturity, *(~ des Kreditangebotes)* duration of the loan offer, time limit set for the acceptance of the loan offer

Befristungsklausel time limitation clause

Befugnis authority, power

befugt *(~ sein)* to be authorised (entitled, empowered)

befürchten *(einen Rückgang der Aktienkurse ~)* to fear a setback in stock prices

Befürchtung *(~en der Anleger)* investor concerns (fears)

befürworten **1.** *(empfehlen)* to recommend **2.** *(unterstützen)* to support, to back, to endorse

Befürwortung **1.** recommendation **2.** support, backing, endorsement

begebbar negotiable, marketable

begeben **1.** *(emittieren)* to float, to issue, to launch, *(auf zinsvariabler Basis ~)* to issue on a floating rate basis **2.** *(negoziieren)* to negotiate

Begebung **1.** floating, flotation, issue, launch, *(~ von Teilschuldverschreibungen)* issuance of notes, *(~ im Versteigerungsverfahren)* issue by tender **2.** negotiation

Begebungs / ~fähigkeit **1.** flotation power **2.** negotiability; **~konsortium** selling group; **~kosten** flotation (issuing) costs; **~kurs** issuing (offering) price; **~vermerk** endorsement

begegnen *(der höheren Volatilität durch Sicherungsgeschäfte ~)* to counter (to respond to) higher volatility by hedging transactions

Beginn beginning, outset, opening, *(~ der Vereinbarung)* inception (commencement) of the agreement

Beginnvaluta initial value date

beglaubigen to certify, to legalise, *(eine Unterschrift ~)* to certify (to legalise) a signature, to attest (to) the authenticity of a signature, *(eine Unterschrift ~ lassen)* to have a signature certified, *(beglaubigte Abschrift)* certified true copy

Beglaubigung certification, legalisation

begleichen to settle, to pay

Begleichung settlement, payment, *(~ der fälligen Zins- und Tilgungsleistungen)* settlement of interest and principal payments falling due

Begleit / ~dokumente supporting documents, documents in support, companion (accompanying) documents; **~gesetz** Supplementary Act; **~papiere** → Begleitdokumente; **~schäden** incidental damages; **~schreiben** covering (accompanying) letter; **~umstände** *(die ~ dieser Transaktion)* the circumstances surrounding this transaction

Begleitung *(~ von Kapitalaufnahmen)* support during fund raising transactions

begrenzen **1.** to limit, to confine, *(das finanzielle Engagement ~)* to limit the fi-

B

nancial exposure, *(weitere Erhöhungen ~)* to place a cap on further increases, *(die Kreditschöpfung ~)* to rein in credit creation, *(die Risiken sind auf ein geringes Zinsrisiko begrenzt)* exposure is confined to a small interest risk 2. *(nach oben ~)* to cap, to put an upper limit on, to set an upward limit, *(die Anrechnung auf 60 % ~)* to cap recognition at 60 %
(den Zinssatz nach oben ~) to cap the interest rate, to put a ceiling on the interest rate, *(die Verschuldung nach oben ~)* to limit (to put a lid on) outstanding debt
3. *(nach unten ~)* to set a downward limit, to take out a floor, *(Verluste nach unten ~)* to put a floor under losses, *(den Zinssatz nach unten ~)* to take out an interest floor

begrenzt *(~e Dispositionsbefugnisse)* limited discretionary powers, *(~e Haftung)* limited liability, *(~e Laufzeit)* limited duration (term), definite maturity, *(~ steuerpflichtige Gebietsfremde)* non-residents subject to limited tax liability □ i.e. taxation is limited to German source income

Begrenzung 1. limitation, *(~ der Bonitäts-/Kreditrisiken)* limiting the exposure to credit risks, *(~ der Kapitalbeteiligungen)* limitation of shareholdings, *(~ des Währungsrisikos)* limiting the currency exposure
2. *(nach oben)* capping, *(~ der Hypothekenkreditaufnahme)* putting a ceiling (a cap) on mortgage borrowing, *(~ des Zinssatzes nach oben)* interest rate capping, taking out an interest rate cap
3. *(nach unten)* setting a downward limit, *(~ des Zinssatzes nach unten)* taking out an interest rate floor

begründen 1. constitute, *(den Beweis des ersten Anscheins ~)* to serve as prima facie evidence, *(eine Forderung ~)* to constitute a claim, *(eine rechtswirksame Zahlung ~)* to constitute a valid payment
2. to substantiate, to justify, to state the reasons for, *(einen Anspruch ~)* to substantiate a claim, *(begründeter Anspruch)* justified (legitimate) claim, *(glaubhaft begründetes Interesse)* credibly substantiated interest, *(begründete Stellungnahme)* reasoned statement
3. to create, to set up, to establish, to found, *(einenAnspruch ~)* to give rise to a claim, *(eine Position ~)* to establish (to open, to set up, to initiate) a position, *(durch ein Rechtsgeschäft ~)* to create by a legal transaction, *(ein Schuldverhältnis ~)* to create an obligation (a debt), *(eine Steuerverpflichtung ~)* to give rise to a tax liability

Begründer founder, organiser, promoter

Begründetheit justification, *(~ eines Widerspruchs)* merits of an appeal

Begründung 1. constitution, creation, establishment, *(~ des Eigentums)* constituting ownership, *(~ vertraglicher Rechte)* inception of contractual rights
2. substantiation, justification, statement of reasons, reasoned (explanatory) statement, *(~ zu einem Gesetz)* official reasoning, *(ohne zur ~ einer Kreditkündigungsentscheidung verpflichtet zu sein)* without being obligated to justify the decision to call in the loan
3. *(zu einem Gesetzentwurf)* explanatory memorandum

begrüßen *(am Markt ~)* to welcome in the market

begünstigen 1. *(bevorzugen)* to prefer, to give preference to, to favour
2. *(unterstützen)* to support, to back, to foster

Begünstigter *(im Zahlungsverkehr)* beneficiary, payee, *(Konto des Begünstigten)* beneficiary's account, receiving account

Begünstigung 1. preference, preferential treatment, backing **2.** designation as beneficiary, entitlement to payment of the proceeds **3.** *(steuerliche ~)* tax privilege

Begünstigungs / ~klausel beneficiary clause; **~konzept** concept of preferential treatment; **~tarif** preferential rates

begutachten to evaluate, to appraise, to give an expert opinion

Begutachtung evaluation, appraisal, expert opinion

behaftet *(mit einem hohen Bonitätsrisiko ~ sein)* to carry a high credit risk, *(mit Zins- und Währungsrisiken ~ sein)* to be exposed to currency and interest rate risks

behalten to keep, *(das Eigentum an den Waren bis zur vollständigen Bezahlung ~)* to retain title to the goods until payment in full, *(eine Minderheitsbeteiligung ~)* to retain (to keep) a minority stake

Behaltensfrist *(gesetzliche ~)* legal retention period

behandeln to treat, to deal, *(als Betriebsaufwand ~)* to charge to operating expenses

Behandlung 1. *(bilanzielle/steuerliche ~)* accounting/tax treatment **2.** *(einer Reklamation)* handling of a complaint

behaupten 1. *(erklären)* to declare, to state, to maintain
2. *(sich ~, sich durchsetzen)* to hold up well, to hold (to stand) one's ground, *(die Aktie konnte sich in den letzten Monaten gut ~)* the stock has borne up well over the last few months, *(Börsentendenz: behauptet)* maintained, steady

Behauptung 1. declaration, statement, affirmation **2.** *(~ am Markt)* holding one's ground in the market

behebbar *(~er Leistungsverzug)* remediable default

beheben to remedy, to remove, *(einen Mangel ~)* to remedy a deficiency, *(das Ungleichgewicht ~)* to redress the imbalance, *(eine Vertragsverletzung ~)* to cure a breach of contract, *(den Zahlungsverzug ~)* to make good (to cure) the default

Behebung 1. remedy, cure, redress **2.** elimination, removal

beherrschen to control, to dominate, to have a hold over, to be in control of, *(beherrschte Gesellschaft)* controlled company, *(einen ~den Einfluss ausüben)* to exercise a dominant (controlling) influence, *(~der Aktionär)* controlling shareholder, shareholder-controller, *(~de Beteiligung)* controlling interest (stake)

Beherrschung control, domination

Beherrschungsvertrag controlling (domination) agreement, *(Beherrschungs- und Gewinnabführungsvertrag)* control and profit transfer agreement

behindern to impede, to obstruct, *(den freien Kapitalverkehr ~)* to hamper (to constrain, to hold back) free capital movements

Behinderung impediment, obstruction, hindrance

behutsam *(~es Vorgehen)* cautious approach

beibehalten to retain, to keep (up)

Beibehaltung *(~ der Kontrolle)* retention of control, *(~ einer Kreditfazilität)* upkeep of a loan facility

beibringen *(den Verschiffungsnachweis ~)* to furnish (to procure, to produce) evidence of shipment

Beibringung *(~ einer Garantie)* furnishing a guarantee

Beibringungsgrundsatz principle to submit all relevant facts

beiderseitig mutual, reciprocal, *(im ~en Einverständnis)* by mutual consent

beifügen to enclose, to attach, to annex

Beihilferecht State Aid Law

beilegen 1. to enclose, to attach **2.** to settle, to resolve, *(gütlich ~)* to settle amicably, *(durch einen Vergleich ~)* to settle by a composition (a compromise)

B

B

Beilegung 1. enclosing **2.** settlement, *(~ durch ein Schiedsgericht)* settlement by arbitration, *(~ durch eine außergerichtliche Vereinbarung)* settlement by an out-of-court arrangement

beimessen 1. *(Bedeutung ~)* to attach (to attribute) importance to, *(der einer Sicherheit beigemessene Wert)* value ascribed to a security **2.** *(Gewicht ~)* to give weight to

beimischen *(dem Portefeuille ~)* to add to the portfolio mix, to admix

Beinahe-Geld near-money

Beine *(das angeschlagene Unternehmen wieder auf die ~ bringen)* to restore the floundering company to health

beinhalten 1. to contain **2.** *(einschließen)* to include, to comprise **3.** *(implizieren)* to imply

Beiordnung assignment, *(beigeordneter Anwalt)* assigned (appointed) lawyer

Beipackzettel *(zu Finanzprodukten)* factsheet, key informaton document (KID)

Beirat advisory council, Board of Advisors

bei Sicht at sight, *(~ zahlbare Dokumente)* documents payable at sight

Beistand *(finanzieller ~)* financial assistance (aid)

Beistandskredit stand-by credit (facility)

Beistellpflicht → Mitwirkungs- und Beistellpflichten

beisteuern *(zum Gewinn ~)* to contribute to the profit

Beitrag 1. contribution, amount contributed **2.** *(Anteil)* share, contribution **3.** *(Mitgliedsbeitrag)* subscription, *(IWF)* quota **4.** *(Versicherungsbeitrag)* insurance premium

beitragen to contribute to, to make a contribution, to add to

Beitrags / ~aufkommen premium income; **~depot** premium deposit account □ investment used to honour the policyholder's regular payment commitments

beitragsfrei non-contributory, exempt from contributions

Beitragsleistung contribution, payment of a contribution

beitragsorientierter Plan *(betriebliche Altersversorgung)* defined contribution plan, → leistungsorientierter Pan

Beitragspflicht liability to pay contributions

beitragsrelevant *(~e Passiva)* subscription relevant liabilities, → Bankenabgabe, → Restrukturierungsfonds

Beitrags / ~rückstand contributions in arrears; **~satz** contribution rate; **~zeitraum** premium-paying period

beitreibbar recoverable, collectible, enforceable

beitreiben to collect, to recover, to enforce a payment, *(eine Darlehensforderung gerichtlich ~)* to recover a loan by legal process

Beitreibung 1. recovery, collection, enforcement of payment, *(~ von Zahlungsrückständen)* collection (pursuit) of payment arrears **2.** *(~ einer Zwangsvollstreckung)* levying execution

Beitreibungsverfahren recovery proceedings

beitreten 1. to join, *(einem Schuldverhältnis ~)* to enter into (to join) an existing obligation, to assume the liability of a co-debtor
2. to accede to, *(einem Vertrag ~)* to accede to a treaty

Beitritt joining, entering into, *(~ zu einem Kreditvertrag)* accession to a loan agreement

beizulegender Zeitwert *(zum beizulegenden Zeitwert bewerten)* to measure at fair value

bekämpfen *(die Inflation ~)* to combat inflation

Bekämpfung *(~ der Geldwäsche)* combat against money laundering

bekannt 1. known, noted, *(~e Schadenfälle)* reported claims **2.** *(wie Ihnen sicherlich ~ sein dürfte)* as you are no doubt aware, as you will certainly know

Bekanntgabe 1. release, announcement **2.** disclosure

bekanntgeben 1. to release, to make known, to announce, *(das Jahresergebnis ~)* to release the results for the year **2.** *(offenlegen)* to disclose, *(die Konditionen der neuen Emission ~)* to unveil the terms of the new issue

Bekanntmachung 1. (official, public) announcement **2.** *(Offenlegung)* disclosure

Beklagter defendant

bekleiden *(ein Amt ~)* to hold an office

bekräftigen *(seine Entschlossenheit ~)* to confirm (to reaffirm) one's determination

bekunden *(Interesse ~)* to express (to manifest) interest

Belange *(die ~ des Kunden wahren)* to represent (to safeguard) the customer's interests

belangen *(den Schuldner gerichtlich ~)* to institute legal proceedings against the debtor, to sue the debtor

belasten 1. to burden, *(den Aktienmarkt ~)* to depress (to weigh down, to plague) the stock market, *(die Bilanz ~)* to burden (to dog, to strain) the balance sheet, *(die Ertragslage ~)* to be a drag on earnings, to place a burden on earnings
(den Markt zusätzlich ~) to put added pressure on the market, *(stark ~)* to place a great burden upon, *(mit hohen Verbindlichkeiten belastet sein)* to be burdened by heavy debt
2. *(mit einem Pfandrecht ~)* to charge, to encumber, *(ein Haus hypothekarisch ~)* to mortgage a house
3. *(rechnerisch)* to debit, to charge, *(dem Betriebsergebnis ~)* to charge to income (to operations), *(das Konto des Kreditnehmers ~)* to debit (to enter to the debit of) the borrower's account, *(Zinsen vierteljährlich ~)* to debit (to charge) interest every three months

belastend *(sich ~ auswirken)* to prove burdensome, to have a detrimental effect, *(die Auflagen weniger ~ gestalten)* to make the requirements less onerous

Belastung 1. burden, strain, *(~ der Eigenkapitalquote)* strain on the capital ratio, *(~des Marktes)* strain (pressure) coming to bear on the market, *(starke ~ der Finanzmärkte)* severe financial market strains
2. load, charge, *(~ mit EEV-Steuern)* income, profit and property tax load, *(~ aus der Fremdkapitalaufnahme)* debt charge (load), *(~ en aus dem Kreditgeschäft)* charges from lending operations, *(~ der Zinserträge mit Quellensteuer)* incidence of withholding tax on interest income
(ohne steuerliche ~) without attracting tax, *(~ der Zinsspanne)* charge against the interest margin, *(~ mit Zins und Tilgung)* debt service load, interest and redemption burden
3. *(dingliche)* charge, encumbrance, mortgage, *(~ mit einer Hypothek)* mortgage charge, taking out a mortgage, taking a mortgage charge over a property, *(~ einzelner Vermögenswerte)* charge over specific assets
4. *(rechnerische/bilanzmäßige) (~ des Betriebsgewinnes)* charge against operating profit, *(~des Jahresergebnisses)* charge against the result for the year, *(~ eines Kontos)* account debit, debiting an account, *(~ einer Kreditkartenzahlung)* charge transaction
(~ aus Einzelwertberichtigungen) charge for specific loan loss allowances, *(~en im außerordentlichen Geschäft)* extraordinary charges (mainly loan losses or securities write-downs), *(~ aus Wertpapierabschreibungen)* charge from securities writedowns

Belastungs / ~anzeige debit advice (note); **~buchung** debit entry; **~ermächtigung** charge authority, debit authorisation; **~faktoren** *(Börse)* depressive factors, market depressants, detrimental (negative) factors

B

Belastungs / ~festschreibung establishment of fixed interest and principal payments; **~grenze** encumbrance limit; **~urkunde** charge certificate, deed of charge

belaufen *(sich ~ auf)* to amount to, to run into, to total, to come to, to stand at

beleben 1. to revive, to reinvigorate, to stimulate, *(die Börsensitzung ~)* to enliven the session

Belebung *(~ der Konjunktur)* revival of economic activity, *(~ der Kreditnachfrage)* upturn (revival) in loan demand

Beleg 1. *(im Zahlungsverkehr)* voucher, slip **2.** proof **3.** *(pl)* supporting documents, documentary evidence

belegen 1. *(auferlegen)* to impose, *(Kapitalerträge mit einer Steuer ~)* to impose (to levy) a tax on income from capital investments, *(mit Mindestreserven ~)* to establish (to impose) minimum reserve requirements, *(mit einer Eigenkapitalanforderung von 10 % belegt sein)* to carry a 10 % capital charge
2. *(ausmachen)* to account for, *(langfristige Ausleihungen ~ 40 % des Kreditvolumens)* long-term lendings account for 40 % of the loan portfolio
3. *(nachweisen)* to prove, to furnish proof, to support by, to document, *(durch Schriftstücke ~)* to evidence through documents
4. *(nutzen)* to use, *(das Rediskontkontingent mit 30 % ~)* to use 30 % of the rediscount quota
5. *(reservieren)* to book, to reserve, to fill

Belegerstellung making out a voucher

beleggebunden → beleghaft

beleghaft *(~ erteilte Überweisungen)* paper-based credit transfers

beleglos *(~es Abrechnungssystem)* paperless (voucherless) settlement system, *(~es Scheckinkasso/Scheckeinzugsverfahren)* truncated cheque collection/truncated cheque collection procedure (for cheques below € 6,000), *(~e Übertragung)* paperless transfer *(~er Überweisungsverkehr)* paperless credit transfers (money transmission), *(~es Zahlschein-Überweisungsverfahren)* paperless cash-linked credit transfer system, *(~er Zahlungsverkehr)* paperless payments, paperless transfer of funds

Belegschaft staff, personnel, workforce

Belegschafts / ~aktien staff shares, employee shares (stock); **~produktivität** *(~ je Mitarbeiter)* staff productivity; **~programm** employee stock ownership plan, staff (employees') share scheme; **~stärke** staffing level

Belegverkehr paper-based transactions

Belehrung *(jur.)* instructions, caution

beleihbar eligible as collateral, *(~e Forderungen)* receivables qualifying as security for loans, eligible accounts receivable

Beleihbarkeit eligibility as collateral

beleihen to lend against (on), to advance money against, *(Grundbesitz ~)* to lend against real (landed) property, *(das Umlaufvermögen bis zur Hälfte ~)* to lend up to half of the current assets, *(Wertpapiere mit 60 % ~)* to lend up to 60 p.c. of the securities' market value

Beleihung lending on (against), *(~ von Forderungen)* lending against receivables, *(~ gewerblich genutzter Grundstücke und Gebäude)* commercial property lending

Beleihungsauslauf loan-to-value ratio

beleihungsfähig eligible as collateral (security), loanable, *(~er Betrag)* loanable amount, market value of the collateral less safety margin, *(~e Wertpapiere)* securities eligible as collateral, securities acceptable to the bank as collateral

Beleihungs / ~fähigkeit eligibility (suitability) as collateral; **~grenze** lending limit, exposure limit, *(~ von*

60 %) lending is limited to 60 % of the property's (collateral's) market value; **~grundsätze** lending principles, principles of lending against collateral (security)

Beleihungs / ~höchstsatz lending limit; **~kriterien** lending criteria; **~objekt** property serving as security (collateral), mortgaged property

Beleihungs / ~prüfung assessment (appraisal) of the property serving as collateral, collateral assessment; **~quote** loan-to-value ratio, percentage advanced (e. g. against the market value of securities), *(bei börsennotierten Wertpapieren)* loan-to-value ratio on listed securities

Beleihungs / ~raum lending margin, *(erststelliger ~)* margin for lendings against first-rank security, *(Sicherung im nachrangigen ~)* provision of security by a junior property charge; **~richtlinien** lending guidelines

Beleihungs / ~satz → Beleihungsquote; **~stopp** lending freeze; **~vertrag** lending agreement; **~verzeichnis** register of properties serving as security

Beleihungswert lendable (lending) value, value assigned for security purposes, *(~ der vom Kreditnehmer verpfändeten Vermögenswerte)* lendable value of the assets pledged by the borrower

Beleihungswert / ~abschlag valuation haircut; **~berechnung/~ermittlung** determination of the lendable value; **~grenze** lending limit (derived from the lendable value)

beleumundet *(gut ~es Unternehmen)* well-reputed company

beliebig *(~verfügbare Mittel)* freely available funds

belieferbar *(~er Terminkontrakt)* futures contract based upon a cash instrument

Belieferung delivery, *(~ eines Terminkontraktes)* delivery against a futures contract, *(~ eines Verkaufs)* making delivery under a selling transaction (under a short position), *(~ eines Wertpapiergeschäftes)* delivering securities to clear a trade

bemessen 1. to calculate, to measure, to assess **2.** to fix, to establish

Bemessung 1. calculation, measurement, *(~ des aufsichtsrechtlichen Eigenkapitals)* measuring the regulatory capital for banks
2. *(~ der Länderlimite)* fixing (establishing) country limits

Bemessungs / ~basis der Eigenmittel capital (equity) measurement basis; **~grundlage** basis of measurement (assessment, calculation), *(die als ~ dienenden Ausleihungen)* lendings taken as basis for calculation

bemühen to seek, to be anxious, to strive, *(sich um Kapitalbeteiligungen ~)* to solicit financial commitments, *(sich um finanzielle Unterstützung ~)* to seek financial assistance (backing), *(sich um die Zustimmung der Aktionäre ~)* to seek shareholder approval

Bemühen/Bemühung endeavour, effort, *(~ um eine Fremdfinanzierung)* seeking external funding, *(~en um eine Kostenbegrenzung)* drive (endeavours) to hold down costs

benachrichtigen to notify, to advise, to inform

Benachrichtigung notification, notice, advice, information

Benachrichtigungs / ~pflicht notification requirement (duty), obligation to notify; **~zeitraum** period for notification

benachteiligen to disadvantage, to put (to place) at a disadvantage, to discriminate against, *(Gläubiger ~)* to prejudice creditors, *(wettbewerbsmäßig stark ~)* to put at a severe competitive disadvantage

Benachteiligung disadvantage, *(~ von Gläubigern)* prejudice to creditors, *(~ bestimmter Kreditnehmer)* discrimination against specific borrowers

B

Benachteiligungsvorsatz wilful intent to discriminate

Benehmen *(~ herstellen; bei einer Emission)* to agree on the bond terms (on the coupon)

benennen to nominate, to name, to appoint, to designate, *(bei Akkreditiven: benannte Bank)* designated (nominated) bank

Benennung *(~ als Inkassobank)* designation as collection bank

benutzbar usable, available, *(das Akkreditiv ist durch Trattennegoziierung ~)* the documentary credit is available by negotiation of drafts, *(Bank, bei der das Akkreditiv ~ gestellt ist)* bank where the credit is available, *(gegen Vorlage der folgenden Dokumente ~)* available against presentation of the following documents

benutzbar stellen to make available, *(einen Kredit ~ bei … ~)* to allow drawings against (on) the loan with …

Benutzer / **~anforderungen** user requirements; **~berechtigung** user (use) authority; **~kennung** user ID

beobachten to observe, to watch, *(genau ~)* to keep a close watch on, to pay close attention to

Beobachtungsfehler observation error (bias)

bepreisen to price, to set a price, *(richtig bepreister Titel)* correctly priced security, *(adäquat bepreiste Kreditrisiken)* adequately priced credit risks

Bepreisung *(~ von Kreditengagements)* loan pricing

beraten 1. to advise, to counsel, to consult **2.** *(debattieren)* to deliberate, to confer, to debate

Berater advisor, consultant, counsellor

Berater / **~haftung** advisor liability; **~honorar** consultancy fee

Beratung 1. counselling, consultancy, guidance, *(~ in Anlagefragen)* (giving) investment advice, investment consultation (counselling), investment advisory service, *(~ der Kunden)* counselling of customers
2. deliberation, debate

Beratungs / **~ansatz** advisory concept, *(beratender Verkaufsansatz ~)* consultative selling approach; **~anspruch** entitlement to counselling; **~bedarf** counselling requirement(s); **~dienste** advisory (counselling, consultancy) services; **~entgelt** advisory fee

beratungsfrei *(~e Auftragsausführung)* counselling-free order execution

Beratungs / **~funktion** advisory (counselling) function; **~gebühr** advisory (counselling) fee; **~geschäft** → Beratungsdienste; **~gespräch** consultation, advisory meeting, consultation (counselling) interview; **~haftung** counselling liability, liability for advice given; **~honorar** counselling (consulting) fee

Beratungs / **~kompetenz** advisory competence (skills), expertise in consultancy, counselling competencies; **~kosten** advisory expenses (cost); **~leistungen** → Beratungsdienste; **~mandat** advisory mandate (assignment)

Beratungs / **~nachweis** proof of counselling; **~pflicht** duty to advise (customers properly), counselling requirement (mandate); **~protokoll** consultation record, advisory report

Beratungs / **~qualität** advisory quality, quality of the counselling service; **~stelle** advisory bureau; **~unterlagen** consultation documents, documentation of consultancy; **~unternehmen** consultancy firm; **~vertrag** *(in der Vermögensverwaltung)* advisory management agreement; **~verzicht** counselling waiver, waiver of the counselling requirement

berechnen 1. *(belasten)* to charge, to bill **2.** *(erheben)* to levy, to assess **3.** *(errechnen)* to calculate, to compute, *(zuviel berechnete Gebühren)* excess charges, fees charged in excess

Berechnung 1. *(~ von Kontoführungsgebühren)* charging account maintenance fees, *(halbjährliche ~ von Zinsen)* charging interest every six months 2. assessment 3. calculation, computation, *(~ der Mindestkapitalanforderungen)* calculation of minimum capital requirements

Berechnungs / **~annahmen** calculation (actuarial) assumptions; **~fehler** calculation error, error of calculation (computation); **~grundlage** basis of (for) calculation; **~methode** method of calculation (computation), method of (for) determining the value

Berechnungs / **~stelle** *(bei Swap-Transaktionen)* calculation agent, party that calculates settlement amounts owing between the parties; **~verfahren** method of calculation; **~zeitraum** period of computation, charge period

berechtigen to authorise, to entitle, to empower, *(zu Verfügungen über ein Konto ~)* to authorise to draw on an account

berechtigt 1. to be authorised (entitled, empowered), to be eligible for, to qualify for 2. *(gerechtfertigt)* justified, warranted, *(~ verweigern)* to be justified in refusing 3. *(rechtmäßig)* legitimate, lawful, (~e *Belange des Kreditnehmers)* borrower's legitimate interests

Berechtigte(r) 1. person entitled, legitimate (rightful) claimant 2. *(Begünstigter)* beneficiary 3. *(Verfügungsberechtigter)* person authorised (e. g. to draw on an account)

Berechtigung 1. eligibility 2. *(Ermächtigung)* authorisation, authority, entitlement 3. *(Recht)* right, title 4. *(Rechtfertigung)* justification 5. *(Vollmacht)* power, authority

Berechtigungs / **~alter** eligibility age; **~kriterien** eligibility (qualifying) criteria; **~nachweis** proof of eligibility (entitlement), eligibility certificate, legitimation; **~schein** *(Börse)* scrip; **~träger** officer holding approval powers

Bereich 1. field, area (of competence) 2. range, region, *(im hohen fünfstelligen ~)* in the high five-figure range 3. *(Sektor)* branch, sector, *(Ausleihungen im kurz-/langfristigen ~)* short-term/long-term lendings, *(Entwicklungen im Bereich Privatkunden)* developments in the retail banking sector, *(in andere ~e des Marktes umschichten)* to switch into other sectors (segments) of the market, *(Notierungen im kurzfristigen ~)* quotations (prices) at the short end of the market 4. *(Unternehmensbereich)* division, *(Neuausrichtung des ~s Inlandskredite)* realignment of the domestic lending division

Bereichs / **~abschluss** divisional accounts; **~berichterstattung** divisional reporting

bereichsbezogen *(~es Rechnungswesen)* divisional acounting

Bereichs /**~clearing** area (district) clearing; **~erfolg**/**~ergebnis** divisional performance (results); **~ergebnisrechnung** divisional income statement

Bereichs / **~leiter** Division Head, Divisional (Area) Manager; **~leitung** division (divisional) management

bereichsübergreifend *(~e Steuerung)* cross-divisional management

Bereichs / **~verantwortung** divisional (area) responsibility, divisional performance responsibility; **~vorstand** Divisional Board Member, Divisional Managing Director, Divisional CEO

bereinigen 1. *(berichtigen)* to adjust, to correct, to rectify, to revise, *(bereinigt um Währungsverschiebungen)* adjusted for currency movements 2. *(neu ordnen)* to realign 3. *(Schuld)* to settle, to clear 4. *(Statistik, Index)* to adjust 5. *(Wertpapiere)* to revalidate

bereinigt *(~e Bilanzsumme)* adjusted total assets, total assets less intangible assets, *(~e Eigenkapitalbildung)* net equity formation, *(~es Ergebnis je Aktie)* diluted earnings per share, *(~er Index)* adjusted index, *(~e Zinsspanne)* adjusted interest margin □ ratio of interest received to a bank's total assets adjusted for interbank business

Bereinigung 1. adjustment, correction, *(nach ~ um saisonale Einflüsse)* after adjusting for seasonal influences, *(~ des Index)* adjustment of the index **2.** *(~ des Produktprogrammes)* realignment of the product range, *(~ des Portefeuilles von Problemkrediten)* removing distressed loans from the portfolio **3.** *(~ eines Schuldverhältnisses)* settlement of an obligation, debt discharge

bereithalten *(Sicherheiten ~)* to hold collateral in readiness

Bereithaltung supply, provision, commitment, standby, → Bereitstellung

Bereithaltungskosten standby cost

Bereitschaft willingness, readiness, *(~ zu Aktienengagements)* investors' willingness to become involved in the equity market, *(~ zur Gewährung von Krediten)* willingness to extend loan facilities, *(~ zur Kreditaufnahme)* propensity to borrow

Bereitschaftskredit standby credit

bereitstehen *(zur Anlage ~de Mittel)* funds available for investment

bereitstellen 1. to provide, to supply, to make (to hold) available, *(eine Deckungslinie ~)* to provide a support (backup) line, *(Haushaltsmittel ~)* to appropriate budget funds, *(der Kredit wird auf einem Sonderkonto bereitgestellt)* the loan proceeds will be credited to (will be made available on) a special loan account **2.** extend, *(auf gedeckter Basis ~)* to extend on a secured basis, to extend (to lend) against collateral, *(gegen die Garantie der Muttergesellschaft ~)* to extend against the parent's guarantee, *(zusätzliche Sicherheiten ~)* to put up extra security **3.** to commit, *(10 Mio € an Kapital ~)* to commit € 10m in capital, *(zur Unterstützung ~)* to commit in support

Bereitstellung 1. provision, supply, delivery, appropriation, *(~ des Kreditbetrages)* provision of the loan amount, loan disbursement, *(~ von Mitteln auf ungesicherter Basis)* provision of funds on an unsecured basis, *(~ der ersten Tranche)* provision (payment) of the first tranche **2.** extension, accommodation, *(~ eines Festsatzkredites)* extending a fixed rate loan, accommodation of a fixed-rate loan, *(~ zusätzlicher Kredite)* extending further credit, granting additional finance **3.** commitment, *(~ des erforderlichen Kapitals)* commitment (allocation) of the necessary capital

Bereitstellungs / ~fonds appropriation fund; **~kosten 1.** cost of supply **2.** commitment (availability) fee; **~provision** commitment commission, availability fee, *(bei Deckungslinien)* standby fee; **~verpflichtung 1.** commitment to provide funds, lending commitment, → Bereitstellungszusage **2.** obligation to provide (e.g. additional security)

Bereitstellungs / ~zeitraum *(für einen Kredit)* commitment (availability, drawdown) period; **~zinsen** interest on undrawn loan funds, commitment interest; **~zusage** commitment undertaking

Berg *(die Gesellschaft ist über den ~)* the company has turned the corner

bergen *(Derivate ~ besondere Risiken ~)* derivatives carry special risks

Bericht report, account, *(~ erstatten)* to report on, to give an account of, *(~ über das Geschäftsjahr)* business report, annual report

berichten to report, *(~des Unternehmen)* reporting company

Berichterstatter reporter, rapporteur

Berichterstattung reporting, *(~ nach außen)* external reporting, *(~ in der*

Presse) press coverage, *(~ der Unternehmen)* corporate reporting

Berichterstattungspflichten reporting requirements

berichtigen 1. to correct, to rectify, to adjust, to straighten out, *(berichtigte Anschaffungskosten)* adjusted cost price, *(berichtigte Buchung)* corrected entry, *(berichtigter Buchwert)* adjusted carrying value, adjusted basis **2.** *(stornieren)* to reverse

Berichtigung 1. correction, rectification, adjustment, straightening out, *(~ des Buchwertes)* adjustment of (to) the book value **2.** *(Stornierung)* reversal **3.** *(~ nach oben/nach unten)* upward (downward) reassessment

Berichtigungs / ~aktien bonus shares; **~aktienemission** capitalisation issue, scrip issue; **~bedarf im Kreditgeschäft** required loss allowances

Berichtigungs / ~buchung rectifying (adjustment) entry, *(Storno)* reversal entry; **~posten** *(~ zum Eigenkapital)* equity adjustment item

Berichts / ~lasten reporting burden; **~linie** reporting line

Berichtspflicht 1. reporting requirement(s), reporting obligation, duty to report **2.** accountability, duty to render account

berichtspflichtig subject to reporting requirements, *(~es Geschäft)* reportable deal (transaction)

Berichts / ~termin *(im Insolvenzverfahren)* reporting date, first meeting of the insolvency creditors; **~verantwortlichket** line (reporting) responsibility; **~währung** reporting currency, currency used in preparing the financial statements

Berichts / ~wege reporting channels (lines); **~wesen** reporting system; **~zeitraum** reporting period, period under review, period covered by the report, reference period

berücksichtigen 1. to take into account (consideration), to consider, to make allowance for, to bear in mind **2.** *(im Erfolg ~)* to report in net income **3.** *(im Grundsatz II ~)* to include in Principle II

Berücksichtigung consideration, *(nach ~ der berechtigten Belange des Kunden)* after duly considering the customer's legitimate interests, *(unter ~ einer angemessenen Kündigungsfrist)* allowing for an adequate period of notice, *(unter ~ des hohen Zinsniveaus)* taking into account the high interest level

berücksichtigungsfähig *(~ als hartes Kernkapital)* qualifying for inclusion in common equity, → Kernkapital, *(~e Sicherheiten)* eligible collateral

berufen 1. *(bestellen)* to appoint, to nominate, *(in den Vorstand ~)* to appoint to the Board **2.** *(Bezug nehmen auf)* to refer to **3.** *(sich auf ein Recht ~)* to invoke a right

Berufsbild job description

Berufshaftpflichtversicherung professional liability (indemnity) insurance

Berufshandel professional traders (operators)

berufsständisch *(~e Regelungen)* professional rules

Berufung 1. appeal, *(~ einlegen)* to appeal, to lodge an appeal **2.** appointment, nomination **3.** *(unter ~ auf)* with reference

Berufungs / ~beklagte/r appellee, respondent, party against whom an appeal is taken; **~einlegung** filing (lodging) an appeal; **~erwiderung** response to an appeal

Berufungs / ~gericht appellate (appeals) court, court of appeal; **~gründe** grounds for appeal; **~instanz** court of appeal; **~kläger** party appealing, appellant; **~recht** right of appeal; **~verfahren** proceedings on appeal

beruhen *(~ auf)* to be based upon

beruhigen 1. to calm (down), to stabilise, to consolidate **2.** *(Anleger ~)* to reassure investors

B

B

Beruhigung stabilisation, consolidation, *(~ des Aktienmarktes)* stabilisation (settling down) of the stock market, *(~ des Preisauftriebs)* slowing down of the upsurge in prices

berühren *(die Gültigkeit der übrigen Bestimmungen wird davon nicht berührt)* the validity of the remaining provisions shall not be affected thereby

beschädigen to damage, to harm, to mar, *(beschädigte Wertpapiere)* damaged (defective) securities

beschaffen *(Mittel, Kredite)* to raise, to procure, to generate, to obtain, to take up

Beschaffung raising, procurement, sourcing, generating, *(~ von Geldern auf dem Kapitalmarkt)* raising funds in the capital market, *(~ von Zentralbankgeld)* borrowing (buying) central bank funds

Beschaffungskosten procurement (sourcing) cost, *(der Bank)* cost of funds to the bank

Beschäftigtenzahl *(einer Unternehmung)* headcount, payroll

Beschäftigung 1. employment **2.** activity **3.** capacity, utilisation

Bescheid 1. notification, notice, information **2.** *jur.* directive, ruling **3.** answer, reply

bescheinigen 1. to certify, to attest **2.** *(bestätigen)* to confirm, to acknowledge

Bescheinigung 1. certification, attestation, confirmation **2.** certificate

Beschlagnahme 1. seizure, confiscation, *(~ von Grundbesitz)* seizure of real estate, *(~ von Kapitalerträgen)* distraint of capital income **2.** *(~ beim Drittschuldner)* garnishment

Beschlagnahme / ~beschluss seizure (confiscation) order; **~deckung** confiscation risk coverage

beschlagnahmen to seize, to confiscate, to distrain

Beschlagnahme / ~recht right of seizure; **~verfügung** seizure order, writ of seizure

beschleunigen 1. to accelerate, *(die wirtschaftliche Entwicklung ~)* to speed up economic development, *(den Zusammenbruch ~)* to hasten the collapse **2.** *(der Abwärtstrend beschleunigt sich)* the downward trend is gathering pace (momentum)

Beschleunigung acceleration, speeding up, hastening, pick-up

Beschleunigungsregel acceleration rule

beschließen 1. to resolve, to decide **2.** *(verabschieden)* to adopt, to pass

Beschluss 1. resolution, decision **2.** adoption, passing **3.** *(Gerichtsentscheidung)* ruling, court decision (order)

beschlussfähig *(~ sein)* to constitute a quorum, to be quorate, *(die Gläubigerversammlng ist ~)* the meeting of creditors is quorate, *(nicht ~ sein)* to lack a quorum, *(~e Sitzung)* quorate meeting, *(nicht ~e Sitzung)* non-quorate meeting

Beschlussfähigkeit constituting a quorum, presence of a quorum

Beschlussfassung *(~ mit Stimmenmehrheit)* passing a resolution by the majority of votes, *(~ über die Verwendung des Bilanzgewinnes)* resolution on the appropriation of profits

Beschlussfassungs / ~anforderungen *(gesetzliche)* statutory requirements for passing resolutions; **~pflicht** obligation to pass a relevant resolution; **~unfähigkeit** lack of quorum

Beschlussvorlage draft resolution

beschneiden *(Befugnisse ~)* to trim (to clip, to prune) powers

beschönigen *(die finanzielle Lage ~)* to gloss over (to extenuate) the financial situation

beschränken 1. to restrict, to limit, *(Anlagen auf Anleihen ~)* to confine investments to bonds, *(die Kosten ~)* to limit (to contain) the costs, to rein

in (to control) spending, *(auf ein Minimum ~)* to pare (to pare down) to a minimum
2. to tighten, to curtail, to squeeze, *(die Kreditaufnahme ~)* to tighten up on credit
3. *(sich ~ auf)* to confine o. s. to

beschränkt limited, restricted, *(~ haftender Gesellschafter)* limited partner, *(~er Handel)* restricted dealings, *(~e Konvertierbarkeit)* limited convertibility, *(~er Negoziierungsauftrag)* restricted order to negotiate, *(~e Zuteilung)* limited (scaled down) allotment

Beschränkung 1. limitation, restriction, *(~ der Aktivitäten auf)* confining activities to, *(~ der Deckung)* limiting the cover (e.g. to damage caused by …), *(~ der Haftung)* limitation of liability, restricting the liability to, *(~ des Kapitalverkehrs)* restrictions on capital flows (movements), *(~ des Notenbankkredites)* restrictions on central bank borrowings, *(ohne betragsmäßige oder zeitliche ~en)* without amount or time limitations
2. tightening, squeeze, curtailment, *(~ der Hypothekenkreditaufnahme)* mortgage credit squeeze, tightening of mortgage lending, *(~ der Kreditvergabe)* lending restrictions, credit tightening, loan curbs
3. *(gesetzliche Beschränkungen)* legal constraints

Beschwerde 1. complaint 2. *(Berufung)* appeal 3. *(Forderung)* claim

Beschwerde / ~bearbeitung complaints processing; **~brief** letter of complaint; **~frist** time for appeal; **~führer** appealing party, appellant, petitioner, complainant, party filing a complaint

Beschwerde / ~gericht appellate court, court of review;**~grund** reason (grounds) for complaint; **~management** complaints management; **~ordnung** complaints procedure; **~recht** right to complain, right of appeal; **~verfahren** complaints procedure

beseitigen 1. to remove, to eliminate 2. *(Mängel)* to redress, to remedy

besetzen *(personalmäßig)* to staff, *(eine freie Position ~)* to fill a vacancy

besichern to collateralise, to secure, to provide (to furnish) security, to put up security, to provide collateral, *(durch eine erstrangige Hypothek ~)* to provide security by way of a first-ranking (senior) mortgage, *(nachrangig ~)* to secure by a lower-ranking collateral

besichert *(~ durch eine uneingeschränkte Bürgschaft)* collateralised by an unconditional guarantee, *(Inanspruchnahmen werden durch Forderungen ~)* borrowings are collateralised by receivables, *(~e Kreditaufnahme)* secured (collateralised) borrowing

Besicherung collateralisation, securing, provision of security (collateral), putting up security, *(~ der Ansprüche der Bank)* collateralisation of the bank's claims, *(~ durch Barmittel)* cash collateralisation, *(~ von Fremdwährungskrediten)* provision of security for foreign currency lendings, *(~ durch eine unbedingte und unwiderrufliche Garantie)* security by way of an unconditional and irrevocable guarantee, *(zur ~ hinterlegen)* to deposit for the purpose of collateralisation

Besicherungs / ~anforderungen collateral posting requirements; **~anhang** *(bei Finanztermingeschäften)* credit support annex; **~anspruch** *(~ der Bank)* bank's right (entitlement) to collateral (to collateralisation); **~form** security device, type of collateral, means of security provision

Besicherungs / ~geschäft hedging transaction; **~grad** degree of collateralisation, collateralisation level; **~klasse** collateral category; **~pflicht** obligation to provide collateral (to furnish security); **~quote** collateral ratio, → Besicherungsgrad

Besicherungs / ~recht law on collateral security; **~risiko** collateral risk, risk of collateral impairment; **~umfang**

B

extent of collateralisation; ~**vertrag** collateral agreement; ~**wert** collateral value

Besitz 1. possession, *(in ~ nehmen)* to take possession of, *(wieder in ~ nehmen)* to repossess
2. *(Eigentum, Eigentumsrecht, Rechtstitel)* ownership, title, *(der ~ an der Pfandsache)* title to (ownership of) the pledged asset
3. *(Grundbesitz)* real property
4. *(Wertpapierbesitz)* holdings

Besitz / ~**anspruch** ownership claim, claim of title, possessory claim; ~**aufgabe** surrender of ownership (possession); ~**einheit** unity of ownership, unity of possession; ~**einkommen** unearned income; ~**erlangung** taking possession

besitzen to possess, to own, to be in possession of, to hold

Besitzer owner, proprietor, possessor, holder

Besitzergreifung 1. taking possession 2. seizure, appropriation

besitzgebunden *(~es Pfandrecht)* possessory lien

Besitz / ~**gesellschaft** holding company, owning company; ~**konstitut** indirect possession;~**nahme** entry into possession; ~**pfandrecht** possessory lien; ~**recht** possessory title, right to a property, ownership (property) right

Besitzstandswahrung grandfathering, safeguarding acquired (vested) rights, → Bestandsschutz

Besitzstandswahrungsklausel grandfather(ing) clause

Besitz / ~**störung** 1. tort of trespass 2. wrongful interference with goods; ~**störungsklage** action of trespass; ~**titel** 1. title 2. → Besitzurkunde; ~**übergang** transfer of title (possession)

Besitz/~**übertragung**/~**umschreibung** transfer of title (ownership), property conveyance; ~**urkunde** instrument of title, deed of ownership, title deed; ~**verhältnisse** ownership structure

Besitz / ~**verlust** loss of property, dispossession; ~**verschaffung** delivery of possession; ~**wechsel** change in ownership, *(bei Unternehmen i.w.S.)* change of corporate control; ~**zeit** holding period

besonderes Kursrisiko *(Eigenkapitalanforderungen für das besondere Kursrisiko)* capital requirements (capital charge) for special risks

Besonderheit particularity, *(~ en des inländischen Marktes)* special features of the domestic market, *(die ~ dieser Transaktion)* the special nature (specifics) of this deal

Besorgnis *(~ über hohe Zinssätze)* concern (uneasiness) about high interest rates, alarm at high interest rates

besorgt *(~ sein)* to be alarmed at

besparen to make regular deposits under a savings scheme

besprechen to discuss, to confer, to review

Besprechung meeting, discussion, conference

Besprechungsprotokoll minutes of the meeting

Besserung improvement

Besserungsabrede earn-out agreement, agreement on compensation from future profits

Besserungsklausel earn-out clause

Besserungsschein earn-out certificate, debtor's undertaking to pay compensation (to repay debt in whole or in part) from future profits

Bestallungsurkunde certificate of appointment

Bestand 1. existence, *(Fortbestand)* continued existence
2. *(rechtlicher ~ einer Forderung)* legal validity of a claim
3. inventory, book, portfolio, holding, position, *(~ im kurz- und mittelfristigen Geschäft)* short and medium-term

loan portfolio, *(~ der Händler)* dealer inventories (positions)
(im eigenen ~ halten) to hold in one's own book (portfolio), *(in den eigenen ~ nehmen)* to take on one's own book (portfolio), *(nicht platzierte Titel in den eigenen ~ nehmen)* to inventory (to warehouse) unplaced securities, *(im ~ verbleiben)* to remain on the book
4. *(Saldo)* balance
5. *(Warenbestand)* inventory, stock, *(~ per Jahresanfang/Jahresende)* opening/closing inventory

Bestand an *(~ liquiden Aktiva)* stock of liquid assets, → erstklassige liquide Aktiva, *(~ Festgeldern)* total (aggregate) time deposits, *(~ Fremdwährungen)* foreign currency position (holdings), *(~ Hypothekendarlehen/Hypothekenausleihungen)* mortgage loan portfolio, total mortgage lendings, *(~ festverzinslichen Papieren)* holdings of fixed income securities, *(~ Wertberichtigungen)* total allowance for loan losses, *(~ Wohnungsbaukrediten)* home loan portfolio

Beständigkeit 1. consistency, stability, reliability **2.** permanence

Bestands / ~abbau portfolio reduction, inventory (position) cutbacks; **~abgleich** portfolio reconciliation; **~abschreibung** inventory write-off (write-down); **~absicherung 1.** portfolio hedging **2.** hedging existing positions

Bestands / ~anzeigepflicht inventory notification requirement; **~aufnahme** inventory-taking, position-taking; **~aufstockung** inventory (position) buildup, increase in holdings; **~ausweitung im Kreditgeschäft** increase in total lendings, lending expansion

Bestands / ~betreuung 1. servicing existing customers **2.** *(von Problemkrediten)* managing problem (distressed) loans, problem loan workout; **~bewertung** inventory (portfolio) valuation

Bestands / ~dispositionen inventory (position) management, buying and selling, increasing and/or decreasing holdings; **~erhöhung** → Bestandsaufstockung; **~ermittlung** → Bestandsaufnahme

Bestands / ~finanzierung inventory financing; **~fortschreibung 1.** rollover of a position **2.** portfolio update; **~führung 1.** position-keeping **2.** inventory (portfolio) management; **~führungssystem** portfolio management system

Bestands / ~gefährdung threat to the bank's/company's existence; **~geschäft** existing business, business with existing customers, portfolio business; **~glattstellung** position-squaring, closing out a position, position close-out

Bestands / ~größen stock variables; **~haltung** carrying a position (an inventory), holding a position; **~immobilien** portfolio properties, existing properties

Bestands / ~konten → aktivische/ → passivische Bestandskonten; **~kontrolle** position (inventory) control; **~kosten 1.** inventory cost **2.** *(von Finanzinstrumenten)* carrying charges (cost); **~kraft** validity

Bestandskunden existing customers (clients)

Bestandskunden / ~basis existing customer (client) base; **~betreuung** existing customer support; **~bindung** maintaining existing clients, customer retention; **~geschäft** existing clients business; **~marketing** marketing to existing clients; **~pflege** cultivating the existing customer base; **~zufriedenheit** satisfaction of existing clients

Bestands / ~limit inventory limit; **~mehrung** inventory increase, → Bestandsaufstockung; **~minderung** inventory (portfolio) cutback, decrease in holdings, reducing (cutting down) a position; **~mitteilung** inventory notification

B

Bestands / ~position portfolio (inventory) position, asset item; **~regulierung** position settlement, → Bestandsdispositionen; **~risiko** 1. inventory risk 2. position risk (exposure) 3. → Veritätsrisiko

Bestandsschutz 1. grandfathering, *(~ für Alttransaktionen)* grandfathering of existing transactions, *(für bestehende Regelungen gilt ~ bis ...)* existing arrangements will be grandfathered until ...
2. *(im Kreditgeschäft)* non-callability of a loan during the fixed rate period agreed upon

Bestandsschutz / ~klausel grandfather clause, grandfathering provision □ provision allowing an old rule to apply; **~rechte** grandfather rights; **~regeln** grandfathering rules

Bestands / ~sperrung portfolio freeze, blocking the portfolio (the holdings); **~übertrag** portfolio (position) transfer; **~veränderungen** 1. inventory (portfolio) changes 2. changes in book value

Bestands / ~verzeichnis 1. inventory record 2. position sheet 3. *(im Grundbuchblatt)* list of properties; **~wert** inventory (position) value, value of holdings; **~zuwachs** inventory increase, *(~bei Spareinlagen)* growth in aggregate savings deposits

Bestandteil part, component, constituent, *(Bestandteile des regulatorischen Eigenkapitals)* regulatory capital elements, *(einen ~ dieses Vertrages bilden)* to form part (to be an integral component) of this agreement

bestätigen 1. to confirm, to affirm, *(bestätigtes Akkreditiv)* confirmed documentary credit, *(die bestehende Anleiheeinstufung ~)* to reaffirm the bond's rating, *(eine Entscheidung ~)* to uphold (to reaffirm) a decision, *(die Untersuchungsergebnisse ~)* to corroborate the findings of the analysis, *(ein Urteil ~)* to uphold a sentence
2. *(bescheinigen)* to certify, to attest, *(einen Scheck ~)* to certify a cheque, to guarantee that the cheque will be honoured upon presentation
3. *(billigen)* to approve, to sanction
4. *(den Empfang ~)* to acknowledge receipt
5. *(sich ~)* to bear out, *(falls sich Meinungsumfragen/Übernahmegerüchte ~)* if opinion polls are borne out/if rumours of a take-over come true

bestätigende Bank confirming bank, bank confirming a documentary credit

Bestätigung 1. confirmation, *(~ eines Akkreditivs)* confirming a documentary credit, *(~ der Ordnungsmäßigkeit der Dokumente)* certificate of compliance □ certificate confirming that the documents are in accordance with the terms and conditions of the credit, *(~ der Rechtmäßigkeit)* affirmation of the validity, *(~ der Transaktionsdaten am gleichen Tag)* same-day affirmation of the transaction data
2. certification, attestation, *(~ einer Unterschrift)* attesting to the authenticity of a signature
3. approval 4. acknowledgement

Bestätigungs / ~bank confirming bank; **~code** confirmation code; **~nummer** confirmation number; **~provision** confirming commission; **~schreiben** confirmatory letter, *(einer Kreditgewährung)* facility letter,loan confirmation; **~vermerk** 1. confirmation, acknowledgement 2. *(des Buchprüfers)* audit certificate 3. *(auf einem Scheck)* certification, certification statement, undertaking to pay (to honour) a cheque

Bestbieter highest bidder

bestehen 1. to exist 2. *(~ auf)* to insist on, to persist in 3. *(~ aus)* to consist of, to be made up of, to comprise 4. *(die finanzielle Krise ~)* to overcome (to weather, to survive) the financial crisis 5. *(den Test ~)* to pass (to stand) the test

Bestehen 1. *(~ einer Forderung)* existence of a claim **2.** insistence, persistence

bestehen bleiben 1. to continue to exist, to remain in existence, *(im Hinblick auf eine Unternehmung ferner)* to continue as a going concern, to remain afloat **2.** *(weiterhin Gültigkeit besitzen)* to remain valid, to remain in force

bestehend *(~e Forderung)* existing claim, *(~es Gesetzesrecht)* enacted statutes, *(~e Vorschriften)* provisions in force, current regulations

Bestelldauer *(eines Vorstandsmitgliedes)* term of office

Bestelleingang order intake

bestellen 1. to order, to place an order, to book
2. to create, to constitute, to establish, *(die der Bank bestellten Sicherheiten)* the collateral furnished to the bank, *(eine Hypothek ~)* to create (to take out) a mortgage
3. to appoint, to retain, to engage the services of, *(einen Anwalt ~)* to retain an attorney

Bestellerkredit buyer (buyer's) credit; **~versicherung** buyer credit guarantee (insurance)

Bestellung 1. order, placing an order, booking
2. creation, establishment, *(~ einer Hypothek)* mortgage creation, creation of a mortgage charge, *(~ eines Pfandrechtes)* taking a charge over (upon) assets, creation of a lien, *(~ von Sicherheiten)* provision of collateral, furnishing security, *(~ eines Sicherungsrechtes)* creation of a security interest
3. *(~ eines Bevollmächtigten)* appointment of a proxy

Bestellungs / ~periode term of office; **~urkunde** deed of charge

bestens at best, → Bestens-Order

bestensfalls *(wir erwarten ~ eine Gewinnstagnation)* we are expecting profits to remain flat at best

Bestens-Order order to sell at best, order to sell a security at the best price available

besteuerbar taxable, assessable

besteuern to tax, to levy (to impose) a tax

Besteuerung taxation, levying a tax, *(~ an der Quelle)* taxation at source

bestimmen 1. *(anordnen)* to stipulate, to order **2.** *(ernennen)* to appoint, to designate **3.** *(festlegen)* to determine, to establish, to fix, to specify, *(durch Angebot und Nachfrage bestimmter Kurs)* price determined by supply and demand **4.** *(regeln)* to regulate

bestimmt specific, given, *(zu einem ~en Zeitpunkt)* at a given point in time, *(für einen ~en Zeitraum anlegen)* to invest for a stated period of time, *(für einen ~en Zweck verwenden)* to use for a particular (specific) purpose

Bestimmtheitsgrundsatz principle of clarity, requirement to specify details, *(bei Kreditsicherheiten)* requirement that assets provided as collateral must adequately be defined

Bestimmung 1. *(Bedingung)* condition **2.** *(Ernennung)* appointment, designation **3.** *(Festlegung)* determination, establishment, fixing, *(~ der angemessenen Eigenmittel)* determining capital adequacy **4.** *(eines Vertrages)* provision, clause **5.** *(Vorschrift)* regulation, rule

Bestimmungs / ~hafen port of destination; **~parameter** *(~ der Geldpolitik)* monetary policy parameters (determinants); **~zweck** designated use

bestmöglich *(~e Ausführung von Kundenaufträgen)* best execution of customer orders, *(Verpflichtung zur ~en Ausführung)* best execution obligation, *(~e Konditionen)* best possible terms (rates), *(~er Schätzwert) (im Hinblick auf die → versicherungstechnischen Rückstellungen)* best (central) estimate

bestreben to endeavour, *(um eine Risikoeindämmung bestrebt sein)* to strive (to be anxious) to contain the risk

Bestreben strive, endeavour, effort

bestreiten 1. to contest, to oppose, to call (to put) into question, to doubt, to challenge, *(den Anspruch des Gläubigers ~)* to contest (to dispute) the creditor's claim
2. *(aufkommen für)* to meet, to cover, to pay, *(den Schuldendienst ~)* to meet debt service obligations, to effect (to settle) interest and redemption payments

Bestreiten 1. contesting, contestation, challenge **2.** meeting, payment, *(~ der Kosten)* defrayal of the expenses

Beta Beta □ measure of how closely an individual stock price moves with the market

beteiligen 1. to participate, to take part, to join, to take an interest in, *(sich an den Kosten ~)* to share in the costs, to contribute to the expenses, *(sich an einem Unternehmen ~)* to acquire an interest (a share, a stake) in a company, to take an interest in a company
2. *(jmd. ~)* to give s. o. a share (stake, interest) in

beteiligt 1. *(partizipierend)* to have an interest (a share) in, to hold an interest in, *(am Gewinn ~ sein)* to share in the profit, to have a share in the profit
2. *(betroffen)* involved, to be a party to, *(die ~en Parteien)* the interested parties, the parties concerned (involved in the process), the parties to this agreement

Beteiligte/r person involved, party

Beteiligung 1. *(am Gewinn)* share (participation) in profits, profit-sharing
2. *(an einem Unternehmen)* equity investment, interest, participation, share, stake, shareholding
3. *(verbundenes Unternehmen)* affiliated (associated) company
4. *(Beitrag)* contribution

Beteiligungen *(Bilanzposten)* investments, participating interests, *(~ zum Ankaufswert, abzüglich Abschreibungen)* investments at cost, less amounts written off, *(~ zum Buchwert)* investments at book value (at amortised cost), *(~ an verbundenen Unternehmen)* investments in affiliated companies

Beteiligungsabschreibung write-down of an investment

beteiligungsähnlich *(~es Darlehen)* investment loan

Beteiligungs / ~anzeige notification of interests held, disclosure of participations; **~ausbau** increase in the stake (interest) already held, stakebuilding, → Anschleichen; **~beitrag** income (contribution) from equity investments

Beteiligungs / ~besitz equity investment portfolio, total investments held, private equity holdings; **~bestand** investment portfolio, portfolio of financial and industrial holdings; **~buch** → Beteiligungsportefeuille; **~buchwert** book value of an investment

Beteiligungs / -Controller/-Controlling investment controller/controlling; **~darlehen** → partiarisches Darlehen; **~engagement** equity exposure; **~erträge** investment income, income from trade investments, equity income; **~erwerb** acquiring a shareholding, acquisition of an interest (stake), making an equity investment

Beteiligungs / ~finanzierung equity financing (finance), financing the acquisition of investments; **~fonds** equity fund, venture capital fund; **~fondsgeschäft** equity funds business

Beteiligungs / ~garantie-Gemeinschaft equity guaranteeing society; **~geber** investor, provider of equity, venture capital lender; **~geflecht** cross shareholdings

Beteiligungsgesellschaft 1. *(auf den Erwerb von Beteiligungen spezialisiertes Unternehmen)* private equity company, participation company **2.** *(verbun-*

denes Unternehmen) affiliated (associated) company

Beteiligungs / ~investitionen private equity investments, portfolio investments; **~kapital** private equity, equity capital invested in private companies, *(i. S. von Wagniskapital)* venture capital

Beteiligungs / ~management equity investment management, participations management, management of shareholdings; **~markt** private equity market; **~nehmer** investee company, venture capital borrower; **~option** equity investment option

Beteiligungs / ~paket large shareholding; **~papiere** equity securities, investment securities, equity stock; **~portefeuille** investment (shareholding) portfolio, portfolio of equity participations, total investments (shareholdings); **~positionen** equity investment exposures

Beteiligungs / ~quote percentage of shares (percentage interest) held, stake, *(an einem Konsortialkredit)* syndicate interest; **~rechte 1.** ownership interests **2.** investments

Beteiligungs / ~richtlinie (EU) Qualifying Holdings Directive; **~risiko** equity investment risk, investment exposure, risk from equity holdings; **~risikomodell** equity risk model

Beteiligungs / ~tausch investment swap, swap (exchange) of shareholdings; **~verhältnis** participating interest, participatory relationship, *(Unternehmen, mit denen ein ~ besteht)* affiliated companies, companies in which an equity (participating) interest is held

Beteiligungs / ~verkauf disinvestment, selling off a stake, sell-off, stake sale; **~vermittlung** equity investment service, *(i.w.S.)* merger and acquisition (M&A) activities

Beteiligungs / ~verwaltungsgesellschaft portfolio management company; **~zugänge** investment additions, additions to the investment portfolio, new shareholdings

betonen to stress, to accentuate, to emphasise

Betracht *(in ~ ziehen)* to take into account (consideration)

beträchtlich considerable, sizeable, substantial

Betrachtungsweise *(bei wirtschaftlicher ~)* from a substance-over-form perspective

Betrag amount, sum, *(~ in Worten/Ziffern)* amount in words/figures, *(in einem ~)* in one amount

betragen to amount (to add up) to, to run to (into), *(insgesamt 60 Mio. € ~)* to total (to aggregate) € 60m

betraglich *(~ begrenzte Bürgschaft)* guarantee for a limited (fixed) amount, *(~ unbegrenzte Bürgschaft)* unlimited guarantee, guarantee with no limit on the amount

betragsabhängig *(~e Staffelverzinsung)* balance-related interest payments

betragsgenau *(~e Abdeckung)* cover for an identical amount

betragsmäßig *(~e Begrenzung der einzelnen Emissionen)* limit on the amount of each issue, *(~e Inkongruenz)* mismatch in amount, mismatch in terms of money

Betragsspalte amount column

betrauen *(mit der Verwaltung der Vermögenswerte ~)* to entrust with the management of the assets, *(die mit diesen Aufgaben betrauten Mitarbeiter)* staff members charged with these tasks

Betreff reference, subject

betreffen 1. to affect, *(die am stärksten betroffenen Märkte)* the hardest hit markets **2.** *(angehen)* to concern, to refer to

betreiben 1. to pursue, to conduct, to run, to operate, *(Bankgeschäfte ~)* to conduct banking business (operations), to run a bank
2. to seek, *(die Zwangsvollstreckung ~)*

B

to seek a compulsory enforcement, to initiate (to instigate) a compulsory enforcement, *(aus einer gesicherten Forderung die Zwangsvollstreckung ~)* to initiate compulsory enforcement proceedings by virtue of a secured claim

betreibende Partei moving party

Betreiber 1. operator, operating company **2.** *(wenn identisch mit Eigentümer)* owner

Betreiber / **~entgelt** *(bei Abhebungen vom Geldautomaten)* access fee, ATM service fee; **~immobilie** owner-operated property

Betreibung 1. pursuit, conduct, running, operating **2.** seeking

betreuen 1. *(Kunden)* to service, to serve, to support, *(mittelständische Unternehmen ~)* to cater to the needs of small and medium-sized companies, *(Anzahl der betreuten Kunden)* customers (accounts) serviced
2. to handle, *(Vermögenswerte)* to manage, *(das betreute Volumen)* volume under management, *(betreute Portefeuilles)* portfolios under management, portfolios handled

Betreuer 1. *(Kundenbetreuer in einer Bank)* relationship manager, customer support officer, customer care officer, accounts officer **2.** *jur.* curator **3.** *(börsenmäßiger – einer Aktie)* designated sponsor

Betreuung 1. customer support, customer care, servicing, catering, *i.w.S.* relationship management **2.** management, handling **3.** *(unter gesetzlicher ~ stehende Person)* person under custodianship **4.** *(börsenmäßige – einer Aktie)* sponsoring

Betreuungs / **~aufwand** customer support expense, servicing expenditure; **~intensität** intensity of customer support; **~kapazität** servicing potential; **~konto** curatorship account; **~konzept** customer support concept, servicing blueprint; **~kosten** customer support expense

Betreuungs / **~recht** custodianship law; **~team** customer support team, service team; **~vollmacht** durable power of attorney, health care power of attorney

Betrieb 1. company, business, enterprise, establishment, plant, organisation **2.** running, operating **3.** → Teilbetrieb

betrieblich *(~e Altersversorgung)* occupational pension, *(~e Altersvorsorge)* occupational old age provision, → betrieblicher Pensionsplan, *(~e Ausbildung)* in-house training, *(~er Cashflow)* operative cash flow, *(~ gebundenes Vermögen)* capital employed, *(~er Nettoerlös)* net operating earnings
(~e Nutzungsdauer) operating (useful) life, service life, *(~er Pensionsplan)* company (occupational, employee) pension scheme, retirement benefits plan, *(~es Risikokapital)* operational risk capital, *(~e Schulden)* operating liabilities, *(~e Vermögenswerte)* operating assets

Betriebs / **~abläufe** operational processes, business workflows; **~abrechnungsbogen** cost distribution (apportionment) sheet; **~absprache** company (works) agreement; **~analyse** operations analysis, review of operations

Betriebs / **~aufspaltung** company (corporation) split-up, demerger; **~ausgaben** operating cost (expenses), deductible business expenses, *(Abzugsfähigkeit der ~)* deductibility of operating expenses; **~ausstattung** business equipment, manufacturing facilities

betriebsbedingt *(~er Aufhebungsvertrag)* redundancy agreement, *(~e Kündigung)* redundancy

Betriebs / **~berater** business consultant; **~beratung** business consultancy, business consulting services; **~bereich** operating division; **~einheit 1.** operating unit **2.** business entity;

~**einnahmen** business income, income from operations; ~**einrichtungen** plant facilities, operating equipment; ~**erfolg** operating (company) performance, → Betriebsergebnis

Betriebsergebnis operating result(s), operating profit/loss, income/loss from operations, company performance, *(einer Bank)* operating result □ net interest and commission income less operating expenditure, *(~ vor Afa)* operating profit/loss before depreciation for wear and tear, *(~ nach Risikovorsorge)* operating profit after risk provisions

Betriebsergebnis / ~**quote** profit ratio □ operating profit as a percentage of the average business volume; ~ **rechnung** operating income statement, statement of operations

Betriebs / ~**ertrag** operating earnings, *(einer Bank)* operating income, commission and fee income; ~**ertragsspanne** operating income margin □ expressed as a percentage of the average business volume

Betriebs / ~**erweiterung** plant extension; ~**fortführung** continuance (continuation) of operations

betriebsfremd non-operating, outside, foreign to the business of the company, *(~e Aufwendungen/Erträge)* non-operating expenses/earnings, *(~e Mittel)* outside funds (capital), third-party funds

Betriebs / ~**führung 1.** company management **2.** management (conduct) of operations; ~**geheimnis** trade secret; ~**gesellschaft** operating (managing) company; ~**gewinn** operating (trading) profit

betriebsgewöhnlich *(~e Nutzungsdauer)* operating life expectancy

Betriebs / ~**haftpflichtversicherung** business (premises and operations) liability insurance; ~**handelsspanne** operating margin

betriebsintern *(~es Informationssystem)* in-house information system

Betriebs / ~**kapazität** operating capacity; ~**kapital** working (rolling) capital, → Betriebsmittel; ~**koeffizient** working (operating) ratio; ~**kosten** operating cost, cost of operations; ~**kredit** operating loan, short-term loan, business credit; ~**leistung** operational performance, operating output

Betriebsmittel 1. working (operating) funds, working capital **2.** enterprise resources, rolling capital **3.** operating equipment, production facilities

Betriebsmittel / ~**bedarf** working capital requirements; ~**bereitstellung** provision of operating funds; ~**finanzierung** working capital funding, financing working capital requirements

Betriebsmittel / ~**kredit** operating (business) loan, working capital credit; ~**kreditlinie** operating (working capital) line of credit; ~**planung** enterprise resource planning; ~**rücklage** operating cash reserve; ~**verwaltung** enterprise resource management

betriebsnotwendig *(~es Vermögen)* net operating assets

Betriebs / ~**prüfung 1.** *(intern)* internal audit **2.** *(durch das Finanzamt)* company audit, tax audit of the accounts; ~**rat** staff council; ~**rente** company (occupational) pension; ~**rentenansprüche** occupational pension claims; ~**risiko** operational (operations) risk; ~**schulden** business (operating) debt

Betriebsstätte 1. plant, place of operations **2.** *(in der Steuergesetzgebung)* permanent establishment

Betriebsstätten / ~**finanzamt** tax office competent for the company's place of business; ~**gewinn**/~**verlust** profit/loss of a permanent establishment

Betriebs /~**stilllegung** closing down a plant, discontinuance of operations, works closure; ~**stoffe** operating supplies; ~**störung** business disruption, interruption of business, malfunction

Betriebs / ~**übergang** transfer of company ownership, → Betriebsübertragung; ~**überschuss** net operating income, → Teilbetriebsergebnis; ~**übertragung** transfer of operations (of business)

Betriebs / ~**vereinbarung** company (works) agreement; ~**verfassungsgesetz** German Works Constitution Act;~**verlust** operating loss, loss from operations; ~**vermögen** business (operating) assets, working capital; ~**versammlung** company (works) meeting

Betriebs / ~**wirt** graduate in business administration (economics); ~ **wirtschaft(slehre)** business administration, business economics, business studies

betriebswirtschaftlich *(~e Analyse)* management assessment (analysis), *(~es Instrumentarium)* business tools, *(~e Kennzahlen)* financial and accounting ratios

Betriebszugehörigkeit seniority, length of service (in a company)

betroffen *(~er Kundenkreis)* customers affected by, customers involved (interested in), *(von der Rezession ~ sein)* to be hit (to be affected) by the recession

Betrug **1.** fraud **2.** *(Unterschlagung)* embezzlement

betrügen **1.** to defraud **2.** to embezzle

betrügerisch *(in ~er Absicht)* with intent to defraud, *(~e Gläubigerbevorteilung)* fraudulent preference, *(~es Handeln)* fraudulent trading

Betrugs / ~**absicht** fraudulent intent; ~**abwehr** fraud protection; ~**bekämpfung** combating (fight against) fraud, antifraud measures; ~**erkennung** fraud detection; ~**fall** fraud case; ~**handlung** fraudulent act; ~**quote** *(im Kreditkartengeschäft)* fraud to sales ratio; ~**risiko** risk of fraud; ~**versuch** attempted fraud

beugen *(sich dem Druck ~)* to succumb to the pressure

beunruhigen *(die Finanzmärkte ~)* to disturb (to worry, to unsettle) the financial markets, *(beunruhigt über die hohe Verschuldung)* concerned about (alarmed at) the high debt level, *(beunruhigte Anleger)* disconcerted (worried) investors

beunruhigend *(~ für die Aktionäre)* worrying to shareholders, *(~e Übernahmegerüchte)* disturbing take-over rumours

Beunruhigung concern, worry, disturbance, alarm, uneasiness, *(starke ~ unter den Aktionären)* grave concerns among shareholders

beurkunden to authenticate, to notarise, *(gerichtlich beurkundete Erklärung)* statement authenticated by a court, *(notariell beurkundete Erklärung)* notarised statement (declaration), declaration authenticated by a notary

Beurkundung authentication, *(öffentliche/notarielle)* notarisation

Beurkundungsgesetz German Notarisation Act

Beurkundungspflicht notarisation requirement, mandatory notarisation, obligation to have an agreement/a document notarised

beurteilen to assess, to rate, to evaluate, *(einen Emittenten/Kreditnehmer bonitätsmäßig ~)* to rate an issuer/borrower, to assess an issuer's/a borrower's credit-worthiness, *(erstklassig beurteilter Kreditnehmer)* highly rated (top-rated) borrower, *(einen Kreditantrag ~)* to assess (to appraise) a loan application, *(das Länderrisiko ~)* to assess the country risk, *(einen Mitarbeiter ~)* to appraise a staff member

Beurteilung judg(e)ment, assessment, rating, opinion, *(~ der Angemessenheit des Eigenkapitals)* assessing (measuring) the adequacy of capital, *(~ der Kapitaldienstfähigkeit)* assessment of the borrower's (issuer's) ability to effect the required redemption payments *(~ der Kreditwürdigkeit)* credit appraisal (evaluation), assessment of (assessing) the credit-worthiness, credit evaluation, *(~ der Liquidität)* measurement of liquidity, *(~ am*

Markt) rating in the market, *(~ von Mitarbeitern)* staff appraisal (assessment), merit rating

Beurteilungs / ~gespräch appraisal interview; **~grundlage** rating basis, basis of assessment; **~maßstab** performance benchmark; **~skala** rating scale

beuteln *(der von starken Kursrückgängen gebeutelte Markt)* the market buffeted by heavy price falls

bevollmächtigen to authorise, to empower, to grant a power of attorney, to confer a power

Bevollmächtigte/r attorney, authorised agent, authorised person (signatory), person holding discretionary powers, *(bevollmächtigter Vertreter)* authorised representative, *(Stimmrechts-Bevollmächtigter)* proxy

Bevollmächtigung 1. *(Ermächtigung)* authorisation, granting (conferring) a power **2.** *(Vollmacht)* power of attorney, proxy

Bevorratungskosten stockpiling cost

bevorrechtigen to prefer, to give preference (priority) to (over)

bevorrechtigt preferential, prior, privileged, senior; ~ **sein** to rank prior to, to hold a prior right of payment, to be entitled to preference in payment, to be accorded priority in payment, to hold a superior claim, to have priority of claim, to rank preferentially

bevorrechtigt *(~er Anspruch)* senior claim, *(~e Ausschüttung) (a)* → bevorrechtigte Dividende, *(b) (im Falle einer Unternehmensliquidation)* liquidation preference, *(~e Dividende)* preferred (preferential) dividend, *(~e Forderungen)* preferential debt, prior (priority) claims, preference claims, debts payable in preference to all others, *(~er Gläubiger)* creditor with a preferential right to payment, preferential creditor (BE), prior (preferred) creditor, prior (senior) claimant (AE), *(~e Hypothek)* senior mortgage

Bevorrechtigung priority, privilege, giving preference to, giving priority over, *(~ von Forderungen)* priority of claims, *(~ bestimmter Gläubiger)* privilege of priority enjoyed by certain creditors

bevorschussen to advance, to lend against, *(Forderungen ~)* to lend (to advance funds) against accounts receivable

Bevorschussung *(~ von Dokumenten)* advance against (on) documents, *(~ eines Nachlasses)* probate advance, advance against estate assets, *(~ von Warenbeständen)* inventory lending, lending against stocks

Bevorschussungskredit 1. short-term lending facility **2.** *(in Verbindung mit einem Dokumentenakkreditiv)* anticipatory credit

Bevorschussungsquote advance (lending) rate

bevorstehen to be imminent (forthcoming), to be in the pipeline, to be afoot

bevorstehend *(~e Dividendenzahlung)* upcoming dividend payment, *(~e Emission)* forthcoming (imminent) issue, issue in the pipeline, *(~er Steuertermin)* upcoming tax payment date, *(~e Zinssenkung)* imminent cut in interest rates

bevorzugen to prefer, to give preference over (to), to pay in preference to others

bevorzugt preferred, preferential, possessing a priority, (~e *Ausführung)* priority execution, *(~es Befriedigungsrecht)* preferential right to payment (satisfaction), *(~er Kunde)* preferred (valued, esteemed) customer, *(~e Methode)* method of choice

Bevorzugung preference, preferential treatment, giving preference over

bewahren *(die Unabhängigkeit ~)* to preserve (to retain) independence

bewähren *(sich ~)* to prove successful, to prove its worth, *(bewährte Anla-*

B

B

geform) proven (successful) type of investment, tried and tested form of investment

bewältigen *(die finanziellen Schwierigkeiten ~)* to cope with (to overcome) the financial difficulties

bewegen 1. to move, *(sich in die erwartete Richtung ~)* to move in (into) the anticipated direction **2.** *(sich auf der Höhe des Vorjahres ~)* to be around last year's level **3.** *(sich zwischen 2 und 3 Mrd. ~)* to run at between 2 and 3 bn

beweglich 1. moveable **2.** mobile, flexible, *(~es Vermögen)* moveable property, moveables, chattels

Bewegung movement

Bewegungsbilanz flow-of-funds statement, statement of funds, statement of sources and application

Bewegungsmuster movement pattern

Beweis proof, evidence, *(~ des ersten Anscheins)* prima facie evidence, *(~ durch Augenschein)* evidence by inspection, *(unter ~ stellen)* to give proof of, to be testimony to the fact, *(als ~ vorlegen)* to offer in evidence

Beweis / ~aufnahme hearing of evidence, taking evidence; **~beschluss** order to take evidence

beweisen 1. to prove **2.** *(unterstreichen)* to demonstrate, to exemplify

Beweis / ~kraft conclusive force, conclusiveness, probative force (value), *(für die Bank beweiskräftig dokumentieren)* to give conclusive evidence to the bank; **~last** burden (onus) of proof; **~lastumkehr** reversal of the burden of proof

Beweis / ~mittel evidence, documents produced in evidence; **~recht** Law of Evidence; **~regeln** rules of evidence; **~urkunde** document of proof, documentary proof (evidence); **~würdigung** evaluation (assessment) of evidence

bewerben *(sich ~)* **1.** to apply for **2.** *(bei Ausschreibungen)* to bid for, to tender for, *(sich um das Mandat zur Konsortialführung ~)* to bid for the mandate to lead the group **3.** *(kandidieren)* to stand as a candidate

Bewerber 1. applicant **2.** *(Kandidat)* candidate

Bewerbung 1. application **2.** candidacy

Bewerbungs / ~formular application form; **~frist** period for filing an application, *(bei Ausschreibungen)* tender period; **~schreiben** letter of application; **~unterlagen** application papers

bewerten 1. to value, to measure, *(einheitlich ~)* to value on a uniform basis, *(mit 50 Mio. € ~)* to value at € 50m, *(mit dem 15fachen des Jahresgewinnes ~)* to value at 15times last year's profits, *(zu den Gestehungskosten ~)* to value at cost
(einen Kredit zu den Anschaffungskosten ~) to measure a loan at cost, *(mit dem niedrigeren Wert aus Buchwert oder Marktwert ~)* to value at the lower of carrying value or fair value, *(zum Zeitwert ~)* to measure at fair value
2. *(bonitätsmäßig) (einen Emittenten ~)* to rate an issuer, *(höher ~)* to upgrade, to rate higher, *(niedriger ~)* to downgrade, to rate lower
3. *(kursmäßig)* to price, *(das Papier ist angemessen bewertet)* the stock is fairly priced, *(im Kurs höher/niedriger ~)* to mark up/to mark down
4. *(einschätzen)* to assess, to evaluate, *(die Leistung ~)* to assess (to appraise) the performance, *(die Projekterfolgsaussichten ~)* to evaluate the project's prospects
5. *(das Wertpapierportefeuille täglich neu ~)* to mark the portfolio value to the market each day

Bewertung 1. valuation, measurement, *(~ des Aktienportefeuilles)* stock portfolio valuation, *(~ bei erstmaliger Erfassung)* measurement on initial recognition
(~ von Finanzanlagen) valuation of investments, *(~ des Immobilienbesitzes)* valuation of the property portfolio, *(~ notleidender Kredite)* measurement of impaired (troubled) loans,

(~ zum Marktwert) valuation (measurement) at market value *(~ zum Niederstwertprinzip)* valuation at the lower of cost or market, *(~ der zur Verfügung gestellten Sicherheit)* valuation of the security (collateral) furnished, *(~ zum Wiederbeschaffungspreis)* measurement at replacement cost, *(~ zum beizulegenden Zeitwert)* measurement (valuation) at fair value 2.*(bonitätsmäßige)* rating, assessment, *(~ der neu emittierten Anleihe)* rating of the newly issued bond 3. *(kursmäßig)* pricing, *(~ am Terminmarkt)* pricing in the futures (forward) market 4. appraisal, assessment, evaluation, *(~ der Kreditqualität)* assessment of the loan quality, *(~ durch einen Sachverständigen)* professional valuation, *(keine ~ abgeben)* to express no opinion on the merits of … 5. *(tägliche ~ von Finanzpositionen)* daily marking to the market

Bewertungs / ~**abschlag** haircut, valuation discount (markdown); ~**abweichungen** valuation differences; ~**agentur** rating agency; ~**änderung** 1. change in valuation, measurement change, valuation adjustment 2. rating change

Bewertungs / ~**anomalien** *(zwischen Kassa- und Terminmärkten)* pricing anomalies between cash and futures markets; ~**ansatz** 1. valuation approach 2. *(für Derivate)* exposure measurement for derivatives 3. value quoted

Bewertungs / ~**aufschlag** valuation premium (markup); ~**aufwand** valuation charge (expenditure); ~**bedarf** *(~ im Kreditgeschäft)* charges for bad and doubtful debt, → Wertberichtigungsbedarf

bewertungsbedingt *(~er Aufwand/Ertrag)* valuation-induced expense/income, *(~e Kursverluste)* valuation-induced price losses

Bewertungs / ~**einheit** valuation unit, positions/transactions combined for valuation purposes; ~**ergebnis** net measurement gain (loss), income (loss) from asset valuation, *(Bewertungsergebnis aus Sicherungsbeziehungen)* hedging gains (losses)

Bewertungs / ~**fehler** valuation error; ~**gesetz** German Valuations Act; ~**gewinne** valuation (measurement) gains; ~**grundsätze** valuation (measurement) standards, principles of valuation; ~**gutachten** valuation report (memorandum)

Bewertungs / ~**horizont** assessment (evaluation) period; ~**indikatoren** assessment indicators; ~ **inkonsistenz** accounting mismatch

Bewertungs / ~**kennzahl** 1. assessment (performance) ratio 2. *(bei Wertpapieremissionen)* rating grade, rating symbol; ~**korrektur** valuation adjustment; ~**kriterien** valuation criteria, criteria for judging the …; ~**kurs** valuation price

Bewertungs / ~**maßstab** 1. valuation standard (benchmark) 2. rating standard (scale); ~**modell** valuation model, asset pricing model; ~**pflicht** obligation to value, obligatory (mandatory) valuation; ~**politik** valuation (measurement) policy

Bewertungs / ~**regel** valuation rule; ~**relationen** *(bei Aktien)* pricing ratios; ~**reserve** valuation reserve; ~**risiko** 1. valuation risk 2. *(bei der Umrechnung ausländischer Anlagen)* translation risk

Bewertungs / ~**skala** rating (assessment) scale; ~**stetigkeit** consistency (continuity) of (in) valuation; ~**stichtag** measurement (valuation) date; ~**techniken** valuation techniques (methods); ~**unterschiede** valuation (rating) differences

Bewertungs / ~**verfahren** 1. measurement (valuation) method 2. rating method; ~**verlust** impairment, valuation loss; ~**vorschriften** measurement (valuation) rules, → handelsrechtliche Ansatz- und Bewertungsvorschriften;

~**wahlrecht** measurement (valuation) option; ~**zahl** valuation score; ~**zeitraum** 1. valuation period 2. valuation time bucket

bewilligen 1. *(billigen, genehmigen)* to approve, to permit, to allow 2. *(Gelder gewähren)* to grant, to appropriate

Bewilligung 1. approval, permission 2. grant, *(~ von Haushaltsmitteln)* appropriation of budget funds, *(~ eines Kredites)* loan approval, approving a loan application, granting a loan

Bewilligungs / ~**antrag** appropriation request; ~**ausschuss** 1. *(für Kredite)* loans committee 2. *(für Haushaltsmittel)* appropriations committee; ~**befugnisse**/~**kompetenz** 1. (loan) approval powers 2. power of appropriation 3. discretionary limit; ~**volumen** loans approved (accommodated, granted)

bewirken to cause, to effect, to give rise to, *(eine Renditeverbesserung ~)* to bring about (to lead to) an enhancement in the yield, *(als bewirkt gelten)* deemed to have been effected

Bewirtschaftungskosten *(einer Immobilie)* management and maintenance cost, property's operating expenses

bewusst 1. conscious, aware, *(sich der Risiken der Transaktion ~ sein)* to be aware of the risks inherent in the transaction
2. deliberate, intentional, *(~e Falschdarstellung)* deliberate misrepresentation, *(~ offenlassen)* to leave deliberately open

Bewusstsein awareness

bezahlen to pay, to settle, to clear

Bezahl / ~**karte** payment card; ~**lösung** pay solution; ~**terminal** payment terminal

bezahlt (b) market cleared □ all buying and selling orders were executed at the current published quotation

bezahlt, Brief (bB) further offerings, sellers over

bezahlt, Geld (bG) stocks continued to attract buying interest, buyers over

Bezahltmeldung confirmation (advice) of payment

Bezahlverfahren payment method

bezeichnen to designate, to describe, to mark, to indicate

Bezeichnung designation, description, marking, indication, *(unter der ~ … laufen)* to be issued in the name of …, to bear (to go under) the title of …

beziehen 1. *(Aktien ~)* to subscribe to shares 2. *(ein Gehalt ~)* to draw a salary 3. *(Informationen ~ von)* to draw information from 4. *(erwerben)* to purchase, to buy 5. *(sich ~ auf)* to refer to, to relate to, to concern

Bezieher 1. subscriber 2. recipient

Beziehung 1. *(~ mit dem Kunden)* relationship with the customer 2. *(gute ~en unterhalten)* to maintain good relations (connections, ties, links) 3. *(Hinsicht)* respect

Beziehungs / ~**aufbau** relationship building; ~**management** (customer) relationship management; ~**marketing** relationship marketing

beziffern 1. *(sich ~ auf)* to amount to, to add up to 2. *(den Schaden auf … ~)* to put the damage at …

bezogen 1. *(~e Bank)* drawee bank, bank drawn upon 2. *(währungsbezogen, zinsbezogen)* currency-related, interest-related

Bezogener drawee

Bezug 1. *(von Aktien/Anleihen)* subscription, *(die Anleihe zum ~ anbieten)* to offer the bond for subscription 2. *(Bezugnahme)* reference 3. *(Gehalt, Bezüge)* salary, remuneration package 4. *(Kauf)* purchase

Bezugnahme reference, *(unter ~ auf)* with reference to, referring to

Bezugnahmeprospekt abridged prospectus (based upon a prospectus published only a few months ago)

Bezugs / ~aktien new shares, shares offered under subscription or conversion options; **~angebot** offer for subscription, offer to shareholders to subscribe to new shares, rights offering; **~aufforderung** invitation to subscribe

bezugsberechtigt *(~e Aktionäre) (a)* shareholders entitled to subscribe *(b)* shareholders entitled to dividends

Bezugs / ~berechtigter 1. rightful claimant **2.** *(Begünstigter)* beneficiary; **~erklärung 1.** letter of subscription **2.** exercise notice; **~frist** subscription period, *(bei Kreditverträgen)* loan acceptance period

Bezugs / ~größe reference figure; **~kurs** subscription price; **~leistung** subscription payment

Bezugsrecht subscription right, stock right, *(~e der Aktionäre)* shareholders' subscription (preemptive) rights, *(~ gegen Bareinlagen/Sacheinlagen)* cash/non-cash subscription right, *(mit/ohne ~e)* cum (ex) rights, *(rechnerischer Wert eines ~es)* theoretical value of a right, *(einschließlich der ~e verkaufen)* to sell rights on, to sell cum rights

Bezugsrechts / ~abschlag rights markdown, ex-rights quotation, deduction of subscription rights; **~angebot** rights letter, rights offering; **~ankündigung** rights issue announcement, notice of rights

Bezugsrechts / ~anspruch rights entitlement; **~anwärter** rights candidate; **~ausschluss** exclusion of (excluding, precluding) subscription rights

Bezugsrechts / ~ausübung exercise of subscription rights, take-up of rights, taking up one's subscription rights/one's entitlement; **~ausweis** certificate of subscription (rights) entitlement; **~bedingungen** terms of subscription

Bezugsrechts / ~emission rights issue; **~erlös** rights money, rights issue proceeds; **~gewährung** granting of (providing with) subscription rights; **~handel** rights trading, trading of subscription rights

Bezugsrechts / ~inhaber rights holder; **~konditionen** terms of the rights issue; **~kurs** rights issue price, price at which a rights issue is traded in the market; **~nachweis** evidence of rights entitlement; **~notierung** rights quotation; **~obligation** bond with warrants

Bezugsrechts / ~schein subscription certificate (warrant); **~scheininhaber** warrant holder; **~stelle** rights agent, subscription agent; **~tag** day of subscription; **~verhältnis** *(~ 6:1)* one for six subscription ratio; **~wert 1.** rights value **2.** security (stock) carrying subscription rights

Bezugs / ~währung reference currency; **~zeitraum 1.** reference period **2.** subscription period; **~zinssatz** reference interest rate

bG → bezahlt, Geld

BGB-Gesellschaft civil law association (partnership) □ business/partnershp under the German Civil Code

BGB-Vertrag contract based on the German Civil Code

bieten to bid, to put in a bid, to offer, to tender for

Bieter bidder, offerer, tenderer

Bieter / ~gruppe bidding group (consortium); **~verfahren** bidding (auction) process; **~wettbewerb** bidding contest

Bietfrist bidding period

Bietungs / ~aufkommen total amount of bids, aggregate bidding; **~aval** → Bietungsgarantie

bietungsberechtigt entitled to submit bids

Bietungs / ~ergebnis bidding result; **~garantie** bid bond, tender bond (guarantee); **~höchstbetrag** bid limit; **~konsortium 1.** bidding group (syndicate, consortium) **2.** *(bei Emissionen)* tender panel

Bietungs / ~kurs bidding price; **~satz** bidding rate; **~schluss** bidding close; **~verhalten** *(~ der Banken)* banks' bidding behaviour

Bilanz 1. balance sheet, *(i. S. von Jahresabschluss)* annual financial statements, *(Kurzform)* accounts
2. balance, *(~ ziehen)* to strike a balance

Bilanz / ~aktiva balance sheet assets; **~analyse** balance sheet analysis; **~angaben** balance sheet data, figures entered in (appearing on) the balance sheet; **~anmerkungen** notes to the financial statements

Bilanz / ~ansatz carrying amount, reported value, value (amount) shown in the balance sheet, balance sheet value, reported value; **~aufblähung** inflating the balance sheet

Bilanz / ~ausweis 1. book value, value shown (reflected) in the balance sheet, → Bilanzansatz **2.** recognition (disclosure) in the balance sheet; **~auszehrung** asset depletion

Bilanz / ~belastung balance sheet charge, charge on the accounts; **~bereinigung 1.** restatement of book values **2.** restructuring the balance sheet; **~bewertung** balance sheet appraisal, accounts assessment; **~bonität** balance sheet quality, accounts quality; **~darstellung** statement presentation

Bilanzeid *(zum Geschäftsbericht)* responsibility statement □ statement by the Board of Management that the financial statements give a true and fair view of the company's assets, liabilities, financial position and profit or loss

Bilanz / ~entlastung balance sheet relief, relieving pressure on the accounts, freeing up funds; **~erfordernisse** balance sheet (accounting) requirements

Bilanz / ~forderungen balance sheet receivables; **~format** balance sheet format; **~gewinn** net income for the year, profit available for distribution; **~gewinnausweis** income for the year shown

Bilanz / ~gleichung balance sheet equation, accounting equation; **~gliederung 1.** balance sheet format (breakdown), accounts breakdown (layout) **2.** spreading the balance sheet

bilanziell *(~ ausweisen)* to recognise (to report) in the balance sheet, *(~e Abbildung von Sicherungsgeschäften)* hedge accounting, *(~e Behandlung von Bezugsrechtsemissionen)* accounting (accounting treatment) of rights issues, *(~es Eigenkapital)* equity stated in the balance sheet (shown in the accounts), reported equity (capital)
(~er Fehlbetrag) (a) accounting loss, annual loss *(b)* negative net worth, *(~es Geldgeschäft)* on-balance sheet money market operations, *(~es Kreditgeschäft)* on-balance sheet lendings, lendings reflected in the balance sheet, *(~es Regelwerk)* accounting framework, *(~e Schätzung)* accounting estimate, *(~e Verschuldungskennzahl)* leverage ratio

bilanzieren 1. *(eine Bilanz erstellen)* to draw up a balance sheet, to prepare the accounts
2. *(in der Bilanz ausweisen)* to report (to state, to recognise, to carry, to show) in the balance sheet, *(gesondert als Eigenkapital ~)* to recognise separately under equity, *(bilanziertes Kreditvolumen)* total on-balance sheet lending, *(bilanzierte Verbindlichkeiten)* recognised liabilities

Bilanzierung 1. accounts presentation, statement presentation, preparation of the accounts (of the balance sheet)
2. accounting, accounting treatment, financial reporting, recognition (reporting) in the balance sheet, *(~ zum Erfüllungstag)* settlement date accounting, *(~ nach dem Handelsrecht/nach dem Steuerrecht)* commercial accounting/tax accounting, *(~ nach der Marktwertmethode/zu Marktwerten)* fair value accounting, *(~ notleidender Kredite)* accounting for impaired

loans, *(~ von Sicherungsbeziehungen)* hedge accounting, *(~ zum Zeitwert)* reporting at fair value

Bilanzierungs / ~grundsätze principles (standards) of statement presentation, reporting (accounting) principles; **~hilfe** accounting aid; **~methode** accounting method

bilanzierungspflichtig requiring disclosure in the balance sheet, *(~ e Geschäfte)* on-balance sheet transactions

Bilanzierungs / ~praxis accounts presentation practice, accounting policies (conventions); **~recht** accounting law; **~risiko** reporting risk □ risk of loss due to a change in the accounting methods to be observed by foreign subsidiaries

Bilanzierungs / ~ und Bewertungsmethoden accounting policies; **~vorschriften** accounts presentation rules, legal (statutory) reporting rules; **~wahlrecht** accounting option

Bilanz / ~jahr accounting reference period; **~kennzahlen** balance sheet ratios; **~kennzahlenanalyse** balance sheet ratio analysis; **~kontinuität** consistency in statement presentation, consistency of accounting treatment, accounting continuity

Bilanz / ~kontrollgesetz Financial Reporting Control Act; **~konzept** accounting concept; **~korrektur** accounting adjustment; **~kosmetik** window-dressing; **~kurs** book value; **~lage** balance sheet situation

bilanzmäßig *(~e Ausgliederung)* removing from the balance sheet, *(~es Risiko)* balance sheet risk

bilanzneutral *(~es Absicherungsinstrument)* off-balance sheet hedging vehicle, *(~e Verpflichtungen)* off-balance sheet obligations, obligations not reflected in the balance sheet

Bilanz / ~position 1. balance sheet heading (item, exposure), *(~en unter dem Strich)* headings below the line, *(Absicherung von ~en)* hedging balance sheet exposure; **~präsentation** presentation of the annual accounts, results presentation

Bilanz / ~pressekonferenz accounts press conference; **~publizität** balance sheet disclosure, accounting disclosure; **~qualität** asset quality, quality of the balance sheet; **~recht** accounting law

Bilanzrechtsmodernisierungsgesetz German Accounting Law Modernisation Act □ comprehensive revision of statutory (HGB) accounting principles; designed to internationalise HGB-based accounting law and to strengthen the independence of auditors

Bilanz / ~relationen balance sheet ratios; **~restrukturierung** balance sheet restructuring; **~risiko** balance sheet exposure

Bilanz / ~sanierung balance sheet restructuring; **~schema** standard balance sheet format; **~stärkung** strengthening (boosting) the balance sheet, shoring up the annual accounts

Bilanz / ~steuerrecht tax accounting law; **~stichtag** date of the accounts, balance sheet date, accounting reference date, reporting date; **~stichtagskurs** period-end exchange rate

Bilanz / ~struktur balance sheet structure (pattern); **~strukturmanagement** asset/liability management; **~summe** total assets, balance sheet total; **~summenwachstum** increase in total assets; **~system** accounting regime

Bilanz / ~terminologie accounting terminology; **~transparenz** transparency of the balance sheet; **~umschichtung** regrouping of balance sheet items, restructuring the balance sheet

bilanzunwirksam *(~ darstellen/~ werden lassen)* to take off the balance sheet, to remove from the balance sheet (from the books)

bilanzunwirksam *(~e Finanzierung)* off-balance sheet financing (funding), *(~e Verpflichtungen)* off-balance sheet commitments

B

Bilanz / **~verkürzung** reduction in total assets, contraction (shortening) of the balance sheet; **~verlängerung** stretching (leveraging) the balance sheet; **~verlust** net loss for the year; **~vermerke** items shown below the line

Bilanz / **~verschleierung** window-dressing; **~vorlage** presentation (submission) of the annual accounts; **~vorschriften** balance sheet (accounting) rules ; **~wachstum** increase in total assets; **~währung** accounting currency; **~wert** carrying value (amount), stated value

bilanzwirksam **1.** *adj. (~e Finanzierung)* on-balance sheet financing, financing reflected in the balance sheet, *(~e Kredite)* on-balance sheet loans, lendings recorded on the balance sheet, *(~e Positionen)* on-balance sheet positions, *(~e Transaktionen)* on-balance sheet transactions, *(~e Verschuldung)* on-balance sheet leverage
2. *adv. (~ darstellen/~ werden lassen)* to bring onto the balance sheet

Bilanz / **~zahlen** balance sheet figures, financial statement values; ~ **zusammenfassung** condensed financial statements

bilaterales Netting bilateral netting

Bild *(ein den tatsächlichen Verhältnissen entsprechendes ~ der Vermögens-, Finanz- und Ertragslage der Gesellschaft)* a true and fair view of the net worth, financal position and results of the company

bilden **1.** to form, *(ein Konsortium ~)* to assemble (to arrange, to put together) a syndicate/consortium
2. *(ermitteln)* to determine, *(den Durchschnitt ~)* to calculate (to determine) the average, *(die Zinsen ~ sich frei nach Angebot und Nachfrage)* interest rates are determined by supply and demand
3. to establish, *(Rücklagen/Kreditwertberichtigungen ~)* to set up reserves/ loan loss allowances

Bildschirm / **~feststellung** screen rate determination;~ **handel** screen-based trading

Bildung **1.** formation, assembling, arrangement
2. calculation, determination
3. setting up, establishment, *(~ von Rückstellungen für Kreditverluste)* setting up provisions (providing, making provisions, provisioning) for loan losses, *(~ von Wertberichtigungen) (a)* establishment of valuation allowances *(b) (im Kreditgeschäft)* setting up loan loss allowances

billig **1.** cheap, low-priced, inexpensive, *(~es Geld)* cheap (easy) money, *(~er Kredit)* low-interest loan, *(~e Mittel)* cheap-rate finance
2. *(nach ~em Ermessen)* on the basis of reasonable discretion, using equitable discretion

billigen **1.** to approve, to agree to, to consent to **2.** *(unterstützen)* to back, to endorse, to support

billigend *(~ in Kauf nehmen)* to knowingly accept

Billigkeitsgründe reasons of equiy

Billigkeitsrechte equitable rights (interests), *(billigkeitsrechtlicher Anspruch)* equitable claim

billigst at best

Billigst-Gebot market bid, bid without indication of a bidding price

Billigst-Order at the market buy order, order to purchase securities at the lowest offering price

Billigung **1.** approval, agreement, consent **2.** *(Unterstützung)* backing, endorsement

BilMoG → Bilanzrechtsmodernisierungsgesetz

binäre Option binary option, digital option, fixed return option □ the holder is entitled to a fixed payout if the price of the underlying asset is either above (binary call option) or below (binary put option) the strike price at the time of expiration of the contract

Bindefrist commitment (lock-in, lock-up) period

binden 1. *(festlegen)* to tie up, to freeze, to immobilise, *(Ersparnisse in langfristigen Anlagen ~)* to lock up savings in long-term investments, *(Gelder in Immobilien ~)* to tie up cash in real estate, *(Kapital/Mittel ~)* to tie up (to commit) capital/funds, to make capital/funds unavailable for other purposes, *(durchschnittlich gebundenes Eigenkapital)* average amount of equity tied up, *(längerfristig ~)* to tie up (to invest) for a longer term
2. *(~ an)* to tie to, *(an ein Kurslimit gebunden sein)* to be bound by (to) a price limit, *(an Libor gebundene Zinszahlungen)* Libor-linked interest payments, *(an den Tagesgeldsatz ~)* to tie (to link, to lash) to the overnight rate, *(den Zinssatz an einen Referenzsatz ~)* to link (to peg) the interest rate to a reference rate
3. *(festschreiben) (den Zinssatz ~)* to lock in the interest rate

bindend *(~es Angebot)* binding (firm) offer, *(~es Recht)* binding law, *(eine für den Gläubiger ~e Vereinbarung)* an agreement binding on the creditor, *(rechtlich ~e Zahlungsverpflichtung)* legally binding payment obligation

Bindung 1. tying up, tie-up, freeze, blocking, commitment, *(~ des Kontoguthabens)* tying up (blocking) the account balance, *(~ der Mittel)* earmarking of the funds, allocating (setting aside) the funds for a particular purpose
2. linking to, pegging to, *(~ an einen Index)* linking to an index, indexing, indexation, *(~ der Kreditzusage an eine erstklassige Sicherheit)* pegging (subjecting) the loan undertaking to the provision of first rate collateral
3. locking in, *(~ des Zinssatzes auf fünf Jahre)* locking in the interest rate for five years, arranging a fixed-rate period for five years, *(~ der Zinssätze im Hypothekenkreditgeschäft)* locking in mortgage lending rates, establishment of fixed mortgage loan rates

Bindungsdauer 1. commitment (tying-up) period, fixed rate period, lock-in period **2.** non-withdrawal period

Bindungsfristen *(Hypotheken mit fünfjährigen ~)* mortgages with rates fixed (locked in) for five years, *(Neuzusagen im Baufinanzierungsbereich mit kurzen ~)* new construction lendings carrying short fixed rate periods

Bindungswirkung binding force

Binnenkonnossement inland waterway consignment note

Binnenwert *(einer Währung)* internal value of a currency

biometrische Autorisierung biometric authorisation □ authorisation of a financial transaction that is based on the customer's face, iris, fingerprints, etc.

biometrische Unterschrift biometric signature

blanke Zahlung clean payment

blanko blank, unsecured, *(~ indossierter Wechsel)* bill of exchange endorsed in blank

Blanko / ~abtretung assignment in blank; **~benachrichtigungsschreiben** blank notification letter (form); **~indossament** endorsement in blank; **~kredit** unsecured credit (loan), loan accommodation in blank; **~risiko** unsecured risk; **~scheck** blank cheque

Blanko / ~überziehungskredit unsecured overdraft; **~verkauf** short sale; **~verkäufer** short seller; **~vollmacht** blank (unlimited) power of attorney; **~wechsel** blank bill of exchange; **~zession** → Blankoabtretung

bleiben to remain, to stay, *(für mehrere Jahre investiert ~)* to remain committed for several years

Blindpool blind pool, blind investments □ investors are aware of investment objectives, but not of specific holdings

Blitzhandel flash trading

Blockhandel block trading, trading large amounts of securities, *(der Deutschen Börse für institutionelle Investoren)* block crossing

blockieren 1. *(Gelder ~)* to freeze (to tie up) funds, → binden 2. *(ein Konto/eine Übernahme ~)* to block an account/a take-over

BO/Bobls → Bundesobligation

Boden 1. ground, *(an ~ gewinnen)* to gain ground, *(an ~ gutmachen)* to make up ground, to recover lost ground, *(gegenüber den Hauptwährungen an ~ verlieren)* to lose ground against the major currencies 2. *(Grundbesitz)* land, landed property

Boden / **~bildung** finding a stable base; **~formation** *(Chartanalyse)* bottoming pattern; **~kreditinstitut** mortgage bank, land credit bank; **~nutzungsplanung** land use planning; **~pfandrecht** lien on landed property

Boden / **~richtwert** indicative land value; **~satz** core (permanent) deposits, deposit base; **~wert** land value

BÖGA → Börsengeschäftsabwicklungssystem

Bogen coupon sheet; **~erneuerungsdienst** coupon renewal service

bogenlos *(~e Stücke)* securities without coupon sheet

Bonifikation 1. bonus, commission 2. *(bei Anleiheemissionen)* reallowance, selling commission 3. *(bei Spareinlagen)* interest bonus

Bonifikationsabschlag deduction of (for) selling commission

Bonifikationssperre reallowance restriction period

bonifizieren *(Spareinlagen ~)* to pay (to grant) an interest bonus on savings deposits, *(bonifizierte Spareinlagen)* bonus-carrying savings deposits

Bonifizierung paying an interest bonus, adding a bonus to the usual interest rate

Bonität credit, credit-worthiness, credit (financial) standing, credit quality, *(~ der abgetretenen Forderungen)* quality of receivables assigned, *(~ des Forderungsbestandes)* credit quality of the loan portfolio, *(~ des Kreditnehmers/Emittenten)* borrower's/issuer's credit standing, *(Kunden erster ~)* top-rated customers

bonitätsabhängig *(~e Eigenkapitalanforderung)* credit-related (credit-based) capital requirement (capital charge)

Bonitäts / **~abschlag** credit downgrade; **~anforderungen** credit requirements, credit quality requirements, credit (financial) standing required, conditions as to standing and reliability; **~anspruch** credit quality (rating) required

bonitätsbedingt *(~er Renditeunterschied)* credit spread, *(~e Wertminderung)* credit-related (rating-related) impairment

Bonitäts / **~beeinträchtigung** damage to the credit-worthiness (to the financial standing), impairment of (fall-off in) credit quality; **~befürchtungen** credit concerns (worries), concerns about the borrower's/issuer's financial standing

Bonitäts / **~beurteilung** credit assessment, assessment of the borrower's/issuer's credit-worthiness, determining a loan applicant's credit-worthiness, *(~ durch eine externe Rating-Agentur)* external credit assessment; **~beurteilungskriterien** credit assessment (rating) criteria

Bonitäts / **~bewertung** credit evaluation (rating), → Bonitätsbeurteilung; **~bewusstsein** credit-consciousness, credit-sensitiveness; **~daten** credit particulars

Bonitäts / **~differenzierung** credit differentiation; **~effekt** credit quality effect, impact on the credit quality of a debtor; **~einschätzung** → Bonitätsbeurteilung; **~einstufung** rating, loan grade, → Bonitätsbeurteilung

Bonitäts / ~erfordernisse credit requirements; **~erhöhung** credit enhancement; **~erklärung** statement (letter) of solvency; **~ermittlung** credit assessment, establishing a rating

Bonitäts / ~gefälle credit differential (gap), differential in the financial (credit) standing

bonitätsgerecht *(~e Konditionen)* pricing in line with the borrower's credit rating, credit-based pricing

Bonitäts / ~gesichtspunkte *(unter ~n)* from a credit standpoint; **~gewichtung** credit (credit-based) weighting, *(bonitätsgewichtete Risikoaktiva)* credit-weighted risk assets; **~gewichtungsfaktor** credit weighting factor; **~grad** rating grade

Bonitäts / ~klasse credit (rating) class, credit category; **~kontrolle** *(von Kreditnehmern durch die Bank)* credit control, checking (monitoring) the borrowers' financial standing; **~kriterien** credit criteria (requirements); **~management** credit management

bonitätsmäßig *(~e Bewertung/Einstufung)* rating, credit assessment, quality grading, *(~e Herabstufung)* credit downgrade, *(~e Höherstufung)* credit upgrade, *(~ einwandfreie Kreditnehmer)* borrowers of impeccable credit standing
(~ erstklassiger Emittent) top-rated (top-quality) issuer, triple A rated issuer, *(~ erstklassiger Kreditnehmer)* prime borrower, blue chip borrower, borrower of undoubted financial standing

Bonitäts / ~maßstab credit benchmark, credit quality measure; **~minderung** → Bonitätsbeeinträchtigung ; **~note** credit grade

bonitätsorientiert *(~e Ausrichtung des Kreditgeschäftes)* alignment of lending operations to customer credit-worthiness, credit-geared orientation of lending operations

Bonitäts / ~prüfung credit assessment (analysis), credit investigation, checking the borrower's/issuer's credit-worthiness; **~rating** credit quality evaluation

Bonitätsrisiko 1. credit risk, risk of default by the borrower (issuer, obligor), risk resulting from changes in the financial standing of the borrower
2. *(Kontrahentenrisiko)* counterparty risk

Bonitätsrisikobeurteilung 1. credit risk assessment **2.** assessment of counterparty risk

Bonitätsrückstufung rating (credit) downgrade, downgrading the credit quality

bonitätsschwach *(~e Adresse)* borrower/issuer with a low credit rating

bonitätssensitiv *(~er Markt)* credit-sensitive market

Bonitätsskala rating (credit quality) scale

bonitätsstark *(~e Adresse)* borrower/issuer with a high credit rating, *(~es Kundensegment)* high-credit customer segment, *(unterschiedlich ~e Kunden)* customers of varying credit quality

Bonitäts / ~überprüfung → Bonitätsprüfung; **~überwachung** credit watch, credit monitoring; **~unterschied** credit (rating) differential, divergence (difference) in credit standing

Bonitätsverbesserung credit enhancement, credit quality improvement

Bonitätsverschlechterung credit deterioration, deterioration of (in) the financial standing, deterioration in credit-worthiness, impaired credit rating, *(~ des Forderungsbestandes)* deterioration of credit quality in the loan portfolio

Bonitäts / ~verstärker credit enhancement; **~vorgabe** required credit rating; **~vorsprung** higher credit rating

bonitieren *(hoch bonitiertes Unternehmen)* highly rated company

Bonus bonus, extra payment, *(~ bei Endfälligkeit)* terminal bonus

B

Bonus / ~**karte** bonus card; ~**sparvertrag** bonus-carrying savings scheme; ~**zahlung** bonus payment; ~**zertifikat** bonus certificate

Bordbescheinigung Mate's Receipt

Bordkonnossement shipped on board B/L

Börse 1. *(Wertpapierbörse)* stock exchange, stock market, → Regulierter Markt, → Freiverkehr 2. *(Warenbörse)* commodity exchange (market) 3. *(elektronische Geldbörse)* purse

Börsen / ~**abschluss** bargain, deal, *(Abschlüsse)* trades, business (bargains) done, exchange dealings (transactions); ~**abwicklungssystem** exchange settlement system

Börsen / ~**adressen** 1. listed companies 2. stock exchange members; ~**anbieter** *(einer elektronischen Geldbörse)* purse provider; ~**anbindung** link to a stock exchange

Börsen / ~**anleger** stock market investor(s); ~**aufsicht(sbehörde)** stock exchange regulatory agency, Securities and Exchange Commission (US); ~**aufträge** stock market orders, buy and sell orders; ~**auftragsbuch** stock order book

Börsen / ~**baisse** bear market, slump in the stock market; ~**barometer** stock exchange indicator; ~**bedingungen** exchange trading rules; ~**beginn** start of trading; ~**bericht** stock exchange news, stock market report

Börsen / ~**besuch** *(Zulassung zum ~ mit Handelsbefugnis)* admission to the trading floor; ~**besucher** *(mit Handelsbefugnis)* member of the stock exchange, person admitted to the trading floor; ~**bewertung** 1. stock market valuation 2. *(Marktkapitalisierung)* market capitalisation

Börseneinführung stock market listing (flotation), initial public offering (IPO), launching on the stock market, stock exchange introduction

Börseneinführungs / ~**gebühren** listing (flotation) cost; ~**kurs** flotation price; ~**provision** listing (flotation) fee, listing commission; ~**vorschriften** listing (flotation) rules

Börsen / ~**erholung** rally (upturn) in the stock market, stock market recovery; ~**eröffnung** opening of the session, start of trading

börsenfähig eligible for a stock market listing, qualifying for trading in the regulated or open market

börsenfrei *(~e Option)* over-the-counter (OTC) option

Börsengang going public, initial public offering, stock market flotation, *(Finanzierungsmaßnahmen vor (nach) einem Börsengang)* pre-IPO (post-IPO) financing

börsengängig *(~e Finanzierung)* financing through a stock or bond market flotation (issue), *(~e Papiere)* marketable securities

börsengehandelt *(~es Beteiligungskapital)* public equity, *(~e Derivate)* exchange-traded derivatives, *(~er Indexfonds)* exchange-traded fund (ETF), *(~e Optionen)* exchange-traded options, listed options, *(nicht ~e Optionen)* over-the-counter options, *(~e Wertpapiere)* exchange-traded securities

Börsengerüchte stock market rumours

Börsengeschäft bargain, deal, trade

Börsengeschäfts / ~**abwicklung** settlement of stock trades; ~**abwicklungssystem** computerised settlement system of Deutsche Börse; ~**bedingungen** exchange trading rules; ~**fähigkeit** capacity to trade on the stock exchange; ~**feiertag** non-market day

Börsen / ~**geschehen** stock market activities, trading on the stock exchange; ~**gesetz** German Stock Exchange Act; ~**grundstimmung** underlying market sentiment, basic tone of the stock market

Börsenhandel stock exchange trading (dealings), trading on the stock exchange, *(~ in derivativen Produkten)* on-exchange derivatives trading, *(Zulassung zum ~)* admission to trading on the stock exchange, admission to the trading floor

Börsen / ~händler stock market dealer; **~hausse** bull market, upsurge of prices in the stock market, soaring (rocketing) equity prices; **~index** stock exchange index, market average; **~informationen** stock market news; **~inhaber** *(einer elektronischen Geldbörse)* purse holder

Börseninteresse *(Fahrzeugwerte standen im Mittelpunkt des ~s)* motors held the limelight throughout the session, *(das ~ konzentrierte sich auf Spekulationswerte)* buying interest centered on speculative counters

Börsen / ~kandidat candidate for flotation; **~kapitalisierung 1.** *(eines Unternehmens)* market capitalisation **2.** *(insgesamt)* total market value of listed stocks; **~klima** tone of the market, market sentiment (climate, mood)

Börsen / ~kommissionsgeschäfte stockbroking; **~krach** stock exchange crash, collapse of the stock market; **~kreise** stock market community

Börsen / ~kurs stock exchange price (quotation), market price; **~kursblatt** List of Quotations, *(amtliches)* Stock Exchange List, Stock Exchange Daily Official List; **~kurswert** market value; **~lage** state (tone) of the market; **~makler** stockbroker

börsenmäßig *(~gehandelte Option)* exchange-traded option, listed option; *(~ lieferbare Aktien)* good delivery stock, *(die ~e Lieferbarkeit der jungen Aktien gewährleisten)* to guarantee the delivery of marketable certificates for the new shares

börsenmäßig *(~e Abwicklung)* settlement through the stock exchange, *(~er Optionshandel)* listed options trading, *(~er Verkauf)* selling (sale) through the stock exchange

Börsen / ~mitglied member of the stock exchange, member firm of the Exchange; **~mitgliedschaft** stock exchange membership

Börsen / ~nachrichten stock exchange news (intelligence); **~neuling** newly-listed (newly-quoted) company, newcomer to the stock exchange (to the market)

börsennotiert *(~e Aktien)* listed shares (stock), publicly quoted shares, *(~e derivative Finanzprodukte)* listed derivative financial products, *(~e öffentliche Anleihe)* listed public bond, *(~es Unternehmen)* publicly quoted company, bourse-listed company, listed corporation, *(~e Wertpapierbestände)* holdings of listed securities

Börsen / ~notierung 1. stock exchange quotation, market quotation **2.** stock exchange listing, market listing; **~order** stock exchange order, instructions to buy or sell securities

Börsen / ~ordnung stock exchange rules and regulations; **~organ** body of the stock exchange; **~organisation** stock exchange organisation

Börsen / ~papiere exchange-traded stock, listed (quoted) securities; **~pflichtblatt** official stock exchange gazette, journal for statutory stock market advertisements; **~platz** stock market, market place; **~prospekt** prospectus (accompanying the listing application); **~publikum** stock market investors

Börsen / ~reife *(Erfüllung der Börsenreife)* meeting the requirements for going public; **~saal** trading floor; **~schiedsgericht** arbitration panel of the stock exchange

Börsen / ~schluss 1. trading lot (unit), contract **2.** close (closing) of the session, market close; **~schlusskurs** closing quotation (price), price at the close of the market; **~schwäche** market weakness, subdued market sentiment

Börsen / ~**segment** stock market segment, trading segment, → Freiverkehr, → Regulierter Markt; ~**sitzung** stock exchange session, market hours; ~**spekulant** stock market player, speculator; ~**spekulation** playing the stock market, speculation on the stock exchange

Börsen / ~**stand** pitch, trading post; ~**stimmung** market sentiment, market mood, tone of the market; ~**stunden** trading hours, session

Börsen / ~**tag** trading day, market day, *(börsentägliche Neubewertung)* daily marking to the market; ~**tendenz** stock market trend

Börsen / ~**termingeschäfte** exchange-traded contracts for future delivery, listed options and futures deals, *(Börsentermingeschäfte mit Differenzausgleich in bar)* cash-settled futures and options deals; ~**termingeschäftsfähigkeit** capability to trade in futures and options; ~**terminhandel** listed options and futures trading

Börsen / ~**titel** exchange-traded stock, stock exchange securities; ~**umsätze** stock exchange turnover, activity in the stock market; ~**usancen** customs and usage of the exchange; ~**versammlung** trading session

Börsen / ~**vorgabe** lead given by a stock exchange; ~**vorstand** Stock Exchange Council; ~**wert 1.** *(börsennotiertes Unternehmen)* listed company **2.** *(Kurswert)* stock market value, market price **3.** *(Marktkapitalisierung)* market capitalisation **4.** *(Transaktionswert)* transaction value; ~**zeit** trading hours, session

Börsenzulassung 1. admission to listing on the stock exchange (on the Regulated Market/Open Market), → Regulierter Markt, → Freiverkehr **2.** admission to the trading floor

Börsenzulassungs / ~**antrag** listing application; ~**ausschuss** listing committee, Admissions Office (→ Regulierter Markt), Admissions Committee (→ Freiverkehr); ~**gesetz** Stock Exchange Listing Act

Börsenzulassungs / ~**prospekt** listing prospectus; ~**richtlinie** listing directive; ~**verfahren** listing procedure; ~**voraussetzungen/vorschriften** listing requirements

Börsenzwang obligation to execute a transaction through the stock exchange, mandatory exchange trading

Börsianer stock exchange operator, market operator

börslicher Aktien- und Rentenhandel exchange trading in shares and bonds

böswillig *(~e Herabsetzung)* tort of injurious falsehood

Botengeschäfte dealings for account of another bank

brachliegend *(~e Gelder)* funds lying idle, dormant funds, non-interest-bearing money

Branche branch, sector, line, industry

branchenbezogen *(~ e Kreditrisikokonzentration)* industry-related credit risk concentration

Branchen / ~**Code 1.** sector code **2.** *(im Kartengeschäft)* Merchant Category Code; ~**durchschnitt** sector (industry) average; ~**fonds** sector fund, industry fund □ focus on investments in specific industries or groups of companies

Branchen / ~**gewichtung** sectoral weighting; ~**index** sector (sectoral) index, industry index; ~**kompetenz** sector expertise; ~**risiko** sector risk, industry exposure; ~**standards** industry-wide standards;~**trend** sectoral trend

branchenüblich customary in the trade, in line with the customs of the trade, *(~e Standards)* industry standards

Branchen / ~**unterschiede** sectoral differences; ~**wissen** industry expertise

Brandversicherungsurkunde fire insurance certificate

brechen 1. *(die Vertraulichkeit ~)* to break confidentiality **2.** *(verstoßen gegen)* to violate, to infringe

Bredouille *(finanziell in der ~ sein)* to be in a financial mess (fix), *(der Gesellschaft aus der ~ helfen)* to bail out the troubled company

breit *(~e Abdeckung eines Marktes)* broadly-based coverage of a market, *(~e Anlagenstreuung)* broad portfolio diversification, wide investment spread, *(~es Anlagepublikum)* general investing public, investing public at large, *(~es Privatkundengeschäft)* retail banking, *(~e Privatkundschaft)* retail banking customers, *(~e Unterstützung)* widespread support, *(~e Verteilungsenden)* fat tails

Breite *(~ des Marktes)* breadth of the market

Breitenvorteile economies of scope

breit gestreut *(~e Anlagen)* diversified investments, widely spread investments, broadly diversified (widely disseminated) portfolio, *(~ es Kreditportefeuille)* broadly spread loan portfolio, *(~e Platzierung)* widely spread placement, *(~e Syndizierung)* broad syndication, *(Unternehmen mit ~em Aktienbesitz)* company with substantial ownership among the public, company with a widely dispersed stock ownership

bremsen to curb, to check, *(das Geldmengenwachstum ~)* to put a brake on the rising money supply, *(den Kapitalfluss ~)* to rein in the flow of capital, *(den Zinsauftrieb ~)* to check the upsurge in interest rates

Brief 1. letter **2.** deed, *(Grundschuldbrief)* charge certificate **3.** *(Kurszusatz)* offer, offered, sellers, sellers over, → Briefkurs

Brief / ~ausschluss excluding delivery of a deed (charge certificate); **~erteilung** issuance of a deed, delivery of a charge certificate

Brief / ~grundschuld certificated land charge (charge over property), → Buchgrundschuld (brieflose Grundschuld); **~hypothek** certificated mortgage □ mortgage transferable by a written declaration of assignment

Brief / ~kurs offering price (quotation), offered (selling) rate; **~offerte** → Briefkurs; **~recht** certificated right, deed-based right; **~repartierung** scaling down sell orders; **~schuld** certificated debt

bringen 1. *(zur Auktion ~)* to put up for auction **2.** *(einen hohen Ertrag ~)* to yield (to bring, to generate) high earnings **3.** *(auf den Kapitalmarkt ~)* to bring to the capital market **4.** *(einen hohen Preis ~)* to command a high price **5.** *(eine Verzinsung von 3 % ~)* to earn 3 p.c. interest, to yield a 3 p.c. return **6.** *(mit sich ~)* to bring in its wake

Bruch 1. breakage, rupture, *(~ des vorherrschenden Trends)* trend break **2.** *(Verletzung, Verstoß gegen)* breach, violation, infringement

Bruchteil fraction, portion

Bruchteils / ~eigentum fractional ownership; **~eigentümer** fractional owner, co-owner; **~gemeinschaft** ownership (tenancy) in common; **~stimmrechte** fractional voting rights

Bruchzins broken interest

Brückenbank bridge bank, → Restrukturierungsgesetz, → Kreditinstitute-Reorganisationsgesetz

Brückenfinanierung bridge financing

brutto *adj.* gross, *adv.* in gross terms

Brutto / ~abrechnung → Bruttogeschäft; **~abschreibungen** *(im Kreditgeschäft)* gross charge-offs; **~anlageinvestitionen** gross capital formation, gross investment in fixed assets; **~anlagevermögen** gross tangible assets, tangible assets before depreciation

Brutto / ~ausgleichssystem gross settlement system; **~ausweis** gross recognition (reporting), gross disclosure, stating the gross amount

B

Brutto / ~**bedarfsspanne** gross operating margin □ personnel and other operating expenditure expressed as a percentage of the average business volume; ~ **beiträge** gross premiums written; ~**darlehensbetrag** gross loan principal, loan principal plus discount deducted

Brutto / ~**dividende** gross dividend, pre-tax dividend; ~**dividendenrendite** gross dividend yield

Brutto / ~**eigenkapitalrendite** gross return on shareholder's equity; ~**ergebnis** gross performance, gross profit on sales; ~**erlös** gross proceeds; ~**ertrag** gross earnings (income); ~**ertragsspanne** gross earnings margin □ earnings expressed as a percentage of the average business volume

Brutto / ~**geldvermögen** gross monetary wealth; ~**gesamtschadenquote** gross loss ratio; ~**geschäft** gross transaction □ securities transaction in which the quoted price does not include transaction cost; ~**gewinn** gross profit (income); ~**gewinnspanne** gross margin, gross profit margin

Brutto / ~**inanspruchnahme der Kreditmärkte** gross borrowings in the financial markets; ~**inlandsprodukt** gross domestic product; ~**kapitalbildung** gross capital formation; ~**kapitalertrag** gross investment income

Brutto / ~**leistung** gross performance; ~-**Margining** gross margining, margining based on the gross exposure; ~**methode** gross method □ stating amounts before tax, consolidation adjustments, discounts and rebates

Brutto / ~**rechnung** gross account(ing), gross settlement; ~**reichweite** gross coverage (reach, exposure); ~**rendite** gross yield (return), pre-tax yield; ~-**Risiko-Position** gross exposure, gross risk position; ~**sozialprodukt** *(~ zu Faktorkosten/Marktpreisen)* gross national product at factor cost/ at market prices

Brutto / ~**verarbeitung** gross processing; ~**verzinsung** gross interest return; ~**wert** *(~ in der Unternehmensbilanz)* gross value on the company's balance sheet; ~**wertentwicklung** gross performance; ~**wertschöpfung** gross value added

Brutto / ~**zinsklausel** gross-up (grossing-up) clause; ~**zinsmarge**/~**zinsspanne** **1.** gross interest margin □ interest received less interest paid expressed as a percentage of average total assets **2.** excess spread, → Überschussmarge

BSE → belegloser Scheckeinzug

Buch book, portfolio, *(über Ein- und Ausgänge ~ führen)* to keep track of inflows and outflows, *(negativ/positiv zu ~e schlagen)* to have a negative/ positive impact, *(zu ~e stehen mit …)* to be recorded in the accounts with …, to be carried in the accounts at …, to be entered in the books for …

buchen to enter (in the books), to post, *(als Aufwand ~)* to charge to expenditure, *(als Gewinn ~)* to enter on the profits side, *(die bei uns gebuchten Werte)* the assets entered in our books

Buch / ~**forderungen** accounts receivable, book-entry claims; ~**führungsrichtlinien** accounting standards; ~**geld** deposit (bank) money; ~**gewinn** book (paper) profit, unrealised profit

Buch / ~**grundschuld** registered land charge, non-certificated land charge, → Briefgrundschuld; ~**hypothek** registered mortgage, mortgage charge recorded in the land registry; ~**kapital** book equity; ~**kapitalisierung** book capitalisation; ~**kredit** book credit, current account credit

buchmäßig *(~ regulieren)* to settle by book transfer, *(~e Erfassung)* recognition (entry) in the accounts, *(~e Lieferung)* delivery by book entry, delivery in book-entry form, *(~e Wertpapierübertragung)* book transfer of securities, transfer of securities in book-entry form

Buch / ~**prüfer** auditor; ~**prüfung** audit of the accounts; ~**prüfungsbericht** auditors' report; ~**recht** registered right; ~**rendite** book yield; ~**saldo** book balance; ~**schuld 1.** *(in Verbindung mit Wertpapieren)* book-entry debt **2.** *(Plural)* accounts payable

buchtechnisch *(~e Kapitalerhöhung)* capital increase from reserves, accounting-driven capital increase

Buchübertrag book (book-entry) transfer

Buchung 1. entering (posting) to an account, booking **2.** *(in einem Kontoauszug)* entry

Buchungs / ~**aufgabe**/~**beleg** accounting advice (voucher); ~**betrag** amount entered (booked); ~**fehler** accounting error; ~**gebühr** entry fee, transaction fee, item charge

Buchungs / ~**lauf** settlement cycle; ~**posten** entry, accounting entry; ~**postengebühr** entry fee; ~**schluss** accounting close; ~**schnitt** accounting close (cutoff); ~**stand** balance in the account

Buchverlust book (paper) loss, unrealised loss

Buchwert book value, carrying amount (value), *(~ je Aktie)* book value per share

Buchwert / ~**fortschreibung** rolling forward the book value; ~**minderung** *(~ eines Kredites)* reducing the loan's book value (carrying amount)

Budget budget; ~**ansätze** budget estimates, *(Ermittlung der ~)* budget estimating; ~**erstellung** budget preparation; ~**genehmigung** budget approval

budgetiert *(~e Bilanz)* budgeted balance sheet, *(~e Erfolgsrechnung)* budgeted income (profit) statement, *(~er Vorsorgebedarf)* budgeted provisioning requirements

Budgetierung budgeting

Budgetierungs / ~**befugnisse** budgetary powers; ~**zeitraum** budget period (time-table)

Budget / ~**rechnung** budget accounting; ~**ungleichgewicht** budgetary imbalance; ~**wert** *(~ der geplanten/erbrachten Leistung)* budget cost of work scheduled/performed

Bullen / ~**ausbruchsmuster** bullish breakaway gap; ~**divergenz** bullish divergence; ~**falle** bull trap; ~**flagge** *(Chart-Analyse)* bull flag; ~**formation** bullish pattern (formation); ~**markt** bull market; ~**umkehrmuster** bullish reversal pattern; ~**wimpel** bull pennant

bullisch *(~es Dreieck)* bullish (ascending) triangle, symmetrical triangle in an uptrend

bündeln 1. to bundle, to combine, to concentrate, to pool, *(Finanzdienstleistungen ~)* to bundle financial services **2.** *(kleine Wertpapieraufträge ~)* to bunch small securities orders

Bündelung bundling, bunching, *(~ der liquiden Mittel)* cash pooling

Bundesamt Federal Agency, Federal Office

Bundesanleihe Bund, Federal government bond □ Federal bearer bonds issued with maturities ranging from ten to thirty years. Bunds carry a fixed rate of interest and are issued in book-entry form.

Bundesanleihekonsortium Federal bond syndicate

Bundesanstalt für Finanzdienstleistungsaufsicht (BaFin) Federal Financial Supervisory Authority □ regulator that supervises banks, financial services institutions and insurance undertakings in Germany

Bundesanstalt für Finanzmarktstabilisierung Federal Agency for Financial Market Stabilisation

Bundesanzeiger (Elektronischer ~) Electronic Federal Gazette

Bundesaufsichtsamt für das Kreditwesen/für das Versicherungswesen/für den Wertpapierhandel former regulators replaced by → Bundesanstalt für Finanzdienstleistungsaufsicht

Bundesbank Bundesbank, German Central Bank; ~**ausweis** Bundesbank return; ~-**Direktorium** Bundesbank directorate;~**gesetz** Bundesbank Act; ~-**Girokonto** Bundesbank giro account

Bundes / ~**beauftragter** Federal Commissioner; ~**behörde** Federal Authority (Agency); ~**bürgschaft** Federal government guarantee; ~**datenschutzgesetz** Federal Data Protection Act

Bundesdaueremission Federal tap issue, government securities issued on an ongoing basis

Bundesdeckung Federal government guarantee, Federal guarantee cover, *(bundesgedeckte Ausfuhrgeschäfte)* exports covered by Federal government guarantees, *(bundesgedeckte Kredite)* government-guaranteed loans (credits), loans covered by Federal government guarantees

Bundes / ~**gesetz** Federal Act; ~**gesetzblatt** Federal Law Gazette; ~**leistungen** Federal government payments; ~**oberbehörde** Superior Federal Authority

Bundesobligationen (five-year) Federal notes □ Bundesobligationen (Bobls) carry a fixed rate of interest. Repayment in bullet form.

Bundesobligo *(in Verbindung mit Ausfuhrgewährleistungen)* Federal government exposure (i.e. exposure from the assumption of warranties)

Bundesschatzanweisungen Federal Treasury financing paper □ two-year fixed rate notes issued at regular intervals

Bundesschatzbriefe Federal savings notes □ offered for sale with maturities of six or seven years; scheduled interest rate rises during the life of the bonds, → Daueremission

Bundesschätzchen → Bundesschatzbriefe

Bundesschätze → Bundesschatzanweisungen

Bundesschatzwechsel Federal treasury bill

Bundesschuldbuch Federal debt register

Bundesschuldenverwaltung Federal Debt Administration

bundesverbürgt *(~er Exportkredit)* government-guaranteed export credit, export credit provided with government insurance cover

Bundeswertpapiere Federal Securities, German Government Securities

Bundeswertpapierverwaltung Federal Securities Administration

Bürge surety, *(als ~)* **1.** in his/her capacity as surety **2.** *(Vermerk)* pour aval

bürgen to stand surety, to guarantee, to furnish a surety, *(bürgende öffentliche Stelle)* public agency standing surety

Bürgen / ~**bonität** surety's (guarantor's) standing; ~**einrede** plea by the surety; ~**haftung** liability of the surety

Bürgerentlastungsgesetz Taxpayer Relief Act

Bürgerliches Gesetzbuch German Civil Code

Bürgschaft surety bond, *(~ der öffentlichen Hand)* public sector surety bond, *(~ auf Zeit)* dated surety bond, suretyship limited in time □ Unlike a guarantee, the "Bürgschaft" is an accessory obligation, i.e. it is fully contingent on the principal obligation. → Garantie

bürgschaftsähnlich *(~e Sicherheit für einen Kredit)* surety-type loan collateral

Bürgschafts / ~**bank** surety bank; ~**befreiung** release of a surety bond; ~**bestand** surety book, surety bond portfolio; ~**entgelt** **1.** surety fee **2.** *(Plural i. S. von Einnahmen)* surety fee income; ~**erklärung** contract of suretyship, surety bond

Bürgschafts / ~freigabe surety release, release from suretyship; **~geber** surety bond provider, obligor; **~kredit** surety loan; **~kündigung** calling in a surety bond; **~leistung** furnishing (provision) of a surety bond

Bürgschafts / ~nehmer obligee, beneficiary of a surety bond; **~plafond** surety limit; **~programm** surety bond scheme; **~provision** surety bond commission; **~rahmen** surety line

Bürgschafts / ~schuld obligation under a surety bond; **~übernahme** furnishing a surety bond, assumption of suretyship, → Bürgschaftsversprechen; **~urkunde** surety bond (deed), deed of suretyship

Bürgschafts / ~vergabe surety bonding, → Bürgschaftsleistung; **~verpflichtung** surety commitment (obligation), engagement of suretyship, suretyship undertaking; **~versicherer** surety underwriter; **~versicherung** surety insurance, surety underwriting

Bürgschafts / ~versprechen surety undertaking, declaration (engagement) of suretyship; **~vertrag** suretyship (surety) agreement, contract of suretyship; **~wechsel** surety bill; **~zusage** → Bürgschaftsversprechen

C

C

Cap / ~**darlehen** capped variable rate loan; ~-**Floordarlehen** → Collar-Darlehen; ~**käufer** cap buyer; ~**kredit** capped variable rate credit; ~**prämie** cap premium; ~**verkäufer** cap seller, writer of a cap, → Floor-Darlehen, Collar-Darlehen

Cashflow *(~ aus operativer Geschäftstätigkeit, Finanzierungstätigkeit, Investitionstätigkeit)* cash flow from (net cash provided by) operating/financing/investing activities

Cashflow / ~-**Prognose** cash flow forecast; ~-**Rechnung** cash flow statement; ~-**Risiko** cash flow risk, risk relating to the size of future cash flows; ~-**Überschuss** free cash flow

Chancenverhältnis odds ratio

Chance-Risiko / ~-**Bewusstsein** risk/reward awareness, awareness of opportunity and risk; ~-**Profil** risk/reward profile; ~-**Verhältnis** risk/reward ratio

Chaos *(den Markt ins ~ stürzen)* to throw the market into turmoil (disarray), to create havoc in the market

Chart-Analyse chart analysis

Charter-Konnossement charter-party bill of lading

Chart-Theorie chart theory

CDAX Composite Dax □ German share price index composed of the shares of all domestic companies listed in the → Prime and → General Standard

Chartformation chart pattern (formation)

Chefsyndikus General Counsel

Chemie-Werte chemicals, chemical stocks, *(Chemie-Nebenwerte)* second-line chemicals

Chipgröße chip size

Chipkarten / ~**leser** chip card reader; ~**terminal** chip card terminal

chronologisch *(in ~er Reihenfolge)* in chronological order

Circa-Auftrag near-limit order □ buy or sell order permitting a slight deviation from the limit given

Circa-Kurs approximate price

Clearing / ~**forderungen** clearing receivables; ~**guthaben** clearing balances (assets); ~**konto** clearing account; ~**mitglieder** clearing members, clearing names; ~**stelle** clearing house; ~**verbindlichkeiten** clearing liabilities; ~**verkehr** clearing transactions

Clearstream settlement entity of Deutsche Börse Group □ offers centralised settlement and custody facilities

Collar-Darlehen collared variable rate loan □ loan provided with a rate cap and a rate floor, → Cap-Darlehen, → Floor-Darlehen

Compliance-Beauftragter Compliance Officer

Computer-Handel(ssystem) computerised trading, screen-based trading system

Courtage brokerage, broker's fee, brokerage fee; ~**einnahmen/erträge** brokerage income; ~**rechnung** brokerage statement; ~**satz** brokerage rate

CRD/CRD II/CRD III/CRD IV → Eigenkapitalrichtlinie

Criée-Handel open outcry trading

CVA-Eigenkapitalanforderung CVA capital charge, → Anpassung der Kreditbewertung

D

Dachfonds fund of funds (FoF) □ holds a portfolio of other investment funds (single manager funds)

Dachgesellschaft holding company, umbrella company

Dach-Hedgefonds fund of hedge funds □ invests in several Ziel-Hedgefonds (single hedge funds)

Dachmarkenstrategie umbrella brand strategy

Dachorganisation umbrella (parent) organisation

Dach-Skontro umbrella (central) order book

Dach-Sondervermögen *(~ mit zusätzlichen Risiken)* fund of funds (with additional risks), → Dach-Hedgefonds

Damnum discount, amount deducted from the loan principal

dämpfen to dampen, to curb, to check, to restrain, *(die Hoffnungen auf eine Kurserholung am Aktienmarkt ~)* to dampen (to temper) hopes of a rally in stock market prices, *(die Kreditexpansion ~)* to restrain (to moderate) the credit expansion, *(den Zinsauftrieb ~)* to check (to curb) the upsurge in interest rates

Dämpfer *(~ für Haussiers)* dampener for bulls

Dämpfung dampening, curb, curbing, checking, restriction, moderation

darlegen *(die Vor- und Nachteile ~)* to set out (to explain, to make clear, to state, to point out) the advantages and disadvantages

Darlehen loan, advance

Darlehen *(~ mit kurzen Anpassungsfristen)* loan(s) renegotiable after short periods, *(unter Bürgschaft der öffentlichen Hand gewährte ~)* loans guaranteed by public sector institutions, *(~ aus öffentlichen Fördermitteln)* loan(s) from public development funds, *(~ mit fester Laufzeit)* fixed-term loan(s), *(~ mit Gläubiger-/Schuldnerkündigungsrecht)* loan(s) with embedded call/put option, *(~ mit veränderlichem Zinssatz)* variable rate loan(s), *(~ zur Vor- und Zwischenfinanzierung)* interim and bridging loan(s)

Darlehens / ~**abgeld** loan discount, discount deducted from the loan principal; ~**abruf** calling up the loan funds, drawing on a loan; ~**abwicklung** loan processing, handling a loan commitment

Darlehens / ~**anspruch** loan entitlement; ~**antrag** loan application; ~**art** type of loan; ~**ausbuchung** loan charge-off; ~**ausfälle** loan losses; ~**ausreichung** loan extension (accommodation), extending a loan

Darlehensauszahlung loan disbursement, disbursing a loan, *(die ~ erfolgt auf Konto Nr. ...)* the loan proceeds will be credited to account No. ..., *(Gesamtsumme der ~en)* total amount of loans disbursed

Darlehens / ~**beginn** inception of the loan agreement; ~**belassungserklärung** loan maintenance agreement, undertaking not to withdraw a loan; ~**beschaffung** raising a loan, procurement of loans

Darlehens / ~**beschränkungen** loan (lending) curbs, borrowing restrictions, credit squeeze; ~**bestand** loan portfolio, loan book, total lendings; ~**bestätigung** loan confirmation, facility letter, confirming the extension of a loan facility; ~**beteiligung** loan participation; ~**betrag** loan amount, loan principal, principal sum loaned

Darlehens / ~**bewilligung 1.** *(Genehmigung)* loan approval **2.** *(Gewährung)* loan extension (accommodation); ~**bewilligungsgrenze** loan authorisation limit; ~**dokumentation** loan documentation; ~**einräumung** → Darlehensgewährung; ~**fälligkeit** loan maturity, due date of a loan; ~**fazilität** loan facility

Darlehensforderung bank's claim under a loan agreement, *(~en abzüglich Wertberichtigungen)* loans (loan receivables) less loan loss allowances, *(Abtretung einer ~)* loan assignment, assigning the claim under a loan agreement, *(Handel in ~en)* trading in loans (loan receivables), *(Verkauf einer ~)* loan sale

Darlehens / ~**garantie** loan guarantee; ~**geber** lender; ~**gebühr** loan arrangement fee; ~**gelder** loan funds (finance), loanable funds; ~**geschäft** lending business (operations, activities)

Darlehens / ~**gewährung** loan extension (accommodation), extending a loan; ~**größe** size of a loan; ~**hingabe** → Darlehensgewährung; ~**höchstbetrag** maximum loan amount

Darlehens / ~**konditionen** loan (lending) terms; ~**konto** loan account; ~**kosten** loan charges; ~**kunde** borrowing customer; ~**kündigung** calling in a loan, terminating a loan agreement

Darlehens / ~**laufzeit** life (term) of a loan, loan maturity, loan duration; ~**leistungen** principal and interest payments (on a loan); ~**markt** loans market; ~**mittel** loan funds (finance), loanable funds

Darlehens / ~**nachfrage** loan demand, demand for loans; ~**nehmer** borrower; ~**nennbetrag** loan principal; ~**neugeschäft**/~**neuzusagen** new loans extended, new loan commitments

Darlehens / ~**politik** lending policy; ~**programm** loan (lending) scheme; ~**prolongation** loan extension, extending the date for repayment of the loan facility; ~**rahmen 1.** borrowing limit **2.** general loan agreement; ~**rate** loan repayment rate

Darlehens / ~**restbetrag**/~**restschuld** residual loan amount, principal amount (balance) outstanding; ~**risiko** loan risk; ~**rücknahme** *(aus der Sicht des Kreditgebers)* accepting premature repayment of a loan; ~**rückzahlung** loan repayment

Darlehens / ~**schuld** outstanding principal; ~**schuldner** borrower, loan debtor; ~**sicherheit** loan collateral, security (collateral) provided for a loan; ~**stock** loan portfolio, total lendings

Darlehens / ~**streckung** stretching (extending) the loan maturity, stretching out the loan repayment, loan extension; ~**stundung** deferring repayments due, loan respite, debt deferral; ~**summe** loan principal; ~**tätigkeit** lending activities (operations, business)

Darlehenstilgung loan amortisation (repayment), *(Gesamtsumme der Darlehenstilgungen)* total amount of loans repaid, total repayments

Darlehenstilgungs / ~**plan** loan amortisation schedule; ~**rechner** loan amortisation calculator; ~**satz** loan amortisation rate, principal repayment rate

Darlehens / ~**urkunde** loan deed; ~**valuta 1.** loan proceeds **2.** loan currency; ~**valutierung** loan disbursement, allowing drawdowns on the loan; ~**verbindlichkeiten** loans payable

Darlehens / ~**vergabe** loan accommodation (origination); ~**vergabeprozess** loan origination process; ~**verlängerung** loan extension; ~**vermittler** (business) loan broker; ~**vermittlung** loan brokerage

Darlehens / ~**verpflichtung 1.** *(der Bank)* loan commitment **2.** *(des Kre-*

ditnehmers) borrower's commitments under the loan, principal and interest to be paid by the borrower; ~**vertrag** loan agreement

Darlehens / ~**verzug** loan default, failure to abide by the terms of the loan agreement; ~**voraussetzungen** loan eligibility requirements (criteria); ~**vormerkung 1.** approved loan 2. loan commitment

Darlehens / ~**zins** loan interest; ~**zinssatz** loan interest rate, lending rate; ~**zusage** loan commitment (undertaking), undertaking to extend a loan, lending commitment; ~**zusammenlegung** loan consolidation, consolidating two or more outstanding loans

Darleiher → Darlehensgeber

darniederliegen to languish, to be in the doldrums, *(~de Konjunktur)* flagging economy

darstellbar workable, viable, realisable, feasible, capable of being put into practice

darstellen 1. *(bedeuten)* to constitute, to represent, to mark, *(ein Risiko für das Bankensystem ~)* to pose a risk to the banking system, *(einen Zahlungsverzug ~)* to constitute an event of default
2. *(beschreiben, darlegen)* to describe, to set forth (out), to state, *(die Kursentwicklung graphisch ~)* to chart (to map) the price development
3. *(durchführen)* to carry out, *(die Finanzierung über den Euromarkt ~)* to carry out (to realise, to effect) the financing through the Euromarket
4. *(falsch ~)* to misrepresent, to give an incorrect (misleading) representation
5. *(sich ~ als)* to present itself as

darstellend *(~er Teil, z.B eines Insolvenzplanes)* declaratory part, → gestaltender Teil

Darstellung presentation, description, statement

Darstellungsstetigkeit *(im Rechnungswesen)* consistency of statement presentation

Daten data, information

Daten / ~**abgleich** data reconciliation, data matching; ~**abspeicherung** data storage; ~**anzeige** data display; ~**aufbereitung** preparation (editing) of data, data conditioning; ~**aufzeichnung** data recording

Daten / ~**austausch** data interchange (exchange); ~**auswertung** data evaluation; ~**autobahn** data highway, information superhighway; ~**bank** database, *(datenbankgestützte Klassifizierung)* database-assisted classification; ~**bankpflege** database care

Daten / ~**bearbeitung** data handling; ~**bereinigung** data cleansing; ~**bereitstellung** data deployment (supply); ~**beschaffung** data acquisition; ~**bestand** database, data pool

Daten / ~**echtheitsprüfung** data authentication; ~**eingabe** data input, entering data into (the system); ~**empfang** data downstreaming; ~**erfassung** data capture (gathering, pooling); ~**erhebung** data collection; ~**erkennung** data recognition; ~**exploration** data mining

Daten / ~**fernübertragung** remote data transmission, electronic data interchange; ~**fluss** data (information) flow; ~**format** *(~ für den Zahlungsaustausch)* data format for payment exchanges; ~**gewinnung** data acquisition (mining, collection); ~**lager** data warehouse

Daten / ~**menge** data volume, amount of data; ~**pflege** data maintenance; ~**pool** data pool (warehouse); ~**reihe** data set; ~**rückgewinnung** data (file) recovery; ~**sammelstelle** data repository, → Transaktionsregister; ~**sammlung** data pool; ~**satz** data set (record)

Datenschutz data (information) privacy, data protection; ~**beauftragter** 1. data protection officer (official) 2. *(staatlicher)* Data Protection Commissioner; ~**bestimmungen** data privacy rules, data protection regula-

D

tions; ~**erklärung** privacy policy, data privacy statement; ~**gesetz** Data Protection Act; ~**recht** data privacy law

Daten / ~**sicherung** data backup; ~**sparsamkeit** data economy; ~**speicher** data warehouse; ~**speicherung** data storage

Datenträger data medium (media), data carrier; ~**austausch** data medium exchange, electronic data interchange; ~**austausverfahren** → DTAUS-Dateiformat

Daten / ~**übermittlung** data transmission; ~**überprüfung** data verification; ~**übertragung** data transfer (transmission); ~**verarbeitung** data processing (handling); ~**verdichtung** data compression

Daten / ~**versand** data transfer, data upstreaming; ~**verschlüsselungsstandard** data encryption standard; ~**wiedergewinnung** data recovery (retrieval); ~**zusammenfassung** data aggregation (consolidation)

datieren to date, *(datiert vom 1. Oktober)* dated (dd.) October 1st, under date of October 1

dato *(ein bis ~ nicht realisierter Gewinn)* an as yet unrealised profit

Datowechsel after-date bill

Datum date, *(~ der Ausstellung/Fälligkeit)* date of issue/of maturity, *(vom heutigen ~)* dated this day

Dauer duration, term, length, period, *(auf ~)* indefinitely, *(auf ~ angelegtes Kreditverhältnis)* long-term loan relationship, *(~ der Betriebszugehörigkeit)* length of service, *(für die ~ des Kreditverhältnisses)* for the duration of the loan arrangement

Dauer / ~**anlagen** permanent investments, held-to-maturity investments; ~**anleger** long-term investor; ~**auftrag** standing order; ~**charakter** *(Beteiligungen mit ~)* investments of a permanent nature

Daueremission tap issue, issuance of securities on an ongoing basis, *(~en des Bundes)* Federal tap issues, → Bundesschatzbriefe, → Finanzierungsschätze; *(Mittelaufnahmen durch ~en)* borrowing through the ongoing issue of securities

Daueremittent tap issuer, regular issuer

Dauer / ~**finanzierungsmittel** long-term finance; ~**globalurkunde** indefinite (permanent) global certificate

dauerhaft *(~e Wertminderungen)* permanent impairments

Dauer / ~**konsortium** standing group (syndicate); ~**lastschrift** standing direct debit; ~**nehmer** *(im Geldmarkt)* permanent buyer (borrower); ~**nutzungsrecht** permanent right to use, permanent lease

Dauer / ~**rechtsverhältnis** permanent contractual obligation; ~**schuld** long-term (permanent) debt; ~**schuldentgelte/schuldzinsen** interest expense for long-term debt; ~**schuldverhältnis** long-term (permanent) debt obligation, continuous recurring obligation; ~**überzahlungsbescheinigung** certificate of permanent surplus payments

Davon-Vermerk 'of which' memorandum item

DAX German stock market index, → Deutscher Aktienindex

dazugehören to belong to, to be incidental (appurtenant) to, *(zugehörige Rechte)* appurtenant rights, appurtenances

dazwischentreten to intervene, *(dazwischentretende Pfandrechte)* mezzanine liens

Debet debit; ~**buchung** debit entry; ~**posten** debit entry (item); ~**saldo** debit balance; ~**spalte** debit column; ~**zins** debit interest; ~**zinssatz** lending rate, loan interest rate

Debit-Karte debit card, charge card

Debitoren **1.** *(einer Bank)* loans and advances, lendings **2.** *(einer Industrieunternehmung)* trade (account) debtors, receivables, accounts receivable

Debitoren / ~aufstellung 1. statement of loans extended **2.** list of accounts receivable; **~ausfälle 1.** loan charge-offs, loan losses **2.** trade debt losses, defaulting debtors (customers), credit losses

Debitoren / ~bestand 1. loan (lending) portfolio **2.** debtor (debt) portfolio; **~buchhaltung** sales ledger accounting; **~finanzierung 1.** lending against accounts receivable **2.** debtor financing, financing of receivables

Debitoren / ~geschäft lending business (operations); **~konto** debtor account; **~kontrolle 1.** supervision of loan commitments, monitoring lendings **2.** debt (debtor) control, credit-worthiness checks on customers; **~kunden** borrowing customers, debtors

Debitoren / ~länder debtor (borrowing) countries; **~limit** debtor exposure limit; **~-Management** credit management, debtor management, accounts receivables management

Debitoren / ~risiko credit risk, debtor risk, risk of default (by borrower); **~risikomanagement** debtor risk management; **~sätze** lending rates; **~umschlag** turnover of receivables, receivables (debtor) turnover, debtor ratio

Debitoren / ~verluste loan losses (charge-offs); **~versicherung** credit insurance, accounts receivable insurance; **~verwaltung** credit management; **~ziehung** own drawing, bank bill drawn on a customer

debitorisch *(~es Geschäft)* lending business, *(~es Konto)* debtor (overdraft) account, account kept on a borrowing basis, *(~e Kunden)* borrowing customers, *(~er Saldo)* debit balance

Deckelung fixing a limit, capping, setting a ceiling

decken 1. to cover, to provide cover, to protect, to hedge, to guarantee, *(Einschussverpflichtungen ~)* to cover margin requirements, *(das Risiko ~)* to hedge the risk (exposure), *(am Terminmarkt ~)* to cover in the forward market, *(Zins- und Währungsrisiken ~)* to hedge interest and currency risks (exposure)
2. to meet, to pay, to honour, *(die Kosten ~)* to meet the cost, *(den Refinanzierungsbedarf ~)* to meet (to cover) funding (refinancing) requirements, *(die Nachfrage ~)* to meet (to satisfy) the demand
3. *(versichern)* to insure, to provide insurance cover
4. *(sich ~ mit)* to match (to tally) with, to be in accord with, to conform to, to coincide with

Deckung 1. cover, covering, provision of cover, hedge, prefunding, *(~ von Leerverkaufspositionen)* short covering, *(~ für ausgestellte Schecks)* cover for cheques written, *(~ durch ein Termingeschäft)* forward cover, *(vorherige ~ von Zahlungsverpflichtungen)* prefunding of payment obligations
2. guarantee, *(als ~ dienende Grundpfandrechte)* liens on real estate (charges over property) serving as guarantee (support), *(in ~ genommener Kredit)* loan for which a guarantee has been provided, *(Exportkredite in ~ nehmen)* to provide guarantees for export credits
3. payment, *(~ des Betriebsmittelbedarfs)* meeting (funding) working capital requirements
4. insurance cover (coverage), *(~ veranlassen)* to take out insurance cover, *(in ~ genommene Geschäfte)* transactions insured (covered)
5. matching, *(~ der Kreditfristen auf der Aktiv- und Passivseite)* matching lendings against deposits

Deckung *(die ~ erfolgt auf Konto Nr. …)* cover (reimbursement) will be on account No. …, cover funds will be remitted to account No. …, *(rechtzeitig für ~ sorgen)* to provide cover in due course, *(die Einlösung mangels ~ verweigern)* to refuse payment for lack of cover, to dishonour for want of cover

D

D

Deckungs / ~anforderungen cover (collateral, hedging) requirements; **~anschaffung 1.** provision of cover, remitting cover, *(nicht rechtzeitige ~)* failure to provide cover in time **2.** *(Rückerstattung)* reimbursement; **~anspruch** cover claim, right to coverage

Deckungs / ~antrag 1. cover request (application), application for cover **2.** guarantee application; **~anweisungen** covering (reimbursement) instructions, instructions for providing cover

Deckungs / ~art type of cover, covering (hedging) device, method of reimbursement; **~ausschluss** exclusion from coverage, *(pl)* risk exclusions, exceptions of coverage, risks and perils excluded

Deckungs / ~bedarf cover (hedging) requirements; **~beitrag** contribution margin (rate), profit contribution; **~beitragsrechnung** contribution costing (accounting); **~beitragsziele** contribution margin objectives; **~beschränkungen** cover restrictions

Deckungs / ~bestand asset pool (serving as collateral), cover holdings, *(~ des Stillhalters)* option writer's covering portfolio; **~bestätigung** cover note, note evidencing that insurance cover has been taken out; **~bestimmungen 1.** coverage rules **2.** → Deckungserfordernisse

Deckungs / ~darlehen loan serving as cover, covering loan; **~einkauf** covering purchase; **~erfordernisse 1.** cover (hedging) requirements **2.** *(bei Börsenterminpositionen)* margin requirements

deckungsfähig 1. *(~e Geschäfte)* transactions eligible for cover **2.** *(~e Risiken)* insurable (hedgeable) risks

Deckungs / ~fähigkeit eligibility for cover, insurability; **~fonds** cover fund; **~forderungen** cover (reimbursement) claims; **~garantie** undertaking to cover (to guarantee); **~gegenstand** asset (property) insured; **~geschäft** cover (covering, hedging) transaction

deckungsgleich matching, identical

Deckungs / ~grad 1. cover (covering) ratio, degree (level) of cover **2.** liquidity ratio; **~gleichheit** matching cover; **~grenze** cover (guarantee) limit, collateralisation limit

Deckungs / ~guthaben compensating balances, cover funds; **~höhe** level of cover, coverage level; **~hypothek** mortgage serving as cover; **~kapital** cover (guarantee) funds, cover capital

Deckungskauf covering purchase (transaction)

Deckungskäufe *(~ in Erwartung eines Kursanstiegs)* buying ahead of an upsurge in prices, *(~ zur Glattstellung von Leerverkaufspositionen)* short covering, buying against short positions

Deckungskommunalkredite public sector loans serving as cover

Deckungskongruenz matching cover, *(~ im Hypothekengeschäft herstellen)* to match mortgage lendings against mortgage bonds issued

Deckungs / ~konto cover (reimbursement) account, guarantee account; **~kosten** covering (hedging) cost; **~linie** support line, back-up line

Deckungs / ~lücke 1. shortfall of cover, missing cover, inadequate cover **2.** *(bei einem Finanzierungs-, Pensionsplan)* funding gap **3.** gap between assets and liabilities; **~marge** cover margin; **~masse** cover pool assets, cover funds, coverage capital, assets serving as cover (collateral)

Deckungs / ~mittel 1. cover funds **2.** guarantee funds **3.** *(Haushalt)* receipts, revenue; **~nehmer 1.** policy holder, insured **2.** guarantee; **~papiere** securities pledged as collateral

Deckungs / ~pflicht cover requirement, obligation to provide cover (a guarantee), *(deckungspflichtig)* requiring cover; **~plafond** cover limit;

~politik guarantee policy; ~position hedge (cover) position

Deckungsprinzip cover principle □ principle according to which covered mortgage bonds (Pfandbriefe) outstanding must be covered by mortgage loans of at least equal value and yielding at least an equal interest return

Deckungs / ~prüfung checking the cover; **~punkt** break-even point; **~punktanalyse** break-even analysis; **~quote** cover (covering) ratio, guarantee ratio, *(~ im Kreditgeschäft mit Problemländern)* provisioning ratio for lendings to problem countries

Deckungs / ~rechnung cover calculation; **~register** cover register, register of mortgages serving as cover for mortgage bonds issued; **~rückstellung** *(im Versicherungsgeschäft)* benefits reserve, policy reserve

Deckungs / ~schlusszeit closing cover time; **~schutz** *(Fortbestehen des Deckungsschutzes)* continuation of coverage; **~schutzerweiterung** extension of coverage

Deckungsstock 1. cover pool, cover pool assets, cover (guarantee) funds **2.** *(einer Versicherung)* premium reserve fund

Deckungsstockfähigkeit eligibility as cover funds, *(deckungsstockfähige Wertpapiere)* securities eligible to serve as cover assets, securities eligible as investments for a premium reserve fund

Deckungsstock / ~risiken risks inherent in cover pools; **~treuhänder** cover pool trustee (monitor); **~werte** cover pool assets

Deckungs / ~stopp cover freeze, refusal to provide further cover; **~tranche** (covering) layer; **~umfang** scope (degree) of cover, cover level; **~urkunde** cover note, insurance certificate

Deckungs / ~verfahren funding procedure; **~verhältnis 1.** cover (covering) ratio, guarantee ratio **2.** *(bei Kundenkrediten)* ratio of customer lendings to customer deposits **3.** *(im Interbankgeschäft)* ratio of interbank lendings to interbank borrowings

Deckungs / ~vermögen cover fund(s), cover assets; **~verpflichtung** undertaking to cover, obligation to provide cover (a guarantee); **~verzicht** waiver of cover; **~volumen** volume of business covered

Deckungs / ~werte cover (covering) assets, assets serving as collateral; **~zeitraum** coverage period, term of coverage; **~zusage** cover note

de facto de facto, in fact, in practice, *(de facto und de jure)* in fact and by law

Defekt deficiency, defect, fault

Defektivzinsen → Minuszinsen

definitiv *(~er Kauf/Verkauf)* outright purchase (sale), *(~e Offenmarkttransaktionen) (der EZB)* outright open market transactions

Defizit deficit, deficiency, shortfall, shortage, shortcoming

defizitär adverse, in deficit, *(~e Leistungsbilanz)* current account deficit, adverse current account

Deflationspolitik deflationary policy

Defusionierung demerger

degressiv *(~e Abschreibung)* diminishing (reducing, declining) balance depreciation, *(~er Tarif)* sliding scale tariff

dehnen *(die Bilanz ~)* to stretch the balance sheet

de jure de jure, by law

deklaratorisch *(nur ~e Bedeutung besitzen)* to be merely declaratory

deklarieren to declare, *(zu deklarierende Erträge)* reportable income

dekonsolidieren to deconsolidate, *(dekonsolidierte Einheiten)* deconsolidated companies (entities)

Delegierung *(~ von Kreditkompetenzen)* delegation of loan approval powers

D

D

deliktisch *(~er Anspruch)* tort claim, *(~e Produzentenhaftung)* product liability in tort, *(~e Störung)* tortious interference

Deliktsfähigkeit liability in tort

Deliktsrecht tort law , law of trespass

Delkredere 1. del credere, guaranteeing due payment or performance of the contract, → Delkrederehaftung **2.** *(i. S. von Wertberichtigung auf Forderungsausfälle)* charge-off for bad and doubtful debts

Delkredere / ~abschlag del credere discount, haircut; **~agent** del credere agent □ guarantees to his principal the solvency of the purchaser; **~fall** *(bei Eintritt des ~s)* in the event of the debtor's default (non-payment); **~fonds** contingencies fund

Delkredere / ~geber del credere agent, protection seller, → Delkrederevertreter; **~gebühr** del credere agent's fee (commission); **~haftung** del credere liability, assuming the risk of default (the financial responsibility if the buyer defaults on his payment commitments)

Delkredere / ~kommission del credere agency; **~nehmer** protection buyer; **~provision** del credere agent's commission (fee); **~risiko** credit risk, risk of non-payment; **~rückstellungen** provisions for bad and doubtful debts, loss provisions

Delkredere / ~schutz credit protection, credit risk cover; **~versicherung** trade indemnity insurance, commercial credit insurance, accounts receivable insurance; **~vertrag** del credere agency agreement; **~vertreter** del credere agent, → Delkredereagent

Delta Delta □ measures the rate of change in the option price for a one-unit change in the cash market price of the underlying asset, → Griechen

dematerialisiert *(~e Wertpapiere)* dematerialised securities, securities existing only as (electronic) accounting records

Dematerialisierung dematerialisation

Denomination denomination

denkbar *(~e Finanzierungsmöglichkeit)* conceivable funding option

Deponent depositor

deponieren to deposit, to lodge

Deport backwardation □ descriptive of an inverted market, i.e. a condition in which the spot rate (or cash price for nearby delivery months) of a commodity or financial instrument rises above its forward rate (or price for more distant delivery months), → Report (contango)

Depositalschein deposit (custody) receipt

Depositen deposits; **~banken** *(i.e.S.)* deposit-taking banks, *(in Germany)* commercial banks; **~buch** passbook; **~geschäft** deposit-taking business (operations); **~kasse** city branch; **~vermerk** note indicating the place of deposit

Depot 1. *(Konto)* securities account, custody account, *(~ zu Gunsten Dritter)* third party securities account **2.** *(Portefeuille)* securities portfolio

Depot / ~abrundung portfolio rounding; **~absicherung** portfolio hedging; **~abstimmung** reconciliation of securities (custody) accounts; **~abteilung** custodial (custody) services

Depot / ~anlagen portfolio investments; **~aufbau** → Depotstruktur; **~aufstellung** statement of securities, list of securities held under a securities portfolio (custody account); **~aufteilung** portfolio asset allocation

Depot / ~ausgang securities sold (withdrawn), outgoing securities, delivery of securities, securities delivered; **~ausgangskontrolle** outgoing securities control; **~auszug** securities account statement, custody account statement, statement of securities

Depotbank depositary bank, custodian (custodial) bank, depository

Depotbank / ~**garantie** depositary (custodian) bank's guarantee; ~**mandat** depositary bank (depositary services) mandate; ~**rating** depositary bank rating; ~**vertrag** depositary services agreement

Depot / ~**beimischung** adding to the portfolio; ~**belastung** securities account debit, debiting a securities (custody) account; ~**beleihung** lending against a securities portfolio; ~**beleihungswert** lending value (loanable value) of a portfolio

Depot / ~**berater** portfolio advisor (counsellor), → Depotbetreuer; ~**beratung** portfolio consulting (consultancy), → Depotbetreuung; ~**bescheinigung** deposit (custody) receipt

Depotbestand **1.** portfolio holdings, securities account balance, → Depotwert **2.** *(Bestand an Depotkonten)* total number of custody accounts (securities portfolios) **3.** *(i. S. von verwalteten Vermögenswerten)* assets held under management, assets managed, portfolio holdings

Depot / ~**betreuer** portfolio relationship manager, custodial services manager; ~**betreuung** **1.** portfolio relationship management, custodial services management **2.** provision of custodial services (custody account) services **3.** *(i.w. S. Vermögensverwaltung)* investment management services

Depot / ~**buch** custody accounts ledger; ~**buchführung** securities (custody) accounting; ~**buchhaltung** securities (custody) accounts department; ~**buchung** securities account entry, entering in (posting to) a securities (custody) account

Depot / ~**deckung** securities account cover, *(Depotdeckung anschaffen)* to deliver securities in cover of, to provide securities account cover; ~**dispositionen** portfolio arrangements (management), buying and/or selling of securities

Depot / ~**eingang** securities deposited (purchased), securities added to a portfolio, incoming securities, receipt of securities, securities received; ~**eingangskontrolle** incoming securities control

Depot / ~**einlieferung** deposit of securities, securities deposited for safekeeping; ~**entgelt** safekeeping fee (charge); ~**eröffnung** opening of a securities account; ~**erträge** portfolio income (earnings)

Depot / ~**forderungen** **1.** deposits receivable **2.** *(aus dem in Rückdeckung übernommenen Versicherungsgeschäft)* deposits with ceding undertakings, amounts owed by ceding undertakings, → Depotverbindlichkeiten; ~**führung** **1.** maintenance (administration) of a securities account **2.** *i. w. S.* portfolio management; ~**gebühren** custody charges, safekeeping fee

Depotgeschäft **1.** *(allg.)* custody business (operations, activities), custodial services, administration of securities and safekeeping of valuables
2. *Depot-und Treuhandgeschäft (Geschäftsfeld einer Bank nach Basel II)* Agency Services

Depot / ~**gesetz** German Safe Custody Act; ~**güter** custody items, property (assets) held in safekeeping; ~**gutschrift** securities account credit, crediting a securities account

Depot / ~**handhabung** securities account administration, processing of custody accounts; ~**hinterlegung** deposit into a custody account, placing for safekeeping; ~**inhaber** securities account holder

Depot / ~**karte** securities account card; ~**konto** securities account, custody account; ~**kosten** custody charges, safe custody expenses; ~**kunde** securities account holder (customer); ~**kurswert** portfolio value, portfolio's market value; ~**lastschrift** securities account debit

D

depotmäßig *(~e Verbuchung)* portfolio entry, entry in a securities account, posting to a securities (custody) account

Depot / **~nummer** securities account number; **~optimierung** portfolio optimisation; **~pfändung** portfolio seizure, seizure (attachment) of portfolio assets; **~prüfung** securities account audit, audit of custody operations

Depot / **~schein** deposit (custody) receipt; **~sperre** blocking a securities (custody) account, portfolio blocking; **~stand** custody account balance

Depot / **~stelle** **1.** *(Institut)* depositary bank (agent), custodian, depository **2.** *(Ort)* place of deposit (of custody); **~stimmrecht** **1.** voting right(s) pertaining to shares held in custody accounts **2.** authority of the bank to vote shares held in custody accounts

Depot / **~struktur** portfolio structure, asset classes in a portfolio; **~strukturierung** portfolio structuring, portfolio asset allocation; **~stücke** securities held in a portfolio (in a custody account), items (property) held in safekeeping

Depot / **~tagesauszug** daily securities account statement; **~titel** portfolio securities, → Depotstücke

Depot / **~übereignung** assignment of a securities portfolio; **~übersicht** portfolio (securities account) statement, portfolio status report; **~übertrag** securities account (portfolio) transfer; **~umbuchung** → Depotübertrag; **~umschichtung** portfolio (investment) shift, restructuring a portfolio, portfolio switching

Depot / **~verbindichkeiten** **1.** deposits payable **2.** *(aus dem in Rückdeckung gegebenen Versicherungsgeschäft)* deposits received from reinsurers, amounts owed to reinsurers, → Depotforderungen; **~verpfändung** portfolio pledge, pledging portfolio assets (a securities portfolio)

Depot / **~vertrag** **1.** custody (custodian) agreement **2.** depositary services agreement; **~verwahrung** securities custody, holding in safekeeping (in custody), custodyship, *(depotverwahrte Stücke)* securities held in safe custody (safekeeping)

Depot / **~verwalter** **1.** custodian, depositary bank **2.** portfolio manager; **~verwaltung** **1.** custodial services, administration of securities **2.** portfolio management; **~vollmacht** power of attorney (for a securities account), power to handle (to operate) a custody account

Depot / **~wechsel** bill deposited as security, bill serving as collateral; **~wert** value of a securities portfolio; **~werte** securities held in safekeeping (held under custody accounts), *i.w.S.* portfolio assets (securities); **~wertsteigerung** portfolio appreciation

Depot / **~zinsaufwendungen** interest paid on deposits received from reinsurers, → Depotverbindlichkeiten; **~zinsen** **1.** portfolio (deposit) interest **2.** → Depotzinsaufwendungen; **~zinserträge** interest received from deposits with ceding undertakings, → Depotforderungen

Deregulierung *(~ des Finanzsektors)* deregulation of the financial sector

Derivate derivatives, derivative products, *(~ auf Aktien, Indizes, Rohstoffe)* equity/index/commodity derivatives, *(~ des Bankbuches)* banking book derivatives, *(~ auf Dreimonats-Zinssätze)* derivatives on three-month interest rates, *(~ auf makroökonomische Indikatoren)* macroeconomic derivatives, *(~ mit/ohne Optionscharakter)* option-based/non-option derivatives

Derivate / **~abteilung** derivatives unit, derivatives trading desk; **~abwicklung** **1.** *(Abteilung)* derivatives back office **2.** derivatives processing, derivatives trade settlement

Derivate / **~bereich** derivatives sector (markets), derivatives sales, → Derivateabteilung; ~**bewertung** derivatives pricing, valuation of derivatives; ~**bewertungsmodell** derivative pricing model

Derivate / ~börse derivatives exchange, futures and options exchange; ~**buch** derivatives book (portfolio); ~**eigenhandel** proprietary derivatives trading; ~**fonds** derivative fund, arbitrage fund; ~**handel 1.** derivatives trading **2.** derivatives trading desk; ~**händler** derivatives trader

Derivate / ~markt derivatives market; ~**geschäft** derivatives business, derivatives trading operations; ~**gewinne** derivative gains; ~**obligo** derivative exposure, commitments from derivative instruments (positions); ~**positionen** derivative positions (exposure)

Derivate / ~regulierungsrahmen regulatory framework for the derivative markets; ~**risiko** derivative risk exposure, exposue to loss from derivative instruments; ~**team** derivatives team (unit); ~**verluste** derivative losses, losses on derivative positions (instruments) ; ~-**Verordnung** Derivatives Regulation; ~**vertrieb** derivatives sales

derivativ *(~er Firmenwert)* purchased (derivative) goodwill, *(~e Geldhandelsprodukte)* derivative money market products, *(~e Sicherheiten)* derivative collateral (e. g. letter of comfort, negative pledge clause), *(~e Sicherungsinstrumente)* derivative hedging instruments

designieren *(zum beizulegenden Zeitwert designierte Finanzinstrumente)* financial instruments designated at fair value

Desinvestitionsstrategie divestiture (divest) strategy

destabilisieren to destabilise, to unsettle, *(~de Wirkung)* destabilising impact

detachieren *(Kupons ~)* to detach (to clip) coupons

Detaillierungsgrad level of detail

deutlich marked, pronounced, significant, *(~ niedrigere Erträge)* significantly lower earnings, *(~ schlechter)* significantly (noticeably) worse, *(wie die Ergebnisse ~ machen)* as the results highlight (demonstrate), *(~ übertreffen)* to outperform handsomely, *(~er Anstieg)* marked rise, *(~er Vorteil)* distinct advantage, *(~e Zinssenkung)* noticeable (substantial) cut in interest rates

Deutscher Aktienindex (DAX) □ German stock market index □ tracks the performance of the 30 largest and most actively traded stocks, → MDAX, → SDAX

Deutscher Corporate Governance Kodex German Corporate Governance Code □ statutory regulations for the management and supervision of German companies

Deutscher Rentenindex (REX) German bond index

Deutscher Sparkassen-und Giroverband German Savings Bank Association

Deutsche Vereinigung für Finanzanalyse und Anlageberatung (DVFA) German Association for Financial Analysis and Investment Counselling

Devisen foreign exchange, *(Abkürzungen)* forex, F/X, currency

Devisen / ~abflüsse currency outflow, outflow of foreign exchange; ~**abhängigkeit** sensitiveness to currency movements, ~**abrechnung 1.** forex (currency) clearing **2.** *(Abteilung)* forex back office, forex settlements department **3.** *(Schlussnote)* foreign exchange settlement note; ~**angebot** currency supply

Devisen / ~ankauf buying foreign currencies, currency buying; ~**ankaufskurs** currency buying rate; ~**arbitrage** currency arbitrage, forex arbitrage

Devisen / ~behörden exchange control authorities; ~**bestände 1.** foreign exchange holdings, currency holdings **2.** *(Reserven)* currency reserves;

D

~**bestimmungen** exchange control regulations, currency regulations; ~**bilanz** net foreign exchange movements; ~**börse** (official) foreign exchange market

Devisen / ~**defizit** foreign exchange deficit (shortage); ~**differenzkontrakte** currency CDFs, → Differenzkontrakte; ~**dispositionen** foreign exchange (currency) management, foreign exchange dealing (trading); ~**dispositionsabteilung** forex (currency) trading desk

Devisen / ~**eigenhandel** proprietary FX trading, foreign exchange dealings for own account, own-account currency trading; ~**eingänge** currency inflow, inflow of foreign exchange; ~**einnahmen** foreign exchange receipts (revenue); ~**erwerb** currency buying

Devisen / ~-**Future** currency futures contract; ~-**Futureoption** option on a currency futures contract; ~**geldkurs** currency buying rate; ~**genehmigung** exchange control permit, exchange authorisation

Devisen / ~**gesamtposition** aggregate exchange position; ~**gesetzgebung** exchange control legislation; ~**guthaben** currency (exchange) assets, foreign exchange holdings

Devisenhandel 1. foreign exchange trading (dealings), F/X dealing, currency trading **2.** *(Bereich, Einheit)* forex dealing desk, currency trading desk, dealing room

Devisenhandels / ~**gewinn** foreign exchange trading profit; ~**linie** foreign exchange dealing line, forex trading line; ~**usancen** forex dealing practice (usage); ~**volumen** forex dealing (trading) volume

Devisenhändler foreign exchange dealer (trader), F/X dealer

Devisenkassa / ~**geschäft** spot exchange deal; ~**handel** spot exchange trading; ~**händler** spot exchange dealer; ~**kauf** spot purchase of a currency; ~**kurs** spot exchange rate; ~**markt** spot exchange market; ~**verkauf** spot sale of a currency

Devisen / ~**kaufoption** currency call option; ~**kommissionsgeschäfte** currency brokerage transactions; ~**kontrollbestimmungen** exchange control regulations; ~**kredit** currency loan

Devisenkurs / ~**feststellung** exchange rate fixing; ~**notierung** exchange rate quotation, currency quotation; ~**sicherung** hedging the exchange rate, currency hedge; ~**zettel** rate sheet, currency quotations list

Devisen / ~**leihe**/~**leihgeschäft** currency lending (transaction); ~**makler** foreign exchange (forex, currency) broker; ~**marktintervention** intervention in the foreign exchange market; ~**mittelkurs** mean rate of exchange

Devisen / ~**nachfrage** currency demand; ~**netting** currency netting; ~**option** currency option; ~**optionshandel** currency options trading; ~**optionsschein** currency warrant

Devisen / ~**pensionsgeschäft** currency repo, currency-based repurchase transaction; ~**position** foreign exchange position, currency position; ~**positionsmeldung** exchange position return; ~**provision** foreign exchange commission

Devisen / ~**recht** exchange control regulations, *(devisenrechtliche Genehmigung)* exchange control approval; ~**reserven** foreign exchange reserves, currency reserves; ~**spekulation** currency speculation, playing (speculation on) the foreign exchange markets

Devisen-Swap 1. forex swap deal, foreign exhange swap □ a spot sale (or purchase) and simultaneous forward purchase (or sale) of a currency **2.** *(Währungs-Swap)* currency swap □ a contract to exchange payments denominated in one currency for those denominated in another

Devisen-Swaption currency swaption □ option to enter into a currency swap contract

Devisentermin / ~geschäft forward exchange deal, *(Plural)* currency forwards, forward exchange operations, commercial FX forward, *(~ geschäfte mit Barausgleich)* non-deliverable forwards: **~handel** forward exchange dealings (trading); **~händler** forward forex dealer: **~kontrakt** currency futures contract; **~kurs** forward exchange rate

Devisentermin / ~markt forward exchange market; **~notierung** forward exchange rate (quotation); **~obligo** forward exchange exposure; **~verpflichtungen** forward exchange commitments

Devisen / ~transaktion foreign exchange deal, currency transaction; **~transfer** foreign exchange (currency) transfer; **~verkaufskurs** currency selling rate; **~verkaufsoption** currency put option; **~vorschriften** exchange control regulations; **~wechsel** currency bill; **~zuflüsse** currency inflows

Dezimalstelle decimal place, *(aufgerundet auf die vierte ~)* rounded to the fourth decimal place, *(den Kurs auf fünf ~n kalkulieren)* to calculate the rate to five decimal places

dezimieren *(stark dezimierte Rücklagen)* sharply (drastically) reduced reserves

DFÜ-Abkommen RDT (remote data transmission) Agreement

Dialog *(in einen ~ eintreten)* to engage in (to enter into) a dialogue

Diamant-Formation *(Chart-Analyse)* diamond chart pattern □ reversal pattern at the end of an uptrend

dicht *(~es Filialnetz)* dense (closely-knit) branch network

Dichte density

dienen *(als Sicherheit für einen Kredit ~)* to serve as security (collateral) for a loan

dienendes Grundstück servient tenement, servient estate, → herrschendes Grundstück

Dienstbarkeit *(Grunddienstbarkeit)* easement, real servitude

Dienstleistung service

Dienstleistungs / ~anbieter service provider; **~angebot** range of services offered, service offerings; **~bereich** services sector; **~betrieb** service undertaking; **~bilanz** invisible balance, balance of invisibles; **~entgelte/erträge** fee income, fees earned, fees and commissions from services

Dienstleistungs / ~geschäft servicing activities (transactions); **~marke** service brand: **~palette** range of services offered, services portfolio; **~sektor** services sector, tertiary industry; **~verkehr** service transactions, *(freier ~)* free movement of services

Dienst / ~verhältnis *(bei Beendigung des ~ses)* upon termination of employment; **~vertrag** service contract; **~vertragsrecht** Service Contract Law

Dienstzeit / ~aufwendungen service cost; **~ertrag** service income

Differentialzoll differential duty

differentielle Fehleranalyse differential fault analysis

Differenz 1. difference, discrepancy, *(aus der Währungsumrechnung entstandene Differenzbeträge)* differences from currency translation, translation adjustments **2.** *(Lücke)* gap **3.** *(Meinungsverschiedenheit)* difference of opinion, disagreement, dispute

Differenzarbitrage arbitrage □ based on price anomalies between two different market places

Differenzausgleich *(bei Börsentermingeschäften)* cash settlement, → Barausgleich

D

Differenzbesteuerung margin taxation, taxing the difference between purchase and selling price

Differenzeinwand plea of invalidity of contracts for difference □ German legal provision according to which futures and option contracts (contracts for difference) were regarded as gambling debts and thus not legally enforceable. This provision was abolished in 1989.

Differenzgeschäft → Differenzkontrakt

Differenzgewinne/-verluste gains/losses on contracts of difference

Differenzhaftung compensation liability

Differenzierung 1. differentiation 2. *(~ der Konditionen)* tiering of lending terms

Differenzierungsmerkmal distinguishing feature

Differenzkontrakt contract for difference (CFD) □ agreement between two parties to pay the difference between the opening and closing price of a contract, → Aktiendifferenzkontrakt

Differenzkostenrechnung differential costing

Differenzmethode differential method □ assessing interest withholding tax on the difference between the original purchase price and the sales proceeds, → Pauschalmethode

digital *(~e Geschäftsprozesse)* digital business processes, *(~e Option)* digital (binary) option, *(~e Unterschriftserfassung)* digital signature capture, *(~ unterschriebenes Dokument)* digitally signed document

digitalisieren *(digitalisierte Darlehensakte)* digitised loan file, *(digitalisiertes Zahlungsgeschäft)* digitalised payments

Digitalisierung *(~ von Geschäftsprozessen)* digitising business processes

dilatorische Einrede/Einwendung dilatory plea/defense

dinglich 1. *adj. (~er Anspruch)* real right, right (claim) in rem, *(~e Anwartschaft)* estate in expectancy, *(~er Arrest)* freezing order, Mareva order (injunction) (AE), *(~e Belastungen)* charges over property, property charges, *(~e Einwendungen)* real defenses *(~e Gläubiger)* creditors secured by charges over property, creditors in rem, *(~e Klage)* action in rem, *(~e Rechte) (an Grundstücken)* rights in rem, rights to real estate, *(~e Sicherheit)* real security, security by way of a property charge, *(~e Übertragung)* transfer in rem *(~e Unterwerfungsklausel)* compulsory enforcement clause, → unterwerfen, *(~es Vorkaufsrecht)* preemptive right to real property, *(~e Zinsen)* interest on property charges, *(~er Zinssatz)* property lending rate 2. *adv. (~ ausgestaltete Optionen)* options conferring rights in rem, *(~ berechtigter Inhaber)* owner holding an in rem legal title, beneficiary in rem, *(~ besichern)* to secure by real property, to secure by way of a property charge (mortgage), *(~ gesicherter Kredit)* loan secured by a charge over property, collateral loan

direkt 1. *adj. (~es Aval)* → Direktaval, *(~e Kosten)* direct cost, *(~e Notierung/Quotierung)* direct quotation, → Preisnotierung 2. *adv. (~ platzierte Schuldtitel)* directly placed debt, → Direktplatzierung,

Direkt / ~abbuchung 1. direct debit 2. direct charge-off; **~abschreibung** *(~ uneinbringlicher Kreditforderungen)* direct write-off of irrecoverable loan assets; **~andienung** 1. direct delivery (sale) 2. *(von Dokumenten)* direct tender of documents, direct tendering

Direkt / ~anschaffung *(beim Begünstigten)* direct remittance to the beneficiary; **~aval** direct guarantee (aval), guarantee directly furnished by the bank without calling in a correspondent bank

Direkt / ~banken direct banks; **~bankgeschäft** direct banking; **~besitz** *(Beteiligungen)* directly held interests, direct shareholdings; **~besteuerung** direct taxation

Direkt / ~Clearing-Lizenz direct clearing licence □ entitling members to clear for themselves and their clients; **~emission** direct offering (issue); **~emittent** direct issuer

Direkt / ~-Export/Import-Factoring direct export/import factoring; **~finanzierung** direct financing (funding); **~investitionen** direct (portfolio) investments

Direktion management, board of management

direktional *(~e Handelsstrategie)* directional trading strategy

Direktive guideline(s), instruction(s), directive

Direktkredite 1. *(aufgenommene)* direct borrowings **2.** *(gewährte)* direct lendings

Direkt-Leasing direct leasing

Direktor 1. senior manager **2.** *(geschäftsführender ~)* Managing Director

Direktorium 1. management board, managing (executive) committee, board of management **2.** *(einer Organisation)* Board of Governors, Directorate

Direktplatzierung direct placement (placing), selling a security issue to institutional investors (a limited number of investors) rather than offering it to the public through banks or broker-dealers

Direkt / ~versicherer direct insurer (writer); **~zusageverfahren** direct loan origination

Disaggregation disaggregation, breakdown

Disagio 1. discount, *(vom Darlehensnennbetrag in Abzug gebrachtes ~)* discount deducted from the loan principal **2.** *(im Kreditkartengeschäft)* discount, discount fee, discount rate □ fee(s) charged a merchant by the acquirer/acquiring bank for processing its credit card sale

Disagio / ~abgrenzung accrual of discount(s); **~abrechnung** discount settlement note; **~anleihe** discount bond; **~aufwendungen** discounts paid; **~darlehen 1.** loan extended at a discount **2.** → Disagiozusatzdarlehen

Disagio / ~erstattung refund of discounts deducted (in the event of early loan repayments); **~erträge** discounts received; **~gebühr** discount fee; **~gewinn** gain on redemption

Disagio / ~sätze discount rates; **~staffel** table of applicable (staggered) discounts; **~zusatzdarlehen** additional loan to cover the discount deducted from the loan principal

Discount-Zertifikat discount certificate

Disintermediation disintermediation

Diskont / ~abzug 1. discount, discount deducted **2.** deduction of a discount; **~-Amortisationssatz** discounted rate of return; **~aufwendungen** discounts allowed (paid)

Diskont / ~bank discounting bank (banker); **~einreichung** presentation for discount; **~erlös** discounting proceeds, proceeds of a bill discounted; **~erträge** discounts earned (received)

Diskont / ~fähigkeit discountability, eligibility for discount, *(diskontfähig)* discountable, eligible for discount; **~geber** discounter; **~geschäft** discounting of bills; **~grenze** discount ceiling (limit)

diskontieren to discount, *(diskontierende Bank)* discounting bank, *(auf den Barwert mit aktuellen Zinssätzen ~)* to discount to the present value on the basis of current interest rates, *(einen Wechsel ~ lassen)* to have a bill discounted

D

D

Diskontierung discounting, *(~ von Buchforderungen)* discounting accounts receivable, receivables discounting, *(~ ohne Regress)* discounting without recourse, *(~ von Wechseln)* discounting (of) bills, taking bills on discount

Diskontierungs / **~erlös** discounting proceeds; **~faktor** discount factor; **~linie**/**~rahmen** discounting line, discount facility; **~zins** *(steuerlicher)* discount rate used for tax purposes; **~zusage** undertaking to discount

Diskont / **~kredit** discount credit; **~markt** discount market; **~material** bills, bills presented for discount; **~nota** discount settlement note, statement of discount; **~papier** discounted bond (paper), bond issued at a discount

Diskont / **~politik** discount policy; **~portefeuille** portfolio of bills discounted; **~provision** discount charges (commission); **~rechnung** statement of discount; **~rückvergütung** discount refund

Diskont / **~satz** discount rate; **~spesen** discount charges; **~tage** discount days; **~wechsel** discounted bill; **~zinsen** 1. → Diskontsatz 2. *(Forfaitierungssatz)* forfaiting rate; **~zusage** discount undertaking, undertaking to discount

Diskrepanz discrepancy, difference, disparity

diskretionär *(~e Kosten)* discretionary cost, managed expenditure, *(~e Vermögensverwaltung)* discretionary investment management □ day-to-day investment decisions are delegated to the portfolio manager

Diskretionskonto numbered account

Diskriminanz / **~analyse** discriminant analysis; **~klage** discrimination complaint

Diskussion discussion, debate, *(zur ~ stellen)* to put forward (to bring up) for discussion

Diskussionsentwurf *(für ein Gesetz)* preliminary (discussion) draft

Disparitätsindex disparity index

Dispolimit → Dispositionslimit

Disponent 1. account officer 2. *(im Geld- und Devisenhandel)* dealer, treasury manager

Disponibilität availability

disponieren 1. to arrange, to make arrangements for, to provide for
2. to withdraw, *(über das gekündigte Guthaben ~)* to withdraw (to dispose of) the funds for which notice of withdrawal has been given, *(über ein Konto ~)* to draw on an account
3. *(handeln, investieren)* to deal, to trade, to buy and sell, *(langfristig ~)* to invest for the long term, *(vorsichtig ~)* to trade cautiously

Disposition(en) 1. arrangement(s), *(~ der Aktiv- und Passivmittel)* asset and liabilities management, → Gelddisposition
2. withdrawal, *(~ über ein Konto)* drawings on an account
3. trading, *(~ des Berufshandels)* professional trading, professional buying and selling, *(~ in Fremdwährungen)* currency dealing(s), buying and selling foreign currencies
4. *(zur ~ stehen)* *(a)* to be negotiable *(b)* to be available

Dispositionsbefugnis 1. discretionary (approval) power, power of attorney
2. *(bei Vermögensverwaltungsvereinbarungen)* trading discretion (authority) □ bank's (broker's) authority to buy/sell securities for account of the customer without the customer's prior approval, *(Höhe der ~)* discretionary limit
3. *(~ über das Gesellschaftsvermögen)* power to sell (to dispose of) the company's assets

Dispositions / **~berechtigung** → Dispositionsbefugnis; **~depot** trading portfolio; **~freiheit** discretionary power, liberty to act according to one's judgment, freedom of contract; **~ge-**

pflogenheiten dealing (trading) practices; ~**grenzen** limits on discretionary powers, limiting approval powers

Dispositions / ~**kredit** personal credit line, overdraft limit, drawing credit (facility); ~**limit 1.** drawing (overdraft) limit **2.** buy (sell) limit **3.** discretionary limit, → Dispositionsgrenzen; ~**möglichkeiten** room to manoeuvre, discretionary scope (leeway)

Dispositions / ~**papiere** documents of title; ~**rahmen 1.** *(bei einem Kredit)* drawing line (limit), overdraft limit **2.** *(im Hinblick auf Befugnisse)* discretionary limit, → Dispositionsbefugnis; ~**recht**/~**vollmacht 1.** → Dispositionsbefugnis **2.** *(Veräußerungsrecht)* power of disposal

dispositiv *(~er Bestand)* available-for-sale holdings, *(~e Vorschriften)* → abdingbare Vorschriften

Dispo / ~-**Kredit** personal credit line, → Dispositionskredit; ~-**Zinssatz** overdraft interest rate

Distanzgeschäfte 1. non-face-to-face transactions **2.** non-local transactions

distanzieren *(sich ~ von)* to distance o. s. from

Distanzscheck/~**wechsel** out-of-town cheque/bill

Distributions / ~**dichte** distribution density; ~**kanal** distribution channel; ~**kette** distribution chain; ~**kosten** distribution (distributive) cost; ~**wirtschaft** distribution management

Divergenz divergence; ~**index** divergence index

divergieren to differ, to diverge, *(~de Entwicklungen an den Finanzmärkten)* divergent developments in the financial markets

diversifizierbares Risiko diversifiable risk, unsystematic (idiosyncratic) risk

diversifizieren to diversify, to spread

Diversifizierung/Diversifikation diversification, spreading, *(~ der Anlagen)* asset (portfolio) diversification, spreading of investments, *(~ der Refinanzierungsquellen)* diversification of funding sources

Diversifikations / ~**effekt** diversification impact;~**grad** *(des Kreditportefeuilles)* degree (level) of diversification in the loan portfolio; ~**nutzen** diversification benefits; ~**prinzip** principle of diversification

Dividende dividend, *(~ auf Stammaktien/Vorzugsaktien)* ordinary dividend/preferred dividend, *(ex ~)* ex dividend, coupon detached, *(mit ~)* cum dividend

Dividenden / ~**abgabe** dividend tax; ~**abgrenzungen** deferral of dividends; ~**abrechnung** dividend note; ~**abschlag** quotation ex dividend, ex-dividend markdown, deduction of dividend; ~**abschnitt** dividend coupon

Dividenden / ~**ankündigung** dividend statement (notice); ~**ankündigungstermin** announcement day; ~**anspruch** → Dividendenberechtigung; ~**aufbesserung** dividend enhancement; ~**aufkommen** dividends received

Dividenden / ~**aufwand** dividends paid (distributed); ~**ausfall** passing (omission) of a dividend, dividend omission; ~**ausschüttung** dividend distribution (payout, disbursement); ~**ausstattung 1.** dividend rate, dividend level **2.** carrying dividend rights

Dividenden / ~**bekanntmachung** dividend notice; ~**berechtigung** dividend entitlement (privilege), *(mit ~ ab)* ranking for dividend (carrying dividend rights) as of, *(dividendenberechtigt)* entitled to dividend payments, bearing dividend

Dividenden / ~**berechtigungsschein** dividend warrant (scrip); ~**bogen** dividend coupon sheet; ~**bonus** dividend bonus; ~**deckung** dividend cover (coverage), ratio of earnings to dividends payable

Dividenden / ~**empfänger** shareholder, recipient of dividend income; ~**ent**-

wicklung dividend record; ~**ergebnis** dividend performance; ~**erhöhung** dividend increase (rise); ~**erklärung** dividend statement (announcement); ~**erträge** dividend income, dividends earned (received); ~**erwartungen** expected (anticipated) dividend, dividend expectations

D

Dividenden / ~**fähigkeit** ability to pay a dividend; ~**forderungen** dividends receivable; ~**garantie** dividend guarantee; ~**gutschrift** dividend credit

Dividenden / ~**inkasso** dividend collection; ~**kontinuität** continuity of dividend payments, unbroken dividend record; ~**kürzung** dividend cut, lowering the dividend rate

Dividenden / ~**papiere** shares, dividend-carrying securities, equities; ~**politik** dividend policy; ~**prognose** dividend forecast; ~**recht** dividend entitlement; ~**rendite** dividend yield; ~**rückstände** dividend arrears

Dividenden / ~**satz** dividend rate; ~**schein** dividend coupon; ~**scheinbogen** coupon sheet; ~**senkung** dividend cut, dividend downgrade; ~**stichtag** dividend record date, books closed date; ~**stopp** dividend freeze; ~**summe** dividend amount; ~**stripping** dividend stripping

Dividenden / ~**termin** dividend due date; ~**titel** → Dividendenpapiere; ~**vorrecht** preferential right to dividend payments, entitlement to priority of dividend; ~**vorschlag** proposed dividend, dividend proposal

Dividenden / ~**wachstum** dividend growth; ~**werte** shares, equity securities; ~-**zahlstelle** dividend paying agent, coupon paying agency; ~**zahlung** dividend payment, dividend paid (distributed), *(~en wieder aufnehmen)* to return to the dividend list

Divisionalisierung divisionalisation

Divisionalorganisation divisional organisation

Dokument document, instrument, *(~ des kombinierten Transports)* combined transport document

dokumentär documentary, *(~es Inkasso)* documentary collection, *(~e Zahlung)* documentary payment, payment against documents, *(~e Zahlungsgarantie)* documentary payment guarantee

Dokumentation documentation

Dokumentations / ~**entgelt** documentation fee; ~**pflicht** documentation requirement, duty to document; ~**risiko** documentation risk □ exposure to loss from insufficient/incomplete documents or from errors or omissions in the contract between two parties

Dokumente *(~ gegen Akzept)* documents against acceptance (D/A), *(~ zu getreuen Händen)* documents in trust, *(~ nach dem Ermessen der Inkassobank)* documents against discretion of collecting bank, *(~ des Straßen-, Eisenbahn- oder Binnenschiffstransports)* road, rail or inland waterway transport documents, *(~ ohne Wertpapiercharakter)* non-negotiable documents, *(~ gegen Zahlung)* documents against payment (D/P)

Dokumenten / ~**akkreditiv** documentary credit; ~**andienung** tendering (submitting) documents; ~**ankauf** negotiation of documents; ~**ankaufszusage** undertaking to purchase (to negotiate documents under a documentary credit)

Dokumenten / ~**aufnahme** taking up documents; ~**aufnahmeermächtigung** authorisation to take up documents; ~**aufnahmeprovision** commission for taking up documents

Dokumenten / ~**bearbeitung** handling of documents, processing documents; ~**beglaubigung** certification of documents; ~**bevorschussung** advance (lending) against documents

Dokumenten / ~**einlösung** honouring documents; ~**einreicher** presenter of the documents; ~**einreichung** presentation of documents, presenting documents

Dokumenten / ~freigabe release of documents; **~gegenwert** proceeds of the documents, currency equivalent of the documents; **~geschäft** documentary business (transactions)

Dokumenten / ~inkasso documentary collection, collection against documents, *(Dokumenten-Import-Inkassi)* documentary import collections; **~negoziierung** negotiation of documents; **~prüfung** examination of (checking) the documents; **~schutzzusage** silent confirmation of a documentary credit; **~sendung** remittance of documents

Dokumenten / ~tratte documentary draft; **~übergabe** delivery (surrender) of documents; **~versand** dispatch (forwarding) of documents; **~vorlage** presentation of (presenting the) documents; **~vorschuss** advance against documents

dokumentieren 1. to document, to record **2.** to illustrate, to show **3.** to support by documents

Dollar / ~abfluss dollar drain (outflow); **~anleihe** dollar bond, USD-denominated bond traded outside the US; **~emission** dollar issue (offering), → Dollaranleihe; **~erlös** dollar proceeds; **~kurs** dollar exchange rate, dollar rate; **~mittelkurs** mean dollar exchange rate; **~-Optionsschein** dollar warrant; **~-Rembours** dollar acceptance credit

dollarsensitiv *(~e Werte)* **1.** stocks sensitive to the development of the USD/EUR exchange rate **2.** stocks of companies with a heavy exposure to the United States

Dollar / ~titel dollar securities, dollar debt; **~überhang** surplus dollar holdings; **~zinsen** dollar interest rates; **~zufluss** influx of dollars, dollar inflow

dolose Handlung deliberate tort

Dominoeffekt domino (knock-on) effect

Domizil 1. domicile, residence **2.** *(Zahlstelle)* domicile, paying agent

domizilieren *(einen Wechsel bei einer Bank ~)* to domicile a bill with a bank

Domizilierung domiciliation

Domizil / ~provision 1. domiciliation fee **2.** paying agent's fee; **~stelle** domicile, place for presentation; **~wechsel** domiciled bill, addressed bill

Doppel / ~aktivierungs-Leasing double dip leasing; **~anrechnung** double counting; **~ausfalleffekt** double default effect; **~ausführung** *(~ eines Zahlungsauftrages)* double execution of a payment order

Doppel / ~belastung double charge (charging), *(~ der Einkommen)* placing a double burden on incomes; **~belegung** *(von Eigenmitteln)* double equity charge, double gearing

Doppel / ~besteuerungsabkommen double taxation convention (agreement); **~boden** *(Chart-Analyse)* double bottom, → Doppel-Tief; **~buchung** amount entered twice, double payment

Doppel / ~decker split securities repo transaction, → Doppeltender; **~erfassung** double counting; **~-Hoch** *(Chart-Analyse)* double top □ signals the end of an extended uptrend; **~-Plusankündigung/~-Minusankündigung** → doppelte Plus-/Minusankündigung; **~spitzen** → Doppel-Hoch

doppelstöckige Verbriefung re-securitisation □ securitisation in which at least one of the underlying exposures is a securitisation exposure

doppelstufige Sanierung capital write-down followed by an immediate capital increase

doppelt 1. *adj.* double, *(in ~er Ausfertigung)* in duplicate, *(~e Plusankündigung/Minusankündigung)* uptick/downtick by more than 10 % (shares) or 3 % (bonds)

D

(~e Schriftformklausel) double written form clause □ clause stipulating that any amendments to a contract must be made in writing and any amendment to this written form requirement must also be made in writing
2. *adv.* twice, *(sich ~ so schnell ausweiten)* to expand twice as fast, *(~ gespannter Kurs)* quarter spread of the fixing

Doppeltender split repurchase agreement □ combining a fixed and a floating rate or two tranches with different maturities

Doppel / ~-Tief *(Chart-Analyse)* double bottom □ signals the end of an extended bear trend; **~veranlagung** double assessment

Doppelwährungs / ~anleihe dual currency bond □ interest and redemption payments are made in two different currencies; **~schuldverschreibungen** dual currency notes

Doppel / ~zahlung double payment; **~zählung** double counting

Doppik *(doppelte Buchführung in Konten)* accrual accounting

dosieren 1. *(die Zuführung neuer Mittel ~)* to regulate the injection of fresh funds, to measure out fresh funds **2.** *(das geldpolitische Instrumentarium richtig ~)* to employ (to apply) monetary policy tools in line with market requirements

Dotation allocation, endowment

Dotations / ~kapital capital resources (capital stock) of a public sector bank; **~mittel 1.** funds provided, contribution amounts, → Dotationskapital **2.***(für eine Anleihe)* debt service funds

dotieren to allocate, to endow, to provide funds for, to transfer, *(die Rücklagen ~)* to allocate (to transfer) to the reserves, *(Sparkonten ~)* to invest (to deposit) in savings accounts

Dotierung allocation, provision (transfer) of funds, *(~ der Risikovorsorge)* risk provisioning, allocation (transfer) to risk provisions

drängen 1. to force, to push, to press, to urge, to insist, *(auf vollständige Rückzahlung ~)* to press (to push) for full repayment, *(~de Probleme)* pressing problems **2.** to forge ahead

drastisch drastic, rigorous, sharp, severe, *(~er Kursverfall)* steep (dramatic) fall in share values, *(die Dividende ~ senken)* to slash the dividend

Draufgeld earnest money

drehen 1. to turn, *(die Stimmung am Markt hat sich gedreht)* the market has turned, the mood has veered towards optimism/pessimism **2.** to twist, *(in die gewünschte Zinsbasis ~)* to twist into the required interest rate basis

Drehung turn, *(~ der Zinskurve)* tilt of the interest rate curve

Dreieck *(Formation in der Chart-Analyse)* triangle, → ansteigendes, →absteigendes, → symmetrisches Dreieck

dreifach threefold, treble, triple, *(in ~er Ausfertigung)* in triplicate, *(~e Gebühr berechnen)* to charge three times the ordinary fee, *(~e Plusankündigung/Minusankündigung)* uptick/downtick by more than 20 %

Dreifach-Hoch/Dreifach-Spitzen *(Chart-Analyse)* triple top □ signals a change in trend from up to down

Dreifach-Tief *(Chart-Analyse)* triple bottom □ signals a change in trend from down to up

dreimonatig *(~e Kündigungsfrist)* three months withdrawal notice, *(~es Zahlungsziel)* three months credit

Dreimonats / ~-Abschlag *(Deport im Devisen-Terminhandel)* three-month discount; **~-Aufschlag** *(Report)* three-month premium; **~-EONIA-Swap-Index** three-month EONIA Swap Index; → EONIA-Swap-Index; **~-Eurodollar-Kontrakte** three-month Eurodollar contracts; **~-Euribor** 3 month Euribor interest rate

Dreimonats / ~**Festsatz** 3 month fixed rate; ~**Geld** three-month money; ~-**Reposatz** 3 month repo rate; ~-**Swapsatz** 3 month swap rate; ~-**Terminkurs** three-month forward rate; ~-**Wechsel** three-month bill

Drei-Säulen-Konzept three pillar concept, → Säule 1, 2, 3

dreißig/dreihundertsechzig (30/360) interest calculation method based on 30 days per month and 360 days per year

Dreiwährungsarbitrage triangular (three point) currency arbitrage

dringen *(auf Zahlung ~)* to press for (to demand, to insist on) payment

dringend *(~ empfehlen)* to recommend strongly, *(~er Auftrag)* urgent order, *(~e Nachfrage)* pressing demand, *(~e Warnung)* dire (strong) warning

Dringlichkeit urgency, priority

Dringlichkeitsverfahren emergency procedure

Dritt / ~**auftraggeber** instructing third party, third party originator; ~**ausfertigung** *(Wechsel)* third of exchange; ~**besicherung** third party collateralisation

Dritte *(für Rechnung ~r)* for third party account, for the account of third parties, *(Rechte ~r)* third party rights

Dritt / ~**fälligkeitsklausel** → wechselseitige Vorfälligkeitsklausel; ~**markt** *(einer Börse)* third market; ~**marktpapiere** third-market (third-tier) securities; ~**organschaft** legal representation of a company by persons who are not shareholders/partners

Dritt / ~**parteidokumente** third-party documents; ~**rangmittel** *(Basel II)* tier 3 capital □ to be dropped under the new capital framework → Basel III

Dritt / ~**schuldner** third-party debtor, garnishee; ~**sicherheit** third-party collateral, security (guarantee) provided by a third party; ~**sicherungsgeber** third-party surety

Dritt / ~**sonderverwahrung** individual safekeeping with a third-party custodian; ~**staateneinlagenvermittlung** non-EU deposit broking; ~**vergleichstest** third-party comparison test; ~**verschulden** third-party intervention; ~**vertrieb** third-party sales

Dritt / ~**verwahrer** third-party custodian, sub-custodian; ~**verwahrung** safekeeping with a third party (with a third-party custodian), third-party custodyship □ arrangement under which a bank or depository places customer securities into safekeeping with another bank

Dritt / ~**verzugsklausel** cross default clause; ~**widerspruchsklage** third-party objection writ, third-party action against execution

drohen 1. to threaten **2.** to loom, to be impending, to be imminent, *(dem Markt droht der Zusammenbruch)* the market is in danger of collapsing, the market is on the verge (brink) of collapse, *(drohendes Insolvenzverfahren)* looming insolvency proceedings, *(drohende Zahlungsunfähigkeit)* imminent illiquidity

Drohung threat, warning

Drohverlustrückstellungen troubled loan loss provisions, provisions for potential (foreseeable) losses

drosseln to curb, to curtail, to restrict

Drosselung curb, curbing, curtailment, restriction

Druck pressure, squeeze, *(~ ausüben)* to exert (to exercise) pressure, *(Aktienkurse gerieten verstärkt unter ~)* equity prices came under increasing pressure, *(~ auf das Zinsniveau ausüben)* to put upward *(or: downward)* pressure on interest rates, *(~ auf die Zinsspannen)* squeeze (pressure) on interest margins

drücken to press, to push, to depress, *(steigende Betriebskosten ~ auf die Gewinne)* rising operating expenses are squeezing earnings, *(auf die Börsenstimmung ~)* to depress the sentiment in the stock market, *(ge-*

D

drückte Börsenstimmung) subdued sentiment, *(kräftig gedrücktes Kursniveau)* sharply depressed price level *(die Aktienkurse nach oben ~)* to push (to force) stock prices up, *(die Aktienkurse nach unten ~)* to depress share prices, to force (weigh) down share prices, *(die Konditionen ~)* to bring down (to ratchet down) the pricing, *(die Margen nach unten ~)* to compress margins, *(die Zinssätze nach unten ~)* to nudge (to force) interest rates down

D

drückend *(~e Schuldenlast)* heavy (onerous) debt burden

DTA/DTAUS → Datenträgeraustauschverfahren

DTAUS-Dateiformat file format used by German banks for money exchanges

duale Schnittstellenkarte dual interface card

dubios *(~e Forderungen)* bad (doubtful) debts

dulden 1. to endure, to put up with **2.** to tolerate, to permit, to allow, to condone, *(geduldeter Überziehungskredit)* tolerated overdraft **3.** to acquiesce, to give an implied consent

Duldung toleration, acquiescence, *(~ der Kontoüberziehung/der Zwangsvollstreckung)* tolerating the account overdraft/enforcement proceedings

Duldungs / ~titel → Vollstreckungstitel; **~vollmacht** agency by estoppel

dümpeln *(der Markt dümpelt vor sich hin)* the market is plodding along, a languishing market

dünn *(~e Kapitaldecke)* thin capital base

Duplikat duplicate; **~frachtbrief** duplicate freight bill

Durationsfächer duration ladder

durchbrechen to break (through), *(€ 1,30 nach unten ~ : im €/Dollar-Kurs)* to fall through €1.30, *(die Grenze von 2000 Punkten ~)* to break (through) the 2000 points barrier, *(eine Trendlinie ~)* to penetrate a trendline, *(die psychologisch wichtige Unterstützungsmarke von … ~)* to burst the psychologically important barrier of …

Durchbruch breakthrough, *(einen ~ bei den Verhandlungen erreichen)* to achieve a breakthrough in the negotiations, *(der erhoffte ~ am Rentenmarkt)* the hoped-for breakthrough in the bond market

durchdringen *(einen Markt ~)* **1.** to penetrate a market **2.** to break into a new market

Durcheinander *(~ an den Devisenmärkten)* disarray (havoc) in the currency markets

durcheinanderbringen *(den Markt ~)* to throw the market into disarray (disorder)

durchfallen to fail to go through, to be rejected

Durchflusswirtschaft throughput economy

durchforsten *(die Kostenbudgets werden durchforstet)* cost budgets are coming under scrutiny

Durchfracht throughfreight; **~konnossement** through bill of lading; **~verladung** throughfreight shipment

durchführbar *(~e Finanzierung)* feasible (practicable, viable) financing, *(nicht~)* impossible to implement

Durchführbarkeit feasibility, practicability, viability

durchführen to carry out, to effect, to implement, *(eine Befragung ~) (a)* to conduct a survey *(b)* to hold a referendum, *(eine Bonitätsbeurteilung ~)* to carry out a credit assessment

Durchführung carrying out, execution, implementation, *(ordnungsgemäße ~ von Bankgeschäften)* orderly conduct of banking operations, *(~ des Vertrages)* execution of the agreement

Durchführungs / ~bestimmungen provisions for implementation, implementing regulations; **~richtlinie** EU

Implementing Directive; ~**verordnung** Implementation Ordinance

durchgängig *(~ vollautomatisierte Zahlungsabwicklung von einem Ende der Zahlungskette zum anderen)* end-to-end straight-through processing, *(~ sechs Monate)* six months in succession, *(~ e Verschlüsselung)* end-to-end encryption

durchgehen 1. *(angenommen werden)* to be approved, to be adopted **2.** *(durchlaufen)* to go through **3.** *(prüfen)* to examine, to review

durchgreifend *(~e Erholung)* sustained recovery, *(~e Sanierung)* sweeping (far-reaching, thorough-going) reorganisation

Durchgriffshaftung piercing the corporate veil

durchhalten *(Wertpapiere ~)* to hold securities from issue to redemption

Durchhandeln 1. round tripping **2.** intermediary trading

Durchkonnossement through bill of lading

durchlaufend *(~e Gelder)* funds awaiting settlement, *(~e Kredite)* pass-through loans □ loans extended by a government agency through banks that do not assume any credit risk, → Durchleitkredite, *(~er Posten)* self-liquidating item, on-and-off item, transitory item

Durchlaufkonto pass-through account

Durchlaufzeit *(Verkürzung der ~en)* shortening of throughput times

durchleiten 1. to pass on **2.** *(einen Kredit ~)* to transmit a loan, to extend a loan facility under a public lending scheme

durchleitende Bank fronting (transmitting) bank, mandatory bank, → Durchleitkredite

durchleitender Treuhänder transmitting trustee

Durchleitkredite/durchgeleitete Kredite transmitted loans, loans extended by banks under a public lending scheme □ the banks take on the credit risk, → durchlaufende Kredite

Durchleitungsmarge transmission fee

Durchlieferung *(~ von Geschäften am gleichen Tag)* same-day turnaround

Durchlieferverfahren transactions in securities not eligible for collective safekeeping

durchnummerieren to number consecutively

durchsacken to fall sharply, to slump

Durchsatz throughput

Durchschau / Durchschauverfahren *(i. S. des Investmentgesetzes)* look-through approach

durchschlagen 1. *(auf das Jahresergebnis ~)* to filter through to the annual performance **2.** *(negativ ~)* to have a negative impact

Durchschnitt average, mean, *(im ~ zwischen drei und vier Prozent liegen)* to average between three and four per cent

durchschnittlich *(~ gebundenes Kapital)* average capital tied up, *(~er Kapitalkostensatz)* weighted average cost of capital, *(~e Kosten der Mittelbeschaffung)* average cost of funds, *(~e Kreditausfallquote)* average loan loss rate, *(~e Laufzeit der Ausleihungen/Einlagen)* average asset/deposit maturity

Durchschnitts / ~anschaffungskosten average acquisition cost; ~**bestand** average inventory (position); ~**bilanzsumme** average total assets

Durchschnittskosten / ~effekt average cost effect; ~**methode** average cost method; ~**rechnung** cost averaging; ~**satz** mean cost unit rate

Durchschnitts / ~kurs average price (rate), mid-market rate; ~**kursoption** average rate option; ~**laufzeit** average life (duration, maturity, term); ~**notierung** mid-market price (quote, rate); ~**rendite** average return (yield)

Durchschnitts / ~satz average rate, *(~ für Tagesgelder im Interbankgeschäft)* Overnight Interbank Average, → EONIA; **~valuta** mean value date; **~verfalltag** average due date, average maturity; **~verzinsung** average interest rate (interest return)

Durchschnitts / ~wert average value (figure); **~wertmethode** average value method; **~zinsaufwandssatz** average interest expense rate; **~zinsertragssatz** average interest revenue rate

durchschreiten to go (to pass) through, *(der Abschwung hat die Talsohle durchschritten)* the recession has bottomed out

Durchsetzbarkeit *(~ einer Garantie)* enforceability of a guarantee

durchsetzen 1. *(ausführen, umsetzen)* to carry through, to achieve, *(die Gebührenerhöhung lässt sich nur schwer ~)* the increase in fees is difficult to implement
2. *(seine Ansprüche ~)* to assert (to push through) one's claims
3. *(auf dem Rechtsweg ~)* to enforce by the aid of the law
4. *(sich ~)* to succeed in (with), to gain the upper hand, to prevail, *(sich gegen Konkurrenten ~)* to prove oneself against competitors

Durchsetzung 1. implementation **2.** assertion **3.** enforcement

Durchsicht inspection, perusal, examination, *(bei ~ der Kontounterlagen)* on checking (examining) the account records

durchstehen *(die finanzielle Krise ~)* to weather (to survive, to cope with) the financial crisis

Durchstellgeschäfte *(~ in Devisen)* third-party foreign exchange transactions

durchstreichen to delete, to cross out, to cancel

Durchsuchungsanordnung search order

düster *(~e Aussichten)* gloomy (dismal) outlook, bleak prospects

DVFA/SG-Ergebnis je Aktie income per share □ income established in accordance with DVFA/SG recommendations (DVFA → Deutsche Vereinigung für Finanzanalyse und Anlageberatung/ Schmalenbach-Gesellschaft)

Dynamik 1. dynamics, momentum **2.** strength, vigour

dynamisch dynamic, strong, flexible, *(~er Markt)* fast-growing market, *(~e Tilgung)* redemption rates increasing over the life of the loan, *(~e Währungsumrechnung) (im Kreditkartengeschäft)* dynamic currency conversion, automatic settlement of a credit card transaction in the cardholder's home currency, *(~e Wertpapierdaten)* dynamic securities data, → Termindaten

Dynamisierung 1. dynamisation **2.** *(Indexbindung)* indexation, index-linking **3.** *(bei Sparplänen)* compounding of interest

E

EAEG → Einlagensicherungs-und Anlegerentschädigungsgesetz

ebB/ebG → etwas bezahlt Brief/etwas bezahlt Geld

EBICS-Zugang access to the Electronic Banking Internet Communication Standard

ECA-Deckung cover by Export Credit Agencies (staatliche Exportkreditversicherer)

echtes Factoring old-line (non-recourse) factoring □ factoring without recourse to the seller of the receivables in the event of non-collection of an account

echter Forderungsverkauf *(bei Verbriefungen)* true sale, forfaiting, securitisation based on the sale of the receivables by the originator to a special purpose vehicle

echtes Pensionsgeschäft genuine repurchase transaction □ the lender (transferee) undertakes to return the assets (the securities repoed) on a specified date, → unechtes Pensionsgeschäft

echte Unmöglichkeit der Leistungserfüllung absolute impossibility of performance of contract

Echtheit genuineness, authenticity

Echtheits / ~bescheinigung certificate of authenticity; **~bestätigung** authentication, validating (corroborating) the authenticity; **~beweis** proof of authenticity; **~prüfung** checking the authenticity

Echtzeit / real time, *(Zahlungen in ~ verarbeiten)* to process payments in real time

Echtzeit / abwicklung real-time settlement; **~-Bruttozahlungssystem** Real Time Gross Settlement System; **~informationen** real time data; **~-Risikomanagement** real-time risk management; **~ verarbeitung** real-time processing

Eck / ~daten basic (fundamental) figures; **~pfeiler** *(~ der Geldpolitik)* cornerstone (keystone) of monetary policy; **~punkte** key points, framework, basic elements, cornerstones; **~wert** benchmark, benchmark figure; **~zins** basic rate of interest, base rate

Edelmetall precious metal, *(ausschließlich Gold und Silber)* bullion

Edelmetall / ~handel precious metals trade (trading), bullion trade; **~händler** precious metals trader (dealer); **~konto** precious metals account; **~kredit** precious metals loan; **~leihe** precious metals lending

Edelmetall / ~lombardierung lending against precious metals; **~markt** market in precious metals, bullion market; **~notierungen** precious metal prices; **~optionen** options on precious metals *(e. g. gold/silver options)*

Edelmetall / ~risikoposition risk position in precious metals, precious metals exposure; **~swap** precious metals swap; **~terminkontrakte** futures on precious metals, (e. g. gold/silver futures contracts)

EdW → Entschädigungseinrichtung der Wertpapierhandelsunternehmen

EEV-Steuern income, profit, and property taxes

Effekt effect, impact, result

Effekten securities; **~abrechnung** contract note, bought or sold note; **~abschreibungen** securities write-downs; **~auftrag** securities order, buy or sell order; ~**ausgang** securities delivered (sold), outgoing securities

Effekten / ~**beleihung** lending on (against) securities; ~**diskont 1.** discounting of securities □ bank's purchase of securities coming up for redemption **2.** security discount rate

Effekten / ~**eigengeschäft** own-account securities transaction; ~**eigenhandel** proprietary securities trading, own-account trading in securities, trading securities for own account; ~**eingang** securities received (purchased), incoming securities

E

Effekten / ~**emission** securities issue (offering); ~**gattung** class of securities; ~**geschäft** securities transaction (deal), *(pl)* securities operations (business)

Effekten / ~**girosystem** securities book-entry system; ~**giroverkehr** transactions in securities by book-entry; ~**handel** securities (security) trading; ~**handelsbestand** securities trading portfolio; ~**händler** securities dealer

Effekten / ~**kaufabrechnung** bought note; ~**kaufauftrag** buy order; ~**kommission** securities brokerage; ~**kommissionär** securities broker; ~**kommissionsgeschäft** securities brokerage business, buying and selling securities for account of customers

Effekten / ~**konto** securities account; ~**kredit 1.** loan on (against) securities **2.** loan to purchase stock, securities market credit; ~**leihe** securities lending; ~**lieferung** securities delivery; ~**lombard** lending (advance) against securities

Effekten / ~**pensionsgeschäft** sale and repurchase agreement in securities; ~**platzierung** placing (placement) of securities; ~**portefeuille** securities portfolio; ~**provision** securities commission

Effekten / ~**scheck** securities transfer order; ~**substitution** security replacement; ~**termingeschäft** forward transaction (deal) in securities, securities traded for future delivery; ~**übertragung** transfer of securities

Effekten / ~**verkauf** security sale, selling securities; ~**verkaufsabrechnung** sold note; ~**verkaufsauftrag** sell order; ~**verkehr** *(platzüberschreitender ~)* off-board securities transactions involving two or more trading venues

Effekten / ~**verpfändung** pledging (of) securities; ~**verwahrung** safekeeping of securities, securities custody; ~**verwaltung** securities administration; ~**verzeichnis** securities list

effektiv *(~e Darlehenskosten)* true loan cost, true cost of a facility, *(~es Eigenkapital)* share capital plus disclosed and hidden reserves, *(~er Jahreszins)* effective annual interest rate, *(~er Hebel)* effective leverage, *(~e Kreditkosten)* real cost of borrowing

effektiv *(~e Lieferung)* physical (constructive, actual) delivery, *(~e Rendite)* real rate of return, *(~e Stücke)* physical securities (certificates), *(~e Übergabe)* physical delivery (surrender), *(~er Wert)* actual value, net value, *(~e Zahlung)* actual payment, *(~e Zinsbelastung)* effective interest load

Effektiv / ~**bestand** actual holdings; ~**betrag** actual amount, net cash amount; ~**geschäft** cash market transaction

Effektivitätsprüfung effectiveness test(ing)

Effektivklausel 1. *(in Verbindung mit Bankgarantien)* requirements clause □ states that payment by the guaranteeing bank is dependent on the fulfillment of specific conditions, e.g. proof of non-performance or statement of default
2. *(Währungsklausel)* currency requirements clause □ clause stipulating payment in a specific currency

Effektiv / ~**kosten** true cost, actual expenses, cost (expenses) actually incurred;~**markt** spot market; ~**ren-**

dite actual (effective) yield; ~**steuersatz** effective tax rate

Effektiv / ~**verzinsung** actual (effective, real) interest return; ~**ware** spot commodity; ~**zins** effective (true) interest rate; ~**zinsmethode** effective interest rate method

effizient *(~e Sicherungsbeziehung)* efficient (perfect) hedge

Egalisationspreis parity price

egalisieren to equalise, to equal

E-Geldinstitut electronic money institution, e-money institution

E-Geldrichtlinie (EU) E-Money Directive

EGHGB → Einführung zum Handelsgesetzbuch

Ehegattenbürgschaft spouse's guarantee

Ehegattenkonto spousal account

Ehren / ~**akzept**/~**annahme** acceptance for honour; ~**eintritt**/~**zahlung** payment for honour

EHS → elektronisches Handelssystem

EHUG → Gesetz über elektronische Handelsregister und Genossenschaftsregister sowie das Unternehmensregister

EIB → Europäische Investitionsbank

Eid oath

eidesstattlich *(~e Erklärung/Versicherung)* affidavit, affirmation in lieu of an oath, statutory declaration

eidlich under (on, upon) oath, *(~ versichern)* to affirm under oath, *(~e Aussage)* statement on oath, sworn statement

eigen *(~ e Aktien/Anteile)* treasury shares (stock), stock held in treasury, own stock, *(~e Anteile im Umlaufvermögen)* treasury shares reported as current assets, *(~e Akzepte im Umlauf)* own acceptances outstanding, *(~e Kapitaltitel)* own equity instruments, treasury shares, *(~e Mittel)* own funds, capital resources, internally generated funds *(im ~en Namen und für ~e Rechnung abschließen)* to deal under one's own name and for one's own account, *(~e Schuldverschreibungen) (a)* own notes *(b)* notes (bonds) of our own issue, *(auf ~e Verantwortung)* on one's own responsibility, *(~e Ziehung)* own drawing, promissory note

Eigen / ~**akzept** promissory note; ~**anlagen** own (proprietary) investments; ~**aufsicht** self-supervision; ~**bedarf** personal requirements (needs), *(für den ~)* for owner's use

Eigen / ~**behalt** retention, *(~ des Erstversicherers)* net loss retention; ~**beitrag** own (individual) contribution; ~**besitz** **1.** proprietary possession **2.** own holdings

Eigenbestand proprietary portfolio, own inventory (book, portfolio, holdings), *(Eigenbestände in Finanzinstrumenten)* proprietary positions (inventories) in financial instruments, *(im ~ halten)* to hold in one's own portfolio, *(in den ~ nehmen)* to take on one's own book, *(Wertpapiere für den ~ erwerben)* to buy securities for inventory

Eigenbestands / ~**erwerb** purchasing for one's own inventory (portfolio); ~**veränderung** change in the inventory of (e. g. own bonds)

Eigen / ~**beteiligung** own funds contributed; ~**bewertung** own assessment; ~**deckung** self-insurance, self-hedge; ~**depot** proprietary securities portfolio; ~**dynamik** self-perpetuating momentum, internal dynamism, dynamism of its own, inherent momentum

Eigen / ~**emission** own issue (offering), securities issue directly placed with investors (without a bank's or banking syndicate's intermediary); ~**engagement** own exposure; ~**entwicklung** in-house product development

eigenfinanziert financed with funds generated internally, *(vollständig ~)* with all the funds being provided inhouse

E

E

Eigenfinanzierung financing from funds generated internally, self-financing, internal financing

Eigenfinanzierungs / ~bedarf internal financing needs; **~kraft** self-financing power; **~mittel** self-financing resources, internal resources

Eigen / ~forfaitierung non-recourse purchase of deferred payment claims under letters of credit; **~geldanteil** share of own funds contributed; **~geldmarge** *(Sicherheitsleistung bei Finanzterminen)* margin

eigengenutzt *(~es Haus)* owner-occupied house, *(~er Wohnraum)* owner-occupied accommodation

Eigengeschäft own-account deal, transaction for own account, transaction (trade) on one's personal account

Eigengeschäftsorder proprietary trading order

Eigengeschäftstätigkeit own-account trading, → Eigenhandel

Eigenhandel proprietary trading, proprietary trading activities, trading (dealings) for own account, *(~ in Wertpapieren/Devisen/Edelmetallen)* own-account trading in securities/ foreign exchange/precious metals

Eigenhandels / ~absicht intent to trade on one's own account; **~bestand** proprietary trading position, own-account trading inventory; **~ergebnis/~erfolg** net proprietary trading income (loss), own-account trading performance (record)

Eigenhandels / ~gewinn net proprietary trading income, profit from trading for own account; **~konten** principal accounts; **~provisionen** commissions from proprietary trading activities; **~verlust** net proprietary trading loss, own-account trading loss

eigenhändig 1. in (by) one's own hand **2.** personal, in person, *(~ übergeben)* to deliver to the addressee in person, *(~ unterschreiben)* to sign in one's own hand, *(~e Unterschrift)* autograph signature

Eigenhändler proprietary trader, dealer (trader) for own account, → Kundenhändler

Eigenheim single-family home (dwelling), one-family residence, *(eigengenutztes Haus)* owner-occupied home

Eigenheim / ~finanzierung financing a single-family home; **~förderung** assistance to residential building; **~hypothek** residential mortgage single-family home mortgage loan; **~zulage** tax relief for first-time home owners

Eigeninvestment proprietary investment

Eigenkapital 1. capital, equity, shareholders' (stockholders') funds, shareholders' equity, → Kernkapital **2.** *(eines privaten Bauherrn)* owner's equity, → Eigenleistung

Eigenkapitaladäquanz capital adequacy, → Eigenkapitalanforderungen

eigenkapitalähnlich *(~e Mittel)* near-equity resources

Eigenkapitalallokation equity allocation

Eigenkapitalanforderungen 1. capital requirements, capital (equity) required, → Basel II, Basel III
2. capital charge, *(~ für Ausfallrisiken)* credit (default) risk charge, *(~ zur Deckung operationeller Risiken)* operational risk charge, capital charges (equity charges) to cover operational risks, *(~ für Kredit-, Markt- und Fremdwährungsrisiken)* capital charge for credit, market and currency risks

Eigenkapitalanteil 1. *(Beteiligung)* equity interest (stake) **2.** *(des Bauherrn)* own capital contribution, → Eigenleistung **3.** → Eigenkapitalquote

Eigenkapital / ~äquivalent equity equivalent; **~aufbringung** putting up capital (equity); **~auffüllung** replenishment of the capital stock; **~aufschlag** capital surcharge; **~ausstattung** capital funding, capital resources available, total amount of capital and reserves, total net worth

Eigenkapital / ~basis capital (equity) base; ~**bedarf** capital (equity) requirements; ~**beratung** equity consultancy, *i. w. S.* corporate finance; ~**berechnung** measurement of capital, calculation of capital and reserves

Eigenkapital / ~bereitstellung commitment of equity, capital allocation; ~**beschaffung** raising equity, equity financing; ~**beschaffungsmaßnahmen** equity-raising measures; ~**bestandteil** equity element (component); ~**beteiligung** equity interest (stake)

eigenkapitalbezogen *(~e Anleihe)* equity-driven (equity-linked) bond, *(~e Emission)* equity-related issue, *(~e Finanzierungsinstrumente)* equity-driven (equity-related) financing instruments

Eigenkapital / ~bildung equity (net worth) formation, equity building; ~**charakter** *(Emission mit ~)* issue of a capital nature, *(Produkte mit ~)* products with equity characteristics

Eigenkapital / ~decke equity (capital) base; ~**deckung** capital (equity) cover; ~**definition** definition of capital (equity); ~**derivate** equity derivatives

Eigenkapitalentlastung / ~erleichterung capital (equity) relief, *(das Eigenkapital entlastende Maßnahmen)* measures easing the pressure on capital utilisation, reduction in capital requirements (charges), → Eigenkapitalanforderungen

Eigenkapitalersatz equity substitution, *(eigenkapitalersetzende Gesellschafterdarlehen)* shareholder loans substituting equity

Eigenkapitalerweiterung broadening the equity base

eigenkapitalfinanziert *(~e Investitionen)* equity-financed investments

Eigenkapital / ~finanzierung equity financing, *(~ im Wege einer Kapitalerhöhung)* equity financing through a capital increase; ~**fonds** equity fund; ~**freisetzung** release of regulatory capital, → Eigenkapitalentlastung/-erleichterung; ~**größe** equity measure

Eigenkapitalgrundsätze 1. *(für international tätige Banken)* capital rules, capital adequacy rules (requirements), → Basel II, Basel III
2. *(für Nichtbanken)* net worth requirements
3. *(für Versicherungsunternehmen)* minimum capital requirements, → Solvabilität II

Eigenkapital / ~hilfe equity assistance (aid); ~**hilfedarlehen/~programm** equity assistance loan/scheme; ~**instrumente** equity instruments; ~**investmentgesellschaft** private equity house (bank); ~**investor** private equity investor

Eigenkapital / ~kategorie/~klasse equity (capital) category; ~**komponente** equity (capital) component; ~**konsolidierung** equity consolidation (funding); ~**konvergenz** equity convergence; ~**kosten** cost of equity

Eigenkapital / ~last capital (equity) charge, *(Minderung der ~)* lowering the capital charge; ~**lücke** equity gap (shortage), shortfall of equity

Eigenkapital / ~mangel equity shortage; ~**mehrung** increase in (addition to) shareholders' funds; ~**messgröße** equity measure

eigenkapitalnah *(~e Finanzinstrumente)* near-equity financial instruments

Eigenkapital / ~norm capital standard, → Eigenkapitalstandards; ~**polster** capital cushion; ~**produkte** equity products; ~**puffer** → Kapitalerhaltungspolster

Eigenkapitalquote 1. *(Eigenkapitalunterlegung der risikogewichteten Aktiva)* capital ratio, capital expressed as a percentage of assets weighted according to risk
2. *(bei Baufinanzierungen)* share of own capital contributed, → Eigenleistung

E

Eigenkapital / **~regelungen** capital regulations, → Eigenkapitalgrundsätze; **~rendite/~rentabilität** return on equity, *(Eigenkapitalrendite nach Steuern)* after-tax return on equity

Eigenkapitalrichtlinie (EU) Capital Requirements Directive (CRD) □ CRD Amendments: CRD II – comprising amendments related to own funds, large exposures, supervisory arrangements, liquidity risk management; CRD III – amendments relating to capital requirements for the trading book, re-securitisation exposures and remuneration schemes; CRD IV – introduction of new capital and liquidity standards largely reflecting the framework of → Basel III

E

eigenkapitalschonend *(~e Transaktion)* equity-sparing transaction

Eigenkapital / **~schwäche** capital inadequacy, inadequate position on share capital and reserves; **~spiegel** statement of changes in equity capital

Eigenkapitalstandards *(des Basler Ausschusses für Bankenaufsicht)* capital standards □ adopted by the Basel Committee on Banking Supervision, → Basel II, III

Eigenkapital / **~stärke** capital (equity) strength; **~surrogate** surrogate forms of capital, → Eigenkapitalersatz; **~titel** equity securities (instruments); **~tranche** equity tranche; **~transaktion** equity transaction (deal); **~übereinkunft** capital accord

eigenkapitalungebunden *(~e Erträge)* income not requiring the deployment of equity

Eigenkapitalunterlegung 1. *(zur Abdeckung von Risiken)* capital charge(s), charge against equity, capital needed to back risks, capital required to support market exposures, *(~ für Adressenausfallrisiken)* capital charges for credit (counterparty) risks
(~ des operationellen Risikos) capital charge to cover operational risks, *(Befreiung von der ~)* exemption from capital charges, *(eine ~ von 2 % ergeben)* to translate into a capital charge of 2 %
2. *(i. S. einer Unterstützung durch Eigenkapital)* capital (equity) backing, *(Umfang der erforderlichen ~)* scope of capital backing required, *(eine angemessene ~ gewährleisten)* to guarantee an adequate capital backing

Eigenkapital / **~veränderungsrechnung** statement of changes in equity; **~vergleich** *(bei konzernzugehörigen Betrieben)* equity comparison test; **~versorgung** supply of equity; **~verteuerung** increase in equity cost; **~verzehr** capital depreciation (loss)

Eigenkapital / **~verzinsung** return on equity (on net worth), net worth return, return on shareholders' equity; **~volumen** total capital, total capital resources; **~vorschriften** capital adequacy requirements, → Eigenkapitalquote; **~wert** equity value

Eigenkapital / **~zufuhr/~zuführung 1.** infusion of equity, injection of fresh capital **2.** addition to equity, increase in capital; **~zusammenfassung** consolidation of capital, equity consolidation; **~zuschläge** equity add-ons; **~zwänge** capital (equity) constraints; **~zwischenfinanzierung** equity bridge financing

Eigenkompetenz own authority, own approval powers, *(im Rahmen seiner ~ entscheiden)* to decide within one's own approval powers

Eigenkompetenzkredite loan extensions under own approval powers, loans extended within the scope of the authority vested (e. g. in a loan officer), loans falling within the approval powers of the relevant officer or branch establishment

Eigenleistung 1. own capital contributed, cash equity investment
2. *(bei einer Baufinanzierung)* own funds, personal contribution, equity investment, downpayment, *(erforderliche ~)* required capital contribution,

equity requirement, *(eine ~ von 10 % des Kaufpreises erbringen)* to put down 10 % of the purchase price
3. *(in Verbindung mit Großfinanzierungen)* equity capital invested upfront

eigenmächtig *(~e Entscheidung)* arbitrary decision

Eigenmarke own (private) brand, own label

Eigenmittel 1. *(im allgemeinen Sprachgebrauch)* own funds, capital (equity) resources
2. *(intern aufgebrachte Mittel)* internally generated funds, internal funds, *(Investitionen aus ~n finanzieren)* to finance investments from funds generated internally
3. *(haftende ~ von Kreditinstituten)* liable own funds, *(Begrenzung des Kreditgeschäftes auf das 18fache der haftenden ~)* limiting lending operations to 18times the liable own funds

Eigenmittel / ~anforderungen own funds requirements, → Eigenkapitalanforderungen; **~anlagen** equity investment positions; ~ **aufbringung** raising equity, procurement of own funds; **~ausstattung** equity funding, → Eigenkapitalausstattung

Eigenmittel / ~ belastung capital charge, → Eigenkapitalunterlegung; **~berechnung** measurement of capital, calculating capital requirements; **~definition** definition of own funds; **~einschuss** equity infusion (injection), contribution of own funds

Eigenmittel / ~grundsatz → Grundsatz I; **~kredit** equity investment loan; **~programm** equity finance scheme; **~quote** equity ratio, ratio of equity to total assets

Eigenmittel / ~richtlinie Own Funds Directive □ EU Directive that defines equity components accepted by bank supervisory authorities; **~segment** layer of equity (capital); **~situation** equity position; **~stärkung** strengthening (boosting) the equity base, increasing (stepping up) capital resources

Eigenmittel / ~unterlegung capital backing, equity support; **~unterlegungskosten** cost of equity support; **~vorschriften** capital rules, capital adequacy rules

Eigennutzung owner-occupation

Eigenobligo *(im ~ gewährte Kredite)* loans extended on one's own risk

Eigenorganschaft own pooling of interests

Eigenpositionen *(~ in Finanzinstrumenten)* own positions in financial instruments, → Eigenbestand

Eigenpositionierung own positioning, opening (initiating) positions for own account

Eigenrisiko own risk (exposure), → Eigenobligo

Eigenschaft capacity, *(Merkmal)* characteristic, feature, *(zugesicherte ~ einer Ware)* guaranteed feature, guaranteed (warranted) quality level

Eigenservice-Factoring in-house factoring, bulk factoring, □ customer retains the debtor management, → Fälligkeitsfactoring

eigenständig *(~es Geschäft)* stand-alone transaction, arm's length transaction, *(~ operierende Gesellschaft)* independently operating company, *(~ er Schuldner)* debtor in his/her own right, *(~e Wertpapiere)* stand-alone securites, *(~ es Zahlungsversprechen)* non-accessory payment undertaking

Eigenständigkeit independence, *(~ in der Geschäftsführung)* management autonomy

Eigentum ownership, possession, title, property, *(~ der Gesamthand/zur gesamten Hand)* joint property, *(~ an Grundbesitz)* ownership of real property

Eigentümer owner, proprietor

eigentümerähnlich *(~e Rechte)* rights approximating to ownership

Eigentümererklärung 1. owner's statement 2. *(der Wohnungseigentümer)* commonhold community statement

eigentümergeführt *(~es Unternehmen)* proprietor-managed company

Eigentümer / ~gemeinschaft commonhold association, flat owners' (condominium owners') association; **~grundschuld** owner's land charge □ land charge taken out and recorded in the proprietor's name and assignable by the latter

Eigentümer / ~haftung owner's liability; **~risiko** owner's risk; **~struktur** ownership structure; **~versammlung** 1. owners' (proprietors') meeting 2. *(der Wohnungseigentümer)* flat owners' meeting, meeting of the commonhold association

Eigentums / ~anspruch ownership claim, claim to ownership, title to property; **~anteil** ownership interest (share), proprietary interest; **~aufgabe** relinquishment of ownership (possession)

Eigentums / ~beschränkungen ownership restrictions, restrictions on the ownership of ...; **~bildung** creation (accumulation) of personal property

Eigentums / ~erwerb 1. acquisition of ownership (of title) 2. property purchase; **~herausgabeanspruch** claim to restitution of property

Eigentums / ~kataster juridical cadastre; **~klage** action for restitution of property; **~nachweis** 1. proof of title (of ownership), documentary evidence of ownership, evidence of the right to property (to ownership in property) 2. title certificate, certificate of ownership

Eigentums / ~papiere title documents; **~prüfung** title examination

Eigentumsrecht title (to property), property right, right of ownership, proprietary right (interest), *(die ~e besitzen)* to hold the legal (rightful) title, *(Verletzung von ~en)* proprietary tort

Eigentums / ~schutz/~sicherung title protection; **~titel** title (to property); **~übergang** 1. passing of ownership (of property) 2. point in time when title passes to buyer from seller

Eigentumsübertragung transfer of ownership (of possession), transfer of title, property conveyance, *(~ auf den Gläubiger)* transfer of possession to the creditor, *(~ vom Verkäufer auf den Käufer)* transfer of title from the seller to the buyer

Eigentumsübertragungs / ~urkunde deed of transfer, deed of conveyance; **~verpflichtung** obligation to transfer ownership

Eigentums / ~umschreibung property conveyance, registration of a change in ownership, registration of the new owner; **~urkunde** title deed, deed of ownership

Eigentums / ~verhältnisse ownership structure; **~verleihung** vesting of ownership; **~vermutung** presumption of ownership; **~verzicht** relinquishment of ownership (possession)

Eigentums / ~vorbehalt reservation of title, title retention, reservation of ownership; → einfacher, → erweiterter, → verlängerter Eigentumsvorbehalt; **~vorbehaltsklausel** title retention clause; **~vorbehaltswaren** goods subject to reservation of ownership

Eigentums / ~wechsel change of (in) ownership; **~wert** property value; **~wohnung** freehold flat, commonhold flat

eigenverantwortlich *(~ gewährte Kredite)* 1. loans extended within one's approval powers 2. loans extended on one's own risk

Eigen / ~verwahrung self-custody, *(eigenverwahrte Aktien)* shares held in self-custody, securities held in the owner's own custody

Eigenverwaltung *(des Schuldners im Insolvenzverfahren)* self-administration □ the debtor retains management powers and remains in possession of the assets (similar to the US Chapter 11 concept of debtor-in-possession); a self-administration is supervised by a → Sachwalter

Eigenvorsorge *(~ der Kreditinstitute)* banks' risk provisioning

Eigenwechsel promissory note

eignen *(sich ~ für)* to be suitable for, to be qualified

Eigner proprietor, owner

Eignerkontinuität continuity in (of) ownership

Eignung qualification, aptitude, ability, *(~ als Kreditsicherheit)* suitability as security for a loan

Eignungskriterien qualification (suitability) criteria

Eilüberweisungsverkehr express credit transfer service, express payments

einarbeiten 1. *(in den neuen Vertrag ~)* to include in (to incorporate into) the new agreement **2.** to train, to familiarise o. s./s.o. with, to make o. s./s.o. familiar with

Einbau incorporation into, building into, embedding

einbauen to incorporate (to fit, to build) into, to embed, *(in den Ausgabepreis ~)* to build into the issuing price, *(eine Option ~)* to embed an option, *(eingebaute Rückzahlungsoption)* embedded repayment option (privilege)

Einbehalt retention

einbehalten 1. to retain, *(~er Jahresgewinn)* profit retained for the year **2.** *(Steuern ~)* to withhold (to deduct) taxes, *(~er Betrag)* amount retained (withheld), holdback, retention

Einbehaltsablösungsgarantie retention release bond

Einbehaltung retention, withholding, deduction, *(~ einer Steuer an der Quelle)* taxation at source, withholding tax at source

Einbehaltungsklausel retention clause

einberufen to convene, to convoke, to summon, *(eine Aktionärsversammlung ~)* to convene (to summon) a meeting of shareholders, *(eine Dringlichkeitssitzung ~)* to call an emergency meeting, *(die Gläubiger ~)* to call the creditors together

Einberufung convening, call, convocation

Einberufungsbekanntmachung notice of meeting, convening notice

einbetten to embed, *(fest im Konzern eingebettet)* firmly embedded (enmeshed) in the group, *(eingebettete Derivate)* embedded derivatives

Einbettung embedding, enmeshment

einbeziehen 1. to include, *(in den Jahresabschluss ~)* to include in the annual accounts **2.** to integrate into, *(~ in den Entscheidungsprozess)* to integrate into the decision-making process

Einbeziehung inclusion, integration, *(~ in den amtlichen Handel)* inclusion in official trading, adding to the list of quoted shares, *(~ in den Konzernabschluss)* inclusion in the consolidated financial statements, *(~ in die Risikoaktiva)* inclusion in (counting towards) risk assets

einbinden to include, to integrate, *(~ in den Konsolidierungskreis)* to include in the consolidation (in the group of companies consolidated)

Einbindung 1. inclusion, integration **2.** membership

Einblick *(~ in die finanzielle Lage erhalten)* to get an insight into the financial situation

einbrechen 1. *(Konjunktur, Kurse)* to drop (to fall) sharply **2.** *(in neue Märkte ~)* to make inroads into new markets, to break into new markets

Einbrechen → Einbruch

Einbringbarkeit *(~ der vertraglichen Tilgungszahlungen)* collectibility of the contractual repayments

einbringen 1. to submit, *(eine Entschließung ~)* to propose (to submit, to table, to introduce) a resolution, *(Ideen ~)* to put forward ideas

E

2. *(Gelder/Kapital ~)* to invest (to put up) funds/capital, *(einbringender Gesellschafter)* contributing partner, *(5 Mio. € in die neue Gesellschaft ~)* to put up € 5m of capital for the new company, *(eingebrachte Gelder)* funds invested, amount of capital invested, funds brought into a business
3. *(einen Gewinn ~)* to produce (to yield, to net) a profit
4. *(hinterlegen)* to lodge, deposit, to file

einbringlich *(als uneingeschränkt ~ gelten)* to be deemed fully collectible

Einbringlichkeit *(~ von Kapital und Zinsen)* collectibility of principal and interest

Einbringung 1. submission, *(~ eines Gesetzentwurfes)* introduction (tabling) of a bill
2. investment, *(~ von Kapital durch die Muttergesellschaft)* capital contribution by the parent, parental equity (capital) contribution, *(~ von Know-how in das Gemeinschaftsunternehmen)* contributing know-how to (bringing know-how into) the joint venture
3. *(~ von bereits abgebuchten Kreditforderungen)* recoveries on loans previously charged off
4. *(~ in die Sammelverwahrung)* depositing (lodgement) for collective safe custody

Einbringungs / ~aktie founder's share; **~kapital** capital invested, capital brought into a business; **~quote** *(bei abgeschriebenen Forderungen)* recovery rate; **~vertrag** contribution agreement; **~wert** equity investment value, value of a capital investment

Einbruch 1. fall, plunge, *(~ der Aktienkurse)* sharp fall (heavy drop, plunge) in stock prices, *(~ bei den Immobilienpreisen)* property price slump, *(~ der Konjunktur)* sharp downturn (downswing, plunge) in economic activity
2. *(~ in einen Markt)* inroads into a market

einbuchen 1. to enter into an account, to post to an account **2.** *(einen Kredit ~)* to recognise a loan **3.** *(Sicherheiten)* to record collateral

Einbuchung 1. entry in the account (in the books), posting to an account **2.** recognition

Einbuße loss, damage

einbüßen 1. *(Marktanteile ~)* to lose market shares **2.** *(einige Punkte im Kurs ~)* to shed (to relinquish) some points

eindämmen to contain, to restrain, *(die Ausweitung der Geldmenge ~)* to check (to curb) the expansion of the money stock, *(die Inflation ~)* to dampen inflation, *(das Risiko ~)* to contain the risk

Eindämmung containment, curb, curbing, checking

eindecken 1. *(sich ~) (in Verbindung mit einer Verkaufsposition)* to buy in, to make a covering purchase (transaction), to cover o. s., to obtain cover (cover funds), *(sich billig ~)* to buy in at low prices
2. *(sich in Erwartung eines möglichen Kursanstiegs ~)* to buy ahead of a possible upsurge in prices
3. *(ausgereichte Mittel mit kongruenter Laufzeit wieder ~)* to fund (to cover) lendings at matching maturities

Eindeckung 1. buying in, covering, covering purchase, cover transaction, *(~ von Leerverkaufspositionen)* short covering **2.** buying ahead **3.** *(bei Ausfall des Kontrahenten)* replacement

Eindeckungsaufwand / ~kosten 1. covering cost, cost of the covering transaction **2.** *(bei Ausfall/Insolvenz des Kontrahenten)* replacement cost, cost to replace a defaulted contract

Eindeckungsgeschäft 1. buy-in (covering) transaction **2.** replacement transaction

Eindeckungsrisiko replacement risk □ possible loss incurred when replacing the original transaction at current market prices

Eindeckungsverlust 1. buy-in loss 2. loss upon replacement

eindeutig clear, clear-cut, unambiguous, unequivocal, *(~ bestimmbar)* unambiguously definable

eindringen *(~ in einen Markt)* to make inroads into (to penetrate) a market

Eindruck impression, *(die Börsensitzung stand unter dem ~ politischer Unsicherheiten)* the session was dominated by political uncertainties, *(unter dem ~ eines baldigen Nachgebens der Zinssätze anziehen)* to advance on hopes of an early downturn in interest rates, *(den ~ vermitteln)* to give the impression

eindrucksvoll *(~e Ertragsverbesserung)* impressive improvement in earnings

einebnen to level (off), to flatten

Einebnung *(~ des Zinsgefälles)* levelling off the interest rate differential

einengen 1. to narrow, to squeeze, to tighten 2. to constrain, to restrict, to constrict, *(den Kreditspielraum ~)* to constrain lending

einfach *(~es Anfordern)* simple demand, *(~e Arbitrage)* one-point arbitrage, *(~er Eigentumsvorbehalt)* simple (ordinary) reservation of title □ the seller reserves ownership until complete payment of the purchase price, → erweiterter, → verlängerter Eigentumsvorbehalt, *(~e Fahrlässigket)* simple negligence, failure to use reasonable care, *(~e Finanzierung)* straightforward financing, *(~es Inkasso)* clean collection,
(~e Kurslücke) (in der Charttechnik) common gap, *(~e Mehrheit)* simple majority, *(~e Plusankündigung/Minusankündigung)* uptick/downtick by more than 5% (shares) or 1.5% (bonds), *(~e Sicherungsabrede)* security agreement confined to current claims, → erweiterte Sicherungsabrede

einfahren *(einen hohen Gewinn/ein schlechtes Ergebnis ~)* to turn in a high profit/to turn in poor results, *(hohe Verluste ~)* to run into heavy losses, to incur large losses

Einfamilienhaus single-family home

einfließen *(in die Insolvenzmasse ~)* to accrue to the insolvency assets

Einfluss influence, *(~ ausüben)* to exercise (to exert) influence, *(großen ~ besitzen)* to play an influential role, to have great influence, to have a strong bearing on

Einfluss / ~bereich sphere of influence, *(außerhalb seines ~es)* beyond the reach of his influence; **~faktor** influencing (contributing) factor, determinant; **~größen** influencing variables; **~nahme** exercise of influence, influencing, bringing influence to bear on; **~stärke** quantative impact

einfordern 1. to request, to demand, to claim
2. *(Kapital ~)* to call in (to call up) capital, *(weitere Einzahlungen auf das Aktienkapital ~)* to call for further contributions to the share capital, *(eingefordertes Kapital)* called-up share capital, capital actually paid in plus amounts presently due

Einforderung 1. request, claim
2. call, calling in, *(~ von Barkapital)* cash call, call for cash funds, *(~ von Einschüssen)* margin call, *(~ zusätzlicher Sicherheiten)* demand for additional collateral, *(~ von Sonderbeiträgen)* making a call for special contributions, *(~ ausstehender Zeichnungsbeträge)* call on unpaid subscriptions

einfrieren *(Gelder ~)* to freeze (to block, to immobilise) funds

Einfrieren freeze, blocking, immobilisation, *(~ von Vermögenswerten)* asset freeze

einfügen to insert

Einfuhr import, → Import

E

einführen 1. to introduce, to implement, *(ein Produkt ~)* to introduce (to launch) a product
2. *(in den amtlichen Handel ~)* to admit to official trading, to introduce to official listing, to admit to the Official List, *(Wertpapiere an der Börse ~)* to introduce (to list) securities on the stock exchange, to float securities on the stock market
3. *(in ein neues Aufgabengebiet ~)* to initiate s. o. into a new job
4. *(neue Kontrollen stufenweise ~)* to phase in new controls
5. to import

Einführung 1. introduction, implementation, roll-out, *(~ neuer Anlageprodukte)* introduction (launch) of new investment products, *(konzernweite ~)* roll-out at group level, *(~ am Markt)* launch (roll-out) on the market, *(~ strenger Kontrollen)* introduction of (putting in place) strict controls, *(~ einer neuen Steuer)* introduction of a new tax, bringing in a new tax
2. *(~ an der Börse)* introduction (flotation, listing) on the stock exchange, stock market flotation, *(~ in den* → Regulierten Markt) admission to listing in the regulated market
3. initiation **4.** *(schrittweise ~ neuer Eigenkapitalstandards)* phasing in of new capital standards **5.** import(ing)

Einführungs / ~bekanntmachung flotation announcement; **~gesetz zum Handelsgesetzbuch** Introductory Act to the German Commercial Code; **~kampagne** introductory campaign

Einführungs / ~klausel introductory (preambulatory) clause; **~konsortium** introduction (flotation) syndicate; **~kosten** flotation cost; **~kurs** flotation (issuing, offering) price

Einführungs / ~preis introductory (launching) price; **~prospekt** listing prospectus; **~provision** flotation (listing) commission; **~schreiben** letter of introduction; **~tag 1.** first day of listing **2.** launch date; **~zeitraum** launch period

Eingabe 1. application, petition, submission
2. input, entry, *(manuelle ~ von Daten in das Terminal)* hand keying of data into the terminal, *(~ eines Geschäftes)* bargain input

Eingabe / ~daten input transaction data; **~maske** entry mask; **~tag** input day, *(letzter ~)* input deadline

Eingang 1. *(Ankunft)* arrival
2. *(Erhalt)* receipt, *(~ der Deckung)* receipt of cover funds, *(~ vorbehalten)* due payment provided, subject to final payment, *(~ der Zahlung beim Begünstigten)* receipt of payment by the beneficiary, *(Zinsen bei ~ vereinnahmen)* to recognise interest in the income statement as it is received

Eingänge receipts, income, proceeds, *(~ in bar)* cash receipts, monies paid, cash payments received, *(~ und Ausgänge)* receipts and expenditure, *(~ aus abgeschriebenen Kreditforderungen)* recoveries on loans written off

Eingangs / ~bestätigung acknowledgement of receipt; **~seite 1.** receipt side, → Fondseingangsseite **2.** income side **3.** buy side; **~steuersatz** starting (first-bracket) tax rate

eingeben *(Kundenaufträge ~)* to enter (to key in, to record) customer orders

eingefahren *(~e Anlagegewohnheiten)* ingrained investing habits

eingehen 1. *(abschließen)* to enter into, *(eine Kauf/Verkaufs-Position ~)* to enter into a long/short position, to go long/short, *(eine Optionsposition ~)* to enter into (to establish) an option position, *(einen rechtsverbindlichen Vertrag ~)* to enter into a binding contract
2. *(eintreffen, erhalten)* to arrive, to receive, *(~de Post)* incoming mail, *(~de Überweisungen)* incoming credit transfers, *(~de Wertpapiere)* securities received, incoming securities, *(~de Zahlungen)* incoming payments, payments received
3. *(ein Risiko ~)* to run (to incur) a risk

4. *(in die Risikoposition ~)* to be included in the risk position
5. *(einen Vergleich ~)* to agree to a settlement (compromise)
6. *(eine Verpflichtung ~)* to contract (to enter into) an obligation, to incur an obligation, to undertake a commitment

Eingehen 1. *(~ einer Position)* entering into (initiating, establishing) a position, *(~ eigener Positionen)* running own positions, *(~ einer Kauf-/Verkaufsposition)* going long/short 2. *(~ einer Zahlung)* receipt of payment 3. *(~ eines hohen Risikos)* running (incurring) a high risk 4. *(~ in die Ergebnisrechnung)* inclusion (recognition) in the income statement 5. *(~ einer Verbindlichkeit)* contracting a liability (a debt), incurrence of a liability 6. *(~ eines Vergleichs)* agreeing to (accepting) an arrangement, coming to a settlement

eingeschränkt *(~es Besitzrecht)* restricted title (ownership), *(~e Bestätigung)* conditional (qualified) confirmation, *(~er Bestätigungsvermerk)* qualified audit certificate, *(~e Dispositionsvollmacht)* limited discretionary power, limited discretion
(~e Eigentumsrechte) restricted ownership rights, *(~e Garantie)* qualified (limited) guarantee, *(~es Indossament)* qualified endorsement, *(~e Rembourszusage)* qualified commitment to reimburse, *(~e Vollmacht)* limited power of attorney, power of attorney limited to specific transactions, specific power

eingetragen *(~er Eigentümer)* owner of record, registered owner

eingetrübt *(~es Konjunkturklima)* subdued economic activity

eingleisig *(~e Vertriebsstrategie)* single channel strategy

eingliedern to integrate, to incorporate

Eingliederung integration, incorporation, *(wirtschaftliche und organisatorische ~)* economic and organisational integration

eingreifen 1. to step in, to interfere with, to become involved in 2. *(am Devisenmarkt ~)* to intervene in the foreign exchange market 3. *(in Rechte ~)* to interfere with, to encroach upon

eingrenzen 1. to limit, *(das Zinsrisiko ~)* to limit (to confine) the interest rate risk 2. *(die Wahlmöglichkeiten ~)* to narrow down the choice to

Eingrenzung limiting, limitation, confinement, narrowing down

Eingriff 1. stepping in, interference with 2. *(~ in die Märkte)* intervention in the markets, *(mit negativen Folgen)* disruption of the markets
3. encroachment

eingruppieren to group, to classify

Eingruppierung classification, *(~ in Risikoklassen)* grouping into (in) risk categories

Einhaftung assumption of liability (by the new insurer)

einhalten to comply, to observe, to abide by, to adhere to

Einhaltung compliance with, observance of, abiding by, *(~ der Vertragsbestimmungen)* compliance with the provisions of the contract, *(unter/ohne ~ der Kündigungsfrist)* with due regard to (without observing) the notice period agreed upon

Einheit 1. unity 2. *(im Börsenhandel, Rechnungseinheit)* unit

einheitlich uniform, standardised, *(~er Ansatz)* unified (common) approach, *(~e Geldpolitik)* single monetary policy, *(~ er Markt)* single market, *(~es Vorgehen)* concerted action, *(~e Zinssätze)* uniform interest rates, *(~er Zuteilungssatz) (bei Mengentender)* uniform allotment rate

Einheitliches Europäisches Meldewesen/EU-Reporting Common Reporting (COREP)

Einheitlicher Euro-Zahlungsverkehrsraum Single Euro Payments Area, → SEPA

E

Einheitlicher Raum für Euro-Bargeldverkehr Single Euro Cash Area (SECA)

Einheitliche Richtlinien für auf Anfordern zahlbare Garantien Uniform Rules for Demand Guarantees

Einheitliche Richtlinien und Gebräuche für Dokumentenakkreditive Uniform Customs and Practice for Documentary Credits

E

Einheitliche Richtlinien für Inkassi Uniform Rules for Collections

Einheitlichkeit *(~ der Märkte)* uniformity of the markets

Einheits / ~bewertung uniform valuation (measurement); **~hypothek** consolidated (unified) mortgage; **~konditionen** uniform (standard) terms and rates

Einheits / ~konsortium underwriting and selling group; **~kosten** *(~je Transaktion)* unit cost per transaction; **~kurs** single cash price, single price quotation, standard price; **~kursfeststellung** fixing (establishment) of a single cash price

Einheits / ~markt single-price market □ descriptive of a market in which only one official price is fixed during the trading session; **~satz** standard rate; **~scheck** standardised cheque form

Einheits / ~vertrag standard agreement; **~währung** single currency; **~wert** rateable value, unitary tax value, *(Festlegung des ~es)* determining the rateable value (the tax level for a property); **~zins** uniform interest rate

einhergehen *(die mit diesen Zahlungen ~den Gebühren)* charges that accompany such payments

einholen to obtain, to solicit, to seek, *(das Akzept ~)* to obtain (to procure) acceptance of, to present for acceptance, *(eine Bankauskunft über einen Kunden ~)* to make a status enquiry on a customer, *(Gebote ~)* to solicit bids, to take bids (tenders) for, *(die Genehmigung ~)* to seek the approval of, *(Quotierungen ~)* to obtain quotes

Einholung obtaining, procurement, soliciting

einigen *(sich ~)* to agree, to reach (to come to) an agreement, to come to terms, to settle

Einigkeit unity, harmony, *(~ hinsichtlich der zu ergreifenden Maßnahmen)* agreement (unanimity) with regard to the measures to be taken, *(es besteht ~ zwischen ...)* it is understood and agreed between ...

Einigung agreement, arrangement, settlement, accord

Einigungs / ~formel working agreement; **~vertrag** consensus agreement; **~vorschlag** proposal for an arrangement (a settlement)

einkalkulieren to take into account, to allow for

Einkauf purchase, acquisition

Einkaufs / ~budget purchasing budget; **~karte** purchasing card, procurement card; **~kommission** agency transaction, instructions to buy on a commission basis

Einkaufs / ~kommissionär buying agent □ bank buying securities in its own name but for account of a customer; **~kommittent** principal, securities account holder instructing the bank to buy; **~preis** cost price

einklagbar enforceable (recoverable) at law, legally enforceable, *(~e Forderung)* actionable claim, claim enforceable in a court of law

einklagen 1. *(einen Anspruch/eine Forderung ~)* to file (to assert) a claim in court, to enforce a claim 2. *(eine Schuld ~)* to sue for recovery of a debt

Einklagung judicial enforcement

Einklang *(im ~ mit den Anlagezielen des Kunden)* in line (in accord, in agreement, in keeping) with the customer's investment objectives, *(sich im engen ~ befinden mit)* to be closely in tune with, *(sich weitgehend im ~ befin-*

den) to be largely consistent with, *(sich nicht im ~ befinden)* to be inconsistent with, to be out of line with, to be incompatible with, *(in ~ bringen)* to bring into line with, to reconcile with

einklarieren to clear inwards

Einkommen 1. *(Erträge, Einkünfte)* income **2.** *(Gehalt, Vergütung)* income, remuneration **3.** *(~ aus Unternehmertätigkeit)* income derived from economic activities

Einkommens / ~aufstellung statement of income; **~besteuerung** taxation of income; **~effekt** income effect □ impact of interest rate movements on the interest margin/interest income

Einkommens / ~ermittlung determination (calculation) of income; **~fluss** income stream; **~generierung** income generation, *(einkommensgenerierende gewerbliche Immobilien)* income-producing commercial real estate; **~gruppe** income bracket

Einkommens / ~kreislauf incomes cycle; **~nachweis 1.** proof of income **2.** pay slip; **~niveau** incomes level

Einkommens / ~orientierung *(eines Anlegers)* investor's orientation towards regular income (payments, payouts), *(einkommensorientiertes Depot)* income-oriented portfolio; **~steigerung** *(von Kapitaleinkünften)* income enhancement

Einkommensteuer income tax; **~belastung** income tax load (charge); **~bemessungsgrundlage** basis for income tax assessment; **~bescheid** income tax assessment; **~erhebung** levying (imposition of) income tax; **~erklärung** income tax return

einkommensteuerfrei *(~e Kuponzahlungen)* coupon payments exempt from income tax

Einkommensteuer / ~freibetrag income tax allowance; **~gutschrift** income tax credit; **~klasse** income tax bracket; **~nachlass** income tax relief (concession)

Einkommensteuer / ~pflicht income tax liability, *(einkommensteuerpflichtig)* liable (chargeable) to income tax; **~rückerstattung** income tax refund; **~satz** income tax rate

Einkünfte income, revenue

Einkünfte aus *(~ nichtselbständiger Arbeit)* unearned income, income from employment, *(~ selbständiger Arbeit)* self-employment income, *(~ Gewerbebetrieb)* business income, *(~ Kapitalvermögen)* investment income, income from capital investments *(~ privaten Veräußerungsgeschäften)* income from private sales transactions, *(~ Vermietung und Verpachtung)* income from letting and leasing, rental income, income from rental property

Einladung *(~ zur Jahreshauptversammlung)* invitation to the annual general meeting

Einlage 1. *(bei einem Kreditinstitut)* deposit **2.** *(Kapitaleinlage)* capital contribution, capital invested

Einlagefazilität *(der EZB)* deposit facility □ a standing facility of the Eurosystem available for banks to deposit surplus funds

Einlagen 1. deposits, *(~befristet bis zum nächsten Geschäftstag)* overnight deposits, *(~ mit vereinbarter Laufzeit)* deposits with an agreed maturity, *(~ mit vereinbarter Kündigungsfrist)* notice deposits, deposits redeemable at notice, *(~ verbundener Parteien)* deposits from related parties, *(~ von Privatkunden)* retail customer deposits, *(~ auf Termin)* forward deposits, *(~ bei der Zentralbank)* deposits at (with) the Central Bank
2. capital contributions, *(~ stiller Gesellschafter)* equity contributed by silent partners

Einlagen / ~abfluss deposit drain; **~abgänge** outflow of deposits; **~beschaffung** deposit procurement, *(am Markt)* raising deposits in the market

E

Einlagen / ~bestand total deposits; **~bonifikation 1.** interest bonus 2. paying an interest bonus; **~fristigkeit** maturity pattern of deposits; **~geschäft** deposit banking, deposit-taking business, deposit operations; **~kreditinstitut** deposit-taking credit institution

E

Einlagen / ~kunde depositing customer; **~mix** deposit mix; **~prolongation** deposit rollover; **~rückgewähr** refund of contributions; **~rückgewähransprüche** *(~ der Gesellschafter)* shareholder claims to the repayment of equity

Einlagen / ~schutz deposit protection (insurance); **~sicherheit** safety of deposits; **~sicherung** deposit protection (insurance)

Einlagensicherungs- und Anlegerentschädigungsgesetz German Deposit Guarantee and Investor Compensation Act

Einlagensicherungsfonds des Bundesverbandes deutscher Banken Deposit Protection Fund of the Association of German Banks

Einlagensicherungsrichtlinie (EU) Deposit Guarantee Directive

Einlagensicherungsschutz deposit insurance coverage

Einlagen / ~struktur pattern of deposits; **~termingeschäft** forward deposit transaction; **~überhang/~überschuss** surplus of deposits; **~umschichtungen** shifting of deposits

Einlagen / ~vermittlung deposit brokerage (broking); **~volumen** total deposits, deposit volume, *(je Kunde)* deposits per customer; **~wettbewerb** competition for deposits (depositors)

Einlagen / ~zertifikat certificate of deposit; **~zins** interest on deposits; **~zinssatz** deposit rate; **~zugang/~zuwachs** inflow of deposits, net growth in deposits, net deposit gain

einlagern to warehouse, to store, to put into storage, *(eingelagertes Sicherungsgut)* warehoused collateral, *(eingelagerte Waren)* warehoused goods, *(Beleihung eingelagerter Waren)* warehouse lending

Einlagerung warehousing, storage, storing, *(~ des Sicherungsgutes)* warehousing the collateral, *(~ unter Zollverschluss)* warehousing in bond

Einlagerungs / ~deckung storage cover; **~kosten** warehousing (storage) charges; **~kredit** warehousing loan; **~pflicht** compulsory warehousing (storage); **~wechsel** storage bill

Einlassung defense, statement, response

Einlassungsfrist period for response (and comments)

einläuten 1. *(eine Verkaufswelle ~)* to herald a surge of selling **2.** *(eine starke Wachstumsphase ~)* to usher in a period of strong growth

einlegen 1. *(Berufung ~)* to file (to lodge) an appeal **2.** *(Stücke ins Depot ~)* to deposit securities in the custody account **3.** *(sein Veto ~)* to veto, to exercise one's right of veto

Einleger depositor; **~schutz** depositor protection; **~struktur** depositor pattern

einleiten 1. *(Maßnahmen ~)* to take measures
2. *(ein Sanierungsprogramm ~)* to embark on a restructuring programme
3. *(ein gerichtliches Verfahren ~)* to start (to institute, to initiate) legal proceedings
4. *(Verhandlungen ~)* to open (to enter into) negotiations

einleitend introductory, opening, preliminary

Einleitung 1. institution, opening, starting **2.** introduction, preambula, preface

Einlieferer 1. depositor **2.** submitter

einliefern to deposit, to lodge, to hand in (over), to deliver, *(durch Datenträger ~)* to submit via data media, *(ein-*

gelieferte Stücke) securities delivered into safe custody

Einlieferung deposit, lodgement, handing in (over), delivery, *(elektronische Ein- und Auslieferung)* electronic submission and delivery, *(~ in ein Depot)* placing in a custody account, *(~ in den Sammelbestand)* adding to the collective holdings, *(~ zur Sammelverwahrung)* depositing for collective safe custody

Einlieferungen 1. *(im Abrechnungsverkehr)* incoming remittances **2.** *(im Depotgeschäft)* lodgement of securities, securities delivered into safe custody, securities deposited

Einlieferungs / **~bestätigung** deposit (custody) receipt; **~schein** deposit slip

einlösbar redeemable, payable, cashable

einlösen *(eine Anleihe ~)* to redeem (to repay) a bond, *(eine Kreditzusage ~)* to honour a lending commitment, *(Kupons ~)* to cash (to collect) coupons, *(ein Pfand ~)* to redeem a pledge, *(ein Versprechen ~)* to keep a promise, *(Wechsel bei Fälligkeit ~)* to honour (to pay, to meet) bills as and when they fall due, *(nicht eingelöster Wechsel)* dishonoured bill

einlösende Bank paying bank

Einlösepflicht obligation to honour (to pay, to redeem)

Einlösung 1. redemption, *(~ eines Wertpapiers bei Fälligkeit)* redemption of a securiy upon maturity
2. encashment, collection, *(~ über die Tafel)* encashment over the counter **3.** payment, honouring, meeting, *(~ eines Schecks bei Vorlage)* paying (honouring, cashing) a cheque upon presentation

Einlösungs / **~anzeige** redemption notice, notification of redemption (payment); **~bedingungen** terms of redemption; **~bekanntmachung** redemption notice; **~ermächtigung** authority to pay

Einlösungs / **~fonds** sinking (redemption) fund; **~frist** redemption period (term); **~garantie** payment guarantee, → Einlösungsverpflichtung; **~gebühr 1.** *(bei Schecks)* cashing fee (charge) **2.** *(bei Kupons)* collection fee

Einlösungs / **~gewinn** redemption gain, gain on redemption; **~kurs** redemption (repayment) price; **~mittel** redemption funds; **~provision 1.** payment (cashing) commission **2.** redemption commission

Einlösungs / **~stelle** paying agent, coupon paying agent; **~stopp** payment stop, countermand of payment; **~termin** redemption date; **~verpflichtung** obligation to honour (to meet, to redeem)

Einlösungs / **~versprechen** undertaking to pay (to honour); **~verweigerung** *(a)* non-payment, refusal to pay (to honour) *(b)* refusal to execute a direct debit instruction; **~zusage** undertaking to pay (to honour)

Einmal / **~aufwendungen** non-recurrent expenditure; **~belastung** one-off charge, non-recurrent charge (payment); **~emission** one-off issue; **~emittent** one-off issuer, occasional issuer; **~erträge** non-recurrent income, exceptional income

einmalig *(~e Arrangierungsprovision)* non-recurrent (once-and-for-all) arrangement fee, *(~e Aufwendungen/Erträge)* non-recurrent expenditure/income, *(~er Beitrag)* one-off contribution
(~e Belastung) one-time charge, *(~er Gewinn/Verlust)* one-time gain/loss, *(~er Höchststand)* all-time high, *(~e Wertberichtigung)* one-time valuation allowance, one-time charge against earnings, *(~e Zahlung)* non-recurrent (one-off) payment

Einmal / **~lastschrift** one-off (non-recurrent) direct debit; **~prämie** *(vorab zu zahlen)* upfront premium; **~saldo** balance on non-recurrent items

E

Einmalvalutierungserklärung commitment of the lien holder (holder of a land charge) to use the lien as collateral only for a specific outstanding facility

Einmalzahlung single (non-recurrent) payment

Ein-Personengesellschaft single-member company, *(GmbH)* single-member limited liability company

einmischen to interfere, to intervene

Einmischung interference, *(~ von außen)* outside interference

Einmonats / ~-Gelder one-month monies (funds); **~-Liquiditätskennzahl** one-month liquidity ratio; **~-Pensionsgeschäft** one-month repurchase agreement

Einnahme *(~ kurz-/langfristiger Positionen)* short-term/long-term position taking, *(~ von Positionen an den Terminmärkten)* entering into (opening, establishing) positions in the forward and futures markets

Einnahmen revenue, receipts, earnings; **~fehlbetrag** shortfall in revenue; **~minderung** revenue contraction; **~seite** revenue side; **~überschuss** revenue (financial) surplus, net receipts; **~überschussrechnung** cashflow accounts (accounting)

einnahmenwirksam *(~e Erträge)* earnings recognised in the profit and loss account

Einnahmenzuwachs growth (increase) in revenue

Einnahmequellen revenue sources

einnehmen 1. to adopt, *(eine unnachgiebige Haltung ~)* to adopt an intransigent stance (e. g. in monetary policy), *(eine Kauf-/Verkaufs-Position ~)* to go long/short
2. *(innehaben) (den zweiten Platz ~)* to hold (to take) second place, *(jmds. Position im Aufsichtsrat ~)* to replace s. o. (to take s. o.'s place) on the Supervisory Board, *(den ersten Rang im Grundbuch ~)* to hold first rank
3. *(verdienen)* to earn

einordnen 1. to classify, to categorise, *(unter einer bestimmten Position ~)* to group under a specific heading
2. *(richtig ~)* to put in its proper place (order)
3. *(nachrangig eingeordnet werden)* to be ranked below the rights of others

Einordnung classification, grouping

einpendeln *(der Kurs pendelte sich bei … ein)* the price settled down at …

einplanen 1. to plan, to schedule **2.** to budget for **3.** to take into consideration (into account), to allow for

einpreisen to include, to discount, *(im aktuellen Kurs eingepreiste Faktoren)* factors discounted in the current price

Einpunktklausel *(Incoterms)* single-point clause □ both risks and costs pass to the buyer at the same location, → Zweipunktklausel

einräumen 1. *(gewähren)* to grant, to allow, to accord, *(einen Kredit ~)* to grant (to extend, to accommodate) a loan, *(Vorrang ~)* to give precedence (priority) to, to accord priority to, *(ein dreimonatiges Zahlungsziel ~)* to allow a three months' credit
2. *(zugeben)* to admit, to concede

Einräumung 1. granting, extension, allowance, *(~ von Bezugsrechten)* granting of subscription rights **2.** admission, concession

einrechnen 1. to include, *(in die Kreditlinie ~)* to include in (to add to, to count towards) the credit line
2. *(berücksichtigen)* to allow for, to take into account, *(Finanzierungskosten ~)* to allow for financing costs

Einrede plea, objection, → Einwand, *(frei von ~n Dritter)* free from third-party pleas, *(eine ~ geltend machen)* to put in a plea, to file a complaint (an objection)

Einrede / ~ der Anfechtbarkeit plea of contestability (voidability); **~ der**

Aufrechenbarkeit plea of compensation

Einrede / ~ der höheren Gewalt plea of force majeure; **~ des Mitverschuldens** plea of contributory negligence

Einrede /~ des Rechtsmissbrauchs plea of abuse of rights; **~ der Unzuständigkeit** plea of incompetence, objection to the jurisdiction

Einrede / ~ der Verjährung plea of the Statute of Limitations; **~ des unerfüllten Vertrages** plea of non-performance of contract

Einrede der Vorausklage benefit of discussion □ right of the surety to cause the creditor to exhaust all remedies against the principal debtor before resorting to him, → selbstschuldnerische Bürgschaft, *(die Garantiebank verzichtet auf die ~)* the guaranteeing bank waives the right to the benefit of discussion

einredebehaftet subject to a plea, burdened with pleas, *(~e Forderung)* plea-laden claim

einredefrei *(~er Erwerb)* acquisition with any plea being ruled out, *(~e Forderung)* plea-proof claim, claim free from any pleas

Einredeverzicht waiver of plea

einreichen 1. to present, to submit, to file, *(einen Kreditantrag ~)* to file (to submit) a loan application, *(seinen Rücktritt ~)* to hand in (to tender) one's resignation, *(Schuldverschreibungen zur Wandlung ~)* to surrender (to deliver) bonds for conversion **2.** to deposit, *(Schecks zum Inkasso ~)* to pay in (to deposit) cheques for collection, *(Wertpapiere zur Verwahrung ~)* to deposit (to lodge) securities for safekeeping

Einreicher 1. presenter, presenting party, depositor, sender **2.** *(einer SEPA-Lastschrift)* creditor

Einreicherbank/-institut 1. presenting bank **2.** *(im Dokumentengeschäft)* remitting bank **3.** *(im Kreditkartengeschäft)* acquiring bank

Einreicherobligo *(bei Wechseldiskontierungen)* liability ledger on bills

Einreichung 1. presentation, submission, filing, *(~ zum Akzept)* presentation for acceptance, *(~ der Bilanz)* presentation (submission) of the financial statements, *(~ einer Klage)* filing an action, bringing an action against, *(~ per Swift)* submission via SWIFT, *(~ von Wechseln zum Diskont)* tendering (presenting) bills for discount **2.** deposit, lodgement

Einreichungsfrist presentation period, period for presentation (filing), reporting deadline, *(bei Ausschreibungen)* tender period

Einreichungsgebühr filing fee

Einreichungswertstellung value date identical with the date of presentation

einrichten 1. to open, to establish, to set up **2.** *(sich ~ auf)* to prepare for

Einrichtung opening, establishment, setting up, *(~ eines Akkreditivs)* opening (establishment) of a documentary credit, *(~ eines CP-Programms)* establishment of a commercial paper programme, *(~ eines Kontos)* opening an account, *(~ einer Kreditlinie)* setting up a credit line

Einrichtungsgebühr set-up (opening) fee

Einsatz 1. use, usage, application, *(~ von Fremdmitteln)* use (employment) of external (borrowed) funds, debt usage, *(massiver ~ der Währungsreserven)* massive deployment of currency reserves **2.** effort, commitment **3.** assignment **4.** risk, stake, *(den ~ erhöhen)* to raise the stakes

Einsatz / ~bereitschaft commitment (and initiative); **~erfahrung** experience in the practical use (e.g. of a rating system); **~gebühr** usage fee; **~mittel** required resources

E

einschalten 1. to call in, *(einen Sachverständigen/Vermittler ~)* to call in an expert/a mediator, *(eingeschaltete Bank)* intermediary bank, bank called in, *(in die Transaktion eingeschaltet sein)* to be involved in the transaction 2. *(sich ~)* to intervene in, to step in

Einschaltung calling in, involvement

einschätzen 1. to assess, to judge, to appraise 2. *(bonitätsmäßig)* to rate

Einschätzung 1. assessment, appraisal, *(~ der finanziellen Lage des Unternehmens)* assessment of the company's finances, *(nach meiner ~)* in my view, *(positive ~ des Aktienmarktes)* positive appraisal of the equity market 2. rating

einschießen 1. to contribute, to inject, *(zusätzliche Gelder in das Unternehmen ~)* to invest (to pump) fresh money into the company
2. *(Sicherheitsleistung bei Effektenkrediten bzw. Terminpositionen erbringen)* to deposit a margin

einschlagen *(einen restriktiven Kurs ~)* to embark on (to take, to adopt, to steer) a restrictive course

einschlägig *(~e gesetzliche Bestimmungen)* relevant statutory provisions

einschleichen *(ein Fehler hat sich in die Kalkulation eingeschlichen)* an error has crept into the calculation

einschleusen *(Liquidität in den Markt ~)* to fuel liquidity into the market

einschließen 1. to include, to comprise, *(die Verwaltungsgebühr schließt die Depotkosten ein)* the management fee is inclusive of custodial charges 2. *(umfassen)* to embrace, to encompass

einschließlich including, inclusive, cum, *(~ Auslosungsbetrag)* cum drawing, *(~ Bezugsrechte)* cum rights, rights on, with subscription rights attached, *(~ Dividende)* cum dividend, dividend on, *(Rückzahlungen erfolgen ~ Zinsen)* repayments are made inclusive of interest, *(Zinsvergütung bis ~ 31. Dezember)* payment of interest up to and including 31st December

einschneidend *(~e Sanierungsmaßnahmen)* drastic (radical, far-reaching) reorganisation measures

Einschnitt *(~ in der Unternehmensgeschichte)* turning point (watershed) in the company's history

einschränken 1. to restrict, to limit, to restrain, *(einschränkende Bestimmung)* restrictive clause (covenant), *(einschränkendes Indossament)* restrictive endorsement 2. *(eingrenzen)* to confine to, to narrow down 3. *(verringern)* to cut back (down), to reduce, to curtail, to pare, to pare down 4. *(relativieren)* to qualify, to modify

Einschränkung 1. restriction, restraint, limitation, *(~ der Ausleihungen)* lending squeeze, restrictions on lendings
2. confining to, narrowing down
3. cutting back (down), reduction, curtailment, *(~ der Produktion)* production cutback
4. qualification, reservation, *(unter den üblichen ~en)* with the usual reservations, *(~ des Bestätigungsvermerks)* accounts qualification, adverse opinion, *(~ der Rembourszusage)* qualification of the agreement to reimburse

Einschreibebrief registered letter, *(unter Einschreiben)* registered, under registered cover

Einschuss 1. *(bei Effektenkrediten, Börsenterminpositionen)* margin, *(durch Einschüsse unterlegte Transaktion)* margined transaction
2. *(von Kapital)* capital (equity) injection, infusion of capital, putting up capital
3. *(Investition)* capital invested, equity participation

Einschusserfordernisse/~forderungen margin requirements

Einschussperiode (initial) margining period

Einschusspflicht *(einer täglichen ~ unterworfen sein)* to be subject to daily margin requirements

Einschusszahlung margin payment, *(~ auf Futures)* futures margin, *(~ auf Optionen)* option margin

einschwenken *(~ auf)* to fall into line with

einsehen 1. *(das Grundbuch ~)* to search the land register, to make a search on the land register 2. *(die Kontounterlagen ~)* to examine (to inspect) the account records 3. *(verstehen)* to understand, to appreciate

einseitig 1. *adj.* unilateral, one-sided, *(~es Anfordern der Gläubiger)* unilateral creditor request, *(~e Kündigung)* one-sided termination, *(~e Verpflichtung des Garantiegebers)* unilateral obligation on the part of the guarantor
2. *adv. (die Vereinbarung ~ kündigen)* to terminate the arrangement unilaterally

einsetzen 1. *(anwenden)* to employ, to use, to put to use (to work), to apply, *(in voller Höhe im Grundsatz I ~)* to count in full towards Principle I, *(die Mittel nutzbringend ~)* to deploy the funds profitably
2. *(beginnen)* to set in, to begin, to be underway
3. *(einfügen)* to insert
4. to appoint, to nominate, to designate, *(einen Zwangsverwalter ~)* to appoint an administrator over the property
5. to establish, *(einen Ausschuss ~)* to set up a committee

Einsetzen/Einsetzung 1. employment, use, application 2. *(~ der Rezession)* onset of the recession 3. insertion 4. appointment, nomination 5. establishment, setting up

Einsicht 1. *(Verständnis)* understanding, comprehension 2. → Einsichtnahme

Einsichtnahme inspection, search, examination, *(jedermann zur ~ zur Verfügung stehen)* to be available for inspection by anyone

Einsichtsrecht right of inspection

einsparen 1. to save, to economise, *(bis zu 50 % bei den Provisionen ~)* to save up to 50 % in commissions, *(ungefähr € ... an Zinskosten ~)* to save about € ... in (on) interest costs 2. *(Personal ~)* to retrench staff, to save manpower (staff)

Einsparung 1. saving, economising, *(~en bei den Finanzierungskosten)* savings in funding (borrowing) cost, *(~en durch Konzentration)* economies of concentration, *(~ bei den Provisionen)* savings in (on) commissions
2. *(~en im Personalbereich)* staff retrenchment, headcount cut, staff savings

Einsparungsprogramm 1. cost savings scheme 2. retrenchment programme

Einsprechende/r opponent

einspringen to step in

Einspruch opposition, objection, appeal, veto, *(~ einlegen) (a)* to object to, to raise an objection, to veto a deal, to be opposed to a deal *(b)* to file notice of opposition, to file a complaint, to make a plea

Einspruchs / ~frist time for appeal (for notice of opposition), opposition period; **~grund** ground of (reason for) opposition; **~recht** right of appeal (opposition), veto right; **~schreiben/~schrift** notice of opposition; **~verfahren** opposition proceedings, proceedings on appeal

Einstands / ~kosten *(der Bank)* cost of money, cost of funds, *(auf den ~ basierende Preisgestaltung)* at cost pricing, *(Verteuerung der ~)* increase in the cost of funds; **~kurs** 1. purchase price 2. historical rate

Einstands / ~pflicht liability to assessments; **~preis/~wert** cost price; **~zins** 1. historical interest rate 2. *(~ der Bank)* bank's cost of funds

einstehen to guarantee, to accept responsibility for, to answer for, *(für Gewährleistungsansprüche ~)* to accept responsibility (liability) for warranty claims

einsteigen 1. *(in Aktien ~)* to move into equities, to buy stock **2.** *(sich beteiligen an)* to take part in, to participate in, to take a capital interest (stake) in

E

einstellen 1. to employ, *(zusätzliches Personal ~)* to employ (to recruit, to take on) additional staff
2. to state, *(in die Bilanz ~)* to state (to report) in the balance sheet
3. to stop, to halt, *(die Produktion ~)* to cease production, *(ein Verfahren ~)* to stay (to stop, to discontinue) proceedings, *(Zahlungen ~)* to suspend (to stop) payments, *(die Zinsabgrenzung ~)* to discontinue (to cease) the accrual of interest
4. to transfer, *(in die Rücklagen ~)* to transfer (to allocate) to the reserves, *(in die Gewinnrücklage ~)* to allocate to retained earnings
5. to enter, *(eine Quotierung in das Orderbuch ~)* to enter a quote in the order book
6. *(sich ~, i. S. von auftreten)* to arise, to appear
7. *(sich ~ auf)* to adapt to, to prepare for, *(sich auf eine Baisse ~)* to gear up for a bear market, *(Kreditnehmer sollten sich auf höhere Zinssätze ~)* borrowers should brace (prepare) themselves for higher interest rates

Einstellung 1. employment, recruitment, hiring, staff intake
2. reporting, *(~ zum Bruttowert)* reporting (stating) at the gross value, *(~ in die Ergebnisrechnung)* reporting (recognition) in the income statement
3. stop, halt, stay, *(~ der Börsennotierung)* delisting, discontinuance of listing, *(~ jedweder Finanzierung)* cessation of all funding, *(~ der Geschäftstätigkeit)* cessation of business operations, *(~ des Handels)* halt to dealings *(~ des Schuldendienstes)* suspension of debt service payments, *(~ des Verfahrens)* abatement of action, *(~ der Zinszahlungen)* suspension of interest payments
4. transfer, allocation, *(~ in die Gewinnrücklagen)* allocation to retained earnings, *(~ in das entsprechende Laufzeitenband)* assignment to (slotting into) the appropriate time band, *(~ in die Pauschalwertberichtigung)* transfer to the general loan loss allowance (to the general valuation allowance), *(~ in die Rücklagen)* reserve appropriation, allocation (transfer) to reserves
5. *(persönliche ~en des Systems)* personal system settings
6. *(Haltung)* attitude, stance, line

Einstieg 1. move, *(~ in neue Märkte)* move (moving) into new markets, *(~ in eine neue Unternehmensstrategie)* adoption of a new corporate strategy
2. *(Beteiligung)* participation, taking part in, joining, *(kapitalmäßiger ~)* investing capital, providing funds, taking a capital stake

einstimmig *(~er Beschluss)* unanimous resolution, *(~ wiedergewählt)* unanimously reelected

Einstimmigkeit unanimity

Einstimmigkeitsprinzip principle of unanimity

einstufen 1. to classify, to categorise, to grade, *(einen Kredit als notleidend ~)* to classify a loan as non-performing, to identify a loan as impaired
2. *(unter Bonitätsgesichtspunkten)* to rate, to assign (to award) a rating

einstufig *(~es Auswahlverfahren)* one-stage sampling, *(~e Flächenstichprobe)* single-tier area sample

Einstufung 1. classification, grading, *(~ als Privatkunde)* classification (categorisation) as retail client, *(~ in eine Risikokategorie)* assignment to a specific risk category
2. *(~ einer Anleihe)* rating of a bond, *(~ des Länderrisikos)* rating (assessing) the country risk

einstweilige Einstellung temporary adjournment

einstweiliger Rechtsschutz injunctive relief

einstweiliges Rechtsschutzverfahren proceedings for injunctive relief

einstweilige Verfügung preliminary injunction, temporary relief, temporary restraining order

eins-zu-eins one-to-one, *(~ in die Gesetzesvorlage übernehmen)* to import without change into the bill

Ein-Tages-Umkehrformation *(in der Charttechnik)* one-day reversal pattern

eintägig *(~es Kassageschäft)* overnight (one-day) spot deal

eintauschen to swap, to exchange, *(Aktien gegen Festverzinsliche ~)* to swap shares (equities) for fixed rate debt

einteilen 1. to divide, to classify, to class, to group, to categorise **2.** to organise, to arrange

Einteilung 1. division, classification, grouping, categorisation **2.** organisation, arrangement

Eintrag entry, registration

eintragen to register, to record, to enter, *(sich im Verzeichnis der Aktionäre ~ lassen)* to have one's name entered in the register of shareholders, *(eingetragener Aktionär)* shareholder (stockholder) of record, registered shareholder, *(auf den Namen der Bank ~)* to register to the bank, to register in the bank's name, *(im Grundbuch ~)* to record in the land register, *(eingetragenes Grundpfandrecht)* registered charge over property

einträglich profitable, remunerative

Einträglichkeit profitability, profitableness

Eintragung registration, recording, entering, *(~ des Eigentumsübergangs)* registration of the transfer of title, *(~ einer Gesellschaft)* registration (incorporation) of a company, *(~ im Grundbuch)* registration in (with) the land registry, *(~ im Handelsregister)* entry on (in) the Register of Companies, *(~ der Löschung)* registration of satisfaction, entry of satisfaction of mortgage

Eintragungs / ~antrag application for registration; **~bescheinigung/~bestätigung** certificate of registration; **~bewilligung** registration consent (authority)

eintragungsfähig *(~es Besitzrecht/Sicherungspfandrecht)* registrable title (charge)

Eintragungs / ~gebühr registration (recording) fee; **~pflicht** registration requirement, *(eintragungspflichtig)* registrable, subject to registration; **~stelle** registration office, registry

Eintragungs / ~urkunde registration certificate; **~verfahren** registration proceedings; **~vermerk** note of entry

eintreffen 1. to arrive **2.** to come true, to materialise

eintreibbar *(~e Forderung)* recoverable debt

eintreiben to collect, to recover

Eintreibung collection, recovery, *(~ von Forderungen)* debt recovery

eintreten 1. to enter, *(in eine leichte Rezession ~)* to enter into a light recession, *(in Verhandlungen ~)* to enter into (to open) negotiations
2. to join, to assume, *(als Gesellschafter ~)* to join a company as partner, *(in ein Schuldverhältnis ~)* to assume a debt obligation, *(bei Zahlungsverzug des Kontrahenten ~)* to step in should the counterparty default
3. to occur, to take place, to happen, *(die angestrebte Verbesserung der Unternehmensfinanzen ist nicht eingetreten)* the desired improvement in the company's finances failed to materialise
4. *(in die Rechte einer Person ~)* to succeed to s. o.'s rights
5. *(~ für)* to favour, to advocate

Eintritt 1. entry, entering, *(~ in einen Dialog)* entry into (opening,engaging in) a dialogue, *(~ in eine Verpflichtung)* entry into an obligation

E

2. *(nach ~ in das Unternehmen)* after joining the company
3. occurrence, *(bei ~ eines bestimmten Ereignisses)* upon the occurrence of a specific event, upon the happening of a certain contingency, *(nach ~ des Versicherungsfalls)* following the occurrence of the event insured against, *(~ des Verzugs)* occurrence of default

E

Eintrittswahrscheinlichkeit probability of occurrence

Eintrübung *(deutliche ~ des Konjunkturklimas)* noticeable slowdown in economic activity

Einvernehmen agreement, understanding, *(im gegenseitigen ~)* by mutual agreement, *(einvernehmliche Lösung)* consensual solution

Einverständnis agreement, consent, approval, *(es besteht~)* it is understood, *(Ihr ~voraussetzend)* taking your agreement for granted

Einverständniserklärung letter of consent

Einwand 1. objection **2.** *(jur.)* defense, demurrer, *(Verzicht auf den ~ der Unterversicherung)* waiving the defense of underinsurance, *(~ erheben)* to raise an objection, to voice opposition → Einrede

einwandfrei *(~er Beweis)* incontestable proof, *(~e Bonität)* irreproachable (immaculate) credit standing, *(~e Kontoführung)* proper conduct of an account, impeccable account maintenance, *(~er Zustand)* perfect (flawless) condition

einweisen to instruct in, to initiate into, to introduce, to brief

Einweisung instruction, introduction, briefing

einwenden to object, to raise an objection

Einwendung objection, challenge

Einwendungsausschluss excluding objections

einwendungsfrei free from any objections

Einwendungsfrist time allowed for objections

einwilligen to agree to, to consent to, to accept

Einwilligung agreement, consent, acceptance

Einwilligungs / ~erklärung declaration of consent; **~klausel** agreement clause

einwirken 1. *(auf jmd. ~)* to influence s. o., to exert influence (pressure) on s. o. **2.** *(die Maßnahmen ~ lassen)* to allow the measures to take effect (to feed through)

Einwirkung 1. influence **2.** effect, impact

einzahlen to deposit, to pay into, *(auf ein Konto ~)* to pay into an account

Einzahler depositor

Einzahlplan deposit scheme

Einzahlung 1. payment, paying in, deposit, inpayment, *(regelmäßige ~en auf ein Konto)* regular deposits (payments) into an account, *(~ aus der Veräußerung von Finanzanlagen)* proceeds (receipts) from the sale of financial investments, *(Einzahlungen und Auszahlungen)* deposits and withdrawals (disbursements), paying and receiving funds
2. contribution, *(~ auf das Aktienkapital)* contributions to the share capital

Einzahlungs / ~aufforderung call to pay up, call letter; **~automat** cash deposit machine (CDM), → Geldautomat, Geldausgabeautomat; **~beleg** paying-in slip, deposit (credit) slip

Einzahlungs / ~dauer savings period;**~funktionen** depository functions; **~mechanismus** deposit mechanism; **~pflicht** *(~ der Aktionäre)* stockholders' call liability

Einzahlungs / ~quote 1. percentage paid up **2.** required deposit; **~überschuss** net deposits, surplus of deposits; **~verpflichtung** call liability (commitment), capital contribution commitment, *(~en auf nicht voll eingezahlte Aktien)* commitments for uncalled payments on partly paid shares, *(~en aus der Kapitalerhöhung)* call commitments resulting from the capital increase

Einzel / **~abschluss** **1.** single entity (stand-alone) financial statements, separate accounts **2.** individual contract (trade); **~abschreibung** separate (individual) write-off; **~abtretung** assignment of a specific claim

Einzeladresse single name, *(einzeladressenbezogene Kreditrisikokonzentration)* single-name credit risk concentration

Einzeladressen-CDS single-name CDS (credit default swap)

Einzelaktien-Futures single stock futures

Einzel / **~aktionär** individual (single) shareholder, *(der größte ~)* the biggest single shareholder; **~anzeige** individual report (notification); **~aufstellung** individual (separate, detailed) statement, itemisation

Einzel / **~auslosungsrecht** special drawing right □ i.e. number-linked drawings as opposed to series-linked drawings; **~beschluss** individual resolution; **~betrag** single (individual) amount, individual item

Einzelbewertung separate (individual) valuation, valuation on an individual basis, individual measurement, microvaluation, *(~ von Finanzanlagen)* valuation on an item-by-item basis, *(~ von Wertminderungen)* individual assessment of impairments

Einzel / **~bilanzen** separate balance sheets (accounts); **~deckung** single transaction cover, specific (scheduled, individual) coverage; **~engagement** **1.** individual loan commitment, individual (separate) exposure **2.** individual investment

Einzel / **~factoring** single debtor (individual) factoring; **~fall** individual (specific) case, *(im ~)* in a given case, *(einzelfallbezogene Kreditprüfung)* loan review on a case-by-case basis; **~firma** sole proprietorship; **~ forderungsabsicherung** individual credit insurance, specific account policy

Einzel / **~geschäftsführungsbefugnis** sole management authority; **~geschäftslimit** individual transaction limit; **~gesellschaft** individual group company; **~großkredit** single large exposure (loan)

Einzel / **~haftung** individual (several, sole) liability; **~-Hedgefonds** single hedge fund, → Dach-Hedgefonds

Einzelheiten details, particulars, *(~ der Zahlung/der Transaktion)* payment/transaction details, *(technische ~)* technical details, technicalities

Einzel / **~investition** *(die größte ~)* the biggest single investment; **~kalkulation** unit calculation; **~kaufmann** sole trader; **~kompetenz** individual decision-making authority, individual loan approval powers

Einzel / **~konto** single (individual) account; **~kontrahierung** individual contracting, concluding individual deals (contracts)

Einzelkredit individual loan (loan exposure), lending to a single borrower

Einzelkredit / **~geber** single lender; **~höchstgrenze** single exposure ceiling, individual exposure limit, limit for lendings to a single borrower; **~nehmer** individual borrower; **~nehmerlimite** individual borrower limits

Einzelkredit / **~risiko** individual (specific) loan exposure, individual (specific) credit risk; **~versicherung** individual credit insurance, specific credit insurance policy □ policy to cover large or excessive exposure to a single customer

Einzelmeldung separate notification, individual report

einzeln *(~abwickeln/bearbeiten)* to settle/to process on a case by case basis, *(entweder ~ oder in der Summe be-*

werten) to assess either alone or in aggregate, *(~ haften)* to be individually (severally) liable, to be liable alone, *(~ ermittelte Wertberichtigung)* individually assessed allowance for loan losses, *(Zahlungen ~ regulieren)* to settle payments individually, to settle on a transaction by transaction basis

E

Einzel / ~**preis** unit price; ~**prokura** individual power of representation, general power of attorney (to act for the company); ~**prokurist** executive holding a general power of attorney

Einzel / ~**prüfung** *(~ aller Anträge)* case-by-case consideration of all applications; ~**rating** stand-alone (separate) rating; ~**rechtsnachfolge** singular succession

Einzelrisiko specific risk (exposure), *(Einzelrisiken im Kreditgeschäft)* specific (individual) lending risks

Einzelrisiko / ~**rückversicherung** single risk reinsurance, specific reinsurance; ~**versicherung** named peril coverage; ~ **vorsorge** specific risk provisioning

einzelschuldbuchfähig eligible for transfer to an individual debt register account

Einzel / ~**schuldbuchforderung** individually inscribed debt, ~**schuldbuchkonto** individual debt register account; ~**schuldner 1.** individual debtor **2.** single counterparty

einzelstaatlich *(~e Rechtsvorschriften)* national legal provisions

Einzel / ~**stücke 1.** *(im Börsenhandel)* odd lots **2.** *(im Depotgeschäft)* securities held separately; ~**stückelung** single denomination; ~**unternehmung** sole proprietorship; ~**urkunde 1.** separate (individual) certificate **2.** *(bei Teilschuldverschreibungen)* definitive note

Einzel / ~**verbriefung 1.** issuance of separate share certificates **2.** separate securitisation; ~**verfügungsberechtigung** *(über ein Bankkonto)* individual signature authority, authority (power) to draw singly on an account

Einzel / ~**vermögen** individual fund, → Sondervermögen; ~**verpflichtung** individual (several) obligation; ~**vertretungsberechtigung** individual (sole) power of representation, authority to act singly (on behalf of the company)

Einzel / ~**verwahrung** individual custody (safekeeping), *(einzelverwahrte Stücke)* securities held separately, securities held under individual custody accounts; ~**verwaltung** *(von Vermögenswerten)* individual investment management

Einzel / ~**vollmacht 1.** specific (special) power of attorney **2.** → Einzelverfügungsberechtigung; ~**vollstreckung** individual (separate) enforcement, levy upon individual assets

Einzel / ~**vorschuss 1.** special (separate) advance **2.** individual advance (e.g. against export receivables); ~**währungsposition** individual currency position

einzelwertberichtigt *(~e Forderungen)* lendings for which specific loan loss allowances have been set up

Einzelwertberichtigung specific valuation allowance, *(im Kreditgeschäft)* specific loan loss allowance, *(~en zu Aktivpositionen)* valuation allowances against specific assets, specific loan loss allowances, *(~ in Höhe des möglichen Verlustes)* specific valuation allowance reflecting the scale of the possible loss, *(-en auf Verlustrisiken)* specific allowances against loss exposure

Einzelzahlungsvertrag single payments contract

Einzelzeichnung sole signature

Einzelzeichnungs / ~**berechtigter** signatory (person) authorised to sign alone; ~**berechtigung** power (authority) to sign alone, single signing authority, sole signing power

Einzel / ~**zession** → Einzelabtretung; ~**zinsposition** individual interest exposure; ~**zwangsvollstreckung** individual compulsory enforcement, individual debt enforcement proceedings

einziehen 1. to collect, to recover, *(Außenstände ~)* to collect (to recover) trade receivables, *(auf dem Rechtsweg ~)* to collect by taking legal action, *(einen Scheck ~)* to collect (to cash) a cheque
2. to retire, to withdraw from circulation, *(Wertpapiere ~)* to retire (to call in) securities
3. *(beschlagnahmen)* to seize, to confiscate
4. *(Erkundigungen ~)* to make inquiries

Einzug 1. collection, *(~ von Forderungen)* debt collection (recovery), collecting receivables, *(~ der fällig werdenden Kupons)* collecting (encashment of) coupons falling due for payment, *(~ zum Nennwert)* par collection, *(~ von Steuern)* collection of taxes
(~ im Wege des Abbuchungs-/Lastschriftverfahrens) pre-authorised debit, collection by direct debit, *(im ~ befindliche Werte)* cash items in the process of collection
2. *(~ von Banknoten)* calling in (retirement of) bank notes, withdrawing bank notes from circulation
3. confiscation, seizure

Einzugs / ~auftrag 1. collection order, instructions to collect **2.** direct debit order, → Einzugsermächtigung; ~**bank** collecting bank; ~**bedingungen** terms of collection; ~**erlös** collection proceeds

Einzugsermächtigung collection authorisation (mandate)

Einzugsermächtigungs / ~lastschrift direct debit (under a collection authorisation), → Abbuchungslastschrift; ~**verfahren** collection authorisation system

Einzugs / ~gebiet catchment area; ~**gebühr** collection fee; ~**indossament** collection (proxy) endorsement; ~**kette** chain of collecting agencies; ~**kosten** collection charges; ~**liquidität** acid-test ratio; ~**papiere** collection items (documents)

Einzugs / ~system collection (direct debit) system; ~**verfahren 1.** collection process, method of collection **2.** → Einzugsermächtigungslastschrift, Abbuchungslastschrift; ~**verkehr** collections, collection operations; ~**vollmacht** authority to collect; ~**weg** collection channel

Einzweckgesellschaft single purpose company (vehicle), single purpose entity

Eisberg-Order iceberg order □ displaying only a portion of a large buy or sell order in order to conceal the actual order quantity

Elan *(Börse)* momentum

Elastizität flexibility, elasticity

elektronisch 1. *adj.* *(~e Auftragserteilung)* electronic order placing, *(~er Bundesanzeiger)* Federal Electronic Gazette, *(~er Datenaustausch für Verwaltung, Handel und Verkehr)* electronic data interchange for administration, commerce and transport (EDIFACT), *(~er Einkommensnachweis/Entgeltnachweis)* electronic remuneration certification
(~e Einreichung) electronic presentation (submission), *(~es Geld)* electronic money, e-money, e-cash, *(~e Geldbörse)* electronic purse, electronic wallet, *(~er Geschäftsverkehr)* electronic commerce, E-Commerce, *(~es Handelsregister)* electronic commercial register, → EHUG, *(~es Handelssystem)* electronic trading system □ automated system providing order routing, quotation, clearing, and settlement services
(~er Handelsplatz) electronic trading venue, *(~e Initiierung von Zahlungen)* electronic payment initiation, *(~er Kontoauszug/Kontoinformation)* electronic account statement/information, *(~es Lastschriftverfahren)* electronic direct debit, *(~e Legitima-*

E

E

tion) electronic ID verification, *(~er Massenzahlungsverkehr)* electronic retail payments, *(~es Orderleitsystem)* electronic order routing system *(~e Rechnungstellung)* e-Invoicing, *(~es Rückverfolgungssystem)* electronic tracking system, *(~er Schalter)* electronic counter arrangement, *(~e Signatur/Signierung)* electronic signature/signing, *(~e Sperrliste)* electronic stoplist, electronic warning bulletin, *(~es Übertragungssystem)* electronic transmission (delivery) system *(~e Unterschrift)* electronic signature, *(~e Unterschriftenerfassung)* electronic signature capture, *(~er Verkaufspunkt)* electronic point of sale (EPOS), *(~e Wertpapierhandelsplattform)* Electronic Communication Networks, *(~er Zahlungsverkehr)* electronic funds transfer, *(~es Zahlungsverkehrssystem)* electronic funds transfer system (EFTS), electronic payments system, *(~es Zugriffsrecht)* electronic access right, *(~es Zuordnungssystem)* electronic matching system **2.** *adv. (~ übermitteln)* to forward by electronic means, *(~ zuordnen)* to match electronically

Elektrowerte electricals, electrical shares (stocks)

Elena → elektronischer Einkommensnachweis/Entgeltnachweis

Elferausschuss Central Capital Market Committee

ELV → elektronisches Lastschriftverfahren

Embargo embargo, ban

Emission 1. issue, offering **2.** *(Vorgang)* issuance, issuing, offering, launching an issue **3.** emission

Emissionen *(~ im Dollarbereich)* dollar-denominated issues, *(~ am Euroanleihemarkt)* issues in the Eurobond market, *(~ der öffentlichen Hand/öffentlicher Schuldner)* public sector issues, *(~ im Tenderverfahren)* issues by tender, *(~ festverzinslicher Werte)* issues of fixed income securities, fixed rate offerings, straight bond issues

Emissions / ~abteilung new issues department; **~adresse** name, *(erstklassige Emissionsadresse)* top-quality name in the primary market, prime issuer; **~agio 1.** issuing premium **2.** *(Eigenkapitalposition)* share premium account

Emissions / ~angebot 1. securities offering **2.** offer to handle a flotation (a securities issue); **~ankündigung** new issue announcement; **~aufgeld** → Emissionsagio; **~aufstockung** topping up an issue

Emissions / ~bank 1. underwriting house, issuing bank, investment bank **2.** *(Notenbank)* bank of issue; **~bedarf** new issue requirements; **~bedingungen** terms of an issue, offering terms, bond features, *(~ am Markt)* issuing conditions in the market

Emissionsberechtigung emission allowance, *(Handel in ~en)* trading in emission allowances, *(Überschuss an ~en)* excess emission allowances

Emissionsbetrag 1. amount of an issue, principal **2.** issuing total, *(Emissionsbeträge, die nicht bei Anlegern untergebracht werden konnten)* securities not taken up by investors

Emissions / ~dauer issuing (offering) period; **~disagio** issuing discount; **~erlös** proceeds of an issue, issuing proceeds (receipts), proceeds of the flotation

emissionsfähig *(~es Unternehmen)* company able to access the capital market, company able to gain financing in the public bond market, *(für Commercial Paper)* corporation qualifying as CP issuer

Emissionsfähigkeit debt issue ability, ability to access the capital market, ability to launch an issue in the capital market

Emissions / ~fahrplan issuing timetable (calendar), timetable of new issues, running order of new issues;

~**flaute** standstill in the new issue market; ~**flut** flood of new issues

Emissions / ~**form** 1. issuance procedure (method) 2. type of offering; ~**führerschaft** lead management

Emissions / ~**genehmigung** issuing approval, authorisation to issue; ~**genehmigungsverfahren** issue authorisation procedure; ~**geschäft** debt and equity origination, issuing business (operations), new issue activities; ~**gläubiger** issuing creditor, bond creditor

Emissionshandel emissions trading, *(Deutsche Emissionshandelsstelle)* German Emissions Trading Authority

Emissions / ~**haus** issuing (underwriting) house; ~**höchstgrenze** issuing limit (cap); ~**höhe** size (magnitude) of an issue; ~**inventar** emissions inventory; ~**jahr** year of issue

Emissions / ~**kalender** issuing timetable (calendar), calendar of new issues, schedule of upcoming offerings; ~**käufer** investor, buyer of an issue; ~**konditionen** terms of issue, issuing (offering) terms

Emissions / ~**konsortium** issuing (underwriting) syndicate; ~**kontrolle** new issue control, primary market control; ~**kosten** issuing (flotation) cost, issuance (offering) cost, debt issuance cost

Emissionskredit 1. *(des Emittenten)* issuer's credit, standing (rating) of an issuer 2. *(der Emissionsbank)* standing of the issuing house (of the underwriter) 3. *(Kreditvergabe an den Emittenten einer Neuemission)* loan against newly issued securities

Emissions / ~**kurs** issuing (issue, offering) price, coming-out price; ~**mandat** mandate to arrange an issue, flotation (issuance) mandate; ~**markt** new issue market, primary market; ~**merkmale** features (characteristics) of an issue, bond features

Emissions / ~ **minderung** emissions reduction; ~**minderungszertifikat** emission reductions certificate

Emissions / ~**nebenkosten** ancillary issuance cost; ~**obergrenze** issuing ceiling (cap), ceiling on the issuing amount; ~**paket** issue package; ~**pause** halt in new issues, temporary issuing freeze; ~**platzierung** placing (of) an issue; ~**politik** new issue policy

Emissions / ~**preis** issuing (offering) price; ~**prospekt** issuing (underwriting) prospectus, offering prospectus, *(vorläufiger Prospekt)* red herring; ~**quote** underwriting share, share in an issue; ~ **rating** issue credit rating

Emissionsrechte emission allowances, *(am Terminmarkt gehandelte ~)* emission allowances traded in the forward market; ~**handel** emission allowance trading

Emissions / ~ **reihe** issuing series; ~**rendite** issuing yield, yield upon issue; ~**risiko** issuing (underwriting) risk; ~**schuldner** issuing (bond) debtor; ~**sperre** ban on new issues, issuing freeze

Emissions / ~**staffelungsregelung** staggering arrangements for new issues; ~**standing** issuer's (issuing) credit, issuer's standing; ~**stelle** fiscal agent; ~**syndikat** issuing syndicate

Emissions / ~**tätigkeit** issuing (new issue) activities, *(~ am Eurokapitalmarkt)* issuing activity (underwriting operations) in the Eurobond market; ~**technik** issuing techniques; ~**tranche** issue (offering) tranche

Emissions / ~**überhang** oversupply of new issues; ~**übernahme** underwriting (of) an issue, *(~ auf Kommissionsbasis)* taking up an issue on a commission basis, *(~ zur Verkaufsvermittlung)* sale of a security issue on a best efforts basis; ~**übernahmeverpflichtung** commitment to take up an issue, underwriting commitment, undertaking to underwrite

Emissions / ~**umfang** issue (issuing) size, size of an issue; ~**umlauf** securities (bonds/notes) outstanding; ~**unterbringung** placing (placement of)

E

E

an issue; ~**unternehmer** issuing (underwriting) house

Emissions / ~verfahren issuing method (procedure), offering method; ~**vertrag** *(mit dem Konsortialführer)* letter of engagement, underwriting agreement; ~**volumen** *(einer Anleihe)* total amount issued, issuing total (volume); ~**vorhaben** new issue project

Emissions / ~währung issuing (offering) currency; ~**warteliste** queuing list for new issues; ~**warteschlange** new issue queue; ~**welle** spate (flood, surge) of new issues; ~**wert** face value (principal) of an issue

Emissions / ~zeitpunkt date of issue, launching date, *(den ~ abstimmen)* to agree on the timing of the issue, *(zum ~)* at the time of issuance; ~**zertifikate** emissions certificates; ~**zins** issuing coupon, interest rate upon issue

Emittent issuer, *(~ des öffentlichen Sektors)* public sector issuer

Emittenten / ~bonität issuer's credit standing; ~**gruppe** group of issuers; ~**rating** issuer credit rating; ~**risiko** issuer risk, issuer-related risk, possibility that an issuer fails to pay interest and/or principal when due

emittierbar issuable

emittieren to issue, to offer, to launch, to float, *(mit Laufzeiten von drei oder mehr Jahren ~)* to issue for terms of three years or more, *(als Namenspapier/Inhaberpapier ~)* to issue as a security in registered form/in bearer form
(über pari ~) to issue above par, to offer at a premium, *(unter pari ~)* to issue below par, to offer at a discount, *(zu pari/zum Nennwert) ~* to issue at par, to offer at par, *(auf dem Submissionsweg ~)* to issue by tender

Empfang 1. receipt **2.** welcome

Empfänger recipient, *(auf Verschiffungsdokumenten)* consignee, *(im Zahlungsverkehr)* recipient, payee, remittee; ~**bank** recipient (receiving) bank; ~**konto** receiving account, beneficiary's account; ~**land** recipient country

empfangsberechtigt authorised to accept (to receive)

Empfangs / ~berechtigter authorised recipient; ~**bevollmächtigter** authorised receiving agent; ~**datum** date of receipt

Empfangs / ~konnossement received for shipment bill of lading; ~**schein 1.** *(allgemein)* receipt **2.** *(bei Übernahme der Güter an Bord)* mate's receipt **3.** *(bei Abladung am Kai)* quay receipt

empfehlen 1. *(Anlagen ~)* to recommend investments, to make investment recommendations **2.** *(raten)* to advise **3.** *(es empfiehlt sich)* it is advisable

empfehlenswert advisable, expedient, *(~e Anlage)* recommendable investment

Empfehlung 1. recommendation, *(auf ~ von)* at (on) the recommendation of **2.** *(Rat)* advice **3.** *(Referenz) (erstklassige ~en)* first-class references

Empfehlungsschreiben letter of recommendation (of reference)

emporschießen/emporschnellen *(Kurse)* to soar, to rocket, to zoom

EMZ → elektronischer Massenzahlungsverkehr

End / ~abnehmer ultimate buyer (user); ~**abrechnung** final (closing) statement, final account; ~**ausschüttung** final distribution (payout)

End / ~begünstigter ultimate beneficiary, ultimate party to be credited; ~**bestand 1.** closing balance **2.** closing inventory; ~**betrag** total amount, total

Ende end, close, *(die Aufgabe zu ~ bringen)* to take the task to its conclusion, *(die Hausse scheint zu ~ zu gehen)* the bull run appears to peter out, *(am kurzen/langen ~ des Marktes)* at the short/long end of the market

enden 1. to end, to come to an end, to run out, *(der Kreditvertrag endet am*

...) the loan agreement runs out (expires) on ... **2.** to close

Ende-zu-Ende Abwicklung end-to-end settlement

endfällige Anleihe bullet bond (issue) □ bond issue with a single repayment of the principal on the maturity date

endfälliges Darlehen maturity (bullet) loan, interest-only loan □ the borrower makes monthly interest payments with the total principal due at final maturity

endfällige Kapitalerträge investment income paid wholly on the maturity date

Endfälligkeit final maturity, maturity date, stated maturity, *(bis zur ~ gehaltene Finanzinvestitionen)* financial investments held to maturity

endgültig 1. *(~e Antwort)* definite (conclusive) answer, *(~e Entscheidung)* final (irrevocable, non-appealable) decision, *(~ finanzierender Darlehensgeber)* ultimate lender, *(~e Finanzierung)* permanent financing, *(~es Zertifikat)* definitive certificate, *(~er Zahlungsausgleich)* final payment (settlement)
2. *(~e Käufe/Verkäufe)* outright transactions, *(~e Offenmarktgeschäfte)* outright open market transactions

Endgültigkeit finality, definitiveness, *(~ des Zahlungsausgleichs)* settlement finality, → Richtlinie über die Endgültigkeit von Zahlungen

End / ~kapital principal upon maturity, capital repayable upon maturity; **~kreditnehmer** ultimate (final) borrower; **~kundenbetreuung** servicing end customers; **~kundengeschäft** business to customer (B2C) transactions

End / ~kursquotierung quotation of the final price; **~phase** *(in die ~ eintreten)* to enter its final phase; **~saldo 1.** final balance **2.** net balance; **~valuta** final value date

Energie / ~darlehen/~kredit energy loan; **~derivate** energy derivatives; **~finanzierung** *(Finanzierung erneuerbarer Energien)* renewable energy financing; **~terminkontrakte** energy futures; **~werte** energy stock, resource stock

eng 1. *adj. (~e Geschäftsbeziehung)* close business relationship, *(~er Markt)* narrow (thin, limited) market, *(~e Spanne)* narrow (tight) margin
2. *adv. (~ zusammenhängen mit)* to be closely associated with, *(eng verbundene Währungen)* closely correlated currencies, *(~gefasste Geldmenge)* narrow monetary aggregate, → Geldmenge M1

Engagement 1. commitment, *(~ ausländischer Anleger)* foreign investors' involvement, *(zu hohes ~ am Aktienmarkt)* overcommitment in stocks, *(~ im Privatkundenbereich)* involvement in retail banking, *(~s mit hohem Risikocharakter)* high-risk commitments, *(~ am Terminmarkt)* forward market commitments
2. *(Kreditengagement)* loan commitment, loan (lending) exposure, *(~ im Hypothekenbereich)* mortgage loan exposure (commitments), mortgage lendings, mortgage loan portfolio, *(~ am Interbankenmarkt)* exposure in the interbank market
(~ in langfristigen Krediten) long-term loan exposure, long-term lendings, *(Gesamtsumme der ~s gegenüber Nichtbanken)* total lendings to non-bank customers, *(~ gegenüber Problemschuldnerländern)* exposure (commitments) to problem debtor countries
3. *(Wertpapierinvestment)* investment, holdings, exposure, *(~ in Aktien/am Aktienmarkt)* exposure (investment) in stocks, stock market exposure, share (equity) investments, *(~ in Dollartiteln)* investment in dollar securities, buying of dollar securities, *(~ in Rentenwerten)* bond exposure, investments in bonds

E

E

Engagement / ~bewertung exposure assessment; **~obergrenze** exposure limit; ~ **prüfung** checking the credit-worthiness of a borrower, credit investigation (assessment); **~überwachung** exposure monitoring, monitoring a loan commitment, exposure control

engagieren 1. *(sich ~)* to commit o.s., to get (to be) involved, *(sich stark in Aktien ~)* to pile money into equities, *(sich stärker im Firmenkundengeschäft ~)* to expand the corporate banking activities, *(sich mit neuen Krediten ~)* to increase the loan exposure, to extend fresh money, *(sich am Markt ~)* to commit funds to the market, to invest funds in the market
2. *(anstellen)* to employ, to recruit, to hire, to take on

engagiert *(stark in Aktien ~ sein)* to be heavily invested (weighted) in equities, *(wir sind mit ca. 3 Mio. € ~)* our exposure totals approximately € 3m, we are committed with approximately € 3m, *(~er Mitarbeiter)* committed staff member

Enge narrowness, tightness

Engpass bottleneck

Enkelgesellschaft sub-subsidiary, second-tier subsidiary

entbinden 1. *(von der Haftung ~)* to release (to relieve) from liability
2. *(von der Leistungspflicht ~)* to relieve of the duty to perform, *(von einer Verpflichtung ~)* to discharge (to release) from an obligation, to dispense from an obligation

Entbindung release, discharge, relief, *(~ von der Leistungspflicht)* discharge of performance

enteignen to expropriate

Enteignung expropriation, compulsory purchase, taking by eminent domain, condemnation

Enteignungsbeschluss/~verfügung expropriation order, compulsory purchase order

entfallen 1. to account for, *(30 % der Neuausleihungen ~ auf langfristige Kredite)* long-term loans account for 30 p.c. of new lendings, long-term loans make up 30 p.c. of new lendings
2. to attribute,to allot, *(die auf Aktien ~den Bezugsrechte)* subscription rights attributed to shares, *(die auf das folgende Jahr ~den Diskonterträge)* discount earnings relating to the following year, *(einschließlich der darauf ~den Zinsen)* including interest accruing thereon, *(auf jmd. ~)* to be allotted to s. o.
3. *(wegfallen)* to be dropped (omitted, cancelled)

entfalten to display, to unfold, to exhibit, *(umfangreiche Aktivitäten ~)* to develop considerable activities

entflechten to demerge, to decentralise, to divest, to decartelise

Entflechtung demerger, decentralisation, divestiture

entgegengesetzt contrary, opposite, *(~ sein)* to be contrary (opposed) to, *(~e Interessen)* conflicting interests, *(~e Wirkung)* opposite effect, *(sich in die ~e Richtung entwickeln)* to go into the reverse

entgegenkommen 1. *(einem Kunden/Kreditnehmer ~)* to accommodate (to oblige) a customer/borrower, *(entgegenkommender Weise haben wir die Bereitstellungsprovision um 10 % reduziert)* we have obligingly reduced the commitment commission by 10 p.c.
2. to make concessions

Entgegenkommen 1. accommodation, favour, goodwill, obligingness **2.** concession

Entgegennahme acceptance, receipt, *(~ von Kauf- oder Verkaufsorders)* order taking

entgegennehmen 1. *(Gelder/Einlagen ~)* to accept funds/deposits **2.** *(eine gerichtliche Zustellung ~)* to accept service of process

entgegensetzen *(der Übernahme keinen Widerstand ~)* to put up no resistance to the takeover

entgegenstehen 1. *(im Widerspruch stehen zu)* to conflict with, to be in contrast with, *(~ de Interessen)* conflicting interests, *(~de Vereinbarungen)* agreements to the contrary
2. *(behindern)* to impede, to bar, *(einer Kurserholung ~)* to stand in the way of (to preclude) a price rally

entgegenwirken to counter, to counteract, to run counter to, *(dem Trend durch Rationalisierungsmaßnahmen ~)* to counter the trend through rationalisation measures, *(dem Zinsanstieg ~)* to counter (to take steps against) the rise in interest rates

entgehen 1. *(der Insolvenz ~)* to escape (to avoid) insolvency
2. *(übersehen)* to miss, to fail to notice, *(es ist uns entgangen)* we failed to notice, it escaped our notice
3. *(verlieren)* to forego, *(entgangener Gewinn/entgangene Zinserträge)* foregone (lost) profit/interest income

Entgelt 1. (monetary) consideration **2.** *(Gebühr)* fee, charge, *(Entgelte für Schulden)* interest expense **3.** *(Prämie)* premium **4.** *(Vergütung)* fee, remuneration, *(erhaltene Entgelte)* fee income

Entgelt / ~abzug deduction of a fee, fee deducted (withheld); **~belastung** debiting (charging) a fee; **~berechtigung** fee entitlement; **~ einnahmen** fee income, premiums received

Entgelt / ~erstattung reimbursement of a fee, fee refund; **~forderung** remuneration claim, *(pl)* fees receivable; **~grenze** fee cap; **~konzept** remuneration concept; **~leistungspflicht** fee payment obligation

entgeltlich against payment, for good and valuable consideration

Entgelt / ~offenlegung fee disclosure; **~pflichtiger** payor; **~regelung** fee assessment rules; **~sätze 1.** tariff of charges **2.** premium rates; **~teilung** fee sharing; **~umwandlung** *(i. S. einer Gehaltsumwandlung)* conversion of salary entitlements into pension entitlements; **~zahlung** payment of a monetary consideration

enthaften to discharge (to release) from liability

Enthaftung liability discharge

Enthaftungs / ~erklärung liability release form, release from liability statement; **~ klausel** disclaimer, hold harmless (non-responsibility) clause

enthalten 1. to contain, to include, *(ein Kreditrisiko ~)* to contain (to involve) a credit risk **2.** *(umfassen)* to comprise **3.** *(sich der Stimme ~)* to abstain from voting

entheben *(jmd. eines Amtes ~)* to relieve s. o. of a post, to remove s. o. from office

Entherrschungsvereinbarung decontrolling agreement

entkonsolidieren to deconsolidate

Entkonsolidierungs/~erfolg/~gewinn deconsolidation gain; **~stichtag** deconsolidation date

entladen to unload, to discharge, *(eine Geldkarte ~)* to unload a paycard

Entladung unloading, discharge

entlassen 1. *(aus einem Arbeitsverhältnis ~)* to dismiss, to lay off **2.** *(aus einer Verpflichtung ~)* to release (to discharge, to relieve) from an obligation, *(den Garantiegeber aus der Haftung ~)* to discharge (to release) the guarantor from liability

Entlassung 1. dismissal, laying off, redundancy
2. release, discharge, *(~ der Bank aus ihrer Garantie)* releasing the bank of (from) its guarantee, *(~ des Bürgen aus seiner Haftung)* discharge of the guarantor from liability, *(~ aus der Wechselhaftung)* discharge (release) from liability on a bill

Entlassungsabfindung severance payment, redundancy compensation

E

E

entlasten 1. to relieve, to unburden, to ease (to alleviate, to lower, to lighten) the burden, *(die Bilanz ~)* to relieve the balance sheet, to take off the books (the balance sheet), to relieve the pressure on the balance sheet, *(finanziell ~)* to provide financial assistance, to ease the financial strain, to extend fresh money, to reduce the debt load, *(steuerlich ~)* to reduce the tax burden
2. *(die Amtsführung billigen)* to grant discharge, to approve of the conduct of office, *(mit entlastender Wirkung)* with discharging effect
3. to clear from a charge, to exonerate

Entlastung 1. relief, relieving, easing (reducing) the burden, *(~ von Altverbindlichkeiten)* debt relief, reducing the existing debt load, → Entschuldung, *(~ der Bilanz)* balance sheet relief, taking off the books, *(~ der Eigenkapitalrelation)* easing the pressure on the capital ratio, *(~ der Grundsätze I und II)* easing the regulatory requirements stipulated under Principles I and II
2. granting discharge, giving approval, formal approval of s.o.'s conduct of office/activities, *(~ des Vorstandes)* discharge of (granting discharge to) the Board of Management, *(Verweigerung der ~)* refusal to grant discharge

Entlastungs / ~betrag allowance, tax relief; **~gesetz** German Tax Relief Act

entleihen to borrow, *(entliehene Wertpapiere)* securities borrowed

Entleihen *(von Wertpapieren)* borrowing of securities

Entleiher borrower (of securities)

Entleiherposition borrowing position, borrower's position (exposure)

Entleihgebühr borrowing fee

Entlohnung *(~ auf Honorarbasis)* fee-based remuneration

Entmaterialisierung *(~ von Wertpapieren)* dematerialisation of securities, converting physical shares to securities in electronic form

Entnahme 1. withdrawal, drawing, *(~ aus einem Depot)* withdrawal from a securities account, sale against (transfer from) a securities account, *(~ der Gesellschafter)* drawings by the partners, distributions to the partners *(~ aus einbehaltenen Gewinnen)* transfer from retained profits, *(~ von Kapital)* capital takedown, capital withdrawal, drawing on the capital account, *(~ aus Rücklagen)* reserve drawings
2. *(~ von Stichproben)* taking samples

Entnahmeplan withdrawal plan

entnehmen 1. to draw, to withdraw, *(aus der gesetzlichen Rücklage/der Kapitalrücklage/der Tilgungsreserve ~)* to draw on the legal reserve/on the capital reserve/on the redemption reserve *(entnommener Gewinn)* profit (income) withdrawn, distributed profit, *(nicht entnommener Gewinn)* retained (undistributed) profit, *(entnommene Stücke)* securities sold (withdrawn), securities transferred
2. *(Stichproben)* to sample, to take samples

entrichten to pay, to settle, *(im voraus ~)* to pay in advance, *(voll ~)* to pay in full

Entry Standard segment of the exchange-regulated unofficial market (→ Freiverkehr) of Deutsche Börse; established for mid caps seeking a share listing with less stringent requirements. → Prime/General Standard, → First/Second Quotation Board

entschädigen 1. to indemnify, to compensate for, to make up for, *(für einen Verlust ~)* to compensate for a loss
2. *(zurückerstatten)* to refund, to repay

Entschädigung 1. indemnity, indemnification, *(~ für die vorzeitige Rückzahlung)* prepayment indemnity, *(~ für erlittene Verluste)* compensation for losses sustained 2. *(Rückerstattung)* refund, repayment 3. *(Schadenersatz)* damages 4. *(Vergütung, Entgelt)* remuneration

Entschädigungsanspruch right to indemnification (to compensation)

entschädigungsberechtigt entitled to compensation (an indemnity)

Entschädigungseinrichtung deutscher Banken German Banks' Compensation Scheme

Entschädigungseinrichtung der Wertpapierhandelsunternehmen Securities Trading Firms' Compensation Scheme

Entschädigungs / ~fonds compensation (indemnification) fund; **~forderung** claim for indemnification, compensation claim; **~garantie** letter of indemnity

Entschädigungs / ~klage action for damages; **~klausel** indemnification (compensation) clause; **~leistung** indemnification, → Entschädigungszahlung

Entschädigungs / ~pflicht duty to compensate (for loss), obligation to indemnify, *(entschädigungspflichtig)* liable to pay compensation; **~schuldverschreibung** indemnification bond; **~summe** indemnity, amount of compensation; **~vorrisiko** aggregate first loss risk

Entschädigungszahlung compensation payment, payment of damages, *(~ für eine vorzeitige Vertragsbeendigung)* break-up fee, breakage cost

entschärfen *(die Liquiditätskrise ~)* to alleviate (to mitigate, to ease) the liquidity crisis

Entschärfung alleviation, mitigation, easing

entscheiden 1. to decide (e. g. on a loan application) 2. *(beilegen)* to settle 3. *(festlegen)* to determine 4. *(urteilen)* to rule, to judge, to pass judgment 5. *(sich ~ für)* to make up one's mind, to elect, to opt for

entscheidend 1. *adj.* *(~er Einfluss)* decisive influence, *(~er Faktor)* crucial (deciding) factor, *(~e Stimme)* decisive (casting) vote 2. *adv.* *(~ von der Zinsentwicklung abhängen)* to depend crucially (essentially) on the direction of interest rates, *(~ für das Ergebnis sein)* to be crucial to the outcome, to be pivotal to the performance, *(~ für das Unternehmensimage)* central to the company's image

Entscheidung 1. decision, *(hinsichtlich der Kreditverlängerung zu einer ~ kommen)* to come to (to arrive at) a decision as to the renewal of the loan facility 2. *(Entschlossenheit)* determination 3. *(Urteil)* ruling, judgement, court decision

Entscheidungs / ~baum decision tree; **~befugnis** authority to decide, decision-making power (authority), *(eines Kreditsachbearbeiters)* approval powers, lending authority, *(entscheidungsbefugt sein)* to hold the decision-making authority; **~ebene** decision-making level

Entscheidungs / ~findung decision-making; **~freiheit** freedom of decision; **~gewalt** decision-making authority; **~gremium** decision-making body; **~kompetenz** decision-making power; **~rechnung** decision accounting; **~träger** decision-maker; **~wege** decision-making channels

Entschließung resolution, *(mit Stimmenmehrheit verabschiedete ~)* majority resolution, resolution passed by the majority of votes

Entschließungsentwurf draft resolution

Entschlossenheit determination, firmness, decidedness

Entschlüsselung decoding, decryption

Entschlüsselungsschlüssel decryption key

Entschluss decision, resolution

entschulden 1. *(vollständig)* to clear (to repay) the debt, to disencumber 2. *(teilweise)* to ease the debt burden, to ease the level of indebtedness, to reduce the debt load, to deleverage

E

Entschuldung 1. debt clearance (repayment), repayment of debt, disencumbrance, remission of debt **2.** debt relief, deleveraging, decreasing the financial leverage, easing the debt burden

Entschuldungs / ~prozess debt relief process, deleveraging process; **~verfahren 1.** debt discharge proceedings, disencumbrance proceedings **2.** → Entschuldungsprozess

entsenden to delegate to, *(in den Verwaltungsrat ~)* to appoint to the Board

Entsendungsrecht power of appointment (of delegation)

Entspannung *(~ an den Devisenmärkten)* easing (lessening) of tension in the currency markets

entsprechen 1. to correspond with (to), to conform (to be in conformity) with, to match, to be in line with, *(dem aktuellen Marktwert ~)* to match the current market value, *(die Zinssätze ~ den Marktgegebenheiten)* interest rates reflect the conditions in the market
2. *(erfüllen)* to meet, to satisfy, *(den Bonitätsanforderungen ~)* to meet the required credit (financial) standing, *(den Bonitätsanforderungen nicht ~)* to fall short of (to fail to meet) the required credit standards, *(den Erwartungen der Aktienanleger ~)* to meet (to match, to live up to) the expectations of equity investors, *(der Marktnachfrage ~)* to meet market demand
3. *(sich halten an)* to comply with, to observe, to abide by, *(den Akkreditivbedingungen ~)* to comply with (to observe) the terms and conditions of the documentary credit, *(den gesetzlichen Formalitäten ~)* to comply with the legal formalities, *(den Gesellschaftsstatuten ~)* to observe the articles of association

entsprechend 1. *adj* corresponding, *(~e Ansparung)* commensurate (adequate) savings, *(~e Buchung)* corresponding entry, *(Rückkauf zu einem dem Marktwert ~en Preis)* repurchase at a price equal to the market value
2. *adv.* correspondingly, *(den Zinssatz ~ erhöhen)* to raise the interest rate accordingly, *(~ anwenden)* to apply accordingly, *(Abschnitt 4 gilt ~)* section 4 shall apply mutatis mutandis
3. *prep.* according (pursuant) to, *(~ Ihren Anweisungen)* in accordance (in line, in compliance) with your instructions, *(den Risiken ~)* commensurate with the risks involved

Entsprechenserklärung statement of compliance

entstehen 1. to emerge, to develop, to spring up **2.** *(hervorgehen)* to arise, to result from **3.** to incur, to accrue, *(die dem Kreditgeber ~den Kosten)* the costs incurred by the lender

Entstehen 1. emergence, development, *(~ eines CP-Marktes)* emergence of a commercial paper market, *(ein im ~ begriffener Markt)* a market in the making
2. origination, *(~ einer Forderung)* origination of a claim (debt), *(~ eines Grundpfandrechtes)* creation (origination) of a charge over property, *(~ eines Zahlungsanspruchs)* origination of a claim to payment
3. *(~ des Klageanspruchs)* accrual of the cause of action, *(~ einer Verpflichtung)* accrual of an obligation

Entstehungskurs *(zum ~)* at the rate prevailing at the time of purchase or sale

entwerfen 1. *(eine Strategie ~)* to design (to devise, to map out, to work out) a strategy **2.** *(einen Vertrag ~)* to draft (to draw up) an agreement

entwerten 1. *(ungültig machen)* to invalidate, to cancel, to obliterate **2.** *(im Wert mindern)* to devalue, to depreciate

Entwertung 1. invalidation, cancellation **2.** devaluation, depreciation

entwickeln 1. to develop, to evolve, to grow **2.** to design, to devise **3.** *(sich entfalten, entstehen)* to unfold, to emerge, to arise

Entwicklung 1. development, evolution, growth, progress, *(~ en im Privatkundengeschäft)* developments in retail banking **2.** design **3.** performance, *(~ des Aktienkurses)* share price performance **4.** trend, *(Unsicherheit über die weitere ~der Zinssätze)* uncertainty over the further trend in interest rates

Entwicklungs / ~abteilung research and development (R&D) division; **~aufwand** expenditure on research and development; **~bank** development bank, development finance institution; **~darlehen** development loan; **~finanzierung 1.** development finance **2.** microfinance

entwirren to disentangle, to unravel, to straighten out

Entwurf 1. *(eines Vertrages/Vortrages)* draft **2.** *(Konzept)* concept, plan, design, blueprint **3.** *(Entwerfen)* drafting, mapping out, working out, *(~ des Nachtragshaushaltes)* draft of the supplementary budget

entziehen 1. withdraw, to deprive of, *(die Unterschriftsberechtigung ~)* to revoke the signing power (signature authority)
2. to drain, to skim (to siphon) off, *(dem Bankensystem Liquidität ~)* to drain (to sap) liquidity from the banking system
3. *(sich ~)* to evade, to dodge, *(sich dem negativen Trend ~)* to buck the negative trend, *(sich seinen Garantieverpflichtungen ~)* to evade (to disavow) one's obligations under the guarantee

Entziehen/Entzug 1. withdrawal, *(~ der Vollmacht)* revocation of the power of attorney, *(~ des Nutznießungsrechtes)* deprivation of enjoyment **2.** drain, skimming off **3.** *(Enteignung)* dispossession

EONIA Euro Overnight Index Average □ EONIA, the reference interest rate for the euro, is computed as the weighted average of all overnight unsecured lending transactions in the interbank market

EONIA Feststellung EONIA fixing

EONIA Future □ based on the EONIA monthly average

EONIA Spread □ spread between EONIA and the key policy rate (zentraler Leitzins) of the European Central Bank, i.e. the minimum bid rate (Mindestbietungssatz) in the Eurosystem's main refinancing transactions

EONIA Swap □ descriptive of an interest rate swap where fixed rate payments are swapped against variable interest rate payments linked to EONIA rates

EONIA Swap Index Average average rate of the daily quotations of prime panel banks for EONIA swaps; benchmark for euro moneymarket derivatives

EÖ-Verfahren *(elektronische Öffnung)* electronic access procedure

EPG → Europäische Privatgesellschaft

ERA → Einheitliche Richtlinien und Gebräuche für Dokumentenakkreditive

erachten *(für notwendig ~)* to consider (to deem) necessary

Erb / ~anspruch 1. *(Forderung)* claim to an inheritance **2.** *(Recht)* right of inheritance; **~anteil** share in an inheritance; **~ausschlagung** → Erbverzicht

Erb / ~bauberechtigter holder of a building lease; **~baugrundbuch** register of leasehold interests; **~baurecht** hereditary building right, building lease; **~bauzins** ground rent

Erb / ~berechtigter 1. heir **2.** legitimate successor; **~berechtigung** right of inheritance, title to an inheritance, *(erbberechtigt)* entitled (by law) to inherit

Erbe 1. heir, successor **2.** *(Erbschaft)* inheritance, estate, estate assets

Erbeinsetzung appointment (institution) of an heir

erben to inherit, to take by inheritance, to come into an inheritance, to succeed to

Erben / **~gemeinschaft** community of heirs, heirs to an estate; **~haftung** liability of the heirs

erbfähig capable of inheriting, qualified to inherit

E

Erb / **~fähigkeit** capacity (qualification) to inherit; **~folge** **1.** succession, *(im Wege der ~ übergehen)* to pass by way of succession **2.** order of succession, legal order of succeeding; **~folgerecht** law of succession

Erb / **~lasser/~lasserin** testator, testatrix, descendent; **~lasserschulden** testator debts; **~masse** estate assets; **~nachweis** proof of inheritance, grant of probate; **~pacht** building lease; **~pflichtteil** statutory (forced) share; **~recht** **1.** right of inheritance, title to an inheritance **2.** law of succession

erbrechtlich *(~ e Ansprüche)* claims under inheritance law, inheritance rights

erbringen **1.** *(bereitstellen)* to furnish, *(den Nachweis ~)* to submit (to produce) evidence, to furnish proof, *(eine Sicherheitsleistung ~)* to furnish (to deposit) collateral, *(bei Börsentermingeschäften)* to put up a margin, *(erbrachte Gegenleistung)* value given (furnished)
2. *(einbringen)* to yield, to net, *(einen angemessenen Gewinn ~)* to yield a fair return, *(eine 6%ige Rendite ~)* to offer (to bring, to carry) a 6 p.c. yield
3. *(leisten)* to render, to effect, to perform, *(Leistungen ~)* to render (to provide) services, *(Provision für erbrachte Dienstleistungen)* commission for services rendered

Erbringung rendering, *(~ von Finanz-/Wertpapierdienstleistungen)* provision (performance) of financial services/investment services

Erbschaft inheritance

Erbschafts / **~annahme** acceptance of an inheritance; **~anspruch** claim to an inheritance; **~antritt** accession to an estate, entering upon an inheritance; **~aufteilung** distribution of an estate

Erbschafts / **~ausschlagung** disclaimer of inheritance; **~besteuerung** taxation of an estate, levying inheritance tax (succession duty); **~schulden** estate debts; **~steuer** inheritance tax, succession duty; **~steuererklärung** inheritance tax return

Erbschaftssteuer- und Schenkungsgesetz German Inheritance and Gift Tax Law

Erb / **~schein** certificate of inheritance; **~teil** share in an inheritance; **~teilung** division of an estate; **~unfähigkeit** incapacity to inherit; **~verzicht** waiver of right of inheritance, renunciation of inheritance

erdient *(~e Leistungsansprüche)* earned entitlements, vested (accumulated) benefits

Erdienungszeitraum vesting (accumulation) period

ereignen *(sich ~)* to happen, to occur

Ereignis event, occurrence, *(~ se höherer Gewalt)* force majeure events, *(~ se nach dem Bilanzstichtag)* events after the balance sheet date

ereignisbestimmt *(~e Vertragsklauseln)* event-driven covenants (contract provisions)

ereignisgesteuert *(~e Abwicklungs-/Prozesskette)* event-driven settlement/process chain

Ereignisrisiko event risk □ exposure to loss arising from a fall in a customer's/borrower's credit quality or rating due to unanticipated events (e.g. takeover, natural disaster) or changes in the market environment

erfahren *adj.* experienced, skilled, well-versed, *(~e Marktteilnehmer)* experienced market operators, old market hands
v. **1.** *(durchlaufen)* to experience, *(einen neuen Auftrieb ~)* to experience a new upsurge

2. *(erleiden)* to sustain, to undergo, *(hohe Verluste ~)* to sustain heavy losses, *(eine Wertminderung ~)* to suffer a depreciation
3. *(Kenntnis erhalten)* to learn, to hear, to come to know, *(aus zuverlässiger Quelle ~)* to learn from a reliable source

Erfahrung 1. experience, *(~ im Kreditgeschäft)* lending experience
2. *(mit umfangreicher ~ im Finanzsektor)* with a proven track record in the financial sector

Erfahrungsaustausch exchange of experience

erfahrungsgemäß as past experience has shown, to know from experience

Erfahrungskurve experience (learning) curve

Erfahrungswert experience, empirical value, *(die Annahmen basieren auf ~en)* assumptions are based on past experiences, *(auf der Basis historischer ~e ermitteln)* to determine on the basis of historical experiences, *(~e aufgrund früherer Forderungsausfälle)* past loss experience, *(~ e mit Kreditausfällen)* historical loss experience

erfassen 1. to capture, to include, to cover, *(alle Bereiche des Marktes wurden von der Aufwärtsbewegung erfasst)* all market sectors were caught up in the buoyancy, *(elektronisch ~)* to capture electronically, *(das Gesamtrisiko ~)* to capture (to catch) the total exposure, *(im Grundsatz I ~)* to cover by (to include in) Principle I
2. *(bilanzmäßig)* to recognise, *(als Aufwand ~)* to recognise as expense, *(in der Bilanz ~)* to report (to state, to recognise) in the financial statements, *(direkt im Eigenkapital ~)* to recognise directly in equity
3. to register, to record, *(in den Unterlagen der Bank ~)* to record on the books of the bank

Erfassung 1. capture, inclusion, including 2. registration, recording, *(~ als Ertrag oder Aufwand im Gewinn oder Verlust)* recognition as income or expense in profit or loss

Erfolg success, performance, profit, *(das Unternehmen arbeitet mit ausgezeichnetem ~)* the bank has an excellent performance record, *(die Emission wurde mit ~ begeben)* the issue was successfully launched, *(mit seinen Forderungen ~ haben)* to succeed in one's claims, *(die Neuemission verzeichnete einen großen ~)* the new issue was extremely well received

erfolgen to occur, to take place, *(Abschlüsse ~ in vier Währungen)* contracts are traded in four currencies

erfolglos *(~e Sanierungsbemühungen)* unsuccessful (failed, abortive) restructuring efforts

erfolgreich *(~e Handelsaktivitäten)* successful (thriving, prolific) trading activities

erfolgsabhängig *(~e Gebührenstruktur)* performance-linked pricing (fee) structure, *(~e Vergütung)* performance fee

Erfolgs / ~analyse profit (performance) analysis; **~aussichten** prospects of (for) success; **~ausweis** income reporting, *(periodengerechter ~)* reporting profit on an accrual basis; **~beitrag** profit contribution, *(~ beiträge aus Handelsgeschäften)* profit contributed from trading activities; **~beteiligung** profit-sharing, profit-sharing scheme

erfolgsbezogen *(~ e Vergütung)* performance-based remuneration

Erfolgs / ~bilanz performance record, track record; **~controlling** performance controlling; **~faktoren** profit factors (determinants); **~honorar** 1. success (performance) fee 2. *(eines Anwalts)* contingency fee; **~honorarvereinbarung** contingency fee agreement

Erfolgs / ~indikatoren performance indicators; **~kalkulation** performance accounting; **~kennzahl** performance

E

measure (indicator); ~**konsolidierung** consolidation of earnings; ~**konto** income (revenue) account; ~**kontrolle** performance control

Erfolgs / ~**maßstab** profit (performance) measure, benchmark (criterion) for performance; ~**messung** performance measurement

erfolgsneutral neutral in its effect on profits, *(~ ausgewiesen) (a)* shown with no effect on the net profit *(b)* not recorded in the income statement, *(~ erfassen)* to recognise with no effect on income, to recognise directly in equity

erfolgsorientiert *(~ er Anleger)* performance-focused investor

Erfolgs / ~**plan** profit plan (budget); ~**planung** profit planning; ~**quote** success rate

Erfolgs / ~**rechnung** **1.** income statement (account), profit and loss account, *(Erstellung einer ~)* profit accounting **2.** performance summary; ~**risiken** *(einer Bank)* performance risks □ credit, interest and currency risks; ~**verbuchung** revenue recognition

erfolgswirksam **1.** *adj. (~ e Verbuchung)* recognition in the income statement, treating as income, *(~e Verbuchung von Dividendenzahlungen)* income recognition of dividend payments, *(~ e Zuschreibung)* writeup taken to the income statement
2. *adv. (~ erfassen)* to recognise through profit and loss, to recognise in the income statement, to charge/ to credit to the profit and loss account

Erfolgsziffer **1.** performance measure **2.** profit ratio

erfolgversprechend promising

erforderlich required, necessary, requisite, *(nicht unbedingt ~)* not a mandatory requirement, *(die für die Fortsetzung unseres Engagements unbedingt ~en Tilgungszahlungen)* the repayments essential to continuing our loan accommodation *(die nach dem Verzug des Kreditnehmers ~en Maßnahmen)* the measures necessary to respond to the default of the borrower, *(~er Betrag stabiler Refinanzierung)* required amount of stable funding (RSF), → Strukturelle Liquiditätsquote

erfordern to require, to demand, to necessitate

Erfordernis requirement, condition, demand, necessity

erfragen to inquire, to make an inquiry

erfüllen **1.** to meet, *(die strengen Auflagen ~)* to meet (to observe, to comply with) the stringent requirements, *(die Erwartungen nicht ~)* to fail to live up to the expectations, to fall short of expectations, *(den Schuldendienst aus dem Cashflow ~)* to meet debt service payments out of internal cash flow
2. to perform, to fulfil(l), to discharge, *(seine vertragsgemäßen Verpflichtungen ~)* to fulfil (to perform) one's duties under the contract, to carry out one's contractual obligations, *(seine Verpflichtungen nicht ~)* to fail in one's obligations, to default on one's obligations, *(einen Vertrag ~)* to perform (to fulfil) a contract, *(die Zulassungsvoraussetzungen ~)* to satisfy the listing requirements, *(seinen Zweck ~)* to serve (to fulfil) its purpose
3. to settle, *(ein Börsengeschäft ~)* to settle (to clear) a stock exchange trade, to meet one's settlement obligations, *(einen Terminkontrakt physisch ~)* to settle a futures contract through delivery of the underlying instrument

Erfüllung **1.** meeting, compliance, *(~ von Lieferverpflichtungen)* meeting delivery commitments, *(~ der Mindestkapitalanforderungen)* compliance with the minimum capital requirements, *(~ der Stillhalterverpflichtungen)* meeting the delivery commitments under a short option position, *(~ einer Zielvorgabe)* meeting a target **2.** performance, fulfil(l)ment, discharge, *(~ der Bürgschaftsschuld)* discharge of the guarantee indebtedness, guarantee discharge, *(~ einer Verpflichtung)* performance (discharge) of an obligation, *(~ eines Vertrages)* performance of a contract, fulfilment of the obligations under a contract, compliance with (discharge of) contractual obligations, *(in ~ des Vertrages)* in satisfaction of the contract 3. settlement, *(~ zwei Arbeitstage nach Abschluss)* settlement two business days after trade date, *(~ im Ausland/im Inland)* settlement abroad/in Germany, *(~ durch Barausgleich)* cash settlement, *(~ von Börsengeschäften)* settlement of stock trades, *(~ durch Einigung)* settlement by mutual agreement, *(stückemäßige ~)* physical (non-cash) settlement, *(~ per Termin)* forward settlement, *(~ des Verkaufs)* making delivery under a selling transaction (under a short position)

Erfüllungs / **~ablehnung** refusal to perform; **~anspruch 1.** claim to performance, right to claim performance **2.** settlement claim; **~betrag** settlement amount; **~bürgschaft** performance guarantee

Erfüllungs / **~frist** settlement period; **~garantie 1.** performance guarantee (bond, warranty) **2.** settlement guarantee **3.** delivery guarantee

Erfüllungs / **~gehilfe** vicarious agent, → Verrichtungsgehilfe; **~geschäft** transaction in satisfaction of a contract of sale, delivery and/or payment under the contract

erfüllungshalber *(~ annehmen)* to accept with a view to performance, to accept conditionally, *(Leistung ~)* service with a view to performance □ i.e. full discharge of the debt/obligation is subject to final payment or to the creditor's satisfaction, → Erfüllungs Statt

Erfüllungs / **~hindernisse** impediments to performance; **~klage** action for specific performance; **~mangel** failure to perform (of performance)

Erfüllungs / **~ort** place of performance; **~periode 1.** settlement period **2.** *(im Hinblick auf zu unterhaltende Mindestreserven)* maintenance period; **~pflichten** performance obligations

Erfüllungsrisiko settlement (performance) risk, delivery risk □ risk of loss when a party fails to make a promised delivery or complete an agreed transaction, *(Erfüllungsrisiken bei Pensionsgeschäften)* settlement risks inherent in repurchase transactions

Erfüllungs statt *(an ~)* in discharge of, *(Leistung an ~)* accord and satisfaction □ full discharge of a debt/an obligation by a performance/service other than that which was originally required, → erfüllungshalber *(Leistung ~)*

Erfüllungs / **~tag/~termin** date of performance, settlement day, maturity (payment) date; **~theorie** performance theory □ requires delivery of the goods in conformity with the contract

Erfüllungs / **~verpflichtungen** settlement (delivery, payment) obligations; **~ verweigerung** refusal to perform, non-performance, repudiation of contract; **~wahl** *(des Insolvenzverwalters)* right to accept or to decline performance; **~währung** settlement currency; **~zeitpunkt** settlement date

ergänzen 1. to supplement, to complement, to add, *(sich produktmäßig ~)* to complement each other in the product range **2.** *(das Lager ~)* to replenish the stock **3.** *(vervollständigen)* to complete

ergänzend supplementary, complementary, additional, further, *(~es Eigenkapital)* → Ergänzungskapital

Ergänzung 1. supplement, complementing, addition **2.** replenishment **3.** completion

Ergänzungs / **~bestimmungen** supplementary provisions; **~darlehen** complementary loan (facility)

Ergänzungskapital *(under → Basel II rules)* Tier 2 capital, supplemen-

E

tary capital, → Ergänzungskapital 1.Klasse/2. Klasse

Ergänzungskapital 1. Klasse upper tier 2 capital □ consists of instruments that are essentially permanent in nature/ **2. Klasse** lower tier 2 capital □ consists of instruments that are not permanent in nature, e.g. term subordinated debt. The division of the tier 2 capital into upper and lower Tier 2 capital will be dropped under the new capital framework → Basel III

E

Ergänzungskapital *(under →Basel III rules)* Tier 2 capital □ consists largely of instruments that meet the relevant inclusion criteria, but are not included in Tier 1 Capital (→ Kernkapital, → Gesamtkapital). Given the objective to provide loss absorption on a gone-concern basis, Tier 2 Capital is also described as Gone-Concern capital.

Ergänzungs / ~kapitalanleihe supplementary capital bond; **~kredit** supplementary loan, fresh money; **~wahl** election to fill a vacancy

ergeben 1. *(entstehen)* to arise, to happen, *(sich aus dem Vertrag ~)* to arise from the contract **2.** *(führen zu)* to result in **3.** *(zeigen)* to show, to produce

Ergebnis 1. result, outcome, *(im ~)* on balance, as a result, in the final analysis, *(sich im ~ um 3 % erhöhen)* to increase on balance by 3 %
2. profit, income (or loss), performance, *(~ pro Aktie)* income/loss per share, per share performance, *(~ der gewöhnlichen Geschäftstätigkeit)* profit/loss on ordinary activities, earnings from current operations, *(~ nach Steuern und Anteilen Dritter)* income after taxes and minority interests
3. performance, *(~ im Kreditgeschäft)* performance of lending operations, *(~ im Privatkundenbereich)* performance in retail banking, figures on the retail business, *(ein gutes/schlechtes ~ erzielen)* to perform well/badly
4. *(Rendite, Verzinsung)* yield, return
5. *(Wirkung, Folge)* effect, impact, consequence

Ergebnis aus *(~ Anteilsbesitz/Anteilen an verbundenen Unternehmen)* net income (loss) from equity investments, *(~ der außerordentlichen Rechnung)* income (loss) from extraordinary accounts, *(~ dem Beteiligungs- und Wertpapierbestand)* net result on investments and securities portfolio, *(~ Derivaten)* net profit (loss) on derivatives
(~ dem Eigenhandel) profit/loss from proprietary trading activities, *(~ Finanzanlagen)* net investment income, net income (loss) from investment securities, *(~ der gewöhnlichen Geschäftstätigkeit)* result from (on) ordinary activities, earnings from current operations, *(~ Sicherungszusammenhängen)* net result on hedge accounting, *(~ Sondergeschäften)* gain/loss on exceptional transactions
(~ der Veräußerung von Sachanlagen) profit (loss) from the sale of fixed assets, *(~ dem Versicherungsgeschäft)* net profit (loss) from insurance operations, *(~ dem Wertpapiergeschäft)* securities trading income/loss, *(~ dem Wertpapier-Liquiditätsbestand)* result from liquidity portfolio operations

Ergebnisabführung profit transfer

Ergebnisabführungsvertrag profit and loss transfer agreement

ergebnisabhängig *(~e Ausschüttung)* results-based distribution (payout), *(~e Vergütung)* performance-related compensation, performance-linked fee

Ergebnis / ~analyse performance (profit) analysis; **~anreiz** profit incentive, incentive to strong performance; **~ausweis** *(~ des Konzerns)* group's statement of income; **~auswirkungen** consequences for (impact on) the company's performance

Ergebnis / ~beitrag profit contribution, contribution to profits (to earnings, to the performance); **~belastung** charge against earnings, burdening the performance, *(sich ergebnisbelastend auswirken)* to be a drag on earnings; ~**bewertung** performance assessment (measurement)

Ergebnis / ~**einbruch** sharp decline in the company's performance; ~**erwartung** expected performance, expected profit (loss); ~**erwartungswert** expected monetary value; ~**generierung** delivery of results; ~**glättung** smoothing of earnings

Ergebnis / ~**kennzahl** performance indicator, income ratio, *(pl)* key earnings figures; ~**kontrolle** performance (profit) control; ~**korrektur** performance adjustment, upgrading/downgrading the performance (the results); ~**liste** rankings

ergebnislos *(~ verlaufen)* to end inconclusively (without result), *(~e Bemühungen)* fruitless efforts, *(~e Gespräche)* inconclusive talks

ergebnisneutral with no effect on the income statement, excluding from the revenue results

ergebnisorientiert *(~e Gewinnbeteiligung)* results-based (performance-linked) profit-sharing scheme, *(~er Portefeuille-Manager)* performance-focused (performance-oriented, results-driven) portfolio manager

Ergebnis / ~**periodisierung** accrual basis of accounting; ~**plan** profit budget (plan); ~**planung** profit budgeting (planning), performance planning; ~**potenzial** *(~ eines Marktes)* market's profit potential; ~**publizität** publishing (disclosure of) the annual performance

Ergebnis / ~**qualität** earnings quality; ~**quote** ratio of profits before tax to average business volume; ~**rechnung** income statement, profit and loss account; ~**rückgang** decline in earnings (in performance); ~**rücklage** revenue reserve; ~**rückschlag** setback in performance

Ergebnis / ~**schwankungen** earnings volatility, fluctuations in performance (in the results); ~**steigerung** increase in performance, profit rise; ~**steuerung** performance control; ~**träger** performance pillar, mainstay of performance; ~**transparenz** transparency of results

Ergebnis / ~**übernahmevertrag** profit and loss pooling agreement; ~**überwachung** performance control, monitoring the performance; ~**unterschiede** *(~ bei Aktien und Anleihen)* divergence of performance between equities and bonds

Ergebnis / ~**verantwortung** performance responsibility, *(ergebnisverantwortlich)* responsible for the performance,accountable for the results; ~**verbesserung** improvement in the performance, enhanced performance, increase in profits; ~**verschlechterung** deterioration in performance; ~**verwendung** appropriation of the profit

Ergebnis-Vorab preferential profit share

ergebniswirksam 1. *adj. (~e Bereitstellung)* making available from the profits, *(~e Verrechnung)* inclusion in the revenue results, *(nicht ~)* not recognised in income
2. *adv. (direkt ~ abschreiben)* to write off directly against income, *(~ abwerten)* to reduce the value with a charge to the income statement, *(sich ~ auswirken)* to be reflected in the profit and loss account, to impact the revenue results
(~ belasten) to charge to the income statement, *(~ erfassen/verrechnen)* to include in the revenue results (in net income), to recognise in the profit and loss account, *(Erträge ~ erfassen)* to take to income, to credit to operations

Ergebnis / ~**wirksamkeit** income recognition; ~ **ziel** profit (performance) target

ergiebig profitable, remunerative, lucrative, productive, *(sich als ~e Fi-*

E

nanzierungsquelle erweisen) to prove a fruitful funding source

ergreifen 1. *(einen Beruf ~)* to take up a profession 2. *(Besitz ~)* to take possession of 3. *(eine Gelegenheit ~)* to seize (to grasp, to avail o. s. of) an opportunity 4. *(Maßnahmen ~)* to take measures

E

Erhalt receipt, *(bei ~)* on (upon) receipt, *(nach ~)* when received

erhalten 1. to receive, *(~e Anzahlungen)* payments (advances) received 2. *(erlangen)* to obtain, to gain, to achieve, *(eine klare Vollmacht ~)* to be given a clear authority, *(die Unterstützung von … ~)* to win the support (backing) of 3. *(bewahren)* to maintain, to keep, *(das investierte Kapital ~)* to preserve the capital invested

Erhaltung 1. maintenance 2. preservation, *(~ des Kapitalbetrages)* preservation of the principal

Erhaltungs / ~aufwand *(für Sachanlagen)* maintenance cost (expenditure); **~marge** maintenance margin

erheben 1. *(einen Anspruch ~)* to claim s.th., to lay claim to 2. *(einen Einwand ~)* to raise an objection 3. *(eine Klage wegen Vertragsbruch ~)* to bring an action against s.o.for breach of contract 4. *(Kontoführungsgebühren ~)* to charge account-maintenance fees 5. *(eine Verkaufsgebühr ~)* to assess (to levy) a sales charge 6. *(einen Protest ~)* to lodge a protest 7. *(eine Steuer ~)* to levy (to impose) a tax, *(die auf den Gewinn erhobene Steuer)* the tax levied (imposed) upon the profit

erheblich 1. considerable, substantial, appreciable 2. *(wesentlich)* material, essential

Erhebung 1. *(Berechnung)* charging 2. *(Einzug)* collection, levying 3. *(von Gebühren, Steuern)* imposition, levying 4. *(einer Klage)* lodgement of an action, bringing an action 5. *(Umfrage)* survey, poll 6. *(Zählung)* census

Erhebungszeitraum 1. *(Statistik)* reporting period, period under survey (review) 2. *(Steuern)* taxation period

erhoffen *(erhoffte finanzielle Unterstützung)* hoped-for financial backing

erhöhen 1. to increase, to lift, to advance, *(die Umsatzerlöse erhöhten sich von … auf …)* sales revenue climbed (moved ahead) from … to … 2. *(aufschlagen)* to mark up 3. *(verstärken)* to strengthen, to intensify, *(den Druck ~)* to step up the pressure 4. *(wertmäßig)* to improve (to enhance) the value

Erhöhung 1. increase, rise, advance 2. *(Aufschlag)* markup, premium 3. *(Verstärkung)* strengthening, intensification 4. *(Verbesserung)* improvement, enhancement

erholen 1. *(sich ~)* to recover, to rally, to stage a recovery, to improve, *(sich geringfügig ~)* to pick up slightly, to recover marginally, *(sich nach Käufen des Berufshandels ~)* to rally on professional buying, *(die Konjunktur beginnt sich zu ~)* economic activity begins perking up 2. *(sich auf die ausländische Bank ~)* to obtain reimbursement from the foreign bank, *(sich durch Belastung des Kundenkontos ~)* to reimburse o. s. by debiting the customer's account

Erholung 1. recovery, rally, upturn, *(~ am Aktienmarkt)* stock market rally, recovery (rally, pick-up) in equity prices 2. obtaining reimbursement

Erholungs / ~ansätze indications (signs) of a recovery; **~phase** recovery phase; **~potenzial** recovery potential

ERI → Einheitliche Richtlinien für Inkassi

erinnern *(sich ~)* to remember, to recall, to recollect, *(den Kreditnehmer an fällige Tilgungsleistungen ~)* to remind the borrower of redemption payments due

Erinnerungs / ~posten memorandum item, reminder entry; **~schreiben** reminder; ~ **test** recall test; **~werbung** reminder advertising; **~wert** residual (notional) value

erkennbar 1. discernible **2.** visible, *(~e Risiken aus dem Darlehensgeschäft)* recognisable (discernible) risks from lending operations

erkennen 1. to recognise, to discern, to perceive, to identify **2.** *(ein Konto ~)* to credit an account, to enter to the credit of an account **3.** *(auf Schadenersatz ~)* to award damages

Erkennen 1. recognition, discernment, perception **2.** identification, *(~ eines Kreditrisikos)* identifying a credit risk

Erkenntnis perception, finding, knowledge, *(zu der ~ kommen)* to come to the conclusion, to realise

erklären 1. to explain **2.** to declare, to state, to announce, to express, *(die Bereitschaft zur Bürgschaftsübernahme ~)* to state (to express) one's willingness to furnish a guarantee, *(eine Dividende ~)* to declare a dividend

erklärt *(eindeutig ~ er Verzicht)* clearly avowed waiver, *(unser ~es Ziel ist die Rückführung des Engagements)* our stated (professed) goal is to reduce the exposure

Erklärung 1. explanation **2.** statement, declaration, announcement, *(durch schriftliche ~ an den Kreditnehmer)* by delivering written notice to the borrower, *(~ zur Unternehmensführung)* corporate governance statement

Erklärungs / ~irrtum mistake of expression;**~tag** *(bei Optionskontrakten)* declaration day

erklimmen *(einen neuen Höchststand ~)* to soar (to climb) to a new high

erkunden to explore, to sound out, to investigate

Erkundigung inquiry, investigation, *(~en einziehen)* to make inquiries

Erkundung exploration, investigation

Erkundungsstudie exploration study

erlahmen to wane, to decline, to sag, *(~des Anlegerinteresse)* waning investor interest, *(~de Wirtschaftstätigkeit)* flagging (sagging) economic activity

erlangen to obtain, to attain, to reach, *(das Eigentum an den Waren ~)* to acquire possession of the goods

Erlass 1. *(Freistellung)* exemption, exoneration **2.** *(eines Gesetzes)* enactment **3.** *(einer Schuld)* remission of a debt, debt waiver **4.** *(Verordnung)* decree, order

erlassen 1. *(freistellen)* to exempt, to exonerate, to release **2.** *(ein Gesetz ~)* to enact **3.** *(eine Gebühr ~)* to remit a fee, *(eine Schuld ~)* to remit (to waive) a debt **4.** *(eine Verordnung ~)* to decree, to issue a decree

Erlassvertrag *(im Hinblick auf Verbindlichkeiten)* remission agreement, deed of remission

Erlaubnis / ~freiheit exemption from the licensing requirement; **~pflicht** authorisation (licensing) requirement; **~verfahren** authorisation (licensing) procedure; **~vorbehalt** *(des KWG)* licence proviso

erläutern 1. to explain, to clarify, to disclose **2.** to comment on

Erläuterung 1. explanation, disclosure **2.** comment, *(~en zum Konzernabschluss)* notes on the consolidated financial statements

Erläuterungspflicht disclosure duty, duty to describe (to explain)

erledigen 1. to settle, to carry out (through) **2.** *(bearbeiten, sich kümmern um)* to attend to, to deal with

erleichtern 1. *(Kreditbeschränkungen ~)* to ease (to relax) credit restrictions, *(die Steuerlast ~)* to alleviate (to ease) the tax burden **2.** *(den Zugang zu den internationalen Kapitalmärkten ~)* to facilitate access to the international capital markets

Erleichterung 1. easing, relaxation. alleviating **2.** facilitating **3.** *(steuerliche ~)* tax relief

erleiden to suffer, to sustain, to experience, *(einen 20%igen Ertragsrückgang ~)* to suffer a 20 % fall in profits, *(einen Verlust ~)* to suffer (to sustain) a loss, *(starke Verluste ~)* to incur heavy losses, to take a battering (hammering)

Erlös 1. proceeds, return, receipts, *(~ aus einer Bezugsrechtsemission)* rights issue proceeds, *(~ aus zum Verkauf stehenden Wertpapieren)* proceeds from ongoing securities sales
2. revenue, *(~e aus dem Emissionsgeschäft)* underwriting revenue, *(~e aus Zahlungsverkehrsleistungen)* revenue from money transmission services

erlösabhängig *(~ e Betriebskosten)* revenue-related operating cost

Erlösauskehr payment of the proceeds

erlösbar *(~ er Sicherheitenwert)* realisable value of collateral

Erlös / ~berichtigung revenue adjustment; **~beteiligung** revenue sharing

erloschen 1. *(abgelaufen)* expired, lapsed, *(~e Kontovollmacht)* lapsed authority (to operate the account), *(~e Option)* expired option
2. *(aufgelöst)* extinct, dissolved, liquidated, *(~er Anspruch)* extinct claim, *(~e Schuld)* discharged (extinct) debt, *(~es Unternehmen)* defunct (dissolved) company

erlöschen 1. *(ablaufen)* to expire, to run out, to lapse, to terminate, to cancel
2. *(nicht mehr bestehen)* to cease to exist, to be extinguished, to become extinct, *(das Pfandrecht erlischt mit der Rückzahlung des Kredites)* the lien is extinguished by (upon) repayment of the loan

Erlöschen 1. expiration, lapse, *(~ einer Garantie)* expiration (termination) of a guarantee, *(~ einer Option)* expiration (lapse) of an option
2. extinguishment, extinction, cancellation, *(~ eines Anspruchs)* forfeiture of a right, *(~ einer Forderung)* extinguishment of a debt, *(einen Anspruch zum ~ bringen)* to have a claim extinguished, *(~ kraft Gesetzes)* extinguishment by operation of law
(~ eines Pfandrechtes) extinguishment of a lien, lien defeasance, *(~ einer Schuld/eines Schuldsaldos)* extinguishment (discharge) of a debt, *(~ durch Verfall)* extinguishment by lapse of time

erlösen *(€ … aus dem Verkauf einer Anleihe ~)* to receive (to net, to generate) € … from the sale of a bond

Erlös / ~erfassung revenue recognition; **~funktion** revenue function; **~gutschrift** credit of the proceeds; **~konto** revenue account; **~-Kosten-Relation** earnings-cost ratio; **~minderung** revenue shortfall, decrease in revenue

Erlös / ~optimierung optimising the revenue stream; **~planung** revenue planning; **~potenzial** revenue potential; **~quote** recovery rate (from the realisation of collateral)

Erlös / ~realisierung revenue recognition; **~rechnung** revenue accounting; **~rendite** revenue yield, ratio of operating income to revenue; **~schmälerung** → Erlösminderung; **~sicherung** securing revenue streams; **~verteilung** distribution of the proceeds

ermächtigen to authorise, to entitle, to empower, *(zu Verfügungen über das Konto ~)* to authorise to draw on the account (to operate the account)

Ermächtigung authorisation, entitlement, authority, power, *(~ zur Einzelvertretung des Unternehmens)* authority to represent the company alone, *(~ der Hauptversammlung)* authorisation given by the annual general meeting, *(~ zur Zahlung)* authorisation of payment

Ermächtigungs / ~beschluss resolution to authorise (*e.g.* the Directors to …), **~formular** authorisation form; **~rahmen** *(~ für weitere Kapitalerhöhungen)* general authorisation for additional increases in capital; **~schreiben** authorisation letter

ermangeln to lack, to be lacking

Ermangelung *(in ~ ausreichender Sicherheiten)* for lack (want) of adequate collateral

ermäßigen to reduce, to cut, *(die EZB ermäßigte ihren Leitzins auf ...)* the ECB lowered its key policy rate to ..., *(AB ermäßigten sich um ... auf ...)* AB slipped (gave up) ... to ...

Ermäßigung reduction, lowering, cut

ermessen 1. *(abschätzen, beurteilen)* to assess, to estimate, to judge **2.** *(erkennen)* to realise, to appreciate

Ermessen judg(e)ment, discretion, opinion, option, *(nach seinem/ihrem billigen ~)* as he/she reasonably sees fit, *(im ~ der Bank liegen)* to be a matter of judgment for the bank, *(die Bank wird nach pflichtgemäßem ~)* the bank will in the proper exercise of its discretion *(eine nach dem alleinigen ~ der Bank angemessene Sicherheit für die Verbindlichkeiten)* a security which in the sole judgment of the bank is good and adequate to secure the obligations, *(nach dem ~ des Emittenten)* at the option (discretion) of the issuer

Ermessens / ~ausübung exercise of discretionary powers; **~befugnisse** discretionary powers; **~entscheidung** discretionary decision (judgment); **~fehler** error of judgment; **~frage** matter of discretion

Ermessens / ~missbrauch abuse of discretionary powers; **~spielraum** discretionary leeway; **~überschreitung** exceeding discretionary powers; **~vollmacht** discretionary power(s), power of discretion

ermitteln 1. *(errechnen)* to calculate, to determine
2. *(feststellen)* to determine, to establish, to ascertain, *(den Sachverhalt ~)* to establish the facts, *(den Schaden ~)* to ascertain (to evaluate) the damage
3. *(untersuchen)* to inquire into, to investigate, to make an inquiry into, *(von Amts wegen ~)* to investigate ex officio

Ermittlung 1. calculation, determination, *(~ des Beleihungswertes)* determination of the lending value, *(bei ~ des Eigenkapitalbedarfs)* when (in) calculating equity requirements
2. establishment, ascertainment, *(~ des Schadens)* ascertainment of the damage (loss)
3. inquiry, investigation

E

Ermittlungsverfahren preliminary proceedings, judicial inquiry

ermöglichen 1. to make (to render) possible, to enable **2.** to allow

ermutigen to encourage, *(~des Signal)* encouraging signal

ernennen to appoint, to nominate, to designate

Ernennung appointment, nomination, designation, *(~ zum Bevollmächtigten)* appointing as proxy (mandatory)

Ernennungs / ~recht power of appointment; **~urkunde** certificate of appointment

erneuerbar renewable

erneuern 1. to renew **2.** *(verlängern)* to prolong **3.** *(ersetzen)* to replace

Erneuerung 1. renewal **2.** prolongation **3.** replacement

Erneuerungs / ~gebühr renewal fee; **~konditionen** terms of renewal; **~provision** *(im Versicherungsgeschäft)* renewal commission; **~schein** renewal coupon

erneut 1. *adj.* renewed, fresh, new, *(~e Kapitalspritze)* fresh capital injection
2. *adv.* anew, afresh, *(~ nachgeben) (Kurse)* to retreat afresh

Ernst *(~ der finanziellen Lage)* gravity of the financial situation

ernsthaft *(~e finanzielle Schwierigkeiten)* serious (grave) financial difficulties

Ernte *(die ~ aus einer Investition einfahren)* to reap the rewards (benefits) of an investment

Ernüchterung *(~ der Anleger)* disenchantment by investors

E

erobern *(einen größeren Marktanteil ~)* to capture a bigger market share

eröffnen 1. to open, *(geringfügig schwächer ~)* to open a shade lower, *(bei lebhaften Umsätzen fester ~)* to open higher in brisk trading, *(im Auftrag unseres Kunden ~ wir hiermit unser unwiderrufliches Akkreditiv zu Ihren Gunsten)* by order of our customer we hereby open our irrevocable documentary credit in your favour
(ein Insolvenzverfahren ~) to open (to initiate) insolvency proceedings, *(eröffnetes/eigentliches Insolvenzverfahren)* opened insolvency proceedings, → vorläufiges Insolvenzverfahren, *(ein Testament ~)* to open (to read) a will
2. *(errichten)* to set up, to establish, *(Repräsentanzen im Ausland ~)* to set up representative offices abroad
3. *(mitteilen)* to notify, to inform, to disclose

Eröffnung 1. opening, *(~ des Insolvenzverfahrens)* opening of judicial insolvency proceedings, *(~ einer Position)* opening (initiating) a position **2.** setting up, establishment

Eröffnungs / ~antrag application to open proceedings; **~auktion** opening auction; **~bank** opening (issuing) bank; **~beschluss** order for relief, order initiating insolvency proceedings; **~bestand** opening (initial) inventory

Eröffnungs / ~bilanz opening balance sheet, opening financial accounts; **~buchung** opening entry; **~geschäft** opening trade (transaction); **~kapital** opening (initial) capital

Eröffnungs / ~kurs/~notierung 1. *(zu Beginn der Börsensitzung)* opening price **2.** *(Einführungskurs)* issuing price, introductory price; **~position** *(bei einer Kombinationsposition)* opening leg (position), front leg

Eröffnungs / ~schreiben *(bei Akkreditivgeschäften)* advice of the credit; **~sitzung** opening (initial, inaugural) meeting; **~stand** opening level; **~transaktion** opening transaction (trade)

erproben to test, to put to the test, to try (out), *(erprobtes Verfahren)* tried and tested procedure

ERP-Sondervermögen ERP Special Fund

errechnen to calculate, to compute, *(es errechnet sich ein Ausgabepreis von ...)* the offering price works out at ...

Errechnung calculation, computation

erreichen to reach, to arrive at, to achieve, *(die Exporte erreichten nahezu ...)* exports came to nearly ..., *(einen neuen Höchststand ~)* to reach a new peak (record level), *(das angestrebte finanzielle Ziel nicht ~)* to fall short of the aspired financial goal

Erreichen 1. *(~ der Gewinnschwelle)* reaching the break-even point **2.** *(~ eines Ziels)* attainment of a goal, achievement of an objective

errichten to establish, to found, to set up

Errichtung establishment, foundation, setting up

Errichtungsfinanzierung set-up financing

Ersatz 1. replacement, substitute, surrogate **2.** *(Entschädigung)* indemnification, indemnity **3.** *(Erstattung)* restitution, refund **4.** *(Schadenersatz)* damages

Ersatz / ~anspruch compensation claim, right to compensation (to damages); **~aussonderung** *(im Insolvenzverfahren)* substitutional segregation, **~aussonderungsrecht** right to substitutional segregation; **~autorisierung** stand-in authorisation

Ersatz / ~bescheinigung replacement certificate; **~deckungswerte** assets serving as substitute cover, substitute cover assets; **~investitionen** expenditure on plant replacements

Ersatz / ~leistung 1. *(des Entleihers an den Verleiher für entgangene Wertpapiererträge)* manufactured payment

2. compensation; ~ **pflicht** obligation to provide compensation; ~**scheck** replacement cheque; ~ **sicherheit** substitute security (collateral); ~**stücke** *(für verloren gegangene Wertpapiere)* replacement certificates

ersatzweise 1. as a replacement (substitute) 2. as compensation, by way of compensation 3. alternatively

Ersatzwert replacement value

erscheinen to appear, *(Aktien attraktiv für Anleger ~ lassen)* to make equities look attractive to investors, *(in der Bilanz ~)* to appear (to be shown) in the balance sheet

Erscheinen 1. appearance 2. *(Veröffentlichung)* publication 3. *(Handel per Erscheinen)* pre-IPO trading, dealings on a when-issued-basis

Erscheinungsbild *(~ der Unternehmung)* corporate identity

erschließen to develop, *(einen neuen Markt ~)* to open up a new market

Erschließung development, *(~ von Finanzierungsquellen)* opening up new financial sources, financial sourcing, *(~ von Grundstücken)* land development

Erschließungsgarantie development guarantee

erschöpfen 1. to deplete, to use up, *(erschöpfte Kapitalquellen)* depleted capital resources 2. *(die liquiden Mittel ~)* to exhaust (to drain) the liquidity

erschöpfend *(~e Auskunft)* complete (exhaustive) information

Erschöpfung depletion, exhaustion, draining

Erschöpfungslücke *(Chart-Analyse)* exhaustion gap □ occurs after the end of a steep uptrend or downtrend and signals a reversal of this trend

erschüttern *(den Aktienmarkt ~)* to send a shiver through the stock market, to send the stock market into disarray, *(das Unternehmen ~)* to rock the company, *(das Vertrauen der Anleger ~)* to shock (to upset) investors, to shake investor confidence

erschweren 1. to aggravate, to make more difficult (more complicated) 2. *(behindern)* to obstruct, to impede

ersetzen 1. to replace 2. *(die Kosten ~)* to refund (to reimburse) the expenses 3. *(eine Person ~)* to replace s. o., to take s. o.'s place, *(hochverzinsliche Kredite durch Schuldtitel ~)* to replace high-cost borrowing with debt securities 4. *(den Schaden ~)* to compensate for (to indemnify for) the damage

ersichtlich evident, obvious

Ersitzung *(Erwerb von Eigentum durch ~)* acqusition of title by adverse possession

Ersparnis saving(s), *(~se der privaten Haushalte)* private household savings, retail savings; ~**bildung** formation of savings, *(~ durch Lebensversicherungen)* saving through life assurances

Erste Abwicklungsanstalt First Workout Entity

erste Adresse 1. *(Emittent)* top-rated (prime) issuer, prime name 2. *(Kreditnehmer/Schuldner)* first-rate (high-quality) borrower, highly rated credit 3. *(Kunde)* blue-chip (highly valued) customer

erstes Anfordern *(Zahlung auf ~)* payment upon first demand

Erst / ~**absatz** *(im Wertpapiergeschäft)* new issue business, *(~ von Pfandbriefen)* sale of newly issued mortgage bonds; ~**abschreibung** initial (first-year) depreciation, initial allowance

Erst / ~**aktionäre** first-time shareholders; ~**anleger** first-time (novice) investors; ~ **ansatz** *(in der Bilanz)* first-time (initial) recognition; ~**anspruch** priority claim, *(einen ~ auf die Vermögenswerte besitzen)* to have a first priority claim to the assets; ~ **anwendung** first-time application

Erstarrung *(~ des Marktes)* stiffening (paralysis) of the market

E

erstatten 1. *(die Auslagen ~)* to refund (to return, to reimburse) the expenses **2.** *(einen Bericht ~)* to report on **3.** *(den Verlust ~)* to compensate for the loss

Erstattung refund, reimbursement, compensation

Erstattungs / ~anspruch refund (reimbursement) claim, right to a refund; **~antrag** refund (reimbursement) application

erstattungsfähig refundable, reimbursable

Erstausfall / ~absicherung first-default protection; **~-Kreditderivat** first-to-default credit derivative □ specifies payments when any of the reference entities defaults (→ Kreditereignis), whereupon the contract will be terminated; → Zweitausfall-Kreditderivat; **~position** → Erstausfalltranche, **~risiko** first loss risk; **~tranche** first loss piece (tranche) □ usually the top-yield tranche, but in the event of losses (→ Kreditereignis) the holders would incur these losses first

Erstausfertigung 1. original **2.** *(eines Wechsels)* first of exchange

Erstausgabe *(im Emissionsgeschäft)* initial offering; **~aufschlag** first-day premium, initial offering premium; **~preis** issuing (subscription) price, initial offering price; **~zeit** initial offering period

Erstausreichung *(im Kreditgeschäft)* initial extension (accommodation)

Erstbegünstigter/~bezugsberechtigter first (primary) beneficiary, first name insured

ersteigern to buy at an auction

Ersteinlage initial deposit, maiden contribution

Ersteinschuss initial margin

erstellen 1. *(Bilanz, Plan)* to prepare, to draw up, to establish **2.** *(Kontoauszug)* to issue, to prepare, to make out **3.** *(Strategie)* to work out, to map out, to devise

Erst / ~emission initial public offering; **~emittent** first-time issuer, newcomer to the equity/bond market; **~erfassung** initial (first-time) recognition; **~erwerb 1.** first purchase, original acquisition **2.** *(im Emissionsgeschäft)* purchase of newly issued securities

Erst / ~erwerber first purchaser (holder), first-time buyer; **~finanzierer** initial financing institution; **~finanzierungsrunde** first-stage financing; **~gebot** first (initial) bid

erstklassig first-rate, top-quality, first-class, *(~ geführtes Unternehmen)* superbly-run operation, *(~e Anlagemöglichkeiten)* high-quality investment opportunities, *(~e Anleiheadresse)* first-rate name in the bond market, prime issuer
(~e Bonität) unquestionable financial standing (soundness), first-rate credit, *(~er Kreditnehmer)* prime (first-rate) borrower, borrower with an impeccable credit rating

erstklassige liquide Aktiva high-quality liquid assets □ Cash and unencumbered liquid assets, which are easily convertible into cash in periods of severe market stress, must be held by banks according to the liquidity coverage ratio (→ Mindestliquiditätsquote) set out in the → Basel III framework. There are two categories of assets: → Aktiva der Stufe 1/ Stufe 2

Erst / ~konsolidierung first-time consolidation; **~lastschrift** initial direct debit

erstmalig *(~er Kreditnehmer)* first-time borrower

Erstplatzierung 1. initial placement **2.** primary offering

Erstrang / ~-Finanzierer lender (provider of funds) against first-rank security;**~-Gläubiger** first-rank creditor, creditor secured by a first-rank mortgage; **~-Hypothek** first mortgage

erstrangig first, first-rank, *(einen ~en Anspruch auf den Erlös besitzen)* to have first priority on the proceeds, *(~ es Grundpfandrecht)* senior charge

Erstrangigkeit first rank, *(Anspruch auf ~)* right of being placed in first rank, *(Einräumung der ~)* according first rank

Erstrangkredit first lien credit facility, loan secured by a first mortgage

Erstrangteil *(eines Hypothekendarlehens)* senior portion (tranche) of a mortgage loan

erstreiten to sue, to contend, *(erstrittenes Urteil)* judgment rendered on appeal

Erstrisiko first loss; ~**schuldner** primary (principal) debtor; ~**versicherung** first loss cover (insurance, policy), first risk insurance

erststellig *(~ besichertes Darlehen)* loan secured by a first-rank charge over property, *(~e Grundschuldabsicherung)* provision of security by a first lien on land (senior land charge), *(~es Hypothekendarlehen)* first lien mortgage loan, *(~ es Sicherungsrecht)* first lien, first position security interest

Erst / ~**verbuchung** initial recognition; ~**verlusttranche** → Erstausfalltranche; ~**verpflichteter** party primarily liable, primary debtor; ~**versicherer** primary insurer (underwriter), direct insurance company; ~**versicherung** primary insurance (policy), underlying insurance

Erst / ~**verwahrer** original custodian, original depository; ~**votierer** initial decision-making body, first decision-maker; ~**zulassung** initial admission to trading

ersuchen 1. to ask for, to request **2.** to apply for

erteilen 1. *(Anweisungen ~)* to instruct, to give instructions **2.** *(Auskunft ~)* to give information **3.** *(einen Grundschuldbrief ~)* to execute a land charge deed **4.** *(Gutschrift ~)* to credit to an account, to credit s. o. with **5.** *(eine Kauf-/Verkaufsorder ~)* to place a buy/sell order **6.** *(eine Löschungsbewilligung ~)* to grant a mortgage discharge **7.** *(einen Rechnungsabschluss ~)* to issue an account balancing statement

Ertrag 1. earnings, revenue, income, profit, gain, *(~ der laufenden Periode)* current period earnings, *(~ nach/vor Risikovorsorge)* earnings after/before provisioning **2.** *(Erlös)* proceeds **3.** *(Rendite)* yield, return, *(~ für den Anleger)* return to the investor, *(~ aus dem investierten Kapital)* return on investment, *(~ aus einer Kontoverbindung)* account profitability, earnings from an account relationship, *(~ aus Planvermögen)* return on plan assets

ertragbringend *(~e Geldanlage)* profitable (productive) investment

Erträge aus *(~dem Abgang von Gegenständen des Anlagevermögens)* gains on disposal of fixed assets, *(~ dem Aktivgeschäft)* earnings from asset operations, *(~ der Auflösung von Sonderposten mit Rücklagenanteil)* gains from writing back special reserves *(~ der Auflösung von Rückstellungen)* gains on the reversal of provisions (from provisions written back), *(~ Beteiligungen)* investment (equity) income, *(~ dem Beratungsgeschäft)* advisory revenues, *(~ dem Devisenhandel)* earnings (revenues) from foreign exchange trading, *(~ Dienstleistungsgeschäften)* earnings (revenues) from service transactions, service revenues

Erträge aus *(~ dem Eigengeschäft)* earnings from own account dealings, *(~ dem Emissionsgeschäft)* earnings from issuing activities, origination revenues, *(~ dem Finanzgeschäft)* earnings from financial activities, *(~ gewerblich genutzten Grundstücken)* commercial property income, *(~ Grundbesitz und Kapitalanlagen)* earnings (income) from property and capital investments *(~ dem Handelsbestand)* income from the trading book (portfolio), *(~aus Kapitalanlagen)* investment income,

E

(~ *Kapitalmarktgeschäften)* earnings (income) from capital trading operations, *(~ dem Kreditgeschäft)* earnings from lendings (lending operations), *(~ Kredit- und Geldmarktgeschäften)* income from lending and money market operations

Erträge aus *(~ Termingeschäften)* income from forward transactions, *(~ Treuhandgeschäften)* trust (fiduciary) income, *(~ der Veräußerung von Sachanlagen)* gains on the sale of fixed assets, *(~ dem Vermittlungsgeschäft)* revenues from agency operations *(~der Währungsumrechnung)* translation gains, *(~ Wertpapieren)* income from securities, *(~dem Wertpapiergeschäft)* earnings (gains) from securities operations, *(~ dem Wertpapierleihegeschäft)* revenues from securities lending

E

ertraglos *(~ gestellte Engagements)* loans put on a non-accrual basis

Erträgnis / ~**abrechnung**/~**aufstellung** **1.** *(bei Dividenden-/Zinszahlungen)* income statement **2.** *(bei festverzinslichen Wertpapieren)* coupon statement; ~**ausschüttung** income payout, distribution of earnings; ~**gutschrift** income credited, dividend, coupon (interest) payment; ~**schein** coupon

ertragreich profitable, lucrative, productive

Ertrags / ~**abbildung** earnings mapping; ~**abgrenzung** income recognition on an accrual basis, deferment of income

ertragsabhängig *(~e Gewinnausschüttung)* earnings-related distribution of profits, *(~e Steuern)* income-linked taxes

Ertrags / ~**absicherung** income hedging; ~**anteil** income share, share in revenues; ~**ausfall** loss of earnings, revenue shortfall; ~**ausfallversicherung** loss of income insurance

Ertrags / ~**ausgleich** income equalisation (netting); ~**ausgleichsverfahren** income equalisation proceedings; ~**ausschüttung** distribution of earnings (income); ~**aussichten** earnings prospects

Ertrags / ~**belastung** charge on (against, to) earnings, burden on earnings; ~**besserung** improvement in earnings; ~**besteuerung** taxation of capital investments; ~**beteiligung** revenue sharing

Ertrags / ~**defizit** revenue shortfall; ~**delle** dent in earnings; ~**druck** pressure on earnings, revenue pressure; ~**einbruch** sharp drop (setback) in earnings; ~**entwicklung** earnings performance (history), performance record, development in earnings, earnings trend

Ertrags / ~**erfassung** recognition of income; ~**ergebnis** earnings performance; ~**erholung** earnings recovery; ~**erwartungen** profit expectations, anticipated earnings (income); ~**erzielung** making (generating) a profit

Ertrags / ~**fähigkeit** earnings capacity, profitability, productiveness, *(ertragsfähiges Geschäft)* profitable business, fee-earning transactions; ~**feststellung** determination of income; ~**gesichtspunkte** profitability considerations

Ertrags / ~**gewichtung** weighting of earnings, *(ertragsgewichtetes Depot)* earnings-weighted investment portfolio; ~**historie** earnings record (history); ~**höhe** earnings (performance) level

Ertrags / ~**impuls** stimulus to earnings; ~**indikatoren** earnings indicators; ~**kennzahl** earnings ratio; ~**konsolidierung** consolidation of income; ~**kontinuität** earnings continuity; ~**konto** revenue account

Ertrags / ~**kraft** earnings power, profit-earning capacity; ~**lage** earnings situation (position), *(die ~ wurde als zufriedenstellend bezeichnet)* earnings were termed satisfactory

Ertrags / ~**management** yield management; ~**marge** earnings margin (spread); ~**maximierung** maximisation of earnings, maximising earnings; ~**messung** earnings measurement; ~**minderung** drop (fall) in earnings, earnings shortfall, *(ertragsmindernd)* earnings-dilutive

Ertrags / ~**optimierung** optimising earnings; ~**orientierung** earnings orientation, *(ertragsorientiertes Portefeuille)* income-oriented portfolio

Ertrags / ~**papiere** yield instruments; ~**perspektiven** earnings (performance) outlook; ~**position** earnings item; ~**potenzial** earnings potential; ~**profil** earnings (reward) profile; ~**prüfung** performance review

Ertrags / ~**qualität** earnings quality; ~**quelle** source of earnings; ~**rechnung** income statement; ~**rückgang** earnings decline (setback), downturn in earnings

Ertrags / ~**schätzung** earnings (income) estimate, expected (budgeted, anticipated) earnings; ~**schein** coupon; ~**schwäche** weakness in earnings power; ~**schwelle** pay-off stage

Ertrags / ~**spanne** earnings margin (spread) □ earnings expressed as a percentage of the average business volume; ~**sprung** leap in earnings (profitability); ~**stagnation** slackness in earnings

Ertrags / ~**stärke** strength in earnings power, *(ertragsstarke Einheit)* unit strong in earnings power, profitable unit; ~**stärkung** boost to earnings; ~**steigerung** increase in earnings, earnings rise (surge), *(ertragssteigernde Maßnahmen)* earnings-enhancing (earnings-accretive) measures

Ertrag(s)steuer income tax; ~**ansprüche** current tax assets; ~**aufwand** income tax expense; ~**belastung** income tax load (burden); ~**entlastung** income tax relief; ~**schulden** current tax liabilities

Ertrags / ~**steuerung** earnings control, *(~ der Niederlassungen)* control of branch earnings; ~**ströme** revenue flows; ~**synergieeffekte** earnings synergies; ~**thesaurierung** retention (reinvestment) of earnings; ~**überschuss** net earnings; ~**untergrenze** earnings floor

Ertrags / ~**verbesserung** improvement in earnings, earnings enhancement; ~**verlauf** earnings performance, development of the earnings situation; ~**verwässerung** diluting earnings; ~**vorschau** earnings forecast

Ertrags / ~**wachstum** earnings growth; ~**wert** **1.** productive (earnings) value **2.** *(Rendite)* return, yield **3.** *(einer Immobilie)* net income value, property yield; ~ **wertverfahren** income approach, income capitalisation approach; ~**wiederanlage** reinvestment of income distributed

ertragswirksam *(~ verbuchen)* to credit to earnings, to recognise in current earnings, to include in the operating profit

Ertrags / ~**wirkungen** consequences for (impact on) earnings; ~**zinsen** interest received; ~**zinssatz** interest rate receivable; ~**zuwachs** earnings gain (rise), growth in earnings

eruieren *(neue Finanzierungsquellen ~)* to explore (to sound out) new funding sources

erwachsen *(Verpflichtungen, die aus einer Garantie ~)* obligations arising (accruing, resulting) from a guarantee

erwägen **1.** to consider, to weigh **2.** *(planen)* to intend, to contemplate **3.** *(prüfen)* to examine, to check

Erwägung consideration, *(nach sorgfältiger ~)* after due consideration, *(sachfremde ~en)* considerations extraneous to the case, *(in ~ ziehen)* to take into consideration (account)

Erwägungsgründe *(einer Verordnung)* considerations given, recitals page, initial implementation considerations

erwähnen **1.** to mention **2.** *(sich beziehen auf)* to refer to

E

erwähnenswert to be worth mentioning

Erwähnung mention, reference

erwärmen *(sich für die neuen Anlageprodukte ~)* to warm up to the new investment products

erwarten to expect, to anticipate

E

erwartet *(~e Ausfallhäufigkeit)* expected default frequency, *(~e Ausfallhöhe)* exposure at default (EAD), *(~e Nutzungsdauer)* expected useful life, *(~er Kreditbedarf)* projected borrowing requirements
(~e Rendite) expected yield, *(~e Senkung der Zinssätze)* anticipated cut in interest rates, *(~er Verlust)* expected loss (EL), *(~er Verlust einer Forderung bei Ausfall des Kontrahenten)* loss given default, loss in the event of default, amount of loss after the counterparty/the borrower has defaulted
(Marge zur Abdeckung des ~en Verlustes) expected loss premium, *(~e langfristige Verlustquote)* expected long-run loss rate, *(~er positiver Wiederbeschaffungswert)* expected positive exposure (EPE)

Erwartung expectation, anticipation, *(in ~ Ihrer Antwort)* looking forward to receiving your reply, awaiting your reply, *(in ~ von Kursrückgängen)* in anticipation of price falls, *(hohe ~en setzen in)* to place high expectations on
(das Ergebnis im Privatkundengeschäft ist hinter den ~en zurückgeblieben) the performance of retail operations has fallen short of expectations (failed to meet the expectations)

Erwartungseffekt expectation bias

Erwartungswert expectation (expectancy) value, expected value, *(monetärer ~)* expected monetary value, *(~ des tatsächlichen Verlustes im Zeitpunkt des Ausfalls)* loss given default

erweisen to prove, to show, *(sich als Erfolg ~)* to turn out to be a success, *(sich als wirtschaftliche Kraft ~)* to manifest itself as an economic force, *(sich als vorteilhaft ~)* to prove beneficial

erweitern to extend, to enlarge, to broaden, to widen, *(die Kapitalbasis ~)* to expand the capital base

erweitert *(~ e Anzeigepflicht)* extended notification duty, *(~e Bandbreiten)* widened parity bands, *(~e Deckungsklausel)* extended coverage clause, *(~er Eigentumsvorbehalt)* enlarged title retention, extended reservation of title □ transfer of title depends on the settlement of all outstanding receivables
(~er Geldhandel) money market dealings between banks and non-banks, *(~e Geldmenge)* extended money stock, *(~e Haftungsrisiken)* extended warranty (liability) exposure, *(~ es Produkt)* augmented (enhanced) product
(~e Strukturanpassungsfazilität) (des IWF) Enhanced Structural Adjustment Facility, *(~ e Sicherungsabrede)* extended security agreement □ includes also future claims arising from the relationship between lender and borrower, → einfache Sicherungsabrede
(~ er Versicherungsschutz) extended coverage, *(~er Zinsüberschuss einer Hypothekenbank: laufende Zinsen zuzüglich Saldo aus abgegrenzten Damnen)* net interest income plus net deferred discounts, *(~ er Zugang zu den Fondsmitteln des IWF)* enlarged access to the IMF's resources

Erweiterung 1. extension, enlargement, expansion, *(~ der Dienstleistungspalette)* extension of (extending) the range of services offered, *(~ des Versicherungsschutzes)* extension to the cover, extended coverage, *(~ der Vollmachten)* extension of powers granted
2. widening, *(~ der Zinsmarge)* widening of the interest margin, *(~ der Finanzierungsbasis/Kapitaldecke)* broadening (of) the funding base/equity base

Erweiterungs / ~aufwendungen expansion expenses; **~emission** supplemental issue; **~finanzierung** expansion financing; ~**investitionen** expansion capital expenditures, expansion investments

Erwerb purchase, acquisition, *(~ der Eigentumsrechte)* acquisition of legal ownership, *(~ einer Mehrheitsbeteiligung)* acquisition of a majority interest, *(~ für fremde Rechnung)* purchase for third-party account, *(~ eines Rechtsanspruchs)* acquiring a legal title to

erwerben 1. to purchase, to buy, to acquire, *(eine 30%ige Beteiligung ~)* to take a 30 p.c. shareholding in ., to acquire a 30 p.c. stake in ..., *(die Eigentumsrechte ~)* to acquire (to take) title to, *(eine Option ~)* to buy (to take out) an option, to open a long option position
2. *(erworbene Ansprüche)* established (vested) rights

Erwerber purchaser, buyer, acquirer

Erwerbs / ~charakter *(Unternehmen ohne ~)* non-profit enterprise; ~**einkommen** earned income, wage and salary income; ~**frist** *(für Wertpapiere)* subscription period; ~**gesellschaft** acquiring company

Erwerbs / ~methode *(im Rechnungswesen)* purchase method, acquisition accounting; ~**position** long position; ~**steuer** acquisition VAT, *(~ auf den innergemeinschaftlichen Erwerb von Waren)* tax on intra-EU acquisitions

erwerbstätig *(~ e Bevölkerung)* gainfully employed population

Erwerbstätigkeit gainful activity (employment)

erwerbswirtschaftlich *(~es Unternehmen)* commercial enterprise

erwidern 1. to reply, to answer **2.** *(eine Gefälligkeit ~)* to return (to reciprocate) a favour

Erwiderung 1. reply, answer **2.** return, returning, reciprocating

erwirken to obtain, to secure, to procure, *(gegen den Schuldner ein Gerichtsurteil ~)* to obtain a court judgment against the borrower, *(einen Zahlungsbefehl ~)* to take out a default summons

erwirtschaften to generate, to earn, to produce, *(erwirtschaftete Erträge)* income generated, *(erwirtschafteter Mehrwert)* economic value added

Erwirtschaftung *(~ von Erträgen)* generating income, production of income

erzeugen 1. *(herstellen)* to manufacture, to produce **2.** *(eine Baissestimmung ~)* to bring about (to give rise to) a bearish sentiment

Erzeuger producer, manufacturer; ~**preisindex** producer price index

Erzeugung production, manufacture

erzielbar *(~e Konditionen)* obtainable terms

erzielen to obtain, to achieve, to reach, to score, *(ein hervorragendes Ergebnis ~)* to perform strongly, *(bessere Konditionen ~)* to win better financial terms, *(einen hohen Preis ~)* to fetch a high price, *(eine endgültige Regelung über die beabsichtigte Kreditaufnahme ~)* to reach (to come to) a final agreement on the intended borrowing

erzwingen to force, *(eine Zahlung ~)* to enforce a payment

EsAeG → Einlagensicherungs- und Anlegerentschädigungsgesetz

Eskalations / ~leiter escalation ladder; ~**pfad** escalation path, → Eskalationswege; ~**prozess** escalation process; ~**stufe** escalation level ; ~**verfahren** escalation procedure; ~**wege** escalation channels; 1st, 2nd, 3rd level support

eskomptieren to discount, to anticipate, *(im derzeitigen Kurs eskomptiert)* discounted in the current price

etablieren to establish, to set up

Etablierung *(~ eines CP-Programms)* establishment of a commercial paper programme

Etat budget, → Haushalt

E

ethisch-ökologisch *(~ e Anlagen)* socially responsible investments

etwas bezahlt Geld / Brief *(Kurszusatz)* only some limited buy/sell orders were filled at the current published quotation

EU-einheitliche Regelung uniform regulation within the European Union, uniform set of rules in the EU

EU-Investmentanteile UCTIS fund shares, → OGAW-Richtlinie

Euler Hermes Deckung cover by the Federal government, → Exportkredit

EUREPO benchmark for secured money market transactions in the Eurozone, i.e. the rate at which prime banks offer funds in the interbank market in exchange for first-rate securities

Euribor euro interbank offered rate

Euro-Anleihe 1. euro-denominated bond **2.** Eurobond □ bond issued in a specific currency outside the jurisdiction of the currency's domicile

Euro-Anleihemarkt 1. euro-denominated bond market **2.** Eurobond market

Euro-Dollar / ~einlagen Eurodollar deposits □ USD deposits held by banks outside the United States; not subject to US banking regulations; **~kredit** Eurodollar borrowing; **~markt** Eurodollar market; **~termineinlagen** Eurodollar time deposits

Euro / ~-Emissionen euro-denominated issues; **~-Großbetragszahlungssystem** euro large-value payments system; **~-Länder** eurozone countries; **~-Währungsgebiet** eurozone; **~-Zahlungsverkehrsraum** Euro payments area, →SEPA; **~-Zinsmethode** actual/360; **~-Zone** *(Finanzinstitute der ~)* euro (eurozone) financial institutions

Europa-GmbH → Europäische Privatgesellschaft

Europäische Aufsichtsbehörden European Supervisory Authorities (ESAs) □ ***Europäische Aufsichtsbehörde für das Versicherungswesen und die betriebliche Altersversorgung*** European Insurance and Occupational Pensions Authority ***Europäische Bankaufsichtsbehörde*** European Banking Authority ***Europäische Wertpapier- und Börsenaufsichtsbehörde*** European Securities and Markets Authority

Europäischer Ausschuss für Systemrisiken European Systemic Risk Board

Europäische Bank für Wiederaufbau und Entwicklung European Bank for Reconstruction and Development (EBRD)

Europäische Finanzstabilitätsfazilität European Financial Stability Facility (EFSF)/Europäischer Finanzstabilitätsmechanismus (EFSM) □ established in 2010 to provide temporary financial assistance to eurozone members in difficulty; will expire in mid-2013 and be replaced by the permanent bail-out fund, the European Stability Mechanism, → Europäischer Stabilitätsmechanismus (ESM)

Europäischer Fonds für währungspolitische Zusammenarbeit European Monetary Cooperation Fund (EMCF)

Europäische Fondsrichtlinie → OGAW-Richtlinie

Europäisches Gemeinschaftsrecht European Community Law

Europäische Gesellschaft European Company, Societas Europaea

Europäisches Komitee für Bankenstandards European Committee for Banking Standards

Europäische Option European option, European-style option □ call or put that can be exercised only on the expiration date

Europäischer Pass European passport □ authorises banks and securities houses to provide services and to operate branches in other EU member states without having to go through a separate application procedure

Europäischer Pass für Verwaltungsgesellschaften EU management company passport

Europäische Privatgesellschaft European Private Company

Europäischer Stabilitätsmechanismus European Stability Mechanism (ESM) □ designed to safeguard the stability of the eurozone as a whole; will take over from the → Europäische Finanzstabilitätsfazilität expiring in 2013

Europäische wirtschaftliche Interessenvereinigung European Economic Interest Grouping

Europäischer Zahlungsverkehrsrat European Payments Council □ manages all → SEPA-related activities

Europäische Zentralbank European Central Bank (ECB)

Europäisches Zentralbankensystem European System of Central Banks (ESCB)

Euro-Referenzkurse Euro reference rates of the European Central Bank

Euro-Rettungsschirm Euro rescue (bailout) fund, → Europäischer Stabilitätsmechanismus

Euro-Zahlungen *(bargeldlose ~)* cashless payments in Euro

Eurozone-Länder eurozone countries

Eventual / ~fazilität contingent loan facility; **~fonds** contingency fund; **~forderungen** contingent assets (receivables), *(~ gegenüber Kunden)* contingent claims on customers; **~gewinn** contingent gain; **~haftung** contingent liability

Eventual / ~obligo contingent commitment(s), contingent exposure; **~positionen** contingency items; **~risiko** contingent risk; **~verbindlichkeiten** contingent liabilities, *(Rücklage für ~)* contingent reserve; **~verlust** contingent loss; **~verpflichtung** *(~ zur Mittelbereitstellung)* contingent funding obligation

Evidenzkonten *(bei Gegengeschäften)* evidence accounts

Evidenzzentrale 1. evidence centre, credit reporting agency, *(~ für Millionenkredite)* central register for loans of € 1.5 million or more
2. *(im Kreditkartengeschäft)* registration centre

EWB → Einzelwertberichtigung

ewig *(~e Renten)* government perpetuals, undated government bonds

ex ante (ex post) Bewertung pre-measurement, ex ante evaluation (post-measurement, ex post evaluation)

ex / ~Ausschüttung (exA) ex distribution; **~Berichtigungsaktien (exBA)** ex scrip issue, ex capitalisation issue (x.cp.); **~Bezugsrecht (exB/exBr)** ex rights (x.r.); **~Bonusrecht (exBo)** ex bonus rights

ex / ~Dividende (exD) ex dividend, ex coupon (x.d.), *(ex Dividende notiert werden)* to go ex dividend, to be quoted ex dividend; **~Split (exSP)** ex splitting; **~Ziehung (exZ)** ex drawing; **~Zinsen (exZS)** ex interest

exekutieren *(einen schwebenden Kontrakt ~)* to liquidate an open contract (upon the customer's failure to meet margin calls)

Exekutiv / ~ausschuss executive committee; **~funktionen** executive functions; **~organ** executive (governing) body

existenzfähig *(~e Betriebe)* viable operations

Existenz / ~förderung promoting (funding) business start-ups; **~gefährdung** endangerment of a bank's existence, → Restrukturierungsgesetz; **~gründer** business start-ups, new entrepreneurs

Existenzgründung business start-up

Existenzgründungs / ~beratung start-up consultancy (counselling); **~ darlehen** business start-up loan; **~zuschuss** start-up subsidy

Exit / ~erlöse exit income, income from the sale of investments; **~klausel** exit clause (option); **~wege** exit channels

Exklusiv / ~recht exclusive right; **~vertriebsrechte** sole (exclusive) distributorship rights; **~vertriebsvereinbarung** exclusive distributorship agreement

exotische Optionen exotic options, options that differ from standard options in terms of exercise and/or payoff features

expandieren to expand, to spread into

Expansion expansion, extension, spreading into

Expansions / ~bemühungen *(die ~ verstärken)* to step (to ramp) up expansion efforts; **~finanzierung** expansion financing; **~kapital** expansion capital; **~kurs** *(auf ~ gehen)* to steer an expansionary course

expansiv *(~ e Geldpolitik)* expansionary monetary policy, *(~es Kreditgeschäft)* continually (steadily) expanding lending operations, *(~e Wirkung)* expansionary effect

Expertenbefragung expert opinion survey, key informant technique

Expertise 1. expertise, expert's report **2.** legal opinion

explizit *adj.* express, explicit, *adv.* explicitly, in express terms

exponentiell 1. *adj. (~e Glättung)* exponential smoothing, *(~ er Trend)* exponential trend **2.** *adv. (~ geglättete gleitende Durchschnitte)* exponentially smoothed moving averages

exponieren *(mit 2 Mio. € exponiert sein)* to be committed with €2m

Export export, exportation

Export / ~-Akkreditiv export documentary credit; **~bewilligung** export licence; **~-Dokumenten-Inkasso** export documentary collection; **~ergebnis** export performance; **~erlöse** export revenue

Export-Factoring export factoring □ descriptive of the collection of debt by a factoring company operating in a correspondent relationship with an import factor in the buyer's country

Export / ~finanzierung export financing; **~finanzierungsprogramm** (ERP) export financing programme; **~flaute** flagging exports, lull in exports; **~forderungen** export receivables; **~forderungsabtretung** assignment of export receivables; **~förderung** export promotion, promotion of (assistance to) exports

Export-Forfaitierung forfaiting of export receivables □ non-recourse sale of export receivables to a forfaiting company without recourse to seller in the event of the debtor's default

exportinduziert *(~e Erholung)* export-led recovery

Export / ~kommissionär export agent; **~konditionen** export credit terms

Exportkredit export credit (loan), *(bundesgedeckte ~e)* export credits covered by Federal guarantees, *(ECA-gedeckte ~ e)* export credits guaranteed by Export Credit Agencies, *(Konditionen für ~e)* export credit terms

Exportkredit / ~garantie export credit guarantee, → Euler-Hermes Deckung; **~versicherer** (staatlicher ~) Export Credit Agency; **~versicherung** export credit insurance

exportlastig *(~e Wirtschaft)* economy heavily dependent on exports

Export / ~-Leasing export leasing; **~linie** export credit line, export finance facility; **~lizenz** export licence (permit); **~sicherungsvertrag** assignment of export trade receivables

Export / ~träger mainstay of exports, main export earner; **~überschuss** export surplus; **~vorfinanzierung** pre-financing of exports; **~vorschuss** export facility, advance against export receivables

Export / ~wechsel export bill of exchange; **~-Wechsel-Inkasso** export bill collection; **~wert** export value; **~werte** export stocks; **~wirtschaft** export sector (activities)

extern *(~e Bonitätsbeurteilung)* → externes Rating, *(~e Bonitätsverbesserung)* external credit enhancement, third party credit enhancement, provision of additional collateral by a third party *(~er Finanzierungsbedarf)* external funding requirements, *(~ es Rating)* external rating, external credit assessment, rating made by a private or public sector agency, *(~ e Rating-Agentur)* external credit assessment institution *(ECAI)*, *(~ es Rechnungswesen)* external accounting

Externalisierung *(~ von Kosten)* externalisation of cost, offloading cost to a third party

exterritorial *(~er Finanzmarkt)* offshore financial market

extrem *(~e Kursschwankungen)* sharp (erratic) price swings, price gyrations

Exzedentenversicherung excess insurance

exzessiv *(~e Verschuldung)* excessive indebtedness

EZB / **~-Basiszins** ECB basic interest rate; **~-fähig** eligible for repo funding with the ECB; **~-Direktorium** ECB Executive Board; **~-Leitzinsen** ECB key interest (lending) rates, → Zinssatz für die Einlagefazilität, → Zinssatz für das Hauptrefinanzierungsgeschäft, → Zinssatz für die Spitzenrefinanzierung

EZB / **~-Rat** ECB Governing Council; **~-Referenzkurse** ECB reference exchange rates; **~-Repofähigkeit** eligibility for repo funding with the European Central Bank, ECB repo eligibility; **~-Schuldverschreibungen** ECB debt certificates; **~-Sicherheiten** ECB collateral, eligible assets

EZBS → Europäisches Zentralbankensystem

F

Fach 1. *(Geschäftszweig)* line of business, trade, branch **2.** *(Zuständigkeitsbereich)* province, field, line

Fach / **~abteilung** competent department; **~ausbildung** professional training; **~ausschuss** panel of experts, expert committee; **~beirat** advisory board; **~beratung** professional advice (counselling)

Fächer/Fächerformation fan/fan pattern □ signals a weakening downward or upward trend and a possible trend reversal

Fach / **~kenntnisse** professional (specialised, expert) knowledge, professional skills, trade knowledge; **~kompetenz** special expertise; **~kräfte** qualified staff, specially trained staff; **~kreise 1.** professional circles, *(in ~n)* among experts 2. financial community

fachkundig *(~e Beratung)* competent (specialised) counselling, expert advice

fachlich *(~e Qualifikationen)* professional qualifications, *(~e und technische Aspekte)* functional and technical issues, *(~e Weisung)* functional directive, *(~es Weisungsrecht)* functional authority, authority to issue directives, *(~e Zuständigkeit)* functional responsibility

Fach / **~personal** → Fachkräfte; **~tagung 1.** trade (professional) conference **2.** banking conference (congress); **~verantwortung** functional responsibility; **~verband** professional (trade) association; **~wissen** functional expertise, business skills (knowledge)

Façonwert goodwill

Factor → Factoring-Gesellschaft

Factoring factoring □ selling accounts receivable to a third party at a discount; differs from invoice discounting in the sense that discounting refers to the process of borrowing funds using the receivables as collateral

Factoring / **~entgelt** factorage, factoring charge, factor's fee; **~erlös** factoring proceeds, factor's advance; **~finanzierung** factoring funding; **~gebühr** → Factoringentgelt; **~gesellschaft**/**~institut** factor, factoring company

Factoring / **~kosten** cost of factoring, → Factoringentgelt; **~kunde** factor's client, business entity that sells its receivables to the factor; **~limit** factoring facility limit; **~makler** factoring broker; **~prüfung** factor's verification process; **~rahmen** factoring line

Factoring / **~unternehmen** → Factoringgesellschaft; **~vereinbarung** factoring arrangement; **~verhältnis** factoring relationship; **~vertrag** factoring agreement

fähig 1. able, capable **2.** *(qualifiziert)* qualified, competent

Fähigkeit 1. ability, capability **2.** *(Befähigung)* qualification, aptitude, competence **3.** *jur.* capacity

fahnden to search, to investigate

fahren *(tiefer in die roten Zahlen ~)* to slide deeper into the red

fahrlässig 1. *(jur.) adj.* negligent, careless, *(~e Irreführung)* negligent misrepresentation
2. *adv.* through (by) negligence, *(~ abdisponieren lassen)* to permit drawings by negligence

Fahrlässigkeit negligence, failure to exercise ordinary care, *(grobe Fahrlässigkeit)* gross negligence

Fahrnis chattels, ~**hypothek** chattel mortgage; ~**pfandrecht** lien over moveables

Fahrplan *(im Emissionsgeschäft)* issuing calendar (timetable)

Fahrt *(an ~ gewinnen)* to gather (to gain) momentum, to gather steam, to pick up speed

Fahrzeugwerte motors

Faksimile-Unterschrift facsimile signature, *(per Faksimile unterzeichnete Dokumente)* facsimile signed documents

faktisch *(~e Unmöglichkeit der Leistungserfüllung)* → praktische Unmöglichkeit

Faktor factor; ~**einkommen** factor income; ~**einsatzmenge** factor input; ~**ertragsmenge** factor output; ~**kosten** factor cost

Faktura invoice

Fakturierung invoicing, billing

Fakturierungswährung invoicing currency

fakultativ *(~e Lieferung des Basiswertes)* optional delivery of the underlying instrument, *(~e Rückversicherung)* facultative reinsurance, reinsurance of individual risks by offer and acceptance

Fakultativklausel optional clause

Fall 1. *(Angelegenheit)* matter, case, affair, issue, *(im günstigsten/schlimmsten ~)* under the best (worst) of circumstances **2.** *(Rückgang)* decline, fall, drop, decrease **3.** *(einen Vertrag zu ~ bringen)* to frustrate (to thwart, to wreck, to derail) an agreement

fallbezogen on a case-by-case basis

fallen 1. to decline, to fall, to drop, to decrease, *(die Aktienkurse sind um mehr als ein Viertel gegenüber dem Jahreshöchststand gefallen)* stock prices have fallen by more than one quarter from this year's high, *(die Anleihekurse sind in den zurückliegenden zwei Jahren stark gefallen)* bond prices have come down sharply over the past two years **2.** *(unter die Bestimmungen eines Gesetzes ~)* to come within the provisions of an Act, to fall within the scope of a law *(unter die Kompetenz von … ~)* to be within the competence of …, to come (to fall) within the province of … **3.** *(aufgehoben werden)* to be repealed, to be revoked

fällen *(ein Urteil über die Bonität des Kunden ~)* to give an assessment of the customer's credit-worthiness

fallend *(~es Dreieck) (Chart-Analyse)* → absteigendes Dreieck, *(~er Keil)* falling wedge □ bullish chart pattern, *(~e Tilgungsleistungen)* decreasing principal payments

fallen lassen *(einen Anspruch ~)* to waive (to abandon) a claim, *(eine Klage ~)* to drop an action

fällig *(~ bei Sicht)* due (payable) on demand, *(~ dreißig Tage nach Inanspruchnahme)* payable 30 days from drawdown, *(~ bei Vorlage)* due (payable) upon presentation *(~e Darlehensforderung)* loan falling due for repayment, claim maturing under a loan agreement, *(~er Kapitalbetrag)* principal due for repayment (redemption), *(~e Rückzahlungen)* repayments due, scheduled repayments (redemptions), *(~e Stücke)* securities due for redemption, *(~e Tilgungsleistung)* principal payment falling due, maturing repayment (repayment obligation), current maturity, *(~e Zahlung)* payment due

fällig stellen to call, *(einen Kredit ~)* to call in a loan, *(zur sofortigen Rückzahlung ~)* to call for immediate repayment, *(die Restschuld zur sofortigen Rückzahlung ~)* to declare the unpaid balance of principal to be immediately due and repayable

fällig werden to fall (to become) due, to mature, to run out, *(wenn die durch die Garantie gesicherten Ansprüche der*

F

Bank ~) when the bank's claims secured by the guarantee fall due, *(zur Rückzahlung ~)* to fall due for repayment

Fälligkeit 1. maturity, due date, *(Titel mit unterschiedlichen ~en)* bonds with maturities of varying lengths, *(~ der Darlehenssumme)* principal maturity, *(~ eines Kupons)* coupon due date, *(~ drei Monate nach Ausstellungsdatum)* maturity three months after date of issue
2. *(bei ~)* at maturity, when due, *(die Zinsen bei ~ vereinnahmen)* to recognise interest in the income statement as it becomes due, *(zahlbar bei ~)* payable at maturity, *(vor ~)* prior to maturity

F

Fälligkeiten / **~liste** maturity schedule; **~streckung** → Fälligkeitsstreckung

Fälligkeits / **~aufschub** deferring the maturity, extension of maturity; **~bereich** maturity range; **~betrag** amount payable at maturity

Fälligkeits / **~darlehen** bullet loan □ no principal repayments are made during the loan period, i.e. the entire loan is repayable upon maturity as one lump sum payment, → Annuitätendarlehen; **~divergenzen** maturity discrepancies

Fälligkeits / **~fächer** range of maturities, maturity range; **~-Factoring** maturity factoring □ factor assumes the debtor management and pays the amount of each invoice as it falls due

Fälligkeits / **~gliederung** maturity breakdown (spacing); **~hypothek** mortgage falling due on a fixed date; **~kurs** price (rate) payable upon maturity

Fälligkeitsmitteilung maturity notice □ a public notary's notice to the property buyer that the agreed prerequisites for the property conveyance have been met and that the purchase price is due for payment

Fälligkeits / **~monat** *(eines Terminkontraktes)* delivery month; **~option** maturity option; **~plan** maturity schedule; **~reduzierung** shortening the maturity; **~rendite** maturity yield

Fälligkeits / **~spektrum** maturity range (spectrum); **~streckung** extending (stretching, lengthening) the maturity; **~struktur** maturity pattern

Fälligkeits / **~tabelle** maturity ladder; **~termin** maturity date, due date, date of maturity, *(im Optionshandel)* expiry date; **~verkürzung** shortening the maturity, retracting the maturity date; **~verlängerung** extending the maturity, → Fälligkeitsstreckung

Fälligkeits / **~wert** maturity value; **~zeitpunkt** *(Erträge zum ~)* income at maturity; **~zinsen** late interest, *(berechnete Fälligkeitszinsen)* interest charged after the payment's due date

fallweise *(~ entscheiden)* to decide on a case-by-case basis

falsch 1. *adj.* wrong, *(irrtümlich)* erroneous, mistaken, *(ungenau)* inaccurate, *(unwahr)* untrue, false, *(~e Angaben)* wrong (incorrect) information, misinformation, false statements, *(~e Darstellung)* misrepresentation, fraudulent (deceptive) representation, *(~e Wertstellung)* wrong value date
2. *adv. (~ angegebener Betrag)* amount stated incorrectly, *(~ berechnen)* to miscalculate, *(~ handeln)* to act wrongly

Falschberatung *(Ansprüche aus ~)* claims based on misselling

Falschbuchung wrong (erroneous) entry, misentry

fälschen 1. *(Banknoten, Schecks, Wertpapiere)* to counterfeit, to forge 2. *(Bilanz, Kontounterlagen)* to falsify, to fake

Fälscher forger, counterfeiter

Falschgeld counterfeit money

Fälschung forgery, counterfeit(ing), falsification

Fälschungsschutz protection from forgery, counterfeit protection

fälschungssicher forgery-proof

Familien / ~erbfolge succession by the next of kin; **~unternehmen** family concern, family-owned company

Farbklausel *(im Akkreditivgeschäft)* green/red clause

fassen 1. *(abfassen)* to draw up, to formulate **2.** *(einen Beschluss ~)* to carry (to adopt) a resolution, to resolve

Fassung 1. version **2.** *(Wortlaut)* wording

fauler Kredit bad (sour) loan, → notleidender Kredit

Faustpfand pawn, pledge; **~kredit** advance against moveables pledged as collateral

favorisieren to favour, to support, to back, *(favorisierte Titel)* market favourites, *(Bankenwerte wurden favorisiert)* banks were in strong demand

Fazilität facility, loan (credit) facility, *(~ zur Kompensations- und Eventualfinanzierung) (des IWF)* Compensatory and Contingency Financing Facility

FAZ-Index FAZ stock index □ Market index of 100 leading shares calculated and published by the Frankfurter Allgemeine Zeitung

federführend *(~ arrangieren/zeichnen)* to arrange as lead manager, to lead, to lead-manage, *(~e Bank)* lead bank, lead manager

Federführer lead manager (arranger), lead bank, syndicate manager

Federführung lead management, leadership, *(mit der ~ beauftragen)* to be awarded the lead-arranger mandate, *(ein Konsortium unter ~ von …)* a syndicate led by …

Fehl / ~anzeige nil, nil return, negative answer; **~berechnung** miscalculation; **~bestand** shortage, deficiency; **~betrag** deficit, shortage, short amount, loss, *(~ in der Gelddisposition)* liquidity shortage (shortfall)

Fehl / ~bewertung 1. misjudgement, miscalculation, *(bonitätsmäßig)* wrong assessment (rating) **2.** *(kursmäßig)* mispricing; **~buchung** wrong entry (posting), amount posted to the wrong account, misposting; **~disposition** *(im Anlagebereich)* wrong investment decision; **~einschätzung** → Fehlbewertung

fehlen to be missing (lacking), to be absent

Fehlen *(~ gesetzlicher Bestimmungen)* absence of legal provisions, *(~ einer zugesicherten Eigenschaft)* lack of a guaranteed feature

fehlend *(~e Anlagebereitschaft)* unwillingness to invest, *(~e Anschlussaufträge)* lack of follow-through support, *(~e Deckung)* lack of cover, lacking cover, *(~e Einverständniserklärung)* failure to agree (to consent), *(~es Interesse der privaten Anleger)* lacking retail investment interest, *(~e Unterlage)* missing document

Fehl / ~entscheidung wrong decision; **~entwicklung** development (trend) into the wrong direction, undesirable development

Fehler 1. mistake, error, fault **2.** flaw, *(~ in der neuen Unternehmensstrategie)* flaws in the new corporate strategy

fehlerfrei *(~e Titelübertragung)* correct (accurate, flawless) transfer of title

Fehlergrenze error limit, tolerance

fehlerhaft 1. faulty, deficient, wrong **2.** *(ungenau)* incorrect, inaccurate **3.** *(Produkt)* defective, *(~e Finanzierungsberatung)* misselling, bad financial advice

Fehlerhaftigkeit 1. faultiness **2.** incorrectness, inaccuracy **3.** defectiveness

Fehl / ~gewicht short weight, shortage (deficiency) in weight; **~investition** misinvestment, misdirected investment; **~kalkulation** miscalculation

fehlleiten 1. *(Börsenorder)* to misroute **2.** *(Sendung)* to miscarry **3.** *(Investitionen)* to misdirect

Fehlleitung misrouting, miscarriage, misdirection

fehllenken *(Kapitalströme ~)* to misdirect capital flows

Fehl / ~lenkung → Fehlleitung; **~orientierung** misorientation, misguidance; **~prognose** wrong forecast

Fehlschlag failure

fehlschlagen to fail, to end in failure, to turn out to be a failure, to fall through, to go wrong, to founder

F

Fehl / ~schluss wrong (erroneous) conclusion; **~spekulation 1.** poor speculation, misspeculation **2.** *(falsche Annahme)* wrong assumption; **~start** *(einer Neugründung)* unsuccessful take-off; **~verhalten 1.** wrongdoing, misdemeanour **2.** (financial) misconduct, wrongful conduct

Feiertag public (statutory) holiday, bank holiday, non-business day

feindlich *(~e Übernahme)* hostile takeover, *(~er Übernahmeversuch)* hostile bid (offer)

Feinkörnigkeit *(~ des Portfolios)* portfolio granularity

Feinsteuerung fine tuning

Feinsteuerungsoperationen *(des EZBS)* fine-tuning operations □ liquidity-absorbing or liquidity-providing operations of the Eurosystem to adjust liquidity in the market

Feinunze troy ounce, fine ounce

Fernabsatz 1. *(~ finanzieller Dienstleistungen)* (long) distance selling of financial services **2.** *(im Kartengeschäft)* card-not-present (CNP) transactions □ credit card purchases made over the telephone or internet, etc.

Fernabsatz / ~gesetz Distance Selling Act; **~richtlinie** (EU) Distance Selling Directive; **~vertrag** distance contract

Fern / ~geschäfte distance trading, non-face-to-face transactions; **~zugang** remote access; **~zugangszahlungsinstrument** remote access payment instrument

fertigen to manufacture, to produce

Fertigerzeugnisse finished goods (manufactures), *(fertige Erzeugnisse und Waren)* finished goods and merchandise

Fertigstellung completion, accomplishment

Fertigstellungsgarantie performance (completion) bond

Fertigung manufacturing, production

Fertigungs / ~bereich manufacturing division; **~betrieb** manufacturing operation (concern), production facility; **~gemeinkosten** manufacturing (production) overheads; **~kosten** manufacturing cost; **~vorbereitung** production engineering

Fertigwarenbestände finished goods in stock

fest 1. *adj.* *(~e Börse)* strong (buoyant, firm) market, *(~es Einkommen)* regular income, *(~e Grundstimmung)* firm undertone (underlying sentiment), *(~e Kurse)* firm (strong) prices, *(~er Markt)* buoyant market, *(~e Paritäten)* fixed parities, *(~e Rückzahlungsverpflichtung)* fixed repayment obligation *(~er Schluss)* firm closing, *(geringfügig ~er gegen Schluss der Börsensitzung)* marginally higher at the close of the session, *(~e Übernahme)* firm underwriting (commitment), *(~er Wechselkurs)* fixed exchange rate
2. *adv.* *(die Aktienkurse tendierten weiterhin ~)* equities continued (remained) firm, *(die Ausleihungen ~ refinanzieren)* to fund the lendings at a fixed rate, *(bei lebhaften Umsätzen ~er tendieren)* to turn (to edge) higher in active trading, *(fest zugesagte Fazilität)* committed facility

Fest / ~angebot firm (binding) offer; **~auftrag** firm order; **~besitz** *(der nicht im ~ befindliche Teil des Aktienkapitals)* free float; **~betragshypothek 1.** → Bankvorausdarlehen **2.** mortgage for a specific amount

Fest / ~darlehen 1. *(mit fester Laufzeit)* fixed term loan, loan extended for a fixed period **2.** *(mit Festzins)* fixed rate loan; ~**finanzierungskosten** cost of fixed rate funding; ~**gebot** firm bid

festgefahren *(~e Gespräche)* deadlocked (stalled) talks

Festgeld time deposit(s), fixed term (fixed) deposit

Festgeld / ~anlage time deposit investment; ~**konto** time deposit account; ~**rendite** time money yield; ~**sperre** time deposit freeze; ~**verlängerung** extending a time deposit, time (term) deposit rollover

Festgeschäft 1. firm contract (transaction, deal, bargain)
2. *(i. S. von Termingeschäft)* forward transaction
3. *(Festzinskredite)* fixed rate lendings

festhalten 1. to adhere to, *(an Aktien ~)* to hold on to equities, *(an seinen Fusionsplänen ~)* to adhere to (to stand firm on) one's merger plans, *(an unveränderten Wechselkursparitäten ~)* to stick to unchanged parities
2. to put on record, to record, *(schriftlich ~)* to keep a written record of
3. to persist, *(an der Ablehnung des Kreditantrages ~)* to persist in the refusal of the loan application

Festhalten adherence, observance, *(~ an bestimmten Bonitätserfordernissen)* adherence to specific credit standards, *(~ an einer Entscheidung)* sticking to a decision

Festhypothek fixed date mortgage □ mortgage arrangement whereby the entire principal falls due on a fixed date

festigen *(seine Marktposition ~)* to strengthen (to stabilise, to consolidate, to solidify) one's market position

Festigkeit *(~ des Marktes)* firmness (stability) of the market

Festigung *(~ der Eigenkapitalbasis)* strengthening (stabilisation) of the equity base

Fest / ~jahre 1. fixed term **2.** *(kündigungsfreie Jahre)* call-free years, period during which a bond cannot be called in; ~**kapital** fixed capital; ~**kauf** firm purchase; ~**konditionen** fixed terms, fixed rate(s), *(festkonditionierte Finanzierung)* fixed rate financing (funding), financing on fixed terms

Fest / ~kosten fixed cost; ~**kostenbelastung** fixed cost charge; ~**kredit** fixed rate loan; ~**kurs 1.** fixed price (quotation) **2.** fixed exchange rate; ~**kurssystem** fixed exchange rate system; ~**laufzeit** fixed term (maturity), fixed lifespan, *(festlaufende Sparbriefe)* fixed term savings bonds

festlegen 1. to fix, to stipulate, *(die Bedingungen/die Einzelheiten ~)* to spell out the rules/the details, *(die Berichtspflichten ~)* to lay down (to stipulate) the reporting requirements, *(die genauen Konditionen in einem Kreditvertrag ~)* to set out the full terms in a loan agreement
2. to tie up, to lock up, to invest (to deposit) for a fixed period, *(Barmittel für längere Zeiträume ~)* to invest (to tie up) cash for longer periods
3. *(sich festlegen)* to commit o. s.

Festlegung 1. fixing, stipulation, *(~ der Anleihekonditionen)* establishment of the bond terms, bond pricing, pricing a bond issue, *(~ der Bereitstellungsprovision)* fixing the commitment fee, *(~ des Emissionszeitpunktes)* timing of an issue, *(~ der Kreditkonditionen)* establishment of the loan terms, fixing (setting out) the terms of a credit facility
2. lock-up, *(~ der Spareinlagen auf vier Jahre)* tying up the savings for a period of four years, *(~ der Vertragsbedingungen)* stipulation of the contract terms, laying down the terms of the agreement
3. commitment
4. *(~ einer Zinsobergrenze)* capping an interest rate, fixing an interest rate cap, *(~ einer Zinsuntergrenze)* setting (placing) a floor under an interest rate, fixing an interest rate floor

Festlegungsdauer 1. investment term **2.** fixed investment period, blocking period

F

Festpreis firm (fixed) price

Festpreis / ~angebot fixed quotation, fixed price offer (tender); **~geschäft** fixed price deal (transaction); **~verfahren** fixed price offer(ing), marketing a new issue at a preset fixed price

Festsatz fixed rate, locked-in (locked-up) rate

Festsatz / ~bereich fixed rate lendings, fixed rate lending (loan) sector; **~bond** fixed rate bond, straight bond; **~-Dollarbonds** dollar straights; **~emission** fixed rate deal, fixed rate debt issue, straight issue

Festsatz / ~empfänger fixed rate receiver, fixed receiver □ party receiving a fixed rate under a swap contract while paying a floating rate; **~finanzierung** fixed rate funding (financing); **~garantie** fixed rate guarantee

Festsatz / ~hypothek fixed rate mortgage; **~kondition(en)** fixed interest rate, terms based on a fixed rate of interest, *(~ anbieten)* to offer a fixed rate of interest (fixed interest payments); **~kredit** fixed rate loan; **~mittel** fixed rate funds, fixed funds

Festsatz / ~risiko fixed rate risk □ risk resulting from a surplus of fixed rate assets/positions; **~titel** fixed coupon debt, straight debt securities, straights; **~verbindlichkeit** fixed rate liability (debt)

Festsatz / ~vereinbarung fixed rate agreement, agreement on fixed rate payments, locking in to fixed interest payments; **~verzinsung** payment of a fixed interest rate; **~zahler** fixed rate payer, fixed payer □ party paying a fixed rate under a swap contract while receiving a floating rate of interest

festschreiben 1. *(die neuen Regeln ~)* to fix (to establish) the new rules and regulations **2.** *(einen Zinssatz ~)* to lock in to a fixed rate of interest

Festschreibung 1. fixing, *(~ der Konditionen)* establishing fixed loan terms, locking in the loan terms, *(~ der Kontrolle durch den Hauptaktionär)* entrenching the control of the principal shareholder, *(~ der Währungsparitäten)* fixing of parities
2. blocking, *(~ von Wertpapieren) (a)* blocking (of) securities *(b)* registration of securities in their owners' names
3. *(~ des Zinssatzes auf zwei Jahre)* locking in (up) the interest rate for two years, establishing a fixed interest rate for two years

Festschreibungsfrist fixed rate period, locking-in period

festsetzen 1. to fix, to establish, to lay down, to set, to determine, *(festgesetzter Anspruch)* established claim **2.** *(Steuer, Abgabe)* to assess

Festsetzung 1. fixing, *(~ einer Frist)* setting a term (time) limit, *(~ des Libor-Satzes)* Libor rate setting **2.** *(von Abgaben, Steuern)* assessment

Festsetzungs / ~bescheid 1. *(steuerlicher)* assessment notice **2.** *(Zuschussgewährung)* notice of allowance; **~frist** *(steuerliche)* tax assessment period; **~verfahren 1.** assessment procedure **2.** method of (for) determining

feststehen 1. to be fixed, to be certain **2.** *(feststehendes Recht)* vested interest

feststellbar determinable, ascertainable, assessable

feststellen 1. to ascertain, to conclude, to state, *(die Beschlussfähigkeit ~)* to ascertain a quorum, to fix, to state, *(einen Kurs ~)* to fix (to determine) a price
2. to establish, *(die Identität des Karteninhabers ~)* to establish the cardholder's identity, *(gerichtlich festgestellte Ansprüche)* court-established claims, *(im Insolvenzverfahren festgestellte Forderungen)* acknowledged (accepted) claims, *(rechtskräftig festgestellte Forderungen)* legally effective claims
3. *(den Jahresabschluss ~)* to approve (to establish) the annual accounts
4. *(den Schaden ~)* to assess the damage

Feststellung 1. ascertainment, conclusion, statement, *(~ der Beschlussfä-*

higkeit) ascertainment of a quorum, *(Antrag auf ~ der Beschlussfähigkeit)* call to quorum, *(~ der Zahlungsunfähigkeit)* statement of insolvency
2. fixing, *(~ des amtlichen Kurses)* official price fixing, *(~ des Eröffnungskurses)* fixing the opening price, *(~ der Erträge)* determination of income, *(~ eines Sicherungsrechtes)* determination of a security interest, *i.w.S.* lien search
3. establishment, *(~ einer Forderung)* establishment (acknowledgement, allowance) of a claim, *(~ der Insolvenzmasse)* establishment of the debtor's property, *(~ des Schuldnerverzugs)* establishment of the debtor's default
4. *(~ des Jahresabschlusses)* approval of the annual accounts
5. *(~ des Schadens)* assessment of the damage

Feststellungs / ~**klage** declaratory action, action for a declaratory ruling; ~**last** *(~ für die Richtigkeit)* burden of ensuring the correctness; ~**stelle** *(für die Feststellung eines Kreditereignisses)* Determination Agent; ~**urteil** declaratory judgment (ruling); ~**verfahren** *(bei Konkursforderungen)* approval procedure

Festübernahme *(Emission)* firm underwriting

festverzinslich *(~e Anleihe)* → Festzinsanleihe, *(~e Kapitalanlagen)* fixed income investments, *(~ anlegen)* to invest at a fixed rate of interest

Festverzinsliche fixed income (fixed interest) securities, fixed income debt

Festzins fixed interest rate

Festzins / ~**aktiva** fixed rate assets; ~**aktivüberhang** net long fixed rate position; ~**anleihe** fixed income (fixed coupon) bond, straight bond; ~**ansprüche** claim to fixed rate payments, → Festzinsempfänger; ~**arbitrage** fixed-income arbitrage; ~**derivate** fixed rate (fixed income) derivatives

Festzins / ~**empfänger** *(bei Swapkontrakten)* fixed rate receiver, swap seller □ party that receives fixed rate and pays floating rate cash flows in a swap; ~**empfänger-Swap** receiver swap, *(Option auf einen Festzinsempfänger-Swap)* receiver swaption

Festzins / ~**hypothek** fixed rate mortgage; ~**kredit** fixed rate loan; ~**kreditgeschäft** fixed rate lending operations; ~**kreditportefeuille** fixed rate loan book; ~**lücke** fixed-rate gap; ~**nehmer** → Festzinsempfänger

Festzins / ~**passiva** fixed rate liabilities; ~**passivüberhang** net short fixed rate position; ~**satz** fixed interest rate; ~**schulden** fixed interest debt (liabilities); ~ **schuldtitel** fixed income debt securities

Festzins / ~**seite** *(eines Swap-Kontraktes)* fixed leg; ~**sparen** fixed rate saving; ~**teil** fixed rate component, → Festzinsseite; ~-**Tender** fixed rate tender

Festzins / ~**überhänge** **1.** surplus of fixed rate positions **2.** fixed interest surplus; ~**vereinbarung** fixed rate agreement; ~**verpflichtungen** fixed interest payment obligations, fixed rate payment commitments

Festzins / ~**zahler** *(bei Swapkontrakten)* fixed rate payer, swap buyer □ party that pays fixed rate and receives floating rate cash flows in a swap ; ~**zahler-Swap** payer swap, *(Option auf einen Festzinszahler-Swap)* payer swaption, call swaption; ~**zahlungen** fixed interest payments

Feuerwehrfonds → Einlagensicherungsfonds

FFG → Finanzmarktförderungsgesetz

fiduziarisch *(~e Abtretung)* fiduciary assignment

fiktiv *(~e Anleihe) (Basiswert eines Zins-Terminkontraktes)* fictitious (notional) bond, *(~e Dividende)* fictitious (sham) dividend

Filial / ~**bank** multibranch bank, multiple office bank; ~**bankensystem**

branch banking, multiple office banking; ~-**Debitoren** branch debtors

Filiale branch, branch office, branch establishment

Filial / ~**geschäft** multibranch banking, *(filialgestützte Bankgeschäfte)* branch-based banking operations; ~**kostenrechnung** branch costing; ~-**Kreditoren** branch creditors; ~**leiter** branch manager

F

Filial / ~**netz** branch network; ~**prokura** authority to act for a branch establishment; ~**steuerung** branch control; ~**vertrieb** branch sales

Finalitätsrichtlinie (EU) Settlement Finality Directive

Finanz / ~**abschreibungen** financial write-offs; ~**abteilung** finance department (division); ~**aktiva** financial assets, *(Finanzaktiva im Bankbestand)* financial assets in the banking book

Finanz / ~**ampel** traffic light labelling for financial products; ~**amt** tax office, revenue office (authorities)

Finanz / ~**analyse** financial (investment) analysis, analysis of a company's financial statements, *i.w.S.* investment research; ~**analyseverordnung** Analysis of Financial Instruments Regulation; ~**analyst** financial analyst, investment (research, securities) analyst

Finanz / ~**anlageergebnis** income (loss) from financial investments, result on financial investments; ~**anlagen** investments, investment securities, long-term investments, financial assets

Finanz / ~**anlagenvermittler** investment intermediary, financial investment broker; ~**anlagenvermittler- und Vermögensanlagerecht** Investment Intermediary and Asset Investment Law; ~**anlagenvermittlung** investment intermediation, financial investment brokerage; ~**anzeige** financial advertisement; ~**apparat** financial system

Finanz / ~**aufkommen** budgetary receipts, state revenue; ~**aufsicht** financial supervision, financial services supervision; ~**aufsichtsbehörde** financial supervisory authority, Financial Services Authority (UK), → BaFIN

Finanz / ~**aufwendungen** finance expenditure, financial charges; ~**ausgleich** financial equalisation (adjustment); ~**ausschuss** finance committee (commission)

Finanz / ~**ausstattung** financial (capital) resources, availability of financial resources; ~**ausweis** financial accounts

Finanz / ~**bedarf** borrowing (finance) requirements; ~**behörde** revenue office (authority); ~**beihilfe** financial assistance (aid); ~**beitrag** financial contribution

Finanz / ~**berater** financial advisor (consultant); ~**beratung** financial advice (consultancy), financial advisory service; ~**bereich** financial (finance) sector; ~**berichterstattung** financial reporting

Finanz / ~**beteiligung** financial interest (stake), *(pl)* financial investments, interests (investments) in the financial sector; ~**bewegungsrechnung** source and application of funds

Finanz / ~**daten** financial data; ~**deckung** financial cover; ~**derivate** financial derivatives, derivative financial products; ~**dienstleister** financial services company (provider)

Finanzdienstleistungen financial services

Finanzdienstleistungs / ~**aufsichtsgesetz** Financial Services Supervision Act; ~**industrie/sektor** financial services industry (sector); ~**institut** financial services institution

Finanz / ~**differenzgeschäft** financial contract for difference, → Aktien-Differenzgeschäft; ~**direktor** (Senior) Finance Manager, (Senior) Treasurer, → Finanzvorstand; ~**disposition** treasury (financial) management;

~**engpass** financial straits, liquidity squeeze

Finanzen finance(s), financial means

Finanz / ~**ergebnis** 1. financial results, financial performance 2. *(im Jahresabschluss)* non-operating result; ~**erträge** financial income; ~**fachmann** financial expert; ~**flussrechnung** funds statement, financial flow statement

Finanz / ~**garantie** financial guarantee; ~**gebaren** 1. financial management (policy), handling of financial matters 2. management of public finances; ~**geflecht** financial net (web)

Finanz / ~**gericht** Fiscal Court; ~**gerichtsbarkeit** fiscal jurisdiction; ~**geschäfte** financial transactions (operations); ~**geschehen** financial activities; ~**gruppe** financial group, group of investors

Finanz / ~**hedging** hedging in the financial markets; ~**hilfe** financial aid (assistance), financing aid; ~**hoheit** fiscal prerogative; ~**holdinggesellschaft** financial holding company

finanziell 1. *adj. (~e Absicherungen)* financial safeguards, *(~e Belastung)* financial charge (strain, burden), *(~es Engagement)* financial commitment (exposure), financial involvement, *(~e Ferngeschäfte)* financial non-face-to-face transactions, *(~e Gesundung)* financial revitalisation (recovery), *(~es Gleichgewicht) (a)* financial equilibrium *(b)* sound financial footing (basis)
(~e Leistung) financial performance, *(~e Mittel)* financial resources (funds), *(~e Neuordnung/Sanierung)* financial reconstruction (rehabilitation, restructuring), *(~e Rechnungslegung)* financial accounting, *(~es Risiko)* financial risk (exposure), *(~e Schwierigkeiten)* financial difficulties (embarrassment, woes)
(~e Sicherheit) financial security, *(~e Unterstützung)* financial backing (support), financial assistance, funding (financing) support, *(~e Verbindlichkeiten zu Handelszwecken)* financial liabilities held for trading, *(~e Verpflichtungen)* financial obligations, *(~e Wertschöpfungskette)* financial value chain
2. *adv. (ein Projekt ~ absichern)* to ensure the provision of funds for a project, to provide financial backing for a project, *(die Gruppe ~ sanieren)* to restructure the group financially, *(die Tochtergesellschaft ~ unterstützen)* to support (to back) the subsidiary financially
(~ angeschlagenes Unternehmen) financially stricken (distressed, troubled) company, *(~ gesundes Unternehmen)* financially sound company, *(~ schwaches Unternehmen)* financially weak company, cash-strapped company, *(~ sicher)* financially secure

Finanzier financier, provider of finance (funds), investor

finanzierbar *(längerfristig ~e Investitionen)* investments capable of being financed over the longer term

finanzieren to finance, to fund, to payroll, *(bis zu 90% ~)* to finance up to 90% (to the extent of 90%), *(mit Bankkrediten ~)* to finance with bank debt (with bank borrowings), to finance (to fund) through bank facilities, *(weitgehend aus Barguthaben ~)* to finance largely from cash resources *(aus dem verfügbaren Einkommen ~)* to finance from disposable income, *(über den Kapitalmarkt ~)* to fund (to source) through the capital market, to fund through tapping the capital market, to finance through the issuance of bonds, *(aus Kreditmitteln ~)* to finance from loan funds, *(mit staatlichen Mitteln ~)* to finance through governmental funding
(das Programm finanziert sich durch regelmäßige Beiträge) the scheme is funded by regular contributions, *(sich aus verschiedenen Quellen ~)* to draw finance from a number of sources, *(den laufenden Schuldendienst ~)* to

F

finance ongoing debt service payments

Finanzierung *(~ durch Aktien)* equity (stock) financing, *(~ des Anlagevermögens)* fixed asset financing, *(~ durch Bankkredite)* financing through borrowings with banks (through bank loans), *(~ aus Betriebsgewinnen)* financing out of operating earnings, *(~ außerhalb der Bilanz)* off-balance sheet financing, financing off the balance sheet
(~ aus Eigenmitteln) financing from funds generated internally (from internal earnings), financing (funding) out of own resources, *(~ durch Forderungsabtretung)* accounts receivable financing, *(~ durch Fremdmittel)* financing with outside capital (borrowed funds), *(~ über Geldmarktpapiere)* funding through money market debt, *(~ langlebiger Gebrauchsgüter)* financing consumer durables
(~ aus einer Hand) one-stop financing package, *(~ von Investitionen)* capital investment financing, *(~ durch private Kapitalgeber)* private capital funding, *(~ des Kreditgeschäfts)* funding of lending operations, *(~ aus einbehaltenen Mitteln)* funding from retained earnings
(~ durch Pensionsgeschäfte) financing with repurchase agreements, *(Kredite zur ~ von Übernahmen)* loans to finance corporate takeovers, *(~ des Umlaufvermögens)* current asset financing, *(~ von Vorratsvermögen)* inventory financing, financing inventories

Finanzierungs / ~abschnitt 1. funding tranche **2.** financing (funding) phase, **~alternativen** financing alternatives, *(die dem Kunden zur Verfügung stehenden ~)* financing (funding) options available to the customer

Finanzierungs / ~angebot offer to finance, financing offering; **~arrangeur** finance arranger; **~aufwand** financing (borrowing) cost(s), finance charges

Finanzierungs / ~basis funding base; **~baustein 1.** funding component, financing block **2.** *(Beitrag)* funding contribution

Finanzierungsbedarf financing (funding) needs, borrowing requirements, *(~ der Emittenten)* issuers' borrowing requirements, issuers' capital needs, *(~ der öffentlichen Hand)* public borrowing requirements

Finanzierungs / ~bedingungen financing terms, terms of finance, funding conditions; **~beitrag** contribution to financing; **~bereitschaft** willingness to finance (to provide funds); **~bilanz** financing statement, statement of sources and application of funds

Finanzierungs / ~dauer financing (finance) period, life (term) of the financing; **~defizit 1.** financing (funding) deficit, funding shortage, shortage of funds, *(~ der Unternehmen)* corporate financial deficit **2.** net borrowing of the government; **~einheit** financing unit

finanzierungsfähig eligible for funding, capable of being financed

Finanzierungs / ~fazilität finance facility; **~form** form (method, way, type) of financing, funding vehicle; **~frage** funding (finance, financial) problem; **~fundament** funding base

Finanzierungs / ~grenze funding limit; **~gesellschaft** finance company; **~hilfe** financial aid (assistance); **~instrument** financing (funding) tool, funding vehicle

Finanzierungs / ~kennzahl financial ratio; **~-Know-how** financing expertise; **~ kompetenz** expertise in financing; **~konditionen** financing terms, terms of finance

Finanzierungs / ~konsortium finance consortium, consortium to finance (to fund); **~konstruktion** financing arrangement; **~konzentration** concentration of funding; **~konzept** financing (funding) blueprint, finance concept; **~kosten** financing (borrowing) cost(s), finance charges (costs, expenditure), total cost of credit

Finanzierungs / ~lasten financing charge(s), burden of financing; **~leasing** finance leasing; **~lösungen** financing solutions; **~lücke** financing gap (shortage), funding gap (shortfall)

Finanzierungs / ~marge funding margin; **~mechanismus** financing mechanism; **~mittel** finance, financial resources, finance capital, *(Angebot an ~n)* funding supply, *(unbesicherte ~)* unsecured funding; **~-Mix** funding mix, multi-product financing mix; **~modalitäten** financing terms

Finanzierungs / ~modell financing (funding) model, way of financing; **~möglichkeiten 1.** financing (funding) opportunities, openings for finance, ways (forms) of raising finance **2.** *(Fähigkeiten, Kapazitäten)* funding capabilities (capacities) **3.** *(Optionen)* financing (funding) options

Finanzierungs / ~objekt asset (project) being financed; **~obligo** financial commitment (exposure); **~offerte** financing offer

Finanzierungs / ~paket financing (funding) package, loan package, funding deal; **~palette** range of credit facilities (funding instruments) offered; **~papiere** financing (funding) instruments □ money market paper issued by government agencies and local authorities to cover their borrowing requirements

Finanzierungs / ~phase financing round, phase of financing; **~plan** finance (financing) plan, financial planning statement; **~programm** financing (funding) scheme, finance program

Finanzierungs / ~quelle funding source, source of financing (of funds); **~rechnung** cash flow statement; **~regeln** financing rules (standards), funding rules; **~rückhalt** financial backing (support)

Finanzierungsschätze *(des Bundes)* Federal Treasury financing paper □ short-term notes (maturities up to two years) issued on a tap basis; interest is paid by way of a discount from the purchase price

Finanzierungs / ~schwerpunkt emphasis of funding activities; **~schwierigkeiten** funding difficulties, financial distress, difficulties in providing the necessary funds (finance); **~sicherheit** *(als ~ dienen)* to serve as collateral for the financing; **~struktur** funding pattern, financing structure

Finanzierungs / ~technik financing techniques, finance (financial) engineering, mechanics of finance; **~titel** debt security; **~träger** financing (funding) institution, organisation providing the funds for …; **~überschuss** financial surplus

Finanzierungs / ~vereinbarung financing (funding) arrangement; **~verpflichtung 1.** obligation to finance **2.** liability to provide financial support; **~vertrag** finance (financing) agreement

Finanzierungs / ~volumen 1. financing (funding) volume **2.** total loan amount, total lendings; **~vorschlag** financing (funding) proposal; **~wechsel** finance (credit) bill

Finanzierungs / ~zusage undertaking (commitment) to finance, commitment to fund, finance (funding) commitment; **~zusageprovision** loan commitment fee; **~zwänge** financing constraints

Finanz / ~innovationen financial innovations; **~institut** financial institution, finance company; **~instrument** *(~e des Handelsbuches)* financial instruments in the trading book; **~interessen** financial interests

Finanz / ~intermediäre financial intermediaries □ banks, investment funds, insurance companies; **~intermediation** financial intermediation, intermediation between users and sellers of financial services; **~investitionen** financial investments, *(als ~ gehaltene Grundstücke)* investment properties; **~jahr** fiscal year

F

Finanz / ~kapital 1. finance capital **2.** *(im bilanziellen Kontext)* equity and long-term borrowings; **~kennzahl 1.** financial ratio (measure) **2.** *(durch den Kreditnehmer einzuhaltende Finanzkennzahlen)* financial covenants; **~kennzahlenanalyse** financial ratio analysis

Finanz / ~klemme financial straits (squeeze); **~kommissionsgeschäft** financial brokerage business, financial broking services, finance agency transactions

F

Finanz / ~konglomerat financial conglomerate, diversified financial group; **~konglomerat-Richtlinie** EU Financial Conglomerates Directive; **~konsortium** financial (finance) consortium, finance syndicate

Finanz / ~kontrolle financial control (supervision); **~konzept** funding concept (blueprint); **~kraft** financial strength (muscle, clout), funding power (capabilities); **~kraft-Ratings** financial strength ratings

Finanzkredit 1. finance facility (loan), finance facility linked to a specific transaction, loan to finance (e. g. the takeover of a company)
2. *(gebundener Finanzkredit)* buyer credit □ a domestic bank lends directly to the foreign buyer

Finanzkredit / ~bürgschaft buyer credit surety (for public sector borrowers); **~deckung** buyer credit cover; **~garantie** buyer credit guarantee (for private sector borrowers)

Finanz / ~kreise financial community (circles); **~lage** financial situation (condition, position), *(die ~ des Unternehmens)* the company's financial situation, state of the company's finances

Finanz / ~lasten financial burden, financial expenditure burden; **~leistungen** financial services; **~makler** finance broker; **~management** financial management

Finanzmarktaufsicht (regulatory) supervision of financial markets

Finanzmarktförderungsgesetz (Viertes ~) Fourth Financial Markets Development Act □ The Act aims at strengthening Germany as a financial centre. It contains comprehensive amendments to the Stock Exchange Act and Securities Trading Act.

Finanzmarktliberalisierung liberalisation (deregulation) of financial markets; **~regulierung** financial market regulation

Finanzmarktrichtlinie (Richtlinie über Märkte für Finanzinstrumente) EU Markets in Financial Instruments Directive (MiFID) □ Replaced the EU Investment Services Directive (Wertpapierdienstleistungsrichtlinie) to reflect changes in the financial markets. Principal objectives: harmonisation of investment services regulations across jurisdictions, strengthening the protection of consumers/investors and enhancing financial transparency. Institutions falling within the scope of MiFID also have to comply with the Capital Requirements Directive (CDR). → Eigenkapitalrichtlinie

Finanzmarktrichtlinie-Umsetzungsgesetz MiFID Implementation Act

Finanzmarktstabilisierungsanstalt Financial Market Stabilisation Agency □ manages the → Finanzmarktstabilisierungsfonds (SoFFin)

Finanzmarktstabilisierungsbeschleunigungsgesetz Financial Market Stabilisation Acceleration Act □ aims at accelerating the implementation of recapitalisation measures

Finanzmarktstabilisierungsergänzungsgesetz Supplementary Financial Market Stabilisation Act □ allows the Government to expropriate the shareholders of systemically important banks that are in financial distress and require support under the rescue package set out in the → Finanzmarktstabilisierungsgesetz

Finanzmarktstabilisierungsfonds (Sonderfonds Finanzmarktstabilisierung/ SoFFiN) Financial Market Stabilisation Fund □ designed to support the financial markets by providing guarantees for newly-issued refinancing instruments/debt securities and equity investments

Finanzmarktstabilisierungsfondsgesetz Financial Market Stabilisation Fund Act

Finanzmarktstabilisierungs-Fortentwicklungsgesetz Bad Bank Act, Act on the Further Development of Financial Market Stabilisation □ Enacted in 2009, the Bad Bank Act aims at supplementing the framework established by the → Finanzmarktstabilisierungsgesetz. It enables banks to transfer risk positions/problem loans to an external unit (Bad Bank) and thus remove these positions from their balance sheets. → Konsolidierungsmodell, → Zweckgesellschaftsmodell

Finanzmarktstabilisierungsgesetz Financial Market Stabilisation Act □ aims at restoring confidence in the financial sector. It was enacted in 2008 and authorises the government to seize control of banks whose failure would pose a threat to the financial system. It includes the → Finanzmarktstabilisierungsfondsgesetz and the Finanzmarktstabilisierungsbeschleunigungsgesetz.

Finanzmittel 1. *(Bilanzposition)* cash and cash equivalents **2.** *(allg.)* financial means (resources), funds

Finanzmittel / **~abfluss** cash outflow; **~bedarf** required funds; **~fonds** cash and cash equivalents, *(zahlungswirksame Veränderung des ~)* net change in cash and cash equivalents; **~überschuss** net cash flow; **~zufluss** cash inflow

Finanz / **~ordnung** financial system (regulations); **~papiere** financial securities; **~passiva** financial liabilities; **~plan** financial (budget) plan, financial planning statement; **~planung** financial (budget) planning, financial budgeting

Finanzplatz financial market place, financial centre, *(Finanzplatz Deutschland)* Germany as a financial centre, *(Stärkung des Finanzplatzes Deutschlands)* enhancing (strengthening) Germany's position (role) as a financial centre

Finanz / **~portal** financial (finance) portal; **~portfolioverwaltung** financial portfolio management; **~polster** financial cushion; **~rückversicherung** financial reinsurance; **~schulden** financial liabilities, borrowings

finanzschwach *(~es Unternehmen)* financially weak company

Finanz / **~schwierigkeiten** financial (funding) difficulties, shortage of funds; **~sektor** financial sector; **~sicherheit** financial collateral; **~sicherheiten-Richtlinie** (EU) Financial Collateral Arrangements Directive

Finanz / **~sponsor** financial sponsor; **~spritze** capital injection, infusion of capital, fresh funding

finanzstark *(~es Unternehmen)* financially strong (sound) company

Finanz / **~status 1.** financial statement **2.** *(eines Kreditantragstellers)* statement of assets and liabilities, affordability status **3.** → Finanzübersicht; **~-Swap** financial swap

Finanz / **~terminkontrakt** financial futures contract, financial future; **~terminmarkt** financial futures market

Finanz / **~titel 1.** financial instrument, debt instrument (security) **2.** *(börsennotierte Finanztitel)* financials; **~transaktion** financial transaction (operation, deal); **~transfergeschäft** money transmission services; **~übersicht** *(Konten- und Depotübersicht)* net worth statement; **~unternehmen** financial enterprise

Finanz / **~verbund 1.** financial network (association) **2.** → genossenschaftli-

F

cher Finanzverbund; ~**verfassung** financial system; ~**vermögen** financial assets; ~**vermögensverwaltung** financial assets management

Finanz / ~**vertrieb** financial services distribution; ~**verwaltung** revenue authorities; ~**vorstand** Chief Financial Officer, Finance Director

Finanz / ~**wechsel** finance bill; ~**werte** financials, financial shares (stocks); ~**wirtschaft** *(öffentliche)* public finance; ~**zentrum** financial centre, → Finanzplatz; ~**zuweisungen** allocation of funds

FinDAG → Gesetz über die integrierte Finanzaufsicht

finden *(einen Käufer ~)* to find (to locate) a buyer

Firma **1.** business, company, firm, concern **2.** *(in der Anschrift)* Messrs

Firmen / ~**anteil** share in a business, partnership share, business interest; ~ **ausfallrisiko** corporate default exposure; ~**bezeichnung** firm (business) name, style of the company

Firmen / ~**bonds** corporate bonds; ~**briefbogen** headed paper; ~**bürgschaft** corporate guarantee; ~**eigentum** company property, corporate assets

Firmen / ~**geschäft** *(einer Bank)* corporate banking; ~**inhaber** owner (proprietor) of a business, company owner; ~**kapital** company's capital, capital stock; ~**karte** company card, business credit card; ~**konto** business account

Firmenkredit business loan (credit), commercial (corporate) loan, *(Konditionen für ~e)* business loan rates

Firmenkredit / ~**buch** corporate loan book; ~**engagement** corporate credit exposure; ~**geschäft** corporate lending business; ~**karte** → Firmenkarte; ~**portefeuille** corporate (commercial) loan book

Firmenkunde **1.** business customer, corporate customer (client), *(pl)* corporates, *(große Firmenkunden)* large corporate customers, large caps, *(kleine Firmenkunden)* small firm customers **2.** *(Kontoverbindung)* business (corporate) account relationship

Firmenkunden / ~**abteilung** Corporate Customer Desk, Corporate Accounts Department (Desk), Corporate Banking; ~**bereich** corporate banking sector (market), *(im ~)* on the corporate banking side, in the corporate banking market

Firmenkunden / ~**betreuer** corporate relationship manager, *i.e.S.* corporate accounts officer; ~**betreuung** **1.** corporate relationship management, relationship banking, *i.e.S.* servicing (and counselling) corporate customers **2.** → Firmenkundenabteilung

Firmenkunden / ~**einlagen** corporate deposits, corporate customer deposits; ~**geschäft** **1.** *(allg.)* corporate banking, corporate customer business (operations), wholesale banking, *(elektronisches Firmenkundengeschäft)* corporate electronic banking **2.** *(Geschäftsfeld einer Bank nach Basel II)* Commercial Banking

Firmenkunden / ~**kredit** business (corporate) loan; ~**kreditgeschäft** corporate lending operations; ~**profitabilität** *(Messung der ~)* measuring corporate customer profitability; ~**termineinlagen** corporate time deposits

Firmen / ~**lastschrift** → SEPA-Firmenlastschrift; ~**mantel** corporate shell; ~**neugründung** business start-up; ~**sitz** registered office

Firmen / ~**übernahme** company (corporate) takeover, *(~ durch den Erwerb von Unternehmensanteilen/Anlagen)* share/asset deal; ~**übernahmefinanzierung** corporate acquisition financing, financing corporate takeovers

Firmen / ~**vermögen** company (business) assets, corporate assets; ~**wert** goodwill, *(erworbener Firmenwert)* acquired surplus; ~**zusammenschluss** merger of companies, business combination

firmieren to trade under the name of…

First/Second Quotation Board Subsegments of the → Freiverkehr (Open Market) of Frankfurter Wertpapierbörse. While the First Quotation Board has been established for companies seeking an initial listing in the Open Market, the Second Quotation Board has been designed for companies whose shares are already listed on another national or international exchange. → Regulierter Markt

fiskalisch *(~e Anreize)* fiscal stimuli (incentives), *(~e Vorteile)* tax advantages, tax relief

Fiskalvertreter fiscal representative (of a foreign company in Germany)

fixe Seite *(eines Swap-Kontraktes)* fixed leg

Fixkosten fixed cost; **~belastung** fixed cost charge; **~remanenz** excess of fixed costs

Fixum fixed allowance (remuneration)

flach *(~e Hierarchie)* flat hierarchy, *(~e Zinskurve)* flat (humped) yield curve

flächendeckend *(~e Vertretung)* nationwide representation, *(~er Vertrieb)* nationwide sale, national coverage

Flächen / ~instandhaltungskosten facilities maintenance cost; **~management** space management; *i.w.S.* facility management; **~nutzungskataster** land use cadaster; **~nutzungsplan** land use plan, development plan

Flaggenformation *(Chart-Analyse)* flag pattern (formation) □ short-term continuation pattern

flankierend *(~e Maßnahmen)* accompanying (supporting) measures

flau *(~es Geschäft)* sluggish (slack) trade, *(~er Immobilienmarkt)* flat (dull) property market

Flaute dullness, sluggishness, stagnation

Flexibilität flexibility

flexible *(~ Inanspruchnahme eines Kredites)* flexible borrowing, flexible drawings, availment at the discretion of the borrower, *(~ Konditionengestaltung)* flexible pricing, *(~ Planungsrechnung)* flexible budgeting, *(~ Wechselkurse)* flexible exchange rates

fließen to flow, to pour, *(auf den Kapitalmarkt ~)* to flow into the capital market, *(umfangreiche Mittel in das Projekt ~ lassen)* to pour (to channel) substantial funds into the project

Fließhandel continuous trading, trading stock continuously

floatfrei *(~e Geldverrechnung)* float-free settlement of payments

Floatgewinn float, float profit, profit from varying value dates

floatinduziert *(~er Zinsverlust)* float-induced loss of interest

Floatnutzen → Floatgewinn

Floor / ~-Darlehen floored variable rate loan; **~käufer** floor buyer; **~prämie** floor premium; **~verkäufer** floor seller, writer of a floor, → Cap-Darlehen, Collar-Darlehen

florieren to thrive, to flourish, to prosper, to boom, *(florierender Markt)* thriving (burgeoning) market

flottantes Material freely tradeable stock

Flottenleasing fleet leasing

Fluchtgelder flight capital

Flugzeug / ~finanzierung aircraft financing; **~fonds** aircraft fund; **~hypothek** aircraft mortgage; **~pfandbriefe** Aircraft Pfandbriefe □ Pfandbriefe (Covered Bonds) secured against aircrafts

Fluktuation fluctuation, oscillation, variation

fluktuieren to fluctuate, to oscillate, to vary

Flur cadastral area; **~karte** cadastral map, subdivision map; **~stück** parcel, plot; ~**stückskennzeichen**/~**nummer** parcel identifier

Fluss flow, flux, *(sich im ~ befinden)* to pass through a period of flux, to be in flux

Flussgrößen flow variables

flüssig 1. liquid **2.** available, *(~ sein)* to hold ample liquid funds (resources), *(~e Mittel)* liquid funds (resources), liquidity

F

Flussladeschein/Flusskonnossement inland waterway consignment note

Flut *(~ von Neuemissionen)* glut (surge, welter) of new issues

FMSA → Finanzmarktstabilisierungsanstalt

FMSterG → Finanzmarktstabilisierungsergänzungsgesetz

FMStFG → Finanzmarktstabilisierungsfondsgesetz

FMStG → Finanzmarktstabilisierungsgesetz

Fokussierung focussing, placing special emphasis on

Folge 1. *(Ergebnis, Wirkung)* consequence, result, *(~n für den Kapitalmarkt)* consequences for (implications for, repercussions on, impact on) the capital market
2. *(Reihenfolge)* order, succession, *(AB ließ die Dividendenzahlungen zum zweiten Mal in ~ ausfallen)* AB has passed its dividend for the second year running, *(Umsatzsteigerung für das dritte Jahr in ~)* sales increase for the third year in succession
3. *(Fortsetzung, Sequenz)* continuation, sequence

Folge / ~**abtretung** consequential assignment; ~**änderungen** consequential (subsequent) amendments; ~**aufträge** *(Börse)* repeat (follow-up) orders, follow-through support

Folge / ~**belastung** subsequent charge; ~**berichterstattung** follow-up reporting; ~**bewertung** subsequent valuation (measurement)

Folge / ~**emission** follow-up (subsequent) issue, seasoned public offering; ~**finanzierung** subsequent financing; ~**geschäfte** follow-up (subsequent) business; ~**kosten** consequential charges

folgen 1. to follow, *(unmittelbar auf die Sanierung ~)* to come hard on the heels of the restructuring **2.** *(~ aus)* to ensue, to result from

folgend *(~er Geschäftstag Usance)* following business day convention □ i.e. payment/settlement date that falls on a non-business/non-settlement day rolls forward to the next business day, *(~e Rechnungsperiode)* subsequent accounting period

folgern to conclude, to infer, to deduce

Folgerung conclusion

Folge / ~**schaden** consequential damage (loss); ~**tranche** subsequent tranche; ~**wirkungen** repercussions

Fonds fund, investment fund, mutual fund, unit trust, → OGAW, → Sondervermögen, → Spezial-Sondervermögen, → Publikums-Sondervermögen, *(Fonds ohne Ausgabeaufschlag)* no-load fund, *(Fonds für allgemeine Bankrisiken)* Fund for General Banking Risks

Fonds / ~**anlagen 1.** fund's investments **2.** investments in unit trusts; ~**anteil** unit, share; ~**anteilsbestand** unitholding, shareholding; ~**anteilseigner** unitholder, shareholder; ~**ausgabe** issuance of mutual fund shares, fund sales; ~**ausgabeaufschlag** front-end load, sales charge

Fonds / ~**ausgangsquellensteuer** withholding tax on the fund distribution side; ~ **ausgangsseite** fund distribution side; ~**ausschüttung** distribution by a fund, fund's payout; ~**betreiber** fund manager

Fonds / ~**eingangsquellensteuer** withholding tax on the fund receipt side; ~**eingangsseite** fund receipt side; ~**einlagen** fund deposits;~**entnahmen** fund withdrawals; ~**entnahmeplan**

fund withdrawal plan; ~**familie** family of funds

fondsgebunden *(~es Anlageprodukt)* unit-linked investment product, *(~e Vermögensverwaltung)* fund-based asset (portfolio) management

Fonds / ~gesellschaft investment company; ~**handel** (closed-end) funds trading

Fonds-im-Fonds-Konzept fund-in-fund concept

Fonds / ~initiator fund initiator; ~**kaufmann/kauffrau** investment fund professional; ~-**Leasingfinanzierung** financing by way of fund leasing; ~-**Manager** fund manager

Fonds / ~mittel funds, fund assets, fund's resources; ~**notierung** unit quotation, quotation of unit (share) prices; ~**platzierung** placement of units (shares); ~**police** unit-linked policy

Fonds / ~rating mutual fund rating; ~**richtlinien** fund's investment policy guidelines; ~**rücknahme** fund (unit) redemption; ~**rücknahmeabschlag** back-end load, deferred sales charge, fund redemption fee

Fonds / ~sparplan mutual fund savings scheme; ~**vermittler** (mutual) fund broker; ~**vermittlung** fund brokerage; ~**vermögen** fund assets; ~**vertrieb** fund sales, mutual fund distribution

Fonds / ~verwalter fund manager; ~**verwaltung** fund management; ~**verwaltungsgesellschaft** fund management company; ~**zeichner** subscriber to units (shares)

forcieren 1. *(den Absatz ~)* to push sales **2.** *(beschleunigen)* to step up, to accelerate

Förder / ~bank development bank; ~**datenbank** funding database

förderfähig eligible for assistance, → förderungsfähig

Förder / ~fonds development fund; ~**gebiet** development area, region (area) assisted; ~**geschäft** development lending business; ~**institut 1.** development agency **2.** public development bank, *(Förderinstitute des Bundes)* development agencies of the Federal Government

Förder / ~kredit development loan, state-aided loan; ~**kreditprogramm** funding scheme, development loan scheme; ~**kriterien** assistance criteria, eligibility requirements

förderlich advantageous, beneficial, conducive to

Förder / ~maßnahmen assistance (support, development) measures, measures designed to assist (to promote, to further); ~**mittel** development (support) funds, *(Zuschuss)* subsidy, grant

fordern to demand, to call for, to request, to ask, to claim, *(eine Entschädigung ~)* to claim compensation, *(eine zu hohe Provision ~)* to ask too high a fee, *(eine Untersuchung ~)* to call for an investigation, *(die sofortige Zahlung der geschuldeten Summe ~)* to demand immediate payment of the amount owed

fördern 1. to promote, to assist, to further, to support, to sponsor, *(den Absatz ~)* to promote (to spur on) sales, *(Investitionen ~)* to encourage (to promote, to foster) investments
2. *(gefördert werden)* to enjoy the support of, to be sponsored by **3.** *(entwickeln)* to develop

Förderprogramm 1. development (assistance) scheme, support programme **2.** funding scheme, *(~ mit Eigenkapitalcharakter)* funding scheme with equity capital feature

Forderung 1. demand, request, call, *(~ nach Bereitstellung zusätzlicher Sicherheiten)* call for the provision of additional collateral, call for a collateral enhancement
2. *(Anspruch)* claim, *(~aus der Grundschuld)* claim arising from the land charge, *(~ gegenüber dem Kreditnehmer)* claim on (against) the borrower
3. *(Kreditforderung)* *(a)* loan asset,

F

(~ *zum Zeitpunkt des Ausfalls)* exposure at default *(b)* claim under a loan agreement
4. *(Schuld)* debt
5. *(Warenforderungen)* trade receivables, accounts receivable

Förderung 1. promotion, assistance, furtherance, encouragement, *(~ der gewerblichen Wirtschaft)* development of trade and industry, promoting trade and industrial development
2. (financial) funding, financial assistance

F

Forderungen an (~ *Kreditinstitute*) claims on banks, due from banks, lendings to banks, loans and advances to banks, *(~ Kunden)* claims on (due from) customers, lendings to customers, loans and advances to non-bank customers, *(~ öffentliche Haushalte)* claims on (lendings to) local authorities, *(~ Privatkunden/imRetailkreditgeschäft)* retail lendings, retail exposures, claims on retail customers
(~ Staaten/staatliche Schuldner) claims on sovereigns, claims on (lendings to) sovereign borrowers, *(~ öffentliche Stellen)* claims on (lendings to) public sector entities, *(~ verbundene Unternehmen)* due from affiliated companies, *(~ Wertpapierhäuser)* claims on securities firms, *(~ Wirtschaftsunternehmen)* claims on corporates

Forderungen aus *(~ einem Akkreditiv)* claims under a documentary credit, *(~ Aktienzeichnungen)* receivables from share (stock) subscriptions, *(~ Finanzierungsverträgen)* receivables (claims) under funding agreements
(~ Inkassogeschäften) collection claims, *(~ Kapitalzeichnungen)* receivables from capital subscribed, receivables from equity subscriptions, *(~ Kreditgeschäften)* receivables from lending transactions
(~ Lieferungen und Leistungen) trade receivables, trade debtors, *(~ gezogenen Salden)* claims from (under) balances struck, *(~ Teilzahlungsgeschäften)* receivables (balances outstanding) under hire purchase agreements, *(~ Termingeschäften)* claims from contracts for future delivery, claims under future contracts (forward agreements)
(~ Umschuldungsvereinbarungen) amounts due under rescheduling agreements, *(~ Vermögenseinlagen)* receivables from assets contributed, *(~ Warenlieferungen)* trade receivables, accounts receivable,trade, *(~ Wertpapiergeschäften)* receivables from securities transactions, *(~ Zeichnungen)* subscription receivables, *(~ Zinsabgrenzungen)* accrued interest receivables

Forderungen gegenüber *(~ Banken)* claims on banks, due from banks, lendings to banks, *(~Dritten)* claims against third parties, receivables from third parties, *(~ Konzerngesellschaften)* claims on group companies, amounts owed by (due from) group companies, intragroup receivables

Forderungs / ~abschlag debt discount; **~abschreibung** *(einer Bank)* writing off a loan, loan write-off (charge-off), credit write-off; **~absicherung** receivables hedge, hedging receivables; **~abtretung** assignment of receivables, assignment (transfer) of a claim

Forderungs / ~anerkennung allowance of a claim; **~ankauf** purchase (buying) of receivables, → Factoring; **~anmeldeformular** (proof of) claim form; **~anmeldung 1.** asserting (filing) a claim, submission of a claim **2.** *(im Insolvenzverfahren)* proof of debt, proving a debt, lodgement of (filing) a proof of claim

Forderungs / ~aufstellung receivables schedule; **~ausbuchung** charging off a claim, deleting a claim (debt) from the books

Forderungsausfall *(im Kreditgeschäft)* loan loss (default)

Forderungsausfall / ~quote loan loss experience, loan charge-off ratio, loan loss ratio, default rate, default experience on loans; **~risiko** credit risk, default risk, loan loss risk, risk of bad debt losses

Forderungsausfall / ~verhältnis → Forderungsausfallquote; **~versicherung** commercial credit insurance, credit loss insurance, accounts receivable insurance, indemnity insurance

Forderungs / ~begleichung settlement of a claim (debt), payment of a debt; **~beitreibung** debt recovery (enforcement), recovery of a debt (of a loan)

forderungsberechtigt entitled to claim (to a claim)

Forderungsberechtigte/r 1. beneficiary **2.** rightful claimant

forderungsbesichert *(~e Wertpapiere)* asset-backed securities

Forderungsbesicherung 1. providing security for a claim (for receivables) **2.** loan security, collateralisation of a loan, *(durch gewerbliche Immobilien besicherte Forderungen)* claims secured by commercial real estate

Forderungsbestand 1. receivables portfolio, sales (debtors') ledger, inventory of receivables **2.** *(im Kreditgeschäft)* loan book (portfolio) **3.** existence of a claim, legal validity of a claim

Forderungsbetrag 1. outstanding amount (debt), *(gegenüber einer Versicherung)* claim amount **2.** loan amount, exposure

Forderungs / ~bevorschussung lending (advancing money) against receivables; **~bewertung** valuation of claims; **~buchwert** carrying value of the loan asset; **~deckung** credit risk cover

Forderungs / ~einzug collection of receivables, debt collection; **~entstehung** origination (creation) of a claim; **~erlass** debt waiver, waiver (remission) of claims; **~erlös** proceeds from receivables sold

förderungsfähig *(~e Investitionen)* investments qualifying for grants/subsidies, investments qualifying for funding

Forderungs / ~feststellung determination (establishment) of a claim, *(im Insolvenzverfahren)* acknowledgement (acceptance) of claims; **~finanzierung** receivables financing

forderungsgewichtet *(~e durchschnittliche Verlusthöhe im Schadenfall)* exposure-weighted average loss given default, *(~e Durchschnittslaufzeit)* exposure-weighted average maturity

Forderungs / ~höhe amount of the debt, debt level, *(Forderungshöhe zum Zeitpunkt des Ausfalls)* exposure at default; **~inhaber 1.** owner of receivables **2.** holder of a claim, rightful claimant; **~inkasso** debt collection

Forderungs / ~kategorie asset category (class); **~käufer 1.** buyer of receivables (of loan assets) **2.** forfaiting company; **~kaufvertrag** receivables purchase agreement; **~klasse** *(i. S. von Kreditforderungen)* asset class, exposure class; **~kontrolle** credit control, sales ledger control

Forderungs / ~liquidation 1. settlement (liquidation) of a claim **2.** debt collection; **~ management** receivables management, debt management, **~nachweis** proof of claim, proof of debt, documents supporting the claim; **~papiere** debt securities

Forderungspfändung debt attachment, garnishment

Forderungspfändungs /~beschluss garnishee order; **~verfahren** garnishee proceedings

Forderungs / ~pool pool of receivables, receivables (exposure) pool; **~prüfung** verification of a claim; **~recht 1.** right to claim **2.** *(gesetzlicher Anspruch)* legal claim **3.** *(Besitzrecht)* claim to ownership, proprietary interest; **~regulierung** settlement (liquidation) of a claim

F

Forderungs / ~sicherung → Forderungsbesicherung; **~teilung** split-up of a claim, dividing (splitting up) a claim; **~tilgung** debt redemption (repayment)

Forderungs / ~übergang passing (devolution) of a claim, passage (transfer) of a claim, point in time when the claim passes (e.g. from the customer to the bank); **~umwandlung** debt conversion, converting a debt

forderungsunterlegt *(~e Wertpapiere)* asset-backed securities

Forderungsverkauf 1. sale of accounts receivable **2.** *(im Kreditgeschäft)* loan sale, asset sale **3.** *(bilanzwirksamer ~ im Rahmen einer Verbriefung)* true sale

Forderungsverkäufer 1. seller of receivables **2.** *(von Kreditforderungen)* asset seller **3.** *(im Rahmen einer Verbriefung)* originator, entity assigning receivables in a securitisation transaction

Forderungs / ~verluste bad debt losses; **~verwalter 1.** accounts receivable manager **2.** servicer; **~verwaltung 1.** receivables management **2.** *(im Rahmen einer ABS-Finanzierung)* servicing; **~verwässerung** claim dilution

Forderungsverzicht debt waiver (foregiveness), waiver of debt repayments, renunciation of a claim, *(Forderungsverzicht mit Besserungsabrede)* debt waiver linked to an earn-out agreement, debt waiver linked to an agreement on compensation from future profits

Forderungswertberichtigung 1. bad debt allowance **2.** loan loss allowance, → Einzelwertberichtigung, → Pauschalwertberichtigung

förderungswürdig *(~es Projekt)* project worth backing

Forderungszession assignment of a claim, assignment of receivables

Forfaiteur forfaitist

forfaitierbar forfaitable, eligible for forfaiting, *(~e Forderungen aus Lieferungen)* forfaitable trade receivables

forfaitieren *(die Akkreditivforderung ~)* to forfait the claim under (arising out of) the documentary credit

Forfaitierung forfaiting □ purchase of trade receivables at a discount and without recourse to the supplier/exporter

Forfaitierungs / ~erlös forfaiting proceeds; **~geschäft** forfaiting transaction, forfait deal; **~gesellschaft** forfaiting company, forfaiter; **~kosten** forfaiting cost; **~marge** forfaiting margin

Forfaitierungs / ~markt forfait market; **~material** forfait paper; **~satz** forfaiting rate, discount deducted upon purchase of the receivables; **~techniken** forfaiting techniques; **~volumen** forfaiting portfolio; **~zusage** undertaking to forfait

Form 1. form, shape, design, *(~und Inhalt)* form and content *(e. g. of annual reports), (in der gesetzlich vorgeschriebenen ~)* in the form required (prescribed) by law, *(in mündlicher ~)* orally, verbally, *(in schriftlicher ~)* in writing
2. *(Verfassung, z.B. des Marktes)* shape, condition
3. *(Version)* version, form

formal *jur.* formal, *(~e Haftung)* formal liability, *(~e Voraussetzungen)* formal prerequisites

Formalität formality, technicality, *(gesetzlich vorgeschriebene ~en)* formalities required by law, legal formalities

Format 1. format, size **2.** stature, calibre

Formation *(in der Chart-Analyse)* pattern, formation

Formel formula

formell *(~er Beschluss)* formal (official) resolution, *(~e Zusage)* formal commitment

Formerfordernisse formal requirements, requirements as to proper form

Formfehler error in form, formal defect

formgerecht *(~e Vollmacht)* power of attorney drawn up (executed) in due form

formgültig valid in form

förmlich *(~e Erklärung)* formal declaration

formlos *(~e Kreditabsprache)* informal loan agreement, *(~er Vertrag)* contract requiring no specific form, informal contract

Formsache matter of form

Formular 1. form **2.** *(Fragebogen)* questionnaire; **~satz** set of forms; **~vertrag** standard form agreement

formulieren 1. to phrase, to formulate, to word, to state **2.** *(einen Vertrag ~)* to draft (to formulate, to draw up) a contract

Formulierung wording, drafting

Formvorschriften requirements of form, requirements relating to the form in which ...

formwidrig *jur.* contrary to formal (legal) requirements

Fortbestand continuation, *(~ der Garantie)* continued existence (continuation) of the guarantee, *(~ des Unternehmens)* continuation of the company as a going concern

fortbestehen to continue to exist, *(~de Unternehmensbereiche)* continuing operations, operations remaining afloat, *(~de Verpflichtungen)* continuing obligations

Fortbildung 1. further education (training) **2.** *(berufliche)* continuation training, advanced training **3.** *(innerbetriebliche)* internal (on-the-job, in-house) training

Fortbildungslehrgang continuation course, in-house training course

fortbleiben *(vom Markt ~)* to stay away (to be absent) from the market

Fortdauer continuation, continuance

fortdauern to continue, to persist, to last, *(~de Rezession)* continuing (persisting) recession, *(~der Zinsanstieg)* continuous (continual, unbroken) rise in interest rates

fortentwickeln 1. to develop further **2.** *(verbessern)* to enhance, to improve **3.** *(wachsen)* to grow, to expand

Fortentwicklung 1. further development, enhancement, improvement, *(stetige ~)* continuous improvement process **2.** growth, expansion

Fortfall 1. abolition **2.** discontinuance

fortführen 1. to continue, to carry on, **2.** *(wiederaufnehmen)* to resume

Fortführung 1. continuation, *(~ einer Kreditvereinbarung)* continuation of a loan agreement **2.** *(Wiederaufnahme)* resumption

Fortführungsgrundsatz going concern principle

Fortführungswert going concern value

Fortgang 1. *(Entwicklung)* progress, development **2.** *(Fortsetzung)* continuation

fortgeführt *(zu den ~en Anschaffungskosten bilanzieren)* to state at amortised cost, *(~e Unternehmensbereiche)* continuing operations

fortgeschriebener Barwert updated present value

fortgeschrittener Bemessungsansatz *(zur Bemessung der operationellen Risiken)* advanced measurement approach □ most advanced method of calculating capital requirements for a bank's operational risks

fortgeschrittene elektronische Signatur advanced electronic signature

fortgeschrittener IRB-Ansatz *(Modell eines auf internen Ratings basierenden Ansatzes)* advaned IRB approach □ advanced method to calculate a bank's capital requirements for credit risks on the basis of internal data

F

fortgesetzt continued, continuous, constant

fortlaufend 1. *adj.* *(~e Aktualisierung)* continuous updating, *(~e Anpassung an die Marktkonditionen)* adjustment to market rates on an ongoing basis, *(~e Auktion)* continuous auction trading, *(~er Handel)* continuous trading, trading on an ongoing basis, *(~e Kursstellung)* continuous price-setting
(~e Notierung) continuous (variable price) quotation, quoting prices continually, *(~e Notierung von Zinssätzen)* quoting (posting) interest rates on a continuous (on an ongoing) basis, *(~e Nummerierung)* consecutive numbering, *(~e Nummern)* consecutive (running) numbers, *(~e Überwachung eines Engagements)* continuous monitoring of an exposure
2. *adv.* *(~ notiert werden)* to be continually listed, *(~ nummerieren)* to number consecutively, *(~ überwachen)* to monitor continually

fortschreiben 1. to update **2.** *(eine Optionsposition)* to roll forward **3.** *(neu bewerten)* to reassess, to reappraise **4.** *(Statistik)* to extrapolate, to adjust

Fortschreibung 1. (continuous) updating **2.** roll-over, rolling forward (over), *(~ einer Optionsposition)* rollover of an option position from one delivery month to another **3.** reassessment, reappraisal **4.** extrapolation, current adjustment

Fortschreibungs / ~budgetierung rolling budgeting; **~zeitraum 1.** rollover period **2.** extrapolation period

fortschreiten 1. to progress, to advance, *(~de Abschwächung der Konjunktur)* progressing downturn in economic activity **2.** *(zunehmen)* to increase, to rise

Fortschritt 1. progress, advance, step forward, stride, *(~e machen)* to make progress, to progress with, to make headway, *(geringe ~e machen)* to make little progress, *(~e hinsichtlich der Rückzahlung)* progress towards repaying the debt
2. *(Verbesserung)* improvement, enhancement

Fortschrittszahlung progress payment

fortsetzen 1. to continue, to carry on, to advance, *(die Aufwärtsbewegung sollte sich ~)* the upward trend is likely to continue (to persist) **2.** *(wiederaufnehmen)* to resume

Fortsetzung 1. continuation **2.** resumption **3.** *(Folge)* sequel

Fortsetzungs / ~formation *(in der Chart-Analyse)* continuation pattern □ indicating a continuation of the current stock price trend; **~lücke** continuation gap

fortwähren to continue, to persist, to last

fortwährend *adj.* continual, continuous, *(~e finanzielle Unterstützung)* continual (lasting) financial support

fortwälzen *(eine Steuer ~)* to shift forward (to pass on) a tax

fortwirken *(z. B. von Zinserhöhungen)* to continue to have effect (repercussions)

fortzahlen to continue to pay

Fortzahlung continuation of payments

Forum 1. platform, forum **2.** *(von Fachleuten)* panel of experts

Forward / ~-Aufschlag forward premium; **~-Darlehen** forward loan □ commitment to extend a loan at a future point in time and at a rate specified at the time of the transaction; **~-Periode** forward period □ time span between conclusion of the loan agreement and commencement of the loan; **~-Swap** forward swap, forward (delayed) start swap; **~-Zinskurve** forward interest rate curve

Fracht 1. *(Kosten)* carriage, freight, freightage, freight charges, *(~ bezahlt)* freight prepaid, *(~ zahlbar am Bestimmungsort)* freight payable at destination
2. *(Ladung)* cargo, freight

Frachtbrief waybill, freight bill, *(Eisenbahnfrachtbrief)* rail consignment note (BE), railroad waybill, railroad bill of lading (AE), *(Luftfrachtbrief)* air consignment note, airway bill, *(Straßengüterverkehr)* road waybill; ~**doppel** waybill duplicate; ~**original** original waybill

Frachtenaval freight guarantee

frachtfrei carriage paid to (CPT), freight prepaid

frachtfrei versichert carriage and insurance paid to (CIP)

Fracht / ~führer carrier; ~**kosten** carriage, freight, freight (transportation) charges; ~**papiere** forwarding (shipping) documents; ~**vermerk** freight notation; ~**vertrag** contract of carriage, freight contract; ~**zahlungsvermerk** freight payment notation

Frage 1. question **2.** issue, point, problem, *(für staatliche Garantien in ~ kommen)* to qualify for state guarantees, *(in ~ stellen)* to call into question, to cast doubt on, to challenge (e.g. the validity)

Fragebogen questionnaire

Fragenkomplex issue, complex of questions

fraglich *(~e Angelegenheit)* matter in question, *(~e Zinssenkung)* uncertain (doubtful) cut in interest rates

fragmentiert *(~er Markt)* fragmented market

fragwürdig *(~es Finanzgebaren)* questionable (dubious) financial practice

Fraktionshandel trading in fractions

Franchise franchise, *(in ~ vergeben)* to franchise

Franchise / ~-Geber franchisor; ~**-Gebühr** franchise fee; ~**-Nehmer** franchisee, franchised dealer; ~**-Vertrag** franchise agreement

Franchising franchising; ~**-Unternehmer** franchise operator

Frankatur Incoterm

franko 1. *(frachtfrei)* carriage paid, freight prepaid **2.** *(als Handelsklausel)* free

frei 1. *adj.* *(~e Aktionäre)* outside shareholders, *(~e Berufe) (als Kundengruppe eines Kreditinstitutes)* professional customers, professionals, professional market (sector), *(~ er Cashflow)* free cash flow □ cash flow from operations, plus interest payments, minus capital expenditures

(~e Gelder) uncommitted funds, *(~er Goldmarkt)* free-tier gold market, *(~es Guthaben) (a)* (freely) available funds *(b)* unblocked funds, *(~e Kapazitäten)* spare capacities, *(~er Kapitalverkehr)* free flow of capital, freedom of capital movements

(~e Liquiditätsreserven) free liquidity reserves, *(~er Markt) (a)* open market *(b) (außerbörslich)* free market, over-the-counter market, off-board market, *(~e Rücklagen) (a)* free reserves (surplus), unallocated reserves *(b)* retained earnings

(~e Sparkassen) non-public (private) savings banks, → Sparkasse, *(~es Spiel der Marktkräfte)* free play of market forces, *(~e Stücke) (Börse)* freely marketable stock, *(~e Übertragbarkeit)* free transferability, *(~e Wechselkursbildung)* free determination of exchange rates

2. *adv.* *(~ ausgehandelte/aushandelbare Provisionssätze)* freely negotiated/negotiable commission rates, *(~ finanziertes Projekt)* privately financed project, unsubsidised project, project financed without government funds (without recourse to government-assisted lending schemes), *(~ floatende Wechselkurse)* freely floating exchange rates, *(~ handelbare Wertpapiere)* freely tradeable stock

(~ konvertierbare Währung) freely convertible currency, *(~ negoziierbares Akkreditiv)* freely negotiable (unrestricted) documentary credit, *(~ vereinbare Kurse)* freely negotiable prices (rates), (~ *verfügbar) (a)* freely

F

(unconditionally) available *(b) (frei veräußerbar)* freely disposable *(c) (frei verfügbarer Einzahlungsüberschuss)* free cash flow, *(~ von Belastungen)* free and clear, unencumbered
3. *(Incoterms) (~Bestimmungshafen)* free port of destination, *(~ an Bord des Schiffes)* free on board (FOB), *(~ an Bord des Flugzeuges)* free on aircraft, *(~ Dock)* free delivery to dock, *(~ Frachtführer)* free carrier (FCA), *(~ Längsseite Schiff)* free alongside ship (FAS), *(~ LKW Abgangsort)* free on truck, *(~ Schiene)* free on rail, *(~ Schiff)* free on board, free on steamer, *(~ Waggon Abgangsort)* free on rail, free on wagon

F

Frei / ~**aktien** bonus shares; ~**berufler** self-employed, *(freiberufliche Sozietät)* limited liability partnership; ~**betrag** personal tax allowance, tax-exempt amount

freibleibend without any obligation, without engagement, on a non-binding basis, *(freibleibendes Angebot)* open (uncommitted) offer, offer subject to confirmation (subject to prior sale)

Freiexemplar complimentary (free) copy

Freigabe 1. release, unblocking, lifting *(~ der Abtretung)* release of assignment, retransfer of rights under the assignment, *(~ der Dokumente)* release of documents, *(~ der Garantie)* guarantee release, releasing a guarantee, *(~ von Geldern)* unblocking (of) funds
2. *(Deregulierung)* deregulation, decontrol
3. floating, *(~ des Wechselkurses)* floating (of) the exchange rate, currency floatation

Freigabe / ~**anspruch** *(~ des Sicherungsgebers)* assignor's claim to release; ~ **bescheinigung** release notice, notification of release; ~**klausel** release clause; ~**pflicht** *(hinsichtlich einer Sicherheit)* obligation to release the security (collateral), mandatory release; ~**verfahren** approval process

freigeben 1. to release, to lift, *(Gelder ~)* to free up funds 2. to deregulate, to decontrol 3. to float

Freigrenze exemption limit (threshold)

frei halten *(eine bestimmte Rangstelle ~)* to reserve (to retain) a specific rank

freihändig *(~er Ankauf/Rückkauf)* purchase/repurchase in the open market (at market rates), *(~er Verkauf)* sale in the open market, market sale, *(eine Sicherheit ~ verwerten)* to foreclose on collateral

Freijahre *(Tilgungsfreijahre)* redemption-free years, capital repayment holiday

freimachen *(den Weg für eine neue Kreditvereinbarung ~)* to clear the way (to prepare the ground) for a new credit agreement, *(den Weg für niedrigere Zinssätze ~)* to pave the way for lower interest rates

Freimakler unofficial (free) broker
□ Freimakler act as intermediaries on the German stock exchanges and transact business for their own account; they deal mainly in securities listed in the unofficial markets

freisetzen *(Kapital/Liquidität ~)* to release (to unlock) capital/liquidity, *(regulatorisches Eigenkapital ~)* to free up regulatory equity

Freisetzung setting free, *(~ festgelegter Gelder)* freeing blocked (committed) funds, *(~ gebundenen Kapitals)* release of tied-up capital

freisprechen to acquit, to clear

Freispruch acquittal

freistehendes Derivat stand-alone derivative

freistellen 1. *(befreien)* to exempt (to exonerate) from, *(dem Inhaber ist es freigestellt)* the holder is free to, *(von Offenlegungsvorschriften ~)* to exempt from disclosure requirements
2. *jur.* to release, to relieve, to indemnify, *(die Bank von allen Ansprüchen*

~) to indemnify (to hold safe and harmless) the bank against (from) any claims, *(von der Haftung ~)* to release (to relieve, to discharge) from liability

Freistellung 1. exemption, exoneration, *(~ von der Mindestreservepflicht)* exemption from minimum reserve requirements
2. release, relief, indemnification, holding safe and harmless

Freistellungs / ~anspruch right to exemption (to indemnification), **~auftrag** tax exemption request, application for tax exemption; **~berechtigung** entitlement to exemption; **~bescheinigung** exemption certificate

Freistellungserklärung 1. liability release form, release from liability statement 2. indemnity bond 3. tax exemption certificate 4. *(~ für Waren im Dokumentengeschäft)* letter of release

Freistellungs / ~klausel exemption (relieving) clause, save harmless clause; **~ vereinbarung** 1. hold harmless agreement 2. exemption agreement; **~verpflichtung** obligation to indemnify (to hold safe and harmless), indemnity bond; **~volumen** tax exemption total

Freitextfeld blank (free) text field

Freiverkauf *(bei einem öffentlichen Zeichnungsangebot)* public sale, selling publicly

Freiverkehr 1. *(an der Frankfurter Wertpapierbörse)* Open Market □ The Open Market, the second trading segment (first segment → Regulierter Markt) of the Frankfurt Stock Exchange, was established in 1987 after the merger of "geregelter" and "ungeregelter Freiverkehr" as Regulated Unofficial Market and renamed Open Market in 2005.
Listing and trading: shares issued by small and medium-sized German companies, international shares, warrants and certificates. Sub-segments: → First/Second Quotation Board, → Entry Standard
2. *(außerbörslicher Handel)* over-the-counter (OTC) trading, off-board trading

Freiverkehrs / ~ausschuss Admissions Committee; **~derivate** OTC derivatives; **~handel** 1. trading on the Open Market 2. OTC dealings; **~kurs** 1. Open Market price 2. OTC quotation

Freiverkehrs / ~markt → Freiverkehr; **~richtlinien** Open Market Rules; **~werte** securities traded on the Open Market ; **~zulassung** admission (of securities) to the Open Market

frei werden to be released, *(frei werdende Gelder)* funds becoming available, funds approaching maturity

Freiwerden release, unblocking, *(das ~ des Bürgen von seinen Verpflichtungen)* the guarantor's release (discharge) from his liabilities

freiwillig *(~e Beiträge)* voluntary contributions, *(~e Gerichtsbarkeit)* non-contentious jurisdiction, *(~e Kreditverlängerung)* discretionary credit extension, *(~e Liquidation)* voluntary liquidation (winding up), *(~e Rücklagen)* voluntary (non-obligatory) reserves, retained earnings

freizeichnen *(sich von der Haftung ~)* to discharge o. s. from liability

Freizeichnung exemption (discharge) from liability, liability discharge

Freizeichnungsklausel non-liability (non-warranty) clause, escape clause, disclaimer

Freizone free zone

Freizügigkeit *(~ des Kapitalverkehrs)* freedom of capital movements

fremd foreign, outside, external, third party, *(~e Gelder) (a)* external (outside) funds, borrowings *(b) (einer Bank)* deposits and borrowed funds, *(~e Währung)* foreign currency, *(für ~e Rechnung)* on behalf of a third party, for third party account

Fremdabhebung cash withdrawal at another bank's ATM □ withdrawing

F

money from cash dispensers/ATMs not operated by the bank where the customer maintains his account or not connected to an interbank network, *(Gebühr für ~en an Geldautomaten)* ATM usage fee, access fee

Fremd / **~besitz** third party property, property held in the name (on behalf) of a third party, *(Anteile im ~)* minority interests; **~bestände** third party holdings; **~bezug** *(von Leistungen)* external procurement of services; **~emission** issue through a bank (through an issuing house)

F

fremdfinanzieren to finance with outside capital (with borrowed funds)

fremdfinanziert *(~e Firmenaufkäufe)* debt-financed acquisitions of companies, leveraged corporate acquisitions, *(~e Investitionen)* debt-financed investments, *(ein in hohem Maß ~es Unternehmen)* highly leveraged (highly geared) company, *(~e Unternehmensübernahme)* leveraged takeover, leveraged buyout

Fremdfinanzierung debt financing, external financing (funding), financing with borrowed (outside) funds, *(Einsatz von ~)* use of leverage, *(~ von Investitionen)* leveraging of investments

Fremdfinanzierungs / **~bedarf** borrowing (debt) requirements, external funding (financing) requirements, external financing needs; **~kosten** debt financing cost, cost of debt finance, cost of borrowing; **~mittel** external funds

Fremdgrundschuld land charge registered in favour of a third party (creditor), → Eigentümergrundschuld

Fremdkapital debt capital, outside capital, external funds

Fremdkapitalanteil share of borrowed funds (of debt capital), gearing, gearing level, leverage, *(mit einem hohen ~ arbeiten)* to operate with a high degree of financial leverage, *(mit einem zu hohen ~ arbeiten)* to overleverage, *(mit einem hohen ~ finanzierte Übernahme)* highly leveraged takeover, *(den ~ erhöhen/verringern)* to leverage up/down, to increase/to reduce the share of outside capital, to increase/to lower debt financing

Fremdkapital / **~beratung** debt advisory; **~beschaffung** generation (procurement) of outside capital; **~einbringung** bringing in outside capital; **~geber** debt investor, provider of outside capital, capital (financial) backer; **~instrumente** debt instruments

Fremdkapital / **~kosten** borrowing cost; **~markt** debt market; **~verringerung** deleveraging, reducing the debt burden (the financial leverage); **~zinsen** interest on debt capital; **~zuführung** addition (injection, infusion) of outside funds

Fremdleistungen outside services

Fremdleistungskosten cost of external supplies (outside services)

Fremdmandat mandate for account of a third party

Fremdmittel outside (external) funds, borrowed funds, debt finance, *(einer Bank)* deposits and borrowed funds

Fremdmittel / **~bedarf** borrowing requirements, external fund (funding) requirements; **~bedienung** servicing outside capital; **~beschaffung** generation (procurement) of external funds; **~kosten** cost of external funds (of debt finance); **~zufluss** inflow of deposits; **~zuwachs** increase (growth) in deposits

Fremdorganschaft → Drittorganschaft

Fremdvaluta foreign currency

Fremdverfügung **1.** cash withdrawal at another bank's ATM, → Fremdabhebung **2.** account drawing by an unauthorised third party

Fremdvergleichsprinzip arm's length principle □ principle according to which transactions between affiliated or related parties must be made on prevailing market terms (i.e. the parties must deal independently and on an equal footing)

Fremdverschuldung gearing, indebtedness, debt burden

Fremdwährung foreign currency, *(Engagement in ~en)* currency exposure, holdings of (exposure in) foreign currencies

Fremdwährungs / ~aktiva foreign currency assets; **~anleihe** foreign currency bond; **~aufwandskonten** currency expense accounts; **~ausleihungen** foreign currency lendings

Fremdwährungs / ~bestand foreign currency holdings, currency portfolio; **~einlagen** foreign currency deposits; **~engagement** 1. currency exposure 2. foreign currency loan (lending); **~ertragskonten** currency income accounts

Fremdwährungs / ~finanzierung foreign currency funding; **~forderungen** 1. foreign currency lendings 2. receivables in foreign currencies; **~guthaben** foreign currency balances (deposits); **~konto** foreign currency account

Fremdwährungs / ~kredit foreign currency loan; **~kreditaufnahme** taking out a foreign currency loan, foreign currency borrowing; **~kreditgeschäft** foreign currency lending, currency lending operations

Fremdwährungs / ~-LCR foreign currency LCR (liquidity coverage ratio), → Mindestliquiditätsquote; **~-Minus-Position** short foreign exchange position; **~passiva** foreign currency liabilities; **~-Plus-Position** long foreign exchange position; **~position** foreign exchange position, currency position

Fremdwährungs / ~risikoposition foreign currency exposure; **~saldo** 1. net foreign exchange position 2. net foreign currency balance; **~spread** currency spread

Fremdwährungs / ~termingelder foreign currency time deposits; **~titel** foreign currency debt, securities denominated in foreign currencies

Fremdwährungs / ~verbindlichkeiten 1. foreign currency borrowings, foreign currency debt 2. payables in foreign currencies; **~wechsel** foreign currency bill

freundlich *(~e Grundstimmung) (Börse)* cheerful undertone (sentiment)

frisieren *(die Bilanz ~)* to dress up (to fake) the balance sheet

F

Frist term, time, period of time, period set (given), time limit, deadline, *(~ für Einwendungen)* time allowed for objections, *(innerhalb der gesetzten ~)* within the prescribed limit of time, within the specified time frame
(die ~ für die Kreditrückzahlung) time allowed for repayment of the loan, loan repayment period, *(eine letzte ~ setzen)* to set a final deadline, *(die ~ für die Zeichnung der neuen Stücke)* the period set for subscribing to the new securities

Fristablauf expiry of the period set (fixed)

Fristen / ~analyse ageing analysis; **~asymmetrie** mismatched maturities, → Fristeninkongruenz; **~entsprechung** → Fristenkongruenz

Fristen / ~gliederung maturity breakdown, breakdown according to maturities, maturity spacing; **~inkongruenz** 1. mismatched maturities 2. mismatch in timing, maturity mismatch

fristenkongruent (at) matching maturities, *(~e Abdeckung)* hedging a transaction at matching maturities, *(~e Refinanzierung der Hypothekenausleihungen)* funding (refinancing) of mortgage lendings at matching maturities

Fristen / ~kongruenz 1. matched (matching) maturities 2. matching of maturities, maturity matching; **~raum** maturity range; **~schutz** maturity hedging; **~struktur** *(~ des*

Kreditgeschäftes) maturity pattern of lendings

Fristen / ~symmetrie matched maturities, → Fristenkongruenz; **~transformation** maturity (time) transformation, *(Risiken aus der ~)* maturity transformation risks; **~vereinbarungen** maturities agreed upon, maturities fixed

fristgemäß/fristgerecht timely, within the specified period, *(~e Vorlage der Dokumente)* presenting the documents on the date (within the period) agreed upon, *(~e Zahlung)* payment (paying) on the date agreed upon, payment at (on) maturity, timely payment

F

Fristhypothek fixed date mortgage

Fristigkeit 1. maturity **2.** maturity pattern, *(~en verzinslicher Einlagen)* maturities (maturity pattern) of interest-bearing deposits

Fristigkeitenfächer/Fristigkeitstabelle maturity ladder

fristlos immediate, without notice, *(die Garantie ~ kündigen)* to terminate the guarantee without giving notice, *(~e Kündigung)* termination (cancellation) without notice, *(~ e Vertragsaufkündigung)* immediate termination (repudiation) of contract

Frist / ~setzung setting a time limit (deadline); **~überschreitung** non-compliance with (infringement of) a time limit, exceeding the time limit (deadline); **~verkürzung** shortening the period (the maturity)

Frist / ~verlängerung extension of time (of maturity), extension of the period set (e. g. for payment, for subscribing to the new shares); **~versäumnis** default, failure to comply with a time limit; **~wahrung** observing the time limit (deadline) set for, compliance with a time limit

Front *(die Aktienkurse zogen auf breiter ~ an)* equity prices firmed broadly, stock prices moved higher across the board (across a broad front)

frostig *(~es Konjunkturklima)* chilly economic climate

Früchte *(~ tragen)* to bear fruit

Fruchtlosigkeitsbescheinigung certificate of ineffectiveness

FRUG → Finanzmarktrichtlinie-Umsetzungsgesetz

früher *(~er Inhaber)* former (previous) holder

Früherkennung *(~ potenzieller Risiken)* early risk detection

frühestmöglich *(~er Anleihe-Kündigungstermin)* earliest possible call date

Früh / ~indikator *(~en der Umsatzentwicklung)* early sales indicators; **~phasenfinanzierung** early stage financing: **~zeichnerrabatt** early subscription discount

FuE-Kosten research and development expenditure

fühlbar *(~e Verschlechterung)* noticeable deterioration

führen 1. to keep, *(ein Konto ~)* to keep (to maintain) an account, *(das Protokoll ~)* to keep the minutes
2. to conduct, *(einen Prozess/Rechtsstreit ~)* to carry on (to conduct) a lawsuit, to litigate, to engage in litigation, *(Verhandlungen ~)* to conduct (to hold) negotiations, *(den Vorsitz ~)* to be in the chair, to preside
3. to lead, *(ein Konsortium ~)* to lead (to lead-manage) a syndicate, *(ein Unternehmen ~)* to run (to manage) a company, *(als Kommanditgesellschaft geführtes Unternehmen)* company organised (run) as a limited partnership
4. *(führen zu)* to lead to, to result in, to bring about, to trigger

führend *(~e Börsenwerte)* leading shares (stocks), leaders, Blue Chips, *(~e Chemiewerte/Industriewerte)* leading chemicals/industrials, *(~er Marktteilnehmer)* leading player, *(~e Rolle)* leading role, *(~e Stellung)* leading (prominent) position

Führung 1. maintenance, *(kostenlose ~ eines Kontos)* maintaining an ac-

count free of charge, *(ordnungsgemäße ~ eines Kontos)* proper conduct (maintenance) of an account
2. conduct, *(~ der Geschäfte)* conduct of business, management of affairs
3. lead, leadership, management, control, guidance, *(ein Banken-Konsortium unter der ~ von)* a bank syndicate led by, *(Wertpapieremission unter der ~ von)* securities issue lead-managed by ... (under the lead management of ...)
(die ~ im Neuemissionsgeschäft übernehmen) to take the lead in new issue activity, *(~ eines Unternehmens)* *(a)* company management *(b)* running (managing) a company, *(die alleinige ~ des Unternehmens behalten)* to retain sole stewardship of the company

Führungs / **~aufgaben** management duties, managerial functions, executive responsibilities (duties); **~auftrag** management brief; **~bank** lead (leading) bank, lead manager, front bank, managing bank, bank running the books, → Führung (3)

Führungs / **~ebene** management level, *(Verringerung der ~n)* delayering; **~eigenschaften** leadership qualities (capabilities); **~gesellschaft** holding company, lead company

Führungs / **~gruppe** 1. management team 2. *(bei einer Emission)* lead management group; **~informationssystem** management (executive) information system; **~instrumente** management tools

Führungs / **~kontinuität** management continuity; **~kraft** 1. executive 2. *(Plural)* management staff, executive officers; **~position** 1. managerial (executive) position, 2. *(~ am Markt)* leadership position

Führungs / **~provision** lead management fee; **~qualitäten** leadership qualities (skills); **~rolle** 1. leading role 2. leadership position (e. g. in a market); **~spanne** → Leitungsspanne; **~spitze** top management

Führungs / **~stil** leadership style; **~struktur** managerial structure; **~verhalten** leadership behaviour; **~wechsel** change in leadership; **~zeugnis** character certificate, certificate of good conduct

Fuhrunternehmer carrier, haulage contractor

Fülle abundance, *(eine ~ neuer Emissionen)* a wealth of new issues

Fundament foundation(s), basis, groundwork, bedrock

Fundamental / **~-Analyse** fundamental analysis; **~-Daten** *(~ eines Marktes)* market fundamentals; **~-Datenderivate** macroeconomic derivatives □ allow traders to take positions on macroeconomic data; **~-Untermauerung des Kursniveaus** underpinning the price level by fundamentals

fundieren 1. *(begründen)* to substantiate, *(fundierte Hoffnungen auf eine Kurserholung)* well-founded hopes for a price recovery 2. to consolidate, to fund

Fundierungsanleihe/~schuldverschreibung funding debenture

fünffach *(~e Erhöhung)* fivefold increase, *(in ~er Ausfertigung)* in quintuplicate

Fungibilität fungibility, interchangeability (resulting from standardisation)

fungible *(~ Finanzanlagen)* fungible financial investments, *(~s Kapital)* fungible (freely transferable) capital, *(~ Wertpapiere)* fungible securities □ securities that are interchangeable with other securities

fungieren to act as, to assume the duties of, *(als Reservewährung ~)* to act as reserve currency

Funktion 1. function, activity 2. duty, office, position, *(in leitender ~ tätig sein)* to hold an executive position

funktional *(~e Organisation)* functional organisation, *(~es Weisungsrecht)* functional authority, *(~e Zuordnung)* functional assignment

Funktionen / ~etat functional budget; **~plan** functional plan; **~teilung** division of responsibilities

funktionieren to function, *(ein gut funktionierender Markt)* an efficiently functioning market

Funktionieren *(das ~ des Marktes)* functioning (workings, operation) of the market

funktionsabhängig *(~e Kreditkompetenzen)* position-linked loan approval powers

F

Funktions / ~abläufe functional processes; **~analyse** functional analysis; **~ ausgliederung** functional outsourcing; **~bereich** area of activity, functional area, business unit

Funktions / ~beschreibung *(a)* functional specifications, functional specification document, functional description *(b)* job description; **~ebene** functional level; **~einheit** functional (executive) unit

funktionsfähig *(~er Sanierungsplan)* workable restructuring plan, *(~er Sekundärmarkt)* viable (well-functioning) secondary market, *(~er Wettbewerb)* effective competition

Funktions / ~fähigkeit functional effectiveness, → Funktionstüchtigkeit, *(~ des Kapitalmarktes)* viability (proper functioning, workability) of the capital market; **~kostenanalyse** functional cost analysis, functional costing

Funktions / ~nachfolge functional succession; **~profil** functional (feature) profile; **~spezifikationen** functional specifications, functional specs, *(funktionsspezifische Lösung)* function-specific solution; **~stufe** functional level

Funktions / ~träger office holder, functional executive; **~trennung** functional separation, segregation of duties; **~tüchtigkeit** *(~ des Aufsichtssystems)* effectiveness of the supervisory system

funktionsübergreifend *(~e Steuerung)* cross-functional control

Funktions / ~verlagerung *(a)* relocation (transfer) of functions, business relocation, *(b)* transfer of goodwill; **~verlagerungsverordnung** Functions Transfer Regulation

fürchten *(um die Zahlungsfähigkeit des Unternehmens ~)* to fear for the solvency of the company

Fusion merger, amalgamation

Fusions / ~abkommen merger agreement; **~arbitrage** merger arbitrage; **~beschluss** merger resolution, decision to merge; **~bilanz** merger accounts; **~ genehmigung** merger clearance; **~kontrolle** merger control; **~vertrag** merger agreement, deed (contract) of merger

Fuß *(Bemühungen, auf einem Markt ~ zu fassen)* efforts to gain access (entry) to a market

Fußnote *(als ~ zur Bilanz ausweisen)* to state as a note to the balance sheet, to record on a memorandum basis

Future futures contract, → Kontrakt

Futures / ~abrechnungspreis futures settlement price; **~börse** futures exchange; **~handel** futures trading, trading in futures; **~kaufposition** long futures position; **~kontrakt** futures contract; **~liefertermin** futures delivery date; **~notierung** futures quotation (price)

Futures / ~option futures option, option on a futures contract; **~position** futures position, *(Einschusszahlung auf eine ~)* futures margin, *(Risiko aus ~en)* futures exposure; **~preis** futures price, price of a futures contract; **~preisbildung** futures pricing; **~verkaufsposition** short futures position

FZ *(finanzielle Zusammenarbeit)* **-Finanzierung** funding with financial cooperation funds

G

G → Geld

-G → gestrichen Geld

GA/GAA → Geldautomat/Geldausgabeautomat

galoppierend *(~e Inflation)* runaway inflation

Gamma gamma □ descriptive of the rate of change in an option's → delta for a one-unit change in the price of the underlying asset

Gang *(Verlauf)* course, *(~ an die Börse)* going public, initial public offering, stock market flotation, *(~ der Verhandlungen mit den Gläubigern)* course (progress) of the negotiations with the creditors, *(die derzeit im ~ befindliche Neustrukturierung)* the restructuring currently underway, *(in ~ bringen/setzen)* to set in train (motion)

gangbar *(~e Finanzierungsregelung)* feasible (practicable) financing arrangement

gängig 1. current, common, *(~e Konditionen)* current (prevailing) terms and conditions
2. regular, usuual, *(~e Fälligkeiten)* regular (standard) maturities, *(~e Stückelung)* customary denomination **3.** marketable, major, *(~e Emissionen)* seasoned (marketable) securities

ganzheitlich *(~er Beratungsansatz)* holistic approach in advisory services, *(~e Lösung)* holistic solution

ganzjährig *(~er Kupon)* annual coupon

Garant guarantor

Garanten-Delkredereversicherung guarantor indemnity insurance

Garantie 1. guarantee (BE), guaranty (AE), bond, surety, *(Garantie auf erstes Anfordern)* first demand guarantee □ The guarantee is a non-accessory undertaking, i.e. it is, unlike a → Bürgschaft (surety bond), not dependent on the principal obligation.
2. *(Gewährleistung)* warranty **3.** *(Sicherheit)* security, collateral **4.** *(Zusicherung)* guarantee, assurance, undertaking

Garantie / ~abkommen guarantee agreement; **~abrede** guarantee clause

garantieähnlich *(~e Verpflichtung)* undertaking similar in nature to a guarantee, *(~e Willenserklärung)* declaration (letter) of intent similar to that of a guarantee

Garantie / ~aktien 1. shares deposited as security (collateral) **2.** qualification shares; **~angebot** guarantee offer; **~anspruch** claim under a guarantee, guarantee claim; **~aufkündigung** (notice of) determination of guarantee

Garantie / ~auftrag guarantee order (request); **~auftraggeber** customer, guarantee applicant, requesting party, principal under the guarantee; **~ausbuchung** deletion of a guarantee, guarantee release

Garantie / ~ausfertigung 1. execution of a guarantee **2.** guarantee deed; **~ausfertigungsgebühr** guarantee issuing fee; **~ausstellung** execution (issuance, delivery) of a guarantee

Garantie / ~bank guaranteeing (guarantor) bank; **~bedingungen** guarantee (warranty) terms; **~befristung** limitation of the guarantee period, limiting the life (term) of the guarantee; **~begünstigter** guarantee, party to whom a guarantee is made, warrantee

Garantie / ~beschränkungen restrictive provisions of a guarantee, guarantee restrictions; **~bestand** guarantee portfolio; **~bestätigung** confirmation of a guarantee, guarantee commitment; **~bestätigungsschreiben** guarantee commitment letter

Garantie / ~bestellung taking out a guarantee; **~betrag** guarantee amount, amount guaranteed; **~brief** deed of guarantee, guarantee (warranty) certificate, letter of guarantee

Garantie / ~deckung guarantee cover; **~deckungskonto** guarantee cover account; **~dividende** guaranteed dividend; **~dokument** → Garantiebrief

Garantie / ~einbehalt retention money; **~erfüllung** meeting the obligations under a guarantee, paying up under a guarantee; **~erklärung** guarantee (surety) bond, guarantee letter

garantiefähig *(~ sein)* to have full power and authority to enter into a guarantee

Garantie / ~fähigkeit power to enter into guarantees, power to guarantee the obligations of others; **~fall** guarantee event, *(bei Eintritt des ~es)* when the debtor (borrower, obligor) has defaulted, in the event that the guarantor is called upon, should the borrower default

Garantie / ~fazilität 1. guarantee facility **2.** backup (support) line; **~fonds 1.** guarantee fund, indemnification fund **2.** *(zur Einlagensicherung)* deposit insurance fund, guarantee scheme; **~form** type of guarantee (bond); **~freigabe** release of a guarantee; **~frist** life (term) of a guarantee, guarantee (warranty) period

Garantiegeber guarantor, warrantor, surety, *(Ansprüche der Bank gegen den ~)* the bank's claims (rights) against the guarantor, *(Haftung des ~s)* guarantor's liability, liability on the part of the guarantor (warrantor), warrantor's liability, *(den ~ zur Erfüllung bei Verzug des Hauptschuldners verpflichten)* to bind the guarantor to performance in the event of non-performance by the principal obligor

Garantie / ~geberhaftung *(die ~ übernehmen)* to assume the responsibility of a guarantor; **~gegenstand** subject matter of the guarantee; **~geschäft** *(der Bank)* bank's guarantee operations, assumption of guarantees and warranties

Garantie / ~gruppe 1. guaranteeing syndicate (group) **2.** *(Gruppe, die die Bonität des Emittenten garantiert)* stand-by group (syndicate) **3.** *(Garantie- und Übernahmekonsortium)* underwriting group; **~gültigkeit** validity of a guarantee

Garantie / ~haftung liability on (under) a guarantee, *(Übernahme der ~)* assumption of liability under a guarantee; **~hinauslegung** provision of a guarantee, furnishing a guarantee

Garantie / ~hinterlegung *(bei der Bank)* depositing (lodging) a guarantee with the bank; **~höhe** amount guaranteed, guarantee level; **~inanspruchnahme 1.** guarantee availment, calling upon the guarantor, call to pay up under a guarantee **2.** amount requested under the guarantee furnished

Garantie / ~kapital guarantee funds □ share capital plus reserves; **~klausel** guarantee (indemnity, warranty) clause, clause containing the undertaking given by the guarantor; **~konsortium** → Garantiegruppe; **~kosten** guarantee charges

Garantie / ~laufzeit guarantee duration (period), term (life) of a guarantee; **~leistung** furnishing (providing) a guarantee, delivery of a guarantee; **~mittel** guarantee funds, funds serving as collateral; **~nehmer** guarantee, party to whom a guarantee is given

Garantie / ~obligo guarantee exposure, commitment (exposure) under a guarantee; **~produkte** (capital-) guaranteed products, guaranteed investment products; ~**provision** 1. guarantee commission 2. *(bei Neuemissionen) (a)* underwriting commission *(b)* standby commission

Garantie / ~**rahmen** guarantee line; ~**rahmenvertrag** master guarantee agreement, guarantee override agreement; ~**recht** Law of Guarantees

garantieren to guarantee, to furnish a guarantee, to warrant, *(die ordnungsgemäße und pünktliche Rückzahlung ~)* to guarantee the due and prompt repayment, *(gegenüber dem Kreditgeber die Erfüllung aller Verbindlichkeiten ~)* to guarantee (to warrant) to the lender the fulfillment of all obligations and liabilities

garantierend *(~e Bank)* guaranteeing bank, *(~e Gesellschaft)* guarantor corporation

Garantie / ~**rücklagen** guarantee reserves; ~**schein** guarantee (warranty) certificate; ~**schreiben** guarantee commitment letter, guarantee facility letter

Garantie / ~**stellung** furnishing (provision of) a guarantee, *(garantiestellende Bank)* guaranteeing bank, bank furnishing a guarantee; ~**summe** amount guaranteed, amount (principal) of the guarantee

Garantie / ~**text** guarantee text, wording of the guarantee; ~**träger** guarantor, guarantor corporation, supporting institution (organisation); ~**übernahme** furnishing (assuming) a guarantee; ~**urkunde** guarantee deed (bond)

Garantie / ~**vereinbarung** guarantee arrangement (agreement); ~**verpflichtung** guarantee obligation (commitment), warranty commitment, obligation (liability) under a guarantee commitment

Garantie / ~**versicherung** guarantee insurance; ~**versicherungsgesellschaft** guarantee association (society); ~**versprechen** guarantee undertaking (commitment), undertaking (covenant) to guarantee; ~**vertrag** contract of guarantee, guarantee agreement

Garantie / ~**verzinsung** guaranteed return; ~**wechsel** guarantee bill; ~**wert** value of a guarantee; ~**zeit** guarantee (warranty) period; ~**zertifikat** 1. guarantee certificate 2. guarantee investment contract

Gastgeberland *(Aufsichtsbehörde des ~es)* host state regulator

Gattung category, *(Aktien der gleichen ~)* shares of the same class

Gattungsschuld 1. class obligation, generic debt
2. *(in Verbindung mit Pensionsgeschäften)* obligation of the pledgee to return securities of the same kind and quality

Gattungsvollmacht class power of attorney, power of attorney restricted in its application to a specific class of transactions

GdbR → Gesellschaft des bürgerlichen Rechts

geben *(im Geldhandel)* to sell, to lend

Geber seller (lender) of funds; ~**bank** selling (lending) bank; ~**land** lender country; ~**position** lending position; ~**währung** lender currency

Gebiet 1. region, area, territory, district 2. *(Bereich)* field, sphere, sector 3. *(Zuständigkeit)* province, line of business

Gebietsansässige residents, *(gebietsansässige Kreditinstitute)* resident financial institutions

Gebietsfremde non-residents, *(gebietsfremde Anleger)* non-resident investors

Gebietskörperschaften regional and local administrative authorities, *(örtliche Gebietskörperschaft)* local authority, *(under → Basel II/III)* non-central public sector entities

Gebot 1. bid, offer, *(gebotener Kurs)* price bid 2. *(Notwendigkeit)* necessity 3. *(Vorschrift)* (binding) rule

Gebots / ~**frist** bidding period; ~**satz** bidding rate

Gebrauch 1. use, utilisation, usage, application **2.** *(i. S. von Marktgepflogenheiten)* customs, practice

Gebrauchs / **~güterfinanzierung** financing consumer durables; **~muster** utility model; **~mustergesetz** German Utility Models Act; **~wert** utility value

gebrochen *(~e Laufzeiten)* broken maturities, *(~er Termin) (im Devisenhandel)* broken (odd) date

Gebühr 1. charge, fee **2.** *(Bearbeitungsgebühr)* service charge, handling fee

G

Gebühren / **~abgrenzung** fee deferral; **~anzeige** display of fees (charges); **~aufschlag** additional (supplementary) fee, surcharge, extra charge; **~aufstellung** statement of fees; **~aufteilung** fee apportionment, allocation of charges

Gebühren / **~befreiung** exemption from charges (from a fee), remission of fees; **~begrenzung** fee cap, limiting the fees; **~belastung 1.** debit of charges (fees), debiting a fee **2.** burden of charges; **~berechnung 1.** charging of fees, fee(s) charged **2.** calculation of charges, calculating a fee

Gebühren / **~einnahmen** fee income (revenue); **~erhebung** levying a fee (charge); **~erhöhung** fee increase, increase in charges; **~erlass** remission of fees (of charges); **~ermäßigung** fee reduction, reduction in (lowering of) charges; **~erstattung** refund of fees (charges); **~erträge** fee income

gebührenfrei *(~e Debit-Karte)* non-fee debit card, *(~e Transaktion)* cost-free (non-chargeable) transaction, *(einen Auftrag ~ bearbeiten)* to handle an order free of charge

Gebühren / **~gestaltung** establishing the fee structure, pricing; **~ordnung** fee schedule, standard scale of charges (fees); **~pauschale** flat rate charge; **~politik** *(der Bank)* pricing policy

Gebühren / **~rechnung** bill of charges, fee sheet; **~recht** law on fees and charges; **~regelung** fee rules; **~satz** rate of charges; **~senkung** → Gebührenermäßigung; **~struktur** fee structure, pricing pattern; **~tabelle**/**~tarif**/**~verzeichnis** table of fees and charges, fee table, tariff of charges

gebunden 1. bound, committed, controlled, *(an eine Zahlungszusage ~ sein)* to be bound by a payment undertaking
2. blocked, *(~e Mittel)* blocked (frozen) funds, tied-up capital, *(~es Vermögen) (eines Versicherers)* restricted assets
3. linked, *(~e Aktie)* vinculated share, *(~er Finanzkredit/Bestellerkredit)* buyer credit, *(~er Zinssatz)* interest rate linked to a reference rate, *(zweckgebundener Kredit)* transaction-linked loan, loan tied to a specific project
4. *(~es Vermögen)* restricted assets (of an insurance company)

gedämpft *(~e Nachfrage)* muted demand

gedeckt 1. secured, *(~er Kredit)* secured (collateralised) loan (borrowing), *(~e Schuldverschreibung) (a) (Pfandbrief bzw. pfandbriefähnlicher Titel)* covered bond *(b) (allgemein)* secured bond, secured note
2. covered, *(~e Option)* covered option, *(~er Optionsschein)* covered warrant, *(~er Optionsverkäufer)* covered option writer, option writer who owns the underlying instrument, *(~e Stillhaltergeschäfte)* covered option writing, *(~es Termingeschäft)* covered forward contract

gedeihen 1. to prosper, to flourish **2.** to make progress

gedrückt *(~er Aktienmarkt)* depressed (muted) equity market, *(~e Stimmung)* subdued sentiment (tone)

Geduld patience, *(~ der Kreditgeber)* lenders' forebearance

geduldet *(~er Überziehungskredit)* tolerated overdraft □ *(i. S. des Verbraucherkreditgesetzes)* overdraft not agreed to, but tolerated by the bank

geeignet 1. suitable, appropriate, *(~e Sicherheit)* appropriate collateral **2.** qualified for, capable of

Geeignetheitstest *(i. S. der MiFID)* suitability test (check)

Gefahr danger, risk, hazard, *(~ laufen)* to run (to incur) a risk, to be exposed to a risk, *(auf Kosten und ~ von)* at the risk and cost of

gefährden to endanger, to jeopardise, to threaten, to imperil, to put at risk, *(die Aussichten auf eine Erholung ~)* to place the prospects of recovery in jeopardy

gefährdet *(~es Engagement/~er Kredit)* troubled loan commitment (exposure), loan (commitment) vulnerable to default, risky loan, *(stark ~es Engagement)* high-risk loan commitment, *(~e Kreditinstitute)* endangered (ailing) credit institutions, *(~e Zahlungen)* imperiled payments

Gefährdung 1. endangerment, hazard, imperilment **2.** exposure

Gefährdungs / **~haftung** strict (absolute) liability, strict liability in tort; **~indikator** exposure indicator

Gefahren / **~klasse** class of risk; **~übergang** passing of a risk; **~übernahme** risk taking, assumption of a risk

Gefälle differential, gap

Gefälligkeits / **~annahme** accommodation acceptance; **~indossament** accommodation endorsement; **~wechsel** accommodation bill, non-value bill

Gefolge *(im ~ der Zinserhöhung)* in the wake of the rise in interest rates

gefragt *(~ sein)* to be in demand, *(Bankwerte waren weiterhin ~)* banks remained in demand (in support), banks continued to find support, *(Finanzwerte waren lebhaft ~)* financials encountered lively interest

Gefüge pattern, structure

gegebenenfalls 1. if applicable, as the case may be **2.** if possible, if the occasion arises **3.** if necessary

Gegebenheiten *(konjunkturelle ~)* economic conditions, given facts in the economy

Gegen / **~akkreditiv** countervailing credit, back-to-back credit; **~angebot** counteroffer; **~anspruch** counterclaim; **~antrag** countermotion, counterproposal

Gegen / **~bestätigung** counterconfirmation; **~bestrebungen** counterefforts; **~beweis** counterevidence, rebutting evidence, proof to the contrary; **~buchung 1.** *(Ausgleichsbuchung)* offsetting (balancing) entry **2.** *(Stornobuchung)* reverse (reversing) entry

Gegen / **~bürge** counterguarantor, countersurety; **~bürgschaft** counterguarantee, countervailing bond of indemnity; **~einrede** plea in reconvention, cross-complaint, counterplea; **~erklärung** counterstatement, counterdeclaration; **~forderung** counterclaim; **~garantie** counterguarantee; **~gebot** counterbid

gegengerichtet *(~er Swap-Kontrakt)* offsetting (mirror, reverse) swap

Gegengeschäft 1. countertransaction **2.** *(im Außenhandel)* countertrade, countertrade deal (transaction) **3.** *(zur Positionsglattstellung)* offsetting transaction (trade), reversing trade, *(eine Futures-Position durch ein ~ schließen)* to close out a futures position through an offsetting transaction **4.** *(Gegengeschäfte, die eine Bank einer Korrespondenzbank einräumt)* reciprocal business

Gegengeschäfts / **~verpflichtung** countertrade commitment; **~vertrag** countertrade agreement

Gegengewicht counterweight, counterbalance, *(ein ~ zu dem starken Auslandsengagement bilden)* to counterbalance (to serve as a counterweight to) the strong international exposure

Gegen / **~gutachten** counteropinion; **~klage** cross-action, cross-complaint,

G

countersuit; ~**kontrakt** → gegenläufiges Geschäft

Gegenlaufen counterrunning □ countertrading for own account in a financial instument on account of advance knowledge of upcoming customer transactions, *(Verbot des ~s)* ban on counterrunning, → Mitlaufen, Vorlaufen

gegenläufig *(~es Geschäft) (zur Positions-Glattstellung)* offsetting trade (transaction), *(~e Positionen an zwei Märkten)* opposite positions in two markets, *(~es Swap-Geschäft)* → Gegen-Swap, *(~es Termingeschäft)* offsetting forward deal (transaction), counterforward deal

Gegen / ~leistung 1. service rendered in return, return service **2.** consideration, *(als ~)* for good and valuable consideration; **~partei 1.** counterpart, other side **2.** *jur.* opposing party, adverse party (in litigation), opposite side in a lawsuit

Gegen / ~position 1. opposite position **2.** offsetting (matching) position; **~posten 1.** counter item, offsetting item **2.** *(Gegenbuchung)* balancing (offsetting) entry

Gegensatz contrast, difference, opposition, *(im ~ zu)* contrary to, in contrast with, as opposed to, *(im ~ dazu)* by contrast, *(im ~ stehen)* to contradict, to be in opposition to, to contrast with

gegensätzlich 1. opposite, opposing, conflicting, divergent, *(~e Bestimmungen)* conflicting (opposing) rules, *(~e Stellungnahme)* opposite comment (opinion)
2. *(widersprüchlich)* contradictory

Gegenseite 1. opposite (opposing) party **2.** *(bei Finanzgeschäften)* counterparty

gegenseitig mutual, reciprocal, *(~es Garantieversprechen)* reciprocal guarantee undertaking, mutual guarantee, *(~e Kapitalbeteiligung)* cross-shareholding, reciprocal shareholding, *(~e Notierung)* cross-listing, *(~e Verpflichtungen)* mutual obligations, reciprocal debts, *(im ~en Einverständnis)* by mutual consent

Gegenseitigkeit reciprocity, mutuality

Gegenseitigkeits / ~gesellschaft mutual company; **~klausel** reciprocity clause; **~prinzip** reciprocity principle

Gegensicherungsgeschäft counterhedge, counterhedging transaction

Gegenstand 1. object, *(~ des Unternehmens)* corporate purpose, objectives of the company
2. subject, matter, topic, *(~ der Diskussion)* subject under discussion, *(~ des Streitfalles)* matter at issue (in controversy, in dispute), *(~ des Vertrages)* subject matter of the contract
3. *(Gegenstände des Umlaufvermögens)* current assets

gegenständlich 1. *(~ beschränkter Erbschein)* certificate of inheritance relating to specific assets (e.g to the assets held in Germany) **2.** *(im ~en Fall)* in the case at hand

gegenstandslos 1. to be no longer valid, invalid **2.** *(unbegründet)* unfounded, groundless

gegensteuern *(bei den Kosten ~)* to counter the rise in costs

Gegensteuerung counteraction(s)

Gegen / ~stimme dissenting vote, *(ohne ~ verabschieden)* to adopt unanimously; **~strömung** countercurrent

Gegen-Swap reverse swap, mirror swap

Gegenteil opposite, contrary, *(bis zum Beweis des ~s)* failing proof to the contrary, until the contrary is proved

gegenteilig contrary, opposed, opposite, *(~e Bestimmung)* provision to the contrary, *(sofern nichts ~es durch die Parteien vereinbart wurde)* unless otherwise agreed by the parties

gegenüber *(~ dem Euro fallen)* to fall against (versus) the Euro, *(eine deutliche Verbesserung ~ dem letzten Jahr)* a marked improvement on the last year, *(eine ~ dem Vorjahr unveränderte Di-*

vidende) a dividend unchanged from the previous year

gegenübersehen *(sich ~)* to be confronted (to be faced) with

gegenüberstehen **1.** *(einer steigenden Verschuldung ~)* to face (to be confronted with) mounting debt **2.** *(ablehnend ~)* to disapprove of **3.** *(positiv ~)* to approve of, to take a positive view, to support

gegenüberstellen **1.** to contrast with **2.** to confront with **3.** *(im Orderbuch ~)* to match in the order book

Gegen / **~verpflichtung** counterobligation, counterliability; **~vorschlag** counterproposal

gegenwärtig *(die ~e finanzielle Lage)* the present (current) financial situation, *(unter den ~en Marktbedingungen)* under the present (prevailing, prevalent) market conditions

Gegenwartswert current (present, actual) value, → Zeitwert

Gegenwert **1.** equivalent, *(der ~ aus Pensionsgeschäften)* money equivalent of repurchase transactions, *(der ~ auf der Basis des derzeitigen Wechselkurses)* the equivalent amount at the current rate of exchange, *(in Höhe des ~es ausstellen)* to issue for the equivalent amount
2. *(Erlös)* proceeds, *(~ der Dokumente)* proceeds of the documents, *(~ eines Wechsels)* bill proceeds, *(wir bitten um Anschaffung des ~es auf unser Konto)* please remit the proceeds to our account
3. *(Transaktionswert)* transaction value

Gegen / **~wertmittel** *(ERP)* counterpart funds; **~wertverrechnung** settlement of the proceeds; **~zeichnung** countersignature

Gegner **1.** opponent (e. g. of capital controls) **2.** *jur.* opposing party, opponent

gegnerisch *(~er Anwalt)* opposing counsel, *(~e Partei)* opposing party (side)

Gehalt **1.** salary, remuneration, earnings, pay, *(i. S. von Gesamtvergütung)* salary (remuneration) package, *(Gehalt und Nebenleistungen)* compensation and benefits
2. content, *(wirtschaftlicher ~)* economic substance

gehalten *(~ sein)* to be obliged, to be bound

Gehalts / **~abtretung** salary assignment; **~ansprüche** salary (remuneration) requested; **~bescheinigung** pay certificate; **~empfänger** salary earner(s), salaried employee(s)

G

Gehalts / **~entwicklung** salary progression; **~erhöhung** salary increase, pay rise; **~forderung** salary (remuneration) requested; **~konto** payroll account; **~kosten** *(gesamte ~)* compensation and benefit expense, total payroll and benefit expense; **~liste** payroll

Gehalts / **~pfändung** attachment of earnings; **~stufe** salary bracket (grade); **~tabelle** pay scale; **~wunsch** remuneration (salary) request; **~zulage** additional (extra) pay, bonus

geheim *(~ halten)* to keep secret, *(~e Wahl)* secret ballot (vote)

Geheimhaltung **1.** secrecy **2.** *(Vertraulichkeit)* confidentiality

Geheimhaltungs / **~bestimmungen** obligation of secrecy provisions; **~pflicht** obligation of secrecy, obligation (duty) to maintain secrecy, *(~ im Bankgewerbe)* obligatory secrecy in banking

Geheimhaltungs / **~vereinbarung** secrecy (non-disclosure) agreement, confidentialty agreement; **~verpflichtung** confidentialty and non-disclosure commitment, → Geheimhaltungspflicht

Geheimkonto secret (numbered) account

Gehilfenhaftung vicarious liability

gehobenes Kundensegment higher-income (upscale) customer segment, → gehobene Privatkunden

gehobener Mittelstand *(im Firmenkundengeschäft)* upper mid-market enterprises

gehobenes Preissegment upper price range

gehobene Privatkunden upper retail customers, higher-income private customers, upscale customers, → vermögende Privatkunden, *(gehobenes Privatkundengeschäft)* private banking, business serving higher-income private customers

G

gehören to belong to, *(zu einem Konzern ~)* to be part of a group

gehörig *(~e Erfüllung/Leistung)* proper performance, performance as specified by the contract

geistig *(~e Eigentumsrechte)* intellectual property rights

gekappt *(~e Optionsscheine)* capped warrants

gekoren *(~e Orderpapiere)* documents made out to bearer, securities transferable by endorsement

gekreuzt *(~es Orderbuch)* crossed order book

gekündigt *(~er Betrag)* amount for which notice of withdrawal has been given, *(~e Stücke)* securities called for redemption, securities for which notice of redemption has been given

gelangen *(zu einer Vereinbarung ~)* to reach (to arrive at) an agreement

Geld 1. money, *(~ haltender Sektor)* money holding sector, *(~ von heute bis zum nächsten Geschäftstag)* overnight money, *(~ von morgen auf übermorgen/den übernächsten Geschäftstag)* tom/next money
2. *(Bargeld)* cash
3. *(Gelder, Mittel)* funds, capital, financial resources (means)
4. *(Kurszusatz)* bid, buyers, buyers over

Geld / ~abgänge/abflüsse outflow of funds (of deposits); **~angebot** money supply; **~angebotsmultiplikator** money supply multiplier; **~anhäufung** accumulation of funds; **~anlageberatung** investment advisory

Geldanlagen 1. cash investments, *(~ von Gebietsfremden)* non-resident deposits (investments)
2. *(im Geldhandel)* placing of deposits, short-term lendings in the interbank market, *(~ bei anderen Kreditinstituten)* deposits placed with other banks

Geld / ~anschlussrisiko transformation risk, risk of loss resulting from the non-availability of follow-up funding; **~anspannung 1.** liquidity squeeze **2.** tightness in the money market; **~anspruch 1.** money (monetary, pecuniary) claim **2.** right to payment; **~anweisung** money order

Geldaufnahmen 1. borrowings, fundraising, *(~ am Euromarkt)* borrowings in the Euromarket, *(~ bei anderen Instituten)* borrowings with other banks
2. *(im Geldhandel)* taking of deposits, *(~ im Interbankgeschäft)* borrowing overnight or term money in the interbank market, short-term fund-raising in the interbank market, *(~ mit Laufzeiten von einem Tag)* overnight borrowings

Geldausfuhr export of money, capital exports

Geldausgabeautomat cash dispenser, cash dispensing machine, → Geldautomat, → Einzahlungsautomat

Geld / ~ausgaben 1. cash outlays (disbursements) **2.** expenditure; **~ausgänge** cash drawings, withdrawal of funds; **~ausleihungen** cash lendings, *(~ im Interbankgeschäft)* short-term lendings in the interbank market; **~ausweitung** monetary expansion

Geldautomat automated teller machine (ATM), cash machine, *(~ innerhalb des Bankgebäudes)* on premise ATM, lobby ATM, *(~ an einem Standort außerhalb des Bankgebäudes)* off premise ATM, *(~ an der Außenfront des Bankgebäudes)* through-the-wall ATM

Geldautomaten / ~entgelt ATM usage fee, access fee; **~netz** interbank network, ATM network; ~**gebühren** → Geldautomatenentgelt

Geld / ~basis monetary basis □ money in circulation plus bank reserves; ~**bedarf** cash requirements, capital needs; ~**beitrag** financial contribution; ~**belastung** cash debit; ~**beschaffung** fund-raising, procurement of funds, raising (generating) funds

Geldbeschaffungs / ~kosten cost of funds, fund-raising cost, cost of obtaining credit, *(~ der Banken)* cost of funds to the banks, funding costs of the banking system; ~**möglichkeiten** opportunities (avenues) for raising funds; ~**papiere** fund-raising instruments

Geld / ~besicherung cash collateralisation; ~**bestand 1.** *(einer Unternehmung)* cash in (on) hand, cash assets, monetary holdings **2.** *(einer Volkswirtschaft)* money stock; ~**betrag** amount (sum) of money

Geld / ~bewegungen monetary movements; ~**bewilligung** granting (appropriation) of funds; ~**-Brief-Spanne** bid/offer spread; ~**buchung** cash entry, entry in the money account

Geld / ~deckung 1. cash cover, cover funds **2.** availability of cash (funds) **3.** *(~ prüfen)* to check the availability of adequate funds, to check the cover; ~**defizit** shortage of liquid funds, liquidity shortage (shortfall)

Geld / ~disponent treasurer; ~**disposition 1.** *(i.e.S)* money dealings **2.** *(i.w.S.)* managing the cash position, cash (and liquidity) management, treasury management; ~**durchhandel** borrowing and relending funds at an interest markup, round tripping

Geld / ~eingang 1. receipt of funds, cash receipts **2.** *(Geldeingänge)* inflow of funds (of deposits), *(auf abgeschriebene Kreditforderungen)* recoveries on loans written off; ~**einheit** monetary (currency) unit

Geld / ~einnahmen cash receipts (takings); ~**einstandskosten** cost of money; ~**einzahlung** cash deposit, depositing cash; ~**einzahlungsautomat** automated (auto) depositor

Geld / ~entschädigung cash compensation (indemnity), indemnification in cash; ~**entwertungsrate** inflation rate; ~**ersatz** money substitute, token money

Geld / ~flussrechnung cash flow statement; ~**forderung** money claim, amount owed, amount due, *(Geldforderungen)* monetary receivables; ~**frage** question of money, financial matter (question); ~**fülle** abundance (glut) of cash assets

geldgebende Bank 1. *(am Geldmarkt)* selling bank **2.** *(kreditgebende/finanzierende Bank)* lending bank

Geldgeber 1. (money) lender, funder, supplier of funds, donor **2.** *(Finanzier)* financier, financial backer **3.** *(bei Pensionsgeschäften)* cash provider, party providing cash

Geld / ~geschäft 1. cash transaction **2.** *(unter Banken)* interbank money dealings, interbank placements; ~**gutschrift** cash credit; ~**haltungssektor** money holding sector

Geldhandel money dealings (trading), dealings in the money market, borrowing and lending in the money market

Geldhandels / ~abteilung money desk, money dealing operation (unit); ~**adresse** money market participant; ~**ertrag** income from money market dealings; ~**forderungen** overnight and term money lendings, due from money market operators

Geldhandels / ~linie money dealing line, money market facility; ~**verbindlichkeiten** overnight and term money borrowings

Geld / ~händler money dealer; ~**institut** financial institution; ~**kapital** monetary capital; ~**kapitalbildung** formation of monetary capital; ~**karte** paycard, stored value card; ~**kartengeschäft** cash card operations;

~**kaufkraft** purchasing power of the currency

Geld / ~**knappheit** shortage (scarcity) of funds, monetary tightness; ~**konto** money account; ~**kreislauf** monetary (money) circulation; ~**kurs** bid, bid price (quotation), bid rate

Geld / ~**leihe 1.** cash loan, cash advance **2.** overnight borrowing; ~**leihekosten** cost of borrowing overnight; ~**leistung 1.** payment in cash **2.** cash benefit

geldlich monetary, pecuniary, financial, *(~e Abwicklung/~e Regulierung/ ~e Verrechnung)* money (monetary) settlement

Geldmakler money broker; ~ **geschäfte** money broking

Geldmarkt money market

Geldmarkt / ~**abschluss** money market deal (transaction); ~**adresse** money market name, borrower in the money market; ~**alimentierung** feeding the money market

Geldmarkt / ~**anlagen** money market investments; ~**anspannung** tightness in the money market; ~**buchforderungen** registered money market claims; ~**derivate** money market derivatives; ~**eigengeschäfte** money market dealings for own account

geldmarktempfindlich sensitive to rate fluctuations in the money market

Geldmarkt / ~**fälligkeiten 1.** money market maturities **2.** money market commitments; ~**fonds** money market fund; ~**fondsanlagen** investments in money market funds

Geldmarkt / ~**forderungen** *(~ an ausländische Banken)* lendings to foreign banks in the money market; ~**fristigkeiten** money market maturities; ~**-Futures** money market futures

geldmarktgebunden *(~e Zinssätze)* interest rates linked to money market rates

Geldmarkt / ~**geschehen** money market activities, trading in the money market; ~**gleichgewicht** money market equilibrium; ~**intervention** intervention in the money market; ~**konto 1.** money market account **2.** same as → Tagesgeldkonto; ~**kredit** money market loan; ~**mittel** money market funds

geldmarktnah *(~er Fonds)* near-money market fund, *(~e Konditionen)* near-money market terms (pricing)

Geldmarkt / ~**papiere** money market securities (instruments), money market debt securities; ~**rendite** money market yield; ~**satz** money market rate, *(Geldmarktsätze unter Banken)* interbank money market rates; ~**teilnehmer** money market operator (participant, player)

Geldmarkt / ~**titel** money market securities (instruments); ~**transaktionen** money market transactions, short-term money dealings; ~**-Usancen** money market practice (customs); ~**verschuldung** money market indebtedness; ~**wechsel** money market bill

Geldmenge money supply (stock), *(~ in der weitesten Abgrenzung)* broad monetary aggregate, broad money supply, → M3, *(~ in der engeren Definition)* narrow monetary aggregate, narrow money supply, → M1

Geldmenge M1 *(im ESZB)* narrow monetary aggregate, Money Stock M1 □ cash (bank notes and coins) and overnight deposits (balances which can easily be converted into cash)

Geldmenge M2 intermediate monetary aggregate, Money Stock M2 □ M1 deposits with a maturity of up to two years and deposits redeemable at a period of notice of up to three months

Geldmenge M3 broad monetary aggregate, Money Stock M3 □ M2 and marketable instruments (money market fund shares, money market paper, and repurchase agreements) issued by monetary financial institutions

Geldmengen / ~**aggregate** monetary (money) aggregates; ~**expansion**

monetary expansion; ~**größe/-kennzahl** money stock measure, measure of the money supply; ~**kontraktion** monetary contraction; ~**kontrolle** money supply control

Geldmengen / ~**steuerung** money supply control; ~**wachstum** monetary growth, money supply growth, growth in (expansion of the) money stock; ~**zahlen** money supply figures, monetary aggregates; ~**ziele** money targets, monetary aggregate targets

Geld / ~**mittel** funds, financial resources (means), capital; ~**mittelfluss** flow of funds; ~**nachfrage** demand for money (capital), money demand

geldnah *(~e Aktiva)* near-money assets, *(~e Anlagen)* near-money investments, investments that are readily convertible into cash

Geldnehmer 1. borrower 2. *(im Interbanken-Geldhandel)* borrowing (buying) bank 3. *(bei Pensionsgeschäften)* cash taker, party receiving cash

Geldofferte *(im Geld- und Devisenhandel)* bid, buying rate

Geldpolitik monetary policy, *(eine antizyklische/expansive/restriktive ~ fahren)* to steer an anticyclical/an expansionist/a restrictive (tight) monetary policy course

geldpolitisch *(~er Handlungsrahmen)* framework for monetary policy operations, *(~es Instrumentarium)* instruments of monetary policy, monetary policy tools, *(~er Kurs)* monetary policy course (stance)

Geld / ~**position** cash position; ~**quellen** financial (funding) sources ; ~**repartierung** *(im Effektenhandel)* scale-down of buy (purchase) orders; ~**schöpfungssaldo** net money creation; ~**schwemme** money surge, glut of money

Geld / ~**sendung** cash remittance, → Geldtransfer; ~**sicherheit** cash security (collateral); ~**spritze** money infusion, cash injection; ~**stabilität** monetary stability; ~**stelle** money desk, money dealing unit

Geld / ~**stromanalyse** flow-of-funds analysis, money flow analysis; ~**transfer** funds transfer, money transmission; ~**transferdienstleister** money transmitter; ~**-transfer-Verordnung** Funds Transfer Directive

Geld / ~**überhang** surplus money supply, *(Überschüsse in der täglichen Gelddisposition)* day-to-day surplus of funds; ~**überweisung** funds (money) transfer; ~**umlauf** money in circulation, monetary circulation, notes and coins in circulation; ~**umlaufgeschwindigkeit** velocity of monetary circulation; ~**umstellung** currency conversion

Geld / ~**verbilligung** 1. *(der Geldeinstandskosten)* lowering the cost of funds 2. *(der Kreditkosten)* lowering borrowing cost; ~**verfassung** *(nationale ~)* national monetary statutes (system); ~**verkehr** monetary movements; ~**verknappung** monetary contraction (tightness), scarcity of funds; ~**verlust** loss of money, pecuniary loss

Geldvermögen cash assets, cash and cash equivalents; *i.w.S.* financial assets, monetary wealth, *(~ der privaten Haushalte)* financial assets of the personal sector

Geldvermögens / ~**bestände** holdings of financial assets; ~**bildung** formation of financial assets; ~**erträge** income from financial assets

Geld / ~**verrechnung** cash (money) settlement, settlement of the proceeds; ~**verrechnungskonto** money account; ~**verrechnungsverkehr** money clearing operations; ~ **volumen** money supply

Geld / ~**wäsche** money laundering; ~**wäschebekämpfung** fight against money laundering; ~**wäschegesetz** Money Laundering Act

geldwert *(~e Leistungen) (a)* benefits in kind *(b) (Vereinbarung über ~e Leistungen)* soft dollar arrangements, *(~e*

Nebenleistungen) perquisites, perks, *(~er Vorteil)* non-cash benefit

Geld / **~wert** value of money, monetary value; **~wertminderung** monetary depreciation, inflation; **~wertstabilität** monetary stability; **~wesen** monetary system, money and finance

Geld / **~zahlung** payment of money, cash payment; **~-Zinssatz** bid rate; **~zuflüsse** inflow of funds (of deposits); **~zuweisung** appropriation of funds

Gelegenheitsgesellschaft temporary joint venture

G

gelegentlich *(~e Stützungskäufe)* occasional support buying

geliefert *(~ Grenze)* delivered at frontier (DAF), *(~ ab Kai (verzollt))* delivered ex quay (duty paid) (DEQ), *(~ ab Schiff)* delivered ex ship (DES), *(~ unverzollt)* delivered duty unpaid (DDU), *(~ verzollt)* delivered duty paid (DDP)

gelingen to succeed (to be successful) in, *(nicht ~)* to fail in

Gelingen success, *(das ~ der Sanierungsbemühungen)* the successful outcome of the restructuring efforts

gelten 1. *(gültig sein)* to be in force, to be effective (valid), *(unsere Kreditzusage gilt weiterhin)* our loan undertaking shall continue in force (shall remain operative), *(die Vereinbarungen ~ unverändert fort)* the agreements shall continue to apply unchanged
2. *(maßgebend sein)* to prevail, to be governing, to apply
3. *(zutreffen)* to apply to, to be applicable, *(das gleiche gilt für langfristige Kreditaufnahmen)* the same holds true for long-term borrowings, *(die neuen Zinssätze ~ ab)* the new interest rates apply from
4. *(~ als)* to be considered as, to pass for, *(als nicht eingelöst ~)* to be deemed unpaid, *(die Leistungsstörung gilt als eingetreten)* non-performance is deemed to have occurred, *(als uneinbringlich ~)* to be considered uncollectible *(als vertrauenswürdiger Kreditnehmer ~)* to be regarded as trustworthy borrower, *(als berechtigte Unternehmen ~)* to qualify as authorised entities, *(der Auszug gilt als Unterrichtung des Kunden)* the statement shall be deemed to constitute notification to the customer, *(die Zustimmung gilt als erteilt)* consent is deemed to have been given
5. *(~ lassen)* to accept, to admit

geltend valid, in force, current, prevailing, *(~e Bestimmungen)* provisions in force, current regulations, *(~es Recht)* law in force, governing (prevailing, applicable) law, *(~er Zinssatz)* prevailing (current) interest rate, *(der jeweils ~e Zinssatz)* the interest rate as valid (charged) from time to time

geltend machen *(einen Anspruch ~)* to assert (to put forward) a claim, *(einen Anspruch gerichtlich ~)* to assert a claim in court, to enforce a claim, *(nicht geltend gemachte Ansprüche)* unexhausted claims
(Einfluss ~) to exercise (to exert) influence, *(Einwände ~)* to put forward (to raise) objections, *(steuerlich ~)* to claim a tax deduction (tax allowance) for, *(einen Verlust im laufenden Jahr ~)* to claim a loss in the current year

Geltendmachung 1. *(~ von Ansprüchen)* assertion of claims, *(~ einer Garantieforderung)* asserting a claim under a guarantee, *(gerichtliche ~ von Ansprüchen)* asserting claims in court, legal enforcement of claims
2. *(von Einwänden)* putting forward (raising) objections

Geltung 1. *(Ansehen)* credit, standing, authority, *(zur ~ kommen)* to show, to stand out, *(sich ~ am Markt verschaffen)* to assert o. s. in the market, to increase one's standing (to gain recognition) in the market
2. *(Gültigkeit)* validity, force, applicability, effect, operation

Geltungsbereich 1. *(Anwendungsbereich)* scope (sphere) of application, validity, *(~ dieser Bestimmungen)*

purview of these terms and conditions
2. *(geografischer ~)* territorial validity, geographical limits, *(~ eines Gesetzes)* territorial scope of an Act
3. *(einer Versicherung) (a)* policy territory, territorial limits *(b)* coverage

Geltungsdauer term (duration) of validity

gemäß *(~ den Anweisungen des Kunden)* in accordance with (according to, pursuant to) the customer's instructions

gemeiner Wert current (ordinary) value, market value (worth)

Gemeinkosten overheads, overhead cost (expense); **~wertanalyse** overhead value analysis

gemeinnützig non-profit making, *(~e Körperschaft/Organisation)* non-profit corporation/organisation, *(~er Status)* public benefit status

gemeinsam 1. *adj.* *(~e Absichtserklärung)* joint letter of intent, joint statement of interest, *(~e Aufsichtsorgane)* shared regulatory bodies, *(~e Haftung)* joint liability, *(auf ~e Rechnung)* for joint account, *(~es Vorgehen)* joint (concerted) action
2. *adv.* *(~ besitzen)* to own (to possess, to hold) jointly, *(~ haften)* to be jointly (collectively) liable, *(~ zeichnen)* to sign jointly

Gemeinschaft community, *(~ zur gesamten Hand)* joint partnership under civil law

gemeinschaftlich 1. *adj.* *(~e Bevollmächtigung)* joint power, *(~e Bürgschaft)* joint guarantee □ the guarantors bind themselves both jointly and individually, *(~es Eigentum)* joint property, jointly owned (held) property, community property, *(~e Rechnung)* joint account *(~e Verfügungsberechtigung über ein Konto)* joint authority to draw, joint authority to operate an account, *(~ es Wohneigentum)* co-ownership of residential property, *(~e Zeichnungsberechtigung)* joint signatory power
2. *adv.* *(~ geführtes Unternehmen)* jointly managed (controlled) company, *(~ handelnde Personen)* parties acting jointly (acting in concert), *(~ über ein Konto verfügen)* to operate (to draw) jointly on an account
(~ zur Erfüllung der Verbindlichkeiten verpflichtet sein) to be jointly bound to fulfil the obligations under the contract, *(~ vertreten)* to represent jointly, *(~ zeichnungsberechtigt)* authorised to sign jointly

Gemeinschafts / ~depot joint securities account, joint portfolio; **~eigentum** joint property, *(bei einer Eigentumswohnungsanlage)* common elements, common ownership; **~eigentümer** joint owner (proprietor); **~emission** joint issue

Gemeinschafts / ~finanzierung joint financing (funding), syndicated finance; **~fläche** common area; **~konto** joint account, bank account held in joint tenancy; **~kredit** syndicated (joint) loan, joint loan extension (accommodation); **~kreditgeschäft** syndicated (joint) lending operations

Gemeinschafts / ~plattform (single) shared platform;**~recht** community law; **~schuldner** joint debtor, codebtor; **~sparen** collective saving; **~unternehmen** joint venture

Gemeinschuldner insolvent debtor

gemessen *(~ am Eigenkapital)* measured by (in terms of) capital and reserves, *(~ am Vorjahresergebnis)* measured against last year's performance

gemischt *(~er Fonds)* mixed fund, asset allocation fund, balanced fund, *(~ genutzter Grundbesitz)* mixed real property □ property used for commercial and residential purposes, *(~e Immobilien)* mixed usage properties *(~e Hypothekenbank)* mixed mortgage bank □ mortgage bank which also offers general banking services, *(~ es Sondervermögen)* mixed fund, → Sondervermögen, → Spezial-Sondervermögen, → Publikums-

G

Sondervermögen, *(~es Unternehmen)* mixed-activity enterprise

genau 1. *adj.* *(~e Abschrift)* true copy, *(~e Angaben)* exact (accurate) details, full details, complete particulars, *(~e Einhaltung)* strict observance of, strict adherence to, *(~e Kenntnis)* precise (detailed) knowledge, *(~e Übereinstimmung der Dokumente)* exact match of the documents
2. *adv.* *(~ überwachen)* to monitor closely, to maintain a close watch over

G

Genauigkeit accuracy, exactness, precision

Genauigkeitsgrad degree of accuracy, accuracy level

genehm *(ein der Bank ~er Lagerhalter)* a warehousing company acceptable to the bank

genehmigen 1. *(billigen)* to authorise, to approve, *(eine Kapitalerhöhung ~)* to authorise a capital increase, *(einen Kredit ~)* to sanction a loan, to consent to a loan (facility), *(genehmigter Überziehungskredit)* authorised (negotiated) overdraft
2. *(erlauben)* to permit, to allow, to authorise, to clear 3. *(zustimmen)* to agree to, to consent to, to accept

genehmigt *(~es Kapital)* authorised capital, *(~es Kapital durch Sacheinlagen)* authorised capital through contributions in kind

Genehmigung 1. authorisation, approval, *(~ durch die Aktionäre)* shareholder approval, *(~ des Kreditantrages)* sanction (approval) of the loan application, *(um die ~ der Kreditgeber nachsuchen)* to seek the lenders' approval, *(~ eines Kreditkartengeschäftes)* authorisation of a credit card transaction, *(~ durch Schweigen)* tacit approval
2. permission, clearance, *(~ durch die Behörden)* clearance by the authorities, (*die ~ zur Bereitstellung zusätzlicher Gelder erhalten)* to obtain (to receive) permission to provide additional funds
3. agreement, consent, licence

Genehmigungs / ~anfrage *(im Kreditkartengeschäft)* authorisation request, merchant's request for authorisation of a credit card sales transaction; **~antrag** sanction request, application for approval (permission); **~befugnisse** *(im Kreditgeschäft)* approval powers; **~behörde** authorising agency

Genehmigungs / ~bescheid 1. letter of approval 2. *(im Kreditkartengeschäft)* authorisation (approval) response 3. clearance certificate; **~betrag** authorised amount; **~ergebnis** → Genehmigungsbescheid; **~gebühr** authorisation fee

Genehmigungs / ~kompetenz approval authority; **~nachweis** *(als ~ dienen)* to serve as proof of authorisation; **~nummer** authorisation code, authorisation ID □ numerical code that indicates approval of a credit card transaction

genehmigungspflichtig *(~e Termingeschäfte)* forward deals subject to approval (requiring approval) of

Genehmigungs / ~verfahren approval (sanctioning) process, authorisation procedure; **~vermerk** authorisation note (stamp), note of approval

General / ~bevollmächtigter 1. general manager 2. generally authorised agent, representative (person) holding a general power; **~direktor** managing director, general manager; **~klausel** blanket clause

General / ~police blanket floater, all-risks insurance policy; **~prokura** general power to represent the company; **~versammlung** 1. general meeting (assembly) 2. *(einer Genossenschaft)* members' meeting; **~vollmacht** general power

genießen *(Kredit ~)* to enjoy credit, *(die Rechte voll ~)* to enjoy the rights in their entirety, *(einen guten Ruf ~)* to enjoy a good reputation, *(einen beträchtlichen Spielraum ~)* to enjoy considerable freedom

Genossenschaft cooperative, cooperative society

genossenschaftlich *(~er Finanzverbund)* Cooperative Banking Group, financial network of Germany's cooperative banks, *(~e Kreditinstitute)* cooperative credit institutions

Genossenschafts / ~anteile shares in a cooperative society; **~bank** cooperative bank; **~bankensektor** cooperative banking sector; **~gesetz** German Cooperatives Act; **~kapital** cooperative capital; **~register** Cooperative Society Register, → EHUG

Genossenschafts / ~ring giro network of credit cooperatives, network operated by the cooperative banking sector; **~vertrag** articles of a cooperative society; **~wesen** cooperative system; **~zentralbank** Central Cooperative Bank

genügen 1. to be sufficient (adequate) **2.** *(den hohen Bonitätsanforderungen ~)* to satisfy (to meet, to fulfil) the high credit standards

genügend sufficient, adequate

Genuss 1. *jur.* enjoyment, *(~ von Rechten)* enjoyment of rights, *(in den ~ einer Steuererleichterung kommen)* to enjoy a tax relief **2.** *(Nießbrauch)* usufruct

Genussrecht participation right, profit-sharing right, jouissance (participatory) right

Genussrechts / ~inhaber holder of participation rights (of jouissance rights); **~kapital** jouissance rights capital, participatory capital

Genussschein participation certificate, profit-sharing certificate □ hybrid financial instrument between debt and equity

Genussschein *(~ mit ergebnisabhängiger Ausschüttung)* participation certificate with income-linked payout, *(~ mit fester Ausschüttung)* fixed income participation certificate, *(~ mit/ohne Optionsscheine)* participation certificate cum/ex warrants, *(~ mit Wandelrechten)* participation certificate with conversion rights

Genussschein / ~emission issue of participation certificates; **~inhaber** holder of a participation certificate; **~kapital** participation certificates outstanding; **~verbindlichkeiten** liabilities from participation certificates outstanding

geordnet *(~e bilanzielle Verhältnisse)* well-ordered balance sheet situation, *(~e finanzielle Verhältnisse)* sound financial situation, *(~er Markt)* regular (organised) market, *(einen ~en Markt garantieren)* to guarantee a fair and orderly (a well-regulated) market

gepaart *(~e Stichprobe)* matched sample

Gepflogenheiten (business) practices, customs, customary terms, *(die ~ im internationalen Wertpapierhandel)* customary practices in international securities trading

geradlinig *(~e Entwicklung)* linear (straight) trend

geraten *(unter Abgabedruck ~)* to come under selling pressure, *(in finanzielle Schwierigkeiten ~)* to run into financial difficulties (straits), *(mit seinen Zahlungen in Rückstand ~)* to fall behind with one's payments

gerecht werden to meet, to satisfy, to live up, *(den Anforderungen der Position ~)* to meet (to fulfil) the job requirements

gerechtfertigt *(~e Ansprüche)* justified (legitimate) claims

geregelter Freiverkehr → Freiverkehr

geregelter Markt regulated market □ former second market segment of the German stock exchange; closed and transferred to → Regulierter Markt in 2007

gereizt *(~e Stimmung an den internationalen Finanzmärkten)* irritable mood (edgy sentiment) in the international financial markets

gerichtlich *(~e Anordnung)* court order, writ, *(~e Beurkundung)* certification by a court, *(~e Liquidation)* liquidation subject to supervision of a court, *(~er Pfändungsbeschluss)* writ of attachment, *(~e Überprüfung)* judicial review, *(~er Vergleich)* court-approved scheme of arrangement, court settlement
(~ beitreibbare Schuld) debt recoverable in law, debt enforceable in court, *(~ bestellter Treuhänder/Zwangsverwalter)* judicial trustee, court-appointed trustee/administrator, *(~ geltend machen)* to enforce a claim, to assert a claim in court, *(~ vorgehen)*to institute legal proceedings

G

Gerichts / ~**barkeit** jurisdiction, *(einer ~ unterliegen)* to be subject to the jurisdiction of; ~**beschluss** court order, ruling, writ; ~**entscheid** court (judicial) decision; ~**kosten** legal costs, court fees; ~**kostengesetz** German Court Fees Act

Gerichtsstand venue, forum, place of jurisdiction, *(Gerichtsstand und Erfüllungsort)* venue and place of performance, *(Gerichtsstand und Rechtswahl)* venue and choice of law

Gerichtsstands / ~**klausel** forum selection clause, legal venue (choice of forum) clause; ~**vereinbarung** venue agreement, forum agreement; ~**wahl** choice of venue, forum selection

Gerichts / ~**urteil** judg(e)ment; ~**verfahren** legal (judicial) proceedings, lawsuit; ~**vollzieher** court bailiff, enforcement agent

gering *(~e Abgaben)* small selling (offerings), *(~es Anlegerinteresse)* little investor interest, *(~er Kapitaleinsatz)* low equity commitment, *(~es Käuferinteresse)* small buying interest, *(~e Nachfrage)* sluggish demand, *(~e Umsätze) (Börse)* sparse (thin) trading

geringfügig insignificant, minor, slight, trifling, *(~ fester)* slightly firmer, *(~ im Geld)* marginally in the money, → im Geld, *(~ schwächer nach Gewinnmitnahmen)* slightly off (lower) on profit-taking, *(~er Betrag)* trifling amount, *(~es Guthaben)* insignificant credit balance (deposits)

geringwertig of inferior (low) quality, of minor (little) value, *(~e Sachanlagen)* low-value fixed assets, *(~e Wirtschaftsgüter)* minor-value (low-value) assets

Gerüchte *(~ hinsichtlich einer bevorstehenden Dividendenerhöhung)* rumours (whispers) of an imminent dividend rise

gerundet *(~es Bezugsverhältnis)* rounded (rounded off) subscription ratio

gesamt total, entire, whole, *(zur ~en Hand zustehen)* to own collectively, *(auf den ~en Kredit anwenden)* to apply to the whole of the loan

Gesamt / ~**abtretung** global assignment; ~**aktie** global share; ~**aktivbestand** total assets, aggregated long position

Gesamtanrechnungsbetrag *(~ für Adressenrisiken)* total capital charge for counterparty risks

Gesamt / ~**aufwand** total (aggregate) expenditure; ~**aufwandsquote** total expense ratio; ~**ausfallrisiko** aggregate exposure; ~**ausleihungen** aggregate loan portfolio, total lendings

Gesamt / ~**bankkontrolle** bank-wide control (monitoring); ~**bankrisiko** aggregate bank-wide risk; ~**bankrisikoposition** bank's overall risk position; ~**banksteuerung** total bank management, bank-wide risk management; ~**belastung** total charges, total (aggregate) encumbrance

Gesamt / ~**bestand** aggregate holdings,*(~ an langfristigen Ausleihungen)* total long-term lendings; ~**betrag** total (aggregate) amount, *(~ des Darlehens zahlbar zum Endfälligkeitstermin)* total principal due at final maturity

Gesamtbetriebsergebnis *(Teilbetriebsergebnis plus Eigenhandelsergebnis*

sowie sonstiger laufender Aufwendungen und Erträge) aggregate operating result □ partial operating result plus own-account trading profit and other current income and expenditure items

Gesamt / ~bewertung global valuation, macrovaluation; **~börsenkapitalisierung** aggregate market capitalisation; **~börsenumsatz** aggregated national stock exchange turnover; **~buchgroßkredite** aggregated large exposures; **~budget** master (overall, summary) budget

Gesamt / ~dotierung aggregate remuneration, remuneration package; **~eigentum** joint property; **~eigenkapitalquote** overall equity ratio; **~einlagenquote** aggregate deposit ratio; **~emission 1.** issue of identical debt securities **2.** global issue

Gesamt / ~engagement aggregate (total) commitments, aggregate loan exposure; **~engagementgrenze** total exposure threshold; **~ergebnis** overall performance, aggregate income (loss); **~erledigungsklausel** full execution clause; **~erlöse** *(~ aus langfristigen Aufträgen)* contract revenue

Gesamtertrag aggregate (total) earnings, total return, *(~ des Kreditgeschäftes)* aggregate earnings from lending operations

Gesamtertrags-Swap Total Return Swap (TRS) □ Unlike a → Kreditausfallswap, which provides protection against specific credit events, the Total Return Swap provides protection against loss in asset value insofar as one party (protection buyer) sells the total return (income and capital appreciation or depreciation) of a reference asset (e.g. bond, loan, equity index) against regular fixed or floating interest rate payments made by the other party (protection seller).

gesamtfällige Anleihe bullet bond □ the principal of the bond is repaid in one amount upon maturity

Gesamt / ~fälligkeit / ~fälligkeitstermin total (bullet) maturity; **~fälligstellung** *(eines Darlehens)* calling in the entire loan; **~finanzierungsangebot** all-in financing offer, all-in funding package

Gesamt / ~gebühr all-in fee; **~geschäftsführungsbefugnis** joint management authority; **~gläubiger** joint creditor; **~grundschuld** collective land charge; **~gut** joint property; **~haftung** joint liability; **~haftungsverpflichtung** joint liability undertaking

Gesamthand / ~eigentum joint property, jointly owned property; **~-GbR** joint partnership under civil law; **~gemeinschaft 1.** joint owners, tenancy in common, common ownership **2.** *(Gesellschafter)* joint partners **3.** *(Erben)* joint heirs

Gesamthand / ~gläubiger joint creditor; **~schuld** joint debt; **~schuldner** joint debtor; **~vermögen** joint property, jointly owned assets

Gesamt / ~heit 1. entirety, totality, as a whole **2.** general public; **~hypothek** collective mortgage; **~inanspruchnahme** total drawings (utilisation); **~investitionen** total (aggregate) capital expenditure

Gesamtkapital 1. *(eines Kreditinstituts nach* → Basel III) total capital □ consists of Tier 1 capital (→ Kernkapital) and Tier 2 Capital (→ Ergänzungskapital). Total capital will need to equal 8% of a bank's risk-weighted assets. **2.** *(i. S. von Gesamtkapitalisierung einer Unternehmung)* aggregate capitalisation, funding from both debt and equity sources

Gesamtkapital / ~betrag *(einer Anleihe)* aggregate principal amount; **~quote** aggregated capital ratio; **~rentabilität** all-in equity return (earnings rate)

Gesamtkosten total (aggregate, all-in) cost, *(~ für den Emittenten)* all-in cost to the issuer, *(~ der Kreditinanspruchnahme)* aggregate cost of the credit

G

Gesamtkostenquote *(eines Fonds)* total expense ratio □ ratio of total operating cost to the fund's net assets

Gesamtkredit aggregate loan facility

Gesamtkredit / **~aufnahme** total funds raised, total borrowings; **~engagement/~linie** **1.** aggregate facility (credit line) **2.** aggregate loan exposure; **~risiko** aggregate credit risk, **~volumen** **1.** total lending(s) **2.** *(eines Kreditnehmers)* total borrowings, all facilities granted to the borrower

G

Gesamt / **~laufzeit** aggregate life, overall duration, entire runtime; **~leistung** *(Umsatzerlöse, Bestandsveränderung)* aggregate operating performance; **~liquidität** *(einer Bank)* total liquid assets (means); **~liquiditätsstandards** overall liquidity standards, → Basel III

Gesamt / **~markt** market as a whole; **~marktrisikoposition** overall market risk position; **~nachfolger** sole (universal) successor; **~nennbetrag** *(einer Anleihe)* aggregate principal amount (face value); **~nutzungsdauer** total useful life

Gesamt / **~obligo** total (aggregate) exposure, aggregate liability, total commitments; **~passivbestand** aggregate liabilities □ deposits and other liabilities; **~performance** aggregate performance, total return □ interest income plus capital gains

Gesamt / **~plan** master plan; **~portefeuilleanalyse** overall portfolio analysis; **~position** aggregate exposure; **~prämienaufkommen** total premium income; **~preis** all-in price

Gesamt / **~profitabilität** aggregated profitability; **~prokura** joint authority to represent (to bind) the company, authority to act jointly for a company; **~prokurist** authorised officer holding joint power of representation, executive authorised to act jointly for a company

Gesamt / **~rechnung** *(volkswirtschaftliche)* national accounting; **~rechtsnachfolge** universal succession, succession to the entire property (estate); **~rendite** aggregate yield, all-in return

Gesamt / **~risiko** aggregate exposure (risk); **~risikoposition** aggregate net open position; **~rückzahlung** repayment in one sum, bullet repayment, → gesamtfällige Anleihe

Gesamt / **~schuld** joint and several debt; **~schuldner** joint and several debtor

gesamtschuldnerisch **1.** *adj.* *(~e Bürgschaft)* joint and several guarantee, *(~e Haftung)* joint and several liability **2.** *adv.* *(~ haften)* to be jointly and severally liable, *(wir verpflichten uns ~)* we obligate ourselves jointly and severally

Gesamt / **~schuldverhältnis** joint and several obligation; **~sparleistung** net growth in savings deposits and savings bond sales; **~summe** total, total amount, *(~ aller liquiden Mittel)* cash float

Gesamt / **~tilgung** → Gesamtrückzahlung; **~überschreitungsposition** aggregate excess exposure; **~überschuss** total surplus, aggregate excess exposure, *(~ im operativen Geschäft)* total income from operating business

Gesamt / **~umsatz** total sales, *(Börse)* aggregate turnover; **~unterlegungsbetrag** *(für das operationelle Risiko der Bank)* total capital charge for the bank's operational risks

Gesamt / **~verantwortung** overall responsibility; **~verfügungsrahmen** aggregate drawing line; **~verhältnisse** *(einer Unternehmung)* overall economic and financial position; **~verlust** total loss; **~verlustverteilung** aggregated loss distribution; **~vermögen** total property (assets)

Gesamt / **~verpflichtungen** total amounts payable, total liabilities, → Gesamtverschuldung; **~verschuldung** aggregate indebtedness (debt), aggregate volume of debt (stock of debt), total borrowings (debt); **~versicherung** all-loss (all-risks) insurance

Gesamt / ~**vertretungsbefugnis** *(für ein Unternehmen)* joint power to represent (to bind) the company; ~**verzinsung** total return on an investment, all-in return; ~**vollmacht** joint power of attorney

Gesamtvollstreckung collective (comprehensive, general) enforcement, levy upon the entire property

Gesamtvollstreckungs / ~**ordnung** collective enforcement regulations; ~**verfahren** collective enforcement proceedings

Gesamt / ~**volumen** **1.** total volume, aggregate amount **2.** balance sheet total plus endorsement liabilities and credits by way of guarantee; ~**vorstand** group management board

Gesamt / ~**wert** total (aggregate) value; ~**wertberichtigung** total loan loss allowance, aggregate amount of valuation adjustments; ~**wertpapierumsatz** aggregate securities turnover; ~**wirtschaft** economy as a whole, national (overall) economy

gesamtwirtschaftlich *(~es Gleichgewicht)* general economic equilibrium, *(~e Leistung)* overall economic performance (output), *(~e Nachfrage)* aggregate (economy-wide) demand, *(~e Sparquote)* overall savings ratio, *(~es Umfeld)* macro-economic environment (scenario), *(~e Vermögensbildung)* aggregate capital formation, *(~es Wachstum)* overall economic growth

Gesamtwirtschaftsvolumen total economic activity

Gesamtzeichnungsberechtigung joint signatory (signing) power, *(gesamtzeichnungsberechtigt sein)* to be authorised to sign jointly with others

Gesamtzins / ~**belastung** total interest charge (burden), aggregate interest payments; ~**position** aggregate interest position (exposure); ~**spanne** aggregate interest margin; ~**überschuss** aggregate net interest income

geschädigt *(~e Partei)* aggrieved party, complainant

Geschäft **1.** business, transaction, *(~ mit Firmenkunden)* corporate banking, *(~ mit vermögenden Privatkunden)* private banking for high net worth individuals **2.** *(Unternehmen)* business, company

Geschäfte *(~ auf Kommissionsbasis)* transactions on a commission basis, agency transactions, *(~ am offenen Markt)* open market transactions, transactions in the open market, *(~ auf eigene Rechnung)* transactions (business) for own account, *(~ auf fremde Rechnung)* transactions for account of a third party

geschäftlich *(~ erfahren)* experienced in business, *(~e Angelegenheiten)* business (commercial) matters

Geschäfts / ~**ablauf** business process; ~**abschluss** **1.** deal, transaction, trade **2.** conclusion of a trade (deal), striking a deal **3.** *(Jahresabschluss)* results for the year, annual accounts; ~**abschlusstag** *(bei Börsengeschäften)* trade (contract) date

Geschäfts / ~**abwicklung** **1.** trade settlement, trade processing **2.** conduct of business; ~**adresse** business address; ~**anteil** share (interest, stake) in a business, shareholding, participation

Geschäfts / ~**aufgabe** sale of a business, retirement from business, giving up a business; ~**auflösung** liquidation (dissolution, winding up) of a business; ~**aufschwung** business upturn (revival), increase in business activity; ~**aufsicht** *(~ verhängen)* to place under management supervision

Geschäfts / ~**ausführung** *(eines Börsenauftrags)* execution of a trade, filling an order; ~**ausgaben** business expenses (expenditure); ~**aussichten** business (sales) prospects, business (economic) outlook

Geschäfts / ~**bank** commercial bank; ~**bedingungen** **1.** business conditions, terms of business, *(Allgemeine ~)* General Business Conditions 2. trading conditions

Geschäfts / ~beginn commencement of business, *(Börse)* start (commencement) of trading, start of the trading session; **~belebung** business upturn (revival), *(an der Börse)* upturn in trading (dealings)

Geschäftsbereich 1. *(~ einer Unternehmung)* division, *(Abschluss eines ~es)* divisional accounts (statements), divisional performance, *(Erfolgsrechnung eines ~es)* divisional income statement, *(Ergebnis eines ~es)* divisional performance, *(Gliederung nach ~en)* divisional breakdown, *(Zusammenlegung von ~en)* divisional merger
2. *(Branche)* business sector (branch)
3. *(Sparte, Segment)* business line (segment)
4. *(Zuständigkeit)* competence, province

Geschäftsbereichsaktien tracking stock

Geschäftsbereichskennung *(Teil der SEPA → Gläubiger-Identifikationsnummer)* creditor business code, → Kundenkennung

Geschäfts / ~bericht annual (business) report; **~besorgungsvertrag** agency contract (agreement), service agreement; **~bestätigung** trade confirmation, transaction acknowledgement, confirmation of a deal; **~beteiligung** → Geschäftsanteil

Geschäftsbetrieb 1. business, business (commercial) enterprise, *(Aufrechterhaltung des ~s)* (ensuring) business continuity, *(Finanzierung des laufenden ~s)* financing current business operations, *(im gewöhnlichen ~)* in the normal course of business (activities)
2. running a business

Geschäfts / ~beziehung 1. business relationship (relations) **2.** *(geschäftsmäßig)* working relationship; **~brauch** business (commercial) practice; **~bücher** books, business (corporate) records

Geschäfts / ~eingabe *(eines Wertpapiergeschäftes)* bargain input; **~einlage** capital brought into a business, capital (money) invested, partnership share, (amount of) capital contributed by a partner

Geschäfts / ~entgelt transaction fee (service); **~entwicklung** development of business, business trend; **~erfahrung** business (commercial) experience; **~erfassung** trade capture; **~erfüllung** trade settlement, settling the obligations arising from a trade/contract

Geschäftsergebnis performance, business (trading) performance, results, *(das ~ der Bank im abgelaufenen Geschäftsjahr)* the bank's performance over the past twelve months, *(Verbesserung des ~ses)* improvement in performance, improved results, *(das laufende Jahr wurde mit einem wesentlich verbesserten ~ abgeschlossen)* the company came out of the current year with noticeably improved figures

Geschäfts / ~entwicklung business development, **~entwicklungsfinanzierung** development financing, provision of development capital

geschäftsfähig *(~ sein)* to have capacity to contract, to be of contractual capacity

Geschäfts / ~fähigkeit capacity to contract, contractual capacity; **~feld** business line (segment); **~feldrechnung** segment reporting; **~flaute** business slump, dullness in trading

geschäftsführend *(~er Ausschuss)* executive (managing) committee, *(~er Direktor)* managing director, *(~er Gesellschafter)* managing partner

Geschäftsführer managing director; **~-Kollegium** Board of Managers

Geschäftsführung 1. management of a company, business management, conduct of business (of operations), running a business

2. *(Leitung)* company management, senior management
3. *(Geschäftsführung ohne Auftrag)* agency without mandate

Geschäftsführungs / ~**befugnis** management authority, power to manage the affairs of the company; ~**vertrag** management agreement

Geschäfts / ~**gang** 1. *(Entwicklung)* business (sales) trend, business development 2. *(gewöhnlicher ~)* ordinary course of business; ~**gebaren** business management (practice, policy); ~**gegenstand** business (corporate) purpose, *(bei Börsentermingeschäften)* underlying instrument

Geschäfts / ~**geheimnis** trade (business) secret; ~**gewinn** business profit, trading profit (income); ~**girokonto** business account; ~**grundlage** 1. basis of (for) business 2. *(eines Vertrages)* basis of the agreement; ~**gründung** company formation, incorporation, establishment of a business

Geschäfts / ~**guthaben** 1. operating (working) balances 2. *(einer Genossenschaftsbank)* members' capital contributions; ~**herr** principal; ~**inhaber** owner (proprietor) of a firm

geschäftsinitiierend *(~er Bereich)* originating unit

Geschäfts / ~**interessen** business (financial) interests; ~**inventar** operating and office equipment; ~**jahr** business (fiscal) year

Geschäfts / ~**kapital** business (trading, working) capital; ~**kontakte** business contacts; ~**konto** business account; ~**kredit** business loan; ~**kreise** business community (circles)

Geschäfts / ~**lage** business (financial) situation; ~**leitung** → Geschäftsführung; ~**leitungsbetriebsstätte** primary place of management; ~**limit** transaction limit

Geschäfts / ~**minderwert** negative goodwill; ~**möglichkeiten** business (trading) opportunities; ~**nachbearbeitung** post-processing; ~**ordnung** internal regulations, rules of business (operation)

Geschäftspartner 1. business partner (associate) 2. *(Geschäftspartner der Europäischen Zentralbank)* counterparties to the Eurosystem's operations (meeting the eligibility criteria set by the Eurosystem)

Geschäfts / ~**partnerschaft** corporate partnership; ~**plan** business plan; ~**politik** business (corporate) policy; ~**prozessoptimierung** business process (work flow) optimisation

Geschäfts / ~**räume** offices, office (business) premises; ~**risiko** business (trading) risk; ~**rückgang** decline in business, slowing down of business activities, *(Börse)* downturn in trading, drop-off in turnover

Geschäfts / ~**schließung** closing (shutdown) of a business; ~**schulden** business liabilities (debts); ~**sinn** business acumen; ~**sitz** registered office, head (principal) office, headquarters

Geschäfts / ~**sparte** business segment; ~**stelle** 1. branch, office, agency 2. *(des Gerichts)* Registry of the Court; ~**stellennetz** branch network; ~**steuerung** business management, running a business

Geschäfts / ~**stunden** business (office) hours; ~**tag-Konvention/Usance** business day convention; ~**tätigkeit** business (commercial) activity

Geschäfts / ~**umfang** *(eines Einzelgeschäftes)* size of a transaction, magnitude of a deal, *(der Börsenumsätze)* trading volume, volume of dealings, level of business; ~**umfeld** general economic environment, trading environment; ~**umsatz** total sales (turnover), *(Börse)* (trading) turnover

geschäftsunfähig *(~ sein)* to lack the capacity to contract, to be under legal incapacity

Geschäfts / ~**unfähigkeit** incapacity to contract, legal (contractual) incapacity; ~**unterlagen** business records, transaction documents; ~**verbindung**

business relationship, *(in ~ stehen)* to maintain business relations, to do business with, *(in ~ treten)* to enter into (to establish) business relations

Geschäfts / ~verkehr 1. business transactions (dealings) **2.** *(im Rahmen eines ordnungsgemäßen ~s)* in the course of ordinary business transactions; **~verlagerung 1.** shifting of deals **2.** *(geographische)* relocation of a business; **~verlauf** business (sales) trend, development of business

G

Geschäfts / ~verlegung relocation of a business; **~verlust** business (trading) loss; **~vermögen** business property (assets); **~verpflichtungen** business commitments (liabilities); **~verteilung** allocation of duties, distribution of responsibilities (and accountability)

Geschäfts / ~volumen 1. *(einer Bank)* business volume □ balance sheet total plus endorsement liabilities **2.** *(eines Einzelgeschäftes)* bargain volume; **~vorfall/~vorgang** business transaction, *(~ zwischen unabhängigen Geschäftspartnern)* arm's length transaction; **~weg** *(auf dem üblichen ~)* through the usual business channels; **~wertbeitrag** economic value added

Geschäfts / ~zeichen reference number; **~zeit** business (office) hours; **~zunahme** *(an der Börse)* increase in trading (turnover); **~zweck** business (corporate) purpose; **~zweig** business sector (branch)

Geschehen *(am Aktien-/Rentenmarkt)* trading (turnover, dealings) in the equity/bond market, equity/bond market activity

Geschicke *(~ des Unternehmens)* the company's fortunes (destiny)

geschickt *(~er Anleger)* shrewd (clever) investor

geschlossen *(~er Immobilienfonds)* closed-end real property fund, closed-end property investment company, real estate investment trust, *(~er Investmentfonds)* closed-end fund □ an investment company whose equity capitalisation remains constant, *(~e Position)* closed position

Geschmacksmuster registered design; **~gesetz** Registered Designs Act

Geschossflächenzahl floor space ratio

geschuldet *(~e Leistung)* performance due

Gesellschaft 1. company, firm, corporation, *(~ in Gründung)* company in the stage of foundation, *(~ in Liquidation)* company in liquidation **2.** *(Personengesellschaft)* partnership

Gesellschaft des bürgerlichen Rechts civil law partnership, association under civil law

Gesellschaft mit beschränkter Haftung (GmbH) limited liability company, private company limited by shares

Gesellschaft mit beschränkter Haftung und Compagnie Kommanditgesellschaft (GmbH & Co. KG) limited partnership with a limited liability company as general partner

Gesellschaft mit beschränkter Haftung mit nur einem Gesellschafter – Mini-GmbH/Unternehmergesellschaft single-member private limited company, entrepreneurial company

Gesellschaft mit/ohne eigene Rechtspersönlichkeit legal entity/unincorporated entity

Gesellschaft öffentlichen Rechts statutory corporation

Gesellschafter 1. *(einer Personengesellschaft)* partner **2.** *(einer Kapitalgesellschaft)* shareholder, stockholder **3.** *(einer Genossenschaft)* member

Gesellschafter / ~anteil partnership share (interest), partner's interest, member's shareholding; **~beschluss** shareholder resolution, resolution by the partners, corporate resolution

Gesellschafter / ~darlehen shareholder loan, loan made by a partner (shareholder) to the company; **~einlagen** partners' capital contributions, capital paid in by the partners (shareholders, members), funds invested (put up) by the partners

Gesellschafterfremdfinanzierung shareholder debt financing, *(Regeln zur Gesellschafterfremdfinanzierung)* thin capitalisation rules □ limit the tax deductibility of interest paid on shareholder loans, i.e. interest paid on loans above a specific debt-equity-ratio is treated as a constructive dividend payment and therefore non-deductible

Gesellschafter-Geschäftsführer single managing member

Gesellschafter / ~haftung shareholder liability, liability of the partners; **~kreis** shareholders, shareholder group, *(zum ~ gehören)* to be one of the shareholders (partners); **~mittel** shareholder funds; **~rechte** shareholder (membership) rights, rights of membership

Gesellschafter / ~verhältnisse ownership structure; **~versammlung** partners' (shareholders', members') meeting; **~verzeichnis** register of shareholders (members); **~wechsel** change in ownership

Gesellschafts / ~anteil **1.** share (stake, interest) in a company **2.** partnership interest; **~blätter** newspapers authorised to publish company announcements; **~eigentum** → Gesellschaftsvermögen; **~entwicklung** company record (development), company performance

Gesellschafts / ~form form of business corporation, corporate form, legal form of a company; **~gründer** founder of a company; **~gründung** foundation (establishment) of a company

Gesellschafts / ~kapital company capital (equity); **~mantel** corporate shell; **~mittel** company's financial resources, financial means (resources) of a company, corporate funds; **~organe** corporate bodies of the company

Gesellschafts / ~recht company (corporate) law; **~siegel** company seal; **~sitz** corporate domicile, company's registered office

Gesellschafts / ~statuten **1.** *(einer Personengesellschaft)* deed of partnership **2.** *(einer Kapitalgesellschaft)* memorandum and articles of association of a company (UK), company byelaws (US); **~steuer** tax levied on companies seeking a stock exchange listing

Gesellschafts / ~unterlagen company records; **~vermögen** company assets (property), partnership property; **~vertrag** **1.** *(bei Personengesellschaften)* deed of partnership, partnership agreement **2.** *(bei Kapitalgesellschaften)* articles of association; **~zweck** corporate purpose, purpose of a company, corporate business

Gesetz law, Act, statute

Gesetz gegen *(~ den unlauteren Wettbewerb)* Fair Competition Act, *(~ Wettbewerbsbeschränkungen)* Antitrust Act, Act against Restraints of Competition

Gesetz über *(~ elektronische Handelsregister und Genossenschaftsregister sowie das Unternehmensregister)* Law on Electronic Commercial Registers, Cooperative Society Registers and the Company Register, *(~ die integrierte Finanzaufsicht)* Act on Integrated Financial Services Supervision *(~ Kapitalanlagegesellschaften)* German Capital Investment Companies Act, abgelöst durch das → Investment-Gesetz, *(~ über Schuldverschreibungen aus Gesamtemissionen)* German Bond Act, *(~ Unternehmensbeteiligungsgesellschaften)* Equity Investment Companies Act

Gesetz zur *(~ Förderung von Wagniskapitalbeteiligungen)* Act to Promote Venture Capital Participations, *(~ Fortentwicklung des Pfandbriefrechtes)* Act to Devleop the Law on Covered Bonds, *(~ Kontrolle und Transparenz im Unternehmensbereich)* Corporate Control and Transparency Act, *(~ Kontrolle von Unternehmensabschlüssen)* Financial Reporting Control Act

(~ Modernisierung der Rahmenbedingungen für Kapitalbeteiligungen) Act to Modernise the Conditions for Venture Capital and Private Equity Investments, *(~ Modernisierung des GmbH-Rechts und zur Bekämpfung von Missbräuchen)* Act to Modernise the German Limited Liability Company Law and to Combat Misuse
(~ Regelung von öffentlichen Angeboten zum Erwerb von Wertpapieren und von Unternehmensübernahmen) Securities Acquisition and Takeover Act, *(~ Regelung des Rechts der Allgemeinen Geschäftsbedingungen)* → AGB-Gesetz, *(~ Reorganisation von Kreditinstituten)* → Kreditinstitute-Reorganisationsgesetz
(~ Stärkung der Finanzmarkt- und Versicherungsaufsicht) Act to Strengthen the Regulatory Supervision of Financial Markets and Insurance, *(~ Stärkung des Anlegerschutzes und Verbesserung der Funktionsfähigkeit des Kapitalmarktes)* Act to Strengthen Investor Protection and Improve the Functionability of the Capital Market, *(~ Umsetzung der Aktionärsrechterichtlinie)* Act to Implement the Shareholder Rights Directive
(~ Unternehmensintegrität und Modernisierung des Anfechtungsrechts) Act on Corporate Integrity and Modernisation of Rescission Rules, *(~ zur Vorbeugung gegen missbräuchliche Wertpapier- und Derivategeschäfte)* Act relating to the prevention of Abusive Securities and Derivatives Trading

Gesetzentwurf bill

Gesetzes / ~änderungen legal changes, amendments to an Act; **~aufhebung** abolition (repeal) of an Act; **~begründung** explanatory memorandum, introductory statement; **~kraft** legal force, *(~ erlangen)* to become law, to pass into law

Gesetzes / ~lücke loophole in the law; **~recht** legislative law; **~text** wording of the Act; **~verstoß** violation (infringement) of an Act; **~vorlage** government bill; **~vorrang** precedence of statutes, statutes taking precedence over …

gesetzgebend *(~e Körperschaft)* legislative body

gesetzgeberisch *(~e Maßnahmen)* legislative measures

Gesetzgebung legislation

gesetzlich 1. *adj. (~er Anspruch)* legal claim (title), *(~e Ausführungsbestimmungen)* regulatory rules and regulations, regulatory legislation, *(~e Bestimmungen)* legal (statutory) provisions, *(~er Einlagenschutz)* statutory protection for deposits, *(~er Erbe)* legal (lawful) heir, heir at law
(~e Erbfolge) legal order of succession, *(~e Haftung)* legal (statutory) liability, *(~e Kündigungsfrist) (a)* statutory notice period *(b) (bei Spareinlagen)* legal (statutory) withdrawal notice, *(~es Nießbrauchrecht)* legal usufruct, *(~es Pfandrecht)* lien by operation of law, statutory lien
(~e Prüfung) statutory audit, *(~e Rahmenbedingungen)* regulatory framework, *(~e Rechte)* statutory rights (powers), *(~e Rücklage)* statutory (legal) reserve, *(~e Überbesicherung)* statutory overcollateralisation, *(~e Verjährungsfrist)* statutory period of limitation
(~ es Schuldverhältnis) obligation(s) imposed by law, *(~e Verpflichtung)* legal (statutory) obligation, *(~er Vertreter)* legal representative, *(~e Vorschriften)* legal (statutory) provisions, *(~es Zahlungsmittel)* legal tender, *(~er Zinssatz)* statutory rate of interest
2. *adv. (~ genehmigtes Kapital)* statutorily authorised capital, *(~ geregelt)* regulated by law, *(~ haftbar)* to be legally liable, *(~ untersagt)* prohibited by law, *(~ verpflichtet)* to be legally bound (obliged), required by law, *(~ zur Offenlegung verpflichtet)* to be legally obligated to disclose, *(~ vorgegeben/vorgeschrieben)* required (set) by law, legally required
(in der ~ vorgeschriebenen Form) in

the form prescribed by law (by statute), *(innerhalb der ~ vorgeschriebenen Frist)* within the legally (statutorily) prescribed period, *(~ vorgesehen)* legally provided for, *(~ zulässig)* permitted by law, authorised (warranted) by the law
(~ zulässige Höchstgrenze) limit allowed by law, lawful maximum, *(~ zulässige Verschuldungshöchstgrenze)* statutory debt limitation, *(~ zulässiger Höchstzinssatz)* maximum rate of interest permitted to be charged under applicable law, *(soweit ~ zulässig, im ~ zulässigen Rahmen)* to the extent permitted by law

gesetzmäßig 1. legal, lawful, legitimate 2. according to law, in accordance with the relevant legal provisions

gesetzwidrig illegal, contrary to the law, unlawful

gesichert *(~e Anleihe)* collateralised (secured) bond, *(~e Forderung)* secured claim (debt), *(~er Kredit)* secured loan, *(~e Zahlungsströme)* hedged cash flows

Gesichtspunkt view, viewpoint, aspect, consideration, angle

gesondert *(~ ausgewiesen)* shown separately in the balance sheet, *(~ berechnen)* to charge separately, *(~ offenlegen)* to disclose separately, *(~e Absprache)* separate agreement

gespalten *(~er Kurs)* two-way price, *(~er Markt)* two-tier market, *(~er Wechselkurs)* split rate of exchange

gespannt *(~e Beziehungen)* strained relations, *(~e Liquiditätssituation)* tight liquidity position, *(~er Wechselkurs)* mid-point of the bid/offer spread, mean spread of the fixing

gesperrt *(~e Guthaben)* frozen (tied-up, blocked) funds

gespiegelt *(~es symmetrisches Dreieck) (Chart-Analyse)*, → umgekehrtes Dreieck

Gespräche talks, negotiations, *(~ aufnehmen)* to open (to enter into) talks, *(~ führen)* to hold (to be in, to conduct) talks

Gesprächsrunde 1. round of talks 2. meeting

gestaffelt *(~e Einführung)* staggered (phased) introduction, *(~e Einlagenzinsen)* staggered (tiered) interest rates on deposits, *(~e Rückzahlungsraten)* stepped (graduated) repayment rates

Gestalt shape, form, *(die Sanierung nimmt ~ an)* the restructuring is taking shape

gestalten 1. to structure, to arrange, to organise, to work out, *(ein Darlehen/eine Finanzierung ~)* to structure a loan/a financing, *(ähnlich gestaltetes Kreditprogramm)* loan scheme operating (structured) along similar lines, *(individuell gestaltetes Portefeuille)* portfolio structured to the customer's requirements, individually structured portfolio
2. *(entwerfen)* to design, to devise
3. *(formen)* to shape, to form, to mould

gestaltend *(~er Teil, z. B. eines Insolvenzplanes)* constructive part, → darstellender Teil

Gestaltung 1. structuring, arrangement, organisation, working out, *(~ der Kreditkonditionen)* structuring (working out) the loan terms, loan pricing, *(~ der langfristigen Projektfinanzierung)* structuring (arranging) the long-term funding of the project
2. design, formation, *(~ der Geldpolitik)* shaping monetary policy

Gestaltungs / ~freiheit freedom to (e.g. determine the conditions of a contract/to shape and organise a business); **~klage** action for a judicial modification; **~recht** right to transform (e.g. an existing legal relationship)

Gestehungskosten 1. cost price, cost of acquisition 2. cost of production

gestrichen no official price fixing, no quotation, *(~ Geld/Brief)* no offi-

G

cial price fixing, only buyers/sellers, *(~ Geld/Brief/Taxe)* estimated bid/offered price

gestückelt *(~e Titel)* securities issued in denominations of …

Gesuch request, petition, application

gesucht *(Finanzwerte blieben ~)* financials attracted renewed demand (fresh support), *(AB wurden zu € 25 ~)* AB were wanted at € 25

gesund *(~e finanzielle Lage)* strong (sound) financial position, *(~es Unternehmen)* strong (viable) company, soundly based company, financially sound company

G

gesunden to recover, *(den finanziell angeschlagenen Konzern wieder ~ lassen)* to restore health to the financially stricken group

Gesundheitszertifikat *(Warenbegleitdokument)* health certificate

Gesundung *(~ des Kreditnehmers)* recovery (revitalisation) of the borrowing company

Gesundungskonzept recovery (rescue) scheme, financial reconstruction scheme

geteilt *(~er Meinung sein)* to be divided over, to be of a different opinion

getragen **1.** *(das positive Ergebnis wird durch das Wertpapiergeschäft ~)* the positive development is sustained by the securities business **2.** *(der Trend wird von hohen Investitionen ~)* the trend is fuelled by high investments

getrennt **1.** *adj. (~e Abrechnung)* separate settlement, *(~er Ausweis)* separate statement (reporting), *(~e Haftung)* several liability, *(~e Rechnungslegung)* separate accounting, *(~e Veranlagung)* separate assessment, *(~e Verwahrung von Wertpapieren)* segregated custody, segregation of securities
2. *adv. (~ ausweisen)* to state (to report) separately, to separate (to segregate) in the financial statements, *(~ ausgewiesene Positionen)* separately stated items, *(~ haftbar sein)* to be severally liable, *(~ notiert)* quoted separately, *(~ zur Einkommensteuer veranlagen)* to assess separately for income tax, *(~ verwahrte Wertpapiere)* securities held separately, securities segregated in custody

getreu *(~e Darstellung der finanziellen Verhältnisse)* fair presentation (true and fair view) of the financial situation

gewagt *(~e Spekulation)* risky speculation

Gewähr **1.** guarantee, warranty **2.** liability, responsibility

gewähren **1.** *(einräumen)* to grant, to accord, to extend **2.** *(gestatten)* to allow, to permit

gewährleisten to guarantee, to ensure, to warrant, *(einen geordneten Markt ~)* to ensure an orderly market, *(die Erfüllung des Vertrages ~)* to guarantee performance of the contract, *(die Zahlung bei Fälligkeit ~)* to guarantee (to warrant) payment upon maturity

gewährleistend *(~e Bank)* guaranteeing (guarantor) bank

gewährleistet *(~e Risikoaktiva)* risk assets carrying the guarantee of …, *(~e Wertpapiere)* guaranteed securities, securities carrying a guarantee as to principal and interest payments

Gewährleistung **1.** guarantee **2.** *(des Verkäufers)* warranty, *(übernommene ~en)* guarantees assumed (furnished), *(~ durch eine Anstalt des öffentlichen Rechts)* guarantee by a public sector institution, *(~ für Ausfuhrgeschäfte)* guarantee for exports
(Kredite mit kommunaler ~) loans guaranteed by a public sector agency, *(~ der Zahlungsbereitschaft)* guaranteeing (ensuring) solvency, *(die ~ hinsichtlich der Zins- und Tilgungsleistungen übernehmen)* to assume the guarantee for interest and redemption payments

Gewährleistungs / **~anspruch** warranty claim; **~ausschluss** exclusion of warranty; **~aval** guarantee; **~bruch**

breach of warranty; ~**bürgschaft** warranty bond; ~**deckung** warranty coverage; ~**erklärung** declaration of warranty; ~**frist** guarantee (warranty) period

Gewährleistungs / ~**garantie** 1. warranty, warranty bond 2. *(Erfüllungsgarantie)* performance bond 3. *(im Exportgeschäft)* export credit guarantee; ~**geber** 1. warrantor 2. *(bei Kreditderivaten)* protection provider (seller); ~**klage** action for warranty; ~**klausel** guarantee (warranty) clause

Gewährleistungs / ~**nehmer** 1. warrantee 2. *(bei Kreditderivaten)* protection taker (buyer); ~**pflicht** obligation of warranty, obligation to furnish a warranty (guarantee); ~**recht** warranty law

Gewährleistungs / ~**übernahme** warranty assumption; ~**verpflichtungen** guarantee (warranty) commitments, warranty obligations; ~**vertrag** guarantee (warranty) agreement, indemnity agreement; ~**vorschriften** warranty regulations

Gewahrsam *(im ~ der Bank)* in the bank's custody

Gewährträger guarantor, warrantor

Gewährträgerhaftung guaranty obligation, public (statutory) guarantee □ under this obligation the owners of savings banks (local authorities) are jointly and severally liable to the creditors of the bank

Gewährträger / ~**verband** guaranteeing local authority; ~**versammlung** guarantors' meeting

Gewährung 1. granting, accordance, provision, *(~ von Bezugsrechten)* rights distribution, *(~ eines Kredites)* granting of a loan, loan accommodation, *(~ neuer Mittel)* providing fresh funds (money)
2. allowance, *(~ einer Zahlungsfrist)* allowing additional time for payment

Gewährvertrag warranty deed

Gewerbe 1. trade, business 2. commercial (gainful) activity

Gewerbe / ~**betrieb** trade, business enterprise, commercial undertaking (operation), ~**darlehen** commercial loan; ~**ertrag** trading profit, income derived from a commercial activity; ~**ertragssteuer** trade earnings tax; ~**fläche** business space, premises for commercial use

Gewerbeimmobilie commercial property, non-residential property

Gewerbeimmobilien / ~**darlehen** commercial mortgage loan, *(Verbriefung von ~)* commercial mortgage-backed securitisation (CMBS); ~**preise** commercial property prices

Gewerbe / ~**kapital** trading capital; ~**kapitalsteuer** trading capital tax; ~**kredit** business loan; ~**kreditgeschäft** commercial loan operations, business lending; ~**kunden** commercial customers

Gewerbe / ~**ordnung** Trade and Industry Code; ~**park** industrial park; ~**schein** trading licence; ~**steuer** local business tax; ~**steuergesetz** German Local Business Tax Act

gewerbesteuerlich *(~e Organschaft)* fiscal unity for trade tax purposes, → Organschaft

Gewerbetätigkeit trading (commercial) activity

gewerbetreibend carrying on a trade (a business, a gainful activity)

Gewerbeverlust trading loss

gewerblich 1. *adj.* *(~er Anschaffungskredit)* capital investment loan, *(~e Beleihungen)* lendings against (loans granted on) commercial properties, *(~e Beteiligungen)* trade and commercial interests, *(~e Einkünfte)* trade (business) income, *(~e Finanzierung)* commercial finance, business loans, *(~es Finanzierungsinstitut)* commercial finance company
(~e Hypothek) commercial (industrial) mortgage, *(~er Hypothekenkre-*

G

dit) commercial mortgage loan, *(~e Immobilienfinanzierung)* commercial property financing, funding (financing) commercial properties, *(~er Immobilienkredit)* commercial property loan, *(~es Immobilienkreditgeschäft)* commercial property lending business *(~es Immobilienvermögen)* commercial property assets (portfolio)
(~er Kleinkredit) small business loan, *(~er Kredit)* business (commercial) loan, *(~es Kreditgeschäft)* business lendings, commercial lendings (lending operations), *(~er Kreditnehmer)* commercial (business) borrower
(~es Kreditneugeschäft) new business lendings, *(~e Kundschaft)* business (commercial) customers, *(~er Realkredit)* (long-term) commercial property loan, industrial mortgage loan, *(~er Rechtsschutz)* protection of industrial property, *(~e Wirtschaft)* trade and industry
2. *adv. (~ genutzte Objekte)* commercially used properties

G

Gewerkschaft union, *(gewerkschaftlich organisiert)* unionised

Gewicht 1. weight, weighting, *(~ des Garanten im Rahmen der Risikoerfassung)* weighting assigned (given) to the guarantor
2. *(Bedeutung)* significance, importance, weight, *(ins ~ fallen)* to be of importance, to carry weight, *(an ~ gewinnen/verlieren)* to gain/to lose in significance, *(besonderes ~ legen auf)* to put special emphasis on

gewichten to weight, to assign a weighting, *(mit 0 v.H. ~)* to apply a zero weighting, *(offene Devisen-Positionen mit 100 % ~)* to give (to apply) a 100 % weighting to net open foreign exchange positions, *(Forderungen gegen Banken werden mit 25 % gewichtet)* claims on banks are weighted at 25 %, claims on banks carry a 25 % weighting, *(pauschal mit 30 % ~)* to apply a flat-rate weighting of 30 %

gewichtet *(~er Durchschnitt)* weighted average, *(ein mit 50 % ~es Kreditrisiko)* loan exposure weighted 50 %, loan commitment attracting a 50 % weighting, *(niedriger gewichtet werden)* to be given a lower weighting
(~er Kapitalkostensatz) weighted average cost of capital, *(~e Risikoaktiva einer Bank)* weighted risk assets of a bank, *(~er Zinssatz) (bei einem amerikanischen Zinstender)* weighted allotment rate, *(~e Zuteilung)* weighted allotment

gewichtig significant, important, influential

Gewichtsverlagerung shift in importance

Gewichtung *(~ der Risikoaktiva einer Bank)* weighting of a bank's risk assets

Gewichtungs / ~faktor weighting factor; **~satz** weighting percentage

gewillkürt *(~e Erbfolge)* testate succession, *(~e Orderpapiere)* registered securities made endorsable by a special clause

Gewinn profit, income, gain, earnings, return, *(~ je Aktie)* earnings per share, *(~ je MAK/Mitarbeiterkapazität)* profit per FTE/full-time equivalent

Gewinn aus *(~ Anlageabgängen)* gain on the disposal of assets, *(~ Anteilsbesitz)* income from equity investments, *(~ dem Eigenhandel)* profit (income) from trading for own account, *(~ der Einlösung von Wertpapieren)* gain on redemption of securities
(~ Finanzanlagen) investment profit, *(~ dem laufenden Geschäft)* income from current operations, *(~ Glattstellungen)* gain on position-squaring, *(~ Kurssicherungsgeschäften)* foreign exchange (currency) hedging gains, *(~ Neubewertung)* revaluation gain (surplus)
(~ Termin- und Derivatgeschäften) gains on forward and derivatives transactions, *(~ der Veräußerung von Beteiligungen)* gain on sale of investments, *(~Wechselkursschwankungen)* gain (surplus) on exchange rate fluc-

tuations, *(~ Wechselkursumrechnungen)* translation gains

Gewinn vor *(~ außerordentlichem Ergebnis)* income before extraordinary items, *(~ vor Steuern)* earnings before tax (EBT), pre-tax profits, *(~Zinsen und Steuern)* earnings before interest and taxes (EBIT)

Gewinnabführung profit transfer (remittance)

Gewinnabführungsvertrag profit transfer agreement

gewinnabhängig *(~e Vergütung)* profit-related (performance-linked) remuneration

Gewinn / **~abschöpfung** skimming off profits, absorption of income; **~abweichung** profit variance; **~analyse** profit analysis; **~anspruch** profit entitlement, profit-sharing claim; **~anstieg** increase (rise) in profits

Gewinnanteil profit share, share in the profits, *(Gewinnanteil der Minderheitsaktionäre)* profit applicable to minorities; **~schein 1.** coupon **2.** profit participation certificate; **~scheinbogen** coupon sheet

Gewinn / **~aufstellung** statement of income; **~ausfall** loss of earnings; **~ausschüttung** distribution of profits, profit (income) distribution; **~aussichten** profit(s) outlook, prospects of earnings; **~ausweis 1.** statement of income **2.** profit(s) shown **3.** income reporting, profit recognition

Gewinn / **~begrenzung** limitation of profits, income ceiling; **~beitrag** profit contribution; **~belassungserklärung** profit retention undertaking; **~belastung** charge on earnings

gewinnberechtigt 1. participating, entitled to a share in the profits **2.** *(~ ab 1. Juli)* ranking for dividend as from July 1, *(~ für das laufende Geschäftsjahr)* carrying dividend rights for the current business year

Gewinn / **~berechtigung** entitlement to profits, entitlement to a share in the profits; **~beteiligung** profit-sharing, share in the profits, participation in profits, *(Gewinnbeteiligung der Managementgesellschaft)* carried interest

Gewinn / **~beteiligungsplan** profit-sharing scheme; **~beteiligungsrecht** profit participation right, entitlement to a share in profits, dividend right; **~bewertung** profit valuation

gewinnbezogen profit-related, profit-linked

gewinnbringend 1. profitable, lucrative, *(~e Anlagen)* profitable (lucrative) investments
2. income-producing, profit-earning, *(~e Dienstleistungen)* income-producing services, *(~e Tätigkeit)* gainful activity

Gewinn / **~chance** *(Börse)* opportunity for profit, opportunity to realise a profit, profit potential; **~egalisierung** offsetting of profits; **~einbehaltung** profit retention

gewinnen to win, to attain, to reach, to obtain, *(Baissiers gewannen die Oberhand)* bears gained the upper hand, *(Aufwärtsbewegung gewann an Fahrt)* the advance in stock prices picked up (gathered) speed

Gewinn / **~entwicklung** earnings performance (history), profit record; **~ergebnis** profit turnout; **~ermittlung** determination of profits, income recognition, establishing the profit (income), *(steuerliche ~)* profit determination for tax purposes

Gewinn / **~erwartung** profit expectation(s), anticipated profit(s); **~erzielung** realisation of a profit; **~erzielungsabsicht** intention to make a profit (to derive profits from …)

Gewinn / **~festschreibung** locking in a profit; **~gemeinschaft** profit pool, profit pooling agreement; **~gestaltung** earnings management

Gewinn / **~kalkulation** calculation of the profit (income); **~kennzahl** profit (earnings) ratio; **~kontrolle** profit control; **~marge** profit margin; **~ma-**

ximierung profit maximisation, maximising the profit from (the return on)

Gewinn / ~minderung diminishing the profit (income), profit reduction; **~mitnahmen** profit-taking, *(~ des Berufshandels)* profit-taking by professional traders, *(~ gegen Schluss der Börsensitzung)* late profit-taking

gewinnneutral earnings neutral, having no effect (impact) on earnings

Gewinn / ~nivellierung evening out profits; **~offenlegung** earnings disclosure; **~optimierung** → Gewinnmaximierung; **~orientierung** profit orientation, *(gewinnorientiert)* profit-oriented, profit-directed; **~potenzial** profit potential, potential for generating profits; **~prognose** profit forecast

G

Gewinn / ~realisierung *(von Kursgewinnen)* realising (realisation of) stock price gains; **~rechnungsperiode** income statement period; **~revision** revision of a profit forecast, *(nach oben/unten)* profits upgrade/downgrade

Gewinn / ~rückführung repatriation of profits; **~rückgang** profit decline (reduction), decrease in profits, profits fall; **~rücklagen** revenue reserves, appropriated (earned) surplus, retained earnings

Gewinn / ~saldo 1. net profit **2.** profit (credit) balance; **~schätzung** profit estimate; **~schrumpfung** shrinkage of profits; **~schuldverschreibung** income bond, participating bond, bond carrying an entitlement to profits; **~schwelle** pay-off stage, break-even point, *(die ~ erreichen)* to break even

Gewinn / ~spanne profit margin, *(~n der Unternehmen)* corporate profit margins; **~spannenerweiterung** widening of the profit margin; **~spannenverringerung** narrowing (shrinkage) of the profit margin

Gewinn / ~sparbrief income savings bond; **~sprung** leap in earnings; **~steigerung** increase (rise) in profits; **~streben** search (quest) for profits

Gewinn / ~tantieme profit share; **~thesaurierung** profit retention, reinvestment of income; **~träger** strong contributor to profits; **~überschuss** profit surplus, net profit

gewinnunabhängig *(~e Steuer)* non-profit-related tax

Gewinn- und Verlustrechnung profit and loss account, statement of income

Gewinn- und Verlustübernahmevertrag profit and loss pooling agreement

Gewinn / ~verantwortung profit accountability; **~verfall** dramatic profits fall, nosedive in profits; **~verschleierung** concealment of profits; **~verteilung** profit distribution, sharing out the profit

Gewinn / ~verwendung profit appropriation; **~verwendungsvorschlag** proposal on the appropriation of profits; **~vorausberechnung** profit projection, forward earnings projection; **~vortrag** profit brought forward; **~vorzug** preferential right to profits; **~wachstum** profit growth

Gewinn / ~ziel profit objective (goal); **~zone** *(in die ~ zurückkehren)* to be back in the black, to return to profitability; **~zunahme/~zuwachs** profit increase (growth), rise in profits; **~zuschlag** profit markup; **~zuweisungen** profit appropriations

gewissenhaft *(~e Einhaltung)* conscientious observance

gewogen *(~er Anschaffungspreis)* weighted purchase price, *(~es Mittel)* weighted average, *(~er Zuteilungssatz)* weighted allotment rate

gewöhnlich 1. usual, customary, habitual

2. ordinary, normal, *(~e Bürgschaft)* ordinary guarantee □ the guarantor has the right to cause the creditor to exhaust all remedies against the principal debtor before resorting to him as guarantor, *(~e Geschäftstätigkeit)* ordinary course of business, ordinary activities, *(~e Insolvenzgläubiger)* ordinary creditors

gewohnheitsmäßig *(~es Recht)* right by custom, → vertragsmäßiges Recht

Gewohnheitsrecht 1. customary law, law established by long usage
2. right by custom
3. *(betriebliches Gewohnheitsrecht)* established company use

gezielt targeted, *(~e Akquisition)* pinpointed acquisition

Giralgeld bank (cheque) money, deposit (checkbook) money

girieren to endorse

Giro 1. endorsement 2. credit (bank) transfer, money transmission, giro

Giro / **~einlagen** demand deposits, current account deposits; **~geschäft** payment and settlement operations;**~guthaben** current account balance; **~gutschrift** 1. current account credit 2. *(im Effektengiroverkehr)* securities credit

Giro / **~kette** chain of endorsements; **~konto** current account; **~kontoinhaber** giro account holder; **~netz** giro network, money transmission and clearing network

Girosammel / **~anteil** share in a collective securities account; **~bestand** collective securities holdings; **~depot** collective securities account, portfolio of securities held collectively; **~depotgutschrift** collective securities account credit

Girosammel / **~ermächtigung** authorisation to hold securities under a collective securities account; **~stücke** securities held under collective securities accounts; **~verwahrung** collective custody (safekeeping), holding under a collective securities account, *(girosammelverwahrfähig)* eligible for collective custody (safekeeping), *(girosammelverwahrte Aktien)* stocks held under collective securities accounts

Giro / **~verkehr** money transmission and clearing operations; **~zentrale** Central Savings Bank □ acting as clearing house and liquidity manager to the savings banks

glanzlos *(~es Ergebnis)* lacklustre performance

glatt *(~er Termin)* regular forward date, *(~e Zahlung/Zahlungsverkehr)* clean payment, clean payment transactions

glätten *(die Auswirkungen von Zinsschwankungen ~)* to smooth out (to even out) the effects of interest rate movements, *(große Preisschwankungen ~)* to flatten out large fluctuations in prices

glattstellen 1. to liquidate, to close, to square, *(Bestände ~)* to liquidate holdings, to square positions, to sell off, *(eine Futures-Position ~)* to close (to close out) a futures position, *(mit Gewinn ~)* to close out (to unwind) at a profit, *(zum aktuellen Marktkurs ~)* to close out (to liquidate) at the current market price
2. to settle, *(ein Konto ~)* to settle (to balance) an account, to repay the debit balance

Glattstellung 1. liquidation, closing, close-out, squaring, *(~ durch den Berufshandel)* professional liquidation, *(~ von Beständen)* book-squaring, liquidating holdings, *(~ von Kauf-/Verkaufspositionen)* long/short liquidation, *(~en zum Monatsende)* end-of-month position-squaring, *(~ einer Optionsposition durch ein Gegengeschäft)* closing out a position in the options market through a countertransaction (an opposite transaction)
2. settlement, *(~ von Spitzenbeträgen)* settlement of (settling) fractions, *(~ der Überziehung)* settlement of the overdraft, repaying the debit balance

Glattstellungs / **~befugnis** *(bei Futures-Positionen)* (banks') authority to close out futures positions; **~geschäft** closing trade (transaction); **~gewinn/~verlust** gain/loss on closing out a position

Glättung smoothing, evening out

Glaube *(in gutem ~n kaufen)* to purchase in good faith, *(Inhaber in gutem ~n)* holder in good faith

Gläubiger creditor; **~abfindung** paying off a creditor, satisfaction of creditors; **~anspruch** creditor's claim; **~aufruf** call on creditors; **~ausschuss** creditors' committee

Gläubiger / **~bank** creditor bank; **~begünstigung** fraudulent preference (of a creditor); **~benachteiligung** impairment of creditor interests, prejudice to creditors, fraudulent conveyance; **~forderungen** creditor claims

Gläubiger / **~identifikationsnummer** (SEPA) creditor identifier, creditor ID; **~interesse** creditor's interest, → Leistungsinteresse

Gläubiger / **~klasse** class of creditors; **~kündigungsrecht** 1. *(eines Kreditgebers)* lender's right to call in a loan, lender's right to request repayment of a loan 2. *(eines Emittenten)* call option □ option giving the issuer the right to redeem the issue before maturity

Gläubiger / **~land** creditor country; **~papiere** debt securities; **~position** 1. creditor position 2. *(im Geldhandel)* selling (lending) position, to be sellers; **~rangfolge** ranking of creditors; **~schutz** *(im Insolvenzverfahren)* creditor protection in insolvency proceedings

Gläubiger / **~versammlung** creditors' meeting; **~vertreter** representative of the creditors; **~verzicht** foregiveness of indebtedness, waiver on the part of the creditor(s)

glaubwürdig creditable, reliable, trustworthy

Glaubwürdigkeit creditibility, reliability

gleich 1. *adj.* equal, same, *(einheitlich)* uniform, *(kongruent)* identical, matching, *(~e Rechte für alle Aktionäre)* equal rights for all shareholders, *(mit ~em Schreiben)* under same cover, *(zu ~en Teilen ausschütten)* to distribute in equal parts (shares), to distribute equally, *(~e Währung)* matching (identical) currency, *(~e Wettbewerbsbedingungen)* level playing field, *(~e Ziele am Markt verfolgen)* to follow (to pursue) identical goals in the market 2. *adv.* equally, alike, in the same way, *(das Gleiche gilt)* the same applies to, the same holds true for, *(alle Kreditnehmer ~ behandeln)* to treat all borrowers alike (in the same way, in like manner), to put all borrowers on an equal footing

gleichbedeutend *(~ mit einer Kreditzusage)* equivalent to a loan commitment

Gleichbehandlung equal treatment

Gleichbehandlungs / **~gesetz** Equal Treatment Act, Non-Discrimination Act; **~grundsatz** principle of equal treatment; **~klausel** → Gleichstellungsklausel

gleichberechtigt *(~e Kreditgeber)* lenders with equal rights, lenders enjoying equal rights, lenders ranking equally (pari passu)

Gleich / **~berechtigung** equality of rights (of status); **~besicherungsklausel** pari passu clause, equally secured clause

gleich bleiben to remain the same, to stay unchanged

gleichbleibend invariable, unchanging, constant, steady, *(~e Annuität/Zins- und Tilgungsleistung)* invariable interest and redemption payments, level debt service, *(~e monatliche Zahlungen)* level monthly payments, *(~er Zinssatz)* fixed (invariable) interest rate

gleichermaßen *(die Bestimmungen gelten ~)* the provisions apply in like measure to

gleichförmig *(~e Entwicklung)* uniform development

gleichgerichtet *(~e Kursbildung)* parallel pricing

gleichgestellt *(~e Forderungen)* equally-ranking claims

Gleichgewicht balance, equilibrium, *(~ zwischen Angebot und Nachfrage)* equilibrium of supply and demand, *(sich im ~ befinden)* to be in balance, *(ins ~ kommen)* to come into balance, *(den Markt aus dem ~ bringen)* to shake the market out of its balance, *(den Markt durch Arbitrage wieder ins ~ bringen)* to bring the market back into line through arbitrage dealings, *(das Unternehmen wieder ins ~ bringen)* to bring the company back into balance, to put the company back on track

Gleichgewichts / ~preis equilibrium price; **~störung** *(~ des Marktes)* market disequilibrium; **~wechselkurs** equilibrium rate of exchange; **~zinssatz** equilibrium rate of interest

Gleichheitsprinzip principle of equality

Gleichklang harmony, *(sich im ~ mit dem Index entwicklen)* to move in step (in unison) with the index, → Gleichschritt

gleichkommen *(einer Zinserhöhung ~)* to amount to (to be equivalent to) an increase in interest rates

Gleichlauf *(der ~ von Kassa- und Terminmärkten)* correlation (synchronous movements, convergence) of cash and futures markets

gleichlaufen to run parallel to (with)

gleichlautend *(~e Buchung)* identical entry, *(~e Garantie)* identical (identically worded) guarantee, *(~er Wechsel)* identical bill, bill of the same tenor

gleichmäßig 1. *adj.* equal, *(~e Befriedigung der Forderungen)* equal satisfaction of all claims, *(~e Rendite)* level rate of return
2. *adv.* evenly, in equal parts, *(~ unter den Aktionären aufteilen)* to split equally among the shareholders, *(~ verteilt sein)* to be equally spread, *(die Risiken ~er verteilen)* to spread the risks more evenly

Gleichordnungskonzern horizontally organised group

Gleichrangabkommen pari passu agreement

gleichrangig *(~e Gläubiger)* creditors of equal rank, equal-ranking creditors, creditors ranking pari passu, *(~e Grundschulden/Lasten)* charges of equal rank, charges ranking pari passu (possessing the same priority), *(~e Sicherheit)* security (collateral) ranking pari passu

Gleichrangrahmen limit (room) for charges of equal rank

Gleichrichtung *(~ der Geldpolitiken)* harmonisation of monetary policies

gleichschalten to bring into line, to synchronise

Gleichschritt *(im ~)* in pace (hand in hand, step in step) with, *(die Zinssätze im ~ erhöhen)* to increase interest rates simultaneously and at the same rate

gleichseitig *(~es Dreieck) (Chart-Analyse)* symmetrical triangle

gleichsetzen *(~ mit)* to equate with

gleichstehen to be on an equal footing, to be on a par, *(im Rang ~)* to rank equally

gleichstellen to put on an equal footing, to grant equality of rank (of status), to equalise, *(gleichgestellte Gläubiger)* creditors ranking equally with each other

Gleichstellung equal treatment, putting on an equal footing, equalisation

Gleichstellungsklausel/~revers *(hinsichtlich einer Gläubigergleichstellung)* pari passu clause (covenant, statement)

gleichtägig *(~e Abwicklung)* same-day settlement, *(~e Anschaffung)* same-day remittance, *(~es Geschäft)* same-day transaction, *(~e Regulierung)* same-day settlement

Gleichung equation

gleichwertig equal, of the same value, *(~er Ersatz)* substitute of equal value, *(~ e Rechtsstellung)* equivalent legal

G

position, *(~e Sicherheit)* equivalent collateral

gleichzeitig simultaneous, concurrent, synchronous, *(~e Grundbucheintragung)* simultaneous recording in the land registry, *(~er Handel)* simultaneous trading, *(~e Käufe und Verkäufe von Wertpapieren)* concurrent purchases and sales of securities

gleichziehen 1. *(mit den anderen Banken ~)* to draw (to pull) level with the other banks 2. *(sich anschließen)* to follow suit

G

gleiten *(in eine Rezession ~)* to slide into a recession

gleitend *(~e Arbeitszeit)* flexible (staggered) working hours, flexitime, *(~e Bandbreiten)* gliding bands, *(~er Durchschnitt)* moving average, *(~e Lohnskala)* sliding pay scale, *(~e Marge)* floating margin

Gleit / **~klausel** escalator (indexation) clause; **~parität** crawling peg; **~zins** floating (variable) interest rate; **~zinsdarlehen** floating rate loan, variable interest loan

gliedern 1. to break down, to divide 2. *(klassifizieren)* to classify, to class, to group 3. *(strukturieren, untergliedern)* to structure, to subdivide 4. *(die Bilanz ~)* to spread the balance sheet

Gliederung 1. breakdown, *(~ nach Fristigkeiten)* breakdown by maturities, *(geographische ~ des Umsatzes)* geographical breakdown of turnover (of sales) 2. classification, segmentation, subdivision 3. structuring

Gliederungs / **~bogen** spread sheet; **~schema** *(der Bilanz)* classifications in the balance sheet, prescribed format

global global, world-wide, *(~e Kurssicherung)* macrohedging

Global / **~abtretung** global assignment; **~aktie** global (multishare) certificate; **~anleihen** global bonds □ bonds that are issued simultaneously in the Euro, US and Far Eastern markets and traded globally

Global / **~belastung** global (floating) charge; **~betrag** aggregate (global) amount; **~emission** global issue (offering), cross-border offering, → Globalanleihen; **~finanzierung** global (block) financing; **~grundschuld** global (blanket) land charge

Globalisierung *(~ der internationalen Kapitalmärkte)* globalisation of international capital markets

Global / **~kredit** comprehensive loan facility, global loan; **~sicherheit** floating charge (lien); **~rückstellungen** global provisions; **~urkunde** global note (lodged with a central depositary bank and evidencing the rights under a security issue), *(globalverbriefte Schuldverschreibungen)* notes represented by a global note

Global / **~versicherung** all-loss (all-risks) insurance; **~vorschuss** global advance; **~zession** global assignment, assignment of all current and future claims

GmbH & Co. KG partnership with a limited liability company as general partner

GmbH-Gesetz Limited Liabilities Companies Act

GmbH-Recht Limited Liability Company Law

Gold / **~agio** gold premium; **~aktien** gold shares (stocks), gold equities (mines); **~barren** gold bar(s), gold bullion; **~bestand** gold holdings; **~bezugsrecht** gold warrant

Gold / **~darlehen** gold loan; **~deckung** gold cover (backing); **~-Derivate** gold derivatives, gold futures, options and warrants; **~devisenstandard** gold exchange standard

goldene Bankregel principle of matching the maturities of assets and liabilities (if you borrow short, don't lend long)

Gold / **~gehalt** gold content, percentage of gold; **~gewicht** troy weight; **~handel** gold trading, dealing in gold bullion; **~händler** bullion dealer

Gold / **~kassahandel** spot gold trading; **~käufer** buyer of gold bars; **~kernwährung** gold bullion standard; **~legierung** alloy of gold; **~leihe**/**~leihgeschäft** gold lending, gold lending transaction; **~-Lombardkredit** lending against gold

Gold / **~markt** gold market; **~minenwerte** gold mines; **~münzen** gold (bullion) coins; **~notiz** gold quote (price)

Gold / **~option** gold option; **~optionsschein** gold warrant; **~parität** gold parity; **~preis** gold price; **~preisfestsetzung** gold fixing; **~reserven** gold reserves, reserves of gold coins and bullion held by a central bank; **~standard** gold standard

Gold / **~terminbörse** gold futures exchange; **~termingeschäft** gold forward deal (contract); **~terminhandel** **1.** gold forward trading **2.** *(Futures-Handel)* gold futures trading; **~terminkontrakt** gold futures contract; **~terminverkäufe** selling gold forward

Gold / **~umlaufwährung** gold specie standard; **~verkäufe** *(~ am freien Markt)* gold sales in the open market; **~verleihrate** gold lease rate; **~währung** gold standard; **~zertifikat** gold certificate

Grad **1.** *(Ausmaß, Umfang)* degree, extent **2.** *(Stufe)* grade, rank **3.** *(Verhältnis)* ratio

Gradmesser criterion, indicator, gauge, benchmark, yardstick, standard, *(~ für den Anlageerfolg)* performance benchmark, *(~ für das Verhalten der Anleger)* gauge of investor attitude

graduell *(~e Besserung)* gradual improvement

granular *(~es Portfolio)* granular portfolio, well-diversified portfolio

Granularität granularity, fineness of detail, *(~ eines Kreditportefeuilles)* credit portfolio granularity □ concentration risk measure of a loan portfolio

Granularitätsanpassung granularity adjustment

Gratifikation bonus, bonus payment

gratis *adj.* free, cost-free, *adv.* free of charge

Gratis / **~aktien** capitalisation (scrip) issue; **~exemplar** complimentary (free) copy; **~genussschein** bonus participation certificate

grau *(~er Kapitalmarkt)* grey (semi-regulated) capital market, *(~e Zinsen)* interest paid in the grey capital market

greifbar **1.** tangible, *(~es Ergebnis)* tangible result **2.** *(~e Stücke)* physical securities **3.** *(verfügbar)* available

greifen to take hold (root), *(das Kostensenkungsprogramm beginnt zu ~)* cost-cutting measures are taking hold (are feeding through), *(wenn die Erholung zu ~ beginnt)* when (once) the recovery takes root

Gremium committee, body

Grenze border, frontier, boundary, limit, bound(s), *(an die ~n der finanziellen Belastbarkeit des Unternehmens gehen)* to go to the limits of the company's financial capacities, *(den inflationären Druck in ~n halten)* to contain the inflationary pressure, *(die Investitionen in ~n halten)* to keep investment in (within) bounds, *(die Umsätze hielten sich in ~n)* turnover stayed low, *(die Volatilität in ~n halten)* to hold down volatility

grenzen *(an einen finanziellen Zusammenbruch ~)* to be little short of (to verge on) a financial breakdown

Grenz / **~ertrag** marginal earnings, marginal return; **~ertragswert** *(~ der Investitionen)* marginal earnings value of investments; **~kosten** marginal cost; **~kostenprinzip** margin cost of funds concept; **~kostenrechnung** marginal costing

Grenz / ~**leistungsfähigkeit** *(~ des Kapitals)* marginal efficiency of capital; ~**nutzen** marginal utility; ~**rate** *(~ der Substitution/Transformation)* marginal rate of substitution/transformation; ~**rendite** marginal yield; ~**steuersatz** marginal tax rate

grenzüberschreitend *adj. (~er Kapitalverkehr)* cross-border capital movements, *(~e Kreditvergabe)* cross-frontier lending (loan extension)
adv. (~ koordinieren) to coordinate across borders

G

Grenzwahrscheinlichkeit marginal probability

Grenzziehung *(von Grundstücken)* delineation, demarcation, marking out boundaries

Griechen Greeks □ Greek letters used in the valuation of options, →Delta, Gamma, Kappa, Rho, Theta

Griff grip, grasp, handle, hold, *(die steigenden Kosten in den ~ bekommen)* to get a handle (to get a grip) on the mounting expenditure, *(die finanziellen Probleme in den ~ bekommen)* to come to grips with the financial problems, *(den Markt fest im ~ haben)* to have a firm (strong) hold on the market, *(den ~ lockern)* to loosen the grip (hold)

grob 1. *adj. (~e Fahrlässigkeit des Verwahrers)* gross negligence on the part of the custodian, *(~er Fehler)* serious (grave) mistake, blunder
2. *adv. (~ vergleichbar mit)* roughly comparable with

GroMiKV → Groß- und Millionenkreditverordnung

groß *(~e Auswahl) (z.B. an Zinssteuerungsinstrumenten)* large (great) variety of interest management products, *(~e Kapitalgesellschaften)* (nach → EGHGB/BilMOG) large corporations □ total assets above € 19.25m; sales above € 38.5m; headcount: above 250, → Großunternehmen
(~er Kupontermin) major coupon payment date, *(~er Steuertermin)* major tax payment date □ date on which big tax bills fall due, *(~e Stücke)* bonds with a face value of € 1,000 and above, *(~e Stückelung)* large denomination

Groß / ~**abnehmer** bulk buyer; ~**adresse** *(Kreditnehmer/Emittent)* blue chip borrower/issuer, wholesale market operator; ~**aktionär** big (large, major) shareholder; ~**anleger** large-scale investor, wholesale investor; ~**auftrag** large (sizeable) order

Groß / ~**bank** big (large) bank; ~**betragsscheck** large-value cheque; ~**betragsüberweisungsverkehr** bulk credit transfers; ~**betragszahlungsverkehr** → Großzahlungsverkehr

Größe 1. size, extent **2.** dimension(s) **3.** *(Größenordnung)* magnitude, *(ein Unternehmen mittlerer ~)* medium-sized company

Groß / ~**emission** jumbo deal (offering); ~**engagement** large exposure, large-volume loan, → Großkredit

Größenordnung magnitude, order of magnitude, size, volume involved, *(in einer ~ von 10 Mio.)* to the tune of 10m, *(eine Neuemission dieser ~)* a new issue deal of this magnitude

Größenvorteile economies of scale

Groß / ~**finanzierung** large-scale financing, big-ticket financing; ~**firmenkunde** large corporate client; ~**geschäft 1.** large-volume deal (transaction), big-ticket deal **2.** wholesale operations; ~**handel** wholesale trade

Großhandels / ~**betrieb** wholesale trading operations; ~**finanzierung** wholesale financing; ~**preisindex** wholesale price index; ~**werte** big volume stock, big-ticket stock

Groß / ~**händler** wholesaler; ~**industrie** large-scale (big) industry

Großkredit large exposure, large-scale loan, high individual loan commitment □ lending to a customer or group of related customers where the value is equal or exceeds 10 % of the credit institution's own funds

Großkredit / ~**anzeige** large exposure notice (report), reporting a large exposure to the Bundesbank/Financial Supervisory Authority; ~**begrenzung** large exposure limit; ~**einzelobergrenze** individual large exposure limit; ~**gesamtobergrenze** aggregate large exposure limit

Großkredit / ~**geschäft** large-scale lendings, wholesale lending operations; ~**konsolidierung** large exposure consolidation; ~**kontrolle** large exposure monitoring

Großkredit / ~**meldung** large exposure report; ~**obergrenze** large exposure limit; ~**regelung** large exposure regulations; ~**richtlinie** Large Exposure Directive □ EU directive limiting a bank's exposure to a particular client

Großkredit / ~**risiken** large credit risks (exposures); ~**überwachung** monitoring large exposures; ~**vorschriften** large exposure regulations (rules), large-scale loan provisions

Großkunde *(Firmenkunde)* large corporate customer, large cap, wholesale client (customer), key account

Großkunden / ~**betreuer** wholesale relationship manager, wholesale banker, key account manager; ~**betreuung** wholesale relationship management, key account management, servicing large corporate customers

Großkunden / ~**einlagen/gelder** wholesale deposits/funds; ~**geschäft** wholesale banking, wholesale customer business, large-cap corporate banking

Groß / ~-**Leasing** **1.** big ticket leasing **2.** full-service leasing; ~**lebensversicherung** ordinary life assurance; ~**stücke** large-denomination certificates (securities); ~**teil** *(~ der Umsätze)* bulk of turnover; ~**unternehmen** big corporation(s), large companies, large-scale enterprise(s), → große Kapitalgesellschaften

größtmöglicher Verlust worst case loss

großvolumig *(~er Abschnitt)* large-sized tranche, *(~e Anleiheemission)* jumbo bond issue, *(~e Offerte)* high-volume offering, *(~e Zahlungen)* large-scale (large-volume) payments, bulk payments

Groß / ~ **zahlungssystem** large-value (wholesale) funds transfer system, large- value payment system (LVPS); ~zahlungsverkehr large-value payment transactions, wholesale funds transfer, bulk payments; ~ zeichner **1.** large subscriber **2.** wholesale investor

Grund **1.** ground, land, landed property **2.** *(Ursache, Veranlassung)* reason, motive, cause, *(aus gutem ~)* for good cause, *(gute Gründe für die Aufrechterhaltung)* cogent reasons for maintaining, *(~ für die Nichteinlösung)* reason (grounds) for dishonouring (non-payment)
(auf ~ der starken Kursrückgänge) as a result of the sharp price falls, *(den finanziellen Problemen auf den ~ gehen)* to get to the bottom of the financial problems, *(das Unternehmen von ~ auf kennen)* to know the business from top to bottom, *(von ~ auf sanieren)* to rebuild from the ground

Grund / ~**akkreditiv** basic documentary credit; ~**akte** master property file, *(pl)* real property records; ~**bedarf** basic requirements (needs); ~**bedingung** basic condition, prerequisite

Grundbesitz **1.** landed property, real property, freehold property, *(Erwerber von ~)* property buyer, person acquiring the legal title to a property **2.** real estate ownership, *(Eigentumsrechte an ~)* ownership rights of freehold properties; ~**abgabe** property levy; ~**bewertung** property valuation

Grundbesitzer property owner, landowner, owner of real estate, freeholder

Grundbesitz / ~**gesellschaft** property partnership; ~**rechte** real property rights, rights of land tenure; ~**wert** property value

Grundbilanz *(Leistungsbilanz plus Bilanz des langfristigen Kapitalverkehrs)* basic balance

Grundbuch land register (BE), land records (AE)

Grundbuch / **~abschrift** *(beglaubigte ~)* certified land register copy; **~amt** Land Registry, Land Records Office, Land Registration Office; **~auszug** extract from the Land Register, office copy of the Land Register, abstract of title

Grundbuch / **~beamter** land registry official; **~belastungen** encumbrances entered in the land register; **~berichtigung** record adjustment, amending the entry in the land register; **~bescheinigung** certification by the land registration office; **~blatt** (land register) folio

Grundbuch / **~eigentümer** registered property owner (proprietor); **~einsicht** search (inspection) of the land register; **~eintragung** entry (record) in the land register, registration at (with) the Land Registry, *(die Richtigkeit der im Grundbuch eingetragenen Eigentumsrechte)* the correctness of titles recorded on the land register

Grundbuch / **~führung** land register maintenance, keeping the land register; **~gebühr** land registry fee; **~gesetz** Land Registration Act; **~kosten** registration (recording) fees

grundbuchlich *(~ gesicherte Kredite)* loans secured by charges entered in the land register

grundbuchmäßig *(~e Absicherung/Sicherung)* collateralisation (provision of security) by way of a registered charge, *(~e Bezeichnung)* land description, description in the Land Registry

Grundbuch / **~ordnung** Land Registration Code; **~recht** Land Registration Law; **~richter** land register judge; **~schuld** registered land charge; **~sperre** registration freeze

Grundbuch / **~stand** *(unzutreffender ~)* incorrect entry in the land register; **~system** land registration system; **~umschreibung** entering the change of ownership in the land register, registration of the transfer of title from ... to ...; **~unterlagen** public land records; **~vermerk** entry in the land register

Grund / **~deckung** basic coverage; **~dienstbarkeit** real servitude, land easement; **~dividende** basis (basic) dividend; **~eigentum** real property, real estate, realty, landed property; **~eigentümer** → Grundstückseigentümer

gründen 1. to found, to establish, to set up
2. *(die Zinssenkungshoffnungen ~ sich auf)* hopes for a cut in interest rates are based upon

Gründer founder, promoter; **~aktie** founder's share; **~haftung** founder's liability; **~versammlung** founders' meeting

Grund / **~erwerb** purchase of real estate, acquisition of land (landed property); **~erwerbssteuer** real estate (realty) transfer tax; **~flächenzahl** site occupancy ratio; **~gebühr** basic fee (charge), blanket charge

Grund / **~gehalt** base (basic) salary; **~gesamtheit** population; **~geschäft** underlying transaction; **~geschäftsvertrag** underlying contract, contract of delivery, contract of sale; **~haltung** basic stance (attitude)

Grund / **~kapital** share (nominal, registered, authorised) capital, capital stock; **~kredit** land credit, mortgage loan, lending on (against) real property; **~kreditanstalt** real estate credit institution, public sector mortgage bank

Grundlage basis, base, footing, foundation, groundwork *(als ~ dienen)* to serve as a basis, *(gesunde wirtschaftliche ~)* sound economic base, *(das Engagement auf eine sichere ~ stellen)* to put the facility on a secure footing, *(auf eine neue ~ stellen)* to put on a new footing, to restructure

grundlegend *(~e Daten)* fundamental (basic) data, fundamentals

gründlich *(~e Analyse)* thorough (careful) analysis, *(~e Kenntnisse)* profound knowledge

Gründlichkeit thoroughness, profoundness

Grundmietzeit *(bei Leasing-Verträgen)* base lease term

Grundpfand / ~brief deed of charge, charge certificate; **~darlehen/~kredit** real estate loan, mortgage loan; **~gläubiger** lien creditor, holder of a real estate lien

Grundpfandrecht real estate lien, charge on (over) property, lien on landed property, lien upon real property, real property lien, mortgage interest

grundpfandrechtlich *(~e Absicherung/Unterlegung)* collateralisation by way of a property charge (of a real estate lien), provision of a real estate lien, *(~ gesichertes Darlehen/unterlegter Kredit)* loan secured by a charge over property, loan secured by a lien on the borrower's/debtor's property, real-estate-secured loan

Grundpfandrechts / ~abtretung assignment of a property charge; **~bestellung** creation of a real estate lien; **~brief** deed of charge; **~gläubiger** lien creditor; **~inhaber** holder of a real estate lien, lienor; **~schuldner** lien debtor

Grundpfand / ~schulden lien debt, property charges; **~titel** title deed, mortgage interest; **~verwertung** lien enforcement

Grundpfeiler *(~ der Geldpolitik)* cornerstone (keystone) of monetary policy

Grundrelationen *(monetäre ~)* basic monetary relationships

Grundrendite basic yield

Grundrissplan floor plan

Grundsatz principle, tenet, *(~ der Bilanzkontinuität)* principle of accounting consistency, *(~ der Erstrangigkeit)* principle of holding first rank, principle of priority, *(~ der Fristenentsprechung)* principle of matching maturities, *(~ der Gegenseitigkeit)* principle of reciprocity
(~ der Periodenabgrenzung/der periodengerechten Gewinnermittlung) accrual principle, *(~ der Stetigkeit)* principle of consistency, *(~ der Unternehmensfortführung)* going concern principle, *(~ der wirtschaftlichen Betrachtungsweise/Zuordnung)* substance over form principle

Grundsätze *(~ ordnungsgemäßer Buchführung)* principles of orderly accounting, generally accepted accounting standards, *(~ der betrieblichen Übung)* principles of corporate custom and practice

Grundsatz I *(Eigenmittel-/Solvabilitätsgrundsatz)* Principle I □ replaced by the → Solvabilitätsverordnung (Solvency Regulation) in January 2007

Grundsatz II *(Liquiditätsgrundsatz)* Principle II □ replaced by → Liquiditätsverordnung (Liquidity Regulation) in January 2007

Grundsatz / ~entscheidung basic decision, decision in principle, *jur.* leading decision; **~erklärung 1.** statement of principles understood **2.** key policy statement

grundsätzlich 1. *adj.* basic, fundamental, *(~e Einigung)* agreement in principle **2.** *adv.* fundamentally, as a matter of principle, *(~ billigen)* to approve in principle, *(ein ~ gesundes Unternehmen)* a basically (fundamentally) sound company, *(ein ~ positiver Trend)* a basically positive trend

Grundschuld land (property) charge, charge over land (property) □ Although both, the Grundschuld (land charge) and the Hypothek (mortgage) entitle the creditor to payment of a specific amount against the land serving as collateral, *Grundschuld* and *Hypothek* can be distinguished in that the Hypothek is accessory (linked to a specific debt) whereas the Grundschuld is non-accessory/abstract, i.e.

G

it is a stand-alone security that is not dependent on a claim to be secured.

Grundschuld / ~**absicherung** security (collateralisation) by way of a land charge; ~**abtretung** assignment of a land charge; ~**besicherung** → Grundschuldabsicherung; ~**bestellung** creation of a land charge, creating a charge over property; ~**bestellungsurkunde** deed of charge, document creating the charge; ~**brief** land charge deed, charge certificate; ~**eintragung** entering a property charge in the land register, recording a land charge

G

grundschuldgesichert *(~er Anspruch)* claim secured by a land charge

Grundschuld / ~**gläubiger** holder of a land charge, mortgagee; ~**haftung** liability under a property charge; ~**inhaber** holder of a land charge; ~**kapital** principal represented by the charge; ~**kosten** charge recording fee

Grundschuld / ~**löschung** extinguishment (release) of a land charge; ~**nominalbetrag** (registered) amount of the land charge; ~**schuldner** mortgagor, party (person) providing the land charge as collateral; ~**sicherung** → Grundschuldbesicherung

Grundschuld / ~**umschreibung** transferring (conveying) a land charge; ~**valutierung** provision of a land charge as collateral; ~**verwertung** foreclosure (enforcement) of a land charge

Grundschuld / ~**verzinsung** creating an interest-related property charge, → Grundschuldzinsen; ~**zinsen** interest-related property charge □ recorded in the Land Registry; serves as collateral for the bank's interest claims and possible enforcement charges

Grund / ~**sicherheit** real estate collateral, security interest in land; ~**steuer** real property tax, land tax; ~**steuergesetz** German Land Tax Act

Grund / ~**stein** *(den ~ für eine erfolgreiche Sanierung legen)* to prepare the ground (to lay the foundations) for a successful restructuring; ~**stimmung** basic tone (sentiment); ~**stock** basic stock, basis, foundation

Grundstück plot, land, landed property, piece (parcel) of land, *(~ zu Anschaffungskosten)* land valued at cost, *(~ und grundstücksgleiche Rechte)* landed property and equivalent titles to land

Grundstücks / ~**abtretung** property assignment, assignment of land; ~**anteil** interest in land; ~**auflassung** property conveyance, conveying a plot (a piece of land); ~**aufteilung** property apportionment

Grundstücks / ~**belastung** **1.** property charge(s), charge(s) over property, encumbrances (charges) on land **2.** encumbrancing (mortgaging) land; ~**beleihung** lending against land (against a property), advancing money on land; ~**beleihungswert** property's lendable value

Grundstücks / ~**beschreibung** plot (property, land) description; ~**bestandteile** appurtenances, appurtenant items running with the land; ~**bewertung** property (land) valuation

Grundstücks / ~**eigentum** plot (property) ownership, ownership of a piece of land; ~**eigentümer** plot owner (holder), lot owner, landowner, proprietor of the land

Grundstücks / ~**erschließung** plot (property) development; ~**erträge** property income; ~**erwerb** buying a plot (a piece of land), property purchase, purchase of land; ~ **fläche** plot area (size), property area (size)

grundstücksgleich *(~e Rechte)* rights equivalent to real property

Grundstücks / ~**grenzen** plot (property) boundaries; ~**größe** plot size; ~**kaufvertrag** real estate purchase contract, land contract, contract for deed; ~**lage** plot (property) location; ~**lasten** property (land) charges

Grundstücks / ~**markt** real estate (property) market; ~**parzelle** land parcel, plot; ~**plan** plot (site) plan; ~**rechte** rights in (on) land, property rights, interests in property; ~**reserven** property revaluation reserves

Grundstücks / ~**sondervermögen** 1. special property fund, → Sondervermögen 2. special (segregated) real property; ~**teilung** partitioning real property, division (partition) of land

Grundstücks / ~**überlassung** property transfer, surrender of property; ~**übertragung**/~**umschreibung** property conveyance, conveyance of land

Grundstücks/~**veräußerung**/~**verkauf** selling a plot (a piece of land), property sale; ~**verkehr** real estate transactions (dealing); ~**verkehrsgesetz** German Real Estate Transactions Act; ~**vermessung** surveying a plot of land, property surveying

Grundstücks / ~**wert** property (land) value, real estate value; ~**wertminderung** property depreciation, loss in property value

Grundton *(Börse)* basic tone (sentiment)

Gründung 1. foundation, constitution, setting up 2. *(einer Unternehmung)* establishment, formation, incorporation

Gründungs / ~**aufwand** preliminary expenses; ~**beratung** start-up counselling (consultancy); ~**bericht** formation report, minutes of the statutory meeting; ~ **bilanz** start-up accounts

Gründungs / ~**darlehen** business start-up loan; ~**finanzierung** start-up financing; ~**förderung** 1. start-up assistance, promotion of business start-ups 2. *(finanzielle)* start-up funding; ~**formalitäten** incorporation formalities; ~**gesellschafter** founding partners

Gründungs / ~**kapital** initial (original) capital, start-up capital, seed capital; ~**konsortium** founding group; ~**kosten** incorporation (organization) expenses, start-up expenditure

Gründungs / ~**mitglied** founder member, incorporator; ~**protokoll** minutes of incorporation; ~**prüfung** formation (incorporation) audit; ~**urkunde** 1. foundation charter 2. certificate of incorporation

Gründungs / ~**vermögen** founders' (seed) assets; ~**versammlung** statutory (constituent) meeting, founders' meeting, organization meeting; ~**wert** real property value; ~**zins** ground rent; ~**zuschuss** start-up subsidy

Gruppe 1. group, category, *(Gruppe der Zentralbankpräsidenten und Leiter der Bankenaufsichtsinstanzen)* Group of Central Bank Governors and Heads of Supervision □ governing body of the Basel Committee of Banking Supervision 2. *(Konzern)* group

gruppenangehörig *(~ es Unternehmen)* group enterprise (entity)

Gruppen / ~**besteuerung** group taxation, consolidated corporate tax base, → Organschaft; ~**ebene** *(auf ~)* at group level; ~**ergebnis** group income (loss), group performance

gruppenfremd *(~e Beteiligungen)* unconsolidated (non-group) affiliations

Gruppengewinn group income (profit), consolidated income

gruppenintern *(~e Kredite)* intragroup (internal group) lending

Gruppen / ~**leiter** Section Head, Desk (Team) Manager; ~**leitung** 1. Desk (Team) Management 2. Group Management, Group Management Board; ~**rechnung** group (consolidated) accounts; ~**struktur** group structure; ~**träger** group parent; ~**umsatz** group turnover (sales)

Gruppen / ~**versicherung** group insurance; ~**zugehörigkeit** affiliation with the group, group membership, *(gruppenzugehörige Beteiligungen)* consoli-

G

dated affiliations, (interests in) companies affiliated with the group

GS-Gutschrift → Girosammeldepotgutschrift

GT → gestrichen

Guichetprovision → Schalterprovision

gültig 1. valid, in force, applicable, *(~ bleiben)* to remain valid (in force), *(~ sein) (a)* to be valid, to be in force, *(nicht mehr ~ sein)* to be no longer valid, to cease to have effect, to be no longer applicable
2. good, *(~ bis Ultimo) (Börsenorder)* good this month, buy or sell order valid till the end of the month, *(~ bis auf weiteres)* valid until further notice, *(~ bis auf Widerruf)* good-till-cancelled order, GTC order, *(~ nur heute)* day order
3. prevailing, ruling, *(zu dem am Abschlusstag ~en Wechselkurs)* at the exchange rate prevailing on the transaction date, *(zu dem dann ~en Wechselkurs)* at the exchange rate ruling at the time, *(zum ~en Zinssatz)* at the prevailing (current) interest rate
4. *(gesetzlich)* legal, lawful, *(die jeweils ~ en gesetzlichen Bestimmungen)* the relevant legal provisions as amended from time to time
5. *(allgemein ~)* generally accepted

G

Gültigkeit 1. validity, force 2. lawfulness, legality

Gültigkeits / ~bereich scope of validity; **~dauer** 1. validity, period of validity 2. *(Laufzeit)* life, term; **~erklärung** validation, certificate of validation; **~klausel** validity (applicability) clause; **~kontrolle/~prüfung** validation test, validity check; **~verlängerung** validity extension, extending the validity period

Gunst *(Saldo zu Ihren ~en)* balance in your favour

günstig *(~es Angebot)* favourable (advantageous) offer, *(die günstigste lieferbare Anleihe)* cheapest-to-deliver bond □ the least expensive bond to deliver into a futures contract, *(~e Konjunkturaussichten)* favourable economic outlook (prospects), *(zu einem ~en Zinssatz ausleihen)* to lend at a favourable rate of interest

gut 1. *adj. (~e Adresse)* borrower/issuer of good standing, *(sehr gute Adresse)* prime (first-rate) issuer/borrower, *(~e Anlagemöglichkeit)* interesting (fine, good, promising) investment opportunity, *(~es Geschäftsergebnis)* good results, profitable performance
(für den angefragten Betrag ~ sein) to be good for the amount in question (for the amount indicated in your inquiry), *(finanziell und wirtschaftlich in einem ~en Zustand)* in a good economic and financial shape
2. *adv. (~ abschneiden)* to show up well, to fare well, to have a good record, *(die Emission wurde am Markt ~ aufgenommen)* the issue was well received in the market, *(~ behauptete Aktienkurse)* well-maintained equity prices

Gut 1. *(Vermögenswert)* asset, property 2. *(Ware)* product

Gutachten (expert) opinion

Gutachter expert, appraiser, professional valuer, *(Bewertung durch einen ~)* expert assessment

Gutachter / ~ausschuss 1. panel (committee) of experts, appraisal committee, evaluation team 2. review panel; **~gebühr/~kosten** expert's (appraiser's) fee, appraisal cost; **~kommission** → Gutachterausschuss; **~verfahren** expert assessment process

Gutbefund *(Dokumente zum ~ weiterleiten)* to send documents for approval

gutbringen *(einem Konto ~)* to credit to an account, to place in (into) an account

Güte quality; **~grad/~klasse** quality grade; **~klasseneinteilung** grading

Güter goods, articles, property

Güter / ~austausch goods traffic, exchange of goods; **~fernverkehr** long haul, long-distance goods traffic; **~ge-**

meinschaft 1. community of property 2. property owned in common, joint ownership of property; ~**kraftverkehr** road haulage, freight hauling

Güter / ~**recht** law of property; ~**stand** matrimonial property regime; ~**strom** goods flow; ~**trennung** 1. separation of property 2. separate ownership; ~**verkehr** goods (freight) traffic; ~**versand** dispatch (shipment) of goods

Gütestelle conciliation office (board)

gutgehend *(~es Wertpapiergeschäft)* thriving (flourishing) securities business

gutgläubig 1. *adj. (~er Besitz)* possession in good faith, *(~er Eigentümer)* bona fide owner, owner (holder) in good faith, *(~er Erwerb)* acquisition in good faith, *(~er Erwerber)* bona fide purchaser, purchaser in good faith
2. *adv. (~ erwerben)* to acquire (to purchase) in good faith

Gutgläubigkeit *(~ des Erwerbers)* buyer's good faith

Guthaben 1. credit, *(das ~ auf Ihrem Konto beläuft sich auf ...)* the credit balance in your account amounts to ..., the amount standing to your credit totals ...
2. balance, deposits, *(~ bei Kreditinstituten)* balances with banks, cash in (with) banks, *(~ bei Zentralbanken)* balances (deposits) with Central Banks, *(~ in laufender Rechnung/auf Kontokorrentkonten)* current account balances, balances (deposits) in current (checking) accounts

Guthaben / ~**basis** *(das Konto wird ausschließlich auf ~ geführt)* the account is exclusively kept in the credit (on a non-borrowing basis); ~**forderungen** claims arising from credit balances (from deposits), balances due

Guthaben / ~**konto** account kept on a non-borrowing basis, creditor account; ~**posten** credit entry (item); ~**saldo** credit balance; ~**überträge** transfer of credit balances; ~**zinsen** credit (creditor) interest

gütlich 1. *adj. (~er Vergleich)* amicable settlement, out-of-court settlement 2. *adv. (einen Rechtsstreit ~ beilegen)* to settle a litigation amicably

gutmachen *(Aktien konnten verlorenen Boden ~)* equities recovered lost ground

gutschreiben to credit to an account, to enter (to pass) to the credit of an account

Gutschrift credit, credit entry, *(~ in Wertpapierrechnung)* securities account credit (for securities purchased and deposited abroad), *(wir haben den Scheck zur ~ hereingenommen)* we have accepted the cheque for credit to your account

Gutschrifts / ~**anzeige** credit advice (note); ~**träger** credit voucher (advice); ~**verfahren** credit note process

GWB → Gesetz gegen Wettbewerbsbeschränkungen

GwG → Geldwäschegesetz

H

Haben credit; ~**buchung** credit entry, entry to the credit of an account; ~**konto** creditor account, account in the credit; ~**saldo** credit balance; ~**zinsen** credit (creditor) interest

haftbar liable, responsible, *(gesetzlich gegenüber dem Kunden ~)* legally liable to the customer, *(für Verluste ~ machen)* to hold liable (to make accountable) for losses

H

Haftbarkeit liability, responsibility

Haftbarmachung *(~ der Bank)* holding the bank liable

haften 1. to be liable (responsible) for, *(gegenüber der Bank ~)* to be liable to the bank, *(die Bank haftet nicht für Schäden aus ...)* the bank shall not be liable for damage resulting from ..., *(aus einer Bürgschaft/einem Wechsel ~)* to be liable on (under) a surety bond/a bill, *(als Gesamtschuldner ~)* to be jointly and severally liable
2. *(als Sicherheit dienen)* to serve as collateral (security), *(die hinterlegten Wertpapiere ~ für alle Kreditansprüche der Bank)* the securities deposited serve as collateral for all claims of the bank arising from the loan

haftend *(~es Eigenkapital)* liable equity capital, *(~e Eigenmittel)* liable own funds, *(~es Gesellschafterdarlehen)* committed shareholder loan, *(~e Mittel)* liable funds, *(unbeschränkt ~er Gesellschafter)* fully liable (unlimited) partner, general partner, *(die für den Kredit ~en Vermögenswerte)* the assets serving as security for the loan

Haftkapital → haftendes Eigenkapital

Haftpflicht liability, third party liability; ~**versicherer** liability underwriter; ~**versicherung** third party liability insurance, indemnity insurance

Haftrücklass retention money; ~**garantie** retention (money) bond

Haftsumme liability amount, warranty amount, commitment

Haftsummenzuschlag addition of members' uncalled liabilities to capital and reserves

Haftung liability, responsibility, accountability, *(~ aus der Bestellung von Sicherheiten)* liability from collateral furnished, guarantee commitments, *(~ aus einer Bürgschaft)* liability under (on) a guarantee, *(die ~ ist auf die Kapitaleinlage begrenzt)* liability is limited to the amount of capital contributed *(unter ~ der Muttergesellschaft hinausgelegte Garantie)* guarantee furnished under the liability of the parent company, *(die vollständige ~ übernehmen)* to take over 100 % of the liability, *(den Garantiegeber aus seiner ~ entlassen)* to release (to discharge) the guarantor from his guarantee (warranty)

Haftungs / ~ansprüche liability claims; ~**ausschluss** liability exclusion (waiver), non-liability, disclaimer of responsibility (liability), avoidance of liability, *(Plural)* liability exclusions; ~**ausschlussklausel** liability exclusion clause, non-liability (non-warranty) clause, no bailout clause, exculpatory clause

Haftungs / ~basis *(~ des Unternehmens)* corporate liability base; ~**befreiung** liability discharge, discharge (exemption, release) from liability; ~**begrenzung** limitation of liability, liability cap (limit), → Haftungsbeschränkungen; ~**begrenzungsklausel** limited liability (loss) clause

Haftungs / ~beschränkungen restrictions on liability, *(bei Gewährleistungsgarantien)* warranty limitations; **~betrag** guarantee amount, liable amount

Haftungs / ~dach liability umbrella, maximum liability limit; **~dauer** period of liability, guarantee (indemnity, warranty) period; **~deckelung** liability cap (capping); **~durchgriff** enforcement of liability, piercing the corporate veil

Haftungs / ~eintritt assumption of liability; **~entgelt** liability fee; **~entlassung** release from liability; **~erklärung** liability undertaking (bond), undertaking (declaration) of liability; **~erleichterung** liability relief; **~erweiterung** extension of liability; → Kontokorrentvorbehalt

Haftungs / ~feststellung ascertainment (determination) of liability; **~folgen** liability implications, effects (impact) of liability; **~fonds** guarantee (indemnity) fund; **~frage** liability issue; **~freistellung** liability discharge, exemption (discharge, release) from liability; **~freizeichnungsklausel** non-liability (non-warranty) clause

Haftungs / ~garantie liability guarantee, → Haftungszusagen; **~gebot** obligation to assume the liability; **~grenze** liability limit (threshold), exposure (guarantee) limit, → Haftungssumme

Haftungs / ~kapital → haftendes Eigenkapital; **~klage** liability action, action for liability; **~klausel** **1.** liability clause **2.** disclaimer; **~masse** total liable funds (available to the company)

Haftungs / ~ minderungsklausel liability reduction clause; **~obergrenze** liability cap, *(je Schadenereignis)* per occurrence limit, → Haftungsgrenze; **~obligo** liability exposure, liability under a warranty deed

Haftungs / ~quote liability rate (share); **~rahmen** liability limit; **~rangfolge** **1.** ranking of potentially liable persons **2.** ranking of liable funds; **~recht** tort law, *(haftungsrechtlich)* in terms of liability, *(haftungsrechtliche Bestimmungen)* legal liability provisions; **~regelungen** liability regulations, accountability rules

Haftungs / ~risiko liability risk, *(insgesamt)* liability (warranty) exposure; **~rücklassgarantie** retention money bond; **~rückstellung** provision against a specific liability, *(pl)* liability risk provisions, provisions for contingent liabilities

Haftungs / ~summe **1.** warranty amount, commitment **2.** *(maximale ~ des Bürgen/der Kautionsversicherungsgesellschaft)* penal sum of the bond, penalty bond amount; **~teilung** liability sharing, sharing out the liability; **~träger** guarantor, party liable

Haftungs / ~übernahme assumption of liability, taking on the liability; **~umfang** scope (degree, extent) of liability; **~verbund** **1.** liability sharing agreement, risk-sharing (loss-sharing) agreement
2. *(der Sparkassen-Finanzgruppe)* joint liability scheme □ guarantee fund of the German savings banks

Haftungs / ~vergütung fee for assuming (unlimited) liability; **~verhältnisse** *(im Jahresabschluss)* contingent liabilities, contingencies and commitments; **~vertrag** liability (warranty) deed, indemnity agreement; **~verwirklichung** **1.** enforcing a liability undertaking, calling upon the warrantor **2.** → Haftungsübernahme

Haftungs / ~zeitraum liability (warranty) period; **~zusagen** **1.** liability undertakings **2.** committed liable funds; **~zuschlag** **1.** → Haftsummenzuschlag **2.** warranty premium

halbbar *(~e Zahlung)* semi-cash payment

Halbeinkünfteverfahren half income system □ taxation of dividend income at half the regular tax rate

Halbfertigerzeugnisse semi-manufactured goods, semi-manufactures

halbieren *(die Dividende ~)* to halve the dividend, *(der Gewinn hat sich halbiert)* the income has been halved

Halbjahres / ~abrechnung 1. mid-year settlement, semi-annual balancing **2.** mid-year closing statement; **~ausweis** mid-year return; **~bilanz** mid-year financial statements, mid-year accounts

Halbjahres / ~dividende half-yearly (semi-annual) dividend; **~ergebnis** mid-year performance; **~geld** six-month money; **~kupon** semi-annual coupon

H

halbmonatlich *(~e Abrechnung)* half-monthly settlement, settlement every fortnight

halbstaatlich *(~er Emittent)* semi-sovereign issuer

Hälfte half, *(der Gewinn verringerte sich um mehr als die ~)* the profit dropped by more than half, *(die Kosten zur ~ tragen)* to pay (to bear) half the cost

hälftig *(~ anrechnen)* to take into account at half the value

Hals *(eine hohe Schuldenlast am ~ haben)* to be saddled with a high debt burden

haltbar 1. *(~es Argument)* tenable argument **2.** *(~e Konsumgüter)* durable consumer goods, durables

Haltbarkeit 1. tenability **2.** durability, stability

Halte / ~bestand *(an Kreditengagements)* final hold; **~dauer** holding period; **~ empfehlung** hold recommendation; **~kosten** cost of carry, carrying charges

halten 1. *(aufrechterhalten, beibehalten)* to maintain, to hold, to keep, *(die Dividende ~)* to hold the dividend, to maintain the dividend payout, *(bis Fälligkeit ~)* to hold until maturity, *(bis zur Fälligkeit gehaltene Kredite)* held-to-maturity loans
(den Gewinn ~) to stay level on profits, *(sich am Markt ~)* to stay in the market, *(seine führende Position ~)* to retain one's leading position, *(sich umsatzmäßig an der Spitze ~)* to stay at the top in terms of volume
2. *(besitzen)* to hold, *(als Pfand ~)* to hold in pledge, *(in seinem Portefeuille ~)* to hold in one's portfolio, *(eine offene Position ~)* to maintain an open position (a net exposure), *(Wertpapiere langfristig ~)* to hold securities over the long term
3. *(festhalten an) (Aktien ~)* to hold on to shares, *(es lohnt sich die Aktie zu ~)* the stock is well worth holding
4. *(halten für)* to consider (to regard) as
5. *(sich halten an) (sich an den Garantiegeber ~)* to call on (to turn to) the guarantor, to hold the guarantor liable, *(sich an die Vertragsbedingungen ~)* to abide by (to comply with) the terms of the contract
6. *(sich über Kundenwünsche auf dem laufenden ~)* to keep abreast of customer requirements

Halte / ~periode holding period; **~position** shares (securities) worth holding; **~ strategie** retention strategy

Haltung attitude, position, line, *(~ in der Geldpolitik)* monetary stance, *(~ zu Zinssenkungen)* stance on interest rate cuts, *(eine härtere ~ einnehmen)* to take a tougher line, *(eine neutrale ~ einnehmen)* to take a neutral stance

Hand *(aus einer ~)* from a single source, *(Finanzierung aus einer ~)* one-stop financing, *(Verfügungen von hoher ~)* acts of public authorities, *(freie ~ haben)* to be given free rein

Hände *(in die ~ von XY übergehen)* to pass into the hands of XY

Handel 1. *(Devisen-/Wertpapierhandel)* trade, trading, *(~ per Erscheinen)* pre-IPO trading, trading on a when issued basis, *(~ in kurzen Fälligkeiten)* short-term money dealings, *(~ per Kasse)* dealings for cash, cash dealings (trading)
(~ in Kurz- bzw. Langläufern) dealings in shorts/longs, *(~ in Options-*

und Terminkontrakten) options and futures trading, *(~ im Sekundärmarkt)* secondary market dealings, *(~ per Termin)* trading for future delivery, forward trading, *(~ in amtlich notierten Werten)* trading in listed securities, *(~ mit Wertpapierblöcken)* block trading
2. *(Geschäftsfeld einer Bank nach Basel II)* Trading and Sales
3. *(Bereich, Abteilung)* trading desk (unit, department), dealing desk (room)
4. *(Händler)* traders, dealers, dealing community
5. *(Gewerbe)* trade, business

handelbar trad(e)able, marketable, *(~e Forderungen)* negotiable receivables

Handelbarkeit trad(e)ability, marketability

handeln 1. to trade, to deal, *(Aktien wurden lebhaft gehandelt)* stocks were actively traded, equities encountered lively interest, *(die Anleihe wurde mit einem Aufschlag gegenüber ihrem Emissionskurs gehandelt)* the bond traded at a premium to its issue price, *(die Emission wurde mit einem Abschlag von ca. 1 % gehandelt)* the issue traded at a discount of around 1 p.c.
2. to act **3.** *(sich ~ um)* to concern, to refer to

Handeln 1. trading, dealing **2.** acting, action

Handelsabsicht trading intent, *(mit ~ gehaltene Finanzinstrumente)* financial instruments held for short-term profit trading, *(mit ~ gehaltene marktgängige Wertpapiere)* trading securities

Handels / ~abteilung → Handel (3); **~adresse** name, market operator (player), trading name; **~aktiva** *(eines Kreditinstitutes)* trading assets, financial assets held for trading purposes □ securities, precious metals and derivative financial instruments with a positive fair value

Handels / ~akzept trade acceptance; **~algorithmus** trading algorithm; **~ausweitung 1.** increase in trading **2.** trade expansion

handelsbedingt *(~er Personal- und Sachaufwand)* trading-related staff and operating expenditure

Handels / ~bedingungen 1. trading conditions **2.** trade terms; **~befugnis** *(i. S. von Dispositionsbefugnis)* trading authorisation; **~beschränkungen** trading (trade) restrictions; **~bereich** → Handel (3)

Handels / ~bestand trading portfolio (account, book), dealing inventory; **~bestandsbewertung** trading account valuation; **~bestimmungen** trading (trade) regulations; **~beteiligungen** trade investments

handelsbezogen trade-related, *(~e Fazilität) (für Entwicklungsländer)* trade facility, *(~ e Zinsen)* trading-related interest

Handelsbilanz 1. *(eines Landes)* trade balance **2.** *(einer Unternehmung; im Unterschied zur Steuerbilanz)* commercial accounts, financial statements, accounts prepared for financial reporting purposes

Handelsbilanz / ~defizit trade balance deficit, merchandise trade deficit; **~gewinn/~verlust** accounting profit (loss); **~überschuss** trade balance surplus, merchandise trade surplus

Handelsbrauch dealing (trading) practice

Handelsbuch trading book □ a bank's (financial institution's) proprietary positions in financial instruments held for short-term trading

handelsbuchfähig eligible for the trading book

Handelsbuch / ~gesamtposition aggregated trading book position (exposure); **~institut** trading book institution, bank (financial institution) maintaining a significant proprietary trading portfolio; **~nettoposition** net trading book exposure; **~positionen** *(Anrechnungsbeträge für die ~)* capital charges for trading book risk positions

Handelsbuch / ~**risiken** trading book risks, *(Eigenkapitalvorschriften zu ~)* capital rules governing trading book exposures; ~**risikoposition** trading book risk position (exposure); ~**sicherheit** trading book collateral;~**vorschriften** trading book regulations

Handels / ~**büro** trading desk, trading (dealing) office; ~**derivate** trading derivatives; ~**effekten** marketable debt; ~**einheit** trading unit, unit of trading

Handels / ~**erfahrung** trading (dealing) experience; ~**erfolg** trading performance; ~**erfolg/ergebnis** trading performance (gains), net trading income (loss); ~**erlaubnis** trading (dealing) licence

Handels / ~**finanzierung** commodity trade financing, commodities finance; *(Konditionen für Handelsfinanzierungen)* trade finance rates; ~**gegenstand** *(eines Terminkontraktes)* trading unit, underlying instrument; ~**geschäfte** **1.** commercial transactions **2.** trading transactions, stock exchange deals

Handels / ~**gesellschaft** trading company (corporation); ~**gesetzbuch** German Commercial Code; ~**gewinn** trading income (profit)

Handels / ~**hindernisse** trade obstacles, impediments to trade; ~**immobilien** retail properties; ~**instrumente** instruments held for trading purposes; ~**intermediär** trading intermediary

Handels / ~**kammer** Chamber of Commerce; ~**kapital** trading capital, stock-in-trade; ~**klauseln** trade clauses, Incoterms; ~**kosten** trading cost (expenses); ~**kredit** trade credit, business (trade) loan; ~**kreditbrief** commercial letter of credit (CLC)

Handels / ~**linie** dealing limit (line); ~**makler** mercantile broker; ~**marge** **1.** trading margin (commission) **2.** → Händlerspanne; ~**marke** **1.** trademark **2.** private brand (label), distributor's brand; ~**muster** trading pattern; ~**name** trade name

Handels / ~**papiere** negotiable instruments; ~**passiva** trading liabilities, liabilities from trading activities, liabilities from short sales and derivative financial instruments with a negative fair value; ~**phase** trading phase

Handels / ~**plattform** trading platform; ~**platz** **1.** trading venue, place of trading, market place **2.** stock market (exchange); ~**position** trading position; ~**raum** dealing office, trading desk; ~**recht** commercial law

handelsrechtlich under (in terms of) commercial law, under the German Commercial Code (HGB), *(~e Ansatz- und Bewertungsvorschriften)* statutory (HGB-based) recognition and measurement rules, *(~e Bilanzierung)* statutory (HGB-based) accounting, treatment in the financial statements, → Bilanzrechtsmodernisierungsgesetz
(~e Bilanzierungsvorschriften) statutory (HGB-based) accounting rules, *(~es Ergebnis)* net income (loss) stated in the financial statements, net income (loss) according to statutory accounting rules

Handels / ~**register** Commercial Register, Register of Companies; ~**registerauszug** extract from the Register of Companies, certificate of incorporation; ~**ring** trading pit; ~**risiko** commercial (trading) risk, trading exposure

Handels / ~**schluss** close of trading; ~**schlusskurs** closing price (quote); ~**schlussnote** contract note; ~**segment** trading segment

Handels / ~**spanne** **1.** *(Rohgewinn)* gross profit, trade margin □ difference between the net sales price and the cost price
2. *(von Kursen)* trading range, difference between day's high and low
3. → Händlerspanne

Handels / ~statistik trade statistics (returns); **~stopp** trading halt, suspended dealings; **~ströme** trade flows; **~stunden** trading hours; **~tag** trade (trading) date; **~techniken** trading techniques

Handels / ~überschuss net income from trading operations; **~überwachung** trade monitoring, trading surveillance; **~überwachungsstelle** trading supervisory authority (office)

handelsüblich customary, customary in trade, in line with commercial practice, *(~e Größe)* normal trading unit

handelsunabhängig *(~e Bereiche)* units not dependent on trading

Handels / ~unternehmen 1. trading company **2.** commercial undertaking (enterprise); **~usance** dealing (trading) practice, trade (commercial) usage; **~verbot** trading ban; **~verlust** trading loss

Handels / ~vertrag trade agreement; **~vertreter** commercial (mercantile) agent; **~vertretung** mercantile agency; **~volumen 1.** trading (dealing, transaction) volume **2.** total goods traffic

Handels / ~währung dealing currency; **~wareneinsatz** cost of materials; **~wechsel** trade bill; **~wert** commercial (market) value; **~zeit** trading session; **~zwecke** *(zu ~n gehaltene Finanztitel)* financial instruments held for trading purposes, *(zu ~n gehaltene Wertpapiere)* trading securities

Handhabe *(rechtliche)* available remedies, grounds for taking action, legal basis

handhaben to handle, to manage

Handhabung handling, management, administration, *(~ der Rechnungslegung)* accounting treatment

Händler 1. *(an den Finanzmärkten)* dealer, trader **2.** *(im Kreditkartengeschäft)* merchant

Händler / ~bank 1. dealing bank, *(Platzeur)* dealer **2.** *(im Kreditkartengeschäft)* merchant; **~bestand** dealer inventory (portfolio), dealer's position, dealer's book; **~bonifikation** dealer's concession

Händler / ~evidenzzentrale merchant registration centre; **~geschäft 1.** dealer transaction **2.** transaction for own account; **~gewinn** → Händlerspanne

Händler / ~interventionen dealer (desk) interventions; **~karte** retailer (retail) card; **~kennnummer** merchant identification code; **~konto** *(im Kreditkartengeschäft)* merchant account; **~kreise** dealing (trading) community

Händler / ~organisation dealer organisation; **~provision** dealer allowance, dealing commission, dealer's turn; **~raum** dealing room; **~spanne** dealing spread, dealer's margin, dealer's turn, dealership margin

Händler / ~tisch trading desk; **~vertrag** merchant agreement; **~vertragsbank** acquirer; **~zettel** dealing slip

Handlung act, action

Handlungs / ~bedarf need for (further) action; **~bevollmächtigter 1.** authorised agent **2.** *(Funktion im Kreditgewerbe)* assistant manager, assistant treasurer, officer

Handlungs / ~fähigkeit (legal) ability to act, capacity to act (to contract), *(handlungsfähig)* legally competent, capable of acting; **~freiheit** full discretion, freedom to act, *(volle ~ haben)* to have full liberty to act

Handlungs / ~pflichten *(in Kreditverträgen)* affirmative covenants; **~rahmen** framework for action, policy framework; **~spielraum** room to manoeuvre, leeway

Handlungs / ~unfähigkeit (legal) inability to act; **~verbot** interdiction to act; **~vollmacht 1.** commercial power of attorney (power of representation), → Handlungsbevollmächtigter **2.** *(allgemein)* authority (power) to act; **~weise 1.** *(Vorgehen)* handling of a matter, procedure, action, mode of dealing, dealings **2.** *(Verhalten)* conduct, behaviour

handschriftlich *(~e Unterschrift)* autograph (hand-written) signature

harmonisieren to harmonise, *(harmonisierter Verbraucherpreisindex)* harmonised index of consumer prices

Harmonisierung *(~ der Zulassungsvorschriften)* harmonisation of listing rules

hart *adj.* hard, strong, firm, severe, rigorous *adv.* *(~ umkämpfter Markt)* hotly (strongly) contested market

H

hartes Kernkapital *(under* → Basel III rules) Common Equity Tier 1 Capital, Tier 1a Capital □ consists largely of common shares issued by the bank, stock surplus, and retained earnings. On 1 January 2015, Common Equity Tier 1 will need to equal at least 4.5% of a bank's risk-weighted assets. → zusätzliches Kernkapital, → Kernkapital

harte Patronatserklärung hard (unconditional) letter of comfort □ representing a legally binding commitment

harte Währung hard (strong) currency

Härte **1.** firmness, hardness, stability **2.** difficulty **3.** rigidity **4.** severity, rigorousness; **~fall** *(als ~ gelten)* to qualify as hardship; **~fonds** hardship fund; **~klausel** hardship clause

Hartgeld coined money

hartnäckig *(~es Festhalten an)* tenacious (persistent) adherence to, *(~e finanzielle Probleme)* nagging (intractable) financial problems

Hartwährungsland hard currency country

hauchdünn *(~e Marge)* razor-thin margin

häufen **1.** *(sich ~)* to accumulate, to occur frequently, to roll (to pile) up, to increase **2.** *(anhäufen)* to amass

Häufigkeit *(~ der Meldungen)* reporting frequency, *(~der Zinsanpassungen)* rate change frequency

Haupt / **~aktionär** principal (majority) shareholder; **~anspruch** principal claim; **~augenmerk** primary focus

Haupt / **~bankverbindung** key relationship bank, lead bank; **~bestandteile** *(des Vertrages)* principal (main) components of the contract; **~datei** master file; **~ertragsquelle** principal source (mainstay) of earnings; **~finanzierungsquelle** main (principal) source of funding; **~forderung** principal debt (claim)

Haupt / **~geschäft** **1.** core business (operations), mainstream activities **2.** → Hauptgeschäftssitz; **~geschäftsführer** general manager; **~geschäftssitz** principal place of business; **~gewicht** main emphasis, focus; **~gläubiger** principal creditor

Haupt / **~handelsphase** main trading phase; **~investor** lead investor; **~kommissionär** principal agent; **~konto** **1.** principal account **2.** *(Sammelkonto)* master account; **~kostenstelle** main cost centre

Haupt / **~last** *(die ~ der Rezession tragen)* to bear the brunt of the recession; **~merkmale** main features, principal characteristics; **~niederlassung** head office, principal place of business, company headquarters, *(einer Großbank)* Main Branch; **~nutznießer** primary beneficiary; **~police** master policy

Haupt / **~refinanzierungsgeschäfte** main refinancing operations (MROs) □ weekly refinancing operations in the form of standard tenders (→ Standardtender) designed to provide the euro area banking system with liquidity, → Leitzins, → EONIA Spread

Haupt / **~schuld** principal debt (obligation), primary obligation; **~schuldner** principal debtor (obligor), primary obligor; **~schuldverhältnis** principal (primary) debt obligation

Haupt / **~sitz** headquarters, principal place of business, *(mit ~ in Großbritannien)* headquartered in Great Britain; ~**stütze** *(~ der Wirtschaft)* mainstay of economic activity; ~**tender** main tender operation; ~**unternehmer** head contractor

Haupt / ~**veranlagung** general tax assessment; ~**verbindlichkeit** principal liability; ~**verpflichtung** primary obligation; ~**versammlung** general meeting; ~ **versammlungspräsenz** attendance at general meetings; ~**verwaltung** head office

Haupt / ~**wechselschuldner** principal bill debtor, person (party) primarily liable on a bill; ~**zahlstelle** principal paying agent; ~**ziel** prime objective, principal goal, main target; ~**zinstermin** principal coupon date

Hausbank key relationship bank, principal (prime) banker, principal (main) banking connection

Hausbanken / ~**haftung** guarantee provided (liability assumed) by the principal banker; ~**marge** principal banker's fee; ~**prinzip** principle of a close borrower-lender (bank-customer) relationship

Hausbank / ~**funktion** *(die traditionelle ~)* traditional primary bank function; ~**verbindung** prime banker relationship; ~**verfahren** customer access mechanism

hauseigen *(~es Finanzierungsinstitut)* captive (in-house) finance company, *(~er Investmentfonds)* in-house investment fund

Haushalts / ~**ansätze** budget appropriations (estimates); ~**ausgaben** budget expenditure; ~**befugnisse** budgetary powers; ~**bewilligung** budget appropriation; ~**bewilligungsrecht** appropriations power

Haushalts / ~**defizit** budget deficit; ~**einnahmen** budget (budgetary) receipts; ~**entlastung** budget relief; ~**führung** *(straffe ~)* stringent budget policy; ~**gleichgewicht** budget equilibrium

Haushalts / ~**kontrolle** budget control; ~**kürzungen** cuts in budget expenditure, budget trimming; ~**lage** budget situation; ~**mittel** budget funds

Haushalts / ~**plan** budget plan; ~**politik** budget policy; ~**verabschiedung** passage of the budget; ~**voranschläge** budget estimates; ~**vorlage** budget bill

Haus / ~-**Konnossement** house bill of lading; ~-**Sammelverwahrung** in-house collective custody

Hausse bull market, sharp rise in equity/bond prices, *(auf ~ kaufen)* to buy (to go) for a rise, to bull the market

Hausse / ~-**Dreieck** *(Chart-Analyse)* ascending triangle; ~-**Formation** *(Chart-Analyse)* bull pattern (formation);~-**Markt** bull market, market characterised by sharply rising prices; ~-**Muster** bullish pattern ~-**Phase** bull market phase, bull run, *(sich in einer längerfristigen ~ befinden)* to be in a longer-term bull track; ~-**Position** bull account (position)

Hausse / ~-**Spekulant** → Haussier; ~-**Spekulation** speculation for a rise, buying long; ~-**Spread** bull spread, *(mit Kauf-/Verkaufsoptionen)* bull call/bull put spread; ~-**Stimmung** bullish sentiment, bullishness, *(den Aktienmarkt in ~ versetzen)* to trigger off a bull run in equities

Haussier bull, bull operator, bullish player (market operator)

haussieren to rise sharply, to rocket, to soar

Hausüberweisungsverkehr *(einer Filialbank)* intrabank (intragroup) transmission services

HBG → Hypothekenbankgesetz

HBV → Hausbankverfahren

HDAX German share index □ composed of the shares of all 110 companies from the → DAX, → MDAX and → TecDAX

Hebel lever; ~**produkte** leveraged products; ~**wirkung** leverage, leverage effect

heben *(stille Reserven ~)* to unlock (to realise) hidden reserves, *(die Stim-*

H

mung am Aktienmarkt ~) to lift stock market sentiment

Hedge / ~-**Effizienz** hedging efficiency; ~-**Faktor** hedge ratio; ~-**Fonds** hedge fund, → Dach-Hedgefonds; ~-**Geschäft** hedge (hedging) transaction; ~-**Kosten** hedge cost, cost of hedging

heftig 1. *(adj.) (~e Kursausschläge)* erratic price swings, *(~er Preiswettbewerb)* fierce price competition 2. *(adv.) (~ kritisieren)* to be fiercely critical of

heilen *(einen Mangel ~)* to remedy (to redress) a defect

H

Heimatland-Prinzip *(Prinzip der Heimatlandkontrolle/aufsicht)* principle of home country control (supervision) □ principle according to which internationally operating banks are subject to home country supervision

Heimfall 1. reconveyance (of property), retransfer (of a building lease to the owner)
2. *(~ von Vermögenswerten an den Staat)* reversion of property to the state, escheat

Heimfall / ~**anspruch** reconveyance (reversionary) claim; ~**klausel** reconveyance (reversionary) clause; ~**recht** right of reconveyance (of reversion), reversionary interest

heimfallen to revert (to the previous owner/to the state)

hektisch *(~e Käufe)* frenzied (frantic) buying, *(~e Kursausschläge)* erratic price swings

hemmen 1. to hamper, to impede, to obstruct, to block, *(die Emissionstätigkeit ~)* to constrain bond issuance, *(Fortschritte ~)* to hamper (to hold back, to block) progress
2. *(unterbrechen)* to interrupt, to suspend, *(die Verjährungsfrist ~)* to suspend the statute of limitations, to stretch the limitation period

hemmende Einrede dilatory plea

Hemmnis impediment, hindrance, obstacle

Hemmschuh *(~ für die Konjunktur)* drag on the economy, *(als ~ wirken)* to act as a brake

Hemmung obstruction, impeding, blocking, *(~ der Verjährungsfrist)* suspension of the statute of limitations

herabkonvertieren to lower the coupon rate through a bond conversion

herabsetzen 1. *(verringern)* to lower, to reduce, to cut back, to bring down 2. *(das Kapital ~)* to reduce (to write down) the capital 3. *(die Leistung ~)* to belittle (to run down) the achievement

Herabsetzung 1. lowering, reduction, cutback 2. write-down, writing down 3. belittling

Herabsetzungsverhältnis *(bei einem Kapitalschnitt)* write-down ratio

herabstufen *(bonitätsmäßig)* to downgrade, to lower the rating

Herabstufung downgrading, *(~ um eine Stufe)* one notch downgrade

herannahen *(der ~de Steuertermin)* the approaching (imminent) tax payment date

heranreichen *(an das Ergebnis des Vorjahres ~)* to come near last year's performance

heranziehen 1. to call on (upon), *(die Aktionäre ~)* to call upon the shareholders
2. *(ausbilden)* to train, *(als Nachfolger ~)* to raise (to train) as successor
3. *(konsultieren)* to consult
4. *(nutzen)* to call on, to use, to avail o. s. of, *(Daten ~)* to draw on data from, *(Garantien mit 20 % ~) (im Rahmen der Adressengewichtung)* to count guarantees at 20 % of their value, *(die neuesten Wirtschaftsdaten ~)* to call on the latest economic figures

heraufkonvertieren to raise the coupon rate through a bond conversion

heraufsetzen to increase, to lift, to raise, to mark up, *(die Provisionssätze ~)* to put commission rates up

Heraufsetzung *(~ der Leitzinsen)* increase in (lifting) key lending rates

herausbilden *(die Usance hat sich im Verlauf mehrerer Jahre herausgebildet)* the practice has evolved (developed) over a number of years

herausbringen *(ein neues Produkt ~)* to come out with (to launch, to bring out) a new product

herausfinden 1. to discover, to find out **2.** *(aus den finanziellen Engpässen ~)* to find a way out of the financial straits

herausfordern 1. to challenge **2.** to provoke

Herausgabe 1. *(Aushändigung)* delivery, surrender, *(die ~ des Sicherungsgutes verlangen)* to claim surrender of the collateral
2. *(Rückgabe)* restitution, return, *(Klage auf ~)* action for restitution, replevin action
3. *(Veröffentlichung)* publication

Herausgabe / ~anspruch restitution (surrender) claim, right to restitution of property, right to repossess property; **~pflicht** duty to restitute; **~vollstreckung** execution of a writ of restitution

herausgeben 1. *(aushändigen)* to surrender, to deliver **2.** *(veröffentlichen)* to publish **3.** *(zurückgeben)* to return, to restitute

heraushalten *(aus der Bilanz ~)* to keep off the balance sheet (off the books)

herausholen 1. to get **2.** *(einen Gewinn ~)* to extract (to make) a profit **3.** *(einen höheren Preis ~)* to wrest a higher price from

herauskristallisieren *(sich ~)* to take shape

herauslegen *(einen Kredit ~)* to extend (to grant) a loan

Herauslegung extension, granting

herausragen to stand out, *(bei lebhaftem Geschäft ~)* to stand out in brisk trading, *(Finanzwerte ragten mit einem deutlichen Kurssprung heraus)* financials stood out (featured) with a sharp rise

herausragend *(~e Eigenschaft)* distinguishing feature, *(~es Ergebnis)* salient (splendid) performance, *(~er Punkt) (in der Unternehmensentwicklung)* milestone

herausrechnen to deduct, *(die Personalkosten ~)* to segregate staff expenditure

herausstellen *(das Ergebnis des letzten Jahres ~)* to highlight (to feature) last year's performance

herbeiführen *(eine Wende ~)* to bring about a turnaround

hereinholen 1. *(Aufträge ~)* to win (to solicit) orders
2. *(bereits abgeschriebene Kreditforderungen wieder ~)* to recover loans already charged off
3. *(Verluste wieder ~)* to recoup losses

Hereinnahme accepting, acceptance, taking on, *(~ in den eigenen Bestand)* warehousing, taking on one's own books, *(~ von Einlagen)* deposit-taking, taking (taking in) deposits, *(~ eines neuen Gesellschafters)* taking on a new partner
(~ zum Inkasso) taking (accepting) for collection, *(~ einer Sicherheit)* acceptance of a security, *(bei ~ des Schecks)* upon acceptance of (when accepting) the cheque

Hereinnahmesatz rate paid, purchase (discounting) rate

hereinnehmen 1. to accept, to take in (on), *(zum Inkasso ~)* to accept for collection, *(hereingenommene Dividendenscheine/Wechsel)* coupons accepted for encashment/bills accepted for discount, *(hereingenommene befristete Mittel)* term funds taken in, term funds taken on deposit
2. to book, *(Kaufaufträge in Höhe von 5 Mio. € wurden im vergangenen Monat hereingenommen)* buying orders worth €5m were booked last month
3. to warehouse, *(~ in den eigenen Bestand)* to warehouse, to inventory

H

Hergabe **1.** delivery, handing over, *(~ von Eigenkapital)* provision of capital (equity) **2.** *(Leihe)* lending

herkömmlich *(~e Finanzierungsinstrumente)* traditional (established, conventional) funding instruments, *(~ e Option)* plain vanilla option

Herkunfts / ~ nachweis/~zeugnis certificate of origin; **~staat** *(EU-Aufsichtsrecht)* home member state; **~ staatsprinzip** home member state doctrine, home country principle, → Heimatlandprinzip

herleiten to derive, to infer, to deduce, *(einen Anspruch auf Zahlung ~)* to derive a claim to payment

H

Hermes Hermes □ Germany's export credit insurance agency

Hermes-Deckung/-Garantie Hermes cover, government export credit guarantee, *(Hermes-gedeckte Exportfinanzierung)* Hermes-covered (Hermes-backed) export financing

herrschen **1.** to dominate, to control, to rule **2.** *(vorherrschen)* to prevail

herrschendes Grundstück dominant tenement, land that profits from an easement, → dienendes Grundstück

herrschendes Unternehmen controlling company

herrühren to stem from, to emanate from, to be attributable to

herstellen **1.** *(fertigen)* to manufacture, to produce **2.** *(Geschäftsbeziehungen ~)* to establish (to open) business relations

Hersteller manufacturer, producer; **~marke** producer brand, manufacturer's brand

Herstellung **1.** manufacture, production **2.** establishment, opening

Herstellungs / ~kosten cost of production, manufacturing cost(s), *(im Gewinnausweis)* cost of goods sold; **~verfahren** manufacturing process

herunterbrechen to break down *(die vorgegebenen Limits ~)* to subdivide the limits set

herunterfahren **1.** to shut down **2.** *(die Erwartungen ~)* to scale down expectations

herunterhandeln **1.** *(einen Preis ~)* to beat down a price **2.** *(... € vom geforderten Preis ~)* to lop € ... off the asking price

herunterschleusen *(die Produktion ~)* to scale down production, to bring production into line with the order book, *(die Zinssätze ~)* to cut down interest rates

herunterschrauben *(Forderungen ~)* to moderate (to scale down) demands

herunterschreiben *(das Aktienkapital ~)* to write down the share capital

heruntersetzen *(die Kreditzinsen ~)* to lower (to reduce) lending rates

herunterspielen *(die mögliche Zahlungsunfähigkeit ~)* to play down the threat of insolvency

hervorbringen to produce, to bring forth, to launch, *(innovative Produkte ~)* to spawn innovative products

hervorgehen **1.** to show, to prove, *(aus der Kreditakte geht hervor)* the loan file shows, it appears from the loan file **2.** *(sich ergeben aus)* to arise (to result) from

hervorheben **1.** to emphasise, to underline **2.** to distinguish, *(hervorgehobener Hinweis)* highlighted reference

hervorragend *(~es Geschäftsergebnis)* excellent (splendid, outstanding) business performance

hervorrufen to cause, to trigger, to bring about, to provoke

heute gültig *(Börsenauftrag)* good this day □ buy or sell order valid for one day only

Hexen-Sabbat *(an der Terminbörse)* witches' hour, triple witching day

HGB-Abschluss financial statements prepared in accordance with the German Commercial Code

hier abtrennen *(Kupons)* tear along this line

Hierarchiestufe level of authority

hierarchisch *(~ e Eskalation)* hierarchical (vertical) escalation

Hilfe *(dem Unternehmen zu ~ kommen)* to come to the company's rescue

Hilfsgeschäfte ancillary business

hinaufgehen 1. *(im Kurs/Preis ~)* to rise, to climb, to advance **2.** *(den Preis erhöhen)* to put up the price

hinaufschnellen *(von Kursen/Preisen)* to soar, to climb sharply, to zoom

hinaufschrauben *(Forderungen ~)* to step up demands

hinaufsetzen *(den Preis ~)* to increase (to raise, to lift, to put up) the price

hinauftreiben *(die Aktienkurse ~)* to force up (to push up) equity prices, to send stock prices higher

hinausgehen *(über seine Kreditkompetenz ~)* to exceed (to go beyond) one's loan approval powers

hinauslegen *(ein Aval ~)* to furnish a guarantee, *(ein Dokumentenakkreditiv ~)* to open (to issue) a documentary credit, *(einen Kredit ~)* to grant (to extend) a credit

hinausreichen → hinauslegen

hinausschieben to defer, to postpone, to put off, to shelve, *(hinausgeschobene Zahlung)* deferred payment

hinausschießen *(über ein Ziel ~)* to overshoot a target

hinausziehen *(eine Entscheidung über die Finanzierung ~)* to protract a decision on the funding

hinauszögern to delay, to stall, → hinausziehen

hindern 1. to hamper, to hinder **2.** *(~ an)* to prevent from, to debar (e.g. from concluding a contract)

Hindernis obstacle, hindrance, impediment, stumbling block, *(~ für eine deutliche Erholung)* obstacle to a significant recovery, *(~ für die Vertragserfüllung)* impediment to contract performance, *(~ für einen weiteren Rückgang der Zinssätze)* hindrance (impediment) to a further downturn in interest rates, *(~se in den Weg legen)* to put obstacles in the way of, *(auf ~se stoßen)* to encounter difficulties

hindeuten to point to, to signal, to herald, *(alle Anzeichen deuten darauf hin)* all the signs are, *(auf steigende Zinsen ~)* to point to rising interest rates

hineinschlittern *(in eine Rezession ~)* to slip towards (to drift into) a recession

hineinziehen 1. *(in die Krise des Unternehmens ~)* to drag into the company's crisis **2.** *(in die Krise hineingezogen werden)* to become embroiled (involved) in the crisis

hinfällig 1. *(abgelaufen)* lapsed, expired **2.** *(ungültig)* invalid, void

hinhalten *(die Gläubiger ~)* to put the creditors off, to keep the creditors waiting

hinkend *(~es Inhaberpapier)* qualified bearer certificate □ i.e. a financial institution has the right but not the obligation to make payments to the presenter of the instrument

hinnehmen *(eine Kontoüberziehung ~)* to tolerate (to accept) an overdraft

hinreichend 1. *(genügend)* sufficient, adequate **2.** *(reichlich)* ample

hinschleppen to drag on, *(sich ~de Verhandlungen)* long-drawn-out (protracted) negotiations

Hintergrund *(vor dem ~ einer schwächeren Konjunktur)* against the background (backdrop) of a weaker economic environment, *(in den ~ treten)* to recede into the background, to become insignificant

Hintergrundinformationen background information, background brief (notes)

hinterherhinken 1. *(der Indexentwicklung ~)* to lag behind the performance of the index **2.** *(in einem Wettbewerb)* to trail behind **3.** *(mit seinen Zahlungen ~)* to be behind with one's payments

hinterherschicken *(eine weitere Emission ~)* to follow up with another issue

hinterlassen *(vererben)* to leave, to bequeath

Hinterlassenschaft estate, bequest, property left (bequeathed)

hinterlegen 1. to deposit, to lodge, to place, to surrender, *(auf einem Anderkonto ~)* to place (to put) into an escrow account, *(bei einer Bank ~)* to deposit at a bank, to lodge with a bank, *(als Sicherheit ~)* to deposit (to post) as collateral (security), *(durch den Schuldner hinterlegte Sicherheit)* borrower-posted collateral
2. *(einen Bericht ~)* to file a report
3. *(in Verwahrung geben)* to lodge for safekeeping, to commit to safe custody, *(Wertpapiere bei einer Bank ~)* to deposit shares with a bank, to place shares into safe custody with a bank

H

Hinterleger depositor

Hinterlegung deposit, lodgement, placement, filing, *(~ der Eigentumsurkunden)* deposit (deposition) of the title deeds, *(~ einer Sicherheit)* deposit of collateral (security)

Hinterlegungs / ~bestätigung/~schein deposit (custody) receipt; **~stelle** depository, depositary (lodging) agent, custodian; **~tag** date (day) of deposit; **~vertrag** deposit (safekeeping, custody) agreement

Hintermann subsequent endorser

Hintertreffen *(am Markt ins ~ geraten)* to fall behind in the market

hinterziehen to embezzle, to defraud

hinweghelfen *(über die gegenwärtigen Liquiditätsschwierigkeiten ~)* to tide over the current liquidity squeeze

hinwegtäuschen *(~ über die tatsächliche finanzielle Lage)* to obscure (to gloss over) the real financial situation

Hinweis 1. information, notice
2. *(Anzeichen)* indication, clue, signal, *(einen deutlichen ~ geben)* to send a strong signal
3. *(Empfehlung)* advice, recommendation, hint
4. *(Verweis)* reference

hinweisen 1. *(~ auf)* to point to **2.** *(ankündigen)* to signal, *(auf eine Zinserhöhung ~)* to signal (to herald) a rise in interest rates **3.** *(jmd. aufmerksam machen)* to draw s. o.'s attention to, to alert s. o. to **4.** *(verweisen auf)* to refer to

hinziehen to drag on, *(die Gespräche haben sich hingezogen)* the talks have dragged on

hinzufügen/hinzuschlagen *(Zinsen dem Kapital ~)* to add interest accrued to the principal, to roll up interest accrued

hinzurechenbar *(dem Kernkapital ~)* eligible for inclusion in Tier 1 capital

hinzurechnen to add (back), to include, *(Instrumente, die dem Kernkapital nicht hinzugerechnet werden können)* instruments that do not meet the criteria for inclusion in Tier 1 capital

Hinzurechnung inclusion, add-back, addition, *(steuerliche ~)* tax addition

Hinzurechnungsbesteuerung add-back taxation, taxation of foreign-sourced income, German CFC (controlled foreign companies) rules

Hinzurechnungssatz addback rate

hinzuziehen to consult, *(ein Beratungsunternehmen ~)* to call in consultants

Historie track record

historisch 1. *adj.* *(~er Anschaffungswert)* historical cost, *(~e Ausfallquote)* historical loss experience, historical default rate, *(~er Erfahrungswert)* historical experience, *(~es Schlusshoch)* all-time closing high, *(~e Simulation)* historical simulation
adv. *(~ gesehen)* by historical standards

Hoch *(~s und Tiefs des Aktienmarktes)* ups and downs of the equity market

Hochfrequenzhandel algorithmic trading, high frequency trading

hochgesteckt *(~e Erwartungen)* high hopes, *(~es Wachstumsziel)* high-pitched growth target

hochhalten to keep (to maintain) at a high level, *(den Kurs künstlich ~)* to support (to peg) the price

hochkapitalisiert *(~es Unternehmen)* highly capitalised company

hochkarätig *(~es Finanzberater-Team)* high-powered team of financial experts

Hochkonjunktur economic boom, high level of economic activity

Hochkuponpapiere high-coupon (high-interest) securities

hochliquid *(~e Anlagen)* highly liquid assets, *(~er Markt)* highly liquid market, *(~e Sicherheit)* highly liquid collateral

Hochprägung embossing □ printing raised letters or logos on a plastic card, *(hochgeprägte Karte)* embossed card, *(hochgeprägte Zeichen/Buchstaben)* embossed (raised) characters/letters

Hochprozenter high-coupon bond

hochrechnen *(für das Gesamtjahr ~)* to project for the year as a whole

hochrentierliche Anleihen high-yield bonds

hochreden *(den Kurs ~)* to talk the price higher

hochschätzen to esteem (to appreciate) highly, *(hochgeschätzter Kunde)* highly valued (esteemed) customer

hochschnellen to soar, to rocket, to rise suddenly and sharply

Höchstbetrag maximum amount, limit

Höchstbetragsbürgschaft fixed liability surety bond, surety bond with a preset maximum liability □ the guarantor's liability is limited to the amount guaranteed plus interest and charges

Höchstbetragshypothek fixed liability mortgage □ the liability under the mortgage is limited to the debt recorded in the land register plus interest and charges

Höchst / ~bietender highest bidder; **~bindungsfrist** maximum fixed rate period; **~ entschädigung/~entschädigungsleistung** maximum indemnity payment; **~ertrag** maximum return

Höchst / ~gebot highest bid; **~grenze** upper limit, ceiling, cap, *(Höchstgrenze für Einzelkredite)* limit for exposures to a single client, single exposure ceiling; **~kurs** high, highest price, peak price (rate); **~preisverordnung** ceiling price regulations

höchstrangig *(~e Tranche)* most senior tranche

Höchststand highest level, all-time high, *(einen ~ erreichen)* to peak, *(auf einen neuen ~ klettern)* to surge to a new high

Höchst / ~stimmrecht maximum voting power; **~zins** maximum rate of interest, cap rate; **~zinsvereinbarung** cap agreement

hochtreiben *(Kurs, Preis)* to force up, to push up

hochverschuldet highly (deeply) indebted, *(~es Unternehmen)* debt-ridden company

Höchstverschuldungsquote **1.** maximum debt ratio, maximum leverage **2.** *(under* → Basel III rules) leverage ratio □ ratio of Tier 1 capital to total assets plus off-balance sheet exposures; current proposals would limit banks to lending 33 times their capital; → Mindestliquiditätsquote

hochverzinslich *(~e Anleihe)* high-coupon bond, *(~es Konto)* high-interest account, *(~e Titel)* high-interest securities, high yielders

hochvolatil *(~er Index)* high-volatility index, *(~e gewerbliche Realkredite) (Basel II)* High-Volatility Commercial Real Estate

hochwertig *(~e Anlagen)* high-quality (high-grade) investments

Hochzins / ~anleihe high-yield bond; **~periode(~phase)** period of high interest rates; **~politik** high interest rate

H

policy, dear-money policy; ~**währung** high interest rate currency

Hoffnung *(~en auf eine anhaltende Erholung)* hopes (prospects) for a sustainable recovery

Hoffnungsschimmer glimmer (ray) of hope

hoh *(~e Auflagen)* onerous clauses, *(~er Investitionsaufwand)* heavy investment spending, *(~e Kreditaufnahme)* heavy borrowing, *(~e Rückstellungen)* steep provisions, *(~e Schuldenlast)* high debt burden, pile of debt, high level of borrowing, *(Gesellschaft mit einer ~en Schuldenlast)* debt-laden company, *(~e Umsatztätigkeit)* high level of dealing activity

H

Höhe 1. height **2.** *(Stand)* level **3.** *(Umfang)* extent, degree, *(~der Entschädigungszahlung)* amount of damages, *(sich umsatzmäßig auf gleicher ~ befinden)* to run equal (to run level) in terms of turnover, *(Importe in ~ von … Mio. €)* imports worth (imports to the tune of) € …m, *(in die ~ schießen)* to soar, to zoom, to shoot up, *(die restriktiven Maßnahmen könnten die Zinssätze weiter in die ~ treiben)* the restrictive measures could well push the interest rates further up

hoheitlich *(~er Emittent/Schuldner)* sovereign issuer/borrower

Hoheitsrisiko sovereign risk

Höhenflug *(die Aktienkurse setzten ihren ~ weiter fort)* equity prices continued on their record-breaking run

Höhepunkt height, *(den ~ der Bemühungen markieren)* to mark (to represent) the culmination of efforts to, *(der ~ der Hausse ist überschritten)* the bull market has topped out *(~ einer Verkaufswelle)* panic bottom, *(der ~ der Währungskrise)* the height (apogee) of the currency crisis, *(der Zinsauftrieb erreichte seinen ~ in …)* the upsurge in interest rates peaked (culminated) in …

höher *(~e Gewalt)* Act of God, force majeure, *(~e Instanz) (a)* higher authority *(b) (Gericht)* higher (superior) court *(~ bewerten) (a)* to increase in value, to revalue *(b) (bonitätsmäßig)* to rate higher, to upgrade, *(~ bieten)* to make a higher bid, to outbid, *(~ notieren)* to trade higher, to mark up, *(~ rentierliche Anleihen)* higher-yielding bonds, *(~ verzinsliche Anlagen)* investments offering a higher (better) interest rate

Höherbewertung *(~ des Dollar)* appreciation (higher valuation) of the dollar, *(~ eines Wertpapiers) (a) (bonitätsmäßig)* upgrading of a security, debt upgrading *(b)* trading a security at a higher price

Höher / ~bewertungspotenzial 1. revaluation (appreciation) potential **2.** upgrading potential, ~**einstufung** *(bonitätsmäßig)* upgrading; ~ **notierung** uptick; ~**verzinsung** paying a higher interest rate

Holding-Gesellschaft holding company

Holgeld borrowed funds, borrowings

holländische Auktion Dutch auction, descending-price auction □ an auction in which the price is continuously lowered until one of the auction participants responds

holländisches Zuteilungsverfahren → Zinstender *(holländisches Zuteilungsverfahren)*

Honorar fee, remuneration; ~**basis** *(auf ~)* on a fee basis

Honorarberatung fee-based counselling (advisory)

honorieren 1. *(Dokumente, Wechsel, Schecks)* to honour, to pay, to meet **2.** to reward

Honorierung 1. honouring, payment **2.** reward, remuneration

horizontal *(~e Portfolio-Diversifikation)* horizontal portfolio diversification, diversification limited to the same asset class, *(~er Spread)* horizontal spread, time (calendar) spread □ involving call and put options of the same type with the same strike price, but different expiration dates

HRG → Hauptrefinanzierungeschäft

HR-Kennzahlen human resource (HR) metrics

HtM-Vermögenswerte *(bis zur Endfälligkeit gehaltene Vermögenswerte)* held-to-maturity assets

Huckepack-Verfahren piggybacking

Humankapital / **~bewertung** human capital assessment; **~vermögen** human capital resources

Hunderter-Einheit *(Börsenhandel)* round lot

hundertprozentig *(~e Rückzahlung bei Fälligkeit)* 100 % repayment upon maturity

Hürde hurdle, obstacle

Hut *(unterschiedliche Standpunkte unter einen ~ bringen)* to reconcile opposing stances

hybrid *(~e Finanzierungsinstrumente)* hybrids, hybrid financing instruments, → Hybridkapital, *(~e Wertpapiere)* hybrid securities

Hybridanleihen hybrid bonds □ high-yielding subordinated securities that combine features of traditional debt securities and equities

Hybridderivate hybrid derivatives □ combining risks and features from different instruments and/or markets

Hybridfonds hybrid fund □ denotes a type of balanced fund where the fund managers change the mix of assets at their discretion

Hybridkapital hybrid capital □ hybrid of debt and equity capital

Hybridterminal hybrid terminal □ terminal accepting both magnetic stripe cards and chip cards

Hyperinflation hyperinflation, runaway inflation

Hypothek mortgage □ differs from the → Grundschuld in that it is accessory to the existence of a claim

Hypothek *(~ mit fester Verzinsung)* fixed rate mortgage, *(~ mit fünfjähriger Zinsfestschreibung)* mortgage carrying a fixed interest rate for five years, *(~ mit variabler Verzinsung)* variable rate mortgage, floating rate mortgage

hypothekarisch 1. *adj.* *(~e Belastung)* mortgage charge, *(~e Beleihung)* mortgage lending, lending against mortgages, *(~e Haftung)* mortgage liability, *(~e Rechte)* mortgage rights, *(~e Sicherheit)* mortgage collateral, security by way of mortgage, *(~e Verschuldung)* mortgage indebtedness
2. *adv.* *(~ belasteter Grundbesitz)* mortgaged property, *(~ gedeckte Wertpapiere)* mortgage-backed securities, *(~ gesicherte Forderungen)* mortgage-backed claims (receivables), *(~ gesicherte Schuldverschreibung)* mortgage-secured note

Hypothekarkredit mortgage loan, real estate loan, *(~e auf Wohngrundstücke)* residential mortgage loans

Hypothekarkredit / **~geber** mortgage lender; **~geschäft** mortgage lending business, mortgage banking; **~gewährung** granting of a mortgage loan

Hypotheken / **~ablösung** mortgage discharge (retirement), mortgage redemption (repayment), satisfaction of mortgage; **~antrag** mortgage application; **~aufnahme** taking out a mortgage

Hypotheken / **~ausfall** mortgage default (loss); **~ausfälle** defaulted mortgage loans; **~ausfallrate** mortgage default rate; **~auszahlung** disbursement of a mortgage loan, *(Hypothekenauszahlung erfolgt auf Konto ...)* the mortgage proceeds will be credited to account ...

Hypothekenbank mortgage bank, mortgage credit institution, mortgage lending institution; **~geschäft** mortgage banking operations; **~gesetz** German Mortgage Bank Act; **~sektor** mortgage banking sector

Hypotheken / ~**bedienung** mortgage servicing, servicing a mortgage loan, principal and interest payments on a mortgage; ~**bedingungen** mortgage terms; ~**belastung** mortgage encumbrance (charge); ~**bestand** *(eines Kreditinstitutes)* mortgage loan portfolio

Hypotheken / ~**bestellung** taking out a mortgage, mortgage creation; ~**bestellungsurkunde** mortgage deed; ~**brief** mortgage certificate, charge certificate; ~**briefausstellung** issuance of a mortgage certificate

Hypotheken / ~**damnum** mortgage discount; ~**darlehen** mortgage loan; ~ **deckungsmasse** mortgage cover pool; ~**derivate** derivative mortgage products; ~**durchlaufkredit** pass-through mortgage loan; ~**eintragung** mortgage registration (recording)

Hypotheken / ~**fälligkeit** mortgage maturity, mortgage due date; ~**finanzierung** mortgage financing; ~**forderung** 1. mortgage claim 2. *(Plural)* mortgage lendings, mortgage loans outstanding, mortgage receivables

Hypotheken / ~**gelder** mortgage funds; ~**geschäft** mortgage lending business (operations); ~**gewinnabgabe** mortgage levy; ~**gläubiger** mortgage creditor, mortgagee, creditor on mortgage

Hypotheken / ~**haftung** liability under the mortgage; ~**kapital** mortgage equity; ~**konditionen** 1. mortgage loan terms 2. mortgage rates; ~**kosten** mortgage (borrowing) cost

Hypothekenkredit mortgage loan, real estate loan, mortgage advance (credit), mortgage borrowing

Hypothekenkredit / ~**aufnahme** mortgage borrowing, *(Begrenzung der ~)* mortgage squeeze; ~**geschäft** mortgage lending business; ~**gewährung** extending a mortgage loan, mortgage loan accommodation; ~**nachfrage** demand for mortgage credit

Hypothekenkredit / ~**portefeuille** mortgage loan portfolio, mortgage book; ~**summe** mortgage loan principal; ~**versicherung** mortgage protection insurance, mortgage guarantee insurance; ~**volumen** mortgage loan portfolio (loan book); ~**zusage** mortgage loan undertaking

Hypotheken / ~**kündigung** mortgage termination, calling in a mortgage for repayment; ~**laufzeit** mortgage term (period), mortgage maturity; ~**löschung** mortgage discharge, satisfaction (release) of mortgage, dismortgage, extinguishment of a mortgage; ~**löschungsbestätigung** satisfaction of mortgage certificate

Hypotheken / ~**makler** mortgage broker; ~**mittel** mortgage finance (funds); ~**nachfrage** demand for mortgage credit; ~**nebenkosten** incidental mortgage charges; ~**neugeschäft/neuzusagen** new mortgage lendings, new mortgage commitments

Hypothekenpfandbriefe Mortgage Pfandbriefe, Covered Mortgage Bonds □ Bonds issued by German mortgage banks to refinance their lendings against residential and commercial real estate

Hypotheken / ~**rang** mortgage rank; ~**rangordnung** ranking of mortgages, priority of mortgages; ~**rangstelle** mortgage rank; ~**refinanzierung** funding of mortgage loans

Hypotheken / ~**register** mortgage register, register of mortgages serving as cover for mortgage bonds issued; ~**restschuld** residual mortgage debt; ~**rückzahlung** mortgage repayment (redemption, retirement)

Hypotheken / ~**schuld** mortgage debt; ~**schuldner** mortgage debtor, mortgagor; ~**schuldverschreibung** collateral mortgage note

Hypotheken / ~**sicherheit** mortgage collateral (security); ~**sicherungsschein** mortgage coverage certificate □ insurer's confirmation that payments to the insured are subject to the mortgagee's approval; ~**summe** mortgage principal

Hypothekentilgung mortgage redemption (amortisation)

Hypothekentilgungs / ~**darlehen** amortising mortgage loan; ~**rate** mortgage amortisation rate; ~**versicherung** mortgage redemption insurance

Hypotheken / ~**übernahme** mortgage assumption; ~**übertragung** mortgage transfer (assignment); ~**urkunde** mortgage deed (certificate); ~**valuta** mortgage proceeds; ~**valutierung** disbursement of a mortgage loan

Hypotheken / ~**verbriefung** mortgage securitisation, securitisation of mortgage lendings; ~**verlängerung** mortgage extension; ~**verpfändung** mortgage pledge, charging a mortgage

Hypotheken / ~**verschuldung** mortgage indebtedness; ~**versicherung** mortgage protection (indemnity) insurance, mortgage protection policy; ~**vertrag** mortgage agreement (indenture)

Hypotheken / ~**verzug** mortgage default, failure to abide by the terms of the mortgage agreement, defaulting on a mortgage; ~**verwertung** mortgage realisation (liquidation); ~**volumen** mortgage portfolio (book); ~**vorrang** mortgage priority

Hypotheken / ~**zinsen** mortgage interest; ~**zinssatz** mortgage rate, mortgage lending rate; ~**zusage** mortgage loan undertaking, mortgage commitment, *(pl)* mortgage loan exposure (loan portfolio), aggregate mortgage lending, *(~ für den Wohnungsbau)* residential mortgage lendings

Hypotheken / ~**zusammenlegung** mortgage consolidation; ~**zwangsvollstreckung** mortgage foreclosure; ~**zwangvollstreckungskosten** mortgage foreclosure cost

hypothetisch *(~er Kapitalbetrag)* notional principal amount

I

idealtypisch *(~e Anleihe)* notional bond

Identifizierungspflicht identification duty, obligation to identify a customer

Identitätsnachweis *(einen ~ erbringen)* to furnish proof of identity

idiosynkratisch *(~e Risiken)* idiosyncratic (non-systematic) risks

I

IFRS International Financial Reporting Standards, *(Ansatz- und Bewertungsvorschriften nach ~)* IFRS recognition and measurement rules

illegal illegal, unlawful

Illegalität illegality, unlawfulness

illiquid 1. non-liquid, illiquid **2.** *(gesperrt)* frozen, blocked

Illiquidität illiquidity

Illiquiditätrisiko risk of illiquidity

imagegestützt *(~er Scheckeinzug/~es Scheckeinzugsverfahren)* image-based cheque collection/collection procedure, → belegloser Scheckeinzug

im Geld in-the-money □ an option is in-the-money when the market price of the underlying instrument is higher (for calls) or lower (for puts) than the strike price of the option, → aus dem Geld, → am Geld

Immaterialgüterrechte intellectual property rights

immateriell *(~e Anlagewerte)* intangible assets, intangibles, *(~e Einbußen)* non-material losses, losses of a non-pecuniary nature, *(~er Geschäftswert)* goodwill, *(~e Güter)* intangible goods, *(~e Kosten)* intangible (non-monetary) costs
(~er Schaden) immaterial damage (loss), non-material damage, *(~e Unterstützung) (a)* immaterial support *(b) (durch einen Investor)* smart money, *(~e Wirtschaftsgüter)* → immaterielle Anlagewerte

Immobiliar / ~kredit loan secured by a property charge; **~sicherheit** real estate collateral; **~sachenrecht** land law; **~vermögen** real estate assets; **~zwangsvollstreckung** execution against (levy upon) real estate

Immobilien real estate, real property, realty, *(~ des Finanzanlagenbestandes/ als Finanzinvestition gehaltene ~)* investment properties

Immobilien / ~abschreibungen property writedowns, impairments of real estate; **~ aktien** property company shares; **~aktiengesellschaft** property company (corporation), real estate company, Real Estate Investment Trust (REIT)

Immobilien / ~anlage 1. property (real estate) investment **2.** investing in real estate; **~anlageprodukt** real estate investment product; **~anleihe** real property bond

Immobilien / ~beleihung real estate lending, mortgage lending; **~beratung** real estate advisory services, property consultation; **~besitz** → Immobilienbestand/~eigentum; **~bestand** real property portfolio (holdings)

Immobilien / ~bewerter property valuer (appraiser); **~bewertung** property valuation, valuation of real estate, real estate appraisal; **~buch** real estate portfolio

Immobilien / ~darlehen mortgage loan, real estate loan, *(Forderungen aus ~)* mortgage loan receivables, *(Risiken aus gewerblichen ~)* commercial real estate loan exposure; ~**darlehensvertrag** mortgage loan agreement

Immobilienderivate real estate derivatives, property derivatives □ these index-based derivatives usually take the form of a real estate call/put option or total return swap, → Immobilien-Swap

Immobilienderivate / ~**handel** property derivatives trading, trading synthetic real estate; ~**kontrakt** property derivative contract

Immobilien / ~**eigentum** **1.** real estate ownership **2.** real estate owned, real property assets; ~**eigentümer** property owner, real estate owner; ~**erstfinanzierung** initial real property financing; ~**erträge** real property income; ~**erwerb** → Immobilienkauf

Immobilienfinanzierung real estate financing (funding), property finance

Immobilienfinanzierungs / ~**geschäft** property funding operations (activities); ~**kosten** property finance cost; ~**markt** property finance market

Immobilienfonds property fund, property unit trust, real estate investment fund; ~**anteil** property fund share

Immobilien / ~**geschäft** real estate activities (operations); ~**gesellschaft** real estate company (corporation), building and property company; ~**gewinne** real property gains, real property appreciation; ~**gutachter** property valuer, valuation surveyor, land valuer; ~**handel** real property business (sector, industry), real estate operations

Immobilien / ~**index** property index, *(für Gewerbeimmobilien)* commercial property index, *(für Wohnimmobilien)* residential property index; ~**indexderivate** property index derivatives, → Immobilienderivate; ~ **investment** real estate (property) investments; ~**investmentfonds** → Immobilienfonds

Immobilien / ~**kapitalgesellschaft** real estate corporation; ~**kauf** property purchase, purchase of real estate; ~**kredit** real estate loan; ~**kreditbestand** real estate loan portfolio (loan book)

Immobilien / ~-**Leasing** real estate financial leasing, property leasing; ~-**Leasingfonds** property leasing fund; ~**makler** real estate agent (broker), estate agent, realtor; ~**management** facilities management; ~**markt** property market, real estate market

Immobilien / ~**objekt** property; ~**ökonomie** real estate economics; ~-**Partizipationsanleihe** property bond with warrants attached; ~**personengesellschaft** real estate partnership

Immobilien / ~**pfändung** seizure of real property, property seizure; ~**portefeuille** real estate portfolio, property portfolio; ~**preise** property prices, real estate prices; ~**projektentwickler** property developer, real estate development (property development) company

Immobilien / ~**recht** real property law; ~**rechte** real property rights, rights inherent in real estate ownership; ~**rendite** return on property, yield on real estate; ~**risiken** real property risks (exposure)

Immobilien / ~**sachverständiger/schätzer** property valuer, real estate appraiser; ~**schätzung** real estate appraisal (valuation), expert appraisal of real estate; ~**schätzwert** property's appraised value; ~**sicherheit** real estate collateral, collateral in the form of real estate

Immobilien-Sondervermögen *(i. S. des Investmentgesetzes)* Real Property Fund, Real Estate Fund, → Sondervermögen

Immobilien-Spezialfonds special property fund

Immobilien-Swap real estate swap, property total return swap □ swap in which regular cash flows tied to a real estate price index are exchanged for cash flows based on a fixed or floating interest rate, → Immobilienderivate

Immobilienverbriefung real estate securitisation, property securitisation □ securitisation of real property assets as opposed to the securitisation of mortgage loan receivables, i.e. originators are real estate owners and not lending institutions

Immobilien / ~verkehr real property transactions (operations); **~vermögen** real property assets, real estate holdings; **~verwalter** property manager; **~verwaltung** property management; **~verzehrplan** home equity release plan; **~volumen** property portfolio, real estate holdings

I

Immobilien / ~wert real property value; **~werte 1.** real property assets **2.** *(Aktien von Immobiliengesellschaften)* property shares, properties; **~wertermittlung** property valuation, determining the value of a specific property

Immobilien / ~wirtschaft 1. real estate management, business property management **2.** real estate sector; **~zertifikat** property fund share; **~zweitmarktfonds** second real estate fund

Immobilisierung *(von Wertpapieren)* immobilisation of securities □ securities held by a securities depository at all times

immun *(~ gegen Marktschwankungen)* immune to market fluctuations

Immunisierung *(eines Portefeuilles)* immunisation of a portfolio, elimination of portfolio (market) risks

Imparitätsprinzip imparity principle □ mandatory recognition of expected losses

Implementierungsinstrumentarium tools for implementation, execution tools

implizit 1. *adj.* implicit, implied, *(~e Garantie/Gewährleistung)* implied guarantee (warranty), *(~e Option)* embedded option, *(~e Steuer)* implicit tax, *(~er Terminsatz)* implied forward rate, *(~e Volatilität)* implicit (expected) volatility, volatility implied in the price of a financial instrument **2.** *adv.* implicitly, by implication

Import import, importing; **~-Akkreditiv** import documentary credit; **~dokumenteninkasso** import documentary collection

Import / ~erstfinanzierung advance import finance facility □ short-term funds raised by a domestic bank abroad on behalf of the importer and directly placed at the exporter's disposal; **~factoring-Gesellschaft** import factor

Import / ~finanzierung import finance (financing); **~kommissionär** import agent; **~kredit** import financing (finance) facility; **~rechnung** import bill (accounts); **~sicherungsvertrag 1.** import security agreement **2.** assignment of imported goods

Import / ~vorschuss import facility, lending against imported goods; **~waren** imported goods; **~wechselinkasso** import documentary bill collection

Impuls stimulus, impetus, impellent, fillip, *(neue/zusätzliche ~e verleihen)* to give new impetus to, to give added stimulus to, *(dem stagnierenden Aktienmarkt neue ~e verleihen)* to reinvigorate (to liven up) the sluggish stock market

Inaktivität *(~ am Markt)* inactivity (inertness) in the market

Inangriffnahme starting on (with), *(~ der finanziellen Probleme)* tackling the financial problems

Inanspruchnahme 1. availment, use, usage, *(~ von Bankdienstleistungen)* availment of bank services, *(~ eines Kredites)* availment of a loan, *(vor einer weiteren ~ der Fazilität)* before making additional use of the facility, *(aktuelle Inanspruchnahme)* current outstandings
2. drawing, drawdown, *(~ eines Akkreditivs)* drawing(s) under a docu-

mentary credit, *(~ bis zur vereinbarten Höhe)* drawing up to the agreed limit, *(~ der Rücklagen)* drawing on the reserves, *(~ des Kredites über Konto ...)* drawdowns are to be effected against account No. ..., the loan is to be utilised against account No. ..., *(Zeitraum der ~)* drawdown period **3.** *(in Anspruch genommener Betrag)* amount drawn upon, *(die Zinsberechnung erfolgt auf die tatsächliche ~)* interest will be charged on the amount drawn upon (on the actual takedown) **4.** calling on, taking recourse to, tapping, *(~ aus einer Garantie)* call to pay up under a guarantee, enforcing a guarantee, *(~ des Garantiegebers)* calling upon the guarantor, *(~ des Kapitalmarktes)* call on the capital market, tapping the capital market, *(ohne ~ des Kapitalmarktes)* without resorting to (without tapping) the capital market, *(~ öffentlicher Mittel)* recourse to public funds, *(~ von Nachfristen)* recourse to grace periods **5.** *(Beanspruchung)* demands, strain

Inanspruchnahmeprovision utilisation fee, drawdown fee

Inaugenscheinnahme examination, inspection

inbegriffen including, inclusive of, *(Kosten ~)* costs (expenses) included

Inbesitznahme *(~ des Sicherungsgegenstandes)* taking possession of the collateral

Inbetriebnahme commencement of operations (of business), commissioning, putting into operation

Indeckungnahme providing cover, provision of cover, *(~ von Exportkrediten)* providing cover (providing guarantees) for export credits

Index index, average

Index / ~abbildung index tracking; **~aktualisierung** index updating, continuous updating of the index; **~anleihe** index (index-linked) bond; **~anpassung** index adjustment; **~arbitrage** index arbitrage; **~aufnahme** inclusion in the index, adding to the index; **~berechnung** index calculation (pricing); **~bereinigung** index adjustment

indexbezogen *(~e Transaktionen)* index-driven transactions, *(~e Verzinsung)* indexed interest payment

Indexbindung index-linking, indexing, indexation, *(~ des zurückzuzahlenden Kapitalbetrages)* capital indexing

Index-Derivate index derivatives □ index options, futures, warrants

Index-Differenzkontrakte / Index CFDs index contracts for difference, → Differenzkontrakt

indexfähig eligible for inclusion in the index

Index / ~fonds (exchange-traded) index fund; **~future** index future

indexgebunden *(~e Anleihe)* index-linked bond, indexed bond, *(~er Hypothekenzins)* index-linked mortgage rate

Index / ~gewichtung index weighting; **~gewinn** index gain, rise (increase) in index value; **~handel** index trading

indexieren to link (to tie) to an index, *(indexierte Verzinsung)* index-linked interest payment, index-linked coupon

Indexierung linking to an index, indexation

Index / ~kaufoption index call option; **~klausel** indexation (escalator) clause; **~korb** index basket, basket of underlying constituent securities;**~multiplikator** index multiplier

Index / ~nachbildung index tracking, replication of an index; **~notiz** index quotation (quote); **~option** index option; **~optionsschein** index warrant; **~portefeuille** index portfolio, portfolio of stocks identical or similar to those on which the underlying index is based

I

Index / ~stand index level, index value; **~streichung** dropping from the index, deletion of component stocks

Index-Swap index swap □ swap in which the return of an (equity) index is exchanged for cash flows based on the development of a short-term interest rate index

Index / ~terminhandel index futures trading; **~terminkontrakt** index futures contract; **~titel** → Indexwerte

Index / ~veränderungen 1. *(im Indexstand)* changes (movements) in the index level **2.** *(in der Indexzusammensetzung)* changes in index composition; **~verkaufsoption** index put option; **~verlust** index loss (decline); **~volatilität** index volatility

Index / ~währung index-based currency; **~wert** index value; **~werte** index components, index component (constituent) stocks, index (average) stocks, stocks included in the index, underlying constituent securities; **~zahl** index number; **~zertifikat** index certificate; **~zusammensetzung** index composition

indifferentes Geschäft non-lending and non-deposit transactions □ largely fee-related business, such as transmission of funds, custody operations, collections

indikativ *(~e Kursstellung)* indicative quote (quotation), quotation on a purely indicative basis

Indikator indicator, barometer, predictor

Indikatorqualität quality as an indicator

indirekt *(~es Aval)* indirect guarantee □ guarantee furnished by the bank on behalf of a customer through the agency of a second bank, *(~e Devisenarbitrage)* indirect (compound) arbitrage, *(~e Erlöse)* indirect earnings *(~es Hypothekengeschäft)* mortgage lending □ with the bank holding the title to land but not entering into its ownership, *(~e Kosten)* indirect cost, *(~e Notierung)* → same as Mengennotierung, *(~e Parität)* cross rate

Individual / ~abrede individual agreement; **~fonds** → Spezialfonds; **~haftung** personal liability; **~kunden** *(einer Bank)* high-income customers

Individual / ~portfolio individually managed portfolio; **~zahlungssystem** individual payment system; **~zahlungsverkehr** individual payments

individuell 1. *adj.* *(~e Anlageberatung)* personalised investment advice, *(~e Auftragsabwicklung)* individual (trade-for-trade) settlement, *(~e Bewertung)* evaluation on a case-by-case basis, *(~e Finanzierung)* customised financing, *(~e Konditionengestaltung)* individually negotiated terms and rates, tailoring the loan terms to the borrower's specific requirements *(~e Kundenbetreuung)* personal banking service, personal contact with the customer, customised relationship management, *(~e Vermögensverwaltung)* customised asset management, individual (private) portfolio management, investment management geared to the customer's specific investment objectives
2. *adv.* *(~ abgestimmt)* individually adjusted, *(~ ausgerichtet)* tailored to individual requirements, *(~ festlegen)* to fix on a case-by-case basis

Indiz *(~ für eine weitere Zinssenkung)* sign (indication) of a further cut in interest rates

indizierte Transaktionsnummer indexed transaction authentication number (iTAN)

Indossament endorsement

Indossamentenkette chain of endorsers

Indossaments / ~haftung liability on an endorsement; **~provision** endorsement commission; **~reihe** order of endorsers; **~verbindlichkeiten** *(aus weitergegebenen Wechseln)* endorsement liabilities from rediscounted bills

Indossant endorser

Indossatar endorsee

indossierbar endorsable, transferable by endorsement

indossieren to endorse

Indossierung endorsement

Industrie / ~adresse 1. *(am Emissionsmarkt)* industrial issuer **2.** *(Kreditnehmer)* industrial borrower; **~aktien** industrial equities (shares, stocks); **~aktienindex** industrial average, industrial stock index; **~anleihe** industrial (corporate) bond

Industrie / ~besitz industrial holdings; **~beteiligungen** industrial interests (investments, shareholdings), *(~ der Banken)* banks' industrial assets, banks' holdings in industry; **~beteiligungsgesellschaft** industrial holding company; **~betrieb** industrial undertaking

Industrie / ~clearing *(Geldhandel zwischen Industrieunternehmen)* intercompany money dealings; **~darlehen** capital investment loan; **~ emittent** industrial issuer; **~erzeugerpreise** industrial producer prices

Industrie / ~finanzierung industrial financing, financing of industrial projects; **~förderung** assistance to industry, industrial development; **~geldmarkt** corporate money market; **~güter** industrial goods; **~güterklassifizierung** industrial goods classification

Industrie / ~hypothek industrial mortgage; **~immobilien** industrial property, commercial and industrial real estate; **~immobilienrendite** return on industrial property

Industrie / ~kassamarkt cash market in industrial stocks; **~komplex** industrial complex (agglomeration); **~kredit** industrial loan (lending), business loan; **~kreditgeschäft** industrial (corporate) lending business; **~kreditnachfrage** corporate demand for credit

industriell *(~e Leistungserstellung)* industrial output, *(~er Realkredit)* industrial property loan

Industrie / ~schuldverschreibung industrial bond (note); **~unternehmung** industrial enterprise (undertaking, corporation); **~werte** industrials, industrial issues, *(führende Industriewerte)* blue chip industrials, top-quality industrials

inflationär *(~er Druck)* inflationary pressure, *(~e Konjunktur)* inflationary state of the economy, *(~er Preisauftrieb)* inflationary price upsurge

Inflationsangst dread of inflation, inflation jitters

inflationsbedingt *(~er Kreditbedarf)* inflation-fed (inflation-induced) borrowing requirements

inflationsbereinigt *(~e Erträge/Kapitalmarktrendite)* inflation-adjusted earnings/ capital market yield

Inflations / ~derivate inflation derivatives □ derivatives used to hedge inflation risks, → Inflationsswap; **~eindämmung** curb on inflation; **~erwartungsrate** expected inflation rate; **~gefälle** inflation differential

inflationsindexierte Anleihe linker, inflation-indexed bond

Inflations / ~rate inflation rate, *(Anziehen der ~)* pick-up in inflation; **~schub** inflationary push; **~schutz/~sicherung** hedge (protection) against inflation, inflation hedge, inflation backstop; **~spirale** inflationary spiral

Inflations-Swap inflation swap, inflation-linked swap □ swap in which regular cash flows linked to a price index are exchanged for cash flows based on a fixed or floating rate of interest, *(Option auf einen ~)* inflation swaption □ confers the right to enter into an inflation swap

Inflations / ~tempo inflationary pace, pace of inflation; **~ursachen** inflationary causes; **~verlangsamung** slowdown (deceleration) of (in) the inflation rate; ~**währung** inflationary currency; ~**wirkung** impact of inflation

inflatorisch *(~e Lücke)* inflationary gap, *(~es Preisgefälle)* inflationary price differential

Information 1. information, *(~en über den Kreditnehmer einholen)* to make inquiries about the borrower, to gather information on the borrower, *(~en über Verlustrisiken)* information on exposure to loss
2. *(Marktinformationen)* market intelligence (news)

Informations / ~**aufenthalt** fact-finding stay; ~**barrieren** information barriers, *(zur Verhinderung von Insidergeschäften/Interessenkonflikten)* Chinese Walls; ~**bedarf** information needs (requirements); ~**bereitstellungskette** information supply chain

Informations / ~**blatt** factsheet, handout; ~**bringschuld** obligation to provide (to disclose) information; ~**dienst** intelligence service; ~**fluss** flow of information; ~ **freiheitsgesetz** Freedom of Information Act; ~**funktion** information (informing) function

Informations / ~**gehalt** informational content; ~**gesuch** request for information; ~**gewinnung** obtaining (gathering) information; ~**güte** informational quality, quality of information (intelligence)

Informations / ~**inhalt** informational content; ~**material** informative material (literature), factsheet; ~**merkblatt** *(zu Risiken bei Termingeschäften)* risk disclosure statement; ~**pflicht** duty to inform (to notify), notification (disclosure) duty, *(~en des Kreditnehmers)* borrower's reporting covenants

Informations / ~**reise** fact-finding trip (mission); ~**sicherheit** information security; ~**system** information system; ~**verbreitung**/~**weitergabe** dissemination of information

informell *(~e Kreditzusage)* informal loan undertaking, informal commitment to lend

Infrastruktur infrastructure; ~**investitionen** investments in infrastructures; ~**kredit** infrastructure-financing loan; ~-**Sondervermögen** infrastructure fund, → Spezial-Sondervermögen, → Publikums-Sondervermögen

Ingangsetzung starting, putting into operation

Inhaber 1. *(Eigentümer)* owner, proprietor **2.** *(eines Kontos)* holder **3.** *(von Schecks, Wechseln, Wertpapieren)* bearer, holder, owner

Inhaber / ~**aktie** bearer share; ~**anleihe** bearer bond; ~**grundschuld** bearer land charge; ~**indossament** bearer endorsement; ~**klausel** bearer clause; ~**konnossement** bearer bill of lading

Inhaber / ~-**Optionsanleihe** bearer bond with warrants attached, bearer warrant issue; ~-**Optionsschein** bearer warrant; ~**papier** bearer instrument, *(verfügbar als ~)* available in bearer form

Inhaber / ~-**Sammeloptionsschein** global bearer warrant; ~-**Sammelschuldverschreibung** global bearer note; ~-**Sammelurkunde** global bearer certificate ; ~**scheck** bearer cheque; ~**schuldtitel** bearer debt instrument, bearer debt security; ~**schuldverschreibungen** bearer notes

Inhaber / ~**vorzugsaktien** bearer preference shares; ~**wechsel 1.** bearer bill **2.** *(Eigentümerwechsel)* change of (in) ownership; ~**zertifikat** bearer certificate

Inhalt contents, *(inhaltlicher Unterschied)* difference in content

Inhalte-Anbieter content provider

inhärent *(~e Vertretungsmacht)* inherent authority, *(Wertberichtigung für ~e Risiken)* valuation allowance for inherent risks (exposure)

initiieren to initiate, *(vom Kunden initierte Geschäfte)* customer-originated transactions

Inkasso *(~ von Forderungen)* collection of accounts receivable, debt collection, collecting debt, *(~ von Lastschriften)* direct debt collection, *(~ von Schecks/Kupons)* collection of cheques/coupons, *(~ unter dem üblichen Vorbehalt)* collection under the usual reserve, *(zum ~ hereinnehmen/übersenden/vorlegen)* to accept/to remit/to present for collection

Inkasso / **~abteilung** collection desk (unit, department); **~anweisungen** collection instructions; **~auftrag** collection order; **~bank** collecting banker; **~beauftragter** collection agent; **~bedingungen** terms of collection; **~befugnis** collection authority

Inkasso / **~benachrichtigung** advice of collection; **~büro** debt-collecting agency; **~einholungsauftrag 1.** collection authority **2.** remittance for collection; **~erlös** collection proceeds, *(Zession des ~es)* assignment of the collection proceeds

Inkasso / **~ermächtigung** collection authority; **~gebühren** collection charges; **~geschäft 1.** *(einzelnes)* collection transaction **2.** *(Gesamtheit)* collection business; **~indossament** collection endorsement; **~mandat** collection authority (mandate)

Inkasso / **~papiere** collection items; **~posten** item(s) in course of collection; **~provision** collection commission; **~risiko** collection risk, risk that documents of title are lost in the mail; **~scheck** cheque (remitted) for collection; **~spesen** collection charges; **~stelle 1.** collecting bank, collecting agency (agent) **2.** debt-collecting agency

Inkasso / **~tage** collection days; **~tarif** terms (rates) of collection; **~übergabe** transfer to a collection agency; **~verkehr** collections, collection operations; **~vollmacht** collection authority, power of collection (collecting)

Inkasso / **~währung** collection currency; **~wechsel** bill (remitted) for collection; **~weg** collection channel (route); **~zession** assignment for collection

Inkaufnahme accepting, putting up with

inklusiv *(~e Zinsen)* including interest, inclusive of interest

inkongruent mismatched, *(~ refinanziertes Kreditgeschäft)* lendings funded at mismatched maturities

Inkongruenz mismatch, *(~ der Laufzeiten)* mismatched maturities, mismatch of maturities, *(~ der Währungsposition)* mismatched currency position (exposure)

inkongruenzbereinigt adjusted for mismatches

Inkongruenzrisiko mismatch risk □ possible loss arising from differences, e.g. in the fixed rate periods of assets and liabilities or in the maturities of long and short positions

Inkraftsetzung putting into force (effect)

Inkrafttreten coming into force (effect), inception, *(Tag des ~s)* inception date, date of commencement, effective date, initiation date, *(zum Zeitpunkt des ~s dieses Vertrages)* at the time such agreement comes into efffect

Inkrafttretungsklausel operative clause

Inländer resident, national; **~konvertibilität** resident convertibility

Inlands / **~absatz** domestic sales, sales in the domestic market; **~anlagen** domestic investments; **~anleihe** domestic bond; **~aval** domestic guarantee

Inlands / **~bedarf** domestic (home) demand; **~beteiligungen** domestic investments (interests); **~geschäft** *(einer Bank)* domestic banking (operations); **~kreditgewährung** domestic lending

I

Inlands / ~**nachfrage** domestic (home) demand; ~**obligo** domestic exposure (liabilities); ~-**Rentenmarkt** domestic bond market; ~**valuta** domestic (national) currency; ~**vermögen** domestic assets; ~**verwahrung** safekeeping of securities at home

Inlands / ~**wechsel** domestic (inland) bill; ~**werte** domestic (home) securities; ~**zahlungsverkehr** domestic payments, domestic money transmission services, domestic funds transfer

innehaben *(ein Amt ~)* to hold an office, *(den Vorsitz ~)* to be in the chair, to preside over

Innen / ~**finanzierung** internal financing (funding), *(voll innenfinanziert)* fully funded from internal resources; ~**finanzierungsmittel** internal funding resources; ~ **provision** internal commission (fee payment)

Innen / ~**revision** in-house audit, internal audit (auditing function), *(Abteilung)* internal audit unit; ~**umsatzerlöse** internal sales; ~**verhältnis** internal relationship, *(im ~)* internally, inter se, between (among) themselves

innerer Wert **1.** net asset value **2.** *(einer Option)* intrinsic value □ amount by which an option is in the money, (→ im Geld)

innerbetrieblich *(~e Ausbildung)* in-house (internal) training, *(~e Lagerung)* in-plant warehousing, *(~er Verrechnungspreis)* internal transfer price

Innertages / ~**kredit** intraday credit, daylight credit (overdraft); ~**liquidität** intraday liquidity; ~-**Sollsalden** intraday debit positions; ~**überziehungen** intraday overdrafts

innewohnend *(das einer Anlage ~e Risiko)* risk inherent in an investment

Innovationsfreude propensity for innovation

innovativ *(~e Finanzierungsquellen)* non-traditional funding sources, *(~e Kreditpolitik)* innovative approach towards lending, innovative lending policy

Inpfandnahme *(~ von Aktien)* accepting stocks in pledge

Inrechnungstellung invoicing, billing

Insel / **Inselumkehrformation** island reversal pattern □ signals a trend reversal

Insider insider □ persons (directors, officers and/or employees of a company) with access to inside (non-public) information

Insider / ~**handel** insider trading (dealings); ~**handelsverbot** insider trading ban; ~**informationen** insider (inside) information, non-public information; ~**käufe** insider buying; ~**meldepflicht** notification duty with respect to directors' dealings

Insider / ~**papiere** insider securities; ~**überwachung** insider monitoring; ~**vergehen**/~**verstoß** insider offence; ~**verkäufe** insider selling; ~**verzeichnis** insider list □ list of persons with access to inside information

Insolvenz insolvency

Insolvenzanfechtung avoidance in insolvency, avoidance of post-petition transfers, insolvency transaction avoidance

Insolvenzanfechtungs / ~**klage** avoidance action; ~**risiko** risk of loss resulting from an insolvency transaction avoidance; ~**vorschriften** insolvency transaction avoidance rules

Insolvenz / ~**antrag** insolvency petition, *(einen ~ stellen)* to file (to petition) for insolvency; ~**antragspflicht** obligation (requirement) to file for insolvency; ~ **antragstellung** filing for insolvency

Insolvenz / ~**anzeige** insolvency notice; ~**auflage** insolvency restriction order

insolvenzbefangen *(~e Vermögenswerte)* assets forming part of the insolvency estate, assets subject to insolvency proceedings

Insolvenz / ~beschlag seizure; **~bilanz** debtor's statement of affairs; **~delikt** insolvency offence; **~dividende** insolvency distribution rate; **~eröffnung** opening (commencement) of insolvency proceedings, commencement of administration; **~eröffnungsbeschluss** receiving (receivership) order

Insolvenzferne insolvency remoteness, *(insolvenzferne rechtliche Einheit)* insolvency-remote legal entity

Insolvenzfestigkeit insolvency-proof character, *(insolvenzfeste Übertragung von Vermögenswerten)* insolvency-proof (insolvency-resistant) transfer of assets

Insolvenzforderungen claims (debt) provable in insolvency, claims against the insolvency estate

insolvenzfrei *(~es Vermögen)* insolvency assets exempt from seizure

insolvenzgefährdet *(~es Unternehmen)* company threatened with insolvency

Insolvenz / ~geld insolvency benefits; **~gericht** Insolvency Court; **~gläubiger** insolvency creditors □ holding claims that arose prior to the opening of insolvency proceedings. → Masseansprüche/Massegläubiger

Insolvenz / ~gründe grounds for an insolvency petition; **~hauptverfahren** main insolvency proceedings □ proceedings in the main jurisdiction (centre of main interest); **~masse** insolvency estate (assets)

Insolvenz / ~ordnung German Insolvency Statute; **~plan** insolvency plan; **~planverfahren** insolvency plan proceedings □ aims at restructuring the insolvent company; **~quote** dividend (distribution rate) in insolvency proceedings

Insolvenz / ~recht insolvency law; **~rechtspfleger** insolvency registrar; **~richter** insolvency judge; **~schuldner** insolvency debtor

Insolvenz / ~tabelle insolvency schedule, claims register, schedule of debt provable in insolvency, record of the creditors' claims; **~tatbestand** insolvency offence; **~verfahren** insolvency proceedings, *(das ~ eröffnen)* to open insolvency proceedings; **~ vermögen** insolvency assets

Insolvenz / ~verschleppung wilful or grossly negligent delay of insolvency proceedings, (tort of) deepening insolvency, fraudulent trading; **~verwalter** insolvency administrator (receiver, practitioner), trustee (AE)

Insolvenz / ~verwaltung insolvency administration, receivership, *(unter ~ stellen)* to place under receivership; **~verwaltungskosten** insolvency expenses; **~verzicht** insolvency waiver; **~vorrecht** preferential right in insolvency proceedings

instabil unsteady, *(~er Markt)* unstable (jumpy) market

Instabilitätsfaktoren factors of instability

installieren *(eine Kreditlinie ~)* to establish (to set up) a credit line

Instanz 1. stage, instance **2.** authority

Instanzen / ~pyramide management pyramid; **~weg 1.** channels (stages) of appeal **2.** official channels **3.** chain of command

Institut institute, (financial) institution

institutionell *(~e Anleger)* institutional investors, *(~es Depot)* institutional investment portfolio, *(~es Geschäft)* dealings with institutional investors, *(~e Nachfrage)* institutional demand

Instrument tool, *(~ für die Inanspruchnahme) (im Dokumentengeschäft)* operative credit instrument

Instrumentarium der Geldpolitik monetary policy instruments (tools)

instrumentell *(~e Produktmerkmale)* functional product features

Intakthalteerklärung support agreement, → Kapitalintakthalteerklärung

integral *(einen ~en Bestandteil des Kreditvertrages bilden)* to form a constituent component of the loan agreement, to form part and parcel of the loan agreement

integrierte Finanzaufsicht 1. integrated financial supervision 2. *(Behörde)* integrated financial services supervisory authority, → Bundesanstalt für Finanzdienstleistungsaufsicht

integrierte Finanzprodukte integrated (cross-sectoral) financial products

Intensität 1. intensity 2. *(Stärke)* vigour, strength 3. *(Gründlichkeit)* thoroughness

intensiv intensive, vigorous, *(~e Betreuung)* intensified (strong) support, *(~er Handel)* active trading (dealings)

I

Intensivbetreuung personalised (intensified) support

intensivieren 1. *(die Bemühungen ~)* to increase (to step up) the efforts 2. *(die Geschäftsbeziehung ~)* to intensify (to strengthen, to extend) the business (account) relationship

Intensivierung intensification, increase, strengthening

Interbanken / **~aktiva** interbank lendings, lendings in the interbank market; **~-Aktivposition** interbank lending position; **~-Angebots/-Briefsatz** interbank offered rate; **~-Devisenmarkt** interbank forex market; **~einlagen** interbank deposits

Interbankenentgelt 1. *(zu zahlen von der Händlerbank an die kartenausgebende Bank)* interchange fee, debit interchange □ paid by the acquiring bank (merchant's bank) to the issuing bank (customer's bank)
2. *(zu zahlen bei Fremdabhebungen)* ATM usage fee, → Fremdabhebung

Interbanken / **~finanzierung** wholesale funding, financing in the interbank market; **~forderungen** interbank lendings, claims on banks, due from banks, → Interbankengeschäft ; **~geld** wholesale (interbank) funds

Interbanken / **~geschäft**/**~handel** wholesale funding transactions, wholesale banking, interbank dealings (business, transactions), borrowings and lendings among banks in the interbank market; **~kredit** interbank loans, interbank borrowings

Interbanken / **~markt** wholesale market, interbank market; **~mittel** wholesale funds, interbank funds; **~passiva** interbank borrowings, borrowings in the interbank market, → Interbankengeschäft; **~-Passivposition** interbank borrowing position

Interbanken / **~rate** wholesale funding rate, interbank rate (→ EURIBOR, → LIBOR); **~refinanzierung** wholesale funding, funding in the interbank market; **~status** balance on interbank transactions; **~-Terminhandel** interbank forward dealing; **~-Terminmarkt** interbank forward market

Interbanken / **~-Überweisungssystem** interbank funds transfer system; **~verbindlichkeiten** interbank borrowings, due to banks; **~verrechnungssystem** interbank clearing system

Interbanken / **~-Zahlungsverkehr** interbank payments; **~-Zahlungsverkehrsgebühr** multiple interchange fee; **~-Zahlungsverkehrskonvention** Interbank Convention on Payments

Interdependenz *(~ der Finanzmärkte)* interdependence of financial markets

Interesse interest, attention, *(~ der privaten Anleger)* retail investment interest, retail buying interest, *(im ~ der Aktionäre liegen)* to be in the best interest of the shareholders, *(für die neue Emission bestand kaum ~)* the new issue was poorly received in the market, *(auf großes ~ der Anleger stoßen)* to attract wide investor interest, *(starkes ~ zeigen)* to exhibit a keen interest

Interessen / **~abstimmung** co-ordination of interests, **~bereich** sphere of interests; **~divergenz** diversity of interests; **~gemeinschaft** community of interests; **~gruppe** 1. interest grouping, group of interested parties **2.** pressure group

Interessen / ~käufe 1. speculative buying, special-purpose buying **2.** stock purchases designed to acquire a majority; **~kollision/~konflikt** conflict (clash) of interests;**~vereinigung** interest group

Interessen / ~wahrung *(Wahrung des Kundeninteresses)* safeguarding the customer's interests; **~zusammenführung** pooling (uniting) of interests; **~zusammenführungsmethode** pooling-of-interests method, merger method of accounting

interessieren 1. *(sich ~ für)* to be interested in, to take an interest in **2.** *(rechtlich/wirtschaftlich interessiert sein)* to hold a legal/an economic interest

interimistisch *(~e Globalurkunde/Sammelurkunde)* temporary (interim) global certificate □ to be exchanged against definitive securities at a later stage

Interims / ~abschluss interim accounts; **~dividende** interim dividend; **~konto** suspense (interim) account; **~schein** scrip, interim certificate, provisional certificate of title; **~vereinbarung** temporary (provisional) agreement; **~zinsen** interim interest

Intermarkt-Spread intermarket spread, intercommodity spread □ Denotes an arbitrage transaction where an investor tries to profit from expected or existing changes in the usual price difference between two different, but related financial or commodity futures by buying the undervalued contract and selling the overvalued contract of the same delivery month.

Intermediär *(~ am Kapitalmarkt)* intermediary in the capital market; **~bank** intermediary bank

Intermediation intermediation □ raising or investing funds through a bank

Internalisierung *(im Wertpapiergeschäft)* internalisation □ filling orders from the institution's own inventory

international 1. *adj.* *(~e Aktienemission/Kapitalofferte)* international equity issue, *(~er Zahlungsverkehr)* international funds transfer, international money transmission services, *(~e Zinsusance)* international day count convention, → Zinsberechnungsmethode
2. *adv.* *(~ operierendes Kreditinstitut)* internationally operating bank (financial institution), global (international) player

Internationale Bankkontonummer International Bank Account Number (IBAN)

Internationale Bankleitzahl Bank Identifier Code (BIC)

Internationale Rechnungslegungsstandards International Financial Reporting Standards (IFRS)

Internationale Vereinigung von Swap- und Derivatehändlern International Swap and Derivatives Association (ISDA)

Internationale Vereinigung der Versicherungsaufsichtsbehörden International Association of Insurance Supervisors (IAIS)

Internationale Vereinigung der Wertpapieraufsichtsbehörden International Organization of Securities Commissions (IOSC)

Internationaler Währungsfonds International Monetary Fund (IMF)

Internationale Zahlungsanweisung International Payment Instruction (IPI)

Internationaler Zentralverwahrer International Central Securities Depository

interner Bemessungsansatz *(Basel II – zur Bemessung des operationellen Risikos)* internal measurement approach (IMA) □ method to measure operational risk; incorporates a bank's internal loss data into the required capital charge

interne Bewertung/Bonitätsanalyse in-house assessment, internal credit assessment, internal rating method

I

interne Bonitätsverbesserung *(bei einer Verbriefungstransaktion)* internal credit enhancement (e.g. by way of a subordination, recourse commitment or spread account)

Internes Kapitaladäquanzverfahren Internal Capital Adequacy Assessment Process (ICAAP) □ designed to ensure an efficient risk-based capital management

Interne Kapitalverzinsung Internal Rate of Return (IRR)

Interne Modellmethode Internal Model Method (IMM) □ internal model for measuring risk

internes Rating internal rating, internal credit assessment, a bank's own assessment of the credit risk, *(auf internen Ratings basierender Ansatz zur Bemessung des Kreditrisikos)* internal ratings based approach (IRBA)

internes Rechnungswesen managerial (management) accounting

interpretieren to interpret, to construe

intervenieren 1. to intervene, to support, *(am Markt ~)* to intervene in the market, to step into the market, to support a price (rate)
2. *(vermitteln)* to mediate, to intermediate

Intervention intervention, intervening, support, *(~ am freien Markt)* intervention in the open market, *(~ zur Marktberuhigung)* intervention to smooth the market, *(~ durch die Zentralbanken)* intervention from the central banks

Interventions / ~bestände intervention holdings (stock); **~finanzierung** intervention financing; **~käufe** support buying, supporting purchases; **~klage** third-party intervention; **~kurs** intervention rate (price); **~niveau** intervention level

Interventions / ~pflicht obligation to intervene (to support); **~punkt** intervention (support) point; **~recht** right of intervention; **~salden** intervention balances; **~schwelle** intervention threshold

Intramarket-Spread intramarket spread, interdelivery spread □ Denotes an arbitrage transaction where an investor tries to profit from existing or expected changes in the usual price difference between two different delivery months of the same financial or commodity future by opening a long futures position expiring in one month and a short position expiring in another month.

Inventar inventory, stock; **~bewertung** inventory (stock) evaluation; **~frist** period for filing the estate inventory list; **~wert 1.** inventory value **2.** *(eines Fondsanteils)* net asset value of a share (of a unit)

Inventur 1. inventory **2.** stock-taking

inverse Rendite-/Zinsstruktur inverted yield structure, inverse slope of the yield curve, inverse interest rate structure (pattern) □ market in which short-term interest rates are higher than rates at the long end of the market

inverse Terminkurve inverted forward curve, → Deport

investieren to invest, to make an investment, *(investiertes Kapital)* capital employed (invested)

Investition investment, capital expenditure (spending)

Investitions / ~abzugsbetrag investment allowance; **~anreiz** investment incentive, stimulus (inducement) to invest; **~antrag** capital expenditure request (proposal); **~aufwand** capital expenditure, investment cost; **~beihilfe** investment aid (subsidy), capital investment grant; **~bewertung** investment appraisal, capital expenditure rating

Investitions / ~bewilligung capital expenditure authorisation, capital appropriation; **~budget** investment budget, capital expenditure budget; **~darlehen** investment credit (loan), capital investment loan; ~**drosselung** investment curb (restrictions)

Investitions / ~**entscheidung** investment (capital expenditure) decision; ~**finanzierung** investment financing, financing capital expenditure(s), investment funding, ~**förderprogramm** investment promotion scheme; ~**förderung** promoting (furthering) investments; ~**freibetrag** investment allowance incentive

Investititons / ~**genehmigung** authorising capital expenditure, capital appropriation; ~**güter** capital goods; ~**haushalt** capital expenditure budget

Investitions / ~**kontrollbericht** capital expenditure performance report; ~**kontrolle** investment (capital expenditure) control; ~**kosten** investment cost; ~**kredit** investment credit, capital investment loan; ~**kürzungen** capital spending cuts

Investitions / ~**mittel** funds for capital investments, development funds, investible funds; ~**obligo** amounts committed for future capital expenditure; ~**rechnung** capital budgeting; ~**rendite** investment return; ~**risiko** investment risk (exposure)

Investitions / ~**volumen** investment total, aggregate (total) investments, aggregated capital commitments; ~**vorhaben** capital investment (expenditure) project, *(Bewertung eines ~s)* investment appraisal; ~**vorlage** capital expenditure proposal

Investitions / ~**zulagengesetz** Investment Subsidies Act; ~**zusage** investment undertaking; ~**zuschuss** investment aid (allowance, grant)

investiv *(~e Ausgaben)* capital expenditure

Investment / ~**aktiengesellschaft** investment stock corporation; ~**analyse** investment analysis (research); ~**anlage** investing in mutual funds; ~**anteil** unit, share; ~**aufsicht 1.** investment supervision, *(der ~ unterliegen)* subject to the investment regulatory framework 2. investment supervisory authority; ~**ausschüttung** fund payout, income distributed by a fund; ~**berater** investment counsellor (advisor); ~**beratung** investment counselling; ~**erträge** investment income

Investmentfonds investment fund, mutual fund, unit trust, *(OGAW-Fonds/EU-richtlinienkonformer Investmentfonds)* UCITS fund □ investment fund that has been established in accordance with the (EU) UCITS Directive (OGAW-Richtlinie), → Sondervermögen, → Spezial-Sondervermögen, → Publikums-Sondervermögen

Investmentfonds / ~**anteile** units, (mutual) fund shares, share certificates; ~**richtlinie** *(neugefasste ~)* → OGAW-Richtlinie IV; ~**sparplan** unit-linked savings scheme

Investment / ~**gesellschaft** investment company; ~**gesetz** German Investment Act; ~ **kaufmann/kaufleute** investment fund professional(s); ~**qualität** investment grade

Investment / ~**rechnungslegungs- und Bewertungsverordnung** Investment Accounting and Valuation Regulation; ~**recht** investment fund law; ~**sparen** saving through investment funds; ~**steuergesetz** German Investment Tax Act

Investment / ~**vermögen** *(nach dem Investmentgesetz)* investment fund, investment asset pool, *(ausländische/inländische ~)* domestic/foreign funds; ~**zertifikat** share certificate

Investor investor, financier, provider of funds

Investoren / ~**auswahlverfahren** investor selection process; ~**gemeinschaft** community of investors; ~**gruppe** group of investors (financial backers); ~**kreise** investing community

InvG → Investmentgesetz

InvMaRisk → Mindestanforderungen an das Risikomanagement der Investmentgesellschaften

I

InvStG → Investmentsteuergesetz

IRBA-Position IRBA exposure, → internes Rating

irreführen *(Anleger ~)* to mislead (to deceive) investors

irreführende Angaben 1. misleading (false) information
2. *(vorsätzlich)* fraudulent (deceptive) information, misrepresentations

Irreführung 1. misleading, misdirection, misguidance
2. *(vorsätzliche)* wilful (fraudulent) misrepresentation, intentional misleading, deceipt, deception

irritieren *(die Anleger ~)* to unsettle (to confuse) investors

I

Irrtum error, mistake, *(Irrtümer und Auslassungen vorbehalten)* errors and omissions excepted

Irrtumswahrscheinlichkeit error probability

irrtümlich *adj.* erroneous, wrong, *adv.* by mistake, erroneously

ISE → imagegestützter Scheckeinzug

isoliert *(~e Grundschuld)* non-accessory land charge

Ist / ~-Ausfallquote actual default rate; **~-Kosten** *(~ der erbrachten Leistung)* actual cost of the work performed; **~-Leistung** actual performance; **~-Versteuerung** taxation on cash receipts basis

iTAN → indizierte Transaktionsnummer

IWF → Internationaler Währungsfonds

IZV-Zahlung domestic payment

J

Jahresabschluss 1. *(Bilanz)* annual accounts, annual financial statements **2.** *(eines Kontos)* year-end balancing (closing) of an account; ~ **prüfung** audit of the annual accounts

Jahres / ~**bilanz** annual financial statements, annual statement of condition; ~**dividende** annual dividend; ~**durchschnitt** annual average, *(jahresdurchschnittliches Geschäftsvolumen)* average business volume for the year

Jahres / ~**endabrechnung 1.** year-end settlement (balancing) **2.** year-end closing statement; ~**endbestand** year-end position; ~**ergebnis** profit/loss for the year; ~**fehlbetrag** net loss for the year, net deficit recorded in the accounts, annual deficit

Jahres / ~**gebühr** annual fee; ~**gehalt** annual salary; ~**geld** one-year funds, twelve-months money; ~**hauptversammlung** annual general meeting; ~**hoch** annual high; ~**leistung** annual interest and redemption payments; ~**mittelkurs** *(einer Währung)* annual mean rate

Jahres / ~**rendite** annual yield (return); ~ **steuergesetz** Annual Tax Act; ~-**Swapsatz** annual swap rate; ~**tief/tiefstand** annual low, current year low; ~**tilgungsquote** annual redemption rate

Jahres / ~**überschuss** net income for the year, net income recorded in the accounts, *(~ je Aktie)* net income per share; ~ **ultimodispositionen** end-of-year trading (liquidity) arrangements; ~**ultimoglattstellung** end-of-year position squaring

Jahres / ~**umsatz** annual turnover (sales); ~**vergleichsrate** year-on-year rate; ~**verzinsung** annual interest return; ~**zuwachsrate** annual growth rate

Jährling yearling

jederzeit kündbar callable at any time, terminable on demand (at will)

jeweilig *(zu dem zum ~en Zeitpunkt gültigen Kurs abrechnen)* to settle at the rate valid (prevailing) at the respective point in time

Jubiläumszuwendungen long-service awards (payments)

Jumbo-Emission jumbo deal

Jumbo-Pfandbrief Jumbo Pfandbrief, jumbo covered bond, large-issuance covered bond

jung *(~e Aktien)* new shares, *(~er Markt)* fledgling market

Jungschein scrip, provisional bond (stock) certificate

Jungschein / ~**giroverkehr** scrip clearing; ~**guthaben** scrip balances, scrips receivable; ~**konto** scrip account

Junktimierung linkage

juristisch 1. *adj.* legal, juridical, judicial, *(~e Absicherung)* legal cover, *(~er Berater)* legal adviser (counsel), *(~e Person)* legal entity (person), *(~e Person des öffentlichen Rechts)* public entity, entity (corporation) under public law, *(~er Sachverständiger)* legal expert, *(~e Überprüfung)* legal review
2. *adv.* legally, from a legal point of view, in terms of law, *(~ abgesichert)* legally covered

K

kaduzieren to forfeit, *(kaduzierte Aktien)* forfeited shares, *(kaduzierter Aktionär)* shareholder whose shares have been forfeited

Kaduzierung forfeiture of shares, disqualification of shareholders

Kalender *(für Neuemissionen)* issuing calendar (timetable)

Kalender-Spread time (horizontal, calendar) spread □ the simultaneous purchase and sale of options of the same class (either Calls or Puts) having the same strike price but different expiry dates

kalibrieren to calibrate, *(kalibriertes Ratingsystem)* calibrated rating system □ ensures a far-reaching correspondence between forecast default probabilities and actual loss rates

Kalibriertheit calibrative status

Kalibrierung *(~ der Ausfallwahrscheinlichkeiten)* calibration of default probabilities, assignment of default probabilities to rating classes, *(~ von Optionspreismodellen)* calibration of option pricing models

Kalkulation calculation, computation

Kalkulations / ~fehler calculating error, miscalculation; **~grundlage** basis of calculation, computation basis; **~methode** method of calculation; **~sicherheit** costing security; **~zinssatz** calculatory interest rate

kalkulatorisch *(~e Abschreibung)* imputed depreciation, *(~er Gewinn)* calculatory profit, *(~e Größe)* imputed variable, *(~e Kosten)* imputed (calculatory) cost, *(~e Zinsen)* imputed interest

kalkulierbar *(~es Risiko)* calculable risk (exposure)

kalkulieren to calculate, to compute

Kaltakquise cold calling

kalter IPO cold IPO, reverse IPO □ acquisition of a publicly traded company by a private company to avoid the regulatory requirements connected with an initial public offering

Kammer *(~ für Handelssachen)* Panel for Commercial Matters, Commercial Ligitation Panel

kämpfen *(mit Liquiditätsproblemen ~)* to wrestle with (to grapple with) liquidity problems, *(um Marktanteile ~)* to vie (to struggle) for market shares

kanalisieren *(Investitionen ~)* to channel (to funnel) investments into

Kandidat candidate

kandidieren *(für den Aufsichtsrat ~)* to stand (to run) as a candidate for the Supervisory Board

Kann / ~leistungen 1. discretionary services 2. voluntary contributions 3. discretionary (voluntary) benefits; **~vorschrift** discretionary clause (provision)

KAP → Konsolidierungsausgleichsposten

KapAEG → Kapitalaufnahmeerleichterungsgesetz

Kapazitäts / ~abbau capacity cut, scaling down capacities; **~abweichung** capacity variance; **~ausnutzung** capacity utilisation (usage); **~ausnutzungsgrad** capacity utilisation rate, capacity usage ratio; **~effekt** *(der Investitionen)* capacity effect of investments

Kapazitäts / ~engpässe capacity constraints; **~erweiterung** extension of (increase in) capacities, expanding capacities; ~**kosten** capacity cost; ~**lenkung** capacity control (management); ~**messung** capacity measurement; ~**steuerung** → Kapazitätslenkung; ~**überhang** excess (surplus) capacity

KapCo-Gesellschaft Qualifying Partnership (Personengesellschaft) with a limited company as general partner → Kapitalgesellschaften-und Co-Richtliniengesetz

KapCoRiLiG → Kapitalgesellschaften-und Co-Richtliniengesetz

Kapital 1. capital, equity **2.** *(Darlehens-/Anleihekapital)* principal

Kapital / ~**abfluss** outflow of capital, capital efflux; ~**abgabe** capital levy; ~**abruf** capital call; ~**abschöpfung** capital absorption; ~**absorptionsfähigkeit** ability to absorb capital

Kapital / ~**abwanderung** capital drain (exodus); ~**abzug** withdrawal of capital (funds); ~**abzüge** *(under* → Basel III rules) capital deductions □ minority interests, deferred tax assets, mortgage servicing rights; ~**adäquanzmessgröße** measure of capital adequacy

Kapital / ~**allokation** capital allocation, allocation of invested funds; *(~ für operationelle Risiken)* allocation of capital against operational risks; ~**anbieter** supplier(s) of capital (of funds)

Kapital / ~**anfangsrendite** initial return on investment; ~**anforderungen** capital (equity) requirements, *(~ für das Ausfallrisiko/Kontrahentenrisiko)* default risk capital charge/CCR (counterparty credit risk) default risk charge, *(~ an Kreditinstitute und Wertpapierfirmen)* capital requirements for credit institutions and securities firms; ~**angebot** capital supply, supply of funds

Kapitalanlage investment; / ~**aufwendungen** investment expense; ~**berater** investment advisor (counsellor); ~**beratung** investment counselling (advice); ~**beratungsvertrag** investment advisory agreement

Kapitalanlage / ~**gesellschaft** capital investment company; ~**konto** capital investment account; ~**politik** investment policy; ~**streuung** diversification of investments

Kapital / ~**anleger** investor; ~**anlegermusterverfahrensgesetz** Act regulating the proceedings for actions brought by investors; ~**anlegerziele** investor aims; ~**ansammlung** accumulation of capital

Kapital / ~**anteil** equity share (interest), capital share, shareholding; ~**anteilscheine** equity share certificates; ~**anteilsmethode** equity method; ~**aufbringung** putting up capital, contributing (providing) capital

Kapitalaufnahme capital (equity) raising, raising capital (funds), equity borrowing, *(~ über die Börse)* raising funds on the stock market, *(~ durch eine Anleiheemission)* raising capital through a bond issue

Kapital / ~**aufnahmeerleichterungsgesetz** Capital Procurement Relief Act; ~**aufstockung** capital increase; ~**aufwand** capital expenditure, capital spending (outlay), outlay of funds; ~**aufzehrung** capital depletion, gradual capital reduction, using up the capital invested

Kapital / ~**ausfallrisiko** *(bei Kreditgewährungen)* loan loss risk, principal risk (exposure); ~**ausfuhr** capital export(s); ~**ausfuhrland** capital exporting country; ~**ausgaben** capital spending; ~**ausstattung** capital resources, capitalisation, capital base; ~**ausstattungsverordnung** Solvency Regulation; ~**auszahlung 1.** capital paid out, → Kapitalentnahme **2.** disbursement of capital (principal)

Kapital / ~**basis** capital (equity) base; ~**bedarf** capital needs (requirements), capital (funds) required, *(~ für Marktrisiken)* capital charge for market risks; ~**bedarfsrechnung** capital re-

K

quirements statement; **~bedienung** debt servicing; **~belassungserklärung** → Kapitalintakthalteerklärung

Kapitalbereitstellung provision of capital, providing funds, commitment of capital (of funds), capital appropriation, capital funding

Kapitalbereitstellungs / ~kosten capital commitment charges; **~verpflichtung** capital (equity) commitment letter

Kapitalberichtigung *(~ im Verhältnis 6:1)* one-for-six capitalisation issue

Kapitalbeschaffung raising capital (funds), capital (fund, equity) raising, generation (procurement) of capital, capital procurement, funding, *(~ zu Festzinskonditionen)* raising fixed rate funds

K

Kapitalbeschaffungs / ~kosten cost of funds, cost of equity raising; **~maßnahmen** capital-raising (fund-raising) operations, ways (methods) of obtaining equity, → Kapitalmaßnahmen

Kapital / ~besitz equity ownership, shareholding(s); **~bestandteile** capital components

Kapitalbeteiligung equity interest (holding, share, stake), equity participation (investment), shareholding, share in the capital

Kapitalbeteiligungs / ~erwerb acquiring a shareholding, making an equity investment; **~finanzierung** equity participation financing; **~gesellschaft** equity investment company, venture capital company (firm); **~vereinbarung** private equity partnership agreement

Kapital / ~betrag principal, amount of capital, capital sum; **~bewegungen** capital movements; **~bewertung** capital rating; **~bilanz** capital account; **~bildung** capital formation, accumulation of capital, *(kapitalbildende Maßnahmen)* capital-building measures

Kapitalbindung capital commitment, capital lockup, tying up funds, *(~ durch das Kreditportefeuille)* funds tied up in the loan portfolio

Kapitalbindungs / ~dauer/~frist capital commitment period; **~kosten** capital commitment cost

Kapital / ~budget capital budget, planned capital expenditure; **~decke** capital (equity) base, capital cover; **~deckenerweiterung** broadening (strengthening) the capital base

Kapitaldienst principal repayments, repayment of the principal, debt servicing

Kapitaldienst / ~fähigkeit financial ability (capacity) to repay the loan, capacity to meet principal repayments; **~hilfe 1.** assistance in the repayment of principal **2.** *(Zuschüsse zum Schuldendienst)* debt service subsidies

Kapital / ~effizienz capital efficiency, ratio of output to capital expenditure; **~eigner** shareholder, equity holder; **~eignerseite** shareholder side; **~einbringung** capital contribution, bringing in capital, putting up capital, contributing funds, → Kapitaleinlage

Kapital / ~einbuße loss of capital; **~einforderung** capital call; **~einkommen/~einkünfte** investment income, capital income, income (revenue) from invested assets

Kapital / ~einlage capital (equity) contribution, amount of capital invested (contributed), capital brought into the business, capital invested (put up); **~einsatz** employment (use) of capital, capital employed, capital deployment, → Kapitaleinlage

Kapital / ~einschuss capital (equity) injection; **~einzahlung** capital contribution, capital contributed (paid in); **~einzahlungsverpflichtung** undertaking to contribute capital; **~emission** capital issue

Kapital / ~entlastung capital relief; **~entnahme** withdrawal (drawing) of funds, capital take-down; **~entwer-**

tung capital depreciation (impairment), loss in capital value

Kapitalerhalt(ung) preservation of capital, capital maintenance, *(Vorschriften zur ~)* rules on capital preservation

Kapitalerhaltungspolster *(Basel III)* capital conservation buffer □ designed to absorb losses during periods of economic and financial stress; to be met with common equity (hartem Kernkapital)

Kapitalerhaltungsvorschriften capital maintenance provisions

Kapitalerhöhung capital increase, → Kapitalmaßnahmen, *(~ im Verhältnis 6:1)* one-for-six capital increase, *(~ durch die Ausgabe neuer Aktien)* increase in capital through the issuance of new shares
(~ gegen Bareinlagen) cash capital increase, capital increase for cash, *(~ aus Gesellschaftsmitteln)* capital increase out of retained earnings, *(~ aus genehmigtem Kapital)* capital increase from authorised capital
(~ durch die Umwandlung von Rücklagen) increase in capital through the conversion (incorporation) of reserves, *(~ gegen Sacheinlagen)* capital increase through non-cash contributions

Kapitalerhöhungs / ~beschluss resolution on a capital increase; **~gesetz** Capital Increase Act

Kapital / ~erleichterung *(z. B. regulatorische ~ im Rahmen des Standardansatzes)* regulatory capital relief, reduced capital charge; **~ersatz** equity substitution, *(kapitalersetzende Gesellschafterdarlehen)* equity-substituting shareholder loans; **~ersatzrecht** equity substitution law

Kapital / ~ersparnis capital savings; **~ertrag** investment income, *(Kapitalerträge aus Wertpapieren)* income from securities; **~ertragsbilanz** investment income account; **~ertragssteuer** capital gains tax, investment income tax; **~ertragssteuerentlastung** capital gains tax relief

Kapital / ~erweiterung capital widening, broadening the capital base; **~fälligkeit 1.** principal maturity, maturing principal payment **2.** repayment of principal falling due; **~fehlbetrag** → Kapitalunterdeckung; **~fehlleitung** misdirection of capital, misinvestment

Kapital / ~flucht capital exodus (flight), massive transfer of capital abroad; **~fluss** capital (cash) flow, flow of funds; **~flussrechnung** cash flow statement, funds statement, flow-of-funds analysis

Kapital / ~fonds *(eines Unternehmens)* capital fund, aggregate capital resources, equity and debt capital; **~forderungen 1.** capital (equity) claims **2.** monetary receivables **3.** *(Darlehensforderungen)* funds loaned, loans; **~freisetzung** release of equity (funds), freeing up capital (capital funds)

Kapitalgarantie capital guarantee, guaranteed return of the principal at maturity, guaranteeing the capital invested, *(Anlageprodukte mit Kapitalgarantie)* capital-guaranteed investment products, *(kapitalgarantierte Schuldtitel)* principal-protected notes

Kapitalgeber investor, supplier of capital (of funds), funder, equity provider; **~land** donor country

kapitalgedeckt *(~e Altersvorsorge)* funded old age provision scheme, *(~e Leistungsansprüche)* funded benefit entitlements

Kapitalgesellschaft corporation, → kleine/→ große/→ mittelgroße Kapitalgesellschaften

Kapitalgesellschaften-und Co-Richtliniengesetz German Qualifying Partnership Act □ law that extends accounting standards to be observed by corporations to qualifying partnerships (→ KapCo-Gesellschaften)

Kapitalgesellschaftsanteil corporate share

Kapitalgewinn capital gain (appreciation), *(~e aus Immobilienvermögen)* capital gains derived from the sale of real estate; ~**besteuerung** taxation of capital gains

Kapital / ~**herabsetzung** capital reduction (write-down); ~**hergabe** provision of capital, providing funds; ~**herkunft** source of capital

Kapital / ~**hilfe** capital assistance (aid), assistance in the provision of capital (equity) to companies; ~**hunger** heavy equity requirements, heavy capital needs; ~**indexanleihe** capital-indexed bond

Kapitalintakthalteerklärung equity maintenance agreement, capital support agreement, undertaking not to sell or assign the capital interest in a company, undertaking (covenant) to maintain the capital unchanged

K

Kapitalintakthalteklausel equity maintenance clause

Kapital / ~**intensität** capital intensity, *(kapitalintensiver Betrieb)* capital-intensive operation(s); ~**intensivierung** strengthening (broadening) the capital base; ~**interessen** capital (equity) interests; ~**investition** capital investment

kapitalisierbar capitalisable

kapitalisieren to capitalise, *(die Kreditkosten ~)* to capitalise the finance charge(s), to add the total finance charge to the amount borrowed, *(die Rücklagen ~)* to capitalise reserves, to convert reserves into share capital, *(kapitalisiert durch die Ausgabe von Berichtigungsaktien)* capitalised on scrip issue, *(kapitalisierter Marktwert)* capitalised market value

Kapitalisierung capitalisation, *(~ eines Unternehmens)* company's capitalisation, total amount of capital invested in a company (i.e. shares, loan capital, capital reserves, bank borrowings), *(die ~ beläuft sich auf ungefähr …)* capitalised (on the market) at around

Kapitalisierungs / ~**faktor** capitalisation rate; ~**grad**/~**kennzahl** capitalisation ratio, capital expressed as a percentage of assets; ~**zinsfuß** capitalisation rate

Kapital / ~**knappheit** shortage of capital (of funds), lack of funds; ~**koeffizient** capital output ratio; ~**konsolidierung** capital consolidation; ~**kontenkonsolidierung** consolidation of capital accounts; ~**konto** capital account

Kapital / ~**kosten** cost of capital; ~**kostenentlastung** capital cost relief; ~**kostenreduzierung** lowering the cost of capital; ~**lebensversicherung** endowment policy; ~**lenkung** capital investment control, channelling of investments

Kapitalmarkt capital market, wholesale funding market, *(Emittenten am ~)* issuers operating in (on) the capital market

kapitalmarktabhängig *(~e Konditionen)* terms linked to wholesale funding rates

Kapitalmarkt / ~**adresse** *(erste ~)* prime borrower in the wholesale funding market; ~**anlagen** investments in capital market instruments; ~**ausschuss** capital market issues committee

kapitalmarktbasiert *(~e Finanzierung)* funding through the capital market, wholesale funding, *(~e Finanzierungsinstrumente)* equity-linked products

Kapitalmarkt / ~**beanspruchung** borrowing on the capital market, tapping the capital market; ~**deregulierung** deregulation of the capital market; ~**derivate** capital market derivatives, fixed income derivatives; ~**effizienz** capital market efficiency; ~**erträge** income from capital market transactions

Kapitalmarkt / ~**fähigkeit** ability to access the capital market, *(kapitalmarktfähig)* able to access the capital market, eligible to tap the capital market; ~**fi-**

nanzierung capital market financing, funding through issues in the capital market, bond and/or equity financing, wholesale funding

Kapitalmarkt / **~marktgeschäft** *(Bereich)* Debt & Equity Markets; **~gleichgewicht** capital market equilibrium; **~gleichgewichtsmodell** capital asset pricing model; **~konditionen** capital market rates, wholesale funding rates; **~lenkung** capital market control; **~liberalisierung** liberalisation (deregulation) of the capital market; **~ordnung** capital market system

Kapitalmarkt / **~orientierung** capital market orientation, gearing (tailoring) to wholesale funding rates, *(kapitalmarktnahe/-orientierte Lösung)* capital-market-driven solution, *(kapitalmarktorientiertes Unternehmen, i. S. des HGB)* capital-market-oriented corporation; **~papiere** capital market instruments (debt); **~politik** capital market policy

Kapitalmarkt / **~recht** capital market law; **~rendite** capital market yield, yield in the capital market; **~satz** capital market rate, long-term interest rate; **~verhältnisse** conditions in the capital market, wholesale funding conditions; **~verschuldung** capital market debt, borrowing(s) in the capital market; **~zins** capital market rate; **~zugang** access to the capital market

kapitalmäßig *(~ unterlegen)* to back up with capital, *(~e Bindungen)* equity links, shareholding links (ties), *(~e Verflechtung)* cross-shareholdings, *(~er Verlust)* capital loss

Kapitalmaßnahmen corporate actions □ all measures that affect the capital (equity or debt) issued by the corporation, e.g. capital increases/write-downs, bonus issue of shares, buyback of shares, splits, mergers, reorganisations, schemes of arrangement

Kapital / **~mehrheit** majority of shares, majority shareholding; **~mehrung** capital addition (appreciation); **~mittel** capital (equity) funds, capital (financial) resources; **~mobilisierung** mobilising capital

Kapital / **~nachfrage** demand for capital; **~nachfrager** demanders of capital; **~nehmer 1.** capital user **2.** borrower; **~neuordnung** capital reorganisation (restructuring); **~nutzungskosten** capital user costs

Kapital / **~offerte** equity offering, equity issue; **~polster** equity cushion, capital backing; **~prämie** capital bonus; **~produktivität** capital productivity; **~puffervorgabe** capital buffer requirement

Kapital / **~quellen** capital (equity) resources; **~quote** capital ratio, → hartes Kernkapital, → Gesamtkapital; **~rationierung** capital rationing, restrictions on new investments; **~rechnung** statement of shareholders' equity; **~reduzierung 1.** capital reduction (write-down) **2.** principal reduction

Kapital / **~rendite** return on capital, capital yield; **~restschuld** residual debt, residual (remaining) principal, principal balance; **~risiko** capital risk, principal exposure

Kapital / **~rückfluss 1.** reflux (reflow) of capital **2.** recovery of capital; **~rückflussdauer** payback period, time required to recover the initial investment in a project; **~rückflussmethode** payback method; **~rückführung 1.** repatriation of capital **2.** repayment of principal

Kapital / **~rücklage** additional paid-in capital, capital surplus; **~rückwanderung** reflux (reflow) of capital; **~rückzahlung** capital repayment, repayment of principal, principal repayment (redemption), amortisation (payback) of principal

Kapital / **~saldo** principal balance; **~sammelstellen** financial intermediaries, institutional investors; **~sanierung** capital (financial) reconstruction, capital overhaul, revamping the capital structure; ~**sanierungsprogramm** capital reconstruction scheme

Kapital / ~**schnitt** capital write-down; ~**schöpfung** creation of capital; ~**schutz** capital protection, *(Anleihe mit ~)* capital-protected bond (note); ~**schutzregeln** capital protection rules; ~**schwäche** thin (frail) capital base, inadequate capitalisation; ~**schwund** shrinkage of funds

Kapital / ~**segment** layer of capital; ~**sicherheit** safety of the capital invested; ~**sicherung** preservation of capital; ~**situation** capital position; ~**spritze** capital infusion, equity injection

Kapital / ~**steuer** capital levy; ~**steuerung** capital control; ~-**Strip** *(Anleihemantel, Kapitalansprüche)* principal-only strip, → Stripping; ~**ströme** capital (equity) flows

K

Kapital / ~**struktur** capital structure, mix of debt and equity financing, relationship of debt to equity; ~**strukturregel** *(vertikale)* debt to equity rule □ requiring a specific ratio of debt to equity; ~**subventionen** capital investment subsidies

kapitalsuchend *(~e Emittenten)* capital-seeking issuers, *(~es Unternehmen)* capital-seeking company

Kapital / ~**tilgung** → Kapitalrückzahlung; ~**transaktionen** capital transactions, → Kapitalmaßnahmen; ~**transfer** capital transfer, transfer of capital funds; ~**transferbeschränkungen** restrictions on capital transfers

Kapital / ~**überlassung** capital commitment, provision of capital (equity); ~**überlassungsdauer** capital commitment period; ~**überschuss** capital surplus, surplus of funds; ~**übertragung** capital transfer

Kapital / ~**umlauf** 1. circulation of capital 2. capital issued; ~**umlenkung** diversion of capital; ~**umschichtung** regrouping of capital (of funds); ~**umschlag** capital turnover

Kapital / ~**unterdeckung** capital deficiency, shortage of capital funds; ~**untergrenze** capital (equity) floor, minimum capital requirements; ~**unterlegung** capital charge, capital backing, → Eigenkapitalunterlegung; ~**unterlegungsvorschriften** capital adequacy rules, requirements on banks to hold capital against exposure; ~**unterstützung** capital support

Kapital / ~**veränderung** change in capital; ~**veränderungsrechnung** statement of changes in capital accounts (in shareholders' equity); ~**verbrauch** capital consumption

Kapital / ~**verflechtung** cross-shareholding, shareholding (equity, capital) links; ~**verhältnisse** capital situation (position), capital structure, *(Neuordnung der ~)* capital reorganisation (restructuring)

Kapitalverkehr capital movements (transactions), *(Freizügigkeit des ~s)* freedom of capital movements

Kapitalverkehrs / ~**beschränkungen** restrictions on capital movements; ~**bilanz** capital account; ~**steuer** capital transfer tax

Kapital / ~**verlagerung** shift of capital, *(~ ins Ausland)* shifting capital (funds) abroad; ~**verlust** capital loss, principal loss, fall in value of the capital invested; ~**verlustrisiko** exposure to (risk of) capital losses, principal exposure

Kapital / ~**verminderung** capital reduction, capital write-down; ~**vermittler** financial intermediary; ~**vermögen** capital assets; ~**verpflichtungen** 1. capital commitments 2. principal repayment commitments

Kapital / ~**verstärkung** strengthening (broadening) the capital base, injection of fresh (additional) funds; ~**verteilung** capital allocation (distribution)

Kapital / ~**vertreter** shareholders' representatives (side); ~**verwaltung** investment management; ~**verwaltungsgesellschaft** capital investment company

Kapital / ~**verwässerung** capital (equity) dilution, stock watering, reduction in share value resulting from the issuance of additional stock or the conversion of convertible securities; ~**verwässerungsschutz** dilution protection, antidilutive provisions, provisions to protect an equity position in the event of a further equity issue

Kapital / ~**verwendung** use of capital, appropriation of capital (funds); ~**verzehr** capital depletion (depreciation), capital consumption; ~**verzicht** capital repayment waiver

Kapital / ~**verzinsung** **1.** *(des eingesetzten Kapitals)* return on equity (on capital invested) **2.** *(von Einlagen)* interest paid on deposits; ~**volumen** **1.** aggregated capital **2.** total capital raised

Kapital / ~**wachstum** capital growth (appreciation); ~**wachstumsfonds** capital growth fund; ~**wachstumsrate** capital growth rate

Kapital / ~**wert** **1.** capital value, principal value **2.** *(Barwert)* present value; ~**wertpapiere** stocks and bonds; ~**wertzuwachs** capital (equity) appreciation, rise in market value; ~**wiedergewinnungsdauer** payback period

Kapital / ~**zinsen** interest on capital; ~**zufluss** inflow of capital; ~**zuführung** capital injection (addition), injection of fresh capital; ~**zuordnung** capital allocation, → Kapitalallokation

Kapital / ~**zusage** capital commitment, undertaking to provide capital; ~**zusammenlegung** capital consolidation (merger), regrouping of capital; ~**zusammensetzung** capital structure, → Kapitalstruktur; ~**zuwachs** capital growth, capital appreciation, increase in capital; ~**zuwachsanleihe** capital growth bond

Kappa Kappa □ descriptive of a movement in the option price in response to a 1 % change in volatility

kappen *(Kapazitäten ~)* to cut back capacities

Karenz / ~**frist** **1.** waiting (qualifying) period **2.** *(Nachfrist)* grace period; ~ **entschädigung** waiting allowance

Karriere career; ~**entwicklung** career development

Kartei card index, file

Kartell cartel; ~**abrede** cartel agreement, restrictive agreement; ~**behörde** antitrust agency (authority); ~**bildung** formation of cartels, cartelisation; ~**entflechtung** decartelisation; ~**gesetz** Antitrust Act

Kartell / ~**recht** antitrust law (legislation), *(kartellrechtlich)* under antitrust law; ~**register** register of restrictive agreements; ~**verbot** ban on restrictive agreements (on cartels); ~**verfahren** antitrust lawsuit; ~**vertrag** cartel (restrictive) agreement

Karten / ~**abrechnung** credit (debit) card statement; ~**akzeptant** (~**akzeptanzstelle**) merchant, card acceptor, acceptor; ~**akzeptanzvertrag** merchant agreement; ~ **aufbewahrung** card safekeeping; ~**ausgabe** card issuance, *(kartenausgebende Bank)* card-issuing bank, issuer; ~**ausfallquote** card default rate

Karten / ~**authentifizierung** card authentication, ~**authentifizierungsverfahren** card authentication process, process to ensure that a credit card is genuine; ~**besitzer** card holder; ~**betriebssystem** card operating system

Karten / ~**echtheitsprüfung** card authentication; ~**eigentümer** card owner (holder); ~**element** card component; ~**emittent** card issuer; ~**genehmigung** authorisation for use of a credit card

kartengestützt *(~e Zahlungen)* card-based payments

Karten / ~**guthaben** credit card balance; ~**herausgeber** card issuer; ~**inhaber** *(Legitimationsprüfung von ~n)* cardholder verification; ~**inhaberhaftung** cardholder's liability

Karten / ~**leistungsbeleg** sales slip, charge slip; ~**leser** card reader; ~**missbrauch** card abuse, *(Haftung für ~)* liability for abuse of the card

Karten / ~**personalisierung** card personalisation, *(Rückgängigmachung der ~)* depersonalisation; ~**programm** card scheme; ~**prozessor** card processor; ~**prüfnummer** card validation code; ~**prüfung** card verification (authentication)

Karten / ~**rückbelastung** card chargeback; ~**sicherheitscode** Card Security Code; ~**sperre** card blocking; ~**umsätze** card transactions

Karten / ~**verarbeitung** card processing; ~**verfügung** payment by credit card; ~ **verifizierungscode**/~**wert** card verification code/value; ~**zahlungssysteme** card payment systems

Karusellgeschäft / Karusellbetrug missing trader fraud, carousel fraud □ claiming input tax credits for value-added tax (VAT) that has been charged, but never paid

Kassa / ~**auktion** cash auction (for stocks); ~**betrag** *(bei einem Devisen-Swap)* spot amount; ~**devisen** spot exchange (currency), spot forex, exchange for spot delivery; ~**dollar** spot dollar

Kassa / ~**engagements** spot market commitments (exposure); ~-**Futures-Arbitrage** cash futures arbitrage □ looking for arbitrage opportunities between the two markets

Kassa / ~**geschäft 1.** *(Devisen)* spot deal (transaction) **2.** *(Wertpapiere)* regular way purchase or sale, cash deal (bargain), transaction against cash settlement; ~**gold** spot gold

Kassa / ~**handel 1.** *(Devisen/Edelmetalle)* spot trading (dealings) **2.** *(Wertpapiere)* cash trading (dealings); ~**instrument** *(an einem Kassamarkt gehandeltes Finanzinstrument)* cash instrument

Kassa/ ~**kauf** regular way purchase, purchase in the spot (cash) market; ~**konditionen 1.** spot terms **2.** cash dealing terms; ~**kurs 1.** *(Devisen)* spot rate **2.** *(Wertpapiere)* cash settlement price, cash quotation; ~**leerverkäufe** short sales, → Leerverkäufe per Termin

Kassamarkt 1. spot market **2.** cash market; ~**konditionen** spot/cash market terms; ~**papiere** securities listed on the cash market

Kassa / ~**mittelkurs** *(Devisen)* mean (middle) spot rate; ~**notierung 1.** spot quotation **2.** cash quotation; ~**option** cash option; ~**order** cash market order

Kassa / ~**papiere** securities traded for cash, cash securities (instruments), cash bonds; ~**portefeuille** cash securities portfolio; ~**position** cash position, position in the spot/cash market

Kassa / ~**regulierung** spot/cash settlement; ~**rücktransaktion** cash closing transaction; ~**umsätze** spot/cash trading volume; ~**valuta** spot currency □ foreign currency bought and sold for delivery two business days after the deal has been negotiated

Kassa / ~**valutierung 1.** spot, spot value date **2.** fixing the spot value date; ~**verkauf** regular way sale; ~**verrechnung** cash clearing; ~**ware** spot commodity; ~**wert** cash asset; ~**wertpapiere** cash securities

Kasse 1. cash, *(~ gegen Dokumente)* cash against documents, *(die Aktionäre zur ~ bitten)* to call on the shareholders
2. *(Bilanzposten)* cash on hand and in the bank, cash assets
3. *(Kassenschalter)* cashier's office, teller's counter

Kassen / ~**abhebungen** cash drawings; ~**anweisung** cash voucher; ~**aufnahme 1.** balancing the till (cash) **2.** *(Prüfung)* cash audit; ~**ausgänge** cash disbursements; ~**ausweis** cash statement

Kassen / ~**bedarf** cash requirements; ~**beleg** cash voucher; ~**bericht** cash report; ~**bestand** 1. *(Bilanzposition)* cash on hand, cash assets 2. till money, notes and coins in the till; ~**defizit** cash deficit (shorts), till shortage; ~**disposition** cash management

Kassen / ~**eingänge** cash receipts; ~**einnahmen** cash revenue; ~**finanzierung** 1. financing cash requirements 2. funding short-term public borrowing requirements; ~**führung** cashkeeping, cash accounting; ~**guthaben** cash on hand, cash assets; ~**haltung** cash management

Kassenkredit 1. *(kurzfristiger Barkredit)* cash advance, cash facility 2. *(Kassenkredite, i. S. von kurzfristigen Krediten an die öffentliche Hand)* facilities to fund short-term public borrowing requirements, short-term loans raised by public authorities, *(aus der Sicht eines Kreditinstitutes)* short-term lendings to public authorities

Kassen / ~**lage** cash position; ~**liquidität** tier 1 liquidity, cash ratio; ~**obligationen** public notes □ fixed rate notes issued by the Federal Government, government agencies and specific public sector banks with maturities of up to four years

Kassen / ~**plan** cash budget; ~**planung** cash planning; ~**prognose** cash forecast; ~**prüfung** cash audit; ~**quittung** 1. cash receipt 2. receipt of deposit, deposit slip 3. *(bei Wertpapier-Emissionen)* scrip, provisional certificate, subscription money receipt

Kassen / ~**schein** discounted note; ~**terminal** point-of-sale terminal; ~**überschuss** 1. cash surplus 2. overs in tills account; ~**vorschuss** cash advance

kassenwirksam *(~ erfasste Erträge)* earnings reflected (recognised) in the cash position

Kassenzuflüsse *(~ aus der laufenden Geschäftstätigkeit)* cash provided by operations

Kataster cadastre

Kataster / ~**amt** cadastral authority; ~**buch** cadastral records

katastermäßig *(~e Bezeichnung)* cadastral description

Kataster / ~**nummer** cadastral number; ~**papiere** cadastral records; ~**plan** cadastral (survey) map; ~**vermessung** cadastral survey(ing); ~**verwaltung** cadastral authority

Katastrophen-Anleihe Catastrophe Bond, Cat Bond, Act-of-God Bond □ high-yield bond whose principal is partly or fully forgiven in the event of a specified catastrophe

Katastrophen-Option 1. Catastrophe Option, Cat Option □ entitles the purchaser of the option against a premium payment to a compensatory cash payment if a specified index of catastrophe losses exceeds a pre-determined level (strike price) 2. Catastrophe Equity Put □ entitles the purchaser of the put to sell equities at a pre-determined price in the event of a catastrophic loss (conflagration, earthquake, windstorm)

Katastrophen / ~**rückversicherung** catastrophe reinsurance, catastrophe excess of loss treaty

Kategorie category, class

Kategorie-1/Kategorie-2-Sicherheiten Tier 1/Tier 2 assets, assets eligible as collateral for ESCB monetary policy operations □ Tier 1: marketable assets meeting uniform eligibility criteria; Tier 2: market and nonmarketable assets that are of particular importance to national banking systems

Kauf purchase, acquisition, buying

Kauf *(~ per Kasse)* cash purchase, buying for cash, *(im Devisenhandel)* spot purchase, buying outright, *(~ einer Option)* buying an option, opening a long option position *(~ auf eigene Rechnung)* purchase for own account, *(~ auf feste Rechnung)* firm purchase, buying firm, *(~ für fremde Rechnung)* purchase for third party account, *(~ auf Termin)* purchase for forward (future) delivery

Kauf / ~abrechnung *(bei Wertpapieren)* bought note; **~auftrag** buy order, *(limitierter ~)* limited buy order, stop buy order

Käufe *(Börse)* buying, *(~ des Berufshandels)* professional buying, *(~ auf ermäßigter Kursbasis)* buying at a reduced price level

Kaufempfehlung buy recommendation

kaufen to buy, to purchase, *(Finanzpositionen eröffnen)* to go long, to open (to take) a long position, *(für den eigenen Bestand ~)* to buy for own account, *(an der Börse ~)* to buy in the market, *(am Markt ~ und verkaufen)* trading in and out of the market, *(gegen den Markttrend ~)* to buy anti-marketwise

Käufer buyer, purchaser, *(~ per Termin)* forward buyer

K

Käufer / ~abruf buyer's call; **~bank** buying bank; **~interesse** *(Börse)* buying interest; **~mangel** lack of buying orders, absence of buyers; **~markt** buyer's market

Käufer / ~publikum buyers, investing public; **~seite** buy side, *(auf der ~)* on the buyer's side, as buyers

Käufer- und Verkäufermarkt (liquid) two-way market

Kauf / ~formation buy chart pattern; **~geschäft** buy trade; **~gewährleistungsrecht** warranty law

Kauf-Hedge long hedge, buying hedge □ buying a future or option contract to protect a cash position against a possible price rise in the underlying commodity

Kaufinteresse buying interest (attention), *(das ~ konzentrierte sich auf spekulative Werte)* buying interest centered on speculative counters, speculative counters stood in the limelight

Kauf / ~kraft purchasing power, spending power; **~kraftschwund** shrinkage in purchasing power; **~kurs** buying rate; **~limit** buy limit; **~mann** businessman, *(Kaufmann/Kaufleute i. S. des HGB)* merchant(s)

kaufmännisch *(nach vernünftiger ~er Beurteilung)* in accordance with sound (prudent) business judgment

Kauf / ~mitteilung buy advice, notice of purchase; **~motiv** buying motive; **~neigung** buying interest, propensity to buy

Kaufoption call option, call, *(~ auf einen Terminkontrakt)* futures call option, *(Erwerb einer ~)* buying a call, taking a long call position, *(erworbene Kaufoptionen)* long calls, *(Erwerber/Inhaber einer ~)* call buyer/holder, *(Verkauf einer ~)* selling (writing) a call, opening a short call position, *(verkaufte Kaufoptionen)* short calls, calls written, *(Verkäufer/Stillhalter einer ~)* call writer, seller of a call

Kauf / ~optionsschein call warrant, *(bei Index-Optionsscheinen)* bull warrant; **~ order** buy order, purchase order; **~position** long position, *(über eine ~ verfügen)* to hold a long position, to be long, *(Glattstellung einer ~)* closing out a long position, *(Inhaber einer ~)* long position holder

Kauf / ~preis purchase price, purchase money (consideration); **~preisfinanzierung** financing the purchase price; **~signal** buying signal, signal to buy; **~verhaltensmuster** purchasing pattern; **~verpflichtung** obligation (undertaking) to buy, purchase commitment

Kauf / ~vertrag purchase agreement, contract of sale, contract for purchase and sale; **~welle** *(an der Börse)* welter of buying, buying surge, spate of new buying; **~zurückhaltung** *(an der Börse)* buying restraint

Kausalzusammenhang causal link, causality

Kaution surety, deposit, guarantee, bail, bail bond

Kautions / ~effekten securities deposited (lodged) as collateral; **~erklärung**

surety bond, bail bond, declaration of suretyship

kautionsfähig able to put up security

Kautions / ~hinterlegung → Kautionsleistung; **~kreditgeschäfte** lendings against assets pledged as collateral; **~leistung** payment of a deposit, provision of surety (of a bail bond); **~summe** → Haftungssumme

Kautions / ~verpflichtungen surety commitments; **~versicherung** surety insurance; **~versicherungsgesellschaft** surety company, bonding company; **~wechsel** guarantee bill, bill serving as collateral

KBV → Kurs/Buchwert-Verhältnis

KCV → Kurs/Cashflow-Verhältnis

Kehrseite *(~ der Hausse)* reverse side (the other side) of the bull run

Keil/Keilformation *(Chart-Analyse)* wedge, wedge pattern □ a formation in which the price fluctuations are within converging straight lines, *(nach oben laufender ~)* upward wedge, upward sloping wedge pattern □ indicates a market weakness following a bull run, *(nach unten laufender ~)* downward wedge, downward sloping wedge pattern □ indicates an upward trend following a bear run

Kellerwechsel wind bill, kite

Kennnummer identification (code) number

Kenntnis knowledge, awareness, *(von etwas ~ erhalten)* to learn s.th., *(von der Abtretung ~ nehmen)* to acknowledge the assignment, *(jmd. in ~ setzen)* to inform s. o. about (of, on), to notify s. o.

Kenntnisnahme 1. information, notice **2.** taking note of, *(zu Ihrer ~)* for your information (guidance)

Kennung → Kundenkennung

Kenn / ~wort password; **~zahlensystem 1.** ratio system **2.** scoring system → Kredit-Scoring; **~zahlenvergleich** ratio comparison; **~zeichen 1.** code, identification number **2.** characteristic, distinguishing feature (mark)

kennzeichnen to mark, to distinguish, to label, *(Wertpapiere ~)* to identify

Kennzeichnung identification, marking, labelling, *(~ des Lastschriftsgläubigers)* identification (indication) of the creditor (Teil der SEPA – → Gläubigeridentifikationsnummer)

Kennziffer 1. index (code) number **2.** *(betriebswirtschaftliche Kennzahl)* ratio

Kern / ~geschäft core (mainstream) business, mainstream (traditional) activities;**~geschäftsfeld** core business line

Kernkapital Tier 1 capital, core capital □ Under → Basel III rules, Tier 1 Capital consists of Common Equity Tier 1 Capital (→ hartes Kernkapital) and Additional Tier 2 Capital (→ zusätzliches Kernkapital). On 1 January 2015, Tier 1 Capital will need to equal 6% of a bank's risk-weighted assets at all times. Given the objective that Common Equity Tier 1 must help a bank remain a going concern, it is also described as going-concern capital. → Gesamtkapital

Kernkapitalfähigkeit eligibility for inclusion in the core capital, *(kernkapitalfähige Instrumente)* instruments eligible for inclusion in the core capital

Kernkapitalquote Tier 1 capital ratio □ ratio of a bank's Tier 1 capital expressed as a percentage of total risk-weighted assets

Kernkompetenz core competence (competencies), core qualifications (skills, strength)

Kernleistungen *(einer Bank)* mainstream banking, traditional banking services

Kernstück 1. *(~ des Unternehmensplans)* centrepiece of the business plan **2.** *(z. B. des Eurobond-Marktes)* bedrock of the Eurobond market

3. *(das ~ der Gruppe)* the heart (core) of the group

Kerzenchart candlestick chart □ Chart that represents the price movements of a stock during a trading session or any other specified period. Candlesticks consist of the body/rectangular box (Körper) representing the range between opening and closing price and of lower and upper shadows/wicks (oberer und unterer Schatten/Docht bzw. Lunte) representing the high and low of the session. If the stock closed above the opening price, the body is white, green or blue (bullish signal); it is plotted in black or red if the stock closed below the opening price (bearish signal). In addition to the aforementioned basic patterns, there are multiple forms of candlestick patterns.

K

Kerzenchart / **~analyse** candlestick chart analysis; **~formation/-muster** candlestick chart pattern; **~technik** candlestick charting techniques

KfW *(Kreditanstalt für Wiederaufbau)* German Reconstruction Loan Corporation

KfW / **~-Darlehen** KfW loan; **~-Entwicklungsbank** KfW development bank; **~-Fördermittel** KfW development funds; **~-Förderprogramm** KfW assistance (development) scheme; **~-Gründerkredit** KfW start-up loan; **~-Mittelstandsbank** KfW SME bank; **~-Unternehmerkredit** KfW business loan

Kfz / **~-Darlehen** auto loan, car loan; **~-Darlehensvertrag** car loan agreement; **~-Finanzierung** auto (car) financing; **~-Finanzierungsrechner** auto (car) loan calculator

KGV → Kurs/Gewinn-Verhältnis

Kickback-Zahlung kickback payment □ commission paid (1) by investment companies to financial advisors or banks for fund marketing (2) in consideration of the referral of customers (3) to secure a profit or service

Kinderschuhen *(der Markt steckt noch in den ~)* the market is still in its infancy (still a fledgling market)

klagbar *(~er Anspruch)* actionable claim

Klage 1. action, suit, lawsuit, charge, *(~ auf Leistung)* action for performance **2.** *(Beschwerde)* complaint

Klage / **~abweisung** dismissal of an action, *(Antrag des Beklagten auf ~)* defendant's motion to dismiss; **~ausschlussfrist** limitation of actions; **~befugnis** right of action; **~begründung** substantiation of a case, statement of claim; **~beitritt** joinder (in an action)

Klage / **~erhebung** filing of an action (a suit), bringing an action against; **~erweiterung** extension of an action (of the plaintiff's claim); **~erwiderung** statement of defense; **~grund** cause (ground) of action, ground for bringing an action against

klagen to sue, to bring an action (to take legal action) against, *(auf Schadenersatz ~)* to sue for damages, *(aus einem Vertrag ~)* to sue on a contract, *(auf Zahlung ~)* to sue for payment

Kläger plaintiff, claimant; **~bürgschaft** plaintiff bond; **~gemeinschaft** community of plaintiffs; **~vertreter** plaintiff's legal counsel

Klage / **~recht** right of action, right to bring action (to file a complaint), right to sue in a court of law; **~schrift** statement of claim, complaint, writ; **~verbindung** joinder of causes of action; **~verwirkung** forfeiture of the right of action

Klage / **~verzicht** waiver of the right of action, *(vertraglich vereinbart)* covenant not to sue; **~weg** *(Forderungsbeitreibung auf dem ~)* recovery of a debt by taking legal action; **~zustellung** service of the statement of claim

klären *(einen Sachverhalt ~)* to clear up (to clarify) a matter

Klarheit clarity, clearness

Klärung clearing up, clarification, *(~ der Rechtslage)* clearing up the legal position

Klasse 1. category 2. *(Aktiengattung/Aktionärsgruppe/Gläubigergruppe)* class 3. *(bonitäts-/qualitätsmäßig)* rating, grade 4. *(Eigenkapital-Klasse)* tier 5. *(Gehalts-/Steuerklasse)* bracket

klassifizieren 1. to classify, to class, to categorise 2. *(bonitätsmäßig)* to grade, to rate

Klassifizierung/Klassifikation 1. classification 2. grading, rating

klassisch *(~e Finanzierungsform)* traditional (standard-type, classical) form of financing (funding), *(~ e Option)* plain vanilla option

Klausel 1. clause 2. *(Bestimmung)* provision, stipulation, condition, covenant 3. *(Vorbehalt)* proviso

kleine Stücke *i.w.S.* odd lots, securities order for less than the normal trading unit, *i.e.S.* bond/notes with a nominal value below € 500

kleine Stückelungen small denominations

kleinere und mittlere Unternehmen small and medium-sized (midsized) enterprises, SME enterprises, *(kleinere Kapitalgesellschaften nach* → EGHGB/BilMOG) small corporations □ total assets: below € 4.84m; sales: below € 9.68m; headcount: below 50

Klein / ~aktionär small shareholder; **~anleger** retail investor, small (small-scale) investor; **~auftrag** odd lot order, small market order, *(kleinste handelbare Einheit)* minimum trading unit

Klein / ~beteiligtenprivileg *(im Insolvenzverfahren)* minority shareholder privilege □ exempts shareholder loans with a stake of less than 10 % from subordination and voidability in insolvency; **~betriebsfinanzierung** small business financing

Klein / ~gedrucktes fine print; **~kredit** small loan, *(gewerblicher)* small business loan; **~order** → Kleinauftrag; **~sparer** small saver

kleinteilig *(~es Firmenkundengeschäft)* small-sized corporate banking, *(~es Kreditgeschäft)* small-sized lending business, retail lending

Kleinunternehmen small business (company), → kleinere und mittlere Unternehmen, *(Kreditvergabe an ~)* small firm lending

Kleinunternehmerförderungsgesetz Small Businesses Support Act

kleinvolumige Forderungen low-value (smaller-balance) loan assets

Kleinzahlungsverkehr low-value payment transactions

Klemme *(sich finanziell in der ~ befinden)* to be in financial straits

klettern to climb, to move up, to rise, *(um mäßige 2 % ~)* to climb by a moderate 2 %, *(AB kletterten um 4 auf 50 €)* AB jumped (rose, climbed) 4 to € 50

Klima 1. *(an der Börse)* tone, sentiment, mood 2. *(konjunkturelles)* climate, environment

Klima-Futures climate futures □ futures on emissions allowances and other environmental products

Kluft *(~ zwischen Soll- und Ist-Ergebnis)* wide gap (gulf) between planned and actual performance

Klumpen cluster; **~auswahlverfahren** cluster sampling; **~risiko** cluster risk; **~stichprobe** cluster sample

KMU → kleinere und mittlere Unternehmen

KMU-Kredite/Finanzierungen lendings (credit exposures) to SMEs

knapp 1. *adj.* tight, scarce, scant, *(~e Kapitalausstattung/Liquiditätsausstattung)* scant equity/liquidity resources, *(~e Konditionen)* tight pricing (terms), *(~e Spannen)* tight margins 2. *adv.* *(~ kalkuliert)* tightly priced, *(~ bleiben)* to remain in short supply

Knappheit shortage, scarcity, scantiness

Knebelungsvertrag illegal tie-in (tying) arrangement

Koeffizient ratio, coefficient

kollegial *(~er Führungsstil)* collegiate management style

Kollegialprinzip principle of collective responsibility

kollektiv *(~ ermittelte Wertberichtigung)* collectively assessed allowance for loan losses

Kollektiv / **~abschreibung** flat depreciation; **~bewertung** collective assessment (valuation); **~prokura** → Gesamtprokura; **~verantwortung** principle of collective responsibility

Kollektiv / **~versicherung** group insurance; **~vertretung** joint agency; **~vollmacht** joint power of attorney; **~zeichnung** joint signature, signing jointly

K

kollidieren to collide (to clash) with, *(kollidierende Sicherungsrechte)* conflicting security interests

Kombi-Karte combi card □ combining both contact and contactless technology on one card

Kombinationsfinanzierung multiple-component financing

Kombinationsgeschäft → Kombinationsorder

Kombinationshandel combination trade (trading), → Kombinationsposition

Kombinationsorder 1. OCO (one cancels other) order □ two orders placed simultaneously; when one order is executed, the other order is automatically cancelled
2. OCA (one cancels all) order □ when one order is executed all remaining orders are automatically cancelled

Kombinationsposition *(kombinierte Optionsposition)* combination □ buying or selling both a call and a put on the same underlying instrument with different strike prices and/or different expiry dates, → Spread-Handel

kombinieren to combine, to put (to group) together

kombiniert *(~es Konsortial- und Tenderverfahren)* combined syndicate and tender procedure, *(~e Schadenkostenquote)* combined ratio, *(~es Transportdokument)* combined transport bill of lading, *(~es Übernahme- und Begebungskonsortium)* combined underwriting and selling group, *(~er Zins- und Währungs-Swap)* cross currency interest rate swap □ agreement combining interest rate and foreign currency swap transactions

Kombizinsanleihe step-up bond

Kommandit / **~anteil**/**~beteiligung** interest in a limited partnership, limited partner's share; **~einlagen** equity contributions by the limited partners, amount of capital put up (capital invested) by the limited partners

Kommandit / **~fonds** property bond fund run as a limited partnership; **~gesellschaft** limited partnership; **~gesellschaft auf Aktien** partnership limited by shares

Kommanditist limited partner

Kommanditvertrag limited partnership agreement

Kommentar comment, commentary

kommentieren to comment on

kommerziell *(~es Auslandsgeschäft)* foreign commercial operations, *(~e Ausleihungen)* commercial (corporate) lendings, *(~es Bankgeschäft)* commercial (corporate) banking, *(~es Kreditgeschäft)* commercial lending operations, *(~e Kunden)* corporate customers, *(~es Realkreditgeschäft)* commercial property lending

kommissarisch *(~e Verwahrung)* provisional custody, temporary safekeeping, *(~er Vorstandsvorsitzender)* acting chief executive

Kommission 1. *(Auftrag)* agency, commission, *(in ~ geben)* to consign, to deliver for custody or sale, *(in ~ nehmen)* to take on commission

2. *(Ausschuss)* committee, commission
3. *(Provision)* commission, fee

Kommissionär agent, commission agent, broker

Kommissionsbasis *(auf ~ tätig werden)* to operate on an agency basis (on commission)

Kommissionsbericht committee report

Kommissionsgeschäft 1. *(Wertpapierkommissionsgeschäft)* brokerage (agency) transactions, orders executed for customer account
2. *(pl)* brokerage business, broking services, brokerage (agency) transactions

Kommissions / ~gut consigned goods, goods on consigment; **~handel** brokerage (agency) trading, trading on an agency basis; **~kauf** buying on commission; **~verkauf** sale (selling) on commission; **~vertrag** agency (brokerage) agreement

Kommissions / ~vertreter commission agent; **~verwahrung** safekeeping in one's own name but for account of a third party; **~ware** goods on commission

kommissionsweise on an agency basis, *(~ Übernahme einer Emission)* selling an issue on a best efforts basis, taking up and selling an issue on an agency basis

Kommittent principal, consignor

Kommunalanleihen municipal bonds, → Kommunalobligationen

Kommunaldarlehen loans to public sector entities □ in a narrower sense: lendings made by private and public sector banks to townships, municipalities or public sector institutions; the term includes in a broader sense also loans to the Federal Government, the Land governments and government agencies

Kommunal / ~deckung cover through the guarantee of a public sector agency; **~finanzen** local government finance; **~investitionen** local government investments; **~kredit** → Kommunaldarlehen

Kommunalobligationen / kommunale Kassenobligationen municipal bonds/notes, munis □ bonds/notes issued by private mortgage banks and public sector credit institutions against their lendings to the public sector, → Kommunaldarlehen

Kommunalpfandbrief Municipal Pfandbrief, Municipal Covered Bond, → Pfandbrief

Kommunalverband association of municipalities

kommunalverbürgt *(~e Kredite)* bank lendings against public sector guarantees

Kommunen local governments, public authorities, *(Finanzbedarf der ~)* finance requirements of local governments, *(Schuldenaufnahme der ~)* local government borrowings

Kommunikations / ~beratung communication consulting; **~fähigkeit** communicative (communication) skills; **~kompetenz** communicative competence; **~stärke** strength in communication, *(kommunikationsstark)* to be a good communicator, to have good communication skills

Kompensation 1. *(Entschädigung)* compensation, indemnity, indemnification 2. *(Verrechnung)* set-off, offset, offsetting, netting, pairing, *(~ von Aufwands- und Ertragspositionen)* netting of expenditure and income items, *(~ von debitorischen und kreditorischen Salden)* netting of debit and credit balances

Kompensations / ~abkommen compensation (netting) agreement; **~anspruch** compensation (indemnity) claim; **~betrag** compensation (offsetting) amount; **~geschäft** 1. offsetting transaction 2. *(im Außenwirtschaftsverkehr)* compensation transaction (deal)

Kompensations / ~handel compensation trade; **~schlussnote** settlement note; ~**verpflichtungen** compensation commitments

kompensatorisch *(~e Darstellung)* showing a netted result, *(~e Kosten)* compensatory cost

kompensieren 1. *(entschädigen)* to compensate, to indemnify
2. *(verrechnen)* to set off, to offset, to net, *(mit dem laufenden Konto ~)* to set off (to net, to apply) against the current account, *(XY konnte die Verluste des Vortages ~)* XY succeeded in recovering from yesterday's losses
3. *(im Börsengeschäft)* to match, to pair, *(Kauf- und Verkaufsaufträge ~)* to match (to pair) buy and sell orders, to set off buy orders against sell orders

kompensierend *(~e Risikopositionen)* offsetting (compensating) risk positions, *(~e Transaktion)* closing transaction

K

kompensiert *(~e Bilanzsumme)* consolidated total assets after intragroup balances

kompetent 1. *(befähigt, qualifiziert)* qualified, competent 2. *(bevollmächtigt)* authorised 3. *(zuständig)* competent

Kompetenz 1. competence, skills, qualification(s), expertise
2. *(im Kreditgeschäft)* approval powers, lending authority
3. *(Zuständigkeit)* competence, province, *(unter die ~ des Vorstandes fallen)* to fall within the competence (to come within the province) of the Manangement Board

Kompetenz / ~anforderungen competency requirements; ~**bereich** competence, province, area (sphere) of responsibility; ~**bewertung** competence (skills) assessment; ~**bilanz** competence record; ~**bilanzierung** skills analysis; ~**bündelung** pooling (bundling) of competences

Kompetenz / ~ebene level of authority; ~**entwicklungsmodell** competency (skills) development model; ~**feststellungsverfahren** competence assessment process: ~**gewinn** competence gain, added competence; ~**grenzen** limits of authority (of approval powers)

Kompetenz / ~inventar competence (skills) inventory; ~**kette** lending authority chain; ~**konflikt** conflict of competence; ~**landkarte** competence map; ~**liste** list of approval powers; ~**management** competency (skills) management; ~**messung** measuring competencies, skills (competency) measurement; ~**missbrauch** abuse of appoval powers

Kompetenz / ~ordnung 1. decision-making hierarchy, division of responsibilities 2. system of approval powers; ~**profil** competence profile; ~**regeln** competence rules, → Kompetenzordnung; ~**steigerung** enhancement of competence, skills enhancement

Kompetenz / ~streitigkeiten conflicts (controversies) of competence; ~**stufe** level of authority; ~**träger** person in authority, executive (officer) holding powers of approval, authorised person

Kompetenz / ~überschneidung overlapping of powers; ~**überschreitung** exceeding (overstepping) one's authority (brief), *(kompetenzüberschreitende Darlehensausreichungen)* loan extensions exceeding the approval powers of the officer concerned; ~**überwachung** monitoring approval powers

Kompetenz / ~vermittlung imparting skills; ~**verteilung** distribution (allocation) of competences (approval powers); ~**zentrum** center of competence; ~**zuordnung** assignment of responsibilities (of approval powers)

komplementär *(~es Produkt)* complementary product

Komplementär general partner, personally liable partner

Komplementärfinanzierung complementary financing

Komplementär-GmbH General Partner GmbH □ acts as general partner in a → GmbH & Co. KG

komplettieren *(das Leistungsangebot ~)* to round off (to complete) the range of services offered

Komplett / ~konto all-in-one account; **~lösung** all-round solution, one-stop solution

komplex 1. complex, many-sided **2.** *(schwierig)* intricate, complicated

Komplex 1. complex **2.** issue

Komplexität *(~ des Handels)* complexity (intracacies) of trading

Kompositgeschäft composite insurance business, property and casualty insurance operations

Komposit / ~versicherer composite insurance company, composite underwriter, multiline insurer; **~versicherung** composite insurance, composite policy

Kompromiss compromise; **~bereitschaft** *(~ signalisieren)* to signal willingness to compromise; **~formel** compromise formula; **~klausel** arbitration clause; **~lösung** compromise solution; **~vorschlag** offer of compromise

Komptant / ~geschäft cash deal (trade), delivery (of securities) versus payment; **~kurs** cash price

Konditionalität conditionality □ criteria for the use of IMF resources

Konditionen 1. terms, pricing, terms and conditions, *(~ im Aktivgeschäft)* loan pricing, loan terms, lending rates, *(~ von Anleiheemissionen)* bond terms, bond pricing, *(~ für Festgeldanlagen)* interest rates paid on time (term) deposits, *(~ für Hypothekenkredite)* mortgage loan rates (terms), *(die besten verfügbaren ~)* the finest pricing available, *(jmd. die besten ~ einräumen)* to grant s. o. one's very best terms
2. *(für Bankdienstleistungen im allgemeinen)* fees and commission rates
3. *(für Warengeschäfte)* payment and delivery terms

Konditionen / ~absprache terms arranged (agreed upon), agreement on the terms of the facility; **~änderung** change of (in) loan terms, repricing, reviewing (modification of) the loan terms; **~änderungsklausel** repricing clause

Konditionen / ~angebot terms (rates) offered; **~anhebung** rate (pricing) increase; **~anpassung** pricing adjustment, rate adjustment, adjustment of the loan terms, *(~ an die veränderte Marktlage)* adjusting the terms (the loan rate) to the changed conditions in the market; **~anpassungsklausel** terms (rate) adjustment clause

Konditionen / ~aufstellung rate sheet, → Konditionenblatt; **~befristung** limiting the duration of the terms (the rate) offered

Konditionenbindung 1. *(i. S. einer Festschreibung des Zinssatzes)* establishment of a fixed interest rate (of fixed loan terms), locking in the interest rate
2. *(i. S. einer Bindung an einen Referenz-Zinssatz)* linking (indexing) the interest rate to a reference rate

Konditionen / ~blatt 1. *(bei Kreditausreichungen)* term sheet, rate sheet **2.** *(bei Schuldtitelemissionen)* pricing supplement; **~druck** pricing pressure, competitive pressure on terms and rates

Konditionenfestlegung pricing, fixing the terms and conditions, *(~ für Bankdienstleistungen)* pricing of banking services, *(~ im Kreditgeschäft)* loan pricing, fixing the loan terms, establishing the terms for (e. g. borrowings in the Euromarket, overdraft facilities, etc.), *(~ für Neuemissionen)* new issue pricing

Konditionen / ~festschreibung → Konditionenbindung; **~findung** pricing, → Konditionenfestlegung; **~frage**

pricing issue; ~**gefälle** interest rate differential, pricing differential

Konditionen / ~**gestaltung** *(im Kreditgeschäft)* pricing of loans, *(von Bankdienstleistungen)* pricing of banking services; ~**liste** → Konditionentableau; ~**nachlässe** pricing concessions; ~**palette** range of rates and terms offered; ~**politik** pricing policy, policy on rates and fees

Konditionen / ~**regelung** → Konditionenfestlegung; ~**spielraum** pricing leeway; ~**spreizung** tiering the loan terms; ~**tableau** schedule of (interest rates and) fees charged, rate sheet; ~**transparenz** transparency in pricing; ~**überprüfung** pricing review, reviewing the loan terms

Konditionen / ~**varianten** pricing alternatives (options); ~**vereinbarung** term sheet; ~**verschlechterung** deterioration in lending rates (in pricing); ~**wettbewerb** pricing competition; ~**zugeständnisse** rate (pricing) concessions

K

Konditionsdifferenzversicherung difference in conditions coverage, DIC insurance

Konferenz conference, meeting

konferieren to confer, to hold a conference (a meeting)

Konfidenz / ~**intervall** confidence interval; ~**niveau** confidence level

Konflikt conflict, clash; ~**ursache** cause of conflict

konform conforming, coinciding, matching, *(~ gehen mit)* to agree with, to be in agreement with

Konformität *(~ mit EU-Standards)* conformity with EU standards

Kongress convention, congress, conference

kongruent 1. *adj.* *(~e Aktivbestände)* matching long (asset) positions, *(~e Deckung)* matching cover, *(Grundsatz der ~en Deckung)* principle of matching cover, *(~e Laufzeit)* matching maturity (life, term), *(~e Refinanzierung)* funding (refinancing) at matching maturities, *(~e Währungsdeckung)* matching currency cover
2. *adv.* *(~ refinanziertes Kreditgeschäft)* lendings funded at matching maturities, *(~rückgedeckt)* funded with matching cover

Kongruenz *(Herstellung einer ~ im Laufzeitenbereich/im Währungsbereich)* maturity matching/currency matching

Kongruenzprinzip matching principle

Konjunktur business (economic) activity, state of the economy

Konjunktur / ~**abschwächung** receding economic activity; ~**abschwung** economic downswing, downturn (slump) in business; ~**ankurbelung** stimulation of economic activity, economic pump priming

Konjunktur / ~**anreiz** stimulus to economic activity; ~**anspannung** economic (cyclical) strains; ~**aufschwung** economic upswing, upturn in business; ~**aussichten** economic (business) prospects

Konjunktur / ~**barometer** economic (business) indicator; ~**belebung** economic revival (recovery), upturn in business; ~**bremsung**/~**dämpfung** checking (curb on) excessive economic activity; ~**einbruch** sharp setback in business activity, economic slump

konjunkturell cyclical, economic

konjunkturempfindlich sensitive to cyclical fluctuations (to fluctuations in business activity), *(~e Aktien)* economically sensitive shares

Konjunktur / ~**entspannung** easing of economic strains; ~**entwicklung** economic trend, development of business activity; ~**flaute** lull (slackness) in business, slackening of economic activity; ~**förderprogramm** economic stimulus package

Konjunktur / ~**impulse** economic stimuli, business incentives; ~**indikatoren** economic indicators, indicators of business activity; ~**lage** economic situation, state of the economy (of economic activity); ~**motor** primary mover of economic activity, economic engine

Konjunktur / ~**phase** business (economic) cycle; ~**politik** economic policy; ~**reagibilität** sensitiveness to cyclical swings; ~**rückgang** economic downturn, decline in economic activity; ~**rückschlag** setback in economic activity

Konjunktur / ~**sachverständiger** economic research expert; ~**schwäche** flagging economy, downturn in business activity; ~**schwankungen** economic (cyclical) fluctuations, swings in the economic cycle

Konjunktur / ~**spritzen** government measures (e. g. tax reliefs) designed to stimulate economic activity, economic stimulus package; ~**tief** economic (cyclical) low; ~**überhitzung** overheating the economy; ~**unsicherheiten** economic uncertainties

Konjunktur / ~**verlangsamung** economic slowdown, slowdown in business activity; ~**verlauf** economic trend, development of business activity; ~**wende** turnaround in economic activity, break in the economic trend; ~**zyklus** business (economic) cycle

konkludent 1. *adj.* *(~e Einwilligung)* implied (implicit) consent 2. *adv.* *(~ annehmen)* to accept implicitly

konkret *(~e Fortschritte)* concrete (tangible) progress, *(~e Kreditzusage)* precise (firm) loan undertaking

konkretisieren 1. *(die Vorschläge ~)* to put the proposals into concrete (definite) terms, → präzisieren
2. *(sich ~)* to take shape

Konkretisierung putting into concrete terms, precise definition

Konkurrent competitor, rival

Konkurrenten / ~**klage** action for unfair competition; ~**schutz** protection of competing entities; ~**streitverfahren** unfair litigation proceedings

Konkurrenz competition

Konkurrenz / ~**anbieter** competitor, rival firm; ~**angebot** competing offer, rival bid; ~**ausschlussklausel** non-compete clause, covenant not to compete; ~**bedingungen** terms of competition, competitive situation; ~**druck** competitive pressure, pressure of competition

konkurrenzfähig competitive, able to compete, *(~ sein)* to stand any competition, *(~es Angebot)* competitive quotation, *(~e Produkte)* competitive products, *(preislich)* competitively priced products

Konkurrenz / ~**fähigkeit** competitiveness, competitive power; ~**firma** competitor, rival firm; ~**klausel** competitive clause

konkurrenzlos unrivalled, without competition

Konkurrenz / ~**marken** competing (rival) brands; ~**unternehmen** rival (competing) firm, competitor; ~**vorteil** competitive advantage (edge); ~**werbung** competitive advertising; ~**wirtschaft** competitive economy

konkurrieren *(mit etablierten Marktteilnehmern ~)* to compete (to vie) with established market players

Konkurs bankruptcy → Insolvenz

Konnossement bill of lading, B/L, *(~ einer Linienreederei)* liner bill of lading

Konnossements / ~-**Ausfertigung** B/L copy; ~-**Garantie** B/L letter of indemnity; ~-**Klausel** B/L clause; ~**vermerk** notation on the bill of lading

Konsensbildung consensus building

konsensorientiert *(~er Ansatz)* consensus-oriented approach

Konsensualvertrag consensus agreement

konsequent *(~e Umsetzung)* consistent implementation

Konsequenz consequence, effect, *(~en für die Geldpolitik)* consequences for (impact on, repercussions on, impli-

K

cations for) monetary policy, *(die ~en tragen)* to face (to acknowledge) the consequences

konservativ *(~e Anlagestrategie)* conservative (prudent) investment strategy, *(~e Schätzung)* conservative estimate

Konsignant *(im Außenhandel)* principal

Konsignations / ~lager consignment stock (inventory); **~verkauf** consignment sale

Konsignator *(im Außenhandel)* commission agent

konsolidieren to consolidate, *(im Konzernabschluss voll konsolidiert werden)* to be fully consolidated in the financial statements

konsolidiert *(~e Bedingungen)* integrated conditions, → nicht konsolidierte Bedingungen, *(~e Bilanz)* consolidated balance sheet (financial statements), *(~e Gewinn-und Verlustrechnung)* consolidated statement of income *(~e Kapitalrechnung)* consolidated statement of shareholders' equity, *(~e Rechnungslegung)* consolidated accounting, *(eine ~e Rechnungslegung unterhalten)* to run a consolidated book, *(~er Reinertrag)* consolidated net income

Konsolidierung **1.** consolidation, strengthening, *(~ am Aktienmarkt)* consolidation in the equity market, *(~ des Haushalts)* budget consolidation
2. *(bilanzmäßig)* consolidation, *(~ auf nachgeordneten Ebenen)* sub-consolidation
3. debt consolidation, combining two or more loans into one loan facility, conversion of short-term loans into long-term borrowings

Konsolidierungs / ~anleihe consolidation bond; **~ausgleichsposten** → aktiver/passiver Konsolidierungsausgleichsposten; **~darlehen** consolidation loan; **~differenzen** *(Bereinigung von ~)* consolidation adjustments

Konsolidierungs / ~kredit debt consolidation loan; **~kreis** companies included in consolidation, basis of consolidation, group of consolidated companies, *(aufsichtsrechtlicher ~)* scope of regulatory consolidation, *(Veränderungen im ~)* changes in the scope of consolidation (acquisitions and divestitures)

Konsolidierungsmodell consolidation model □ Unlike the → Zweckgesellschaftsmodell, the consolidation model enables a bank to transfer a wide range of risk positions to a winding-up institution (→ Abwicklungsanstalt) that will be established by the FSMS (→ Finanzmarktstabilisierungsanstalt) upon the bank's request. → Finanzmarktstabilisierungs-Fortentwicklungsgesetz

Konsolidierungsmuster *(in der Charttechnik)* consolidation pattern

Konsolidierungspflicht consolidation requirement, duty to prepare consolidated financial statements, *(konsolidierungspflichtige Beteiligungen/Tochterunternehmen)* equity investments/subsidiaries requiring consolidation

Konsolidierungs / ~phase period of consolidation; **~pflicht** consolidation requirement; **~richtlinie** Consolidation Directive □ EU directive laying down rules for the consolidated supervision of financial groups

Konsolidierungs / ~risiko *(bei der Umrechnung der Unternehmensabschlüsse von Auslandsniederlassungen)* consolidation (translation) risk; **~verfahren bei Großkrediten** consolidation procedure for large exposures

Konsorte syndicate member, underwriter

Konsortial / ~abteilung syndicate (syndication) desk; **~anteil** syndicate (underwriting) share, underwritten amount; **~banken** syndicate banks, underwriting banks; **~beteiligung** → Konsortialanteil; **~bindungen** syndication commitments; ~**finanzierung** syndicated financing

Konsortialführer lead manager, syndicate leader (manager), *(konsortialführende Bank)* lead bank, lead manager, managing bank, syndicate leader (manager)

Konsortialführung lead management, management group, *(mit der ~ betrauen)* to award the lead management to, to entrust with the lead management, *(die ~ innehaben)* to run the books

Konsortial / ~geschäft syndicate (underwriting) business; ~**gestaltung** syndicate set-up; ~**konto** new issue account; ~**kredit** syndicated loan, consortium loan; ~**kreditgeschäft** syndicated loan business, syndicated lendings

Konsortial / ~mitglied syndicate member, syndication participant, member of the lender consortium; ~**nutzen** underwriting spread; ~**provision** underwriting commission, syndicate fee

Konsortial / ~quote underwriting share, underwriter's share, underwriting commitment, syndicate share (interest); ~**rechnung** syndicate account (accounting)

Konsortial / ~sitzung meeting of the syndicate members, underwriters' meeting; ~**spanne** underwriting spread (margin); ~**tranche** syndication tranche, → Konsortialquote

Konsortial / ~vergütung underwriting commission; ~**verhältnis** syndicate relationship; ~**vermögen** syndicate assets; ~**vertrag** syndicate (syndication) agreement, underwriting agreement

Konsortium 1. *(von Banken)* banking syndicate, group of banks **2.** *(von Nicht-Banken)* consortium, group of companies

Konstellation situation, circumstances, pattern, set-up

konstituieren to constitute, to set up, *(~de Sitzung)* constituent meeting

Konsultations / ~papier consultation paper (document); ~**verfahren** consultation procedure (process)

Konsumentenfinanzierung consumer finance

Konsumentenkredit consumer loan, *(Konditionen für ~e)* consumer loan rates (terms)

Konsumentenkredit / ~geschäft consumer lendings, consumer lending business; ~**versicherung** consumer credit insurance; ~**volumen** consumer lending portfolio

kontaktbehaftet *(~e Chipkarte)* contact chip card (smart card)

Kontaktfläche contact surface (of a chip card)

kontaktieren to contact, to approach

K

kontaktlos *(~es Bezahlsystem)* contactless payment system, *(~e Chipkarte)* contactless chip card (smart card), *(~e Identifizierung)* contactless (contact-free) identification

Konten / ~aufgliederung breakdown (classification) of accounts; ~**kompensation** account netting; ~**konzentration** account concentration, account pooling; ~**pfändung** seizure of the account balance; ~**plan** chart of accounts; ~**rahmen** accounting system; ~**sparen** deposit account saving; ~**sparer** account depositor; ~**sperre** account freeze

Kontingent quota; ~**erhöhung** quota increase

kontingentfrei quota-free

kontingentieren 1. to fix quotas **2.** to ration

Kontingentierung 1. fixing of quotas, quota fixing **2.** rationing

Kontingentierungs / ~kartell quota ring; ~**system** quota system; ~**vertrag** quota agreement

kontinuierlich 1. *adj.* continuous, steady, *(~es Preisfestsetzungsverfahren)* continuous auction market **2.** *adv.* *(~ steigen)* to rise steadily (continuously)

Kontinuität continuity

Konto account, *(i. S. von Geschäftsverbindung)* relationship; ~ **pro Diverse** sundries (suspense) account

Konto / **~abfrage** account inquiry; **~abgleich** account reconciliation; **~abschluss 1.** balancing an account (e. g. quarterly, half-yearly account balancing), periodical closing (up) of an account **2.** *(Auflösung)* closing out an account

Konto / **~abstimmung** account reconciliation (verification); **~akte** account file; **~angaben** account information (data); **~auflösung** closing out (liquidating) an account, account close-out

Kontoausgleich 1. *(Rückzahlung des Sollsaldos)* settling (repaying) the debit balance of an account **2.** *(Rückführung der Überziehung)* settling the account overdraft **3.** *(i. S.von Saldierung)* account balancing

K

Konto / **~auszug** statement of account, bank statement; **~auszugsdrucker** statement printer; **~belastung** account debit, debit to an account, amount debited to an account; **~berichtigung** account adjustment, correction of an account; **~bestätigung** confirmation of balance

Konto / **~betreuer** account(s) officer, *i.w.S.* relationship manager; **~betreuung** servicing an account, *i.w.S.* relationship management; **~bewegungen** account movements, movements (transactions) routed through an account; **~bezeichnung** title of an account, account heading

Konto / **~deckung** account cover, *(vorbehaltlich ~)* provided that there is sufficient credit in the account; **~dispositionen** account drawings, drawings on the account; **~einrichtung** opening (establishment) of an account; **~einzahlung** payment (paying) into an account, deposit

Kontoeröffnung account opening

Kontoeröffnungs / **~antrag** account opening application; **~formular** account opening form; **~schreiben** account opening confirmation, letter confirming the opening of an account; **~vertrag** account opening agreement

Konto / **~freigabe** release of a blocked account; **~führer/~in** account(s) officer, → Kontobetreuer, *(kontoführende Stelle)* account-maintaining office

Kontoführung account maintenance, account-keeping, maintaining (running, operating) an account, conduct of an account, *(~ auf Guthabenbasis)* keeping an account in the credit, maintaining an account on a non-borrowing basis

Kontoführungsgebühren account maintenance charges, account-keeping fees, charges for running an account

kontogebunden *(~e Geldkarte)* account-linked money card, → kontoungebundene Geldkarte

Konto / **~guthaben** credit balance of (in) an account; **~gutschrift** account credit, amount credited to an account, crediting an account; **~inhaber** account holder

Kontokorrent current account

Kontokorrent / **~abrede** current account agreement; **~abschluss** balancing a current account, making out the account balancing statement, → Kontoabschluss

Kontokorrent / **~einlagen** demand (checking) deposits, deposits on current accounts; **~forderungen** current account claims; **~geschäft** current account business

Kontokorrent / **~guthaben** current account balance, balance (funds) available in a checking account; **~inanspruchnahmen** current account drawings; **~konto** current account (BE), checking account (AE)

Kontokorrent / **~kredit** advance (borrowing) on current account, overdraft facility, drawing credit; **~kreditzin-**

sen current account borrowing rates; ~**leistungen** *(~ für Privatkunden)* current account services for personal customers

Kontokorrent / ~**periode** current account settlement period; ~**saldo** current account balance, balance in a current account; ~**schuld** current account debt; ~**schuldzinsen** debt interest on current account

Kontokorrent / ~**überziehung** overdraft on current account; ~**verhältnis** current account relationship, *(Ansprüche aus einem ~)* claims arising from a current account relationship; ~**verkehr** current account transactions; ~**vorbehalt** extended reservation of title

Konto / ~**kündigung** termination of an account, terminating the account relationship; ~**name** title of an account; ~**nummer** account number; ~**pfändungsschutz** exempting the (basic) account balance from seizure, → Pfändungsschutzbetrag; ~**regulierung** account settlement; ~**rentabilität** account return, relationship profitability

Konto / ~**saldo** account balance, balance on (in) the account; ~**sparvertrag** investment account savings scheme; ~**sperre** blocking an account, account freeze

Konto / ~**stand** balance in (of) an account, *(aktueller ~)* current account balance; ~**standsabfrage** balance inquiry; ~**tagesauszug** daily statement of account; ~**übertrag** account transfer, transfer to account …; ~**überwachung** account monitoring

Konto / ~**überziehung** **1.** account overdraft, amount overdrawn **2.** overdrawing an account; ~**überziehungskredit** overdraft facility, personal credit line; ~**überziehungsprovision** overdraft commission

Konto / ~**umsatz** account movements, turnover on the account, transactions routed through the account; ~**umschreibung** transferring the account to the name of, change in the title of an account

kontoungebunden *(~e Geldkarte)* standalone card, white card □ card not linked to the holder's bank account

Konto / ~**unterlagen** account records; ~**verbindung** account relationship, banking connection, account maintained (kept) with

Konto / ~**verfügung** drawing (signing) on an account, withdrawal of money from an account; ~**verfügungsberechtigung** authority (power) to draw on an account, authority to operate an account, signature authority; ~**verpfändung** pledge over a bank account; ~**verrechnung** account settlement, settlement through debit/credit to the account

Konto / ~**vertrag** account maintenance agreement; ~**vollmacht** power of attorney, signature authority, → Kontoverfügungsberechtigung; ~**vortrag** account balance brought forward; ~**zeichnungsberechtigung** signature authority, authority to sign on (for) an account; ~**zugangsbeschränkung** account hold, limiting the account holder's access to his/her account

KonTraG → Gesetz zur Kontrolle und Transparenz im Unternehmensbereich

Kontrahent **1.** *(Gegenseite im Handel mit Finanzinstrumenten)* counterparty, party to a trade **2.** *(allgemein)* contracting party, party to an agreement

Kontrahentenausfall counterparty default, *(Verlust bei ~)* loss given default of the counterparty, *(Anpassung für den erwarteten Verlust aus einem ~)* counterparty default adjustment

Kontrahentenausfallrisiko counterparty credit risk (CCR), credit exposure to counterparties □ risk that the other party to a transaction will default prior to the settlement of the transaction

Kontrahenten / ~**gewichtung** counterparty weighting; ~**limit** counterparty credit limit; ~-**Netting** counterparty netting; ~**obligo** counterparty exposure; ~-**Rating** counterparty rating

Kontrahenten / ~**risiko** counterparty credit risk (CCR), *(Bewertung des ~s)* counterparty risk assessment, *(~ im Handelsbuch)* counterparty risk in the trading book; ~**verzug** counterparty default

kontrahieren to contract, to make a deal, to conclude a contract, *(telefonisch ~)* to contract over the phone

Kontrahierungs / ~**mix** pricing mix, *i.w.S.* pricing and delivery terms; ~**politik** contracting policy; ~**zwang** contracting requirement, duty to contract

K

Kontrakt (derivative, futures) contract, *(~e auf Einzelaktien)* single stock futures, *(~e auf Tagesgeldsätze)* contracts on overnight rates, *(~e auf Währungen)* currency futures, *(~e auf Wirtschaftsdaten)* economic derivative contracts

Kontrakt / ~**abrechnungspreis** contract settlement price; ~**abschluss** taking out a contract, buying/selling a contract; ~**belieferung** making delivery under a contract, contract settlement; ~**bestand** contract portfolio

Kontrakt / ~**einführung** contract launch; ~**einschuss** contract margin; ~**erfüllung** meeting the obligations under a contract; ~**erwerb** *(im Futures-/Optionshandel)* buying a contract, going long; ~**fälligkeit** contract (transaction) maturity

kontraktgebundenes Sparen scheme-linked saving

Kontrakt / ~**fälligkeit** contract maturity; ~**gegenstand** *(im Futures-/Optionshandel)* underlying instrument; ~**glattstellung** *(im Futures-/Optionshandel)* liquidating (selling) a contract, contract closing, closing out a contract position

Kontrakt / ~**größe** contract size, amount (quantity) of the underlying instrument, unit of trading; ~**handel** contract trading

kontraktiv *(~ wirken)* to have a contractionary impact, *(~e Geldpolitik)* tight monetary policy

Kontrakt / ~**laufzeit** contract period (maturity), life of a contract; ~**liefertag** contract delivery date; ~**monat** contract (delivery) month, *(der nächste auslaufende Kontraktmonat)* front month, spot month

Kontrakt / ~**qualität** *(im Warenterminhandel)* contract grade; ~**regulierung** contract settlement; ~**schluss** unit of trading; ~**spezifikationen** contract terms (specifications)

Kontrakt / ~**umsätze** → Kontraktvolumen; ~**verfall** expiry of a contract, contract maturity; ~**verkauf** *(im Futures-/Optionshandel)* selling a contract, going short

Kontrakt / ~**volatilität** contract volatility; ~**volumen** volume (number) of contracts traded; ~**wert** **1.** contract value **2.** *(bei Futures/Optionen)* unit of trading

konträr **1.** *adj.* contrary, opposite, *(~e Spekulation)* trading against the trend **2.** *adv.* *(~ zum Markttrend verlaufen)* to go counter to the market trend, to buck the trend

Kontroll / ~**abschnitt** counterfoil, stub; ~**abteilung** audit (auditing) department; ~**aufgaben** supervisory responsibilities (duties); ~**ausschuss** control (supervisory, inspection) committee; ~**befugnis** authority to control; ~**beleg** counterfoil, transaction record, voucher in support

Kontrolle **1.** control, *(außer ~ geraten)* to run (to spin, to slip, to drift) out of control, to get out of hand
2. *(Prüfung)* audit, check
3. *(Überwachung)* control, supervision, monitoring, surveillance, *(~ der Ausleihungen)* controlling (monitoring) lendings

Kontroll / ~funktion supervisory function; **~häufigkeit** monitoring frequency

kontrollierbar controllable, checkable

kontrollieren 1. to control, to supervise, to monitor **2.** to audit, to check, to examine

Kontroll / ~instanz → Kontrollorgan; **~maßnahme** control (supervisory) measure; **~mehrheit** controlling majority; **~organ** control (supervisory) body

Kontroll / ~recht right of control, right to supervise (to oversee); **~verfahren** surveillance procedure; **~vermerk** endorsement, check mark, control stamp; **~vollmachten** supervisory powers

Kontrollwechselklausel change of control clause □ permits the termination of an employment contract, bond indenture or loan agreement in the event of a change in the control of the employing, issuing or borrowing organisation

Kontroverse controversy, dispute

Konventionalstrafe contractual penalty, penalty for non-performance of the contract

Konventionalstrafen-Garantie penalty bond

Konvergenz *(~ der Aufsichtspraxis)* supervisory convergence, *(im Futures-Handel)* convergence, movement of a futures price towards the price of the underlying cash instrument as delivery approaches

Konvergenz / ~bericht convergence report; **~länder** emerging economies; **~lösung** convergence solution, systems integration; **~validität** convergence validity

konvergieren to converge

Konvertibilität convertibility

konvertierbar *(~e Währung)* convertible currency

Konvertierbarkeit convertibility

Konvertierung 1. *(einer Anleihe)* conversion, exchanging an outstanding bond for a new security **2.** *(einer Währung)* conversion, exchange

Konvertierungs / ~angebot conversion offer; **~anleihe** conversion bond; **~bestimmungen** conversion regulations; **~faktor 1.** conversion factor □ factor on the basis of which off-balance sheet transactions are converted to a credit equivalent, → Kreditäquivalenzbetrag **2.** → Preisfaktor

Konvertierungs / ~kurs conversion price; **~recht** right of conversion, conversion (exchange) privilege; **~risiko** conversion risk, → KT-Risiko; **~soulte** difference between the repayment price of the old bond and the issuing price of the new security; **~verhältnis** conversion ratio

Konvexität convexity, rate of change in the price of a financial instrument for a given change in yield

Konvexitätsrisiko convexity risk, risk of loss due to yield changes

Konzentration *(~ auf das Kerngeschäft)* focus on the core business, *(~ von Kreditrisiken)* concentration of credit risks

Konzentrationsprozess concentration process

Konzentrationsrisiko concentration risk □ exposure to loss from focussing one's activities on individual borrowers/group of borrowers or from concentrating investments on one specific stock or market

konzentrieren 1. to concentrate on, to focus on, to centre on, *(die Erwartungen ~ sich auf eine Zinssenkung)* expectations centre on an interest rate cut **2.** *(das Interesse konzentrierte sich weitgehend auf Aktien)* attention was largely directed at (largely focus(s)ed) on equities

Konzentrierung concentration, *(~ auf das Kerngeschäft)* focussing on one's core business

Konzept 1. concept, blueprint, *(~ der Periodenabgrenzung)* accruals concept, *(~ der funktionalen Währung)* functional currency concept **2.** *(einer Rede, eines Vertrages)* draft

Konzept / ~beratung concepts counselling; **~generierung** concept (idea) generation, ideation

Konzeption conception, *(konzeptioneller Rahmen)* conceptual framework

Konzeptphase concept (idea, pre-feasibility) phase

Konzern group; **~absatz** group sales; **~abschluss** consolidated accounts; **~abschlussüberleitungsverordnung** Group Financial Statements Reconciliation Regulation

konzernangehörig *(~e Unternehmen)* group members, affiliated companies

K

Konzern / ~anhang notes to the consolidated financial statements; **~ausfallrisiko** group credit risk; **~bereich** group division; **~betriebsergebnis** group operating result; **~betreuer** group relationship manager

Konzern / ~bilanz consolidated balance sheet (financial statements); **~bilanzgewinn** consolidated profit for the year; **~bilanzierung** consolidated accounting, **~bilanzsumme** consolidated total assets, consolidated balance sheet total, group's total assets

Konzern / ~bildung formation of a group; **~bindung** affiliation with a group, group relationship; **~darlehen 1.** group loan facility, lending to a group **2.** intragroup loan; **~ebene** group level, *(Risikomessung auf ~)* risk measurement on a groupwide basis

konzerneigen group-owned, belonging (pertaining) to the group, *(~e Wertpapiere)* securities held by the group, group's securities portfolio

Konzern / ~eigenkapital group equity; **~eigenmittel** group's share capital and reserves, consolidated shareholders' funds; **~einbindung** integration into the group, → Konzernbindung; **~einheit** group unit

konzerneinheitlich *(~e Bilanzierungs- und Bewertungsmethoden)* uniform accounting and valuation methods throughout the group, *(Finanzierung nach ~en Grundsätzen)* valuation according to uniform group standards

Konzern / ~engagement *(Gesamtausleihungen an einen Konzern)* group exposure, loans extended to a group; **~entflechtung** demerger; **~ergebnis** group income/loss, consolidated income/loss, group performance; **~ertragsrechnung** group's (consolidated) statement of income

Konzern / ~fehlbetrag consolidated loss, loss of the group for the year; **~forderungen** claims on group companies, intragroup receivables

konzernfremd *(~en Gesellschaftern zustehender Gewinn)* minority interest income, profit (loss) attributable to minority shareholders, *(~e Unternehmen)* non-affiliated (non-group) companies

konzerngebunden *(~e Hypothekenbank)* group mortgage bank, captive mortgage bank

Konzern / ~geschäftsvolumen group's business volume; **~gesellschaft 1.** group company **2.** *(in Verbindung mit dem Konzernabschluss ferner)* company included in the consolidation; **~gewinn** group income for the year, consolidated profit (income)

Konzern / ~hintergrund *(~ des Kreditnehmers)* the borrower's (the borrowing company's) parentage; **~holding** group holding company; **~hypothekenbank** group mortgage bank

konzernintern *(~e Anteilsübertragungen)* intragroup share transfers, *(~e Erträge/Aufwendungen)* intragroup earnings/expenditure, *(~e Finanzierung)* intragroup funding, *(~er Kredit)* intragroup loan (lending)

Konzern / ~kapitalflussrechnung consolidated cashflow statement; **~klau-**

sel corporate group clause; ~**kreditengagement** group loan exposure; ~**lagebericht** group management report, report on the group's state of affairs

Konzern / ~**neuordnung** realignment (reorganisation) of the group; ~**obergesellschaft** group parent; ~**obligo** group exposure, *(Steuerung des ~s)* managing group risks

Konzernrechnungslegung group accounting, group financial reporting

Konzernrechnungslegungs / ~**pflicht** reporting requirement for groups, *(konzernrechnungslegungspflichtig)* required to prepare consolidated financial statements; ~**vorschriften** group accounting rules

Konzern / ~**sparte** group division; ~**stab** central staff management; ~**steuerumlage** group tax allocation; ~**steuerung** group control, steering of the group's activities;~**tochter** group subsidiary

Konzern / ~**überschuss** consolidated net income; ~**umsatz** group turnover (sales); ~**unternehmen** group company (enterprise); ~**verbund** group, group of companies, *(konzernverbundenes Unternehmen)* group company

Konzern / ~**verlust** group loss for the year, consolidated loss; ~**vermögen** group assets (property), consolidated assets; ~**verschuldung** group debt (borrowings), indebtedness of the group

konzernweit *(~e Risikosteuerung)* groupwide risk management

Konzernzugehörigkeit group affiliation

konzertiert *(~e Aktion)* concerted action

Konzert / ~**zeichner** stag; ~**zeichnung** stagging, speculative oversubscription of a securiy issue

Konzession 1. licence (BE), license (AE) 2. *(Zugeständnis)* concession

Konzessionär licensee, concessionary

konzipieren 1. *(entwerfen)* to draw up, to draft 2. *(erdenken)* to conceive, to map out 3. *(strukturieren, gestalten)* to structure 4. *(neu ~)* to re-define

Kooperation cooperation, collaboration

Kooperationsabkommen cooperation agreement

Koordinator coordinator

koordinieren to coordinate, to orchestrate, to dovetail, *(mit anderen Banken ~)* to coordinate (to act in concert) with other banks, *(die Börsenbegebung ~)* to coordinate (to orchestrate) the flotation, *(die verschiedenen Interessen ~)* to reconcile the diverging interests

Koordinierung coordination, orchestration, reconciliation,*(~ der Wirtschaftspolitik)* economic policy coordination

Kopf *(pro ~ Einkommen)* per capita income

Kopffiliale regional head office, main branch

Kopf-Schulter-Boden *(Chart-Analyse)* head and shoulders bottom, inverse head and shoulders □ bullish reversal pattern, buy signal

Kopf-Schulter-Gipfel head and shoulders top □ bearish pattern; sell signal

koppeln 1. to couple, to join
2. to tie, to peg, *(an den jeweils gültigen Marktsatz ~)* to link to (to tie to) the prevailing market rate, *(seine Währung an den Euro ~)* to peg (to lash) one's currency to the Euro, *(gekoppelt an die geltenden Marktsätze)* linked (pegged) to the prevailing market rates

Kopplung tying (linking, pegging) to

Kopplungsgeschäft 1. package deal
2. *(illegales)* tie-in transaction
3. *(im Außenwirtschaftsverkehr)* counterpurchase transaction

Kopplungsklausel tie-in clause

K

Korb / **~option** basket option □ option whose underlying is a basket of commodities or financial instruments; **~währung** basket currency; **~zertifikat** basket certificate, → Korboption

Körperschaft body, body corporate, corporation, *(~ des öffentlichen Rechts)* public law corporation

Körperschaftssteuer corporate income tax, corporation tax, *(~ auf Dividendenerträge)* corporate income tax on dividends received

Körperschaftssteuer / **~-Anrechnungsbetrag** corporation tax credit; **~-Bemessungsgrundlage** *(konsolidierte)* consolidated corporate tax base; **~-Gesetz** German Corporate Income Tax Act

körperschaftssteuerliche Organschaft fiscal unity for corporate income tax (and trade tax) purposes

K

Korrealhypothek consolidated (collective) mortgage

Korrektur correction, rectification, adjustment, *(~ der Gewinnprognose)* (upward/downward) revision of the profit forecast

Korrektur / **~buchung 1.** rectifying (adjustment) entry **2.** *(Storno)* reversal entry; **~maßnahmen** corrective action (measures); **~posten** adjustment item

Korrelation correlation □ degree to which two related positions move in tandem

Korrelations / **~annahmen** correlation assumptions; **~handel** correlation trading, dispersion trading □ trading in products/credit derivatives that are based on a basket of correlated instruments of varying credit quality

Korrelations / **~produkte** correlation products, → Korrelationshandel; **~risiko** wrong-way risk, correlation risk □ risk *(a)* that prices of two related positions do not move in tandem, *(b)* default risk and credit exposure increase together, *(c)* counterparty credit exposure is negatively correlated with the transaction value

korrelieren to correlate, to move in close step with, *(hochkorrelierte Risiken)* highly correlated risks

Korrespondentennetz network of correspondents (of correspondent banks)

Korrespondenz / **~bank** correspondent, correspondent bank, *(Darlehen von ~en)* correspondent loans, *(Guthaben bei ~en)* correspondent balances, due from correspondent banks; **~bankengeschäft** correspondent banking; **~zentralbank-Modell** correspondent central banking model

korrespondieren *(übereinstimmen)* to correspond (to agree) with, to match, *(~de Aktivposition)* matching asset item

Korridor 1. range **2.** band

Korridor-Optionsschein corridor warrant, range warrant □ the holder receives a fixed amount when the spot price of the underlying instrument is within a certain range on pre-specified dates

korrigieren to correct, to rectify, to amend, *(nach oben/nach unten ~)* to revise upwards/downwards, to adjust up/to adjust down

Kosten cost, charge(s), expense(s), expenditure, *(auf ~ von)* at the expense of, *(ohne zusätzliche ~)* at no extra charge
(~ für Erwerb und Betrieb) total cost of ownership, *(~ für den Kreditnehmer)* borrower's cost of funds, *(~ der Mittelbeschaffung für kurz- und langfristige Kredite)* cost of funds for short and long-term loans, *(~ der umgesetzten Leistung)* cost of sales, *(~ je Produkteinheit)* costs per unit of output, *(~ und Fracht) (Incoterms)* cost and freight (CFR), *(~, Versicherung und Fracht)* cost, insurance and freight (CIF)

Kosten / **~abbau** cost cutting (reduction); **~abgrenzung** cost deferment (accruals); **~absetzung** cost deduction; ~**abweichung** cost variance; ~**aktivierung** cost capitalisation; ~**analyse** cost analysis (study)

Kosten / ~**anfall** accrual of costs, incurring costs (expenses); ~**angaben** cost particulars; ~**anteil** share in the cost (expenses); ~**aufstellung** statement of charges, cost schedule, cost sheet; ~**aufteilung** **1.** cost breakdown (classification), classifying costs **2.** *(Umlage)* cost (expense) allocation

Kosten / ~**aufwandsquote** expense ratio; ~**ausgangsbasis** cost baseline; ~**ausgleich** payment (settlement) of the costs; ~**ausgleichsvereinbarung** cost equalisation agreement

Kosten / ~**begrenzung** limiting (capping) the cost, cost capping; ~**beitrag** cost contribution, contribution towards the expenses; ~**belastung** cost load, cost (expenditure) burden

Kosten / ~**berechnung** **1.** calculation (computation) of the cost, cost calculation **2.** *(Inrechnungstellung)* charging expenses to …; ~**beschränkung** cost containment, limiting the expense; ~**bestimmungsfaktor** cost determinant

Kosten / ~**beteiligung** **1.** cost (expense) sharing **2.** share in the costs; ~**bewusstsein** cost consciousness, *(kostenbewusster Ansatz)* cost-conscious approach; ~**budget** cost budget; ~**dämpfung** dampening the cost rise; ~**deckung** cost (expense) covering, cover for the costs; ~**deckungsmethode** cost recovery method; ~**deckungsquote** cost/income ratio; ~**druck** cost pressure

Kosten / ~**einheit** cost unit; ~**einsparung** cost saving, cost economies; ~**empfindlichkeit** expense sensitivity; ~**entlastung** reducing (lowering) the cost burden, cost relief; ~**entwicklung** cost development (trend); ~**erfassung** cost recording

Kosten / ~**ermittlung** cost determination, cost calculation (ascertainment); ~**ersparnis** costs saved, → Kosteneinsparung; ~**erstattung** refund of costs (expenses)

Kosten / ~**festsetzung** **1.** cost determination, fixing the cost **2.** *(der Gerichtskosten)* taxation of costs; ~**freiheit** cost exemption, exemption from charges; ~**gesichtspunkt** *(unter ~ en)* from a cost point of view; ~**gliederung** breakdown of costs, expenditure spread

kostengünstig **1.** *adj.* cost-effective, *(~e Finanzierung)* low-cost finance, *(~e Option)* option attractive in terms of cost
2. *adv.* *(~ absichern)* to hedge at a favourable (low) price, to hedge on favourable terms, *(~ beschaffen)* to raise on cheap terms

Kosten / ~**inflation** cost inflation, cost-push inflation; ~**intensität** cost intensity, *(kostenintensive Dienstleistung)* cost-intensive service; ~**kalkulation** cost calculation, calculation (computation) of the cost; ~**kontrolle** cost control; ~**last** cost burden (charge)

kostenlos cost-free, free of charge, charge-free

Kosten / ~**management** cost management; ~**minimierung** minimising costs; ~-**Nutzen-Analyse** cost-benefit analysis; ~**obergrenze** expenditure limit (cap, ceiling), *(Festlegung einer ~)* cost capping; ~**optimierung** cost optimising; ~**orientierung** cost orientation, *(kostenorientiert)* cost-oriented

Kosten / ~**plan** cost (expense) budget; ~**planung** cost planning (budgeting); ~**projektionen** cost projections; ~**rechnung** **1.** cost accounting, costing **2.** bill of costs; ~**rechnungsanalyse** costing study; ~**rückstellungen** expense accruals

Kosten / ~**senkung** cost cutting, expenditure cut; ~**senkungsmaßnahmen** cost-cutting measures; ~**sockel** cost base, basis cost; ~**steigerung** increase of (in) costs; ~**stelle** cost center; ~**stellenrechnung** cost center accounting

Kosten / ~**struktur** cost pattern (structure); ~**synergien** cost synergies; ~**tabelle** scale of charges, fee table; ~**träger** cost unit; ~**trägerrechnung** cost unit accounting; ~**treiber** cost drivers

Kosten / ~**übernahme** meeting (paying) the expenses, cost absorption; ~**überwälzung** shifting (passing) on the cost; ~**umlage**/~**umlegung** cost allocation (apportionment)

Kosten / ~**vergütung** cost refund, reimbursement of expenses; ~**verlauf** cost pattern (trend); ~**verrechnung** settlement of the costs involved, → Kostenübernahme, Kostenumlage; ~**verteilungsschlüssel** cost allocation formula; ~**verursacher** cost driver

Kosten / ~**voranschlag** cost estimate, quotation; ~**vorauszahlung** advance payment of cost; ~**vorgaben** cost projections, budgeted expenses; ~**vorteile** cost benefits; ~**zuschuss** contribution to the costs

K

Kraft force, strength, power, *(außer ~)* invalid, *(außer ~ setzen)* to repeal, to abolish, to abrogate, to override, *(außer ~ treten)* to cease to have effect, to become invalid, *(in ~)* in force, valid, *(in ~ bleiben)* to remain in force, to continue to have effect
(in ~ setzen) to carry into effect (into operation), to put into force, *(in ~ treten)* to come into force, to take effect, to become operative, *(rückwirkend in ~ treten)* to come into force with retroactive effect

kraft *(~ seines Amtes)* by virtue of his office, *(~ Gesetz entstehendes Pfandrecht)* lien conferred by operation of law

Kraftfahrzeugfinanzierung → Kfz-Finanzierung

kräftig 1. *adj. (~e Erholung) (von Kursen)* strong recovery (rally) 2. *adv. (~ steigen)* to soar, to rise sharply, to move up strongly

kräftigen 1. *(Kapitaldecke)* to strengthen, to buttress, to reinforce 2. *(Konjunktur)* to invigorate

Kräftigung 1. strengthening 2. invigoration

kraftlos invalid, null and void, *(für ~ erklären)* to annul, to void, to declare null and void, to repeal, to abolish, *(Wertpapiere für ~ erklären)* to invalidate (to destroy) securities

Kraftloserklärung invalidation, annulment, declaration of invalidity, *(~ im Aufgebotsverfahren)* invalidation through public notification

Kredit 1. loan, credit, facility, advance, lending 2. *(i. S. von Engagement)* commitment, exposure

Kredite *(~ im Anlagebuch)* banking book exposures, *(~ an Bund, Länder und Gemeinden)* lendings to the Federal, Land Governments and Local Governments, *(~ an Firmenkunden)* lendings to corporate customers, corporate exposures
(~ gegen Forderungsabtretung) loans against assignment of receivables, *(~ an Kleinunternehmen)* small business loans, *(~ zu günstigen Konditionen)* borrowings on favourable terms, *(~ mit fester Laufzeit)* fixed-term lendings (loans)
(~ aus öffentlichen/nicht-öffentlichen Mitteln) loans from public/non-public funds, *(~ an Privatkunden)* retail lendings (loans), retail exposures, retail portfolio, lendings to private customers, *(~ in laufender Rechnung)* current account credits, advances on current account, *(unter unserem eigenen Risiko dargestellte ~)* lendings (loans extended) at our own risk
(~ an staatliche Schuldner) lendings to sovereign borrowers, *(~ an verbundene Unternehmen)* loans to affiliated companies, *(~ in Verzug)* past-due loans, *(~ mit Zinsbindung)* fixed rate loans (lendings), *(~ mit Zinsobergrenze)* capped loans, *(~ mit variablem Zinssatz)* variable interest (floating rate) loans, variable rate facilities

Kredit / ~**abdeckung** loan repayment, repayment of a credit facility; ~**ab-**

kommen loan (lending) agreement; ~**ablehnung** rejection of (turning down) a loan application, denial of a loan request; ~**ablösung** loan repayment

Kredit / ~**abschnitt** loan tranche; ~**abschreibungen** loan writedowns; ~**abschreibungsbedarf** loan writedown requirements; ~**absicherung** → Kreditsicherung; ~**absprache** loan (credit) arrangement

Kredit / ~**abteilung** loan department, lending desk; ~**abwicklung** loan processing (administration), *(eines Problemkredites)* loan workout; ~**abwicklungsfonds** loan workout fund, debt processing fund

kreditähnlich *(~e Beteiligung)* debt-linked equity investment

Kredit / ~**akte** loan file (envelope); ~**aktiva** loan assets; ~**anbahnung** loan origination; ~**anbieter** lender

Kredit / ~**angebot** **1.** loan offer, offer of credit **2.** *(Gesamtheit)* credit supply, credit availability **3.** *(i. S. von Produkt)* lending product; ~**angebotsverhalten** credit supply behaviour; ~**annahme** accepting (acceptance of) the loan offer

Kredit / ~**anreiz** incentive to borrow; ~**ansprüche** borrowing requirements; ~**anstalt für Wiederaufbau** → KfW; ~**anteil** loan participation, facility share, share in a facility

Kreditantrag loan application (request), borrowing request, *(Bearbeitung/Überprüfung des ~es)* processing/examining (reviewing) the loan application

Kredit / ~**antragsteller** loan applicant, applicant for the loan; ~**anzeige** loan report, → Großkreditanzeige; ~**apparat** banking (credit) system

Kreditäquivalent credit equivalent

Kreditäquivalenzbetrag credit equivalent amount □ off-balance sheet items involving credit risks are converted into credit equivalent amounts by multiplying them with predetermined weighting factors (Kreditumrechnungsfaktoren), *(Kreditäquivalenzbeträge von Derivaten/Wertpapierpensionsgeschäften)* credit equivalent amounts of derivatives/securities repurchase agreements, *(kreditäquivalentes Volumen)* credit equivalent volume

Kredit / ~**art** type of loan (lending); ~**auflagen** loan covenants, specific conditions attached to a loan, restrictive loan provisions

Kreditaufnahme borrowing, raising (taking out) a loan, *(~ im Ausland)* overseas borrowing, borrowing abroad, *(~ am Eurodollarmarkt)* Eurodollar borrowing, borrowing in the Eurodollar market, *(~ durch die öffentliche Hand)* public sector borrowings, borrowing by public authorities *(~ der privaten Haushalte)* private household borrowings, *(~ am Kapitalmarkt)* borrowings in the capital market, wholesale funding, tapping the capital market, *(~ per Termin)* forward borrowing, *(vorübergehende ~ in Form eines Überziehungskredites)* temporary borrowing by way of an overdraft

Kreditaufnahme / ~**beschränkung** tightening up on credit, credit contraction (squeeze); ~**fähigkeit** borrowing capacity

Kredit / ~**aufschlag** credit spread; ~**aufstockung** increase in the loan amount, facility increase; ~**auftrag** borrowing request (application)

Kreditausfall loan (credit) loss, loan default, *(höchstmöglicher Kreditausfall)* credit value at risk, *(Kreditausfälle abzüglich Eingänge auf Forderungsabschreibungen)* loan losses net of recoveries

Kreditausfallereignis credit event, credit default event, → Kreditereignis

kreditausfallgefährdet *(~e Transaktion)* transaction at risk of default

K

Kreditausfalloption Credit Default Option, Credit Default Swaption □ Option to either buy protection or sell protection on a specified future date. → Kreditausfallswap

Kreditausfallquote loan loss ratio, loan default rate, charge-off rate, delinquency rate on loans, loan loss experience

Kreditausfallrisiko credit default risk

Kreditausfallswap Credit Default Swap (CDS) □ Instrument that allows the transfer of an asset risk from one party (protection buyer who either owns the underlying asset, e.g. corporate or sovereign bond, or speculates on a default of that asset) to another party (protection seller).
In consideration of the periodic fee/premium (CDS spread) paid by the protection buyer on the agreed nominal amount to the seller, the seller undertakes to pay the buyer a specified compensation upon occurrence of a specific credit event (e.g. borrower's/issuer's insolvency, default, rating downgrade, restructuring, etc.). → Gesamtertrags-Swap

Kreditausfallswap-Index CDS index □ reflects the CDS spreads/performance of a basket of single name Credit Default Swaps

Kreditausfallswap-Prämie CDS spread, → Kreditausfall-Swap

Kreditausfallversicherung 1. → Kreditausfallswap 2. → Restschuldversicherung

Kreditausfallverteilung credit loss distribution

Kredit / ~ausgestaltung loan features, loan terms; **~auskunft** credit information, credit position report, banker's reference

Kredit / ~ausreichung loan extension (accommodation), extending (granting) a loan, *(kreditausreichende Stelle)* lending bank (office); **~ausschuss** loans committee; **~ausweitung** credit expansion, increase in the volume of lendings

Kreditauszahlung loan disbursement, disbursement of the loan proceeds, crediting the loan proceeds to the customer's account, *(~ zu 100 %)* full disbursement of the loan, with the loan proceeds being paid in full

Kredit / ~banken private commercial banks; **~bearbeitung** loan processing (servicing), loan administration, *(kreditbearbeitende Stelle)* loan processing office; **~bearbeitungsgebühr** loan processing charge (servicing fee)

Kreditbedarf *(~ der öffentlichen Hand)* public borrowing requirements, *(~ der privaten Haushalte)* private household (consumer) borrowing requirements, *(~ der Unternehmen)* corporate (companies') borrowing requirements

Kredit / ~bedienung 1. servicing a loan 2. *(aktueller Stand der~)* loan performance status; **~bedingungen** loan terms, terms of a credit

Kredit / ~befugnis 1. *(des Kreditnehmers)* borrowing authority, borrowing powers 2. *(des Mitarbeiters eines Kreditinstitutes)* loan approval powers, lending authority; **~begrenzung** 1. limitation of lending activities, lending cap 2. loan ceiling

Kredit / ~beitreibung loan recovery; **~belastung** debt charge (load); **~beratung** loan (credit) counselling; **~berechtigung** loan eligibility, eligibility to receive a loan; **~bereich** lending sector

Kreditbereitschaft 1. *(seitens der Banken)* willingness to lend, willingness of the banks to provide finance
2. *(seitens der Kreditnehmer)* willingness to contract debt, propensity to borrow (to raise bank finance)

Kreditbereitstellung extension (granting) of a loan, making a loan available, loan arrangement, *(für die Dauer der ~)* as long as the facility is available,

(~ zu Vorzugskonditionen) making loans available at preferential terms

Kredit / ~**bereitstellungsprovision** arrangement (commitment) fee; ~**beschaffung** procurement of credit facilities (of loan funds), fund raising; ~**beschaffungskosten** fund-raising cost; ~**beschränkungen** lending restrictions (constraints), lending squeeze

Kreditbesicherung provision of security for a loan, putting up (providing) security for a loan, collateralisation of a loan (of a facility)

Kreditbesicherung durch *(~ die Abtretung von Forderungen)* loan collateralisaton by way of an assignment of accounts receivable, *(~ die Belastung von Immobilienwerten)* collateralising the loan by a charge on (over) real property

Kreditbesicherungs / ~**garantie 1.** loan guarantee, facility guarantee **2.** letter of credit; ~**instrumente** loan collateralisation instruments

Kredit / ~**bestand** loan portfolio, loan book, credit portfolio, total lendings; ~**bestätigung** loan confirmation, confirmation of the facility (loan) granted; ~**bestätigungsschreiben** loan confirmation, facility letter; ~**bestimmungen** loan (credit) terms, provisions of the loan agreement

Kredit / ~**beteiligung** loan participation, interest (stake) in a loan commitment; ~**betrag** loan amount, loan principal, *(akutell in Anspruch genommener ~)* loan amount currently drawn

Kredit / ~**beurteilung** loan (credit) assessment, credit (loan) appraisal; ~**beurteilungsverfahren** credit assessment procedure; ~**bewerber** loan applicant; ~**bewertungsagentur** credit rating agency

Kredit / ~**bewilligung** loan approval, credit sanction; ~**bewilligungsausschuss** loan committee, sanctioning committee; ~**bewilligungsgrenze** sanctioning limit, lending authority limit

Kredit / ~**beziehung** debtor/creditor relationship, financial relationship; ~**bilanz** financial statements; ~**bodensatz** hard core lendings; ~**bonität** credit, credit (financial) standing

Kredit / ~**bremsen** credit brakes; ~**brief** letter of credit; ~**bündel** loan basket, loan bundle; ~**bürgschaft** loan guarantee; ~**bürgschaftsprogramm** loan guarantee scheme; ~**büro** loan office (department)

Kredit / ~**daten** loan particulars; ~**derivate** credit derivatives □ instruments designed to transfer credit risk from one party to another party, *(Kreditderivate im Handelsbuch)* credit derivatives in the trading book, → Kreditausfallswap

Kredit / ~**disagio** loan discount, amount deducted from the loan principal; ~**dokumentation** loan documentation; ~**drosselung** credit crunch (squeeze), credit contraction

Kredit / ~**einräumung** extension (granting) of a loan, loan accommodation, *(krediteinräumende Stelle)* lending office (branch); ~**einräumungsschreiben** loan confirmation (undertaking), facility letter; ~**einrichtungsgebühr** loan arrangement fee

Kredit / ~**einschätzung** loan assessment; ~**einweisung** loan approval (undertaking), loan commitment; ~**engagement** loan commitment (exposure); ~**entscheidung** loan decision, decision on a loan application

Kreditereignis credit event □ failure of the debtor/borrower to meet his obligations, e.g. payment default, moratorium, opening of insolvency proceedings, restructuring, or any other pre-specified event, e.g. rating downgrade, *(Eintritt eines bestimmten ~ses)* occurrence of a specific credit event, → Kreditausfallswap

K

Kredit / ~erleichterungen 1. *(der Kreditpolitik)* easing of the tight credit policy **2.** *(bei einem Engagement)* easing (mitigating, tempering) the loan terms; **~ermächtigung** borrowing authorisation; **~ermächtigungsrahmen** general credit facility

Kredit / ~erneuerung loan renewal, renewal of a credit facility (line); **~eröffnung** loan account opening; **~ersatz** credit (loan) substitute; **~ersatzgeschäft** credit substitute operations (business), e.g. securitising loan receivables or acquiring credit-equivalent interests

Kredit / ~ersuchen loan (borrowing) request; **~erweiterung 1.** increase in a loan facility (credit line) **2.** *(i. S. von Bonitätserhöhung)* credit enhancement; **~expansion** credit expansion, growth in lendings

K

Kredit / ~fähigkeit 1. legal capacity to borrow, capacity to contract debts, ability to raise funds **2.** credit-worthiness; **~fälligkeit** loan maturity; **~fazilität** credit (loan, borrowing) facility

kreditfinanziert *(~e Expansion)* debt-financed expansion, *(~e Übernahmen)* debt-financed acquisitions, acquisitions financed through bank borrowings (bank debt), *(~e Wertpapierkäufe)* buying (purchase) of securities with borrowed funds

Kredit / ~finanzierung financing through bank borrowings (bank credits), financing through loans; **~finanzierungsquote** borrowing ratio

Kreditforderung 1. loan, lending *(Plural, im bilanziellen Kontext einer Bank)* assets, loan receivables, *(Handel mit ~en)* loan asset trading, *(zur Veräußerung bestimmte ~en)* loans (assets) held for sale
2. claim arising from a loan, claim against the borrower

Kreditforderungs / ~bestand loan portfolio, loan book; **~pool** pool of loan assets; **~verkauf** loan sale, asset sale

Kreditfrist loan period (duration), *(Kreditfristen der Aktiv- und Passivseite)* maturities of lendings and deposits

Kreditgarantie loan (credit) guarantee; **~gemeinschaft** credit guarantee society; **~programm** loan guarantee scheme

Kredit / ~gebaren lending policy (practice); **~geber** lender, credit grantor; **~geberkonsortium** lender consortium, *(kreditgebende Bank)* lending bank; **~gebühren** loan (credit) charges; **~gefährdung** jeopardising the borrower's credit (borrower's financial standing), damage to creditworthiness

Kreditgenehmigung loan (credit) approval, loan (credit) sanction, *(der Kredit muss zuvor durch unsere zuständigen Kreditausschüsse genehmigt werden)* the loan must have the prior approval of our senior loan committees

Kreditgenehmigungs / ~kompetenz loan approval powers, credit approval authority; **~verfahren** credit approval process, credit sanctioning procedure

Kreditgenossenschaft credit cooperative, *(genossenschaftlicher Bereich)* cooperative banking sector

Kreditgeschäft lendings, lending business (operations), *(~ mit Firmen-/Privatkunden)* lendings to corporate/private customers, corporate/retail lendings, *(~ im Inland)* domestic lending operations, *(~ mit mittelständischen Kunden)* lendings to small and medium-sized enterprises (companies), SME lendings

Kreditgesuch loan application, loan (borrowing) request, borrowing proposition

Kreditgewährleistung credit guarantee

Kreditgewährung extension (granting) of a loan, loan (credit) accommodation, lending, *(~ der Banken an den privaten Sektor)* bank lendings to the private sector, *(kreditgewährendes*

Institut) lending bank (institution), *(~ per Termin)* forward lending

Kreditgewährungs / ~spielraum scope for (further) lendings; **~zusage** loan undertaking, lending (loan) commitment, credit (facility) undertaking

Kredit / ~gewerbe banking industry, banks, banking business; **~grundsätze** lending principles; **~hebel** leverage; **~herabsetzung** reduction of the loan principal, loan reduction

Kredit / ~hergabe → Kreditgewährung; **~höchstgrenze** credit (lending) ceiling, *(aus der Sicht des Kreditnehmers)* borrowing limit; **~höhe** *(~ im Zeitpunkt des Ausfalls) (Basel II)* exposure at default (EAD)

kreditierbares Akkreditiv negotiable documentary credit

kreditieren 1. to lend, to extend (to grant) a loan **2.** *(gutschreiben)* to credit

kreditierende Bank lending bank, *(bei einem Dokumentenakkreditiv)* negotiating bank

Kreditierung 1. lending, loan accommodation, *(~ der erforderlichen Vorauszahlungen)* providing the funds for the advance payments to be made
2. *(Gutschrift)* crediting

Kreditinanspruchnahme 1. loan availment (takedown), drawing on a loan, drawing against a credit, availment of a credit facility, *(Zeitraum der ~)* takedown period
2. *(der in Anspruch genommene Betrag)* takedown, amount drawn, amount taken down

Kredit / ~inflation credit-induced inflation; **~institut** financial (credit) institution, banking organisation

Kreditinstitute-Reorganisationsgesetz Bank Reorganisation Act □ Sets out special rules to save ailing banks in the financial system. It is based on the following three-tier system of pre-insolvency measures, → Sanierungsverfahren, → Reorganisationsverfahren, → Übertragungsanordnung

Kreditinstitutsgruppe group of financial institutions, banking group

Kreditinstituts-Rechnungslegungsverordnng Regulation on the Accounting of Credit Institutions

Kredit / ~instrumentarium lending instruments (tools); **~interessent** potential borrower, would-be-borrower; **~kapazität** lending capacity (power)

Kreditkarte credit card

Kreditkarten / ~abrechnung credit card statement; **~akzeptanzvertrag** merchant agreement; **~antrag** credit card application; **~ausfallquote** credit card default rate; **~betrug** credit card fraud; **~-Emittentenbank** card issuing bank

Kreditkarten / ~forderungen credit card receivables, *(durch ~ gedeckte Wertpapiere)* credit card asset-backed securities; **~gesellschaft** credit card company

Kreditkarten / ~organisation credit card organisation; **~prozessor** credit card processor □ authorises and settles credit card payments; **~umsätze** credit card sales; **~verbriefung** securitisation of credit card receivables; **~verlust** credit card loss

Kredit / ~kauf instal(l)ment buying, purchase on credit, credit sale; **~klemme** credit crunch; **~knappheit** loan shortage, credit stringency; **~kompetenz** loan approval powers, lending authority; **~kompetenzgrenze** loan approval limit, sanctioning limit

Kredit / ~konditionen loan terms, terms of a credit, loan prices, lending rates, *(Festlegung der ~)* loan pricing, fixing the loan rates (loan terms); **~konsortium** loan (lending) syndicate

Kredit / ~konto loan account; **~kontrolle** credit (loan) control, supervising (monitoring) a loan commitment; **~kontrollsystem** loan monitoring system; **~konversion** credit conversion; **~konversionsfaktor** credit conversion factor, → Kreditumrechnungsfaktor

Kredit / ~kosten borrowing cost, cost of credit, finance charge, funding costs, *(Kreditkosten der Unternehmen)* corporate borrowing cost; **~kunde** borrowing customer; **~kündigung** calling in a loan, loan termination; **~kündigungsschreiben** loan termination notice

Kreditlaufzeit term (life) of a credit, loan period, loan duration (maturity), *(die am Ende der ~ fälligen Zinsen)* interest due at the end of the life of the loan; **~-Deckungsgrad** loan life cover ratio

Kredit / ~leihe 1. lending one's credit **2.** guarantee credit; **~lenkung** credit control; **~lieferant** credit supplier; **~limit** borrowing limit, credit cap; **~limitierung** setting a loan limit, → Kreditplafondierung

K

Kreditlinie credit line, *(jederzeit kündbare ~)* uncommitted credit line, *(zugesagte, aber nicht in Anspruch genommene ~n)* committed, but undrawn credit lines, *(Aufstockung einer ~)* increase in a credit line, providing fresh (additional) funds, *(Einräumung einer ~)* extending (granting) a credit line, *(Erneuerung einer ~)* line renewal, renewing a credit line, *(Verlängerung einer ~)* extending the maturity of a credit line, line rollover, *(~n des Mengengeschäftes)* retail exposures

Kredit / ~lockerung easing the tight credit policy, easing of loan restrictions; **~mangel** credit shortage; **~marge** credit spread; **~margenverfall** sharp drop in credit spreads

Kreditmarkt loan (credit) market; **~modell** credit market model

kreditmäßig *(~ unterstützen)* to support by way of a loan, to back up by loan funds, *(~e Beurteilung)* credit rating, *(~e Unterstützung)* credit support

Kredit / ~mediation credit mediation; **~mediationsverfahren** credit mediation procedure; **~mediator** Credit Commissioner (appointed by the Federal Government)

Kredit / ~migration credit migration, change in credit-worthiness, rating change; **~mittel** borrowed funds, loan funds, loan finance; **~mittler** credit (loan) broker; **~mittlerfunktion** credit brokerage function, credit intermediation

Kredit / ~modalitäten loan (credit) terms; **~möglichkeiten 1.** borrowing options **2.** sources of finance, loan resources

Kreditnachfrage loan demand, demand for credit (for bank finance), *(~ der öffentlichen Hand)* public sector demand for credit, *(~ des privaten Sektors)* private sector demand for credit, *(~ der Unternehmen)* corporate loan demand, corporate demand for bank finance

kreditnah *(~e Beteiligung)* credit-equivalent interest

Kreditnebenkosten loan-related cost, non-interest charges

Kreditnehmer borrower, *(~ mit einem hohen Finanzierungsbedarf)* borrower(s) with large funding needs, *(~ mit niedriger Bonität)* borrowers with a poor (low) credit rating

Kreditnehmer / ~ausfall borrower default; **~bewertung** rating of a borrower, borrower assessment (evaluation); **~bonität** borrower's credit standing, credit-worthiness (solvency) of a borrower

Kreditnehmer / ~einheit borrower unit; **~position** borrowing position, *(kreditnehmerbezogene Gesamtposition)* borrower-related aggregate position; **~staat** sovereign borrower

Kredit / ~neugeschäft new lendings; **~neuzusagen** new loan commitments; **~obergrenze** borrowing limit, credit cap; **~obligo 1.** *(aus der Sicht eines Kreditgebers)* total lending commitments (lending exposure) **2.** *(aus der Sicht eines Kreditnehmers)* aggregate borrowing commitments; **~of-**

ferte loan offer; ~**option** loan (borrowing) option

Kreditoren 1. *(von Banken)* deposits 2. *(von Nichtbanken)* accounts payable, trade payables; ~**zuwachs** growth in deposits

kreditorisch *(~es Konto)* creditor account, account kept in the credit, account maintained on a non-borrowing basis, *(~e Kontoführung)* account maintenance on a non-borrowing basis, *(~e Kunden)* non-borrowing customers, *(~er Saldo)* credit (creditor) balance

Kreditplafond 1. *(aus der Sicht eines Kreditgebers)* lending (credit) ceiling 2. *(aus der Sicht eines Kreditnehmers)* borrowing limit

Kreditplafondierung setting a limit on bank borrowings, setting an asset ceiling, *(Begrenzung des Kreditangebotes der Kreditwirtschaft)* setting a limit on the banks' credit supply, limiting credit supply

Kreditpolitik credit policy, lending policy

kreditpolitisch *(~e Beschlüsse zur Konjunkturankurbelung)* credit policy measures designed to stimulate economic activity, *(~e Lenkungsmittel/~es Instrumentarium)* credit policy instruments (tools)

Kredit / ~**portefeuille**/~**portfolio** loan (credit) portfolio, lending book, total lendings (lending assets); ~**portfoliober ichterstattung** loan portfolio reporting;~**portfoliosteuerung** loan portfolio management; ~**potenzial** lending power, lending capacities

Kredit / ~**praxis** lending practice(s); ~**preis** cost of borrowing, loan cost; ~**preispolitik** loan pricing policy; ~**produkt** loan product

Kredit / ~**programm** lending (loan) scheme; ~**prolongation** extending the maturity of a loan, renewal of a loan commitment; ~**protokoll** loan record; ~**provision** loan commission

Kredit / ~**prüfung** loan review; ~**prüfungsausschuss** loan review body; ~**prüfungsverfahren** (internal) loan review procedure

Kredit / ~**punktbewertungssystem** credit scoring system; ~**pyramiden** *(im Bankgewerbe)* shifting of loans extended by the parent to subsidiaries and associated companies

Kredit / ~**qualität** asset quality, *(Minderung der ~)* loan impairment; ~**quellen** borrowing sources; ~**quote** 1. loan tranche 2. loan participation

Kreditrahmen credit line, borrowing arrangement, *(gesamter ~)* total credit availability; ~**vertrag** general (master) loan agreement, credit override agreement

Kredit / ~**rationierung** credit rationing; ~**refinanzierungsgeschäft** loan funding operations; ~**regelung** credit arrangement; ~**restriktionen** credit (lending) restrictions, credit squeeze, loan curbs

Kredit / ~**revalutierung** re-establishing (re-opening) a loan facility; ~**revision** loan review, reviewing the loan commitment, loan account audit; ~**richtlinien** loan directives, lending guidelines (criteria)

Kreditrisiko credit risk, loan exposure, risk of default by borrower or issuer, risk that a loan will not be repaid, *(Kreditrisiken im Anlagebuch)* credit risks in the banking book

Kreditrisiko / ~**äquivalent** credit risk equivalent; ~**aufschlag** credit spread

kreditrisikobehaftet *(~ e Forderungen)* assets subject to credit risk, credit risk exposures

Kreditrisiko / ~**beurteilung** credit risk assessment; ~**erfassung** capturing credit risks; ~**ermittlung** calculating (determination of) the credit risk

Kreditrisiko / ~**gewichtung** credit risk weighting, *(kreditrisikogewichtete Aktiva)* credit risk weighted assets; ~**grad** degree of credit risk; ~**handel**

K

trading credit risk (in the secondary market)

Kreditrisiko / ~**indikator** credit risk indicator; ~**konzentration** credit risk concentration; ~**korrelationen** credit risk correlations

kreditrisikolastig *(~es Engagement)* high risk exposure

Kreditrisiko / ~**management** credit risk management; ~**messung** credit risk measurement, measurement of credit exposure; ~**minderung** credit risk mitigation, lowering the credit risk, *(kreditrisikomindernde Instrumente)* instruments designed to reduce credit risk

Kreditrisiko / ~**quantifizierung** quantifying credit risk; ~**rating** credit risk rating; ~-**Standardansatz** standardised approach to credit risk □ risk measuring techniques based on external credit assessments; ~**transfer** credit risk transfer; ~**vorsorge** provisioning for credit risk

Kreditrückflüsse repayment on loans (lendings), loans repaid

Kreditrückführung 1. *(i. S. von Rückzahlung)* loan repayment **2.** *(i. S. einer Verringerung der Kreditsumme)* reduction of the loan principal, partial repayment of the loan

Kreditrücklauf → Kreditrückflüsse

Kreditrückzahlung loan repayment, repayment of (paying down) a loan, *(wir stellen hiermit den Kredit zur sofortigen Rückzahlung fällig)* we hereby call in the loan for immediate repayment

Kredit / ~**sachbearbeiter** loan (lending) officer; ~**sanierung** loan workout (restructuring); ~**schädigung** damage to the borrower's credit standing, damage to credit-worthiness; ~**schöpfung** credit creation; ~**schöpfungsprozess** credit creation process

Kredit / ~**schraube** credit screw; ~**schuldner** borrower, loan debtor, → Kreditnehmer; ~-**Score-Berechnung** credit score calculation; ~-**Score-Rechner** credit score calculator; ~-**Scoring** credit scoring □ method to assess the credit-worthiness of a customer

Kredit / ~**sekretariat** *(Kreditabteilung)* loan office, lending desk; ~**sektor** loan sector; ~**sekundärmarkt** secondary loan market (loan sales, loan trading); ~**sicherheit** loan collateral, security for a loan

Kreditsicherung providing security (collateral) for a loan, putting up security for a loan, collateralisation of a loan

Kreditsicherungs / ~**fazilität** credit backup facility, support facility; ~**garantie** loan guarantee, standby letter of credit (AE); ~**instrumente** loan collateral instruments; ~**vereinbarung**/~**vertrag** loan security (loan collateral) agreement

Kredit / ~**sonderkonto** special loan account; ~**spanne** credit margin; ~**sparte** lending segment; ~**spread** credit spread, risk premium on a security with a higher credit risk

Kredit / ~**spielraum** scope for (further) borrowings/lendings; ~**status** statement of assets and liabilities; ~**stopp** ban on new lendings, credit (lending) freeze; ~**streckung** stretching the maturity of a loan

Kredit / ~**streuung** loan diversification, diversification of lendings; ~**struktur** lending pattern, structure of lending operations, set-up of borrowing customers; ~**stundung** loan respite, debt deferral; ~**substitut** credit substitute, *(Positionen mit Kreditsubstitutscharakter)* positions in the nature of credit substitutes

kreditsuchend *(~es Unternehmen)* loan-seeking company, loan applicant

Kredit / ~**summe** loan amount (principal), principal of a loan; ~**syndizierung** loan syndication, syndication of a credit facility; ~**syndizierungsgeschäft** loan syndication business

Kredit / ~**tarife** loan rates, loan pricing; ~**termingeschäft** forward loan contract (transaction); ~**tilgung** loan repayment; ~**tranche** loan (credit) tranche, loan instalment; ~**transparenz** transparency in lending transactions

Kredit / ~**überlassung** loan extension, → Kreditvergabe; ~**überschreitung** **1.** exceeding a borrowing limit (a credit line), overdrawing a credit line **2.** amount by which a credit line is overdrawn; ~**übersicherung** overcollateralisation of a loan

Kredit / ~**überwachung** credit control, credit screening, policing (monitoring) loan commitments, loan monitoring; ~**überwachungssystem** credit control (loan review) system; ~**überziehung** overdrawing a credit (a loan facility), overdraft; ~**überziehungsprovision** overdraft commission;~**umfang** loan size

Kredit / ~**umrechnung** credit conversion; ~**umrechnungsfaktoren** credit conversion factors □ factors used to convert off-balance sheet commitments into credit exposure equivalents, *(~ für außerbilanzielle Geschäfte)* credit conversion factors for off-balance sheet exposures

Kredit / ~**umschuldung** renegotiation (rescheduling, refunding) of a loan; ~**umwandlung** **1.** loan/equity conversion, converting loans into equity **2.** → Kreditumrechnung

Kredit / ~**unterbeteiligung** loan subparticipation; ~**unterlagen** loan records, loan documents; ~**unterlegung** credit (loan) support, → Kreditbesicherung

kreditunwürdig without adequate credit standing, not credit-worthy

Kredit / ~**valuta** **1.** loan proceeds, disbursed loan amount **2.** loan (lending) currency; ~**valutierung** loan disbursement, disbursement of the loan funds

Kredit / ~**verbesserung** credit enhancement, increase in credit quality; ~**verbilligung** **1.** lowering of lending rates, lowering the cost of credit **2.** *(Gewährung von Zinssubventionen)* granting of interest rate subsidies

Kredit / ~**verbriefung** loan securitisation, securitisation of loan receivables (assets); ~**vereinbarung** loan agreement, loan (credit) arrangement; ~**verfügbarkeit** availability of loans, credit availability

Kreditvergabe loan extension (accommodation), lending, loan origination, granting a loan (a facility), credit granting

Kreditvergabe *(~ der Banken)* bank lending, lending by banks, *(~ an die öffentliche Hand/an öffentliche Haushalte)* lendings to the public sector (to public sector entities), *(auf Sachwerte abgestellte ~)* asset-based lending *(~an den privaten Sektor)* lendings to the private sector, *(~ im kurz-/langfristigen Bereich)* short-term/long-term lendings, *(~ an Nicht-Banken)* lendings to non-banks, *(auf zukünftige Zahlungsströme abgestellte ~)* future cash flow-based lending

Kreditvergabe / ~**entscheidung** credit granting decision; ~**kosten** cost of lending; ~**praxis** lending conventions, loan origination practices; ~**prozess** credit granting process, loan origination process; ~**standards** lending standards

Kreditverhältnis debtor-creditor relationship (arrangement), loan arrangement, *(Kündigung des ~ses)* calling in the loan, terminating the loan agreement, *(nach Beendigung des ~ses)* upon repayment of the loan, upon termination of the loan agreement

Kredit / ~**verkauf** loan sale, asset sale; ~**verkehr** lending operations (transactions); ~**verknappung** credit squeeze, credit crunch, shortage of loan funds; ~**verlängerung** extending the maturity of a loan, renewal of a credit line (of a credit facility), rollover of a loan

Kreditverlust loan loss (charge-off), loan write-off, *(Kreditverluste abzüglich eingegangener Beträge)* loan losses net of recoveries; ~**quote** loan loss ratio, charge-off rate, default rate, *(in den USA ferner)* delinquency rate

Kredit / ~vermittler credit (loan) broker; ~**vermittlung** credit (loan) brokerage; ~**vermittlungskosten** loan brokerage cost; ~**vermittlungsvertrag** loan brokerage agreement

Kredit / ~verpflichtungen 1. loan commitments, committed credit lines **2.** obligations under a loan agreement; ~**versicherung 1.** credit (loan) insurance, payment default policy **2.** → Kreditausfallswap

Kredit / ~versorgung loan (credit) supply; ~**versprechen** loan undertaking, commitment (undertaking) to extend a loan, facility undertaking (letter); ~**verteuerung** increase in the cost of credit, rise in borrowing costs

K

Kreditvertrag loan agreement (contract), facility agreement, *(kreditvertragliche Regelungen)* contractual loan arrangements, provisions of the loan agreement, → Auflagen

Kreditvertrags / ~ausfertigung execution of the loan agreement; ~**dokumentation** loan documentation

Kreditverwendung application of the loan funds

Kreditverzug credit default, loan default, failure to abide by the terms of the loan agreement, inability to pay interest or principal when due or to otherwise meet the loan terms

Kredit / ~volumen loan portfolio, total lendings, loan book, aggregate lendings; ~**voraussetzungen** loan eligibility requirements; ~**vorlage 1.** loan application **2.** loan under consideration

Kredit / ~vormerkung 1. loan commitment, approved credit line, loan (credit facility) held available, *(Volumen der ~en)* volume of loan commitments **2.** noting a loan undertaking in the bank's records; ~**votum** lending decision, credit granting decision

Kredit / ~wachstum lending growth, asset growth; ~**weiterbearbeitung** further processing of the loan

Kredit / ~wertberichtigung loan loss allowance, allowance for loan (credit) losses, → Einzelwertberichtigung, → Sammelwertberichtigung; ~**wertminderung** credit impairment; ~**wertminderungsaufwand** credit impairment loss

Kredit / ~wesen banking industry, banking business; ~**wesengesetz** German Banking Act; ~**wettbewerb** competition in lending operations; ~**wirtschaft** banking industry, banking business, banks; ~**wünsche** loan requests, borrowing requirements

kreditwürdig credit-worthy, *(~ in Höhe des angefragten Betrages)* credit-worthy to the extent of the loan required

Kreditwürdigkeit credit, credit-worthiness, credit creditibility, *(~ der öffentlichen Hand)* public credit

Kreditwürdigkeits / ~anforderungen credit standards, requirements as to credit-worthiness; ~**prüfung** credit assessment (investigation), credit analysis

Kreditziehung → Kreditinanspruchnahme

Kreditzinsen 1. loan interest, interest charged on a loan **2.** *(Zinssatz)* lending rate, loan interest rate

Kreditzusage loan commitment (undertaking), lending commitment, facility undertaking, *(~n des Handelsbuches)* lending commitments in the trading book, *(zugesagte Kreditlinien)* committed credit lines

Kreditzusage / ~schreiben facility letter, line letter, loan confirmation; ~**volumen** total loan (lending) commitments

Kreditzusammenlegung loan consolidation

Kreis 1. circle, group, range **2.** class, category **3.** *(Banken-, Börsenkreise)* community, *(der ~ der betroffenen Anleger)* the group of investors concerned, *(der ~ der erfassten Produkte)* the range of products covered

Kreislauf circulation, cycle

Kreissparkasse county savings bank

kreuzen to cross, *(gekreuzter Scheck)* crossed cheque

Kreuzkurs cross rate

Kreuzungspunkt *(in der Charttechnik)* crossover

Krise crisis, *(krisenanfällige Währung)* crisis-prone currency, currency susceptible (vulnerable) to crises, *(krisenfeste Anlage)* crisis-proof (fail-safe) investment, *(krisengeschüttelte Branche)* crisis-ridden sector

Krisen / ~mechanismus *(dauerhafter ~)* permanent crisis mechanism, → Europäischer Stabilitätsmechanismus; **~szenario** stress scenario; **~tests** stress test(ing), → Bankenstresstests

Kriterium criterion

kritisch *(~e finanzielle Lage)* precarious (critical) financial situation, *(~er Punkt)* critical (crucial) point

krumm *(~er Betrag)* odd amount, *(~es Bezugsverhältnis)* unusual (odd) subscription ratio, *(~e Börsenaufträge)* odd lot orders, buy or sell orders for an amount of stock less than the normal trading unit, *(~er Termin)* broken (odd) date

KSA-Risikogewicht/-Risikoklasse CRSA (credit risk standardised approach) risk weight / CRSA exposure class, → Kreditrisiko-Standardansatz

KT-Risiko *(Konvertierungs- und Transferrisiko)* conversion and transfer risk □ risk of loss arising from actions preventing the conversion of currency or the transfer of payments

Kulanzgründe *(aus ~n)* in order to accommodate (oblige) s. o., *(aus ~n berechnen wir keine Zinsen)* as a gesture of goodwill we will charge no interest

Kulanzleistung / ~regelung ex gratia settlement, goodwill settlement, accommodating arrangement

kulanzweise *(~ handeln)* acting solely on goodwill

Kulanzzahlung ex gratia payment, → Kulanzleistung

Kulisse 1. unofficial market 2. professional traders

Kulissenwerte securities traded in the unofficial market, off-board securities

kümmern *(sich um den Finanzbedarf kleiner Unternehmen ~)* to cater to the borrowing requirements of small companies

kumulativ *(~e Ausfalldichte)* cumulative default density, *(~e Ausfallrate)* cumulative default rate, *(~er Betrag)* aggregate amount, *(~e Dividende)* cumulative dividend, *(~er Ertrag)* cumulative return, *(~e Finanzierungslücke)* cumulative funding gap, *(~ revolvierendes Akkreditiv)* cumulative revolving documentary credit *(~er Schuldbeitritt)* assumption of a joint and several liability, *(~es Stimmrecht)* cumulative voting right, *(~e stimmrechtslose Vorzugsaktien)* non-voting cumulative preferred stock, *(~e Verteilungsfunktion)* cumulative distribution function, *(~e Verzinsung)* cumulative interest return

Kumulhaftung cumulative liability

kumulieren to accumulate, *(kumulierte Abschreibungen)* accumulated depreciation, *(kumulierter Effekt aus Änderungen der Bilanzierungsmethoden)* cumulative effect of accounting changes, *(kumulierte einbehaltene Erträge)* cumulative retained earnings *(kumulierter übriger umfassender Periodenerfolg)* accumulated other comprehensive income, *(kumulierte Unterschiedsbeträge aus der Währungsumrechnung)* cumulative translation adjustment

Kumulierung accumulation, *(~ von Emissionen)* bundling of issues, *(~ von Risiken)* accumulation of risks

Kumul / ~risiko accumulation risk, risk of loss arising from a large number of correlated risks; ~**schaden** cumulative loss

kündbar 1. *(~e Einlagen)* deposits subject to call (subject to a withdrawal notice)
2. *(Kredit, Darlehen) (jederzeit ~er Kredit)* call loan, loan subject to being called in for payment at any time, loan terminable at the discretion of the lender at any time, uncommitted loan
3. *(zum Nennwert ~)* callable at par, *(~e Anleihe; kündbar durch den Anleiheschuldner/Emittenten)* callable bond, *(kündbar durch den Anleihegläubiger/Anleger)* puttable bond
4. *(Vertrag)* terminable, rescindable, *(~e Leasingvereinbarung)* cancellable lease agreement, *(jederzeit ~er Vertrag)* contract terminable (rescindable) at will, → kündigen, → Kündigungsfrist

K

Kündbarkeit 1. callability **2.** terminableness

Kunde customer, client, account

Kunden / ~**abrechnung** customer account settlement; ~**abwerbung** customer poaching, touting customers; ~**akquisition** new business development, soliciting customers, seeking out new business (new accounts)

Kunden / ~**akte** customer file; ~**akzeptanz** customer acceptance; ~**ansprache** contacting the customer, customer approach; ~**aufgabe** customer statement

Kunden / ~**auftrag** customer (customer's) order, *(im ~ übernommene Garantien)* guarantees entered into on behalf of customers, *(im ~ tätig werden)* to act on a customer's behalf (request); ~**ausfall** customer default; ~**bedarf**/~**bedürfnisse** customer needs (requirements)

kundenbedient *(~e Terminals)* customer-operated terminals

Kunden / ~**befragung** customer survey, client interviews; ~**berater** customer advisor, → Kundenbetreuer; ~**beratung** customer counselling, counselling of customers, advisory services for customers, customer advisory

Kunden / ~**beschwerde** customer complaint; ~**beschwerdestelle** customer complaints desk, ombudsman; ~**bestände** customer portfolios (holdings, positions)

kundenbestimmt *(~e Preisbildung)* customer-driven pricing

Kundenbetreuer account(s) officer, customer service officer, relationship manager (officer), *(für vermögende Privatkunden)* account executive (manager)

Kundenbetreuung 1. customer support, customer care, servicing and counselling of customers, *i.w.S.:* relationship management, relationship banking
2. *(Abteilung, Mitarbeiter der Kundenbetreuung)* customer accounts desk, customer relations staff, customer support staff

Kundenbeurteilung customer rating (assessment)

Kundenbeziehung customer relationship, *(Ausbau der bestehenden ~en)* developing the portfolio of existing clients, developing existing accounts, *(langfristiger Wert einer ~)* customer lifetime value

Kundenbeziehungs / ~**management** customer relationship management; ~**pflege** customer relationship building, cultivation of customer relations; ~**zyklus** customer relationship cycle

Kundenbindung customer (client) retention, retaining customer loyalty

Kundenbindungs / ~**kosten** customer retention cost; ~**grad** customer retention level

Kunden / ~**bonität** (customer's) credit quality; ~**debitoren** lendings to customers; ~**depot** customer portfolio, securities held for third party account

Kunden / ~**eigenleistung** *(bei einer Baufinanzierung)* customer equity; ~**einlagen** customer deposits, deposits by customers; ~**einlagenbestand** customer deposit portfolio; ~**einstufung** customer classification (categorisation)

Kunden / ~**engagement 1.** customer commitment (involvement) **2.** customer exposure; ~**entgelt** service fee, → Interbankenentgelt

Kunden / ~**erfolg 1.** customer (account) profitability; *(i.e.S.)* earnings from an account **2.** customer success; ~**ertragswert** *(langfristiger Kundenwert)* customer lifetime value

Kunden / ~**fluktuation** customer turnover; ~**fokussierung** customer focus, focussing on customer wants and needs, customer-centric approach; ~**forderungen 1.** lendings to customers, loans and advances to customers, claims on customers **2.** customer requirements; ~**freundlichkeit** customer friendliness, *(kundenfreundliches Image)* customer-friendly image

Kunden / ~**gelder** client money, clients' funds; ~**geldkonto** customer money account; ~**geschäft 1.** *(Kreditgeschäft)* retail lending **2.** *(im Wertpapiergeschäft)* retail trading, customer trades **3.** *(Gesamtheit)* customer business, customer-driven business; ~**gespräch** customer meeting, customer talks

Kunden / ~**haftung** customer liability; ~**handel** agency trading, trading for customer account, → Eigenhandel; ~**händler** agent trader; ~**hinweis** notice to customers, customer alert (notice)

kundenindividuell personalised, customised, tailored to the customer's requirements

Kunden / ~**information** customer information, customer (client) briefing, → Kundenhinweis; ~**kalkulation** customer (account) calculation; ~**karte** customer card, private label card, white label card, (retailer's) proprietary card

Kunden / ~**kennung** customer ID (i.e. account number (IBAN) and bank identifier code (BIC), *(~ des Zahlers)* payor ID; ~**klasse** customer (client) class; ~**konto** customer account

Kunden / ~**kreditnachfrage** customer loan demand, customer demand for credit; ~**kreditvolumen** customer lending book; ~**kreis 1.** customers, customer portfolio **2.** group of customers; ~**marge** customer margin; ~**nachfrage** customer demand

kundennah *(~e Beratung)* personalised counselling, → kundenorientiert

Kunden / ~**nähe** customer proximity, closeness to the customer; ~**nutzen** customer value, benefits (value) to customers; ~**obligo** customer liability; ~**orders** customer orders

kundenorientiert *(~es Geschäftsmodell)* customer-driven business model, *(~e Preisgestaltung)* perceived-value pricing, *(~e Strategie)* customer-oriented (customer-focused) strategy

Kunden / ~**orientierung** customer focus (orientation); ~**pflege** cultivating existing accounts (connections), customer care

Kunden / ~**portefeuille** customer portfolio; ~**präsentation** customer presentation; ~**profil** customer profile; ~**profitabilität** customer (account) profitability; ~**profitabilitätsanalyse** customer profitability analysis; ~**rückgewinnung** customer recovery

Kunden / ~**schnittstelle** customer interface; ~**segment** customer segment; ~**sicherheiten** collateral furnished by customers; ~**sicht** *(aus ~)* from the customer's perspective; ~**sorgfaltspflichten** *(i. S. der Geldwäschebekämpfung)* duties with respect to the idemnification and monitoring of customers

Kunden / ~**stamm** customer (client) base, regular (standing) clientele, regular clients; ~**stammnummer** basic customer account number; ~**termingelder** customer term (time) deposits

Kunden / ~**verbindlichkeiten** liabilities to customers, customer deposits;

~**verbindung** customer (account) relationship, *(Ertrag aus einer ~)* customer profitability; ~**verhalten** customer behaviour; ~**vertrauen** client trust, customer confidence; ~**vorgabe** customer requirement (specifications)

Kunden / ~**wahrnehmung** client perception, customer experience; ~**wechsel** trade bill; ~**werbung** canvassing, winning new customers; ~**wert** customer value, → Kundenertragswert; ~**zufriedenheit** customer satisfaction; ~**zufriedenheitsbefragung** customer (client) satisfaction survey; ~**zuführung** client referral

kündbar terminable, *(jederzeit ~)* terminable at will, *(kurzfristig ~)* terminable on short notice, *(kurzfristig ~e Gelder)* deposits at short notice, *(~ mit zehntägiger Kündigungsfrist)* terminable on 10 days' notice

K

kündigen 1. to give notice, *(Einlagen ~)* to give notice of withdrawal for funds deposited, *(dreißig Tage im voraus ~)* to give notice 30 days beforehand (in advance), to give 30 days' advance written notice, *(termingerecht ~)* to give notice within the required period
2. to terminate, *(ein Arbeitsverhältnis mit einer Frist von vier Wochen zum Quartalsende ~)* to terminate an employment with four weeks' notice to the end of the respective quarter
(die Kontoverbindung ~) to terminate the account relationship, *(den Vertrag unter Beachtung einer dreimonatigen Kündigungsfrist ~)* to terminate (to cancel) the agreement on a three months' notice
3. to call in, *(eine Anleihe ~)* to call in a bond, to give notice on a bond, *(einen Kredit ~)* to call in a loan, *(zur sofortigen Rückzahlung ~)* to call in for immediate repayment, *(gekündigte Engagements)* commitments called in, *(Wertpapiere zum Nennwert ~)* to call securities at par

Kündigung 1. giving notice, *(~ von Einlagen)* giving notice of withdrawal, *(nur nach vorheriger ~ rückzahlbar)* repayable only after the specified period of notice has been given, *(ohne vorherige ~)* without prior notice
2. termination, *(~ des Kreditverhältnisses mit sofortiger Wirkung)* terminating the loan relationship (loan agreement) with immediate effect, *(~ des Arbeitsverhältnisses)* termination of employment, *(freiwillig)* quitting, giving notice, *(unfreiwillig)* dismissal, *(~ im beiderseitigen Einvernehmen)* termination by mutual agreement, *(~ wegen Leistungsverzug)* default termination, *(~ eines Vertrages aus wichtigem Grund)* termination for good cause
3. call, calling in, *(auf tägliche ~)* on (at) call, *(die vollständige oder teilweise ~ der Emission)* calling in the issue in part or in its entirety, *(~ vor Fälligkeit)* calling in prior to maturity, *(~ aller ausstehenden Titel)* clean-up call

Kündigungs / ~**absicht** intention to give notice; ~**aufgeld** call premium; ~**bedingungen** conditions for termination (for calling in, for dismissal); ~**bestimmung** termination clause (provision), call provision, call feature

Kündigungs / ~**darlehen** medium-term call loan; ~**ereignis** event of default, → Ausfallereignis; ~**freijahre** call protection, call deferment period, non-callable period, call-free years

Kündigungsfrist 1. notice period, *(nicht eingehaltene ~)* period of notice not observed, days of short notice, *(ohne Einhaltung der ~)* without giving notice, without observing the termination (withdrawal) notice, *(unter Einhaltung der ~)* with due regard to the termination (withdrawal) notice
(der Kreditnehmer kann den Kredit mit dreimonatiger ~ jederzeit zurückzahlen) the borrower has the option to give three months' notice of repayment at any time, *(Tilgungen sind unter Beachtung einer sechsmonatigen ~ möglich)* redemptions are permitted on a six months' notice
2. *(bei Einlagen)* withdrawal notice

Kündigungs / ~gebühr termination (cancellation) fee; **~gelder** notice deposits, deposits at notice; **~geldkonten** notice deposit accounts; **~grund** 1. cause (reason) for termination 2. reason for dismissal

Kündigungs / ~hypothek callable mortgage; **~interesse** *(kein berechtigtes ~ besitzen)* to have no legitimate right to terminate the contract

Kündigungs / ~klausel 1. termination clause 2. *(eines Anleihe-, Kreditvertrages)* call provision, call feature, optional redemption clause; **~kurs** call price; **~möglichkeit/~option** call privilege (option, facility); **~quote** termination rate

Kündigungsrecht 1. right to give notice, right of termination, right to terminate (to repeal)
2. *(bei Anleihen)* call right (privilege)
3. *(bei Krediten) (a) (~ der Bank)* bank's right to call in a loan, *(b) (~ des Kreditnehmers)* borrower's right to terminate the loan agreement, *(vorzeitiges Recht)* borrower's early repayment privilege, borrower's right to repay the loan prematurely

Kündigungs / ~regelung notice (termination) arrangements; **~risiko** termination (callability) risk; **~schreiben** 1. termination (call) notice, letter (notice) of termination 2. withdrawal notice; **~schutz** 1. *(bei einer Anleihe)* call protection 2. *(eines Arbeitnehmers)* notice protection, protection against unjustified dismissal; **~schutzklage** dismissal suit

Kündigungs / ~sperrfrist 1. waiting period 2. *(bei Anleihen)* non-call period 3. *(bei Einlagen)* period during which no withdrawal notice can be given; **~termin** 1. *(bei einer Anleihe)* call date 2. *(bei Einlagen)* date on which notice of withdrawal must be given; **~vorschriften** notice requirements

Kupon coupon, *(mit ~)* cum coupon, *(ohne ~)* ex coupon

Kupon / ~bogen coupon sheet; **~einlösung** collection (encashment) of coupons, coupon payment; **~inhaber** coupon holder; **~strip** interest strip, → Stripping; **~swap** plain vanilla interest rate swap; **~termin** coupon date, coupon payment date

Kurs 1. *(einer Aktie/Anleihe)* price, quotation; *(~ ex Bezugsrechte)* rights-off share price, *(~ gestrichen)* no dealings, no quotation, non-quoted, *(~ im nachbörslichen Handel)* price in after-hours trading, *(~ über dem Nennwert)* price above par, premium price, *(~ unter dem Nennwert)* price below par, discount price, *(~ vor dem Aussetzen der Notierung)* pre-suspension price
2. *(einer Devise)* exchange rate
3. *(Richtung)* direction, course, line, policy, *(die Wirtschaft wieder auf ~ bringen)* to get the economy back on track

K

Kurs / ~abbröckelung crumbling of prices; **~abschlag** 1. *(Festsetzung eines niedrigeren Kurses)* price markdown 2. *(Abgang eines Bezugsrechtes/einer Dividende)* quotation ex rights/dividend 3. discount, → Deport, → Disagio

Kurs / ~abschwächung *(am Aktienmarkt)* easing (sagging) of prices in the equity market, stock price decline; **~absicherung** → Kurssicherung; **~abstriche** price markdowns; **~abwärtsbewegung** downward trend (drift) in prices

Kurs / ~änderung price change (variation), rate change; **~anfrage** quote request, price indication request; **~angabe** price indication, quotation; **~anomalie** price aberration, price anomaly, → Kursungleichgewichte; **~anpassung** price adjustment, rate adjustment

Kursanstieg price increase (rise, run-up), advance in prices, *(~ des Dollar gegenüber dem Euro)* dollar rise against the Euro, *(~ auf breiter Front)* buoyancy of prices across the board, broad price advance, *(~ durch Übernahmegerüchte)* bid-inspired rise, *(starker ~ bei Aktien)* upsurge in equities, sharp rise in share (stock) prices

Kurs / ~anzeigetafel quotations board, price indicator board; **~aufschlag** 1. price markup 2. premium, → Report, → Agio; **~aufschwung** *(am Aktien-/Rentenmarkt)* upturn in equity/bond prices

Kurs / ~auftrieb price upsurge (boost); **~ausschläge** sharp price fluctuations, price gyrations; **~aussetzung** suspension from quotation

kursbedingt *(~e Abschreibungen auf Wertpapiere)* price-related write-downs on securities

kursbeeinflussend *(~e Faktoren)* factors influencing the price, price determinants

K

Kursbefestigung strengthening (stiffening) of prices, price advance, *(~ des Euro gegenüber den meisten anderen Hauptwährungen)* appreciation (firming up) of the Euro against most other major currencies

Kurs / ~besserung *(~ am Aktienmarkt)* improvement in stock prices, stock price recovery; **~beständigkeit** firmness (steadiness) of prices

Kursbewegungen price (rate) movements, *(keine nennenswerten ~ bei Aktienwerten)* featureless trading in equities, *(geringe ~ bei den Hauptwährungen)* the major currencies moved within a fairly narrow range

Kurs / ~bildung price (rate) determination, → Kursfestsetzung; **~bildungsfaktoren** price (rate) determinants; **~blasé** stock price bubble; **~blatt** quotations list, stock exchange list

Kurs / ~-Buchwert-Verhältnis price/book ratio □ ratio of a stock's market value to the book value per share

Kurs / ~-Cashflow-Verhältnis price/cash flow ratio □ ratio of cash flow per share to stock price, ratio designed to measure the earnings power of a company

Kurs / ~chancen price appreciation potential, upward price potential; **~diagramm** (commodity/stock) price chart

Kurs / ~differenz price difference (discrepancy); **~differenzkontrakt** contract for difference, → Differenzkontrakt; **~druck** *(im Bankenbereich)* pressure on bank stocks, *(~ auf den Euro)* pressure coming to bear on the Euro; **~durchschnitt** 1. average price, price average 2. mean rate, rate average

Kurs / ~einbruch *(bei Aktienwerten)* downslide in equity prices, sharp setback in stock prices, *(einer Valuta)* sharp fall in the value of a currency; **~einbußen** 1. *(Devisen)* exchange loss, loss on exchange 2. *(Wertpapiere)* (stock) price losses

Kurs / ~einschätzung price assessment; **~entwicklung** price development (performance), development in prices/rates, *(~ an den Wertpapiermärkten)* price trends in the securities markets, stock/bond market trend

Kurs / ~erholung *(am Aktienmarkt)* stock price recovery, rally in equities, *(Kurserholung des Euro gegenüber dem Dollar)* recovery (improvement) of the Euro against the dollar; **~errechnung** price-finding, rate-finding, calculating the price (the rate); **~explosion** sharp upsurge in stock prices, rocketing (zooming) equity prices

Kurs / ~festsetzung/~feststellung/~findung 1. price fixing, price determination, price-setting 2. *(des amtlichen Wechselkurses/des Goldpreises)* rate fixing/fixing; **~flaute** flagging prices

Kurs / ~fluktuationen price fluctuations; **~freigabe** *(~ des Wechselkurses)* floating of the exchange rate; **~garantie** *(Devisen)* forward exchange guarantee (cover, protection); **~gebot** quote, price quote (bid), *(Aufforde-*

rung zur Abgabe eines ~es) price request; ~**gefälle** price differential

kursgesichert rate-hedged, *(~ durch ein Termingeschäft)* covered forward, *(~e Dollars)* dollars hedged (covered) forward, *(~e Aufwendungen/Erträge)* rate-hedged expenses/income, *(~e Währungsanleihe)* rate-hedged currency bond

Kursgewinn 1. *(bei Wertpapieren)* price gain **2.** *(bei Devisen)* exchange profit, gain on exchange; ~**chancen** price (appreciation) potential

Kurs/Gewinn-Verhältnis price earnings ratio, P/E ratio

kursgünstig *(~e Anschaffung) (von Devisen)* buying a currency amount at a favourable rate, *(von Wertpapieren)* buying securities at a favourable (low) price, buying on favourable terms

Kurs / ~**höhe** price level, rate level; ~**index** share (stock) price index, market average; ~**indikation** indicative quote (price); ~**information** price information, dissemination of market prices

Kurs / ~**korrektur** *(nach oben/unten)* upward/downward price correction, upward/downward adjustment in prices, *(~ nach den Verlusten des Vortages)* technical rebound after yesterday's losses; ~**kosmetik** price (rate) window-dressing

Kurs / ~**limit** price limit; ~**lücke** price gap; ~**makler** official broker; ~**manipulation** price (rate) manipulation, rigging a price (rate), market rigging; ~**neuordnung** *(der Wechselkurse)* realignment of exchange rates; ~**niveau** *(am Aktienmarkt)* stock price level

Kurs / ~**notierung 1.** *(Devisen)* exchange rate quotation, → Mengennotierung, → Preisnotierung **2.** *(Aktien)* stock price quotation, quotation in the stock (equity) market **3.** *(Form)* price notation (e.g. comma or point for decimal separator); ~**notiz** quote, quotation

Kurs / ~**obergrenze** price cap (ceiling), maximum price, upper price limit, rate limit (cap); ~**offerte** quotation, price (rate) offered

Kurs / ~**optimismus** *(~ am Aktien-/Rentenmarkt)* upbeat mood (bullish sentiment) in the equity/bond market; ~**pessimismus** *(~ am Aktien-/Rentenmarkt)* downbeat mood (bearish sentiment) in the equity/bond market

Kurspflege 1. market-smoothing operations, carrying out smoothing operations in the market, *(~ für eine Emission)* secondary market support, stabilising the price of an issue by buying and selling in the open market **2.** *(i. S. von Kursstützung)* price support, price-regulating interventions

Kurspflege / ~**bestände** portfolios maintained for market support; ~**konsortium** price support syndicate; ~**mittel** funds for price-supporting purchases

Kurs / ~**reagibilität** price (rate) sensitiveness; ~**regulierung** price intervention (support); ~**rendite** price yield; ~**reserve** upside price potential

Kursrisiko price risk, exchange risk, downside risk, *(~ bei Aktienanlagen)* price risk inherent in equity investments, equity market exposure, *(~ nach unten)* downside risk

Kursrisikobegrenzung limiting downside risk

kursrisikotragend *(~e Titel)* securities carrying a price risk

Kursrückgang decline (fall, drop) in prices, price decline, *(~ am Aktienmarkt)* fall (drop, decline) in equity prices, price slippage, *(~ des Dollar gegenüber dem Euro)* dollar fall against the Euro, *(~ auf breiter Front)* fall in prices across the board, *(~ bei geringen Umsätzen)* prices turning lower in thin trading

Kurs / ~**rücknahme** marking down a stock, *(Kursrücknahmen zu Beginn der Börsensitzung)* opening markdowns; ~**rückschlag** *(~ am Rentenmarkt)* setback in bond prices; ~**rutsch** *(~ am Aktienmarkt)* slide in equity prices

Kurs / ~schnitt price fraud; → Mindestkursschritt; **~schwäche** weakness of prices; **~schwankungen** price swings (fluctuations), ups and downs of the market, rate fluctuations, *(starke ~)* sharp price swings, gyrations; **~schwankungsintensität** *(~ des Aktienkurses)* stock price volatility, *(~ eines Wechselkurses)* rate volatility, volatility of the exchange rate

kurssensitiv *(~e Informationen)* price-sensitive information

Kurssicherheit guaranteeing the price (rate), assurance as to the price

kurssichernd *(~e Abschlüsse)* price-hedging (rate-hedging) transactions

Kurssicherung price hedge, *(~ von Fremdwährungseinlagen)* hedging (securing) the exchange rate of currency deposits, *(~ durch ein Futures-/Optionsgeschäft)* futures/option hedge, *(~ durch ein Termingeschäft)* forward cover

Kurssicherungs / ~aufwand hedging charges (expenditure); **~ergebnis** hedging performance, rate-hedging result; **~geschäft** hedge, price (rate) hedging transaction

Kurssicherungs / ~gewinn hedging profit (gain); **~kosten** hedge cost, rate-hedging cost; **~möglichkeiten** hedging options; **~programm** hedging scheme

Kurssicherungs / ~strategie hedging strategy; **~technik** hedging techniques; **~verhalten** hedging policy, exposure management; **~verlust** hedging loss

Kurs / ~spanne price range (spread), range between high and low prices over a given period; **~spekulation** **1.** speculation on the stock exchange, market playing **2.** currency speculation

Kurs / ~spielraum *(nach oben)* upside potential, price (rate) appreciation potential; **~sprünge** *(~ am Aktienmarkt)* jumps in equity prices

Kurs / ~stabilisierung price (rate) stabilisation, steadying of the market; **~steigerung** price (rate) appreciation, *(~ am Aktienmarkt)* increase (advance) in equity prices, firming up of stock prices

Kurs / ~stellung quotation, quote, *(~ im Sekundärmarkt)* quotation in the secondary market; **~sturz** steep plunge, heavy drop (nosedive) of prices, price slump

Kursstützung **1.** price support, price-supporting purchases, price propping **2.** intervening in support of a currency, rate support

Kursstützungs / ~käufe support buying, price-supporting purchases; **~konsortium** price support syndicate; **~niveau** price support level

Kurs / ~tafel quotations board; **~tendenz** price trend (tendency), trend in prices, market trend

Kurs / ~umkehrformation *(in der Chartanalyse)* price reversal pattern; **~-Umsatz-Verhältnis** price-to-sales ratio; **~umschwung** rebound (turnaround) in prices

Kursungleichgewichte price imperfections, *(~ zwischen zwei Märkten)* price anomalies, out-of-line price relationship between two different market places, pricing inefficiencies in different markets

Kurs / ~unsicherheiten uncertainties over (about) the further trend in prices, uncertainty over the development of the exchange rate, currency uncertainties; **~untergrenze** price (rate) floor, minimum price (rate), lower price limit, down limit; **~unterschied** price difference (disparity)

Kurs / ~variabilität price volatility; **~veränderungen** price (rate) changes, price variations, *(~ nach oben/unten)* upward/downward price (rate) changes

Kurs / ~verbreitung price dissemination; **~verfall** price collapse, heavy fall in prices, free fall of the market, stock market crash; **~verlust** **1.** price loss,

K

(starke ~e am Aktienmarkt) heavy stock price losses, hefty losses in the equity market **2.** exchange loss

Kurs / ~verzerrung price distortion; **~volatilität 1.** price volatility, volatility of stock (equity) prices **2.** exchange rate volatility; **~vorgabe 1.** *(i. S. von Festlegung)* setting a price (a price limit) **2.** *(~ durch Wall Street)* price lead from Wall Street

Kurs / ~wechsel change in policy direction; **~wert 1.** market value **2.** value quoted; **~wertberichtigungen** write-downs on (value adjustments to) securities holdings (portfolios)

Kurs / ~zacken *(Charttechnik)* ripples; **~zettel** list of quotations, quotations (stock exchange) list; **~ziel** upside price objective, upside target; **~zusatz** price supplement (annotation)

Kurve *(Rendite-/Zinskurve)* curve

kurz *(im ~en Bereich)* at the short end of the market, *(am ~en Ende des Laufzeitenspektrums)* at the short end of the maturity range

kurz *(~e Laufzeit)* short life (maturity), *(~e Termine)* short dates, maturities of less than 30 days, *(~e Zinsbindung)* fixed interest rate for a short period, locking in the interest rate for a short term

Kurzakkreditiv short form bill of lading

Kurzakzept blank acceptance

Kürze *(~ des Berichtszeitraumes)* brevity of the period under review

kürzen 1. *(verringern)* to reduce, to cut, to cut back (down) **2.** *(die Laufzeit ~)* to shorten the maturity

Kurzfassung short (abridged) version, *(~ der Bilanz)* summary financial statements, abbreviated accounts

Kurzform-Konnossement short form (blank) bill of lading

kurzfristig 1. *adj.* *(~e Adressenausfallrisiken)* short-term credit risks (i.e. settlement and clearing risks), *(~e Ausleihungen)* short-term lendings, *(Volumen der ~en Ausleihungen)* short-term loan book, *(~e Finanzanlagen)* current investments (intended to be held for up to one year), *(~e Finanzierungskosten)* short-term financing cost, *(~e Finanzierungsmittel)* short-term finance

(~es Fremdkapital) short-term debt capital, *(~e Geldaufnahmen)* short-term borrowings, *(~e Geldausleihungen)* short-term cash lendings (overnight, tomnext, spot next), *(~e Geldhereinnahmen)* acceptance of short-term deposits, *(~e Geldpolitik)* near-term monetary policy, *(~er Kreditbedarf)* short-term borrowing requirements

(~es Kreditgeschäft) short-term lendings, *(~e Kapitalanlage)* short-dated investment, investing for the short term, *(~e monetäre Posten)* short-term monetary items, *(~e latente Steueransprüche)* current deferred tax assets, *(~e Liquiditätsvorschau)* short-range liquidity forecast, *(~e Mittelaufnahme)* short-term borrowing

(~es Nettovermögen) working capital, *(~e monetäre Posten)* short-term monetary items, *(~e Planung)* short-term (short-run) planning, *(~er Schuldschein)* short note, *(~e Verbindlichkeiten)* current liabilities, short-term debt, *(~e Verbindlichkeiten gegenüber Banken)* current bank borrowings, *(~er Währungsbeistand)* short-term monetary support

2. *adv.* *(sehr ~ abrufen)* to call at a very short notice, *(~ aufnehmen)* to raise at short notice, to borrow for the short term, *(~ fällig werdende Teile der langfristigen Verbindlichkeiten)* current portion of long-term debt, *(~ fällig werdende Verpflichtungen)* near-term commitments

Kurzfrist / ~kredit short-term loan (credit), short loan, short-term borrowing facility; **~trend** *(in der Chart-Analyse)* minor trend

Kurz / ~indossament blank endorsement, endorsement bearing only the name of the endorser; ~**informationsblatt** factsheet; ~**konnossement** → Kurzform-Konnossement

kurzlaufend *(~e Bankschuldverschreibungen)* short-dated bank notes

Kurzläufer short, short bond, short-dated issue (security), short maturity

Kurzläufer-Rendite yield on shorts

kurzlebig *(~e Investitionsgüter)* short-lived capital goods

Kürzung 1. abridgement, shortening 2. reduction, cut, cutback

KWG → Kreditwesengesetz

L

Labilität *(~ des Marktes)* instability (shakiness) of the market

Lade / **~betrag** loading amount, loadable amount; **~hafen** shipping port, port of lading (loading); **~kosten** cost of loading; **~liste** **1.** freight (loading) list **2.** *(im Schiffsverkehr)* manifest, shipping bill

laden **1.** *(eine Geldkarte ~)* to load a money card **2.** *(vorladen)* to summon

Ladeschein consignment note

Ladung **1.** cargo, shipment, consignment **2.** loading **3.** *(Vorladung)* summons

ladungsfähig *(~e Anschrift)* address for service, legal address

Ladungspfandrecht cargo lien

Lage **1.** situation, state, condition(s), circumstances, *(finanzielle ~ des Unternehmens)* company's financial situation (position) **2.** *(Standort)* location **3.** *(Liquidität)* position

Lagebericht Management Report, Management Discussion and Analysis

Lager **1.** inventory, stock **2.** warehouse,storage location, depository

Lager / **~abbau** stock reduction (rundown), destocking; **~bestand** inventory, goods in stock, stock position; **~bestandsfinanzierung** inventory financing; **~bewertung** stock (inventory) valuation; **~dauer** stockholding (warehousing) period; **~empfangsschein** warehousekeeper's receipt

Lager / **~finanzierung** inventory (stock) financing; **~finanzierungskredit** inventory loan; **~geld** storage (warehousing) charges, warehouse fee; **~gut** warehoused goods (merchandise)

Lager / **~halter** warehousekeeper; **~halter-Konnossement** custody bill of lading; **~halter-Pfandrecht** warehousekeeper's lien; **~haltung** stock management; **~investitionen** inventory (stock) investment, inventory spending; **~land** country of deposit

lagern to store, to warehouse, to stock, to take in stock, *(getrennt vom Sicherungsgut ~)* to store separately from the collateral

Lager / **~ort** **1.** storage location **2.** *(von Wertpapieren)* depository, place of deposit; **~risiko** inventory (stockholding) risk; **~schein** warrant, warehouse warrant, warehousekeeper's warrant; **~scheininhaber** warrant holder, bearer of a warrant; **~stellenverzeichnis** list of depositories; **~umschlag** stock turnover

Lagerung storage, warehousing, storing

lahmen to trail behind, *(~de Konjunktur)* sluggish state of the economy

lähmen *(die Wirtschaft ~)* to paralyse (to cripple) the economy

Lambda descriptive of the option's leverage □ determined by dividing the percentage change in the option price by the percentage change in the price of the underlying asset, → Griechen

Land **1.** country **2.** *(Bundesland)* Land, State **3.** *(Grund und Boden)* land, landed property

Länder / **~anleihe** Land bond, State government bond; **~ausfallwahrscheinlichkeit** likelihood of a country default; **~bewertung/~beurteilung** country assessment, sovereign rating; **~bonität** country's credit (credit-worthiness), country's financial standing

Länder / ~engagement 1. country commitment 2. *(Gesamtobligo)* country exposure, country loan portfolio, *(Aufstellung unserer ~s)* list of our exposures (lendings) to sovereign borrowers; **~forderungen** claims on (due from) sovereign borrowers

Länder / ~gewichtung country weighting; **~-Jumbo** large bond issued jointly by several Federal States (Länder); **~klassifizierung** 1. country grading (rating) 2. country risk score

Länderkredit country loan (debt), sovereign loan, *(Rückstellungen für ~e)* provisions for lendings to sovereign borrowers, country debt provisioning, *(Umschuldung von ~en)* country debt rescheduling

Länder / ~limit country limit, limit (ceiling) on lendings to a specific country; **~obligation** → Länderanleihe; **~obligo** 1. country exposure (commitments) 2. country exposure list; **~rating** country rating (assessment)

Länderrisiko country risk (exposure), sovereign risk, risk from lending funds to or making investments in a specific country

Länderrisiko / ~bewertung country risk assessment, sovereign risk rating; **~engagement** country risk exposure; **~gewichtung** country risk weighting; **~gewichtungsfaktor** country risk weighting factor

Länderrisiko / ~messung country risk measurement; **~steuerung** country risk management; **~überwachung** monitoring country risk; **~verordnung** Country Risk Ordinance; **~vorsorge** country risk provisioning

Länderusance custom (practice) prevailing in a specific country, *(in der länderusancegemäßen Form)* in the form prescribed by local practice

Länderwertberichtigungen country valuation allowances, country-specific loan loss allowances, charges against sovereign loans (sovereign lendings, country debt)

Landesaufsichtsbehörde State supervisory authority

Landesbank Landesbank □ Public sector bank acting as the central credit institution, clearing house and liquidity manager for municipalities and the State's public savings banks. Moreover, Landesbanken engage in all types of commercial and investment banking activities.

Landes / ~bürgschaft Land (State) guarantee, guarantee furnished by a Land (State) government; **~schatzanweisungen** Land (State) discount notes; **~schuldbuch** Land debt register

landesverbürgt *(~e Anleihe/~es Darlehen)* bond/loan guaranteed by a Land (State) government

Landes / ~währung national (domestic) currency; **~zentralbank** Regional Bundesbank Office

landesweit *(~es Filialnetz)* nationwide branch network

Landgericht Regional Court

ländlich *(~e Kreditgenossenschaft)* rural credit union

landwirtschaftlich *(~e Genossenschaftsbank)* rural (agricultural) cooperative bank, farm credit bank, *(~er Kredit)* agricultural loan, farm credit, *(~es Vermögen)* agricultural property, farming stock

lang *(im ~en Bereich)* at the long end of the market, *(~e Kasse)* forex deals maturing within a period of one week, *(~e Laufzeit)* long life (maturity), *(~er Tender)* longer-term tender, *(~e Zinsbindung)* interest rate fixed for a long period, locking in the interest rate for a long term

Länge *(~ des Absatzweges)* channel length

länger *(~e Laufzeiten)* long-range maturities, *(über einen ~en Zeitraum hinweg)* over a prolonged period of time

längerfristige Refinanzierungsgeschäfte *(des EZBS)* longer-term refinancing operations □ liquidity-providing reverse transactions (→ befristete Transaktionen) designed to provide additional longer-term liquidity; carried out in the form of monthly standard tenders

Langform full-length form

langfristig 1. *adj. (~e Ausfallrate)* long-term default rate, *(~e Ausleihungen)* long-term lendings, *(Volumen der ~en Ausleihungen)* long-term loan book, *(~e Einlagenverzinsung* interest rate(s) paid on long-term deposits, *(~e Emission)* long-dated issue, *(~e Fertigungsaufträge)* long-term construction contracts, *(~e Finanzanlagen)* long-term investments, *(~e Finanzierungsmittel)* long-term finance
(~e Forderungen) non-current receivables, *(~es Fremdkapital)* long-term debt capital, *(~e Kapitalanlage)* long-dated investment, *(~e Kapitalbildung)* formation of long-term capital, *(~er Kreditbedarf)* long-term borrowing requirements, *(~e Kreditzinsen)* long-term lending rates, *(~e Kundenforderungen)* long-term lendings to (long-term claims on) customers, *(~e latente Steueransprüche)* non-current deferred tax assets, *(~e Umschuldung)* rescheduling (renegotiation) into a long-term loan
(~e Verbindlichkeiten) non-current liabilities, long-term debt, *(~e Verbindlichkeiten gegenüber Banken)* non-current bank borrowings, *(~e Vermögensteile)* non-current assets, *(~er Wechsel)* long-dated bill, long bill, *(~e Wertpapieranlage)* long-term securities investment, *(~e Zinsbindung)* fixing the interest rate for (over) a long period
2. *adv. (~ investieren)* to invest for the long term, *(~ orientierte Anleger)* buy and hold investors, *(Wertpapiere ~ halten)* to hold securities over the long term

Langfristigkeit 1. long maturity **2.** long-term nature (feature)

Langfrist / ~kredit long-term loan, long credit; **~kreditportefeuille** long-term loan book (portfolio); **~planung** long-term (long-range, long-run) planning; **~trend** *(in der Chart-Analyse)* primary (major) trend; **~vergleich** comparison over a longer period of time; **~zins** long-term interest rate, interest rate for long-term lendings

langjährig *(~e Geschäftsverbindung)* long-standing business relationship, *(~er Kunde)* customer for (of, over) many years

langlaufend *(~e Terminkonten)* long-term time deposits (deposit accounts)

Langläufer long, long bond, long-dated issue (security), long maturity

Langläufer-Rendite long bond yield, yield on longs, long-term bond yield

langlebig *(~e Wirtschaftsgüter)* durable economic goods

Langlebigkeit *(~ der Rezession)* longevity of the recession

langwierig *(~es Verfahren)* lengthy (long drawn-out, protracted, time-consuming) process

Langzeit-LE long-term supplier's declaration

Langzeitprognose long-range forecast

Last 1. *(Belastung)* burden, charge, load **2.** *(Gewicht)* weight, load **3.** *(Grundstückslast)* charge, encumbrance

lasten to weigh (to lie, to bear) upon, *(die auf dem Unternehmensvermögen ~den Schulden)* the debt (the charges) weighing upon the company's assets, encumbrances on corporate assets

Lasten 1. charges **2.** *(eine Dividende zu ~ der Rücklagen zahlen)* to pay a dividend out of the reserves, *(zu ~ Ihres Kontos einlösen)* to pay (to honour) to the debit of your account, *(Eintragungsgebühren gehen zu ~ des Kreditnehmers)* registration fees will be debited to the borrower's account

lastenfrei unencumbered, clear of encumbrances, unmortgaged, *(das Ei-*

gentum ~ übertragen) to transfer the property (ownership) free from/of encumbrances (free of liens)

Lasten / ~**heft** performance (product) specification(s); ~**übergang** transfer of liabilities (or duties); ~**verzeichnis 1.** schedule of charges (of encumbrances) **2.** → Lastenheft

Lastschrift 1. *(im Abbuchungsverfahren)* direct debit, direct withdrawal **2.** *(Kontobelastung)* debit, debit entry **3.** *(Belastungsanzeige)* debit advice (voucher)

Lastschrift / ~**abkommen** direct debit agreement; ~**auftrag** direct debit instruction (DDI), direct debit order; ~**auftraggeber** payor; ~**ausführung**/~**bearbeitung** processing direct debits; ~**beleg** direct debit note

Lastschrift / ~**einlösung** payment of direct debits; ~**einreicher** payee, direct debit creditor; ~**einreichung** direct debit origination, presenting a direct debit for payment, ~**einzug** → Lastschriftinkasso

L

Lastschrift / ~**ermächtigung** direct debit authorisation (mandate); ~**garantie** direct debit guarantee; ~**gebühr** direct debit charge; ~**gläubiger** direct debit creditor; ~**inkasso** direct debit collection; ~**mandat** direct debit mandate; ~**obligo** direct debit limit (line)

Lastschrift / ~**retoure**/~**rückgabe** returned direct debit, DD return, rejected item; ~**valutierung** fixing the value dates of direct debits; ~**verfahren** direct debiting scheme; ~**verkehr** direct debit payments; ~**vordruck** direct debit form; ~**zahlung** payment by direct debit

latent *(~e Ertragssteuerverpflichtungen)* deferred income tax liabilities, *(~e Kreditausfälle)* latent losses in the loan portfolio, *(~es Kreditrisiko)* latent (hidden) credit risk, *(~er Steueraufwand)* deferred tax expenses, *(~e Steuerforderungen/Steueransprüche nach Wertberichtigung)* deferred tax assets, net of valuation allowance

laufen 1. *(Gültigkeit besitzen)* to run, to be valid, to be in force (in effect), *(die Vereinbarung läuft drei Jahre/läuft bis ...)* the agreement runs for three years/is valid till ..., *(die Zinsen ~ ab 1. Jan.)* interest accrues (runs) from January 1 **2.** to work, to function, to run

laufend 1. *adj.* continuous, *(~er Dividendenertrag)* current dividend yield, *(~e Emission)* tap issue, *(~es Ergebnis aus Beteiligungen)* current result on investments, *(~e Erträge)* current income (earnings), earnings from current operations, *(~e Ertragssteueransprüche)* current income tax assets, *(~e Ertragssteuerverpflichtungen)* current income tax liabilities *(~e Geschäftstätigkeit)* *(a)* current operations *(b)* ordinary course of business, day-to-day business (operations) *(c)* *(im bilanziellen Kontext)* continuing operations, *(~e Gewinnrechnung)* current period earnings, *(~e Kalendertage)* running days *(~es Konto)* current account (BE), checking account (AE), *(~e Kontoverbindung)* ongoing account relationship, *(~e Kosten)* running cost (charges), *(~er Kreditbedarf)* ongoing borrowing requirements, *(~er Kupon)* current coupon, *(~e Kursfeststellung)* continuous price-setting, *(~e Obligokontrolle)* continuous monitoring of the exposure *(für ~e Rechnung kaufen)* to buy for current account, *(~e Rechnungsperiode)* current accounting period, *(~e Tilgung)* regular redemption payments, *(~er Verfall)* current maturity, *(~e Verzinsung)* current return, *(~e Zinsen)* interest accrued, *(~e Zinszahlungen)* regular interest payments **2.** *adv.* continuously, on an ongoing basis, *(sich ~ um Verbesserungen bemühen)* to be constantly seeking improvements, *(~ emittieren)* to issue on tap (in tap form), to issue continuously, to issue on an ongoing basis, *(~ überwachen)* to monitor (to supervise) on a continuing (an ongoing) basis

Laufzeit 1. term, life, duration, period, tenor, *(Anleihen mit zehnjähriger ~)* ten-year bonds, *(zinsvariable Anleihe mit vierjähriger ~)* four-year floater, *(Einlagen mit fester ~)* fixed-term deposits, *(die ~ des Kredites ist zunächst bis TMJ begrenzt)* the initial term of the credit expires on DMY, *(während der ~ der Kreditvereinbarung)* for (during) the lifetime of the credit arrangement
2. maturity, *(Emission mit einer ~ von acht Jahren)* issue with an eight-year maturity, *(Schuldtitel mit fester ~)* debt security of a fixed maturity
3. *(Gültigkeitsdauer)* validity, period (term) of validity

laufzeitabhängig *(~e Kreditkosten)* maturity-linked (maturity-driven, term-linked) cost of the credit

Laufzeitband maturity band (bracket), time bucket

laufzeitbedingt *(~e Renditedifferenz)* maturity-related yield differential

Laufzeitbegrenzung limiting the duration, maturity cap, putting a maturity cap on, *(~ des Kredites)* limiting the term (life) of the loan, *(Schuldtitel ohne ~)* perpetual debt, undated securities (debt)

laufzeitbezogen maturity-driven, *(~e Zinssätze)* maturity-related interest rates, *(~e Zuschläge)* maturity-related add-ons

Laufzeit / ~bindung locking in to a fixed term (life), agreeing on a fixed duration; **~divergenzen** maturity discrepancies; **~ende** *(am kurzen ~)* at the short end of the market

Laufzeiten / ~angebot range of maturities offered; **~bereich** maturities (life) range, maturities spectrum, *(im kurzen ~)* at the short end of the market

Laufzeiteninkongruenz mismatched maturities, maturity mismatch □ e.g. using short-term funds to finance long-term lendings (or investments), *(~ zwischen Forderungen und Sicherheiten)* mismatches in the maturities of the loans and the corresponding collateral

laufzeitenkongruent *(~e Ausleihungen)* lendings at matching maturities, *(~e Deckung der Aktiv- und Passivpositionen)* matching maturities of lendings and deposits, *(~e Kauf- und Verkaufspositionen)* long and short positions with matching maturities, *(~e Refinanzierung)* funding (refinancing) at matching maturities

Laufzeitenkongruenz matched maturities, *(Herstellen einer ~ zwischen Aktiva und Passiva)* matching the maturities of assets and liabilities (of lendings and deposits)

Laufzeiten / ~mix maturity mix; **~schutz** maturity hedging (protection); **~spektrum** → Laufzeitenbereich; **~staffelung** staggering (tiering) of maturities; **~streckung** extending (stretching, stretching out) the maturity

Laufzeiten / ~struktur maturity pattern, *(~ beim Erstabsatz von Neuemissionen)* maturity pattern of new offerings; **~transformation** maturity transformation (intermediation); **~verkürzung** shortening of maturities; **~verlängerung** → Laufzeitenstreckung

Laufzeit / ~fächer maturity range (spectrum); **~fonds** fixed maturity fund, limited duration fund, fund launched for a limited period of time

laufzeitgerecht *(~ am Geldmarkt refinanzieren)* to fund (to refinance) at matching maturities in the money market

Laufzeit / ~gewichtung maturity (duration) weighting, *(laufzeitgewichtet)* maturity-weighted; **~gliederung** maturity breakdown

laufzeitkonstant *(~er Ertrag)* constant yield to maturity

laufzeitlos *(~es nachrangiges Darlehen)* undated subordinated loan

Laufzeit / ~methode original exposure method; **~obergrenze** maturity cap, maximum maturity (duration, period); **~segment** maturity band, long/short end of the market

Laufzeit / ~unterdeckung mismatched maturities; **~untergrenze** maturity floor, minimum maturity (duration, period); **~zone** maturity zone; **~zuschlag** *(für Langfristkredite)* maturity markup for long-term loans

lauten 1. to read, *(wie folgt ~)* to read as follows
2. *(~ auf)* to be denominated in, to be made out to, *(auf Euro ~)* to be denominated (to be issued) in Euro, *(auf den Inhaber ~)* to be made out (to be issued) to bearer

L-DAX/L-MDAX/L-SDAX late indices of the German benchmark indices, → DAX, → MDAX, → SDAX

L

Leasing / ~anbieter leasing provider (company); **~aufwand** leasing (lease) expenses; **~bedingungen** lease terms, terms of the lease; **~beginn** lease commencement date; **~bestand** leasing portfolio

Leasing / ~dauer leasing period, lease term (duration); **~einnahmen** leasing (lease) revenue; **~erträge** leasing (lease) income, *(~ aus Weitervermietung)* sublease rental income; **~finanzierung** lease financing; **~fonds** leasing fund

Leasing / ~forderungen *(Verbriefung von ~)* securitisation of lease receivables; **~geber** lessor; **~gegenstand** leased asset (property); **~gesellschaft** leasing company; **~nehmer** lessee; **~objekt** leased asset

Leasing / ~quote leasing ratio □ share of leasing in total equipment spending; **~rate** lease rental; **~verpflichtungen** lease (leasing) commitments; **~vertrag** lease agreement

Leben 1. *(das Unternehmen am ~ erhalten)* to keep the company afloat **2.** *(die Vereinbarung mit ~ erfüllen)* to fill the agreement with substance

Lebens / ~dauer *(von Wirtschaftsgütern)* service (useful) life, durability; **~erwartung** life expectancy

lebensfähig *(~er Markt)* viable market

Lebens / ~haltungskosten cost of living, *(Index der ~)* cost-of-living index; **~lauf** curriculum vitae, personal record; **~versicherung** life assurance (insurance); **~versicherungspolice** life policy; **~zeit** lifetime, *(Besitzrecht/Einkommen/Rente auf ~)* life estate/income/annuity

lebhaft 1. *adj. (~e Börse)* brisk (lively) market, *(bei ~en Umsätzen anziehen)* to advance (to move ahead) in active trading, *(~er Wertpapiermarkt)* lively (buoyant) securities market
2. *adv. (~ expandieren)* to expand vigorously, *(~ gehandelte Aktien)* actively traded equities, active (high-volume) stocks, *(AB wurden ~ gehandelt)* AB traded busily

leer *(~e Stücke) (a)* stripped bonds *(b)* bonds ex warrants/ex rights, *(die Aktionäre gingen ~ aus)* the shareholders went empty-handed

Leer / ~aktien unpaid and partly paid shares; **~standsdauer** void period; **~verkauf** short sale (selling), *(leerverkaufte Aktien)* stock sold short, *(Leerverkäufe per Termin)* forward short selling; **~verkäufer** short, short seller

legal *adj.* lawful, legal, *adv.* legally, by lawful means

Legalisierung *(~ von Dokumenten)* legalisation (authentication) of documents

Legat legacy, bequest

Legatar legatee

legitim legitimate, lawful

Legitimation 1. (furnishing) proof of identity **2.** identity verification (authentication) **3.** credentials

Legitimations / ~aktionär nominee shareholder; **~prüfung** identity check, *(~ von Karteninhabern)*

cardholder verification; **~urkunde** **1.** proof of identity **2.** proof of title

legitimieren **1.** to legitimate, to confer legitimacy **2.** *(sich legitimieren)* to prove one's identity

Legitimität legitimacy

leicht **1.** *adj.* light, slight, *(~e Aktien)* low-priced equities (stock), *(~e Kurserholung bei Aktien)* slight rally in equities, *(~e Fahrlässigkeit)* ordinary negligence, *(~e Papiere)* low-priced securities
2. *adv.* *(~ abgeschwächt)* slightly lower, *(~ anziehen)* to edge higher, to firm up, *(~ liquidisierbar)* readily (easily) convertible into cash, *(~ nachgeben)* to turn slightly lower, to turn (to drift) a shade easier, *(~ realisierbar)* readily realisable (marketable), *(~ transferierbar)* easily transferable, *(~ verwertbare Sicherheit)* readily realisable collateral, *(~ zugängliche Refinanzierungsquellen)* readily accessible funding sources

leichter *(~ eröffnen)* to open lower, to be lower at the start of trading, *(~ schließen)* to close lower, to close on retreating prices, *(~ tendieren)* to ease, to slither, to turn lower, to lose ground, *(~ nach Glattstellungen durch den Berufshandel)* lower on professional liquidation, *(auf breiter Front ~)* lower across the board, *(geringfügig ~)* slightly (marginally) lower

leiden to suffer from, to be adversely affected by, *(der Aktienmarkt litt unter negativen Unternehmensnachrichten)* the stock market was hit by negative corporate news, *(unter den schwierigen Marktbedingungen ~)* to be afflicted by the difficult market conditions, *(stark unter der Zinserhöhung ~)* to be badly mauled (to be hard hit) by the rise in interest rates

leihbar *(~e Wertpapiere)* lendable securities

Leihdevisen short-term currency borrowings by banks

Leihe lending, loan, → Wertpapierleihe

Leihe / ~entgelt lending rate; **~geber** lender; **~gebühr** lending fee; **~gegenstand** item (securities/currency) lent; **~geschäft** *(Devisen-, Wertpapierleihgeschäft)* lending operation (transaction), *(~e in sachbezogenen Werten)* lendings in pyhsical assets

Leihe / ~markt lending market; **~nachfrage** lending demand; **~nehmer** borrower; **~programm** lending scheme; **~satz** lending rate

leihen to lend

Leih / ~gebühr rental; **~geld** funds borrowed in the money market; **~geldlinie** short-term borrowing facility, credit line; **~kapital** loanable funds

leihweise Überlassung *(von Wertpapieren)* lending (loaning out) securities

Leiste renewal coupon

leisten **1.** *(ausführen)* to perform, to effect, to carry out, *(eine Anzahlung ~)* to pay down a deposit, to make a downpayment, *(einen Ergebnisbeitrag ~)* to make a contribution (to contribute) to profits, *(Zahlung ~)* to make (to effect) payment
2. *(bereitstellen)* to provide, to furnish, to put up, *(eine Garantie/Sicherheit ~)* to furnish a guarantee, to put up security, to stand surety for, *(Einschusszahlungen ~)* to put up margin, *(Rembours ~)* to provide reimbursement

Leistenschein renewal coupon

Leistung **1.** service, performance, *(vertragliche ~en)* contractual services (obligations), services under the agreement, contracted services, *(~ erfüllungshalber/~ an Erfüllungs statt)* → erfüllungshalber, → Erfüllungs statt
2. *(Ergebnis)* achievement, accomplishment, results
3. *(Gegenleistung)* consideration
4. *(Lieferung/Zahlung)* delivery/payment
5. *(Versicherungs-/Versorgungsleistungen)* benefits

leistungsabhängig performance-related, performance-linked

Leistungs / ~abnahme acceptance of delivery (performance); **~analyse** performance (output) analysis; **~anbieter** service provider; **~angebot** service offer, range of services (facilities) offered, spectrum of services

Leistungs / ~anreiz 1. performance incentive **2.** merit bonus **3.** *(Mitarbeitervergünstigungen)* perks; **~anspruch 1.** right to performance, right to discharge of contract **2.** *(eines Versicherten)* right to draw benefits, entitlement to benefits, *(pl)* benefit entitlements

leistungsäquivalent *(~er Preis)* price commensurate with the performance (service)

Leistungs / ~aufgabe *(im Rahmen des Zins- und Tilgungsdienstes)* statement of interest and principal payments; **~ausschluss 1.** exclusion from coverage **2.** exclusion of benefits; **~austausch** exchange of goods and services; **~aval** performance guarantee

L

leistungsbedingt performance-related, performance-based, *(~e Abschreibung)* sum-of-the-units method

Leistungs / ~befreiung discharge (exemption) from performance; **~befugnis** authority to make payment (or delivery); **~beginn 1.** commencement of services **2.** benefit commencement date

Leistungs / ~beleg *(bei einer Kreditkartenzahlung)* sales slip, sales draft, charge slip, ticket, hard copy; **~berechtigter** beneficiary, person entitled to benefits; **~bereitschaft** commitment

Leistungs / ~bericht performance report (record); **~beschränkung** limitation of performance, restrictions on the provision of services; **~beschreibung** performance specification

Leistungs / ~bestimmungsrecht right to specify performance; **~beurteilung/~bewertung** *(Mitarbeiterbeurteilung)* performance appraisal, merit rating, performance assessment (rating); **~bewertungsskala** performance (appraisal) scale

leistungsbezogen *(~e Vergütung)* performance-related pay

Leistungsbilanz 1. current account **2.** *(Erfolgsrechnung)* income account (statement); **~defizit** current account deficit; **~überschuss** current account surplus

Leistungs / ~budget performance budget; **~controlling** performance controlling; **~dokumente** delivery (performance) documents; **~empfänger 1.** service recipient **2.** beneficiary, benefit recipient; **~entgelt** service fee (charges), remuneration

Leistungs / ~erbringer service provider; **~erbringung** provision of services, rendering services; **~erfordernisse 1.** service (delivery) requirements **2.** performance requirements **3.** job requirements

Leistungserfüllung performance of a contract, discharge of an obligation, *(vertragsgemäße ~)* discharge of contract, performing one's duties under the contract, *(nachträgliche Unmöglichkeit der ~)* subsequent impossibility of performance, impediments to performance arising after conclusion of the contract

Leistungs / ~ersteller service provider; **~erstellung** production, provision of services; **~erstellungsprozess** production process

leistungsfähig efficient, productive

Leistungs / ~fähigkeit 1. efficiency, effectiveness, productivity **2.** capacity, power, potential; **~förderung** performance development (improvement); **~fortschrittsmessung** performance control measurement; **~frist** delivery period, performance time limit, time for performance

Leistungs / ~garantie performance bond (guarantee); **~gegenstand 1.** subject matter of the agreement **2.** delivery item, *(pl)* deliverables

leistungsgesteuert *(~e Terminplanung)* performance-driven scheduling

leistungsgestört *(~er Kredit)* impaired loan, sub-performing loan, *(i. S. von notleidender Kredit)* non-performing loan, *(~e Kreditforderungen)* impaired (distressed) loan assets

Leistungs / ~grad performance level, efficiency level; **~gratifikation** performance bonus; **~grenze** capacity (performance) limit; **~hindernis** impediment to performance of contract

Leistungs / ~indikatoren performance indicators; **~inhalt** specification of services (deliverables); **~interesse** interest in receiving performance; **~kennzahl** performance ratio (measure)

Leistungs / ~klage action for performance of (or desistance from) a certain act; **~kontrolle** performance control, performance monitoring; **~kurve** performance graph

Leistungs / ~messung performance measurement; **~motivation** performance motivation; **~nachweis** **1.** proof of performance (of delivery) **2.** performance record, certificate (record) of achievement

leistungsorientiert performance-minded, performance-oriented, performance-driven, *(~er Plan)* defined benefit plan

Leistungs / ~orientierung performance orientation, commitment to perform; **~ort** place of performance (delivery)

Leistungspflicht **1.** duty to perform, obligation under the contract, contractual obligation to pay or to deliver **2.** obligation to pay benefits **3.** claims settlement obligation, *(Befreiung von der ~) (a)* discharge from contract, *(b)* claims discharge

Leistungs / ~prämie performance (merit) bonus; **~prinzip** performance principle, principle of achievement; **~programm** product (service) range; **~prüfung** performance test

Leistungs / ~rate *(bei Krediten)* (monthly, quarterly) interest and principal payments; **~rechnung** performance (results, output) accounting; **~rückgang** decline in performance, drop in efficiency

Leistungs / ~schein **1.** service level agreement, service description **2.** renewal coupon; **~schuldverschreibungen** depositary receipts, bearer certificates representing foreign stocks; **~schwankungen** fluctuations in performance

Leistungs / ~sicherung performance guarantee (maintenance); **~soll** performance (production) target; **~spektrum** range of products and services, → Leistungsumfang; **~stand** performance level; **~steigerung** performance increase, increase in performance (in efficiency)

Leistungsstörung **1.** *(Nichterbringung einer bestimmten vertraglichen Leistung)* non-performance, impairment to performance, defective performance, default in performance, failure to perform properly, → leistungsgestörter Kredit
2. *(im Hinblick auf die Bedienung von Kreditverbindlichkeiten)* default on repayment commitments, default on a loan
3. event of default

Leistungsstörungsrecht default in performance law

Leistungs / ~termin date of payment; **~test** (benchmark) test; **~tiefe** depth of the product (service) range; **~träger** **1.** high (top) performer, key player **2.** benefits agency; **~treiber** performance driver

Leistungs / ~umfang service level, range of services offered, scope of performance; **~unterlassung** failure to perform, non-performance; **~unterschiede** differences in performance, performance discrepancies

Leistungs / ~verbesserung improvement (enhancement) of performance, improved performance; **~vereinba-**

L

rung service level agreement (SLA); ~**vergütung** benefit payment

Leistungs / ~**verhalten** performance behaviour; ~**verkehr** *(~ mit dem Ausland)* current transactions with non-residents; ~**verpflichtung** performance obligation; ~**verrechnung** *(innerbetriebliche)* transfer pricing

Leistungs / ~**verweigerung 1.** refusal to perform **2.** repudiation of contract, repudiatory breach of a contract; ~**verweigerungsrecht** right to refuse (to withhold) performance of the contract; ~**verzeichnis** service specifications, → Preis- und Leistungsverzeichnis; ~**verzögerung** delay in performance

Leistungsverzug non-performance, failure to perform, failure to meet an obligation, default (e. g. by a contracting party), contract default, *(~ des Schuldners)* failure of the debtor to perform, *(in ~ geratene Vertragspartei)* defaulter, defaulting party

Leistungs / ~**vorgabe** performance target; ~**wertanalyse** earned value analysis; ~**zeitpunkt 1.** time of performance **2.** date of delivery; ~**zeitraum 1.** service (performance) period **2.** benefit period, period of benefit payments

Leistungs / ~**ziele** performance (output) objectives; ~**zulage** merit (performance) bonus; ~**zusage 1.** performance undertaking **2.** delivery commitment, payment undertaking

Leitbörse leading stock exchange

leiten 1. to lead, to manage, to run, to be in charge of, to direct, *(ein Unternehmen ~)* to run (to manage) a company, to conduct operations
2. to route (to pass) through, *(über eine ausländische Bank ~)* to route through a foreign bank
3. *(den Vorsitz innehaben)* to be in the chair, to preside
4. *(in die Wege leiten)* to initiate, *(Verhandlungen in die Wege ~)* to initiate (to pave the way for) negotiations

leitend managing, executive, leading, *(~er Angestellter)* senior executive, *(pl)* managerial staff, *(~e Stellung)* executive position

Leiter 1. manager **2.** *(einer Abteilung)* head of department, *(Leiter Finanzabteilung)* Chief Financial Manager, *(Leiter Operatives Geschäft)* Chief Operating Officer **3.** *(Vorsitzender)* chairman

Leiteroption ladder option □ enables the option holder to lock in gains once the price of the underlying asset has reached certain thresholds

Leitparität central parity

Leitung 1. *(Führung)* management, conduct, direction
2. *(Unternehmensleitung)* Senior Management, Management Board
3. *(Vorsitz)* chairmanship, presidency

Leitungs / ~**aufgaben** management (executive) duties; ~**befugnis** line authority, power of direction, authority to issue directives; ~**ebene** management level; ~**erfahrung** executive (leadership) experience; ~**gremium** governing body, management board, executive committee

Leitungs / ~**instanz** → Leitungsstelle; ~**kompetenz** leadership competence; ~**organe** executive bodies; ~**spanne** span of control, span of management; ~**stelle** line (executive) position; ~**struktur** management structure; ~**tiefe** management depth, depth of control

Leit / ~**währung** key (anchor) currency; ~**währungsfunktion** role of key currency; ~**wegänderung** routing change

Leitzins benchmark interest rate, *(pl)* key interest rates, *(zentraler Leitzins des Eurosystems)* key policy rate of the Eurosystem, i.e. the minimum bid rate (→ Mindestbietungssatz), → EONIA Spread

lenken 1. *(führen)* to guide, to manage, to govern **2.** *(steuern)* to control, to

L

steer, to direct 3. *(Gelder in ein Projekt ~)* to channel funds into a project

Lenkung 1. guidance, management, governance 2. control, steering, direction 3. channelling

Lenkungs / ~ausschuss steering committee, governing body; **~funktion** guiding function; **~maßnahmen** regulatory measures; **~modell** governance model; **~spanne** → Leitungsspanne

Letztbegünstigter ultimate beneficiary

Letztkreditnehmer ultimate borrower

Liberalisierung *(~ des Kapitalverkehrs)* liberalisation (deregulation) of capital movements

Liberierung payment for securities subscribed

LIBOR / London Interbank Offered Rate *(Finanzierung zu ~)* LIBOR funding, *(Finanzierung zu einem Satz unter ~)* sub-LIBOR funding, *(Geldbeschaffungskosten zu ~)* LIBOR-based cost of funds, *(Schuldtitel mit an ~ gekoppelter Verzinsung)* LIBOR-based debt

LIBOR-Aufschlag spread over LIBOR, *(ohne Aufschlag)* Libor flat

LIBOR-Festsetzung/Feststellung LIBOR rate setting, LIBOR fixing, *(nachträgliche ~)* LIBOR fixing in arrears

LIBOR-Konditionenbindung LIBOR-linked pricing

LIBOR-Marktmodell LIBOR market model □ used for pricing interest rate derivatives

LIBOR/OIS Spread spread between 3-month Libor and the overnight indexed swap (OIS) rate □ The latter is an interest rate considered less risky than Libor. Therefore, the spread is a risk premium to be paid for 3-month Libor and denotes the credit risk perceived in the interbank lending market, i.e. the higher the spread, the higher the concerns about credit risk. → Übernachtindex-Swap

Lieferansprüche delivery claims (rights), *(~ aus Termingeschäften/Wertpapierkäufen)* claims to delivery under forward transactions/under securities purchased

Lieferant supplier

Lieferanten / ~erklärung supplier's declaration; **~kredit** (short-term) supplier loan, trade credit; **~pfandrecht** supplier's lien; **~rabatte/~skonti** suppliers' discounts; **~wechsel** supplier's bill; **~ziel** accounts payable period

Liefer / ~anweisungen delivery instructions; **~anzeige** advice of delivery, delivery note, *(bei der Belieferung aus Derivate-Kontrakten)* notice of intended physical settlement; **~art** method of delivery; **~auftrag** delivery order

lieferbar 1. deliverable 2. *(vorrätig, verfügbar)* in (on) stock, available

lieferbare Bundesanleihe *(im Futures-Handel)* deliverable Bund, Bund eligible to be delivered against a specific Bund futures contract

lieferbare Stücke 1. *(effektive Wertpapiere)* deliverable securities, securities available as physical certificates 2. *(mängelfreie Stücke)* securities constituting good delivery, *(nicht lieferbare Stücke)* *(a)* undeliverable securities *(b)* securities issued in book-entry form, dematerialised securities

Lieferbarkeitsbescheinigung certificate of deliverability, certificate of good delivery

Liefer / ~bedingungen terms of delivery; **~beschränkungen** supply restrictions (cut); **~firma** supplier, supplying company, contractor; **~frist** delivery time; **~garantie** delivery (performance) guarantee, supply bond

liefergebunden *(~er Finanzkredit)* buyer credit (finance) tied to a specific delivery

Liefermonat *(im Futures-/Optionshandel)* contract (delivery) month, month in which a futures or option contract expires

liefern 1. to deliver, to supply **2.** *(einbringen)* to yield **3.** *(zur Verfügung stellen)* to furnish, *(aus dem Sammelbestand ~)* to deliver from collective holdings

Liefer / ~nachweis delivery evidence; **~option** *(im Futures-Handel)* delivery option; **~ort** place of delivery; **~preis** supply price

Liefer / ~schein delivery note; **~termin** delivery date, day of delivery, *(im Terminhandel)* delivery date, prompt date, settlement date

Lieferung 1. delivery, supply, *(~ der effektiven Stücke)* physical delivery, delivery of the actual (physical) securities, *(~ des Vertragsgegenstandes) (im Futures-/Optionshandel)* delivery of the underlying instrument, *(~ gegen Zahlung)* delivery versus payment (DVP)
2. *(i. S. von Abwicklung, Regulierung)* settlement
3. *(Bereitstellung)* provision, furnishing
4. *(Sendung)* consignment

L

Lieferungen *(~ aufgrund von Ausübungen und Zuteilungen im Optionsgeschäft)* deliveries as a result of exercises and assignments, *(~ aus vorhandenen Beständen)* deliveries from available holdings

Lieferungs / ~annahme acceptance of delivery, *(die ~ verweigern)* to refuse to take delivery; **~stelle** Delivery Agent

Lieferverpflichteter *(bei Wertpapieren, Devisen)* obligor

Lieferverpflichtung delivery commitment (obligation), settlement obligation, obligation to deliver, *(~en aus Optionsgeschäften)* delivery obligations under option contracts, *(~en aus Wertpapierverkäufen)* deliveries to be made under securities sold, securities delivery obligations, *(Überhang an ~en)* net delivery commitments

Liefer / ~versprechen undertaking to deliver, delivery (supply) pledge; **~vertrag** delivery contract, contract for delivery, supply agreement; **~verzögerung** delay in delivery (settlement); **~verzug** default in delivery (settlement); **~wert** delivery value, value delivered; **~zeit** time of delivery

liegen *(bei ca. € … ~)* to be (to stand) around € …, to run around (to be close to) € …, *(im Ermessen der Bank ~)* to be at the bank's discretion, to be up to the bank, *(vor den Konkurrenten ~)* to be ahead of one's competitors, *(über/unter dem Marktdurchschnitt ~)* to outperform/to underperform the market, to be above/below the market average *(das Neuemissionsvolumen wird bei ungefähr … Mio. ~)* the volume of new issues will be in the range (in the region) of …, *(umsatzmäßig an vierter Stelle ~)* to be lying in fourth place in terms of volume transacted, *(unter den Planwerten ~)* to be short of plan, *(die Haftung liegt bei dem Garantiegeber)* the liability lies (rests) with the guarantor

Liegenschaften landed property, real estate (property)

Liegenschafts / ~amt cadastral authority; **~buch** cadastral register, **~karte** cadastral map; **~kataster** real estate cadastre, cadastral records; **~recht** property law; **~rechte** property rights

Liegenschafts / ~vermögen real property assets; **~verwaltung** property management; **~vollstreckung** levy of execution against real estate; **~zins** real property yield

Limit 1. limit **2.** *(Kurslimit)* price limit **3.** *(Obergrenze für Kreditinanspruchnahmen)* limit, line **4.** *(Überziehungsmöglichkeit)* overdraft facility, *(an ein ~ gebunden sein)* to be bound by (to) a limit

Limit / ~anrechnung counting towards the limit (line); **~auftrag** → limitierter Auftrag; **~auslastung/~ausnutzung** limit usage (utilisation), drawing against a limit (on a line); ~**ausschöpfung** *(volle ~)* making full use of a limit (line)

Limit / ~**einhaltung** compliance with a limit, observing the limit set; ~**entgelt** limit fee; ~**erhöhung** increase in the limit; ~**festsetzung** establishment of a limit, setting (fixing, establishing) a limit; ~**führung** limit maintenance; ~**gebot** limit bid; ~**genehmigung** limit approval

limitieren to limit, to set (to fix) a limit

limitiert *(~er Auftrag)* **1.** *(im Kurs)* limit order, order to buy or sell at a limited price **2.** *(zeitlich limitierte Order)* time order, buy or sell order to be executed at a specified time

Limitierung limiting, setting (fixing) a limit, limitation

Limit / ~**inanspruchnahme** drawing against a limit; ~**protokollierung** **1.** noting a limit **2.** obtaining limit approval; ~**überprüfung** limit check; ~**überschreitung** overstepping a limit, exceeding the specified limit (the limit set), limit overrun

Limit / ~**überwachung** limit control (surveillance), monitoring the limit set; ~**überziehung** → Limitüberschreitung; ~**vormerkung** making a limit (a line) available

lindern *(die Auswirkungen der hohen Zinssätze ~)* to alleviate (to mitigate) the impact of high interest rates

Linderung alleviation, mitigation

linear *(~e Abschreibung)* straight-line depreciation (amortisation), *(~e Planungsrechnung)* linear programming, *(~es Verantwortungsdiagramm)* linear responsibility chart, *(~e Zinsberechnung)* straight-line interest computation

Linie (credit) line

Linien / ~**absicherung** providing security for a credit line; ~**absprache** credit line agreement; ~**abteilung** line department; ~**aufstockung** increase in a credit line; ~**chart** bar (line) chart

Linien / ~**einräumung** accommodation (granting) of a credit line; ~**führungskräfte** line managers; ~**funktion** line function, *(Inhaber einer ~)* line manager; ~**inanspruchnahme** availment of a credit line, drawing on a credit facility; ~**reederei** *(Bedingungen der ~en)* liner terms

Linien / ~**organisation** line organisation; ~**streichung** line cancellation; ~**vereinbarung** arranging a credit line, borrowing arrangement; ~**verlängerung** line renewal, extending the maturity of a credit line

Linksunterzeichner signatory to the left

liquid **1.** liquid, *(~e Aktiva)* liquid assets, assets that can easily be turned into cash, → erstklassige liquide Aktiva, *(~e Anlagen)* liquid investments, *(~er Markt)* liquid market, permanent availability of bid and asked prices, *(~e Mittel)* liquid funds, *(~e Sicherheiten)* liquid security
(~e Unterlegung) collateralisation with liquid assets, cash collateral, provision of liquid security, provision of liquid assets as security for a loan (e. g. cash, savings/time deposits and/or quickly realisable assets)
2. *(zahlungsfähig)* solvent
3. *(~e Einrede)* conclusive and provable plea

Liquidation **1.** *(~ eines Unternehmens)* winding-up (liquidation, dissolution) of a company **2.** *(~ einer Position)* liquidating (closing out) a position **3.** *(Regulierung)* settlement

Liquidations / ~**antrag** winding-up application (petition); ~**beschluss** winding-up resolution; ~**bilanz** winding-up accounts, liquidation accounts; ~**erlös** winding-up (liquidation) proceeds; ~**eröffnung** opening of winding-up proceedings; ~**eröffnungsbilanz** opening winding-up accounts

Liquidations / ~**gebühr** **1.** winding-up (settlement) fee **2.** *(bei der Rück-*

nahme von Fondsanteilen) liquidation (redemption) fee; ~**gesellschaft** liquidator, liquidating (liquidation) company; ~**gewinn** winding-up profit; ~**kasse** clearing agency (organisation)

Liquidations / ~**kompetenz** power to close out a position; ~**konto** realisation (settlement) account; ~**kurs** liquidation (settlement) price; ~**masse** total assets of a company in liquidation

Liquidationsnetting close-out netting, netting by close-out, open contract netting, default netting □ netting that occurs after the occurrence of predefined events such as default (→ Kreditereignis); all outstanding contracts are terminated.

Liquidations / ~**ordnung** winding-up rules; ~**rate** liquidating dividend, dividend in liquidation; ~**schlussbilanz** closing winding-up accounts; ~**überschuss** surplus assets (on winding-up); ~**verfahren** winding-up (liquidation) proceedings

L

Liquidations / ~**vergleich** winding-up by creditors, liquidation under assignment; ~**verkauf** winding-up sale; ~**verlust** loss on winding-up; ~**versicherung** business liquidation insurance; ~**verzug** liquidation preference

Liquidationswert 1. liquidation (break-up) value, gone-concern value 2. *(von Börsengeschäften)* settlement (liquidation) value 3. *(bei einer Zwangsversteigerung)* forced sale value

Liquidator liquidator

liquidierbar 1. *(verwertbar)* realisable 2. *(liquidisierbar)* convertible into cash, *(kurzfristig ~e Aktiva)* quick assets, assets that can easily be turned into cash

Liquidierbarkeit 1. realisability 2. possibility to turn assets into ready cash

liquidieren 1. to wind up (to dissolve, to liquidate) a company
2. to square the books, to close out (to liquidate) a position, *(sich selbst ~der Kredit)* self-liquidating loan
3. to sell, to sell off, to realise

Liquidierung 1. winding-up, dissolution, liquidation, taking to liquidation 2. closing out, *(~en des Berufshandels)* book squaring by professional traders, *(~ offener Positionen)* liquidating (closing out) open positions
3. sale, selling, realisation

Liquidierungskosten *(~ des Kontraktes)* liquidation cost, cost of liquidating the contract

Liquidisierbarkeit convertibility into cash (liquidity), *(liquidisierbare Posten)* assets/items convertible into cash (liquidity)

liquidisieren to turn (to convert) into cash (liquidity), *(liquidisierende Offenmarktgeschäfte)* liquidity-providing open-market transactions

Liquidisierung turning (converting) into cash

Liquidität liquidity, liquid funds, *(~ des Bankenapparates)* liquidity in (of) the banking system, *(~ der Unternehmen)* corporate liquidity

Liquidität I (ersten Grades) cash ratio □ ratio of liquid assets to current liabilities

Liquidität II (zweiten Grades) acid-test-ratio, quick ratio □ ratio of liquid assets plus short-term receivables to current liabilities

Liquidität III (dritten Grades) current ratio □ ratio of current assets to current liabilities

Liquiditäts / ~**abfluss** efflux (outflow) of liquidity, cash outflow; ~**ablaufbilanz** funding matrix; ~**abruf** withdrawal of liquidity; ~**abschöpfung** liquidity absorption, absorbing (skimming off) liquidity, draining liquidity from the banking system, *(liquiditätsabschöpfende Maßnahmen)* liquidity-absorbing measures

Liquiditäts / ~**absicherung** liquidity hedging, ~**absicherungslinie** liquidity backup line; ~**abzug** liquidity drain, withdrawing liquidity; ~**adäquanz** adequacy of liquidity

Liquiditäts / ~angebot liquidity supply, supply of liquid funds; **~anlagen 1.** investments in liquid assets, liquid investments **2.** quickly realisable assets; **~annahmen** liquidity assumptions

Liquiditäts / ~anreicherung liquidity enhancement, boosting liquidity, measures designed to increase liquidity; **~anspannung** strains on liquidity, tightness of liquidity, liquidity squeeze

Liquiditäts / ~aufbau building up liquidity, liquidity buildup; **~aufnahme** raising liquidity; **~ausstattung** liquidity position, availability of liquid resources

Liquiditäts / ~ausgleich liquidity equalisation, *(kurzfristiger ~ zwischen Marktmitgliedern)* short-term liquidity transfers between market members; **~ausweis** liquidity return; **~ausweitung** liquidity expansion, increase in liquid funds; **~auswirkungen** impact (repercussions) on liquidity, liquidity effects

Liquiditäts / ~bedarf liquidity requirements, *(den kurzfristigen ~ decken)* to meet short-term liquidity needs; **~belastung** charge on liquidity; **~bereitstellung** liquidity supply, provision of liquidity; **~beschaffung** liquidity procurement, raising liquidity, generation of liquidity

Liquiditäts / ~bestand stock of liquid assets, liquidity holdings; **~beurteilung** liquidity assessment (rating); **~bilanz** *(Saldo der ~)* net liquidity balance

Liquiditäts / ~bindung tying up liquidity, committing liquid funds (assets), *(liquiditätsbindende Offenmarktpapiere)* open market instruments absorbing (mopping up) liquidity; **~bindungsdauer** liquidity commitment period; **~bodensatz** liquidity base

Liquiditäts / ~defizit shortfall of liquidity, liquidity shortage; **~disposition** liquidity management; **~dispositionsergebnis** liquidity management performance

Liquiditäts / ~engpass liquidity squeeze (crunch), tight liquidity position; **~entzug** liquidity drain, drain on liquidity (on liquid funds); **~erfordernisse** liquidity requirements

Liquiditäts / ~erhaltung preservation of liquidity; **~erhöhung** increase in liquidity, liquidity enhancement; **~fazilität** liquidity facility, facility used solely for liquidity purposes; **~fehlbetrag** liquidity shortfall

Liquiditäts / ~freigabe/~freisetzung unlocking (freeing up) liquidity, release of liquidity; **~fristentransformation** liquidity maturity transformation; **~fristentransformationsrisiko** structural liquidity risk; **~fülle** abundance of liquidity (of liquid assets), → liquiditätsstark

Liquiditäts / ~garantie 1. guaranteeing the availability of liquid funds **2.** debt service guarantee □ issued by a parent company to assist a subsidiary in raising funds; **~generierung** generating liquidity

liquiditätsgetrieben *(~e Hausse)* liquidity-driven upsurge in prices

Liquiditäts / ~grad liquidity ratio, → Liquidität I/II/III; **~grundsätze** liquidity adequacy rules □ laid down by the Banking Supervisory Authority to safeguard bank liquidity

Liquiditäts / ~haltekosten cost of liquidity; **~haltung 1.** liquidity maintenance, maintaining liquid assets to cover cash flow needs, liquidity management, *(hohe Liquiditätshaltung)* maintaining a high level of liquid assets **2.** form in which liquidity is held

Liquiditäts / ~hilfe liquidity aid, measures designed to increase liquidity, *(~ im Wege eines Offenmarktgeschäftes)* liquidity support by way of open market transactions; **~inkongruenzen** mismatched liquid positions

Liquiditäts / ~kennzahl liquidity ratio (measure); **~kontingent** liquidity quota; ~**kosten** cost of liquidity; ~**kredit** liquidity facility, facility (loan) to cover cash flow needs; ~**krise** liquidity crisis

Liquiditäts / ~**lage** liquidity position (situation); ~**linie** liquidity line (facility), liquidity backup (support); ~**management** liquidity management

liquiditätsmäßig *(~e Entlastung des Unternehmens)* taking the liquidity strain off the company, *(~e Grundversorgung)* basic liquidity supply, *(~e Unterstützung)* liquidity support, liquidity backing (backup), *(~e Verpflichtungen)* commitments to provide liquidity

Liquiditätsmaßstab measure of liquidity, liquidity benchmark

liquiditätsnah *(~e Werte)* near-liquidity securities

Liquiditätsneigung *(~ der Anleger)* investors' preference for liquid funds

L

liquiditätsneutral without impact on liquidity

Liquiditäts / ~**normen** liquidity standards; ~**papiere** liquidity instruments (paper); ~**planung** liquidity planning; ~**politik** liquidity policy (management), *(liquiditätspolitische Instrumente)* liquidity policy tools

Liquiditäts / ~**polster** liquidity cushion (buffer); ~**pool** liquidity pool; ~**position** *(Stärkung der ~)* strengthening (enhancing) the liquidity position; ~**posten** liquidity items; ~**potenzial** liquidity potential, potential liquid resources; ~-**Put** liquidity put □ right (option) to request conversion of an instrument into liquidity

Liquiditäts / ~-**Rating** liquidity rating, assessment of the liquidity position; ~**rechnung** liquidity budgeting; ~**relationen** liquidity ratios; ~**reserve** liquidity reserve; ~**reservehaltung** liquidity reserve management

Liquiditäts / ~**richtsätze** → Liquiditätsgrundsätze; ~**risiko** liquidity risk (exposure), exposure to loss arising from a lack of adequate liquidity; ~**risikomanagement** liquidity risk management; ~**rückhalt** liquidity backup (support); ~**rücklage** liquidity reserve; ~**schatzwechsel** liquidity treasury bill

liquiditätsschonend *(~e Transaktion)* liquidity-sparing transaction

Liquiditäts / ~**schöpfung** liquidity creation, generation of liquidity; ~**schraube** liquidity screw; ~**schwankungen** liquidity swings, fluctuations in liquid assets; ~**schwemme** surge (welter) of liquidity

Liquiditäts / ~**sicherung** safeguarding (ensuring) liquidity, *(i. S. von Unterstützung)* liquidity backup (support, enhancement); ~**sicherungsmaßnahmen** liquidity safeguards; ~**spanne** liquidity margin; ~**spritze** injection of fresh funds, infusion of liquidity

liquiditätsstark *(~es Unternehmen)* cash-rich company, company flush with liquidity (liquid funds)

Liquiditäts / ~**stärkung** strengthening liquidity, boost to liquidity, liquidity enhancement; ~**status** liquidity status report, statement of liquid assets; ~**steuerung** liquidity control, liquidity management; ~**störungen** liquidity disruptions

Liquiditäts / ~**stützung** liquidity support (backup), bolstering liquidity, *(~ des Geldmarktes)* channelling liquidity into the money market; ~**stützungslinie** liquidity support line; ~**überhang** surplus liquidity; ~**überschuss** excess liquidity, surplus funds (resources)

Liquiditäts / ~**überträge** liquidity transfers; ~**umschichtung** liquidity switching, regrouping the stock of liquid assets, shifting liquid funds; ~**ungleichgewicht** liquidity imbalance; ~**unterstützung** liquidity support (backing)

liquiditätsunwirksam *(~e Posten)* items not impacting liquidity, *(~er Zahlungsaufwand)* non-cash expenses

Liquiditäts-U-Schätze liquidity discount paper

Liquiditäts / ~**verbesserung** liquidity enhancement; ~**verbund 1.** liquidity pool **2.** liquidity pooling agreement; ~**verknappung** liquidity squeeze; ~**verlust** loss of liquidity; ~**verringerung** rundown (decrease) in liquid assets

Liquiditäts / ~**verordnung** Liquidity Regulation; ~**vorhaltung** commitment of liquid funds; ~**vorschriften** liquidity rules; ~**vorsorge** liquidity provisioning, safeguarding liquidity supply, setting up a liquidity reserve

liquiditätswirksam *(als ~ gelten)* to be regarded as liquid assets (as having an impact on liquidity), *(~e Aufwendungen)* liquidity-related expenditure, *(~e Leistungen)* services requiring liquidity (requiring cash payments), *(~e Posten)* items impacting liquidity

Liquiditäts / ~**wirkung** impact on liquidity; ~**zufluss** inflow of liquidity, cash inflow; ~**zufuhr** supply of fresh liquid funds, injection (infusion) of liquidity, *(liquiditätszuführende Geschäfte)* liquidity-providing transactions (operations); ~**zusage** liquidity undertaking, commitment of liquid funds

Liquiditäts / ~**zuteilung** liquidity allotment, *(~ der nationalen Zentralbanken)* liquidity allocated to financial institutions by the national Central Banks; ~**zuwachs** liquidity buildup; ~**zwänge** liquidity constraints

Lizenz license; ~**bestimmungen** license terms; ~**bürgschaft** license bond; ~**dauer** license term, licensing period; ~**einnahmen** licensing income (revenue);~**erteilung** licensing, granting (issuance) of a license

Lizenzierung licensing

Lizenz / ~**freigabe** license approval; ~**geber** licenser, licensor; ~**gebiet** (licensed) territory; ~**gegenstand** licensed object; ~**gewährung** grant of license; ~**inhaber** license holder; ~**marke** licensed brand; ~**nehmer** licensee; ~**vergabe** licensing, grant of license; ~**vertrag** license agreement

lockern 1. *(Beschränkungen ~)* to ease (to relax) restrictions **2.** *(die Kreditauflagen ~)* to relax the loan covenants, to loosen restrictive loan provisions

Lockerung easing, relaxation, loosening, *(~ der Kreditbremsen/der kreditpolitischen Zügel)* loosening the credit reins, easing the credit squeeze

lohnend *(~e Kapitalanlage)* profitable (remunerative, lucrative) investment, *(~ erscheinen lassen)* to make it seem worthwhile

Lohn / ~**forderungen** pay claims; ~**gefälle** pay differential; ~**kosteninflation** wage-cost (wage-push) inflation; ~**pfändung** wage garnishment, attachment of wages, execution against wages, earnings arrestment; ~**stückkosten** unit labour costs

Lohn / ~**- und Gehaltsaufwand** payroll cost, → Personalaufwand; ~**- und Gehaltskonten** payroll accounts

Lokal / ~**finanzierungen** transactions (assets) funded in the national currency of the issuer/borrower; ~**markt** local stocks, market in local securities

lokal *(~e Bankverbindung)* local banking relationship, *(~e Usancen)* local practice

loko *(~ verkaufen)* to sell for spot delivery

Loko / ~**-Geschäfte** spot dealings in commodities; ~**-Markt** spot market

Lokomotive 1. *(~ des Aktienmarktes)* stock market's locomotive **2.** *(~ der Konjunktur)* prime mover (engine) of the economy

Loko / ~**-Preis** spot rate (price); ~**-Ware** spot commodity

Lombard / ~**ausnutzung** drawing on a Lombard facility; ~**depot** securities portfolio serving as collateral for a loan, pledged securities portfolio

lombardfähige Wertpapiere securities eligible for Lombard borrowings,

→ Lombardkredit, *(i.w.S. beleihbare Wertpapiere)* eligible securities, securities acceptable to banks as collateral for loans

Lombardgeschäft collateralised lendings, lendings against security

lombardieren to lend money against securities or goods pledged as collateral

Lombardierung lending (advancing money) against securities or commodities

Lombardkredit 1. loan (advance, credit) against securities or commodities 2. *(Geldbeschaffungsmöglichkeit der Kreditinstitute bei der Bundesbank bis Ende 1998)* Lombard facility, emergency funding facility for banks ; replaced by the ECB's → Spitzenrefinanzierungsfazilität

Lombardsatz 1. rate for advances against securities 2. Lombard rate □ one of Bundesbank's key lending rates; superseded by the ECB's marginal lending facility rate, → Zinssatz für die Spitzenrefinanzierungsfazilität

L

Londoner Interbanken-Angebotssatz London Interbank Offered Rate, LIBOR rate, → LIBOR

Loro / ~-Effekten loro securities, securities held by one bank for account of another bank; **~-Valuta-Konto** loro currency account

löschen 1. *(annullieren, schließen)* to cancel, to annul, *(ein Konto ~)* to close out an account
2. *(streichen)* to delete, *(in einem Register ~)* to delete in (to strike off) a register 3. *(entladen)* to unload, to discharge 4. *(tilgen)* to redeem, *(eine Hypothek ~)* to discharge (to release) a mortgage, to remove a mortgage charge, to enter a satisfaction of mortgage
5. *(widerrufen)* to revoke, *(eine Vollmacht ~)* to revoke a power of attorney

Löschung 1. cancellation, annulment 2. deletion 3. unloading 4. discharge, liquidation, *(~ einer Hypothek)* satisfaction of mortgage, mortgage discharge, *(~ eines Pfandrechtes)* lien discharge 5. revocation

Löschungs / ~anspruch right to discharge (to release) of mortgage, *(gesetzlicher Löschungsanspruch)* statutory right to satisfaction of mortgage, *(des Vormerkungsberechtigten)* cautioner's right to cancellation of a prior encumbrance; **~antrag** mortgage release request

Löschungs / ~anzeige notice of satisfaction, mortgage release notice; **~auftrag** 1. *(für eine Hypothek)* mortgage release instructions, instructions to enter a satisfaction of mortgage 2. *(für ein Konto)* order to close an account

Löschungs / ~bestätigung certificate of discharge, release certificate; **~bewilligung** mortgage release authority, deed of release; **~frist** deletion period; **~gebühr** (deed) release fee, discharge fee

Löschungs / ~klage legal action to cancel; **~klausel** release clause; **~urkunde** release deed; **~verfahren** procedure for discharge; **~vermerk** entry (memorandum) of satisfaction

Löschungs / ~voraussetzungen prerequisites for discharge (release); **~vormerkung** priority notice securing the right to mortgage release (or any other charge over property)

Lose-Blatt-Information loose-leaf information

lösen 1. *(abbrechen, einstellen)* to break off, to discontinue 2. *(die finanziellen Probleme ~)* to solve (to sort out) the financial problems 3. *(eine Krise ~)* to resolve a crisis 4. *(einen Vertrag ~)* to terminate (to rescind, to repudiate) a contract 5. *(sich ~ von)* to disengage from

Lösung 1. breaking off, discontinuance 2. solution, answer 3. termination, rescission

Lot *(wieder ins ~ bringen)* to put back on track, to set matters right again

LRG → längerfristige Refinanzierungsgeschäfte

Lücke 1. *(in der Finanzierung)* financing gap **2.** *(in der Steuergesetzgebung)* tax loophole

lückenlos *(~e Indossamentskette)* uninterrupted (complete) chain of endorsements

Luftfahrt-Pfandbrief Aircraft Pfandbrief, covered aircraft bond □ the cover assets are loan assets secured by registered aircraft mortgages

Luftfahrtwerte aviation stocks, aircrafts, airline equities

Luftfracht / ~brief airway bill, air consignment note; **~führer** air freight carrier

lustlos *(~er Aktienmarkt)* dull (listless) equity market, *(~e Stimmung)* dull (flat) sentiment

M

M1/M2/M3 → Geldmenge M1/M2/M3

Machbarkeitsstudie feasibility (viability) study

MaComp → Mindestanforderungen an Compliance

Magnetstreifen-Kartenleser magnetic stripe card reader, (credit) card swipe reader

MaH → Mindestanforderungen an das Betreiben von Handelsgeschäften; superseded by → MaRisk

Mahn / ~bescheid order for payment, summary order to pay; **~brief** dunning (arrears) letter, reminder, backbill

mahnen to dun, to remind s. o. of a payment, to demand payment, to press for payment

Mahn / ~gebühren dunning fee, reminder (delinquency) charges; **~lauf** dunning procedure; **~schreiben** dunning letter (note); **~stufen** dunning stages

Mahnung (payment) reminder, warning

Mahnverfahren dunning procedure, reminder proceedings

MaIR → Mindestanforderungen an die Ausgestaltung der internen Revision der Kreditinstitute, superseded by → MaRisk

Majoritätskäufe *(Börse)* buying designed to acquire or to increase a majority shareholding

MaK 1. → Mitarbeiterkapazität
2. → Mindestanforderungen an das Kreditgeschäft der Kreditinstitute; superseded by → MaRisk

Makler 1. *(Börsen-/Versicherungsmakler)* broker, intermediary **2.** *(Immobilienmakler)* real estate agent

Makler / ~firma brokerage house (firm); **~gebühr** brokerage, broker's fee, agent's fee, agency commission; **~gesellschaft** broker house, brokerage company; **~kammer** brokers' association

Makler / ~ordnung brokers' code of conduct; **~provision** brokerage; **~schaft** broking community; **~skontro** → Skontro; **~vertrag** brokerage agreement

Makro-Derivate macroeconomic derivatives, economic derivatives, → derivatives linked to the performance of macroeconomic indicators

Makro-Hedge macro hedge □ reducing or eliminating risks on an aggregated basis

makroökonomisch *(~e Indikatoren)* macroeconomic indicators, *(~es Risiko)* macroeconomic risk

makroprudenziel *(~le Aufsicht)* macroprudential supervision (aims at identifying systemic risks)

mal *(drei~ so hoch wie üblich)* three times above the normal level

Management / ~bewertung 1. management assessment **2.** management performance appraisal; **~ebene** management level; **~erfolg** management (managerial) success, *(pl)* achievements; **~erfolgsrechnung** management result accounts

Management / ~fähigkeiten management skills; **~funktionen** management (managerial) functions; **~informationssystem** management information system; **~kontinuität** continuity in management; **~kompe-**

tenz managerial competency; ~**konzept** management concept (blueprint)

Management / ~**leistung** management performance; ~-**Pass** → Europäischer Pass für Verwaltungsgesellschaften; ~-**Pyramide** management pyramid; ~**risiko** management risk, loss from potential management errors; ~**techniken** management techniques

Managerhaftpflichtversicherung directors' and officers' insurance

Mandant client

Mandantenschutzklausel client confidentiality clause

Mandat **1.** *(Aufsichtsratsmandat)* board membership, seat on the supervisory board, directorship **2.** *(Amtszeit)* term of office **3.** *(Auftrag)* mandate, order, brief **4.** *(Vollmacht)* power of attorney

mandatieren to commission, to mandate

Mandats / ~**auftrag** engagement letter, letter of mandate; ~**betreuung** mandate support (management); ~**brief** letter of engagement; ~**dauer** term of office; ~**dokument** engagement letter; ~**erneuerung** renewal of the term of office (of a directorship); ~**erteilung** awarding the mandate (e. g. to arrange the loan/issue)

Mandats / ~**führer** lead manager; ~**führung** **1.** lead management **2.** case conduct (management); ~**referenz** *(Ermächtigung zum SEPA-Lastschrifteinzug)* unique mandate reference; ~**vereinbarung** → Mandatsbrief; ~**vergabe** awarding the mandate to (e.g. arrange the loan); ~**vermittlung** mandate brokerage

Mangel **1.** shortage, scarcity **2.** *(Defekt)* defect, fault, shortcoming **3.** *(Fehlen)* want, lack, absence

Mängel / ~**ansprüche** deficiency claims; ~**anzeige** notice of defect, letter of complaint

mängelbehaftet *(~e Erfüllung eines Vertrages)* defective (imperfect) contract performance

Mängelbehebung remedying defects

Mangel / ~**ersatz** replacement of defective products; ~**folgeschaden** consequential damage

mängelfrei free from defects, flawless

Mängelfrist defect(s) notification period

Mängelgewähr warranty against defects, guaranteeing against defects

Mängelgewährleistungs / ~**ansprüche** maintenance bond claims; ~**bürgschaft** maintenance bond, warranty bond; ~**rechte** warranty rights, statutory warranties

mangelhaft *adj.* **1.** faulty, defective, *(~es Akkreditiv)* faulty letter of credit, *(~e Erfüllung)* deficient performance, *(~e Ware)* defective (deficient) goods **2.** insufficient, imperfect, *(~e Angaben)* insufficient (inadequate) information **3.** unsatisfactory, *(~es Ergebnis)* poor performance
adv. *(~ erfüllen)* to fail to perform properly

Mangelhaftigkeit **1.** faultiness, deficiency, defectiveness **2.** imperfection, insufficiency

Mängel / ~**haftung** liability for defects; ~**haftungsgarantie** defects liability bond; ~**klausel** defects clause; ~**meldung** defect notification

mangeln to be lacking (missing), to be short (to be in want) of, *(mangelnde Nachfrage)* lacking demand

Mängelrüge complaint, notice of defect

mangels *(~ Annahme/Bestätigung des Akkreditivs)* for lack of acceptance/confirmation of the documentary credit, *(~ Deckung/Guthaben zurückgeben)* to return for lack of cover/funds *(~ einer schriftlichen Vereinbarung)* in the absence of a written agreement, failing a written agreement, *(~ Zahlung)* failing payment, in default of payment, *(~ Zahlung protestieren)* to protest for non-payment

Manipulation *(von Aktienkursen)* manipulation of stock prices, market rigging

manipulieren to manipulate prices, to rig the market

Manko 1. deficiency, shortage **2.** *(Fehlbetrag)* deficit

mannigfaltig *(~e Anlagemöglichkeiten)* manifold (various, diverse) possibilities of investment

Mannstunden / Manntage man-hours/ man-days

manövrieren to manoeuvre

Manövriermöglichkeit room for manouevre, leeway

Mantel 1. *(bei Wertpapieren)* corpus, share (bond) certificate **2.** *(einer Unternehmung)* corporate shell

Mantel / ~deckung comprehensive export credit insurance (for a specific country); **~gesellschaft** shell company, dormant limited liability company

Mantelkauf acquisition of a shell company; **~regelung** loss trafficking rules □ rules on the utilisation of current losses and loss carryforwards of a shell company, → Verlustabzugsbeschränkung

M

Mantel / ~titel principal strip, → Stripping; **~vertrag** blanket agreement; **~verwendung** shell activation; **~zession** blanket (general) assignment

manuell *(~e Auftragsbearbeitung)* manual order processing, *(~e Eingabe)* hand keying, *(~e Meldung)* manual notice (notification)

Marathonläufer securities carrying extremely long maturities

Marge 1. *(im Kreditgeschäft)* (lending) margin, *(Geschäfte mit niedrigen Margen)* low-margin volume business
2. *(Aufschlag auf einen Referenz-Zinssatz)* spread, margin
3. *(Unterschied zwischen Geld- und Briefkurs)* spread □ spread (margin) between buying and selling rate
4. *(Sicherheitsmarge bei Sicherheitenstellungen)* haircut, collateral valuation haircut □ amount deducted from the market value of a collateral
5. → Margin

Margen / ~anforderungen margin requirements; **~anpassung** margin adjustment; **~anpassungsklausel** margin ratchet; **~aufschlag** spread; **~ausgleich** margin call

Margen / ~besteuerung margin taxation; **~bewusstsein** margin awareness; **~deckung 1.** answering a margin call **2.** covering a margin deficiency; **~druck** margin squeeze

Margen / ~einbruch sharp fall in margins; **~einengung** narrowing of margins, margin squeeze; **~erhöhung 1.** spread increase **2.** margin increase; **~ermäßigung** spread cut, lowering of margins

Margen / ~ermittlung margin calculation (determination); **~erosion** margin erosion, shrinkage of spreads; **~erträge** margin income; **~erweiterung** widening of a spread; **~festschreibung** spread lock, locking in the spread, establishing a fixed margin

Margen / ~geschäft margin transactions; **~kontraktion** → Margenverengung; **~kredit** spread loan □ loan carrying interest at a rate composed of a reference rate plus a specific spread

margenschwach/margenstark *(~es Geschäft)* low-margin/ high-margin operations

Margen / ~spreizung tiering of margins; **~verengung** narrowing (tightening) of a spread, narrowing of margins; **~verfall** sharp drop in margins; **~zahlung** margin payment; **~zuschlag** loan spread

Margin *(Sicherheitsleistung bei Börsentermingeschäften)* margin

marginal *(~er Kapital-Koeffizient)* marginal capital-output ratio, *(~e Refinanzierungskosten)* marginal cost of funds, *(~ er Swapsatz)* marginal swap point quotation, *(~es Wachstum)* slight (negligible) growth, *(~er Zinssatz)* marginal interest rate, *(~er Zuteilungssatz)* marginal allotment rate

Margin / ~anforderung margin requirement, margin call; **~ausnutzung**

availment of a margin limit; ~**handel** margin trading; ~**limit** margin limit

marginpflichtig *(~e Geschäfte)* transactions subject to margin requirements, marginable transactions

Marginzahlung margin payment

MaRisk → Mindestanforderungen an das Risikomanagement

Marke 1. mark, *(sich der 2000er ~ nähern)* to approach (to test) the 2,000 mark **2.** brand, trademark

Marken / ~**artikel** branded goods; ~**artikel-Sortiment** branded product range; ~**barometer** brand barometer; ~**bewusstsein** brand awareness (perception); ~**bildung** brandbuilding; ~**eigenschaften** brand properties; ~**erweiterung** brand extension; ~**familie** brand family; ~**führer** brand leader; ~**führung** brand management

Marken / ~**gesetz** Trademark Act; ~**kern** brand core value; ~**name** brand name; ~**produkte** branded goods; ~**recht** trademark law; ~**rechte** trademark rights ~**treue** brand loyalty; ~**vermittlung** trademark brokerage; ~**wechsler** brand switcher; ~**wert** brand equity

markieren to mark, *(eine Wende ~)* to mark a turnaround

Markt 1. market **2.** (a) Front Office, *(b)* Loan Origination, (c) Trading *(Markt und Marktfolge)* front office and back office, → Marktfolge/Marktfolgebereich

Markt *(auf den ~ kommen)* to come on to the market, *(die auf den ~ kommende Neuemission)* the new issue coming onto the market, *(die Emission kam zu 102% auf den ~)* the issue entered the market at 102%, *(Wertpapiere aus dem ~ nehmen)* to take (to buy) up securities, to repurchase securities offered, *(am ~ sein) (a)* to operate (to intervene) in the market *(b)* to tap the market, *(am ~ gut eingeführt sein)* to be well introduced (entrenched) in the market

Markt für *(~ derivative Produkte)* derivatives market, *(~ Kurzläufer/Langläufer)* short/long end of the market, *(~ Neuemissionen)* primary market, *(~ im Umlauf befindliche Papiere)* secondary market, *(~ Zentralbankgeld)* central bank funds market, federal funds market (AE)

Markt / ~**abdeckung** market coverage; ~**abschwächung** weakening of the market

marktabweichend *(~e Sätze)* rates deviating from the market level

Markt / ~**akteure** market operators (players); ~**analyse** market analysis; ~**anomalien** market discrepancies, mispricings; ~**ansatz** market (market-based) approach; ~**anspannung** market strains (constraints, tightness)

Markt / ~**anteil** market share, share (slice) of the market; ~**antritt** → Marktansatz; ~**aufgaben** Front Office functions (jobs); ~**aufnahmefähigkeit** market receptivity (capacity); ~**aufsicht** market supervision, monitoring the market, controlling (overseeing) market activity; ~**aufteilung** market sharing (partitioning), market carve-up

Markt / ~**ausgleich** market clearing, balancing the order book; ~**ausgleichsphase** market clearing phase; ~**ausreißer** market outlier; ~**aussichten** market prospects (outlook); ~**barometer** market indicator (barometer); ~**beanspruchung** tapping (calling on) the market

markbedingt market-induced, brought about by market forces

Markt / ~**bedingungen** market conditions, conditions in the market; ~**befestigung** market consolidation, stabilisation of the market; ~**beherrschung** market dominance (domination), market control, *(marktbeherrschend)* dominating (controlling) the market

Markt / ~**belebung** market recovery (revival); ~**beobachter** market observer(s), market watcher(s); ~**beobachtung 1.** market observation **2.** market survey; ~**bericht** market report (news)

marktbestimmend *(~e Anleihe)* bellwether (benchmark) bond, *(~e Faktoren)* market determinants

marktbestimmt *(~e Finanzinnovationen)* market-driven financial innovations

Markt / ~beteiligte market participants (operators, members); ~**beurteilung** market assessment (appraisal); ~**bewegungen** market movements (moves, fluctuations)

Markt / ~bewertung 1. → Marktbeurteilung **2.** valuation based on the fair market price **3.** *(einer Futures-Position)* marking a futures position to the market; ~**bewertungsmethode 1.** current exposure method **2.** mark-to-the-market method

marktbezogen *(~e Wertansätze)* market-related carrying values

M

marktbreit *(~e Aktien)* stock with a widely dispersed ownership, → Streubesitz, *(~er Index)* broad (broadly-based) index, broad average, index covering a wide range of stocks

Markt / ~breite breadth of the market; ~**chancen** market prospects (opportunities); ~**chaos** market turmoil; ~**dispositionen** buying and selling (trading) in the market

Markt / ~durchdringung market penetration; ~**durchschnitt** market average, *(über/unter dem ~ liegen)* to outperform/to underperform the market, to be above/below the market average; ~**dynamik** dynamics of the market

Markt / ~einbruch market slump, market's steep plunge; ~**einführung 1.** market introduction (launch), introduction on (to) the market **2.** time to market; ~**einführungsphase** market introductory phase

Markt / ~eingriff market intervention, intervention in the market; ~**einschätzung** market assessment, analysis of market prospects, *(~ der Zinsentwicklung)* market perception of interest rate moves; ~**eintrittsschranken** barriers to market entry

marktempfindlich sensitive to market fluctuations

Markt / ~enge tightness (narrowness) of the market, market constraints, tight market conditions, *(marktenge Wertpapiere)* illiquid securities; ~**entwicklung** market trend (development); ~**erfordernisse** market requirements; ~**erholung** market recovery (rally)

Markt / ~erkundung market research (exploration); ~**erschließung** market development, opening up a market; ~**erschöpfung** depletion of the market

Markt / ~erwartungen market expectations; ~**erweiterung/~expansion** market expansion, broadening of the market

marktfähig marketable, acceptable to the market, *(~ e Instrumente)* marketable instruments (e.g. money market fund shares, money market paper, repurchase agreements), *(~e/notenbankfähige Sicherheiten)* marketable/eligible securities

Markt / ~fähigkeit marketability, tradeability, *(am Geldmarkt)* marketability (negotiability) in the money market; ~**faktor** market factor; ~**festigung** market consolidation (stabilisation); ~**finanzierung** financing through borrowings in the market, raising funds in the market

Marktfolge / Marktfolgebereich *(bei größeren Kreditinstituten)* Middle Office, *(bei Banken/Sparkassen mittlerer Größe)* Back Office
(i.e.S. Marktfolge Aktiv bzw. Marktfolge Kredit) Loan Administration, Credit Support, *(Marktfolge Passiv)* Back Office, Transaction Management, *(i.w.S.)* credit risk management

Marktfolgeaufgaben Middle Office (Back Office) functions

Markt / ~**förderung** market-boosting measures, market development; ~**forschung** market research

marktführend leading in the market

Marktführer market leader, *(einer der ~)* one of the leading players in the market

marktgängig 1. marketable, merchantable, *(~e Beteiligungspapiere)* marketable equity securities
2. *(aktuell)* current, prevailing, *(~e Konditionen)* current terms, prevailing market rates, terms reflecting the current market situation

Markt / ~**gängigkeit** marketability; ~**gebiet** market, market territory, outlet; ~**gefüge** market structure (setup); ~**geltung** market standing; ~**gepflogenheiten** market conventions, market practice

marktgerecht 1. *adj.* *(~e Ausstattung einer Anleihe)* bond terms (bond features) in line with general market conditions, *(~e Konditionengestaltung)* market-oriented pricing, fixing the rates/terms in accordance with the prevailing market rates, pricing in line with market conditions
(~es Entgelt) remuneration customary in the market, *(~er Preis) (a)* price in line with market rates, fair market price, *(b)* arm's length price, *(~er Zinssatz)* interest rate consistent with the market situation, fair market rate, fair return on investment
2. *adv.* *(~ bewerten) (a)* to value on the basis of market prices *(b)* to mark to the market

Markt / ~**gerechtigkeitskontrolle** monitoring compliance with market conditions; ~**geschehen** market activity, activity (operations) in the market; ~**gesundung** market revitalisation; ~**gewichtung** market weighting; ~**gleichgewicht** market equilibrium; ~**größe** market size (dimension)

Markt / ~**instrumentarium** market instruments (tools); ~**interdependenz** market interdependence; ~**intermediation** market intermediation; ~**intervention** market intervention, intervention in the market

Markt / ~**kapazität** market capacity; ~**kapitalisierung** market capitalisation; ~**kennziffer** market measure (index); ~**klima** tone (sentiment) of the market, market climate; ~**kompetenz** market expertise; ~**konditionen** market terms, rates/terms ruling in the market

marktkonform → marktgerecht

Markt / ~**konstellation** market setup (configuration), market conditions; ~**korrektur** market (price) correction; ~**kräfte** market forces; ~**kreise** market community, market operators (players); ~**kurs** market price, market rate, *(Bewertung zu ~en)* market valuation

Markt / ~**lage** state of the market, situation in the market; ~**lenkung** market control (regulation); ~**liquiditätsrisiko** market liquidity risk; ~**macher** market maker

marktmäßig *(~ verzinst werden)* to attract interest at market rates, *(~e Neuverschuldung)* new borrowing in the market

Markt / ~**mechanismus** market mechanism, mechanics of the market; ~**meinung** market view, view on the market; ~**messgrößen** market metrics;~**missbrauchsrichtlinie** (EU) Market Abuse Directive

Markt / ~**mitarbeiter** front office employee, *(pl)* front office staff, → Markt (2); ~**mitläufer** market follower; ~**mittel 1.** market funds, funds raised in the market **2.** funds borrowed/lent at market rates; ~**mittler** market agent, market intermediary; ~**monopol** market monopoly

Markt / ~**nachfrage** market demand; ~**neuling** newcomer to the market, market entrant; ~**nische** market niche; ~**notierung** market quotation

Markt / ~**ordnung** market organisation; ~**orientierung** market orientation (trend), *(marktorientierte Preisbestimmung)* market-oriented pricing, going-rate pricing

Markt / ~periode market life; **~perspektiven** market prospects (outlook); **~pessimismus** market gloom

Marktpflege market support, market price regulation, market management, market-regulating (market-smoothing) operations, *(zur ~ reservieren)* to set aside for market support

Marktpflege / ~bestand market support (management) stock; **~betrag/~quote** **1.** *(bei Neuemissionen)* amount/share set aside for market support measures **2.** amount/share retained by the Central Bank for market intervention activities; **~verkäufe** support-driven sales

Markt / ~position market position, position in the market; **~positionierung** market positioning; **~preis** market price, current (ruling) price, → Marktwert; **~preisänderungsrisiken** market price risks; **~prognose** market forecast (outlook)

M

Markt / ~reaktion market reaction (response); **~regulierung** market regulation; **~reife** maturity of the market; **~rendite** market yield; **~richtungsindikator** market movement indicator

Marktrisiko market risk (exposure), risk inherent in the market, exposure to market movements, *(Marktrisiken im Anlagebuch/Handelsbuch)* market risks in the banking/trading book, *(mit einem ~ behaftete Positionen)* market risk positions, positions (items) subject to market risk, *(~ aus dem Wertpapiergeschäft)* securities market exposure

Marktrisiko / ~abschlag discount (deduction) for market risks; **~ausweis** market risk disclosure; **~meldungen** market risk reporting; **~position** market risk exposures

Markt / ~rückzug withdrawal from a market, pulling out of a market; **~sättigung** market saturation; **~satz** market rate, prevailing (current, going) rate; **~schutzvereinbarung** market protection agreement

Markt / ~schwäche market weakness (depression, softness); **~schwankungen** market fluctuations (swings), ups and downs in the market, swings in the market; **~segment** market segment; **~segmentierung** market segmentation

Markt / ~stabilisierung market stabilisation, stabilising a price by buying and selling in the market; **~stabilität** market stability, steadiness of the market

Markt / ~standort market position; **~stellung** market standing (position), position in the market; **~steuerung** market control, steering of the market

Marktstörungs / ~fazilität market disruption facility; **~klausel** market disruption clause

Markt / ~strategie market strategy; **~struktur** market structure (pattern, setup); **~strukturverschiebung** shift in market structure

Markt / ~studie market study (analysis); **~sturz** slump in the market; **~stützung** market support; **~stützungskosten** cost of market support; **~stützungsmaßnahmen** measures designed to stabilise the market

markttechnisch *(~e Abwärts-/Aufwärtsbewegung)* adjusting drop/rise, *(~e Erholung) (nach überdurchschnittlichen Abgaben)* technical rally from oversold positions

Markt / ~teilnehmer market participant (operator, player), participant in the market, *(auf dem Börsenparkett)* trading crowd; **~tendenz** market trend (tendency), development of (in) the market, *(konträr zur ~)* anti-marketwise

Markt / ~tiefe market depth; **~transparenz** market transparency; **~turbulenzen** market upheavals, market turmoil (turbulence)

Markt / ~übersicht market survey, overview of the market; **~überwachung** market supervision (control), market vetting, surveillance of the market, overseeing market activities

marktüblich in line (in conformity) with the market, usual (customary) in the market, *(~er Kauf/Verkauf)* regular way purchase (sale), *(Transaktion zu ~en Bedingungen)* arm's length transaction, *(zu den ~en Sätzen emittieren)* to issue at prevailing market rates

Marktumschwung break in the market, turn of the market, rebound in market prices

marktunabhängig unaffected by market movements, independent of the market (the front office), → Markt (2)

Markt / ~unbeständigkeit instability (unsteadiness) of the market; **~ungleichgewicht** market imbalance (disequilibrium, imperfection), imbalance in the market

Markt / ~unsicherheit market uncertainty, market unease, concerns of market operators over future developments; **~unterstützung** market support, propping up the market; **~untersuchung 1.** market research **2.** market study

marktunüblich *(~e Konditionen)* mispricing, pricing not in conformity with market conditions

Markt / ~unvollkommenheiten market imperfections; **~usancen** market customs, current market practice; **~veränderungen** market changes (variations), changes in the market situation; **~verfassung** state of the market, market sentiment (tone)

Markt / ~verflechtung interpenetration (interdependence) of markets; **~verhaltensregeln** accepted market practices, market conduct rules; **~verhältnisse** market conditions

Markt / ~verlagerung/~verschiebung 1. market shift (dislocation) **2.** switching into other markets; **~vermittler** market agent (intermediary); **~verschuldung** market debt, debt contracted through capital market issues

Markt / ~versorgung market supply, supplying the market; **~verunsicherung** unsettling the market; **~verwerfung** market disruption; **~wachstum** market growth; **~wahrnehmungsrisiken** market perception risks

Marktwert 1. market value (price), market worth
2. fair value, *(Absicherung des ~es)* fair value hedge, *(positive ~e aus Derivaten)* positive fair values from derivatives, *(zum ~ ausweisen)* to recognise at fair value, *(zum ~ bewertete Anlagen/Engagements)* mark-to-market assets/exposures

Marktwert / ~absicherung fair value hedge; **~ansatz** fair value approach; **~bestimmung/~ermittlung** fair value computation (measurement); **~modell** fair value model; **~risiko** fair value risk; **~wertverlust** *(einer Finanzposition aufgrund einer Neubewertung)* mark-to-market loss, credit value adjustment, *(Risiko von ~en)* risk of mark-to-market losses; **~verteilung** fair value distribution

Marktwiderstandsfähigkeit market resilience

Marktwirtschaft market economy, *(marktwirtschaftliche Ausrichtung)* market orientation

Markt / ~zerrüttung disintegration of the market; **~zersplitterung** market fragmentation; **~zins** market (current) interest rate

Markt / ~zugang market access (entry); **~zusammenbruch** market collapse; **~zuwachs** growth in the market share

maschinell 1. *adj.* *(~e Anlagen)* machinery and equipment, *(~er Buchungsaufdruck)* computerised booking imprint, *(~e Meldung)* mechanical notice, *(~es Übertragungsverfahren)* cash concentration (pooling) system, concentration account system
2. *adv.* *(~ ausgedruckt)* issued in computerised form, *(~ eingelesene Geschäf-*

te) transactions in machine-readable form, *(~ erstellt)* mechanically issued, produced by mechanical means

Maschinen *(~ und maschinelle Anlagen)* machinery and equipment

Maschinenbau mechanical engineering, engineering industry; **~werte** *(Börse)* engineering stocks, engineerings

maschinenlesbare Karte machine-readable card

Maß 1. measure, measurement **2.** *(Abmessung)* dimension **3.** *(Größe)* size **4.** *(Umfang)* extent, degree

Masse 1. mass, bulk, *(die ~ der Anleger)* the bulk of investors
2. *(Insolvenzmasse)* insolvency estate, assets in insolvency, insolvent's estate,

Masseansprüche preferential claims □ fees charged by the insolvency administrator/insolvency court, claims from contracts concluded by the administrator after the opening of insolvency proceedings in the performance of his duties

M

Masse / ~armut insufficiency of assets in insolvency; **~darlehen** loan raised by the insolvency administrator to maintain company operations, debtor-in-possession financing (AE)

Masse / ~forderungen 1. *(allgemein)* claims against the insolvent's estate, administrative claims (AE) **2.** → Masseansprüche; **~gegenstände** assets in insolvency

Masse / ~gläubiger preferential creditors, creditors holding preferential claims, → Masseansprüche, → Insolvenzgläubiger; **~gutachten** professional valuation (appraisal) of the insolvent's estate

Masse / ~kosten cost of insolvency proceedings; **~kostenvorschuss** advance to cover cost of the proceedings; **~kredit** → Massedarlehen; **~losigkeit** lack of assets in insolvency; **~mehrung** appreciation of insolvency assets; **~minderung** impairment of insolvency assets

Massen / ~geschäft *(der Banken)* mass retail banking, mass retail financial services; **~zahlungsverkehr** mass retail payments, bulk payments, bulk funds transfer; **~zahlungsverkehrssystem** retail (bulk) funds transfer system, (electronic) low-value funds transfer system

Masseschulden → Masseverbindlichkeiten

Masseunzulänglichkeit → Massearmut

Masseverbindlichkeiten preferential debt (liabilities) □ → Massedarlehen possibly extended, cost of the proceedings and liabilities (debts) contracted by the administrator in the performance of his duties

Masseverzeichnis schedule of insolvency assets, inventory of property

Maßgabe 1. on the condition that, with the proviso that, *(mit der ~ einer erneuten Vorlage des Kreditantrages)* subject to (on the understanding of) a fresh review of the loan application, *(mit der ~ erwerben)* to purchase subject to the condition
2. *(nach ~ der Kreditbedingungen)* under the terms of (as provided for in) the loan agreement, *(nach ~ der gesetzlichen Bestimmungen)* pursuant to the statutory provisions

maßgebend 1. *(einflussreich)* influential
2. *(entscheidend)* decisive, deciding, *(~er Faktor)* determining (determinative) factor
3. *(gültig)* prevailing, ruling, *(die am Tag des Abschlusses ~en Konditionen)* the rates prevailing on the date of contract, *(die deutsche Version des Kreditvertrages ist ~)* the German version of the loan agreement shall prevail, *(~ sein)* to apply
4. *(zuständig)* authorised, competent

maßgeblich 1. considerable, sizeable, substantial, *(~e Beteiligung)* sizeable shareholding □ as a rule any stake exceeding 25 % of the capital
2. prominent, leading, *(eine ~e Rolle bei der Börseneinführung spielen)* to

play a prominent (an active) role in the flotation
3. applicable, authoritative, *(~es Eigenkapital einer Bank)* bank's relevant liable capital, *(~es Recht)* applicable (governing) law

Maßgeblichkeit relevance, authoritativeness

Maßgeblichkeitsprinzip authoritative principle

maßgeschneiderte Finanzierung financing structured to the needs of the customer, financing tailored to the borrower's specific requirements, customised financing concept

maßgeschneiderte Option customised (custom-made) option, option tailored to the customer's requirements

massieren to accumulate, to pile up

Massierung 1. accumulation 2. *(Zusammenfassung)* concentration, bunching

mäßig *(~er Kursanstieg)* moderate price advance, *(~e Umsätze)* moderate trading (turnover)

mäßigen *(die Kreditexpansion ~)* to restrain (to moderate, to check) the expansion in credit

massiv *(~e Abgaben)* heavy selling, excessive sales, bear hammering, *(~er Kurseinbruch)* deep plunge (sharp fall, drop) in stock prices, *(~ in Aktien investieren)* to pile money into equities

Maßnahme 1. measure, *(~ zur Eigenkapitalbeschaffung)* equity-raising measure (exercise), *(~n ergreifen)* to take measures 2. *(Entscheidung)* decision 3. *(Schritt)* move, step, action

Maßnahmenbündel package of measures

Maßstab 1. scale
2. measure, benchmark, yardstick, standard, rule, *(~ für den Anlageerfolg)* benchmark for the investment performance, *(~ für die Nachfrage)* gauge of the demand, *(konservative Maßstäbe anlegen)* to apply conservative standards

Maßstabszinssatz benchmark (reference) interest rate

Master-Fonds master fund □ uses several independent feeder funds to achieve a broad asset allocation and risk diversification

Material 1. material 2. securities, securities (stocks) on offer 3. *(Unterlagen)* literature, documentary material, supporting documents (literature) 4. *(Wechsel)* bills

Material / ~abgaben selling of securities; **~aufnahmen** buying (taking) up securities; **~mangel** shortage of offerings

materiell 1. material, substantive, *(~es Eigenkapital)* tangible common equity, *(~es Recht)* substantive law, *(~e Wirtschaftsgüter)* tangible assets
2. financial, pecuniary, *(~e Kreditwürdigkeit)* loan repayment capacity, borrower's financial ability to repay the loan

maximal *(~e Belastung)* maximum (maximum permissible) charge, *(~er Beleihungswert)* maximum lending (lendable) value, *(~es Kursrisiko)* maximum downside risk

Maximal / ~betrag maximum (highest) amount; **~haftung** *(der Bank)* bank's maximum liability; **~hypothek** → Höchstbetragshypothek; **~preis** maximum price, price limit

Maxime maxim

Maximierung *(~ der Gewinne)* maximisation of (maximising) profits

MDAX German share price index □ tracks the performance of 50 mid-sized companies listed in the Prime Standard; these companies rank in terms of trading volume and market capitalisation immediately below the companies included in the → DAX; → SDAX

Medio / ~gelder funds repayable (loans due) at mid-month; **~geschäft** transaction for mid-month settlement; **~liquidation** mid-month settlement

Mehr / ~aufwendungen 1. → Mehrkosten **2.** *(steuerlich absetzbare ~)* deductible additional expenses; **~augenprinzip** multiple control principle, → Vieraugenkontrolle; **~bedarf** additional requirements

Mehr / ~belastung additional burden (charge); **~einnahmen** surplus revenue; **~erlös** surplus proceeds; **~ertrag** surplus income, additional (incremental) income

Mehrfach / ~arbitrage compound arbitrage; **~belastung** multiple charge; **~belegung** *(von Eigenmitteln)* multiple charge against equity, multigearing; **~besteuerung** multiple taxation; **~deckung** multiple coverage; **~unterstellung** multiple subordination

Mehr / ~familienhaus multiple family home; **~gewinn** surplus profit

mehrgleisig *(~er Vertrieb)* multi-tier distribution

Mehrheit majority

M

mehrheitlich *(~e Kapitalbeteiligung)* majority equity holding, *(~e Übernahme)* acquiring a majority stake, *(~ beteiligt sein)* to hold a majority interest

Mehrheits / ~aktionär majority (controlling) shareholder; **~beschluss** majority resolution, resolution taken by a majority of votes; **~besitz** majority ownership; **~beteiligung** majority holding (stake, interest)

Mehrheits / ~eigner majority shareholder; **~gesellschafter** majority partner; **~gruppe** group of shareowners holding a majority; **~kosten 1.** additional cost (expenses) **2.** *(bei Projektfinanzierungen)* cost overruns, *(Finanzierung der ~)* overrun financing, funding overruns

Mehr / ~leistung 1. surplus performance (output) **2.** additional payment **3.** *(einer Versicherung)* additional benefits; **~mandantendienstleister** multi-client service provider

Mehr / ~markenstrategie multibrand strategy; **~mütterorganschaft** multiparent fiscal unity; **~produktbetrieb** multiproduct (multiline) company; **~quellenfinanzierung** multisource funding

mehrstellig *(~e Umsatzsteigerung)* multidigit increase in sales

Mehrstimmrechtsaktie plural (multiple) voting share, multi-voting share

mehrstöckig *(~e Immobiliengesellschaft)* multi-level real estate company, *(~e Kapitalstruktur)* multi-tiered capital structure

mehrstufig *(~er Aufbau)* multi-tier structure, *(~e Flächenstichprobe/Stichprobenerhebung)* multi-stage area sample/sampling

Mehrung *(~en auf der Aktivseite)* additions to (increase in) assets

Mehrwährungs / ~arbitrage compound currency arbitrage; **~klausel** multi-currency clause

Mehrwert 1. added value **2.** *(Wertsteigerung)* capital appreciation; **~leistungen** value-added services; **~steuer** value-added tax (VAT)

Mehr / ~zuteilung surplus allocation; **~zuteilungsoption** *(bei einer Börsenplatzierung)* greenshoe option; **~zweckdarlehen** multi-purpose loan

meiden to eschew, to shy away from, to shun

Meilenstein milestone, *(~ in der Geschichte des Unternehmens)* landmark in the company's history; **~planung** milestone planning (scheduling)

Meinung opinion, view, point of view

Meinungs / ~forschung public opinion research, polling; **~käufe/~verkäufe** *(Börse)* speculative buying (selling); **~umfrage** opinion poll

Meinungsverschiedenheit dispute, *(~ unter den Aktionären)* shareholder dissension (controversy), *(~ hinsichtlich der Unternehmensstrategie)* disagreement over the business strategy

Meist / ~**ausführungsprinzip** principle of the highest volume transacted; ~**begünstigungsklausel** most-favoured nation clause; ~**bietender** highest bidder

meistern *(die finanziellen Schwierigkeiten ~)* to overcome the financial difficulties

Meistgebot highest bid

meistgehandelt *(~e Aktie)* volume leader

Melde / ~**adresse** notify address; ~**befreiung** exemption from reporting requirements; ~**bestand** reorder point (level); ~**bestimmungen** reporting (notification) requirements

Melde / ~**dichte** frequency of notifications; ~**format** reporting format; ~**formular** reporting form; ~**freigrenze** reporting exemption limit; ~**grenze** reporting threshold

melden **1.** to report **2.** *(mitteilen)* to inform, to notify, to advise **3.** *(vermelden, ankündigen)* to announce

Meldepflicht **1.** *(gegenüber EZB/Finanzbehörden)* duty to report (to notify), reporting obligation, *(Plural)* notification (reporting) requirements **2.** obligatory registration

meldepflichtig *(~e Partei)* party obligated to notify, party subject to reporting requirements, *(~e Transaktion)* reportable (notifiable) transaction

Melde / ~**schwelle** notification threshold; ~**stichtag** reporting date; ~**system** reporting system; ~**termin** reporting date; ~**verfahren** reporting (notification) procedure; ~**vorschriften** reporting (notification) provisions, notification rules; ~**wesen** reporting system

Meldung **1.** report, notification, notice, *(~en nach dem Außenwirtschaftsgesetz)* reports filed in accordance with the Foreign Trade Act, *(~ zur Eigenmittelausstattung)* capital adequacy report, *(~ von Großkrediten)* large exposure reporting, *(~ des* → *Kreditereignisses)* credit event notice, *(~ von Wertpapiergeschäften)* securities transactions reporting
2. announcement, news

Meliorationskredit improvement loan

Memorandum memorandum, paper

Menge **1.** quantity, number **2.** *(Betrag)* amount **3.** *(Vielzahl)* great number, host, multitude **4.** *(Volumen)* volume

Mengen / ~**abweichung** volume variance; ~**beschränkungen** quantitative restrictions; ~**gerüst** volume parameters; ~**geschäft** *(eines Kreditinstitutes)* retail banking, retail business

mengenmäßig *(~er Absatz)* volume sales, *(~e Reduzierung)* reduction in terms of volume, quantitative reduction

Mengennotierung *(von Devisenkursen)* indirect quotation □ indicates the number of units of foreign currency per unit of domestic currency

mengenorientiert *(~es Privatkundengeschäft)* volume-driven retail banking

Mengentender fixed rate tender, volume tender, → Zinstender

Mengenwachstum/~zuwachs increase in volume sales, volume growth

Merkblatt factsheet, leaflet

merklich *(~e Abschwächung)* noticeable weakening, *(~er Verlust)* considerable (sizeable) loss

Merkmal characteristic, trait, *(~e einer Anleiheemission)* features of a bond issue

Merkposten nominal (memorandum) entry

messbar measurable, quantifiable, *(~er Verlust)* quantifiable loss

Messbarkeit measurability

messen to measure, to gauge, to evaluate, *(am Ergebnis ~)* to measure by the performance

Mess / ~**fehler** measurement error; ~**größe** measure, standard, parameter, *(~ für ein ausreichendes Eigenka-*

pital) parameter for measuring capital adequacy, *(~ der Wahrscheinlichkeit)* measure of probability

Mess / **~latte** *(~ für den Anlageerfolg)* performance benchmark; **~methodik** measurement methodology

Messung measurement, gauging, evaluation, *(~ des Anlageerfolgs)* performance measurement, *(~ von Risiken)* risk measurement

Mess / **~verfahren** measurement approach; **~zahl 1.** measure **2.** index

Meta / **~geschäft** transaction on joint account (with profit and loss sharing); **~kredit** joint loan extension

Metisten parties to a joint transaction

Mezzanin-Darlehen mezzanine loan

Mezzanin-Finanzierung mezzanine financing □ combines characteristics of debt and equity financing, e.g. subordinated debt, convertibles, preferred equity instruments

Mezzanin-Geber mezzanine investor (lender), → Mezzanin-Kapital

M

Mezzanin-Kapital mezzanine capital, → Mezzanin-Finanzierung, *(überwiegend eigenkapitalähnlich)* equity mezzanine capital, *(überwiegend fremdkapitalähnlich)* debt mezzanine capital

Mezzanin-Kreditgeber mezzanine lender

Mezzanin-Nehmer mezzanine borrower

Midcap-Fonds Midcap Fund □ investment fund investing in listed medium-sized companies

Midcap Market Index German share price index □ composed of the → MDAX and → TecDax shares

Miet / **~aufwendungen** rental expenditure; **~ausfall** loss of rent; **~ausfallversicherung** rent guarantee policy; **~aval**/**~bürgschaft** → Mietkaution; **~dauer** lease term (duration, period), duration of a tenancy (rental) agreement

Miete rent, rental

Miet / **~einnahmen** rental income, rental (rent) receipts; **~einzug** rent collection, collection of lease rentals

mieten 1. to rent, *(leasen)* to lease **2.** *(Fahrzeug)* to rent, to hire

Mieter tenant, lessee; **~haftung** tenant's (lessee's) liability

Miet / **~erträge** rental income; **~forderungen** rent(s) due, rent(s) receivable; **~immobilien** rental properties; **~kauf** hire purchase, lease purchase; **~kaution** rent deposit guarantee, rental payment guarantee, lease security deposit; **~kautionskonto** rent deposit acount

Miet / **~kosten** rent, rental (lease) expenditure; **~objekte** rental properties; **~pfändung** seizure of goods for non-payment of rent, distress for rent; **~preis** rent, rental, lease rental; **~recht 1.** tenancy law **2.** *(dingliches Mietrecht)* leasehold interest (title); **~rückstände** rent arrears

Miet / **~sache** leased property (asset); **~ und Pachtvertragsrecht** tenancy law; **~verhältnis** tenancy, lease, landlord and tenant relationship; **~verlängerung** lease extension, extending a lease (rental) agreement; **~verpflichtungen** lease commitments

Miet / **~vertrag 1.** rental (tenancy) agreement, lease **2.** commercial lease; **~vertragsabschluss** entering into a lease, signing a rental (tenancy) agreement; **~vorauszahlung** advance rental

Miet / **~wert** rental value; **~zahlung** rental payment, lease rental (payment); **~zeit** → Mietdauer; **~zins** rent, rental

MiFID → Finanzmarktrichtlinie

Migrationsrisiko (credit) migration risk, risk of loss resulting from the issuer's/borrower's rating downgrade

Mikro / **~absicherung** microhedge, hedge designed to cover a specific risk; **~finanzierung** microfinancing, microlending, extending loans to small, newly established companies; **~kredit**

microloan, very small loan; ~**kreditgeber** microlender, microfinance institution, microcredit provider

mikroprudenziell *(~e Aufsicht)* microprudential supervision, bank-specific supervision, *(~e Regelung)* microprudential (bank-level) regulation

mildern to mitigate, *(den Inflationsdruck ~)* to mitigate the inflationary pressure, *(die Kreditrestriktionen ~)* to ease (to relax, to lessen) the credit restrictions, *(ein Risiko ~)* to mitigate a risk, *(die Schuldenlast ~)* to alleviate the debt burden

Milderung mitigation, alleviation, easing, lessening

Million million, *(Abkürzung: m)*

Millionenkredit loan of € 1.5m or more (to a particular client)

Millionenkredit / ~anzeige/~meldung large exposure notification, reporting exposures of € 1.5 m and more; ~**verordnung,** → Großkredit- und Millionenkreditverordnung

Minder / ~bestand deficit; ~**betrag** short amount, deficit, shortfall; ~**bewertung** undervaluation; ~**einnahmen** shortfall in receipts (in revenues); ~**erlös** shortfall proceeds; ~**ertrag** reduced return (earnings), shortfall in earnings

Minderheit minority, *(minderheitliche Überkreuzbeteiligung)* cross minority shareholding

Minderheitenausweis disclosure of minority interests

Minderheits / ~aktionär minority shareholder (stockholder); ~**anteile** minority interests, *(~n zurechenbarer Konzernüberschuss)* consolidated surplus attributable to minority interests

Minderheits / ~besitz minority ownership; ~**beteiligung** minority interest (holding, investment); ~**verlangen** motion by minority shareholders; ~**votum** minority vote, dissenting (minority) opinion

Minder / ~jährige(r) minor; ~**konditionen** lending rates below market rates, concessional rates; ~**leistung** reduced performance, shortfall in output (performance); ~**lieferung** short delivery, quantity delivered short, short shipment

mindern 1. to reduce, to diminish, to decrease
2. *(beeinträchtigen)* to impair, to depreciate, *(die Attraktivität der Aktie ~)* to dull the stock's appeal

Minderumsatz reduced sales (turnover), reduction in sales

Minderung 1. diminution, *(~ der Kreditsumme)* reduction in the principal amount **2.** *(Wertminderung)* impairment, depreciation, decrease in value

Minderungsanspruch right to a price reduction

minderverzinslich *(~e Einlagen)* low-interest deposits, deposits carrying a low rate of interest

minderwertig inferior, of inferior quality

Minderzahl minority

Mindest / ~abschlag *(vom Sicherheitenwert)* minimum haircut; ~**absicherungsniveau** minimum coverage level

Mindestanforderungen an das Betreiben von Handelsgeschäften/an das Kreditgeschäft der Kreditinstitute minimum requirements for the trading activities of credit institutions/minimum requirements for the credit business of credit institutions □ former regulations superseded by → Mindestanforderungen an das Risikomanagement

Mindestanforderungen an Compliance (und die weiteren Verhaltens-, Organisations- und Transparenzpflichten nach WpHG) Minimum Requirements for Compliance (and Additional Rules of Conduct, Organisational and Transparency Obligations according to the Securities Trading Act)

Mindestanforderungen an das Kernkapital/Gesamtkapital minimum Tier 1 capital requirements/minimum total capital requirements, → Kernkapital, → Gesamtkapital, → Basel III

Mindestanforderungen an das Risikomanagement (MaRisk)/der Investmentgesellschaften (InvMaRisk) Minimum Requirements for Risk Management/of Investment Companies

Mindest / ~anlagedauer minimum investment period; **~anzahlung** minimum deposit; **~ausschüttungsverpflichtung** minimum distribution requirement

Mindest / ~ausstattung *(~ an Eigenmitteln)* minimum capital resources, minimum level of own funds; **~ausübungsbetrag** *(z. B. bei Optionsscheinen)* minimum exercise amount

Mindest / ~belegung minimum filling; **~bestand** minimum (safety) stock; **~bietkurs** minimum bidding price; **~bietungssatz** *(~ für* → Hauptrefinanzierungsgeschäfte) minimum bid rate in the Eurosystem's main refinancing operations

M

Mindest / ~eigenkapital minimum capital (equity); **~eigenkapitalquote** minimum capital ratio, minimum ratio of capital to risk-weighted assets; **~eigenkapitalstandards** minimum capital standards

Mindest / ~einlage 1. minimum deposit **2.** minimum capital contribution, minimum share capital requirement; **~einschuss** *(bei Börsentermingeschäften)* minimum margin, maintenance margin; **~einschusspflicht** minimum margin requirement

Mindest / ~gebot minimum bid; **~gebotssatz** minimum bidding rate; **~gebühr** minimum fee (charge); **~geschäftsvolumen** minimum transaction volume; **~gewinnspanne** bottom-line profit margin

Mindest / ~haltefrist minimum holding period; **~handelsbetrag** minimum trading amount; **~handelsgröße** minimum trading size

Mindestkapital minimum capital (equity)

Mindestkapital / ~anforderung minimum capital requirement (MCR) □ minimum level of capital to be held by an insurance company, → Solvabilität II; **~ausstattung** minimum capital resources; **~erfordernisse** minimum capital required, minimum equity level requirement, capital adequacy requirements

Mindest / ~kernkapital minimum core capital; **~kondition** minimum rate, minimum pricing; **~kurs** floor (minimum) price, **~kursschritt** tick, minimum price movement; **~laufzeit** minimum term (life, duration)

Mindestliquiditätsquote *(*→ Basel III) Liquidity Coverage Ratio (LCR) □ requires banks to maintain a buffer of high-quality liquid assets (→ erstklassige liquide Aktiva) that is sufficient to cover net cash outflows over a thirty-day liquidity stress period, → Strukturelle Liquiditätsquote

Mindest / ~marge minimum margin, *(~ über Libor)* minimum spread above Libor; **~nennbetrag** minimum face value, minimum principal, minimum nominal value; **~normen** *(~ für die Eigenkapitalausstattung)* minimum equity requirements

Mindest / ~ordergröße minimum order size; **~quotierungsgröße** minimum quotation size; **~preis** minimum price, *(bei Bietungsverfahren)* minimum bidding price; **~rendite** minimum yield

Mindestreserve minimum reserve □ compulsory interest-bearing deposits to be held by credit institutions with the national central banks

Mindestreserve / ~anforderung (minimum) reserve requirement; **~basis** reserve base; **~berechnung** calculation of the reserve requirement;

~**dispositionen** minimum reserve arrangements, reserve management

Mindestreserve / ~**erfordernisse** reserve requirements; ~**erfüllungsperiode** reserve maintenance period; ~**erhöhung** increase in the reserve requirements (ratios)

mindestreservefrei *(~e Beschaffung von Geldern)* reserve-exempt procurement of funds, *(~e Einlagen)* reserve-exempt deposits, deposits exempt from reserve requirements, *(~e Refinanzierung)* reserve-exempt funding

Mindestreserve / ~**freiheit** exemption from reserve requirements, reserve exemption; ~**guthaben** reserve holdings (balances); ~**haltung** maintenance of minimum reserves; ~**kosten** reserve cost; ~**last** reserve charge (burden); ~**periode** (minimum) reserve period; ~**pflicht** (minimum) reserve requirement

mindestreservepflichtig *(~e Einlagen)* reserve-carrying deposits, *(~es Kreditinstitut)* bank subject to reserve requirements

Mindestreserve / ~**satz** reserve ratio; ~**soll** reserve requirement

Mindestschluss *(Börse)* minimum trading unit, minimum contract, minimum lot, minimum acceptable trading quantity; ~**größe** minimum trading size

Mindest / ~**sparzeit** *(bei Bausparverträgen)* minimum savings period □ time span between conclusion of a → Bausparvertrag and allocation of a loan; ~**stückelung** minimum denomination; ~**transaktionsgröße** minimum transaction size

Mindest / ~**valutierung** minimum loan amount; ~**verzinsung** minimum interest rate, minimum return, → Mindestzins; ~**vorsorge** minimum reserve provisions; ~**wertschwankung** *(bei Terminkontrakten)* minimum price fluctuation; ~**zeichnung** minimum subscription

Mindest / ~**zins 1.** minimum interest rate, *(bei Schuldtiteln ferner:)* minimum coupon **2.** *(Zinsuntergrenze)* interest rate floor; ~**zinsvereinbarung** floor agreement; ~**zinszertifikat** floor certificate; ~**zuteilungsbetrag** minimum allotment

Minenwerte mining stock (shares)

Mini-GmbH → Unternehmensgesellschaft

minimal *(~es Kursrisiko)* minimal downside risk, *(~e Schwankungen)* minuscule fluctuations (variations)

Minimierung *(~ der Erfüllungsrisiken)* minimising settlement risks

Minimum-Solvenzkapital *(eines Versicherers)* minimum solvency capital, → Solvabilität II

Minorität minority

Minoritätsrechte minority shareholders' rights

Minus deficit, shortage, *(mit ~ ankündigen) (im Kurs)* to mark down, to trade sharply lower, to downgrade

Minus / ~**ankündigung** downtick, price markdown, → einfache, → doppelte, → dreifache Minusankündigung; ~**bestand** → Minusposition; ~**betrag** shortage; ~**korrektur** downward adjustment, markdown; ~**marge** negative margin; ~**notierung** downtick, minus tick

Minus / ~**position 1.** net liabilities position **2.** *(im Devisen-/Wertpapierhandel)* short position, net sold position, sales exceeding purchases; ~**saldo** debit balance; ~**zeichen** markdown; ~**zinsen 1.** negative interest **2.** interest paid by the issuer until commencement of the coupon payment period

Mischberechnung mixed calculation

mischen to mix, to blend

Misch / ~**fazilität** mixed facility, → Mischfinanzierung; ~**finanzierung** mixed financing □ descriptive of a financing arrangement based on two or more sources; ~**fonds** balanced fund

Misch / ~**kurs** mixed rate; ~**nutzung** mixed use; ~**refinanzierung** mixed refinancing (funding); ~**satz** *(bei Risikogewichtungen)* composite weighting; ~**system** *(ökonomisches)* mixed economy

Mischung mix, blend, *(~ der Vermögensanlagen)* asset mix, *(~ von festen und variablen Zinsverpflichtungen)* blend of fixed and floating rate liabilities

Mischzinssatz composite rate of interest, blended interest rate

Misere *(wirtschaftliche ~)* economic plight

missachten *(das Zahlungsziel ~)* to disregard (to ignore, to pay no attention to, to fail to observe) the deadline set for payment

Missachtung disregard, disrespect, failure to observe, non-observance, *(~ des Gerichts)* contempt of the Court

Missbrauch 1. abuse, *(~ der Ermessensfreiheit/der Kreditkompetenz)* abuse of the discretionary power/approval powers, *(~ der Vertretungsmacht)* abuse of the power of representation **2.** *(fehlerhafter Gebrauch)* misuse

M

missbrauchen 1. to abuse **2.** to misuse

missbräuchlich *(~e Anfechtungsklage)* abusive avoidance (opposition) action, *(~e Leerverkäufe)* abusive short selling, *(~e Wertpapier- und Derivategeschäfte)* abusive securities and derivatives transactions, *(~e Verwendung)* misuse, improper use

Misserfolg failure, lack of success, *(~ am Markt)* failure in the market, market flop

Misskredit disrepute, discredit, *(den Schuldner in ~ bringen)* to discredit the debtor, to bring the debtor into discredit

misslich *(~e Lage)* difficult situation, predicament

misslingen to fail, to prove unsuccessful, to turn out badly, *(misslungener Sanierungsplan)* failed (aborted, abortive) rescue plan

Misstrauen *(~ der Anleger)* investors' distrust

Missverhältnis 1. disproportion **2.** *(fehlende Kongruenz)* mismatch

missverständlich *(~e Angaben)* misleading information (particulars)

Missverständnis misunderstanding

missverstehen 1. to misunderstand **2.** to misinterpret

Misswirtschaft mismanagement

Mitantragsteller co-applicant

Mitarbeit cooperation, collaboration, → Mitwirkung

mitarbeiten to cooperate, to collaborate, → mitwirken

Mitarbeiter 1. collaborator **2.** assistant **3.** *(eines Unternehmens)* staff member(s), staff, personnel

Mitarbeiter / ~**beteiligungsprogramm** employee share ownership programme, employee profit-sharing scheme; ~**beteiligungs-Sondermögen** employee participation fund; ~**beurteilung** staff rating (appraisal), performance appraisal, evaluating the job performance

Mitarbeiter / ~**fonds** employee fund; ~**förderung** staff development; ~**geschäfte** employee (staff) transactions; ~**kapazität** (MAK) full-time equivalent (FTE), one staff person working full time for one year

Mitarbeiter / ~**kapitalbeteiligung** employee equity participation; ~**kompetenz** staff competence; ~**schulung** staff training; ~**vergütungsplan** staff remuneration scheme; ~**zahl** staff, number of persons employed, headcount

Mit / ~**begründer** co-founder, joint founder; ~**berechtigter** joint beneficiary; ~**besitz** joint possession, co-ownership

mitbesitzen to own (to hold, to possess) jointly

Mitbesitzer joint owner (holder), co-owner, coproprietor

mitbestimmen to co-determine

Mitbestimmung 1. industrial co-determination, co-determination by managers and elected workers' representatives
2. *(Mitleitung)* joint management
3. *(kooperativer Führungsstil)* participative management, → Mitsprache

Mitbestimmungs / ~gesetz Co-Determination Act; **~recht** right of co-determination

Mit / ~bevollmächtigter jointly authorised person, joint proxy; **~bewerber** competitor, rival; **~bürge** joint guarantor, co-guarantor; **~bürgschaft** co-guarantee, co-suretyship

Miteigentum co-ownership, joint ownership (property); **~ nach Bruchteilen** tenancy in common, two or more persons holding fractional shares in the same property

Miteigentümer co-owner, joint owner (proprietor)

Miteigentums / ~anteil co-ownership share (interest), *(~ am Girosammelbestand)* co-ownership in (of) collective holdings, title to co-ownership of collective securities holdings; **~erwerb** acquisition of co-ownership

Mit / ~erbe joint heir; **~erwerber** joint purchaser

mitfinanzieren to co-finance, to contribute to (to share in) the financing

Mitfinanzierung co-financing, participation in a financing scheme

Mit / ~führer *(bei Emissionen)* joint lead manager, co-lead manager; **~führung** joint lead management, co-lead management; **~gesellschafter** joint partner; **~gläubiger** joint creditor, co-creditor

Mitglied 1. *(einer Börse)* member, member firm **2.** *(einer Genossenschaft)* member

Mitglieder / ~haftung members' liability; **~versammlung** members' meeting; **~zuwachs** increase in membership

Mitgliedsbeitrag membership fee, subscription

Mitgliedschaft membership

Mitglieds / ~institut member institution; **~klausel** new members clause; **~land** member country; **~quote** *(IWF)* members' quota subscription

mithaften to be jointly liable (responsible), *(mithaftender Kontoinhaber)* jointly liable account holder, *(mithaftender Schuldner)* co-debtor, co-obligor

Mithaftung joint liability (responsibility)

mithalten to hold its own, *(mit dem allgemeinen Kursaufschwung ~)* to keep pace with the general upturn in prices

Mithilfe assistance, backing, support

Mit / ~inhaber joint owner, co-owner, co-proprietor, *(von Konten, Wertpapieren)* joint holder, co-holder; **~käufer** joint purchaser, co-purchaser; **~konsorte** co-underwriter

Mitlaufen parallel running □ using knowledge of customer transactions for simultaneous own account deals, *(Verbot des ~s)* ban on parallel running

Mitnahme *(~ von Kursgewinnen durch den Berufshandel)* professional profit-taking

mitnehmen *(Kursgewinne ~)* to cash in on profits, to take profits

mitrechnen to include, *(anrechnen)* to count towards

Mitschuld contributory negligence

Mitschuldner joint debtor (obligor), co-debtor, co-obligor

Mitsprache *(in der Unternehmensführung)* say in the management of the company

Mitspracherecht *(ein ~ besitzen/einräumen)* to have/to give a say in

mitteilen to inform, to advise, to notify

Mitteilung information, advice, notice, *(~ an den Optionsverkäufer)* notification to the option writer

Mitteilungspflicht duty to notify, *(pl)* notification duties (requirements)

Mittel 1. *(Geldmittel)* funds, financial resources (means), *(~ auf Festsatzbasis/~ auf zinsvariabler Basis)* fixed rate funds/floating rate funds, *(~ der finanziellen Zusammenarbeit)* financial cooperation funds, *(~ aus der Kapitalerhöhung)* funds stemming from the capital increase, funds available as a result of the capital increase
2. *(Durchschnitt)* mean, average, *(arithmetisches ~)* arithmetic mean
3. *(Instrument)* instrument, tool, method
4. *(Rechtsmittel, Abhilfe)* remedy

Mittel / ~abfluss cash outflow, outflow of funds, *(~ aus der Investitionstätigkeit)* net cash used in investing activities; **~abschöpfung** skimming off liquidity, **~abstrom** → Mittelabfluss; **~anlage** investment of funds; **~aufkommen 1.** funds raised (generated) **2.** *(einer Kapitalanlagegesellschaft)* sales revenue

M

Mittelaufnahme borrowing, raising funds, *(~ am Interbankenmarkt)* borrowing(s) in the interbank market, funding operation in the interbank market, *(~ am Kapitalmarkt)* fund-raising (borrowing) in the capital market, *(~ des privaten Sektors)* private sector borrowings

Mittelausstattung financial (equity) resources, availability of funds

mittelbar *(~er Besitz)* indirect ownership, constructive possession, *(~es Bezugsrecht)* indirect subscription right, *(~e Haftung) (a)* indirect liability *(b) (des Arbeitgebers)* vicarious liability, *(~e Kapitalanteile)* indirectly held shares

Mittelbedarf borrowing requirements, funding needs

Mittelbereitstellung *(langfristige ~)* provision of long-term funds

Mittelbeschaffung raising (generating) funds, fund-raising operation, *(~ im Ausland)* borrowings abroad, funds (loans) raised abroad, *(~ über Wertpapieremissionen)* fund-raising through security issues, *(Kosten der ~ für Kreditinstitute)* cost of funds to financial institutions

Mitteleinsatz 1. employment (deployment, use) of funds, funds usage **2.** funds used in operations

Mittelfreisetzung freeing up funds, release of funds

mittelfristig *(~e Anlage)* medium-term (medium-range, mid-range) investment, *(~e Anleihen)* medium-dated bonds, mediums, *(~e Fälligkeiten)* intermediate maturities, *(~e Finanzplanung)* medium-term financial planning
(~er Kredit) medium-term loan (credit), intermediate-term credit, *(~e Liquiditätsvorschau)* medium-range cash forecast, *(~e Schuldtitel)* medium-term (intermediate-term) notes, middle-maturity debt issues, middle maturities, medium-dated issues

Mittelfristtrend *(in der Chart-Analyse)* secondary (intermediate) trend

mittelgroß medium-sized, *(~e Kapitalgesellschaften)* midsized corporations □ total assets: between € 4,84m and € 19.25m;sales between € 9.68m and € 38.5m; headcount: between 50 and 250, *(pl)* midcaps

Mittelhereinnahme 1. deposit-taking, taking deposits **2.** accepting funds for investment

Mittelherkunft *(Kapitalflussrechnung)* funds provided

mittelkapitalisiert *(~e Unternehmen)* midcaps

Mittelkurs 1. *(Devisen)* middle rate, middle market quotation, median bid and ask quotation, mean rate of exchange **2.** *(Wertpapiere)* average price, mid-market price

mittelmäßig *(~es Ergebnis)* moderate (medium, average) performance, *(abwertend)* mediocre performance, *(~e Umsätze)* moderate turnover

Mittelnachfrage demand for funds

Mittelpunkt hub, centre, *(im ~ des Anlegerinteresses stehen)* to be the focus of investors' attention, *(im ~ der Strategie stehen)* to be at the centre (to be the centre point) of the strategy, *(~ des Unternehmensplanes)* centrepiece of the business plan, *(in den ~ rücken)* to come to the fore

Mittelrückfluss 1. reflow of funds
2. *(~ aus dem Kreditportefeuille)* repayments on lendings
3. *(bei Kapitalanlagegesellschaften)* units (shares) repurchased

Mittelsmann intermediary, middleman

Mittelstand 1. *(KMUs)* small and medium-sized enterprises (SMEs), mid-sized companies, small and middle-tier companies, *(oberer/unterer ~)* upper/lower range of mid-sized companies
2. *(als Kundensegment aus der Sicht eines Kreditinstituts)* SME customers, middle-market corporate customers, mid-sized corporate customers, mid-cap segment

mittelständisch *(~es Unternehmen)* mid-sized company, *(Eigenkapitalausstattung der ~en Wirtschaft)* equity capital funding of SMEs

Mittelstands / ~bank *(Geschäftsbereich eines Kreditinstituts)* SME division; **~bereich** → Mittelstand (2)

Mittelstands / ~einlagen SME deposits; **~entlastungsgesetz** German SME Relief Act □ designed to ease the administrative and regulatory burden of small and medium-sized enterprises

Mittelstands / ~finanzierung SME finance (financing), funding small and medium-sized enterprises; **~fonds** SME fund, small and midcap equity fund; **~förderprogramm** SME development (assistance) scheme

Mittelstandskredit SME loan, *(Garantieprogramm für ~e)* SME loan guarantee scheme

Mittelstandskredit / ~geschäft SME lendings, lendings to small and mid-sized enterprises; **~programm** SME lending scheme; **~volumen** SME loan portfolio

Mittelstandskunden *(eines Kreditinstitutes)* → Mittelstand (2)

Mittel / ~überlassung conceding funds, → Mittelvergabe; **~umlenkung** shifting of funds; **~umverteilung** reallocation of financial resources; **~valuta** mean value date; **~vergabe** extension (accommodation) of funds

Mittel / ~verwendung application (employment) of funds, funds usage, *(Kapitalflussrechnung)* funds applied, funds used in operations ; **~wert** mean, mean value, average, median quote

Mittelzufluss 1. cash inflow, inflow of funds, flow of funds (into), *(~ aus betrieblicher Geschäftstätigkeit/aus Investitionstätigkeit)* net cash provided by operating/ investing activities
2. *(bei Kapitalanlagegesellschaften)* sales revenue

Mittelzuweisung appropriation (allocation) of funds

mittlere *(~ Aktiengesellschaften)* mid-caps, *(~ Einkommensschichten)* middle-income brackets, *(~ Fälligkeit)* mean maturity, *(~ Firmenkunden)* mid-sized corporate customers, *(~es Firmenkundengeschäft)* mid-sized (midcap) corporate banking, *(~ Führungsebenen)* middle layers of management, middle level executives
(~ Geldmenge) intermediate monetary aggregate, → Geldmenge M2, *(~ Gesellschaft)* medium-sized company, mid-sized (middle-market) company, *(~ Laufzeit)* intermediate-term maturity, mid-range maturity, *(~r Laufzeitenbereich)* medium-maturity range, *(im ~n Laufzeitenbereich)* in the intermediate maturity area, *(~ Qualität)*

medium quality, middling, *(~ Valuta)* mean value date

Mittler mediator, broker, go-between

mittragen *(die Kosten ~)* to share (in) the costs

Mitunternehmer co-entrepreneur; **~risiko** co-entrepreneurial risk

mitunterschreiben/~zeichnen 1. to sign jointly, to add one's signature **2.** *(gegenzeichnen)* to countersign

Mit / ~unterzeichner joint signatory, co-signatory; **~unterzeichnung 1.** joint signature **2.** countersignature; **~verantwortung** joint responsibility (liability); **~verkäufer** joint vendor; **~verpflichteter** co-debtor, co-obligor, party also liable; **~verpflichtung Dritter** joint liability (joint obligation) of a third party

Mit / ~verschulden contributory negligence, contributing cause of injury, negligence (misconduct) by the injured party; **~versicherer** co-insurer; **~verursachung** contributory causation; **~verwaltung** joint administration (management)

mitwirken 1. *(an einem Kreditprogramm/einer Emission ~)* to participate (to take part) in a lending scheme/an issue **2.** *(Beitrag leisten)* to contribute to **3.** *(mitarbeiten)* to cooperate, to collaborate

Mitwirkung 1. participation, involvement **2.** contribution **3.** cooperation, collaboration, assistance

Mitwirkungsbefugnis/~recht right of participation, right to participate

Mitwirkungspflicht duty to cooperate, *(Mitwirkungs- und Beistellpflichten)* cooperation and supply duties

mitzählen → mitrechnen

mobil *(~es Bezahlterminal)* mobile pay terminal, *(~er Vertrieb)* mobile sales force (sales organisation), *(~e Zahlung)* mobile payment, M-payment

Mobiliar / ~hypothek chattel mortgage; **~kredit** lending (loan) against moveable property; **~pfandrecht** lien upon moveable property

Mobiliar / ~sicherheit moveable property collateral, chattel mortgage; **~vermögen** moveable property, moveables; **~vollstreckung** levy upon moveable property

Mobilien moveable property, moveables, *(Gläubigerrechte an ~)* creditor rights in moveable assets

Mobilien-Leasing moveable equipment leasing

mobilisierbar mobilisable

mobilisieren *(Kapital ~)* to mobilise capital

Mobilisierung *(~ des in Effekten angelegten Kapitals)* mobilisation of capital invested in stocks, *(~ von Reserven)* realisation of reserves

Mobilisierungspapiere mobilisation instruments (paper), Treasury bills and Treasury discount paper

Mobilisierungswechsel mobilisation bill

Mobilität *(~ der Arbeitnehmer/der Produktionsfaktoren)* mobility of labour/factors of production

Mobilzahlungsanbieter mobile payments provider

Modalitäten 1. terms, procedure(s), arrangement(s) **2.** *(einer Anleihe)* features, terms

Modell 1. model **2.** design **3.** *(Modellfall)* specimen case

Modellbewertung marking to model

Modellierung *(~ von Marktrisiken)* modelling of market risk

Modell / ~preis *(zu ~en bewertete Positionen)* marked-to-model exposures; **~risiko** modelling risk; **~validierung** model validation

moderat *(~es Wachstum)* moderate growth

Modernisierungs / ~darlehen property improvement (rehabilitation) loan; **~programm** improvement (modernisation, rehabilitation) scheme

modifizieren 1. *(abändern)* to modify, to alter, to amend **2.** *(einschränken)* to qualify (e.g. an indemnity bond)

modifizierte „folgender Geschäftstag" Usance modified following business day convention □ i.e. a payment/ settlement day that falls on a non-business day rolls forward to the next business day

Modifizierung 1. modification, alteration, amendment **2.** qualification

Modus method, means, way

möglich 1. possible, *(soweit rechtlich ~)* as far as the law permits **2.** *(durchführbar)* feasible, practicable **3.** *(potenziell)* potential, *(~er Anleger)* potential (would-be) investor

Möglichkeit 1. possibility, *(~ der vorzeitigen Verfügung) (über Termingelder)* possibility of early withdrawal, early withdrawal option
2. *(Aussichten)* outlook, prospect(s)
3. *(Durchführbarkeit)* feasibility, practicability
4. *(Gelegenheit)* opportunity, *(wenn sich eine ~ bietet)* should an opportunity present itself

MoMiG → Gesetz zur Modernisierung des GmbH-Rechts und zur Bekämpfung von Missbräuchen

Momentum *(in der Chart-Analyse)* momentum □ intensity of an upward or downward movement in stock prices

Momentumindikator momentum indicator □ measures price changes by comparing a stock's current price to its average over a longer period

Momentumstrategie momentum strategy □ portfolio strategy that relies on the purchase of stocks with an excellent past performance record and frequent portfolio rebalancing

monatlich *adj.* *(~e Belastung/Leistung)* monthly interest and redemption payments *adv.* monthly, on a monthly basis, every month

Monats / ~abschluss 1. monthly settlement **2.** *(Abrechnung)* monthly balancing statement; **~ausweis** monthly return; **~ausweisverordnung** Monthly Reporting Ordinance; **~bilanz** monthly statement of condition

Monats / ~endstand end-of-month balance; **~geld** one-month money (funds), funds borrowed for one month; **~prolongation** monthly prolongation, renewal on a monthly basis

monetär *(~e Aggregate)* monetary aggregates, → M 1/2/3, *(~e Ausweitung)* monetary expansion, *(~e Finanzinstitute)* monetary financial institutions, *(~e Forderungen) (a)* monetary claims (assets) *(b) i.w.S.:* lendings, *(~e Konvergenz)* monetary convergence, *(~e Posten)* monetary items, monetary assets/liabilities, *(~e Vermögenswerte)* monetary assets, *(~e Versorgung)* monetary supply

monetarisieren to monetarise, to convert, *(Wertpapiere ~)* to convert securities into cash

Monopol / ~preis monopoly price; **~stellung** monopoly position

Moratorium moratorium, payments standstill, grace on debt(s), period of grace allowed in capital repayments

Motiv reason, ground, motive

Motivation *(~ der Mitarbeiter)* employee (staff) motivation

Motivations / ~fähigkeiten motivational skills (abilities); **~kraft** motivational strength (power); **~schreiben** letter of motivation; **~training** motivational training

motivieren *(hochmotivierte Führungsmannschaft)* highly motivated executive team

Multibank-Plattform multibank platform

Multifunktionskarte multipurpose (multifunctional, multiapplication) card

Multikanal / ~**ansatz** multichannel approach; ~**bank** multichannel bank; ~-**Banking** multichannel banking

multilateral *(~e Absichtserklärung)* multilateral memorandum of understanding, *(~er Handelsplatz)* multilateral trading venue (platform), *(~e Handelssysteme)* multilateral trading facilities (systems), *(~es Netting)* multilateral netting, netting between multiple counterparties

multimodal *(~er Transport)* multimodal transport

multiple *(~ Giralgeldschöpfung)* multiple bank deposit creation

Multiplikator multiplier; ~**effekt** multiplier effect

Multitranchen-Anleihe multitranche bond

Mündel ward; ~**geld** ward money

mündelsicher *(~e Wertpapiere)* securities eligible for investment of trust funds (of ward money), trustee securities (stock), trust stock

Mündel / ~**sicherheit** eligibility for investment of ward money, eligibility as trustee stock; ~**vermögen** ward property

Mündigkeit legal (full) age, majority

mündlich 1. *adj.* verbal, oral, *(~e Vereinbarung)* verbal agreement 2. *adv.* verbally, by word of mouth, *(~ vereinbarte Konditionen)* terms agreed verbally

Münz / ~**auszahler** coin dispenser; ~**einzahler** coin depositor, coin deposit machine; ~**fälschung** counterfeiting coins; ~**gewinn** seigniorage; ~**hoheit** → Münzregal; ~**prägung** coinage, minting, mintage; ~**regal** coinage prerogative, right of minting coins; ~**stätte** mint; ~**umlauf** coins in circulation; ~**zeichen** mintmark

Mussbestimmung/~**klausel** mandatory provision (clause)

Muster 1. *(Beispiel)* example, specimen 2. *(Form)* design 3. *(Modell)* model 4. *(Norm)* standard 5. *(Warenprobe)* sample

Muster / ~**bilanz** model financial statements; ~**prozess** test case; ~**satzung** model (standard) bye-laws; ~**schutz** 1. legal protection of designs 2. registration of designs; ~**vereinbarung** model (standard) agreement; ~**verfahren** test case (suit)

mutlos *(~e Anleger)* dispirited (discouraged) investors

mutmaßlich allleged, presumed, *(~e Kenntnis)* deemed knowledge

Muttergesellschaft parent company

M

N

nach 1. *(zeitlich) (~ Ablauf)* upon expiration of, at the end of, *(~ Eingang)* upon (following) receipt, *(~ Schluss der Börsensitzung)* after close of the trading session
2. *(gemäß) (~ deutschem Recht)* under German law, *(~ den Umsätzen/Volumina)* in terms of turnover/volume, *(Gebühren ~ dem Marktwert berechnen)* to charge fees according to the market value, *(der Marktstimmung ~ zu urteilen)* to judge by the sentiment (tone) of the market
3. *(Richtung) (~ oben/unten gerichteter Trend)* upward/downward trend

Nachaktivierung retroactive capitalisation

Nachbearbeitung post-processing, further handling

nachbelasten/nachberechnen 1. *(nachträglich)* to debit (to charge) subsequently 2. *(zusätzlich)* to charge (to claim, to debit) in addition

Nachbelastung 1. *(nachträglich)* charging in arrears, subsequent debit (billing) 2. *(zusätzlich)* additional debit (charge), extra charge

Nachberechnung 1. → Nachbelastung 2. ex post calculation

Nach / ~besicherung provision of additional collateral; **~besicherungsanspruch der Bank** bank's right to demand additional collateral, → Nachdeckung; **~besitzer** subsequent owner, successor owner

nachbessern to improve, to rework, to cure, to remedy a defect

Nachbesserung (subsequent) improvement, reworking, remedying a defect, remedial action, → Nacherfüllung

Nachbesserungs / ~frist cure period, period for remedying deficiencies; **~pflicht** obligation to remedy a defect, duty to rework

Nach / ~bestellung follow-up order, reorder, additional (supplementary) order; **~besteuerung** 1. subsequent taxation 2. additional taxation; **~bezugsrecht** *(bei Dividenden)* claim to subsequent payment (to cumulative dividends), deferred payment claim

nachbilden *(einen Index ~)* to track (to replicate) an index

Nachbildung index tracking (replication)

Nachbildungs / ~fehler tracking error; **~güte** tracking quality

Nachbörse after-hours market

nachbörslich *(~ fest)* strong in after-hours trading, *(~er Handel)* after-hours trading, post-bourse trading, *(~es Interesse für Finanzwerte)* after-hours support for financials, *(~er Kurs)* price after hours

Nachbürge secondary surety, party standing surety for a guarantor

Nachbürgschaft secondary surety □ a secondary surety is given to assure the performance of a priority surety bond

Nachbürgschaftsverpflichtungen secondary surety obligations

nachdatieren to antedate

Nachdatierung antedating

Nachdeckung 1. provision of additional cover, reestablishing the required security level 2. *(~ im Markt) (a)* subsequent covering in the market *(b)* obtaining replacement cover in the market

Nachdeckungspflicht obligation to provide additional cover, obligation to reestablish the required margin of security

Nachdruck stress, emphasis, firmness, *(~ legen auf)* to emphasise, to stress, to attach special importance to, *(~ verleihen)* to add weight to, to give emphasis to, *(seinen Forderungen ~ verleihen)* to press one's claims, to add bite to one's claims, *(mit ~)* firmly, flatly, emphatically

Nachemission follow-up (supplemental) issue

Nacherfüllung post-performance, subsequent performance (to correct deficiencies), cure

Nacherfüllungs / ~anspruch → Nacherfüllungsrecht; **~frist** period for subsequent performance, cure period; **~pflicht** (statutory) post-performance obligation; **~recht** right to post-performance, right to cure; **~verweigerung** refusal of post-performance

nachfällig *(~e Posten)* post-maturity debit or credit entries

N

Nachfinanzierung supplementary financing, follow-up funding (financing)

Nachfolge succession

Nachfolge / ~ereignis succession event; **~gläubiger** successor creditor; **~institut** successor institution; **~investitionen** follow-up investments; **~kreditnehmer** successor borrower

nachfolgen to succeed to

nachfolgend subsequent, following, *(~er Eigentümer)* subsequent (successor) owner, successor in interest, *(~er Rechtsinhaber)* successor in title

Nachfolge / ~partei successor party to a contract; **~planung** succession planning

Nachfolger successor

Nachfolgestaat successor state

nachfordern 1. *(nachträglich)* to claim (to demand) subsequently, to lodge a claim subsequently **2.** *(zusätzliche Gelder einfordern)* to call in additional funds

Nachforderung 1. subsequent claim, subsequent lodgement of a claim **2.** *(der Steuerbehörde)* supplemental assessment **3.** extra charge

Nachforderungs / ~bescheid supplemental assessment notice; **~management** claim management; **~zinsen 1.** additional interest charge 2. interest on the supplemental assessment value

nachforschen to inquire, to make inquiries, to investigate, to conduct an investigation

Nachforschung investigation, inquiry

Nachfrage 1. demand, *(~ nach Bankkrediten)* demand for bank finance (financing), *(~ nach Firmenkundenkrediten)* corporate loan demand, *(die neue Emission stieß auf geringe ~)* the new issue found little support
2. *(Ersuchen)* request
3. *(Recherche)* inquiry
4. *(Kurszusatz Geld)* bid

Nachfrage / ~ausweitung increase in (expansion of) demand; **~belebung** upturn in demand, demand recovery; **~beruhigung** slowdown in demand; **~dämpfung** curbing (checking) the demand; **~deckung** covering (meeting) the demand, demand coverage; **~druck** demand pressure; **~dynamik** strength of demand, demand dynamics

Nachfrage / ~einbruch sharp drop in demand; **~empfindlichkeit** sensitiveness to changes in demand; **~erholung** pick-up in demand; **~flaute** sluggishness in demand, sluggish (flat) demand; **~impulse** incentives (factors) stimulating demand, demand stimuli; **~inflation** demand-pull inflation; **~lücke** demand gap

nachfragen 1. to ask, to request **2.** to inquire, to query

Nachfrage / ~rückgang decline (downturn) in demand; **~schub** surge in demand; **~schwäche** weakness of (in) demand; **~schwankungen** fluctuations in (of) demand; ~**seite** *(auf der ~)* on the demand side; ~**sog** demand pull; ~**stagnation** slackness in demand; ~**stau** pent-up (accumulated) demand; ~**steuerung** demand side management

Nachfrage / ~**struktur** demand pattern, structure of demand; ~**überhang 1.** surplus demand, excess of demand **2.** *(an Kauforders)* surplus of buy orders (of bids); ~**verlagerung** shift in demand; ~**wachstum** growth in demand

Nachfrist 1. additional time for payment, extension of the time for payment, respite, period of grace **2.** additional period for performance, → Nacherfüllungsfrist

Nachgang *(im ~ zu unserem Schreiben vom TMJ)* further (with reference) to our letter dd. DMY

Nachgangshypothek junior (subsequent) mortgage

nachgeben 1. to give in, to back down, to make concessions, to give ground, *(dem Druck des Marktes ~)* to bow (to succumb, to yield) to the pressure of the market
2. to drop, to slip, to give way, *(bei fehlenden Anschlussaufträgen ~)* to drift lower (easier) on lack of follow-through support, *(Finanzwerte gaben bei geringen Umsätzen nach)* financials turned lower (lost ground) in thin trading, *(gegen Schluss der Börsensitzung ~)* to skid late in the session

nachgehen 1. *(im Rang ~)* to rank after (behind), to have a lower order of priority, to be subordinate to the claims of a prior lien **2.** *(einer Tätigkeit ~)* to pursue, to attend to

nachgehend *(~e Kreditverbesserung)* subordinate credit enhancement, *(~e Lasten)* junior charges, lower-ranking charges and servitudes, *(im Rang ~e Sicherheit)* subordinated collateral, *(der ersten Hypothek im Rang ~e Rechte)* rights subordinate to the first mortgage

nachgelagert *(~e Ebene/~e Einheit)* downstream level/unit, *(~e Prozesse)* downstream (follow-up) processes, *(~es System)* downstream system, *(~e Verordnungen)* ancillary ordinances

nachgeordnet subordinated, junior, *(~es Darlehen)* subordinated loan, *(~e Dokumentation)* supporting documents, *(~e Gesellschaft)* subordinated corporation, downstream company, *(~es Institut)* subordinated institution, → nachrangig

Nachgeschäftserlöse knock-on business proceeds

nachgestellt *(dem Recht eines anderen ~ sein)* to be inferior to the interest of another (e.g. in the same property), *(allen anderen Verpflichtungen ~ sein)* to be subordinated to all other obligations

Nach / ~**girant** subsequent endorser; ~**giro** → Nachindossament

Nachhaftung extended liability

Nachhaftungs / ~**ansprüche** extended liability claims; ~**klausel** run-off clause; ~**zeit 1.** extended liability period **2.** continued existence of a guarantee

nachhaltig 1. *adj. (dauernd, anhaltend)* lasting, sustainable, sustained, permanent, *(~e Schuldenbereinigung)* lasting debt settlement, *(~e Entwicklung)* sustainable development, *(~e Kurserholung)* sustained recovery in prices, *(~e Substanz der Bank)* sustainable assets of the bank, *(~e Trendumkehr)* durable reversal, key reversal, *(~es Wachstum)* sustained growth, *(~e Wertschöpfung)* sustainable creation of value
2. *adv.* permanently, sustainably, *(die Unternehmensergebnisse ~ beeinflussen)* to materially affect the company's results

Nachhaltigkeit sustainability

Nachhaltigkeits / ~**ansatz** sustainability approach; ~**beitrag** sustainability contribution; ~**berichterstattung** sustainability reporting; ~**management** sustainability management

Nachhandelstransparenzpflichten post-trading transparency requirements

Nachhinein *(im ~)* in retrospect, in arrears, a posteriori, *(im ~ festgelegter Zinssatz)* backset rate, *(Zinszahlungen erfolgen jährlich im ~)* interest payments are made annually in arrears

Nachholbedarf pent-up (accumulated) demand

nachholen 1. to catch up on **2.** to obtain later (afterwards)

Nachindossament 1. subsequent endorsement **2.** post-maturity endorsement

Nachkalkulation ex post calculation

nachklingend *(~e Befürchtungen der Anleger)* lingering investor fears

Nachkommastelle digit after the decimal point

nachkommen to comply with, to abide by, to satisfy, to fulfil, *(einer Aufforderung zur Sicherheitenbereitstellung ~)* to meet a collateral call, *(Zahlungsverpflichtungen absprachegemäß ~)* to meet (to honour) payment obligations as agreed upon, *(Zahlungsverpflichtungen nicht ~)* to fail to meet (to fail to comply with) one's payment obligations, to default in the payments agreed upon

N

Nachlagerung downstreaming

Nachlass 1. *(Erbschaft)* estate **2.** *(Nachlassvermögen)* estate assets **3.** *(Rabatt)* rebate, discount

Nachlass / ~abwicklung settlement of an estate; **~anteil** share in an estate; **~depot** estate portfolio

nachlassen 1. *(vom Preis)* to grant a discount (rebate)
2. *(schwächer tendieren, zurückgehen)* to recede, to ease off, to subside, to give way, to slow down, *(in der Leistung ~)* to fall off (to weaken) in the performance, *(der Druck auf die Zinssätze hat nachgelassen)* pressure on interest rates has subsided (moderated, waned)

Nachlassen drop, decrease, *(~ des Preisauftriebs)* slowdown (decline) in the upsurge of prices, *(~ der Spannungen)* easing (relaxation) of the tension

nachlassend *(~es Anlegerinteresse)* fading (waning, shrinking) investor interest, *(~er Auftragseingang)* dropping (decreasing) order intake, *(~e Investitionstätigkeit)* receding (slackening) investment activity, *(~e Nachfrage)* weakening (flagging) demand

Nachlass / ~forderung claim against an estate; **~gegenstand** estate asset; **~gericht** Probate Court, Surrogates Court; **~gläubiger** creditor of an estate; **~guthaben** balance in the estate account, *(i.w.S.)* estate assets

Nachlass / ~insolvenzverfahren probate insolvency proceedings; **~inventar** estate inventory; **~klage** administration suit; **~konto** estate account; **~pfleger** administrator (curator) of an estate

Nachlass / ~rechnungslegung estate accounting; **~recht** probate law; **~richter** probate judge; **~sache** estate (probate) matter; **~schulden** debts of an estate; **~teilung** division (distribution) of an estate

Nachlass / ~überschuldung insolvency of an estate; **~verbindlichkeiten** liabilities of an estate; **~verfahren** probate proceedings; **~vermögen** estate assets, property of the estate

Nachlass / ~versteigerung auction of the estate assets, succession sale; **~verwalter** administrator; **~verwaltung** administration of an estate; **~verzeichnis** estate inventory; **~wert 1.** value of an estate, probate value **2.** *(Nachlasswerte)* estate assets

Nachlauf *(~ zum Ablieferungsort)* on-carriage to the place of delivery; **~kosten** on-carriage cost

Nachmann subsequent endorser

Nachmarkt *(nach erfolgter Emission)* aftermarket

Nachmittagshandel afternoon (after-hours) trading

Nachnahme *(gegen ~)* against cash on delivery

nachordnen to subordinate

Nachordnung subordination, ranking below the rights of others, *(zur ~ von Rechten aufgefordert werden)* to be asked to subordinate one's rights

Nachpfändung complementary seizure (attachment)

Nachrang / **~abrede** subordination agreement; **~beleihung** lending against junior security; **~darlehen** subordinated loan (debt), junior loan (debt); **~darlehensgeber** provider of a subordinated loan; **~finanzierung** second lien financing, financing based on lower-ranking collateral

nachrangig junior, junior in right of payment, of lower rank, secondary

nachrangig *(~es Anleihekapital)* subordinated loan capital, *(~e Darlehen; i. S. eines Eigenmittelbestandteils)* subordinated loan capital, *(~e Belastung)* lower-ranking charge, junior property charge, *(~er Gläubiger)* junior (secondary) creditor, *(~e Grundschuld)* junior (subordinated) land charge *(~e Forderungen* subordinated claims, *(~es Fremdkapital)* subordinated (junior) debt capital, *(~es Haftkapital)* subordinated liable capital, subordinated equity, *(~e Haftung)* subordinated liability, *(~e Haftungsansprüche)* subordinated (junior) liability claims, *(~e Hypothek)* junior (subordinated, secondary) mortgage, *(~es Hypothekendarlehen)* junior mortgage loan, → Nachrangkredit *(~er Hypothekengläubiger)* junior mortgagee, *(~e Mittelaufnahme)* subordinated borrowing, *(~es Pfandrecht)* junior lien, *(~es Recht)* junior right (interest), *(~e Schuldverschreibungen)* subordinated notes, *(~e Sicherheit)* junior security, *(~e Verbindlichkeiten)* subordinated liabilities

Nachrangigkeit subordination, ranking below the rights of others

Nachrangigkeitsstufe subordination level

Nachrang / **~kapital** subordinated capital; **~kredit** second lien loan, loan secured by a junior security, junior loan; **~teil** *(~ eines Hypothekendarlehens)* junior tranche (subordinated portion) of a mortgage loan; **~tranche** subordinated tranche; **~vereinbarung** subordination agreement

nachreichen to file at a later date, to hand in (to surrender) later

Nachricht 1. news, information, message, notification 2. *(Avis)* advice

Nachrichten / **~abgleich** matching of messages, data reconciliation; **~authentifizierungscode** message authentification code; **~benutzergruppe** message user group

Nachrichten / **~datei** message file; **~dienstleistungen** messaging services; **~dringlichkeit** message priority; **~feld** message field; **~format** message format; **~klasse** message class (category)

nachrücken to advance, to be advanced, to move up

Nachrückungsrecht *(in der Hypothekenrangfolge)* right of a creditor to be brought forward in the order of claiming

Nachschauprüfung follow-up audit

nachschießen 1. *(zusätzliche Mittel bereitstellen)* to put in extra funding, to provide fresh funds
2. *(zusätzliche Sicherheiten bereitstellen)* to furnish additional security
3. *(die Höhe der ursprünglichen Einschusszahlung wiederherstellen)* to remargin

Nachschussforderung 1. *(für abgeschlossene Börsentermingeschäfte/aufgenommene Effektenkredite)* margin call, remargining request 2. request for additional contributions

nachschüssig *(~e Tilgung)* redemption at the end of the respective instalment period, *(~e Zinsen)* interest charged in arrears, *(~e Zinszahlung)* interest payment at the end of the interest period

Nachschusspflicht 1. additional funding commitment (obligation), commitment to put up further capital, obligation to provide extra funds, obligation to make additional contributions 2. *(bei Börsentermingeschäften/Effektenkrediten)* additional margin commitment(s), remargining commitment (obligation), obligation to put up further margin (security)

nachschusspflichtig *(~e Aktien)* contributing shares, *(~er Gesellschafter)* contributory partner, partner liable to contribute additional funds, *(~er Kreditnehmer)* borrower liable (a) to furnish additional security (b) to put up further margin, *(~e Versicherung)* assessment insurance

Nachschussverbindlichkeiten additional funding commitments, → Nachschusspflicht

Nachschusszahlung 1. subsequent (additional) payment 2. further margin, additional security, *(~en fordern)* to assess for additional payments, to request further margin, *(~en leisten)* → nachschießen

N

nachsenden to forward, to send on, to redirect

Nachsicherungsrecht right to request additional security (collateral enhancement)

Nachsicht / **~akkreditiv** deferred payment credit; **~betrag** after-sight amount; **~frist** 1. *(nach deren Ablauf Zahlung zu leisten ist, z. B. bei Nachsichtakkreditiven)* after-sight period 2. *(im Wechselrecht)* grace period

Nachsicht / **~tratte** term bill, usance bill (draft), after sight bill, bill of exchange payable at a certain date (e. g. 30, 60 or 90 days after sight); **~zahlung** payment after sight

nachstellen *(im Rang ~)* to subordinate, to place in a junior (lower) rank, to rank below the rights of others, → nachgestellt sein

nachstellig *(~er Beleihungsraum)* lending limit for junior mortgages, → nachrangig

Nachstellung subordination

Nachsteuer / **~-Gewinn** after-tax profit (income), **~-Rendite** after-tax yield, yield net of taxes

nächstfällig *(~er Kontraktmonat)* spot month, front month, nearest expiring month

nächstgelegen *(~e Filiale)* nearest branch, the branch nearest at hand

nächstmöglich *(~er Zahlungstermin)* next possible date for payment

nachsuchen to apply for, to request, to seek

Nachteil 1. disadvantage, detriment, drawback, shortcoming 2. *(Schaden)* damage 3. *(Verlust)* loss, *(zum ~ von)* to the disadvantage (detriment) of

nachteilig 1. *adj.* detrimental, disadvantageous, unfavourable, adverse, *(~ für die Kreditwürdigkeit des Schuldners)* detrimental to the debtor's creditworthiness (financial standing) 2. *adv.* *(~ beeinflussen)* to affect adversely, to have an harmful effect

Nachtrag 1. *(~ zu dem Vertrag)* addendum (supplement) to the agreement dd. 2. *(Anhang)* appendix 3. *(Buchung)* additional entry, updating entry 4. *(zum Haushalt)* supplementary estimates 5. *(zu einer Versicherungspolice)* policy rider

nachträglich 1. *adj (a)* subsequent, *(~e Unmöglichkeit der Leistungserfüllung)* impediments to performance arising after conclusion of the contract *(b)* *(rückwirkend)* retroactive 2. *adv.* subsequently, retroactively, in arrears, *(~ berechnen)* to charge (to bill) subsequently, to charge in addition, *(~ zahlbar)* payable in arrears

Nachtrags / **~bewilligung** *(von Geldern)* supplementary appropriation of funds; **~buchung** → Nachtrag (3);

~forderungen claims for supplementary payments (budget funds); ~**haushalt** supplementary budget (estimates); ~**urkunde** supplemental instrument, rider

Nachveranlagung supplemental assessment, back assessment

nachvertraglich *(~ es Schuldverhältnis)* post-contractual debt obligation

nachvollziehbar *(wirtschaftlich ~)* economically plausible

nachvollziehen *(zurückverfolgen)* to track (e. g. disbursement of the funds)

Nachweis proof, evidence, supporting documentation, *(~ für die Einhaltung)* proof of compliance, *(~ über ausreichende eigene Mittel)* evidence of sufficient own funds, *(~ über eine Eintragung im Grundbuch)* evidence of an entry in the land register, *(~ über die Nichteinlösung)* proof of dishonour (non-payment)

nachweisbar provable, *(mit ~er Erfahrung)* with proven track record

Nachweisbarkeit provableness

nachweisen to prove, to furnish proof, to substantiate, *(ordnungsgemäß nachgewiesene Kosten)* duly documented cost, *(den Anspruch mit Dokumenten ~)* to support the claim with specific documentation, *(seine Forderungen glaubhaft ~)* to credibly substantiate one's claims, *(die Zahlung ~)* to prove (to evidence) payment

Nachweiserbringung provision of proof

Nachweispflichten documentation requirements

nachwirken to reverberate, to linger, to have repercussions

Nachwirkungen *(~ der Zinserhöhung)* repercussions (aftermath, after-effects, reverberations) of the rise in interest rates

Nachwuchsführungskräfte junior executive staff

nachzahlbar cumulative, → Vorzugsaktien ohne nachzahlbaren Vorzug

nachzahlen 1. *(zusätzlich)* to pay in addition, → nachschießen **2.** *(später)* to pay later **3.** *(im Nachhinein)* to pay in arrears

Nachzahlung additional (supplementary) payment, back pay, subsequent payment, payment in arrears

Nachzahlungsanspruch 1. entitlement to payment of arrears (to a subsequent payment) **2.** *(im Hinblick auf Dividendenausschüttungen)* deferred payment claim

Nachzahlungspflicht obligation to cover the deficiency (shortfall), *(nachzahlungspflichtige Dividende)* cumulative dividend

nachziehen *(sich anschließen)* to follow suit

Nachzugsaktien deferred shares, *(Inhaber von ~)* deferred shareholders □ receive a dividend after the preferred shareholders have received their payout in full

Nachzugsrechte deferred rights

Nackenlinie *(in der Chart-Analyse)* neckline

nah *(~er Liefermonat) (im Futures-/Optionshandel)* near delivery (contract) month, *(~e an das Vorjahresergebnis herankommen)* to come close to last year's performance

nähern to approach, to near, *(sich der 2000er Grenze ~)* to approach the 2,000 mark

näherrückend *(~er Fälligkeitstermin)* approaching maturity date

Näherungsverfahren approximation method

Näherungswert approximate value

nahestehend 1. *(~e Personen/Unternehmen) (i. S. des Aktienrechts)* related parties
2. *(ein uns ~es Unternehmen)* a company closely associated (connected) with us

nähren *(Hoffnungen auf eine Zinssenkung ~)* to nourish hopes for a cut in interest rates, *(die Hausse/Baisse ~)* to fuel the upturn/downturn in prices

nahtlos *(~e Fortsetzung)* seamless continuation, *(~er Übergang an der Unternehmensspitze)* smooth (friction-free) change in the top management

Name 1. name, *(im eigenen ~)* under one's own name, *(auf den ~n lautend)* registered **2.** *(Bezeichnung)* denomination **3.** *(Ruf)* renown, reputation

Namens / ~aktie registered share (stock); **~aktiengesetz** Registered Shares Act; **~aktionär** registered shareholder (stockholder); **~konnossement** straight bill of lading

Namens / ~papiere registered securities (notes); **~pfandbrief** registered mortgage bond; **~schuldverschreibung** registered bond (note); **~zertifikat** registered certificate

namentlich *(~e Abstimmung)* vote by roll-call

nationales Identifikationsmerkmal national identifier (Teil der SEPA → Gläubiger-Identifikationsnummer)

N

natürlich *(~e Person)* individual, natural person

Neben / ~abrede accessory (ancillary) agreement, *(vertragliche Nebenabreden)* covenants; **~absprache** side letter; **~einkommen** additional (extra, surplus) income; **~erzeugnis** by-product

Neben / ~folgen collateral consequences, side (secondary) effects; **~forderung** ancillary claim; **~gebühren** incidental (extra) charges; **~intervenient** intervenor

Nebenintervention 1. third party intervention (in support of plaintiff or defendant)
2. *(i. S. des Aktiengesetzes)* third-party intervention in support of a minority group

Neben / ~klage accessory suit; **~klausel** subsidiary (collateral) clause; **~konto** *(bei einem Cash-Management-Verfahren)* sub-account, slave account; **~kosten** incidental costs (expenses)

Nebenleistungen 1. accessory services, *(i. S. von Mehrwertleistungen)* added-value services
2. *(einer Bank)* related banking services
3. *(des Schuldners)* borrower's additional duties
4. *(eines Unternehmens für seine Mitarbeiter)* benefits

Neben / ~leistungsaufwand *(des Arbeitgebers)* benefit costs; **~markt** *(Börse)* market in second-line stocks, side-line market; **~papier 1.** → Bogen **2.** → Nebenwerte; **~pflichten** ancillary duties; **~platz** secondary bank place; **~produkt** by-product, secondary product

Neben / ~stelle *(einer Bank)* sub-branch, city branch; **~vereinbarung** side letter (agreement); **~verpflichtung** accessory (ancillary) obligation; **~vertrag** accessory (ancillary) contract

Neben / ~währungen second-line currencies; **~werte 1.** *(nicht zu den Standardwerten zählende Werte)* secondary counters (issues), second-line (second-tier) stock, second liners **2.** *(kleinere und mittlere Kapitalgesellschaften)* small and midcaps

Neben / ~wirkungseffekte *(~ der Zinserhöhung)* knock-on (side) effects of the rise in interest rates; **~zahlstelle** sub-paying agent

negativ 1. *adj.* *(~e Börsenstimmung)* depressed (bearish) market sentiment, *(~er Cash-Flow)* negative cash flow □ cash needs exceed cash intake, *(~es Eigenkapital)* negative net worth *(~er Goodwill)* negative goodwill, badwill □ the price paid for a company is less then the value of the assets acquired, *(~e Haltekosten)* negative cost of carry (e.g. financing charges exceed the yield on financed securities), *(~e Hebelwirkung)* downside leverage

(~e Hypothekenklausel) → Negativklausel,*(~es Kapital)* negative capital, liabilities exceeding assets, *(~es Nettoergebnis aus Finanzgeschäften)* net loss from financial transactions, *(~er Marktwert)* negative fair value, *(~e Orderklausel)* not-to-order clause *(~e Quittung, Nichtversand einer Nachricht/eines Zahlungsauftrages)* negative acknowledgement, *(~er beizulegender Zeitwert)* negative fair value, *(~er Zinssaldo)* net interest loss **2.** *adv.* *(~ beantworten)* to reply in the negative, *(~ schließen)* to close at a loss (deficit)

Negativ / **~auslese** adverse selection; **~erklärung 1.** → Negativklausel **2.** nil statement

Negativklausel negative pledge clause, covenant of equal coverage □ borrower's undertaking not to pledge assets nor to furnish security to other creditors without prior written consent by the lender

Negativ / **~quittung** negative acknowledgement; **~revers** → Negativklausel; **~test** clearance certificate; **~wirkung** negative impact (effect); **~zinsen** negative interest, → Vorschusszinsen

negoziierbar *(~es Akkreditiv)* negotiable credit

negoziieren to negotiate, *(negoziierende Bank)* negotiating bank, *(ohne Regress auf den Aussteller ~)* to negotiate without recourse to the drawer

Negoziierung *(~ von Tratten und Akkreditiven)* negotiation of drafts and documentary credits

Negoziierungs / **~akkreditiv** authority to negotiate; **~antrag/~auftrag** negotiation request, order to negotiate; **~erlös** negotiation proceeds; **~ermächtigung** authority to negotiate; **~kredit** negotiation credit, drawing authorisation

Negoziierungs / **~linie** negotiation line □ indicates the bank's willingness to purchase documentary drafts; **~provision** negotiating commission; **~verpflichtung** commitment to negotiate; **~zusage** undertaking to negotiate

nehmen *(Tagesgeld)* to buy, to borrow, *(aus dem Markt ~)* to take up, to buy up, to absorb (to drain) from the market

Nehmer borrower, *(~ im kurzfristigen Bereich)* borrower at the short end of the market, *(~ am Geldmarkt)* buyer (borrower) of short-term funds

Nehmer / **~bank** buying (borrowing) bank; **~land** borrowing country; **~position** borrowing position

neigen to have a propensity for, *(zu einer Verschärfung der Geldpolitik ~)* to lean (to tend) towards tightening monetary policy

Neigung 1. propensity, leaning, inclination **2.** *(Tendenz)* tendency, trend **3.** *(~ der Renditestrukturkurve)* slope of the yield curve

NE-Metalle non-ferrous metals

Nennbetrag nominal amount, principal

Nennbetragsmethode principal method □ accounting concept according to which a mortgage loan extended at a discount is carried at its principal value in the lending institution's accounts; the discount is recognised as deferred income.

nennen 1. to name, to indicate, to quote, to state **2.** *(benennen)* to appoint, to nominate, to designate

nennenswert 1. noteworthy, worth mentioning **2.** appreciable, noticeable

Nenner *(der geringste gemeinsame ~ in der Zinspolitik)* the lowest common denominator in interest rate policy

Nennung 1. naming, indication, *(unter ~ von)* setting forth, stating **2.** appointment, nomination, designation

Nennwert face amount, nominal (face) value, principal, par, *(über, unter, zum ~)* above (below, at) par

nennwertlose Aktie no-par stock

nervös *(~er Aktienmarkt)* jumpy equity market, stock market prone to jitters, *(der Markt bleibt ~)* the market remains skittish

Nervosität *(~ der Anleger)* nervousness of stock market investors, *(~ des Marktes)* jumpiness of the market

netten *(Derivatekontrakte ~)* to net obligations from derivative contracts

Netting netting □ offsetting mutual obligations between two or more counterparties, offset of payables against receivables, *(~ durch Novation)* netting by novation, replacement of two contracts by one single contract, → Novationsnetting, *(~ von Währungspositionen)* currency netting

Netting / **~-Teilnehmer** netting scheme participant; **~-Vereinbarung** netting arrangement (scheme)

netto net, in net terms

Nettoabrechnung net settlement, settling on a net basis □ denotes a securities transaction where the quoted purchase price/selling proceeds include brokerage and/or sales commission

Nettoabrechnungs / **~salden** net settlement balances; **~system** net settlement system

N

Netto / **~absatz** net sales, *(~ eines Investmentfonds)* net sales, sales net of redemptions; **~abschreibungen** *(im Kreditgeschäft)* net charge-offs, charge-offs (write-offs) net of recoveries; **~aktivposition 1.** net asset position, surplus position **2.** *(im Geldhandel)* net sellers, net lenders, net selling position

Netto / **~anlagevermögen** net fixed assets; **~auflösungen** *(von Wertberichtigungen)* net reversals; **~aufnahme** *(von Wertpapieren)* net take-up of securities

Nettoaufwand net expense(s), *(~ aus der außerordentlichen Rechnung)* net charges from the extraordinary account, *(~ für bezogene Waren und Dienstleistungen)* net cost of goods and services purchased, *(~ aus Finanzgeschäften)* net expenses from financial operations, *(~ für die Risikovorsorge)* net charge for risk provisioning

Netto / **~ausfallquote** net charge-off ratio □ loans charged off as bad debt in the current period less recoveries collected from prior charge-offs; **~ausfallrisiko** net exposure

Netto / **~ausgleich** net settlement; **~auslandsverschuldung** net external indebtedness; **~ausleihungen** net lendings; **~ausweis** net income/loss, net recognition, net disclosure

Netto / **~bankenposition** net interbank position; **~barausschüttung** net cash distribution; **~bedarfsspanne** net expense margin □ ratio of administrative expenditure less net commission income to total assets; **~bestand** net holdings, net position; **~beteiligungsposition** net investment position

Netto / **~betriebsgewinn** net operating income, net trading profit, net results of operations; **~betriebsvermögen** net operating assets; **~bewertungsaufwand** net valuation charge (expenditure); **~buchwert** net book value, net carrying value

Netto / **~darlehen** net loan, loan principal less discount (→ Disagio); **~devisenposition** net currency position (exposure); **~dividende** net dividend ; **~einnahmen** net receipts (revenue)

Netto / **~einsatz** net cash investments, net employment (outlay) of funds; **~emissionserlös** net issuing (offering) proceeds; **~engagement gegenüber Kontrahenten** net counterparty exposure

Netto / **~ergebnis** *(~ aus Finanzgeschäften)* net income (net loss) from financial transactions, *(~ aus Sicherungsbeziehungen)* net profit (loss) on hedges; **~erlös** net proceeds, net avails

Netto / **~ersparnisbildung** *(~ der privaten Haushalte)* net personal savings; **~ertrag** net income from the trading portfolio, *(~ aus Wertpapiergeschäften)* net profit from security operations; ~faktoreinkommen net factor income; ~fehlbetrag net deficit (loss)

Netto / ~**finanzaufwand** net finance charges; ~**finanzierungsbedarf** net financing (net funding) requirements; ~**finanzverschuldung** net financial indebtedness; ~**forderungsausfall** *(bei Krediten)* net loan charge-offs, net loss experience on loans

Netto / ~**geldvermögen** net monetary assets; ~**geschäft** net transaction, → Nettoabrechnung; ~**gewinn** net profit, net income, *(~ aus Handelsgeschäften)* net trading profits, *(~ nach Steuern)* net after-tax profit (income); ~**gewinnspanne** net profit margin (percentage), net spread (turn)

Netto / ~**gläubigerposition** net lending position, *(im Geldhandel)* net selling (lending) position, to be net sellers; ~**habenposition** net credit position

Netto / ~**inanspruchnahme 1.** *(des Kapitalmarktes)* net availment of the capital market, new issues net of repayments **2.** *(eines Kredites)* net drawings, net drawdown; ~**kapitalanlageergebnis** net investment income; ~**kapitalbildung** net capital formation

Netto / ~**kassaposition** *(in einer Fremdwährung)* net spot position; ~**käufer** *(als ~ am Markt fungieren)* to operate as net buyers in the market; ~**kaufposition** net long position

Netto / ~**kreditaufnahme** net borrowing(s), *(~ bei Banken)* net borrowings from the banking system, *(~ am Kapitalmarkt)* net borrowings in the capital market; ~**kreditgewährungen** net lendings, new lendings less (net of) repayments

Netto / ~**kurs** net price, → Nettoabrechnung; ~**kursgestaltung** net pricing; ~**leerverkaufsposition** net short position; ~**liquiditätszufluss** net liquidity inflow; ~**marge 1.** net margin **2.** net profit (turn)

Netto / ~**mittelabfluss** net cash outflow; ~**mittelaufnahme** net borrowings, new funds raised net of repayments; ~**mittelzufluss** net cash inflow, cash receipts net of cash payments, *(eines Fonds)* net sales revenue

Netto / ~**neugeschäft** *(im Kreditgeschäft)* new lendings in net terms, → Nettokreditgewährungen; ~**passivposition** *(im Geldhandel)* net buyers, net borrowers, net borrowing position; ~**position** net position, net holdings, ~**provisionserträge** net commissions received

Netto / ~**reichweite** net coverage (audience); ~**rendite** net yield, after-tax yield; ~**rentenabsatz** net bond sales, bond sales net of redemptions; ~**restschuld** net balance, payoff balance, net payoff

Netto / ~**risikoposition** net exposure; ~**risikovorsorge** net risk provisioning □ new provisions less reversals; ~**sachanlagen** net tangible assets; ~**saldo** net balance; ~**satz** net interest rate □ no additional commissions or fees are charged; ~**schuldenrückführung** net debt repayments

Netto / ~**schuldnerposition 1.** net borrowing position **2.** net buying position **3.** *(im Geldhandel)* to be net buyers (borrowers), net buying (borrowing) position; ~**sollposition** net debit position; ~**sparaufkommen** net savings inflow, net new savings, new savings deposits received less withdrawals

Netto / ~**terminposition** net forward position; ~**tilgung am Kapitalmarkt** net redemptions in the capital market

Netto / ~**überschuss** net surplus; ~**umlaufvermögen** net current assets, net working capital, current assets less current liabilities; ~**umsatzerlöse** net sales □ gross sales less returns, rebates,allowances; ~**veräußerungserlös** net sales proceeds; ~**veräußerungsgewinn** net capital gain

Netto / ~**verbindlichkeiten** net liabilities, net amount owed; ~**verdienst** net earnings; ~**verkaufsposition** net short position; ~**verkaufspreis** net sales price, net aggregate consid-

N

eration; ~**verlust** *(~ in konsolidierter Rechnung)* net consolidated loss

Netto / ~**vermögen** net assets, *(~ je Stammaktie)* net assets per ordinary share; ~**verschuldung** net indebtedness, net amount owed; ~**verschuldungsgrad** net debt leverage; ~**verzinsung** net interest return

Netto / ~**währungsposition** net currency position; ~**waren- und -materialeinsatz** net cost of goods purchased; ~**wert** net value, net worth; ~**wertzuwachs** net appreciation; ~**wiederbeschaffungskosten** net replacement cost; ~**zeitwert** net fair value

Nettozins / ~**aufwand** net interest charge (expense), net interest payable; ~**differenz** net interest gap; ~**erträge** net interest received, interest received net of interest expense, net interest revenue; ~**spanne** net interest margin □ gross interest margin less operating margin (personnel and operating expenses)

Nettozuführung 1. net allocation, *(~ zur Wertberichtigung)* net allocation to loan loss allowances, net increase in the charge for bad and doubtful debts
2. net increase, net addition(s), *(~ zum Eigenkapital)* net increase in equity, *(~ zur Risikovorsorge)* net increase in bad debt provisioning

Nettozuführungsquote net addition rate

Netz net, network, *(~ von Industriebeteiligungen)* web of industrial holdings

Netzgeldgeschäft network cash operations

Netzwerkgeld network money, electronic money transferred via telecommunications networks

neu 1. *adj. (~e Mittel)* fresh funds, *(auf ~e Rechnung)* for new account, relating to the new accounting period
2. *adv.* (*~ emittierte Aktien)* newly issued shares, *(fällige Titel ~ auflegen)* to roll over maturing debt, (*~ bewerten)* to reappraise, to reassess, to revalue, *(die Positionen werden täglich neu bewertet)* positions are daily marked to market, (*~ fassen)* to rewrite, to rephrase, *(~ festlegen)* to reestablish, to rearrange, to reset (e.g. the interest rate), (*~ verhandeln)* to renegotiate

Neuabschlüsse new business (contracts), (*~ im Kreditgeschäft)* new loans extended, new lendings, new lending commitments, (*~ sind mit fünfjähriger Bindungsfrist ausgestattet)* new lendings carry fixed rates for five years

Neu / ~**absprache** 1. re-arrangement 2. fixing a new lending rate; ~**akquisitionen** acquisition of new business; ~**ansatz** *(von Vermögenswerten)* restatement of assets

Neu / ~**aufbau** rebuilding, restructuring; ~**aufnahme** *(~ von Geldern)* new borrowing, fresh credit, taking out fresh funds; ~**aufteilung** redistribution; ~**aushandlung** *(~ der Kreditkonditionen)* renegotiation of the loan terms

Neuausrichtung realignment, reorientation, refocussing, redirection, (*~ der Erwartungen)* readjustment of expectations, (*~ des Filialnetzes)* reshaping of the branch network, (*~ des Kreditgeschäfts)* realignment (repositioning) of lending operations

Neubautätigkeit new building starts

Neubepreisung *(~ des Kredites)* loan repricing

Neuberechnung recalculation

Neubewertung 1. revaluation, remeasurement, *(~ der Kreditsicherheit)* revaluation of the loan collateral (of the security furnished for a loan accommodation, (*~ offener Positionen)* marking open positions to the market, revaluation of open positions to reflect current market prices, (*~ von Vermögenswerten)* remeasurement of assets
2. reassessment, reappraisal, (*~ der Kreditrisiken)* reassessment of the loan risks

Neubewertungs / ~gewinn revaluation gain (surplus), gain on remeasurement (on revaluation), *(neubewertungsinduzierte Wertsteigerung)* revaluation-induced appreciation; **~rücklage** revaluation allowance (reserve); **~überschuss** revaluation surplus; **~verlust** revaluation loss

Neubildung *(von Kreditwertberichtigungen)* establishment of new loan loss allowances

Neue *(das ~ an dieser Dienstleistung)* the novel element of this service

Neu / ~einschätzung reassessment, reappraisal; **~einstellungen** new employees, new staff members; **~einstufung** new rating, new grading

Neue Kreditvereinbarungen *(IWF)* New Arrangements to Borrow

Neuemission 1. new (fresh) issue, *(Festsetzung der Kurse für ~en)* new issue pricing **2.** *(i. S. von Erstemission)* first-time issue, initial public offering

Neuemissions / ~angebote offerings of new issues; **~bereich** *(im ~)* on the new issuing side; **~markt** new issue market, primary market; **~tätigkeit** new issuance activity; **~volumen** new issuing volume

Neu / ~engagements 1. *(~ an der Börse)* fresh orders, fresh buying **2.** *(~ im Kreditgeschäft)* new lendings **3.** new investments (commitments); **~erwerbung** new acquisition, newly acquired company; **~fassung** new (revised) version, revision

Neufestsetzung 1. refixing, re-establishment, *(~ der Wechselkurse)* realignment of exchange rates
2. resetting, *(~ des Hypothekenzinssatzes alle fünf Jahre)* repricing the mortgage loan (renegotiation of the mortgage rate) every five years, *(~ des Zinssatzes einer Anleihe)* coupon reset, coupon refixing, resetting the interest rate of a bond

Neufinanzierung fresh funding (financing)

Neugeschäft new lendings, new loan accommodations, *(~ im Hypothekenbereich)* new mortgage lendings, new mortgage commitment activity, *(Refinanzierung des ~es)* funding new lendings, *(Rückgang des ~es bei Krediten für Privatkunden)* decline in new personal loans, decrease in new credits extended to private customers, *(Wachstum des ~es)* growth in new lendings

Neugeschäftsvolumen volume of new business (of new loan accommodations)

Neu / ~gestaltung restructuring, *(~ von Geschäftsabläufen)* business reengineering, process reorganisation, *(~ einer Strategie)* reshaping of a strategy; **~gliederung** regrouping, reclassification; **~gründung** business start-up, new establishment, new business setup

Neu / ~investitionen new investments, new investment activity; **~kalibrierung** *(~ der Prognosen)* recalibration of forecasts (probability estimates); **~konzeption** new conception, reshaping, redesigning

Neukredit new loan, new advance, new facility, fresh funds; **~bedarf** new borrowing requirements; **~gewährung** extending a new loan, new lending; **~volumen** volume of new lendings

Neuordnung 1. reorganisation, restructuring, revamping, *(~ der Bilanzstruktur)* balance sheet restructuring, *(~ der Kapitalverhältnisse)* capital reconstruction (reorganisation), restructuring the capital base
(~ des Kreditgeschäftes der Bank) reorganisation of the bank's lending business, restructuring lending operations (activities), *(~ der Kreditverhältnisse einer Unternehmung)* loan restructuring, debt reorganisation, restructuring of borrowings, → Neuregelung, *(~ der Unternehmensstruktur)* corporate restructuring
2. *(~ der Währungsparitäten)* realignment of exchange rates

Neuorientierung/~positionierung reorientation, refocussing, repositioning, redirection

Neuregelung 1. new arrangement **2.** enactment of a new statute **3.** *(~ eines Kreditengagements)* rearrangement of a loan commitment, renegotiation of a loan facility, loan (facility) restructuring **4.** *(~ der Haftung)* restatement of liability rules

neutral *(~e Chartformation)* indeterminant formation (pattern), *(~e Leistungen) (einer Bank)* non-banking services, *(~e Partei)* disinterested party

neutralisieren *(das Marktrisiko ~)* to neutralise the market risk (exposure)

Neuvalutierung *(Übernahme eines Grundpfandrechtes)* re-use of a land charge □ assumption of a real estate lien already entered in the land register, → Nichtvalutierungserklärung

Neu / ~verteilung redistribution, reallocation; **~verschuldung** new borrowing (fund-raising), new debt(s) contracted, *(~ der Unternehmen)* new corporate borrowings; **~wert** replacement (reinstatement) value, full replacement cost; **~wertversicherung** reinstatement value insurance; **~zugänge** additions, new purchases

N

Neuzusagen new lendings (commitments), new loans extended

Neuzusagen *(~ an Festzinshypotheken)* new fixed rate mortgage lendings, *(~ bei Wohnungsbaukrediten)* new home loan commitments, *(Volumen der ~)* volume of new loans extended

NE-Werte non-ferrous metals stock

nicht / ~abgeschrieben *(~e Agiobeträge)* unamortised premiums; **~abgesprochen** *(~e Überziehung)* unauthorised (non-agreed) overdraft; **~ablösbar** *(~e Belastung)* irredeemable charge; **~absetzbar/abzugsfähig** *(~e Aufwendungen)* non-allowable (non-deductible) expenditure

nicht / ~absicherbar *(~e Risiken)* unhedgeable (uncoverable) risks; **~akzessorisch** *(~e Kreditsicherheit)* non-accessory loan collateral, → Garantie, → Grundschuld; **~amtlich** *(~er Handel)* unofficial trading (dealings), **~anerkennungsfähig** *(~er Anspruch)* disallowable claim, *(~e Kosten)* non-eligible costs, *(~e Wertpapiere)* ineligible securities; **~anrechenbar** not eligible for inclusion in

nicht / ~ausgabenwirksam *(~e Posten)* non-cash items; **~ausgefallen** *(Ratingstufen für nicht ausgefallene Schuldner)* rating grades for non-defaulted obligors (borrowers)

nicht / ~ausgewiesen *(~e Gewinne)* undisclosed profits; **~ausgezahlt** *(~er Kapitalbetrag)* undisbursed capital, **~ausschüttbar** *(~e Rücklagen)* undistributable reserves

nicht / ~bankfähig *(~e Sicherheit)* unbankable collateral, collateral (security) not acceptable to banks; **~begebbar** *(~er Seefrachtbrief)* non-negotiable seaway bill; **~beitreibbar** *(~e Forderungen)* irrecoverable debt(s), uncollectible accounts (receivables)

nicht / ~besitzgebunden *(~es Pfandrecht)* non-possessory lien; **~bevorrechtigt** *(~e Forderung)* ordinary (non-preferential) debt, *(~ er Gläubiger)* ordinary (non-preferential) creditor, general creditor

nicht / ~bilanzwirksam *(~e Geschäfte)* off-balance sheet transactions; **~börsenfähig** *(~er Titel)* non-marketable security; **~börsennotiert** *(~e Wertpapiere)* unlisted securities

nicht / ~derivativ *(~e außerbilanzielle Aktiva)* non-derivative off-balance sheet assets; **~diskontierbar** *(~er Wechsel)* undiscountable bill; **~diversifizierbar** *(~es Risiko)* non-diversifiable risk, systematic risk; **~dokumentär** *(~e Zahlungen)* clean payments, non-documentary payments

nicht / ~eingefordert *(~es Kapital)* uncalled capital; **~eingelöst** *(~e Kupons)* unclaimed coupons, *(~e Schecks/Wechsel)* unpaid (dishonoured) cheques/bills; ~**eingezahlt** *(~es Kapital)* unpaid capital

nicht / ~**einklagbar** unenforceable in law; ~**emissionsfähig** *(~es Unternehmen)* company unable to access the capital market; ~**entgeltfähig** *(~e Leistung)* non-chargeable service; ~**entnommen** *(~e Gewinne)* undrawn profits, retained income

nicht gedeckt *(~e Forderungen)* unsecured receivables (claims), *(~e Optionsposition)* naked (uncovered) option position, *(~es Risiko)* uncovered risk, unhedged exposure, *(~e Terminfälligkeiten)* unhedged (unmatched) forward maturities

nicht / ~**genannt** *(~e Menge)* unspecified quantity; ~**gehörig** *(~e Leistung)* deficient (faulty) performance; ~**genehmigt** *(~e Inanspruchnahmen/Überziehungen)* unauthorised drawings/overdrafts

nicht / ~**gewerblich** *(~e Einkünfte)* non-commercial income, *(~e Vereine)* non-economic associations; ~**gezeichnet** *(~e Aktien)* unsubscribed shares (stock), shares not subscribed; ~**girosammelverwahrfähig** *(~e Titel)* securities not eligible for collective safekeeping

nicht / ~**kapitalgedeckt** *(~e Leistungsansprüche)* unfunded benefit entitlements; ~**konsolidiert** *(~er Anteilsbesitz)* non-consolidated shareholdings, unconsolidated trade investments, *(~e Bedingungen)* long-form conditions

nicht / ~**konsolidierungspflichtig** *(~e Gesellschaft)* company exempt from consolidation requirements; ~**konvertierbar** *(~e Währung)* non-convertible currency; ~**kumulativ** *(~ revolvierendes Akkreditiv)* non-cumulative revolving credit

nicht / ~**kündbar** *(~e Anleihe)* **1.** non-callable bond, bond not callable during its life **2.** irredeemable bond, bond with no fixed date of redemption □ intended to be a permanent debt; ~**laufzeitkongruent** *(~e Refinanzierung)* mismatched funding

nicht lieferbar *(~e Stücke/Wertpapiere)* **1.** non-deliverable securities **2.** *(nur als Wertrechte verfügbar)* securities issued in book-entry form, dematerialised securities **3.** *(mit Mängeln behaftet)* securities in a condition not constituting good delivery **4.** *(nicht verfügbar)* unavailable securities

nicht / ~**liquiditätswirksam** *(~er Aufwand)* non-cash charges; ~**lombardfähig** *(~e Wertpapiere)* securities not qualifying as collateral

nicht / ~**marginpflichtig** *(~e Geschäfte)* non-marginable transactions; ~**monetär** *(~e Kennzahlen)* non-monetary ratios, *(~e Vermögenswerte/Verbindlichkeiten)* non-monetary assets/ liabilities

nicht / ~**notenbankfähig** non-central bank eligible; ~**notiert** *(~e Aktie)* unlisted (unquoted) share; ~**notifiziert** *(~es Factoring)* undisclosed factoring; ~**pfändbar** *(~e Vermögensgegenstände)* non-leviable assets, property exempt from seizure

nicht / ~**realisierbar** *(~e Vermögenswerte)* unrealisable (unmarketable) assets; ~**realisiert** *(~e stille Reserven)* unrealised latent reserves, *(~er Kapitalgewinn)* unrealised capital appreciation

nicht / ~**rechtsfähig** *(~e Stiftung)* foundation without legal personality (capacity), *(~er Verein)* unincorporated association; ~**rediskontfähig** *(~e Wechsel)* bills not eligible for rediscount

nicht / ~**reservepflichtig** *(~e Verbindlichkeiten)* liabilities free from reserve requirements, liabilities not subject to reserve requirements; ~**säumige Partei** non-defaulting party, performing party; ~**staatlich** *(~e Adresse)* non-sovereign borrower/issuer

nicht / ~**strategisch** *(~e Geschäftseinheiten)* non-core business operations;

~**streitig** *(~es Verfahren)* non-contentious proceedings; ~**testiert** *(~er Abschluss)* unaudited accounts; ~**transparent** *(~er Fonds)* non-transparent fund

nicht übertragbar *(~es Akkreditiv)* non-transferable (non-assignable) documentary credit, *(~er Anspruch)* non-transferable claim, *(~er Rechtstitel)* unalienable title

nicht / ~unterbringbar *(~e Buchungen)* irreconcilable entries; ~**unternehmenstragend** *(~e Aktiva)* non-core assets

nicht / ~verarbeitungsfähig *(~e Datei)* non-processable file; ~**veräußerbar** *(~e Vermögenswerte)* unalienable (unrealisable) property; ~**verbrieft** *(~e Forderungen)* uncertificated claims; ~**verbunden** *(~e Drittanteilseigner)* unrelated third-party investors; ~**vertretbar** *(~e Wertpapiere)* non-fungible securities

nicht / ~voll eingezahlt *(~e Aktien)* partly paid shares; ~**vollständig gezeichnet** *(~e Emission)* undersubscribed issue; ~**voll stimmberechtigt** *(~e Aktien)* shares that do not carry full voting rights; ~**wiederkehrend** *(~e Belastungen)* non-recurrent charges

nicht / ~zahlungswirksam *(~e Vermögenswerte)* non-cash assets; ~**zinsabschlagspflichtig** *(~e Kapitalerträge)* investment income exempt from flat rate withholding tax; ~**zinskongruent** *(~ refinanzierte Aktivgeschäfte)* lendings funded at mismatched rates, mismatched lendings

nicht / ~zinstragend *(~e Aktiva)* non-earning assets; ~**zinswirksam** *(~e Posten)* non-interest items, positions not entailing interest payments; ~**zutreffend** inapplicable, *(~ in der Praxis)* not borne out in practice

nicht zweckgebunden *(~e Ausleihungen)* non-purpose lendings, *(~es Darlehen)* untied loan, *(~e Finanzierung)* financing (funding) not tied to a specific purpose

Nichtabnahme 1. *(~ einer Kreditlinie)* non-availment (non-utilisation) of a credit line 2. *(~ einer Lieferung)* non-acceptance of delivery, refusal to take delivery, failure to take up goods dispatched

Nichtabnahmeentschädigung *(bei Krediten)* non-availment fee (indemnity, penalty), non-utilisation fee, compensation for non-availment of a credit line

Nicht / ~abzugsfähigkeit non-deductibility; ~**akzeptierung** non-acceptance; ~**andienung** non-tender; ~**anerkennung** *(~ von Ansprüchen/Forderungen)* disallowance of claims, *(~ von Verbindlichkeiten)* repudiation of debt (liabilities)

Nicht / ~ansatz *(~ in der Bilanz)* non-recognition (non-disclosure) in the balance sheet; ~**anzeige** non-notification, non-reporting, *(~ der Abtretung)* non-notification (non-disclosure) of an assignment, *(bei ~)* in default of notification

Nicht / ~aufnahme *(~ der Dokumente)* failure to take up the documents; ~**ausführung** *(~ von Zahlungsanweisungen)* non-execution of payment instructions; ~**ausführungsanzeige** notification of non-execution

Nichtausübung non-exercise, *(~ von Bezugsrechten innerhalb des vorgeschriebenen Zeitraumes)* failure to exercise subscription rights within the specified period, *(~ einer Option)* option abandonment

Nichtbanken non-banks, non-financial corporations, non-bank customers

Nichtbanken / ~beteiligungen investments in non-banks; ~**einlagen** non-bank deposits, wholesale funds; ~**engagements** non-bank commitments (exposure); ~**geschäft** non-banking business; ~**kundschaft** non-bank customers; ~**schuldner** non-bank debtor (borrower); ~**sektor** non-banks, non-bank sector

N

Nicht / ~beachtung non-observance, non-compliance, failure to observe; **~bestreitbarkeit** non-repudiability; **~bezahltmeldung** advice of non-payment, notice of dishonour, notice of default

Nicht / ~Clearingmitglied non-clearing member; **~dividenwerte** non-equity securities; **~eingang** non-receipt, *(~ der Bestätigung)* failure to receive the confirmation

Nichteinhaltung non-observance, non-compliance, *(~ einer Bestimmung)* failure to comply with (to observe) a provision, *(~ der Kündigungsfrist)* non-observance of the period of notice, *(~ des Rückzahlungstermins)* non-compliance with the date set for repayment

Nichteinlösung *(~ eines Wechsels)* non-payment of a bill, dishonouring a bill, failing to meet (to pay, to honour) a bill upon maturity

Nichterfüllung non-performance, failure to perform, non-fulfilment, *(~ der Akkreditivbedingungen)* non-compliance with the terms and conditions of the documentary credit, *(im Falle der ~)* in the event of non-performance; *(bei ~ durch den Hauptschuldner)* in the event of non-performance by the principal debtor, on default of the principal obligor, *(~ einer Leistung)* non-performance *(~ einer Nachschussverpflichtung)* failure to remargin, *(~ der Vertragsverpflichtungen)* non-discharge of contractual obligations, defaulting on one's contractual obligations, failing to discharge one's obligations, failure to perform a contract, *(~ einer Zahlungsverpflichtung)* default in payment, failure to meet a payment obligation, failure to settle (to pay) a debt upon maturity, non-payment of a debt

Nicht / ~erscheinen failure to appear, default of appearance; **~fertigstellung** non-completion, failure to complete; **~finanzkunden** non-financial customers; **~finanzunternehmen** non-financial corporate entities; **~firmengeschäft** non-corporate banking, personal banking

Nichthandels / ~aktiva non-trading assets; **~bestand** non-trading asset portfolio; **~buchinstitut** non-trading book institution □ bank maintaining an insignificant proprietary trading portfolio; **~zwecke** *(Positionen zu ~n)* positions for non-trading purposes

nichtig invalid, void, null and void, → null und nichtig

Nichtigkeit invalidity, nullity, voidness

Nichtigkeits / ~einrede plea in nullity; **~erklärung** annulment, defeasance; **~gründe** reasons to invalidate a resolution; **~klage** nullity suit, action for annulment

Nicht / ~inanspruchnahme *(~ einer Kreditlinie)* non-availment of a credit line, non-utilisation of a loan facility; **~kerngeschäft** non-core activities (business operations); **~konvertierbarkeit** inconvertibility, non-convertibility

Nicht / ~leistung non-performance, non-execution, → Nichterfüllung; **~lieferung** non-delivery, failure (failing) to deliver; **~offenlegung 1.** non-disclosure **2.** *(Nichtanzeige)* non-notification; **~regulierung** non-settlement, failure to settle

Nicht / ~übereinstimmung 1. disagreement, discord **2.** non-compliance; **~übernahmeklausel** non-assumption clause; **~übertragbarkeit** non-transferability, non-negotiability

Nichtvalutierung *(der Grundschuld)* confirmation that a real estate lien does no longer serve as collateral for the liabilities of the vendor, but is now binding on the buyer of the property to secure the buyer's debt

Nicht / ~veranlagungsbescheinigung non-assessment certificate; **~verfügbarkeit** unavailability, *(~ der Leistung)* non-availability of performance;

~**vermögensschaden** non-pecuniary damage

Nicht / ~**vorlage** non-presentment, non-presentation, failure to present; ~**zahlung** non-payment, failure to make payment; ~**zahlungsrisiko** risk of default, non-payment risk; ~**zahlungstatbestand** protracted default

Nicht / ~**zustandekommen** *(~ eines Kaufvertrages)* failure to conclude a contract of sale; ~**zustellung** non-delivery; ~**zutreffendes streichen** delete whichever is inapplicable, delete as required

Niedergang *(~ des Unternehmens)* decline in the company's fortunes

niedergedrückt *(~e Börsenstimmung)* depressed sentiment in the market

niederlassen to settle, to establish o. s.

Niederlassung 1. branch, branch establishment, offshoot **2.** settlement

Niederlassungs / ~**freiheit** freedom of settlement; ~**kompetenz** branch approval powers; ~**leiter** branch manager; ~**netz** branch network

N

niederlegen 1. *(aufgeben)* to abandon, to relinquish **2.** *(ein Amt ~)* to resign from office **3.** *(die Arbeit ~)* to stop work, to go on strike **4.** *(schriftlich ~)* to put down in writing

Niederlegung 1. abandonment, relinquishment **2.** resignation **3.** cessation of work

niederschlagen 1. *(sich in der Bilanz ~)* to be reflected (mirrored) in the balance sheet, *(sich deutlich im Ertrag ~)* to have a marked impact on earnings, to come through strongly in the earnings, *(sich in geringeren Erträgen ~)* to be reflected in lower earnings, *(sich in höheren Kursen ~)* to feed through into (to result in) higher prices, *(sich in den Unternehmensgewinnen ~)* to show itself in the profits of the company
2. *(das Verfahren ~)* to quash (to drop) the proceedings

Niederschrift 1. record, notes **2.** *(Protokoll)* minutes

Niederstwert lower of cost or market, *(nach dem Niederstwertprinzip bewerteter Wertpapierbestand)* securities portfolio valued at the lower of cost or market

niedrig 1. *adj.* *(~e Anfangsbelastung)* low initial debt service □ starting with low interest and redemption payments, *(~er Fremdkapitalanteil)* low share of borrowed funds, low gearing (leverage)
(~ere Instanz) inferior (lower) court, *(zum ~eren Einstands- oder Marktwert ausweisen)* to state at cost or market value whichever is lower, *(der ~ste Stand)* the lowest-ever-level, *(~ volatiler Index)* low-volatility index
2. *adv.* *(~ bewertete Aktie)* low-priced share, *(~ eingestufte Schuldtitel)* low-rated debt (bonds), *(~er notieren)* to trade lower, to be marked down, *(~ verzinst werden)* to carry a low rate of interest

niedrighalten *(Zinsen ~)* to keep interest rates down

niedrigkapitalisiert *(~es Unternehmen)* low-capitalised company

Niedrigkupon-Titel → niedrigverzinsliche Schuldtitel

niedrigmargig *(~er Kredit)* low-margin loan

Niedrigstkurs bottom price (rate), *(absoluter ~)* all-time low, rock-bottom price

niedrigverzinslich *(~er Kredit)* low-interest loan (credit), *(~e Kurzläufer)* low-coupon shorts, *(~e Schuldtitel)* low-interest-paying debt securities

Niedrigzins / ~**periode** period of low interest rates; ~**politik** policy of low interest rates, cheap-money policy; ~**währung** low-interest currency

Nießbrauch usufruct, usufructuary right, beneficial interest (use), right of enjoyment (of usufruct)

Nießbraucher usufructuary, beneficial user, person holding the right to enjoy the property in question

Nießbrauch / ~**empfänger** → Nießbraucher; ~**geber** usufruct grantor; ~**gewährung** granting of a usufruct; ~**konto** usufruct account; ~**recht** usufruct, usufructuary right; ~**vertrag** usufruct contract (agreement)

Nießbrauchsbegünstigter → Nießbraucher

Nischen / ~**bank** niche, niche bank; ~**strategie** niche strategy

Niveau level, standard, *(sich auf hohem ~ bewegen)* to run at a high level, *(auf hohem ~ bleiben)* to continue at high levels, *(die Umsätze auf hohem ~ halten)* to keep activity high

nivellieren to level, to even out

Nominal / ~**abschreibungen** scheduled depreciation; ~**beteiligung** nominal (notional) interest; ~**betrag** nominal amount, *(einer Swap-Transaktion)* notional amount (notional principal) of a swap □ principal balance underlying a swap transaction; used to compute swap payments

Nominal / ~**einkommen** nominal income; ~**kapital** nominal capital; ~**verzinsung** nominal interest return; ~**wert** nominal (face) value, par value; ~**zins** nominal rate of interest

nominell nominal, notional, *(~er Kapitalbetrag)* notional amount, notional principal, *(~e Gebühr)* notional charge, *(~er Kurs)* notional (fictitious) price, *(~er Zins)* notional interest (coupon rate)

nominieren to nominate, to designate, to appoint

Nominierung nomination, designation, appointment

Nominierungs / ~**recht** right to nominate (of nomination); ~**verfahren** nominating process

Norm 1. standard, rule 2. *(Maßstab)* measure, yardstick

normal normal, ordinary, standard, *(~ e Kurslücke) (in der Chart-Analyse)* common gap, *(~e Marktsituation)* carrying charge market, → Report

Normal / ~**ausstattung** *(einer Anleihe)* standard terms; ~**konditionen** standard rates, standard terms and conditions, standard fees; ~**leistung** standard level of output; ~**verteilung** normal distribution; ~**zins** standard rate of interest; ~**zuteilung** standard allocation

normiert *(~er Kredit)* standardised loan, *(~es Kreditgeschäft)* standardised lendings (lending operations), *(~e Vorgabekosten)* standard cost

Normkontingent standard quota

Nostro / ~**bestand** proprietary holdings; ~**dispositionen** nostro transactions; ~**effekten** nostro securities, securities owned by the bank; ~**geschäfte** *(~ in Wertpapieren)* proprietary (own-account) trading in securities

Nostro / ~**guthaben** nostro balances, balances with other financial institutions, due from banks; ~**konto** nostro account, our account with you, account maintained by a bank at another bank; ~**verpflichtungen** nostro commitments, funds borrowed

N

Not leidend → notleidend

Nota 1. note, memo(randum) 2. *(Rechnung)* invoice

Not / ~**adresse** address in case of need; ~**anzeige** advice of dishonour

Notar notary; ~- **Anderkonto** notary trust account, client account

Notariat notary's office

Notariats / ~**gebühren** notarial charges (cost), notary's fee; ~**siegel** notarial (notary's) seal; ~**urkunde** notarial deed (act)

notariell *(~es Schuldanerkenntnis)* notarised acknowledgement of debt, *(~e Vollmacht)* notarised power of attorney, power of attorney certified (attested) by a notary public, *(~ abschließen)* to draw up before a notary, *(~ beglaubigen/beurkunden)* to notarise, *(notariell beglaubigt)* notarised, to be certified (authenticated, attested) by a notary public

Note 1. *(Banknote)* (bank) note, bill (AE) **2.** *(Mitteilung)* memorandum, note

Noten / ~aufruf calling in (withdrawal of) bank notes; **~ausgabe** note issue, issue of bank notes

Notenbank 1. Central Bank **2.** *(Notenausgabebank)* Bank of Issue; **~ausweis** Central Bank return

notenbankfähig central bank eligible, *(~e Sicherheiten)* eligible assets, → Kategorie-1/Kategorie-2-Sicherheiten, *(als ~ einstufen)* to class as eligible (e.g. for rediscount with the Central Bank)

Notenbank / ~fähigkeit central bank eligibility; **~gouverneure** Central Bank governors; **~guthaben** Central Bank balances; **~kredit** Central Bank credit (lending), Central Bank facility (loan); **~politik** Central Bank policy; **~refinanzierung** *(~ der Banken)* banks' borrowings from the Central Bank; **~zinsen** Central Bank rates, → Leitzinsen

N

Noten / ~deckung note coverage; **~privileg** note-issuing privilege (power); **~umlauf** notes in circulation

notieren 1. to note, to take note of **2.** *(an der Börse)* to list, to quote, *(Finanzwerte notierten geringfügig schwächer)* financials were a fraction easier, *(weiterhin fest ~)* to remain firm, *(am grauen Markt ~)* to quote on the grey market

Notierung listing, quotation, price, *(~ je Feinunze)* price per fine ounce, *(~ im* → Freiverkehr) quotation in the Open Market, over-the-counter quotation, *(~ im* → Regulierten Markt) listing in the regulated market, *(~ im Telefonverkehr)* off-board quotation, *(aus der ~ nehmen)* to suspend the quotation, to delist

Notierungs / ~aufnahme commencement of listing, first listing; **~aussetzung** suspending the quotation (the listing)

notierungsgesteuert *(~es System)* quote-driven system

Notierungs / ~größe quotation size; **~kosten** listing expense; **~zusatz** → Kurszusatz

notifizieren to notify, to report, *(notifiziertes Factoring)* disclosed factoring, *(notifizierte Position)* notified position, position notified for delivery

Notifizierung notification, reporting

Notifizierungs / ~pflicht notification duty (requirements); **~tag** notification day; **~verfahren** notification procedure; **~vorschriften** notification (reporting) requirements

Notiz 1. note, notice, memo(randum) **2.** *(Kursnotierung)* quote, quotation

Not / ~klausel escape clause; **~lage** emergency situation, dire straits, *(~ des Unternehmens)* company's predicament (distressed state)

notleidend non-performing, distressed, *(~e Aktiva/Forderungen)* distressed assets, *(~e Anleihe)* non-performing (defaulted, dishonoured) bond, *(~e Immobilienkredite)* non-performing property loans, non-performing real estate lendings, *(~e Inkassi)* dishonoured collections, *(~e Investitionen)* distressed investments
(~e Kredite) non-performing loans (NPLs), distressed (troubled) debt □ loans being in default for 90 days or more, *(umgangssprachlich ferner)* bad (sour) loans, *(Handel mit notleidenden Krediten)* distressed debt trading, *(Umstrukturierung notleidender Kredite)* NPL restructuring, distressed debt restructuring
(~e Positionen) positions (exposures) in default, *(~er Wechsel)* dishonoured bill, *(~e Wertpapiere)* distressed securities, non-performing debt securities, securities in default

Not / ~limit *(bei Wertpapieraufträgen)* stop limit, **~liquidation** emergency sale (liquidation), forced sale

notwendig 1. necessary, required, requisite 2. *(unerläßlich)* indispensable 3. *(unvermeidbar)* inevitable 4. *(wesentlich)* essential, vital, *(~ machen)* to necessitate, *(~ werden)* to become necessary, *(für ~ erachten)* to deem (to consider) necessary, *(sich als ~ erweisen)* to turn out to be necessary

Notwendige *(das ~ veranlassen)* to make the necessary arrangements, to see to the necessary

Notwendigkeit necessity

Novation novation □ substitution by mutual agreement of an obligation (contract) for another whereby the previous obligation or debt is extinguished; substituting new partners to an existing contract

Novationsnetting netting by novation, obligation netting □ parties calculate their net obligations to each other and replace the existing contracts by one single net contract

Novelle draft amendment

novellieren to amend

n.s.b.-Kredite *(nicht schriftlich bestätigte Kredite)* loans not confirmed in writing

null *(als ~ und nichtig ansehen)* to consider as null and void, *(einen Vertrag für ~ und nichtig erklären)* to nullify a contract, to declare a contract null and void, *(ein Wertpapier für ~ und nichtig erklären)* to invalidate a security, to declare a security null and void

Null *(auf ~ gestelltes Konto)* zero balance account

Nullbogen zero coupon sheet

Nullkosten / ~**absicherung** zero cost hedge; ~**option** zero cost option, collar

Nullkupon zero coupon, deep discount bond; ~**-Anleihe** zero bond; ~**-Swap** zero coupon swap

Nullstellung *(von Konten)* zero balancing

Numismatik numismatics

nummerieren to number

Nummerierung numbering

Nummern / ~**buch** securities code ledger; ~**konto** numbered account; ~**skontrierung** updating of security code numbers; ~**verzeichnis** list of securities deposited

Nur-Notar plain notary, exclusively a notary

nur zur Verrechnung 'and company', 'account payee only'

nutzbar usable, utilisable

Nutzbarmachung utilisation, exploitation

nutzbringend profitable, remunerative

Nutzeffekt gain, advantage, useful effect

nutzen 1. to use, to utilise, to employ, *(eine Kreditlinie voll ~)* to make full use of a credit line, *(Wissen und Fähigkeiten von … ~)* to harness the skills and knowledge of …
2. *(profitieren)* to benefit (profit) from, to capitalise on, *(Arbitragemöglichkeiten ~)* to exploit arbitrage opportunities, *(das niedrige Zinsniveau ~)* to take advantage of low interest rates

N

Nutzen 1. *(Gewinn, Ertrag)* profit, gain, returns, reward 2. *(im Kreditgeschäft)* margin 3. *(Vorteil)* usefulness, advantage, *(wirtschaftlicher Nutzen)* economic benefits

Nutzen / ~**messung** utility measurement; ~**schwelle** break-even point; ~**übergang** transfer of rights (benefits); ~**vergleich** utility measurement (comparison); ~**versprechen** value proposition; ~**wert** utility value

Nutzer / ~**authentifizierung** user authentication; ~**freundlichkeit** user friendliness; ~**verhalten** user behaviour

Nutz / ~**faktor** utilisation (utility) factor; ~**fläche** usable floor space, useful area

nützlich 1. useful 2. *(gewinnbringend)* profitable, remunerative 3. *(vorteilhaft)* beneficial, advantageous

Nützlichkeit 1. usefulness, utility 2. profitableness 3. benefit, advantage

nutzlos 1. useless, futile 2. *(unergiebig)* unprofitable, unproductive 3. *(vergeblich)* wasted, fruitless

Nutzlosigkeit uselessness, futility, unproductiveness

nutznießen to enjoy (the benefit of property)

Nutznießer beneficial user, beneficiary

Nutznießung *(von Vermögen)* beneficial use (enjoyment) of property, usufruct

Nutzung 1. use, utilisation, usage 2. *(~ einer Kreditlinie)* availment of a credit line, drawing on a credit line 3. *(Verwertung)* exploitation, taking advantage of, capitalising on

Nutzungs / ~**ausfall** loss of use, downtime; ~**berechtigter** authorised user, → Nutznießer; ~**beschränkung** limiting the use (of property); ~**bestimmungen** terms (conditions) of use; ~**dauer** useful (service) life, *(steuerliche ~)* tax life, *(wirtschaftliche ~)* economic life; ~**gebiet** area of use (usage), territory; ~**grenze** user limit

Nutzungs / ~**herausgabe** restitution of benefits received; ~**intensität** use intensity; ~**recht** 1. right of enjoyment, right of use, → Nießbrauch 2. *(Grunddienstbarkeit)* easement, servitude; ~**vereinbarung** usage agreement; ~**verlust** loss of usufruct; ~**wert** utility value; ~**zahlen** user (usage) numbers

Nutzwert utility value, user (economic) value; ~**analyse** utility (cost-benefit) analysis

NV-Bescheinigung → Nichtveranlagungsbescheinigung

N

O

OA m.O./OA o.O. → Optionsanleihe mit/ohne Optionsschein

oben *(nach ~ zeigender Ergebnistrend)* upward performance trend, *(nach ~ berichtigte Prognose)* upward-revised forecast *(nach ~ tendieren)* to move in an upward direction, to be on an upward trend, *(Ausleihungen von ~ nach unten)* downstream lendings, lendings by a central banking organisation to its member banks (or by a parent company to its subsidiaries)

ober *(~er Interventionspunkt)* upper intervention point, *(~es Limit des Zielkorridors)* upper limit of the target range, *(am ~en Ende des Marktes)* at the top end of the market

Obergesellschaft ultimate parent company, ultimate holding company, dominant company, → Organträger

Obergrenze upper limit, ceiling, cap, *(~ für Ausleihungen)* lending ceiling, *(~ für Gebote)* bidding cap, *(~ für Großkredite)* upper limit on the size of large loan exposures, *(~ für einen Zinssatz)* interest rate cap, *(Festlegung einer ~)* putting a cap on, capping, setting an upper limit (upward limit, a ceiling)

Obergutachten senior expert opinion

Oberhand *(die ~ gewinnen)* to gain the upper hand, to get the better of

Oberlandesgericht Higher Regional Court

Objekt 1. object, asset 2. property, building 3. *(Projekt)* project

Objekt / ~bewertung property valuation; **~bonität** property (project) quality; **~einkünfte** property income; **~ entwicklungsgesellschaft** property developer, property (project) development company; **~finanzierung** object finance, property (property-specific) financing

Objektgesellschaft 1. special purpose company, company established for a specific purpose (for one specific venture) 2. property company (partnership), property development (management) company

objektiv objective, impartial, unbias(s) ed, *(~ e Unmöglichkeit der Leistungserfüllung)* objective impossibility of performance □ legal defense since no one can perform the contract, → subjektive Unmöglichkeit der Leistungserfüllung

Objektivität objectivity, impartiality

Objekt-KG limited property partnership

Objektkosten object cost (expenditure), asset-related cost

Objektkredit 1. project-tied loan (lending), purpose loan □ loan facility repaid through the cash flow generated by the assets financed 2. real property loan

Objektmanagement property (facility) management

Objektprüfung 1. project evaluation 2. property valuation (assessment), valuation of the property offered as security for a loan

Objekt / ~rentabilität property yield; **~risiken** property risks (exposure), risks connected with a property; **~volumen** properties under management; **~wert** property value; **~wertermittlung** property valuation

obliegen to be responsible for, to be incumbent upon, *(die Gesamtverantwortung obliegt dem Vorstand)* the ultimate responsibility rests with the Management Board, (*Überwachungspflichten ~ der Aufsichtsbehörde des Heimatlandes)* supervisory duties rest with (fall within the province of) the home country's supervisory authority

Obliegenheit obligation, duty

Obliegenheitsverletzung failure to comply with an obligation

Obligation debenture, bond

Obligationär debenture holder, bondholder

obligationenähnlich (*~e Titel)* debenture-like securities

Obligationen-Fonds bond fund

Obligations / **~gläubiger** bond creditor; **~schuld** debenture debt; **~schuldner** bond debtor; **~zinsen** debenture (bond) interest

obligatorisch obligatory, mandatory, compulsory, *(~ es Schlichtungsverfahren)* mandatory conciliation procedure

Obligo liability, exposure, commitment, *(sich im ~ befinden)* to be committed, to be liable, to be exposed to, *(wir befinden uns mit … im ~)* our exposure (liability) totals …, *(im ~ bleiben)* to remain liable (committed)

O

Obligo aus *(~ Fremdwährungs-Positionen)* currency exposure, exposure in foreign currencies (foreign exchange), *(~ Gewährleistungen)* warranty exposure, *(~ unter unserer Haftung hinausgelegten Krediten)* liability on loans extended against guarantees furnished by us, *(~ kurzfristigen/langfristigen Kreditengagements)* short-term/long-term lending exposure

(~ Problemkrediten) problem exposure, exposure from problem loans, *(~ der Übernahme von Garantien)* exposure from guarantee commitments (undertakings), *(~ Vertragsabschlüssen)* contract exposure, *(~ diskontierten Wechseln)* liability on bills discounted

Obligo / **~anrechnung** counting towards the exposure; **~begrenzung** limitation of liability, limiting the exposure; **~beurteilung** exposure rating (assessment); **~buch** commitment ledger; **~erfassung** recording the exposure; **~kontrolle** monitoring the liabilities (e. g. on bills), exposure control

Obligo / **~limit** exposure (position) limit; **~übernahme** assumption of liability, taking on the exposure (the liability); **~überwachung** monitoring the exposure; **~verringerung** exposure reduction, lowering the exposure

obsiegende Partei prevailing party

oD/oDb → ohne Dividendenschein/Dividendenscheinbogen

Oder-Konto joint account with individual drawing powers

offen 1. open **2.** *(blanko)* blank, in blank **3.** *(öffentlich)* public **4.** *(unbesetzt)* vacant **5.** *(unbezahlt)* unpaid, unsettled **6.** *(ungeklärt)* unclear, unsettled, open

offen *(~ es Absetzen)* deduction on the face of the balance sheet, *(~ e Ankaufszusagen)* undrawn purchase commitments, *(~er Buchkredit)* open account credit, *(~es Depot)* standard custody account

(~es Factoring) notification factoring, *(~e Handelsgesellschaft)* general partnership, *(~er Immobilienfonds)* open-ended property fund, *(~es Indossament)* blank endorsement, *(~ es Interesse)* open interest, open contracts, number of unliquidated derivatives contracts

(~er Investmentfonds) open-end fund □ an investment company without a fixed capitalisation, i.e. it offers and redeems shares continuously, *(~e Kreditlinie)* unused or partially used credit line, *(~ es Orderbuch)* open order book, *(~e Police)* open cover (policy)

(~ e Position) (a) open position, open commitment *(b) (nicht regulierte Position)* unsettled position, uncleared item *(c) (nicht durch ein Gegengeschäft gedeckte bzw. glattgestellte Position)* open (unmatched) position, unliqui-

dated position, *(auf ~e Rechnung liefern)* to deliver on open account, *(~e Rücklagen)* disclosed (general) reserves, surplus
(~er Saldo) open (outstanding) balance, *(~ e Selbstfinanzierung)* funding from disclosed retained earnings, *(~es Treuhandkonto)* open trustee account □ account kept in the name of a notary or solicitor at a bank, but clearly identified as a client's account
(~ e Währungsposition) outstanding (unmatched) currency position, *(~e Wechselbürgschaft)* direct bill guarantee □ providing a guarantee by signing the bill and adding "as guarantor"; → verdeckte Wechselbürgschaft, *(~e Wertpapierleihgeschäfte)* free-market (over-the-counter) securities lending □ as opposed to lending through security clearing organisations
(~ es Wertpapierpensionsgeschäft) open repurchase transaction, open repo, repo with no definite maturity □ may be terminated by the borrower or lender at any time, *(~e Zession)* disclosed assignment, assignment on a notification basis, *(~ e Zinsforderungen)* **1.** uncollected interest **2.** unsettled interest receivables

Offenbarungseid debtor's oath

offen bleiben 1. *(nicht gedeckt durch ein Gegengeschäft)* to remain unmatched **2.** *(offenbleiben für)* to remain open

offen halten to keep open, *(die Kreditlinie ~)* to keep the credit line (facility) open, *(die Möglichkeit ~)* to hold out the possibility (prospect), *(eine Position ~)* to keep a position running

offenkundig obvious, apparent, *(eine ~ politische Zinssenkung)* an overtly political cut in interest rates

offenlassen *(die Entscheidung ~)* to leave the decision open, to leave the matter undecided

offenlegen 1. *(die wirtschaftlichen Verhältnisse ~)* to disclose the financial situation **2.** *(das hohe Risiko ~)* to reveal (to expose) the high risk

Offenlegung disclosure, revelation, *(~ der Abtretung)* disclosure of the assignment, disclosure of assigned claims, *(~ des Kreditrisikos)* credit risk disclosure, *(~ des Marktwertes)* fair value disclosure

Offenlegungs / ~anforderungen disclosure requirements; **~pflicht** duty to disclose, disclosure requirement (obligation); **~recht** right to disclosure; **~verordnung** Disclosure Regulation; **~vorschriften** disclosure rules (provisions)

offenmarktfähig eligible for open-market operations

Offenmarkt / ~-Geschäfte open-market operations (transactions); **~-Käufe** buying in the open market, open-market purchases; **~-Papiere** open-market paper (securities); **~-Politik** open-market policy

offensichtlich obvious, apparent, *(~ e Nichtigkeit)* manifest nullity

offenstehen to be outstanding, to remain unpaid (unsettled), *(~de Forderung)* outstanding (unsettled) claim, *(~de Rechnung)* unpaid invoice, unsettled account

öffentlich *(~e Aktiennotierung)* public equity listing, *(~es Angebot)* public offer, *(~e Anleihen)* public sector bonds, government bonds □ bonds issued by the Federal Government, by State and Local Governments, *(~e Anleiheemission)* issue of public sector bonds, public debt issue, *(~er Anleihemarkt)* public debt market
(~e Banken) public sector banks, *(~es Baudarlehen)* public housing loan, *(~e Begebung)* public offering, public flotation, *(~e Bekanntmachung)* gazetting, public notification (advertisement), official notice, *(~e Betriebe)* → öffentliche Unternehmen, *(~e Beurkundung)* attestation by a notary public
(~e Darlehensnehmer) public sector borrowers, *(~ e Deckungsmasse)* public sector cover pool, *(~e Einnahmen)* public revenue, *(~e Emission)* public

issue (offering), *(~e Finanzen)* public finance, public sector finances, *(~e Fördermittel)* public funds (funding), *(~es Förderprogramm)* public development (assistance) scheme, *(~e Gelder)* public (government) funds
(~e Hand) public sector, public authorities, *(Kreditwürdigkeit der ~ en Hand)* public credit, *(Verschuldung der ~ en Hand)* public debt, *(~e Haushalte)* public sector entities (bodies), *(~es Kaufangebot)* public offering, *(~e Körperschaft)* public entity, public sector corporation
(~es Kreditprogramm) public (government) lending scheme, *(~e Lasten auf einem Grundstück)* public easements, public charges on land, *(~ e Pfandbriefe)* Public Covered Bonds, Public Pfandbriefe □ Pfandbriefe secured against public sector loans, *(~e Platzierung)* public placing
(~er Schlüssel) public key, *(~ e Schuldenverwaltung)* public debt management, *(~er Sektor)* public sector, *(~e Stellen)* public-sector entities, public agencies, *(~e Unternehmen/Wirtschaftsbetriebe)* **1.** public sector corporations, public undertakings (enterprise) **2.** *(Versorgungsbetriebe)* public utilities, *(~e Urkunde)* public deed, deed drawn up before an official agency or notary public
(~er Vertrieb) public distribution, sale of securities to the general public, *(~e Wertpapieremission)* public securities offering, publicly offered securities, *(~es Wohnungsbaudarlehen)* public housing loan, *(~es Zeichnungsangebot)* public offering, public offer for sale, public issue by prospectus

öffentlich bestellt *(~er und vereidigter Sachverständiger)* officially appointed and sworn expert

öffentlich gefördert government-assisted, government-aided, promoted with public funds, *(~e Darlehen zur Existenzgründung)* government-subsidised business start-up loans, business start-up scheme, *(~er Wohnungsbau)* government-assisted housing construction

öffentlich gehandelt *(~e Wertpapiere)* publicly traded securities

öffentlich-privat *(~e Partnerschaft)* public-private partnership (PPP)

öffentlich-rechtlich *(~e Grundkreditanstalt)* public sector mortgage bank, *(~e Körperschaft)* public law corporation, *(~e Kreditinstitute)* public sector banks, credit institutions incorporated under public law (owned mostly by municipalities and municipal associations), *(~es Kreditwesen)* public sector banking, *(~es Sondervermögen)* public fund, *(~er Träger)* public guarantor, *(~es Unternehmen)* public law entity

öffentlich verbürgt *(~e Darlehen/Kredite)* loans secured by a government (local authority) guarantee

Öffentlichkeit public, *(breite ~)* general public

Offerte **1.** *(Kreditofferte)* loan offer **2.** *(Zeichnungsangebot)* offer, offering

Offertgarantie bid bond

Offizialverteidiger court-appointed attorney

offiziell *(~e Ankündigung)* official (formal) announcement

öffnen *(sich internationalen Anlegern ~)* to open up to international investors

Öffnung **1.** opening **2.** *(~ der Zinsschere)* widening of the interest rate gap

OGAW → Organismen für gemeinsame Anlagen in Wertpapieren

OGAW-konformer Fonds UCITS compliant fund

OGAW-Richtlinien I-IV UCITS Directives I-IV □ EU rules designed to allow investment funds authorised in one Member State to market its units in another Member State. Key features: range of products into which UCITS are able to invest, introduction of a management company passport, simplified prospectus. UCITS IV, in particular, aims at improving the single market framework for UCITS compliant funds by entity asset pooling through master-feeder structures and at establishing a uniform high standard for the protection of investors.

OHG → Offene Handelsgesellschaft

ohne *(~ Dividendenschein/Dividendenscheinbogen)* without coupon/coupon sheet, *(~ jedwede Gewähr/Obligo)* without any liability/responsibility, *(~ Rückgriff)* no (without) recourse

OIS → Übernachtindex-Swap

Ökonomie **1.** economics **2.** *(Sparsamkeit)* economy

ökonomisch **1.** economic **2.** *(sparsam)* economical

ökonomisch *(~es Kapital) (i. S. von Basel II)* economic capital □ capital required to cover unexpected losses from risk positions, *(~e Kapitalentlastung)* economic capital relief, *(~er Mehrwert)* economic value added

Ombudsmannverfahren ombudsman scheme

Omega same as → Kappa

Omnibusbefragung multi-client survey, omnibus survey (interview)

Online-Autorisierung online authorisation

operationell *(~es Risiko) (i. S. von Basel II)* operational risk □ exposure to loss from inadequate or failed internal processes or from external events

operativ *(~e Einheit)* operating unit, *(~es Ergebnis)* earnings before interest and taxes (EBIT), operating performance, *(~e Erträge)* operating revenue, *(~e Gesellschaft)* operating company, *(~e Holding)* operative holding company, *(~e Verfahren)* operational procedures

ÖPP Projektgesellschaft PPP project company

Opportunitätsfonds opportunity (opportunistic) fund

Opportunitätskosten opportunity cost

Opposition opposition, *(von Schecks/Wertpapieren)* stop, stop order, *(mit ~ belegen)* to stop payment, *(mit ~ belegte Wertpapiere)* stopped securities, *(auf ~ stoßen)* to run into opposition

Oppositionsliste list of securities invalidated or stopped

optieren *(zur Regelbesteuerung ~)* to opt for standard taxation

optimal *(~ nutzen)* to make the best possible use, *(~e Bestellmenge)* optimal order quantity (size), *(~e Konditionen)* best possible terms (rates)

Optimierung *(~ des Kreditgeschäfts)* optimising lending operations

Optimismus optimism, bullishness, upbeat mood

optimistisch optimistic, bullish, upbeat, *(~ hinsichtlich des Aktienmarktes)* to be (to feel) optimistic about the equity market, to be bullish (cheerful) about the outlook for equities, *(~e Beurteilung)* upbeat assessment (e. g. of economic trends), *(~e Prognose)* upbeat forecast, bullish forecast, *(~e Stimmung)* upbeat mood, buoyant tone

Option option, *(Kaufoption)* call, *(Verkaufsoption)* put

Option auf *(~ Aktien/einen Aktienindex)* stock (equity) option/stock index option, *(~ einen Festzinsempfänger-Swap)* receiver swaption, put swaption, *(~ einen Festzinszahler-Swap)* payer swaption, call swaption, *(~ eine andere Option)* compound option *(~ vorzeitige Rückzahlung)* pre-payment option, *(~ einen Terminkontrakt)* futures option, option on a futures contract, *(~ Umwandlung einer Festsatzverpflichtung in eine zinsvariable Verpflichtung)* floating rate pricing option, *(~ eine Zinsbegrenzungsvereinbarung)* caption, *(~ einen Zins-Swap)* swaption

optionsähnlich *(~e Zinsinstrumente)* interest rate instruments similar in nature to options

Options / ~anleihe bond with warrants, bond cum warrants, cum-warrant-bond, warrant-linked bond, *(nach Abtrennung des Optionsscheines)* bond ex warrants; **~aufgabe** option abandonment, allowing an option to expire; **~ausübung** option exercise, exercising (taking up) an option

Options / ~basispreis option exercise (strike) price; **~bedingungen** option terms; **~bewertung** option valuation; **~bewertungsmodell** option valuation model; **~börse** options exchange, options market

Options / ~darlehen loan carrying a conversion option □ e. g. option to reschedule into a long-term facility; **~erklärung** option exercise notice; **~erwerb** buying an option, option purchase, taking out an option, opening a long option position; **~erwerber** option buyer (taker)

Options / ~fonds option fund, fund specialising in option investments; **~frist** option period, life of an option; **~gegenstand** option instrument, underlying instrument; **~geschäft** option contract (bargain, deal); **~handel** options trading; **~inhaber** option holder

Options / ~käufer option buyer; **~klasse** option class; **~konsortium** optional underwriting group □ underwriting arrangement whereby a banking group underwrites only one tranche of an issue with the option to underwrite further tranches; **~kontrakt** option contract; **~laufzeit** → Optionsfrist

Options / ~nehmer option buyer, option taker, optionee; **~papiere 1.** *(veroptionierte Papiere)* optioned securities **2.** *(Titel mit Optionsscheinen)* securities with warrants

Optionsposition option position, *(Eröffnung einer ~)* opening an option position, *(einer Kaufposition)* going long, buying a call/a put, *(einer Verkaufsposition)* going short, selling a call/a put, *(Eröffnung und Schließung einer ~)* round turn, round trip

Optionsprämie option premium, *(erhaltene ~n)* option premiums earned, premiums from options written

Optionspreis option premium, option money; **~bildung** option pricing; **~modell** option pricing model

Optionsrecht option, option right, right conveyed by an option, *(~ auf den Bezug von Aktien)* stock purchase option, equity warrant, *(~ auf den Bezug von Anleihestücken)* bond warrant

Optionsschein warrant, *(~ auf eine Aktie/einen Aktienindex)* equity warrant/ stock index warrant

Optionsschein / ~aufgeld warrant premium; **~ausübung** warrant exercise, exercising a warrant; **~bedingungen** warrant terms; **~-Emission** warrant issue; **~fonds** warrant fund; **~handel** warrant trading

Optionsschein / ~inhaber warrant holder; **~kosten** warrant cost; **~kurs** warrant price; **~markt** warrant market; **~preis** warrant price; **~serie** warrant series; **~wert** warrant value

Options / ~schuldner *(bei Optionsscheinen)* warrant debtor; **~schuldverschreibung** → Optionsanleihe; **~serie** option series □ all option contracts on the same instrument with the same delivery date, the same exercise price and the same expiry date

Options / ~stelle *(bei Optionsscheinen)* warrant agent; **~strategie** option strategy; **~titel** warrant debt; **~übertragung** option transfer

Options / ~verfall expiry of an option; **~verfalltag** expiry date of an option; **~verkauf** option sale, writing options, *(von Kaufoptionen)* call writing, *(von Verkaufsoptionen)* put writing; **~verkäufer** option writer (seller), option grantor; **~volatilität** option volatility; **~wert** option value

ordentlich 1. proper, *(~er Kaufmann)* conscientious (orderly) businessman, → ordnungsgemäß
2. *(planmäßig)* ordinary, regular, *(~e Abschreibung)* regular depreciation,

O

(*~es Betriebsergebnis)* ordinary operating profit/loss, *(~e Deckung)* ordinary cover, *(~es Ergebnis)* result on ordinary activities
(~e Erträge) (eines Investmentfonds) ordinary income (interest and dividends), *(~e Geschäftstätigkeit)* ordinary business, *(~e Hauptversammlung)* ordinary general meeting
(~es Insolvenzverfahren) regular insolvency proceedings □ split into → vorläufiges Insolvenzverfahren, → eröffnetes Insolvenzverfahren, *(~e Kapitalherabsetzung)* regular capital write-down

Order *(Börsenorder)* order, *(an ~ von)* to the order of, *(an ~ lautend)* made out to order, *(an fremde ~)* to the order of a third party, *(gemäß Ihrer ~)* as per your order

Order / **~abwicklung** order processing (handling), settlement of buy and sell orders; **~annahme** acceptance of orders; **~aufbereitung** order documentation; **~aufkommen** total buy and sell orders, volume turnover

Order / **~ausführung** execution of an order, executing (filling) an order, → Ausführungsgrundsätze; **~buch** order book, *(Orderbuch des Skontroführers)* order book of the lead broker; **~eingang** order intake, incoming orders

ordergeleitet *(~er Auktionsmarkt)* order-driven auction market

ordergesteuert *(~er Handel)* order-driven system

Order / **~klausel** order clause; **~konnossement** order bill of lading; **~lagerschein** order warehouse warrant; **~leitsystem** order routing system; **~mangel** *(Börse)* shortage of buy orders (of buying interest)

Order / **~papiere** instruments made out to order, to-the-order instruments, registered securities; **~scheck** cheque to order, order cheque; **~schlussnote** order contract note; **~schuldverschreibung** bond payable to order, order bond; **~streichung** cancelling an order

Order / **~tätigkeit** buying activity; **~-Übermittlungssystem** order routing system; **~volumen** *(Börse)* total buy orders; **~weiterleitung** order routing, passing on orders; **~zusammenführung** matching of orders

ordnen **1.** *(arrangieren)* to arrange, to classify **2.** *(regeln)* to regulate **3.** → Ordnung, in ~ bringen

Ordnung **1.** order **2.** *(Anordnung)* classification, arrangement **3.** *(Rang)* rank **4.** *(Reihenfolge)* order, sequence, *(die Finanzlage in ~ bringen)* to set the finances right, to straighten out (to sort out, to disentangle) the financial problems

Ordnungsfunktion regulative function

ordnungsgemäß **1.** *adj.* proper, due, regular, *(~e Abwicklung)* proper settlement, *(~e Dokumente: im Akkreditivgeschäft)* documents in accordance with the terms and conditions of the documentary credit, *(~e Erfüllung)* satisfactory performance, *(~er Handel)* fair and orderly trading
2. *adv.* properly, in due form, *(~ ausgefertigte Garantie)* duly executed guarantee, *(~ ausgeführt)* properly carried out (transacted), duly effected, *(~ ausgestellt)* properly issued (drawn up), drawn up in due form, *(~ bediente Kredite)* performing loans, properly serviced loans, satisfactory loans, *(nicht ordnungsgemäß bediente Kredite)* impaired loans, *(~ bevollmächtigter Vertreter)* duly authorised representative (agent), *(~ zur Zahlung vorgelegt)* duly presented for payment

Ordnungsmäßigkeit regularity, correctness, *(die ~ des Akkreditivs feststellen)* to note (to be satisfied) that the terms and conditions stipulated in the documentary credit have been complied with

Ordnungsrahmen regulatory framework (environment)

Ordnungswidrigkeit administrative offence

Organ 1. body, institution **2.** governing body, Board Member

Organ / ~befugnisse executive powers; **~bereich** scope of a group, scope of consolidation; **~bestellungsrecht** right to appoint board members; **~ertrag** income from controlled companies

Organgesellschaft 1. dependent (controlled) company, group member, subsidiary corporation
2. tax group subsidiary, → Organschaft

Organhaftung management liability

Organigramm organisational (organisation) chart, org chart

Organisation organisation

Organisations / ~abläufe organisational (and administrative) processes, organisational flows; **~anweisungen** organisational directives; **~beratung** organisational consultancy (counselling); **~ebene** organisational level; **~einheit** organisational unit

Organisations / ~kontrolle organisation control; **~kosten** organisational cost; **~optimierung** organisational process optimisation; **~plan/~schema** organisation(al) chart, org chart; **~richtlinien** organisational guidelines (directives); **~struktur** organisational structure (pattern)

organisatorisch *(~er Aufbau)* organisational setup, *(~e Fähigkeiten)* organisational skills, *(~e Silos auflösen)* to break down silos, *(~er Umbau)* organisational restructuring (overhaul)

organisieren to organise, to arrange, *(Handel an einem organisierten Markt)* trading in an organised market

Organisierte Handelsfazilitäten Organised Trading Facilties (OTFs) □ according to EU Commission proposals any system/facility operated by a securities or brokerage firm that facilitates the buying and selling of financial instruments

Organismen für gemeinsame Anlagen in Wertpapieren (OGAW) Undertakings for the Collective Investment in Transferable Securities (UCITS)

Organ / ~klage institutional litigation; **~kredite** loans (lendings) to senior management staff and related parties; **~kreis 1.** consolidated companies, scope of consolidation **2.** tax group, → Organschaft

Organ / ~mitglieder 1. board members **2.** tax group members; **~mutter** parent company

Organschaft *(steuerrechtlich)* fiscal unity, tax group, tax consolidation □ tax pooling arrangement between a domestic parent company and its domestic subsidiaries, i.e. all companies are treated as an integrated fiscal unit (one taxable entity), *(Organschaft für Körperschafts-, Gewerbe-, Umsatzsteuerzwecke)* fiscal unity for corporate income/trade income/value added tax purposes

organschaftlich *(~e Einbindung)* integration into the group, *(~e Stellung)* position in the group, *(~e Vertreter einer Gesellschaft)* authorised representatives, *(~e Vertretung)* representation by the company's authorised representatives

Organschaftserklärung 1. → Organschaftsvertrag
2. letter of comfort □ group parent's undertaking towards the subsidiary's lending bank not to terminate the controlling agreement without the lending bank's prior approval

Organschafts / ~kette fiscal unity chain; **~mitglieder** board members; **~modell** concept of fiscal unity, concept of a single entity for tax purposes; **~vertrag** fiscal unity (tax consolidation) agreement, agreement on treatment as a single entity for tax purposes, → Organschaft

Organ / ~stellung management position; **~töchter** tax group subsidiaries; **~träger** parent company, dominant entity, lead business entity

Organ / ~vergütung remuneration of board members; **~verhältnis** → Organschaft; **~verlust** loss incurred by a controlled company; **~vertrag** → Organschaftsvertrag; **~vertreter** management representative

originär *(~er Firmenwert)* non-purchased (self-generated) goodwill, *(~es Schuldinstrument (zu einem eingebetteten Derivat)* host debt instrument

originieren *(~de Bank)* originating (originator) bank

orientieren *(die Aktiennotierungen in Frankfurt orientierten sich an Wall Street)* German equities took their cue from Wall Street, *(am Kapitalmarkt orientierte Anleiheausstattung)* bond pricing orientated at (geared to) the prevailing capital market rates
(an der Leistung orientierte Ausschüttung) performance-linked (performance-geared) payout, *(die Zinssätze ~ sich an den Geldmarktsätzen)* interest rates take their lead (take their bearings) from money market rates

Orientierung 1. orientation, bearing(s), direction 2. guidance, information, *(zu Ihrer ~)* for your guidance (information)

Orientierungs / ~größe benchmark; **~hilfe** *(~ geben)* to provide (to give) guidance; **~konditionen** guiding rates (terms); **~marke** benchmark

Original original; **~-Konnossement** original bill of lading; **~urkunde** original document (deed); **~wechsel** first bill of exchange

Ort place, site, *(~ der Lieferung/Zahlung)* place of delivery/payment, *(vor ~ verfügbar)* to be on hand locally

Orts / ~ausschuss *(im Freiverkehr)* supervisory body for the unofficial market, → Freiverkehr; **~basisrisiko** locational basis risk; **~geschäft** local transaction; **~zahlungsverkehr** town payments

Oszillator oscillator □ indicator that measures a stock price relative to its high/low range; signals overbought or oversold situations

OTC-Derivatehandel OTC (Over-the-Counter) derivatives trading

OTC-Derivateverordnung OTC Derivatives Regulation

P

Paarvergleichstest paired comparison test

Pacht lease; ~**besitz** leasehold property, leasehold land and buildings

pachten to lease, to take on lease

Pächter leaseholder, tenant

Pacht / ~**erträge** lease income; ~**vertrag** lease, tenancy agreement; ~**zins** rental rate

Paket *(Aktienpaket)* large block (of shares), share block

Paket / ~**abschlag** large-block discount □ discount on the market price for a large block of shares sold; ~**angebot** block offer; ~**aufschlag** large-block premium □ for a large block of shares bought; ~**besitz** large shareholding □ holding more than 5% of the company's capital

Paket / ~**handel** large-block trading, off-board trading in large blocks; ~**lösung 1.** package (comprehensive) solution **2.** *(zusammenhängende Lieferungen und Leistungen)* bundled sales arrangement; ~**transaktion** large-block trade (transaction); ~**zuschlag** → Paketaufschlag

Palette range, spectrum, *(~ der Anlagemöglichkeiten)* range (spectrum) of investment vehicles, *(~ der Dienstleistungen)* range of services offered

PAngV → Preisangabeverordnung

Panik / ~**käufe** panic buying; ~**kurse** panic prices; ~**verkäufe** sellout, panic (distress) selling

Papier 1. *(Urkunde)* document **2.** *(Wechsel)* paper, bill **3.** *(Wertpapier)* security, stock, *(~e erster Adressen)* securities issued by prime (first-rate) companies

Papierform *(in ~ zur Verfügung stellen)* to provide in hard copy (on paper)

Papier / ~**geld** paper money; ~**währung** paper currency (standard); ~**wert** paper (fictitious) value

Paragraph paragraph, section

parallel *adj. (~er Trendkanal)* parallel trend channel *adv. (sich ~ entwickeln)* to move in tandem

Parallel / ~**anleihen** parallel bonds □ identical bonds floated by the issuer in several countries; ~**finanzierung** parallel financing; ~**geschäft 1.** parallel deal (contract) **2.** → Mitlaufen; ~**kredit** parallel loan, back-to-back credit; ~**markt** parallel market; ~**währung** parallel standard

Parameter parameter; ~**einstellungen** parametric settings

Parantelen-Erbfolge per stirpes succession

paraphieren to initial

Paraphierung initialling

Pari / ~**-Bezugsrecht** par rights issue; ~**-Emission** issue at par, par issue; ~**-Kurs** par price; ~**-Rückzahlung** redemption (repayment) at par, *(weit unter ~ notierende Anleihen)* deeply discounted bonds

Parität parity, exchange rate between two currencies

Paritäten-Gitter parity grid

paritätisch equal, composed of equal numbers

Paritäts / ~**änderung** parity change; ~**klausel** parity clause; ~**kurs** parity price (rate); ~**prüfung** parity check

Pariwert par value

parken *(Gelder ~)* to park funds, to invest (to deposit) temporarily, to place on temporary deposit, → Parkplatz

Parkett *(Börse)* floor, *(auf dem ~ gehandelte Aktien)* floor-traded stocks

Parketthandelssystem floor trading system, open outcry trading

Parkplatz temporary repository (short-term home) for funds

Partei 1. *(in einem Rechtsstreit)* party (to a lawsuit), *(beklagte ~)* defending party, defendant, *(klagende ~)* plaintiff, claimant, *(gegnerische ~)* opposing (adverse) party
2. *(Vertragspartei)* contracting party, party to a contract (to an agreement), *(beteiligte ~)* party in interest, interested party

parteifähig capable of being party to a lawsuit

parteiisch partial, bias(s)ed, prejudiced

Parteilichkeit partiality, bias

parteilos 1. independent, non-party, non-aligned **2.** *(unvoreingenommen)* unbias(s)ed, impartial

Partenreederei ship-owning partnership

partiarisch *(~es Darlehen)* loan linked to an equity kicker □ i.e. the lender is given a share in the borrower's capital, profit or sales

Partie 1. *(Los)* lot **2.** *(Sendung)* consignment

partienweise *(~ Freigabe)* lot-by-lot release

Partikularinsolvenzverfahren separate (territorial) insolvency proceedings

Partizipations / ~recht right of (to) participation; **~schein/~zertifikat** participation certificate (warrant)

partizipieren to participate, to partake, *(an einer Emission ~)* to take part in an issue, *(zu gleichen Teilen ~)* to take equal shares

Partner partner, associate; **~banken** partner banks; **~schaft** partnership

Partnerschaftsgesellschaft professional partnership

Partnerschaftsgesellschaftsgesetz German Professional Partnership Act

Parzelle lot, parcel, plot

parzellieren to parcel out, to divide into lots

Parzellierung parcelling (out), division into lots, subdivision

passen *(zu der neuen Strategie ~)* to fit (to tie) in with the new strategy

passiv *(~e Anlagestrategie)* passive investment strategy □ e.g. investing in portfolios (index funds) that replicate the performance of an index
(~er Konsolidierungsausgleichsposten) negative consolidation difference, *(~e latente Steuern)* deferred tax liabilities, *(~e Leistungsbilanz)* current account deficit, *(~es Portefeuille)* passive (index-linked) portfolio, → passive Anlagestrategie
(~e Rechnungsabgrenzungsposten) deferred income (revenue) □ income received but for which the material/services have not yet been supplied, → abgrenzen, *(in die ~ e Rechnungsabgrenzung einstellen)* to show under deferred items on the liabilities side; *(~e Rückversicherung)* → Rückdeckung, *(~e Scheckfähigkeit)* capacity to have cheques drawn on oneself
(~er Unterschiedsbetrag) → passivischer Unterschiedsbetrag, *(~er Verrechnungssaldo)* clearing deficit, negative clearing balance, *(~e Wirtschaftsgüter)* liabilities and economic charges

Passiva 1. liabilities **2.** *(Bilanz-Passivseite)* shareholders' equity and liabilities

Passiv / ~ausweis disclosure under equity and liabilities; **~devisenposition** short currency position; **~engpass** shortage of deposits; **~finanzierung** debt and equity financing, → Aktivfinanzierung

Passiv / ~gelder deposits; **~geschäft** *(der Kreditinstitute)* deposit banking,

P

deposit operations, deposit-taking business

passivierbar eligible for expensing

passivieren to expense, to recognise as (in) liabilities, to carry (to report) as a liability, to enter (to state) on the liabilities side, *(als Rückstellung ~)* to recognise (to carry) as a provision

Passivierung 1. expensing, carrying (reporting) as liabilities, entry on the liabilities side **2.** trend towards a deficit

Passivierungs / ~fähigkeit eligibility for expensing; **~gebot/~pflicht** requirement to expense (to enter on the liabilities side); **~wahlrecht** option to report as a liability, expensing option

passivisch 1. *adj.* *(~e Bestände)* short positions, *(~e Bestandskonten)* liability accounts, *(~e Festzinslücke)* liabilities-related fixed rate gap, *(~e Festzinsposition)* fixed rate position on the liabilities side, *(~e Posten)* liability items, *(~es Terminrisiko)* liabilities-related time risk □ loss to the bank resulting from the premature withdrawal of deposits
(~er Unterschiedsbetrag) deficit, negative difference, balancing item on the liabilities side
2. *adv.* *(~ ausweisen)* to state (to report) on the liabilities side

P

Passiv / ~klage action as defendant, *(im Insolvenzrecht)* action brought against the insolvency estate; **~konditionen** deposit rates, interest rates paid on deposits; **~kundschaft** depositors, savers

Passiv / ~management liabilities management; **~mehrungen** liability additions; **~minderungen** liability cuts

Passiv / ~position short position; **~prozess** litigation as defendant, → Passivklage, *(Aufnahme von ~ en)* joinder of pending actions as defendant; **~saldo** adverse (debit) balance, deficit

Passiv / ~seite liabilities side, liabilities section of the balance sheet; **~steuerung** liabilities management; **~-Swap** liability swap; **~tausch** debt-for-debt swap

Passiv / ~überhang 1. net deficit, net liability position, surplus of liabilities
2. *(im Devisenhandel)* net short position
3. *(im Geldhandel)* net borrowing position, net borrowings, net borrowing position in interbank dealings
4. *(Zinsbindungsbilanz)* net fixed rate position, payable

Passiv / ~umlauf liabilities outstanding; **~vorlauf** *(im Hypothekengeschäft)* issuance of covered mortgage bonds without matching lending transactions; **~wechsel** bills payable; **~zins 1.** deposit rate, interest paid on deposits **2.** interest payable

Patronats / ~erklärung letter of comfort, keep well agreement; **~geberin** guarantor; **~haftung** parent company's (guarantor's) liability

patroniert *(~es Unternehmen)* supported enterprise, company for which a letter of comfort has been issued

Patronin guarantor

pauschal lump-sum, all-in, *(~e Abschreibung des Firmenwertes)* flat-rate amortisation of goodwill, *(~er Bewertungsabschlag)* *(a)* general valuation discount *(b) (Sicherheitsabschlag)* general haircut, *(~ in Rechnung stellen)* to charge a flat fee (a flat rate, a lump sum), *(~ wertberichtigen)* to set up a general valuation allowance

Pauschal / ~abschlag flat deduction (haircut); **~betrag** lump sum; **~deckung** blanket cover (coverage), whole-turnover cover

Pauschale lump sum, flat fee, → Pauschalvergütung/~zahlung

Pauschal / ~gebühr all-in fee, flat fee (charge), blanket charge; **~gewichtung** flat rate weighting

pauschalieren 1. to fix a lump sum, to fix (to assess) a flat rate, to pool
2. to estimate (e. g. the tax charge)

3. *(pauschalierte Einzelwertberichtigungen)* collective specific valuation allowances

Pauschalierung fixing a lump sum (a flat rate)

Pauschal / ~methode flat rate method; **~prämie** flat rate premium; **~preis** lump-sum price, all-inclusive price; **~satz** flat rate; **~vergütung** flat rate remuneration, lump-sum compensation

Pauschal / ~wertberichtigung 1. general valuation allowance **2.** *(im Kreditgeschäft)* general loan loss allowance, general allowance established against the loan portfolio; **~zahlung** lump-sum payment; **~zuweisung** lump-sum appropriation

Pauschbetrag flat allowance (relief), standard deduction, non-itemised tax deduction

PD-Schätzung estimating the probability of default

pendeln 1. *(zwischen ... und ... ~)* to fluctuate between ... and ... **2.** *(um den Stand von ... ~)* to hover around ...

Pension 1. pension **2.** → Pensionsgeschäft, *(in ~ gegebene Wertpapiere)* securities sold under agreements to repurchase, *(in ~ genommene Wertpapiere)* securities purchased under agreements to resell, *(in Pension genommene und gegebene Wertpapiere)* securities repoed in and out

Pensions / ~anwartschaften pension entitlements; **~aufwendungen** pension cost; **~bedingungen** repo terms, terms of a repurchase agreement

pensionsfähig *(~e Papiere)* securities eligible for repo transactions

Pensionsgeber pledgor, transferor, borrower

Pensionsgeschäft repurchase agreement, repo arrangement (agreement) □ the borrower pledges or sells specific assets to the lender but simultaneously undertakes to repurchase the same assets at a later date, → echtes, → unechtes Pensionsgeschäft, *(~ in Devisen)* currency repurchase agreement

Pensionsgut item (instrument) pledged, *(bei einem Wertpapierpensionsgeschäft)* security repoed

Pensions / ~kasse pension fund, staff pension scheme; **~leistungen** pension benefits; **~nehmer** pledgee, transferee, lender; **~satz** repo rate; **~sondervermögen** pension fund

Pensions / ~treuhand contractual trust arrangement; **~verpflichtungen 1.** pension liabilities **2.** liabilities under repurchase agreements, repo liabilities; **~wechsel** bill pledged (or sold) under a repurchase agreement

per *(~ Aval)* pour aval, *(~ Erscheinen)* if and when issued, *(~ 31. Januar)* as at 31st January

perfekt *(~e Sicherungsbeziehung)* perfect hedge □ derivative position that exactly offsets any gains or losses from the underlying cash position

Perioden / ~abgrenzung accrual accounting, *(Grundsatz der ~)* accrual principle, accrual method of accounting; **~aufwand** expenditure for the period; **~durchschnittskurs** average rate for the period

periodenecht *(~er Gewinn)* real (actual) profit for the period under review

Periodenerfolg / ~ergebnis net income for the period (under review), results for the period

periodengerecht 1. *adj.* *(~e Bilanzierung)* accrual basis of accounting, *(~e Einkommensermittlung)* determination of income on an accrual basis, *(~er Erfolgsausweis/Gewinnermittlung)* reporting profits on an accrual basis, period profit accounting, *(~e Rechnungslegung)* accrual basis of accounting, *(~e Zurechnung von Einnahmen und Ausgaben)* accrual of income and expenses
2. *adv.* *(~ ermitteln)* to determine on an accrual basis, *(~ verbuchen)* to record as it accrues

P

Perioden / ~**gerechtigkeit** accrual accounting; ~**gewinn** period profit

periodengleich *(~e Gewinnvereinnahmung)* in-period recognition of income

Perioden / ~**kosten** period cost; ~**rendite** period yield

periodenrichtig → periodengerecht

Perioden / ~**satz** periodic rate; ~**topf** time bucket; ~**vergleich** period comparison

periodisch **1.** periodic(al), *(~e Aufwandsverrechnung)* periodic expensing, *(~e Zinsanpassung)* regular interest rate reset
2. *(wiederkehrend)* recurring, recurrent

periodisieren to periodise, *(periodisierte Zugänge)* accrual-based additions

Periodisierungsprinzip accrual principle

permanent *(~e Differenzen)* permanent differences □ differences between book income and taxable income that will not be reversed over subsequent accounting periods

Personal **1.** staff, personnel **2.** human resources

Personalabbau laying off staff, staff reduction (trimming), reduction in staff levels (in staffing), job cuts, payroll cut, labour shedding, workforce reduction, *(~ um 500 Stellen)* laying off 500 staff, *(~ auf natürlichem Wege)* headcount reduction through natural fluctuation

Personal / ~**abteilung** Human Resources (HR) Division, HR unit, personnel department; ~**akte** personnel file; ~**analyse** personnel (manpower) audit; ~**anforderung** staffing request, HR (manpower) requisition

Personalarbeitskosten human resource (HR) cost, *(Personalarbeitskosten je MAK)* HR cost per FTE (full-time equivalent)

Personal / ~**aufwand** compensation and benefits, total payroll and benefit costs, human resource costs; ~**aufwandsquote** compensation ratio, ratio of compensation and benefits expense to net revenues; ~**ausstattung** staffing

Personal / ~**bedarf** staff (manpower) requirements; ~**bedarfsprognose** manpower requirements forecast; ~**berater** human resource consultant; ~**beratung** human resource consultancy

Personal / ~**beschaffung** HR (manpower) recruitment, manpower resourcing, staff procurement; ~**bestand** headcount, payroll, staffing level, total staff, personnel strength, manpower

Personal / ~**beurteilung** merit rating, performance appraisal, staff (personnel) rating; ~**bewegungen** staff changes, staff (personnel) turnover; ~**bogen** personal history sheet

Personal / ~**darlehen** → Personalkredit; ~**dienstleistungen** HR services; ~**einsparung** personnel (manpower) saving, headcount savings; ~**einstellung** employment of staff, HR (staff) recruitment

Personal / ~**entwicklung** human resources development (HRD); ~**fluktuation** human resource (employee, staff) turnover; ~**fluktuationsrate** HR turnover rate; ~**führung** human resources management (HRM), personnel management

personalintensiv *(~e Dienstleistungen)* staff-intensive services

Personalisierung *(~ von Kreditkarten)* personalisation of credit cards

Personal / ~**kennzahlen** human resource (HR) metrics; ~**knappheit** staff (manpower) shortage; ~**kosten** personnel expenditure, staff costs, → Personalaufwand

Personal / ~**kredit** unsecured loan, personal loan, personal drawing credit; ~**kreditgeschäft** personal lending operations

Personal / ~**leiter** HR manager, personnel (staff) manager; ~**leitung** human

P

resources management, personnel (staff) management; ~**organkredite** lendings to general partners, senior executives, members of supervisory bodies and their family members

Personal / ~planung personnel (manpower) planning, HR planning; ~**ressourcen** human (personnel) resources; ~**sicherheit** personal security; ~**stand**/~**stärke** headcount, payroll, staff level; ~**statut** staff regulations

Personal / ~union 1. management and/or staff sharing, two or more firms sharing management and staff **2.** one person holding two or more offices; ~**unterlagen** staff files (records)

Personal / ~vermögen personal property, personalty; ~**versorgungskasse** staff provident fund; ~**vertreter** staff representative; ~**vertretung** staff representation; ~**verwaltung** staff administration; ~**wirtschaft** personnel management; ~**zuwachs** staff increase, increase in the payroll

personenbezogen *(~er Datenschutz)* personal data privacy

Personen / ~depotbuch personal custody ledger; ~**handelsgesellschaft** commercial (trading) partnership; ~**tage** man days

Personen / ~unternehmen unincorporated business; ~**vereinigung** group of shareholders, group of individuals regarded as an entity (pursuing a common purpose)

persönlich 1. *adj. (~es Anschaffungsdarlehen)* consumer loan, *(~er Anspruch)* claim in personam, *(~e Beziehung zum Kunden)* person-to-person relationship, *(~e Dienstbarkeit)* personal easement, *(~er Dispositionskredit)* personal drawing credit, personal overdraft facility, *(~es Engagement)* personal commitment, *(~er Freibetrag)* personal allowance *(~e Kennnummer)* personal identification code/number (PIC/PIN), *(~e Kundenbetreuung)* individual counselling of customers, personal banking service, *(~er Kundenkontakt)* personal contact with the customer, *(~er Ratenkredit)* personal instalment loan, *(~er Service)* personalised service, *(~e Übergabe)* hand delivery, *(~es Vermögen)* personal effects (articles) **2.** *adv. (~ bekannt)* known personally, *(~ haftender Gesellschafter)* personally liable partner

Pessimismus *(~ am Markt)* pessimism (downbeat mood) in the market

pessimistisch pessimistic, bearish, *(~e Beurteilung)* downbeat assessment, *(~e Stimmung)* bearish mood, downbeat tone, *(~ schließen)* to end on a downbeat note, *(sich ~ zeigen)* to take a pessimistic (bearish) view, to paint a pessimistic picture

pfadabhängige Option path-dependent option □ payout upon exercise or expiration depends on the average value of the underlying instrument over a pre-determined period of time

Pfand 1. pawn, pledge **2.** *(Pfandrecht)* lien **3.** *(Sicherheit)* deposit, surety, guarantee

Pfand *(als ~ für alle bestehenden und künftigen Ansprüche der Bank dienen)* to serve as pledge (collateral) for all existing and future claims of the bank, *(in ~ geben)* to pawn, to pledge, to hypothecate, → Pfandkredit, *(als ~ hereingenommene Vermögenswerte)* assets taken in pledge (accepted as pledge)

Pfandauslösung pawn redemption, redemption of a pledge, redeeming the pledged property

pfändbar seiz(e)able, distrainable, attachable, *(~e Vermögensgegenstände)* leviable (attachable) assets

Pfandbestellung pawning, pledging, hypothecation

Pfandbestellungs / ~urkunde deed of pledge; ~**vertrag** pledge (hypothecation) agreement, memorandum of pledge

Pfandbrief Pfandbrief, Covered Bond □ Pfandbriefe are issued by private and public sector credit institutions or mortgage banks and are collateralised by a so-called cover pool consisting of high-quality mortgage loans or public sector loans. In the event of an issuer insolvency, the cover pool assets are separated from the issuing bank's other assets.

Pfandbrief / ~ausstattung Covered Bond terms; **~bank** Pfandbrief Bank □ credit institution licensed to engage in Pfandbrief operations, **~besicherung** collateralisation of Covered Bonds

Pfandbrief / ~deckungsstock Pfandbrief cover pool; **~deckungswerte** Pfandbrief cover assets; **~emittent** Pfandbrief issuer; **~fonds** Pfandbrief Fund □ invests exclusively in German Covered Bonds

Pfandbrief / ~geschäft Pfandbrief business, issuance of Covered Bonds; **~gesetz** German Pfandbrief Act, German Covered Bond Act; **~gläubiger** Pfandbrief (Covered Bond) creditor; **~index** German Pfandbrief Index (PEX) □ measures the performance of German Covered Bonds; **~inhaber** Pfandbrief (Covered Bond) holder

P

Pfandbrief / ~institut → Pfandbriefbank; **~markt** German Covered Bond market; **~nennwert** principal amount of the Pfandbrief; **~privileg** prerogative (right) to issue Pfandbriefe (Covered Bonds)

Pfandbrief / ~refinanzierung refinancing (funding) through the issue of Covered Bonds; **~rendite** Pfandbrief yield; **~spread** Pfandbrief spread, yield differential between government bonds and Pfandbriefe

Pfandbrief / ~umlauf Pfandbriefe (Covered Bonds) outstanding; **~verbindlichkeiten** Pfandbrief liabilities; **~zins** Pfandbrief (Covered Bond) coupon

Pfand / ~depot pledged securities account; **~effekten** pledged securities □ securities pledged as collateral for a loan; **~errichtung** creation of a pledge

pfänden to seize, to attach, to distrain, to levy a distress on, *(gepfändete Waren)* distressed goods

Pfandfreigabe release (discharge) of a pledge, releasing the pledged asset (item)

Pfandgeber pledgor, person (party) delivering goods in pledge

Pfandgegenstand pledged property (asset), pawned item, property subject to a lien, *(Befriedigung aus dem ~)* selling pledged property in satisfaction of a debt

Pfandgläubiger pledgee, person (party) to whom goods are delivered in pledge, *(Befriedigung der Ansprüche des ~s)* satisfaction of the pledgee's claims

Pfand / ~hergabe surrender of the pledge (pawned item); **~hinterlegung** pawning, depositing in pawn; **~indossament** endorsement for pledge, pledging endorsement; **~klausel** pawn (lien)clause

Pfandkredit *i.e.S.* pawnbroker loan, → Pfandleihe *i.w.S.* any loan against collateral (security)

Pfandkredit / ~betrieb pawnbroking institution; **~vertrag** pawnbroking agreement

Pfand / ~leihanstalt public pawnbroker; **~leihe** pawnbroker loan, short-term loan against goods delivered in pledge; **~leiher** pawnbroker; **~leiherverordnung** Pawnbroking Regulation; **~leihgeschäft** pawnbroking

Pfand / ~missbrauch unlawful use of a pledge; **~objekt** → Pfandgegenstand; **~nehmer** pledgee, → Pfandgläubiger; **~pool** collateral pool

Pfandrecht lien, charge, *(~ der Bank)* banker's lien, *(~ an Grundstücken)* real estate lien, charge over property, lien (encumbrance) upon property,

(*~e an Immobilien)* property (real estate) liens, *(~ an beweglichen Sachen)* lien on (charge over) moveables, *(~ zur Sicherung eines Anspruchs)* right of lien to secure a claim, *(~ des Verkäufers)* vendor's lien, *(durch Vertrag begründetes ~)* lien by agreement, lien acquired by contract

Pfandrechts / ~**begründung** constitution of a lien (charge); ~**bestellung** creation of a lien (charge), taking out a lien, creating a lien on property, creating a charge over property; ~**bestellungsurkunde** deed of lien, deed (instrument) of charge

Pfandrechts / ~**freigabe** lien release; ~**gläubiger** lien creditor; ~**inhaber** lienholder, lienor; ~**löschung** lien discharge, extinguishment of lien, lien defeasance; ~**schuldner** lien debtor; ~**verwertung** lien enforcement, realising a lien

Pfand / ~**reife** conditions allowing the realisation of a pledge; ~**rückgabe** restitution of a pledge, returning the pawned item

Pfand / ~**sache** → Pfandgegenstand; ~**schein** pawn ticket □ evidences receipt of the pawned item; ~**schuld** debt secured (collateralised) by a lien; ~**schuldner** pledgor

Pfändung attachment, seizure, distraint, *(~ des Garantieanspruchs)* attachment of the guarantee claim, *(~ einer Immobilie)* property attachment, *(~ von Löhnen)* wage garnishment

Pfändungs / ~**ankündigung** distraint warning, provisional seizure; ~**beschluss** attachment order, writ of attachment, distress warrant

pfändungsfrei *(~e Forderungen)* claims exempt from seizure (execution), non-distrainable claims, *(~e Vermögenswerte)* exempt property, property exempt from seizure (execution), non-leviable (non-seizable) assets (property)

Pfändungs / ~**freiheit** exemption from seizure; ~**gläubiger** attaching (distraining) creditor; ~**grundfreibetrag** → Pfändungsschutzbetrag; ~**pfandrecht** lien by enforcement, execution lien; ~**protokoll** minutes of attachment

Pfändungs / ~**schutzbetrag** basic deposit exempt (privileged) from seizure, non-seizable (non-attachable) account balance; ~**schutzkonto** account maintained with a basic non-seizable balance; ~**verfügung** writ of seizure

Pfand / ~**schutz** exemption from seizure; ~**verfahren** attachment proceedings, *(bei Forderungen)* garnishee proceedings; ~**verkauf** sale of pledged property, enforced sale

Pfand / ~**vermittler** pawnbroker; ~**vertrag** deed (memorandum) of pledge; ~**verwahrung** safekeeping of pledged (pawned) property; ~**verwertung** realisation (enforcement) of pledged property, selling pawned property

Pflege 1. *(~ von Kundenbeziehungen)* customer relationship building, cultivating existing accounts
2. *(von Anwendungsprogrammen)* maintenance of application programmes

pflegen *(den persönlichen Kontakt mit dem Kunden ~)* to cultivate the personal contact with the customer

Pfleger curator, guardian (conservator) appointed by the court

Pflegschaft curatorship

Pflegschaftskonto curatorship account

Pflicht 1. duty, obligation, *(~ zur bestmöglichen Ausführung)* duty of best execution (when executing customer orders)
2. *(Funktion)* office, function

Pflicht / ~**aktien** qualifying (qualification) shares; ~**angaben** *(in Emissions-/Verkaufsprospekten)* mandatory disclosures in prospectuses; ~**angebot** *(an die restlichen Aktionäre)* mandato-

P

ry offer (to the remaining shareholders)

Pflicht / ~beiträge obligatory contributions; **~bekanntmachung** statutory company announcement (notice), statutory (obligatory) public advertisement; **~ beteiligungen** mandatory participating interests

Pflicht / ~blatt journal for statutory stock market notices; **~einlage/einzahlung** mandatory (obligatory) capital contribution; **~feld** mandatory field

Pflichtenheft requirements specification

Pflicht / ~kommunikation mandatory notice; **~mitteilungen** statutory company statements; **~prüfung** statutory audit; **~reserven** statutory reserves

Pflicht / ~teil *(im Erbrecht)* statutory share, legal right; **~text** mandatory wording; **~verletzung** breach of duty, *(pflichtwidriges Verhalten)* breach (neglect) of duty; **~wandelanleihe** mandatory convertible bond; **~wandlung** mandatory conversion

Phantasie 1. imagination **2.** speculative hopes, → Zinsphantasie; **~werte** bazaar securities

Phase 1. phase, stage **2.** *(konjunkturelle)* cycle

phasengleich *(~e Vereinnahmung)* in-phase (in-period) recognition of income

physisch *(~e Abwicklung eines Future-Kontraktes/~e Andienung)* physical delivery □ settlement of a futures contract by delivering the underlying instrument, *(~es Kapital)* physical capital, machinery and equipment

PIB → Produktinformationsblatt

P-Konto → Pfändungsschutzkonto

plädieren to plead for

Plafond 1. ceiling, upper limit, line **2.** borrowing limit

plafondieren to set (to impose) a limit, to cap

Plan 1. *(Absicht)* intention, plan **2.** *(Entwurf)* design **3.** *(Programm, Projekt)* programme, project, scheme **4.** *(Unternehmensplan)* plan, budget **5.** *(Zeitplan)* time schedule

Plan / ~abweichungen budget (plan) variances; **~ansätze** budget estimates; **~bewegungsbilanz** planned funds statement; **~bilanz** budgeted (projected) balance sheet

Plan / ~daten planned (budgeted, projected) figures; **~deckungsbeitrag** planned profit contribution; **~dividende** planned dividend; **~einnahmen** budgeted (planned, projected) revenue

planen 1. to plan, to project, to organise, *(geplante Aktivitäten)* pipeline activity **2.** *(beabsichtigen)* to intend, to envisage

Plan / ~erfolg/~ergebnis budgeted (planned) income, projected performance, profit target; **~ergebnisrechnung** budgeted (projected) income statement, statement of estimated revenue and expenditure

Plan / ~erlöse budgeted (planned, projected) proceeds; **~erstellung** setting up a plan, budget preparation; **~fortschreibung** plan (budget) rollover; **~genehmigung** budget approval

Plan / ~-Ist/-Abweichung variance of performance to budget; **~-/Ist-Leistungsverhältnis** relationship between budgeted figures and actual performance; **~jahr** budget year

Plan / ~kontrolle budgetary control; **~korrekturen** budget amendments; **~kosten** budgeted (planned) cost; **~kostenrechnung** budgeting, budget accounts (accounting); **~leistung** planned performance

planmäßig 1. *adj.* *(~e Abschreibung)* regular (scheduled) depreciation, *(~e Rückführung)* repayment as agreed upon, *(~e Tilgung)* scheduled (regular) redemption, *(~e monatliche Tilgungsleistung)* scheduled monthly payment of principal and interest, *(~e Zahlungen)* scheduled payments

P

2. *adv.* as planned (scheduled), *(~ zurückzahlen)* to repay as agreed upon, to repay according to schedule

Plan / ~**periode** planning (budget) period; ~**revision** plan review, budget adjustment; ~**überschreitungen** budget overruns; ~**umsatz** planned (budgeted) sales

Planungs / ~**ansatz** planning approach; ~**ausschuss** planning committee; ~**größe** planning variable; ~**horizont** planning horizon; ~**instrumentarium** planning tools; ~**kontinuität** planning continuity

Planungs / ~**periode** budget (plan) period; ~**rechnung** budgetary accounting; ~**sicherheit** planning security; ~**stadium** *(im ~)* to be in the planning stages; ~**tiefe** planning depth; ~**zeitraum** planning period, planning horizon

Plan / ~**unterschreitungen** budget underruns; ~**vermögen** plan assets; ~**werte** → Planzahlen; ~**zahlen** planned (budgeted) figures, target figures, *(hinter den ~ zurückbleiben)* to be short of the budgeted figures; ~**ziel** target, goal, planned performance

Plattformgeschäfte stand-in transactions

Platzabrechnungen local (town) clearings

Platzakkreditiv local documentary credit

platzen 1. *(scheitern)* to fail, to fall through 2. *(einen Scheck ~ lassen)* to return a cheque unpaid, to dishonour a cheque

Platzen *(~ der spekulativen Blase)* burst of the speculative bubble

Platzeur dealer □ bank or securities house that buys securities from the issuer and places them in the market

Platz / ~**geschäfte** local transactions; ~**giroverkehr** town clearing

platzieren to place, (*mit einem Agio/Disagio ~*) to place at a premium/discount, (*beim Publikum ~)* to place with the public, to market to the general public, (*Schuldtitel privat bei institutionellen Anlegern ~*) to place debt securities privately with institutional investors

Platzierung placing, placement, *(~ über die Börse)* placement through the stock market, *(~ von Schuldtiteln)* debt placement, *(~ im Sekundärmarkt)* placement in the secondary market

Platzierungs / ~**agent** placement agent; ~**bank** dealer, dealer bank; ~**beschränkungen** restrictions on placement; ~**bestand** placement inventory; ~**erlös** placement proceeds; ~**fazilität** placement facility; ~**form** mode (type) of placement

Platzierungs / ~**garantie** placement guarantee; ~**gebühr** placement fee ; ~**geschäft** placement business; ~**gewinn** placement profit; ~**gruppe** placing (selling) group; ~**institut** placing bank (agent)

Platzierungs / ~**konsortium** selling group; ~**kraft** placing power, product placement power; ~**kurs** placement price, placing (offering) price; ~**memorandum** placing memorandum; ~**nutzen** placement fee

Platzierungs / ~**provision** dealership fee, placement commission; ~**rendite** placement yield; ~**risiko** placing risk; ~**verpflichtungen** placement (placing) commitments; ~**vertrag** placing (selling) agreement

Platz / ~**institut** local bank; ~**scheck** town (local) cheque, locally drawn cheque; ~**spesen** local charges

platzübergreifend *(~es Clearing)* interexchange clearing

Platz / ~**überweisung** local transfer, local money transmission, transfer between local banks; ~**usancen** local (town) practices; ~**verkehr** local payments; ~**verlust** local charges

Plausibilitäts / ~**prüfung** plausibility (reasonability) check; ~**kontrolle**

plausibility control, reasonableness test

plötzliches Ausfallrisiko *(der Gegenpartei/des Kreditnehmers)* jump-to-default risk

plus *(~ Stückzinsen)* plus interest accrued, accrued interest added

Plus 1. *(Nettogewinn)* net income (gain) **2.** *(Vorteil)* benefit, advantage **3.** *(Zunahme)* increase, rise, *(Bankaktien wurden mit ~ angekündigt)* banks were marked up, banks improved sharply, *(AB erzielten ein ~* von 5 Punkten) AB registered a gain of 5 points

Plus-Ankündigung uptick, price markup, upgrading, → einfache, → doppelte, → dreifache Plus-Ankündigung

Pluskorrektur upward adjustment, markup

Plusposition 1. net bought position, net asset position **2.** *(im Devisenhandel)* long position, *(Unterhaltung einer ~)* going long (in a currency)

Police policy

Policen / **~darlehen** policy advance, lending against an insurance policy, loan on policy; **~inhaber** policy holder; **~laufzeit** policy term; **~nachtrag** rider, policy endorsement; **~rückkaufswert** surrender value of a policy

policieren to issue an insurance policy; *i.w.S.* to provide insurance coverage, to underwrite

Policierung policy issuance

Politik *(~ des billigen Geldes)* cheap (easy) money policy, *(~ des knappen Geldes)* tight money policy, policy of monetary contraction, *(~ des teuren Geldes)* dear money policy, policy of high interest rates, *(~ der Risikostreuung)* risk diversification policy, policy of spreading risks

Polster *(~ gegen unerwartete Kreditverluste)* buffer (cushion) against unexpected loan losses

Pönale penalty

Pool pool, syndicate; **~-Abkommen** pooling agreement; **~-Konsortium** pool syndicate; **~-Kreditlinie** pool credit line

Portefeuille portfolio, holdings

Portefeuille / **~beleihungswert** portfolio's loanable value; **~dispositionen** portfolio arrangements, buying and selling portfolio assets; **~ergänzungen** portfolio additions; **~erträge** portfolio income; **~glattstellung** portfolio liquidation, liquidating a portfolio

Portefeuille / **~gliederung** portfolio breakdown; **~granularität** portfolio granularity □ level of portfolio diversification, numbers of exposures in the portfolio; **~papiere** portfolio securities; **~rendite** portfolio yield, return on a portfolio

Portefeuille / **~stabilität** portfolio stability; **~umsätze** portfolio turnover; **~wert** portfolio value; **~wertsteigerung** portfolio appreciation; **~zusammensetzung** portfolio mix, composition of a portfolio

Portfolio / **~abgänge** portfolio disposals; **~absicherung** portfolio hedging (insurance), *(~ gegen Zinsänderungsrisiken)* portfolio hedge of interest rate risks; **~analyse** portfolio analysis; **~ansatz** portfolio approach, **~ausrichtung** portfolio orientation (focus, design)

Portfolio / **~bausteine** portfolio building blocks; **~beimischung** rounding off the portfolio, adding to the portfolio mix; **~beratung** portfolio consultancy (management); **~bereinigungen** portfolio adjustments, streamlining the portfolio

Portfolio / **~bestand** portfolio holdings; **~bewertung** portfolio assessment (evaluation); **~bindung** *(an einen Index)* portfolio indexing; **~diversifikation** portfolio diversification, investing in different asset classes

Portfolio / **~ergebnis** portfolio performance; **~erträge** portfolio income;

P

~**geschäft** portfolio trade (transaction) □ several securities traded as a single lot

Portfolio / ~**gesellschaft** portfolio company, enterprise in which a private equity firm invests; ~**gewichte** portfolio asset weights; ~**gewichtung** portfolio weighting

Portfolio / ~**immunisierung** portfolio immunisation □ measures taken to safeguard the capital invested and the expected portfolio return; ~**investitionen** portfolio investment, acquisition of (foreign) financial assets

Portfolio / ~**management** portfolio management; ~**mix** portfolio's asset mix; ~**optimierung** portfolio optimisation, optimising the portfolio return for a given risk; ~**planung** portfolio planning, allocating resources to asset classes/business units

Portfolio / ~**risiko** portfolio risk, risk attaching to a portfolio, *(Portfoliorisiken aus dem Kreditgeschäft)* portfolio lending risks; ~**sensitivitätsanalyse** portfolio sensitivity analysis

Portfolio / ~**steuerung** portfolio management (control); ~**strategie** *(zielgerichtete ~)* focused, active portfolio strategy; ~**strukturierung** asset allocation, portfolio structuring

Portfolio / ~**techniken** portfolio techniques; ~**theorie** portfolio (selection) theory; ~**umschichtung** portfolio restructuring, portfolio shake-up (switching), redeployment of capital; ~**umschlag** portfolio turnover rate

Portfolio / ~**varianz** portfolio variance, measure of portfolio risk (variance); ~ **verhalten** portfolio (investor) behaviour; ~**versicherung** portfolio insurance □ trading/hedging strategy designed to safeguard the portfolio value

Portfolio / ~**verluste** portfolio losses, financial losses on a portfolio; ~**volatilität** volatility of an investment portfolio; ~**wertberichtigung** portfolio value adjustments; ~**zugänge** portfolio additions, additions to the investment portfolio

Position 1. *(Bestand)* position, inventory, book(s), *(auf/in ~ nehmen)* to take on one's books, to warehouse (e. g. a swap), to take on one's own inventory
2. *(Bilanz-/Rechnungsposten)* item
3. *(Engagement)* commitment, interest
4. *(Stellung, Amt)* post, position

Positionen *(~ des Eigenhandels)* proprietary trading positions, *(~ des Handelsbuches)* positions in the trading book, *(zu Handelszwecken gehaltene ~)* positions held for trading purposes (held with trading intent), *(~ aus dem Kundengeschäft)* positions from client servicing (customer operations)

Positionenaufrechnung position netting, payment netting

positionieren to position, *(gut positioniert sein)* to be well placed (positioned)

Positionierung *(~ am Markt)* positioning in the market

Positions / ~**absicherung** hedging a position, exposure (position) hedge; ~**aggregation** exposure aggregation; ~**aufbau** → Positionseröffnung; ~**auflösung** unwinding (liquidating) a position, position close-out

Positions / ~**bereinigung 1.** position adjustment **2.** → Positionsglattstellung; ~**bewertung** exposure assessment (evaluation); ~**eindeckung** covering a position, exposure cover

Positions / ~**erhöhung** position (inventory) buildup; ~**eröffnung** opening (initiating) a position, opening transaction, *(einer Kauf-/Verkaufs-Position)* opening a long/short position, going long/short, *(Positionseröffnung und Glattstellung)* round turn

Positions / ~**fortschreibung** position rollover; ~**führung** position management (maintenance), position-keeping; ~**glattstellung** position squaring (close-out), liquidating a position

Positions / ~haltung carrying a position, position-keeping; **~handel** position trading; **~händler** position trader, long duration trader; **~kennung** position identifier, position code

Positions / ~kladde position book; **~kontrolle** position monitoring, exposure conrol; **~limit** position limit; **~liquidierung** → Positionsauflösung; **~nahme** *(z. B. am Terminmarkt auf die zukünftige Geldpolitik)* taking positions (e.g. on the future course of monetary policy)

Positions / ~prolongation position rollover; **~risiko** position (exposure) risk, risk of changes in the market value of a position, risk that prices or exchange rates move adversely after the deal is struck

Positions / ~schließung 1. position close-out, closing (closing out, liquidating) a position **2.** gap closure; **~sensitivität** sensitiveness of a position to market fluctuations; **~sicherung** hedging a position (an exposure); **~steuerung** position management, exposure control

Positions / ~überwachung position monitoring, exposure control; **~verantwortlicher** position manager; **~volatilität** exposure of a position to volatility; **~wert** exposure amount

P

positiv 1. *adj. (~es Ergebnis)* positive results (performance), *(~e Haltekosten)* positive cost of carry □ financing cost is below the yield on the assets/securities being financed
(~e Marktwerte aus Derivaten) fair values arising from derivatives, *(~e Quittung/Ausführung eines Zahlungsauftrages)* positive acknowledgement, *(~e Reaktion)* positive (favourable) response, *(~e Steigung der Zinsstrukturkurve)* positive slope of the yield curve, *(~e Vertragsverletzung)* deficient performance, non-performance *(~es Zeichen für den Markt)* positive sign for the market, *(~er beizulegender Zeitwert)* positive fair value, *(~er Zinssaldo)* net interest income
2. *adv. (~ reagieren)* to respond positively to, to react favourably to

Posten 1. *(Amt, Stellung)* office, position, post **2.** *(Betrag)* amount **3.** *(Buchungsposten)* entry, item, *(Positionen unter dem Strich) (a)* items below the line *(b)* off-balance sheet items **4.** *(Rechnungsposten)* item **5.** *(Warenpartie)* lot

Postengebühr entry fee

Post / ~laufkredit mailing (mail) credit; **~laufrisiko** mailing risk, mail loss risk; **~versandnachweis** postal receipt, certificate of posting; **~vollmacht** authority to collect mail

Potenzial potential, capacity

potenziell potential, possible, *(~es Ausfallrisiko)* potential exposure, *(~es Bargeld) (i.e.S.)* demand deposits, *(i.w.S.)* quickly realisable assets, *(~er Kunde)* potential (prospective) customer, prospect

Präambel preamble, recital (commencement) clause, recitals

Prädikats-Rating prime rating

Präferenz preference, *(~ für den Inlandsmarkt)* home bias

Präferenz / ~relationen preference ratios; **~segmentierung** preference segmentation; **~spanne** preference margin; **~zölle** preferential duties

Präge / ~anstalt mint; **~gebühr** mintage; **~kosten** minting expenses

prägen 1. *(Münzen)* to mint, to coin **2.** *(Beziehungen)* to mould, to shape

Präge / ~recht coinage prerogative, right of coinage; **~stempel** mint mark (die)

Prägung minting, coinage

präjudizieren to predetermine, to anticipate, to set a precedent, *(präjudizierter Scheck)* invalidated (stale) cheque

Präklusions / ~ frist preclusion period; **~ vorschriften** preclusion rules

praktikabel practicable, feasible, viable

Praktikant intern

Praktikum internship, practical studies (training)

Praktikumsbescheinigung evidence of internship

praktisch 1. *adj.* (*~e Erfahrung*) practical experience, (*~e Unmöglichkeit der Vertragserfüllung*) practical impossibility of performance 2. *adv.* (*auf ~ allen Finanzmärkten*) in virtually all financial markets, (*~ unverändert*) virtually unchanged

Prämie 1. premium 2. *(Optionsprämie)* option premium, option money 3. *(Vergütung)* bonus, remuneration

Prämien / **~abrechnung** premium statement (account); **~anleihe** premium bond; **~anpassung** premium adjustment; **~aufkommen** premium income; **~aufschlag** premium load (ing), amount added to the premium

prämienbegünstigt *(~er Sparvertrag)* bonus-carrying savings scheme

Prämien / **~bemessung** premium assessment; **~berechnung** calculation of the premium; **~betrag** premium amount

Prämien / **~depot** premium prepayments; **~einnahmen** premium income, premiums received (written); **~einziehung** premium collection; **~erhöhung** premium increase

Prämien / **~fälligkeit** premium maturity; **~festsetzung** fixing the premium; **~freijahre** premium holiday; **~guthaben** scheme-linked deposits (balances); **~korrektur** premium adjustment

Prämien / **~markt** premium market; **~notierung**/**~quotierung** premium quotation (quote); **~rabatt** premium rebate; **~rechnung** premium account; **~rückerstattung**/**~rückgewähr** premium refund; **~rückstände** premium arrears

Prämien / **~satz** premium rate; **~tabelle** premium scale; **~verzug** premium default; **~wert** premium amount

Prämien / **~zahlung** premium payment, *(bei Abschluss/Fälligkeit zu leistende Prämienzahlung)* upfront/back-end premium; **~zahlungszeit** premium-paying period; **~zuwachs** increase (growth) in premium income

Prämisse *(unter der ~)* provided that, *(das Programm basiert auf der ~)* the scheme is based on the premise that

Pränumerandozahlung payment in advance

Präsentation 1. presentation, roadshow 2. *(Vorlage)* presentation, presentment, submittal

Präsentationsfrist presentation period

präsentieren *(vorlegen)* to present, to submit

Präsenz 1. presence, (*~ am Kapitalmarkt)* presence in the capital market 2. *(Teilnahme)* attendance

Präsenz / **~börse** floor trading system; **~geld** attendance fee; **~geschäft** *(im Kartenzahlungsverkehr)* point-of-sale (stationary, card present) business; **~handel** floor trading; **~liste** attendance list (sheet)

präsidieren to be in the chair, to preside

Präsidium executive committee, board of directors

Präsumtiverbe heir presumptive

Präventivmaßnahmen preventive measures

Praxis 1. practice 2. *(Brauch/Usance)* custom, use, usage 3. *(Erfahrung)* experience; **~erfahrung** practical experience

Präzedenzfall precedent, test case, case in precedent

präzis precise, accurate, exact

präzisieren to state (to define, to specify) precisely

Präzision precision, accuracy, exactness

Preis 1. price 2. *(Kosten)* cost, charges 3. *(Wert)* value

Preis / **~absprache** price agreement (arrangement), agreement on prices (charges), *(wettbewerbswidrige ~)* price collusion, price ring (association); ~**änderungsrisiko** price risk

Preis / ~**angabe** price indication, quotation of a price, disclosure of charges; ~**angabenverordnung** Price Indication Regulation; ~**angebot 1.** quotation **2.** price bid; ~**anpassungsklausel** price adaptation (escalator) clause

Preis / ~**anstieg** → Preissteigerung; ~**anzeige** price display; ~**aufschlag** additional price (charge), surcharge, markup; ~**auftrieb** price upsurge, price surge (boost); ~**aushang** notice (schedule) of charges, display of prices; ~**auszeichnung** price marking (labelling)

preisbestimmend *(~e Faktoren)* price determinants

Preis / ~**bestimmung** price fixing, pricing, determination (calculation) of a price, fixing prices; ~**bietungsverfahren** bidding procedure; ~**bildung** price formation, price determination, pricing, → Preisgestaltung; ~**bildungsfaktoren** price determinants

Preis / ~**bindung** price maintenance (control), price fixing agreement, *(~ der zweiten Hand)* resale price maintenance; ~**bindungsklausel** price maintenance clause; ~**dämpfung** dampening the upsurge in prices, *(preisdämpfende Maßnahmen)* price-curbing measures

Preis / ~**deflation** price deflation; ~**differenz** price difference, difference in prices; ~**differenzierung** price differentiation (discrimination)

Preis / ~**einbruch** sharp drop in prices, slump in prices; ~**elastizität** *(~ der Nachfrage)* price elasticity of demand; ~**empfehlung** price recommendation; ~**entwicklung** price development (trend); ~**erhöhung** price increase (rise, hike); ~**erhöhungsspielraum** leeway for price increases; ~**ermittlung** price determination (calculation), pricing

P

Preis / ~**fächer** price range; ~**faktor 1.** price factor (determinant) **2.** *(im Hinblick auf die Belieferung von Zins-Terminkontrakten)* price factor □ factor that brings the various deliverable bonds, which differ in terms of coupon and maturity, onto a common basis

Preis / ~**festigkeit** firmness (stability) of prices; ~**feststellung** price fixing, *(~ im* → Regulierten Markt) fixing of prices in the regulated market; ~**findung** price determination (establishment), pricing; ~**findungsprozess** price discovery

Preis / ~**fixierung** price fixing; ~**freigabe** decontrol (freeing) of prices, price liberalisation; ~**führerschaft** price leadership; ~**gabe 1.** *(Aufgabe, Verzicht)* abandonment, relinquishment **2.** *(Offenlegung)* disclosure

preisgeben 1. *(aufgeben)* to abandon, to relinquish, to give up **2.** *(Informationen ~)* to disclose (to divulge, to give out) information

Preis / ~**geber** rate provider; ~**gefälle** price differential; ~**gefüge** price pattern

Preisgestaltung pricing, *(gleichgerichtete ~)* parallel pricing, *(~ im kurzfristigen/langfristigen Kreditgeschäft)* pricing of short-term/long-term lendings, *(~ im Mengengeschäft)* pricing of retail banking transactions

Preis / ~**gleichgewicht** price equilibrium; ~**gleitklausel** price escalator clause; ~**grenze** price limit, price cap (ceiling), maximum price

preisgünstig *(~er Anbieter)* low-cost supplier

Preis / ~**herabsetzung** price reduction, lowering of prices; ~**höhe** price level; ~**index** price index; ~**kalkulation** price calculation (computation); ~**kartell** restrictive agreement on prices, price ring (association); ~**klasse** price category (line), price range

Preis / ~**kontrolle** price control; ~ **korrekturen** *(~ bei Bankdienstleistungen)*

upward (downward) revision in bank pricing schedules; ~**korridor** price range; ~-**Kosten-Schere** price-cost gap; ~**lage** price line, price range

Preis-Leistungs-Verhältnis price-value relationship

Preis- und Leistungsverzeichnis product and service price list, schedule of services and charges

Preis / ~**lenkung** price control; ~**limit** price limit, *(preislimitierte Order)* order limited in price; ~**mechanismus** price mechanism (machinery); ~**nachlass** discount, price reduction, rebate

Preis / ~**nehmer** rate taker; ~**niveau** price level; ~**notierung** direct quotation □ indicates the number of units of domestic currency in terms of a single unit of a foreign currency, → Mengennotierung; ~**obergrenze** price ceiling, ceiling price, price limit (lid)

Preispolitik price (pricing) policy, pricing, *(~ im Einlagengeschäft)* pricing of deposit transactions, *(~ im Kreditgeschäft)* loan pricing policy

Preis / ~**regulativ** price regulator; ~**rückgang** price decline, fall (drop) in prices; ~**rutsch** price slide; ~**schwankungen** price fluctuations; ~**senkung** price reduction, lowering of prices (charges), price cut

Preis / ~**sensitivität** sensitivity to price fluctuations ; ~**sicherungsinstrument** price-hedging instrument; ~**spanne** price spread; ~**sprung** jump in prices; ~**stabilitätspolitik** policy for price stability

Preis / ~**steigerung** price increase (advance, rise, hike); ~**steigerungsrate** price increase rate; ~**stellung** price quotation; ~**stopp** price freeze; ~**stufe** price line; ~**stützung** price support; ~**tabelle** price schedule, scale of charges

Preis /~**ungleichgewichte** price imbalances (imperfections); ~**untergrenze** price floor; ~**unterschied** price difference (gap, differential), difference in prices; ~ **verordnung** pricing regulation; ~**volatilität** price volatility

prekär *(~e finanzielle Lage)* delicate (critical) financial situation, *(die finanzielle Lage bleibt ~)* the financial situation remains precarious

Presseverlautbarung press release

Prima / ~-**Ausfertigung** first of exchange; ~-**Bankscheck** prime banker's draft; ~-**Nota** day book; ~-**Papiere** prime (first-rate) acceptances, prime paper; ~-**Wechsel** first of exchange

primär *(~e internationale Liquidität)* currency reserves held by Central Banks, (~er *Trend) (in der Chart-Analyse)* long-term (primary) trend

Primär / ~**aufwand** primary input; ~**banken** *(im Genossenschaftsverbund)* local credit cooperatives; ~**geschäft** new issue business, dealings in newly issued securities; ~**haftung** primary liability

Primär / ~**insider** primary insiders □ members of the Board of Management, of the Supervisory Board and their spouses; ~**liquidität** tier-1 liquidity, cash (primary) liquidity, primary liquid assets, → Liquidität ersten Grades; ~**liquiditätsreserven** primary liquidity reserves

Primärmarkt primary market, new issue market

Primärmarkt / ~**geschäft** primary market transactions □ issuance, allotment and subscription of financial instruments; ~**rendite** new issuance yield

Primärmarkt / ~**segmente** *(Deutsche Börse)* primary market segments □ EU → Regulierter Markt: → Prime Standard/General Standard; börsenregulierter Markt: → Entry Standard, → Freiverkehr (Open Market); ~**versteigerung** primary market auction

Primär / ~**reserven** primary reserves, cash holdings and liquid assets; ~**schuldner** primary debtor

Prime Standard/General Standard Primary Market Segments of the EU

P

Regulated Market of Deutsche Börse (→ Regulierter Markt) □ While the Prime Standard segment is composed of companies that meet global standards of corporate governance and target international investors, the General Standard segment is oriented at small and medium-sized companies that have to meet only the minimum admission requirements. → Entry Standard, →First/Second Quotation Board

Prinzip principle, *(~ der getreuen Darstellung)* principle of fair presentation, *(~ der kongruenten Deckung)* principle of matching cover, *(~ der Heimatlandkontrolle)* principle of home country rule, → Heimatland-Prinzip, *(~ der Periodenabgrenzung)* accrual principle, accruals concept

prinzipiell in (on) principle, as a matter of principle

Priorität **1.** priority, preference, *(~ einräumen)* to prioritise, *(höchste ~ einräumen)* to give maximum priority to, to be on the top of the agenda, to accord the highest priority to **2.** *(Selbstbehalt des Erstversicherers)* retention of loss

Prioritäts / ~aktien priority shares (stock), preference (preferential) shares; **~anspruch** priority claim; **~folge** order of priority; **~obligationen** priority (preference) bonds, priorities; **~prinzip** principle of priority

P

privat **1.** *adj.* *(~es Anlagekapital)* private investment capital, *(~e Bankkunden)* retail banking customers, *(~es Beteiligungskapital)* private equity, *(~e Ersparnisse zur Altersvorsorge)* private savings as provisions for old age, *(~e Gelder)* private sector funds *(~e Geschäftsbanken)* private commercial banks, *(~e Hypothekenbanken)* private sector mortgage banks, *(~es Hypothekengeschäft)* residential mortgage lending, *(~e Investitionen)* private sector investment, *(~e Investitionsausgaben)* private investment spending *(~e Kapitalgeber)* private equity investors, *(~es Publikum)* private (retail) investors, *(~er Schlüssel)* private key, *(~e Sparkapitalbildung)* formation of private savings, *(~e Veräußerungsgeschäfte)* private sales transactions □ proceeds are taxable when the assets are sold during the statutory holding period *(~e Veräußerungsgewinne)* private capital gains, *(~er Wohnungsbau)* private housebuilding sector, *(~e Wohnungsbaukredite)* residential mortgage loans **2.** *adv.* *(~ finanzierter Altersvorsorgeplan)* privately funded pension scheme, *(~ platzierte Schuldtitel/Wertpapiere)* privately placed debt/securities

Privat / ~adresse private borrower/investor; **~anleger** private (retail) investor(s); **~anlegerderivate** retail derivatives; **~banken** private banks; **~bankier** private banking house; **~besitz** *(im ~ stehende Bank)* privately owned bank; **~darlehen** personal loan

Privatdiskonten prime bankers' acceptances □ traded until 1991 on the Frankfurt Stock Exchange

Privat / ~entnahmen *(eines Gesellschafters)* personal drawings; **~erbfolge** private succession; **~girokonto** personal current (checking) account, consumer checking account; **~insolvenz** personal insolvency; **~insolvenzverfahren** personal insolvency proceedings; **~investoren** private investors

privatisieren **1.** *(ein staatliches Unternehmen ~)* to privatise **2.** *(eine Publikumsgesellschaft in eine Personengesellschaft umwandeln)* to take a corporation private

Privatisierung privatisation, putting into private ownership (into private hands), taking private, *(~ der Währungsreserven)* increasing shift of currency reserves to the private sector

Privatkunde **1.** *(eines Kreditinstitutes)* retail (personal) customer, retail account **2.** *(gehobener ~)* private customer (client), private banking customer **3.** *(vermögender ~)* high-income customer, high net worth customer (individual)

Privatkunden / **~abteilung** retail (personal) banking department, retail (personal) customer service; **~beratung** advising (counselling) retail customers; **~bereich** retail banking division

Privatkunden / **~betreuer** customer service officer, personal accounts officer; **~betreuung** customer servicing; **~depot** retail customer portfolio; **~einlagen** retail deposits, *(when calculating the liquidity coverage ratio (→ Mindestliquiditätsquote) retail deposits are divided into → stabile Einlagen, → weniger stabile Einlagen*

Privatkundengeschäft retail banking, retail banking segment, retail business, personal banking, → gehobenes Privatkundengeschäft, *(das Ergebnis im ~)* performance on the retail banking side (in the personal market)

Privatkundenkonto retail account, personal account

Privatkundenkredit retail loan, personal loan, *(Zinssätze für ~e)* retail loan rates

Privatkundenkredit / **~bestand** retail loan portfolio; **~geschäft** retail lending business (operations), lendings to retail customers; **~nachfrage** retail lending demand, demand for retail (personal) loans; **~portfolio/volumen** retail loan book (portfolio), total retail exposures

Privatkunden / **~markt** retail banking market; **~stamm** retail client base; **~vertrieb** retail banking sales

Privatkundschaft retail customers, personal customers

Privat / **~personen** private individuals; **~platzierung** private placement, private offering, *(~platzierung nicht bezogener Aktien)* rump placement; **~platzierungsregime** EU private placement regime; **~publikum** retail (private) investors

privatrechtlich *(~es Kreditinstitut)* private sector bank, *(~es Sanierungsverfahren)* private law restructuring proceedings; *(~e Vereinbarung/Vertrag)* agreement under private law, private law contract

Privat / **~sektor** private sector; **~vermögen** private property, private means (wealth); **~wirtschaft** private enterprise sector

privatwirtschaftlich *(~ organisiert)* organised (established) as a private sector organisation, *(~e Adresse)* private sector borrower/issuer, *(~e Investitionen)* private sector investment

Probe **1.** *(Muster)* sample, specimen **2.** *(Versuch)* test, trial, *(auf eine harte ~ stellen)* to put to an acid test

Probe / **~bilanz** trial balance; **~exemplar** specimen (advance) copy; **~zeit** qualifying (trial) period

Problematik problems (difficulties) involved, problematic nature, complex of problems

Problemengagement problem exposure, → Problemkredit

Problemimmobilien distressed (troubled) real estate

Problemkredit problem loan (credit), troubled loan, *(gegebenenfalls → notleidender Kredit)*, *(pl)* problem assets, distressed debt, *(Handel in Forderungen aus ~ en)* distressed debt trading

Problem / **~-Länderkredite** distressed sovereign debt, problem country debt (PCD); **~lösung** solving a problem, finding a solution to a problem; **~obligo** problem exposure

Produkt *(eines Kreditinstitutes)* product, service, *(~e für Privatkunden)* private (personal) banking products, banking services specifically geared to personal customers

Produkt product; **~akzeptanz** product acceptance; **~aufgabe** product deletion (discontinuation); **~aussage**

product positioning claim; ~**aussonderung** product pruning (elimination)

Produkt / ~**basisrisiko** product basis risk □ risk of loss arising from mismatches in quality between the asset and the hedging instrument; ~**bedingungen** product specifications; ~**beschreibung** product description (specification); ~**betreuung** product guidance; ~**bewertung** product assessment (evaluation, rating)

produktbezogen *(~e Gebührenberechnung)* product-related (product-driven) pricing, *(~e Kontrollrechnung)* product profitability measurement

Produkt / ~**bündelung** product bundling; ~**deckungsbeitrag** product profit contribution; ~**eigenschaften** product attributes (properties, features); ~**einführung** product launch

Produkt / ~**erfolg** product success (performance); ~**erprobung** product testing; ~**expertise** product expertise; ~**flankierung** product flanking; ~**gattung** product class; ~**gestaltung** product design

Produkt / ~**gruppensegmentierung** product group segmentation; ~**haftung** product liability; ~**haftungsgesetz** Product Liability Act; ~**haftungsrisiko** product liability risk; ~**informationsblatt** product factsheet

Produktion 1. *(Herstellung)* production, manufacturing **2.** *(Ausstoß)* production, output

Produktions / ~**anlage** production plant (facilities); ~**ausfallversicherung** production disruption insurance; ~**bereich** production line (division); ~**betrieb** manufacturing company (unit); ~**budget** production budget

Produktions / ~**einschränkung** production cutback, cut in production; ~**kosten** cost of production, manufacturing cost(s); ~**leistung** output; ~**rückgang** drop (decrease, decline, fall) in production; ~**schwerpunkt** principal line of manufacture, production emphasis (focus)

Produktions / ~**standort** production site; ~**stätte** plant, place of manufacture; ~**steigerung** increase (rise) in production; ~**steuerung** production control; ~**unternehmen** manufacturing firm; ~**verlagerung** relocation of (moving) the production site

Produktivitäts / ~**erträge** productivity returns; ~**gefälle** productivity differential; ~**messung** productivity measurement

Produktivitäts / ~**verbesserung** improvement in productivity, productivity enhancement; ~**vermögen** productive assets; ~**zuwachsrate** productivity growth rate

Produktiv / ~**kapital** productive capital; ~**kostenrechnung** product costing; ~**kredite** corporate lendings

Produkt / ~**lebensdauer** product life; ~**lebenszyklus** product life cycle; ~**linie** product line; ~**linienerweiterung** product line extension (stretching); ~**nutzen** product utility, product benefits; ~**nutzungsintensität** intensity of product use

Produkt / ~**paketlösung** product package solution; ~**palette** product range (programme), range of services offered; ~**pass** product passport; ~**pflege** product care; ~**positionierung** product positioning; ~**rentabilität** product profitability; ~**risikoklasse** product risk category

Produkt / ~**sparte** product segment, product department (division); ~-**Spread** commodity product spread □ transaction involving the purchase of a primary commodity and the simultaneous sale of a by-product from that commodity (or vice-versa)

produktübergreifend *(~e Aufrechnungsposition/Aufrechnungsvereinbarung)* cross-product netting position/agreement

Produkt / ~**validierung** product validation; ~**verantwortung** product

P

stewardship, product responsibility; ~**vereinbarung** product agreement; ~**wahrnehmung** product perception; ~**wert-Management** product value management; ~**wissen** product knowledge

Produzenten / ~**markt** producer market; ~**rente** producer's surplus

produzieren 1. *(herstellen)* to produce, to manufacture 2. *(vorlegen)* to produce, to furnish

professionell (*~e Anleger/Marktteilnehmer)* professional investors/market operators

profitieren to profit (to benefit, to gain) from, to reap the benefits from, (*Goldwerte profitierten von spekulativer Nachfrage)* golds profited from speculative support

Proforma / ~-**Bilanz** pro forma balance sheet; ~-**Rechnung** pro forma invoice

Prognose forecast, prediction, projection. (*~ über die weitere Zinsentwicklung)* forecast of the future trend in interest rates

Prognose / ~**fähigkeit** predictive ability; ~**fehler** forecast error; ~**genauigkeit** forecasting accuracy; ~**güte** quality (accuracy) of a forecast, forecasting (predictive) quality; ~**kapitalbedarf** projected fund (capital) requirements

Prognose / ~**rechnung** forecast calculation, forecasting; ~**risiken** risks inherent in forecasts; ~**umsatz** forecast (projected) turnover; ~**wert** forecast (predictive) value; ~**zeitraum** forecast period

prognostizierbar (*~es Risiko)* foreseeable risk

prognostizierte Ausfallwahrscheinlichkeit forecast PD (probability of default)

prognostizierte Verlustquote forecast LGD (loss given default)

Programm *(Kredit-/Vermögensbildungsprogramm)* scheme, programme

Programm / ~**handel** program trading; ~**kredit**/~**darlehen** scheme loan, standardised loan (lending); ~**sparen** scheme-linked saving

progressiv (*~e Abschreibung)* depreciation on a rising scale, progressive amortisation, (*~e Steuer)* progressive tax

Projekt 1. project 2. *(i. S. von Objekt)* property

Projekt / ~**abwicklung** execution of the project, project delivery (management); ~**analyse** project analysis (evaluation); ~**beginn** project launch (start-up); ~**beratung** project counselling (consultancy); ~**beteiligte** project participants, parties involved in the project, *i.w.S.* project stakeholders

Projekt / ~**betreuung** project support (management); ~**bewilligungsverfahren** project authorisation procedure; ~**budget** project budget; ~**entwicklungskosten** project development cost; ~**fertigstellungsrisiko** project completion risk; ~**finanzierung** project financing, long-term financing of industrial projects/large infrastructure facilities

projektgebunden (*~e Ausleihungen)* project-tied (project-linked) lendings, (*~e Investitionsfinanzierung)* project-linked investment financing

Projektkredit project line of credit, loan tied to a specific project

Projektmehrkosten project overruns, *(Finanzierung der ~)* overrun financing

Projekt / ~**mittel** project finance; ~**rentabilität** project return; ~**studie** project study (analysis); ~**träger** project sponsor; ~**wert** 1. property value 2. project value

projizieren to project

Pro-Kopf-Einkommen per capita income

Prokura 1. general power of attorney (to act for the company) 2. proxy

Prokura-Indossament proxy endorsement, power of collection

Prokurist 1. executive holding a general power of attorney (to act for the company) 2. *(in der Hierarchie eines Kreditinstitutes)* Assistant Vice President

Prolongation 1. extension, renewal, rollover 2. *(~ eines Wechsels)* renewal (prolongation) of a bill, extension of the time for payment of a bill

Prolongation *(~ auslaufender Kreditvereinbarungen)* extension (renewal) of loan agreements falling due, *(zur ~ anstehende Positionen)* rollover of positions coming up for renewal

Prolongations / **~abschnitt** renewal bill; **~frist** renewal period, period of extension; **~gebühr** renewal fee; **~geschäft** 1. loan extensions 2. *(im Terminhandel)* contango transaction; **~risiko** *(bei einer nicht rechtzeitigen Kapitalrückzahlung)* 1. extension risk 2. repricing risk

Prolongations / **~satz** 1. renewal rate 2. rollover rate; **~schreiben** letter of renewal; **~-Swap** renewal swap; **~tag** contango day; **~wechsel** renewal bill; **~zusage** commitment to extend, renewal undertaking

prolongierbar renewable, continuable, *(~er Swap)* extendible swap

P

prolongieren 1. to renew, to extend the time for payment, to roll over 2. *(fortschreiben)* to roll over

Promesse 1. undertaking, commitment, guarantee 2. promissory note

Promille per mil(le), one tenth of 1 percent

Promotions-Preispolitik promotional pricing

prompt *(~e Regulierung)* prompt (punctual) settlement, *(~e Ware)* spot commodity

Promptgeschäfte dealings for cash (for immediate settlement)

Properhandel dealings for own account, own account trading

proportional proportional, pro rata, → anteilsmäßig

Prorogation/Prorogationsvereinbarung prorogation agreement, forum selection clause

Prospekt 1. *(Emissionsprospekt)* (issuing) prospectus, *(~ für die Zulassung zum Börsenhandel)* listing prospectus 2. *(Broschüre)* brochure, prospectus, factsheet

Prospekt / **~angaben** information given in the prospectus, statements made in the prospectus; **~befreiung** exemption from the prospectus requirements, *(prospektfreie Einführung)* prospectus-exempt listing

Prospekthaftung prospectus liability, liability for statements made in the prospectus

Prospekthaftungs / **~ansprüche** prospectus-based liability claims; **~regeln** prospectus liability rules; **~versicherung** prospectus liability insurance (coverage)

Prospekt / **~inhalt** contents of a prospectus, → Prospektangaben; **~pflicht** prospectus requirement. *(prospektpflichtige Wertpapieremission)* securities issue requiring the publication of a prospectus; **~prüfung** prospectus vetting; **~richtlinie** Prospectus Directive

Prospekt / **~veröffentlichung** publication of a prospectus; **~verordnung** Prospectus Regulation; **~zwang** → Prospektpflicht

prosperieren to prosper, to flourish, to thrive

Protest protest *(nicht zu verwechseln mit 'noting', dem in Großbritannien üblichen Vorprotest)*, *(~ mangels Annahme)* protest for non-acceptance, *(~ mangels Zahlung)* protest for nonpayment, *(zu ~ gehen lassen)* to have a bill protested (for non-payment/non-acceptance)

Protestanzeige advice (notice) of protest, advice of dishonour

Protestat defaulting drawee, defaulting party

Protest / **~aufnahmegebühr** protest recording fee; **~beamter** protesting official; **~erhebung** protesting, levying the protest against the defaulting drawee, *(Rückgriff nach ~ nehmen)* to take recourse once the bill has been protested; **~erlass** waiver of protest; **~erlassklausel** protest waiver clause

protestfähig protestable

Protest / **~frist** time allowed for protesting a bill; **~gebühr** protest fee

protestieren 1. to protest, to enter a protest **2.** *(Wechsel)* to protest a bill, to have a bill protested

Protestierung protesting, protest of a dishonoured bill

Protest / **~kosten** protest charges; **~liste** list of bills protested; **~lokal**/**~ort** place of protest □ i.e. the drawee's premises; **~urkunde** certificate (memorandum) of protest, protest certificate

Protest / **~vermerk** note of protest; **~verzicht** waiver of protest, waiver of the right of protest; **~zeit** protesting hours

Protokoll 1. minutes, (official) record of proceedings **2.** *(zu einem Vertrag)* protocol

Protokoll / **~annahme** approval of the minutes; **~aufnahme** recording (drawing up) the minutes, → Protokollierung; **~auszug** excerpt from the minutes; **~buch** minute-book; **~führer** recorder, secretary, keeper of the minutes

protokollieren 1. to record, to take down on record, to put on record (before a notary public)
2. to keep the minutes, to minute, to enter in the minutes
3. *(eine Kreditlinie ~)* to grant (to note) a credit line

Protokollierung 1. recording, putting on record, *(notarielle ~)* notarial recording **2.** keeping the minutes, entry (entering) in the minutes **3.** noting

Protokollierungsgebühr recording fee

Provision 1. commission, fee, *(~en aus dem dokumentären Zahlungsverkehr)* commissions from documentary payment transactions
2. *(Courtage)* brokerage

provisionsabhängig *(~es Geschäft) (der Kreditinstitute)* commission-earning (fee-earning) business

Provisions / **~anspruch** commission entitlement, entitlement to a commission payment; **~aufkommen** *(aus dem Privat- und Firmenkundengeschäft)* (fee and) commission income from retail and corporate banking operations

Provisions / **~aufteilung** commission sharing (splitting); **~aufwand** fee and commission expense, commissions and fees payable

Provisions / **~basis** *(auf ~)* on a commission basis, on a fee basis, on a fee-earning basis; **~beratung** *(provisionsbasierte Beratung)* commission-based counselling (consultancy); **~berechnung 1.** charging a commission (a fee) **2.** calculation of the commission, fee calculation

Provisions / **~einnahmen** commissions received, (fee and) commission revenue; **~ergebnis** net commission income; **~erträge** fee and commission income (revenue); **~forderungen** commissions and fees receivable

provisionsfrei free of commission, exempt from commission payment

Provisionsgeschäft commission and fee-earning business, *(~ mit Wertpapieren)* **1.** securities broking **2.** commission-bearing securities operations (business)

Provisions / **~höhe** commission level (amount); **~mehreinnahmen** surplus in fee revenue; **~nachlass** commission rebate (discount); **~nutzen** (fee and) commission income; **~offenlegung** disclosure of fees

provisionspflichtig subject to payment of a fee

Provisions / ~saldo net commission income; **~satz** commission rate; **~spanne** commission margin, ratio of net commission income to average business volume

Provisions / ~tabelle commission scale, table of (fees and) commissions charged; **~überschuss** net (fee and) commission income, *(~ aus dem Wertpapiergeschäft)* net commission income on (from) securities transactions; **~vergütung** commission payment

Provisions / ~zahlung commission payment, payment of a fee; **~zugeständnisse** fee concessions, pricing concessions

provisorisch provisional, temporary, interim

Provisorium temporary arrangement, provisional (temporary) solution

Prozent 1. percent, p.c., *(einen siebenprozentigen Anstieg verzeichnen)* to record a 7 p.c. rise, *(mit 4 % verzinst werden)* to bear 4 p.c. interest
2. percentage, *(Cash Flow in ~ vom Umsatz)* cashflow as a percentage of turnover

Prozenter *(Vier-Prozenter)* bond carrying a 4 p.c. coupon

P

Prozent / ~notierung percentage quotation; **~punkt** percentage point; **~satz** percentage

prozentual *(~e Abweichung)* percentage deviation, *(~er Anteil)* percentage share, *(~e Veränderung)* percentage change, *(~ gesehen)* on a percentage basis, expressed in (as) percent

Prozess 1. *(Ablauf)* process
2. *(Rechtsstreit)* suit, lawsuit, case, litigation
3. *(Verfahren)* trial, proceedings

Prozess / ~aval → Prozessbürgschaft; **~bausteine** process modules; **~bevollmächtigter** attorney of record; **~bürgschaft** judicial bond, court bond □ bond required of litigants in civil or criminal court actions; **~ebenen** process levels; **~entwurf** process design

prozessfähig capable of suing/of being sued

Prozessfähigkeit legal capacity to conduct a lawsuit

prozessführend *(~e Parteien)* parties to the proceedings, contending (litigant) parties

Prozess / ~führung conducting a lawsuit, conduct of the case; **~führungsbefugnis** right of action; **~garantie** court bond (guarantee); **~gegner** opposing party; **~ gericht** enforcement court

prozesshindernde Einrede preliminary objection, → prozessuales Hindernis

Prozesskette process chain

Prozesskosten 1. cost of litigation (of a lawsuit), cost of the proceedings
2. process cost(s)

Prozesskosten / ~analyse process cost analysis; **~hilfe** litigation assistance, legal aid (help), help at court; **~rechnung** activity-based accounting; **~vorschuss** suit fee, advance payment on litigation cost

Prozess / ~partei party to a lawsuit (to an action), party to litigation; **~risiken** litigation risks; **~straffung** streamlining processes

prozessual *(~er Anspruch)* case at law, case in (under) dispute, *(~e Fristen)* procedural time limits, *(~es Hindernis)* impediment to litigation, → prozesshindernde Einrede

Prozess / ~verantwortliche/r process owner; **~vergleich** court settlement; **~vertretung** representation in court; **~verwaltung** process administration, task management (scheduling);**~vollmacht** power of attorney to appear in court; **~zinsen 1.** interest income awarded by legal process **2.** interest on claims during litigation

pro-zyklisch *(~es Investieren)* procyclical investing, following the market trend, i.e. buying in an uptrend, selling in a downtrend

Prozyklizität procyclicity □ positively correlated performances between two or more business lines or between individual industrial sectors and the overall state of the economy

prudenziell *(~e Aufsicht)* prudential supervision

Prüfauftrag audit mandate

Prüfbescheinigung 1. verification certificate, certificate of inspection 2. *(hinsichtlich der Prospekterstellung)* letter of comfort 3. audit certificate

prüfen 1. to examine, to inspect, to investigate, to vet, *(genau ~)* to subject to close scrutiny, to scrutinise, *(den Kreditantrag ~)* to examine the loan application, *(die Kreditwürdigkeit ~)* to check (to examine) the creditworthiness, *(die Vorwürfe der Gläubigerbegünstigung ~)* to inquire into the allegations of preferential transfer
2. to audit, to verify, *(den Abschluss/die Bilanz ~)* to audit the accounts/the balance sheet
3. *(abwägen)* to consider, to sound out, *(seine Kreditmöglichkeiten ~)* to weigh up one's borrowing options
4. *(erproben)* to test

Prüfer 1. examiner 2. auditor

Prüf / ~phase screening stage; **~rechte** rights of inspection, audit rights; **~stand** *(eine Strategie auf den ~ stellen)* to put a strategy to the test

Prüfung 1. examination, inspection, investigation, review, *(~ der Bank)* inspection of the bank by the supervisory authority, *(~ der Eigentumsrechte)* examination of title, investigating a person's claim to be the owner of, *(~ der finanziellen Lage)* examination of the financial situation, making an investigation into the financial affairs of
2. audit, verification, *(~ der Bücher einer Unternehmung)* audit of the books and accounts of a company, *(~ der Unterschrift des Scheckausstellers)* checking the genuineness of the cheque writer's signature

Prüfungs / ~aufforderung audit (verification) request; **~auftrag** audit mandate; **~ausschuss** audit committee, review body; **~bericht** 1. audit (auditors') report 2. verification report; **~bestätigung** → Prüfbescheinigung

Prüfungs / ~feststellungen audit findings; **~kosten** audit fee, auditing charges; **~pflicht** duty to inspect (to examine) the books, duty to have the books audited, control (review) requirement, *(prüfungspflichtiger Bericht)* auditable report

Prüfungs / ~recht right of examination, right of scrutiny; **~richtlinien** 1. auditing standards (guidelines) 2. guidelines for examining (checking) (e. g. the accuracy of the documents)

Prüfungs / ~stichprobe audit sample; **~stelle** auditing agency; **~termin** *(im Insolvenzverfahren)* verification meeting □ verification of the claims lodged by creditors

Prüfungs / ~verband auditing body; **~verbund** audit association; **~verfahren** auditing method, verification (review) process; **~vermerk** audit certificate, audit opinion; **~vorschriften** auditing rules; **~wert** verification value

Prüfziffer check digit

Pseudonymisierung aliasing

psychologisch *(~ wichtige Marke)* psychologically important mark (level)

Publikationsorgane *(offizielle ~)* newspapers or journals publishing statutory notices

Publikum *(Anleger)* investing public, *(das breite ~)* retail investors, general investing public, investing public at large, *(das ~ blieb vorsichtig)* investors continued to take a cautious view, *(das ~ verhielt sich abwartend)* retail investors remained on the sidelines

Publikums / ~aktionäre retail equity investors; **~fonds** publicly offered fund, general fund, retail investment fund, fund open to the general public; **~geschäft** retail banking operations, business with the general public

Publikums / ~gesellschaft public company, publicly held corporation, corporation with substantial ownership among the public; **~immobilienfonds** retail real estate fund; **~interesse** investor interest, retail interest; **~käufe** public buying

Publikums / ~nachfrage retail investor demand; **~öffnung** *(eines Unternehmens)* going public; **~papiere** securities offered for public subscription

Publikums-Sondervermögen *(nach dem Investmentgesetz)* mutual fund, public fund □ comprises all investment funds that are not → Spezial-Sondervermögen, → Sondervermögen

Publikums / ~streuung → Streuung; **~verkehr** office hours, opening hours; **~werte** popular stocks, stocks favoured by retail investors

publizieren 1. *(bekanntmachen)* to publicise, to give publicity to, to make public, to advertise 2. *(veröffentlichen)* to publish

Publizität 1. publicity 2. *(i. S. von Veröffentlichung, z. B. Zwischenberichtspublizität)* publication of interim reports 3. *(i. S. von Offenlegung der Unternehmensergebnisse)* disclosure of company results

Publizitäts / ~effekt publicity effect; **~gesetz** German Publicity Act

Publizitätspflicht publication (disclosure) requirement, duty (obligation) to publish annual accounts and other relevant company information, transparency obligation

publizitätspflichtig *(~es Unternehmen)* company subject to publication requirements

Publizitätsvorschriften disclosure (publication) requirements, disclosure rules

Punkt point, score, *(der Index gab um zwei ~e nach)* the index edged two points down, *(um einige ~e höher schließen)* to close a couple of points higher

Punktebewertungsmodell / ~system *(bei Krediten)* scoring model/system

pünktlich *(~e Zahlung)* timely (prompt, punctual) payment, payment on the date agreed upon

Punktwert score

PWB → Pauschalwertberichtigung

Q

Qualifikation 1. qualification, *(berufliche ~en)* professional qualifications (skills) **2.** *(Eignung)* aptitude, ability

Qualifikationsanforderungen/-vorgaben qualification (eligibility) requirements

qualifizierende revolvierende Retailforderung *(Basel II)* qualifying revolving retail exposure (QRRE) □ unsecured revolving exposure to a single individual in the amount of € 100,000 or less

qualifizierte elektronische Signatur qualified electronic signature □ advanced electronic signature based on a qualified certificate and issued by a secure signature creation device

qualifizierte Minderheit / Minderheitsbeteiligung qualified minority (holding) □ minority representing at least 25 p.c. of the equity

qualifizierter Rangrücktritt / qualifizierte Rangrücktrittserklärung qualified subordination/qualified letter of subordination □ the creditor/shareholder declares subordination of his claims to the claims of all other creditors of the company and that in the event of the company's overindebtedness or illiquidity within the meaning of the German Insolvency Code his claims may only be satisfied out of future profits, liquidation surplus or other freely available assets

Qualität quality, *(~ der Aktiva/Ausleihungen/des Kreditportefeuilles)* asset quality, loan book quality

qualitativ *(~ hochwertige Anlageberatung)* high-quality investment counselling, *(~e Kreditverbesserung)* credit enhancement, improvement in asset quality, *(~er Unterschied)* qualitative difference (discrepancy)

Qualitäts / ~anforderungen quality requirements; **~anspruch** commitment to quality; **~beurteilung** quality assessment (rating); **~einstufung** quality grading, *(bei einer Emission)* rating; **~erzeugnisse** high-quality (high-grade) goods; **~kontrolle** quality control

Qualitäts / ~prüfung quality inspection (test), *(~ von Kreditforderungen)* asset quality test; **~sicherung** quality assurance, *(i.w.S.)* quality management; **~stufe** grade, quality level; **~werte** top-quality stocks, investment grade securities, blue chips; **~zeichen** quality mark (label)

Quant-Fonds quant fund, quantitative mutual fund □ investment desicions are based on computational mathematics, algorithmic trading, statistical arbitrage

Quantifizierung *(~ operationeller Risiken)* quantifying operational risks

quantitativ quantitative, in terms of quantity (volume), *(~e Analyse)* quantitative analysis, *(~e Auswirkungsstudie)* (Basel II) quantitative impact study, *(~er Fonds)* → Quant-Fonds

Quanto-Swap differential (quanto) swap □ denotes a swap contract where *(a)* floating interest payments in one currency are exchanged for interest payments in another currency or *(b)* two Libor interest rates are exchanged, e.g. JPY Libor and USD Libor

Quartals / ~abrechnung 1. quarterly settlement, quarterly account balancing **2.** quarterly statement; **~abschluss 1.** quarterly settlement **2.** quarterly accounts; ~**bericht** quarterly report; ~**dividende** quarterly dividend; ~**fälligkeit** quarterly maturity (due date); ~**veränderung** quarter-on-quarter change

quartalsweise quarterly, every quarter, every three months

Quartals / ~ **zahlen** quarterly figures (accounts); ~zahlung quarterly payment

Quasi / ~**eigenmittel** secondary capital; ~**geld** near-money; ~-**Geldmarktfonds** near-money market fund

Quellen / ~**besteuerung** taxation at source; ~**steuer** withholding tax, tax levied at source; ~**steuerentlastung** withholding tax relief

quellensteuerfrei exempt from withholding tax

Quer / ~**klage** impleader; ~ **schnittsanalyse** cross-section analysis; ~**subventionierung** cross-subsidising; ~**verkauf** cross-selling

quittieren to receipt, to acknowledge receipt

Quittung *(~ für die Hinterlegung)* custody receipt

Quittungsverfahren acknowledgement procedure

Quorum quorum, minimum number of people required to be present or represented by proxy to vote at a meeting or make a valid decision, → beschlussfähig

quotal *adj.* *(~e Haftung)* proportional (rateable) liability *adv.* *(~konsolidieren)* to consolidate on a pro-rata basis

Quote **1.** *(Anteil)* share, portion **2.** *(Kontingent)* quota **3.** *(Tranche)* tranche **4.** *(Umtauschquote)* exchange (conversion) ratio **5.** *(Zuteilung)* allocation

Quotelung proportional allocation

Quotenaktie no-par value share

Quoten-Gesellschaft des bürgerlichen Rechts association under civil law with limited personal liability of the partners

Quotenkonsolidierung proportional (pro rata) consolidation, *(quotenkonsolidierte Minderheitsbeteiligungen)* minority interests consolidated on a pro rata basis, *(Quotenkonsolidierungsverfahren)* method of proportional consolidaten

Quoten / ~**rest** *(im Emissionsgeschäft)* unplaced securities; ~**rückversicherung** quota share reinsurance □ reinsuring a defined percentage of all risks held by an insurance company

Quoten / ~**schlüssel** allocation formula; ~**stichprobe** quota sample; ~**stichprobenverfahren** quota sampling; ~**vorrecht** quota privilege; ~**zuteilung** quota allotment

quotieren to quote

Quotierung quotation, quoting rates (prices)

R

Rahmen 1. framework, scope, *(einen allgemeinen ~ festlegen)* to establish a broad framework, *(der für Neuanschaffungen festgelegte ~)* the ceiling set on new equipment spending
2. *(Hintergrund)* background → Rahmenbedingungen
3. **im Rahmen** *(~ seiner Aufgaben)* within the scope of his duties, *(~ der vereinbarten Fazilität erfolgende Inanspruchnahmen)* drawings under the agreed facility, *(~ der üblichen Geschäftstätigkeit)* within the ordinary course of business, *(im ~ des Vertrages)* under the terms of the agreement

Rahmen / **~abkommen** general (master) agreement, framework (basic) agreement; **~aval** guarantee credit line

Rahmen / **~bedingungen** general setting (setup), scenario, general (basic) conditions, *(gesetzliche/rechtliche ~)* legal/statutory framework, *(wirtschaftliche ~)* general economic setting; **~bestimmungen** framework regulations, basic provisions

Rahmen / **~daten** fundamentals, key data; **~fazilität/~kredit** general facility, credit line; **~kreditvertrag** general facility agreement, general (master) loan agreement; **~kreditzusage** facility letter

Rahmen / **~limit** borrowing (credit) limit, e. g. maximum amount up to which a company may borrow by way of cash loans, bills or any other instrument; **~lizenzvertrag** master license agreement

Rahmen / **~richtlinie** (EU) Framework Directive; **~setzung** setting (establishing) the framework; **~vereinbarung** framework agreement, → Rahmenabkommen; **~vertrag** *(~ für Finanztermingeschäfte)* Master Agreement for Transactions in Financial Derivatives; **~zusage** general undertaking, basic commitment

Raiffeisenbank rural credit association, agricultural credit co-operative

Rand 1. edge, margin, *(am ~ vermerken)* to write in the margin
2. brink, verge, *(am ~e der Insolvenz)* on the brink of insolvency

Randaktivitäten fringe (non-core, marginal) activities

Rang 1. *(im Grundbuch)* rank, priority
2. *(Stellung)* position, post 3. *(Güteklasse)* grade, class
im Rang gleichgestellt *(~e Sicherheit)* security ranking equally (concurrently, pari passu)
im Rang nachgehend/nachgeordnet/nachgestellt *(~e Forderung)* subordinated claim, claim ranking after, *(~e Sicherheit)* subordinated (junior) security, subordinated collateral, *(~e Verbindlichkeiten)* liabilities ranking after, subordinated liabilities (debts)
im Rang vorgehend *(~e Forderung)* prior claim, claim ranking ahead (before), claim taking priority (precedence) over (e. g. all other charges), claim of superior priority, claim having priority of (to) payment on default, *(~e Hypothek)* senior (prior) mortgage

Rang / **~abstufung** rank grading; **~änderung** change of rank (of priority), amending the rank (priority) of

Rangfolge priority, order of priority, ranking, *(~ der Forderungen)* priority of claims, *(~ der Gläubiger)* ranking of creditors, *(~ der Hypotheken)* mortgage ranking, *(~ im Insolvenz-*

verfahren) order of payment of debts in insolvency, *(~ der Rechte)* ranking of rights

Ranggleichheit equality of rank, equal rank

Ranggleichstellung 1. accommodating an equal rank, putting on an equal footing **2.** enjoying the same rights

Ranggleichstellungsklausel pari passu clause, equally (rateably) secured clause

ranghöher *(~e Belastung)* prior (senior, higher-ranking) charge

Rang / ~klasse *(von Forderungen im Insolvenzverfahren)* priority, claim category; **~liste** league table

rangniedriger *(~e Forderung)* subordinated claim, claim ranking lower in priority, *(~e Gläubigergruppe)* junior class of creditors, *(~es Grundpfandrecht)* junior (lower-ranking) property charge

Rang / ~ordnung order of priority (of precedence), ranking; **~ordnungsverfahren** ranking system, rank order method

Rang / ~rücktritt subordination; **~rücktrittserklärung** letter (deed) of subordination, subordination agreement; **~rücktrittsklausel** subordination clause; **~stelle** rank; **~stellung** ranking

Rang / ~verhältnis rank, order of priority, ranking order; **~vermerk** entering the rank of a property charge in the land register, rank-related entry in the land register; **~vorbehalt** reservation of a specific rank, reservation of priority, reserving the right to enter a senior charge

R

Rat 1. *(Empfehlung)* recommendation **2.** *(Ratschlag)* advice, counsel **3.** *(Versammlung)* council **4.** *(Vorschlag)* proposal, suggestion

ratB → rationiert Brief

Rate 1. instal(l)ment **2.** *(Satz)* rate

raten *(empfehlen)* to advise, to recommend

Raten / ~anleihe instalment bond; **~finanzierung** instalment financing; **~hypothek** instalment mortgage; **~kauf** hire purchase, buying on hire purchase, buying by instalments

Raten / ~kredit instalment credit, hire-purchase loan; **~kreditvolumen** instalment credit portfolio; **~rückstand** instalments in arrears; **~schuldverschreibung** instalment note; **~tilgung** redemption (repayment) by instalments

ratenweise by (in) instalments

Ratenzahlung 1. instalment, instalment payment **2.** payment by instalments

ratG → rationiert Geld

Ratgeber 1. advisor, counsellor **2.** *(~ zum Kapitalmarkt)* capital market guide

Rating rating, measurement of a borrower's/issuer's creditworthiness, → Ratingstufe

Rating / ~agentur (credit) rating agency, *(under → Basel II/III rules)* external credit assessment institution (ECAI); **~analyse** rating analysis; **~änderung** rating change, → Ratingmigration

ratingbasiert *(~er Ansatz)* rating-based approach, → ratinggestützt

Rating / ~beratung rating advisory (consultancy); **~bewertung** rating assessment; **~-Buchstabencode** rating letter code; **~dynamik** rating dynamcis (momentum) □ further changes in the same direction

Rating / ~einstufung rating assignment (classification); **~ergebnis** rating result (performance); **~ermittlung** rating determination, credit rating establishment, determination of the credit quality; **~faktoren** rating factors, factors relevant to the rating, *(harte/weiche ~)* hard (quantitative) factors/soft (qualitative) factors; **~feststellung** → Ratingermittlung

ratinggestützt *(~e Konditionen)* rating-based (rating-related) rates and terms, rating-based pricing

Rating / ~kategorie rating category; **~kennzahl** rating score; **~klasse** rating class; **~kriterien** rating criteria, → Ratingfaktoren; **~methode** rating method; **~methodik** rating methodology

Rating / ~migration rating migration (change), (positive/negative~) positive (upward) / negative (downward) rating migration, improvement/deterioration in the borrower's/issuer's credit-worthiness; **~migrationsmatrix** rating migration matrix □ denotes past changes in credit quality; **~niveau** rating level; **~note** rating grade, → Ratingstufe

ratingorientiert *(~er Ansatz)* rating-oriented approach

ratingrelevant *(~e Faktoren)* → Ratingfaktoren

Rating / ~skala rating scale; **~stufe** **1.** notch, *(das Rating des Unternehmens um eine Stufe senken)* to cut (to lower) the company's rating by one notch (to e.g. BBB-), *(das Langfrist-Rating um zwei Stufen anheben)* to raise the long-tem rating by two notches **2.** *(allgemein)* rating grade (level); **~system** rating system; **~tabelle** rating schedule (table)

Ratingübergang rating transition

Ratingübergangs / ~häufigkeiten rating transition frequencies; **~matrix** rating transition matrix □ descriptive of the probability of rating changes; **~wahrscheinlickeiten** rating transition probabilities

Rating / ~verbesserung rating upgrade (→ Ratingstufe); **~verfahren** rating process; **~vergabe** rating assignment, rating given (awarded) to ...; **~verschlechterung** rating downgrade, (→ Ratingstufe); **~wanderung** rating migration, → Ratingmigration; **~zusatz** rating notation

rationalisieren to rationalise, to streamline

Rationalisierungs / ~aufwand rationalisation expenditure; **~maßnahmen** rationalisation (streamlining) measures; **~potenzial** rationalisation (cost-cutting) potential

rationieren 1. to ration **2.** *(repartieren)* to scale down

rationiert Brief / Geld *(Kurszusatz)* scaling down of limited sell orders/ limited buy orders

räuberische Anfechtungsklage predatory opposition action

Raumarbitrage market arbitrage, buying and selling the same instrument in different markets to profit from price discrepancies

Raumsicherungsvertrag storage assignment, assignment of goods stored in a specific place

reagibel sensitive (e. g. to interest rate changes), responsive

Reagibilität sensitiveness, responsiveness, susceptibleness

reagieren to react, to respond, *(schnell ~)* to provide a swift response, *(der Aktienmarkt reagierte negativ)* the equity market responded negatively

Reaktionsfähigkeit *(~ auf veränderte Marktbedingungen)* capacity to react to changed market conditions

real 1. *adj.* real, actual, effective, tangible, *(~e Kapitalbildung)* real capital formation, *(~es Volkseinkommen)* real net national income, *(~er Zinsertrag)* real interest return
2. *adv.* in real terms, *(Anstieg um ~ 5 %)* a 5 p.c. increase (growth) in real terms, *(um 2 % ~ fallen)* to fall by a real 2 p.c.

Real / ~darlehen real property loan, → Realkredit; **~einkommen** real income(s); **~einkommenssteigerung** growth in real income(s)

realgedeckt secured by a real property charge

R

Realisations / ~phase implementation phase; **~prinzip** realisation principle □ accounting for revenue when it is earned; **~wert** realisation (liquidation) value

realisierbar *(~er Wert einer Sicherheit)* realisable value of a security (collateral)

Realisierbarkeit realisability

realisieren 1. *(verwerten)* to sell, to realise, to liquidate, *(Kursgewinne ~)* to realise price gains, to cash in on profits, to take profits, *(realisierte Gewinne aus Finanzanlagen)* realised investment profits, *(realisierte Gewinne/Verluste aus Wertpapiergeschäften)* realised security gains/losses 2. *(in die Tat umsetzen)* to realise, to implement, to accomplish

Realisierung 1. sale, realisation, liquidation 2. *(Gewinnmitnahmen)* profit-taking, realising price gains 3. realisation, implementation, accomplishment

Realisierungs / ~erfolge realisation gains ; **~welle** welter (surge) of selling; **~wert** liquidation value, value upon realisation

Real / ~kapital real capital, tangible fixed assets; **~kaufkraft** real purchasing power; **~kosten** real cost

Realkredit real estate loan (lending), (long-term) property loan, loan against real estate, loan secured by a property charge

R

Realkredit / ~ausreichung property loan accommodation, extending a real estate loan; **~geschäft** real estate lending, property lending

Realkredit / ~institute real estate credit institutions □ private mortgage banks and public sector banks authorised to issue → Pfandbriefe and → Kommunalobligationen;**~last** mortgage loan charge; **~portefeuille** real estate loan portfolio (book)

Real / ~last ground rent; **~lohn** real wages; **~recht** real property right; **~rendite** net yield, yield less taxes and inflation rate; **~sicherheit** real property collateral, security on property; **~teilung** division of real property

Real / ~verzinsung effective (real) interest return; **~wert** real value; **~zins** real (effective) interest rate, nominal interest rate less inflation rate, inflation-adjusted interest rate; **~zinsniveau** real interest rate level

Rechenfehler error in calculation, miscalculation

Rechenschaft *(~ abgeben)* to give (to render) an account, to account (to answer) for

Rechenschaftsbericht 1. report, account (of proceedings) 2. annual management report, statement of operations

Rechenschaftslegung rendering an account of, submitting (presenting) a report on

Rechenschaftspflicht 1. duty to account for … 2. *(~ des Vorstandes gegenüber den Aktionären)* accountability of the Board to the shareholders

RechKredV → Kreditinstitute-Rechnungslegungsverordnung

rechnen 1. *(errechnen)* to calculate, to compute 2. *(erwarten)* to expect s.th., to reckon with s.th. 3. *(einkalkulieren)* to take into account 4. *(in Rechnung stellen)* to charge 5. *(~ mit)* to count on, to reckon with 6. *(~ zu)* to number (to count) among

rechnerisch *(~e Anschaffungskosten)* notional (constructed) purchase cost, *(~er Gesamtwert)* arithmetical total, aggregate value, *(~er Gewinn)* book (paper, accounting) profit, *(~e Parität)* calculated parity, *(~e Vergleichsrendite)* notional comparable yield *(~er Verlust)* book (paper, accounting) loss, *(~er Vorteil)* computational advantage, *(~er Wert)* notional (constructed, calculated) value, *(~er Wert der Aktien)* accounting par value of the shares

Rechnung 1. account, *(auf Ihre ~ und Gefahr)* for your account and risk, on your behalf and at your own risk, *(für ~ unseres Kunden)* for account of our customer, *(für eigene/fremde ~)* for own/third-party account, *(für neue ~)* for (on) new account, *(im Auftrag und für ~ von)* by order and for account of **2.** invoice, bill, *(zum Ausgleich Ihrer ~)* in settlement of your invoice
3. *(in ~ stellen)* to charge, to bill, *(dem Kunden in ~ gestellte Kosten)* costs charged (debited) to the customer's account
4. *(~ tragen)* to take into account, *(den erkennbaren Risiken ~)* to make allowance for the discernible risks, *(den Risiken im Kreditgeschäft ~)* to provide for the risks inherent in lending (for non-performing loans), to set up loan loss provisions

Rechnungsabgrenzungsposten *(Aktivseite)* prepayments, *(Passivseite)* deferred income

Rechnungsabschluss 1. *(Saldierung eines Kontos)* account balancing, settlement **2.** *(Schließung)* account closing **3.** *(Abschlussrechnung)* account balancing statement **4.** *(Bilanz)* annual accounts

Rechnungs / **~abschnitt** accounting period; **~aufstellung** statement of account; **~begleichung** settlement of an invoice; **~beleg** *(bei einer Kreditkartenzahlung)* sales slip (draft), charge slip, ticket, hard copy; **~betrag** invoice amount

Rechnungs / **~einheit** unit of account; **~erstellung** invoicing; **~fälligkeit** due date of an invoice; **~führung** accounting, accountancy; **~jahr** accounting year

Rechnungslegung 1. financial accounting (reporting), rendering of accounts, *(vollständige ~)* providing (rendering) full accounts, *(~ der Kreditinstitute)* financial reporting of banks **2.** billing

Rechnungslegungs / **~gesetz** Accounting and Reporting Act; **~grundsätze** accounting principles; **~periode** accounting (reporting) period; **~pflicht** accounting duty; **~recht** accounting law; **~ standards** financial accounting (reporting) standards; **~verordnung** Financial Reporting Regulation ; **~vorschriften** accounting rules

Rechnungs / **~periode** 1. accounting period **2.** billing period; **~posten** item, entry; **~preis** invoice (invoiced) price; **~prüfer** auditor; **~prüfung** audit (of accounts); **~prüfungsausschuss** audit committee; **~schema** accounting scheme

Rechnungs / **~unterlagen** 1. accounting records **2.** billing records; **~vortrag** balance carried (brought) forward; **~währung** invoicing currency; **~wert** invoiced (invoice) value; **~wesen** accounting, accountancy

Recht 1. law, legislation, *(~ der Liegenschaft)* lex situs, *(~ des Wohnorts)* lex domicilii **2.** *(Anspruch)* right, claim **3.** *(Befugnis)* power, authority **4.** *(Option)* option **5.** *(Rechtstitel)* title **6.** *(Vorrecht)* prerogative

Recht auf *(~ abgesonderte Befriedigung)* right to separate satisfaction, *(~ Einsichtnahme)* right of inspection, right to inspect, *(~ Gewinnbeteiligung)* right to a share in the profits, *(~ vollständige oder teilweise Kreditkündigung)* right to call in all or part of the loan
(~ Leistungsverweigerung) right to repudiate the contract, *(~ Nachbesserung)* right to cure, *(~ Nutzung)* right to enjoyment (e. g. of the property), *(~ Offenlegung der Zession)* right to disclosure of the assignment, *(~ vorzeitige Rückzahlung)* right to early repayment of the loan, early repayment (prepayment) option
(~ Umwandlung in Eigenkapital) equity conversion option, *(~ Vertragsrücktritt)* right of rescission, right to repudiate the contract, *(~ Wiederinbesitznahme)* right to recovery (repossession) of property

Rechte *(~ Dritter)* third party rights, *(~ an Grundstücken)* rights over real property, *(~ an Grundstücken und Gebäuden)* rights on land and buildings, *(~ und Pflichten aus dem Vertrag)* rights and obligations under the contract

Rechteck *(Chart-Analyse)* rectangle □ continuation pattern of a bullish trend (rectangle bottom) or of a bearish trend (rectangle top)

rechtfertigen to justify, *(die Annahme ~)* to warrant the assumption

Rechtfertigung justification, warranting

rechtlich 1. *adj.* legal, statutory, *(~e Absicherung)* legal safeguards, *(~er Anspruch)* legal entitlement, *(~es Bestehen)* legal existence (validity), *(~er Eigentümer)* legal owner, *(~e Frage)* question of law, *(Recht auf ~es Gehör)* right to be heard before the Court *(~e Grundlage)* legal basis, statutory base, *(~e Konsequenzen)* legal implications (repercussions), *(~e Rahmenbedingungen)* statutory (regulatory) framework, underlying legal conditions, *(~e Verpflichtung)* legal obligation
2. *adv.* legally, *(~ begründet)* to be justified by law, to be good in law, *(~ bindende Vereinbarung)* legally binding agreement, *(~ durchsetzbarer Anspruch)* legally enforceable right, *(~ feststellbar)* ascertainable at law, *(~ selbstständiges Sondervermögen/Unternehmen)* legally dependent special fund/company *(~ und tatsächlich)* in law and in fact, *(~ teilbar)* legally divisible, *(~ unselbständige Einrichtung)* establishment with dependent legal status, legally dependent establishment, *(~ unwirksam)* legally inoperative, *(~ verpflichtet)* to be bound by law

rechtmäßig 1. *adj.* lawful, rightful, legitimate, *(~er Besitz)* lawful possession, *(~er Besitzer/Eigentümer)* lawful (rightful) owner, *(~er Inhaber)* lawful holder (owner), person lawfully entitled to, holder in due course
2. *adv.* lawfully, legitimately, *(~ bevollmächtigt)* lawfully vested with the power to, duly authorised to

Rechtmäßigkeit lawfulness, legality, legitimacy, justification

Rechts / ~abteilung legal (law) department; **~abtretung** assignment of a right (title); **~angleichung** harmonisation of legal provisions (of laws)

rechtsanhängig pending at law

Rechts / ~anspruch legal claim, title, *(keinen Rechtsanspruch besitzen)* to have no redress at law; **~anwalt** lawyer, solicitor (BE), attorney (AE); **~anwaltsvergütungsgesetz** Attorneys Compensation Act

Rechts / ~anwendung application of a law; **~aufgabe** waiver of a right; **~ausübung** exercise of a right, exercising a right; **~beeinträchtigung** impairment (infringement) of a right; **~behelf 1.** legal remedy (redress) **2.** administrative appeal

Rechts / ~beistand 1. legal assistance **2.** legal advisor (counsel); **~berater** legal advisor; **~beratung** legal advice, legal counselling; **~beschwerde** appeal (complaint) on points of law

Rechts / ~bestand legal validity; **~beziehung** legal relationship, *(~ zwischen den Vertragsparteien)* privity of contract; **~bruch** breach of the law, violation of a right

Rechts / ~charakter legal nature; **~durchsetzung** enforcement of a right, legal enforcement; **~einheit** legal uniformity; **~einwand** defense, legal objection; **~entscheid** legal decision

rechtserhaltende Klausel salvatorius clause, severability clause

Rechtserwerb acquiring a right, acquisition of title

rechtsfähig to have legal capacity (personality), *(rechtsfähiger/nicht rechtsfä-*

higer Verein) incorporated/unincorporated association

Rechts / **~fähigkeit** legal capacity, capacity to act, *(Feststellung der ~)* establishment of the legal capacity; **~fähigkeitsgutachten** capacity opinion; **~folgen** legal consequences; **~folgerung** legal conclusion

Rechts / **~form** *(einer Unternehmung)* legal form, form of business organisation, type of legal entity; **~formalitäten** legal formalities; **~frage** legal matter, point of law; **~geschäft** legal transaction, legal act, *(rechtsgeschäftliches Schuldverhältnis)* contractual obligation; **~gleichheit** legal equality

Rechts / **~grundlage** legal basis, basis in law; **~grundsatz** legal maxim (principle); **~gültigkeit** validity, legality, *(einen Anspruch rechtsgültig abtreten)* to validly assign a claim; **~gutachten** legal opinion

Rechts / **~hängigkeit** pendency (of action), lis pendens, *(rechtshängig)* pending; **~hilfe 1.** legal assistance (aid) **2.** judicial assistance; **~hilfeersuchen** letters of request, letters rogatory (AE)

rechtshindernde Einwendung dilatory defense

Rechts / **~inhaber** title holder, holder of a right; **~kraft** legal (operative) force, validity, *(~ erlangen)* to obtain legal force, *(der Garantie ~ verleihen)* to give legal effect to the guarantee

rechtskräftig legally binding, valid, res judicata, *(~er Beschlusss)* binding, resolution, *(~es Urteil)* final (non-appealable) judgement, *(~ festgestellte Ansprüche)* legally established claims

Rechtsmangel legal deficiency, title defect, deficiency in title, *(rechtsmängelfreier Eigentumstitel)* clear title

Rechtsmängelhaftung liability for title defects, warranty of title

Rechtsmissbrauch abuse of a right (of rights), abuse of the legal system, *(rechtsmissbräuchliche Inanspruchnahme einer Garantie)* unfair calling of a guarantee, *(rechtsmissbräuchliche Klage)* abusive suit

Rechtsmittel 1. legal remedy (redress, recourse), remedial action, remedy at law, remedy provided by law, *(Ausschöpfung aller ~)* exhausting all legal remedies **2.** *(Berufung)* appeal

Rechts / **~nachfolge** legal succession, succession in title; **~nachfolger 1.** legal successor, successor in title **2.** successor party to a contract **3.** assignee; **~norm** legal rule; **~ordnung** legal system

Rechts / **~person** legal entity; **~persönlichkeit** legal personality, *(Gesellschaft ohne ~)* company without legal personality; **~pflege** administration of law (justice); **~pfleger** judicial administrator, senior court officer, *(~ am Nachlassgericht)* probate officer; **~rahmen** legal (regulatory) framework

Rechts / **~pflicht** legal obligation, *(ohne Anerkenntnis einer ~)* without acknowledging any legal obligation; **~risiko** legal risk □ risk of loss due to new legal regulations, risk that a contract cannot be enforced; **~sache** case, legal matter

Rechtsschutz legal protection, *(einstweiliger ~)* injunctive relief, *(gewerblicher ~)* protection of industrial property rights

Rechtsschutz / **~bedürfnis** legitimate interest to claim relief; **~garantie** legal expenses cover; **~gewährung** granting legal protection to …; **~verfahren** relief proceedings; **~versicherung** legal expenses insurance

Rechts / **~sicherheit** legal certainty, *(rechtssicherer Vertrag)* legally binding contract; **~sprechung 1.** jurisdiction **2.** case law, court rulings, legal practice; **~standpunkt** legal point of view

Rechts / **~stellung** legal status; **~ streit** lawsuit, litigation, *(~ bezüglich der Eigentumsfrage)* legal wrangle over the ownership of ..., *(Kosten des ~s)* cost of litigation

Rechts / ~**subjekt** legal person (entity); ~**titel** title, title of property; ~**titelüberprüfung** investigation of title; ~**titelversicherung** title insurance; ~**träger** legal entity

Rechts / ~**übergang** devolution of title, passing of the title, title transfer; ~**übertragung** title transfer, assignment (transfer) of a right; ~**unsicherheit** legal uncertainty, legal uncertainties surrounding the matter (case); ~**unterzeichner** signatory to the right

rechtsunwirksam of no legal value (effect), legally ineffective, null and void

Rechtsunwirksamkeit legal ineffectiveness, voidness

rechtsverbindlich 1. *adj. (~e Verpflichtung)* legally binding obligation, *(~e Zusage)* legally binding undertaking (covenant), *(~ für den Kreditnehmer)* legally binding on the borrower
2. *adv. (~ unterzeichnen/vertreten)* to sign/to represent in a legally binding manner, *(~ unterzeichneter Garantietext)* guarantee text with legally binding signatures affixed thereto

Rechts / ~**verbindlichkeit** legal bindingness, legal obligation; ~**vereinheitlichung** *(europäische ~)* European legal unification; ~**verfolgung** legal pursuit, bringing an action against, pursuit of rights; ~**verfolgungskosten** legal cost (fees), costs of legal pursuit

R

Rechts / ~**verhältnis** legal relationship; ~ **verkehr** legal transactions; ~**verletzung** 1. breach of the law 2. violation (infringement) of a right; ~**verlust** forfeiture of a right; ~**vermutung** legal presumption

Rechts / ~**verordnung** (legal) ordinance, executive order; ~**verpflichtung** legal obligation; ~**verteidigung** legal defense; ~**vertreter** legal representative; ~**verwirkung** forfeiture of a right; ~**verzicht** relinquishment (waiver) of a right

Rechts / ~**vorbehalt** reservation of a right; ~**vorgänger** predecessor in title; ~**vorschrift** 1. statutory regulation 2. legal provision; ~**wahl** choice of law; ~ **wahlklausel** choice of law clause, proper law clause

Rechtsweg *(auf dem ~)* through legal channels, by taking legal action, *(auf dem ~ entscheiden)* to decide by judicial action, *(den ~ beschreiten)* to take legal action, to go to law

rechtswidrig unlawful, illegal, *(~e Inbesitznahme)* unlawful entry, *(~er Besitzanspruch)* tort of conversion

Rechtswidrigkeit unlawfulness, illegality

rechtswirksam 1. *adj.* valid, legally operative, having legal strength (force), *(nicht ~)* legally inoperative, *(~es Pfandrecht/Sicherungspfandrecht)* enforceable lien/security interest, *(~e Urkunde)* operative instrument, *(~er Vertrag)* valid contract
2. *adv. (als ~ anerkennen)* to recognise as effective in law, *(~ werden)* to become operative (legally effective), to operate, to be carried into effect

Rechtswirksamkeit validity, legal force (sufficiency)

Rechtswirkungen legal implications (repercussions)

rechtwinkliges Dreieck *(Chart-Analyse)* ascending triangle □ bullish stock market indicator

rechtzeitig prompt, punctual, *(~e Vorlage der Dokumente)* timely presentation of the documents

Rediskont *(zum ~ hereinnehmen)* to accept for rediscount, *(rediskontfähige Wechsel)* bills eligible for rediscount, rediscountable bills □ *Bundesbank stopped the purchase of bills in December 1998*

Reduktionsklausel 1. de-escalation clause 2. (liability) reduction clause

reduzieren to reduce, to diminish, to cut back, to lower, *(den Bestand ~)* to downsize the holdings

Reduzierung reduction, cut, lowering

Reeder *(Pfandrecht des ~s)* shipowner's lien

Referat 1. *(Abteilung)* unit **2.** *(Bericht)* report **3.** *(Rede)* lecture, address, paper

Referent speaker, reporter

Referentenentwurf first ministry draft, initial draft

Referenz 1. reference, *(~ einer Bank)* banker's reference, *(über ausgezeichnete ~en verfügen)* to hold excellent references (credentials), *(als ~ anführen) (a)* to quote as reference *(b)* to give s. o. as a reference
2. *(Empfehlungsschreiben)* testimonial, recommendation

Referenz / ~aktivum *(das einem Kreditderivat zugrunde liegende Finanzinstrument/der als Sicherheit dienende Vermögenswert)* reference asset; **~einheit** reference entity

Referenz / ~gruppe peer group; **~instrument** reference instrument, → Referenzaktivum; **~marke** benchmark

Referenz / ~nummer reference (file) number; **~periode** reference period; **~portfolio 1.** *(gebündelte Einzelforderungen, z. B. bei einer Verbriefung)* reference portfolio **2.** *(als Vergleichsmaßstab)* benchmark portfolio

Referenz / ~satz reference rate; **~verbindlichkeit** reference liability, → Referenzaktivum; **~währung** reference currency; **~wechselkurs** exchange reference rate; **~zeitraum** reference (base) period; **~zinssatz** reference interest rate

refinanzierbar refinanceable

refinanzieren to fund, to refinance, *(die Bank konnte sich weiterhin zu günstigen Konditionen ~)* the bank kept funding itself on favourable terms, *(sich durch Emissionen am Kapitalmarkt ~)* to fund one's lendings through capital market issues (through tapping the capital market) *(im Kapitalmarkt refinanzierte Kredite)* loans funded in the capital market (wholesale market), *(über Pfandbriefe refinanzierte langfristige Darlehen)* long-term loans funded through the issue of covered bonds, → Pfandbrief, *(mit kurzfristigem Geld ~)* to fund with short-term money, *(sich bei der Zentralbank ~)* to fund one's lendings through Central Bank borrowings

Refinanzierung funding, refinancing, *(~ der Ausleihungen am Interbanken-/Kapitalmarkt)* wholesale funding, funding (refinancing) lendings through borrowings in the interbank (wholesale) market, *(~ zu günstigen Konditionen)* refinancing on favourable terms, *(~ des kurzfristigen Kreditgeschäftes)* funding short-term lending operations, *(~ mit zinsvariablen Mitteln)* floating rate funding

Refinanzierungs / ~basis funding base (basis); **~bedarf** *(~ der Banken)* banks' funding (refinancing) requirements; **~fächer** range of funding instruments

refinanzierungsfähig *(~ im ESZB)* qualifying for use in the ESCB refinancing system, *(~e Sicherheiten)* eligible assets, → Kategorie 1/Kategorie 2 Sicherheiten

Refinanzierungsgeber refinance lender

Refinanzierungsgegenstände *(bei einer True-Sale-Verbriefung)* refinancing assets □ i.e commercial/leasing/loan receivables or registered liens/charges that are eligible for entry in the → Refinanzierungsregister; such assets are insolvency-proof, i.e. the beneficiary may claim separate satisfaction in the case of the originator's insolvency

Refinanzierungs / ~geschäft funding operations, refinancing transactions; **~guthaben** funding assets; **~instrumentarium** funding (refinancing) tools; **~konditionen** funding (refinancing) terms

Refinanzierungs / ~kontingent funding quota; **~kosten** funding cost, cost of refinance; **~kredit** funding

R

facility (loan), refinance credit; ~**linie** refinancing facility (line); ~**mittel** refinance, refinancing funds, funding capital

Refinanzierungsmittler refinancing intermediary □ acquires assets (→ Refinanzierungsgegenstände) from a refinancing enterprise (→ Refinanzierungsunternehmen) for sale to a special purpose vehicle

Refinanzierungs / ~möglichkeiten refinancing options, funding facilities; ~**plafond** refinancing limit; ~**quellen** funding sources, sources of refinance; ~**rahmen** refinancing line

Refinanzierungsregister refinancing register □ register for recording the assets of the refinancing enterprise (originator) for the benefit of creditors, → Refinanzierungsgegenstände, → Refinanzierungsunternehmen

Refinanzierungsregistergesetz German Refinancing Register Act □ introduced the → Refinanzierungsregister into the German Banking Act (KWG)

Refinanzierungsrisiko funding (refinancing) risk, risk that sources required to fund new lendings are not available

Refinanzierungs / ~schwierigkeiten funding difficulties, difficulties in providing the necessary refinance; ~**spielraum** refinancing (funding) scope; ~-**Swap** funding swap

R

Refinanzierungs / ~titel 1. refinanced debt **2.** securities (debt, paper) used/usable in funding transactions; ~**treuhand** refinancing trust

Refinanzierungsunternehmen *(bei True-Sale-Verbriefungen)* refinancing enterprise □ enterprise that sells assets (→ Refinanzierungsgegenstände) to a special purpose vehicle

Refinanzierungs /~verbindlichkeiten liabilities under funding operations, refinancing liabilities; ~**vereinbarung** funding (refinancing) arrangement; ~**verteuerung** increase in funding costs; ~**wechsel** refinance bill; ~**zusage** refinancing undertaking, undertaking (commitment) to refinance

Regal → Münzregal

rege *(~ Nachfrage)* brisk demand

Regel 1. *(Grundsatz)* principle, *(~n der Geldpolitik)* monetary policy principles, *(in aller ~ wird davon ausgegangen)* it is generally assumed **2.** *(Richtlinie)* guideline
3. *(Vorschrift)* rule, ruling, *(Regeln zur Gesellschafterfremdfinanzierung)* thin capitalisation rules, → Gesellschafterfremdfinanzierung

Regel / ~beitragssatz standard premium; ~**bericht** regular (periodical) report; ~ **fall** *(im ~)* normally, as a rule

Regelinsolvenzverfahren regular insolvency proceedings □ consisting of the preliminary insolvency proceedings (vorläufiges Insolvenzverfahren) and the actual (so-called opened) insolvency proceedings (eröffnetes Insolvenzverfahren), → Insolvenzplanverfahren

Regellaufzeit standard maturity

regelmäßig 1. *adj.* regular, scheduled, *(~e Berichte)* regular (periodic) reports, *(~e Dividendenzahlungen)* regular dividend payments, unbroken dividend record, *(~e Einkünfte)* regular income, *(~e Tilgungszahlungen)* regular (scheduled) principal repayments, *(~e Verpfändung)* conventional pledge, *(~e Zinszahlungen)* regular (periodic) interest payments
2. *adv.* regularly, on a regular basis, at regular intervals, *(~ gehandelt werden)* to be traded regularly, to have a steady market

Regelmäßigkeit regularity

regeln 1. *(beilegen)* to settle **2.** *(regulieren)* to regulate, to control **3.** *(Verordnung erlassen)* to rule, to order

Regeltilgungssatz standard repayment rate

Regelung 1. settlement **2.** regulation, regulating **3.** *(Vorschrift)* provision, ruling

Regelungs / **~verfügung** regulatory decree; **~vollmachten** rule-makng powers

Regelverjährung standard limitation period

Regelwerk rules and regulations, regulatory framework, set of rules

Regional / **~bank** regional bank; **~börse** regional stock exchange; **~entwicklungs/~förderprogramm** regional development scheme; **~prinzip** regional principle □ regional competition guidelines prohibiting savings banks from operating outside their local areas

Register **1.** register, record **2.** *(Amt)* registry **3.** *(Inhaltsverzeichnis)* table of contents

Register / **~amt** registry, registration office; **~auszug** extract (excerpt) from the register; **~eintrag** register entry; **~eintragung** registration, entering in a register; **~führer** registrar; **~gericht** Court of Registry, District Court

Registerpfandrecht registered lien □ requires an entry in the corresponding register, e.g. in the register of liens on aircrafts; there is, however, no transfer of title, *(~ an beweglichen Sachen)* registered lien on moveables, *(ein ~verwerten)* to realise a registered lien by way of a foreclosure sale

Register / **~stelle** → Registeramt; **~vormerkung** caution, cavet

REGIS TR *(Transaktionsregister für OTC Derivate)* OTC Derivatives Trade Repository □ global registry for OTC derivative contracts

registrieren to register, to record

Registrierung registration, recording, *(~ im Grundbuch)* registration in (with) the Land Registry

Registrierungs / **~gebühr** registration (recording) fee; **~pflicht** registration requirement, *(Befreiung von der ~)* registration exemption; **~vorschriften** registration (filing) requirements

Reglement regulations

reglementieren to regulate, to regularise, to control, *(stark reglementierter Markt)* heavily regulated market

Regress recourse, redress, *(~ mangels Annahme)* recourse for want of acceptance, *(~ gegenüber Dritten)* recourse against third parties, *(~ mangels Zahlung)* recourse in default of payment, *(in ~ nehmen)* to have recourse to, to obtain redress from

Regress / **~anspruch** right of recourse; **~forderung** recourse claim

regressfrei *(~er Verkauf)* non-recourse sale, à forfait sale, sale without recourse to the seller

Regresshaftung recourse liability

Regressionsanalyse regression analysis

Regressklage action for recourse

regresslos → regressfrei

Regress / **~nehmer** party seeking recourse; **~pflicht** recourse obligation, *(regresspflichtig)* liable to recourse; **~recht** right of recourse; **~schuldner** recourse debtor; **~verzichtserklärung** waiver of recourse

regulär regular, usual, *(~es Bankgeschäft)* mainstream banking, traditional banking activities, *(~es Eigenkapital)* regular liable capital, *(~e Erträge)* regular income, net interest and commission income

regulatorisch *(~e Anpassungen)* regulatory adjustments,adjustments to the regulatory capital, *(~e Eigenkapitalentlastung)* regulatory capital relief, *(~es Kapital)* regulatory capital, □ under → Basel III, banks' regulatory capital consists of Tier 1 capital (→ Kernkapital) and Tier 2 capital (→ Ergänzungskapital)
(~es Risiko) regulatory risk, exposure to loss due to changes in the regulatory requirements, *(~e Risikozuschläge)* regulatory risk add-ons

regulieren **1.** to settle, to pay **2.** to regulate

Regulierer claims adjuster, claims settling agent

Regulierter Markt Regulated Market □ Organised securities exchange established on November 1, 2007 after the merger of the former first market segment (Amtlicher Markt) and the second market segment (Geregelter Markt). Admission requirements are legally regulated. → börsenregulierter Markt, → Freiverkehr

Regulierung 1. settlement, payment , *(~ des Gegenwertes)* settlement of the proceeds (equivalent), (~ *eines Schadens)* settlement of a claim, claims settlement, loss adjustment, (~ *am gleichen Tag)* same-day settlement, *(~ unter Vorbehalt)* settlement under reserve(s) **2.** regulation, control

Regulierungs / **~agentur** regulatory agency; **~anspruch** settlement claim; **~arbitrage** regulatory arbitrage □ *(a)* transacting business in countries offering the best regulatory setting *(b)* making use of discrepancies between regulatory and economic capital

Regulierungs / **~aufgaben** regulatory functions; **~aufwand** claims settlement (loss adjustment) expenses; **~beauftragter** loss adjuster, loss assessor; **~behörde** regulatory authority; **~entgelt** settlement fee; **~ermessen** regulatory discretion

Regulierungs / **~gesetz** Regulatory Act; **~kosten** regulatory cost; **~kurs** settlement price (rate); **~lücke** regulatory gap; **~rahmen** regulatory framework; **~recht 1.** regulatory law **2.** right to regulate, regulatory power; **~risiko** regulatory risk □ risk of loss due to a change in rules or regulations

Regulierungs / **~tag** settlement date; **~verfahren 1.** claims settlement process **2.** regulatory proceedings; **~vollmacht** regulatory (rule-making) power; **~vorgaben** regulatory requirements

reibungslos *(~e Geschäftsübergabe)* smooth handing over of business

reich *(~e Auswahl an Anlagemöglichkeiten)* ample investment opportunities, wide (extensive) selection of investment options (vehicles), *(~e Erfahrung im Wertpapierhandel)* wide (rich) experience in securities trading

reichen 1. *(genügen)* to suffice **2.** *(sich erstrecken über)* to extend, to stretch **3.** *(~ von ... bis ....)* to range from ... to ...

Reichweite *(eines Werbeträgers)* coverage, reach, cumulative audience

Reife *(~ eines Produktes)* product maturity

reifen to take shape, to mature

Reifen taking shape, *(~ eines Marktes)* maturation of a market

reiflich (*~e Überlegung)* careful consideration

Reihe 1. (large) number, *(eine ~ von Treffen)* a series (string, host) of meetings **2.** *(aus den ~n der Aktionäre)* from the ranks of the shareholders **3.** *(Reihenfolge)* order, succession, sequence, *(von Indossamenten)* chain of endorsements

Reihenfolge 1. order, succession, *(in aufsteigender ~)* in ascending order, *(in umgekehrter ~)* in reverse order, *(nach der zeitlichen ~ des Eingangs)* in chronological order of receipt **2.** *(Rangfolge)* ranking, (~ *der Belastungen im Grundbuch)* ranking of charges in the land register

Reihenrückgriff recourse in order of endorsers

rein (~ *Geld)* buyers (bids) only

rein *(~es Ausführungsgeschäft)* execution only, *(~es Konnossement)* clean bill of lading, *(~e Stücke)* good delivery stock, *(~ er Terminkauf)* outright forward purchase, *(~e Transport-/Verschiffungsdokumente)* clean transport/shipping documents, *(~e Zahlung)* clean payment

Rein / **~erlös** net proceeds, net avails; **~ertrag** net earnings (surplus); **~gewinn** net income, net profit, *(~ je Aktie)* net income per share; **~über-**

schuss net balance, net income; ~**vermögen** net worth, net assets

reinvestieren to reinvest, to plough (to plow) back

Reinvestitionsrücklage reinvestment reserve

Reisekostenabrechnung travel expense statement

REIT-AG / REIT-Gesetz REIT Stock Corporation/German REIT Act □ real estate investment trusts in Germany (domestic REITs) are exempted from corporate income tax and trade tax provided that the requirements of the German REIT Act are met

Reiz *(~ für ausländische Anleger)* attraction(s) to foreign investors

Rekapitalisierung recapitalisation, *(~ durch Erhöhung des Fremdkapitalanteils)* leveraged recapitalisation

Reklamation **1.** complaint **2.** *(Nachfrage, Anfrage)* query

Reklamations / ~bearbeitung complaints processing; ~**frist** period for filing a complaint, warranty period; ~**management** complaint management; ~**recht** right to complain; ~**schreiben** complaint letter

reklamieren **1.** to complain, to lodge a complaint, to object to **2.** *(nachfragen)* to query

rekonstruieren *(den Inkassovorgang ~)* to trace back (to reconstruct) the collection

Rekord / ~ergebnis record (record-breaking) performance; ~**gewinn** bumper profit (performance), record profit; ~**höchststand** all-time high; ~**jahr** banner year; ~**kurs** record price (quotation)

Rekord / ~schlusshoch record close, all-time closing high; ~**tiefstand** all-time low, *(die Aktie fiel auf einen ~)* the stock slumped to its lowest-ever level; ~**umsatz** bumper sales (turnover)

Rekta / ~grundschuldbrief registered land charge certificate; ~**konnossement** straight (non-negotiable) bill of lading; ~**papier** registered (non-negotiable) security

Rekta / ~rentenschuldbrief registered annuity bond; ~**scheck** non-endorsable cheque, non-negotiable cheque; ~**wechsel** non-negotiable bill

Relation ratio

Relative-Stärke-Indikator relative strength indicator □ measures a stock's performance to that of a market index

relativieren to qualify, to put into perspective

Relevanz relevance

Rembours reimbursement, *(~ aus einem Akkreditiv erhalten)* to receive reimbursement under a documentary credit, *(~ auf erstes Anfordern)* providing reimbursement on first call

Rembours / ~akkreditiv reimbursement credit; ~**anzeige**/~**avis** reimbursement advice; ~**auftrag** reimbursing instruction; ~**bank** reimbursing bank (banker), accepting bank, *(remboursberechtigte Bank)* bank entitled to claim reimbursement

Rembours / ~ermächtigung reimbursement authority (authorisation); ~**fazilität** reimbursement facility, documentary acceptance facility; ~**geschäft** reimbursement transaction, documentary payment transaction

remboursieren **1.** to reimburse **2.** to claim reimbursement

Remboursierungsanspruch reimbursement claim, right to reimbursement

Rembours / ~kredit reimbursement credit, documentary acceptance credit; ~**leistung** providing reimbursement; ~**linie** reimbursement facility, acceptance credit line; ~**rückgriff** reimbursement recourse

Rembours / ~schreiben reimbursement instructions; ~**schuldner** documentary credit debtor; ~**schutzbrief** reimbursement covering letter; ~**stel-**

le reimbursing bank, reimbursing office

Rembours / ~tratte/~wechsel reimbursement draft; **~zusage** commitment to reimburse, reimbursement undertaking

Remittent *(eines Wechsels)* payee of a bill

Rendite yield, return, *(~ einer Anlage)* investment return, *(~ des Kapitaleinsatzes)* return on capital employed, *(~ von Kurz-/Langläufern)* yield on shorts/longs, short-dated/long-dated bond yield, *(~ am Rentenmarkt)* bond market yield, *(~ am Sekundärmarkt)* secondary market yield, *(~ vor/nach Steuern)* pre-tax/post-tax yield, *(~ auf Verfall)* yield to maturity

Rendite / ~abstand spread, *(~ zwischen drei- und zehnjährigen Anleihen)* yield gap (spread) between three and ten-year bonds; **~abweichung** yield variance; **~angleichung** yield adjustment; **~anstieg** yield increase, yield pick-up, *(~ im kurzen Bereich)* yield increase at the short end of the market

Rendite / ~aufbesserung yield enhancement (improvement); **~aufschlag** spread, *(Renditeaufschläge auf Unternehmensanleihen)* corporate bond spreads □ difference between the yields of corporate and government bonds; **~aussichten** yield prospects

Rendite / ~berechnung yield calculation, computation of the yield; **~bewusstsein** yield awareness; **~depot** income investment portfolio; **~differenz** yield gap

Rendite / ~erhöhung yield increase; **~ermittlung** calculating the yield, yield calculation (computation); **~erwägungen** *(Käufe aufgrund von ~)* buying on yield considerations; **~erwartung** yield expectation, expected yield, expected (anticipated) return

Rendite / ~fächer yield range (spread); **~festschreibung** locking in a yield ; **~garantie** yield maintenance guarantee; **~gefälle** yield differential; **~gefüge** yield pattern; **~immobilien** income properties; **~index** yield index

Rendite / ~kalkulation yield calculation; **~kennziffer** return ratio; **~kontrollrechnung** yield (return) measurement

Renditekurve yield curve □ graphical representation of bond yields against their time to maturity, *(flache/steile ~)* flat/steep yield curve, *(fallende/steigende ~)* downward/upward sloping yield curve, *(positive/negative ~)* positively/negatively sloped yield curve

Rendite / ~liegenschaften investment properties; **~maßstab** yield benchmark; **~maximierung** yield maximisation, maximising the yield (return); **~messung** yield measurement; **~niveau** yield level, *(~ am Anleihemarkt)* yield in the bond market

Renditeobjekt income-producing asset, *(im Immobilienbereich)* investment property, high-yielding investment property, property purchased for investment purposes

Rendite / ~optimierung optimising the yield; **~orientierung** yield orientation (focus), orientation at the yield obtainable in the market, *(renditeorientierte Anlagen)* yield-driven investments, *(renditeorientierter Anleger)* yield-focussed investor

Rendite / ~papiere securities offering an attractive yield, high-yield securities; **~prognose** yield forecast; **~rückgang** decline in yields, yield decrease; **~rutsch** slide in yields

Rendite / ~schätzung yield estimate; **~schere** yield gap; **~schwankungen** yield fluctuations; **~sicherung** yield hedging; **~spanne** yield spread; **~steigerung** yield increase; **~struktur** yield structure (pattern)

Rendite / ~unterschied yield spread, → Renditeaufschlag; **~verbesserung** 1. yield improvement (enhancement) 2. *(verbesserte Rendite)* enhanced return (yield); **~verfall** slump in yields; **~vergleich** yield comparison; **~ver-**

hältnis yield relationship (e. g. between shares and bonds)

Rendite / **~verschlechterung** decline in yields, shrinking yields (returns); **~volatilität** yield volatility; **~vorsprung/~vorteil** yield advantage; **~ziel** return (yield) target, return-on-investment objective

Renommee reputation, renown, repute

renommiert renowned, reputed, high-profile

rentabel profitable, lucrative, remunerative, *(~ anlegen)* to invest at a profit

Rentabilität **1.** profitability, profitableness, *(~ der Kundenverbindung)* customer profitability
2. return on investment, rate of return, *(~ des Kapitaleinsatzes)* return on capital employed, *(~ des Kreditgeschäfts)* return on (profitability of) lending operations

Rentabilitäts / **~analyse** profitability analysis; **~berechnung** calculation of the net return; **~erwartung** expected return (profitability); **~kennzahl/~kennziffer** profitability ratio (measure); **~messung** profitability measurement; **~optimierung** optimising profitability; **~orientierung** profit orientation

Rentabilitäts / **~prüfung** profitability analysis; **~rechnung** **1.** profitability accounting **2.** calculation of the net return **3.** return on investment method; **~risiko** return risk □ risk that the return (yield) falls short of the investor's expectations

Rentabilitäts / **~schwelle** break-even point; **~verschlechterung** deterioration (decline) in profitability; **~vorschau** profitability forecast

Rente **1.** *(Ruhegehalt)* pension **2.** *(regelmäßige Zahlung)* annuity **3.** → Renten

Renten fixed income bonds, fixed interest (fixed rate) securities, fixed rate paper

Renten / **~absatz** fixed income bond sales; **~anlagen** investments in fixed income bonds (securities), bond market investments; **~anleger** bond investor

Renten / **~baisse** sharp drop in bond prices, slump in the bond market (fixed rate paper market), bear run in the bond market; **~bestand** fixed income bond holdings (portfolio); **~depot** bond portfolio, fixed income securities portfolio; **~flaute** stalemate in the bond market, sagging (sluggish) fixed rate paper market

Renten / **~fonds** bond fund, fixed interest securities fund, fund (unit trust) investing only in fixed income securities; **~gewichtung** *(in einem Wertpapierdepot)* portfolio weighting given to fixed income securities

Renten / **~handel** **1.** trading (dealings) in fixed income securities, fixed income bond trading **2.** *(Abteilung)* bond trading desk (unit); **~händler** fixed income bond trader

Renten / **~hausse** bull run in the bond market, strong upsurge in bond prices; **~index** bond market average, → Rentenmarkt; **~indexfonds** bond index fund, fixed-income exchange-traded fund; **~kurse** bond prices; **~leihe** bond lending

Rentenmarkt bond market, fixed income securities market, fixed rate paper market

Rentenmarkt / **~engagement** bond market exposure; **~finanzierung** financing through the bond market; **~investment** bond market investment(s); **~teilnehmer** bond market operator (participant); **~umsätze** turnover in the bond market, level of activity in the bond market

Renten / **~notierungen** bond prices (quotations), prices (quotations) for fixed income securities; **~optionshandel** bond option trading; **~parkett** bond trading floor; **~portefeuille** bond portfolio

Renten / **~quote** *(im Portfolio)* bond allocation, allocation to fixed income

R

securities, *(60%ige Rentenquote)* 60% allocation to bond investments; ~**rendite** (fixed income) bond yield, fixed rate paper yield

Renten / ~schuldforderung annuity land charge; ~**schwäche** weakness in bond prices (in the bond market); ~**umlauf** bonds outstanding; ~**umsätze** turnover (dealings) in bonds, bond transactions; ~**werte** fixed interest (fixed income) securities, fixed rate paper

rentieren 1. *(erbringen)* to yield, to bring in, to return 2. *(sich ~)* to be worthwhile, to pay

Reorganisation *(~ einer existenzgefährdeten Bank)* reorganisation, → Reorganisationsplan, → Reorganisationsverfahren, → Kreditinstitute-Reorganisationsgesetz

Reorganisationsberater reorganisation advisor, → Reorganisationsverfahren

Reorganisationsplan reorganisation plan □ must specify measures with respect to the reorganisation and possible winding-up of the endangered credit institution, → Reorganisationsverfahren, → Kreditinstitute-Reorganisationsgesetz, → Restrukturierungsgesetz

Reorganisationsverfahren reorganisation proceedings □ will be opened if the restructuring proceedings (→ Sanierungsverfahren) of a bank in need of restructuring have failed or are without prospect of success, → Kreditinstitute-Reorganisationsgesetz

R

reorganisieren to reorganise, to restructure

reparieren to repair, to mend (e. g. the rift between … and …)

repartieren 1. to allot 2. *(eine überzeichnete Neuemission von Wertpapieren)* to scale down

Repartierung 1. allotment 2. scaling down

Repartierungsquote *(bei Hauptrefinanzierungsgeschäften)* allotment ratio

repatriieren *(Gelder/Gewinne ~)* to repatriate (to transfer back) funds/profits

Repatriierung *(~ der ins Ausland abgeflossenen Gelder)* repatriation of funds transferred abroad

Repo-Abschlag repo haircut

repofähig *(~e Wertpapiere)* repoable (repo eligible) securities, securities eligible for repo (repurchase) transactions

Repo-Geschäft repurchase agreement, repo transaction

Repo-Käufer repo buyer, transferee

Repo-Rate repo rate □ the difference between purchase and repurchase price in a repurchase agreement; corresponds to the interest due on the funds borrowed/lent

Repo-Verkäufer repo seller, transferor

Report contango □ descriptive of a carrying charge market, i.e. a condition in which the spot rate (or cash price for nearby delivery months) of a commodity or financial instrument is below its forward rate (or price for more distant delivery months), → Deport (backwardation)

reportieren to carry over to the next settlement

Repräsentant representative

Repräsentanz representative office

repräsentativ *(~ für das Kreditgewerbe)* representative of the banking industry as a whole

repräsentieren to represent, to constitute

reprivatisieren to put back into private ownership

Reprivatisierungstransaktion public-to-private deal

Reputations / ~risiko reputation (reputational) risk, exposure to loss from negative publicity; ~**schaden** reputational damage

Reserve 1. *(Rücklage)* reserve 2. *(Vorrat)* supply, supplies

Reserve / **~auflösung** writing back reserves; **~einheit** *(IWF)* reserve unit; **~entnahmen** drawing on reserves; **~guthaben** reserve balances (holdings), reserve deposits

Reserve / **~haltung** reserve maintenance, reserve management; **~meldung** reserve statement; **~mittel** *(IWF)* reserve facility, reserve funds; **~pflicht** reserve requirement

reservepflichtig *(~e Einlagen)* deposits subject to reserve requirements, reservable deposits, *(~e Verbindlichkeiten)* reserve-carrying liabilities, liabilities subject to reserve requirements

Reserve / **~satz** reserve ratio, *(Reservesätze für Sicht-, Termin- und Spareinlagen)* reserve ratios for demand, time and savings deposits; **~soll** reserve requirement, required reserve; **~sollberechnung** calculation of the reserve requirement

Reserve / **~tranche** reserve tranche; **~währung** reserve currency; **~währungsguthaben** reserve currency balances; **~zuweisung** allocation to reserves

reservieren 1. to reserve, to book, to make a reservation **2.** reserved, withdrawn, *(die Anleger verhielten sich reserviert)* investors remained on the sidelines

Residualanspruch *(~ am Reinvermögen)* residual interest in net assets

Residualwert residual (terminal) value

Respektfrist/**~tage** period (days) of grace

Ressort 1. *(Abteilung)* department **2.** *(Zuständigkeitsbereich)* province, sphere, line, competence, preserve, portfolio

Ressourcen resources; **~einsatz** deployment of resources

Restanten/**Restantenliste 1.** unclaimed securities □ relating to securities drawn or called for redemption **2.** unsettled securities transactions

Rest / **~betrag** residual (remaining) amount, → Restschuld; **~buchwert** residual book value, salvage value; **~engagement** residual (remaining) exposure; **~forderung** residual claim; **~guthaben** residual credit balance; **~inanspruchnahme** → Restschuld

Restitutions / **~anspruch** restitution claim; **~klage** action for restitution; **~verfahren** restitution proceedings

Rest / **~kapital** residual capital, → Restschuld; **~kaufgeldhypothek** property charge for payment of the residual purchase price; **~kaufsumme** residual purchase price; **~laufzeit** time (term) to maturity, residual maturity (life), time remaining until expiration

restlich residual, remaining

Restposten 1. *(im Rechnungswesen)* memorandum (residual) item **2.** *(im Emissionsgeschäft)* unplaced securities **3.** *(~ der Zahlungsbilanz)* balancing item of the balance of payments

Restriktion restriction, limitation

Restriktions / **~erleichterungen** easing of (alleviating) restrictions; **~kurs** restrictive course (policy); **~maßnahmen** restrictive measures

restriktiv *(~e Geldpolitik)* tight monetary policy, *(~e Kreditpolitik)* restrictive credit policy

Restrisiko residual exposure, remaining risk, remaining net exposure

restrukturieren to restructure, to reorganise, to reshape

Restrukturierung restructuring, reorganisation, *(~ notleidender Kredite)* troubled debt restructuring

Restrukturierungsaufwand/**~kosten** restructuring cost (charges)

Restrukturierungsfonds restructuring fund □ The fund established under the Restructuring Act to prevent the insolvency of ailing credit institutions will be financed through the bank levy (→ Bankenabgabe) imposed on all German credit institutions. → Restrukturierungsgesetz, → Kreditinstitute-Reorganisationsgsetz

Restrukturierungsfondsgesetz *(Gesetz zur Errichtung eines Restrukturierungsfonds für Kreditinstitute)* Restructuring Fund Act

Restrukturierungsfondsverordnung Restructuring Fund Ordinance □ specifies the rates of the bank levy (→ Bankenabgabe) stipulated in the Restructuring Fund Act

Restrukturierungsgesetz *(Gesetz zur Restrukturierung und geordneten Abwicklung von Kreditinstituten, zur Errichtung eines Restrukturierungsfonds für Kreditinstitute und zur Verlängerung der Verjährungsfrist der aktienrechtlichen Organhaftung)* Bank Restructuring Act (Act on the Restructuring and Orderly Liquidation of Credit Institutions, Establishment of a Restructuring Fund for Credit Institutions and Extension of Corporate Law Management Liability, → Kreditinstitute-Reorganisationsgesetz

Restrukturierungsplan restructuring plan □ must specify the envisaged restructuring measures and the name of the restructuring advisor (→ Sanierungsberater), → Reorganisationsplan

Restrukturierungskredit restructuring loan (facility)

Restrukturierungsrückstellung restructuring provision

R

Restrukturierungsverfahren restructuring proceedings, → Sanierungsverfahren

Restsaldo residual (remaining) balance, remainder, → Restschuld

Restschuld residual debt, outstanding principal balance; **~befreiung** discharge of residual debt; **~versicherung** *(bei Hypotheken)* home mortgage life insurance

Rest / ~summe residual (remaining) amount, → Restschuld; **~tilgung** residual payment (redemption); **~volatilität** residual volatility; **~wert** residual (salvage, terminal) value; **~wertmethode** residual value costing; **~zahlungsgarantie** final payment bond

Resultat result, outcome, findings

resultieren *(~ aus/in)* to result from/in, to be the consequence of

Resümee summary, round-up

resümieren to sum up, to summarise, to round up

Retail / ~anleger retail investor □ individual buying securities for his/her own account; **~bank** retail bank □ financial services provider for consumers and small-sized enterprises

Retail / ~fazilitäten *(Inanspruchnahmen aus ~ verbriefen)* to securitise drawings under retail facilities; **~fonds** retail fund □ shares are sold to individual investors/non-professionals

Retail / ~forderungen retail exposures, retail claims (receivables), *(durch Wohnimmmobilien besicherte ~)* retail exposures secured by residential properties; **~forderungsankauf** purchase of retail receivables; **~forderungspool** pool of retail exposures

Retail / ~geschäft retail operations, retail banking; **~kredit** retail loan (facility); **~kreditgeschäft** retail lending business; **~kunden** retail customers, consumers

Retail / ~portfolio retail portfolio □ portfolio of standardised loans extended to individuals and small-sized companies; **~zahlungsverkehr** retail payments

Retouren cheques and bills returned unpaid

Retourscheck returned cheque

Retrozedent retrocedant, ceding reinsurer

Retrozession retrocession, secondary reinsurance □ transactions ceded by a reinsurer to another reinsurer

Retrozessionar retrocessionaire, assuming reinsurer

retten *(ein Unternehmen ~)* to rescue (to bail out, to salvage) a company

Rettung rescue, bail-out

Rettungserwerb bail-out acquisition

Rettungserwerbe foreclosed assets □ assets acquired to avoid loan default, *(Wertberichtigungen auf ~)* value adjustments to foreclosed assets

Rettungs / ~fond rescue (bailout) fund, → Europäische Finanzmarktstabilisierungsfazilität; **~maßnahmen** rescue measures (package); **~schirm** rescue umbrella

Rettungsübernahmegesetz German Rescue Takeover Act □ allows the nationalisation of endangered financial sector entities

Reugeld *(im Termingeschäft)* forfeit money, premium to be paid upon rescission of a futures contract

revalorisieren to revalorise

Revalutierung revaluation, *(~ einer Grundschuld/Hypothek)* reestablishment of a land charge/a mortgage, *(~ einer Kreditfazilität)* re-establishment (re-opening) of a loan facility

Revers 1. letter, statement, *(Formular)* form **2.** *(Verpflichtung)* undertaking, covenant

revidieren 1. to amend, to modify **2.** to review, to revise

Revirement 1. *(~ an der Konzernspitze)* reshaping the top management **2.** *(währungspolitisches ~)* currency policy realignment

Revision 1. *(Abänderung)* amendment, modification **2.** *(Buchprüfung)* audit **3.** *(jur.)* appeal (on a point of law) **4.** *(Nachprüfung, Überprüfung)* review, examination, check

Revisions / ~abteilung audit department, auditing unit; **~beauftragter** audit officer; **~begründung** setting out the grounds of appeal; **~beklagter** appeal; **~bericht** auditing (auditors') report; **~gericht** Court of Appeal; **~kläger** appellant; **~möglichkeit** appellate remedy; **~pflicht** duty to have the books audited, duty to audit

Revisor auditor, examiner

Revolvierbarkeit *(~ der Fazilität)* revolving nature of the facility

revolvierend *(~es Akkreditiv)* revolving documentary credit, *(~e Aufnahme kurzfristiger Mittel am Geldmarkt)* short-term revolver, revolving borrowings of short-term funds in the money market, *(~er Betriebsmittelkredit)* revolving operating loan *(~e Deckung)* revolving cover (policy), *(~e Interbankeinlagen)* revolving interbank deposits, *(~er Kredit)* revolving credit (loan), bank revolver, *(~e Wertpapierpensionsgeschäfte)* revolving repurchase agreements

REX German Bond Market Index

REXP German Bond Market Performance Index

Rezession recession, economic slump

rezessions / ~anfällig *(~er Wirtschaftszweig)* recession-prone business sector; **~bedingt** *(~e Unternehmensinsolvenzen)* recession-induced company failures (insolvencies), *(~er Rückgang)* recession-driven decline; **~mildernd** alleviating (mitigating) the effects of the recession

rezessiv *(~e Tendenzen)* recessionary tendencies

reziprok reciprocal, mutual, *(~e Verzugsklausel)* cross default clause

Reziprozität reciprocity

Reziprozitätsklausel reciprocity clause

Rho change in option price resulting from a 1 percent change in interest rates, → Griechen

Rhythmus rhythm, pace

Ricambiowechsel redraft

richten 1. *(~ an)* to address to
2. *(~ auf)* to direct to, to concentrate on, to focus on
3. *(sich ~ gegen)* to be directed against, to turn against
4. *(sich ~ nach)* to conform with, to

comply with, to take one's bearings from, *(der Zinssatz richtet sich nach den aktuellen Marktsätzen)* the interest rate floats with the prevailing market rates, the interest rate takes its bearings from current market rates

Richtgröße benchmark

richtig **1.** correct, right, accurate, proper **2.** *(angemessen)* adequate, appropriate **3.** *(berechtigt)* legitimate **4.** *(tatsächlich, echt)* real, genuine, *(das Kreditrisiko ~ einschätzen)* to assess the credit risk accurately

Richtigkeit **1.** correctness, rightness, accuracy **2.** adequacy, appropriateness **3.** legitimacy **4.** genuineness

Richtigkeitsvermutung legal presumption of correctness

richtigstellen to correct, to rectify

Richtigstellung correction, rectification

Richtkurs indicative price (quote)

Richtlinie **1.** guideline, directive **2.** *(Grundsatz)* principle, rule, basic policy

Richtlinie über die Endgültigkeit von Zahlungen (EU) Settlement Finality Directive

Richtlinie über Finanzsicherheiten (EU) Financial Collateral Arrangements Directive

Richtlinie über Märkte für Finanzinstrumente (MiFID) → Finanzmarktrichtlinie

R

Richtlinie über die Verwalter alternativer Investmentfonds (EU) Alternative Investment Fund Managers (AIFM) Directive

Richtlinien / **~kompetenz** authoritative power, policy responsibility; **~preis** indicative (recommended, target, guiding) price; **~vorschlag** draft directive

Richtung **1.** direction, path, tack, *(eine andere ~ einschlagen)* to take a different tack **2.** orientation **3.** *(Tendenz)* trend, tendency

Richtungsindikator directional indicator

Richtungswechsel *(zinspolitischer ~)* change of direction in interest rate policy, interest rate policy shift

richtungsweisend directive, trend-setting, *(~e Anleihe)* benchmark bond, *(~er Zinssatz)* benchmark interest rate

Richtwert **1.** indicative value **2.** benchmark

Richtzinssatz benchmark interest rate

Riesterrente Riester pension □ privately funded, but government-subsidised provision for old age

rigoros *(~e Kostensenkungsprogramme)* rigorous (severe) cost-cutting schemes

Rimesse **1.** bill, draft **2.** remittance, bills (cheques) dispatched

Rimessebrief letter of remittances

Ringhauptstelle main clearing agency □ within the giro network operated by the cooperative banks

Risiko risk, exposure, *(~ einer Änderung des Marktwertes)* market risk, fair value exposure, *(das mit einem Geschäft verbundene ~)* transaction exposure, risk inherent in a transaction, *(mit einem hohen ~ behafteter Kredit)* high-risk loan, high-risk exposure
(einem hohen ~ aussetzen) to expose to a high risk, *(einem zu hohen ~ ausgesetzt sein)* to be overexposed, *(das nicht gedeckte finanzielle ~)* the unhedged financial risk, *(Risiken und Chancen)* risks and rewards

Risiko aus *(~ dem Anlagebuch)* risks from the investment book, *(~ dem Beteiligungsbestand)* investment portfolio risks, risks from equity investments, *(~ bilanzunwirksamen Geschäften)* off-balance sheet exposure (risks), exposure from transactions not reflected in the balance sheet, *(~ Bürgschaftsverpflichtungen)* exposure from surety commitments
(~ Festzinsverpflichtungen) exposure from fixed rate commitments, *(~ dem*

Kreditgeschäft) lending risks, *(~ offenen Positionen)* exposure on open positions, *(~ Stillhalterpositionen)* risks from options written (from short option positions), *(~ Übernahmeverpflichtungen)* underwriting exposure, *(~ Wertpapiergeschäften)* securities exposure

Risiko / ~abbildung risk (exposure) mapping, reflection of the risk involved; **~abdeckung** risk cover, → Risikoabsicherung

risikoabhängig *(~e Kapitalausstattung)* risk-based capital resources

Risikoabschlag haircut, markdown for the risks involved, *(~ vom Zeitwert)* haircut to the fair value, risk allowance on the fair value

Risikoabsicherung risk hedging, hedging (covering) the risk, exposure hedging, *(~ im Freiverkehrsmarkt)* laying off an exposure in the OTC market

Risiko / ~absicherungsbedarf risk (exposure) hedging requirements, need to hedge the risks (exposure), **~abwälzung** passing on the risk (exposure); **~adäquanz** risk adequacy, *(risikoadäquate Konditionen)* rates (terms) in line with the risks involved

risikoadjustiert *(~es Anlageergebnis)* risk-adjusted performance

Risikoaggregation risk aggregation

Risikoaktiva risk assets; **~-Äquivalente** risk-weighted asset equivalents □ capital charges for market risk positions

Risikoanleihen non-investment grade bonds

Risikoanpassung risk adjustment, *(risikoangepasste Eigenkapitalunterlegung)* risk-adjusted capital charges

Risikoanrechnung risk weighting, counting the risk of a specific position towards the aggregate exposure, *(~ der Aktiva)* risk weighting of assets, determining the risk weight of assets, assigning a … p.c. risk weight to claims on (e.g. customers, banks, sovereigns, etc.)

Risikoanrechnungssatz risk weighting factor

Risikoansatz 1. risk approach **2.** *(i. S. von Gewichtung)* risk weighting **3.** → Risikozuschlagsfaktor

Risiko / ~anzeige risk notification, notification of exposure(s); **~äquivalent** risk equivalent; **~arbitrage** risk arbitrage

risikoarm *(~e Anlage)* low-risk investment, defensive (conservative) investment

Risiko / ~aufklärung risk disclosure (disclosure statement); **~aufschlag** risk premium, *(Risikoaufschläge auf Staatsanleihen)* sovereign risk premiums; **~aufwand** risk provisioning expenditure; **~ausgleich** risk compensation, laying off (offsetting) risks, offsetting an exposure, risk offset

Risiko / ~ausleihungen problem lendings; **~ausplatzierung** outplacement of risks; **~ausschaltung** risk elimination, eliminating a risk

Risiko / ~ausschluss exclusion of a risk, *(bei einer Versicherung)* exclusion from coverage, *(Risikoausschlüsse)* policy exceptions (exclusions), risks and perils excluded, exception of coverage; **~ausschlussklausel** exclusion clause

Risiko / ~aversion → Risikoscheu; **~barwert** present value of risk; **~ballung** risk accumulation

risikobasiert *(~e Eigenkapitalforderungen/Eigenkapitalunterlegung)* risk-based capital requirements/capital charge, *(~e Kernkapitalquote)* risk-based tier-1 capital ratio

Risikobegrenzung risk limitation (containment), limiting a risk, limiting the downside risk, minimising the exposure

Risikobegrenzungs / ~gesetz German Risk Limitation Act; **~strategien** strategies reducing or limiting risks

R

risikobehaftet entailing a risk, entailing an exposure to loss, *(~e Aktiva/ Kredite)* risk-carrying assets, problem loans (lendings), *(~e Geschäfte)* transactions (operations) involving risk of loss

Risiko / ~belastung 1. risk burden **2.** degree of risk involved;**~berechnung** calculation of the risk (of the risk charge)

risikobereinigt *(~e Kapitalverzinsung)* risk-adjusted return on capital

Risiko / ~bereitschaft willingness to assume (to incur) risks, willingness to take on a risk, *(~ der Anleger)* the risk investors are prepared to incur, investors' willingness to take risks

Risikoberichterstattung risk reporting

risikoberichtigt risk-adjusted, adjusted for risks of loss

Risikoberichtspflichten risk reporting requirements

Risiko / ~beschränkung → Risikobegrenzung; **~besicherung** risk (exposure) hedging, collateralisation of exposures; **~beteiligung** risk participation; **~beurteilung/~bewertung** risk assessment (measurement, evaluation), risk rating (appraisal), measuring the risk (exposure)

risikobewusst aware of the risks, risk-conscious,risk-sensitive

Risiko / ~bewusstsein risk awareness, awareness of the risks; **~budget** risk budget; **~budgetierung** risk budgeting; **~charakter** *(~ einer Anlage)* risk content of an investment; **~dauer** duration of an exposure; **~deckung** risk hedging, covering (hedging) a risk; **~deckungskapital/masse** risk coverage equity

Risiko / ~determinanten risk determinants; **~diversifikation** risk diversification, risk spreading; **~einschätzung** risk assessment (appraisal), assessing the risk involved

Risiko / ~einstellung risk attitude; **~einstufung** risk grading (classification, rating); **~eliminierung** risk elimination (removal); **~empfindlichkeit** risk sensitivity

Risiko / ~engagement 1. *(Problemkredit)* problem loan (lending) **2.** *(risikoreiches Engagement)* risky investment (commitment) **3.** *(Summe der mit Risiken behafteten Engagements)* risk exposure; **~entlastung** lowering the risk burden, risk relief

Risiko / ~erfassung risk measurement; **~erfassungssystem** risk measurement system; **~erhöhung** risk increase, increase in exposure, *(risikoerhöhende Wirkung)* risk-increasing impact; **~evaluierung** risk evaluation (assessment); **~feststellung** risk identification, identifying (possible) risks

risikofrei *(~e Anlage)* risk-free investment

risikofreudig *(~er Anleger)* risk-loving investor, investor prepared to take risks

Risikofrüherkennung early risk detection (recognition of risks)

Risikogehalt risk content, risk level, degree of risk, *(~ eines Kreditengagements)* risk inherent in a lending transaction, loan exposure, lending risk

risikogerecht *(~e Konditionen)* risk-adequate (risk-based) terms and conditions

Risikogesichtspunkte risk considerations

Risikogewicht *(~ für angekaufte Forderungen)* risk weight for purchased receivables, *(~ für Kontrahentenrisiken aus OTC-Derivaten)* counterparty risk weights for OTC derivatives, *(~ eines Kredites/eines Kreditnehmers)* risk weight of a loan/of a borrower

risikogewichtet *(~e Aktiva des Anlagebuches)* risk-weighted assets of the banking book, *(~es außerbilanzmäßiges Geschäft)* risk-weighted off-balance sheet transactions, *(~e Kapitalunterlegung)* risk-weighted capital backing (capital charge), *(~e Positionswerte)* risk-weighted exposure amounts

Risikogewichtskategorie risk weight category

Risikogewichtung risk weighting, *(~ von Forderungen an Staaten)* risk weighting of claims on sovereigns, *(~ für Kredite im Anlagebuch)* risk weighting of banking book exposures, *(auf Ratings gestützte ~)* discriminatory (ratings-based) risk weighting

Risiko / **~gewichtungsfaktoren** risk weighting factors; **~grad** degree of risk; **~gruppe** → Risikokategorie; **~häufung** risk accumulation; **~indikator** risk (exposure) indicator; **~inventur** risk inventory

Risikokapital risk capital, *(~ für junge Unternehmen)* corporate venture capital

Risikokapital / **~ausstattung** risk capital resources; **~bindung** commitment of risk capital; **~fonds** venture capital fund; **~geber** provider of risk capital; **~unterlegung** risk capital charge

Risiko / **~kategorie** risk (exposure) category, → Risikoklasse; **~kennzahl** risk measure, risk score; **~klasse** risk class, class of risk (of exposure), *(risikoklassenspezifisch)* particular to a risk class; **~klassifizierungssystem** risk classification system

Risiko / **~kompensation** → Risikoausgleich; **~komponente** risk component; **~konzentration** risk concentration, *(~ im Kreditgeschäft)* risk concentration in lending operations; **~konzentrationslimit** risk concentration limit (e.g. per country, industrial sector, etc.)

Risiko / **~kosten** risk cost (expenditure), exposure cost; **~kostenzuschlag** risk cost premium; **~kredit** problem loan (lending), problem exposure; **~kumulierung** risk accumulation; **~lebensversicherung** term life insurance (assurance), term assurance

risikolos risk-free, riskless, without risks, safe, nil risk, zero risk, *(~e Anlage)* risk-free (safe) investment, *(~es Geschäft)* riskless transaction, *(~er Gewinn)* risk-free profit

Risiko / **~losigkeit** *(~ einer Anlage)* risk-free nature of an investment; **~management** risk (exposure) management; **~marge** risk margin

risikomäßig verhaftet to be liable for the risks

Risiko / **~maßeinheit** risk measurement unit; **~maßstab** exposure benchmark, benchmark for measuring risks; **~matrix** risk matrix; **~messgröße** risk measure; **~messung** risk measurement; **~messverfahren** risk measurement method; **~messzahl** risk measure

Risiko / **~minderung** risk mitigation (reduction), lowering (alleviating) the risk; **~minimierung** risk minimisation, risk-minimising, minimising the risk (exposure); **~minimierungsstrategie** risk-minimisation strategy

Risiko / **~mischung** risk exposure mix, *(Grundsatz der ~)* principle of risk diversification; **~modellierung** risk modelling

Risiko / **~nachsteuerung** ex post control; **~neubewertung** reappraising the exposure (the risk); **~neutralisierung** neutralising the risk; **~-Nutzen-Relation** risk/reward ratio

Risiko / **~obergrenze** risk ceiling, overall exposure limit; **~offenlegung** risk disclosure; **~orientierung** risk orientation (focus), *(risikoorientierte Portefeuillesteuerung)* risk-oriented (risk-focused) portfolio management

Risiko / **~politik** risk management policy, *(risikopolitische Leitlinien)* risk policy parameters (guidelines), *(risikopolitische Vorgaben)* risk policy requirements; **~position** risk position, net open position

Risiko / **~potenzial** risk exposure (potential), value at risk, *(~ des Handelsbestandes)* value at risk of the trading portfolio; **~präferenzen** risk preferences; **~prämie** risk premium; **~profil** exposure profile, *(Steuerung des ~s)*

risk profile management; ~**puffer** risk cushion (buffer)

Risiko / ~**qualität** risk quality; ~**quote** risk ratio, *(i. S. von Kreditverlustquote)* loan loss experience (ratio)

Risiko / ~**rahmen** *(~ für Devisentermingeschäfte)* exposure line for forward exchange transactions; ~**reduzierung** lowering the risk (exposure), *(risikoreduzierende Wirkung)* risk-reducing effect

risikoreich *(~e Anlagen)* high-risk investments

Risiko-Rendite-Profil risk/return profile

Risikorückbehalt risk retention

risikoscheu *(~e Anleger)* risk-averse (risk-averting) investors, investors with very low risk tolerance

Risiko / ~**scheu** risk aversion, reluctance (unwillingness) to take on risks, averting risks; ~**schuldnerland** problem debtor country; ~**sensitivität** risk sensitivity, *(risikosensibler Anleger)* investor sensitive to the risks involved, *(risikosensitive Kapitalanforderungen)* risk-sensitive capital requirements; ~**sicherung** risk hedging, collateralisation of the exposure

Risiko / ~**steuerung** risk management (control), exposure management, *(~ des Kreditportefeuilles)* managing the loan portfolio exposure; ~**steuerungsinstrument** risk management tool; ~**steuerungsprozess** risk management process

Risiko / ~**streuung** risk spreading (diversification), diversifying risks, *(risikostreuender Fonds)* risk-diversifying fund; ~**streuungsvorschriften** risk diversification rules; ~**szenarien** *(~ mit hohem Stressfaktor)* highly-stressed risk scenarios

Risiko / ~**teilung** risk sharing, sharing the risk (exposure); ~**toleranz** risk tolerance

risikotragend *(~e Aktiva)* risk-carrying assets, risk assets, *(~es Kapital)* risk (venture) capital

Risiko / ~**tragfähigkeit** risk-bearing (risk-taking) capacity, risk acceptability; ~**transformation** risk (exposure) transformation; ~**treiber** risk driver

Risiko / ~**übergang** passing of the risk, *(bei Versicherungen)* risk attachment; ~**überlegungen** risk considerations; ~**übernahme** assuming a risk, risk assumption, taking on a risk, risk-taking; ~**überwachung** monitoring a risk, risk control, exposure control

Risiko / ~**überwälzung** passing on the risk, shifting the risk; ~**überzeichnung** overexposure, taking on an above-average risk; ~**umfang** degree of risk incurred; ~**umgehung** risk avoidance, avoiding a risk (an exposure); ~**unterbeteiligung** risk subparticipation

Risiko / ~**verlagerung** shifting the risk (exposure) from ... to ...; ~**vermeidung** risk avoidance; ~**verminderung** reducing the risk (the exposure), → Risikominderung; ~**verschlechterung** deterioration in the risk situation

Risiko / ~**verteilung** risk spreading, spreading (diversifying) the risk, *(~ auf eine große Zahl unterschiedlicher Anlageformen)* spreading the risk among a large variety of investment vehicles

Risiko / ~**volumen** **1.** aggregate (total) exposure **2.** total risk assets; ~**vorbeugung** → Risikovorsorge;~**vormerkung** approved risk exposure

Risikovorsorge risk provisioning, providing for risks, bad debt provisioning, *(Aufwendungen für die ~)* risk provisioning expenditure, provisioning expenses, *(hohe ~ für Inlandskredite)* high level of provisioning against domestic loans, *(~ im Konzern)* risk provisioning at group level *(~ im Kreditgeschäft)* setting up loan loss provisions, providing for possible loan losses, providing for non-performing loans, (*~ treffen*) to provide for bad and doubtful debts (for non-performing loans), to set up loan loss provisions

Risikovorsorge / ~aufwand provisioning charge; **~bestand** total loan loss provisions; **~dotierung** transfer to loan loss provisions; **~saldo** net provisioning □ gross provisions less provisions released and loan recoveries

Risiko / ~wahrnehmung risk perception (awareness);**~zuschlag** risk premium, loading for contingencies; **~zuschlagsfaktoren** add-on factors, add-ons □ factors to reflect future exposure

riskant risky, dangerous, perilous

riskieren to risk, (*gefährden*) to jeopardise, to endanger

Riss (*~ in der Unternehmensführung*) rift (split) in the company management

Rivale rival, competitor

rivalisierend (*~e Strategien*) competing (rival) strategies

Rivalität competition, rivalship

Roh / ~bilanz trial balance sheet; **~ertrag** gross income, gross interest and fee income, gross revenue; **~gewinn** gross profit; **~gewinnspanne** gross profit margin

Rohstoff raw material, commodity, (*Roh-, Hilfs- und Betriebsstoffe*) raw materials, consumables and supplies

Rohwaren / ~aktien commodity equities; **~anlagen** investments in commodities; **~ dachfonds** commodities umbrella fund; **~derivate** commodity derivatives (e. g. commodity options, commodity futures)

Rohwaren / ~fonds commodity fund; **~handelsfinanzierung** commodity trade financing □ lending designed to finance inventories or receivables from trade commodities; **~option** commodity option contract; **~optionsscheine** commodity warrants

Rohwaren / ~position (*~en des Anlagebuches*) commodity exposures in the banking book; **~preise** commodity prices; **~risikoposition** commodity risk exposure

Rohwaren / ~swap commodity swap; **~terminhandel** commodity futures trading; **~terminkontrakt** commodity futures contract; **~werte** commodities, commodity stocks

Rolle role, part, (*eine ~ spielen*) to come into play, (*eine wichtige ~ spielen*) to play a vital (crucial) role, to take an active part in

rollierend (*~e Abrechnung*) rolling settlement, (*~e Absicherungsposition*) rolling hedge, (*~er Zinsertrag*) roll yield

Rollover-Kredit rollover credit, rollover loan facility

rot (*in die roten Zahlen geraten*) to plunge (to slide) into the red, (*das Unternehmen aus den roten Zahlen bringen*) to turn the company around, (*weiter in die roten Zahlen abrutschen*) to sink (to move) deeper into the red

Rotation (*~ des Vorsitzes*) rotation of the chairmanship

Rotations / ~plan rotation schedule; **~verfahren** (*im ~*) by rotation

Routine 1. routine **2.** practice, experience

Routine-Geschäftsvorfälle day-to-day transactions, routine transactions

Routine-Swap plain vanilla swap, straight swap

RTF-Berechnung calculation of (an institution's) risk-bearing capacity

Rubrum caption

Rückabtretung reassignment, retransfer

rückabwickeln to reverse, (*einen Vertrag ~*) to rescind a contract, to return to the status pro ante

Rückabwicklung 1. (*~ eines Geschäftes*) reversal of a transaction, reverse transaction **2.** (*~ eines Vertrages*) rescission of contract, restoring (returning) the parties to their status pro ante

Rückandienung re-delivery, → Andienung

Rückauflassung reconveyance, retransfer

Rückauflassungsvormerkung reconveyance notice □ priority notice securing the claim to property reconveyance in the Land Register

rückbelasten to redebit, to charge back

Rückbelastung **1.** *(eines zuvor gutgeschriebenen Betrages)* redebit, **2.** *(im Kreditkartengeschäft)* chargeback □ return of a disputed credit card sale to the acquirer for reimbursement to the cardholder's account

Rückbelastungs / ~ermächtigung authority to redebit (to charge back); **~gebühr** chargeback fee; **~recht** right to redebit (to charge back), chargeback right

Rückbeteiligungen cross-shareholdings

Rückbildung *(~ der Sparquote)* decline in the savings ratio

rückbuchen **1.** *(rückübertragen)* to transfer back, to retransfer **2.** *(stornieren)* to reverse

Rückbuchung **1.** retransfer **2.** reversal, reversing entry **3.** chargeback, → Rückbelastung

Rückbürge countersurety

R

Rückbürgschaft countersurety bond, counterbond, countervailing bond of indemnity □ bond which indemnifies a surety, → Nachbürgschaft

Rückbürgschaftsprovision counterbond commission

rückdatieren to backdate, → rückvalutieren

Rückdatierung backdating, antedating, → Rückvalutierung

Rückdeckung **1.** reinsurance, *(in ~ gegebenes Geschäft/passive Rückversicherung)* outward reinsurance, ceded reinsurance, reinsurance business ceded to another insurer, *(in ~ genommenes Geschäft/aktive Rückversicherung)* inward reinsurance, assumed reinsurance, reinsurance business accepted by an insurer
2. *(i. S. von Absicherungslinie)* backup line
3. *(i. S. von Refinanzierung)* refinancing, funding

Rückdisponierung retransfer

Rückendeckung support, backing, *(mit ~ der Muttergesellschaft)* with the parent's backing

rückerstatten **1.** *(Gelder)* to refund, to reimburse **2.** *(zurückgeben)* to restitute, to return

Rückerstattung **1.** refund, reimbursement **2.** restitution, return, *(~ zuviel gezahlter Gebühren)* refund of charges paid in excess

Rückerstattungsanspruch **1.** right to refund, repayment claim **2.** *(steuerlicher ~)* reclaim entitlement

rückerstattungsberechtigt entitled to a refund

rückerstattungsfähig **1.** refundable, reimbursable **2.** reclaimable

Rückerwerb repurchase, reacquisition

Rückfall reversion, escheat; **~anspruch/recht** reversionary interest

Rückfluss reflux, reflow, *(~ der ins Ausland abgeflossenen Gelder)* reflux of funds transferred abroad

Rückflüsse *(~ aus dem Aktivgeschäft)* repayments on lendings, principal repayments, *(~ von Fondsanteilen)* units (investment fund shares) offered for repurchase
(~ aus Insolvenzverfahren) recoveries from insolvency proceedings, *(~ aus abgeschriebenen Kreditforderungen)* recoveries from loans previously charged (written) off, *(~ aufgrund* von *Regressen)* recoveries under recourse agreements

Rückfluss / ~dauer *(Amortisationsdauer)* payback period; **~erwartungen** recoverability prospects; **~rate**

1. *(to recover the initial capital outlay)* payback rate 2. *(for loans written off)* recovery rate; ~**stücke** securities repurchased (e. g. by the issuing bank to support the price of a new issue)

rückforderbar *(~e Quellensteuer)* reclaimable withholding tax

rückfordern to reclaim, to claim back

Rückforderung 1. reclaiming, recovery claim, claiming back 2. *(~ von Geldern/von Wertpapieren im Rahmen von Wertpapierleihen)* recall of funds/ of securities 3. *(gewährter Vergünstigungen)* recapture

Rückforderungsanspruch 1. right to reclaim, recapture claim, claim for return, *(steuerliche Rückforderungsansprüche)* tax reclaims 2. *(Anspruch auf Rückgabe)* restitution claim 3. *(hinsichtlich eines verpfändeten Gegenstandes)* right of redemption

Rückforderungs / ~bescheid notice to reclaim (e.g. the property), notice of right to reclaim; ~**recht** right to reclaim, → Rückforderungsanspruch; ~**verfahren** recovery proceedings, proceedings to reclaim the ...; ~**vorbehalt** reservation to reclaim

Rückfrage query, further inquiry; ~**klausel** consultation clause

rückfragen to query, to request further details, to inquire again

rückführen 1. *(reduzieren, vermindern)* to reduce, to lower 2. *(repatriieren)* to repatriate 3. *(vollständig zurückzahlen)* to repay 4. *(zurücküberweisen)* to transfer back

Rückführung 1. reduction, *(~ in den vereinbarten Kreditrahmen)* reducing the loan/overdraft to the limit agreed upon, *(~ der Risikovorsorge)* reduction of risk provisions
2. *(~ des investierten Kapitals)* repatriation of the capital invested
3. repayment, *(teilweise ~ des Engagements)* partial repayment of the loan facility, reduction of the loan exposure
4. retransfer

Rückführungs / ~recht right of repatriation; ~**vereinbarung** repatriation agreement

Rückgabe 1. return, *(~ der Papiere vor Fälligkeit)* returning the securities prior to maturity
2. restitution, *(~ an den rechtmäßigen Eigentümer)* restitution (restoration) to the rightful owner, *(~ der als Sicherheit hinterlegten Vermögenswerte)* restitution of property deposited as collateral
3. *(einer Versicherungspolice)* surrender

Rückgabe / ~liquidität *(erforderliche ~)* liquidity required for redemptions; ~ **möglichkeit** return (surrender) option; ~**pflicht** obligation to return (to restitute), redelivery obligation

Rückgabe / ~recht right of return, return privilege, *(Kündigungsrecht des Anleiheinhabers)* put option (right); ~**risiko** surrender risk; ~**verpflichtung** → Rückgabepflicht

Rückgang decline, fall, drop, plunge, downturn, slump, *(~ der Emissionstätigkeit)* slowdown in new issue activity, *(~ der Kurse auf breiter Front)* drop in prices across the board, retreat of prices over a broad front, widespread decline

rückgängig *(~ machen)* 1. to cancel, to annul, to revoke, to rescind 2. *(stornieren)* to reverse

Rückgängigmachung cancellation, annulment, revocation, rescission, reversal

Rückgarantie counterguarantee, back-to-back guarantee

rückgebbar *(~e Papiere)* securities returnable prior to maturity

Rückgewähr 1. refund, reimbursement, *(~ geleisteter Zahlungen)* refund of payments made
2. return, restitution to the owner, *(~ des Sicherungsgegenstandes)* return of the asset pledged as security
3. *(Nachlass)* rebate, discount

4. (~ *einer Grundschuld)* release of a land charge

Rückgewähranspruch 1. reimbursement claim 2. restitution claim, right to restitution
3. *(bei einem Grundpfandrecht)* release claim, right to release of a land charge, equity of redemption

Rückgewährberechtigte/r person/party entitled to the refund/return of …

Rückgewährreife *(bei einer Grundschuld)* fulfillment of the prerequisites for release of the charge

Rückgewährungsverpflichtung duty to return (e.g. the collateral furnished)

Rückgewinnung recovery, retrieval, *(~ der früheren Bonität)* recovery of former credit standing

Rückgrat *(des Konzerns)* backbone of the group

Rückgriff recourse, *(~ nehmen)* to take recourse to, to have recourse to, *(Finanzierung mit eingeschränktem/vollem ~)* limited/full recourse financing

Rückgriff auf *(~ den Aussteller)* calling on the drawer (writer), having recourse against the issuer (drawer), *(~ Dritte)* recourse against third parties, *(~ den Forderungsverkäufer bei einer Verbriefung)* recourse to the originator, *(~ den Kapitalmarkt)* tapping the capital market, borrowing in the capital market, *(~ die Rücklagen)* drawing on the reserves

R

rückgriffsberechtigt holding a right of recourse

Rückgriffs / ~bestimmungen recourse provisions; **~forderung** recourse claim; **~klage** action for recourse

rückgriffslos *(~e Finanzierung)* non-recourse financing

Rückgriffs / ~möglichkeit recourse facility (option); **~rechnung** statement of recourse; **~recht** right of recourse, *(ein ~ gegenüber jeder Wechselpartei besitzen)* to have a right of recourse against any party to the bill; **~risiken** risks from possible recourse claims, recourse exposure

Rückgriffs / ~schuldner recourse debtor; **~vereinbarung** recourse agreement, *(Verpflichtungen aus ~en)* recourse commitments; **~verpflichteter** party liable on the recourse

Rückhaftung counterliability, counterguarantee

Rückhaftungs / ~erklärung counterliability bond; **~vereinbarung** counterliability agreement

Rückhalt *(finanzieller ~ durch die Muttergesellschaft)* financial support (backing) by the parent company

Rückkauf 1. repurchase, reacquisition, buyback, *(~ auf Termin)* forward repurchase 2. *(Einlösung)* redemption, *(~ von Aktien)* share (stock) buyback, repurchase of stock

rückkaufen 1. to repurchase, to buy back, to buy in 2. to redeem

Rückkaufs / ~angebot repurchase offer, buyback offer (tender), offer of redemption; **~disagio** repurchase (redemption) discount

rückkaufsfähig *(~e Papiere)* repurchaseable securities, securities eligible for repurchase

Rückkaufs / ~kurs repurchase (redemption) price, buyback price; **~möglichkeit** repurchase option (feature); **~preis** repurchase price; **~recht** right of repurchase (redemption), buyback option, repurchase privilege

Rückkaufs / ~vereinbarung repurchase agreement, *(Verkauf von Wechseln mit ~)* sale of bills concurrent with an agreement to repurchase the same bills at a later date; **~verlust** loss on repurchase

Rückkaufs / ~verpflichtung repurchase (buyback) commitment, *(~ per Termin)* forward commitment to buy back; **~volumen** (stock) buyback volume; **~wert** repurchase (redemption) value, *(einer Versicherungspolice)* surrender value

Rückkehr return, *(~ in die Gewinnzone)* writing black figures again, recovery into profit, *(~ zu festen Wechselkursen)* return to fixed parities

Rückkonvertierung reconversion, retranslation

Rückkredit 1. counterloan **2.** *(Refinanzierungskredit)* funding (refinancing) facility

Rücklage aus *(~ Aktienaufgeldern)* share premium reserve (account), *(~ der Neubewertung)* revaluation reserve, *(~ der Währungsumrechnung)* reserve from currency translation

Rücklage für *(~ eigene Anteile)* reserve for treasury shares, *(~ Eventualverbindlichkeiten)* reserve for contingencies, *(~ außerordentliche Risiken)* special contingency reserve, *(~ Substanzverlust)* reserve for depletion, *(~ Tilgungsverpflichtungen)* reserve for redemption commitments, redemption reserve, *(~ Verluste aus Währungsabwertungen)* reserve against losses from currency devaluations

Rücklagen / **~auflösung** writing back reserves, reversal (write-back) of reserves; **~bedienung** → Rücklagendotierung; **~bildung** reserve-building, setting up reserves, buildup of reserves, *(~ zur Risikovorsorge)* (prudential) provisioning

Rücklagen / **~dotierung** allocation (transfer) to reserves, reserve appropriation; **~entnahmen** drawings on the reserves; **~erhöhung** increase in reserves, *(~ aus dem Jahresüberschuss)* increase in reserves through allocation from the net income for the year

Rücklagen / **~fonds** reserve fund, contingency fund, reserve for contingencies; **~konto** reserve (surplus) account; **~pflicht** obligation to hold reserves; **~polster** reserve cushion; **~schwund** drain on reserves; **~stärkung** boosting (strengthening) reserves

Rücklagen / **~verzinsung** return on reserves; **~zuführung/~zuweisung** allocation to reserves, reserve appropriation, addition to reserves, taking to reserves

Rücklastschrift dishonoured (returned) direct debit, return debit; **~gebühr** return fee

Rücklauf return, reflux; **~gebühren** *(bei Rückrechnung von Schecks und Wechseln)* return charges

rückläufig declining, *(~e Aktienkurse)* softening (weakening) equity prices, *(~e Ertragsentwicklung)* declining trend in earnings, downturn in earnings, *(~e Konjunktur)* sagging (slumping) economic activity
(~e Margen) receding margins, *(~e Renditen)* diminishing returns, *(~e Tendenz)* downward tendency, *(~e Umsätze)* sluggish turnover, flagging sales, *(Aktienwerte waren weiterhin ~)* stocks crumbled (wilted) further

Rücklauf / **~kupon** return coupon; **~quote** *(bei Befragungen)* response rate; **~stücke** securities repurchased

Rücklieferung redelivery, return delivery

Rücknahme 1. *(von Wertpapieren)* repurchase, redemption, *(~ zum Inventarwert)* repurchase (redemption) at net asset value
2. *(Senkung)* cut, *(~ der Leitzinsen)* lowering of key lending rates
3. *(Widerruf)* revocation, *(~ einer Klage)* withdrawal of an action

Rücknahme / **~abschlag** → Rücknahmegebühr; **~angebot** repurchase offer (offering); **~aussetzung** suspension of redemptions; **~garantie** repurchase (redemption) guarantee; **~gebühr** *(bei Fondsanteilen)* back-end load, exit load, repurchase (liquidation, redemption) charge, deferred sales charge

Rücknahme / **~kurs** → Rücknahmepreis; **~pflicht** → Rücknahmeverpflichtung; **~preis** redemption price, *(bei Fondsanteilen)* bid (call) price, cash-in price; **~satz** repurchase rate

Rücknahme / ~verpflichtung duty to repurchase (to redeem), repurchase (redemption) obligation, repurchase commitment (undertaking), *(~ des Verkäufers)* repurchase commitment on the part of the seller

Rücknahme / ~wert 1. *(von Fondsanteilen)* redemption (bid) value **2.** *(einer Versicherungspolice)* surrender value; **~zusage** *(der Zentralbank)* Central Bank's commitment to repurchase, Bundesbank's repurchase undertaking

Rückrechnung return (back) account, re-account

Rückrechnungsspesen re-account charges

Rückruf 1. *(von fehlerhaften Produkten, Wechseln)* recall **2.** cancellation request; **~gebühren** *(Wechsel)* recall charges; **~recht** right to recall

Rückscheck returned (rubber) cheque

Rückschein return receipt, acknowledgement of receipt

Rückschlagsperre *(im Insolvenzverfahren)* retroactive voidability of certain enforcement measures after the opening of insolvency proceedings

Rückseite reverse, reverse side, back, *(siehe ~)* see overleaf

Rücksicht consideration, *(mit ~ auf unsere langjährigen Geschäftsbeziehungen)* taking into account (in consideration of) our long-standing business relationship, *(mit ~ auf die schwierige finanzielle Lage)* in the light of (making allowance for) the difficult financial situation, *(ohne ~ auf)* without regard to, regardless (irrespective) of

R

Rücksprache consultation(s), *(nach ~ mit der Muttergesellschaft)* having conferred with (following consultation with) the parent company

Rückstand 1. *(an Arbeit/Aufträgen)* backlog of work/orders
2. *(bei Zahlungen)* arrears, arrearage, *(mit mehr als drei Monaten im ~ sein)* to be more than three months in arrears, *(mit den Zins- und Tilgungszahlungen in ~ geraten)* to fall behind with interest and redemption payments
3. *(Lücke)* gap

rückständig *(~e Dividenden)* dividend arrears, dividend payments in arrears, arrearages in dividends, *(~e Raten)* instalment arrears, back instalments, *(~e Tilgungszahlungen)* repayment (redemption) arrears, repayment instalments in arrears, *(~e Zahlungen)* payment arrears, overdue payments, delinquent payments

Rückstellungen provisions, *(in IAS/US-GAAP-Abschlüssen)* (provisions and) accruals, *(~ bilden)* to set up (to make) provisions, to provision, *(zu hohe/zu geringe ~ bilden)* to overprovide, to underprovide, *(Vornahme umfangreicher ~)* making extensive provisions

Rückstellungen für *(~ außerordentliche Aufwendungen)* provisions for extraordinary charges (items), *(~ Ausleihungen an Problemländer)* provisions against problem country debt, *(~ Avale)* guarantee provisions, provisions for indemnity bonds, *(~ Eventualverbindlichkeiten)* accruals for contingencies
(~ dubiose/zweifelhafte) Forderungen bad and doubtful debt provisions, provisions for doubtful accounts, *(~ notleidende Kredite)* provisions for non-performing loans, *(~ Kursverluste)* provisions for price losses
(~ Länderrisiken) country risk provisioning, provisions for country debt, provisions against sovereign risks, *(~ Minderung des Marktwertes)* provisions for diminution in market value, *(~ Pensionen)* accruals for pensions, *(~ Verluste im Kreditgeschäft)* loan loss provisions

Rückstellungs / ~abzinsung discounting of provisions and accruals, *(Erträge/Aufwendungen aus Rückstellungsabzinsung)* income from/expense for discounting provisions; **~auflösung** writing back provisions, reversal (write-back, release) of provisions; ~**aufwand** provisioning charge

Rückstellungsbedarf *(~ im Kreditgeschäft)* loan loss provisions required, provisioning required for lendings, *(~ für risikobehaftete Debitoren)* provisioning needs for doubtful accounts

Rückstellungs / ~**bewertung** valuation of provisions, measurement of provisions and accruals; ~**bilanzierung** provision accounting; ~**bildung** setting up provisions, provisioning; ~**dotierung** transfer to provisions; ~**finanzierung** financing from provisions

Rückstellungs / ~**pflicht** provisioning requirement, obligation to set up provisions; ~**politik** provisioning policy; ~**spiegel** statement of provisions and accruals; ~ **wahlrecht** option to set up a provision, ~**zuführungen** additions to provisions

Rückstufung *(bonitätsmäßig)* downgrading, → Rating

Rücktausch re-exchange

Rücktrag *(~ steuerlicher Verluste)* carryback of tax losses

Rücktritt 1. resignation, *(~ von einem Amt)* resignation from an office, standing down
2. *(~ im Rangverhältnis)* subordination, acceptance of a lower rank
3. *(~ von einem Vertrag)* rescission (abrogation) of contract, nullifying a contract

Rücktritts / ~**klausel** escape clause, abandonment option; ~**recht** right of rescission (of termination), right to rescind a contract; ~**schreiben** letter of resignation; ~ **vorbehalt** escape clause, termination (withdrawal) option, reservation of the right to rescind the agreement

Rückübereignung retransfer of title, → Rückübertragung

Rückübereignungsanspruch 1. claim to repossession **2.** → Rückübertragungsanspruch

rückübertragen to retransfer, to transfer back, to reconvey, to reassign

Rückübertragung 1. retransfer
2. *(von Eigentumsrechten)* reconveyance, resurrender, *(~ an den ursprünglichen Eigentümer)* reconveyance (transferring back) to the original owner, revesting in the original owner

Rückübertragungs / ~**anspruch** claim (entitlement) to reconveyance; ~**pflicht** duty to reconvey, reconveyance requirement, mandatory reconveyance; ~**vereinbarung** agreement to retransfer, reconveyance agreement

Rücküberweisung retransfer

Rückvaluta backvalue, backdated value date

rückvalutieren *(~ auf den Abrechnungstag)* to backvalue to the settlement date

Rückvalutierung backvaluation

rückverbürgen to counterguarantee, to counterindemnify, *(durch die öffentliche Hand rückverbürgte Bankgarantien)* bank guarantees counterguaranteed by public authorities

Rückverfolgung tracking, tracing back

Rückvergleich backtesting

rückvergüten to refund, to reimburse

Rückvergütung 1. refund, reimbursement **2.** *(i. S. eines Vermittlungsentgeltes)* kick-back

Rückverlagerung shifting back, repatriation, *(~ in Festgelder)* switching back into time deposits

Rückversicherer reinsurer, reinsurance (reassurance) company

Rückversicherungs / ~**-Kapitalausstattungsverordnung** Reinsurance Solvency Regulation; ~**provision** reinsurance commission, ceding commission; ~**-Richtlinie** Reinsurance Directive

Rückwälzung backward shifting

Rückwärts / ~**hypothek** reverse mortgage, lifetime mortgage; ~**versicherung** retroactive insurance

R

Rückwechsel re-exchange, dishonoured bill of exchange; ~**provision** re-exchange commission; ~**spesen** re-exchange charges

rückwirkend 1. *adj.* retroactive, *(~e Gesetzgebung)* retrospective legislation, *(~e Wertstellung)* retroactive value, backvalue, backvaluation
2. *adv.* *(~ auf den Kalenderjahresbeginn ausstellen)* to issue retroactively to the beginning of the calendar year, *(~ ausweisen)* to record on a retroactive basis, *(~ berechnete Zinsen)* retroactive interest, *(~ in Kraft treten)* to come into force with retroactive effect, to take effect retrospectively

Rückwirkung 1. retroactive effect, retroactivity, *(steuerliche ~)* retroactive tax effect
2. *(~en auf das Zinsniveau)* repercussions (impact) on the interest rate level

rückzahlbar 1. repayable, *(~ mit einem Abschlag/Aufschlag)* repayable at a discount/premium, *(~ in monatlichen Raten in Höhe von …)* repayable (to be repaid) in monthly instalments of …
2. redeemable, *(~ durch jährliche Auslosungen)* redeemable by annual drawings 3. *(rückerstattungsfähig)* refundable, reimbursable

Rückzahlung 1. repayment, *(~ der Darlehenssumme)* repayment of the loan principal, *(~ in einer Summe)* repayment in one lump sum, *(~ in gleichen Tilgungsraten)* repayment in equal instalments, *(bis zur vollständigen ~ des Kredites)* until repayment in full of the loan
(einen Kredit zur Rückzahlung fällig stellen) to call in a loan for repayment, *(der gesamte Kredit wird sofort zur Rückzahlung fällig)* the whole of the loan accommodation becomes instantly repayable, *(zur Rückzahlung fällig werden)* to fall due, to mature
2. redemption, *(~ über/unter dem Nennwert)* redemption above (below) par, *(~ zum Nennwert plus Stückzinsen)* redemption at par plus interest accrued, *(~ durch Rückkauf)* redemption by way of repurchase

Rückzahlungs / ~agio redemption premium; ~**anspruch** right to repayment (redemption), redemption claim; ~**aufforderung** repayment request, call for repayment

Rückzahlungs / ~bedingungen repayment (redemption) terms, terms of repayment; ~**betrag** 1. repayable amount, amount repaid (to be repaid) 2. redemption money, amount repaid upon redemption of a bond; ~**disagio** redemption discount; ~**ereignis** early repayment event

Rückzahlungs / ~fähigkeit ability to repay, debt repayment capacity (ability); ~**garantie** 1. repayment guarantee (bond), redemption guarantee 2. return-of-money bond; ~**gewinn** gain on redemption

Rückzahlungs / ~kurs redemption (repayment) price; ~**last** debt repayment burden; ~**leistung** 1. repayment, effecting repayment 2. *(auf ein Darlehen)* principal repayment, repayment of principal

Rückzahlungs / ~mittel funds for repayment, redemption funds; ~**modalitäten** terms of repayment (redemption); ~**plan** repayment (redemption) schedule

Rückzahlungs / ~rate principal repayment rate, instalment, repayment (redemption) instalment; ~**recht** 1. *(~ des Kreditnehmers)* borrower's right of repayment 2. *(vorzeitiges ~ des Anleiheschuldners)* call right; ~**rendite** yield to maturity (redemption), redemption yield

Rückzahlungs / ~sperrfrist repayment (redemption) freeze, period (years) of non-redeemability; ~**verhalten** loan repayment behaviour, performance regarding debt repayment; ~**verlust** loss on repayment (on redemption)

Rückzahlungs / ~verpflichtung repayment obligation (commitment), duty to repay (to redeem); ~**versprechen**

R

repayment undertaking, undertaking to repay (to redeem); ~**verzug** default in repayment; ~**vorschlag** repayment proposal

Rückzahlungs / ~wert value upon redemption, redemption value, maturity value, amount paid to the bondholder when the security is redeemed at maturity; ~**zeitplan** timetable for repayment, repayment schedule; ~**zeitraum** repayment period, term of repayment

Rückzinsen back interest, interest refund

Rückzug withdrawal, retreat, climbdown, *(~ von Privatkundeneinlagen)* retail deposit run-off

Rückzugsrate run-off rate (factor) □ assigned to each source of funding for the purpose of calculating the liquidity coverage ratio (→ Mindestliquiditätsquote), *(~ für Privat-/Großkundeneinlagen)* retail/wholesale deposit run-off rate

Ruf reputation, repute, standing

Rufhandel open outcry trading

Rufschädigung reputational damage

ruhen 1. *(~ lassen, aussetzen)* to suspend, *(~de Ansprüche)* dormant (inactive) claims, *(~de Mitgliedschaft)* suspended membership **2.** *(das Projekt ruhte mehrere Jahre)* the project was stalled for several years

ruhig *(~es Geschäft) (Börse)* quiet (thin) trading

ruinös *(~er Wettbewerb)* ruinous (cut-throat) competition

Rumpfgeschäftsjahr rump business year, truncated (abridged) business year

Run run, *(~ auf kurzfristige Anleihen)* stampede into shorts

runder Boden *(Charttechnik)* rounding bottom, saucer bottom □ signals a turn from a bearish bias to a bullish bias

runder Gipfel *(Charttechnik)* rounding top, inverse saucer □ signals a bearish trend

runde Schlusseinheit round trading unit

Runde *(Gerüchte machen am Markt die ~)* rumours are circulating in the market

runden *(auf die nächsten 5% ~)* to round to the nearest 5%, *(auf vier Nachkommastellen ~)* to round to the fourth decimal point

Rundschreiben circular, circular letter

Rundungsdifferenzen differences due to rounding

S

Saatkapital seed capital

Sach / ~anlagen property, plant and equipment, tangible fixed assets; **~anlagenzugänge** additions to tangible fixed assets; **~aufklärung** inquiry into the facts

Sachaufwand *(eines Kreditinstitutes)* non-compensation expenses, general and administrative expense

Sachaufwandsquote non-compensation ratio □ ratio of non-compensation expenses to net revenues

Sach / ~auskehrung return (surrender) of property; **~ausschüttung** non-cash distribution, distribution in kind; **~bearbeiter** *(eines Kreditinstitutes)* junior bank officer (official), *(der zuständige ~)* the competent employee, the employee (officer) in charge of this matter

Sach / ~bezüge non-cash remuneration (benefits, compensation), remuneration in kind; **~bezugswert** *(steuerlicher)* taxable non-cash benefit; **~darlehen 1.** non-cash lending (loan), lending in kind **2.** → Sachkredit; **~dividende** non-cash dividend, dividend payable in kind, commodity dividend

Sache 1. *(Angelegenheit)* matter, issue, subject, problem, point **2.** *(Gegenstand)* thing, property, object, *(bewegliche Sachen)* moveables, moveable property, *(unbewegliche Sachen)* immoveables, immoveable property **3.** *(Rechtssache)* case

Sacheinlagen non-cash contributions, contributions in kind; **~verbot** ban on non-cash contributions

Sachenrecht law of property, body of laws relating to property, *(sachenrechtlich durchsetzbarer Anspruch auf Eigentumsübertragung)* right in rem to the transfer of title

Sach / ~entscheidung decision based on the merits (e. g. of the case, of the project); **~entziehung** deprivation of property; **~forderungen** asset-related (property-related) claims, claims in kind, *(bei Wertpapierleih-/Pensionsgeschäften)* asset claims, claims to the return of securities lent

Sach / ~gründung non-cash incorporation, establishment by non-capital contributions; **~investitionen** fixed asset investments, real investments, equipment spending

Sachkapital real capital; **~erhöhung** capital increase through contributions in kind; **~rendite** real capital return; **~zuführung** additions to real capital

Sach / ~kompetenz expertise; **~konto** real account; **~kosten** operating expenditure, personnel and material costs, → Sachaufwand; **~kredit** loan against collateral, secured loan

Sachkundenachweis evidence of the required qualification, evidence of expertise

sachkundig professionally competent, *(~e Mitarbeiter)* qualified staff

Sach / ~leistungen non-cash benefits (payments), benefits in kind; **~leistungsverpflichtungen** non-cash obligations

sachlich 1. real **2.** *(objektiv)* objective, impartial, unbiased, *(~e Gespräche)* businesslike (matter-of-fact) talks, *(~er Grund)* good reason

Sach / ~mängel material defects; **~mängelhaftung** liability for defects in material (and workmanship), liability for defective performance; **~pfän-**

dung distress; ~**pfändungsauftrag** warrant of distress

Sach / ~schaden property damage (loss), damage to property; ~**sicherheit** real security, security on property, lien on movable or immovable property; ~**steuer** non-personal tax

Sach / ~übergang physical transfer of property; ~**übernahme** tangible asset takeover, taking over available tangible assets; ~**verbindlichkeiten** asset-related liabilities, *(~ aus Wertpapierleihgeschäften)* liabilities from securities lending transactions

Sach / ~verhalt circumstances, issue at hand, facts (of the matter), *(Feststellung des ~s)* factual finding; ~**vermögen** tangible (fixed) property, real assets, fixed capital; ~**vermögensbildung** fixed capital formation; ~**versicherung** non-life insurance; ~**verstand** (skill and) expertise

Sachverständigen / ~ausschuss panel of experts; ~**beweis** expert evidence, evidence by examination of an expert; ~**gutachten** expert opinion (testimony)

Sachverständiger 1. expert **2.** appraiser, valuer **3.** loss assessor

Sachwalter (judicial) trustee, *(bei einer → Eigenverwaltung)* custodian

Sachwert 1. real value, intrinsic value **2.** property's asset value, property's depreciated replacement cost

Sachwerte tangible assets, real properties, *(Inflationsabsicherung durch ~)* tangible inflation hedge

Sachwert / ~anleihe asset-linked bond □ bond whose value is linked to the value of the underlying asset; ~**-Investmentfonds** property fund; ~**klausel** real asset clause

sachwertorientiert *(~e Kreditgewährung)* asset-based lending

Sachwertverfahren cost approach, DRC (depreciated replacement cost) approach

Sackgasse *(Wege aus der gegenwärtigen ~)* ways out of the present impasse

Safe safe, safe deposit box

saisonal *(~er Kreditbedarf)* seasonal borrowing requirements, *(~e Schwankungen)* seasonal fluctuations

Saisonbereinigung seasonal adjustment, *(saisonbereinigt)* seasonally adjusted, adjusted for seasonal influences, *(~ um 3 % steigen)* to rise by a seasonally adjusted 3 p. c.

Saisonkredit seasonal loan

Salden / ~abfrage balance (account) inquiry; ~**abgleich**/~**abstimmung** balance reconciliation; ~**anerkenntnis** acknowledgement of balance; ~**ausgleich 1.** settling a balance, settlement of a (debit) balance **2.** *(Kontoausgleich)* balancing an account

Salden / ~berichtigung rectifying a balance, adjustment of account; ~**bestätigung** confirmation of balance, confirming an account balance; ~**bilanz** trial balance sheet

Salden / ~ermittlung determining (calculating) the balance; ~**feststellung 1.** establishing (determining) the balance **2.** confirmation of balance ; ~**fortschreibung** (continuous) balance rollover; ~**informationssystem** balance reporting system; ~**liste** balance report

saldenmäßig *(~e Aufrechnung)* netting the accounts, offsetting the account balances

Salden / ~mitteilung account statement, statement of account; ~**übertrag** transfer of balances

saldieren 1. *(den Saldo ermitteln)* to balance, to strike the balance, *(saldierter Ausweis)* net balance statement, *(saldierte Position)* balanced position, net position
2. *(schließen)* to close, to close out
3. *(verrechnen, gegeneinander aufrechnen)* to net, to set off, *(Aktiv- und Passivpositionen ~)* to net asset and liability items, *(saldiertes Niederst-*

wertprinzip) netted lower-of-cost-or market principle

Saldierung 1. balancing **2.** *(Abschluss)* closing **3.** *(Verrechnung)* netting, setting off, *(~ der Forderungen an Banken mit den Verbindlichkeiten gegenüber Banken)* setting off due from banks against due to banks

saldierungsfähig nettable, offsettable

Saldierungsgebot/~verbot netting/ non-netting requirement

Saldo 1. balance, *(per ~)* on balance, in net terms, *(per ~ 5 Punkte fester schließen)* to close 5 points higher on balance, to end a net 5 points higher
2. account balance, *(~ zu Ihren Gunsten)* balance in your favour (to your credit), *(~ aus Konsolidierung)* balance arising from consolidation, *(~ aus letzter Rechnung)* balance brought forward from last account, *(~ auf neue Rechnung)* balance carried forward to next account, *(~ der außerordentlichen Erträge und Aufwendungen)* net extraordinary income (charges)
3. *(Restbetrag)* residual amount, remainder

Saldo / ~anerkenntnis confirmation of balance; **~ausgleich** settlement of a balance; **~guthaben** account balance, balance in the account; **~übertrag** balance transfer; **~vortrag** balance brought forward, opening balance; **~ziehung** balancing, striking the balance

salvatorische Klausel severability clause, salvatorius clause

S

Sammel / ~abschreibungen collective writedowns (depreciation); **~aktie** global share; **~auftrag** batch (collective) order; **~bestand** collective holdings; **~bestandsanteil** share in collective holdings; **~bewertung** global valuation

Sammel / ~deckung comprehensive cover; **~depot** collective custody account, collective securities account; **~depotanteil** share in a collective custody account; **~depotbestand** collective securities holdings; **~depotermächtigung** authorisation for collective safekeeping

Sammel / ~einzugsauftrag summary collection order; **~globalurkunde** collective global certificate

Sammel / ~inkasso 1. summary collection **2.** centralised collection; **~klage** class action;**~konnossement** omnibus (combined) bill of lading; **~konto** master account, pool account, concentration account

Sammel / ~ladung consolidated shipment; **~liste** *(~ der mit Opposition belegten Wertpapiere)* list of invalidated securities

sammeln 1. to gather, to collect **2.** *(ansammeln)* to accumulate, to amass

Sammel / ~meldung summary report; **~optionsschein** global warrant; **~position** summary item (heading); **~scheck** summary cheque; **~schuldbuchforderung** collective debt register claim

Sammel / ~überweisung summary payment order, summary remittance; **~urkunde** global certificate; **~verbriefung 1.** collective certification **2.** summary securitisation; **~verrechnung** collective (consolidated) billing

sammelverwahren to hold in collective custody, *(sammelverwahrte Aktienzertifikate)* share certificates held collectively (held in collective safekeeping)

Sammelverwahrer collective custodian (depository)

sammelverwahrfähig *(~e Wertpapiere)* securities eligible for collective safekeeping (collective safe custody)

Sammelverwahrung collective safekeeping (safe custody) of securities, *(Einlieferung von Wertpapieren in die ~)* depositing securities for collective safekeeping, *(Hereinnahme zur ~)* accepting for collective safekeeping

sammelwertberichtigt *(~e Forderungen)* lendings for which a collective valuation allowance has been set up

Sammelwertberichtigung collective valuation allowance, portfolio valuation allowance, *(~ für nicht erkennbare Kreditrisiken)* collective loan loss allowance for undiscernible risks

Sammel / ~zahlungen batch payments; **~zertifikat** global certificate

Sammler summary slip (voucher); **~datei** batch file

Sande *(im ~ verlaufen)* to wither on the vine

sanieren 1. to restructure, to reorganise, to rehabilitate, to revitalise, to revamp, *(das Unternehmen ~)* to turn the company around, to restore health to the company's finances, *(kapitalmäßig)* to recapitalise
2. *(retten)* to rescue, to bail out
3. *(ecol)* to redevelop

Sanierung 1. restructuring, reconstruction, *(erhaltende ~)* corporate reorganisation, *(~ in der Insolvenz)* restructuring (reorganisation) during insolvency, *(finanzielle ~)* financial rehabilitation, *(~ der Kapitalverhältnisse)* capital restructuring (reconstruction), *(~ durch Kapitalherabsetzung)* restructuring by way of a capital writedown, *(~ des Unternehmens durch Zufuhr neuer Mittel)* putting the company back on its feet through the infusion of fresh funds
2. *(Rettung)* rescue, bailout
3. *(notleidender Kedite)* non-performing loans workout
4. *(ecol)* redevelopment, remediation

Sanierungs / ~abteilung *(eines Kreditinstitutes)* restructuring unit, workout unit; **~aufwand** restructuring expense (charge)

Sanierungsbeauftragter restructuring administrator

sanierungsbedürftig *(~es Unternehmen)* company in need of restructuring

Sanierungsberater restructuring advisor □ implements a restructuring plan for an endangered credit institution in close cooperation with the Federal Financial Supervisory Authority (BaFIN), → Sanierungsverfahren, → Kreditinstitute-Reorganisationsgesetz

Sanierungs / ~bilanz reconstruction (reorganisation) accounts, reorganisation statement; **~erlass** Recapitalisation Decree; **~fähigkeit** capability for reconstruction

Sanierungs / ~fusion rescue merger, failing company defense; **~gebiet** redevelopment area; **~gewinn** reorganisation (recapitalisation) gains, surplus on reorganisation

Sanierungsklausel restructuring exemption clause □ offers substantial tax advantages to investors considering an investment in companies threatened with insolvency

Sanierungs / ~konsortium reconstruction (reorganisation) syndicate, rescue group; **~konzept** blueprint for restructuring, rehabilitation concept; **~kosten** restructuring (reorganisation) cost, restructuring charge; **~kredit** reconstruction (reorganisation) loan

Sanierungs / ~management workout management; **~maßnahmen** restructuring measures

Sanierungsplan 1. *(im Insolvenzverfahren)* reorganisation plan (scheme), financial reconstruction plan, financial rehabilitation plan, → Insolvenzverfahren
2. *(für ein gefährdetes Kreditinstitut)* (recapitalisation and) restructuring plan, → Sanierungsverfahren, → Kreditinstitute-Reorganisationsgesetz

Sanierungsprivileg 1. restructuring privilege, → Sanierungsklausel **2.** *(im Insolvenzverfahren)* restructuring privilege □ exempts restructuring loans from shareholders with a stake

S

of less than 10% from subordination and voidability in insolvency

Sanierungs / ~recht law on reorganisations and restructurings; **~träger** redevelopment contractor; **~übersicht** reorganisation statement

Sanierungsverfahren 1. *(außergerichtliches ~)* out-of-court reorganisation proceedings
2. *(für ein gefährdetes Kreditinstitut)* restructuring proceedings □ voluntary proceedings that can be requested by a bank in need of restructuring; requires the appointment of a restructuring advisor (Sanierungsberater), → Kreditinstitute-Reorganisationsgesetz

Sanierungsvergleich reorganisation agreement □ based on an arrangement with creditors

Sanierungs / ~würdigkeit *(Beurteilung der ~ des Unternehmens)* assessment of the extent to which the company is suitable for restructuring; **~zweck** restructuring purpose (objective)

sanktionieren *(billigen)* to sanction, to approve

Sanktionskompetenzen enforcement powers

Satelliten-Portfolio satellite portfolio

sättigen to saturate

Sättigung saturation

Sättigungs / ~grad degree of saturation; **~punkt** saturation point

Satz 1. *(Zinssatz)* rate, *(Sätze im kurzfristigen/langfristigen Bereich)* short-term/long-term lending rates
2. *(von Dokumenten)* set, *(voller ~ reiner Bordkonnossemente)* full set of clean shipped on board bills of lading

Satz / ~findung rate determination; **~format** record format; **~indikationen** indicative interest rates; **~nennungen** rates quoted

Satzung 1. statute(s), byelaws, rules **2.** *(einer Unternehmung)* Articles of Association (BE), Articles of Incorporation (AE)

Satzungsänderung amendment to the Articles of Association

satzungsgemäß/~mäßig 1. *(~e Organe)* statutory (governing) bodies, *(~e Rücklage)* statutory reserve **2.** in accordance with (under) the Articles of Association

satzungswidrig contrary to (contravening) the memorandum of association, in violation of the statute

Säule 1 pillar 1 (of the Basle Capital Accord, → Basel II) □ defines the minimum capital requirements

Säule 2 pillar 2 □ supervisory review process

Säule 3 pillar 3 □ sets up qualitative and quantitative disclosure requirements on risks to strengthen market discipline and enhance transparency

säumig defaulting, in default, *(~er Kreditnehmer/Schuldner)* defaulting (delinquent) borrower/ debtor, *(~er Vertragspartner)* defaulting party, party in default, defaulter

Säumnis delay, default, delinquency; **~urteil** judg(e)ment by default; **~zuschlag 1.** surcharge for delay in payment **2.** late filing penalty

SB-Bankterminal customer-operated terminal, automated teller terminal

Schachtel / ~beteiligung intercorporate equity stake, intercompany participation; **~dividende** intercorporate (intercompany) dividend; **~gesellschaft** affiliated company; **~privileg** *(internationales ~)* international intercorporate privilege □ preferential tax treatment of profits made by foreign affiliated companies (to avoid double taxation)

schaden 1. to damage, to harm **2.** *(von Nachteil sein)* to be detrimental, *(der Bonität ~)* to be detrimental to the credit standing

Schaden 1. damage, injury **2.** *(Havarie)* average **3.** *(Nachteil)* detriment, disadvantage **4.** *(Verlust)* loss **5.** *(Ver-*

S

sicherungsanspruch) claim, *(gemeldete Schäden)* claims reported

Schaden / ~abwendungspflicht duty to avert damage; **~abwicklung** claims settlement (handling, processing); **~anzeige** claims notification, loss advice; **~aufstellung** statement of damages, loss statement; **~aufwand** claims paid

Schaden / ~bearbeitung claims processing; **~begrenzung** damage limitation; **~belastung** loss incidence; **~deckung** loss coverage, covering a loss; **~ entwicklung** loss development; **~ereignis** damage occurrence, loss event (occurrence)

Schadenersatz 1. (compensatory) damages, compensation, *(~ in Höhe von ... € entrichten)* to pay € ... in damages, *(~ fordern)* to seek damages, *(~ wegen Gewährleistungsbruch)* damages for breach of warranty, *(~ wegen Nichterfüllung des Vertrages)* damages for non-performance of the contract, damages for breach of contract, *(~ für den erlittenen Schaden)* damages for the loss (injury) sustained **2.** *(Entschädigung)* indemnity, indemnification

Schadenersatz / ~anspruch 1. *(Forderung)* claim for damages, *(einen Schadenersatzanspruch stellen)* to file a damage claim against **2.** → Schadenersatzberechtigung; **~berechtigung** entitlement to compensation, right to damages, *(schadenersatzberechtigt)* entitled to compensation (to assert damages)

Schadenersatz / ~forderung claim for compensatory damages (for compensation), compensatory damage claim, *(~en wegen Leistungsverweigerung)* damage claims for failure to perform; **~haftung** liability in damages

Schadenersatz / ~klage action for damages, *(~ anstrengen)* to bring an action for damages; **~ leistung** payment of damages; **~pflicht** duty to pay compensation, *(~ des Beklagten)* defendant's liability in tort

schadenersatzpflichtg *(~ sein)* to be liable in damages

Schaden / ~erwartung loss expectancy; **~exzedent** excess of loss; **~exzedentenrückversicherung** excess of loss reinsurance

Schaden / ~fall damage, loss, *(in Verbindung mit finanziellen Vermögenswerten)* loss event; **~feststellung** loss assessment, ascertaining (assessing) the damage; **~freistellung** → Schadloshaltung

Schaden / ~haftung liability for damages; **~häufigkeit** loss rate, damage frequency; **~höhe** extent of damage

Schaden / ~meldung → Schadenanzeige; **~minderungspflicht** obligation to mitigate the damage (loss); **~nachweis** proof of loss, proof (evidence) of damage; **~quote** claims ratio

Schaden / ~regulierer claims adjuster, claims settling agent; **~regulierung** claims adjustment cost, claims settlement (adjustment, handling), loss settlement; **~regulierungskosten** claims settlement expenditure; **~rückstellungen** outstanding claims provisions

Schaden / ~überschuss excess of loss; **~umfang** extent of damage; **~ verhütungspflicht** duty to prevent losses; **~versicherung** non-life insurance, property and casualty insurance

schadhaft 1. defective **2.** damaged

schädigen to damage, to prejudice, to impair, *(geschädigte Partei)* aggrieved (injured) party

Schädiger tort-feasor, author of damage

Schädigung damage, prejudice, harm, impairment

Schädigungsabsicht 1. intent to cause harm/loss **2.** intent to defraud

schädlich damaging, detrimental, disadvantageous, *(~er Beteiligungserwerb) (i. S. des KStG)* harmful acquisition, *(~e Fremdfinanzierung)* harmful debt financing, *(sich als finanziell ~ erweisen)* to prove financially damaging

schadlos *(~ halten)* to indemnify, to hold harmless, to secure against loss or damage

Schadlos / ~bürge indemnitor, indemnifier; **~bürgschaft** indemnity bond, letter of indemnity; **~bürgschaftsnehmer** indemnitee

Schadlos / ~haltung indemnification, *(~ gegen alle Ansprüche)* holding harmless against all claims

Schadloshaltungs / ~erklärung indemnification letter; **~klausel** hold harmless clause; **~vereinbarung** indemnification agreement

schaffen *(die Grundlagen ~)* to lay the groundwork

Schalter counter, *(am ~ in bar auszahlen)* to pay in cash across the counter, *(am ~ einlösen)* to cash over the counter

Schalter / ~ankaufskurs counter buying rate; **~auslieferung** delivery across the counter

Schaltergeschäft 1. *(allgemein)* counter operation(s) 2. *(Wertpapier-Schaltergeschäft)* counter transaction, teller transaction, delivery of securities against cash payment 3. *(Kreditgeschäft)* → Schalterkredit, *(Sätze für Schaltergeschäfte)* counter lending rates

Schalter / ~kredit cash advance, counter lending; **~kurse** counter buying and selling rates; **~nutzen** placing (selling) commission

Schalter / ~personal counter staff; **~provision** placing (selling) commission; **~publizität** duty to hold a company prospectus available at the bank's counters; **~raum** banking hall

Schalter / ~stücke counter stock; **~stunden** banking (business, office) hours; **~terminal** counter terminal; **~vergütung** placing (selling) commission; **~verkaufskurs** counter selling rate; **~verkehr** counter transactions

scharf *(~er Kostendruck)* severe cost pressure, *(~er Protest)* strong (harsh) protest, *(~e Trennung)* strict (rigid, rigorous) division, *(~er Wettbewerb)* tough (fierce, bitter) competition

Schärfe 1. severity, sharpness 2. keenness, fierceness 3. strength 4. strictness, rigidity, *(die ~ nehmen)* to take the edge off

Schattenbankensystem shadow banking

Schatzanweisungen → Bundesschatzanweisungen

Schätzbetrag estimated amount, estimate

Schatzbrief (Federal) savings bond, → Bundesschatzbrief

Schätze → Bundesschatzanweisungen

schätzen 1. to estimate 2. *(taxieren)* to appraise, to value, to assess 3. *(vermuten)* to guess, to reckon, to expect 4. to value, to hold in high esteem, *(geschätzter Kunde)* valued (esteemed) customer

Schätzer appraiser, professional valuer, *(zweiter Schätzer)* reappraiser

Schätz / ~gutachten appraisal, expert opinion; **~kosten** appraisal cost, appraiser's fee

Schatzscheine Treasury certificates

Schätzung 1. estimate 2. appraisal, valuation, assessment

schätzungsweise roughly, approximately, *(~ ein Drittel)* an estimated one third

Schatzwechsel Treasury bill(s) □ issued at a discount and with maturities up to ninety days

Schätzwert appraised (estimated) value, estimate

Schaukelbörse seesaw market

Scheck cheque (BE), check (AE)

Scheck / ~aussteller writer (drawer) of a cheque; **~bearbeitung** cheque processing; **~bestand** cheques in hand;;

S

~**betrug** cheque fraud; ~**bezahltmeldung** advice of payment; ~**bezogener** drawee of (under) a cheque

Scheck / ~**deckung** cheque cover; ~**einlösung 1.** *(durch die Bank)* paying (honouring) a cheque, cheque clearance **2.** *(durch den Kunden)* cashing a cheque; ~**einreichung** cheque presentation, presentation of a cheque for payment

Scheck / ~**einzug** cheque collection, collecting a cheque, *(Hereinnahme eines Schecks zum Einzug)* taking (accepting) a cheque for collection, *(elektronischer Scheckeinzug)* cheque truncation; ~**empfänger** payee of the cheque; ~**fähigkeit** capacity to draw (to write) cheques

Scheck / ~**gegenwert** cheque proceeds; ~**gutschrift** cheque credit; ~**haftung** liability on a cheque; ~**inhaber** bearer (holder) of a cheque; ~**inkasso** → Scheckeinzug; ~**nehmer** person accepting a cheque for payment

Scheck / ~**recht** law relating to cheques; ~**regress** recourse against the writer of a cheque; ~**retoure** returned (dishonoured) cheque, *(Plural)* returns, cheques returned unpaid

Scheck / ~**rückgabe** cheque return, return of an unpaid (dishonoured) cheque, *(~ mangels Deckung)* non-payment of a cheque for lack of cover; ~**rückrechnung** cheque return bill, banker's ticket

Scheck / ~**sperre** stopping a cheque, countermanding payment of a cheque; ~**unterschrift** *(~ prüfen)* to check the genuineness of the drawer's (writer's) signature

Scheck / ~**verfügung** cheque drawing, drawing by cheque; ~**verkehr** cheque payments (transactions); ~**verrechnung** cheque clearing; ~**vorlegungsfrist** presentation period for cheques; ~**zahlung** payment by cheque

scheiden *(aus einem Amt ~)* to resign, to leave office, to retire from office, *(der scheidende Vorstandsvorsitzende)* the outgoing chief executive

Scheideweg *(strategisch an einem ~ stehen)* to be at a crossroads in a strategic sense

Schein 1. *(Banknote)* note **2.** *(Beleg)* slip **3.** *(Bescheinigung)* certificate **4.** *(Bezugsrechtsschein/Optionsschein)* warrant **5.** *(Formular)* form

scheinbar 1. apparent, ostensible, *(~ Berechtigter)* ostensible beneficiary **2.** *(nicht echt)* fictitious, sham **3.** *(nominell)* nominal

Schein / ~**bestandteile** non-permanent property components, temporary (third-party) appurtenances; ~**bilanz** fictitious balance sheet; ~**dividende** sham dividend; ~**gebot** fictitious (straw, rigged) bid

Schein / ~**geschäft** fictitious (feigned) transaction; ~**gesellschaft** fictitious (bogus) company; ~**gesellschafter 1.** fictitious partner **2.** ostensible (nominal) partner; ~**kauf** fictitious (sham) purchase

Schein / ~**kurs 1.** fictitious price **2.** nominal price; ~**vertrag** fictitious (sham, feigned) contract; ~**wechsel** wind bill, kite; ~**zahlung** sham (fictitious, feigned) payment

scheitern 1. to fail, to fall through, to break down **2.** *(zum Scheitern bringen)* to thwart, to frustrate

Scheitern *(~ der Gespräche)* failure (breakdown) of the talks

Schema 1. scheme, pattern **2.** *(graphische/schematische Darstellung)* diagram

Schenkung gift, donation, *(~ unter Lebenden)* gift (donation) inter vivos, absolute gift, *(Eigentumsübertragung durch ~)* conveyance of property by way of a gift

Schenkungs / ~**empfänger** donee; ~**geber** donor, donator; ~**steuer** gift tax; ~**urkunde** deed of donation; ~**versprechen** gratuitous promise

Schere *(z. B. zwischen Kassa- und Terminkursen)* gap (differential) between spot and forward rates

scheuen 1. *(keine Kosten ~)* to spare no expense **2.** *(eine öffentliche Notierung ~)* to eschew a public listing

Schicht 1. layer **2.** *(Gesellschaftsschicht)* class, section, stratum

schichten *(geschichtete Stichprobe)* stratified sample

Schichten / ~bilanz statement of loan and interest maturities; **~bildung** *(Aufteilung einer Grundgesamtheit in kleinere Einheiten)* stratification, *(geschichtete Stichprobenauswahl)* stratified sampling

Schicksal *(~ des Unternehmens)* company's fate (fortunes)

Schieds / ~abkommen arbitration agreement; **~ausschuss** arbitration committee, panel of arbitrators; **~gericht** court of arbitration, arbitration tribunal

schiedsgerichtlich *adj.* arbitral, *adv.* *(~ regeln)* to settle by arbitration

Schiedsgerichts / ~barkeit arbitral jurisdiction; **~entscheidung** arbitration (arbitral) award; **~verfahren** arbitration proceedings

Schieds / ~klausel arbitration clause; **~ordnung** arbitration regulations, → Schlichtungsordnung; **~richter** arbitrator; **~spruch** arbitrator's award; **~verfahren** arbitration proceedings; **~weg** *(auf dem ~)* by arbitration

S

Schieflage *(~ der Gesellschaft)* company's financial distress

Schifffahrtswerte shippings, shipping shares (stocks)

Schiffs / ~bank → Schiffshypothekenbank; **~bauregister** Register of Ships under Construction; **~bauwerkshypothek** mortgage on a ship under construction; **~beleihungsgeschäft** lendings against (on) ships

Schiffs / ~finanzierung ship financing; **~hypothek** ship (vessel) mortgage; **~hypothekarkredit** ship mortgage loan; **~hypothekenbank** ship mortgage bank; **~kaskoversicherung** ship hull policy

Schiffs / ~manifest ship's manifest; **~papiere** ship's papers; **~pfandbriefe** Ship Pfandbriefe □ Covered Bonds secured against ship mortgages; **~pfandrecht** maritime lien; **~registerbrief/~zertifikat** ship's registration certificate

Schirmherrschaft *(unter der ~ von)* under the auspices (patronage) of

Schlagkraft power, clout, prowess

schlagkräftig *(~es Vertriebsnetz)* powerful distribution network

Schlaglicht *(~ werfen auf)* to highlight

Schlange 1. *(Währungsschlange)* currency snake **2.** *(Emittenten stehen ~)* issuers are queueing up

schlank *(~e Organisation)* lean organisation

schlecht 1. *adj (~e Aussichten für den Aktienmarkt)* bleak (poor, gloomy, dismal) prospects for the equity market, *(~e Bonität)* poor credit quality, *(~es Ergebnis)* poor performance, *(~e Marktverfassung)* poor (adverse) market conditions
2. *adv. (~ abschneiden)* to fare poorly, *(~ beraten)* ill-advised, poorly advised

Schlechterbewertung *(bonitätsmäßig)* downgrading, deterioration of (lowering) the rating

Schlechterfüllung *(~ eines Vertrages)* deficient performance

Schlechterstellung *(rangmäßige ~)* holding a lower rank, *(~ eines Gläubigers)* placing a creditor in an inferior position, *(sicherheitenmäßig ~)* holding a junior (lower-ranking) security, *(keine sicherheitenmäßige ~)* no discriminatory treatment in terms of collateralisation

Schlechtleistung deficient (faulty) performance, failure to perform properly

schleichend *(~e Abwertung)* latent devaluation, *(~e Inflation)* creeping (latent) inflation

schleppend *(~es Aktiengeschäft)* sluggish market in equities, *(~e Konjunktur)* flat (flagging) economy, *(~ zahlen)* to be slow in paying

schleusen *(in den Markt ~)* to channel (to funnel) into the market

schlichten 1. to settle **2.** *(durch einen Schiedsspruch ~)* to arbitrate, to settle by arbitration **3.** *(vermitteln)* to mediate

Schlichter conciliator, mediator

Schlichtung conciliation, mediation, dispute resolution (settlement), *(außergerichtliche ~)* alternative (external, extrajudicial) dispute resolution

Schlichtungs / ~antrag request for mediation; **~ausschuss** mediation committee, dispute settlement committee; **~ergebnis** mediation outcome; **~gesetz** Disputes Settlement Act; **~gespräche** mediation (conciliation) talks

Schlichtungs / ~klausel conciliation clause; **~kommission** → Schlichtungsausschuss; **~management** mediation and conciliation management; **~ordnung** conciliation (mediation) rules, dispute resolution regulations

Schlichtungs / ~spruch mediator's proposal, conciliation award; **~stelle** conciliation board, mediation and conciliation service, ombudsman's office

Schlichtungs / ~verfahren conciliation proceedings, dispute resolution procedure, mediative process ; **~versuch** attempt at conciliation, mediation attempt; **~vorschlag** conciliation proposal, mediation scheme, proposed settlement

schließen 1. to conclude, *(einen Vergleich ~)* to compromise, to come to (to reach) a compromise, to arrive at an arrangement (to compound) with one's creditors, *(einen Vertrag ~)* to enter into (to conclude) an agreement
2. to close, to liquidate, *(ein Konto ~)* to close (to close out) an account, *(eine Position ~)* to close (to liquidate, to wind up) a position, *(eine Position durch ein gegenläufiges Geschäft ~)* to close out a position by an opposite transaction
3. to close, to finish, to bring to an end, to terminate, *(einen Betrieb ~)* to shut down a plant, to cease operations, *(die Zeichnungsliste ~)* to close the application (subscription) list
4. *(die Börsensitzung beenden) (fester ~)* to finish (to close) on a firmer note, *(geringfügig schwächer ~)* to close a shade lower, *(um zehn Punkte niedriger/höher ~)* to close ten points down/up
5. *(die Finanzierungslücke ~)* to bridge the financing gap, *(eine Marktlücke ~)* to fill (to plug) a market gap
6. *(schlussfolgern)* to conclude, → Schluss (**3.**)

Schließen / Schließung 1. conclusion **2.** closing, closure, termination, *(~ von Inkongruenzen)* closing out mismatched positions, *(~ offener Positionen)* closing out (liquidating) open positions, *(~ einer Optionsposition)* option closeout

Schließfach safe deposit box, strongbox; **~miete** safe deposit rent

schlimmstenfalls *(~ wird die Dividende ausfallen)* in the worst case (if the worst comes to the worst), no dividend will be paid

schlingern *(der ~de Konzern)* the beleaguered group

schlittern *(in die roten Zahlen ~)* to slide into the red

Schluss 1. close, closing, closure, end, *(~ der Börsensitzung)* close of the session
2. *(Börsen-Handelseinheit)* trading unit, lot
3. conclusion, *(zu dem ~ kommen)* to conclude, to draw (to reach, to arrive at) a conclusion, to infer, to deduct, *(zu einem anderen ~ kommen)* to conclude otherwise

Schluss / ~abrechnung 1. closing (final) statement, final account **2.** final settlement; **~abrechnungspreis 1.** *(für fällige Terminkontrakte)* exchange delivery settlement price **2.** final settlement price

Schluss / **~auktion** closing auction; **~ausführung** concluding statement; **~ausschüttung** final distribution; **~bericht** final (concluding) report; **~bestimmungen** concluding provisions

Schluss / **~bilanz 1.** *(zum Ende eines Geschäftsjahres)* annual accounts **2.** *(bei einer Unternehmensliquidation)* liquidation accounts; **~buchung** closing entry; **~dividende** *(bei einer Unternehmensliquidation)* liquidation (winding-up) dividend; **~einheit** trading unit (lot)

Schlüssel 1. key, clue, formula, *(der ~ zum Erfolg liegt in …)* the clue to success lies in … **2.** *(bei einer Datenverschlüsselung)* encryption key

Schlüssel / **~authentifizierung** key authentication; **~faktor** key determinant, key factor determining the …

schlüsselfertig turn-key

Schlüssel / **~industrie** key industry; **~paar** pair of keys, → öffentlicher, → privater Schlüssel; **~position** key (pivotal) post; **~prüfung** key verification; **~rolle** key role (part), *(eine ~ spielen)* to play a key (pivotal) role (e. g. in developing new products)

Schlüssel / **~verwaltung** key management; **~wiedergewinnung** key recovery; **~zahl** test key, authenticator key ; **~zentrale** key manager authority; **~zertifizierung** key certification

Schluss / **~ergebnis** final result (outcome); **~erholung** recovery towards the close of the session; **~geschäft** *(Börse)* business at the close of the session

schlüssig *(~er Beweis)* conclusive evidence

Schluss / **~kurs 1.** *(Börsenschlusskurs)* closing price (quotation, rate), price at the close of the session **2.** final transaction price; **~note** contract note, settlement note; **~notierung**/**~notiz** closing quotation

Schluss / **~position** *(bei Kombinationspositionen)* closing leg, closing position, back leg; **~rate** final instalment; **~rechnung 1.** *(Abschlussrechnung)* final accounts, settlement (closing) statement **2.** → Schlussnote **3.** *(des Insolvenzverwalters)* realisation and liquidation statement

Schluss / **~saldo** closing (final) balance; **~schein** contract note; **~sitzung** final meeting, closing session

Schlusstag 1. *(Abschlusstag)* trading day **2.** *(Regulierungstag)* settlement day **3.** *(bei einer Ausschreibung)* closing date

Schlusstermin 1. deadline **2.** *(letzte Gläubigerversammlung im Insolvenzverfahren)* final creditors' meeting **3.** *(für die Zeichnung von Wertpapieren)* closing day (date)

Schluss / **~überschuss** terminal dividend; **~verteilung** final distribution; **~verzeichnis** *(im Insolvenzverfahren)* list of creditors entitled to a share in the insolvency estate; **~zahlungsgarantie** retention of money bond

schmälern 1. *(beeinträchtigen)* to impair **2.** *(mindern)* to diminish, to curtail, to clip

Schmälerung 1. impairment **2.** diminution, curtailment

schmutzig *(~es Floaten)* managed (dirty) floating

schnell *(~ realisierbare Vermögenswerte)* quickly realisable assets, assets quickly convertible into cash, *(~ steigende Nachfrage)* rapidly rising demand, *(~e Erholung)* swift recovery, *(~e Zahlung)* prompt payment

Schnellgenehmigungsverfahren fast-track approval procedure

Schnelltender quick tender □ tender procedure used by the European Central Bank for fine-tuning operations with a small number of counterparties

S

Schnitt 1. cut **2.** *(Kapitalschnitt)* capital reduction **3.** *(im ~)* on the average

Schnittstellen / ~kompetenz interface competency; **~management** interface management

schocken *(den Aktienmarkt ~)* to rock the stock market, to send shock waves through the equity market

schonen *(das Eigenkapital ~)* to save (to spare) the equity

schönen *(das schlechte Ergebnis ~)* to gloss over (to embellish) the poor performance

Schönung *(~ der Bilanz)* window-dressing, sprucing up the balance sheet

Schonfrist *(i. S. einer zusätzlichen Zahlungsfrist)* period of grace

Schramme *(~ im Unternehmensergebnis)* dent (scratch) in the corporate performance

Schranke 1. barrier **2.** limit, *(~n setzen)* to put a limit on **3.** *(Hindernis)* impediment

Schreiben *(~ von Optionen)* option sale, option writing

Schrift *(Broschüre)* brochure, leaflet

Schriftform *(Änderungen der Vereinbarung bedürfen der ~)* amendments to the agreement must be made in writing

Schriftformerfordernis written form requirement

schriftlich *(~ bestätigen)* to confirm in writing, *(~ niederlegen)* to put down in writing, *(~e Vereinbarung)* written agreement, *(~ vereinbarte Konditionen)* terms agreed in writing

Schrift / ~satz brief, written pleading; **~stück 1.** paper, document **2.** deed, writ

Schriftwechsel correspondence

Schritt 1. step, stride, move, *(der erste ~ auf dem Weg zu einer Ergebnisverbesserung)* first step towards a performance improvement, *(die Finanzierung einen ~ voranbringen)* to take the financing a step forward **2.** *(in ~en von fünf Punkten notieren)* to quote in intervals of 5 points **3.** pace, *(~ halten)* to keep up with, *(nicht ~ halten können)* to fail to keep pace with

Schrittmacher *(z. B. bei der Einführung innovativer Produkte)* pioneer, pacemaker

schrittweise 1. *adj.* *(~ Annäherung)* progressive approach, *(~ Einführung)* phased introduction, *(~ Erhöhung)* gradual increase **2.** *adv.* gradual(ly), progressive(ly), step by step, *(~ auslaufen lassen/einführen)* to phase out/to phase in, *(~ sinkende Zinssätze)* gradually decreasing interest rates, *(die Schuldenlast ~ reduzieren)* to reduce the debt load little by little (step by step)

schrumpfen to shrink, to dwindle, to contract, to narrow, *(~de Gewinnspannen der Unternehmen)* shrinking corporate profit margins

Schrumpfung shrinkage, dwindling, contraction, diminution, *(~ der Gewinne)* profit shrinkage, dwindling of profits, *(~ der Zinsspannen)* contraction in (narrowing of) interest margins

Schrumpfungsprozess process of contraction

Schub *(z. B. Inflationsschub)* inflationary push

Schubkraft 1. *(wirtschaftliche ~)* economic thrust **2.** *(~ für den Aktienmarkt)* driving force for the equity market

Schufa (Schutzgemeinschaft für allgemeine Kreditsicherung) creditors' protection agency

Schuld 1. debt, amount owed **2.** *(Fehler, Verschulden)* fault **3.** *(Verbindlichkeit)* liability

Schuld / ~ablösung repayment (liquidation) of a debt, debt retirement, discharge of a debt; **~anerkenntnis** acknowledgement of debt; **~aufhebung** debt cancellation, debt discharge

Schuldaufnahme borrowing, contracting (incurring) a debt, *(~ am Kapitalmarkt)* borrowing in the capital market, *(~ aus Rentenemissionen)* borrowing through bond issues

Schuldbedienung debt servicing (service), *(Schulden halbjährlich bedienen)* to service debts every six months

schuldbefreiende Wirkung debt-discharging effect, *(~ besitzen)* to operate as a discharge, to constitute valid discharge of a debt, *(Zahlung mit schuldbefreiender Wirkung)* payment in discharge of a debt, payment implying discharge in full

Schuld / ~befreiung debt discharge; **~beitreibung** debt recovery; **~beitritt** entering into an existing obligation as co-debtor (co-obligor), binding o. s. as co-debtor, assuming joint liability for a debt, collateral promise; **~betrag** amount owed

Schuldbuch debt register, debt book

Schuldbuch / ~eintrag debt book entry, entry in the debt book (register); **~fähigkeit** eligibility for entry in the Federal debt register; **~forderungen** book-entry securities, bonds issued in book-entry form, i. e. the rights of the bondholders (creditors) against the issuer are registered in a so-called debt book

Schuldeinforderung calling in a debt

schulden to owe, *(die Banken aus Umschuldungskrediten geschuldeten Beträge)* amounts owed to banks on rescheduled loans, *(die im Rahmen der Kreditvereinbarungen geschuldeten Gelder)* money owed under the loan (lending) agreements, debt outstanding under the facilities granted

Schulden / ~abbau deleveraging, lowering the debt burden, off-loading debt; **~ablösung** discharge of debts; **~begrenzung** debt limitation, capping the debt (indebtedness), *(Bestimmungen zur ~)* debt capping rules; **~belastung** → Schuldenlast

Schulden / ~bereinigung 1. debt removal, debt elimination **2.** debt reorganisation (settlement) for insolvent consumers; **~berg** debt mountain, pile of debt

Schulden / ~bestand debt level, level of indebtedness, aggregate debt; **~bestandsveränderungen** variations (changes) in the debt level

Schuldendienst debt service, debt servicing, debt service payments, interest and redemption payments, *(Aufrechterhaltung des ~es)* keeping the debt service going, maintenance of debt service payments
(Bereitstellung der für den ~ benötigten Mittel) provision of funds for servicing the debt, *(Einstellung des ~es)* suspension of debt service payments, *(Rückstände im ~)* arrears in debt service payments, debt service arrears

Schuldendienst / ~abkommen debt service accord, agreement on debt service payments; **~aufwand** debt service charge (load), debt servicing cost; **~deckungsgrad** debt service coverage ratio □ ratio of cash flow to debt service requirements

Schuldendienst / ~einstellung suspension of (halt in) debt service payments; **~entlastung** reducing the debt service load; **~erfordernisse** debt service requirements; **~erleichterungen** debt service relief, easing debt service payments

schuldendienstfähig capable of meeting debt service obligations

Schuldendienstfähigkeit debt service capacity, capacity to make interest and redemption payments, capacity to meet debt servicing commitments, ability to repay debt (to service one's debt)

Schuldendienst / ~finanzierung financing (funding) debt service payments; **~last** debt service charge (load), debt servicing burden, burden of debt service payments; **~leistung**

S

debt servicing, servicing a debt, effecting debt service payments

Schuldendienst / ~mittel debt service funds; **~moratorium** debt service moratorium; **~quote** debt service ratio

Schuldendienst / ~reduktion debt service relief, lowering (reducing) the debt service charge; **~relation** debt service ratio, ratio of debt service payments to foreign exchange income

Schuldendienst / ~verpflichtungen debt service commitments (obligations), *(seinen ~ nicht nachkommen)* to default on one's debt service commitments; **~zahlungen** debt service payments, interest and redemption payments

Schulden / ~einzug debt collection; **~erlass** debt remission (waiver), debt foregiveness; **~erleichterung** debt relief; **~fähigkeit** debt capacity, ability to borrow, → Schuldendienstfähigkeit

schuldenfrei unencumbered, unindebted, *(~er Besitz)* unmortgaged (unencumbered) property

Schulden / ~haftung liability on (for) debts; **~höhe** debt level; **~kapitalisierung** converting debt into equity; **~kappung** debt reduction, trimming indebtedness; ~ **konsolidierung** debt consolidation; **~krise** *(internationale ~)* international debt crisis

Schulden / ~last debt burden (load, charge), burden of indebtedness, total debt (liabilities), *(bei Grundbesitz)* encumbrances, property charges; **~löschung** debt repayment, debt discharge

Schulden / ~management debt management; **~masse** total liabilities, aggregate debt (indebtedness); **~moratorium** debt moratorium, standstill agreement on debt repayments

Schulden / ~obergrenze debt ceiling, borrowing cap, ceiling placed on the amount of borrowings; **~reduktion/~reduzierung** debt reduction, lowering the debt load, reducing the debt burden

Schulden / ~refinanzierung debt refinancing, *(bestehende Schulden über einen langfristigen Zeitraum refinanzieren)* to refinance (to fund) existing debt over a long period

Schulden / ~regelung/~regulierung debt settlement (arrangement), debt workout, debt adjusting; **~rückstand** debt arrears

Schulden / ~stand debt level, debt outstanding, level of indebtedness, total borrowings; **~streichung** → Schuldenverzicht; **~-Swap** debt (liabilities) swap

Schulden / ~tilgung debt retirement, discharge (liquidation) of a debt, debt repayment; **~tilgungsfonds** sinking fund

Schuldentlastung easing the debt burden (the debt load), debt relief

Schulden / ~überhang net debt position, overgearing, overleveraging; **~übernahme** assumption of debt; **~übersicht** statement of liabilities; **~überwachung** debt monitoring

Schulden / ~umstrukturierung debt restructuring, restructuring (rescheduling) the outstanding debt; **~umwandlung** debt conversion, converting debt (e. g. into equity)

Schulden / ~verringerung debt reduction, deleveraging, *(Möglichkeiten der ~)* ways to reduce debt (to ease the debt burden); **~verwaltung** debt management; **~verzicht** debt foregiveness, debt waiver

Schuld / ~ersatz/~ersetzung novation, substituting a new obligation (contract) for an existing one, *(in schuldersetzender Weise)* by novation; **~fälligkeit** maturity of a debt; **~feststellung** establishing (determining) a debt; **~forderung** claim, (unpaid) debt; **~forderungsklage** action for recovery of a debt

schuldhaft *(~e Nichterfüllung)* culpable non-performance (non-fulfillment), *(durch kein eigenes ~es Verhalten)* through no fault of his/her own, *(nicht ~es Verhalten)* non-culpable conduct

Schuld / ~haftentlassung release (discharge) from liability; **~kapital** debt capital, borrowed funds; **~mitübernahme** → Schuldbeitritt; **~nachweis** evidence of debt (indebtedness)

Schuldner debtor, obligor, borrower

Schuldner / ~adresse borrowing name, *(erstklassige ~)* prime (top-quality, first-rate) borrower; **~ausfall** debtor default, *(ausstehender Betrag bei ~)* exposure at default, *(Verlust bei ~)* loss given default

Schuldner / ~bank borrowing bank; **~berater** debt counsellor, **~beratung** debtor advice, consumer debt advice, debt counselling; **~beratungsstelle** debt advice bureau (agency)

Schuldner / ~bonität debtor credit rating, borrower's (debtor's) credit standing, creditworthiness of the borrower; **~entlastung** discharge of debtor; **~ermittlung** locating debtors, debtor tracing; **~gesamtheit/~gruppe** group of connected borrowers/issuers

schuldnerische Masse debtor's estate

Schuldner / ~konto debtor account; **~kündigungsrecht** *(bei Emissionen)* call option, issuer's right to redeem a bond issue prior to maturity, *(eines Kreditnehmers)* borrower's right to repay a loan prior to maturity

S

Schuldner / ~land debtor country (nation), obligor country; **~position** borrowing position, *(im Geldhandel)* buying (borrowing) position, to be buyers; **~qualität** borrower's standing; **~rating** debtor rating

Schuldner / ~vermögen assets of the debtor (borrower), *(im Insolvenzverfahren)* debtor's estate; **~verzug** borrower's default, default of the debtor (borrower), *(im Falle des ~s)* in the event that the borrower defaults

Schuldrecht Law of Obligations

schuldrechtlich contractual, under the Law of Obligations, *(~er Anspruch)* contractual claim, ius ad rem, *(~er Rückgewähranspruch)* contractual claim for restitution
(~es Sicherungsgeschäft) contractual hedging transaction, *(~e Verpflichtung)* contractual obligation, *(~e Wirkung)* effect under the Law of Obligations

Schuldrechtsmodernisierungsgesetz Act to Modernise the Law of Obligations

Schuldsaldo debit balance, outstanding balance on an account

Schuldschein 1. promissory note 2. borrower's note, → Schuldscheindarlehen

Schuldscheindarlehen promissory note loan, borrower's note loan, loan against borrower's note □ Medium or long-term loan granted against a note issued by the borrower. These notes are not securities like bonds but undertakings to make interest and principal repayments on specified dates. They can be sold to third parties by written assignments. *(Schuldscheindarlehen des Handelsbestandes)* promissory note loans held in the trading portfolio

Schuldschein / ~forderungen notes receivable; **~geschäft** note business; **~inhaber** note holder; **~markt** note loan market; **~offerte** note tender, note offering; **~verbindlichkeiten** notes payable

Schuldsumme 1. amount owed, amount due 2. *(ausstehender Kapitalbetrag)* principal

Schuldtitel 1. *(Wertpapier)* debt, debt security, debt instrument (obligation), debt issue, *(~ mit Beteiligungscharakter)* equity-linked debt, *(~ der öffentlichen Hand)* public sector debt, debt issued by public sector borrowers
2. *(Vollstreckungstitel)* executory deed

Schuldtitelemission debt issue, *(Kosten einer ~)* debt issuance cost

Schuld / ~übernahme debt assumption, assumption of a debt (an obligation), assuming an obligation; **~übertragung** transfer (assignment) of a debt

Schuld / ~umwandlung 1. debt conversion, *(~ in eine Beteiligung)* debt/equity swap **2.** *(→ Schuldersatz)* novation, *(im Rahmen einer zweiseitigen Nettingvereinbarung)* novation netting, netting by novation **3.** *(Umschuldung)* rescheduling; **~umwandlungsvertrag** contract for novation

Schuld / ~urkunde debt instrument, charge certificate; **~verhältnis** debt obligation, obligation imposed by virtue of law, *(zugrundeliegendes ~)* underlying contractual relationship

Schuldverschreibung bond, debt security, debenture, note, *(~ des Bundes)* Federal debt security, *(~en der EZB)* debt certificates, *(~en im Umlauf)* bonds (notes) outstanding, *(Inhaber einer ~)* bondholder, note holder

Schuldverschreibungsgesetz German Bond Act

Schuldverschreibungsrecht Law on Bonds

Schuld / ~versprechen payment undertaking, debt acknowledgement; **~verzicht** debt foregiveness; **~verzinsung 1.** interest rate charged/paid on a debt **2.** loan interest rate

Schuld / ~wechsel bills payable; **~zinsen** debt (debit) interest, loan interest, interest charge(s), interest payable; **~zinsenabzug** debt interest tax relief, deduction of debt interest expense (from taxable income)

Schulter-Kopf-Schulter Formation *(Chart-Analyse)* shoulder-head-shoulder formation (pattern) □ descriptive of a trend reversal pattern, selling pattern

Schulung *(interne ~)* inhouse (on-the-job) training

Schutz protection, shelter, safeguard(ing), hedge, *(~ gegen Zins- und Währungsrisiken)* hedge against exchange and interest rate risks, *(unter dem ~ der Garantie)* under cover of the guarantee

Schutzbestimmungen 1. safeguarding provisions, protective regulations **2.** *(in einem Kredit- bzw. Anleihevertrag zugunsten der Gläubiger)* protective covenants

schützen to protect, to safeguard, to hedge, *(gegen politische Einflussnahme ~)* to shield from political influence, *(die Kundeninteressen ~)* to protect (to safeguard) customers' interests

Schutz / ~klausel protective clause (provision); **~maßnahmen/~vorkehrungen** protective (safety) measures, safeguards; **~niveau** *(Kunden mit dem höchsten ~)* customers who are afforded the highest level of protection

Schutz / ~rechte industrial property rights; **~vorschriften** → Schutzbestimmungen; **~zoll** protective tariff (duty)

SchVG → Schuldverschreibungsgesetz

schwach *(~e Eigenkapitalbasis)* feeble (weak) equity base, *(~es Ergebnis)* poor performance, *(~e Geschäftstätigkeit) (Börse)* sluggish trading, *(~e Marktposition)* weak (shaky) position in the market, *(~e Verfassung des Marktes)* weak (depressed, frail) state of the market
(schwacher vorläufiger Insolvenzverwalter) weak preliminary insolvency administrator □ has no power of disposal with respect to the debtor's assets; the debtor remains in charge and in possession of the assets, → starker vorläufiger Insolvenzverwalter

Schwäche weakness, feebleness, frailty

Schwächeanfall *(~ des Dollar)* dollar's bout of weakness

schwächen to weaken, to impair, to undermine

schwächer *(~ bei geringen Umsätzen)* lower in light (thin) trading, *(~ ten-*

S

dieren) to drift lower, to tilt downwards, *(schwächer werdende Nachfrage)* weakening (waning) demand

Schwachstelle weak spot

Schwächung weakening, impairment

Schwachwährungsland soft currency country

schwanken 1. to fluctuate, to vary, *(von Bank zu Bank stark ~)* to vary significantly from bank to bank, *(mit den Geldmarktsätzen ~)* to float (to float up and down) with money market rates, *(stark ~de Bewertungen)* widely divergent valuations, *(stark ~de Wechselkurse)* strongly fluctuating exchange rates, gyrating exchange rates **2.** *(zögern)* to waver, to hesitate, to falter

Schwankung fluctuation, variation, swing, *(starke ~en)* gyrations, sharp (severe) swings, *(~en der Aktienkurse)* fluctuations in equity prices, ups and downs in the stock market, *(~en am Devisenmarkt)* fluctuations in (vagaries of) the foreign exchange market

schwankungsanfällig vulnerable (sensitive, susceptible) to market movements, *(stark ~e Anlagen)* high-volatility investments

schwankungsbereinigt *(~er Wert)* volatility-adjusted value

Schwankungs / ~breite 1. band (margin) of fluctuation **2.** variation range **3.** → Schwankungsintensität; **~grad** degree of fluctuation; **~intensität** volatility; **~kurs** variable price

S

Schwankungs / ~marge variation margin; **~markt** variable-price market; **~risiko** fluctuation (variation) risk; **~werte** variable-price securities

schwänzen to corner, to cause a corner situation, to buy up as much as possible of a security/commodity in order to control its price

schwarzer Fonds black fund, intransparent fund □ foreign investment fund that does not meet specific disclosure and reporting requirements

schwarze Zahlen *(~ schreiben)* to operate in the black, to operate at a profit, *(wieder ~ schreiben)* to return to the black, to be back in the black

Schwebe *(in der ~ sein)* to be in the balance, to be unresolved, to be pending, to be in suspense (abeyance), *(rechtlich in der ~ sein)* to be in a legal limbo, *(weiter in der ~ bleiben)* to continue to hang in the balance

schwebend *(~e Geschäfte)* open contracts, open (unsettled) deals, pending contracts (transactions), *(~e Kontroverse)* lingering dispute, *(~es Verfahren)* pending lawsuit, *(drohende Verluste aus ~en Geschäften)* anticipated losses from uncompleted transactions (open contracts), *(~e Verrechnungen)* items in course of settlement, float

Schweigepflicht professional discretion, duty of discretion

Schwelle threshold

Schwellen / ~länder emerging countries (markets); **~marktanleihe** emerging market bond; **~wert** threshold value, escalation trigger

Schwenk swaying over to, *(in der Zinspolitik)* turnaround (U-turn) in interest rate policy

schwer *(~e Papiere)* heavyweights, heavy-priced shares (stocks), highly priced shares, *(~er Schaden)* serious damage, *(~er Verlust)* heavy loss

Schwere *(Bedeutung, Gewicht)* weight, importance, significance, seriousness

schwerfällig *(~er Entscheidungsprozess)* cumbersome decision-making process, *(~er Konzern)* unwieldy group

Schwergewicht *(~ an den Finanzmärkten)* top-rated name (top-quality name, heavyweight) in the financial markets

Schwerpunkt main emphasis, focus, focal point, *(~ in der Geldpolitik)* focus of monetary policy

Schwerpunkt / ~bildung concentration (of efforts); **~setzung** focussing on; **~verlagerung** shift of emphasis

Schwestergesellschaft associated (affiliated) company

Schwierigkeit difficulty, problem, dilemma, *(in finanziellen ~en befindliches Unternehmen)* financially distressed (troubled) company, *(in finanzielle ~en geraten)* to run into (to encounter) financial difficulties

schwinden to decline, to shrink, to wane, to wither away, *(~de Aussichten/Hoffnungen auf eine Zinssenkung)* fading (dwindling) prospects/hopes of an interest rate cut, *(~der Einfluss)* waning influence, *(~de Ertragsmargen)* shrinking profit margins, *(~e Kaufkraft)* declining (decreasing) purchasing power

Schwund 1. decline, shrinkage, diminution **2.** loss **3.** leakage

Schwung drive, impetus, energy, momentum, *(die Konjunktur wieder in ~ bringen)* to reinvigorate the economy, *(an ~ verlieren)* to run out of steam/momentum

Scorecard *(laufende Validierung der ~)* continuous scorecard validation

Scorecard / ~-Bewertung scorecard assessment; **~-Entwicklung** scorecard development

Score-Wert score, score value

SDAX German share price index □ tracks the performance of 50 small and mid-sized companies listed in the → Prime Standard; these companies rank in terms of market capitalisation and trading volume immediately below the companies included in the → MDAX.

Sechsmonats / ~-Geld six-months' money, **~-Libor** six-months' Libor

Second Quotation Board → First/Second Quotation Board

See / ~fracht ocean (maritime) freight; **~frachtbrief** sea waybill, liner waybill; **~frachtführer** marine carrier; **~konnossement** ocean bill of lading; **~pfandrecht** maritime lien

See / ~recht maritime law; **~transport** carriage (shipment) by sea, ocean carriage; **~transportdokument** maritime transport document; **~tüchtigkeit** seaworthiness; **~versicherung** (ocean) marine insurance

Segment (market) segment, *(im oberen ~ des Marktes)* at the top end of the market

Segment / ~aktiva segment assets; **~aufwendungen** segment expenses (expenditure); **~berichterstattung** segment reporting; **~ergebnis** net segment income (loss); **~erträge** segment earnings

Segment / ~passiva segment liabilities; **~rechnung 1.** segment reporting **2.** segment results

segmentspezifisch *(~e Ausfallwahrscheinlichkeit)* segment-specific probability of default

Seite 1. *(Aspekt)* side, aspect **2.** *(Partei)* side, party

Seitwärts / ~bewegung *(~ des Aktienmarktes)* sideways movement of the stock (equity) market; **~markt** sideways market, flat market; **~muster** *(in der Charttechnik)* sideways pattern; **~rendite** sideways yield; **~trend** sideways trend, price movements within a narrow range

Sektor sector, branch, field, *(sektorale Verteilung)* sectoral distribution

Sektoren / ~gliederung breakdown by sectors; **~risiko** sector (sector-related) risk

Sektorfonds investment fund that specialises in investments in specific securities (e. g. warrants, convertibles), specific industries or groups of companies or commodities

Sekunda/Sekunda-Ausfertigung second of exchange

sekundär secondary, peripheral to

Sekundär / ~erhebung secondary survey; **~insolvenzverfahren** secondary insolvency proceedings □ proceedings opened against the debtor's foreign branch establishment

Sekundär / ~**liquidität** secondary liquidity, secondary liquid assets; ~**liquiditätsreserven** secondary liquidity reserves, near-liquid assets

Sekundärmarkt secondary market, market for outstanding securities, *(am ~ gehandelt werden)* to be traded in the secondary market, to go secondary

Sekundärmarkt / ~**abschlag** secondary market discount; ~**handel** secondary market trading; ~**produkte** secondaries; ~**rendite** secondary market yield; ~**trend** secondary (medium-term) trend; ~**umsatz** secondary market turnover, volume transacted in the secondary market

Sekundawechsel second of exchange

selbst *(~ geschaffene immaterielle Vermögensgegenstände)* internally generated intangible assets

Selbstanzeige self-reporting to the Tax Office, self-declaration statement

Selbstauskunft *(~ des Kreditantragstellers)* self-certification of the loan applicant

Selbstbedienungs-Terminal customer-operated terminal, automated teller terminal

Selbstbehalt / ~**beteiligung** **1.** *(des Versicherungsnehmers)* deductible, portion of loss to be borne by the insured, *(des Erstversicherers bei Rückversicherungen)* retention of loss
2. *(des Veräußerers einer Kreditforderung)* first loss piece

S

Selbstbindung self-commitment

Selbstdiskontierung discounting of own acceptances

Selbsteintritt **1.** dealing (acting, contracting) in one's own name, acting as principal, → Selbstkontrahieren
2. front-running, forward trading, → Vorlaufen

Selbstemission direct offering (placement), newly issued securities directly placed by the issuer in the market

selbsterstellt *(~e immaterielle Vermögenswerte)* self-generated intangible assets

Selbstfinanzierung self-financing, financing (funding) from retained earnings, *(~ der Unternehmen)* corporate self-financing

Selbstfinanzierungs / ~**mechanismus** self-funding mechanism; ~**quote** self-financing ratio

Selbstkäufer **1.** buyer for own account
2. underwriter, buyer of an issue □ agrees to purchase unsold securities in a new issue and to sell them under his own name to investors

Selbstkontrahieren self-dealing, acting both as principal and agent, contracting (dealing) in one's own name

Selbstkontrahierungsverbot ban on deals in which a person acts both as principal and agent

Selbstkontrolle self-regulation

Selbstkostenpreis cost price, *(zum ~ ausweisen)* to state (to show) at cost

Selbstliquidation self-liquidation, automatic repayment of capital at a specific date in the future, *(sich selbst liquidierende Dokumentenakkreditive)* self-amortising documentary credits

Selbstnutzung *(von Wohneigentum)* owner-occupation, self-occupancy

Selbstregulierung self-regulation

selbstschuldnerisch *(~ haften)* to be liable in one's own name, to assume a directly enforceable guarantee, → selbstschuldnerische Bürgschaft

selbstschuldnerische Bürgschaft absolute guarantee, directly enforceable guarantee □ guarantee under which the guarantor cannot claim the benefit of discussion, → Einrede der Vorausklage

selbstständig **1.** independent, self-employed, *(~er Unternehmer)* independent contractor, *(Einkünfte aus ~er Erwerbstätigkeit)* self-employment income, *(sich ~ machen)* to set up one's own business, to establish a firm of one's own 2. *(unabhängig)* independent

Selbstständige 1. self-employed 2. *(als Kundengruppe eines Kreditinstitutes)* professional customers, professional sector

Selbstständigkeit 1. self-employment, self-employed business activity 2. independence, *(rechtliche ~)* legal independence, *(Prinzip der rechtlichen ~)* arm's length principle

Selbststeuerungskräfte *(~ des Marktes)* self-regulating forces of the market

selbsttragend *(sich ~er Aufschwung am Aktienmarkt)* a self-sustaining (self-sufficient) upturn in the equity market

Selbst / ~überwachung self-regulation; **~überwachungsorganisation** self-regulatory organisation; **~verpflichtung** voluntary commitment; ~ **verpflichtungserklärung** voluntary undertaking; **~verwahrung** self-custody

senden to send, to forward, to dispatch

Senderbank forwarding (remitting) bank

Sendung 1. sending, forwarding, dispatch 2. *(Lieferung)* delivery 3. *(Warensendung)* consignment, shipment

senken to lower, to reduce, to cut down

Senkung lowering, reduction, cutting down, *(~ der Kreditkosten)* reduction in (of) the borrowing cost, *(~ der Kreditzinsen)* lowering of lending rates

Sensal official broker

sensitiv sensitive (e. g. to interest rate fluctuations)

Sensitivitäts / ~analyse sensitivity analysis; **~berechnung** sensitivity calculation; **~kennziffer** sensitivity ratio; **~maß** sensitivity measure; **~messung** sensitivity measurement

SEPA Single European Payments Area □ i.e. all SEPA-linked payments in the participating countries are treated as domestic payments

SEPA-Basislastschrift SEPA core direct debit (SDD core)

SEPA-Firmenlastschrift SEPA business-to-business direct debit, SEPA B2B direct debit

SEPA-Lastschrift SEPA direct debit (SDD); **~mandat** SEPA direct debit mandate

SEPA-Teilnehmerländer SEPA participating countries

SEPA-Überweisung SEPA credit transfer

separat separate, *(~ in Rechnung stellen)* to charge separately

separieren to separate, *(separierte Vermögenswerte)* segregated (ring-fenced) assets

Separierung separation, segregation

sequentiell *(~e Zahlungsstruktur)* sequential pay structure, sequential tranching

Sequenzanalyse sequence analysis

Sequester trustee in sequestration, preliminary insolvency administrator; **~vermögen** sequestered property

Sequestration sequestration, attachment of property, *(Anordnung der ~)* writ of sequestration

Sequestrationsverfahren sequestration proceedings

sequestrieren to sequester

Serie 1. *(einer Anleihe)* series, issue, tranche 2. *(Satz)* set

Serien / ~anleihe serial bond (issue), bond retired at regular intervals over a period of several years; **~auslosung** series drawing; **~fertigung** series production

serienmäßig *adj.* serial, *adv.* in series

Seriennummer serial number

seriös 1. *(Käufer)* trustworthy, reliable, serious-minded, well-reputed 2. *(Unternehmen)* sound, reliable, of good standing

Seriosität trustworthiness, reliability, soundness

Service / ~anbieter service provider, **~bereitstellung** service delivery, provision of services; ~**empfänger** service recipient; ~**entgelt** service fee (charge); ~**kette** service chain; ~**leistungen** *(zusätzliche)* add-ons

Servitutenbuch record of servitudes

setzen 1. *(auf eine Belebung der Kreditnachfrage ~)* to bank on a revival in credit demand **2.** *(eine Frist ~)* to set (to fix) a deadline **3.** *(außer Kurs ~)* to withdraw from circulation
4. *(auf einen Kursanstieg ~)* to stake funds (to speculate) on a price rise, to reckon with a price rise **5.** *(auf eine bestimmte Marktentwicklung ~)* to take a view on the market **6.** *(auf die Tagesordnung ~)* to put on the agenda **7.** *(ein Ziel ~)* to set a target (goal)

sicher safe, secure, *(~e Anlagemöglichkeit)* safe investment opportunity, safe haven

sicherbar *(~e Rsiken)* hedgeable risks

Sicherheit 1. safety, *(~ einer Anlage/des investierten Kapitals)* safety of an investment/of the capital invested
2. collateral, security, *(für einen Kredit hinterlegte ~)* security provided for a loan, collateral deposited in support of a loan, *(~ in Form von Immobilien)* real estate security (collateral) *(~ in Form börsenfähiger Wertpapiere)* stock market collateral, collateral in the form of marketable securities, *(eine für die Bank annehmbare ~)* a security (collateral) acceptable to the bank, reasonably good security, *(die häufigste ~)* the most common type of collateral
3. *(für Positionen an den Terminmärkten)* margin

Sicherheiten / ~anhang *(für Finanztermingeschäfte)* credit support annex; ~**art** type of security, ~**aufgabe** relinquishment of a collateral

Sicherheiten / ~basis *(auf der Basis der bereitgestellten Sicherheiten)* on the basis of the collateral provided; ~**bearbeitung** collateral processing, ~**beeinträchtigung** lowering the collateral value, impairment of the collateral (security) furnished

Sicherheitenbereitstellung/~bestellung provision of security (collateral), *(Kosten der ~)* cost of collateralisation, *(Unterzeichnung des Kreditvertrages bei ~)* the loan agreement will be signed when the collateral is furnished

Sicherheiten / ~bestand collateral portfolio; ~**bewertung** evaluation of collateral, security evaluation, evaluating the security offered by the borrower

Sicherheiten / ~deckungsgrad collateral cover ratio; ~**depot** securities portfolio pledged as collateral; ~**erfordernisse** collateral requirements; ~**erlös** security proceeds; ~**ersatz** collateral substitute

Sicherheiten / ~form type of collateral; ~**freigabe** release of security, collateral release; ~**geber** collateral provider, guarantor, party providing security (a collateral); ~**gewährung** → Sicherheitenstellung

Sicherheiten / ~hinterlegung deposit of security (of a collateral), posting collateral; ~**instrumente** collateral instruments; ~**klasse** category of collateral

Sicherheiten / ~management collateral management; ~**mappe** security envelope; ~**nachschüsse** remargining; ~**nachschussschwelle** remargining threshold; ~**nehmer** guarantee, taker of collateral, party accepting a collateral

Sicherheiten / ~pool collateral pool; ~**poolvertrag** security pooling agreement; ~**prüfung** collateral assessment, security evaluation

Sicherheiten / ~recht collateral law; ~**regelung** security arrangement, agreement on collateralisation; ~**risiko** collateral (collateralisation) risk, risk that collateral declines in value; ~**rückgabe** collateral return

Sicherheitenstellung providing (putting up) security for a loan, provision of security (of collateral), collateralisation, *(Kreditgewährung gegen Stellung einer erstklassigen Sicherheit)* extension of a loan against a first-rate security

Sicherheiten / ~substitution substitution of collateral; **~swap** collateral swap; ~ **treuhänder** collateral trustee; **~übergang** devolution of collateral; **~überprüfung** → Sicherheitenprüfung; **~überwachung** collateral control, collateral monitoring; **~unterdeckung** collateral shortage, inadequacy of collateral

Sicherheiten / ~verbuchung accounting treatment of collateral; **~vereinbarung** security agreement, collateral arrangement; **~verstärkung** collateral (security) enhancement

Sicherheiten / ~verwahrung safekeeping of a security (collateral); **~verwaltung** administration (handling) of collateral, collateral management; **~verwaltungsgebühr** collateral management fee

Sicherheiten / ~verwertung realisation (liquidation) of collateral, liquidating the security deposited in support of the loan, *(~ bei Zahlungsverzug des Kreditnehmers)* liquidation of the collateral in the event that the borrower defaults; **~wert** collateral (security) value; **~zweck** collateral purpose

Sicherheits / ~abschlag haircut, safety margin (deducted); **~bestimmungen** safety regulations; **~depot** securities account serving as collateral; **~einbehalt** deposit, retention money, *(~des Factors)* factor's reserve; **~einlage** security deposit

Sicherheits / ~erfordernisse 1. *(hinsichtlich der Kreditbesicherung)* collateral requirements, security (collateral) required 2. *(bei Börsentermingeschäften)* margin requirements; **~form** security device, type of collateral

Sicherheits / ~grad degree of security; **~gründen** *(aus ~)* for safety reasons; **~hinterlegung** depositing (lodging) a security, deposit of collateral; **~interesse** security interest

Sicherheitsleistung 1. surety, payment bond, bail
2. collateral, *(~ für einen Kredit)* provision of collateral for a loan, putting up security for a loan
3. *(~für ein Börsentermingeschäft)* margin, margin deposit, *(~ in bar)* cash margin, *(~ in Form von Wertpapieren)* securities margin, margin deposit by way of securities
4. *(~ für die Vertragserfüllung)* performance deposit

Sicherheitsmarge safety margin, *(i. S. v. Sicherheitsabschlag)* haircut

sicherheitsmäßig in terms of security (collateral)

Sicherheits / ~maßnahmen security precautions; **~puffer** safety cushion (buffer); **~rücklage** security reserve, contingency fund, appropriated surplus

Sicherheits / ~versprechen collateral undertaking, guarantee undertaking (commitment); **~vorgabe** security target (requirements); **~vorkehrungen** security precautions

Sicherheits / ~vorleistung collateral furnished in advance; **~vorleistungsrisiko** pre-collateralisation risk; **~vorschriften** security (safety) regulations; **~wechsel** collateral bill, bill serving as collateral; **~zuschlag** risk add-on

sichern 1. to secure, to protect, to guarantee, *(durch eine Grundbucheintragung ~)* to secure by an entry in the land register, *(hypothekarisch ~)* to secure by way of mortgage, *(vertraglich gesicherte Ansprüche)* claims secured by contract
2. to safeguard, to guard, *(Kundeninteressen ~)* to safeguard customer interests
3. to hedge, to provide cover, *(den Devisenkurs durch Termingeschäfte ~)* to

S

hedge the exchange rate by forward covering

sicherstellen 1. to secure 2. *(gewährleisten)* to ensure, to guarantee, to make sure (certain), *(eine angemessene Überwachung ~)* to ensure an adequate supervision

Sicherstellungsvertrag security agreement

Sicherung 1. securing, guaranteeing, *(~ der Bonität)* credit maintenance, safeguarding the financial standing, *(~ der Ertragslage)* securing the earnings position, *(~ des Geldwertes)* securing the value of money
2. collateralisation, security, *(zur ~ aller bestehenden und künftigen Ansprüche der Bank)* as security for all current and future claims of the bank (all claims to which the bank is now or may hereafter be entitled)
3. hedge, hedging, *(~ der Transaktionen über den Terminmarkt)* hedging the transactions in the forward market

Sicherungs / **~abrede** security agreement, security (collateral) clause, → einfache, → erweiterte Sicherungsabrede; ~ **abtretung** security assignment, assignment by way of security, *(die ~ offenlegen)* to disclose the assignment to the debtor; **~anforderungen** security (collateral) requirements

Sicherungs / **~bedarf** security required, need for security (collateral), collateral requirements; **~bedürfnis** *(~ des Anlegers)* investor's security needs; **~beschlagnahme** seizure for security

Sicherungs / **~bestand** collateral (hedging) portfolio; **~bestätigung** insurance guarantee certificate □ securing the creditor's right to insurance payments in the case of loss or damage to the collateral

Sicherungs / **~beziehung** 1. collateralisation 2. hedge, hedging relationship, *(Bilanzierung von Sicherungsbeziehungen)* hedge accounting; **~charakter** *(Position mit ~)* position designed as a hedge; **~derivate** derivative hedging instruments, hedging derivatives

Sicherungs / **~eigentum** non-possessory lien □ although the lender (the bank) becomes the legal owner, the borrower remains in possession of the assets serving as collateral; **~einrichtung** guarantee (protection) scheme, guarantee fund

Sicherungs / **~fall** *(im ~)* in the event of default, *(Eintritt des ~s)* crystallisation of a charge; **~fonds** guarantee fund, → Sicherungseinrichtung; **~form** security device, type of collateral

Sicherungs / **~geber** 1. guarantor, collateral provider 2. assignor 3. *(bei Kreditderivaten)* protection seller, risk taker; **~gegenstand** → Sicherungsgut; **~gehalt** *(die Garantie auf ihren ~ hin überprüfen)* to examine the guarantee as to its solidity

Sicherungs / **~geschäft** 1. secured transaction 2. hedge, hedging transaction; **~gewinn** hedging gain; **~grenze** guarantee (coverage) limit; **~grundschuld** collateral land charge

Sicherungsgut collateral, property subject to a security interest, property assigned (pledged, deposited) as security, asset serving as collateral for a loan, *(Wert des ~es)* collateral value

sicherungshalber *(~ abgetretene Forderungen)* receivables assigned as security

Sicherungs / **~hypothek** debt-securing mortgage; **~instrument** hedging instrument (tool, device); **~kauf** 1. buying protection 2. long hedge **~klausel** 1. security clause 2. protective covenant, negative pledge clause, → Negativklausel

Sicherungs / **~kosten** hedging cost; **~kurs** hedge (hedging) rate; **~maßnahmen** 1. protective measures 2. measures of arrestment; **~mittel** security device; **~mix** hedging mix

Sicherungs / **~nehmer** 1. guarantee, collateral taker, secured party 2. *(bei*

S

Kreditderivaten) protection buyer, seller of credit risk, risk shedder; ~**nießbrauch** usufructuary right registered as security; ~**operation** hedging transaction

Sicherungs / ~**pfandrecht** lien □ charge over property that remains in the debtor's possession; ~**pfändung** seizure for security; ~**position** hedge position

Sicherungsrecht security interest, charge, *(~ an beweglichen Sachen)* security interest in moveable property, *(die mit unseren Geschäftsbedingungen vereinbarten ~e)* security interests agreed under our business conditions

Sicherungs / ~**reserve** guarantee reserve; ~**schein 1.** insurance guarantee certificate, → Sicherungsbestätigung **2.** risk coverage certificate; ~**treuhand** security trusteeship

sicherungsübereignen to transfer the title to property (to transfer the ownership) as security

Sicherungsübereignung transfer of title (of ownership) for security purposes, assignment of ownership, *(aus Gläubigersicht)* acquiring a security interest by having full ownership of the property, *(~ des Lagerbestandes/von Warenbeständen)* assignment of goods in stock, inventory assignment

Sicherungs / ~**übereignungsvertrag** deed of assignment, collateral charge form; ~**vereinbarung** security agreement (arrangement), *(diesbezügliche Klauseln eines Kreditvertrages)* security covenants

Sicherungs / ~**verkauf 1.** sale (liquidation) of a collateral **2.** selling protection **3.** short hedge; ~**verlust** hedging loss; ~**vertrag** security agreement; ~**vorschriften** collateral requirements (standards)

sicherungsweise as security for, security-wise, *(~ abgetretene Warenforderungen)* trade receivables assigned as security, *(~ bestellte Grundschuld)* land charge registered as security

Sicherungs / ~**wert** collateral value; ~**wirkung** hedging effect; ~**zession** → Sicherungsabtretung; ~**zusammenhang** hedging relationship

Sicherungszweck collateral purpose, purpose of the collateral (security) furnished, purpose of the security agreement, *(enger ~)* narrow collateral purpose □ collateral designed to secure a specific claim/loan, *(weiter ~)* broad collateral purpose □ collateral designed to secure all existing and future claims

Sicherungszweckerklärung statement of collateral purpose

Sicht 1. sight, *(bei ~)* at sight, on demand, *(auf lange ~)* in the long run, *(fünf Tage nach ~)* five days after sight
2. view, standpoint, *(aus der ~ der Anleger)* from the investors' standpoint, *(aus der ~ des Kunden)* from the customer's perspective

Sicht / ~**akkreditiv** sight documentary credit; ~**einlagen** demand (sight) deposits, demand balances; ~**kurs** sight rate; ~**negoziationskredit** sight negotiation credit; ~**schuldschein** demand note

Sicht / ~**tratte** sight draft; ~**trattenziehung** drawing of a sight draft; ~**verbindlichkeiten** demand (sight) liabilities; ~**wechsel** sight bill, bill drawn at sight, bill payable on demand; ~**zahlung** sight payment

Siegel seal

Signal *(~ für eine Ergebnisverbesserung)* signal (indication) of an improved performance

signalisieren *(eine Zinssenkung ~)* to herald (to signal, to presage) a cut in interest rates

Signatur / ~**erstellungsdaten** signature creation data; ~**erstellungseinheit** *(sichere ~)* secure signature creation device (SSCD); ~**gesetz** German Signature Act; ~**karte** signature card; ~**prüfdaten** signature verification data; ~**prüfeinheit** signature verification device

Signatur / ~richtlinie (EU) Signature Directive ; **~schlüssel** signature key; **~ schlüsselverwaltung** signature key management; **~tablett** signature pad, pen pad; **~verordnung** Signature Ordinance

Signifikanzprüfung significance assessment check

Silber / ~barren silver bullion; **~bestände** silver holdings; **~-Option** silver option; **~-Preisfeststellung** silver fixing; **~-Terminkontrakt** silver futures contract; **~-Währung** silver standard

Silvester-Anleihe New Year's Eve bond

Silvester-Putz year-end window-dressing

sinken to decline, to drop, to fall, to give way, *(der Index für Industriewerte sank um 14 Punkte)* the industrial average plunged (dropped, fell) 14 points

Sinken decline, drop, fall, plunge

Sinn *(im ~e des KWG)* within the meaning of the German Banking Act

sinngemäß *(~ für alle künftigen Kreditvereinbarungen gelten)* to apply mutatis mutandis to all future loan arrangements

Situation *(wirtschaftliche/finanzielle ~)* economic/financial situation (position)

Sitten *(gegen die guten ~ verstoßen)* to run counter against good morals

sittenwidrig against goods morals, *(~er Vertrag)* contract contra bonos mores

S

Sittenwidrigkeit violation of bonos mores

Sitz seat, *(einer Gesellschaft)* registered seat, Head Office, *(Unternehmen mit ~ in London)* London-based company

Sitzlandprinzip principle of home country control

Sitztheorie seat-of-management rule, → Gründungstheorie

Sitzung 1. meeting, conference**2.** *(Börse)* session **3.** *(Verhandlung)* hearing, sitting

Sitzungs / ~beginn 1. opening of the meeting **2.** *(Börse)* opening of the session; **~bericht** report (record) of the meeting; **~geld** attendance fee (allowance); **~-Halbzeit** *(zur ~)* at mid-session

Sitzungs / ~periode session; **~protokoll** minutes of the meeting; **~schluss** *(Börse)* close of the session; **~vertagung** adjournment of the meeting

Skala scale, spectrum

Skalen / ~analyse scale analysis; **~effekte/~erträge** economies of scale

Skalierungs / ~effekt scaling impact; **~faktor** scaling factor; **~verfahren** scaling method

Skizze sketch, outline, draft

skizzieren to sketch, to draft, to outline, to map out

Skontierung discounting

Skonto discount, rebate, *(~ bei Barzahlung)* cash discount, discount for cash payment; **~aufwendungen** discounts paid; **~erträge** discounts received

Skontration/Skontrierung 1. *(im Wertpapiergeschäft)* running the order book **2.** *(Verrechnung von Forderungen/Verbindlichkeiten)* netting, clearing **3.** *(Lagerwirtschaft)* maintaing a perpetual Inventory

Skontrationsmethode maintaining a perpetual (continuous) inventory system

skontrieren 1. to run the book **2.** to clear, to net **3.** to maintain a perpetual inventory, → Skontration

Skontro/ Skontrobuch order book, stockbroker's register of buy and sell orders

Skontroführer lead broker, book-running broker, pricing intermediary, specialist □ determines prices, has exclusive access to the order book (→ Skontro), *(skontroführender Freimakler)* book-running free broker

Skontroführung lead brokerage, running the order book

Skontromakler → Skontroführer

SMAX tracked the performance of small exchange-listed companies; discontinued in 2003, → MDAX, → SDAX

Sockelbetrag base amount

SoFFin → Sonderfonds Finanzmarktstabilisierung

sofort (*~ fällig stellen)* to call for immediate repayment, (*~ kündbar)* immediately callable, (*~ verfügbare Gelder)* immediately available funds

Sofort / ~abbuchungssystem on-line debit system; **~abschreibung** *(~ eines notleidenden Engagements)* immediate charge-off of a non-performing loan; **~darlehen** immediate loan, → Bankvorausdarlehen; **~finanzierung** immediate financing, immediate loan disbursement

sofortige Tilgungsverrechnung immediate interest-wise application of repayments to the loan principal

Sofort / ~lieferung 1. immediate delivery **2.** spot delivery; **~programm** emergency programme; **~rente** immediate annuity

Solawechsel promissory note

Solidar / ~bürge joint and several guarantor; **~bürgschaft** joint and several guarantee; **~gemeinschaft/ ~gesellschaft** caring society, principle of mutual solidarity; **~haftung** joint and several liability

Solidaritätszuschlag solidarity surcharge

Solidar / ~schuld joint and several debt; **~schuldner** joint and several debtor

solide 1. stable, sound, solid **2.** *(Preise)* reasonable **3.** *(zuverlässig)* reliable, trustworthy, (*~ finanzielle Basis)* sound financial basis

Solidität 1. stability, soundness, solidity **2.** reasonableness, (*~ des Bankensystems)* soundness (health) of the banking system

Soll / ~buchung debit entry; **~ertrag** budgeted (projected) earnings; **~größe** budgeted value; **~-Ist-Kostenvergleich** actual versus projected cost comparison; **~-Ist-Unterschied** difference between projected and actual figures (between projection and outturn)

Soll / ~kosten budgeted (projected) expenditure; **~-Leistung** planned (targeted) performance; **~posten** debit entry (item); **~saldo** debit balance; **~seite** debit side

Soll / ~umsätze debit entries; **~zinsen** debit interest, interest charged (paid); **~zinssatz** debit (debtor) interest rate, interest rate charged, lending rate

Solo-Termindevise outright forward currency

Solo-Termingeschäft outright forward transaction

Solvabilität II Solvency II □ sets out new EU-wide requirements on capital adequacy and risk control management for insurace and reinsurance companies with gross premium income exceeding €5m and technical provisions in excess of €25m. Solvency II, which is similar to → Basel II, is scheduled to be implemented in 2012.

Solvabilitäts / ~anforderungen solvency requirements; **~berechnung** solvency calculation; **~bericht** solvency statement; **~bestimmungen** solvency requirements; **~kapital** solvency capital; **~koeffizient** solvency ratio

Solvabilitäts / ~marge solvency margin □ amount by which the assets of an insurance company exceed its liabilities; **~richtlinie** (EU) Solvency Directive, → Solvabilität II; **~quote** solvency ratio □ ratio of an insurance company's capital to premiums written; **~spanne** solvency margin; **~verordnung** Solvency Regulation

Solvenz solvency, → Solvabilität

Sonder / ~abschreibung 1. special capital (depreciation) allowance **2.** special write-off (write-down); **~aufwand**

special charge; ~**ausgaben** special private expenses, itemised deductions; ~**ausschüttung** special distribution, (payment of a) surplus dividend, superdividend; ~**ausstattung** *(von Wertpapieren)* special terms, special features

Sonder / ~**beauftragter** *(i. S. des KWG)* special commissioner; ~**bedingungen** *(~ für Wertpapiergeschäfte/Termingeschäfte)* Special Conditions for Dealings in Securities/for Forward Transactions

Sonder / ~**belastungen** special (non-recurring) charges; ~**betriebsvermögen** special business assets, assets owned by individual partners; ~**depot** segregated custody account, special securities account

Sonder / ~**eigentum** individual freehold ownership; ~**eigentümer** individual freehold owner; ~**einlage** special deposit (contribution); ~**erträge** special income (revenue)

Sonder / ~**faktoren** special factors, *(EBIT vor ~)* EBIT before special items; ~**finanzierung** special financing (funding)

Sonderfonds Finanzmarktstabilisierung (SoFFin) Special Financial Market Stabilisation Fund, → Finanzmarktstabilisierungsfonds

Sonder / ~**genehmigung** special clearance; ~**gewinn** exceptional (non-recurrent) profit; ~**konditionen** special (preferential) terms, preferential (concessional) interest rate

Sonder / ~**kontingent** special quota; ~**konto** special account; ~**kredit** special facility, special-purpose loan, project-tied facility; ~**kreditprogramm** special lending scheme

Sonder / ~**kündigungsrecht** *(bei einer Anleihe)* special call right; ~**masse** *(im Insolvenzverfahren)* separate (separated) assets; ~**leistungen** 1. special services 2. special benefits (payments); ~**nutzungsrecht** special use right; ~**plafond** special line, special facility

Sonderposten special item, special gain/charge, *(~ für allgemeine Bankrisiken)* special reserve for general banking risks, *(~ mit Rücklagenanteil)* special reserve item, *(~ aus Währungsumrechnung)* unrealised gain/loss from currency translations

Sonder / ~**prüfung** special (exceptional) audit; ~**rechte** special rights; ~**rediskontlinie** special rediscount facility; ~**rücklage** special contingency reserve, surplus reserve

Sonder / ~**tilgung** unscheduled repayment, special redemption payment; ~**tilgungsrecht** extraordinary right of redemption; ~**vereinbarung** special (separate) agreement; ~**vergütung** special allowance, bonus payment

Sondervermögen 1. *(i. S. des Investmentgesetzes)* Fund □ shall be kept separate from the capital investment company's own assets, → Publikums-Sondervermögen, → Spezial-Sondervermögen, *(~ mit zusätzlichen Risiken)* fund with additional risks, i.e. domestic hedge fund, *(Gegenstände des ~s)* fund's assets
2. *(~ des Bundes)* Special Government Fund
3. *(bei einer Verbriefung)* special asset pool, pool of segregated assets (property)

Sonder / ~**verwahrung** segregated custody, individual (separate) safekeeping of securities; ~**vollmacht** special power of attorney, special proxy; ~**wertberichtigung** special valuation allowance, special loan loss allowance, special charge for bad loans

Sonder / ~**zahlung** special (extra, bonus) payment; ~**ziehungsrechte** special drawing rights; ~**zinssatz** special interest rate, *(Vorzugszinssatz)* preferential interest rate

sondieren *(Marktchancen ~)* to sound out (to explore) market prospects

Sondierung sounding out, exploration

Sondierungsgespräche exploratory talks

S

sonstige Finanzanlagen other investments

sonstige Rückstellungen other accruals

sonstige öffentliche Stellen non-central Public Sector Entities

sonstige Sondervermögen other funds, → Sondervermögen

Sorge *(~n der Anleger)* investors' worries, investor concerns

sorgen *(für ausreichende Deckung ~)* to provide for sufficient cover in the account

Sorgfalt 1. care, diligence, *(mit der ~ eines ordentlichen Kaufmanns handeln)* to act with commercial prudence (with the due diligence and care of a conscientious businessman), *(trotz Anwendung der gebotenen ~)* despite exercising the diligence required **2.** *(Genauigkeit)* accuracy, *(sehr große ~)* meticulousness, painstaking care

sorgfältig *adj.* careful, conscientious, prudent *adv.* carefully, with care, conscientiously

Sorgfaltspflicht duty of care, fiduciary duty, *(~ der Bank)* bank's duty to exercise due and reasonable care, prudent behaviour rule, *(Verletzung der ~)* failure to comply with the duty of due care and diligence

Sorte 1. *(Art)* sort, kind **2.** *(Marke)* brand, mark **3.** *(Qualität)* quality, grade

Sorten currency, foreign notes and coin(s)

Sorten / ~ankaufskurs currency buying rate; **~bestand** currency in bank vaults; **~briefkurs** → Sortenverkaufskurs; **~geldkurs** → Sortenankaufskurs; **~geschäfte** transactions in foreign notes and coin(s)

Sorten / ~handel dealings in foreign notes and coin(s), currency dealings; **~händler** currency dealer; **~interbankgeschäft** interbank dealing in foreign notes and coin(s)

Sorten / ~kasse foreign till, till for foreign currencies; **~kurs** exchange rate, currency buying/selling rate; **~lieferung** currency delivery; **~position** foreign till position; **~verkaufskurs** currency selling rate

Sortiment range of services offered, product line (range), assortment

Sortiments / ~breite assortment width; **~erweiterung** increase in the range of services offered; **~straffung** streamlining the product range; **~tiefe** assortment depth, depth of the product mix

soweit *(~ anwendbar)* to the extent applicable, where applicable, *(~ gesetzlich zulässig)* to the extent permitted by law

sozial *(~e Erträge)* social benefits (returns), *(~e Marktwirtschaft)* social market economy, *(~e Schichtung)* social stratification

sozial verantwortliches Investieren ethical investing

Sozial / ~abgaben/~aufwand social security costs (expenses); **~bilanz** social accounting; **~kapital** social overhead capital; **~kosten** social security cost; **~partner** management and labour, employers and employed; **~plan** redundancy scheme

sozialverantwortlich *(~e Anlagen)* social responsible investments

Sozial / ~versicherungsbeiträge social security contributions; **~versicherungsleistungen** social security benefits (benefit payments); **~versicherungsträger** social security fund; **~wesen** social services

Spalte column

spalten to split, to divide, to separate, to break up

Spaltung split(ting), division, *(~ der Gruppe)* breaking up the group, demerger

Spanne 1. margin, spread, *(~ zwischen Ausgabe- und Rücknahmekurs) (bei Fondsanteilen)* bid/offer spread, *(~ zwischen Geld- und Briefkurs)* bid/offer spread, spread between bids and offers, spread between buying and selling rates, *(im Devisenhandel)* forex

spread, *(~n im traditionellen Kreditgeschäft)* spreads (margins) on the traditional forms of lending
2. fee, commission

Spannen / ~denken margin-oriented pricing; **~elastizität** margin flexibility; **~ertrag** margin return; **~erweiterung** widening of a spread, margin increase; **~preis** spread price

Spannen / ~rechnung margin costing; **~reduktion** margin cut; **~veränderung** margin variation; **~verengung** narrowing (tightening) of a spread; **~verringerung** margin cut, → Spannenverengung

Spannkurs mean spread of the fixing

Spar / ~anreiz savings incentive(s); **~aufkommen** volume of saving, net savings; **~bildung** formation of savings; **~brief** savings bond; **~eckzins** base rate for savings deposits, basic savings rate

Spareinlagen savings deposits, savings, *(Zinssätze auf ~)* savings deposit rates

sparen 1. to save, *(30 % gegenüber dem üblichen Preis ~)* to save 30 % off the normal price **2.** *(einsparen)* to economise, to save

Sparen 1. saving **2.** economising

Sparer saver, depositor, savings depositor

Sparer / ~freibetrag saver's tax allowance (tax-exempt interest income), personal allowance on savings; **~schutz** protection of savers (depositors), assuring the safety of depositors' funds

S

Spar / ~fähigkeit saving capacity; **~förderung** encouraging savings, promoting thrift, promoting the idea of thrift in the population

Spar / ~form type of savings, savings facility (vehicle); **~freudigkeit** saving propensity, propensity to save; **~funktion** saving function

Spar / ~gelder savings funds (deposits), savers' funds ; **~geldstrom** savings flow; **~geschäft** savings business, thrift business; **~guthaben 1.** balance in a savings account **2.** *(insgesamt)* deposits (balances) on savings accounts; **~kapitalbildung** formation of savings capital

Sparkasse savings bank (institution) □ *(in Deutschland)* German savings banks are, with a few exceptions, financial institutions incorporated under public law and owned by the municipalities in which they are located, → Regionalprinzip, *(in Großbritannien)* Trustee Savings Bank; *(in den USA – in der Reihenfolge ihrer Bedeutung)* savings and loan association, mutual savings bank, credit union, *(Oberbegriff für diese Institute in den USA)* thrift institutions, thrifts

Sparkassenbrief savings bank certificate

Sparkassen-Finanzgruppe Savings Bank Finance Group

Sparkassen / ~gesetz Savings Bank Act; **~obligationen** savings bank bonds; **~organisation** savings bank system; **~recht** savings bank legislation; **~sektor** savings bank sector, savings banks, → Sparkasse

Sparkassen-Stützungsfonds savings bank guarantee fund

Sparkassen / ~verband Savings Bank Association; **~verbund** network of savings banks; **~verwaltungsrat** Savings Bank Board; **~wesen** savings bank system, thrift institution system, thrifts

Spar / ~konto savings account, thrift account (AE); **~leistung 1.** amount saved, amount paid into a savings account **2.** *(Gesamtsumme)* net savings, new deposits less withdrawals; **~maßnahmen 1.** economising (saving) measures **2.** austerity measures

Spar / ~mittel savings funds, savers' funds; **~plan** contractual savings plan, savings scheme, *(eines Investmentfonds)* accumulation plan; **~quote** savings ratio (rate), ratio of savings to disposable incomes

sparsam 1. thrifty **2.** economical **3.** *(zurückhaltend)* sparing, *(~ mit seinen Interventionsvollmachten umgehen)* to be parsimonious in applying its intervention powers

Sparsamkeit 1. thriftiness **2.** economical use (handling, management) **3.** sparingness

Sparte 1. *(Gebiet)* field, sphere, line **2.** *(Geschäftszweig)* branch, line of business, sector **3.** *(Kategorie)* category, class **4.** *(Unternehmensbereich)* segment, division

Sparten / **~abschluss** divisional (segment) accounts; **~deckungsbeitrag** segment (divisional) profit contribution; **~erfolg** segment (divisional) income; **~ergebnis** segment (divisional) performance; **~ergebnisrechnung 1.** divisional (segment) income statement **2.** segment (segmental) reporting

Sparten / **~erträge** divisional (segmental) earnings; **~gliederung** divisional breakdown, segmentation; **~leiter** divisional (segment) manager; **~organisation** divisional organisation, divisionalisation

Sparten / **~plan** divisional plan; **~rechnung** segment (divisional) accounting; **~struktur** divisional structure; **~zusammenlegung** divisional merger, merger of segments

Spar / **~verhalten** savings behaviour (pattern), *(Veränderung im ~)* change in savings patterns; **~verkehr** savings transactions; **~vertrag** savings scheme (agreement)

Spar / **~zinsen 1.** interest on savings deposits, interest paid (earned) on savings deposits **2.** *(Zinssätze)* saving deposit rates

Spät / **~geschäfte** → Spätschlüsse; **~phase** *(der Hochkonjunktur)* late phase of the boom; **~phasenfinanzierung** later stage financing; **~schlüsse** *(im Börsenhandel)* late trades

Spediteur forwarding agent, *(Frachtführer)* carrier

Spediteur / **~-Durchfrachtbrief** forwarding agent's certificate of transport; **~haftung** carrier's liability; **~-Konnossement** forwarder's bill of lading; **~-Pfandrecht** carrier's lien; **~-Übernahmebescheinigung** forwarder's certificate of receipt

Speditions / **~gewerbe** forwarding trade (industry); **~unternehmen 1.** forwarding agency (company) **2.** shipping company **3.** removal agency

Speicherkarte memory card, store(d) value card

Spektrum range, spectrum, *(~ an Anlagemöglichkeiten)* spectrum of investment vehicles (opportunities), *(~ an Dienstleistungen)* range of services offered

Spekulant speculator, market player, speculative trader

Spekulation speculation, speculating, playing the market, speculative trading, *(~ auf Baisse/Hausse)* speculating on a fall/rise of the market, bear/bull transaction, going for a fall/rise, *(~ in Wertpapieren)* speculation in stocks and shares, playing the securities markets, trading on equity

Spekulations / **~besteuerung** taxation of private capital gains; **~bewegungen** speculative movements; **~druck** speculative pressure; **~frist** tax liability period with respect to capital gains; **~gelder** speculative (hot) funds

Spekulations / **~geschäft** speculative transaction (deal, investment); **~gewinn** speculative gain, windfall profit; **~käufe** speculative buying; **~steuer** capital gains tax

Spekulations / **~verkäufe** speculative selling; **~welle** speculative surge in the market, welter of speculative buying; **~werte** speculative counters, speculatives, hot issues

spekulativ *(~e Anlage)* speculative investment, *(~er Charakter)* speculative nature, *(~e Dispositionen)* speculation-driven buying and selling, *(~er Handel)* speculative trading (dealings)

(*~e Kapitalbewegungen)* speculative flows of capital, (*~e Nachfrage bei geringen Umsätzen)* speculative demand in a thin market, (*~e Zuflüsse)* inflows of a speculative nature

spekulieren to speculate, to play the market, to trade in and out of the market

Sperr / **~anzeige** blocking notice; **~auftrag** **1.** freeze (freezing) order **2.** stop payment order; **~begünstigter** beneficiary of a blocking notice; **~betrag** frozen (blocked) amount; **~depot** **1.** frozen securities portfolio, blocked custody account **2.** special (segregated) securities portfolio

Sperre **1.** *(Auszahlungssperre)* (account) freeze **2.** *(Blockierung)* blocking, immobilisation **3.** *(~ einer Kreditkarte)* blocking a credit card, putting a hold on a credit card **4.** *(Schecksperre)* stop payment order **5.** *(Verbot)* ban

sperren **1.** to freeze, to block, to immobilise, *(gesperrte Kreditkarte)* blocked credit card, hot card
2. to stop, *(einen Scheck ~)* to stop payment on a cheque, to stop a cheque, to countermand payment of a cheque, to put a stop on a cheque

Sperr / **~frist** **1.** freeze (blocking) period, lockup period **2.** *(Karenzzeit)* waiting (qualifying) period; **~guthaben** frozen assets (balances), blocked deposits; **~konto** frozen (blocked) account

Sperr / **~liste** warning bulletin, restricted list, *(von Kreditkarten)* black list, stoplist, hot card list; **~minorität** blocking minority, minority representing at least 25 per cent of the equity

Sperr / **~periode** → Sperrfrist; **~stücke** blocked securities, securities that cannot be resold during a fixed period; **~titel** → Sperrstücke

Sperrung blocking, freeze, immobilisation, close, closing, → Sperre

Sperrvermerk **1.** notice of freeze, blocking notice **2.** *(hinsichtlich der Weitergabe)* non-negotiability clause **3.** *(bei einem Scheck)* orders not to pay, payment countermanded

Sperrverpflichtung obligation to hold blocked, undertaking not to pay, *(in Verbindung mit einer Neuemission)* undertaking not to sell the securities prior to a fixed period

Sperrvorschrift **1.** blocking provision **2.** countermand of payment

Spesen charges, expenses

spesenfrei free of charge(s), all charges paid

Spesen / **~rechnung** statement (bill) of charges; **~vergütung** refund (reimbursement) of charges incurred

Spezialbank specialist bank

Spezialfinanzierung specialised finance, specialised lending, (*Risiken aus ~en)* specialised lending exposures

Spezialfonds **1.** Special Fund, Institutional Fund □ same as → Spezial-Sondervermögen
2. specialised fund, → Sektorfonds

Spezial / **~gebiet** special field (line), specialty; **~institut** specialised institution

Spezialitätenhausse *(Börse)* upsurge in specialties

Spezial / **~investmentaktiengesellschaft** special investment stock corporation; **~investmentvermögen** special investment asset pool, → Spezial-Sondervermögen

Spezial / **~kenntnisse** specialised (expert) knowledge, expertise; **~kräfte** skilled staff, specialists; **~kreditinstitut** specialised bank, specialised financial institution

Spezial-Sondervermögen *(i. S. des Investmentgesetzes)* Institutional Fund, Special Fund □ units are exclusively held by institutional investors/legal entities; all other funds are → Publikums-Sondervermögen

Spezial / **~vollmacht** special power of attorney; **~werte** *(Börse)* specialties

spezifizieren to specify, to detail, to itemise

Spezifizierung specification, itemisation

Spiegel / ~absicherungsgeschäft back-to-back hedge; **~geschäft** mirror trade (transaction)

Spiel *(aufs ~ setzen)* to put at risk

Spielraum scope, margin, leeway, room for (to) manoeuvre, *(~ für einen Kompromiss)* room for a compromise, *(jmd. ~ zur Durchführung der notwendigen Veränderungen geben)* to give s. o. elbowroom to make the necessary changes

Spirale *(Lohn-Preis-Spirale)* wage-price spiral

Spitze 1. top, peak, record, *(an der ~ der Bank stehen)* to be at the helm of the bank, *(an der ~ der Ergebnisliste stehen)* to top the (to come top of the) performance table, *(an der ~ der Sanierungsbemühungen stehen)* to spearhead the restructuring efforts
2. *(Restbetrag)* residual amount, *(bei Wertpapieren)* fraction, fractional share **3.** *(Netto-Minus-/Plusposition)* net short/long position

Spitzen / ~adresse *(an den Finanzmärkten)* top-rated (top-quality) name; **~ausgleich** settlement of fractions, settling fractions; **~bedarf** peak demand, *(im Kreditgeschäft)* peak borrowing requirements; **~beträge** fractions, fractional (residual) amounts

Spitzen / ~ergebnis record performance; **~erzeugnis** top-quality (high-quality, high-grade) product; **~gruppe 1.** top group **2.** *(der Konsortialbanken)* top bracket

Spitzen / ~inanspruchnahme *(im Kreditgeschäft)* peak borrowings; **~institut** central institution, head (umbrella) organisation; **~konto** fractions account; **~kräfte 1.** top executives **2.** leading experts

Spitzenrefinanzierungsfazilität marginal lending facility □ a standing facility of the Eurosystem designed to provide overnight credit to financial institutions against eligible assets, → Ständige Fazilitäten; *(Bedarfsspitzen über die ~ ausgleichen)* to draw on the marginal lending facility to meet peak borrowing requirements

Spitzenrefinanzierungssatz marginal lending rate

Spitzenregulierung settlement of fractions

Spitzenreiter top performer, star performer, *(~ im Umsatzvolumen)* leader (top rider, number one) in terms of volume

Spitzenverband central (top, head, umbrella) organisation, *(Spitzenverbände des Kreditgewerbes)* central associations of the banking industry

Spitzenwerte leaders, leading favourites, Blue Chips

Split-Factoring splitted factoring □ retention of several factoring companies

Spread *(~ auf Unternehmensanleihen)* corporate bond spread, → Renditeaufschlag

Spread-Handel spread trading **1.** *(im Futures-Handel)* denotes arbitrage transactions designed to profit from expected or existing changes in the usual price difference between *(a)* two different, but related financial or commodity futures by buying the undervalued contract and selling the overvalued contract of the same delivery month or *(b)* from changes in the usual price difference between two delivery months of the same financial or commodity future by opening a long futures position expiring in one month and a short position expiring in another month
2. *(im Optionshandel)* buying options and simultaneously selling an equal number of options on the same underlying instrument with *(a)* identical strike prices, but with different expiration dates (calender, time or horizontal spread) or *(b)* with iden-

tical expiration dates, but different strike prices (price, money or vertical spread). Spread positions, which have a limited risk and profit potential, are traded to profit from the relative difference in price changes between the options.

Spread-Risiko spread risk □ exposure to changing spreads between government and non-government yields, → Renditeaufschlag

Spread-Wetten *(finanzielle ~)* financial spread betting □ Betting on the rise above (upbet, going long) or fall below (downbet, going short) the spread (difference between bid and offer price) of a given stock

Spreizung *(~ der Kreditkonditionen)* tiering the loan terms

sprengen *(den Rahmen ~)* to go beyond, to exceed the scope of

Spruchverfahren valuation (assessment) proceedings □ judicial review proceedings to determine the adequacy of a cash/compensation offer to minority shareholders

Spruchverfahrensneuordnungsgesetz Valuation Proceedings Restructuring Act □ shortens judicial review proceedings

Sprung *(ein großer ~ nach vorne)* a great leap forward

sprunghaft precipitous, *(stark schwankend)* volatile, inconsistent, erratic, *(~ steigende Umsatzzahlen)* rocketing (soaring) turnover levels, *(~es Ansteigen der Aktienkurse)* precipitous rise in equities

Sprunghaftigkeit 1. volatility 2. jumpiness 3. inconsistency

Sprungregress recourse to prior endorsers

spürbar 1. perceptible, discernible 2. *(deutlich)* noticeable, appreciable

spüren to feel, to notice, to perceive, *(den Druck der höheren Zinssätze ~)* to feel the pressure of higher interest rates

SRI-Anlagen social responsible investments

staatlich 1. *adj.* *(~e Bürgschaften für Exportkredite)* government guarantees for export credits, *(~es Bürgschaftsprogramm)* government guarantee loan scheme, *(~er Emittent)* sovereign issuer, *(~e Finanzierung)* state (government) financing, *(~e Kapitalmarktbeanspruchung)* government borrowings in the capital market, *(~er Kreditnehmer)* sovereign borrower, *(Ausleihungen an ~e Kreditnehmer)* lendings to sovereign borrowers, sovereign lendings
(~e Mittel) government (state) funds, *(Bereitstellung staatlicher Mittel)* government funding, *(~e Schuldtitel)* government debt securities, *(~es Unternehmen)* state-owned company, government enterprise, *(~e Zuschüsse)* government (state) subsidies, government grants
2. *adv.* *(~ finanziert)* government-financed, *(~ garantiertes Darlehen)* government-guaranteed loan, *(~ gefördertes Kreditprogramm)* government-sponsored loan scheme, *(~ subventionierte Bankkredite)* government-subsidised bank lending

Staats / ~adresse *(an den Kredit-/Kapitalmärkten)* sovereign borrower/issuer, sovereign (state) name; **~anleihe** government bond; **~kreditgeschäft** 1. public sector lendings 2. *(mit dem Ausland)* sovereign lending operations

Staats / ~papiere government securities (stock), governments, gilt-edged securities, gilts (BE); **~schuld** national (sovereign) debt; **~titel** sovereign debt, government bond(s)

stabile Einlagen *(when calculating the runoff rate,* → Rückzugsrate) stable deposits □ retail deposits that are fully covered by a deposit protection scheme, → weniger stabile Einlagen

stabilisieren to stabilise, to consolidate, *(sich auf seinem derzeitigen Niveau ~)*

S

to stabilise at its current level, *(sich bei ca. fünf Prozent ~)* to stabilise at around five p.c., *(der Markt hat sich stabilisiert)* the market has stabilised (steadied), *(stabilisierende Wirkung)* stabilising effect

Stabilisierung stabilisation, consolidation, *(~ der Aktienkurse)* stabilisation of equity prices, steadying of the equity market

Stabilisierungs / ~anleihe consolidation loan; **~faktor** stabilisation factor, stabiliser; **~fonds** stabilisation fund

Stabilisierungs / ~manager *(bei einer Aktienplatzierung)* stabilisation agent; **~maßnahmen** stabilisation measures, government package designed to guarantee (to regain) stability

Stabilität stability, solidity, steadiness, firmness, *(~ des Geldwertes)* monetary stability, *(~ der Kaufkraft)* stability of purchasing power

Stabilitäts / ~erfordernisse stability requirements; **~faktor** factor of stability; **~maßnahmen** measures designed to maintain and to promote stability; **~orientierung** stability bias; **~politik** policy of stability, *(stabilitätspolitische Risiken)* risks to the policy of stability

Stablinienorganisation line and staff organisation

Stabs / ~abteilung/~bereich corporate support unit; **~aufgaben/~funktionen** corporate strategy and support functions

Stadium stage, phase

Stadtanleihe local authority bond

Stadt- und Kreissparkasse municipal savings bank □ German municipal savings banks are backed by municipalities or associations of municipalities

Staffel scale, table

Staffelanleihe graduated-interest loan

staffeln to graduate, to stagger, *(Fälligkeitstermine ~)* to stagger maturities (the due dates), *(gestaffelte Zinszahlungen)* staggered interest payments, *(gestaffelter Ansatz)* layered approach

Staffel / ~preise sliding scale prices; **~provision** sliding scale commission

Staffelung graduation, staggering, tiering

Staffelzins graduated (staggered) interest rate, sliding rate of interest, *(gestaffelte Zinsstruktur)* tiered interest rate structure

Stagnation stagnation, slackness, sluggishness, dullness, lull

stagnieren to stagnate, to be slack (flat), *(~der Absatz)* sluggish sales, *(~de Börse)* sluggish (stale, dull, flat, stagnant) market, *(~de Wirtschaft)* flagging economy

Stahlkammer vault

Stamm *(Kunden/Anleger)* client/investor base

Stammaktien (Stämme) ordinary shares (BE), common stock (AE)

Stammaktien / ~dividende dividend on ordinary shares, common stock dividend; **~emission** ordinary share issue, common stock issue

stammaktiengleich *(~e Papiere)* common stock equivalents

Stammaktien / ~inhaber ordinary shareholder, common stockholder; **~kapital** ordinary share capital, common stockholders' equity; **~umlauf** common stock outstanding

Stamm / ~belegschaft permanent staff, core payroll; **~daten 1.** static securities data, e.g. securities description, issuer's name, etc., → Termindaten **2.** master data, reference data; **~einlagen** *(einer GmbH)* capital contributions (by the shareholders of a limited liability company)

stammen *(herrühren von)* **1.** to stem from, to originate with **2.** to date from

Stamm / ~haus head office; **~kapital** *(einer AG)* share capital, *(einer GmbH)* nominal capital; **~konto** master account; **~kontonummer** master account number; ~**kunde** regular (core) customer; ~**personal** permanent staff

Stand 1. status, level, *(auf den neuesten ~ bringen)* to update, *(den höchsten ~ erreichen)* to reach an absolute high, *(den tiefsten ~ erreichen)* to touch rock bottom, to reach an absolute low **2.** *(Kontostand)* balance

Standard 1. standard **2.** level

Standardabweichung standard deviation □ measures the volatility of a financial instrument

Standardaktien equity leaders, leading (first-line) equities, Blue Chips

Standardansatz *(~ zur Ermittlung der Eigenmittelerfordernisse einer Bank für das Kreditrisiko oder operationelle Risiko)* standardised (standard) approach to determine capital requirements for credit risk or operational risk

Standard-Factoring old-line factoring, full-service factoring, main line factoring, standard factoring

Standardgemeinkosten standard overheads

standardisieren to standardise, *(standardisiertes Kreditgeschäft/Privatkundengeschäft)* standardised lendings/ retail banking

Standard / ~klausel → Standardvertragsklausel; ~**kosten** standard cost; ~**kostenrechnung** standard costing; ~**preissystem** standard price system; ~**produktkosten** standard product cost; ~**risikokosten** standard risk cost, cost of expected losses

Standardtender standard tender □ tender procedure used by the ESCB when operations are open to the whole range of counterparties, → Hauptrefinanzierungsgeschäft, längerfristige Refinanzierungsgeschäfte

Standard / ~termine (standard forward currency transactions at) standard maturities; ~**überweisungsdienst** basic credit transfer service; ~**valutierung** standard value date; ~**vertragsklausel** standard contract clause, boiler plate clause

Standard / ~wert *(Verrechnungswert)* standard value; ~**werte** → Standardaktien; ~**Zinsswap** plain vanilla interest rate swap, generic swap, straight swap, → Zinsswap

Standbein leg, *(ein lange angestrebtes ~ auf dem britischen Markt)* a long-sought foothold in Great Britain

Stand-by / ~-Fazilität stand-by facility; ~**-Geldmarktlinie** stand-by money market facility

Standesorganisation professional organisation

Standfestigkeit firmness, steadiness, stability

standhalten 1. *(spekulativem Druck ~)* to withstand (to resist) speculative pressure **2.** *(einer genauen Prüfung ~)* to stand (to bear) a close scrutiny

ständig 1. *adj.* *(~es Einkommen)* regular income, *(~e Fazilitäten)* standing (permanent) facilities □ facilities of the Eurosystem designed to provide and absorb overnight money, *(~e Inanspruchnahme einer Fazilität)* continuous drawing on a facility, *(~e Überziehung)* hardcore borrowing, *(~er Wohnsitz)* permanent residence **2.** *adv.* constantly, permanently, regularly

Standort location, site, position, *(Standort Deutschland)* Germany as a place for business, Germany as a business centre; ~**bedingungen 1.** local conditions **2.** site requirements; ~**bestimmung** positioning, fixing (determining) a position

standortgebunden site-bound

standortgünstig favourably located

Standort / ~nachteile disadvantages resulting from the geographical location; ~**sicherungsgesetz** Law to secure Germany's place as a business centre; ~**studie** plant location study; ~**wahl** site selection

S

Standpunkt opinion, viewpoint, standpoint

Stapel *(ein ~ schlechter Ergebnisse)* a batch of poor results

Stapelverarbeitung batch processing

stark 1. *adj. (~e Abgaben)* heavy selling, *(~er Anstieg der Aktienkurse)* strong advance in equities, sharp rise of stock prices, *(~er Kursrückgang)* steep fall (plunge) in prices
(starker vorläufiger Insolvenzverwalter) strong preliminary insolvency administrator □ holds power of disposal, → schwacher vorläufiger Insolvenzverwalter
2. *adv. (~ gesuchtes Papier)* stock in high demand, *(~ risikogefährdeter Kredit)* high-risk loan, severely troubled loan, *(~ schwanken)* to vary considerably, to fluctuate strongly, *(~ verschuldet sein)* to be heavily indebted

Stärke 1. strength, force, power, clout, *(die finanzielle ~ der Gruppe)* the group's financial strength (prowess) **2.** *(erfolgreiches Abschneiden)* strong performance

stärken 1. to strengthen, to reinforce, to back, *(die Eigenkapitalbasis ~)* to strengthen (to shore up, to reinforce, to buttress) the capital base, *(die finanzielle Position deutlich ~)* to strengthen the financial position considerably, *(die Rücklagen ~)* to bolster (to boost) reserves, *(das Vertrauen der Anleger in einen Kursaufschwung ~)* to buttress investors' confidence in a price upturn **2.** *(verbessern)* to enhance, *(die Bonität ~)* to enhance the financial standing (credit quality)

Stärkung 1. strengthening, shoring up, reinforcement, boosting **2.** enhancement

starr *(~e Vorschriften)* rigid (stringent) rules

Start start, beginning, commencement

starten *(Unternehmen)* to start, to launch, to set up

Starthilfekredit business set-up loan

stationär *(~er Vertrieb)* stationary sale

statische *(~e Wertpapierdaten)* static securities data, → Stammdaten

statistisch *(~ erfassen)* to record statistically, to cover by statistics, to take a census, *(~e Angaben)* statistical data

Statt *(an Eides ~)* in lieu of an oath, *(an Erfüllungs ~)* in discharge of an obligation, *(an Zahlungs ~)* in lieu (in place) of payment

stattfinden to take place, to happen, to occur

stattgeben 1. *(einem Anspruch ~)* to admit (to allow) a claim **2.** *(einer Berufung ~)* to allow (to uphold) an appeal **3.** *(einer Klage ~)* to sustain an action, to find for the plaintiff **4.** *(einem Kreditantrag ~)* to grant a loan request, to approve of a loan request

statthaft permissible, admissible

Status 1. status, position, rank **2.** *(Vermögensaufstellung)* statement of assets and liabilities, financial statement, statement of condition

Status / ~abfrage status inquiry; **~bericht** status report; **~feststellung** status determination (assessment); **~meldung** status message (report); **~prüfung** status check

Statut(en) 1. statute(s) **2.** *(einer Unternehmung)* articles of association

stecken 1. *(Gelder in ein Unternehmen ~)* to invest money into a business **2.** *(in finanziellen Schwierigkeiten ~)* to be in financial straits, to be stuck (caught) in financial difficulties

stehen *(~ hinter)* to support, to give full backing to

steigen 1. to rise, to increase, to grow, *(bei lebhaften Umsätzen ~)* to advance in active trading, *(um einige Punkte ~)* to gain (to put on) a number of points
2. *(im Wert ~)* to increase in value, to appreciate
3. *(aufsteigen)* to move up, to climb

steigend *(~es Dreieck)* → aufsteigendes Dreieck, *(~er Keil)* → Aufwärtskeil, *(~e Kosten)* rising (mounting) cost,

(*~er Kreditbedarf)* growing (rising) loan demand, *(stark ~e Nachfrage)* burgeoning demand, *(~e Renditekurve)* upward sloping yield curve, *(~e Skalenerträge)* increasing returns to scale

steigern 1. to increase, to raise, to lift **2.** *(verbessern)* to improve, to enhance **3.** *(verstärken)* to intensify, to step up

Steigerung 1. increase, rise, advance, *(eine deutliche ~ gegenüber dem Vorjahr)* a noticeable increase over last year's level
2. improvement, enhancement, (*~ der Attraktivität)* enhancing the appeal of
3. intensification, stepping up

Steigerungs / ~betrag *(Wertsteigerung)* appreciation, increment value; **~faktor** increment factor; **~klausel** escalator clause; **~rate** rate of increase, growth rate; **~tendenz** upward tendency

steil (*~e Abwärtsbewegung)* steep downhill slide, sharp downward trend, (*~er Kursanstieg)* steep (precipitous) increase in prices

Stelle 1. position, place, rank, (*von der Bilanzsumme her an zweiter ~ stehen)* to rank second in total assets, (*an zwölfter ~ unter den ersten 100 stehen)* to rank 12th in the top 100
2. agency, authority, (*bei anderen ~n aufgenommene Kredite)* loans raised from other sources, (*kreditgebende ~n)* lenders, lending offices (sources), (*zuständige ~)* competent authority (agency)
3. *(Standort)* location, site
4. job, position, post, appointment

stellen (*ein Akkreditiv ~)* to open a documentary credit, (*einen Antrag ~)* to file an application, (*Geld- und Briefkurse ~)* to quote two-way prices, (*in die Gewinn- und Verlustrechnung ~)* to take to the profit and loss account, *(einen Kurs ~)* to quote a rate (price), to put a quotation to s.o., (*eine Sicherheit ~)* to put up security, to provide (to furnish) collateral, *(das Geschäftsvolumen stellte sich auf ... €)* volume of business totalled € ...

Stellen / ~abbau laying off staff, reduction in headcount (personnel levels); **~anforderungen** job requirements; **~anforderungsprofil** job profile; **~angebot** job offer (opening), offer of employment; **~ausschreibung** job advertisement, *(betriebsinterne)* job posting

Stellen / ~beschreibung job description (specification); **~besetzung 1.** job recruitment, filling a vacancy **2.** *(Einstellungen)* staffing **3.** *(Verteilung der Aufgaben)* job assignment; **~bewerber** job applicant; **~bewerbung** application for a post; **~bezeichnung** job title

Stellen / ~inhaber job incumbent; **~inhalt** job content; **~markt** job market, job vacancies section, appointments section; **~verantwortung** job responsibilities; **~vermittlung** employment service; **~wechsel 1.** change of position **2.** *(Rotation)* job rotation; **~wert** status, rank, importance, significance, *(einen hohen ~ haben)* to have a high status, to be high on the agenda

Stellung 1. *(Anstellung, Position)* position, post, rank, (*~ am Kapitalmarkt)* position (rating) in the capital market
2. (*~ eines Insolvenzantrages)* filing a petition in insolvency
3. (*~ von Kursen)* rate quotation, quoting rates, price-making, *(~ von Geld- und Briefkursen)* quotation of two-way prices, quoting bid and offered rates/buying and selling rates
4. (*~ von Sicherheiten)* provision of (putting up) security, posting collateral

Stellungnahme 1. comment, statement, commentary **2.** *(~ eines unabhängigen Gutachters)* (reasoned) opinion, fairness opinion

stellvertretend (*~ ausüben) (ein Amt)* to act (to hold an office) as deputy, *(ein Stimmrecht)* to vote as proxy, *(~e*

S

Haftung) → mittelbare Haftung, *(~er Vorsitzender)* deputy chairman

Stellvertreter 1. deputy, substitute 2. *(Bevollmächtigter)* agent, authorised representative, proxy, *(Benennung eines ~s)* appointment of a deputy, *(sich durch einen ~ vertreten lassen)* to be represented by proxy

Stellvertretung 1. substitution 2. representation, agency, proxy, *(offene ~)* direct representation, *(in offener ~ verkaufen)* to sell in the name and for account of the issuer

Stellvertretungs / ~recht agency law; **~vertrag** contract of agency

Stempel 1. stamp 2. *(~ auf Edelmetallen)* hall-mark stamp 3. *(Poststempel)* post-mark 4. *(auf Quittungen)* receipt stamp 5. *(Unterschriftsstempel)* name stamp; **~steuer** stamp duty

stetig 1. *adj. (~er Kursanstieg)* steady rise in prices, *(~e Leistung)* consistent performance, *(~er Mittelzufluss)* continuous supply of funds
2. *adv. (ein sich ~ verbessernder Markt)* a steadily improving market

Stetigkeits / ~gebot consistency requirement; **~prinzip** principle of consistency

Steuer tax; **~abgrenzung** tax deferment; **~abschlag** tax abatement; **~abwehr** tax avoidance, tax planning tools; **~abzug** tax deduction, *(~ an der Quelle)* deduction of tax at source, deduction of withholding tax

Steuer / ~amortisation tax amortisation; **~änderungsgesetz** Tax Amendment Act; **~angleichung** tax harmonisation; **~anrechnung** tax credit; **~ anrechnungsverfahren** tax imputation system; **~ansprüche** 1. tax claims 2. → latente Steueransprüche; **~aufkommen** tax revenue (receipts); **~aufwand** tax expense, tax charge (bill)

Steuer / ~ausfall shortfall of tax revenue, revenue deficit; **~ausgleich** tax averaging (equalisation); **~ausweichung** tax avoidance; **~ausweispflicht** tax reporting requirement; **~aval** tax payment guarantee, tax bond

steuerbar *(~e Risiken)* manageable (governable) risks

Steuer / ~befreiung tax exemption; **~befreiungsanspruch** entitlement to tax exemption

steuerbegünstigt *(~e Anlagen)* tax-privileged investments, tax shelters, *(~e Emission)* tax-privileged (tax-advantaged) issue, *(~e Investitionen)* investments carrying tax relief, *(~e Vermögensbildung)* tax-advantaged accumulation of property

Steuer / ~begünstigung tax privilege, tax relief; **~behörden** tax (revenue) authorities; **~belastung** tax burden, tax charge (load)

Steuer / ~bemessung tax assessment; **~bemessungsgrundlage** tax assessment basis, basis of assessment; **~bemessungswert** assessed base value; **~bereinigung** tax adjustment (revision), *(steuerbereinigt)* tax-adjusted, net of tax; **~bereinigungsgesetz** Tax Revision Act

Steuer / ~bescheid tax assessment notice, notice of assessment, tax bill; **~bescheinigung** tax certificate; **~bilanz** tax accounts, accounts prepared for tax purposes; **~bilanzierungsvorschriften** tax accounting rules; **~bilanzwert** value assigned for tax accounting purposes; **~bürgschaft** tax bond

Steuer / ~effekt *(abzüglich ~e)* net of tax effects; **~einbehaltung** withholding (retaining) a tax, retention of tax; **~einnahmen** tax revenue

Steuer / ~einspruch appeal against a notice of assessment; **~einzug** collection of taxes; **~entlastung** tax relief, lowering the tax burden; **~entlastungsgesetz** Tax Relief Act; **~erhebung** levying a tax, taxation; **~erhebungsrecht** taxing power, revenue-raising power, right of taxation

Steuer / ~erklärung tax return; **~erlass** tax remission; **~erleichterung** tax relief; ~**ersatzansprüche** tax refund claims; ~**ersparnis** tax saving, saving on taxes

Steuer / ~**erstattung** tax refund, refund of a tax; ~**festsetzung** tax assessment; ~**forderungen** **1.** tax receivables **2.** → Steuerersatzansprüche; ~**fortwälzung** forward tax shifting, → Steuerrückwälzung

steuerfrei **1.** *adj.* tax-exempt, tax-free, exempt from tax, tax-sheltered, without attracting tax, *(~e Einkünfte)* tax-exempt (tax-free) income, *(~e Zinszahlungen)* tax-free interest payments, interest payments free of income tax **2.** *adv.* on a tax-exempt basis, on a non-tax basis

Steuer / ~**freibetrag** tax-exempt amount, tax-free allowance, personal tax exemption; ~**freigrenze** tax exemption limit; ~**freiheit** tax exemption; ~**freijahre** tax break (holiday)

Steuer / ~**gelder** tax revenue; ~**gesetzgebung** tax legislation; ~**gewalt** taxing authority; ~**gewinn** taxable profit, gain for tax purposes; ~**gruppe** tax bracket; ~**gutschrift** tax credit

Steuer / ~**harmonisierung** tax harmonisation; ~**heberolle** tax roll, assessment register; ~**hebesatz** tax multiplier; ~**hinterziehung** tax evasion; ~**höchstsatz** maximum tax rate; ~**hoheit** taxing power

Steuer / ~**jahr** tax (fiscal) year, taxation year; ~**kennziffer** tax code; ~**klasse** tax bracket; ~**kraft** revenue-raising power; ~**kurswert** stock price for tax purposes; ~**last** tax charge (bill, load); ~**lastquote** tax load ratio

S

steuerlich *(~er Anreiz)* tax incentive, fiscal boost, *(~e Behandlung von Zinserträgen)* tax treatment of interest income, *(~e Bewertung von Vermögen)* tax valuation of property, *(~er Einheitswert)* unitary tax value, *(~es Ergebnis)* taxable income, *(~e Erwägungen)* tax considerations *(unter ~en Gesichtspunkten)* from a tax standpoint,*(aus ~en Gründen)* for tax reasons, *(~er Schätzwert)* assessed value, tax estimate, *(~e Überleitungsrechnung)* tax reconciliation, *(~er Verlustvortrag/-rücktrag)* tax carryforward (carryback), *(~er Wertansatz)* tax base, carrying amount in the tax accounts

steuerlich absetzbar *(~ er Betrag)* tax-deductible amount, allowable deduction, amount deductible from gross income for tax purposes, *(~e Zinsaufwendungen)* tax-deductible interest expense

Steuer / ~**messbetrag** tax base □ rateable value multiplied by the base rate; ~**messzahl** base rate; ~**mindereinnahmen** tax revenue shortfalls; ~**minderung** **1.** lowering the tax load **2.** tax relief

steuern to steer, to manage, to direct, to control, to regulate

Steuer / ~**nachforderung** additional tax claim; ~**nachlass** tax credit (abatement), *(~ für Zinsaufwendungen)* interest relief; ~**nachteile** adverse tax consequences

steuerneutral *(~e Vermögensübertragung)* tax-neutral transfer of assets

Steuer / ~**nummer** tax ID number; ~**oase** tax haven; ~**offenlegung** tax disclosure

steueroptimierend *(~er Fonds)* tax-efficient fund, tax shelter fund

steuerorientiert *(~e Anlage)* tax-driven (tax-geared, tax-oriented) investment

Steuer / ~**periode** taxation (assessment) period; ~**pfandrecht** tax lien, claim against property for unpaid taxes; ~**pfändung** tax foreclosure, seizure on account of unpaid tax arrears; ~**pflicht** tax liability

steuerpflichtig taxable, subject to tax, chargeable, attracting tax, *(~e Kapitalerträge)* taxable investment income, *(~e Körperschaft)* taxpaying corporation, *(~e temporäre Unterschiede)* taxable temporary differences, *(~e Zinseinkünfte)* taxable interest income

Steuer / ~**pflichtiger** taxpayer; ~**progression** tax progression, bracket creep; ~**prüfung** tax audit, tax inspection; ~**quote** taxation ratio; ~**recht** tax law

steuerrechtlich in (under) tax law, *(~e Ansatz- und Bewertungsvorschriften)* accounting principles used for the preparation of tax accounts, *(~e Bewertung)* valuation for tax purposes, *(~e Erfolgsrechnung)* tax-based income statement

Steuer / ~**rückerstattung** tax refund; ~**rückforderung 1.** *(des Steuerzahlers)* tax reclaim **2.** *(Rückforderung gewährter Vergünstigungen durch die Steuerbehörde)* tax clawback

Steuer / ~**rücklage** taxation reserve; ~**rückstände** tax arrears; ~**rückstellungen** tax accruals, taxation provisions; ~**rückwälzung** backward tax shifting

Steuer / ~**satz** tax rate; ~**säumnis** tax delinquency, failing to pay taxes on the due date; ~**säumniszuschlag** late payment surtax; ~**schätzung** tax appraisal; ~**schraube** tax screw

Steuer / ~**schuld** tax debt, tax(es) payable; ~**schuldner** tax debtor, taxpayer; ~**schuldverhältnis** tax liability (obligation); ~**sparmodell** tax shelter, tax savings scheme; ~**staffelung** sliding scale taxation; ~**stundung** tax deferment; ~**subjekt** taxable entity

Steuer / ~**termin** tax payment date, date on which major tax payments fall due, deadline for taxation payments; ~**tilgung** tax amortisation; ~**überwälzung** tax shifting; ~**umgehung** tax avoidance, dodging tax; ~**umwandlungsgesetz** Tax Reorganisation Act

Steuerung management, direction, control, regulation, operation, *(~ des finanziellen Risikos)* financial risk management (risk control), *(~ des Währungsrisikos)* currency risk (exposure) management, *(~ der Wirtschaft)* steering of the economy, *(~ von Zinsrisiken)* interest rate risk (exposure) management

Steuerungs / ~**datei** controlling file; ~**größen** control (operating) variables; ~**instrumente** regulatory instruments

Steuer / ~**veranlagung** tax assessment; ~**veranlagungszeitraum** assessment period, taxation period; ~**verbindlichkeiten** taxes payable, tax liabilities (obligations); ~**vergehen** tax offense; ~**vergünstigung** tax privilege (relief, concession); ~**vergütung** tax refund

steuerverhaftet taxable

Steuer / ~**verkürzung** tax evasion; ~**verschiebung** tax shifting; ~**verwaltung** revenue authorities; ~**vorauszahlung** tax prepayment; ~**vorteil** tax privilege

Steuer / ~**wert** fiscal (taxable) value, value of a capital asset for tax purposes; ~**widerstände** tax avoidance, tax planning tools; ~**wirkung** tax effects; ~**zuschlag** surtax; ~**zuschuss** tax subsidy

stichhaltig *(~er Grund)* sound (valid) reason

Stichkupon renewal coupon

Stichprobe sample, random check

Stichproben / ~**ansatz** sampling approach; ~**einheit**/~**element** sampling unit; ~**erhebung** sampling survey; ~**fehler** sampling error; ~**größe** sample size; ~**grundlage** sampling basis (frame)

Stichproben / ~**plan** sample design; ~**rahmen** sampling frame; ~**risiko** sampling risk; ~**schätzung** sample estimate; ~**umfang** sample size;~**verfahren** sampling method

Stichtag 1. *(allgemein)* reporting (record) date, reference date, effective (appointed) date, *(~ für Aktienübertragungen/Dividendenausschüttungen)* record date, books closed date □ date on which a register of security owners is closed for the distribution of interest or dividend payments, *(~ der Erhebung)* date of survey

S

2. *(letzter Termin)* deadline, closing date, *(~ für die Anmeldung von Insolvenzforderungen)* deadline for receipt of proofs of claim, *(~ für die Einreichung von Unterlagen)* qualifying (closing) date, deadline for filing the documents
3. *(Bilanzstichtag)* balance sheet date

Stichtagsbewertung fixed date measurement, measurement as of the reporting date (as of a specific date)

stichtagsbezogen on the reporting (agreed) date, as of the reporting (closing) date

Stichtags / ~bilanz *i.e.S.* financial statement (balance sheet) prepared as of a specific date, *i.w.S.* balance sheet date; **~inventur** end-of-period stock taking, annual stocktake

Stichtags / ~kurs reporting date rate, closing (year-end) rate, *(zum ~ umrechnen)* to translate at year-end rates; **~kursmethode** closing rate method; **~methode 1.** reference date method **2.** → Stichtagskursmethode; **~prinzip** reference date principle

Stichtags / ~vergleich year-on-year (quarter-on-quarter) comparison; **~wert** *i.e.S.* value as of the (reporting) date, *i.w.S.* balance sheet value

Stichwort-Akkreditiv proposed letter of credit

stiften 1. *(gründen)* to found, to establish **2.** *(schenken)* to donate

Stifter 1. founder **2.** donor, grantor

Stiftung 1. *(Gründung)* foundation, trust, *(rechtsfähige Stiftung des bürgerlichen Rechts)* foundation under German Civil Law
2. *(Schenkung)* donation

Stiftungs / ~urkunde foundation charter (deed); **~vermögen** foundation property, endowment (trust) funds

still 1.*(geschäftslos)* slack, dull, flat
2. silent, dormant, *(~e Bestätigung von Akkreditiven)* silent confirmation of documentary credits, *(~e Beteiligung)* dormant holding (participation), *(~e Einlage)* silent participation, capital contributions by a dormant partner, *(~e Gesellschaft)* silent (undisclosed, dormant) partnership, *(~er Gesellschafter)* dormant (sleeping, silent) partner
3. undisclosed, hidden, *(~es Factoring)* undisclosed (non-notification) factoring, confidential invoice discounting □ i.e. the factoring relationship is not disclosed to the customer's debtors, *(~er Forderungsverkauf)* undisclosed sale of receivables → stilles Factoring, *(~e Lasten)* hidden liabilities
(~e Rücklagen) (a) hidden (undisclosed) reserves *(b)* embedded (built-in) gains, *(~e Selbstfinanzierung)* funding from hidden reserves, *(~e Vorsorgereserven)* hidden risk provisions, *(~e Zession)* undisclosed (non-notification) assignment

Stille *(Flaute)* dullness, stagnation, slackness

Stille Gesellschaft silent (undisclosed) partnership

Stillhalte / ~abkommen standstill agreement, moratorium; **~klausel** standstill clause; **~kredit** standstill credit

stillhalten *(seitens der Gläubiger)* to postpone claims, to defer payments, to agree to a moratorium

Stillhalter writer (seller) of an option, *(~ in Aktien)* writer of a stock option

Stillhalteregelung standstill agreement

Stillhaltergeschäfte option writing, selling call or put options, call (put) writing

Stillhalterposition short option position, short call/short put, *(Deckung einer ~)* (providing) cover for a short option position

Stillhalterprämie short option premium, *(erhaltene ~n)* short option premiums received, premiums for options written (for short calls/puts)

Stillhalterverpflichtungen commitments from short option positions (from options written)

S

stilllegen 1. *(einen Betrieb)* to close (to shut) down 2. *(einfrieren)* to freeze, to tie (to lock) up, to immobilise 3. *(lahmlegen)* to paralyse

Stilllegung 1. closing down, close-down, shutdown 2. freeze, tying up, immobilisation 3. paralysing

Stillschweigen *(~ gegenüber Dritten wahren)* to observe secrecy towards third parties

stillschweigend 1. *adj.* implicit, implied, tacit, *(~e Garantie)* implied warranty, *(~e Genehmigung)* tacit (implicit) approval, *(~e Verlängerung)* tacit extension, renewal by tacit agreement, *(~es Vertretungsrecht)* implied agency
2. *adv.* implicitly, by implication, by tacit agreement

Stillstand 1. standstill, stoppage, *(die Abwärtsbewegung zu einem ~ bringen)* to bring the downturn to a halt, to stem the decline of
2. *(Festliegen)* immobilisation, tying up, blocking
3. *(Stagnation)* dullness, flatness, sluggishness
4. *(bei Verhandlungen)* deadlock, stalemate, impasse

Stillstandszeit downtime

stillstehen to stand idle (still), to be at a standstill, to be inactive

Stimmabgabe voting, vote, casting of votes, polling, *(~ durch einen Bevollmächtigten)* vote (voting) by proxy

stimmberechtigt 1. to be eligible (entitled) to vote 2. carrying voting rights, *(~er Aktionär)* voting shareholder, *(~es Kapital)* → Stimmrechtskapital, *(~e Stammaktien)* ordinary voting shares, ordinary shares (common stock) carrying voting rights

Stimmberechtigung voting right, right to vote

Stimme 1. vote 2. voice

stimmen *(~ für/gegen)* to vote for/against

Stimmen / ~anteil share (percentage) of the vote(s); **~autorisierung** voice authorisation; **~gleichheit** equality of votes, equal number of votes; **~liste** voting list, list of shareholders represented in a general meeting

Stimmen / ~mehrheit majority of votes, *(mit ~ gefasster Beschluss)* resolution passed (decision taken) by the majority of votes; **~minderheit** minority of votes; **~patt** voting deadlock; **~prüfung** scrutiny of votes

Stimmenthaltung abstention

Stimmerkennung voice recognition

Stimmrecht voting right (power), right to vote

Stimmrechts / ~aktien voting shares, shares carrying voting rights; **~ausgestaltung** powers attached to voting rights; **~ausübung** voting, exercising the voting right, *(~ durch einen Bevollmächtigten)* voting by proxy

Stimmrechts / ~beschränkungen voting right restrictions; **~bevollmächtigter** proxy; **~erweiterung** extension of voting rights

Stimmrechts / ~formular stock power; **~kapital** voting capital, capital (equity) carrying voting rights; **~kontrolle** voting control

stimmrechtslos *(~e Aktien)* non-voting shares, shares carrying no voting rights

Stimmrechts / ~meldepflichten notification duties relating to voting rights; **~treuhänder** voting trustee; **~übertragung** transfer of voting rights, voting right transfer

stimmrechtsverleihend *(~e Finanzinstrumente)* financial instruments entitling the holders to voting rights

Stimmrechts / ~vertreter proxy; **~vertretung** *(~ durch Banken)* proxy voting by banks; **~verwässerung** dilution of voting power; **~vollmacht** voting proxy; **~weisungen** voting instructions

Stimmung sentiment, tone, *(~ unter Aktienanlegern)* sentiment (mood) among stock market investors

S

Stimmungs / ~barometer trend indicator, indicator of market sentiment; **~besserung** improvement in market sentiment; **~umschwung** turnaround (change, reversal) in sentiment; **~verschlechterung** worsening of market sentiment; **~wechsel** → Stimmungsumschwung

stimulieren to stimulate, *(gute Konjunkturnachrichten stimulierten den Aktienmarkt)* favourable economic news propelled the stock market (lifted stock prices, buoyed equities), *(den Wettbewerb ~)* to encourage competition

stocken 1. *(stagnieren)* to stagnate, to slacken, to be slack, to fall off **2.** *(zum Stillstand kommen)* to come to a standstill **3.** *(Verhandlungen)* to be at a deadlock

Stocken *(ins ~ geraten)* to ground to a halt, *(der Aufschwung gerät ins ~)* the recovery is faltering

Stockung 1. stagnation, slackness, lull **2.** standstill, stop, halt **3.** deadlock, stalemate

stolpern *(über Fehlinvestitionen ~)* to stumble over misdirected investments

stopfen *(die finanziellen Löcher ~)* to plug (to fill) the financial holes

Stopp 1. stop, halt **2.** *(Einfrieren)* freeze **3.** *(Embargo)* ban, embargo

stoppen 1. to stop, to halt **2.** to freeze **3.** to ban, *(den Zinsauftrieb ~)* to halt the upsurge in interest rates

Stopp-Kauforder stop buy order □ the order will be executed at the market when the specified security, derivative or currency position trades above the stipulated limit

Stopp-Kurs stop price, → Stopp-Verkaufsorder

Stopp-Limitorder stop limit order □ order to buy or sell a security when the price hits, rises above *(buy)* or falls *(sell)* below the specified price limit

Stopp-Loss-Order / Stopp-Verkaufsorder stop loss order □ the order will be executed when the specified security, derivative or currency position sells at or below the stipulated stop price

stören 1. *(den Handel ~)* to disrupt (to disturb) trading **2.** *(sich einmischen)* to interfere with

Störerhaftung liability of the interferer, aider-and-abettor liability, responsibility for contributing to the infringement of a protected right

stornieren to cancel, to reverse, *(stornierte Belastungen/Gutschriften)* reversed debits/credits

Stornierung cancellation, revocation, reversal, reversing an entry

Stornierungs / ~anforderung reversal request; **~belastung** reversal debit; **~buchung** reversal, reverse (reversing) entry; **~frist** cancellation (revocation) period; **~gebühr** cancellation (revocation) fee; **~gutschrift** reversal credit

Störung 1. disruption, disturbance, *(~ des Betriebs)* business interruption, operational disruptions, *(~ des Handels)* disruption of trading activities
2. interference, harassment, *(~ der Geschäftsgrundlage)* interference with the basis of the agreement
3. *(Defekt)* trouble, failure, breakdown

störungsfrei *(~e Übermittlung von Zahlungsaufträgen)* failure-free transmission of payment orders

stoßen *(auf Einwände ~)* to run up against objections, *(auf spekulative Nachfrage ~)* to meet with speculative demand, *(auf erhebliche Probleme ~)* to encounter (to hit on) considerable problems, *(auf Schwierigkeiten ~)* to run into difficulties, *(XY stießen bei … € auf Interesse)* XY encountered support at € …

STOXX Indizes STOXX indices □ replicating the performance of European equities

strafen *(finanziell ~)* to penalise financially

S

straff *(~e Geldpolitik)* tight monetary policy, *(~e Haushaltsführung)* stringent budget policy, *(~es Kostenmanagement)* strict cost management, clampdown on costs, *(~e Leitung)* firm management, *(~e Organisation)* strict organisation

straffen 1. *(die Dienstleistungspalette ~)* to streamline the range of services offered **2.** *(die Kreditzügel ~)* to tighten the credit reins **3.** *(die Organisation ~)* to streamline the organisational setup, to aim at a lean structure

Straftatbestand constituting a criminal offence

Strafzuschlag penalty surcharge

Straßengüterverkehr road haulage, road carriage

Strategie *(~ im Privat-/Firmenkundenbereich)* retail/corporate banking strategy

Strategie / ~ausrichtung strategy design (orientation); **~entwicklung** developing (devising) a strategy; **~kombination** strategy mix; **~konzept** strategy blueprint (concept); **~papier** strategy paper; **~umsetzung** implementation of a strategy

strategisch *(~e Geschäftseinheit)* strategic business unit (SBU), *(~e Umweltprüfung)* strategic environmental assessment, *(~e Vermögensstrukturierung)* strategic asset allocation, *(~e Ziele)* strategic goals (objectives)

straucheln *(finanziell ~)* to flounder financially

streben *(nach einem höheren Marktanteil~)* to strive for a higher market share

Streben *(~ nach Wechselkursstabilität)* pursuit of exchange rate stability

strecken to extend, to stretch

Streckung extension, stretching, *(~ der Anleihefälligkeiten)* lengthening of bond maturities, *(~ der Bilanz)* stretching the balance sheet, *(~ eines Darlehens)* loan extension, extending the loan maturity, stretching out a loan repayment, *(~ der Kapitalfälligkeiten)* extending the maturity of principal repayments

Streckungsdarlehen 1. advance (loan) granted to cover the discount deducted from a loan **2.** bridge-over loan

streichen 1. *(annullieren)* to cancel, to annul **2.** *(aufheben)* to abolish, to repeal, to revoke **3.** *(durchstreichen)* to delete, to cross out **4.** *(aus einem Register ~)* to strike off (to drop from) a register **5.** *(Stellen ~)* to shed jobs **6.** *(für ungültig erklären)* to invalidate, to declare null and void

Streichung 1. annulment, cancellation **2.** abolishment, repeal, revocation **3.** deletion **4.** striking off **5.** invalidation

Streifband / ~depot individual securities account, jacket custody account; **~depotstücke** securities held under individual securities accounts; **~gebühr** individual custody fee; **~verwahrung** individual safekeeping of securities, jacket custody

Streik 1. strike **2.** *(Arbeitsniederlegung)* stoppage of work, walk-out

streiken 1. to go on strike, to be on strike **2.** to stop work, to walk out

Streit 1. row (e.g. over monetary policy) **2.** *(Meinungsverschiedenheit)* dispute, controversy **3.** *(Rechtsstreit)* lawsuit, litigation, *(Streit verkünden)* to bring (to involve) a third party into a lawsuit, to request s.o. to act as interpleader

Streit / ~beilegung dispute resolution, settlement of disputes; **~ beitritt** intervention

streiten *(über den richtigen Ansatz ~)* to wrangle over the proper approach, *(über die Kosten ~)* to squabble over the cost

Streit / ~fall 1. dispute, conflict, controversy **2.** *(Rechtsstreit)* litigation, case at law, case in (under) dispute; **~frage/~gegenstand** matter at issue (in controversy, in dispute)

Streit / ~helfer intervenor; **~genossenschaft** joinder of parties, *(einfache/notwendige ~)* permissive/compulsory joinder of parties; **~hilfe** third-party intervention

streitig contentious, litigious, in dispute, *(~machen)* to contest, to dispute, *(~es Verfahren)* contentious proceedings, *(~e Vermögenswerte)* property subject to litigation

Streitigkeit 1. dispute, controversy, conflict **2.** *(Rechtsstreit)* litigation

Streit / ~parteien contending (litigant, disputing) parties, parties to a lawsuit (to a dispute); **~punkt** point at issue, point in (under) dispute

Streit / ~schlichtung dispute resolution, *(alternative/außergerichtliche ~)* out-of-court/alternative dispute resolution; **~verfahren** adversary proceedings

Streit / ~verkünder third-party plaintiff, plaintiff-in-interpleader; **~verkündeter** third-party defendant; **~verkündung** third-party notice, interpleader action; **~wert** litigation value, amount in controversy

streng 1. *adj.* strict, severe, hard, *(~e Beleihungskriterien)* stringent (rigorous) assessment criteria
2. *adv.* strictly, severely, *(~ vertraulich)* strictly confidential

Strenge *(~ der Rezession)* severity of the recession

Stress / ~faktor stress factor, *(Szenarien mit hohem ~)* highly stressed scenarios; **~modell** stress testing model; **~test** → Bankenstresstests; **~testannahmen** stress test assumptions

Streubesitz free float, independently held capital, broadly based (widespread) share ownership, public ownership, *(sich im ~ befinden)* to be publicly held, to float freely

Streubesitz / ~dividenden free float dividends; **~faktor** free float factor; **~klausel** free float clause □ ensures that a specific percentage is available to the general investing public; **~quote** free float rate

streuen to spread, to diversify, *(den Aktienbesitz im Publikum ~)* to spread shareholdings amongst the general public, *(Anlagen breit nach Wirtschaftssektoren/Ländern/Schuldnern ~)* to spread investments widely across business sectors/countries/obligors

Streuung spread(ing), diversification, *(~ von Anlagen)* spreading of investments, asset diversification, *(~ der Ausleihungen)* loan diversification, diversification in lending operations, *(~ im Publikum)* spreading amongst the general public

Streuungsrisiko diversification risk

Strich *(Positionen unter dem ~)* below-the-line items, off-balance sheet items, *(unter dem ~ ausweisen)* to show below the line

stripbare Anleihe strippable bond

Stripping stripping □ practice of separating a bond into its principal/corpus (Mantel) and coupons (Zinsscheine) that are then traded separately as principal strips (Kapital-Strips, Mantel-Titel) and interest strips (Zins-Strips, Zinsschein-Titel)

strittig *(~e Forderung)* contested (disputed, litigious) claim, *(~e Punkte)* matters in (under) dispute, points of contention

Strom / ~derivate electricity derivatives; **~futures** electricity futures; **~größen** flow variables

Struktur structure, setup; **~anpassungsfazilität** structural adjustment facility

strukturbedingt structural, structure-induced

Strukturelle Liquiditätsquote Net Stable Funding Ratio (NSFR) □ This measure set out in the → Basel III framework aims at ensuring stable refinancing conditions. It establishes a minimum amount of stable funding based on the liquidity characteristics

S

of the respective bank's assets and activities and stipulates that the ratio between the available amount of stable funding (→ verfügbarer Betrag stabiler Refinanzierung) and the amount of required stable funding (→ erforderlicher Betrag stabiler Refinanzierung) must be greater than 100%.

strukturelles Liquiditätsrisiko funding liquidity risk

strukturelle Operationen structural operations □ open market operations conducted by the Eurosystem to influence the market's liquidity position over a longer period

strukturiert *(~e Befragung)* structured interview, *(~e Handelsfinanzierung)* structured commodity trade finance (financing), *(individuell ~e Emission)* individually structured issue, issue tailored to suit the issuer's specific requirements, *(~e Produkte)* structured products, *(~e Zinsderivate)* structured interest rate derivatives

Strukturierung *(~ einer Finanz-Transaktion)* deal structuring

Strukturierungsentgelt/~gebühr structuring fee

Struktur / ~kredit structural development loan; **~krise** structural crisis; **~verbesserung** structural improvement (enhancement); **~wandel** structural change

Stück 1. piece **2.** *(Einheit)* unit **3.** *(Posten)* item **4.** *(Wertpapier/Aktie)* share → Stücke

Stück / ~aktie no par value share; **~-Aktiengesetz** Law on Individual Share Certificates □ regulates the listing of no-par value shares; **~dividende** dividend per share

Stücke securities, *(im Gegensatz zu stückelosen Wertpapieren)* physical securities, certificated securities, *(zur Rückzahlung fällige ~)* securities (bonds) due for redemption, *(Übergabe effektiver ~)* delivery (surrender) of physical securities

Stücke / ~-Art type of security, **~bewegungen** securities transactions, securities received and delivered; **~lieferung** delivery of securities

stückeln 1. to fix denominations of **2.** to split up, *(klein ~)* to issue in small denominations

stückelos *(~e Abwicklung)* settlement by book entry, *(~es Abwicklungssystem)* book-entry-based clearing system, dematerialised settlement system, *(~e Anleihen)* bonds issued in book-entry form, dematerialised (uncertificated) bonds
(~er Handel) paperless trading, trading in dematerialised securities, *(~e Verrechnung)* → stückelose Abwicklung, *(~e Wertpapiere)* dematerialised securities, *(~e Wertpapierübertragung)* securities transfer by book entry, transfer in book-entry form, non-physical transfer of securities

Stückelung denomination, *(in ~en von 100 € emittieren)* to issue in denominations of €100, *(in ~en von 100 € oder einem Mehrfachen davon)* in denominations of €100 or multiples thereof, *(Wertpapiere in großen ~en)* large-denomination securities

Stückelungsanweisungen denomination instructions

Stückemangel shortage of offerings

stückemäßig *(~e Ein- und Auslieferung von Wertpapieren)* physical deposit and delivery of securities, *(~er Verkehr)* securities transactions involving transfer of the underlying certificates

Stücke / ~nummer certificate number; **~nummernauslosung** drawing of certificate numbers; **~regulierung** delivery of the securities involved, delivery of the underlying certificates

Stückergebnis unit performance

Stücke / ~tausch exchange of securities; **~verzeichnis** list of securities; **~zuteilung** allotment of securities

Stück / ~gebühren unit charges; **~gut** general goods, general cargo, less-than-carload lot; ~**kosten** unit cost; ~**kostenrechnung** unit costing; ~**kostensatz** unit cost rate; ~**kurs** price per share; ~**leistungen** *(einer Bank)* technical banking services (e. g. money transmission services)

stückmäßig *(~er Absatz)* unit sales

Stück / ~**notierung** quotation per share, unit quotation; ~**nummer** share (bond) certificate number; ~**preis** unit price; ~**preisfestsetzung** unit pricing; ~**volumen** unit volume; ~**wert** unit value; ~**wertaktie** share quoted per unit; ~**zahlen** *(hohe ~)* high transaction volumes

Stückzinsen interest accrued, *(Berechnung der ~) (a)* calculation of interest accrued *(b)* adding interest accrued

Stückzins / ~**saldo** accrued interest balance; ~**tage** accrual days; ~**topf** pool of accrued interest

Studie study, analysis

Stufe **1.** degree, notch, level, → Ratingstufe **2.** rank **3.** stage, phase

Stufen / ~**investitionsplan** phased investment plan; ~**kauf** *(Wertpapiere)* scale buying; ~**plan** phased (graduated) plan; ~**preise** staggered prices; ~**swap** step-up swap, accreting swap; ~**system** tiered system; ~**tarif** graduated (progressive) rates

stufenweise **1.** *adj.* gradual, graduated, progressive, *(~ Anpassung)* progressive adaptation, *(~r Ansatz)* phased approach, *(~ Finanzierung)* piecemeal financing, *(~ Zinssenkungen)* interest rate stepdowns, gradual reduction in interest rates
2. *adv.* gradually, step by step, in stages, *(~ einführen)* to phase in gradually

S

Stufenzins staggered (graduated) interest rate

Stufenzins / ~**anleihe** step-up bond, step rate bond; ~**CD** stepped rate certificate of deposit; ~**produkte** stepped rate products

stunden to defer, to grant an extension of time for payment, to grant additional time for payment, *(gestundete Kaufpreiszahlung)* deferred purchase price, *(gestundete Tilgungszahlungen)* deferred repayments, deferred redemption payments

Stundung deferral, deferment, extension of time for payment, respite, *(~ von Tilgungszahlungen)* deferring repayments on loans, debt deferral, *(~ von Zinszahlungen)* deferral of interest rate payments

Stundungs / ~**kreditbetrag** deferred loan principal; ~**vereinbarung** debt deferral agreement, agreement to defer payments, agreement not to call in outstanding loans; ~**vergleich** extension agreement; ~**zins** deferred interest

Sturz *(von Kursen, Preisen)* sharp fall, heavy slump, deep plunge, collapse

Stütze support, backing, buttress

stützen **1.** *(eine Währung/einen Kurs ~)* to support (to peg, to underpin) a currency/a price **2.** *(den Markt ~)* to prop up the market **3.** *(finanziell ~)* to back (to support) financially

Stützung **1.** support, backing, pegging, underpinning **2.** *(Rettung, Sanierung)* rescue, *(Intervention zur ~ der Währung)* intervention in support of the currency, *(Maßnahmen zur ~ der Zinspolitik)* measures designed to prop up the interest rate policy

Stützungsaktion **1.** support operation (measures) **2.** *(~ zur Rettung eines finanziell angeschlagenen Unternehmens)* rescue operation, lifeboat, rescue (bailout) scheme, *(die an der ~ beteiligten Banken)* lifeboat banks

Stützungs / ~**erklärung** letter of support, support agreement; ~**fazilität** backup (support, standby) facility; ~**fonds** support (standby) fund, guarantee fund; ~**käufe** support buying; ~**konsortium** support group, backing syndicate, rescue group

Stützungs / ~**kredit** standby credit, backup facility; ~**kurs** pegged rate (price); ~**linie** **1.** standby line, backup facility 2. *(Chart-Analyse)* support level

Stützungsmaßnahmen 1. support measures, *(finanzielle ~)* financial support package, financial backing 2. *(konjunkturelle ~)* measures designed to boost (to support) economic activity 3. rescue measures

Stützungs / ~programm 1. support scheme 2. rescue scheme; **~verpflichtungen** support commitments, standby obligations

subjektiv *(~e Unmöglichkeit der Leistungserfüllung)* subjective impossibility of performance (not a legal defense), → objektive Unmöglichkeit der Leistungserfüllung

Subkonsolidierung subconsoldiation

Submission invitation to (for) tender

Submissions / ~angebot tender, bid; **~bedingungen** tender (tendering, bidding) terms; **~verfahren** tender procedure, bidding system; **~weg** *(auf dem ~)* by tender

Submittent tenderer, bidding company

Subordination subordination, placing creditors in a lower rank, agreeing to a lower rank

Subordinationserklärung subordination agreement □ agreement that a specific debt (loan, bond) is to be repaid only after another senior debt has been satisfied

Subrogation subrogation, succeeding to the right of another person, substitution of one person in the place of another

Subrogations / ~klausel subrogation clause; **~recht** right of subrogation

subsidiär *(~es Akkreditiv)* secondary credit, *(~es Sicherungsrecht)* junior lien

Subsidiär / ~haftung secondary (derivative) liability; **~klausel** subsidiary clause

Subskribent subscriber

Subskription *(Zeichnung von Wertpapieren)* subscription, subscribing to (for) securities, → Zeichnung

Subskriptions / ~recht subscription right (privilege); **~verhältnis** subscription ratio

Substanz substance, resources, (material) assets

Substanz / ~auskehrung/ausschüttung asset distribution;**~bewertung** net asset valuation; **~erhalt** 1. maintenance (preservation) of assets 2. *(~ des investierten Kapitals)* preservation of capital (principal)

substanzgesichert *(~e Aktie)* stock backed by material assets

substanzielles Recht substantive law

Substanz / ~sicherung → Substanzerhalt; **~steuern** property taxes; **~verkäufe** asset sales; **~verlust** loss of (material) assets

Substanzwert 1. intrinsic (real) value 2. *(Unternehmung)* net asset value (NAV)

Substanzwerte 1. *(einer Unternehmung)* fixed assets 2. *(erstklassige Wertpapiere)* top-quality (first-line) securities

substanzwertorientiert *(~e Anleger)* NAV oriented investors, *(~es Bewertungsmodell)* NAV-based valuation (pricing) model

Substanzzuwachs 1. growth in assets 2. capital appreciation, increase in value

Substituierbarkeit *(~ von Wertpapieren)* substitutability of securities

substituieren to replace, to substitute

Substituierung/Substitution replacement, substitution, *(~ von Sicherheiten)* replacement of one security with another

Substitutions / ~ansatz substitution approach;**~recht** *(im Hinblick auf Kreditsicherheiten)* right of substitution, right to substitute equivalent collateral; **~risiko** substitution (replacement) risk, → Wiedereindeckungsrisiko; ~**risikogewicht** substituted risk weight; ~**vereinbarung** substitution agreement; ~**vollmacht** **1.** power to delegate authority **2.** power of substitution

Subunternehmer sub-contractor

Subvention subsidy, grant

subventionieren to subsidise, to support, to grant subsidies

subventioniert subsidised, *(staatlich ~es Kreditprogramm)* state-subsidised (government-supported) lending scheme

Subventionierung subsidising, subsidisation, granting subsidies, *(~ durch zinsgünstige Kredite)* subsidising through low-interest loans, *(~ von Zinszahlungen)* subsidising interest payments

subventionserheblich eligible for subsidies (within the meaning of the Subsidies Act)

Subventions / ~finanzierung funding through subsidies; ~**gesetz** Subsidies Act; ~ **programm** subsidising scheme; ~**zahlung** subsidy payment

Suche search, quest

sukzessiv **1.** *adj.* successive, *(~e Einführung)* phased-in (progressive) introduction **2.** *adv.* *(~e einführen)* to phase in, *(~e zurückgehen)* to decline progressively

Sukzessivplanung progressive planning

summarisch *(~e Aufstellung)* summary statement, *(~es Verfahren)* summary proceedings, *(~e Versicherung)* aggregated policy

S

Summe sum, amount, *(in der Summe)* on balance

Summen / ~abgleich reconciliation of totals; ~**aktie** share issued for a specific nominal amount; ~**exzedenten-Rückversicherung** surplus reinsurance, reinsurance of risks above a specified amount; ~**mehrheit** majority of totals; ~**saldenliste** list of balances and totals

summieren to sum up, *(sich auf … € ~)* to add up to € …

Superdividende superdividend, surplus dividend

supranational *(~e Emittentin/Kreditnehmerin)* supranational issuer/borrower

Swap swap, → Währungs-Swap, Zins-Swap

Swap / ~-Anbieter swap provider, → Swap-Verkäufer; ~-**Arrangeur** swap arranger; ~-**Aufwendungen** swap expense; ~-**Barwert** net present value of the swap

swap-basiert *(~er Indexfonds)* swap-based index fund

Swap / ~-Bewertung swap valuation; ~-**Bilanzierung** swap accounting; ~-**Buch** swap book, swap portfolio; ~-**Eindeckungskosten** swap replacement cost □ cost incurred when replacing a swap in the event of a counterparty default

Swap ETF swap-based ETF (Exchange-traded Fund) □ Swap arrangement in which the Fund undertakes to deliver the returns of a basket of securities (which may completey be unrelated to the index that the Fund is tracking). At the same time the counterparty undertakes to deliver to the Fund the return of the index.

Swap / ~-Finanzierung swap finance; ~-**Garantie** swap guarantee; ~-**Gebühren** swap fees (charges); ~-**Gegenpartei** swap counterparty

swapinduziert *(~e Emission)* swap-driven issue

Swap / ~-Käufer swap buyer, fixed rate payer, floating rate receiver; ~-**Konditionen** swap terms, swap pricing; ~-**Kurve** swap curve □ denotes the term structure of swap rates; ~-**Laufzeit** tenor (life) of the swap

Swap-Marge swap spread □ difference between the return on a swap and the underlying government bond yield

Swap-Option swaption □ entitles the holder to enter into a swap on a specified future date, at a preset rate and for a specified term

Swap-Position swap position, *(Eröffnung einer ~)* opening (entering into) a swap position, *(Schließung einer ~)* swap closeout, unwinding a swap

Swap / ~-Punkte swap points; → Swap-Satz; **~-Rate** → Swap-Satz; **~-Rendite** swap yield; **~-Risiko** swap risk (exposure), counterparty credit exposure for swaps

Swap-Satz 1. *(bei Devisen-Swaps)* swap points (rate) □ difference between spot and forward rates, i.e. premium over or discount from the spot rate **2.** *(bei Zins-Swaps)* swap rate □ rate paid by the fixed rate payer

Swap-Satzrisiko swap rate risk □ risk inherent in mismatched spot and forward currency positions

Swap / ~-Sekundärmarkt swap secondary market; **~-Valuta** swap currency; **~-Verkäufer** swap seller, fixed-rate receiver, floating-rate payer; **~-Wert** swap value

SWIFT / ~-Nachrichtenstandard SWIFT messaging standard; **~-Nachrichtentyp** SWIFT message type; **~-Satzformat** SWIFT record format; **~-Zahlung** SWIFT payment

Switch-Geschäft *(Wertpapiertauschgeschäft)* switch, switch transaction, buying and selling securities at the same time, exchange of holdings in a portfolio for other securities of similar value

Switch-Klausel *(Möglichkeit der Kreditbereitstellung in einer anderen Währung)* switch clause, switching facility

Switch-Prämie switch premium

Symmetrie symmetry, *(~ im Laufzeitenbereich)* matched maturities

symmetrische Dreiecksformation symmetrical triangle pattern □ based on two converging trendlines; generally, a continuation pattern, but indicating at the same time that a move in either direction is possible

symmetrische Verschlüsselung symmetric cryptography □ the same key is used for both encryption and decryption

Symptom *(~e einer konjunkturellen Erholung)* symptoms (signals) of an economic recovery

Syndikat syndicate, consortium of banks

Syndikatsführung syndicate (lead) management, *(mit der ~ betrauen)* to award the lead management to

Syndikus general counsel, legal adviser of a company

syndizieren to syndicate

syndiziert *(~er Bankkredit)* syndicated bank facility, *(~e Kapitalbeteiligung)* syndicated equity interest, *(~er Kredit)* syndicate (syndicated) loan, large loan arranged by a syndicate (consortium) of banks, *(~e Überbrückungsfazilität)* syndicated bridge facility

Syndizierung syndication, *(die in die ~ eingeladenen Banken)* the banks invited to participate in the syndication

Syndizierungs / ~abteilung syndication desk; **~agent** syndication agent, agent bank; **~gebühr** syndication fee; **~geschäft** syndication operations; **~kosten** syndication cost(s); **~risiko** syndication risk (exposure); **~technik** syndication techniques; **~vereinbarung** syndication agreement; **~verfahren** syndication process

Synergieeffekte/Synergien synergies

synthetische Aktienposition synthetic stock position, synthetic equity portfolio □ replicates the payoff characteristics of an equity portfolio based on a stock index through combining a money market investment and the purchase of a stock index futures contract

synthetischer Future synthetic future □ replicates a futures position by combining Calls and Puts that are

S

based on the corresponding futures contract or on the same underlying instrument. A synthetic Long Futures contract ***(synthetische Futures-Kaufposition)*** is established by combining Long Calls and Short Puts, a synthetic Short Futures contract ***(synthetische Futures-Verkaufsposition)*** is created by combining Long Puts and Short Calls. All positions have identical exercise prices and maturities.

synthetische Verbriefung synthetic securitisation □ contrary to the traditional securitisation there is no true sale of the reference assets (echter Forderungsverkauf), i.e. the assets remain on the bank's balance sheet, only the credit risk is transferred by way of credit derivatives

synthetische Wandelanleihe synthetic convertible bond □ combination of a non-convertible bond with options or warrants that replicates the profile of a traditional convertible issue

System system, (~ *fester/gleitender/ multipler Wechselkurse)* system of fixed/floating/multiple exchange rates

Systemanalyse systems analysis

systematischer Internalisierer systematic internaliser □ investment firm/ market maker executing customer orders against its own book

systematisches Risiko systematic (undiversifiable) risk

System / ~**betreiber** systems operator; ~**entwicklung** systems development; ~**gestaltung** systems design; ~**pflege** systems maintenance; ~**planung** systems design (planning, engineering)

systemrelevante Finanzinstitute systemically important financial institutions (SIFIs)

Systemrisiko systemic risk

Szenario scenario, environment, background; ~**analyse** scenario analysis

S

T

T *(Kurszusatz)* estimated price (no official quotation)

T+0 same-day settlement

T+1/T+2/T+3 settlement of a transaction one/two/three days after the trade date

tabellarisch *adj.* tabulated, tabular, *adv.* *(~ anordnen)* to arrange in tabular form, to tabulate

Tabelle 1. table, list, schedule **2.** chart, diagram

Tafelgeschäft counter transaction

Tafelgeschäfts-Rückkauf repurchase of physical securities at the counter

Tageberechnungsmethode *(bei der Zinsberechnung)* day count convention

Tages / **~abrechnung** daily settlement; **~abschlussverfahren** end-of-day settlement procedure; **~anleihe** day bond; **~auftrag** → Tagesorder; **~auszug** daily statement of account

Tages / **~defizit** *(im Geldhandel)* day-to-day deficit (shortage), deficit at the close of trading; **~dispogrenze** daily drawing limit; **~dispositionen** day-to-day transactions (dealings); **~dispositionslinie** daily drawing (credit) line; **~endauszug** end-of-day statement; **~endposition** end-of-day position; **~fehlbetrag** → Tagesdefizit

Tagesgeld 1. *(fest vereinbarte Laufzeit von 24 Stunden)* overnight money **2.** *(auf b.a.w. Basis)* call money **3.** *(Privatkundeneinlage mit täglicher Verfügbarkeit)* call deposit(s), → Tagesgeldkonto (1) **4.** *(i. S. von Vergütung)* daily allowance, daily benefits

Tagesgeld / **~abgaben** placement of overnight money; **~abschlüsse** overnight contracts (deals), call money deals; **~aufnahmen** overnight borrowings, borrowing overnight money; **~ausleihungen/~forderungen** overnight lendings, call money lendings, call money sold

Tagesgeld / **~handel** overnight dealings, dealings in overnight money (funds), call money dealings; **~hergaben** overnight loans (lendings)

Tagesgeld / **~konto 1.** *(mit täglicher Verfügbarkeit für Privatanleger)* call account, call deposit account, *(Verfügungen über ein ~)* drawings on a call deposit account **2.** *(im Interbanken-Zahlungsverkehr)* overnight money account; **~ koppelung** linking to the overnight rate; ~ kosten cost of borrowing overnight

Tagesgeld / **~markt** overnight (money) market, call money market; **~satz** *(~ am Interbankenmarkt)* overnight rate in the interbank market; **~verbindlichkeiten** overnight borrowings, call money bought

Tagesgeschäft daily operations, day-to-day business

tagesgültig good for the day, → Tagesorder

Tages / **~handel** day trading, buying and selling securities on the same day; **~hoch/~höchstkurs** intraday peak, day's high (peak, best)

tageskumuliert *(~e Zahlungen)* day aggregate of payments

Tages / **~kurs** daily price (quotation), current rate; **~notierung** daily quotation; **~order** *(bei Börsenaufträgen)* day order, order valid for a single trading day; **~ordnung** agenda; **~ordnungspunkt** item on the agenda

T

Tages / ~saldo daily balance; **~schlussposition** end-of-day position; **~schwankungen** daily fluctuations (swings); **~spitze 1.** *(aktivisch)* net long position, surplus at the close of trading **2.** *(passivisch)* net short position, deficit at the close of trading

Tages / ~überschuss *(im Geldhandel)* day-to-day surplus, surplus at the close of trading; **~umsatz** daily transaction volume, daily turnover, daily volume of business

Tages / ~volatilität daily (day's) volatility; **~wert** market price (value); **~zinsen 1.** daily interest **2.** interest for a specific number of days

taggenau *(~e Berechnung)* day specific calculation, *(~e Zinsberechnung)* actual/actual □ interest calculation method based on the actual number of days elapsed in a given interest period and the actual number of days in the year

taggleich *(~e Abrechnung/Abwicklung)* same-day settlement, T+0, *(~er Kauf und Verkauf von Wertpapieren)* intraday trading, *(~e Valuta)* same-day value, *(~e Verbuchung)* same-day accounting

täglich *(~e Nachschussberechnung)* daily remargining, calculation of margin calls if the margin balance drops below the margin requirement level, *(~e Neubewertung von Finanzpositionen)* daily marking to the market, *(~e Sicherheitsnachschüsse)* daily margin calls, → tägliche Nachschussberechnung, *(~e Verarbeitung)* daily processing, *(~er Zahlungsausgleich)* daily settlement, *(~e Zinsberechnung)* daily interest accrual

täglich fällig *(~e Einlagen)* overnight deposits, day-to-day money, *(~e Kundengelder)* customer demand deposits, *(~e Verbindlichkeiten)* liabilities due on demand

täglich kündbar *(~es Repo-Geschäft)* demand repo, open repo

Tagung conference, congress, meeting

Tagwechsel bill payable on a specific date

taktisch *(~es Portfolio)* tactical portfolio □ seeks capital appreciation through investments across global asset classes, *(~e Vermögensstrukturierung)* tactical asset allocation (TAA)

Talfahrt descent, *(~ der Aktienkurse)* nosedive of stock prices, sharp slide in equities, *(~ der Konjunktur)* sharp economic downswing (downturn), plunge into a recession, *(die Konjunktur auf ~ schicken)* to send the economy into a tailspin

Talon 1. *(Kupon-Erneuerungsschein)* renewal coupon **2.** *(Kontrollabschnitt)* counterfoil, stub

Talsohle *(die ~ ist nahezu durchschritten)* the recession is close to bottoming out, *(die ~ verlassen)* to emerge from the trough (doldrums), to climb upwards from the post-recession trough

tangieren to affect, to impact

Tantieme 1. fee, remuneration **2.** *(Aufsichtsratsvergütung)* director's fee **3.** *(Gewinnanteil)* profit share, share in the profits **4.** *(Vergütung)* bonus

Tarif 1. tariff, rates **2.** *(Gebührenordnung)* scale (schedule, tariff) of charges **3.** *(Gehaltstarif)* agreed pay scale **4.** *(Zolltarif)* (customs) tariff

Tarif / ~abkommen 1. agreement on rates **2.** (collective) pay agreement **3.** tariff agreement; **~abschluss** pay settlement, conclusion of a (collective) pay agreement; **~angestellte/r** pay scale employee, employee paid in line with a collective pay scale

Tarif / ~angleichung 1. realignment (standardisation) of rates **2.** realignment (adjustment) of pay scales; **~autonomie 1.** rating prerogative **2.** autonomy in collective bargaining (in negotiating pay agreements) **3.** tariff autonomy

tarifbesteuert *(~e Wertpapiererträge)* income from securities subject to standard taxation rates

Tarif / **~bruch** 1. infringement of rates in force 2. infringement (violation) of a collective pay agreement; **~erhöhung** 1. tariff (rates) increase 2. increase of (in) agreed pay rates

Tarif / **~festsetzung** 1. rate-fixing 2. determination (fixing) of agreed pay rates; **~garantie** rates guarantee; **~gehälter** collectively agreed salaries; **~gesetz** Collective Agreements Act; **~gruppe** 1. rating (tariff) category 2. pay grade, salary bracket

tariflich *(~e Bezahlung)* payment according to an agreed pay scale, *(~e Einstufung)* 1. salary bracket 2. classification into a salary bracket (pay category), *(~e Sonderzahlungen)* (collectively) agreed special payments, special payments stipulated under a collective pay agreement

Tarif / **~parteien/~partner** parties to a collective pay agreement, management and unions, employers and employed; **~politik** 1. rates policy 2. pay policy; **~prämie** standard premium; **~recht** legislation on collective pay agreements; **~runde** pay bargaining round, round of wage bargaining

Tarif / **~senkung** tariff reduction, lowering of rates; **~streit** pay dispute; **~struktur** 1. rate (tariff) structure 2. pay structure

Tarif / **~verhandlungen** collective bargaining, pay negotiations, wage (pay) bargaining process; **~vertrag** (collective) pay agreement; **~werte** *(Börse)* utilities

Tasse-Henkel-Formation cup with handle □ bullish continuation pattern

Taste *(unbeschriftete ~n)* soft keys

tätig *(~er Teilhaber)* active partner, *(im Eurokreditgeschäft ~e Banken)* banks operating (banks active) in the Eurolending business

tätigen 1. to effect 2. *(Abschlüsse ~)* to conclude (to strike, to make) deals, to trade contracts

Tätigkeit 1. activity, operations 2. profession, occupation, job, employment

Tätigkeits / **~analyse** job analysis; **~bereich** province, line, field (sphere) of activity, activities; **~bericht** 1. progress report 2. *(Geschäftsbericht)* business report; **~beschreibung** job specification; **~nachweis** 1. activity report, performance record 2. *(Praktikumsnachweis)* evidence of internship

Tatsachen / **~feststellung** fact-finding, ascertainment of facts; **~vermutung** presumption of facts

tatsächlich *(~e Kosten der Inanspruchnahme)* true cost of borrowing, *(~e Kreditaufnahme)* actual borrowings, *(~e Steuerschulden)* current tax liabilities, *(~e Verzinsung)* effective (true) interest return, *(~er wirtschaftlicher Wert)* actual economic value, *(~er Zinssatz)* effective interest rate, *(der ~ entstandene Schaden)* the loss actually incurred

Tausch exchange, swap; **~anleihe** exchangeable bond; **~depot** exchangeable jacket custody account □ jacket custody account whose owner has authorised the custodian to exchange his stock for identical securities

tauschen to exchange, to swap

täuschen to deceive, to mislead

Täuschung 1. deceipt, deception 2. *(falsche Darstellung)* misrepresentation

Täuschungsabsicht willful intent to deceive

Tausch / **~verwahrung** custody linked to an exchange facility, exchangeable custody; **~vertrag** barter agreement; **~ware** barter goods

Taxator appraiser, valuer

Taxe 1. *(Abgabe)* fee, duty 2. estimated price, price estimate

Taxgebühren appraisal fee

taxieren to appraise, to estimate, to value

Tax / ~**kurs** estimated price; ~**wert** appraised (estimated) value

TecDAX German technology index □ tracks the stock prices of the → Prime Standard's 30 largest technology stocks not listed in the → DAX

technisch (*~e Aktienanalyse)* technical analysis, *(~e Global-/Sammelurkunde)* global bond certificate, *(~e Kurserholung)* technical rally, technical markups, *(~e Reaktion)* technical reaction (rebound, response), adjusting drop (rise) in prices following a sharp upward (downward) trend

Technologiebereich/Technologiewerte technology stocks

Teil 1. part, *(zu gleichen ~en)* in equal parts **2.** *(Anteil)* share, portion **3.** *(Bestandteil)* component, element

Teil / ~**ablösung** partial repayment (redemption); ~**abschreibung** partial write-off (write-down), *(teilabgeschriebene Forderungen)* loans partly charged (written) off

Teil / ~**abtretung** *(~ einer Briefgrundschuld)* partial assignment of a land charge; ~**akzept** partial (restrictive) acceptance; ~**amortisationsvertrag** partial pay-out agreement

Teil / ~**anrechnungsbetrag** *(~ für das allgemeine Kursrisiko)* partial capital charge for general price risks; ~**ausführung** *(eines Börsenauftrages)* partial execution, *(~ möglich)* partial fill allowed

Teil / ~**ausnutzung 1.** *(eines Akkreditivs)* partial drawdown (drawing) on a documentary credit **2.** *(eines Kredites)* → Teilinanspruchnahme; ~**auszahlungszuschlag** partial disbursement (payment) fee

teilbar divisible, severable, *(~ e Leistung)* severable performance, *(~e Verpflichtung)* divisible obligation, *(~er Vertrag)* divisible (severable) contract

Teil / ~**barkeit** divisibility; ~**befriedigung** *(der Gläubiger)* partial satisfaction; ~**betriebsergebnis** partial operating result □net interest and commission income, i. e. interest and commission income less personnel and general administrative expenses

Teil / ~**briefbildung** issuance of a partial charge certificate; ~**bürgschaft** partial surety, surety limited to a specific part of the creditor's claim; ~**deckung** partial cover; ~**eigentum** part (proportional) ownership, shared ownership, co-ownership, *(Wohneinheit)* freehold unit; ~**eigentümer** co-owner

Teil / ~**einkünfteverfahren** partial income procedure □ exempting dividend income from tax to the extent of 40 %; ~**einlösung** partial redemption (repayment); ~**einzahlung** partial payment (deposit), *(teileingezahlte Aktien)* partly paid shares; ~**emission** partial issue, tranche (part) of an issue

teilen 1. to divide, to split (up) **2.** *(Kosten, Ausschüttungen, etc.)* to share

Teil / ~**entlastung** partial discharge; ~**erfüllung** *(~ eines Vertrages)* partial performance, part-performance

teilfinanzieren to part-finance

Teil / ~**finanzierung** partial financing; ~**fonds** sub-fund

teilgedeckt (*~e Optionen)* partially covered options

Teil / ~**haber** partner, shareholder; ~**haberpapiere** shares, equities; ~**haberrecht** ownership right; ~**inanspruchnahme** partial drawing (drawdown), drawing in part, partial utilisation; ~**indossament** partial endorsement; ~**konnossement** partial bill of lading

Teilkonzern sub-group; ~**abschluss** annual sub-group accounts, subgroup financial statements, *(befreiender ~)* exempting annual sub-group accounts; ~**abschlusspflicht** duty to prepare annual sub-group accounts; ~**gewinn** sub-group profit

Teil / ~**kündigung** *(einer Emission)* partial redemption notice, calling in part of an issue, partial call; ~**leistung**

1. partial performance 2. partial payment 3. amount partly paid in (up)

Teil / ~lieferung partial delivery (shipment); **~löschung** partial discharge (release, satisfaction); **~markt** submarket; **~nahme 1.** participation **2.** *(Anwesenheit)* attendance, presence; **~nahmeberechtigung** right to attend

teilnehmen 1. to participate, to take part **2.** to attend, to be present

Teil / ~nehmer participant; **~privatisierung** partial privatisation; **~rahmen** sub-line, sub-facility; **~recht 1.** partial interest **2.** *(bei Wertpapieren)* fractional interest; **~rückführung** partial repayment

Teil / ~schuldverschreibung note □ denotes the method of issuance and the proportionate rights acquired by the bond buyer; **~stichprobe** sub-sample; **~übertragung** *(des Akkreditivs)* partial assignment of the documentary credit

Teilung division, subdivision, partition, split, splitting

Teilungs / ~anspruch → Teilungsrecht; **~erklärung** *(hinsichtlich der eigentumsmäßigen Aufteilung einer Wohnanlage)* commonhold community statement, shared ownership deed; **~genehmigung** subdivision permit; **~klage** action for partition; **~masse** distributable assets (property)

Teilungs / ~plan 1. distribution schedule (for distributing the proceeds from a forced sale) **2.** (property) partition scheme; **~recht** right to partition, right to force a partition and sale

Teilungs / ~urkunde shared ownership deed, → Teilungserklärung; **~versteigerung** partition by way of a public auction; **~unternehmerschaft** commercial co-partnership

Teil / ~valutierung *(eines Kredites)* partial disbursement of a loan; **~valutierungsaufschlag** partial disbursement fee (premium); **~verladung** *(~gestattet/nicht gestattet)* partial shipment allowed/not allowed

teilweise *adj.* partial, *(~ Vertragserfüllung)* partial performance of a contract *adv.* partly, in part

Teilwert 1. *(steuerlicher)* present value **2.** *(Bruchteil)* fractional value

Teilwert / ~abschreibung 1. *(außerplanmäßige Abschreibung)* impairment **2.** *(einer Kreditforderung)* partial write-off; **~absicherung** partial hedge (cover); **~verfahren** *(Verfahren zur Bewertung von Pensionsverpflichtungen)* entry-age normal method; **~versicherung** insurance for less than full value

Teilzahlung 1. part (partial) payment **2.** *(Ratenzahlung)* instalment, payment on account

Teilzahlungs / ~bank instalment credit bank, personal finance company (AE), finance house (BE); **~basis** *(auf ~)* on an instalment basis, on a hire purchase basis; **~finanzierung** instalment financing, hire purchase finance; **~forderungen** instalment receivables (debtors), hire purchase receivables

Teilzahlungs / ~geschäft 1. instalment credit transaction, hire purchase transaction **2.** instalment credit operations (business); **~institut** → Teilzahlungsbank; **~kauf** instalment buying, hire purchase, credit purchase (sale)

Teilzahlungskredit instalment credit, hire purchase loan

Teilzahlungskredit / ~geschäft instalment lending, instalment credit operations; **~institut** → Teilzahlungsbank; **~kosten** instalment credit cost(s); **~vereinbarung/~vertrag** instalment credit agreement, hire purchase agreement

Teilzahlungswechsel instalment credit bill

Teil / ~ziele sub-targets; **~zinsspanne** specific interest margin □ interest margin based upon specific lending and deposit operations; **~zuteilung** partial allotment

Telefonbanking phone banking

Telefonhandel off-floor trading □ descriptive of interbank securities trading

telefonisch *(~e Autorisierung einer Kartentransaktion)* voice authorisation, *(~e Autorisierungsanfrage)* voice request

Tempo *(~ der wirtschaftlichen Erholung)* pace of economic recovery

temporäre Differenzen temporary differences (between the tax base of an asset/liability and its carrying amount in the balance sheet)

Tendenz tendency, trend, *(Umkehr der ~)* trend reversal, turnaround, break

tendenziell *(~e Verbesserung/Verschlechterung)* improvement/worsening in the trend

Tender tender, *(~ für Wertpapierpensionen)* sale and repurchase securities tender

Tender / **~ankündigung** tender announcement; **~ausschreibung** invitation to tender; **~austausch** tender exchange; **~fälligkeit** tender maturity; **~gebot** tender bid

Tender / **~offerte** tender offering; **~satz** tender rate; **~verfahren** tender procedure; → Standardtender, → Schnelltender, *(Emission im ~)* issue through a tender system, *(im ~ anbieten)* to offer for sale by tender; **~zuteilung** tender allocation (allotment)

tendieren to tend, to trend, *(bei geringen Umsätzen uneinheitlich ~)* to be mixed in light (thin) trading, *(nach Glattstellungen des Berufshandels rückläufig ~)* to trend (to head) downward(s) on professional profit-taking

T

Tenor *(jur.)* operative part of the judgment

Termin 1. date, *(vereinbarter ~)* date fixed (set, agreed upon) **2.** *(Fälligkeitstag)* due date, maturity date **3.** *(Frist)* term, period **4.** *(letzter Termin)* deadline, *(per ~ handeln)* to trade for forward (future) delivery, *(per ~ kaufen/verkaufen)* to buy/to sell for forward delivery

Termin / **~abschlag** forward discount; **~abschluss 1.** forward contract (deal), deal for future delivery, → Termingeschäft, → Terminkontrakt **2.** entering into (concluding) a forward deal

Termin / **~absicherung** forward cover (hedge), → Terminsicherung; **~anlagen** term (time) deposit investments; **~aufgeld** forward premium; **~auftrag** forward order, order for future delivery

Termin / **~börse** futures and options exchange; **~börsenfonds** futures fund, fund specialising in futures and option investments; **~briefkurs** forward selling rate

Termin / **~darlehen** forward loan; **~daten** dynamic securities data, e.g. floating interest rate, conversion ratio, → Stammdaten; **~devisen** forward foreign exchange, forward currency, exchange for forward (future) delivery; **~dollar** forward dollar

Termin / **~eindeckung** forward coverage; **~einlagen** term (time) deposits, → Termingeld; **~engagement** forward commitment, forward exposure; **~fälligkeiten** forward maturities; **~forderungen** forward claims

termingebunden tied (linked) to a specific date, *(~e Einlagen)* time deposits, *(~e Zahlung)* payment to be made on a given (specific, preset) date

Termingeld *(Oberbegriff für Fest- und Kündigungsgelder)* term money, time and notice deposits, *(~er mit einer Laufzeit von mehr als zwei Monaten)* term money running for more than two months

Termingeld / **~abschlüsse** term money contracts (deals), term money dealings; **~anlage** *(im Geldhandel)* term money placed, *(durch Kunden)* term deposit investment; **~aufnahmen** term money borrowings

Termingeld / **~bestand** term money holdings; **~geschäfte** term money transactions; **~hergaben** term money lendings; ~**konto** term money account; ~**satz** term money rate

termingerecht *adj.* timely, *adv.* on time (schedule), in due time, on the agreed date

Termingeschäft *(Geschäft mit Erfüllungsverpflichtung zu einem späteren Termin)* forward transaction, forward deal, transaction for future delivery, *(z. B. Devisentermingeschäft)*, FX outright, forex forward, forward currency deal, *zu unterscheiden von* → Terminkontrakt
(*~e mit kurzen/langen Fristigkeiten)* short/long forwards, *(~e mit festverzinslichen Wertpapieren)* forward transactions in fixed-income securities, fixed income forwards

Termingeschäft gegen Termingeschäft *(Kombination von Termingeschäften mit unterschiedlichen Laufzeiten)* forward against forward

Termingeschäfts / ~fähigkeit capacity to buy or sell assets for future delivery, capacity to conclude futures and option deals; ~**gewinne** profits from forward transactions

Termingold forward gold

Terminhandel 1. forward dealings **2.** *(in Börsentermingeschäften)* futures and options trading

terminieren 1. to set (to fix) a date, to set a deadline **2.** to time, to assign a time

terminiert *(~es Tagesgeld)* call money with an agreed term of less than 30 days

Terminintervention intervention in the forward market

Terminkauf forward purchase, purchase for future delivery, buying (e. g. foreign currency) forward, *(Terminkäufe mit Barausgleich)* cash-settled forward purchases

Termin / ~käufer forward buyer; ~**kaufposition** long forward position; ~**kommissionär** futures commission broker

terminkongruent *(~e Refinanzierung von Hypothekendarlehen)* refinancing (funding) mortgage loans with matching maturity dates

Terminkonto 1. time deposit account **2.** forward account

Terminkontrakt futures contract, future □ in contrast to a Termingeschäft (forward contract), futures may be settled through countertransactions, *(~e auf Einzelaktien)* single stock futures, *(Erwerb eines ~es)* buying a future (a futures contract), opening a long futures position, *(Glattstellung eines ~es)* closing out a futures position, *(Verkauf eines ~es)* selling a future, opening a short futures position

Terminkontrakt / ~handel futures trading; ~**markt** futures market; ~**position** futures position, *(Kaufposition)* long futures position, *(Verkaufsposition)* short futures position; ~**preis** futures price (quotation)

Terminkurs forward rate (price); ~**festlegung** forward rate fixing

Terminmarkt 1. forward market, → Termingeschäft **2.** futures and options market, → Terminkontrakt; ~**engagement** forward market exposure; ~**position** position in the forward (futures) market

Terminnotierung 1. forward rate (quotation), quotation for forward delivery **2.** *(eines Terminkontraktes)* futures quotation (price) **3.** *(am Geldmarkt)* term money rate

Termin / ~obligo forward exposure (commitments); ~**option** forward start option; ~**papiere** forward securities, securities traded for forward (future) delivery

Termin / ~planung 1. schedule planning, scheduling **2.** appointment schedule; ~**positionen** forward positions, forward commitments (interests), *(Bestand an ~)* forward book, *(~ unterhalten)* to run a forward book

Termin / ~risiko time risk □ risk of untimely payments, late receipt of principal and/or interest payments; ~**rückkaufsvereinbarung** forward re-

T

purchase agreement; ~ **seite** forward leg

Terminsicherung 1. *(Absicherung eines Kassageschäftes durch ein Termingeschäft)* forward cover (coverage), forward hedge, cover in the forward market, covering (hedging) through a forward transaction **2.** *(Gegensicherung eines Termingeschäftes)* providing cover for a forward transaction

Termin / ~sicherungskosten forward cover (hedging) cost; **~-Swap** forward swap; **~tratte** term (time) draft, usance draft

Termin / ~überschreitung exceeding the deadline (the date fixed), non-compliance with the time limit; **~überwachung** maturity control, monitoring (control) of maturities; **~überwachungsliste** maturity control list

Termin / ~valuta 1. forward currency **2.** forward value date; **~verbindlichkeiten** forward liabilities, liabilities from contracts for future delivery; **~vereinbarung** forward (rate) agreement, agreement for future delivery

Termin / ~verkauf forward sale, sale for future delivery; **~verkäufer** forward seller; **~verlängerung** extending the maturity of; ~ **vertrag** forward agreement

Termin / ~wahrung observing the deadline (the time limit given), compliance with the date fixed; **~waren** forward commodities; **~zinssatz** forward interest rate; **~-Zinsswap** forward interest rate swap, delayed start swap

T

tertiär *(~er Sektor)* tertiary industry (sector)

Testament testament, last will and testament

testamentarisch *(~e Erbfolge)* testamentary order of succession, *(~e Verfügung)* testamentary disposition

Testamentsvollstrecker 1. *(testamentarisch bestimmt)* executor **2.** *(bestimmt durch das Nachlassgericht)* administrator; **~zeugnis 1.** *(where there is a will)* grant of probate **2.** *(where there is no will)* letters of administration

Testat *(des Wirtschaftsprüfers)* audit certificate, auditor's opinion (report), opinion on the financial statements, *(eingeschränktes ~)* qualified opinion, *(uneingeschränktes)* unqualified (clean) opinion

Testat / ~erteilung issuance of the auditor's certificate; **~verweigerung** disclaimer (of an audit opinion)

testieren 1. *(bescheinigen)* to attest, to certify
2. *(ein Testament errichten)* to make (to draw up) a will
3. *(einen Abschluss ~)* to issue an audit report (on the financial statements), *(testierter Abschluss)* audited financial statements, annual accounts provided with an audit certificate

testierfähig testable, to have testamentary capacity

Testierfähigkeit capacity (ability) to make a will

teuer expensive, dear, costly, *(~er werden)* to increase in price, to become dearer, *(~er refinanzieren)* to fund at a higher cost, *(~e Kreditaufnahme)* high-cost borrowing

Teuerung price increase (rise)

Teuerungsrate price increase rate

Text *(eines Gesetzes, Vertrages)* text, wording

Thema subject, topic

Thematik subject matter, issue

thesaurieren to reinvest (income distributed), to plow (to plough) back, *(Gewinn vollständig ~)* to retain income in its entirety, *(thesaurierte Anlageerträge)* reinvested investment income, *(thesaurierter Gewinn)* retained profit (income)

Thesaurierung profit retention, reinvestment (of dividends or interest payments in other securities)

Thesaurierungs / ~begünstigung retention tax credit; **~fonds** growth fund, fund reinvesting its interest income; ~**politik** profit retention policy; ~**quote** retention rate, percentage of earnings (of the annual profit) reinvested in the company

Theta measures time decay of an option

Ticker-Notierung tape quotation

Tick-Größe tick size

Tick-Wert tick value

tief (~ *im/aus dem Geld)* deep in/out of the money

Tief depression, bearish (depressed) sentiment, low

Tiefe *(~ des Marktes)* depth of the market

tiefgestaffelt *(~e Produktpalette)* deeply structured product range

tiefgreifend (~*e Überprüfung)* thorough (thorough-going) review, (~*e Veränderungen/~er Wandel)* profound (sweeping) changes, radical change, sea-change

Tiefpunkt low, bottom, (~ *der Baisse)* bottom of the bear market, (~ *der Rezession)* bottom of the recession (of the trough), *(den ~ erreichen)* to bottom, to touch bottom, *(auf einen absoluten ~ sinken)* to drop to an all-time low, to hit rock-bottom, to hit a record low, to slump to its lowest-ever level

Tiefstand → Tiefpunkt

Tier 1 Kapital *(nach → Basel III)* Tier 1 capital □ consisting of ***Tier 1a capital*** or Common Equity (hartes Kernkapital) that comprises common shares issued by a bank, share premium accounts and disclosed reserves and ***Tier 1b capital*** or Additional Tier 1 capital (zusätzliches Tier 1 Kapital) comprising instruments that meet specific criteria

Tier 2 Kapital *(nach → Basel III)* Tier 2 capital □ consisting of paid-in capital instruments that are subordinated to depositors and general creditors of the bank with a minimum original maturity of at least five years

Tier 3 Kapital/Drittrangmittel *(nach → Basel II)* Tier 3 capital □ short-term subordinated debt, to be dropped under the new capital framework → Basel III

tilgbar redeemable, repayable, amortisable

tilgen to redeem, to amortise, to repay, to pay off (down), to retire

Tilgung redemption, amortisation, repayment, capital repayment, repayment of principal, retirement

Tilgung (~ *durch jährliche Auslosungen)* redemption by annual drawings, (~ *mit einem Aufgeld)* redemption at a premium, *(~ in einem Betrag bei Fälligkeit)* redemption in one lump sum upon maturity, bullet redemption
(~ *vor dem Fälligkeitstermin)* redemption ahead of schedule, repayment prior to maturity, (~ *in voller Höhe)* repayment in full, (~ *zum/über/unter dem) Nennwert* redemption at/above/below par
(~ zum Nennwert zuzüglich Stückzinsen) redemption at par plus interest accrued, (~ *in Raten)* repayment by instalments, (~ *durch Rückkauf am Markt)* redemption by repurchase in the market

Tilgungs / ~ankündigung redemption (call) notice; ~**anleihe** redemption (amortising) bond, bond redeemed in instalments over a number of years; ~**anspruch** redemption claim, claim to repayment

Tilgungs / ~anteil *(an der Kreditbedienung)* capital repayment portion, principal repaid; ~**aufforderung** call for redemption (repayment); ~**aufgeld** redemption (call) premium, premium on redemption

Tilgungs / ~aufschub deferral of redemption (principal) payments, deferring repayments on a loan, respite for principal (debt) repayments; ~**aussetzung** suspension (halt) of redemption payments, redemption break (holiday)

Tilgungs / ~barkredit cash redemption loan; **~belastung** redemption (amortisation) requirements, redemption charge, repayment load (charge); **~betrag** redemption amount, amount (principal) to be redeemed, redemption money

Tilgungs / ~darlehen amortising loan, loan redeemable by scheduled instalments, level payment amortising loan; **~dauer** redemption (repayment) period, term (life) of redemption; **~dienst** redemption service, loan payment service

Tilgungs / ~eingänge repayments received; **~erfordernisse** redemption requirements, repayments required

Tilgungs / ~fähigkeit ability to repay the loan, ability to make the necessary repayments, ability to meet redemption obligations; **~fälligkeit** date of redemption

Tilgungs / ~fonds redemption (amortisation) fund, sinking fund; **~freijahre** redemption-free (capital-repayment-free) years, redemption holiday; **~gewinn** gain on redemption

Tilgungs / ~höhe level of redemption payments; **~hypothek** redemption mortgage, direct reduction mortgage, amortising (amortisation) mortgage, capital repayment mortgage; **~kalender** principal repayment schedule, amortisation schedule

tilgungskongruent (*~e Refinanzierungstitel)* funding instruments at matching redemption rates

T

Tilgungs / ~kosten cost of redemption, amortisation cost; **~kredit** amortising loan facility; **~kurs** redemption (repayment) price, redemption price at maturity

Tilgungs / ~last repayment (redemption) burden, repayment load; **~lebensversicherung** mortgage protection insurance

Tilgungsleistungen repayments, redemptions, redemption payments, debt repayments, repayments on a loan, principal repayments

Tilgungsleistungen (*gleichbleibende monatliche ~ während der vereinbarten Laufzeit des Kredites)* equal monthly repayments over the life of the loan, (*falls der Kreditnehmer mit den ~ in Verzug geraten ist)* if the borrower has defaulted on his payment schedule (on his loan repayment commitments)

Tilgungs / ~mittel redemption funds, funds available for redemptions (repayments); **~modalitäten** repayment terms, terms of redemption (repayment), amortisation features; **~moratorium** standstill on capital repayments

Tilgungs / ~plan redemption schedule, loan repayment schedule (plan), amortisation schedule, schedule of maturities; **~prämie** redemption premium; **~quote** → Tilgungsrate

Tilgungs / ~rate redemption (amortisation) rate, redemption instalment, principal repayment rate; **~rechner** amortisation calculator; **~recht** right of redemption, call right; **~rückflüsse** repayments on loans, principal repayments

Tilgungs / ~rücklage redemption (amortisation) reserve, sinking fund reserve; **~rückstände** redemption (repayment) arrears, arrears of principal, arrears in principal payments

Tilgungs / ~satz repayment (redemption) rate; **~schuldverschreibung** redemption bond; **~streckung** maturity extension, extending the redemption period; **~streckungsdarlehen 1.** additional loan facility for the discount (Damnum, Disagio) deducted from the loan (mortgage) principal **2.** maturity extension loan, repayment-extending loan

Tilgungs / ~ströme redemption flows; **~stücke** securities repurchased, bonds redeemed in the market; **~-Swap** amortising swap □ swap in which the notional principal decreases during the contract period

Tilgungs / ~termin date of redemption; **~überhang** net redemptions (repayments), excess of redemptions

Tilgungs / ~valuta redemption currency; **~verhalten** loan repayment behaviour; **~verpflichtungen** redemption (repayment) commitments; **~verrechnung** interest-wise application of repayments to the loan principal

Tilgungs / ~volumen aggregate (total) redemptions, total of securities redeemed; **~vorbehalt** redemption (amortisation) proviso

Tilgungs / ~währung redemption currency; **~wert** redemption value, value upon redemption (repayment, amortisation)

Tilgungs / ~zahlung redemption payment, *(~en auf Hypothekendarlehen)* principal repayments on mortgage loans; **~zeitraum** redemption period, period of repayment; **~zwang** duty to redeem, obligatory (compulsory) redemption

Titel 1. executory title, enforceable instrument **2.** *(Überschrift)* heading **3.** *(Wertpapiere)* securities, → Stücke, *(~ der zweiten Reihe)* secondary stock (counters)

Titelverfahren contentious proceedings

titulieren to issue an enforceable title, *(titulierte Forderung)* title claim, claim (debt) based on an executory title

Tochtergesellschaft subsidiary, *(hundertprozentige ~)* wholly-owned subsidiary

tot *(~es Kapital)* idle funds, *(~es Konto) (a) (gesperrtes Konto)* blocked account *(b) (umsatzloses Konto)* dormant (inactive) account, *(~e Papiere)* inactive stock, *(~es Portefeuille)* blocked portfolio, *(einen ~en Punkt erreichen)* to reach an impasse, *(den ~en Punkt überwinden)* to break the deadlock

toxisch *(~e Papiere)* toxic securities

traditionell *(~es Geschäft)* mainstream business, core business, traditional line of business, *(~es Kreditgeschäft)* traditional (on-balance sheet) lending, *(~es Spargeschäft)* mainstream savings business

Traditionspapiere documents of title

tragbar *(~e Finanzierung)* viable (feasible) financing, *(~er Kompromiss)* acceptable (reasonable) compromise

träge *(Börsenumsätze)* sluggish, slack, flat

tragen 1. *(abwerfen)* to yield, to bring in, to produce **2.** *(die Folgen/die Verantwortung ~)* to bear the consequences/the responsibility **3.** *(die Kosten ~)* to bear (to meet, to cover, to pay) the cost **4.** *(Rechnung ~)* to take into account, to consider **5.** *(von einer kräftigen Binnennachfrage getragen werden)* to be fuelled by strong domestic demand

Träger 1. holder, bearer **2.** sponsor, sponsoring institution, principal supporter **3.** *(Gewährträger)* guaranteeing organisation, guarantor-owner **4.** *(Pfeiler)* mainstay, pillar

Träger / ~bank 1. sponsoring bank **2.** guaranteeing bank; **~instrument/~kontrakt** host instrument/contract □ contract that includes an embedded derivative; **~kapital** guaranteeing capital, capital subscribed and reserves

Träger / ~schaft 1. sponsorship **2.** ownership; **~unternehmen** sponsoring company; **~versammlung 1.** board of owners (guarantors) **2.** guarantors' (owners') meeting

tragfähig *(~e Grundlage)* solid basis, *(~e Lösung)* viable (workable) solution, *(~e Schuldenregelung)* practicable (acceptable) debt settlement, *(~es Unternehmenskonzept)* viable (tenable, well-founded) corporate concept

Tragfähigkeit 1. viability, tenability, sustainability **2.** carrying capacity **3.** → Risikotragfähigkeit

Tragweite importance, significance, implications, impact, consequences, repercussions

Tranche tranche, *(Finanzierung in mehreren ~n)* multi-tranche financing

tranchieren *(tranchierter Schuldtitel)* debt security issued in tranches, *(tranchierte Verbriefung)* tranched securitisation

Tranchierung tranching, splitting an issue into several classes of notes

Transaktion transaction, deal

transaktionsabhängig *(~es Entgelt)* transaction-based fee, *(~e Kosten)* transaction-related cost

Transaktions / ~abschluss concluding a transaction (a deal); **~autorisierung** transaction authorisation; **~bank** transaction bank, → Transaktionsgeschäft; **~berichterstattung** transaction reporting; **~beteiligter** party to a transaction

Transaktions / ~daten transaction data; **~entgelt** transaction fee; **~erfassung** trade capture; **~erlös** transaction proceeds; **~finanzierung** transactions financing

Transaktions / ~gebühr 1. transaction fee **2.** *(im Kartengeschäft)* item charge, interchange fee;**~geschäft** transaction banking, transaction services □ back office services, domestic and foreign payment services, securities settlement, electronic banking

Transaktions / ~größe transaction size; **~kennnummer** transaction ID; **~kosten** transaction (execution) cost; **~kostenbelastung** transaction cost charge; **~marketing** transaction (transaction-oriented) marketing; **~markt** transaction market, → Transaktionsgeschäft

Transaktionsnummer transaction authentication number (TAN)

Transaktionsregister Trade Repository, Trade Reporting Repository, *(~ für OTC-Derivate)* OTC Derivatives Trade Repository, → REGIS-TR, *(~ für OTC-Zins-Derivate)* Interest Rate Derivatives Trade Reporting Repository

Transaktionsrisiko transaction exposure (risk), potential loss associated with a transaction (e.g. time delay, adverse exchange rate movments)

Transaktions / ~struktur deal structure; **~volumen** volume transacted, bargains struck; **~währung** transaction currency

Transeuropäisches automatisiertes Echtzeit-Brutto-Zahlungssystem Trans-European Automated Real-Time Gross Settlement Express Transfer System (TARGET)

Transfer transfer; **~abkommen** transfer agreement; **~einkommen** transfer income (earnings); **~garantie** transfer guarantee

transferierbar transferable

Transferierbarkeit transferability

transferieren to transfer

Transfer / ~kosten transfer charges, cost of transfer; **~leistungen** transfer payments; **~mechanismus** transfer mechanism; **~moratorium** standstill on interest and capital repayments

Transfer / ~risiko transfer risk □ loss due currency transfer (conversion) restrictions; **~stelle** transfer agent; **~verpflichtung** obligation to transfer; **~zahlungen** transfer payments

Transformation *(~ in nationales Recht)* transformation into national law, *(~ bestehender Verpflichtungen)* transformation (conversion) of existing liabilities

Transformationsvolkswirtschaft transition economy

Transitkonnossement through bill of lading

transparent *(~er Fonds)* transparent (white) investment fund, *(~e Konditionengestaltung)* transparent pricing

Transparenz *(~ in der Kursstellung)* transparency in price-fixing

Transparenz / **~richtlinie** Transparency Directive; **~richtlinieumsetzungsgesetz** Transparency Directive Implementation Act; **~und Publizitätsgesetz** Transparency and Disclosure Act

Transport / **~dokumente** transport documents; **~kosten** cost of transportation, carriage; **~unternehmer** transport operator; **~versicherung** transport insurance, *(im Seefrachtverkehr)* (marine) cargo insurance; **~-Versicherungszertifikat/-Police** (marine) cargo insurance certificate/policy

TransPuG → Transparenz- und Publizitätsgesetz

Trassierungskredit documentary acceptance credit, reimbursement credit

Tratte draft

Tratten / **~ankauf** negotiation of drafts; **~ankaufsermächtigung** authority to take drafts; **~ankaufskredit** negotiation credit; **~einlösungsverpflichtung** undertaking to honour drafts; **~erlös/~gegenwert** draft proceeds

treiben **1.** *(den Dollar in die Höhe ~)* to push the dollar up against other currencies **2.** *(Kurse in die Höhe ~)* to drive (to force, to push) prices up, to propel prices upwards, *(treibende Kraft)* driving force, propellant, mainspring **3.** *(noch tiefer in die roten Zahlen ~)* to push further into the red

Trend **1.** *(Tendenz)* trend, tendency, *(~ zu niedrigeren Konditionen)* downward movement in pricing, *(~ zu einer längerfristigen Verschuldung)* trend towards longer-term debt **2.** *(Kurve)* graph

Trend / **~bereinigung** trend adjustment; **~bestätigungsformation** *(Chart-Analyse)* trend confirmation pattern; **~bestätigungsindikator** trend confirmation indicator; **~bruch** trend break; **~folgeindikator** trend following indicator

Trend / **~kanal** *(Chart-Analyse)* trend channel □ is formed when the stock price oscillates between a resistance and support line; **~linie** trendline; **~studie** trend analysis

Trend / **~umkehr** → Trendwende; **~umkehrformation** trend reversal pattern; **~umkehrsignal** trend reversal signal; **~wende** trend reversal, rebound, turn of the market, turnaround

Trennbankensystem dual banking system

trennbar separable, divisible

trennen **1.** to separate, to segregate, to sever, → getrennt **2.** *(abtrennen)* to detach **3.** *(teilen)* to divide, to split **4.** *(unterscheiden)* to distinguish, to differentiate **5.** *(sich von einer Beteiligung ~)* to sell an interest (stake), to divest, *(sich von Problemengagements ~)* to unload problem assets, to offload problem exposure

Trennung **1.** separation, segregation, severance **2.** detachment **3.** division, split

Trennungsaufwand severance pay

Treppen / **~kredit** graduated-interest loan; **~kupon** graduated coupon, interest rate (coupon) increasing/falling over the life of a loan, step-up/step-down coupon

Tresor strongroom, vault; **~fach** strongbox, safe deposit box; **~räume** vaults; **~vermietung** safe deposit service, hiring out strongboxes

Treu und Glauben *(Grundsatz von ~)* principle of loyalty, equity and good faith, *(Leistung nach ~)* performance in good faith, *(gegen ~ handeln)* to act against good faith

Treue / **~pflicht** duty of loyalty, → Treupflichten; **~verhältnis** fiduciary relationship

Treugeber trustor, trust creator, donor of a trust, settlor, grantor

Treugut trust property

Treuhand / **~abteilung** trust department; **~anlagen** trustee investments; **~auflagen** escrow requirements;

~**bank** trust bank company, trustee bank; ~**depot** → Treuhänderdepot; ~**einlagen** trustee deposits

Treuhänder trustee, fiduciary, fiduciary (escrow) agent, *(als ~ tätig sein)* to act as trustee, to trustee, to act in a fiduciary capacity, *(Ermessensvollmacht des ~s)* trustee discretion

Treuhänder / ~**ausschuss** trustee committee, committee of trustees; ~**depot** trustee portfolio, securities trust account, third-party custody account; ~**haftung** trustee's liability

treuhänderisch 1. *adj.* *(~e Registrierung)* fiduciary registration, *(~e Übertragung)* fiduciary transfer, *(~es Vermögen)* trust assets (property), assets (property) held in trust, *(~e Verpflichtung)* fiduciary duty
2. *adv.* *(~ halten)* to hold in trust (in escrow), *(~ verwahren)* to hold as trustee, to hold in a fiduciary capacity, *(Vermögenswerte ~ verwahren)* to administer assets (property) through a trust, to hold assets in trust, *(~ verwahrte Wertpapiere)* trust-held securities, *(Rechte ~ wahrnehmen)* to exercise rights (powers) in a fiduciary capacity

Treuhänder / ~**rechte** rights of a trustee, powers conferred upon a trustee; ~**schaft** trusteeship; ~**vertrag** *(in Verbindung mit Anleiheemissionen)* fiduciary agent agreement

Treuhand / ~**fonds** trust fund; ~**gebühren** trust fees; ~**gelder** trustee funds, fiduciary funds (deposits), money held in trust (in escrow)

Treuhand / ~**geschäfte** trust (trustee) operations, fiduciary business (activities, operations), *(Erträge aus ~n)* trust (fiduciary) investment income; ~**gesellschaft** trust company, trustee corporation, fiduciary company; ~**giroverkehr** fiduciary book entry transfers

Treuhand / ~**kommanditist** trustee acting as limited partner; ~**konto** trust (trustee) account, escrow account; ~**kredite** trustee loans □ loans extended under public lending schemes; the lending bank does not assume the loan risk; ~**modell** contractual trust arrangement

Treuhand / ~**stelle** trust agency (office); ~**stellung** trustee relationship; ~**urkunde** trust deed, trust indenture (instrument)

Treuhand / ~**verhältnis** trust, trusteeship, *(Begründung eines ~ses)* trust establishment (declaration), *(Aufhebung eines ~ses)* trust voidance; ~**vermögen** trust assets (property), property held in trust (through a trust)

Treuhand / ~**vertrag** trust (fiduciary) agreement, trust indenture, escrow agreement; ~**verwalter** trustee, fiduciary manager; ~**verwaltung** trust administration, fiduciary management, trusteeship, holding property in (on) trust, administration of assets through a trust

Treunehmer trustee, fiduciary debtor

Treupflichten fiduciary duties

triftig *(~er Kreditkündigungsgrund)* strong (valid, plausible) reason for calling in the loan

trotzen *(dem spekulativen Druck ~)* to withstand the speculative pressure

trüb *(~e Aussichten)* dismal (gloomy, bleak) outlook

Trudeln *(finanziell ins ~ kommen)* to fall into a financial tailspin, *(trudelnde Gesellschaft)* stricken (beleaguered) company

Turbulenzen *(~ an den Finanzmärkten)* turmoil (upheaval, disarray, helter-skelter) in the financial markets

Turnus rotation, *(in einem dreimonatigen ~ stattfinden)* to be held every three months, *(nach einem festgelegten ~ überprüfen)* to review at scheduled intervals

turnusmäßig *adj.* *(~e Überprüfung)* regular review, *adv.* in (by) rotation, *(~ ausscheiden)* to retire in rotation, *(~ wechselnder Vorsitz)* rotating presidency

U

Überangebot surplus (excessive) supply

überarbeiten 1. to revise, to review, to redraft **2.** to overhaul

Überarbeitung *(~ der Kreditvereinbarung)* revision of (redrafting) the loan agreement

überbeanspruchen to overstrain, to overstretch, to overstress, to overuse

Überbeanspruchung overstrain, *(~ des Kapitalmarktes durch eine steigende Zahl von Neuemissionen)* overstretching the capital market by a growing number of new issues

Überbeschäftigung overemployment

Überbesetzung *(personalmäßig)* overstaffing, overstrength

überbesichern to overcollateralise, to provide excess security

Überbesicherung *(~ der eingeräumten Fazilitäten)* overcollateralisation of the facilities granted

überbesteuern to overtax, to tax too heavily

Überbesteuerung overtaxing, excessive taxation

überbewerten to overvalue, *(überbewerte Aktie)* overpriced stock, top-heavy share, *(überbewertete Anlagen)* overvalued (overstated) assets, *(überbewertete Währung)* overvalued currency

Überbewertung overvaluation, overpricing, overstating

überbieten 1. to outbid, to overbid, to make a higher bid **2.** *(übertreffen)* to exceed, to surpass

Überblick survey, *(sich einen ~ über die finanzielle Lage verschaffen)* to get a general idea of the financial situation

überblicken to grasp, to understand, to have a clear idea (conception) of s.th.

überbringen to deliver

Überbringer bearer; **~klausel** bearer clause; **~scheck** bearer cheque

überbrücken 1. to bridge over, to fill a gap **2.** *(Meinungsverschiedenheiten ~)* to reconcile differences of opinion

Überbrückungs / ~finanzierung 1. bridge (bridge-over, interim) financing **2.** *(zur Überwindung aktueller Finanzschwierigkeiten)* emergency facility, makeshift loan; **~kredit** bridge (bridging, bridge-over) loan, bridging facility

überdecken 1. to provide surplus (excess) cover **2.** to cover up, to overlay

Überdeckung surplus cover

Überdeckungsstrategie overlay strategy

überdenken 1. *(die Anlagestrategien ~)* to reassess (to reappraise) the investment strategies **2.** *(eine Entscheidung ~)* to reconsider (to review) a decision **3.** *(die Konditionengestaltung ~)* to review (to reevaluate) the pricing policy

Überdividende superdividend, surplus dividend

überdrehen *(die Kreditschraube ~)* to overdo the credit squeeze

überdurchschnittlich *(~e Kursentwicklung)* above-average price performance, *(~e Rendite)* higher-than-average yield

übereignen to assign, to convey the property, to transfer the ownership

Übereignung transfer of title, property transfer (conveyance), transferring the property (ownership), → Sicherungsübereignung

Übereignungs / ~**anspruch** right to transfer of title (property); ~**erklärung 1.** change in ownership statement, ownership transfer statement **2.** declaration of assignment; ~**urkunde** deed of transfer (of conveyance); ~**vertrag** ownership (title) transfer agreement

übereilen to rush, to precipitate, *(übereilte Entscheidung)* overhasty (rash) decision

übereinkommen 1. to agree (upon) **2.** to sign a memorandum of understanding

Übereinkunft/Übereinkommen **1.** agreement, arrangement, accord, convention **2.** memorandum of understanding, *(~ aller Vertragsparteien)* agreement of all parties to the contract, *(zu einer ~ gelangen)* to reach an understanding

übereinstimmen 1. *(mit jmd. ~)* to agree (to concur) with s. o., *(nicht ~)* to disagree with s.o.**2.** *(sich im Einklang befinden)* to be in line with, to match, to be consistent with, to tally with, to harmonise, to dovetail **3.** *(konform gehen)* to conform to, to correspond with **4.** *(beachten, einhalten)* to comply with, to observe **5.** *(zusammenfallen, zeitlich ~)* to coincide

übereinstimmend matching, identical, *(~e Fristenstruktur auf der Aktiv- und Passivseite)* matching maturity pattern of assets and liabilities

Übereinstimmung 1. agreement, *(in ~ bringen mit)* to match, to bring into agreement, to reconcile, to harmonise, *(zeitlich)* to synchronise
2. *(Einhaltung)* compliance, *(in genauer ~ mit den Akkreditivbedingungen vorlegen)* to present in strict compliance with the terms and conditions of the documentary credit
3. *(Einstimmigkeit)* unanimity
4. *(Konformität)* conformity, compatibility, concurrence, accordance, harmony, *(fehlende ~)* lack of conformity (harmony), inconsistency
5. *(Zusammenfallen)* coincidence

Übereinstimmungs / ~**erklärung** compliance statement, declaration of compliance (conformity), compatibility statement; ~**nachweis** certificate of compliance; ~**zertifikat** compliance (compatibility) statement

überempfindlich *(~ gegen Zinsbewegungen)* oversensitive to interest rate movements

Übererlös *(~ aus der Verwertung)* surplus proceeds from the liquidation (realisation sale)

überfällig overdue, past due, unpaid after the date fixed for payment, *(~e Forderungen)* delinquent receivables, *(~er Kredit)* past due loan, delinquent (overdue) loan, *(~e Kurskorrektur)* overdue price correction, *(seit drei Monaten ~e Rückzahlungen)* repayments 90 days past due

überflügeln to exceed, to surpass, to outstrip, to outperform

Überfluss *(~ an Liquidität)* abundance (glut, wealth) of liquidity

überflüssig superfluous, unnecessary

überfluten *(den Markt ~)* to flood (to glut) the market

überfordern to overstrain, to overstretch, to make excessive demands, to overtax

Überforderung *(~ des Marktes)* overstretching the market

Überfremdung *(~ eines Unternehmens)* gradual control by outside (foreign) capital

überführen *(in die Erfolgsrechnung ~)* to transfer to the profit and loss account, *(in die Girosammelverwahrung ~)* to place in collective custody

Übergabe 1. delivery, surrender, handing over, handover, *(~ der Dokumente gegen Zahlung)* handing over the documents against payment
(~ am Schalter) delivery across (over) the counter, *(~ der effektiven Stücke)* constructive (actual) delivery, *(~ der Verantwortung)* handover of responsibility

U

2. *(Eigentumsübertragung)* transfer of title

Übergabevertrag 1. deed of transfer 2. succession treaty

Übergang 1. changeover (switch) to, *(~auf die neue Regelung)* transition to the new rules
2. transfer, devolution, *(~ der Eigentumsrechte)* change (transfer) of ownership, transfer (devolution) of title to property, *(~ von Rechten und Pflichten)* transfer (transmission) of rights and obligations, *(~ des Risikos)* passing of the risk
3. *(~ zwischen Geld- und Kapitalmarkt)* borderline between money and capital market

Übergangs / **~bestimmungen** transitional provisions, temporary regulations; **~periode** transitional period, transition phase; **~regelung** transitional arrangement; **~stufe** transitional stage

übergeben 1. to hand over, to deliver 2. *(anvertrauen)* to entrust to s. o., to commit to the custody of s.o. 3. *(übertragen)* to turn a matter over to, to transfer

übergehen 1. to pass to, to pass into s. o.'s possession, *(auf den neuen Eigentümer ~)* to pass into the hands of (to be transferred to) the new owner, *(kraft Gesetzes ~)* to pass by operation of law, *(vom Verkäufer auf den Käufer ~)* to pass from the seller to the buyer
2. to devolve, *(auf die Erben ~)* to devolve upon (to) the heirs
3. *(hinweggehen über)* to ignore, to pass s.th. over, to omit, to leave out

übergeordnet 1. superior, senior, *(~e Holdinggesellschaft)* parent holding company, *(~e Instanz)* higher authority, *(~es Kreditinstitut)* superordinated financial institution, *(~es Pfandrecht)* senior lien (charge)
2. *(vordringlich, vorrangig)* overriding

Übergewicht 1. overweight 2. *(Überlegenheit)* superiority, predominance, preponderance

übergewichten *(Aktien ~)* to overweight shares, to give an overweighting to shares

Übergewichtung overweighting

Übergewinn *(betrieblicher ~)* economic value added, added value on equity

übergreifen 1. to spread over, *(auf die europäischen Märkte ~)* to spill over into the European markets, *(auf den Rentenmarkt ~)* to feed through into the bond market
2. *jur.* to encroach upon, to infringe

Überhandnahme rapid increase (spread), excessive growth

Überhang 1. surplus, excess, *(~ an Aufträgen)* backlog of orders
2. oversupply, *(~ an alten Festsatzkrediten)* overhang of existing fixed rate loans
3. *(Überhangposition)* surplus position, *(~ an Kauf-/Verkaufs-Positionen)* net long/short positions

überhängig (~e *Emission)* issue not fully subscribed or sold

überhäufen *(mit Aufgaben)* to overburden, to swamp

überhitzen *(überhitzte Konjunktur)* overheated economy

überhöht excessive, *(~es Risiko)* excessive exposure, *(~e Rückstellungen)* overprovisioning

überholen 1. to overhaul 2. *(übertreffen)* to overtake, to surpass, to outstrip

überholt *(~es Abrechnungsverfahren)* outdated (obsolete) settlement procedure

überjährig *(~e Zinszahlung)* interest (coupon) payment for more than twelve months

Überkapazität surplus (excess) capacity

überkapitalisieren to overcapitalise, *(überkapitalisiertes Unternehmen)* top-heavy (overcapitalised) company

Überkapitalisierung overcapitalisation, surplus capitalisation

überkauft *(~er Markt)* overbought market

Überkauft / ~-Indikator *(Chart-Analyse)* overbought indicator; **~-Oszillator** oscillator indicating overbought conditions

überkompensieren to overcompensate

Überkompetenzkredit loan exceeding one's approval powers

Überkreuz / ~beteiligung cross-shareholding; **~kompensation** cross-segment compensation; **~verflechtung** *(~ von Vorstands-/Aufsichtsratsmandaten)* interlocking directorates

überladen 1. to overload **2.** *(überladener Markt)* top-heavy market

überlagern 1. to obscure, to overshadow **2.** to overlay

Überlagerung overlay, overlapping

Überlagerungsstrategie overlay strategy

Überlappung overlapping

überlassen 1. *(jmd. ~)* to leave to s.o (to s.o.'s discretion), to place at s. o.'s disposal, *(den Marktkräften ~)* to leave to the forces of the market
2. *(anvertrauen, übergeben)* to entrust, to hand over, to surrender, to transfer
3. *(abtreten)* to assign
4. *(im Geldhandel)* to sell, to lend, *(überlassende Bank)* selling (lending) bank

Überlassen *(~ der Dokumente)* handing over the documents, delivery of the documents, *(~ von Fremdwährungen)* foreign currency lending, *(~ der Nutzung)* surrender of use, *(~ von Tagesgeld)* selling overnight funds, lending overnight money, lending in the interbank market

U

überlasten to overburden, to overstrain

überleben to survive

Überlebensfähigkeit *(~ eines Unternehmens)* company's ability to survive, company's ability to remain afloat

überlegen *(Konkurrenzunternehmen ~ sein)* to outclass (to outperform) competing companies, *(zahlenmäßig ~)* superior in numbers

Überlegenheit *(~ am Markt)* superiority (preeminence) in the market

überleiten *(zum Cashflow aus der operativen Geschäftstätigkeit ~)* to reconcile to cash flow from operating activities

Überleitung reconciliation, *(~ vom betrieblichen Ergebnis zum Nettoergebnis)* reconciliation from operating results to net income, *(~ von ausgewiesenem Kapital zum anrechenbaren Kapital)* reconciliation of reported capital to eligible capital, *(~ auf den Konzernabschluss)* reconciliation to consolidated accounts

Überleitungsrechnung reconciliation accounts (statement)

Überliquidität surplus (excess) liquidity

Übermacht *(~ im Emissionsgeschäft)* supremacy (preponderance) in the new issue business

übermächtig superior, too powerful

übermäßig *(~ hohe Verschuldung)* excessive (exorbitant) debt

Übermittlungs / ~fehler error in transmission; **~weg** transmission channel

Übernachfrage excess (surplus) demand

Übernacht / ~einlagen overnight deposits; **~fazilität** overnight facility, → Spitzenrefinanzierungsfazilität; **~geld** overnight money

Übernacht-Index-Swap Overnight Index Swap (OIS) □ descriptive of an interest rate swap (→ Zins-Swap) in which the overnight rate is exchanged for a fixed interest rate, → LIBOR/OIS Differenz/Spread

Übernacht / ~kredit overnight credit, overnight lending; **~kreditzinsen** overnight borrowing/lending rates; **~liquidität** overnight liquidity; **~-Pensionsgeschäft** overnight repurchase agreement, overnight repo (with a term of one day)

Übernacht / ~pfandkredit overnight collateralised loan; **~positionen**

overnight positions (e.g. in the forex market); ~**risiko** overnight risk (exposure); ~**sätze** overnight rates

Übernahme 1. takeover, acquisition, purchase, *(~ durch Aktienaufkäufe an der Börse)* takeover through buying in the stock market, *(~ durch ein Konsortium von Investoren)* acquisition by a group of investors
(~ einer Mehrheitsbeteiligung) taking over a controlling interest, *(~ von Swaps auf Position)* taking swaps on one's book, warehousing of swaps, *(~ des Währungsrisikos)* taking on the currency risk
2. *(~ einer Emission)* taking up (underwriting) an issue, *(~ einer Konsortialquote)* taking up (down) a commitment
3. *(~ einer Garantie)* furnishing a guarantee, guarantee undertaking, *(~ der Haftung)* assumption of liability, *(~ einer Schuld)* assumption of a debt, *(~ der Waren zum Versand)* acceptance of goods for carriage
4. *(~ einer Erbschaft)* entrance upon an inheritance, accession to an estate
5. *(~ in nationales Recht)* transposition (translation) into national law

Übernahme / ~**abwehr** takeover defense; ~**angebot** takeover bid, tender offer; ~**finanzierung** acquisition financing, funding (financing) an acquisition

Übernahme / ~**garantie** underwriting commitment (guarantee), undertaking to underwrite (to take up) an issue; ~**gerüchte** takeover (acquisition) rumours, bid talk; ~**gesetz** German Takeover Act; ~**gewinn** gain on takeover

Übernahme / ~**kandidaten** shares of bid-for companies, takeover candidates; ~**klausel** *(in einem Hypothekenvertrag)* assumption clause, ~**kodex** Takeover Code, ~-**Konnossement** received for Shipment Bill of Lading (B/L)

Übernahme / ~**konsortium 1.** purchase group, takeover consortium **2.** underwriting syndicate (group); ~**kosten 1.** underwriting cost **2.** cost of acquisition; ~**kurs 1.** takeover price **2.** underwriting price; ~**ort** place of receipt; ~**provision** underwriting commission

Übernahme / ~**richtlinie** Takeover Directive; ~**risiko** underwriting risk (exposure); ~**strategie** takeover (acquisition) strategy

Übernahme / ~**verlust** loss on takeover; ~**verpflichtung 1.** firm bid **2.** undertaking to take up an issue (a financial instrument), underwriting commitment, *(Emission ohne ~)* non-underwritten issue; ~**verschulden** failure to take delivery; ~**vertrag 1.** purchase (takeover) agreement **2.** underwriting agreement

übernehmen 1. to take over, to purchase, to acquire, *(ein Unternehmen ~)* to take over a company, *(~de Gesellschaft)* acquirer, acquiring (transferee) corporation, *(~der Rechtsträger)* assuming entity, *(~ des Sondervermögen)* acquiring fund, → Sondervermögen
2. to take, *(den Basiswert ~) (bei Termingeschäften)* to take delivery of the underlying instrument, *(in den eigenen Bestand ~)* to take into one's own inventory (books)
3. to accept, to assume, *(zur Depotverwahrung ~)* to accept for (to take into) safekeeping, *(eine Emission ~)* to underwrite an issue, *(eine Garantie ~)* to assume (to furnish) a guarantee, to guarantee, *(übernommene Garantien/Gewährleistungen)* guarantees assumed, undertakings given
(das Obligo ~) to take on the liability, *(das Projektrisiko ~)* to take on (to shoulder) the risk of the project, *(die von den Banken übernommenen Risiken)* the risks taken on by the banks, *(die volle Verantwortung ~)* to assume full responsibility for
4. to receive, *(Waren zur Verschiffung ~)* to receive goods for shipment
5. to enter into, *(eine Position ~)* to enter into (to initiate) a position

U

6. to incorporate, *(in nationales Recht ~)* to incorporate (to translate, to transpose) into national law, *(in die neue Vereinbarung ~)* to incorporate (to import) into the new agreement

überordnen to give priority (precedence) to, → übergeordnet

Überpari-Emission issue above par, issue at a premium

überparteilich impartial, non-partisan, non-aligned

überproportional 1. *adj.* disproportionate, overproportional 2. *adv.* *(~ wachsen)* to grow at a disproportionately rapid pace, to grow overproportionally

überprüfen 1. to check, to examine, to vet, to investigate, to look into, *(die Richtigkeit ~)* to verify the correctness, *(anhand des Unterschriftenverzeichnisses ~)* to check against the list of authorised signatories
2. *(die Bücher ~)* to audit (to inspect) the books
3. to review, to reconsider

Überprüfung 1. check, examination, verification, investigation, *(~ der Bonität des Schuldners)* checking the creditworthiness of the borrower, *(~ der Einhaltung)* verifying compliance with ..., *(~ des Emissionsprospektes)* vetting the issuing prospectus, *(~ vor Ort)* on-site examination
2. audit, *(~ durch eine Aufsichtsbehörde)* regulatory audit (scrutiny)
3. review, reconsideration, *(~ eines Kreditengagements)* loan review

Überprüfungs / ~befugnis power of investigation; **~klausel** review clause; **~recht** right to investigate (to check), inspection right; **~verfahren** review process

überragen *(in der Leistung ~)* to outperform, to outstrip in performance

überragend *(~e Bedeutung)* overriding significance, *(~e Leistung)* outstanding performance

Überreaktion *(~ der Anleger)* overhasty investor response

überreichen 1. to present, to hand over 2. *(in der Anlage ~)* to enclose

überreizen *(die Konjunktur ~)* to overstimulate the economy

Überrendite excess return

übersättigen to oversaturate

Übersättigung *(~ des Emissionsmarktes)* oversaturation of the new issue market

überschatten *(den Markt ~)* to cast a shadow (to put a cloud) over the market, to overhang (to overshadow) the market

überschätzen 1. to overestimate, to overrate 2. *(im finanziellen Wert)* to overvalue, to value too highly, to set too high a value on

Überschätzung 1. overestimation, overrating 2. overvaluation

überschaubar *(~es Engagement)* manageable exposure

überschlagen 1. to make a rough estimate, to calculate approximately 2. *(auslassen)* to omit, to skip

Überschlagsrechnung rough estimate (calculation)

überschneiden 1. to overlap, *(sich ~de Kompetenzen/Vollmachten)* overlapping responsibilities/powers 2. *(zusammenfallen)* to coincide

Überschneidung overlapping, coincidence

überschreiben 1. *(übertragen)* to transfer, to sign over to 2. *(Besitz ~)* to convey, to settle on s. o., to register in s. o.'s name

Überschreibung 1. transfer 2. conveyance

überschreiten 1. to exceed, to be in excess of, to go beyond, to break, *(das Budget ~)* to overstep the budget, *(die vereinbarte Kreditgrenze ~)* to exceed the credit limit agreed upon, *(die Planzahlen ~)* to overrun the budgeted figures, *(das Zahlungsziel um zwei*

Monate ~) to exceed (to stretch) the credit period by two months
2. *(verstoßen gegen)* to violate, to infringe

Überschreitung 1. exceeding, stretching, *(~ des Geldmengenziels)* overshooting the monetary target, *(~ des Kreditrahmens)* exceeding the credit line, *(~ der Widerstandslinie)* breaking the resistance level
2. violation, infringement

überschulden *(überschuldetes Unternehmen)* overleveraged (superleveraged) company, overgeared company

Überschuldung 1. debt overload, overindebtedness, excessive debt burden, excess of debts over assets **2.** overgearing, overleveraging

Überschuldungsbilanz statement of overindebtedness

Überschuss 1. surplus, excess
2. net income, *(~ aus dem Eigenhandel)* net income from proprietary trading, proprietary trading profit, *(~ der Erträge aus dem Dienstleistungsgeschäft)* net income from service transactions
(~ aus dem laufenden Geschäft) net income from (on) current operations, *(~ aus Zinsen und Provisionen)* net interest and commission income
3. *(Saldo)* balance

Überschuss / ~beteiligung policyholder's surplus, *(überschussberechtigter Lebensversicherungsvertrag)* participating life contract; **~betrag** surplus amount, **~gelder** surplus funds, *(Rückführung der ~)* recycling of surplus funds; **~guthaben** surplus balances (funds)

überschüssig excessive, surplus, *(~e Kassenmittel)* surplus funds, *(~e Sicherungsanteile)* excess collateral

Überschuss / ~kapital surplus capital, amount of capital exceeding regulatory capital requirements; **~land** surplus country; **~marge** *(bei einer ABS-Emission)* excess spread □ net interest received from underlying assets after the investors and expenses have been paid

Überschuss / ~position surplus position, net income position, *(~ im Devisenhandel)* net long position; **~rechnung** statement of income; **~rendite** excess return (yield)

Überschuss / ~reserven surplus reserves, freely available liquidity ; **~spanne** → Überschussmarge; **~sparen** arrangement that provides for an automatic transfer of surplus funds from a current account to a savings account

überschwemmen *(den Markt ~)* to glut (to flood, to congest) the market

übersehen *(den Fälligkeitstermin ~)* to overlook (to miss, to fail to observe) the date set for payment, *(der Posten wurde ~)* the item was passed over

übersenden 1. to send, to forward **2.** *(Gelder)* to remit, *(übersendende Bank)* remitting bank

Übersender 1. sender **2.** remitter

Übersicherung → Überbesicherung

Übersicht 1. survey, overview **2.** *(Zusammenfassung)* summary, roundup

übersichtlich *(~e Analyse)* clear (well-structured, clear-cut) analysis

Übersichtszeitraum period under review

überspringen *(den Stand von 2000 ~)* to clear the 2,000 mark

überstehen *(die finanzielle Krise ~)* to weather (to ride out) the financial crisis

übersteigen *(die Erwartungen ~)* to exceed the expectations, *(die Möglichkeiten einer einzigen Gesellschaft ~)* to go (to be) beyond the resources of any one company

übersteigern to outbid

übersteuern *(in der Geldpolitik)* to oversteer monetary policy

überstimmen to outvote, to overrule, to vote against

Überstimmung outvoting, defeat by a majority of votes, overruling

überstrapazieren *(die finanzielle Belastbarkeit ~)* to overstretch the financial resources

überstürzt *(~e Positionenauflösung)* precipitous (rash, overhasty) winding up of positions

überteuern to overcharge, *(überteuerte Aktie)* overpriced stock

Übertrag **1.** *(von Gewinnen oder Verlusten auf die nächste Rechnungsperiode)* carryover, amount carried over, amount brought forward
2. *(Kontoübertrag)* transfer to another account

übertragbar **1.** transferable, *(~es Akkreditiv)* transferable (assignable) documentary credit, *(durch Indossament ~)* transferable (negotiable) by endorsement
2. conveyable **3.** conferrable

Übertragbarkeit *(~ eines Darlehens)* transferability of a loan, *(~ einer Forderung)* assignability of a claim

übertragen **1.** to transfer, to convey, to assign, *(die Besitzrechte ~)* to convey (to transfer) the title to property, *(die Forderungen auf die Bank ~)* to transfer (to assign) the receivables to the bank, *(auf den Namen von AB ~)* to transfer into the name of AB
2. to confer on, to vest in, to delegate, *(ein Anrecht auf einen Dritten ~)* to vest an interest in a third party, *(die dem Bevollmächtigten ~en Vollmachten)* the powers conferred on (vested in) the donee
(dem neuen Eigentümer alle Rechte ~) to vest all rights in the new owner, *(eine Vollmacht ~)* to confer a power, *(aufgrund der mir ~en Vollmacht)* pursuant to the power vested in me
3. *(Zeichnungsberechtigung ~)* to delegate signature authority to …
4. *(Daten ~)* to transmit data

übertragend *(~er Rechtsträger)* transferring (transferor) entity, *(~e Sanierung)* asset deal, transfer/sale of the assets of an insolvent company to a new legal entity, *(~es Unternehmen)* transferor company, *(~es Sondervermögen)* transferring fund

Übertragende/r transferor

Übertragung **1.** transfer, conveyance, assignment, *(~ von Aktien)* stock transfer, *(~ der Eigentumsrechte)* transfer of title (ownership), title transfer, *(~ von Grundbesitz)* conveyance of (conveying) real property, real estate transfer, *(~ durch Indossament)* transfer by endorsement, *(~ mit taggleicher Valuta)* same-day transfer, *(zum Zeitpunkt der ~)* at the time of transfer
2. *(~ von Vollmachten)* conferring (delegation of) powers
3. *(~ der Verwaltung)* entrusting (delegating) the management to
4. transmission of data

Übertragungsanordnung transfer order □ order by which the Federal Financial Supervisory Authority may force an endangered bank to transfer its business to another bank, → Brückenbank, → Restrukturierungsgesetz

Übertragungs / ~anspruch claim (right) to the transfer of the legal title; **~anzeige** notification of transfer (assignment)

Übertragungs / ~berechtigte/r beneficiary holding a claim to transfer of title, party (entity) entitled to transfer of the legal title; **~bilanz** transfer payments account, balance on transfer payments, *(Aktiv-/Passivsaldo der ~)* surplus/deficit on transfer payments

Übertragungs / ~einkommen income from current transfers; **~empfänger** transferee, beneficiary holding a legal claim for transfer of title

Übertragungs / ~gebühr transfer fee (charges); **~genehmigung** authority to transfer, transfer permit (approval)

Übertragungs / ~stelle transfer agent (office); **~urkunde** **1.** deed of conveyance (of transfer), conveyancing instrument, transfer deed (instrument)
2. vesting deed (instrument)

U

Übertragungs / ~vermerk endorsement, notation of transfer, *(~ zugunsten der Bank)* endorsement in favour of the bank; **~verpflichtung** obligation (undertaking, duty) to transfer, covenant to transfer; **~vollmacht** power to transfer

Übertragungs / ~wert value upon transfer, transfer price, value of assets transferred; **~zahlungen** transfer payments

übertreffen to outperform, to outstrip, to outmatch, *(das Ergebnis des Vorjahres ~)* to beat (to better, to outmatch) last year's performance, *(den Index weit ~)* to outperform the index by a wide margin, *(die Prognosen ~)* to surpass (to top) the forecasts

übertreiben to exaggerate, to overdo, *(übertriebene Sicherungsanforderungen)* exaggerated (excessive) collateral requirements

Übertreibung exaggeration, overstatement

übertreten *(Gesetze, Vorschriften)* to infringe, to violate, to contravene

Übertretung infringement, violation, contravention, breach

übertünchen *(die schwierige Finanzlage ~)* to gloss (to paper) over the difficult financial situation

überverkauft *(~er Markt)* oversold market

Überverkauft-Index/Indikator *(Chart-Analyse)* oversold index/indicator

überversichern to overinsure, *(überversichert)* overinsured, insured for more than the real value

überwachen to supervise, to control, to screen, *(den Anlageerfolg laufend ~)* to monitor continuously the investment performance, *(das Kreditgewerbe ~)* to supervise banks and financial institutions, *(die Marktaktivitäten ~)* to oversee market activities

Überwachung supervision, monitoring, control, *(~ durch die Aufsichtsbehörden)* regulatory supervision (scrutiny), *(~ einer Darlehensverpflichtung)* monitoring a loan commitment (an exposure), *(~ der Finanzmärkte)* financial supervision, monitoring (overseeing) operations in the financial markets *(genaue ~ der Risiken)* keeping a close watch on exposures, *(~ der laufenden Tätigkeit)* surveillance of ongoing operations, *(~ des Wertpapiergeschäfts)* supervision (control) of securities operations

Überwachungs / ~aufgaben/~funktionen supervisory duties; **~behörde** supervisory authority, monitoring agency; **~instrumente** monitoring tools; **~kompetenzen** supervisory powers; **~kosten** cost of supervision, supervisory cost(s)

Überwachungs / ~organ supervisory body (authority, agency); **~pflicht** supervisory duty, monitoring duty; **~techniken** techniques of monitoring; **~vorlage** loan monitoring file

überwältigen to overwhelm, *(mit ~der Stimmenmehrheit)* by an overwhelming majority of votes

überwälzen to pass on, to shift

überwechseln *(auf Rentenanlagen ~)* to switch over to bond market investments

überweisen to transfer, to remit, *(~de Bank)* remitting bank, *(elektronisch ~)* to remit electronically

Überweisung (credit) transfer, remittance, money transmission, *(~en aus dem Ausland/aus dem Interbankgeschäft)* credit transfers from abroad/from interbank business

Überweisungs / ~abkommen credit transfer agreement; **~abteilung** payments department, money transmission service; **~auftrag** payment (remittance) order, credit transfer order, money transmission order, funds transfer instruction; **~auftraggeber** remitter, sender, principal, originator; **~ausgänge** outgoing credit transfers

Überweisungs / ~betrag amount transferred, principal amount; **~eingänge** incoming transfers, credit transfers received; **~empfänger** beneficiary, remittee; **~form** method of transfer, form of remittance; **~formular** credit transfer form, transfer form (slip)

Überweisungs / ~gebühren transfer (remittance) charges, money transmission charges; **~geschäft** funds transfer activities, → Überweisungsverkehr; **~gesetz** German Credit Transfer Act; **~gutschrift** credit for payment(s) received; **~system** credit transfer system

Überweisungs / ~träger transfer slip (voucher), credit transfer voucher; **~verkehr** funds transfer, credit transfer operations, credit transfers, money transmission services; **~vordruck** → Überweisungsformular; **~zweck** remittance information

überwiegen to outweigh, to prevail, to predominate, *(Gewinnchancen ~ die Risiken)* profit chances outweigh risks, *(Kursrückgänge überwogen)* falls predominated, declines led (outscored) advances

überwiegend predominant, preponderant, *(~ fester bei lebhaften Umsätzen)* mainly higher in active trading, *(~ schwächer)* predominantly lower, *(zum ~en Teil)* for the most part

überwinden 1. *(eine Reihe von Hindernissen ~)* to surmount a host of obstacles **2.** *(den toten Punkt ~)* to break the impasse **3.** *(finanzielle Schwierigkeiten ~)* to overcome (to get over) financial difficulties

Überzahlerstatus status of surplus payer

U

überzeichnen to oversubscribe, *(die Emission wurde mehr als 6mal überzeichnet)* the issue has been more than 6 times oversubscribed

Überzeichnung 1. *(~ einer Neuemission)* oversubscription, surplus of applications for an issue **2.** *(~ von Finanzrisiken)* overexposure

überzeugen 1. to convince, *(~der Beweis)* substantial (convincing, persuasive) evidence, *(~de Leistung)* convincing performance **2.** *(überreden)* to persuade

Überzeugung conviction, persuasion

Überzeugungskraft persuasive power

überziehen 1. *(ein Konto ~)* to overdraw an account, to go into overdraft **2.** *(eine Kreditlinie ~)* to exceed a credit line, *(das Konto ist um mehr als …€ überzogen)* the account is overdrawn by more than € …

Überziehung 1. overdraft, amount overdrawn, *(60 Tage nach der ersten ~)* 60 days after the first overdraft occurrence **2.** overdrawing an account, exceeding a credit line

Überziehungs / ~genehmigung permission to overdraw; **~kompetenz** overdraft approval powers; **~kredit** overdraft facility, advance on current account; **~limit** overdraft limit, drawing limit

Überziehungs / ~möglichkeit overdraft facility (option), *(~ bis zum dreifachen Nettogehalt)* overdraft line of up to three times net monthly salary; **~provision** overdraft commission; **~rahmen** overdraft facility; **~zinsen** overdraft interest

überzogen *(~e Forderungen)* excessive demands, unreasonably high demands, *(~ restriktiv)* exaggeratedly restrictive, overrestrictive

üblich usual, customary, *(allgemein ~ im Bankgewerbe)* common practice in the banking industry, *(~e Bankpraxis)* established (customary) banking practice, *(zu den ~en Konditionen)* at the usual terms (and rates), *(~e Schlusseinheit)* standard unit of trade, normal trading unit

übriger umfassender Periodenerfolg other comprehensive income

Übung *(betriebliche ~)* corporate custom (and practice), → Grundsätze der betrieblichen Übung

UG → Unternehmergesellschaft

Ultimo 1. *(Monatsultimo)* end-of-month, last trading day of a month 2. *(Jahresultimo)* year-end

Ultimo / ~abrechnung end-of-month settlement; **~ausschläge** end-of-month fluctuations (swings)

ultimobedingt *(~e Glattstellung)* end-of-month position squaring

Ultimo / ~differenz 1. net end-of-month balance 2. difference between settlement and forward rate; **~dispositionen** end-of-month trading arrangements, tidying trading books up for the end of the month; **~fälligkeit** end-of-month maturity

Ultimo / ~geld end-of-month loan □ short-term loan repayable on the last trading day of a month; **~geschäft** transaction for end-of-month settlement; **~glattstellungen** end-of-month position squaring; **~gültigkeit** validity until the end of the month, *(ultimogültige Order)* buy/sell order good till the end of the month

Ultimo / ~handel dealings (trading) for end-of-month settlement; **~kurs** end-of-month quotation; **~regulierung** end-of-month settlement; **~vorbereitungen** *(~ auf der kurzen Seite)* end-of-month dealings at the short end; **~wechsel** bill maturing at the end of the month

umändern to change, to modify, to alter

umarbeiten to revise, to review

Umbau restructuring, reshaping, *(vollständiger ~)* complete shake-up, drastic reorganisation

umbauen 1. to reorganise, to restructure, to reshape 2. *(umbauter Raum)* building volume

Umbauphase reorganisation (restructuring) phase

umbenennen to rename

umbilden to reorganise, *(die Konzernspitze ~)* to reshape (to reshuffle) the group management

Umbruch profound (radical) change, sea-change

umbuchen 1. *(auf ein anderes Konto ~)* to transfer to another account, *(in Gewinn und Verlust ~)* to reclassify to profit and loss
2. *(stornieren)* to reverse an entry

Umbuchung 1. transfer to another account, account transfer, reclassification
2. reversal, reversing an entry, *(~ aus/in Rücklagen)* transfer from (to) reserves

umdisponieren to rearrange, to make new arrangements (plans), to regroup, to reorganise

Umdisposition *(~ von Anlagen)* regrouping (rearrangement, reallocation) of investments, switching over into other forms of investment (e. g. shares, bonds)

Umfang 1. volume, size, magnitude, *(ein Geschäft gleichen ~s)* a deal of the same magnitude, *(~ der Handelsaktivitäten)* volume of trading, *(~ der Verluste)* size of the losses
2. scale, degree, measure, *(in einem geringen ~)* on a small (minor) scale, *(in einem nicht geringen ~ davon abhängen)* to depend in no small measure on, *(Kreditaufnahme in einem großen ~)* large-scale borrowing
(Positionen in einem großen ~ glattstellen) to liquidate positions on a massive scale, *(im ungefähr gleichen ~ anziehen)* to advance at roughly the same pace
3. *(~ einer Versicherung)* coverage, extent of the insured interest
4. *(~ einer Vollmacht)* extent (range) of a power

umfangreich *(~e Investitionen)* extensive investments, *(~e Kreditaufnahme)* sizeable borrowing, *(~e Rücklagen)* ample reserves, *(~e Unterlagen)* copious records

umfassen to comprise, to include, *(eine mehrere Gesellschaften ~de Gruppe)* a group embracing several companies

umfassend *(~e Aktienanalyse)* comprehensive (detailed) analysis of the stock

market, (*~e Bemühungen)* wide-ranging efforts, (*~e Deckung)* comprehensive (global) coverage
(*übriger ~er Periodenerfolg)* other comprehensive income, (*~e Sanierung)* thorough-going restructuring, (*~e Statistik)* comprehensive statistics, (*~e Vollmachten)* wide-ranging (far-reaching, broad) powers

Umfeld environment, background, scenario, (*~ für Banken)* operating environment for banks, banking climate

umfinanzieren to refinance (to reconstruct) debt, to renegotiate an existing debt (payment obligation)

Umfinanzierung debt refinancing (rescheduling), (*~ der bestehenden Verbindlichkeiten)* renegotiating (restructuring) existing debt, reshaping the debt portfolio

Umfirmierung corporate name change

umformen to reshape, to remodel

Umfrage poll, survey, inquiry

Umgang (*im ~ mit Privatkunden)* when dealing with private (retail) customers

umgedreht (*~er Wechsel)* → Umkehrwechsel

umgehen to circumvent, to evade, to side-step, (*den Aktienmarkt ~)* to steer clear of the equity market, (*die Kreditinstitute ~)* to bypass the banking system, (*das Problem ~)* to find a way round the problem, (*eine Steuer ~)* to avoid a tax, (*seine vertraglichen Verpflichtungen ~)* to escape (to evade) one's contractual obligations

Umgehung circumvention, bypassing, evasion, avoidance

Umgehungsgeschäft (*steuerliches)* transaction designed to avoid a tax

umgekehrt 1. *adj.* reverse, opposite, inverted, (*~er Becher/Charttechnik)* inverted bowl, rounding top, (*~es Dreieck)* broadening formation, inverted triangle formation (pattern) □ bearish chart pattern predicting a downward breakout
(*~es Factoring)* reverse factoring, supplier factoring, (*~er Floater)* reverse (inverse) floater □ bond/note whose yield fluctuates inversely to the general trend in interet rates
(*~er Inkassoweg)* reverse (reversed) collection route, (*~e Kopf-Schulter-Formation)* inverse head and shoulders formation □ consolidation or continuation pattern, (*~er Markt)* inverted market condition, → Deport
(*~es Pensionsgeschäft)* reverse repo, reverse repurchase transaction □ repurchase agreement (→ Pensionsgeschäft) seen from the perspective of the party who is buying the securities, (*in ~er Reihenfolge)* in inverse order
(*~e Untertasse)* inverse saucer □ technical chart formation indicating the end of an upward trend, → Untertassenformation, (*~e Zinsstruktur)* inverted interest rate structure □ short-term interest rates are higher than long-term rates
2. *adv.* conversely, vice versa, contrariwise, by the same token

umgestalten 1. to reshape, to revamp, to reorganise 2. to repackage, to reassemble

Umgestaltung 1. reshaping, readjustment, (*~ von Geschäftsprozessen)* business process redesign 2. (*von Anleihen/Krediten)* repackaging of bonds/loans

umgliedern 1. (*Bilanzpositionen)* to reclassify, to restate, (*umgegliederte Finanzinstrumente)* reclassified financial instruments
2. (*den Konzern ~)* to restructure the group

Umgliederung reclassification, restatement, restructuring

umgrenzen (*die Kreditkompetenzen ~)* to define the loan approval powers

umgründen to change a company's legal form

umgruppieren to regroup, to rearrange, to reorganise, to redeploy, to reclassify

Umgruppierung regrouping, rearrangement, reorganisation, redeployment, reclassification

Umkategorisierung *(~ finanzieller Vermögenswerte)* reclassification of financial assets

Umkehr reversal, rebound, turnaround, turning point, *(~ der Beweislast)* reversal of the burden of proof, *(~ des bisherigen Trends)* reversal of the earlier trend, *(~ in der Zinsentwicklung)* interest rate rebound, turnaround in the direction of interest rates

umkehren 1. *(den Abwärtstrend ~)* to reverse the downward trend **2.** *(das Zahlungsbilanzdefizit ~)* to turn round the balance of payments deficit **3.** *(sich ~)* to go into reverse, → umgekehrt

Umkehr / ~formation *(Chart-Analyse)* reversal pattern □ technical chart formation indicating the reversal of a trend, → Kopf-Schulter-Formation; **~linie** return line; **~-Pensionsgeschäft** → umgekehrtes Pensionsgeschäft

Umkehr-Swap reverse (reversal) swap □ counterbalancing the original swap position by entering into another swap agreement identical in terms of maturity, reference rate and notional principal

Umkehrung *(~temporärer Differenzen)* reversal of temporary differences

Umkehr / ~wechsel inverted bill, bill drawn by a supplier and discounted by the drawee (buyer); **~zins** interest rate marking a turn of the market

Umkippen *(~ der Stimmung am Aktienmarkt)* turnaround in stock market sentiment

umklassifizieren *(Kredite in das Anlagebuch ~)* to reclassify loans to the trading book

Umklassifizierung reclassification

Umladekonnossement trans(s)hipment bill of lading

Umladung trans(s)hipment

Umlage 1. *(Abgabe)* levy, rate **2.** *(Beitrag)* contribution **3.** *(~ von Kosten)* cost apportionment (allocation) **4.** *(pl)* operating costs (expenses)

umlagefähig *(~e Kosten)* apportionable cost

Umlage / ~gebühr assessment fee; **~schlüssel** allocation (apportionment) formula

Umlauf 1. circulation, *(im ~ befindliche Banknoten und Münzen)* currency (notes and coins) in circulation, *(in ~ bringen) (a)* to put into circulation *(b) (Banknoten)* to emit (to issue) bank notes, *(aus dem ~ ziehen)* to withdraw from circulation
2. volume outstanding, *(~ der Eigenakzepte)* own acceptances outstanding, *(~ an festverzinslichen Wertpapieren)* fixed income securities (fixed rate bonds) outstanding
3. *(Aktien im freien ~)* free float, publicly held stock

Umlauf / ~beschluss circular resolution (decision); **~verfahren** *(Beschlussfassung im ~)* passing a resolution by (through) circulation

umlaufend *(~e Stammaktien)* ordinary stock in issue, common stock outstanding, current float

umlauffähig 1. negotiable, tradeable **2.** accepted as legal tender

Umlauf / ~geschwindigkeit velocity of circulation; **~grenze** issue limit, issuing ceiling, limit for (on) the number of bonds outstanding

umlaufintensiv *(~er Betrieb)* company with a high proportion of current assets

Umlauf / ~kapital current capital; **~kredit** operating loan; **~markt** secondary market, market for outstanding securities; **~mittel** operating funds

Umlauf / ~rendite current (running) yield, current yield to maturity; **~vermögen** current assets, net working capital; **~volumen** volume outstanding, securities (bonds, stock) outstanding

umlegen to allocate, to apportion

Umlegung *(~ der Kosten)* cost allocation, apportionment of the expenses

umleiten/umlenken *(Kapital ~)* to divert (to redirect) capital

Umleitung/Umlenkung diversion, redirection

Umorganisation reorganisation, restructuring

umorganisieren to reorganise, to restructure

umorientieren to reorientate, to redirect, to reposition

Umorientierung 1. *(~ der Geldpolitik)* reorientation of monetary policy 2. *(~ am Markt)* repositioning in the market

Umplatzierung secondary public offering, *(~ von Fondsanteilen)* shares exchange

umrechnen to convert, to translate, *(in Basispunkte ~)* to translate into basis points, *(zum Durchschnittskurs der Rechnungsperiode ~)* to translate at the average rate for the period *(zum amtlichen Jahresendkurs ~)* to translate at the official year-end rate, *(auf eine Jahresrate ~)* to express as an annual rate, to annualise, *(zu 100 % in ein Kreditäquivalent ~)* to convert at 100 % to a credit equivalent, *(zu den ursprünglichen Wechselkursen ~)* to convert (to translate) at historical rates of exchange

Umrechnung conversion, translation, *(~ ausländischer Vermögenswerte in die Inlandswährung)* translating foreign assets into the national currency, *(~zum Kassakurs des Bilanzstichtages)* translation at the spot rate valid on the balance sheet date

U

Umrechnungs / ~differenzen translation differences (adjustments); **~faktor** *(für die Umrechnung in Kreditäquivalenzbeträge)* conversion factor; **~gewinn** gain on conversion (translation), currency translation gain

Umrechnungs / ~kurs conversion rate (price); **~risiko** translation risk (exposure), risk of loss (risk of a negative impact on the company's financial statements) due to changes in currency exchange rates

Umrechnungs / ~verfahren conversion (translation) method; **~verhältnis** conversion ratio; **~verlust** loss on conversion (translation), currency translation loss

umreißen *(eine Strategie ~)* to sketch (to map out) a strategy

Umsatz turnover, sales

Umsätze *(an der Börse)* trading, dealings, turnover, market activity, *(~ in Finanztiteln blieben gering)* activity in financials remained at a low ebb, *(~ an den Futures- und Optionsmärkten)* transaction volumes (trading) in the futures and options markets *(~ in Kurzläufern)* dealings in shorts, *(~ in Rentenwerten)* bond dealings (sales), *(~ gegen Schluss der Börsensitzung)* late trading (dealings), *(die über das Konto geleiteten ~)* the movements (transactions) routed through the account

Umsatz / ~anstieg → Umsatzsteigerung; **~aussichten** sales prospects; **~belebung/~erholung** pick-up in turnover; **~ergebnisse** sales performance; **~ergiebigkeit** → Umsatzrendite

Umsatz / ~erlöse sales revenue, *(Bilanzposten)* sales, *(~ je MAK)* revenue per full-time equivalent (FTE); **~finanzierung** sales financing; **~flaute** stagnation (slackness) in sales; **~höhe** turnover level; **~information** transaction information

umsatzkongruent *(~es Finanzierungsinstrument)* financing tool matched (geared) to the borrower's turnover

Umsatz / ~kostenverfahren cost of sales accounting method; **~kredit** business (operating) loan

umsatzlos *(~es Konto)* dormant (inactive) account

umsatzmäßig in terms of turnover (of sales)

Umsatz / ~**minderung** → Umsatzrückgang; ~**minus** sales shortfall (deficit); ~**plus** sales increase, → Umsatzsteigerung; ~**provision** sales (turnover) commission; ~**rendite** earnings to sales ratio; ~**rückbelastung** *(im Kartengeschäft)* chargeback

Umsatzrückgang decline in sales, sales setback, *(~ an der Börse)* decline in trading volume, contraction in market volume, volume shrinkage, decline in the number of contracts traded, *(~ am Interbanken-Markt)* decline of activity in the interbank market

umsatzschwach *(~e Aktie)* inactive stock (issue), stock that trades on a very low volume, *(~es Konto)* inactive account, account showing slack movements

Umsatz / ~**schwäche** weakness in turnover; ~**spitzenreiter** *(Börse)* volume leader, most actively traded share (contract); ~**sprung** leap in sales; ~**stagnation** flagging sales

umsatzstark *(~e Aktie)* actively traded stock, high-turnover stock, *(~es Konto)* high-activity account, large-volume account

Umsatzsteigerung sales increase (upturn), *(~ an der Börse)* increase in turnover, upturn in trading (in dealings), increase in market volume (in the number of contracts traded)

Umsatzsteuer value-added tax, turnover tax, *(umsatzsteuerliche Organschaft)* tax group for VAT purposes; ~**erklärung** VAT return; ~**rückvergütung** VAT refund; ~**voranmeldung** advance VAT return; ~ **vorauszahlung** advance VAT payment

Umsatz / ~**träger** mainstay of turnover, main pillar of sales; ~**übertrag** *(im Rahmen einer Cash-Pooling-Vereinbarung)* transfer of debit and credit balances; ~**verlagerung** shift in sales; ~**verlust** sales deficit, → Umsatzrückgang

Umsatz / ~**volumen** sales volume, transaction (trading) volume, aggregate turnover; ~**vorgabe** projected sales; ~**wachstum** growth in sales (turnover); ~**zahlen** sales figures, number of contracts traded

umschichten to regroup, to rearrange, *(Anlagen von Aktien in Rentenwerte ~)* to shift investments from stocks into fixed income securities, *(die Bilanz ~)* to restructure the balance sheet, *(Fördergelder ~)* to reallocate development funds, *(in andere Währungen ~)* to switch into other currencies, *(das Wertpapierportefeuille ~)* to regroup the securities portfolio

Umschichtung regrouping, reallocation, rearrangement, *(~ von Spareinlagen in höher rentierliche Anlageformen)* switching out of savings deposits into higher-yielding investments, *(~ von Wertpapierbeständen)* *(a)* regrouping of securities investments (e.g. reallocations between fixed interest and equity investmens) *(b)* portfolio switching

Umschichtungsfinanzierung debt refinancing (refunding), converting short-term obligations into long-term debt

Umschlag 1. transshipment **2.** *(Umsatz)* turnover

umschlagen to go into the reverse, to change to the contrary

Umschlagshäufigkeit turnover rate (ratio)

umschreiben 1. *(Besitzrechte)* to re-register, to transfer to … **2.** *(neu fassen)* to rewrite, to redraft

Umschreibung transferring to, re-registration, recording a change of ownership

Umschreibungs / ~**bewilligung** reregistration authority; ~**kosten** reregistration expenses (fee)

umschuldbar *(~e Verbindlichkeiten)* debt eligible for rescheduling

umschulden to reschedule (to restructure, to renegotiate) a debt

U

Umschuldung 1. debt rescheduling (restructuring), renegotiating existing loan facilities, *(~ notleidender Kredite)* restructuring troubled loans
2. debt conversion, calling in a high-interest bond or repaying a high-interest loan and replacing it by a low-interest-paying debt

Umschuldungs / ~abkommen rescheduling agreement (accord); **~anleihe** reorganisation (conversion) bond; **~bedarf** debt restructuring requirements; **~engagements** rescheduling commitments (exposure)

Umschuldungs / ~forderungen 1. claims under rescheduling agreements 2. debt to be rescheduled; **~kredit** rescheduling facility; **~land** rescheduling country; **~paket** rescheduling package

Umschuldungs / ~vereinbarung rescheduling agreement, debt restructuring agreement; **~verhandlungen** debt-restructuring negotiations; **~welle** welter of debt restructuring; **~zeitraum** rescheduling period

Umschwung reversal, turnaround, sudden change, (*~ an der Börse)* turn for the better/worse in the market, market rebound, trend reversal, (*~ der Konjunktur)* turnaround in economic activity

umseitig 1. overleaf, *(wie ~ angegeben)* as stated overleaf 2. *(~e Erklärung)* statement on the reverse

umsetzen 1. to sell, to turn over, (*mehr als … Aktien wurden umgesetzt)* more than … shares were traded 2. *(Konzept)* to implement, to realise, to carry (to put) into effect 3. (*in nationales Recht ~)* to transpose (to translate) into national law 4. *(in Barmittel)* to turn (to convert) into cash

Umsetzung 1. turning over 2. implementation, realisation 3. *(~ in nationales Recht)* transposition (translation) into national law 4. conversion

Umsetzungsgesetz Implementation Act

Umsicht prudence, circumspection

umsichtig *(~es Bilanzmanagement)* prudent (conservative) balance sheet management

umsiedeln *(ein Unternehmen ~)* to relocate a company, to move a company to …

umspannen 1. *(umfassen)* to comprise, to embrace 2. *(einen Zeitraum ~)* to span a period of …

Umstände *(unter den gegebenen ~n)* in the circumstances, under the present state of affairs, as matters stand

umsteigen to switch, (*von Aktien auf Renten ~)* to switch from equities to bonds, to switch out of the equity market into bonds, (*auf höher verzinsliche Anlagen ~)* to switch into higher-yielding forms of investment

umstellen 1. to reorganise, to regroup 2. *(Währung)* to convert

Umstellung 1. change, changeover, switch, conversion 2. *(Neuordnung)* reorganisation, regrouping

umstritten *(stark ~e Frage)* highly controversial (hotly debated) issue

umstrukturieren to restructure, to reorganise, to reshape, *(eine bestehende Kreditfazilität ~)* to restructure an existing loan facility, → umschulden

Umstrukturierung (corporate) restructuring, reconstruction, reshaping, reorganisation

Umstrukturierungsprozess restructuring process, process of reorganisation

Umstufung *(~ zum professionellen Kunden)* reclassification as professional customer

Umtausch exchange, swap, conversion

Umtausch / ~aktion exchange, swap transaction; **~angebot** exchange offering (offer), conversion offer, *(umtauschberechtigte Wertpapiere)* securities eligible for exchange; **~anleihe** exchangeable, exchangeable bond □ may be exchanged by its holder for

U

common stock of the same issuer; ~**aufforderung** conversion call

umtauschbar exchangeable, convertible

umtauschen to exchange, to swap, to convert, *(die Zertifikate im Verhältnis 3:1 ~)* to exchange the certificates on a one-for-three basis

Umtausch / ~frist exchange (conversion) period, period allowed for exchange; ~**kurs** conversion price; ~**recht** exchange (conversion) privilege, conversion option

Umtausch / ~stelle exchange (conversion) agent; ~**stichtag** exchange (conversion) record date; ~**verhältnis** exchange (conversion) ratio

umverteilen to redistribute, to reallocate

Umverteilung redistribution, *(~ von Fördergeldern)* reallocation of development funds

umwandelbar convertible

umwandeln 1. to convert, *(Schuldverschreibungen in Aktien ~)* to convert bonds into shares, *(in Bargeld ~)* to turn into cash, *(Verbindlichkeiten in Beteiligungskapital ~)* to convert debt into equity **2.** to reorganise, to transform

Umwandlung 1. conversion, *(~ von Forderungen in Beteiligungskapital)* converting debt into equity, debt-equity swap, *(~ in Namensschuldverschreibungen)* converting into registered notes
2. *(~ eines Unternehmens)* change in the company's legal form, business reorganisation, transformation of a company
3. *(~ von Rücklagen in Grundkapital)* capitalisation of reserves

Umwandlungs / ~abschlag conversion discount; ~**beschluss** resolution (decision) to change the company's legal form; ~**gesetz** Business Reorganisation Act □ Law regulating the transformation of companies

Umwelt / ~risikoprüfung environmental risk check; ~**steuergesetz** Company Reorganisation Tax Act; ~**verträglichkeitsprüfung** environmental impact assessment (EIA), *(umweltverträglich)* environmentally sound (compatible), non-polluting

umwerben 1. *(Anleger ~)* to woo investors **2.** *(das am meisten umworbene Kundensegment)* the most courted customer segment

UmwG → Umwandlungsgesetz

UmwSTG → Umwandlungssteuergesetz

umwidmen to transform, to reclassify

Umwidmung reclassification, change in accounting treatment, *(~ von Anlage- in Umlaufvermögen)* transformation of fixed to current assets, *(~ in den/aus dem Handelsbestand)* reclassification to/out of the trading portfolio, *(~ von Wertpapieren in der Bilanz)* regrouping of securities in the balance sheet

umziehen *(in neue Geschäftsräume ~)* to relocate to new premises

Umzugskosten relocation (moving) expenses

unabdingbar *(~e Voraussetzung für die Auszahlung)* indispensable condition (prerequisite) for the disbursement, *(~e Vorschriften)* mandatory (imperative) provisions

unabhängig *(~ von der Höhe des Zinssatzes)* irrespective of the interest rate, *(~ vom Nennwert)* regardless of the face value, *(~e Einheit)* independent unit, unit not affiliated with ...

unablösbar *(~e Schuld)* irredeemable debt

unabtretbar *(~er Anspruch)* unassignable (untransferable) claim

unanfechtbar *(~er Rechtstitel)* unassailable (incontestable, indefeasible, indisputable, unchallengeable) title

unangefochten *(~er Marktführer)* undisputed (unchallenged) market leader

unangemeldet (*~e Forderung) (im Insolvenzverfahren)* unproven claim (debt), (*~e Vermögenswerte)* undeclared property

unangemessen 1. inappropriate, unsuitable, improper **2.** *(unzureichend)* inadequate, incommensurate, insufficient **3.** (*ein ~ hoher Anteil)* a disproportionately large share

Unangemessenheit 1. inappropriateness, unsuitability **2.** inadequacy, insufficiency

unangetastet (*~e Rücklagen)* undrawn (untouched) reserves

unangreifbar (*~e Stellung am Markt)* unassailable position in the market

unannehmbar (*~e Forderung)* unacceptable claim

unattraktiv (*~e Verzinsung)* unattractive (low) interest/coupon

unaufgefordert (*~e Anlagevorschläge)* unsolicited investment proposals, (*~e Zahlung)* uncalled payment

unaufhaltsam (*~er Kursrückgang)* uncheckable (unstoppable) plunge in prices

unaufschiebbar (*~er Termin)* undeferrable (uncheckable) appointment

unausbleiblich (*~er Anstieg der Finanzierungskosten)* inevitable increase in financing charges

unausgeführt (*~er Auftrag)* unexecuted (unfilled) order

unausgeglichen (*~er Haushalt)* unbalanced budget

Unausgeglichenheit disequilibrium, imbalance

U

unausgenutzt (*~e Kreditfazilität)* unused (undrawn) credit facility

unausgewogen (*~e Geldpolitik)* unbalanced monetary policy

unbar (*~ zahlen)* to pay by cheque (or by money transfer), (*~e Zahlung)* cashless payment, (*~er Zahlungsverkehr)* cashless payments, paper-based funds transfer

unbebaut (*~es Grundstück)* unbuilt property

unbedenklich (*~e Anlage)* absolutely safe investment, safe haven investment, *(für Verbindlichkeiten ~ gut halten)* to consider undoubted for his/her commitments

Unbedenklichkeitsbescheinigung **1.** clearance certificate, certificate of non-objection, (*steuerliche ~)* tax clearance certificate □ confirming the payment of real estate transfer tax or inheritance tax **2.** compliance certificate **3.** certificate of good standing

unbedeutend (*~er Verlust)* minor (insignificant, slight) loss

unbedingt (*~ erforderlich)* imperative, absolutely necessary, (*~e Garantie)* absolute guarantee, (*~es Zahlungsversprechen)* unconditional undertaking to pay

unbefriedigend (*~es Anlageergebnis)* unsatisfactory investment performance

unbefriedigt (*~e Gläubiger)* unsatisfied creditors

unbefristet (*~e Garantie)* guarantee unlimited in time, indefinite guarantee, (*~er Schuldtitel)* undated debt

unbefugt (*~e Kontoinanspruchnahme)* unauthorised drawing on the account

unbeglichen (*~e Rechnung)* unsettled (unpaid) invoice, outstanding account

unbegrenzt (*Garantie in ~er Höhe)* unlimited guarantee, guarantee unlimited as to the amount, (*~e Haftung des Bürgen)* unlimited liability of the surety, (*Kredit für einen ~en Zeitraum)* loan for an indefinite period, (*~e Möglichkeiten)* infinite possibilities, (*Wertpapiere mit ~er Laufzeit)* undated (indefinitely dated) securities

unbegründet (*~e Ansprüche)* unfounded (ill-founded, unwarranted) claims, (*~er Bericht)* groundless (baseless) report, (*~e Zinserhöhungsgerüchte)* unsubstantiated interest hike rumours

unbelastet *(~er Grundbesitz)* unencumbered (unmortgaged) property

unbeleihbar *(~es Wirtschaftsgut)* asset not acceptable (eligible) as collateral

unberechenbar *(~e Kursentwicklung)* unpredictable (incalculable) development in prices

unbeschadet notwithstanding, regardless (irrespective) of, *(~ der Anforderungen des Artikels ...)* notwithstanding the requirements of Article ..., *(~ vorstehender Regelung)* without prejudice to the foregoing provision

unbeschädigt *(~ aus der Rezession kommen)* to emerge unscathed from the recession

unbeschränkt unlimited, unrestricted, without any restrictions, *(~ haftender Gesellschafter)* general (fully liable, unlimited) partner, *(~ steuerpflichtige Aktionäre)* shareholders with unlimited tax liability, *(~es Eigentum)* absolute possession, unlimited ownership, *(~es Eigentumsrecht)* unconditional (absolute) title, *(~er Negoziierungsauftrag)* unrestricted order to negotiate

unbesetzt *(~e Position)* vacant (unfilled) position

unbesichert *(~er Kredit)* unsecured (uncollateralised) loan

unbeständig *(~er Markt)* unsteady (unstable, fluctuating) market

Unbeständigkeit unsteadiness, unstableness, instability, variability

unbestätigt *(~es Akkreditiv)* unconfirmed documentary credit

unbesteuert *(~e Kapitalerträge)* untaxed investment income

unbestimmt *(~e finanzielle Unterstützung)* uncertain (undetermined, vague) financial backing, *(auf ~e Zeit anlegen)* to invest for an indefinite period, *(Verbindlichkeiten mit ~er Laufzeit)* undated liabilities, indeterminate-term liabilities

unbestreitbar *(~er Erfolg)* indisputable (undeniable) success

unbestritten *(~er Anspruch)* undisputed (uncontested) claim

unbeteiligt *(~ an der Finanzierung)* to be not involved in the financing, *(~ am Kapital)* to have (to hold) no capital interest

unbeweglich *(~e Anlagegüter)* immoveable property, immoveables, *(~er Kurs)* sticky price

unbezahlt *(~es Inkasso)* unpaid collection

unbillig *(~e Beeinträchtigung)* unfair prejudice, *(~e Vertragsklauseln)* unfair contract terms

undatiert *(~es Schreiben)* undated letter

Und-Konto joint account, account with joint drawing powers □ all accountholders must sign on any relevant documents, e. g. cheques, payment instructions, etc.

Und/Oder Konto alternate account □ account which two or more individuals can draw against without permission from each other

undurchführbar *(~e Strategie)* impracticable (unfeasible) strategy

Undurchführbarkeit impracticability, unfeasibility

unechtes Factoring recourse factoring □ implies the customer's liability in the event of non-collection

unechtes Pensionsgeschäft non-genuine repurchase transaction □ i.e. the transferee/pledgee is entitled but not obligated to return the assets on a specific date

uneinbringlich *(~e Forderung)* uncollectible (irrecoverable) debt, *(~er Kredit)* irrecoverable loan, dead loan (asset), *(als ~ ausbuchen)* to write off as uncollectible, *(als ~ gelten)* to be deemed uncollectible

Uneinbringlichkeit uncollectibility, irrecoverability

uneingelöst *(~e Kupons)* uncollected (uncashed) coupons, *(~er Wechsel)* dishonoured (unpaid) bill of exchange

uneingeschränkt 1. *adj.* *(~es Akzept)* unconditional (unqualified) acceptance, *(~er Bestätigungsvermerk)* unqualified audit certificate, *(~e Dispositionsvollmacht)* unlimited discretionary power, unlimited power to buy or to sell, *(~er Rechtstitel)* absolute title
(~es Testat) unqualified opinion, *(~e Verfügungsberechtigung)* unconditional power to draw on an account (to operate an account), *(~es Zahlungsversprechen)* unconditional undertaking to pay
2. *adv.* *(~ garantiert durch)* unconditionally guaranteed by, *(~ gültig sein)* to be in full force and effect, *(der Bank ~ zur Verfügung stehen)* to be at the bank's unrestricted (unqualified) disposal

uneinheitlich 1. *adj.* *(~e Entwicklung)* mixed performance, *(~e Gesetzgebung)* differing (non-uniform) legislation, *(~es Rating)* split rating
2. *adv.* *(~ tendierender Markt)* mixed market, *(~ bei geringen Umsätzen)* irregular in light (thin) trading, *(~ bei ruhigen Umsätzen)* quietly mixed, *(~ bis schwächer schließen)* to close mixed to lower

uneinig *(~ über die weitere Vorgehensweise sein)* to be at odds over what action to take

unempfindlich *(~ gegen Konjunktureinbrüche)* invulnerable to (against) economic slumps, *(~ gegen Zinsschwankungen)* insensitive to interest rate fluctuations

unentbehrlich *(~e Rücklagen)* indispensable (vital) reserves

U

unentgeltlich *(~es Inkasso)* free collection, collecting free of charge, *(~e Leistungen)* gratuitous benefits, *(~e Überweisung)* cost-free transfer, *(~e Vermögensübertragung)* gratuitous transfer of property, property transfer without consideration

unentschlossen *(~e Anleger)* undecided (wavering, hesitant) investors

Unentschlossenheit undecidedness, indecision, hesitancy

unentziehbar *(~e Rechte)* irrevocable rights

unerbeten *(~es Übernahmeangebot)* unsought (unsolicited, unwelcome) takeover bid

unerfahren *(~e Marktteilnehmer)* inexperienced (unseasoned) market operators

Unerfahrenheit inexperience, lack of experience

unerfüllt *(~e Verpflichtungen)* unfulfilled obligations

unerheblich *(~e Beteiligung)* insignificant (very small) stake

unerlaubt unauthorised, *(Ansprüche aus ~er Handlung)* claims of wrongdoing

unermüdlich *(~e Bemühungen)* unflagging (untiring, indefatigable) efforts

unerprobt *(~e Strategie)* untested strategy

unerreichbar *(~es Ziel)* unattainable goal

unerreicht *(~es Ergebnis)* unsurpassed (unrivalled, unmatched, unexcelled) performance, bumper performance

unerschöpflich *(~e Reserven)* inexhaustible reserves

unerwartet *(~er Kurssturz)* unanticipated (unexpected) price slump, *(ein ~ schlechtes Ergebnis)* an unexpectedly poor performance

unerwünscht *(~es Anlageangebot)* unsolicited (unrequested) investment offer

unfähig *jur.* incapable, unqualified

unfertig *(~e Erzeugnisse/Leistungen)* work in progress, uncompleted contracts, unfilled orders

unfundiert *(~e Schuld)* floating charge (debt)

ungeachtet *(~ gegenteiliger Bestimmungen)* notwithstanding any provisions to the contrary

ungebremst *(~er Preisauftrieb)* unbridled (unchecked, uncontrolled) upsurge in prices

ungebrochen *(~er Aufwärtstrend)* unbroken upward trend

ungebunden *(~er Finanzkredit)* *(a)* buyer credit not tied to a specific project *(b)* general purpose facility, *(~es Vermögen)* unrestricted assets

ungedeckt *(~er Kredit)* unsecured loan, uncovered advance, *(~e Leerverkäufe)* naked short selling, *(~es Obligo)* uncovered (unhedged) exposure, *(~e Optionsposition)* uncovered (naked) option position □ option position that is not covered by a corresponding cash position in the underlying instrument
(~er Optionsschein) naked warrant, *(~er Optionsverkauf)* naked option writing, *(~er Personalkredit)* unsecured personal loan, *(~es Risiko)* uncovered (unhedged) risk, *(~er Scheck)* dud (uncovered) cheque (check), *(~es Stillhaltergeschäft)* → ungedeckter Optionsverkauf, *(~e Verbindlichkeiten)* unfunded liabilities

ungeeignet 1. unsuitable, inappropriate **2.** *(Person)* unqualified, not qualified

ungefähr approximate(ly), rough(ly), *(die Anlage beläuft sich auf ~ € ... Mio.)* the investment will be in the range of € ... m

ungehindert *(~er Zugang zu ausländischen Kapitalmärkten)* unhindered (free, unimpeded) access to foreign capital markets

ungeklärt *(~er Fehlbetrag)* unaccounted-for deficit, *(~e Frage)* unsettled (uncleared) question, unresolved issue

ungekreuzt *(~er Scheck)* uncrossed cheque

ungekündigt *(~e Anleihe)* uncalled bond, *(~e Einlagen)* deposits for which no notice of withdrawal has been given

ungekürzt *(~er Emissionsbetrag)* full (unreduced) issue amount, *(~er Vertrag)* unabridged agreement

ungelöscht *(~e Hypothek)* undischarged (unextinguished) mortgage

ungenau *(~e Kalkulation)* inaccurate (inexact) calculation

Ungenauigkeit inaccuracy, inexactness

ungenügend *(~e Kapitalausstattung)* inadequate capital resources (equity base)

ungenutzt *(~e Kreditlinie)* unused (undrawn) credit line, *(~e Mittel)* dead capital, *(~es Potenzial)* untapped potential

ungeprüft *(~er Abschluss)* unaudited accounts, *(~e Unterlagen)*unchecked (unexamined, uninspected) records

ungerechtfertigt *(~e Bereicherung)* unjust enrichment, *(~e Forderung)* unjustified (unwarranted) claim, *(~e Garantieinanspruchnahmen)* unfair calling of guarantees

ungeschmälert *(~e Einnahmen)* undiminished (uncurtailed) revenue, *(~e Leistung)* unimpaired performance

ungesetzlich unlawful, illegal

ungesichert *(~es Engagement)* unsecured (unhedged) exposure, *(~er Kredit)* unsecured loan (credit), *(~es Wechselkursrisiko)* uncovered (unhedged) currency risk

ungestört *(~es Wachstum)* uninterrupted (undisturbed, unimpaired) growth

ungeteilt *(~es Besitzrecht)* undivided title

ungetrübt *(~e Marktstimmung)* unclouded (undimmed) market sentiment

ungewiss uncertain, undetermined, doubtful

Ungewissheit uncertainty, lack of certainty, doubt

ungewöhnlich unusual, uncustomary, *(eine ~ ruhige Börsensitzung)* an unusually quiet trading session

ungezügelt *(~e Inflation)* unrestrained (unchecked) inflation, *(~er Wettbewerb)* unbridled competition

ungleich 1. unequal, uneven, *(~e Einkommensverteilung)* unequal distribution of income, *(~e Streuung)* uneven spread **2.** *(verschieden)* different, disparate, varying, divergent

Ungleichbehandlung *(~ von Kreditnehmern)* discriminatory treatment of borrowers

Ungleichgewicht imbalance, disequilibrium, *(~ von Angebot und Nachfrage)* imbalances in supply and demand, *(~e zwischen Kassa- und Terminmarkt)* price disparities between cash and futures markets, *(~e in der Leistungsbilanz)* current account imbalances, *(~e im Markt)* imbalances in the market

Ungleichheit 1. inequality, unevenness **2.** difference, divergence

ungleichmäßig *(~e Tilgungszahlungen)* *(a)* varying redemption payments *(b)* irregular repayments, *(~e Verteilung)* uneven distribution

Ungleichmäßigkeit irregularity, variation, unevenness

ungültig *(~es Aktienzertifikat)* invalid stock certificate, *(~e Vorschrift)* ineffective (inoperative) rule, *(für ~ erklären)* to invalidate, to annul, to declare null and void, to nullify, to render inoperative

Ungültigkeit invalidity, voidness, nullity

ungünstig *(~e Bedingungen)* adverse conditions, *(~e Lage)* inconvenient location, *(~e Marktbedingungen)* adverse market conditions, *(~e Nachrichten)* unfavourable news

unhaltbar *(~ werden)* to become untenable (unsustainable)

uninteressant *(~e Anlagemöglichkeit)* unattractive (uninteresting, unappealing) investment opportunity

Universal / ~bank universal bank, all-purpose (multi-purpose) bank; **~bankkonzept/~system** universal banking concept/system; **~erbe** sole (universal) heir; **~karte** multi-purpose card

unklar *(~e Konjunkturaussichten)* unclear (hazy) economic prospects

Unklarheit lack of clearness (clarity), vagueness

unkompensiert *(~e Bilanzsumme)* total assets before elimination of intragroup balances

unkontrollierbar *(~er Kapitalzufluss)* uncontrollable (uncheckable) inflow of capital

unkontrolliert *(~e Geldmengenexpansion)* uncontrolled (unbridled) monetary expansion

unkonvertierbar *(~e Währung)* inconvertible currency

Unkosten expenses, charges, costs; **~beitrag** contribution to the costs; **~erstattung** refund of expenses incurred

unkündbar *(~ während der Laufzeit der Emission)* uncallable (not callable) for the life of the issue, *(~e Anleihe)* uncallable (irredeemable) bond, *(~e Vereinbarung)* non-terminable agreement

Unkündbarkeit non-callability, irredeemability, non-terminability

Unkündbarkeits / ~frist *(bei Anleihen)* period of non-callability, non-redemption period; **~klausel** non-callability clause

unlauter *(~e Geschäftshandlung)* unfair (deceiving) business practice, *(~er Wettbewerb)* unfair competition

unlimitiert *(~er Auftrag)* unlimited order

unlösbar *(~es Problem)* unsolvable problem

unmissverständlich *(~e Erklärung)* unambiguous statement

unmittelbar 1. *adj.* *(~e Auswirkungen)* immediate (direct) impact, *(~e Emission)* → Selbstemission, *(~e Kapital-*

U

anteile) directly held shares, *(~e Stellvertretung)* direct agency
2. *adv.* directly, immediately, *(~ im Ergebnis verrechnen)* to charge (or: to credit) to operations as incurred

Unmöglichkeit *(~ der Leistungs-/Vertragserfüllung)* impossibility of performance, commercial impracticability, frustration of contract, → objektive Unmöglichkeit der Leistungserfüllung

unnachgiebig *(eine ~e Haltung einnehmen)* to adopt an uncompromising (intransigent, unyielding, unaccommodating) stance, to take a hard line on

unnotiert *(~e Werte)* unlisted (unquoted) securities

unökonomisch *(~er Betrieb)* uneconomic(al) operation

unparteiisch *(~er Vermittler)* impartial mediator

unpfändbar *(~e Forderungen)* non-attachable (non-distrainable) claims, *(~e Vermögenswerte)* unseizable (exempt) property, property exempt from seizure (execution), non-leviable assets

Unpfändbarkeit exemption from seizure, protection from seizure (execution)

unplanmäßig unscheduled

unproduktiv *(~es Kapital)* unproductive (idle) capital

unrealisiert *(~e Erträge)* unearned income

unrechtmäßig *(~er Besitz)* unlawful (illegal, wrongful) possession, *(~er Besitzer)* unlawful owner (holder), wrongful possessor

Unrechtmäßigkeit unlawfulness, illegality

unregelmäßig 1. irregular 2. *(stark schwankend)* erratic, *(~e Zahlungen)* irregular payments

Unregelmäßigkeit irregularity

unrein *(~es Konnossement)* foul (claused, unclean, dirty) bill of lading

unrentabel 1. unprofitable 2. *(unwirtschaftlich)* uneconomical

unrichtig *(~e Angaben)* false (wrong, incorrect) statements, misrepresentations, *(~er Übertragungsvermerk)* wrong endorsement

Unruhe *(~ an den Finanzmärkten)* disturbances (unrest) in the financial markets, *(für ~ unter den Anlegern sorgen)* to sow disquiet among investors

unschlüssig *(~e Anleger)* hesitant (wavering) investors

unselbstständig *(~e Niederlassung)* dependent branch establishment, *(~e Stiftung)* non-autonomous foundation, *(~es Sondervermögen; i. S. des Investmengesetzes)* dependent fund, *(rechtlich ~es Unternehmen)* legally dependent company

unsicher *(~e Börsenstimmung)* unsteady tone of the market, jumpy market, *(~e Wirtschaftslage)* insecure (precarious, unstable) economic situation, *(~e Zukunft des Unternehmens)* company's uncertain future

Unsicherheit uncertainty, lack of security (stability), precariousness, instability, *(~ hinsichtlich der Risiken)* uneasiness about the risks

Unsicherheitseinrede plea of uncertainty

Unsicherheitsfaktor source of uncertainty

unsichtbar *(~e Einfuhren/Ausfuhren)* invisible imports/exports

unstimmig *(~e Dokumente)* inaccurate (imperfect, discrepant) documents

Unstimmigkeit 1. difference, discrepancy, inconsistency 2. disagreement

unstreitig / unstrittig non-contentious, *(~e Ansprüche)* undisputed claims

unsystematisch *(~es Risiko)* unsystematic risk □ e.g. company-specific/investment-specific risk

untadelig *(~e Kontoführung)* immaculate account-keeping

untaxiert (*~e Police)* unvalued policy

unteilbar (*~e Verpflichtung)* indivisible obligation

Unteilbarkeit *(~ eines Rechts)* indivisibility of a right

unten *(nach ~ abgerundet)* downward-revised, *(nach ~drücken)* to drive lower, *(nach ~ gerichtet sein)* to be on a downward path

unter (*am ~en Ende der Erwartungen)* at the bottom of the expectations, (*am ~en Ende der Preisskala)* at the lower end of the price scale, (*~ dem Strich) (a)* on balance *(b) (im Rechnungswesen)* below the line, (*~e Kursgrenze)* bottom rate (price), (*~e Preisgrenze)* price floor, (*~e Renditegrenze)* yield floor

Unterbau base, foundation(s)

Unterbeschäftigung underemployment, underutilisation

unterbesetzt understaffed

unterbesichern to undercollateralise

Unterbesicherung collateral shortage, shortage of security (of cover)

Unterbeteiligter subparticipant

Unterbeteiligung subparticipation, subinterest, subpartnership, (*an einer Emission)* subunderwriting share

unterbewerten 1. *(Aktien ~)* to undervalue (to underprice) stock, (*Anlagen ~)* to undervalue (to understate) assets **2.** to underestimate, to underrate

Unterbewertung 1. undervaluation, understatement, underpricing **2.** underrating

unterbieten to underbid, to underquote, (*einen Preis um 10 % ~)* to undercut a price by 10 p. c.

Unterbietung underbidding

Unterbilanz negative equity (net worth), excess of liabilities over assets, balance sheet insolvency

unterbinden 1. to stop, to put an end to, to prevent **2.** *(verbieten)* to prohibit, to outlaw

unterbrechen 1. to interrupt **2.** *(aussetzen)* to suspend **3.** *(verschieben)* to adjourn

Unterbrechung 1. interruption **2.** suspension **3.** adjournment

unterbreiten to submit, to present, (*ein Angebot ~)* to submit an offer (a quotation), to tender for, (*einen Vorschlag ~)* to make (to set forth) a proposal

Unterbreitung submission, submittal, presentation, putting forward

unterbringbar placeable

unterbringen 1. to place, (*am Markt ~)* to place in the market, (*bei Privatanlegern ~)* to place with (to market to) private investors, (*im freihändigen Verkauf ~)* to place privately with investors
2. *(buchungsmäßig)* to apply, (*wir können Ihre Zahlung nicht ~)* we feel unable to apply (to post) your payment, (*nicht unterzubringende Posten)* uncleared items, items not specifically referable to any particular transaction **3.** *(hinterlegen)* to deposit, to lodge

Unterbringung 1. placing, placement, (*~ einer Emission beim Publikum)* placing an issue with the public, public placing **2.** application, (*~ der Zahlungseingänge*) application of payments received

Unterbringungs / ~möglichkeit placement possibility; **~risiko** placing risk; **~volumen** placement volume

Unterdeckung shortage of cover, short cover, *(kostenmäßige ~)* failure to cover the costs involved, not covering own costs incurred, *(~ von Sicherheiten)* collateral shortage, inadequacy of collateral, *(~ auf einem Treuhandkonto)* escrow deficiency (shortage)

unterdrücken 1. *(Informationen ~)* to suppress information **2.** *(das Wachstum/den Wettbewerb ~)* to stifle growth/competition

U

unterdurchschnittlich *(~e Kursentwicklung)* below-average price performance

Unterfangen attempt, undertaking, venture

unterfinanzieren to underfund, to underfinance

Unterfinanzierung underfunding, financing shortage, inadequate financial resources

Unterfonds subfund

Untergang *(~ von Verlustvorträgen)* forfeiture of tax loss carryforwards

untergehend *(~e Gesellschaft)* transferring company

untergeordnet 1. *(Position, Pfandrecht)* subordinate, inferior **2.** *(in der Bedeutung)* minor, secondary

Untergesellschaft subordinated company, → Organgesellschaft

untergewichten *(Aktien ~)* to underweight shares, to give a low weighting to shares

Untergewichtung underweighting

untergliedern to break down, to subdivide

Untergliederung breakdown, subdivision

untergraben *(das Vertrauen der Anleger ~)* to undermine (to shatter) investor confidence

Untergrenze floor, lower limit, *(~ für Eigenkapitalanforderungen)* required capital floor, required level of own funds

unterhalten to maintain, to keep, to carry, *(Gelder am Euromarkt ~)* to maintain funds in the Euromarket, *(ein ausreichendes Guthaben auf dem Konto ~)* to maintain sufficient funds in the account, *(einen Markt ~)* to make (to maintain) a market, *(eine Position ~)* to run a position

Unterhaltung maintenance, upkeep, *(~ eines hohen Bestandes)* maintaining (carrying) a high inventory, *(~ von Mindestreserven)* maintenance of minimum reserves

unterjährig intra-year, *(~e Erhöhung)* increase during the year, *(~er Zeitraum)* intra-year period, *(~e Zinsrechnung)* intra-year calculation of interest, interest charged (credited) for a period of less than twelve months, *(~e Zinszahlung)* intra-year interest payment

Unterkapitalisierung undercapitalisation, underfunding, thin capitalisation, *(unterkapitalisiertes Unternehmen)* undercapitalised company

Unterkonsolidierung subconsolidation

Unterkonsorte subunderwriter

Unterkonsortium subsyndicate, subconsortium

Unterkonto subaccount, subsidiary account

Unterlage 1. record, document **2.** *(Beleg)* voucher

unterlassen 1. *(sich enthalten)* to refrain (to desist) from **2.** *(auslassen, versäumen)* to omit, to neglect, to fail

Unterlassung 1. refraining (from acting), non-action **2.** omission, neglect, failure **3.** *jur.* injunctive relief

Unterlassungs / ~anordnung → Unterlassungsverfügung; **~anspruch** right to an injunction, *(einen ~ geltend machen)* to apply for injunctive relief, to seek a cease-and-desist order; **~ bescheid** cease-and-desist order

Unterlassungs / ~delikt omission offence; **~erklärung** cease-and-desist undertaking, covenant to cease and desist from, urgent declaratory relief

Unterlassungs / ~klage petition for injunctive relief, action for a cease-and-desist order, declaratory relief action; **~klagengesetz** German Injunctive Relief Act; **~pflichten** *(~ des Kreditnehmers)* restrictive covenants

Unterlassungs / ~verfügung injunctive relief, cease-and-desist order, prohibitory injunction; **~verpflich-**

U

tung cease-and-desist undertaking, → Negativklausel

unterlaufen *(Bestimmungen ~)* to evade (to side-step) regulations

unterlegen 1. *(kapitalmäßig)* to support, to back, *(Kredite mit Eigenkapital ~)* to back lendings with equity, to hold capital in support of lendings, *(Kredit- und Marktpreisrisiken mit Eigenkapital ~)* to provide equity backing for market risks, to apply capital charges to credit and market risks *(Risikoaktiva, die mit Eigenkapital zu ~ sind)* risk assets subject to capital charges, risk assets requiring capital backing, *(unterlegt mit haftendem Eigenkapital)* backed by liable capital **2.** *(sicherheitenmäßig ~)* to secure, to collateralise, to guarantee, *(das Projekt mit Eigenmitteln ~)* to secure the project with own capital resources, *(durch eine erstrangige Hypothek ~)* to collateralise (to back) by a senior mortgage *(Garantien müssen voll unterlegt sein)* guarantees must be supported by the same amount of capital, *(der Kredit wird durch eine Garantie/dingliche Sicherheit unterlegt)* the facility is secured by a guarantee/by real security, *(nicht ~e Papiere)* unbacked paper

Unterlegung 1. support, backing, *(~ durch Kapital)* equity backing (support), support through equity, *(das zur ~ der Marktpreisrisiken erforderliche Kapital)* capital charges for market price risks, capital required to back market price risks, *(~ der Anrechnungsbeträge)* backing of capital charges **2.** provision of security, collateralisation, *(~ einer Bürgschaft)* provision of security for a surety bond, security backing, *(zur ~ der Garantie dienende Verpfändung)* pledge in support of a guarantee *(~ eines Kredites)* credit support, collateral (security) provided for a loan, putting up security in support of a loan, *(~ von Kreditrisiken) (a) (allgemein)* provision of security for lending risks *(b) (i. S. der Basler Kapitalunterlegungsvorschriften)* application of capital charges to credit risks

Unterlegungs / ~bedarf 1. need for capital backing **2.** need for collateral; **~betrag** capital charge, capital backing required

Unterlegungspflicht obligation to provide capital backing (equity support), *(~ für Marktrisiken)* obligation to establish capital charges for market risks

unterlegungspflichtig *(~e Kreditzusagen)* loan commitments requiring equity backing

Unterlieferant subcontractor

unterliegen 1. subject to, *(den Schwankungen des Aktienmarktes ~)* to be subject to the ups and downs (to the vagaries) of the stock market, *(einem Zinsänderungsrisiko ~)* to be exposed to an interest rate risk **2.** governed by, *(der Vertrag unterliegt deutschem Recht)* the agreement shall be governed by German Law (shall be governed and construed in accordance with the Law of the Federal Republic of Germany) **3.** *(jds. Zuständigkeit ~)* to fall (to come) within the province of, to be the responsibility of

untermauern to underpin, to corroborate, to support, to bolster

Untermietvertrag sublease agreement, sandwich lease

unternehmen to undertake

Unternehmen company, corporation, undertaking, enterprise, *(~ des Finanzsektors)* financial sector entities, *(Finanzierungsbedarf der ~)* corporate finance (borrowing) requirements, business funding requirements, *(Gewinnspannen der ~)* corporate profit margins

Unternehmens / ~abschluss company's annual accounts (financial statements); **~ anleihe** corporate bond;

~**anleihefonds** corporate bond fund; ~**auflösung** dissolution of a company

Unternehmens / ~beratung 1. management consultancy **2.** *(Service eines Kreditinstitutes)* corporate consultancy, business advisory service

Unternehmens / ~bereich 1. *(Einzelbereich)* division, business segment **2.** *(gesamter Unternehmensbereich)* corporate sector; ~**bestandssicherung** assuring the continued existence of the company

Unternehmens / ~beteiligung interest (stake, share) in a company, equity (trade) investment, *(pl)* corporate investments; ~**beteiligungsgesellschaft** equity investment company, venture capital company; ~**beurteilung** company assessment

Unternehmens / ~bewertung company valuation, valuation of a business, corporate appraisal; ~**bilanz** company's balance sheet, company (corporate) accounts; ~**bonität** credit rating of a company

Unternehmens / ~einheit business unit; ~**ergebnis** corporate results, corporate (business) performance; ~**erscheinungsbild** corporate design; ~**erträge** corporate earnings; ~**ertragslage** corporate earnings position; ~**ethik** corporate (business) ethics

Unternehmens / ~finanzen company finance; ~**finanzierung** business finance (funding), company (corporate) financing, *(Instrumente der ~)* corporate financing instruments; ~**finanzierung und ~beratung** *(Geschäftsfeld einer Bank nach Basel II)* Corporate Finance; ~**forderungen** exposures to corporates

Unternehmens / ~form corporate form, type (form) of business organisation; ~**fortführung** *(Grundsatz der ~)* going concern principle

Unternehmens / ~führung 1. company management, Management Board, Board of Directors **2.** corporate governance, managing (running) a company; ~**fusion** merger of companies

Unternehmens / ~gegenstand corporate purpose (objective); ~**gesamtwert** aggregate enterprise value; ~**gewinn** corporate (company) profit, corporate (business) income

Unternehmens / ~größe size of a company (of a business); ~ **gründung** company formation; ~**haftung** enterprise liability; ~**identität** corporate identity; ~**immobilienbestand** corporate real estate portfolio; ~**investitionen** business (corporate) investments

Unternehmens / ~kapital company (corporate) equity; ~**kennzahlen 1.** key company data, company highlights **2.** corporate ratios; ~**konzentration** concentration in business

Unternehmens / ~kredite 1. *(Kredite an Unternehmen)* corporate (business) lendings, lendings to companies **2.** *(Kreditaufnahme durch Unternehmen)* corporate borrowings; ~**kultur** corporate culture; ~**kundschaft** *(einer Bank)* corporate customers

Unternehmens / ~leistung 1. corporate (company) performance **2.** *(~en an die Mitarbeiter)* company benefits, *(geldwerte Nebenleistungen)* perks; ~**leitbild** corporate mission; ~**leitung** company management, → Unternehmensführung; ~**liquidation** company liquidation, winding-up of a company; ~**liquidität** corporate liquidity

Unternehmens / ~meldungen corporate news; ~**neugründung** business start-up, corporate venture; ~**neuorganisation** corporate restructuring

Unternehmens / ~organisation company (business) organisation; ~**organkredite** lendings to associated companies, i. e. to companies in which a stake of at least 25 % is held

Unternehmens / ~plan corporate plan, business plan; ~**planung** corporate planning; ~**politik** corporate (business) policy; ~**portal** corporate portal; ~**präsentation** company presentation, roadshow; ~**profil** corporate profile

Unternehmens / ~recht companies legislation, corporate law; ~**rechtsform** legal form of a company, form of business organisation; ~**register** Company Register, → EHUG; ~**rentabilität** company profitability; ~**risiko** corporate risk

Unternehmens / ~sanierung company (corporate) reconstruction, corporate reorganisation; ~**schuldner** corporate borrower (obligor); ~**sitz** principal place of business, company headquarters; ~**sitzklausel** domicile clause

unternehmensspezifisch *(~e Ausfallquote)* entity-specific loss experience

Unternehmens / ~spitze company management; ~**steuerreformgesetz** Business Tax Reform Act; ~**teil** business unit, division

unternehmensübergreifend 1. cross-company, intercompany **2.** across all the company's divisions, covering the company as a whole

Unternehmens / ~übernahme 1. taking over a company, company takeover, corporate acquisition **2.** *(durch das Management/die Mitarbeiter)* management buyout/employee buyout; ~**verbund** group, group of companies, corporate network; ~**verfassung** constitution of a company, *i.e.S.* corporate governance

Unternehmens / ~verflechtung corporate links (ties); ~**verschuldung** corporate debt (indebtedness); ~**vertrag 1.** intercompany agreement, profit and loss pooling agreement **2.** *(mit einer Beteiligungsgesellschaft)* affiliation agreement

Unternehmens / ~wachstum corporate growth; ~**wert** enterprise value, corporate (company) value, going concern value

Unternehmens / ~ziel corporate goal (purpose), company (business) mission, company's objectives; ~**zusammenbruch** company (business) failure, collapse of a company, *(pl)* corporate insolvencies (defaults); ~**zusammenschluss** business combination, merger of companies, corporate amalgamation

Unternehmer entrepreneur, company owner

Unternehmer / ~einkommen entrepreneurial income; ~**investitionen** corporate investments; ~**gedanke** entrepreneurial concept (idea)

Unternehmergesellschaft entrepreneur company □ limited liability company that can be formed without the traditional minimum capital requirement applicable to GmbHs

unternehmerisch entrepreneurial, *(~es Ermessen)* management (managerial) discretion, management's freedom of judgment

Unternehmer / ~leistung company (entrepreneurial) performance; ~**pfandrecht** contractor's lien; ~**rentabilität** return on equity; ~**risiko** entrepreneurial (business) risk; ~**standpunkt** management (employers') standpoint, attitude of the management

Unternehmung 1. → Unternehmen **2.** operation, transaction

Unternehmungslust *(Börse)* activity in the market, *(die ~ wurde durch die Zinsunsicherheit gebremst)* buying interest (investment enterprise) was inhibited by interest rate uncertainties

Unterordnungskonzern vertically organised group

Unterorganisation suborganisation, subsidiary organisation

Unter-Pari-Emission issue below par, issue at a discount

Unterposition subheading

Unterposten subitem

Unterredung talk(s), discussion(s), conversation, interview

Unterrepräsentierung *(~ von Aktien)* underrepresentation (underweighting) of shares in the portfolio

unterrichten to inform, to notify, to give notice, to brief, *(den Kunden regelmäßig über den Markt ~)* to keep the customer regularly informed (advised) on the state of the market

Unterrichtung information, notification, *(ohne vorherige/weitere ~)* without prior/further notice

Unterrichtungspflicht obligation to notify

untersagen to prohibit, to forbid, *(gesetzlich untersagt)* legally prohibited

Untersagung prohibition, ban

unterschätzen 1. to underestimate, to underrate **2.** *(im finanziellen Wert)* to undervalue, to set too low a value on

Unterschätzung 1. underestimation, underrating **2.** undervaluation

unterscheiden to distinguish, to differentiate, *(sich deutlich ~ von)* to differ markedly from, to be distinctly different from, *(sich inhaltlich ~ von)* to differ in content from, *(~de Kompetenz)* distinctive competence

Unterscheidung distinction, differentiation

Unterschied 1. difference, disparity, discrepancy
2. *(Schwankung)* variation
3. *(Trennung)* distinction, *(zum ~ von)* as distinguished from, *(~e in den Konditionen)* differences (disparities) in pricing, *(große ~e im Ergebnis)* wide disparities in earnings

unterschiedlich 1. *adj.* *(~e Berechnungsverfahren)* differing (varying) methods of calculation, *(~e Einflüsse)* contrasting influences, *(~e Erfahrungen)* diversity in experience, *(~e Ergebnisse)* diverging performances, divergent (disparate) financial results *(Emissionen ~en Umfangs)* issues of varying (different) size, *(zwei ~e Verpflichtungen)* two distinct obligations **2.** *adv.* *(~ bewerten)* to value differently, to take a different view, *(sich ~ entwickeln)* to develop divergently

Unterschiedlichkeit diversity, variableness, variability

Unterschiedsbetrag 1. difference (in amount), *(~ aus der Kapitalkonsolidierung)* difference from (due to) capital consolidation, → aktivischer, → passivischer Unterschiedsbetrag
2. balancing item, net amount

unterschlagen 1. to embezzle, to defraud, to misappropriate **2.** *(unterdrücken)* to suppress

Unterschlagung 1. embezzlement, fraud **2.** suppression

unterschreiben to sign, *(blanko ~)* to sign in blank

unterschreiten *(die Mindestkapitalquote ~)* to drop (to fall) below the minimum capital ratio, *(den erforderlichen Satz weit ~)* to fall far short of the required rate

Unterschreitung *(~ der Mindestsätze)* falling (dropping) below the minimum rates

Unterschrift signature

Unterschriften / ~pad signature pad, pen pad; **~prüfung** signature verification, checking the genuineness of a signature; **~verzeichnis** list of authorised signatories

Unterschrifts / ~befugnis signatory power, authorisation to sign; **~beglaubigung** attesting (to) the authenticity of a signature, attestation (authentication, certification) of a signature

unterschriftsberechtigt authorised (entitled, empowered) to sign, *(für ein Konto)* authorised to sign on an account, *(für eine Gesellschaft)* authorised to sign for and on behalf of a company, having signatory power

Unterschrifts / ~berechtigung signing authority, authority to sign, signatory power; **~bestätigung** confirming the genuineness (authenticity) of a signature; **~bevollmächtigter** authorised signatory, authorised signing officer

Unterschrifts / ~erfassung signature capture; **~fälschung** forgery of a signature; ~**karte** signature card; ~**probe** specimen signature; ~**probenblatt** specimen signature card; ~**regelungen** signatory power arrangements; ~**stempel** signature stamp

Unterschrifts / ~**träger** authorised signatory, authorised signing officer; ~**verzeichnis** signature book (index), list of persons given authority to sign on an account (on behalf of the company); ~**vollmacht** authority to sign, signing authority, signatory power

unterschwellig *(~e Börsenstimmung)* undercurrent sentiment in the market

Untersicherung 1. undercollateralisation **2.** underhedging

unterst *(~e Bonitätsstufe)* bottom rating, lowest grade

unterstehen 1. to be subject to, to be controlled by **2.** *(jmd. ~)* to report to s. o., to be subordinate(d) to s. o. **3.** *(direkt ~)* to report directly to, to be directly responsible (answerable) to

unterstellen 1. to subject to, to subordinate to, *(inländischem Recht unterstellte Garantien)* guarantees subject to national law **2.** *(behaupten/vermuten)* to suggest, to suppose, to insinuate, to assume, *(stillschweigend unterstellte Vollmacht)* implied (implicit) authority **3.** *(jmd. ~)* to subordinate s. o. to, *(direkt AB unterstellt sein)* reporting directly to AB

Unterstellung 1. subordination **2.** suggestion, assumption

unterstreichen 1. to underline, to add weight to, to accentuate **2.** to stress, to emphasise **3.** *(erneut bestätigen)* to reaffirm

unterstützen 1. to support, to back **2.** *(billigen)* to endorse, to give endorsement to, *(bei der Finanzierung ~)* to assist with the financing

Unterstützung 1. support, backing, assistance, aid **2.** endorsement

Unterstützungs / ~**funktionen** support functions; ~**kasse** benevolent fund; ~**linie** support level; ~**paket** support package

unterstützungswürdig *(~e Bemühungen)* efforts worth backing

untersuchen 1. to investigate, to inquire, to probe, *(die Finanzlage des Unternehmens ~)* to probe the company's finances **2.** to analyse **3.** *(prüfen)* to examine, to inspect, to verify

Untersuchung 1. investigation, inquiry, probe **2.** analysis **3.** examination, inspection, verification, check, *(eine ~ durchführen)* to conduct an investigation, to hold an inquiry

Untersuchungs / ~**auftrag** research brief; ~**ergebnisse** findings

untertägig *(~e Engagements)* intraday exposures, *(~es Limit)* intraday exposure limit

Untertassenformation *(Chart-Analyse)* saucer bottom, rounding bottom □ technical chart formation indicating the end of a downward trend, → umgekehrte Untertasse

Untervermittler sub-broker, sub-agent

Untervermittlung *(~ von Finanzprodukten)* sub-broking (subnegotiation) of financial products

unterversichern to underinsure, *(unterversichert)* underinsured, insured for less than the real value

Unterversicherung cover shortage, underinsurance

Unterversorgung short supply

Unterverwahrer subcustodian, subdepository

Unterverwahrung subcustody

Untervollmacht subdelegated power

unterwerfen *(sich einem Schiedsspruch ~)* to submit to an arbitral award, *(sich der sofortigen Zwangsvollstreckung in das persönliche Vermögen ~)* to submit to immediate compulsory enforcement on one's personal property, *(Schwankungen unterworfen sein)* to be subject to fluctuations

Unterwerfung *(~ unter eine ausländische Gerichtsbarkeit)* submission to a foreign jurisdiction, *(~ unter die sofortige Zwangsvollstreckung)* submission to immediate enforcement

Unterwerfungs / ~erklärung → Unterlassungserklärung; **~klausel** enforcement clause

unwesentlich *(~er Vertragsbruch)* minor breach of contract

unterzeichnen 1. to sign, to undersign 2. *(eine Emission ~)* to undersubscribe an issue

Unterzeichner/Unterzeichnete signer, signatory, undersigned, *(Rechts-/Linksunterzeichner)* signatory to the right/left

Unterzeichnung 1. signing, signature, *(mit ~ dieser Kreditvereinbarung)* in signing this loan agreement, *(Datum der ~)* signature date, date of signing, *(die Vereinbarung tritt mit rechtsgültiger ~ in Kraft)* the agreement takes effect upon being validly signed 2. *(~ einer Emission)* undersubscription of an issue, *(bei ~ der Emission)* failing subscription of all shares

unterziehen to submit to, *(einer genauen Prüfung ~)* to subject to close scrutiny

untragbar 1. unbearable, *(~e Zinsbelastung)* unbearable interest charge (bill) 2. *(nicht zu rechtfertigen)* unjustifiable, insupportable

untrüglich *(~e Anzeichen einer Kurserholung)* unmistakable signs of a recovery in prices

unüberbrückbar *(~e Meinungsverschiedenheit)* unbridgeable (irreconcilable) dispute

unüberlegt *(~e Anlage)* imprudent (rash) investment

unüberprüfbar *(~e Angaben)* unverifiable information

unübersichtlich *(~e Finanzlage)* unclear (obscure) financial situation

unübertragbar *(~er Bezugsrechtsschein)* untransferable warrant

unübertroffen *(~er Anlageerfolg)* unmatched (unsurpassed) investment performance

unüberwindbar *(~e finanzielle Schwierigkeiten)* insurmountable financial difficulties

unumgänglich *(~er Kapitalschnitt)* inevitable (unavoidable) capital write-down

unumkehrbar/unumstößlich *(~e Entscheidung)* irrefutable (irrevocable, incontestable) decision

unumstritten *(~er Marktführer)* undisputed (uncontested, unchallenged) market leader

ununterbrochen *(~e Dividendenzahlungen)* unbroken (uninterrupted) dividend record, continuous dividend payments

unveränderlich *(~e Grundsätze)* unalterable (unchangeable) principles, *(~er Kursermittlungsfaktor)* constant (invariable, unvarying) price-fixing factor, *(~er Zinssatz)* invariable (fixed) interest rate

unverändert *(~bei … notieren)* to stand unchanged at …, *(~ gegenüber dem zweiten Quartal)* unchanged from the second quarter

unverantwortlich *(~es Finanzgebaren)* irresponsible financial management

unveräußerlich *(~es Recht)* inalienable right, *(~e Vermögenswerte)* unsaleable assets

unverbindlich *(~es Angebot)* non-binding offer, offer (quotation) without any obligation, *(kostenloses, ~es Beratungsgespäch)* free, no-obligation consultation, *(~er Kurs)* non-binding price (rate), price subject to alterations

unverbrieft *(~e Forderungen)* uncertificated claims

unverbürgt *(~es Eigenkapital)* equity at risk

unvereinbar *(~ mit unserer Geschäftspolitik)* incompatible (irreconcilable) with our business policy

Unvereinbarkeit incompatibility, irreconcilability

unverfallbar *(~es Recht)* non-forfeitable (vested) right

unverfälscht *(~er Finanzstatus)* unadulterated (undistorted) statement of assets and liabilities

unverhältnismäßig *(~ hohe/niedrige Umsätze)* extremely (disproportionately) high/low turnover

unverhofft *(~er Kursanstieg)* unexpected (unhoped-for, unanticipated) price increase, *(~e Währungsgewinne)* windfall currency gains

unverjährbar *(~er Anspruch)* indefeasible (imprescriptible) claim

unvermeidbar *(~e Konsequenzen)* inevitable (unavoidable) consequences, *(sich als ~ erweisen)* to prove inevitable

Unvermögen inability, → subjektive Unmöglichkeit der Leistungserfüllung

unveröffentlicht *(~e Zahlen)* unpublished (undisclosed) figures

unverrechnet *(~e Lieferungen und Leistungen)* unbilled contracts

unverrückbar *(~e Finanzierungsregel)* unalterable (unshakable) financing rule

unverständlich *(~e Entscheidung)* incomprehensible (inexplicable) decision

unversteuert *(~e Kapitalerträge)* untaxed investment income

unverteilt *(~er Gewinn)* undistributed (undivided, unappropriated) profit

unvertretbar *(~er Anspruch)* unjustifiable (unwarrantable) claim

unverwässert *(~es Ergebnis)* basic earnings (loss) per share

unverwertbar *(~e Vermögenswerte)* unrealisable assets

unverzichtbar *(~er Anspruch)* unrenounceable claim, *(~e Sicherheit)* indispensable collateral, collateral that cannot be dispensed with

unverzinslich carrying (bearing) no interest, *(~e Einlagen)* non-interest-bearing deposits, interest-free deposits, *(~er Kredit)* interest-free loan

unverzinsliche Schatzanweisungen Treasury discount paper □ discounted notes issued with maturities between six and twenty-four months by the Federal Government and the Land Governments. Interest is paid by way of a discount from the purchase price.

unverzollt *(~e Waren)* uncleared (uncustomed) goods

unverzüglich *(~e Lieferung)* immediate (prompt) delivery, *(~ überweisen)* to remit immediately (without undue delay, at once)

unvollkommen incomplete, imperfect, defective, *(~er Markt)* imperfect market

unvollständig *(~e Angaben)* incomplete information, *(~e Lieferung)* short delivery, *(~er Wettbewerb)* imperfect competition

Unvollständigkeit incompleteness, imperfection

unvoreingenommen *(~er Schiedsrichter)* impartial (unbias(s)ed, unprejudiced) arbitrator

unvorhergesehen *(~e Schwierigkeiten)* unforeseen (unexpected) difficulties

unvorhersehbar unforeseeable, unpredictable, *(praktisch ~)* virtually impossible to forecast

unvorsichtig *(~e Anlage)* imprudent (rash, unwary) investment, *(~e Verwahrung)* careless custody

Unvorsichtigkeit imprudency, rashness, carelessness

unwägbar *(~e Folgen)* imponderable (unforeseeable) consequences

Unwägbarkeit *(konjunkturelle ~en)* economic imponderables (vagaries)

unwahrscheinlich *(~e Zinsentwicklung)* unlikely (unprobable) trend in interest rates

unwandelbar (*~e Schuldverschreibung*) unconvertible bond

unwesentlich (*~ beteiligte Partei*) party holding no material interest, (*~er Beitrag*) insignificant (immaterial) contribution, (*~er Vertragsbruch*) minor breach of contract

unwiderlegbar (*~er Nachweis*) irrefutable (irrebuttable) evidence

unwiderruflich (*~es Akkreditiv*) irrevocable letter of credit, (*~e Kreditzusage*) irrevocable loan undertaking, committed credit facility, (*~e Refinanzierungszusage*) irrevocable undertaking to fund (to refinance), (*der Weltbank*) unqualified agreement to refinance, (*~e Rembourszusage*) irrevocable commitment to reimburse

Unwiderruflichkeit irrevocability, irrevocableness

unwidersprochen (*~er Bericht*) uncontradicted (unchallenged) report

unwiederbringlich (*~er Bonitätsverlust*) irretrievable (irrecoverable) loss in credit standing

unwirksam (*~e Bestimmung*) inoperative (invalid) rule, (*~e monetäre Instrumente*) ineffective monetary tools, (*~e Stabilisierungsbemühungen*) ineffectual (ineffective, fruitless) stabilisation efforts, (*~er Vertrag*) invalid (void) agreement

Unwirksamkeit invalidity, (*~ einer Sicherungsbeziehung*) ineffectiveness of a hedge

unwirtschaftlich (*~er Betrieb*) unprofitable (uneconomical, inefficient) operation

Unwirtschaftlichkeit unprofitability, uneconomicalness, inefficiency

unzählig (*~e Versuche*) countless (innumerable) attempts

Unzufriedenheit dissatisfaction, (*~ der Aktionäre*) shareholder discontent

unzugänglich (*~er Markt*) inaccessible market

unzulänglich inadequate, insufficient

Unzulänglichkeit (*~en in der Kundenbetreuung*) inadequacies in customer counselling

unzulässig inadmissible, not permitted, unlawful, (*~e Einmischung*) inadmissible interference, (*~e Überziehung*) unauthorised overdraft, (*~e Rechtsausübung*) → Rechtsmissbrauch

unzureichend (*~ abgesicherter Gläubiger*) undersecured creditor, (*~e Deckung*) inadequate cover, insufficient funds, (*~e Kapitalausstattung*) inadequate equity base, undercapitalisation, (*~e Sicherheit*) inadequate security (collateral), (*~e Vertragserfüllung*) defective contractual performance (compliance)

unzuständig (*~es Gericht*) incompetent court, court having no jurisdiction

Unzuständigkeit incompetence, lack of jurisdiction (competence)

unzustellbar (*~e Lieferung*) undeliverable consignment (shipment)

unzutreffend **1.** inapplicable, not applicable, (*falls ~ bitte streichen*) delete if not applicable, (*~es streichen*) delete as appropriate
2. (*unbegründet*) unfounded

unzuverlässig (*~er Kreditnehmer*) unreliable borrower

unzweideutig (*~e Kauforder*) clear (unambiguous) buy order

unzweifelhaft (*~e Bonität*) undoubted (unquestionable) credit-worthiness

Urheberrechts / ~gesetz Copyright Act; **~wahrnehmungsgesetz** Copyright Administration Act

Urkunde deed, instrument, document

Urkunden / ~anhang rider, appendix; **~ausfertigung** execution of a deed; **~beweis** documentary evidence; **~einsicht** inspection of documents; **~prozess** summary proceedings; **~register** register of documents, notarial register, registry of deeds

urkundlich (*~er Nachweis*) documentary proof

Urkundsbeamter certifying (authenticating) officer, Registrar

Urlaub *(tariflicher ~)* paid leave (holiday, vacation)

Urlaubsgeld holiday pay, vacation allowance (money)

Ursachenzusammenhang causal relationship, proximate cause

Ursprung 1. origin **2.** source

ursprünglich original, initial, *(eine Hypothek zu den ~en Konditionen übernehmen)* to assume a mortgage on the same rate and conditions as were originally granted, *(~e Unmöglichkeit der Leistungserfüllung)* initial impossibility of performance □ impediments existing already upon conclusion of the contract, → nachträgliche/→ objektive Unmöglichkeit der Leistungserfüllung

Ursprungs / ~erklärung statement of origin; **~geschäft 1.** original contract (deal) **2.** underlying transaction, **~kapital** *(einer Hypothek)* original principal; **~land** country of origin; **~laufzeit** original maturity, original term to maturity; **~zeugnis** certificate of origin

Urteil 1. judg(e)ment, sentence, verdict, ruling **2.** *(Meinung)* opinion, view, judg(e)ment

urteilen to judge, to give (to render) a verdict, to pass judgment, *(nach den jüngsten Konjunkturindikatoren zu ~)* judging by (from) the latest economic indicators

Urteils / ~anerkennung (foreign) judgment recognition; **~aufhebung** reversal (rescission) of a judgment, setting aside a verdict; **~begründung** opinion of the Court, reasons for verdict; **~gläubiger** judgment creditor; **~schuldner** judgment debtor

Urteils / ~spruch judgment, verdict; **~verkündung** rendition (pronouncement) of judgment, rendering judgment; **~vermögen** judgment, ability to judge; **~vollstreckung** enforcement of a judgment (sentence)

Usance 1. custom, usage, *(~ des Marktes)* market custom(s), market practice, established practice in the market **2.** commission (fee) usually charged

usancegemäß 1. by convention **2.** in line (in accordance) with standard market practice, *(~er Betrag)* amount customary in trading

Usance-Handel cross currency dealings

Usance-Kredite drawings on amounts credited due payment provided (e.g. cheques deposited for collection)

Usance-Kurs cross rate □ the exchange rate for one non-USD currency against another non-USD currency

usancemäßig → usancegemäß

U-Schätze → unverzinsliche Schatzanweisungen

UWG → Gesetz gegen den unlauteren Wettbewerb

V

VAG → Versicherungsaufsichtsgesetz

vagabundierend *(~e Gelder)* erring funds

vakant vacant, unoccupied, unfilled, open

Validierungs / ~fehler validation error; **~instanz** validation authority; **~verfahren** validation process

Valoren 1. *(Wertsachen)* valuables **2.** *(Wertpapiere)* securities; **~versicherung** valuables insurance

valorisieren to valorise

Valuta 1. *(Währung)* currency **2.** *(Wertstellung)* value date, *(mit ~ des nächsten Geschäftstages)* for value on the next business day **3.** *(Darlehenserlös)* loan proceeds

Valuta kompensiert same-day value (for delivery and payment)

Valuta / ~-Akzept foreign currency acceptance; **~-Anlagen** foreign currency assets (investments); **~-Anleihe** foreign currency bond, bond issued by a German issuer in a foreign currency; **~forderungen** foreign currency receivables

valutagerecht *(~e Erfüllung von Zahlungsverpflichtungen* meeting payment obligations under good value

Valutageschäft foreign currency transaction, exchange transaction (deal)

valutagleich *(~e Abrechnung)* same-day settlement, settlement under identical value dates

Valutaklausel foreign currency clause

valutakongruent *(~e Kauf- und Verkaufspositionen)* long and short positions with matching value dates, *(~e Refinanzierungen)* funding at matching currencies

Valuta / ~konto foreign currency account; **~kredit** foreign currency loan (lending); **~papiere** foreign currency stock (securities); **~politik** monetary policy; **~position** foreign exchange position

valutarisch *(~er Eingang)* value-wise receipt, *(~er Gewinn) (a)* value-wise profit *(b) (im Scheckzahlungsverkehr der Banken)* float profit, *(~er Saldo)* current balance, value-wise balance, *(~e Überziehung)* value-wise (value-dated) overdraft (debit balance), overdraft resulting from the application of different value dates

Valuta / ~risiko exchange (currency) risk; **~scheck** foreign currency cheque; **~schuld** foreign currency debt; **~schuldschein** borrower's currency note; **~stellung 1.** fixing the value date(s) **2.** value date applied

Valuta / ~tag value date; **~-Tagesposition** daily foreign exchange position; **~trassierungskredit** currency acceptance credit; **~verhältnis** relationship between obligor and beneficiary of a payment, *i.w.S.* underlying obligation

Valuta / ~wechsel currency bill; **~wertsteigerung** currency appreciation; **~zeitraum** additional time for payment

Valuten 1. *(Fremdwährungen)* foreign currencies **2.** *(Fremdwährungskupons)* foreign currency coupons

Valuten / ~arbitrage currency arbitrage; **~durchschnitt** mean value date; **~saldo** → valutarischer Saldo

valutieren 1. *(die Wertstellung festlegen)* to value-date, to fix (to apply) a value date, *(mit dem nächsten Geschäftstag ~)* to value-date for the next business day

2. *(Darlehen/Kredit ~)* to disburse a loan, *(die valutierende Kreditsumme)* the loan amount currently outstanding, *(der Kredit valutiert mit € ...)* the loan amounts to € ..., *(der valutierte Kredit)* the loan amount made available (credited to the borrower's account)
(die Kreditlinie valutiert noch mit € ...) € ... are still outstanding under the credit line, *(solange der Kredit valutiert)* as long as the loan facility is being utilised, *(vollständige valutierte Fazilität)* fully drawn facility
3. *(Garantie/Bürgschaft) (valutierter Gesamtbestand von Bürgschaften und Garantien)* surety bonds and guarantees currently outstanding (furnished)
4. *(Grundschuld) (valutierte Grundschuld)* land charge provided (used) as collateral, *(die Grundschuld kann mit mehreren Darlehen valutiert werden)* the land charge may serve as collateral/security for several loans (up to the maximum amount recorded in the land register)
(die mit € 60 000 bestellte Grundschuld ist mit € 30 000 valutiert) the land charge recorded in the amount of € 60 000 is utilised with € 30 000, *(die Grundschuld ist nicht mehr valutiert)* the land charge is recorded in the land register, but no longer serving as collateral, → Nichtvalutierungserklärung
5. *(auf US Dollar valutierende Verträge)* contracts denominated in USD
6. to set a date for payment/for performance, *(die Anleihe wird am 1. Februar valutiert)* interest on the bond starts to accrue on February 1

Valutierung 1. fixing the value date(s), *(mit gleicher ~)* → valutagleiche Abrechnung, *(~ eingehender Zahlungen)* value date applied to incoming payments, *(mit der ~ wirksam werden)* to take effect on the value date
2. *(im Kreditgeschäft)* loan disbursement, *(bei ~ in Abzug bringen)* to deduct when the loan amount is made available, *(die ~ des Kredites erfolgt nach Genehmigung durch unsere zuständigen Kreditausschüsse)* the loan will be made available (drawdowns will be possible) once our senior loan committees have given their approval
3. *(einer Grundschuld)* provision (use) of a land charge as collateral
4. *(im Devisenhandel: 2-Werktags-Valutierung)* settlement two working days from trade date
5. *(im Wertpapiergeschäft) (a)* start of interest period, date on which interest starts to accrue *(b)* settlement, debiting the amount subscribed to the subscriber's account

Valutierungsbetrag loan amount (made available)

Valutierungstag/~termin 1. *(Wertstellung)* value date
2. *(im Kreditgeschäft)* date of disbursement, date on which the loan is made available (credited to the borrower's account)
3.*(im Devisenhandel)* settlement day
4. *(im Wertpapiergeschäft) (a)* date of payment *(b)* settlement day (date), date on which the amount subscribed will be debited to the subscriber's account

Valutierungsvoraussetzungen prerequisites for disbursement of the loan

VaR value at risk □ maximum expected loss that will not be exceeded

VaR-Abschlag VaR-based haircut

variabel (*~ verzinsliche Anleihe)* floater, floating rate bond, (*~ verzinsliche Hypothek)* variable rate mortgage, adjustable rate mortgage,

variable (*~ Gemeinkosten*) variable overhead expenses, *(~ Mittelaufnahme)* borrowing floating rate funds, *(~ Notierung)* variable price quotation, continuous price-setting, (*~ Werte)* floaters, floating price securities, *(~ Zins-/Swapseite)* floating leg

variabler (*~ Handel*) continuous trading, variable price trading (dealing), *(~ Kurs)* variable price, (*~ Markt)* variable price market, (*Kredit mit*

V

~ *Verzinsung)* variable interest (floating rate) loan

variables (~ *Zinsänderungsrisiko)* floating rate risk

Varianz variance, square of the standard deviation

Varianzanalyse variance analysis

Varianz-Swap variance swap □ Forward contract on the variance of a financial instrument during a pre-specified time period. Payoff profile at maturity: if the realised variance is higher than the pre-agreed level, the holder of a variance swap position makes a profit (the seller a loss). Conversely, if the realised variance is lower the holder makes a loss and the seller a profit.

Varianz-Swapfälligkeiten variance swap maturities

Variations / **~breite** variation range; **~koeffizient** variation ratio; **~rechnung** calculus of variations

VDAX volatility index of the Frankfurt Stock Exchange

Vega same as Kappa

verabschieden 1. *(einen Beschluss ~)* to adopt (to carry, to pass) a resolution **2.** *(einen Gesetzentwurf ~)* to pass a bill, (*mit Stimmenmehrheit* ~) to pass by a majority of votes

Verabschiedung adoption, carrying, passing

Veralterung *(~ von Sachanlagen)* obsolescence of plant and equipment

verändern 1. to alter, to modify, to change **2.** *(schwanken)* to vary, to fluctuate

Veränderung 1. alteration, modification, change **2.** variation, fluctuation, *(~en im Wertberichtigungsbestand)* movements in the total allowance for loan losses

Veränderungsmanagement change management

verankern to embody, to incorporate, to lay down, (*gesetzlich verankert*) enshrined in law, *(fest ~)* firmly established, *(im Gesellschaftsrecht verankerte Grundsätze)* principles set forth (embodied) in corporate law, (*im Markt verankert ~ sein)* to have its roots (to be rooted) in the market

veranlagen to assess, *(gemeinsam/einzeln veranlagt werden)* to be jointly (individually) assessed for tax

Veranlagung *(steuerliche)* assessment, (~ *zur Einkommensteuer)* assessment on income

Veranlagungs / **~basis** basis of assessment; **~jahr** year of assessment; **~satz** rate of assessment; **~zeitraum** assessment period

veranschlagen *(Kosten)* to estimate, to draw up a cost estimate, to appraise, (*auf ca. € ... ~)* to put at around € ..., (*die Kosten wurden mit nahezu € ... veranschlagt)* the cost was estimated to be almost € ...

Veranschlagung estimate, appraisal

verantworten to answer for, to assume the responsibility for

veranwortlich responsible, liable, accountable, answerable, (~ *machen)* to hold liable (responsible) for, to blame, (~ *zeichnen für)* to answer for, to assume (to take) the responsibility for

Verantwortlichkeit responsibility, accountability

Verantwortlichkeitsrechnung responsibility accounting

Verantwortung responsibility, liability

Verantwortungs / **~bewusstsein** sense of duty (responsibility), *(verantwortungsbewusst)* conscientious, responsible; **~freudigkeit** willingness to take (to accept) responsibility; **~losigkeit** irresponsibility

verarbeiten 1. process **2.** *(die Auswirkungen der Zinserhöhung ~)* to digest the repercussions of the interest rate hike

Verarbeitung processing

verarbeitungsfähig *(~e Datei)* processable file

V

Verarbeitungswege *(bei einem Geschäftsvorfall)* transaction trail

Verästelung *(~en eines Konzerns)* ramifications of a group

verauslagen to advance, to spend, to disburse, *(vorab verauslagte Mittel)* funds advanced

veräußerbar *(jederzeit ~e Wertpapiere)* available-for-sale securities

Veräußerer alienor, transferor, *(bei einer Forderungsverbriefung)* originator

veräußern to sell (off), to alienate, to dispose

Veräußerung sale, selling off, alienation, disposal, (*~ von Anlagen)* asset disposal, (*~ von Unternehmen/Unternehmensteilen)* divestiture, disposal of an investment, (*~ von Werten aus dem Deckungsbestand)* selling assets from the asset pool serving as collateral, *(zur ~ stehende finanzielle Vermögenswerte)* available-for-sale financial assets

Veräußerungs / ~befugnis power of sale; **~beschränkungen** restraints on alienation; **~entgelt** disposal proceeds; **~erlös** amount realised, disposal proceeds

Veräußerungs / ~geschäfte sales transactions; **~gewinn** capital gain, gain on the sale (disposal) of; **~gewinnbesteuerung** taxation of capital gains; **~kosten** disposal cost

Veräußerungs / ~recht right of disposal, right to alienate; **~verbot** sales ban, *(allgemeines ~)* general restraint on alienation; **~verlust** capital loss; **~wert 1.** realisable value, sales price **2.** *(einer Beteiligung)* exit value

Verband association, federation

V

Verbandsklagerecht association's right of action

verbessern 1. to improve, to enhance, (*die Aussichten beginnen sich zu ~)* the outlook is brightening **2.** *(berichtigen)* to correct, to amend, to revise **3.** *(sich ~, im Kurs anziehen)* to improve, to pick up, to put on, to advance

Verbesserung 1. improvement, enhancement, *(~ der Ertragslage)* improvement in earnings, *(~ der Kreditqualität)* credit enhancement, (*~ der Sicherheitenregelung)* security enhancement, enhancement of the collateral arrangement, *(~ gegenüber dem Vorjahresergebnis)* improvement on last year's result
2. *(Berichtigung)* correction, amendment, revision
3. *(Kursbefestigung)* advance

verbieten to prohibit, to forbid, to ban, to outlaw

verbilligen 1. to lower (the price), to cheapen, *(die Hypothekenkreditaufnahme ~)* to lower mortgage lending rates
2. *(sich ~, im Kurs fallen)* to fall, to drop, to drift lower

Verbilligung 1. lowering, cheapening, (*~ der Refinanzierung der Banken)* lowering the cost of funds to banks, decrease in funding costs **2.** fall

verbinden 1. to connect, to combine, to join, to couple, to link, → verbunden **2.** *(vereinigen)* to unite

verbindlich 1. binding, *(~e Kreditzusage)* firm loan undertaking, binding commitment to lend, *(~e Kursgebote)* binding quotes
2. *(~ sein)* to be binding, to have binding force, (*nach Billigung ist der Vorschlag für alle Parteien ~)* the proposal, if sanctioned, becomes binding on all concerned
3. *(verpflichtend)* obligatory, compulsory, *(~e Eigenkapitalanforderung)* mandatory minimum capital requirement

Verbindlichkeit 1. binding nature (character), *(Rechtskraft)* binding force **2.** *(Schuld)* liability, debt
3. *(Verpflichtung)* engagement, liability, obligation, commitment

Verbindlichkeiten liabilities, amounts (accounts) payable

Verbindlichkeiten aus (*~ Anleiheemissionen*) bonds payable, (*~ der Bege-*

bung und Übertragung von Wechseln) liabilities from the drawing and endorsement of bills, *(~ Bürgschaften)* liabilities from (on) surety bonds furnished, *(~ Einlagen)* deposit obligations (liabilitics), liabilities to depositors
(~ Lieferungen und Leistungen) trade payables, trade creditors, *(~ Pensionsgeschäften)* liabilities under repurchase agreements, *(~ Sichteinlagen)* demand deposit liabilities
(~ Währungstermingeschäften) liabilities on forward exchange contracts, *(~ Warenlieferungen)* trade payables, accounts payable (trade), *(~ Wertpapiergeschäften)* amounts payable for securities traded, *(~ Wertpapierpensionsgeschäften)* liabilities on (under) securities repurchase agreements

Verbindlichkeiten gegenüber *(~ Banken)* liabilities (due) to banks, exposure to banks, bank debts, liabilities to financial institutions, bank loans and overdrafts, *(~ Kunden)* liabilities to customers, *(~ verbundenen Unternehmen)* amounts owed to group companies

Verbindlichkeiten mit *(~ täglicher Fälligkeit)* liabilities payable on demand, *(~ unbestimmter Laufzeit)* undated liabilities, indeterminate-term liabilities, *(~ vereinbarter Laufzeit)* liabilities subject to an agreed term

Verbindlichkeiten / ~quote ratio of liabilities to total assets; **~spiegel** statement of liabilities

Verbindung 1. connection, link, linkage **2.** (customer) relationship, affiliation, *(enge ~ zu einem Unternehmen)* close affiliation (association) with a company **3.** *(in ~ stehen mit)* to be in contact with, *(in ~ treten zu)* to contact, to liaise with, to establish contacts with

Verbindungs / ~ausschuss liaison committee; **~stelle** liaison agency

Verbleib 1. *(~ des Schecks)* whereabouts of the cheque **2.** *(~ der Sicherheit im Besitz des Kreditnehmers)* collateral remaining in the possession of the borrower

verbleiben to remain, *(im Amt ~)* to remain (to stay, to continue) in office, *(das Eigentum verbleibt bei dem Schuldner)* the ownership is retained by the debtor, *(die Gelder ~ im Unternehmen)* the funds remain invested in the company, *(das Kreditrisiko verbleibt bei der Bank)* the bank retains the credit risk

verborgen *(~e Verbindlichkeiten)* hidden liabilities, *(~e Vermögenswerte)* hidden assets

Verbot prohibition, ban, interdiction

verbrauchen *(die Rücklagen ~)* to use up (to exhaust, to deplete) the reserves

Verbraucher / ~insolvenzverfahren consumer insolvency procedure; **~kredit** consumer credit; **~kreditgesetz** Consumer Credit Act; **~kreditrichtlinie** (EU) Consumer Credit Directive; **~preisindex** cost-of-living index, consumer price index

verbreiten 1. to spread, to proliferate **2.** *(Kurse/Informationen ~)* to disseminate prices/information

verbreitern 1. to broaden, to widen **2.** to strengthen

Verbreiterung *(~ der Finanzierungsquellen)* broadening of funding sources, *(~ der Kapitalbasis)* broadening (strengthening) the equity base, *(~ der Zinsspanne)* widening of the interest margin

Verbreitung 1. spreading, proliferation, increasing use **2.** *(~ von Kursinformationen)* dissemination of price information

verbriefen 1. *(Darlehens-/Hypothekenforderungen)* to securitise loans/mortgages **2.** *(dokumentieren)* to document, to evidence the ownership (an ownership claim), to give conclusive proof of ownership
3. *(urkundlich bestätigen/zusichern)* to certificate, to certify
4. *(ein Recht ~)* to vest a right in

V

verbrieft *(~e Ansprüche)* certificated claims, *(~e Kredite)* securitised loans (assets), *(~e Kreditkartenforderungen)* securitised card receivables, *(~e Hypothekendarlehen)* securitised residential mortgage loans, *(~es Recht)* certificated (vested) right

Verbriefung 1. securitisation, *(~ von Darlehensforderungen)* loan securitisation, packaging loans into securities, *(~ ganzer Geschäftseinheiten oder aller Forderungen/Aktiva)* whole business securitisation, (~ *von Hypothekenforderungen)* mortgage securitisation, *(~ von Immobilien)* real estate securitisation
(~ *von Kreditkartenforderungen)* credit card securitisation, securitisation of credit card receivables, *(~ von Retail-Krediten)* securitisation of retail exposures, *(~ von Sachversicherungsrisiken)* non-life securitisation, *(~ von Verbindlichkeiten)* debt securitisation, *(~ von Versicherungsrisiken)* insurance securitisation, *(~ zukünftiger Zahlungsströme)* securitisation of future cash flows
2. certification, evidencing the ownership, (~ *von Wertpapieren durch Urkunden)* certification of securities, physical representation of securities

Verbriefungs / ~fonds securitisation fund; **~garantie** securitisation guarantee; **~geschäft** securitisation activities; **~gesellschaft** securitisation company; **~liquiditätsfazilität** securitised liquidity facility; **~markt** securitisation market; **~position** securitisation exposure; **~programm** securitisation scheme

Verbriefungs / ~risiko securitisation risk(exposure); **~risikogewicht** securitisation risk weight; **~tranche** securitisation tranche; **~volumen** securitisation portfolio; ~ **zweckgesellschaft** special purpose vehicle (company)

verbuchen 1. to enter, to post, *(auf ein Konto ~)* to post (to pass) to an account, to enter into an account, *(in der laufenden Rechnungsperiode ~)* to recognise in the current accounting period
2. *(registrieren)* to register, to record
3. *(verzeichnen)* to score, (*Kursgewinne ~)* to score (to register) price gains, *(einen Umsatzzuwachs ~)* to register an increase in sales

Verbuchung 1. entry, posting **2.** accounting treatment, recognising **3.** registering, scoring

Verbund 1. association, group **2.**network, linkage

Verbund / ~beteiligungen participating interests (under the cooperative umbrella); **~darlehen** joint loan extension (e. g. by a commercial and a mortgage bank); **~dienstleistungen** association (integrated) services; **~direktorium** joint (interlocking) management; **~effekte** economies of scope, synergies

verbunden 1. associated, connected, linked, (*~e Bankprodukte)* related banking products, *(~e Geschäfte)* related trades, (*Geschäfte mit ~en Parteien)* related party transactions, (*durch gemeinsame Geschäftsinteressen ~ sein)* to be connected through (by) common business interests, *(~e Parteien)* related (connected) parties (*~es Unternehmen)* affiliated (associated) company, group undertaking, *(eng ~e Unternehmen)* closely related (linked) companies, (*eng ~e Währungen)* closely correlated currencies, (~ *mit einem ständig zunehmenden Wettbewerb)* coupled with an ever growing competition
2. attaching to, inherent in, (*die mit Aktien ~en Stimmrechte)* the voting rights attaching to shares, (*die mit dem Geschäft ~en Konditionen)* the conditions attached to the deal, (*das mit Wertpapiergeschäften ~e Risiko)* the risk inherent in securities transactions
3. *(~e Versicherung)* comprehensive insurance
4. *(mit etwas ~ sein, implizieren)* to involve, to entail, (*mit einem hohen*

Kapitalaufwand ~ sein) to entail (to involve) heavy capital expenditure

Verbundenheit **1.** connection **2.** attachment, closeness

Verbund / ~finanzierung joint financing, one-stop financing, all funds being provided by the same institution; **~geschäfte** cross selling; **~gesellschaft** affiliate, associated entity; **~notierung** unified quotation system, composite quotation

Verbund / ~umsätze cross sales; **~vorteile** economies of scope; **~werbung** joint advertising; **~wirtschaft** integrated operations, vertical integration

verbürgen to guarantee, to stand surety, to answer for, to warrant, to vouch for, *(sich für die Rückzahlung ~)* to guarantee the repayment

verdecken to cover, to hide, to mask

verdeckt hidden, secret, *(~es Aufgeld)* undisclosed premium, *(~es Factoring)* non-notification factoring, *(~e Dividendenausschüttung)* constructive dividend, disguised dividend distribution, *(~e Gewinnausschüttung)* hidden profit distribution
(~e Sacheinlagen) hidden non-cash distributions, *(~es Sicherungsrecht)* secret lien, *(~es Treuhandkonto)* undisclosed trustee account □ bank account in the name of a notary or solicitor, *(~e Wechselbürgschaft)* indirect bill guarantee □ accepting liability on a bill by acting as drawer, acceptor or endorser

verdeutlichen to document, to illustrate, to be illustrative of, *(die Kreditrisiken ~)* to highlight the credit risks

verdichten **1.** *(sich zu einem Kreditrisiko ~)* to crystallise into a credit risk **2.** *(zu einem Saldo ~)* to condense into one balance

verdienen **1.** to earn, to gain, *(verdiente Abschreibungen)* earned depreciation, *(verdiente Leistungsansprüche)* earned benefits (entitlements)
2. to deserve, to merit, to be worthy of, *(volles Vertrauen ~)* to deserve full confidence

Verdienst **1.** merit, credit **2.** *(Ertrag)* earnings **3.** *(Gewinn)* gain, profit **4.** *(Gehalt)* salary; **~ausfall** loss of earnings, lost earnings; **~bescheinigung** statement of earnings; **~spanne** profit margin

Verdingungs / ~ausschuss public procurement rules committee; **~ordnung** standard contract terms

verdoppeln to double, *(der Gewinn verdoppelte sich praktisch auf … €)* profits virtually doubled to € …, *(sich im Wert ~)* to double in value

Verdoppelung doubling

verdrängen **1.** to displace **2.** *(vom Kapitalmarkt ~)* to squeeze out (to put out) of the capital market **3.** *(aus einer Position ~)* to drive out of (to oust from) a position

Verdrängung displacement, squeezing out

Verdrängungs / ~preisgestaltung squeeze-out (put-out) pricing; **~wettbewerb** predatory competition

verdreifachen to treble, to triplicate, to increase threefold

Verdreifachung trebling, triplication

Verdrossenheit *(am Markt)* listlessness, disheartened sentiment, sullenness

veredeln to process, to finish, to improve

vereidigen to put s. o. under an oath, to swear s. o. in, *(vereidigter Sachverständiger)* sworn expert

Vereidigung swearing-in

Verein association, society

vereinbar compatible with, *(~ mit dem Geldmengenziel)* consistent with the monetary target

vereinbaren **1.** to agree (upon), to arrange, to stipulate, to fix **2.** to enter into an agreement with s. o. **3.** to reconcile with

vereinbart *(~e Kündigungsfrist)* agreed period of notice, *(~er Zinssatz)* agreed (stipulated) interest rate, *(falls nicht anderweitig ~)* unless otherwise agreed, *(Inanspruchnahme bis zur ~en Höhe)* drawing up to the prearranged limit, *(schriftlich ~)* agreed in writing

Vereinbarung agreement, contract, arrangement, *(~ über die Rückführung des Kredites)* agreement on the repayment of the loan, *(nach ~)* by arrangement, *(zu einer ~ gelangen)* to reach an agreement (understanding), to come to (to enter into) an agreement

vereinbarungsgemäß *(~ zahlen)* to pay as agreed upon

Vereinbarungstreuhand contractual trust

vereinfachen to simplify, to make easier

vereinfacht *(~es Ertragswertverfahren)* simplified income approach, *(~e Kapitalherabsetzung)* simplified capital reduction, *(~e Prospektpflicht)* simplified prospectus requirement, *(~er Verkaufsprospekt)* simplified sales prospectus

Vereinfachung 1. simplification, *(zur ~)* to simplify matters **2.** deregulation

vereinheitlichen to harmonise, to standardise, to level

Vereinheitlichung *(~der Rechnungslegungsgrundsätze)* harmonisation (standardisation) of accounting rules

vereinigen 1. to unify, to unite
2. *(fusionieren)* to merge, to amalgamate
3. *(zusammenfassen)* to combine, to join, to group together
4. *(30 % des Marktes auf sich ~)* to garner 30 % of the market
5. *(eine Stimmenmehrheit auf sich ~)* to poll (to receive) a majority of the votes

V

Vereinigung 1. unification, uniting **2.** merger, merging, amalgamation **3.** combination, grouping together **4.** *(Körperschaft)* body **5.** *(Verein)* association, society **6.** *(Zusammenkunft)* meeting, assembly

vereinnahmen 1. to receive, *(vereinnahmte Netto-Optionsprämie)* net premium received, *(vereinnahmte Steuergutschriften)* tax credits received
2. *(beitreiben, einbringen)* to recover, *(zuvor abgeschriebene Beträge ~)* to recover prior write-offs, *(vereinnahmte Beträge auf abgeschriebene Forderungen)* recoveries on previous charge-offs, recoveries on amounts written off
3. *(einziehen)* to collect, to cash, *(eine Prämie ~)* to collect a premium
4. *(verbuchen)* to recognise, to record, *(sofort ~)* to recognise in current earnings

Vereinnahmung 1. collection **2.** recovery **3.** recognition, *(~ von Erträgen)* income recognition

vereinzelt isolated, rare, *(~ geringfügige Abgaben)* scattered small selling, *(~e Kursgewinne)* scattered gains

vereiteln *(die geplante Übernahme ~)* to thwart (to frustrate, to upset) the planned takeover

verengen to narrow, to tighten

Verengung narrowing, tightening, contraction, squeeze, *(~ des Geldmarktes)* tightening up of the money market, squeeze in the money market, *(~ der Gewinnspannen)* narrowing of profit margins

vererben to leave by will, to bequeath

Verfahren 1. procedure, proceedings, method **2.** *(gerichtliches ~)* court proceedings, litigation, suit

Verfahrens / ~antrag procedural motion; **~beteiligte** parties to the proceedings; **~bevollmächtigter** procedural agent; **~dauer** duration of the proceedings; **~einstellung** abatement of action, overthrow of an action; **~fehler** procedural error

Verfahrens / ~gegenstand subject matter of the suit (of litigation); **~kosten** cost of proceedings; **~mängel** procedural flaws; **~ordnung** rules of procedure; **~partei** party to the proceedings

Verfahrens / ~recht procedural law, adjective law; **~stopp** *(im Insolvenzver-*

fahren) moratorium on all proceedings;~ **verzögerung** procedural delay; ~**wert** litigation value

Verfall 1. *(Ablauf)* expiration, expiry, lapse of time, termination, *(~ einer Garantie)* expiration (determination) of a guarantee, *(~ einer Option)* expiry of an option, *(~ einer Versicherungspolice)* expiration of an insurance policy, termination of a policy by lapse of time
2. *(Fälligkeit)* maturity, due date
3. *(~ der Kurse)* collapse (nosedive, sharp decline) of prices
4. *(Verwirkung)* forfeiture, *(~ eines Rechtes durch Nichtausübung)* forfeiture of a right through neglect to exercise it
5. *(Zusammenbruch)* disintegration

verfallbar *(~er Anspruch/~ es Recht)* forfeitable claim/right

verfallen 1. *(ablaufen)* to expire, to lapse, to come to an end, *(eine Option ~ lassen)* to abandon an option, to let an option expire worthless, to allow an option to lapse
2. *(ungültig werden)* to become invalid (void, worthless, forfeited), to cease to be valid, *(die Rechte ~ bei …)* the rights are forfeited upon …
3. *(zusammenbrechen)* to disintegrate

Verfall(s) / ~erklärung 1. forfeiture statement **2.** calling in for repayment; ~**frist** preclusive period; ~**klausel** forfeiture (determination, expiry) clause; ~**monat** *(im Options-/Futures-Handel)* contract month, delivery month

Verfall(s) / ~rendite yield-to-maturity; ~**tag**/~**termin** expiry (expiration) date, maturity (due) date, *(im Optionsgeschäft)* expiry date; ~**zyklus** *(eines Optionskontraktes)* expiration cycle

verfälschen 1. *(Bilanz, Kontounterlagen)* to falsify, to fake **2.** *(Informationen)* to falsify, to misrepresent

verfassen to write, to draw up, to draft

Verfassung *(einer Gesellschaft)* constitution of a company, *(~ des Marktes)* tone (state) of the market, market sentiment, *(in einer schlechten finanziellen ~)* in a poor financial shape

verfechten 1. to advocate, to fight for, to support strongly **2.** *(einen Anspruch ~)* to assert (to maintain) a claim

verfehlen to miss, to fail, *(die Erwartungen ~)* to fall (to be) short of expectations, *(das Geldmengenziel ~)* to miss the monetary target, *(weit)* to be wildly off the monetary target, *(die gewünschte Wirkung ~)* to fail to have the hoped-for effect

verfehlt 1. unsuccessful, abortive **2.** inappropriate

Verfehlung 1. *(~ des Umsatzziels)* missing (failure to reach) the sales target **2.** *(im Amt)* misdemeanour, offence

verfestigen *(sich ~)* to harden, to firm, to gather momentum

verflachen to flatten, to level off, to slacken

Verflachung 1. *(~ der Renditekurve)* flattening of the yield curve **2.** *(~ der Konjunktur)* levelling off in economic activity

verflechten to entwine, to interweave, to link up, to interlock, to dovetail

Verflechtung entwinement, linkage, links, interrelationship, *(~ der Kapitalmärkte)* entwinement (interpenetration, interlinking) of capital markets, *(die ~ zwischen den beiden Unternehmen)* the links (cross-linkage) between the two companies, *(kapitalmäßige ~)* cross shareholdings, *(kapitalmäßig verflochten)* linked through cross shareholdings

verflüssigen to turn into cash, to sell, to liquidate

Verflüssigung turning (converting) into cash, sale, *(~ des Marktes)* increasing the liquidity in the market, *(~ des Wertpapierbestandes)* liquidation (sale) of the securities portfolio

verfolgen *(eine Politik ~)* to pursue (to follow) a policy

Verfolgungsbehörde enforcement authority

verfügbarer Betrag stabiler Refinanzierung available amount of stable funding (ASF) □ denotes the amount of stable funding that a bank actually holds; consists in the main of the bank's capital, preferred stock with a maturity of one year or more, liabilities with effective maturities of one year or more, → Strukturelle Liquiditätsquote, → Mindestliquiditätsquote

verfügbares Einkommen disposable income

verfügbares Kontoguthaben balance available in the account, freely (unconditionally) available account balance

verfügbare Mittel liquid funds

Verfügbarkeit 1. disposability 2. *(~ langfristiger Kreditlinien)* availability of long-term credit lines

Verfügbarkeitsklausel availability clause

verfügen 1. *(besitzen)* to possess, to hold, to have at one's disposal, *(über große Bestände ~)* to hold (to carry) large inventories, to run (to maintain) a large book, *(über alle Informationen ~)* to be in possession of all the information, *(nicht über die notwendigen Mittel ~)* to lack the necessary funds, *(über breite Unterstützung ~)* to command widespread support
2. *(gerichtlich anordnen)* to rule, to decree
3. *(über Guthaben, Gelder)* to draw, to withdraw, to dispose of, *(über ein Konto ~)* to draw on an account, to withdraw funds from an account, *(durch Scheck über ein Konto ~)* to draw on an account by cheque
4. *(veräußern)* to sell, to dispose of

Verfügung 1. disposal, sale, *(~ über Vermögenswerte)* disposition of assets, *(zur ~ des Kunden halten)* to hold at the customer's disposal, *(zur ~ stehen)* to be available, to be at s. o.'s disposal, *(diese Emissionen stehen nicht mehr zur ~)* these issues are no longer on offer
(für eine Anlage zur ~ stehen) to be available for investment, *(jmd. zur ~ stellen)* to place at s. o.'s disposal, *(dem Zeichner zur ~ stellen)* to make available to the subscriber
2. drawing, withdrawal, *(~en über ein Konto)* drawings on an account, *(~ über den eingeräumten Kredit)* drawings on the loan extended, *(eine kurzfristige ~ über die Mittel)* drawing on the funds (withdrawing the funds) at short notice
3. order, ruling, injunction → einstweiligeVerfügung

Verfügungsanspruch 1. right to seek an injunction 2. → Verfügungsberechtigung

Verfügungsbefugnis *(~ über das Schuldnervermögen)* authority to dispose of the debtor's assets, → Verfügungsberechtigung

verfügungsberechtigt 1. entitled to dispose of 2. *(über ein Konto ~ sein)* to be authorised to draw on an account

Verfügungsberechtigte/r person authorised to draw (to sign) on an account

Verfügungsberechtigung 1. *(Berechtigung zur Veräußerung)* power of alienation (of sale), power to dispose of property (to sell property), right of disposal, *(gesetzliche ~)* power of disposition at law
2. *(Berechtigung zu Kontoverfügungen)* drawing authority (authorisation), authority to operate an account
3. *(Vollmacht)* power of attorney

Verfügungsbeschränkung 1. *(hinsichtlich einer Veräußerung)* restriction of the power of disposition 2. *(bei Konten)* drawing restriction, limitation of drawing powers

Verfügungsgeschäft transaction in satisfaction of a contract

Verfügungsgewalt control, *(~ der Bank)* bank's power of disposal (disposition), *(~ über den Nachlass)* power of disposition over the estate

Verfügungshöchstbetrag drawing (withdrawal) limit

Verfügungsmöglichkeit 1. *(jederzeitige ~ über das Konto)* right (power) to draw on the account at any time 2. *(Kredit)* drawing facility

Verfügungsrahmen 1. *(~ des Kreditnehmers)* drawing limit, line (funds) available for drawings 2. *(~ des Karteninhabers)* credit limit

Verfügungsrecht 1. *(gesetzliche ~e)* powers of disposition at law 2. *(~ des Insolvenzverwalters)* administrator's right to dispose of the debtor's assets

Verfügungsverbot ban on (against) any disposition of assets

Vergabe 1. *(~ eines Auftrages)* placing of an order, awarding a contract, contract award 2. *(~ eines Kredites)* extension (granting) of a loan, loan accommodation 3. *(~ des Syndizierungsmandats)* awarding the mandate to arrange the loan

Vergabe / **~ordnung** contract award rules; **~recht** public procurement law; **~sätze** 1. selling rates 2. lending rates

vergeben 1. *(Auftrag/Mandat)* to place, to award 2. *(einräumen)* to extend, to grant 3. *(ein Rating ~)* to assign a rating 4. *(die Position ist bereits ~)* the post has already been filled

vergeblich *(~e Sanierungsbemühungen)* futile (fruitless) efforts to rescue the company

Vergehen 1. *(z. B. Konkursvergehen)* offence 2. *(~ im Amt)* misdemeanour, malfeasance in office

vergeuden *(Mittel ~)* to squander (to waste, to misspend) funds

vergewissern *(sich ~)* to satisfy o. s.

Vergleich 1. comparison, *(im ~)* by comparison, *(im internationalen ~)* by international standards, *(Aktien im ~ zu Renten)* equities versus bonds, *(im ~ zum Vorjahr)* compared with the same period last year, *(einem ~ standhalten)* to bear comparison with (to)
2. *(mit Gläubigern)* compromise, composition, arrangement, *(gütliche Vereinbarung)* amicable settlement, *(durch einen ~ beilegen)* to settle by a compromise, *(einen ~ schließen)* to compound, to enter into a composition agreement

vergleichbar 1. comparable, *(Emissionen mit ~er Laufzeit)* instruments of comparable maturity, *(ein früheren Jahren ~es Ergebnis)* a performance comparable to that of previous years
2. *(ähnlich)* similar, alike, *(wenig ~ sein)* to bear little resemblance to

Vergleichbarkeit 1. comparability 2. resemblance, similarity

vergleichen 1. to compare with (to), to put against, *(wenn man die Bank mit deutlich größeren Konkurrenten vergleicht)* if the bank is put against much larger rivals
2. *(sich ~)* to compound, to compromise, *(sich mit seinen Gläubigern ~)* to enter into a composition agreement, to compound with one's creditors
3. *(Bücher, Konten)* to reconcile, to check

vergleichend *(~e Abschlüsse)* comparative financial statements

Vergleichs / **~abschluss** comparative statement; **~analyse** 1. comparative analysis 2. peer group analysis; **~angaben** comparative (reference) data; **~angebot** offer of compromise, proposal for a composition; **~antrag** petition for composition proceedings

Vergleichs / **~bedingungen** terms of composition (of a composition agreement); **~bereitschaft** willingness to come to a compromise (to a composition agreement); **~bewertung** comparative valuation; **~bilanz** 1. comparative balance sheet 2. *(in einem Vergleichsverfahren)* statement of affairs

Vergleichs / **~daten** comparative data; **~eröffnung** opening of composition proceedings; ~**fonds** settlement fund; ~**gläubiger** creditor in composition proceedings; ~**grundlage** basis for a settlement

Vergleichs / ~**index** reference index, benchmark; ~**jahr** comparable (reference) year; ~**klausel** 1. composition clause 2. *(Schiedsklausel)* arbitration clause; ~**lösung** compromise solution; ~**maßstab** benchmark

Vergleichs / ~**ordnung** composition rules; ~**periode** comparative period; ~**portefeuille** reference portfolio; ~**quote** dividend in composition; ~**rendite** benchmark return

Vergleichs / ~**tabelle** comparative schedule; ~**vereinbarung** composition agreement (deed), scheme of arrangement, *(Abschluss einer ~)* entering into a composition agreement; ~**verfahren** composition proceedings

Vergleichs / ~**verwalter** administrator (trustee) in composition proceedings, trustee under a scheme of arrangement, *(in den Vereinigten Staaten ferner)* settlement administrator; ~**verwaltung** administration in composition proceedings, settlement administration

Vergleichs / ~**vorschlag** 1. offer of compromise 2. proposal for a composition (an arrangement), proposed settlement; ~**weg** *(auf dem ~ beilegen)* 1. to settle by a compromise 2. to settle by way of an arrangement with one's creditors

vergleichsweise 1. comparatively, *(~ gering)* small in comparative perspective 2. *(~ Regelung)* settlement by way of a compromise

Vergleichs / ~**wert** 1. benchmark 2. comparative (reference) value; ~**wertverfahren** 1. comparison method, valuation based on comparisons 2. sales comparison approach; ~**zeitraum** comparable (reference) period; ~**zwecke** comparative purposes

vergrößern 1. to increase, to expand, to enlarge, to widen 2. *(intensivieren)* to intensify, to enhance, to strengthen 3. *(verschlimmern)* to aggravate, to exacerbate, to worsen, to compound, *(die Spanne ~)* to widen the spread, *(den Vorsprung ~)* to lengthen the lead

Vergrößerung 1. increase, expansion, enlargement, *(~ des Gefälles)* widening the gap (differential) 2. intensification, enhancement, strengthening 3. aggravation, exacerbation, worsening

Vergünstigung 1. preferential treatment, privilege, *(eine besondere ~ einräumen)* to make a special concession 2. *(Ermäßigung)* reduction, allowance 3. *(betriebliche ~en)* fringe benefits 4. *(steuerliche ~)* tax relief

vergüten 1. to pay, to remunerate, *(Dienstleistungen ~)* to remunerate services, *(einen Festzins ~)* to pay a fixed rate of interest 2. *(entschädigen)* to indemnify, to compensate 3. *(zurückzahlen)* to refund, to reimburse

Vergütung 1. remuneration, payment, compensation, *(~ nach Aufwand)* remuneration according to outlay, *(~ auf Honorarbasis)* fee-based remuneration 2. *(Honorar)* fee 3. *(Gratifikation)* bonus 4. *(Rückvergütung)* refund, reimbursement

Vergütungs / ~**antrag** refund application; ~**bestandteile** *(erfolgsbezogene ~)* performance-linked remuneration components; ~**grundsätze** remuneration policy; ~**system** compensation scheme; ~**vereinbarung** fee agreement

verhalten *(~es Kreditwachstum)* restrained (contained) growth in lendings, *(~e Nachfrage nach Aktien)* lacklustre demand for stocks

Verhalten 1. behaviour, conduct, attitude, *(standeswidriges ~)* professional misconduct 2. *(~ der Anleger)* investor behaviour (attitude)

Verhaltens / ~anforderungen conduct requirements; **~kodex** *(der Marktteilnehmer)* code of conduct; **~parameter** behavioural parameters; **~pflichten** *(des Kreditnehmers)* covenants and undertakings; **~regeln** professional rules of conduct; **~scoring** behavioural scoring

Verhältnis 1. proportion, *(im ~ zu) (a)* in proportion (relation) to *(b)* compared with, in comparison with, *(in keinem ~ zu)* out of proportion to **2.** relationship, ratio, *(~ von Eigenkapital zu Fremdkapital)* equity/debt ratio, *(die jungen Aktien zum Preis von 30 € je Aktie im ~ 4:1 beziehen)* to subscribe to the new shares at a price of € 30 per share and at a rate of one new share of every 4 held, *(Kapitalerhöhung im ~ 6:1)* one-for-six capital increase

verhältnismäßig 1. *(anteilsmäßig)* proportional, *(~e Zuteilung)* proportional allotment **2.** *(relativ)* relative, comparative, *(~ geringe Umsatzsteigerung)* comparatively low increase in sales

verhandeln 1. to negotiate, to bargain **2.** to debate, to discuss, to deliberate, to confer **3.** *(vor Gericht ~)* to hear (to try) a case

Verhandlung 1. negotiation(s), talks **2.** negotiating, bargaining, conferring **3.** *(Zivilsache)* hearing, *(Strafsache)* trial

Verhandlungs / ~abbruch breaking off negotiations; **~basis** basis for negotiation; **~beginn** opening of negotiations (of a hearing); **~führung** conduct of negotiations

Verhandlungs / ~geschick negotiating (bargaining) skills; **~lösung** negotiated solution; **~paket** negotiation package; **~partner** bargaining (negotiating) partner; **~position** bargaining position; **~protokoll** record of proceedings, minutes of the negotiations

Verhandlungs / ~runde round of talks; **~sache** matter for negotiation; **~spielraum** scope for negotiations (talks); **~stand** stage of negotiations; **~wege** *(auf dem ~)* by way of negotiation(s)

verhängen 1. *(eine Geldstrafe ~)* to levy a fine **2.** *(Sanktionen ~)* to impose sanctions

verhärten to harden, *(sich in der Haltung ~)* to toughen one's stance

Verhärtung toughening, hardening, stiffening

verhindern 1. to prevent, to impede **2.** *(ausschließen)* to preclude **3.** *(durchkreuzen)* to thwart, to forestall, to frustrate

Veritäts / ~aval/~garantie validity guarantee; **~haftung 1.** liability for the legal validity **2.** liability for providing correct information; **~risiko 1.** validity risk, risk related to the legal validity of purchased receivables **2.** dilution risk

verjährbar *(~er Anspruch)* claim (right) subject to the statute of limitations

verjähren to become statute-barred, to fall under the statute of limitations (statute of repose), to be extinguished by lapse of time, *(der Anspruch gegen den Garantiegeber verjährt nach sechs Jahren)* the claim against the guarantor is barred under the statute of limitations after a period of six years

verjährt *(~e Forderung)* statute-barred (time-barred) claim, debt barred by lapse of time (barred by limitation)

Verjährung falling under the statute of limitations, *(~ eines Anspruchs)* forfeiture of a claim through the statute of limitations, extinction of a claim by lapse of time, *(sich auf ~ berufen)* to plead the statute of limitations, *(der ~ unterliegen)* to be subject to the statute of limitations, to fall under the statute of limitations

Verjährungs / ~bestimmungen statute of limitations; **~frist** limitation period, *(nach Ablauf der ~)* after the limitation period has elapsed

Verkauf sale, *(~ unter Eigentumsvorbehalt)* sale subject to reservation of title, *(~ auf eigene/für fremde Rechnung)*

sale for own account/third party account, *(~ in offener Stellvertretung)* selling on a best efforts basis, *(~ auf dem Submissionsweg)* sale by tender *(~ per Kasse)* spot selling, spot sale, *(~ per drei Monate)* selling three months forward, *(~ per Termin)* forward sale, forward selling, *(zum ~ stehende Vermögenswerte)* assets held for sale (disposal), *(Wertpapiere zum ~ stellen)* to offer securities for sale

verkaufen 1. to sell, *(auf Baisse ~)* to sell on a fall, to sell on a declining market, *(bestens ~)* to sell at best (at the market), *(einschließlich/ausschließlich aller Rechte ~)* to sell cum/ex all rights, *(mit Gewinn ~)* to sell at a profit, *(sich gut ~)* to sell well, to find a ready market, *(auf Kredit ~)* to sell on credit, *(am freien Markt ~)* to sell in the open market, *(gegen den Markttrend ~)* to sell anti-marketwise
2. *(eine Verkaufsposition eingehen)* to go short, to take a short position, *(eine Option ~)* to sell (to write) an option, to open a short option position, → Verkaufsoption, *(per Termin ~)* to sell forward, to sell for future delivery, *(einen Terminkontrakt ~)* to sell a futures contract, to open a short futures position, *(verkaufter Terminkontrakt)* short futures position

Verkäufer seller, vendor; **~abruf** seller's call; **~bank** selling bank; **~darlehen** seller's (vendor's) loan; **~markt** seller's market; **~option** seller's option; **~seite** sell side

Verkaufs / ~abrechnung *(eines Wertpapiergeschäftes)* sold note; **~absicherung** short (selling) hedge;**~angebot** offer for sale; **~argument** selling point (argument); **~auftrag** selling (sell) order, *(zum Kurs limitierter ~)* stop loss order

Verkaufs / ~beschränkungen *(bei einer Neuemission)* selling restrictions, issue not for sale in …; **~druck** selling pressure, *(unter ~ geraten)* to come under selling pressure

Verkaufs / ~empfehlung sell recommendation (advice); **~erfolg** sales performance; **~ergebnis** net income (loss) from sale; **~erlös** sales (realisation) proceeds, amount realised; **~erlöse** sales revenue

Verkaufs / ~finanzierung sales financing; **~frist** selling (subscription) period; **~förderung** sales promotion; **~geschäft** sell trade; **~gruppe** selling group □ dealers or banks selling newly issued shares or bonds to investors on behalf of the underwriters; **~hedge** short hedge; **~höhepunkt** selling climax, washout (cleanout) day

Verkaufs / ~kommission selling commission; **~kommissionär** selling agent; **~kommissionsbank** agency bank; **~konditionen 1.** conditions of sale **2.** selling terms (rates); **~konsortium** selling group; **~kurs** offering (selling) price

Verkaufs / ~limit selling limit; **~mitteilung 1.** advice of sale **2.** *(bei Neuemissionen)* offer for sale

Verkaufsoption put option, *(~ auf einen Terminkontrakt)* futures put option, *(erworbene ~)* long put, *(verkaufte ~)* short put, *(Käufer einer ~)* put buyer (holder), *(Stillhalter/Verkäufer einer ~)* put writer, seller (writer) of a put option

Verkaufs / ~optionsschein put warrant; **~order** sell (selling) order; **~position** short position, *(über eine ~ verfügen)* to hold a short position, to be short

Verkaufs / ~prospekt sales (offering) prospectus; **~prospektgesetz** Securities Sales Prospectus Act; **~prospektverordnung** Sales Prospectus Ordinance □ specifies the minimum information requirements; **~provision** selling commission (concession); **~punkt** point of sale

Verkaufs / ~signal selling signal, signal to sell; **~spanne** sales margin; **~stelle** selling (subscription) agent

Verkaufs / ~vermittlung *(eine Emission zur ~ übernehmen)* to take up an issue (to undertake to sell an issue) on a best efforts basis; ~**verpflichtung** commitment to sell, obligation (undertaking) to sell, *(~ per Termin)* forward commitment to sell

Verkaufs / ~**vertrag** contract of sale, selling agreement; ~**vollmacht** authority to sell, power of sale; ~**volumen** total sales, sales volume; ~**welle** wave of selling, sell-off, selling surge, spate (welter) of selling

Verkaufs / ~**zinssatz** *(bei Diskontpapieren)* rate of discount, discount deducted from the par value; ~**zwang** obligation to sell

Verkehrsfähigkeit marketability, *(~ von Wertpapieren)* fungibility (tradeability) of securities, *(verkehrsfähige Forderungen)* marketable (tradeable) receivables

Verkehrs / ~**hypothek** conventional mortgage; ~**sitte** accepted practice; ~**steuer** transaction tax; ~**wert** fair value, market (current) value; ~**wertansatz** fair value approach

verkennen 1. to misjudge 2. *(unterschätzen)* to underestimate, to undervalue

verklagen to sue, to bring (to file) an action against, to take legal action

verkleinern *(Aktienpositionen ~)* to downsize (to reduce, to scale down) positions in the equity market

Verkleinerung downsizing, reduction, scaling down

verknappen 1. to become scarce (rare) 2. *(das Kreditangebot ~)* to tighten the credit supply

Verknappung 1. scarcity, shortage 2. tightening, *(~ am Geldmarkt)* tightening up of (contraction in) the money market

verknüpfen to connect, to link, to combine, → verbunden

Verknüpfung 1. connection, link, combination 2. *(Interdependenz)* interdependence, interrelation

verkörpern to evidence, to embody, to represent, *(einen Anspruch ~)* to represent a claim, *(durch Zertifikate verkörperte Anteile)* shares embodied (documented) in certificates, shares evidenced by certificates

verkraften to manage, to come to terms with, to absorb, *(das Unternehmen muss eine hohe Zinsbelastung ~)* the company has to cope (to digest) a high interest charge

verkünden 1. to announce 2. *(Gesetz)* to promulgate 3. *(Urteil)* to pronounce, to render, to deliver

verkürzen 1. to shorten, to reduce, to diminish, *(verkürzter Zeitraum)* shortened (truncated) period 2. *(abkürzen)* to abbreviate, to abridge, *(verkürzte Bilanz)* abbreviated accounts, 3. *(beschränken)* to limit, to curtail

Verkürzung 1. shortening, reduction, diminution 2. abbreviation, abridging 3. limitation, curtailment, *(~ der Bilanz)* contraction of the balance sheet, *(~ der Kreditlaufzeit)* shortening the term of the loan, shortening the maturity

Verladekonnossement (shipped) on board bill of lading

verladen *(an Deck des Schiffes ~)* to load on deck of the ship

verlagern 1. to shift, to switch, to move to (into), *(Gelder in Aktienwerte ~)* to shift funds into equities 2. *(anderweitig einsetzen)* to redeploy 3. *(auslagern)* to contract out, to farm out

Verlagerung 1. shift, shifting, switch, *(~ auf Anleihen)* shift towards (move into) bonds, *(~ des Schwergewichtes)* shift in emphasis 2. redeployment 3. contracting out, farming out, outsourcing

verlangen 1. to demand, to request, to ask for 2. *(bestehen auf)* to insist on, to persist

verlängerbar extendable, renewable, capable of being renewed (rolled over), *(~ nach Wahl des Kreditneh-*

mers) renewable at the option of the borrower, *(der Kredit ist jedes Jahr um weitere zwölf Monate ~)* the loan is extendable every year for another twelve months, *(monatlich ~er Vertrag)* monthly rolling contract

verlängern 1. to extend, to roll over, *(den Kredit um ein weiteres Jahr ~)* to extend the loan for another year, *(die Laufzeit auf zehn Jahre ~)* to extend the maturity to ten years, *(das Zahlungsziel ~)* to allow further time for payment, to grant an extension of the time for payment, to extend the credit period
2. to renew, *(sich automatisch um ein Vierteljahr ~)* to be automatically renewed for three months, *(einen Wechsel ~)* to prolong (to renew) a bill
3. to roll over, *(von einem Liefermonat auf den nächsten ~)* to roll over from one contract month to the next, *(bis zum nächsten geltenden Valutatag ~)* to roll into the next value date
4. to stretch, *(die Bilanz ~)* to stretch (to leverage) the balance sheet

verlängerter Eigentumsvorbehalt extended retention of title □ the seller authorises the buyer to re-sell the goods purchased against the buyer's assignment of the corresponding receivable (or of the proceeds from the resale)

Verlängerung 1. extension, *(~ einer Kreditlinie)* credit line extension, *(~ der Versicherungsdauer)* extension of the coverage (of the term of insurance), *(eine ~ der Zeichnungsfrist beantragen)* to seek an extension to the subscription deadline
2. *(~ eines Wechsels)* renewal of a bill, **3.** rollover, *(~ bei Fälligkeit)* rolling over (forward) at maturity

Verlängerungs / ~bedingungen terms of renewal, rollover terms; **~klausel** renewal (rollover) clause; **~kosten** renewal cost, cost of rolling over; **~option** renewal option, rollover option, option for extension, *(mit einer ~)* with the possibility of an extension for e. g. a further two years

Verlängerungs / ~provision renewal fee (commission), rollover (extension) fee; **~termin** rollover date; **~zeitraum** renewal period, rollover period; **~zinsen** extension interest

verlangsamen to slow down, to slacken, to decelerate, *(das Wachstum wird sich weiter ~)* growth will slow further, *(das Wachstum hat sich deutlich verlangsamt)* growth has decelerated significantly

Verlangsamung slowdown, slowing down, slackening, deceleration

Verlauf 1. course, *(~ der Verhandlungen)* course of negotiations, *(im ~ des letzten Jahres)* during the course of last year, *(im ~ der kommenden Monate)* over the coming months
2. development, tendency, trend, *(einen günstigen ~ nehmen)* to take a favourable turn
3. *(~ der Renditekurve)* shape of the yield curve

verlaufen 1. *(konträr zu den Markterwartungen ~)* to move contrary to market expectations
2. *(die Sanierungsbemühungen sind ohne Erfolg ~)* the rescue efforts failed (came to nothing, were of no avail)
3. *(die Hauptversammlung verlief wie üblich)* the general meeting took its usual course

verlautbaren to issue a statement, to announce

Verlautbarung statement, announcement

verlegen 1. *(den Sitz des Unternehmens ~)* to move (to relocate) the company's seat **2.** *(einen Termin ~)* to adjourn, to postpone

Verlegung 1. moving, move, relocation **2.** adjournment, postponement

verleihbar *(~e Titel)* securities eligible for lending transactions, → Wertpapierleihe

verleihen 1. to lend, to loan, to hire out, *(Gewicht ~)* to lend (to add) weight to, *(Glaubwürdigkeit ~)* to lend cred-

itibility to, *(Wertpapiere ~)* to lend (to loan out) securities
2. to confer, *(das Recht ~)* to confer the right, to vest with the right, *(Rechtskraft ~)* to render effective

Verleihen 1. lending, *(~ von Wertpapieren)* securities lending **2.** *(von Befugnissen)* conferring powers, vesting powers in

Verleiher *(bei einer Devisen-/Geld-/Wertpapierleihe)* lender

Verleih / ~gebühr lending fee; **~geschäft** lending transaction; **~rate** *(für Gold)* gold lease, cost of borrowing gold

Verleitung *(~ zum Vertragsbruch)* tortious inducement of breach of contract, tortious interference, interference with contractual relations

verletzen to violate, to infringe, to break, to contravene

Verletzung violation, infringement, breach, contravention, *(~ eines Patentes)* infringement of a patent, *(~ von Rechten/Vertragsbedingungen)* infringement (violation) of rights/of contract terms, *(~ der Sorgfaltspflicht)* tort of negligence, *(~ von Wertpapiergesetzen)* violation of securities laws

verlieren 1. to lose, *(an eine Konkurrenzbank ~)* to lose out to a rival bank, *(ein Recht ~)* to lose (to forfeit) a right **2.** *(an Wert ~)* to fall in value

verloren gehen to be lost (missing), *(verloren gegangene Zertifikate)* lost (missing) certificates, *(verlorene Zuschüsse)* non-repayable subsidies

verlosbar *(~e Wertpapiere)* securities redeemable by drawings

verlosen to draw (by lots)

Verlosungs / ~anzeige notice of drawing; **~kontrolle** monitoring (supervision) of drawings; **~liste** drawing list, list of bonds drawn; **~termin** date of drawing

Verlust 1. loss, *(Kreditverlust)* loan loss, loan charge-off, *(~ bei Ausfall/Verzug des Kontrahenten, Kreditnehmers,Schuldners)* loss given default, loss in the event of default, *(~ bei Risikoereignis)* loss given event
2. *(Defizit)* deficit, shortfall
3. *(Schaden)* damage

Verluste aus *(~ dem Abgang von Gegenständen des Anlagevermögens)* losses on disposal (sale) of fixed assets, *(~ dem Anlagebuch)* losses from the banking book, *(~ Darlehen)* loan losses, losses from loan charge-offs *(~ der Veräußerung von Beteiligungen)* losses on sale of trade investments, *(~ Währungsabwertungen)* losses from devaluations, *(~ Wertpapiergeschäften)* losses on securities traded

Verlust / ~abdeckung covering losses, cover for losses; **~abschluss 1.** closing at a loss **2.** → Verlustbilanz; **~absorbierung** loss absorption, *(verlustabsorbierendes Kapital)* loss-absorbing capital; **~abzug** deducting the loss from current earnings; **~abzugsbeschränkung** restriction on loss utilisation, → Mantelkaufregelung

Verlust / ~anfälligkeit susceptibility to losses; **~ankündigung** announcement of a loss; **~anzeige** loss advice, notice of loss; **~aufteilungsvereinbarung** loss-sharing agreement

Verlust / ~ausgleich loss compensation, compensation for financial losses, *(vollständiger ~)* full absorption of losses; **~ausweis** reporting (showing) a loss

Verlust / ~begrenzung limitation of losses; **~begrenzungsauftrag** protective stop order, stop loss order; **~beteiligung** sharing (share) in the loss; **~betrag** amount of loss, *(bei Ausfall)* loss at default

Verlust / ~bilanz adverse annual accounts, showing a net loss on the balance sheet; **~bringer** *(Bereich, Sparte)* loss-making division; **~ereignis** loss event

verlustig gehen *(eines Anspruchs/Rechtes ~)* to forfeit a claim/right

Verlust / ~kaskade loss waterfall; **~minimierung** minimising losses; **~neutralisierung** neutralising losses; **~potenzial** loss potential, value at risk, probability of loss from a position

Verlust / ~risiko exposure to loss, loss exposure, *(~ aus Währungsumrechnungen)* foreign currency translation exposure, translation risk; **~rückstellung** provision (appropriation) for losses, *(~en für Kreditverluste)* loan loss provisions; **~rücktrag** (tax) loss carryback

Verlust / ~saldo 1. net loss **2.** debit balance; **~situation** loss (loss-making) situation, loss posture; **~spanne** deficit margin; **~tragfähigkeit** loss absorption (loss-bearing) capacity

Verlust / ~übernahme loss takeover, assuming (accepting) a loss; **~übernahmevereinbarung** loss-transfer (loss-sharing) agreement; **~umlage** loss apportionment

Verlust / ~verrechnung loss compensation (set-off); **~verteilungsansatz** *(Basel II)* loss distribution approach (advanced measurement approach to determine capital requirements for operational risk)

Verlust / ~vertrag onerous contract; **~vortrag** loss carryforward (carryover);**~wahrscheinlichkeit** loss probability

Verlust / ~zone 1. *(in die ~ geraten)* to plunge into the red **2.** *(sich aus der ~ lösen)* to emerge from the red; **~zuweisung** loss allocation; **~zuweisungsgesellschaft** tax loss company, loss corporation

vermachen to leave by will, to bequeath

Vermächtnis legacy, bequest

VermAnlG → Vermögensanlagegesetz

vermehren 1. *(das investierte Kapital ~)* to increase (to enlarge) the capital invested **2.** *(vervielfachen)* to multiply

vermelden *(ein ausgezeichnetes Ergebnis ~)* to report an excellent performance

Vermengung *(~ von Geldern)* commingling of funds

Vermerk 1. note, notation, remark, entry, brief statement, memo **2.** *(bilanzieller)* memorandum item

vermerken to note, to put on record, to make an entry, to make a brief written statement

vermieten to lease, to let, *(vermietete Objekte)* tenanted properties, property and equipment rented out

Vermieter lessor, landlord; **~-Pfandrecht** lessor's lien, landlord's statutory lien

Vermietung letting, leasing, *(Einkünfte aus ~ und Verpachtung)* income from letting and leasing

Vermietungsobjekt letting property

vermindern 1. to reduce, to diminish, to ease **2.** *(beeinträchtigen)* to impair **3.** *(einschränken)* to limit, to restrict, to curtail

Verminderung 1. reduction, diminution, decline, drop **2.** impairment **3.** limitation, restriction, curtailment

vermischen to mix, *(mit anderen Vermögenswerten~)* to commingle with other asets

vermitteln 1. to mediate, to act as mediator (go-between), to arbitrate **2.** *(beim Zustandekommen von Wirtschaftsgeschäften)* to broker, to act as agent (intermediary, broker)
3. *(arrangieren)* to arrange, to bring about
4. *(weitergeben)* to convey, to pass on, to impart, to present (e.g. an accurate picture of the financial situation)

vermittelt *(durch uns ~e Darlehen)* loans extended through our agency, *(ein durch die Bank ~er Vergleich)* a compromise settlement mediated (brokered) by the bank

Vermittler 1. mediator, go-between, arbitrator **2.** *(bei Wirtschaftsgeschäften)* agent, intermediary, broker, middleman, *(die als ~ tätige Bank hat …)* the bank, acting as middleman, has …

Vermittler / ~richtlinie (EU) Mediation Directive; **~rolle** office of mediator, mediatorship, intermediary role; **~tätigkeit** brokerage activity

Vermittlung 1. mediation, arbitration, *(um die ~ der Bank nachsuchen)* to seek the good offices of the bank **2.** agency, brokerage, *(durch die ~ der Bank)* through the agency (intermediary) of the bank, *(~ von Anlagen)* investment broking (brokerage), *(~ von Krediten)* loan brokerage **3.** arranging, bringing about, procurement

Vermittlungs / ~agent soliciting agent; **~angebot** offer of mediation; **~funktion** agency function, intermediary role; **~gebühr** agency (intermediation) fee; **~geschäft 1.** agency operations, brokerage transactions **2.** loans extended on a pass-through basis

Vermittlungs / ~ makler intermediary broker; **~marge/~provision** agency fee, brokerage, broker's commission; **~verfahren** conciliation proceedings, arbitration procedure; **~vertrag** agency (brokerage) agreement; **~vorschlag** proposal for a settlement

Vermögen 1. property, assets, fortune **2.** *(Fähigkeit)* ability, capacity

vermögende Privatkunden high net worth individuals (HNWIs), wealthy private clients, wealthy individuals

Vermögens / ~abgabe property levy; **~abtretung** assignment of assets (property); **~anforderungen** asset requirements; **~angelegenheiten** financial matters

Vermögensanlage investment (of assets), *(~ in Immobilien/Wertpapieren)* real estate investment/investment in securities, *(pl, i.S. von Produkten)* investment products

Vermögensanlagegesetz Investment Products Act

Vermögensanlagen-Informationsblatt investment information sheet (factsheet)

Vermögensanlagerecht Asset Investment Law, Law on Investment Products

Vermögens / ~anmeldung declaration of property; **~anspruch** claim to property, possessory title; **~anteil** property share, ownership (participating) interest, share in an estate

Vermögens / ~aufbau asset building; **~aufstellung** asset (property) statement, statement of assets held; **~aufteilung 1.** property distribution **2.** *(im Rahmen eines Portefeuilles)* asset allocation; **~ausbau** further asset building

Vermögens / ~berater investment advisor (counsellor, consultant); **~beratung** investment advice, investment counselling (consultation), wealth advisory service, → Vermögensstrukturberatung; **~beratungskunde** private client, high net worth individual

Vermögens / ~beschlagnahme confiscation (seizure) of property; **~besteuerung** taxation of property; **~bewertung** valuation of assets, property valuation; **~bilanz** property statement, statement of assets and liabilities

Vermögens / ~bildung asset building (accumulation), wealth building, capital formation; **~bildungsprogramm** asset building scheme; **~diversifizierung** asset diversification, property (portfolio) diversification

Vermögens / ~einkommen *(~ der privaten Haushalte)* private property income; **~einlagen** assets (property) brought into a company, *(~ stiller Gesellschafter)* silent partner contributions; **~erhalt** preservation of assets; **~ertrag** property (investment) income; **~erwerb 1.** acquisition of property **2.** *(im Rahmen einer Übernahme)* asset acquisition

Vermögens / ~gegenstand asset, (item of) property; **~gleichgewicht** asset equilibrium; **~interessen** property (financial) interests; **~klasse** asset

V

category; ~**lage** financial (property) situation

Vermögens / ~masse *(im Insolvenzverfahren)* debtor's property (assets); ~**mehrung 1.** increase in personal assets **2.** *(wertmäßige)* property appreciation **3.** *(Zugänge)* asset additions

Vermögens / ~minderung 1. decrease in personal assets **2.** *(wertmäßige)* property depreciation **3.** *(Abgänge)* asset disposals; ~**neubewertung** property revaluation, revaluation (reassessment) of assets

Vermögens / ~offenbarung disclosure of (the debtor's) assets; ~**optimierung** asset optimisation; ~**pfändung** execution against assets; ~**planung** asset planning

Vermögens / ~rechnung 1. property statement, statement of assets **2.** asset accounting; ~**recht** proprietary right; ~**regelung** property settlement; ~**rückgabe** restitution of property (of assets)

Vermögens / ~schaden pecuniary (financial, economic) loss; ~**schaden-Haftpflichtversicherung** pecuniary loss liability insurance; ~**sicherung** asset protection; ~**situation** financial situation

Vermögens / ~status asset status, property (asset) statement, register of assets; ~**steuer** wealth tax, net worth tax; ~**streuung** asset diversification, spreading of investments

Vermögens / ~struktur asset structure; ~**strukturberater** asset allocation advisor; ~**strukturberatung** asset allocation advisory service, portfolio structure advisory, asset structure consultancy; ~**strukturierung** asset structuring, asset allocation; ~**substanz** net asset backing

Vermögens / ~übergang 1. transfer of ownership, property transfer **2.** *(im Nachlassfall)* devolution of assets; ~**übersicht** asset and liability statement; ~**übertragung** transfer of assets (property), property transfer (conveyance), → Vermögenserwerb

Vermögens / ~umschichtung regrouping (rearrangement, redeployment) of assets, portfolio shift; ~**verfall** sharp decline in property values, disintegration of assets; ~**verhältnisse** financial (property) situation; ~**versicherung** asset insurance, portfolio insurance

Vermögensverwalter asset (investment, portfolio) manager

Vermögensverwaltung asset management, wealth management

Vermögensverwaltungs / ~abteilung asset management unit; ~**erträge** asset (investment) management income; ~**gebühr** asset (investment) management fee, portfolio management fee

Vermögensverwaltungs / ~geschäft asset (investment) management operations, portfolio management services; ~**gesellschaft** asset management company, *(vermögensverwaltende Personengesellschaft)* asset-management partnership

Vermögensverwaltungs / ~konto asset management account; ~**pauschale** flat (all-inclusive) management fee; ~**vertrag** investment management agreement, wealth management services agreement

Vermögenswert 1. asset, property **2.** *(Wert eines Wirtschaftsgutes)* asset value; ~**klasse** asset class

vermögenswirksam *(~e Leistungen)* asset-building benefits

Vermögenszuwachs growth in assets, asset growth, capital appreciation

vermuten 1. *(annehmen)* to suppose, to assume, to presume, *(vermutete Kenntnis des Kunden)* assumed awareness of the customer **2.** *(erwarten)* to anticipate, to expect **3.** *(spekulieren)* to surmise, to conjecture

vermutlich 1. presumable **2.** *(~e Zinsentwicklung)* probable (likely) trend in interest rates

Vermutung 1. assumption, *(gesetzliche ~)* statutory presumption 2. expectation, anticipation 3. surmise, conjecture

vernachlässigen to neglect, *(Finanzwerte wurden weiterhin vernachlässigt)* bank stocks remained out of favour

vernetzen *(Betriebe global ~)* to network operations globally, *(vernetzter Vertrieb)* networked sales organisation

Vernetzung *(~ der Kommunikationswege)* networking of communication channels

vernichten *(die entwerteten Wertpapiere ~)* to destroy the invalidated securities

Vernunft *(wirtschaftliche ~)* economic reason (rationale), *(vernünftige kaufmännische Beurteilung)* reasonable commercial judgement

veröffentlichen 1. to publish, to release, *(den Jahresabschluss ~)* to publish the annual accounts, to release the results for the year 2. *(ankündigen)* to announce 3. *(offenlegen)* to disclose 4. *(ein Gesetz ~)* to promulgate a law

Veröffentlichung 1. publication, release 2. announcement 3. disclosure 4. promulgation

Veröffentlichungspflichten disclosure obligations (requirements)

veroptioniert *(~e Aktien)* optioned stock

verordnen to enact, to decree, to order

Verordnung regulation, directive, decree, order, *(~ über die Kapitalausstattung von Versicherungsunternehmen)* Regulation on the Capital Resources of Insurance Companies, *(~ über die Rechnungslegung der Kreditinstitute)* Bank Accounting Directive

verpachten to let, to lease

Verpächter lessor; **~pfandrecht** lessor's lien

Verpachtung letting, leasing

verpassen *(eine Anlagemöglichkeit ~)* to miss out an investment opportunity

verpensionieren *(verpensionierte Wertpapiere)* securities repoed, securities transferred under repurchase agreements

verpfändbar *(~e Vermögenswerte)* pledgeable assets, assets eligible as collateral

verpfänden to pledge, to pawn, to give in pledge, to deliver goods in pledge, to hypothecate, *(Aktien als Sicherheit für einen Kredit ~)* to pledge shares as collateral for (against) a loan, *(der Bank als Sicherheit verpfändete Wertpapiere)* securities pledged to the bank as collateral

Verpfänder pledger, pledgor

Verpfändung pledge, pledging, delivering goods in pledge, hypothecation, *(die durch die ~ gesicherten Ansprüche)* the claims secured by the pledge, *(~ von Forderungen)* pledging accounts receivable, *(~ von Wertpapieren als Sicherheit)* pledging securities as collateral

Verpfändungs / ~anzeige notice (notification) of pledge, notice of hypothecation; **~erklärung** memorandum of pledge (of deposit), letter of pledge (of hypothecation); **~ermächtigung** authority to pledge; **~vertrag** contract of pledge

Verpflegungsaufwendungen subsistence expenses

verpflichten 1. to oblige, to commit, to obligate, to bind, *(Bestimmungen, die den Kreditnehmer ~)* provisions that obligate the borrower to …, *(die Gesellschaft durch eine Garantie ~)* to bind the company in a guarantee *(wir ~ uns unwiderruflich und uneingeschränkt zur Leistung einer Bürgschaft in Höhe von …)* we irrevocably and unconditionally undertake to furnish a guarantee in the amount of …, *(der Kunde ist nicht verpflichtet)* there is no duty on the customer to …
2. *(sich ~)* to commit o. s., to under-

take, to give an undertaking, to contract, to covenant, *(sich gegenüber der Bank ~)* to undertake towards the bank

verpflichtend binding, obligatory, compulsory

verpflichtet (*~ sein)* to be committed to, *(vertraglich ~ sein)* to be bound by contract, (*nicht ~ sein)* to be under no obligation to

Verpflichtete/r obligor, party liable

Verpflichtung obligation, commitment, undertaking, covenant, *(~ der eröffnenden Bank)* undertaking on the part of the issuing (opening) bank

Verpflichtungen aus *(~ dem Darlehensvertrag)* commitments (obligations) under the loan agreement, *(~ Derivatekontrakten)* obligations under derivative contracts, *(~ Rückgriffsvereinbarungen)* obligations under recourse agreements, *(~ Wertpapierpensionsgeschäften)* repo obligations

Verpflichtung zur (*~ Bereitstellung eines erstrangigen Hypothekendarlehens)* undertaking to extend a first-rank mortgage loan, (*~ Sicherheitsleistung)* obligation to provide security, collateral obligation, *(~ Übernahme der Emission)* undertaking to take up (to underwrite) the issue

Verpflichtungs / ~erklärung 1. undertaking, letter of commitment **2.** performance bond; **~fähigkeit** legal capacity to enter into commitments; **~geschäft** contractual obligation, contract (deal) imposing a legal obligation; **~kredit 1.** support (backup) facility **2.** credit by way of guarantee

verprovisionieren to pay commission

verrechenbar *(~er Kontrakt)* nettable contract

verrechnen 1. *(aufrechnen gegen)* to set off (to net) against, to offset, (*im Eigenkapital ~)* to set off against equity, (*über ein Konto ~)* to settle through an account, (*die Kontokorrentschuld mit den Sparguthaben ~)* to set off the debit balance in the current account against the savings deposits, (*als Tilgung ~)* to apply against the principal outstanding, *(direkt mit den Rücklagen ~)* to eliminate directly against reserves
2. *(belasten/gutschreiben)* to charge/ to debit, (*im Betriebsergebnis ~*) to charge (or to credit) to income, to account for (to recognise) in the operating results
3. *(zuordnen)* to match, to pair, *(Kauf- und Verkaufsaufträge miteinander ~)* to pair off buy orders with sell orders

Verrechnung 1. set-off, netting, (*~ mit den Gewinnrücklagen)* setting off against retained earnings, (*~ von Kauf- und Verkaufspositionen)* netting of long and short positions, netting long against short exposures, (*~ mit den Kreditwertberichtigungen)* setting off against loan loss allowances
(*~ von Verbindlichkeiten/Verlusten mit Forderungen/Gewinnen)* setting off (applying) liabilities/losses against receivables/profits, (*~der Tilgungsleistung)* → Tilgungsverrechnung, *(unter ~ von Stückzinsen)* plus/less interest accrued
2. *(Gutschrift/Belastung)* (*~ im Kontokorrent)* crediting/debiting to the current account
3. *(nur zur ~) (Scheckvermerk)* account payee only, for account only

Verrechnungs / ~abkommen clearing agreement; **~ausgleich** settlement, netting; **~bank** settlement (clearing) bank; **~datensatz** clearing data record; **~dollar** clearing dollar; **~einheit** unit of account

Verrechnungs / ~guthaben clearing balances; **~konto 1.** *(zu einem Depot)* cash (money) account **2.** settlement (clearing) account; **~kurs** settlement price

Verrechnungs / ~laufzeit settlement (clearing) period; **~preis** transfer price; **~recht** right of set-off; **~scheck** crossed cheque; **~schulden** clearing debt (liabilities); **~spitzen** clearing balances (fractions); ~**stelle** clearing office

Verrechnungs / ~tage settlement days; ~**verkehr** clearing transactions; ~**währung** clearing currency; ~**wege** clearing channels

Verrichtungsgehilfe servant, → Erfüllungsgehilfe

verringern 1. to reduce, to diminish, to cut back (down), *(das Defizit ~)* to reduce (to bring down) the deficit 2. *(sich ~)* to shrink, to contract

Verringerung reduction, diminution, decrease, cutback, contraction, *(~ des Marktwertes)* depreciation in market value

versammeln *(sich ~)* to meet, to assemble

Versammlung meeting, gathering, assembly, *(~ der Gläubiger)* creditors' meeting

Versand dispatch, shipment, shipping, forwarding

Versand / ~anweisungen forwarding (shipping) instructions; ~**bereitstellungskredit** packing credit; ~**dokumente** forwarding (shipping) documents; ~**hauswerte** mail orders; ~**kosten** forwarding charges, cost of carriage (delivery)

Versand / ~papiere → Versanddokumente; ~**scheck** out-of-town cheque; ~**schein** consignment note; ~**wechsel** bill sent for collection, out-of-town bill

versäumen 1. to miss, to miss out (an opportunity), to omit, to fail 2. to neglect

Versäumnis 1. missing (out), failure, omission 2. neglect; ~**klage** default action; ~**urteil** default judgment, judgment issued by default; ~**zuschlag** 1. late payment fee 2. *(für verspätete Einreichung)* penalty for late filing

Verschachtelung interconnection, interlocking, interpenetration

Verschaffung 1. *(~ des Fremdwährungsbetrages)* delivery (remittance) of the foreign currency amount 2. *(~ des Miteigentums)* securing the co-ownership

verschärfen 1. *(die Überwachung ~)* to tighten the control (the grip on), *(die Zulassungsvorschriften ~)* to tighten (to toughen up) the rules for admission (e. g. to the stock exchange)
2. *(verstärken)* to increase, to intensify, *(sich ~de Spannungen an den Devisenmärkten)* mounting tension in the currency markets, *(der Wettbewerb wird sich deutlich ~)* competition will heighten appreciably
3. *(verschlimmern)* to aggravate, to exacerbate, to worsen

Verschärfung 1. *(~ der Eigenkapitalvorschriften)* tightening of equity requirements (of capital standards), *(~ der restriktiven Kreditpolitik)* tightening the credit screw, tightening up on credit
2. increase, intensification, *(~ der Rezession)* deepening of the recession, *(~ des Wettbewerbs)* stiffening of (increase in) competition
3. aggravation, exacerbation

verschätzen to make a wrong estimate

Verschiebebahnhof *(im Kreditgeschäft)* subsidiary or associated company taking over a loan commitment from the parent

verschieben 1. to postpone, to put off, to defer, to shelve, to adjourn, *(Neuanlagen bis nächstes Jahr ~)* to put off new investments until next year, *(die Sitzung ~)* to adjourn the meeting, *(die Pläne zur Eröffnung einer neuen Repräsentanz wurden verschoben)* plans to set up a new representative office have been shelved 2. *(verlagern)* to shift

Verschiebung 1. postponement, putting off, deferment, adjournment
2. *(~ der Renditestrukturkurve)* shift of the yield curve

verschieden 1. different, distinct, divergent, *(~ sein)* to differ, *(~ in Stückelung und Währung)* varying in denomination and currency, *(~e Inte-*

ressen) different (diverging) interests 2. sundry, miscellaneous, *(~e Kosten)* sundry expenses, *(~e Posten)* miscellaneous items, sundries

verschiedenartig 1. *(vielfältig)* diverse, varying **2.** *(unterschiedlich)* different, disparate **3.** *(gegensätzlich)* opposing

Verschiedenartigkeit *(die ~ der Finanzierungen)* the diversity (variety) of funding transactions

Verschiedenheit 1. difference, disparity, divergence **2.** *(Mannigfaltigkeit)* variety

Verschiffungs / ~anzeige advice of shipment; **~dokumente** shipping documents; **~vorschriften** shipping instructions; **~wert** shipping value

Verschlankung 1. streamlining **2.** *(~ der Geschäftsprozesse einer Bank)* lean banking

verschlechtern to deteriorate, to worsen, *(verschlimmern)* to aggravate, *(sich ~de Aussichten)* worsening prospects

Verschlechterung deterioration, worsening, adverse change, aggravation, *(~ des Kreditportefeuilles/~der Kreditqualität)* deterioration in asset quality, worsening of (in) credit quality

verschleiern 1. to conceal, to hide, to veil, to disguise, to mask **2.** *(schönen)* to window-dress

Verschleierung 1. concealment, disguise, masking **2.** window-dressing, faking

Verschleiß 1. *(Abnutzung)* wear-out, attrition **2.** *(von Sachanlagen)* wear and tear

verschleppen to delay, to protract, to draw out, to obstruct

Verschleppung delay, protraction, obstruction

verschließen to close, to lock, → verschlossen

verschlimmern 1. to exacerbate, *(die Liquiditätsprobleme ~)* to exacerbate (to aggravate) the liquidity problems **2.** *(verschlechtern)* to deteriorate, to worsen, *(die sich ~de Rezession)* the worsening (deepening) recession

Verschlimmerung exacerbation, aggravation, deterioration, worsening

verschlingen *(30 % des Jahresgewinns ~)* to swallow up 30 % of the income for the year

verschlossen *(~es Depot)* closed custody account □ custody arrangement whereby the custodian has no knowledge of type and value of the property deposited, *(~er Emissionsmarkt)* market closed to a specific issuer

verschlüsseln to encode, *(verschlüsselter Zugriff)* encrypted access

Verschlüsselung encoding, encryption

Verschlüsselungsschlüssel encryption key

verschmelzen to merge, to amalgamate

Verschmelzung merger, amalgamation, *(~ der Tochter- auf die Muttergesellschaft/der Mutter- auf die Tochtergesellschaft)* upstream merger/downstream merger

Verschmelzungs / ~bericht merger report; **~beschluss** merger resoluton; **~bilanz** merger accounts; **~gewinn** merger profit; **~kosten** merger expense; **~prüfung** merger audit; **~richtlinie** Merger Directive; **~stichtag** effective date of merger; **~verlust** merger loss; **~vertrag** merger agreement; **~wert** merger value

Verschnaufpause *(die Börse legte eine ~ ein)* the stock market took a breather

verschulden 1. *(sich ~)* to take on debt, to incur a debt, to become indebted, *(sich stark ~)* to borrow heavily, to take on a high level of borrowing, → verschuldet, *(sich in Dollar ~)* to contract a dollar debt
2. *(belasten)* to encumber
3. *(verursachen)* to cause, to be responsible for, to be the cause of

Verschulden fault, *(durch ~ des Kreditnehmers)* through the borrower's fault

verschuldet indebted, in debt, *(~es Unternehmen)* debt-laden (debt-burdened) company, *(stark ~es Unternehmen)* debt-ridden (heavily indebted, highly geared, highly leveraged) company, *(die am stärksten ~en Länder)* the most heavily indebted countries

Verschuldung 1. indebtedness, debt burden (load), debt/equity gearing, leverage, *(bilanzwirksame und außerbilanzielle ~)* on- and off-balance sheet leverage, *(~ in kurzen Fristen)* contracting short-term debt
2. *(Kreditaufnahme)* borrowing, *(~ der privaten Haushalte)* accumulation of debt by private households, → Verschuldungsgrad (2)

Verschuldungs / ~begrenzung debt limitation, debt capping, → Verschuldungsgrenze;**~bereitschaft** propensity to borrow, propensity to contract debt, willingness to take out loans

Verschuldungsgrad 1. *(der privaten Haushalte)* private households' level of indebtedness, income gearing
2. *(einer Unternehmung)* debt/EBITDA ratio, debt leverage, leverage (gearing) ratio

Verschuldungs / ~grenze 1. debt limitation (ceiling), ceiling placed on the amount of borrowings **2.** → Höchstverschuldungsquote *(Basel III)*; **~messgröße** leverage ratio; **~höhe** debt level, → Verschuldungsgrad; **~instrumente** debt instruments; **~krise** debt crisis

Verschuldungs / ~ maßstab measure of indebtedness; **~problem** debt problem; **~rate** debt ratio; **~wünsche** borrowing requirements

Verschweigen *(arglistiges ~)* fraudulent concealment

Verschwiegenheitspflicht/-verpflichtung duty of confidentiality, obligation to observe (to maintain) secrecy, *(~ der Banken)* banks' duty of secrecy, banking secrecy, *(der ~ unterliegen)* to be subject to secrecy requirements

Verschwimmen *(~ der Grenze zwischen Geld- und Kapitalmarkt)* blurring of the line between money and capital market

versechsfachen to sextuplicate, to increase sixfold

versehen to provide (to furnish) with, *(~ mit dem Indossament der Bank)* provided with (bearing) the endorsement of the bank, *(mit einer staatlichen Garantie ~sein)* to carry a government guarantee

Versehen error, mistake, oversight, inadvertent error (omission)

versehentlich *adj.* unintentional, inadvertent, *adv.* by mistake, through an oversight, unintentionally, *(~ fehlgeleitet)* inadvertently misdirected

verselbstständigen to put on an independent footing

versenden to send, to forward, to dispatch

versetzen to transfer, to move, to relocate

versicherbar *(~es Risiko)* insurable (hedgeable) risk

Versicherer insurer, insurance company, underwriter

versichern 1. to insure, to take out an insurance, *(aus Sicht des Versicherers)* to underwrite, *(die Wertgegenstände ~ lassen)* to have the valuables insured **2.** to hedge, *(sich gegen Währungsrisiken ~)* to hedge one's currency risks **3.** *(bestätigen)* to confirm, to affirm **4.** *(zusichern)* to assure, to guarantee **5.** *(sich ~)* to convince o. s., to make sure

Versicherte/r insured, assured

Versicherung 1. insurance, *(aus Sicht des Versicherers)* underwriting **2.** confirmation, affirmation, *(Versicherung an Eides Statt)* statutory declaration **3.** assurance, guarantee

Versicherungs / ~abschluss taking out an insurance; **~aktien** insurance stock; **~antrag** application (proposal)

form; ~**aufsichtsgesetz** German Insurance Supervision Act

Versicherungs / ~beginn policy inception date, commencement of cover, commencement date; ~**begünstigte/r** insurance beneficiary; ~**bestand** insurance portfolio; ~**bestätigung** insurance certificate; ~**beteiligungen** equity investments in insurance companies

Versicherungs / ~darlehen policy loan, loan extended by an insurance company; ~**dauer** policy (insurance) duration, policy term; ~**deckung** insurance cover

Versicherungs / ~derivate insurance derivatives, instruments to hedge exposure to catastrophic losses, → Katastrophen-Anleihe, → Katastrophen-Option; ~**gegenstand** property insured, interest insured, insurance interest

Versicherungs / ~gemeinschaft insurance (underwriting) pool; ~**kosten** cost of insurance, insurance costs, hedging cost; ~**leistungen** insurance benefits, claims payments

versicherungsmathematisch *(~e Bewertungsmethoden)* actuarial valuation methods

Versicherungs / ~nehmer insured, assured, policyholder; ~**pflicht** obligation to take out an insurance, compulsory insurance; ~**police** insurance policy; ~**prämie** insurance premium

Versicherungs / ~schein insurance certificate; ~**schutz** insurance cover (coverage); ~**summe** insurance principal, amount insured, underwritten amount

versicherungstechnisch *(~es Ergebnis)* underwriting result, *(~e Rückstellungen)* technical provisions

Versicherungs / ~träger insurance carrier (underwriter); ~**umfang** scope of insurance, insurance cover, cover provided by an insurance; ~**unternehmen** insurance company, underwriter, underwriting office; ~**verein auf Gegenseitigkeit** mutual insurance association

Versicherungs / ~vermittler insurance intermediary, insurance broker; ~**vermittlerrecht** legislation on insurance intermediaries, law of insurance broking; ~**vermittlerrichtlinie** (EU) Insurance Mediation Directive; ~**vermittlung** insurance mediation, insurance broking

Versicherungs / ~vertrag insurance contract (policy); ~**vertragsgesetz** Insurance Contracts Act; ~**wert** insured value, insurable value; ~**wirtschaft** insurance industry; ~**zertifikat** insurance certificate

versiebenfachen to septuplicate, to increase sevenfold

versiegeln to seal, to affix a seal

versiegen *(einer Kapitalquelle)* to dry up, to peter out

versorgen to supply, to provide with, *(das Bankensystem mit Liquidität ~)* to provide the banking system with liquidity, to pump (to inject) cash into the banking system

Versorgung supply, provision

Versorgungs / ~anrechte pension entitlements; ~**ansprüche** *(Übernahme bestehender ~)* taking over existing service entitlements; ~**leistungen** pension benefits

Versorgungs / ~plan pensions scheme; ~**verpflichtungen** pension obligations (commitments); ~**werte** utilities, utility stocks, ~**zahlungen** benefit payments

verspätet *(~e Vorlage der Dokumente)* late (delayed) presentation of the documents

Verspätung 1. lateness **2.** *(Verzögerung)* delay (e. g. in effecting the payment agreed upon)

versprechen to promise, to undertake, to pledge, to covenant

Versprechen promise, undertaking, pledge, covenant

verständigen 1. *(sich ~ über)* to come to an agreement (understanding), to settle, to agree on 2. *(unterrichten)* to inform, to notify, to advise

Verständigung 1. agreement, understanding 2. *(Kompromiss)* compromise, settlement 3. *(Unterrichtung)* information, notification

Verständigungsbereitschaft willingness to come to a compromise

verstärken 1. to strengthen, to intensify, to increase, to step up, *(den Abwärtsdruck ~)* to add to the downward pressure, *(den Aufwärtstrend ~)* to give further impetus to the upward trend, to buttress the uptrend, *(die Befürchtungen der Anleger ~)* to fuel investor fears, to heighten investor concern *(die Hoffnungen auf eine Kurserholung ~)* to boost hopes of a price recovery, *(die Liquidität ~)* to strengthen (to reinforce) liquidity, *(der Liquiditätsdruck wurde durch die hohen Zinssätze verstärkt)* strain on liquidity has been accentuated by high interest rates
2. to speed up, *(die Auslosungen für diese Anleihen ~)* to accelerate drawings for these bonds
3. to enhance, *(die gestellten Sicherheiten ~)* to enhance the collateral

Verstärkung 1. strengthening, intensification, reinforcement, increase, stepping up, *(~ der Eigenkapitalbasis)* strengthening (reinforcement of) the equity base, shoring up the equity base
2. acceleration
3. *(~ der Sicherheiten)* enhancement of the collateral provided, providing (provision of) additional security

versteckt *(~e Gewinnausschüttung)* hidden profit distribution, *(~e Reserven)* hidden reserves

versteigern to sell by auction, to auction off

Versteigerung auction, public sale

Versteigerungs / ~erlös auction proceeds; **~kurs** auction rate (price)

verstimmen *(die Börse ~)* to unsettle (to upset, to irritate, to disquiet) the market

Verstoß infringement, breach, *(~ gegen die guten Sitten)* violation of bonos mores

verstoßen *(gegen Bestimmungen eines Vertrages ~)* to infringe (to violate, to breach) the terms of an agreement

verstreichen 1. to expire, to lapse, to elapse, *(eine Frist von zwanzig Tagen muss ~)* a twenty-day period must elapse
2. *(eine Möglichkeit ~ lassen)* to pass up (to miss out) an opportunity, *(den Termin ~ lassen)* to allow the deadline to pass

Verstrickungsbruch breach of attachment

vertagen *(eine Sitzung ~)* to adjourn (to postpone) a meeting

Vertagung adjournment, postponement

Verteidigungseinwand defense objection

verteilen 1. to distribute, to divide, *(den Erlös ~)* to distribute (to share out) the proceeds
2. to spread, *(das Risiko auf viele Papiere ~)* to spread the risk across (over) a wide range of securities, *(die Zahlungen über einen Fünfjahres-Zeitraum ~)* to spread (to phase) payments over a five-year period
3. to allocate, to assign, *(auf mehrere Rechnungsperioden ~)* to allocate to several accounting periods

Verteilung 1. distribution, division, *(~ der Ausfallwahrscheinlichkeiten)* default probability distribution, *(~ des Gesellschaftsvermögens)* distribution of the company's property, property share-out, *(~ im Insolvenzverfahren)* distribution of proceeds in insolvency proceedings
2. spreading, *(~ des Risikos auf mehrere Vermögensklassen)* spreading the risk across several asset classes
3. allocation, apportionment

verteilungsfähig distributable, *(~er Überschuss)* surplus for distribution

Verteilungs / ~schlüssel allocation formula; **~termin** distribution hearing (on the distribution of the proceeds); **~verfahren** court proceedings for the distribution of assets

verteuern to increase in price, to become dearer, (*die neue Zinsanhebung wird die Kreditaufnahme weiter ~*) the new interest hike is bound to add to the cost of borrowing, (*AB verteuerten sich um 3 auf 22 €)* AB firmed (hardened, rose) 3 to 22 €

Verteuerung increase in price, (*~ der Kredite)* increase in the cost of borrowing, (*~ der Refinanzierung)* increase in funding costs

vertiefen *(die Liquiditätsprobleme ~)* to deepen (to increase) the liquidity problems

vertikale Diversifikation vertical diversification, diversifying investments across different types of assets

vertikaler Spread vertical spread □ option combination (based on either calls or puts) where one option is purchased and another is sold; the options have different exercise prices but the same expiry dates

Vertikalverbund vertical integration

Vertrag contract, agreement

vertraglich 1. *adj.* (*~er Anspruch)* contractual claim, claim guaranteed by the contract (arising from the contract), (*~e Anzeigepflicht)* contractual notification requirement
(*~e Haftung)* contractual liability, (*~e Rechte)* contractual rights (powers), contract rights, (*~e Verpflichtung)* contractual obligation, obligation arising from the contract
2. *adv.* (*~ binden)* to bind by contract, *(sich ~ binden)* to bind o. s. by contract, to covenant, *(~ gebunden)* to be bound by contract, (*~ festlegen)* to stipulate by contract
(*~ vereinbaren)* to agree by contract, to contract, *(~ vereinbarte Frist)* term stipulated by contract, term agreed upon under the contract, *(~ vereinbarter Zinssatz)* contractual interest rate, *(sich ~ verpflichten)* to contract

Vertrags / ~abrede covenant; **~abschluss** conclusion of contract, entering into an agreement, *(unter dem Vorbehalt des ~es)* subject to contract; **~abschlüsse** contracts signed, new business; **~absprache** contractual arrangement; **~abweichung** deviation (variance) from contract

vertragsähnlich (*~es Rechtsverhältnis)* quasi-contractual relationship

Vertrags / ~anbahnung contract formation phase; **~änderung** contract amendment, amending (modifying) an agreement; **~aufhebung** repudiation (rescission) of contract

Vertrags / ~aufkündigung/~auflösung rescission (repudiation) of contract, *(vertragsauflösende Klausel)* resolutory (dissolving) clause; **~aufsage** *(vorzeitige ~)* anticipatory rescission, anticipatory breach of contract

Vertrags / ~ausfertigung 1. execution of contract **2.** *(Abschrift)* copy of a contract; **~auslegung** interpretation of contract, construing an agreement; **~bedingungen** terms and conditions of contract, contract terms; **~beendigung** termination of contract (of an agreement)

Vertrags / ~beginn commencement of the agreement, inception of contract, commencement date, *(das Vertragsverhältnis beginnt mit der Unterzeichnung des Vertrages durch die Parteien)* the contract goes into effect upon being signed by the parties; **~bestandteil** component (integral part) of the agreement

Vertrags / ~bestimmung contract provision, contractual provision (clause); **~beziehungen** contractual relations, treaty relations; **~bindungen 1.** contractual ties **2.** → Vertragsbedingungen; **~bruch** breach of contract

V

Vertrags / ~dauer contract period, life of contract, life (term, duration) of an agreement; **~dokumentation** contract documentation

Vertrags / ~einhaltung contract compliance, complying with (abiding by, observing) the terms of contract; **~entwurf** draft agreement; **~erfüllung** performance (execution) of contract, contract performance (discharge); **~erfüllungsgarantie** performance guarantee (bond), completion bond, contract collateral

Vertrags / ~erneuerung contract renewal, renewal of an agreement; **~erweiterung** extension to the contract; **~fähigkeit** capacity to contract, contractual capacity; **~forderung** contractual claim, claim under a contract;**~freiheit** freedom to contract

vertragsgebunden *(~es Sparen)* scheme-linked saving

Vertragsgegenstand object of contract, subject matter of the agreement, *(bei Börsentermingeschäften)* underlying instrument, *(vertragsgegenständliche Leistungen)* services that are the subject matter of the contract

vertragsgemäß contractual, *(~e Abwicklung)* settlement as agreed upon under the contract, *(~e Bedienung)* debt service as agreed upon (as stipulated in the relevant loan/bond agreement), *(~ bedienter Kredit)* performing loan, loan serviced as agreed upon, *(~e Leistungserbringung)* contractual performance, discharge of contract

Vertrags / ~gestaltung 1. drafting of the contract (agreement) **2.** documentation; **~grundlage** basis of contract, → Wegfall der Geschäftsgrundlage; **~gültigkeit** validity of contract (of an agreement)

Vertrags / ~haftung contractual liability, liability under the contract; **~hypothek** contractual mortgage; **~klausel** contract clause, contract provision, covenant

Vertrags / ~kündigung rescission (repudiation, termination) of contract; **~kündigungsrecht** right to repudiate (to terminate) a contract, right of rescission, → Vertragsrücktritt

Vertrags / ~laufzeit contract duration, lifetime of a contract; **~leistung 1.** contractual consideration **2.** contract performance

vertragslos *(~er Zustand)* without a contractually binding arrangement

vertragsmäßig *(~e Erfüllungspflichten)* contractual delivery (performance) obligations, *(~es Recht)* right by contract, → gewohnheitsmäßiges Recht

Vertrags / ~partei 1. contracting party, party to an agreement **2.** *(Kontrahent)* counterparty; **~pfandrecht** contractual lien; **~pflichten** contractual duties, duties under a contract; **~preis** contract price, price stipulated by contract

Vertrags / ~recht law of contract(s), contract law; **~rechte** contractual rights; **~regelung** contractual settlement; **~rückabwicklung** contract rescission, returning the parties to the status quo ante;**~rücktritt** avoidance of contract, withdrawal from contract; **~rückversicherung** obligatory reinsurance

Vertrags / ~schuld contract debt; **~schuldner** contract debtor; **~sparen** scheme-linked saving, contractual saving; **~sparplan** contractual savings scheme (plan); **~spediteur** contracting carrier

Vertrags / ~strafe contractual penalty; **~streitigkeiten** disputes arising from a contract; **~summe** amount contracted, contract amount; **~text** wording of a contract, contract terms

vertragstypisch *(~e Pflichten)* duties that are typical for such contracts

Vertrags / ~übernahme assumption of contract; **~umfang** scope of contract, field covered; **~unfähigkeit** contractual incapacity; **~unterlagen** contract documentation, contract documents;

~**unternehmen** **1.** contracting company **2.** *(einer Kreditkartenorganisation)* merchant

Vertrags / ~**unterschrift** signature on a contract; ~**unterzeichner** signatory to a contract; ~**unterzeichnung** signing of the agreement; ~**urkunde** deed

Vertrags / ~**verhältnis** contractual relation (relationship); ~**verlängerung** contract extension, renewal of an agreement, → Vertragsbeginn; ~**verletzung** breach of contract, contract default (infringement); ~**verpflichtung** contractual obligation, obligation (liability) under a contract

Vertrags / ~**vollmacht** power (authority) to conclude a contract; ~**volumen** portfolio of contracts; ~**vorbehalt** contractual reservation; ~**wert** contract value; ~**widrigkeit** contract infringement, *(vertragswidrig)* contrary to the terms of contract

Vertrags / ~**zeit** life (duration) of an agreement, life of contract; ~**zinsen** contractual interest; ~**zusatz** addendum to the agreement; ~**zuteilung** contract allocation; ~**zweck** purpose of contract

Vertrauen confidence, trust

vertrauensbildend *(~e Maßnahmen)* confidence-building measures

Vertrauens / ~**bruch** breach of confidence; ~**missbrauch** abuse of confidence; ~**sache** **1.** matter of confidence (of confidentiality) **2.** confidential matter

Vertrauens / ~**schadenversicherung** fidelity insurance (bond); ~**schutz** **1.** protection of legitimate expectations **2.** protection by grandfathering rules, *(~ für Altverträge)* grandfathering of existing contracts; ~**schwund** decline in (loss of) confidence; ~**würdigkeit** trustworthiness, reliability, *(vertrauenswürdiger Kunde)* trustworthy (reliable) customer

vertraulich confidential, *(streng ~)* strictly confidential, private and confidential, *(streng ~ behandeln)* to treat in strictest confidence

Vertraulichkeit confidentiality, confidential character

Vertraulichkeits / ~**vereinbarung** confidentiality (non-disclosure) agreement; ~ **verhältnis** relationship of trust; ~**zusage** confidentiality undertaking

vertraut familiar with, conversant with, accustomed to, *(sich mit den Einzelheiten ~ machen)* to make o. s. familiar (to familiarise o. s.) with the details

vertreiben to sell, to market, to distribute

vertretbar **1.** justifiable, supportable, warrantable, tenable, *(~es Risiko)* justifiable risk, *(~ unter Risikogesichtspunkten)* acceptable in terms of risk **2.** *(~e Wertpapiere)* fungible securities

Vertretbarkeit **1.** justifiableness, *(~ der Kreditentscheidung)* tenability of the lending decision **2.** fungibility

vertreten **1.** *(für jmd. handeln) (a)* to represent s. o., to act on behalf of s. o., *(b) (als Stellvertreter)* to deputise for, to take s. o.'s place, to replace s. o **2.** *(vor Gericht ~)* to represent in court, to defend, to plead for, *(durch einen Anwalt/Stimmrechtsvertreter ~ sein)* to be represented by counsel/proxy **3.** *(eine Meinung ~)* to hold an opinion, to support a view **4.** *(Interessen ~)* to safeguard (to represent) the interests of

Vertretenmüssen liability requirement, *(ein ~ der Bank)* obligation of liability on the part of the bank

Vertreter **1.** representative, agent, *(ordnungsgemäß bevollmächtigter ~)* properly appointed representative, duly authorised representative (agent) **2.** *(Befürworter)* supporter, advocate **3.** *(Stellvertreter)* deputy, substitute, replacement **4.** *(Stimmrechtsvertreter)* proxy **5.** *(einer Genossenschaft)* member

Vertreterrecht law of agency

Vertretung 1. representation, agency, *(anwaltliche ~)* representation by counsel, *(in ~ von)* acting as representative for, by proxy, *(bei Unterschriften: in ~ von ...)* for Mr/Ms ...
2. substitution, replacement, → Vertreter
3. *(Niederlassung)* representative office, agency

Vertretungsauftrag 1. instructions to represent (to act as agent) **2.** *(Stimmrechtsauftrag)* proxy, proxy statement *(Vertretungsaufträge anderer Banken)* proxies given by other banks (e. g. to exercise voting rights)

vertretungsberechtigt authorised to represent (to act), *(allein/gemeinsam ~ für eine Gesellschaft)* authorised to act singly/jointly for a company

Vertretungsberechtigte/r authorised representative, *(für eine Gesellschaft)* person authorised to act for a company (to bind a company), *(für ein Konto)* person authorised to operate (to draw on) an account

Vertretungsberechtigung 1. authority to represent (to bind a company) **2.** authority to operate (to draw on) an account

Vertretungs / ~macht power of representation, *(~ kraft Amtes)* inherent authority; **~regelung** substitute staffing schedule; **~vertrag** agency contract, contract of agency; **~vollmacht 1.** power of attorney (of representation), agency power **2.** *(Stimmrechtsvollmacht)* power of substitution, proxy

Vertrieb sale, distribution, *(~ von Vermögensanlagen)* placement of investment products

Vertriebs / ~anstrengungen sales efforts; **~anzeige** *(für Fondsanteile)* notification for public distribution; **~aufwand** distribution cost (expenses); **~außendienst** field sales force; **~beauftragte/r** *(under the WpHG/Securities TradingAct)* Placement Officer

vertriebsberechtigt *(~er Fonds)* fund admitted to public distribution

Vertriebs / ~betreuung sales support; **~erfolg/~ergebnis** sales performance; **~gemeinkosten** distribution (selling) overheads; **~gesellschaft** distributor, marketing company; **~intensivierung** stepping up sales efforts

Vertriebs / ~kapazitäten distribution capacities; **~konsortium** *(bei einer Emission)* selling group (syndicate); **~kooperation** sales co-operation, distribution partnership; **~kosten** distribution (selling, distributive) cost; **~kostenrechnung** distributive costing; **~kraft** selling power

Vertriebs / ~leistung sales performance; **~mitarbeiter** sales staff; **~partner** distribution partner; **~stelle** distributor, distributing agent; **~steuerung** *(der Filialen)* control of branch sales; **~unterstützung** sales support; **~verbot** distribution (sales) ban; **~vergütung** sales remuneration; **~weg** distribution channel

verunsichern to upset, to puzzle, to disconcert, to confuse, *(Anleger wurden durch widersprüchliche Prognosen verunsichert)* investors have been puzzled by conflicting forecasts

Verunsicherung upset, confusion, disconcertion

veruntreuen to embezzle, to misappropriate

Veruntreuung embezzlement, misappropriation, fraud

Veruntreuungsversicherung fidelity bond (insurance), employee dishonesty bond

verursachen 1. to cause **2.** *(auslösen)* to prompt, to trigger **3.** *(Kosten ~)* to entail (to involve) expenses

Verursacher / ~haftung perpetrator's liability; **~prinzip** perpetrator principle, causation principle

verurteilen 1. *(zu den Kosten ~)* to sentence to the costs, to be ordered to pay the costs **2.** *(ablehnen)* to condemn, to disapprove of, to denounce the measures

vervollkommnen 1. to refine, to perfect **2.** *(abrunden)* to round off (out)

vervollständigen to complete, to fill

Verwahrart type of custody

verwahren to hold in safe custody (in safekeeping, on deposit), *(verwahrende Bank)* custodian bank, depositary bank, *(depotmäßig verwahrte Wertpapiere)* securities held in (under) custody accounts, securities held in safekeeping, *(im Ausland verwahrte Wertpapiere)* securities held in custody abroad, securities on deposit abroad

Verwahrer custodian

verwahrfähig *(~e Finanzinstrumente)* financial instruments eligible for safe custody

Verwahr / ~kette chain of custodians; **~ort** place of custody (deposit); **~pflichten** custodial duties; **~stelle** *(Bank)* custodian, depositary; **~stück** custody item, item (asset, property) held in safekeeping

Verwahrung custody, safekeeping, holding in safe custody, *(in ~ geben)* to place (to deposit) into safe custody, to deposit (to lodge) for safekeeping, to commit to custody, *(in ~ nehmen)* to receive in (for) safe custody, to take into safekeeping, *(zur ~ hinterlegt)* placed for safekeeping, *(~ bis zur Fälligkeit)* holding until maturity, *(~ bei einer Wertpapiersammelbank)* central depository safekeeping

Verwahrungs / ~buch custody ledger; **~gebühren** custodian fees, safekeeping charges; **~geschäft** custody (safekeeping) transactions; **~ort** (physical) place of deposit, depository; **~quittung** custody receipt; **~vertrag** custody (safekeeping) agreement, deposit agreement

Verwahrvorschriften custody rules, rules for proper safekeeping

verwalten 1. to administer **2.** *(Immobilien, Vermögen)* to manage, *(verwaltete Gelder/verwaltetes Vermögen)* assets/funds under management **3.** *(ein zahlungsunfähiges Unternehmen)* to administer

Verwalter 1. administrator **2.** *(Verwalter von Vermögenswerten)* asset manager, *(wenn sich die Aufgabe auf eine reine Verwahrtätigkeit beschränkt)* custodian of assets **3.** *(Insolvenzverwalter)* administrator, receiver, trustee **4.** *(Immobilienverwalter)* estate manager

Verwaltung administration, management, servicing, *(~ eines Nachlasses)* administration of an estate, *(~ von Vermögenswerten)* asset management, investment management

Verwaltungs / ~abgaben regulatory levies; **~akt** administrative order; **~aufwand 1.** *(eines Kreditinstitutes)* administrative expenses (expenditure) **2.** operating (management) expenses; **~beirat** Advisory Board, Board of Advisors

Verwaltungs / ~ertrag fee and commission income; **~gebühr** administration (management, servicing) fee; **~gemeinkosten** administration (management) overheads; **~gesellschaft** management company, manager; **~gesetze** administrative statutes

Verwaltungs / ~kosten → Verwaltungsaufwand; **~kredite** administered loans □ loans administered by banks for third-party account; **~mandat** management mandate; **~rat** Administrative Board; **~recht** *(einer Kapitalanlagegesellschaft)* management right

Verwaltungs / ~sitz administrative place of business; **~treuhand** administrative trustee agreement; **~verpflichtung** servicing obligation; **~vertrag** management (servicing) agreement, contract of management; **~vollmacht** power to manage (to administer), discretionary power

verwässern 1. *(Kapital ~)* to dilute capital **2.** *(Vorschriften, Bestimmungen ~)* to water (down) regulations,

V

(verwässertes Ergebnis je Aktie) diluted earnings per share □ assumes the conversion into common shares of outstanding stock options/rights and convertible bonds

Verwässerung 1. dilution **2.** watering (down)

Verwässerungs / ~effekt dilutive effect; **~risiko** dilution risk; **~schutz** antidilutive provisions, hedge against dilution; **~schutzklausel** dilution protection clause, clause designed to safeguard the rights of existing bond/warrant holders

verwechseln *(die verschiedenen Zahlungsanweisungen ~)* to confuse (to get mixed up with) the different payment instructions

verwehren *(den Zugang zum Kapitalmarkt ~)* to deny access to the capital market, to bar from the capital market

verweigern to refuse, to decline, to deny, *(die Aufnahme der Dokumente ~)* to refuse acceptance of the documents, to dishonour the documents, *(die Einlösung des Schecks ~)* to dishonour the cheque, *(die Kreditgenehmigung ~)* to decline to sanction the loan, *(die Vertragserfüllung ~)* to repudiate the contract, *(die Zahlung ~)* to refuse payment

Verweigerung refusal, declining, denial, *(~ der Annahme/~ der Akzeptleistung)* non-acceptance, refusal to accept, *(~ des Bestätigungsvermerks)* disclaimer of opinion, *(~ der Entlastung)* denial of discharge, *(~ der Lieferung)* refusal to deliver, *(~ der Zahlung)* non-payment, refusal to pay

Verweis 1. reprimand, censure **2.** reference **3.** → Verweisung

verweisen 1. *(auf Schreiben, etc.)* to refer to **2.** *(an einen Ausschuss, eine andere Instanz)* to refer, to remit

Verweisung referral, *(~ an ein anderes Gericht)* remitting (referring) a case to another court, *(~ an die Schlichtung)* referral for mediation

Verweisungs / ~recht right of referral; **~vertrag** referral agreement

verwenden 1. to use, to employ, to apply, to utilise, *(voll zur Refinanzierung bestehender Kredite ~)* to apply in full to the refinancing of existing loans, *(zur Rückzahlung des Darlehens ~)* to apply (to go) towards repaying (paying down) the loan

Verwendung use, utilisation, application

Verwendungs / ~bereich field of application; **~nachweis** evidence (statement) of use; **~zweck** reference, purpose, designated use, *(Darlehen mit freiem ~)* any purpose loan, *(bei Überweisungen)* reason for payment (transfer)

verwerfen 1. *(ablehnen)* to reject, to turn down **2.** *(Einwände zurückweisen)* to dismiss, to set aside

Verwerfung 1. rejection, turning down **2.** dismissal, setting aside **3.** *(~en an den Kapitalmärkten)* distortions (disruptions) in the capital markets

verwertbar *(~e Sicherheit)* realisable collateral

verwerten 1. *(nutzen)* to use, to make use of, to exploit **2.** *(Sicherheiten)* to realise, to liquidate, to sell

Verwertung 1. use, exploitation
2. realisation, liquidation, sale, *(~ von Bezugsrechten)* sale of subscription rights, *(~ von Grundsicherheiten)* realisation (enforcement) of real estate liens, *(~ einer Hypothek)* mortgage foreclosure, *(~ des Pfandgegenstandes bei Zahlungsverzug)* selling (realising) the pledged property upon default
(~ eines Pfandrechtes) lien enforcement, *(~ des Sicherungsgutes)* liquidation (realisation) of the collateral, security enforcement (liquidation), collateral liquidation, *(~ durch freihändige Verwertung/durch Zwangsversteigerung)* realisation by sale in the open market/by way of a foreclosure sale

Verwertungs / ~aktien → Vorratsaktien; **~befugnis** power of sale (realisation); **~erlös** realisation proceeds, enforcement (foreclosure) proceeds, amount realised (from the sale of assets), *(~ bei einem Ausfall)* recovery proceeds in case of default

Verwertungs / ~fall enforcement event, *(im ~)* in case of realisation; **~kosten** cost of realisation; **~pflicht** duty to realise (to liquidate), compulsory (mandatory) realisation; **~quote** recovery rate

Verwertungs / ~recht right to liquidate (realise), power of sale (of alienation), *(~ des Insolvenzverwalters)* right of enforcement; **~risiko** realisation risk, forced sale risk, risk of loss resulting from being forced to realise a collateral

Verwertungs / ~schwierigkeiten difficulties in liquidating a collateral; **~verfahren** realisation (liquidation) proceedings, *(gerichtliches ~)* judicial foreclosure; **~verlust** loss upon realisation; **~zeitraum** realisation period

verwickeln to involve (to engage) s. o. in, *(in das Verfahren verwickelt sein)* to be party to the lawsuit (to the proceedings), to be involved in the lawsuit

verwirken 1. *(ein Recht/einen Anspruch ~)* to forfeit a right/claim **2.** *(verfallen)* to expire

Verwirkung 1. forfeiture, *(~ von Anwartschaftsrechten)* forfeiture of vested benefits **2.** expiration

Verwirkungsklausel forfeiture clause

verwischen *(die Grenzen ~)* to blur the lines (the distinction) between … and

verwurzelt *(tief ~e Anlagegewohnheiten)* ingrained investing habits

Verzahnung *(~ der Kassa- und Derivatemärkte)* interaction (interpenetration, close connection) of cash and derivative markets

verzeichnen to post, to record, to score, to register, *(hohe Erträge ~)* to post (to register) high earnings, *(Finanzwerte konnten hohe Gewinne ~)* financials scored heavy gains, *(im Grundbuch ~)* to record in the land register

Verzeichnis 1. list, table, schedule, statement **2.** register

verzerren to distort, to falsify, to warp, to misrepresent

Verzerrung distortion, falsification, misrepresentation

Verzicht waiver, disclaimer, renunciation, *(~ auf einen Anspruch)* relinquishment of a claim, *(~ auf die Ausübung einer Option)* option abandonment, *(~ auf Einreden)* waiver of pleas *(~ auf die Einrede der Vorausklage)* waiving the plea of prior proceedings against the principal debtor, waiving the benefit of discussion, *(~ auf einen Rechtstitel)* disclaimer of title, *(~ auf die Schriftform)* waiver of written form, *(~ auf Schuldentilgung)* waiver of debt repayment

verzichten to waive, to disclaim, to relinquish, *(auf die Avisierung wird ausdrücklich verzichtet)* notification is waived expressly, *(auf Forderungen ~)* to waive (to write off) claims *(auf sein Optionsrecht ~)* to abandon one's option, to waive one's right of option, *(auf seine Rechte uneingeschränkt ~)* to renounce one's rights unconditionally, *(auf Zinszahlungen ~)* to forego interest on loans

Verzicht / ~erklärung 1. waiver, *(~ seitens der Banken)* disclaimer from the banks **2.** dispensing notice; **~klausel** waiver clause

verzinsen 1. to pay interest **2.** to bear (to yield) interest, *(die Anleihe wird mit 3 % verzinst)* the bond pays (carries) a 3 p.c. coupon, the bond bears 3 % interest, *(ab Ausstellungsdatum mit 4 % verzinst werden)* to attract (to bear, to carry) 4 % interest from the date of issue, *(Einlagen auf Kontokorrentkonten werden nicht verzinst)* funds in checking accounts earn no interest, *(höher verzinst werden)* to carry a higher rate of interest

verzinslich 1. *adj.* interest-bearing, interest-earning, *(~e Aktiva)* interest-earning (interest-bearing) assets 2. *adv. (hoch ~ anlegen)* to invest at a high rate of interest

Verzinsung 1. *(Zinssatz)* interest rate, *(~ zu Dreimonats-Libor)* interest at three-month Libor, *(die bestmögliche ~)* the highest rate of interest available 2. *(Kupon)* coupon 3. *(Zinszahlung)* payment of interest, *(~ am Geldmarkt)* interest paid on money market investments, *(~ von Festgeldeinlagen)* interest paid on (for) fixed-term deposits, return on time deposits, *(die ~ beginnt am)* interest starts accruing on, *(die ~ richtet sich nach den Kapitalmarktsätzen)* payment of interest is geared to the prevailing capital market rates 4. *(Rendite)* yield, return, *(~ einer Anlage)* return on an investment, *(~ des eingesetzten Kapitals)* return on the capital invested

Verzinsungsbeginn interest commencement date

verzögern 1. to delay, to lag, *(verzögerte Auswirkungen der Zinssenkungen)* lagged effects of interest rate cuts 2. *(hinausziehen)* to protract

Verzögerung 1. delay, lag, holdup 2. protraction

Verzollung customs clearance, payment of customs duties

Verzug default, delinquency, *(in ~ befindliche Kredite)* delinquent loans, *(bei ~ des Kreditnehmers)* in the event of the borrower's default, *(einen ~ anzeigen)* to file notice of default, *(den ~ beheben)* to remedy the default, *(in ~ geraten)* to default, to fail to meet payments due *(mit der Rückzahlung des Kredites in ~ geraten)* to default on the loan, *(der in ~ geratene Kreditnehmer)* the defaulting borrower, *(mit dem Schuldendienst in ~ sein)* to default (to be delinquent) in the payment of interest and capital, *(in ~ setzen)* to put in default

Verzugs / ~anzeige/bescheid default notice, notice (notification) of default; **~bestimmungen** default regulations; **~eintritt** commencement of default; **~erklärung** statement (declaration) of default

Verzugs / ~folgen consequences of default (of late payment); **~gebühren** default (delinquency, late payment) charges; **~klausel** default clause, *(reziproke Verzugsklausel)* cross default clause, clause stipulating that default on one debt obligation triggers default on another debt obligation

Verzugs / ~risiko default risk; **~schaden** 1. loss incurred as a result of the default, loss (damage) caused by the default, loss incurred through default in payment, default-induced loss 2. → Verzugszinsen; **~status** *(eines Darlehens)* delinquency status

Verzugs / ~tage days past due, default days, days in arrears; **~tatbestand** protracted default; **~wahrscheinlichkeit** probability of default, probability that a borrower will default within a stated time period

Verzugs / ~zeitraum period of default; **~zinsen** default interest, *(3% ~ berechnen)* to charge 3% interest on arrears; **~zuschlag** late payment surcharge

verzweigt *(weit ~es Filialnetz)* widely ramified branch network

V-Formation *(Charttechnik)* V formation (pattern) □ trend reversal pattern

vielfach manifold, *(Wertpapiere mit Stückelungen von € 1.000 oder einem V~en davon)* securities in denominations of € 1,000 or multiples thereof

Vielfalt diversity, variety

Vielgefahrenversicherung multiple peril policy

vielseitig *(~e Geschäftsinteressen)* manifold (varied) business interests, *(~er Mitarbeiter)* versatile (all-round) staff member

vielversprechend *(~er Unternehmensstart)* promising (encouraging) business startup

Vielzahl *(~ von Anlagemöglichkeiten)* multitude (wealth) of investment opportunities, *(~ neuer Verordnungen)* a host (a large number) of new directives

Vier-Augen-Prinzip four eyes principle, principle of dual control

vierfach fourfold, *(in ~er Ausfertigung)* in four copies, in quadruplicate, *(eine ~e Steigerung des Umsatzes)* a fourfold increase in turnover, *(den ursprünglichen Schätzwert um das Vierfache übersteigen)* to come to four times the original estimate

Vierteljahres / ~abrechnung 1. quarterly settlement, quarterly closing (balancing) of an account **2.** quarterly closing statement; **~akzept** three months' acceptance; **~ausweis** quarterly return; **~auszug** quarterly statement; **~ergebnis** quarterly performance; **~zahlung** quarterly payment

vierteljährlich *adj.* quarterly, *adv.* quarterly, every three months

Vindikationszession assignment of the right to restitution of property

Vinkulationsgeschäft lending against goods carried by rail

vinkulieren to bind, to limit the transferability, *(vinkulierte Aktien)* registered shares □ transferable only with the issuing company's or the other shareholders' consent

Vinkulierung putting restrictions on the transferability of shares

virtuelles Geld CyberCash

VL → vermögenswirksame Leistungen

VL-Sparvertrag asset building savings scheme

Volatilität volatility, measure of an asset's price variability

Volatilitäts / ~arbitrage volatility arbitrage □ attempts to benefit from differences between forecast(ed) and implied volatilities; **~fläche** volatility surface; **~handel** volatility trading, trading on changes in volatility, → Volatilitätsarbitrage; **~händler** volatility trader

Volatilitäts / ~index volatility index □ replicates volatility in the market; **~indexderivate** volatility index derivatives; **~kurve** volatility curve, *(Asymmetrie der ~)* volatility skew; **~matrix** volatility matrix □ illustrates the variation of implied volatilities

Volatilitäts / ~prognose volatility forecast; **~risiko** volatility risk □ risk of loss resulting from unforeseeable changes in volatility; **~sensitivität** volatility sensitivity; **~spitzen** volatility peaks

Volatilitäts / ~steigerung increase in volatility; **~swap** volatility swap □ exchanging the realised volatility of a financial instrument for a fixed volatility; **~unterbrechung** volatility break (interruption)

Volksbank credit union, commercial credit cooperative

Volkswirt economist

Volkswirtschaft national economy, *(volkswirtschaftliche Gesamtrechnung)* national accounts, *(volkswirtschaftliche Wertschöpfung)* net domestic product

voll 1. *adj. (~e Deckung)* full coverage, *(~er Satz reiner Seekonnossemente)* full set clean on board bills of lading, *(~e Stücke/Teilschuldverschreibungen)* bonds cum warrants, bonds with warrants attached
2. *adv. (~ abzugsfähig sein)* to be fully deductible, *(~ beanspruchte Kreditlinie)* fully drawn credit line, *(~ besichert durch Wertpapiere)* fully collateralised with securities, *(~ dividendenberechtigt)* carrying full dividend rights, *(~ eingezahltes Aktienkapital)* fully paid share capital
(~ gedeckte Optionen) fully covered options, *(~ gedeckte Position)* fully hedged position, *(~ haftbar)* fully lia-

V

ble (accountable), (*~ haftender Gesellschafter)* fully liable partner, (*~ nutzen)* to fully utilise, to exploit to the full, (*~ stimmberechtigte Aktien)* stock carrying full voting rights, (*~ werthaltige Besicherung)* full value collateral

Vollakzept general acceptance

Vollamortisationsvertrag full pay-out lease (agreement)

vollautomatisierte Zahlungsabwicklung straight-through processing

vollberechtigt 1. fully authorised (entitled) **2.** fully qualified

Volleigentum full ownership

vollelektronisch *(~es Handelssystem)* fully electronic trading system

Vollfinanzierung one hundred percent funding, *(voll finanziertes Objekt)* property fully (entirely) financed with borrowed funds

vollgültig *(~e Ermächtigung)* fully valid authority

Voll / ~haftung full (unconditional, unrestricted) liability; **~indossament** unqualified (unconditional) endorsement; **~jährigkeit** full age, legal age, majority, *(Eigentumsübergang bei Erreichung der ~)* transfer of ownership upon coming of age (upon attaining majority)

vollkonsolidiert *(~es Unternehmen)* fully consolidated company

Vollkonvertibilität full convertibility

Vollmacht power, power of attorney, authority, *(Stimmrechtsvollmacht)* proxy, (*~ zur Aufnahme von Krediten)* borrowing authority, (*~, eine Gesellschaft rechtsverbindlich zu vertreten)* power to bind a company (to act on behalf of a company), *(die ihm übertragenen ~en)* the powers vested in him

Vollmacht / ~geber donor, grantor of a power of attorney, party conferring a power (an authority); **~inhaber** donee, holder of a power of attorney, proxy

Vollmachts / ~aktionär proxy share holder; **~beschränkung/en** limitation of an authority (of powers conferred), limitations imposed by the donor, restraining powers, restrictions on a power of attorney

Vollmachts / ~depot discretionary investment portfolio; **~entzug** → Vollmachtswiderruf; **~erteilung** granting a power, vesting powers in s. o., conferring powers on s. o.; **~formular** power of attorney form, proxy form

Vollmachts / ~indossament procuration endorsement; **~indossant** proxy endorser; **~missbrauch** abuse of a power of attorney; **~stimmrecht** proxy voting right; **~überschreitung** excess of powers conferred, exceeding the authority conferred, breach of warranted authority

Vollmachts / ~übertragung conferring a power of attorney, delegation of a power, transfer of authority, vesting of powers; **~umfang** extent of an authority, scope of powers conferred; **~urkunde** power of attorney, proxy deed

Vollmachtsvertrag *(in der Vermögensverwaltung)* discretionary investment management agreement, discretionary account agreement, full management agency agreement (contract) □ the customer gives the bank or the portfolio manager complete control over investment decisions without reference back to him

Vollmachtsverwaltung *(von Vermögenswerten)* discretionary asset management

Vollmachtswiderruf revocation of a power of attorney (of an authority)

vollständig 1. *adj.* complete, full, (*~e Erfüllung der Bürgschaftsschuld)* full discharge of the guarantee, (*~e Rückzahlung)* full repayment, repayment in full, (*~er oder teilweiser Verkauf)* sale in whole or in part

2. *adv.* (*~ ausgezahlter Kredit)* loan amount paid in full, (*~ gezeichne-*

te Anleihe) fully subscribed bond, *(~ übertragen)* to transfer in its entirety, to transfer fully, *(~ zahlen)* to pay in full, to settle completely

Vollständigkeitserklärung statement of completeness

vollstreckbar *(~e Ausfertigung)* enforceable copy, *(~er Titel)* enforceable judicial act

Vollstreckbarkeit *(~ von Sicherungsrechten)* enforceability of security interests

Vollstreckbarkeitserklärung statement of enforceability

vollstrecken 1. to enforce, to execute, *(in das Immobiliarvermögen des Schuldners ~)* to levy execution against the debtor's real property **2.** *(Hypothek)* to foreclose

Vollstreckung 1. execution, enforcement **2.** *(~ aus einer Hypothek)* mortgage foreclosure

Vollstreckungs / ~auftrag enforcement order; **~befehl 1.** writ of execution **2.** foreclosure order; **~bescheid** enforcement order, enforceable default summons; **~gericht** court of enforcement; **~gläubiger** execution (judgment) creditor , foreclosing lender

Vollstreckungs / ~handlung act of enforcement; **~klage** action upon judgment; **~klausel** enforcement (execution) clause; **~kosten** enforcement charges; **~maßnahmen** enforcement measures

Vollstreckungs / ~organe (official) enforcement services; **~pfandrecht** enforcement (execution) lien; **~recht** right of (to) foreclosure, right of execution

V

Vollstreckungs / ~schuld judgment debt; **~schuldner** judgment (execution) debtor; **~tilgungsdarlehen** level payment mortage □ mortgage loan requiring full amortisation of principal and interest

Vollstreckungs / ~titel executory title, enforcement order, title (writ) of execution, *(Europäischer Vollstreckungstitel für unbestrittene Forderungen)* European Enforcement Order for Uncontested Claims; **~verfahren 1.** execution proceedings, enforcement process **2.** foreclosure proceedings

vollumfänglich *(~ für uns verbindlich)* binding upon us in each and every respect

vollwertig *(~e Grundschuld)* full-value property charge, *(~er Kredit)* performing loan, *(~e Sicherheit)* sound (valuable) collateral, full-value collateral, prime security

Vollzeitäquivalent/Vollzeitmitarbeiter full-time equivalent

vollziehen to perform, to carry out

Vollzug *(~ eines Vertrages)* performance of a contract

Volumen 1. *(Börsenhandelsvolumen)* turnover, volume, dealings, *(~ an Neuemissionen)* new issue volume, volume of new issue activity, *(Volumen der Kursverlierer)* total down volume
2. *(Volumen auf der Geldseite/Briefseite)* bid size/ask size
3. *(Kreditvolumen)* loan portfolio, total lendings, *(~ der Neuzusagen)* volume of new commitments, *(~ an niedrigverzinslichen Krediten)* low-interest loan portfolio

volumengewichtet *(~er Auslauf)* volume-weighted loan-to-value ratio, *(~er Durchschnittspreis)* volume-weighted average price

volumenmäßig in terms of volume (turnover), in terms of business transacted, volume-wise, *(~ zurückgehen)* to decrease in terms of volume

Volumen / ~risiko volume risk; **~rückgang** decline in volume; **~steigerung** increase in volume (in dealings), volume enhancement; **~steuerung** volumes control; **~wachstum** volume growth, growth in terms of volume

vorab in advance, *(~ festgesetzter Kurs)* predetermined (preset, prespecified) price

Vorab / ~**ausschüttung** advance distribution; ~**freistellung** *(der Waren)* advance release of the goods; ~**zeichnungsrecht** preferential subscription right; ~**zug** **1.** advance deduction **2.** deduction at source

voranbringen to give fresh impetus to, *(die Harmonisierung weiter ~)* to take harmonisation further down the track

vorangehen **1.** *(im Rang)* → vorgehen **2.** *(zeitlich)* to precede, *(die dem Verfalltermin unmittelbar ~den fünf Tage)* the five days immediately preceding the expiration

vorankommen to progress, to make headway (progress), *(langsam ~)* to make slow progress

vorankündigen to give prior notice

Vorankündigung advance (prior) notice

Voranschlag (cost) estimate

voranstellen *(in der Zahlung/im Rang)* to accord priority in payment, to accord a senior rank to

vorantreiben **1.** *(die Umstrukturierung ~)* to press ahead with the restructuring **2.** *(das Wachstum ~)* to spur growth

Voranzeige pre-advice, prior (advance) notice

Vorausabtretung advance assignment, assignment of future receivables

Vorausabtretungsklausel advance assignment clause

Vorausautorisierung pre-authorisation of a credit card transaction

Vorausavisierung *(~ einer Akkreditiveröffnung)* pre-notification of the opening of a documentary credit

vorausbedingen to stipulate in advance

Vorausbelastung advance debit (charge)

vorausberechnen to project, to calculate in advance

Vorausberechnung projection, advance calculation, precalculation, *(~ künftiger Zinsverpflichtungen)* projection of future interest obligations

vorausbezahlte Kredikarte prepaid credit card, stored value card

Voraus / ~**darlehen** cash advance loan, prefinance facility, bridge-over facility (loan); ~**datierung** postdating; ~**depot** advance deposit;~**ermächtigung** pre-authorisation, authorisation in advance; ~**fakturierung** pre-billing

Voraus / ~**informationen** advance (preliminary) information; ~**inkasso** advance collection; ~**klage** action against the principal debtor before resorting to the guarantor, → Einrede der Vorausklage

Voraus / ~**leistung** advance payment (contribution); ~**lieferung** advance delivery; ~**platzierung** advance placement (selling), preplacement; ~**sage** forecast, prediction

voraussagen *(die weitere Zinsentwicklung ~)* to forecast (to predict) the future trend in interest rates

Voraussagewert predictive value

vorausschicken *(dies vorausgeschickt, vereinbaren die Parteien)* given the above (in consideration thereof, on the basis of the foregoing), the parties agree as follows

voraussetzen **1.** to presuppose, to take for granted **2.** *(annehmen)* to presume, to assume **3.** *(erforderlich machen)* to require

Voraussetzung **1.** prerequisite, requirement, *(~en für die Gewährung des Darlehens)* loan eligibility requirements, *(~en für eine Lockerung der Geldpolitik)* prerequisites for easing monetary policy, *(Erfüllung der gesetzlichen ~en)* meeting the legal (statutory) requirements
2. (*unter der stillschweigenden ~, dass)* with the implicit understanding that
3. qualification, (*die ~ für Zinszuschüsse erfüllen)* to qualify (to be eligible) for interest rate subsidies

voraussichtlich *(~er Emissionstermin)* probable (prospective) issuing date, *(~er Wertzuwachs)* prospective (potential, presumable) capital appreciation

vorauszahlen to pay in advance, to prepay

Vorauszahlung 1. prepayment, advance payment **2.** *(vorausbezahlter Betrag)* amount paid in advance

Vorauszahlungs / ~garantie advance payment guarantee; **~kredit** advance payment credit; **~rabatt** anticipation discount

Voravis pre-advice, prior notice (advice)

Voravisierung *(~ eines Akkreditivs)* preadvising a documentary credit

Vorbedingung prerequisite, *(~ für den Eigentumsübergang)* condition precedent to passing of title

Vorbehalt reservation, reserve, proviso, *(unter ~ glattstellen)* to liquidate (to close out) with reservations, *(unter dem üblichen ~)* with the usual proviso, under the usual reserve, *(unter dem ~ des Eingangs bei der Bank)* subject to receipt of payment by the bank, *(~e anmelden)* to make reservations, *(~e hinsichtlich der Aufnahme der Emission am Markt)* reservations about the issue's reception in the market

vorbehalten to reserve, to retain, *(das Eigentum ~)* to retain title to the property, *(sich die endgültige Kreditentscheidung ~)* to reserve final judgement on the loan, *(alle Rechte ~)* all rights reserved, *(sich alle Rechte ~)* to retain all rights, *(sich ein Widerrufsrecht ~)* to reserve (to o.s.) the right to revoke (e. g. the contract)

V

vorbehaltlich subject to, save, *(~ Änderungen)* subject to (save) alterations, *(~ der nachstehend angeführten Bedingungen)* subject to the requirements hereinafter mentioned
(~ gegenteiliger Bestimmungen) save as otherwise provided, unless expressly otherwise stated herein, *(~ entsprechender Bonität)* adequate credit standing provided, *(~ des Eingangs/der ordnungsgemäßen Einlösung)* due payment provided
(~ eines offensichtlichen Irrtums) save for manifest error, *(~ unvorhergesehener Umstände)* barring unforeseen circumstances, *(~ anders lautender Vereinbarungen)* unless otherwise agreed

vorbehaltlos 1. *adj.* *(~es Akzept)* unconditional (clean) acceptance, *(~e Bestätigung)* unconditional (unqualified) confirmation, *(~er Eingang der Zahlung)* unconditional receipt of payment
2. *adv.* *(~ aufnehmen)* to take up unconditionally, *(~ garantieren)* to carry the unconditional guarantee of, *(~ gutschreiben)* to credit without reservations, to credit unconditionally

Vorbehalts / ~eigentum retention of title (of ownership), retained title; **~gut** → Vorbehaltswaren; **~gutschrift** conditional credit entry, credit subject to reservations

Vorbehalts / ~inkasso conditional collection; **~käufer** buyer acquiring goods subject to a retention of title; **~klausel** saving clause, reservations clause, *(hinsichtlich des Eigentums)* title retention clause; **~rechte** rights reserved

Vorbehalts / ~urteil provisional judgment; **~waren** goods/assets subject to a retention of title (of ownership); **~zahlung** payment under reserve, payment subject to a reservation (proviso), conditional payment

vorbei *(an den Banken ~ handeln)* to bypass the banks

Vorbelastungen prior encumbrances (charges)

vorbereiten to prepare, to gear up to, to set the stage, *(~de Gespräche)* preparatory talks

Vorbereitung *(~ der Börseneinführung)* IPO preparation

Vorbereitungs / ~arbeiten preparatory work; **~stadium** preparatory (preliminary) stage, *(sich noch im ~ befinden)* to be still in the drawing board stage (in the pipeline)

Vorbescheid advance ruling (notice)

Vorbesitzer previous owner (proprietor), *(eines Wechsels, Anteils etc.)* prior holder

Vorbesprechungen exploratory (preparatory) talks

vorbestimmt *(zu einem ~en Kurs)* at a predetermined (preset, prestated) price

vorbeugen 1. to prevent, to guard against, *(vorbeugendes Risikomanagement)* preventive risk management, *(vorbeugende Unterlassungsklage)* preventive injunctive relief **2.** *(ausschließen)* to preclude, to forestall

Vorbeugungsmaßnahmen preventive (precautionary) measures

Vorbörse market before hours, premarket

vorbörslich *(~er Kurs)* pre-market price, quotation in pre-market trading, *(die Anleihe wurde ~ mit einem Abschlag von ca. 1 % gehandelt)* the bond traded at a discount of around 1 % in the pre-market

Vorbote *(~ für eine Lockerung der Geldpolitik)* harbinger of an easing in monetary policy

vorbringen *(Beweise, Argumente)* to put (to bring) forward, to produce, to present

Vorbürge first guarantor (surety)

vordatieren to postdate, *(vordatierter Scheck)* postdated cheque

Vordatierung postdating

Vordergrund *(in den ~ rücken)* to come to the fore, *(im ~ stehen)* to be in the fore (centre) of, to be at the forefront (e. g. of our efforts), to hold the limelight

Vordermann previous endorser, previous holder

Vorderseite face, *(~ des Schecks)* front of the cheque

vordringen 1. to advance, to move ahead, to gain ground **2.** to penetrate, to make inroads

Vordringen 1. growing importance, increasing use **2.** *(~ in einen Markt)* making inroads into a market, market penetration, *(das ~ neuer Produkte)* advance of new (innovative) products

vordringlich urgent, *(~ behandeln)* to give priority to

voreilig *(~e Anlageentscheidung)* rash (hasty) investment decision

Voreingenommenheit bias, prejudice

vorenthalten *(ein Recht ~)* to withhold a right

Vorentwurf preliminary (rough, tentative) draft

Vorfälligkeits / ~entschädigung early repayment penalty, prepayment penalty (indemnity) □ for paying off a loan before its scheduled maturity; **~klausel** prepayment (acceleration) clause; **~option** prepayment option

Vorfeld *(im ~ der Hauptversammlung)* in the run-up (lead-up) to the general meeting

vorfinanzieren to prefinance, to lend against future proceeds, to finance provisionally, to extend a bridge-over loan

Vorfinanzierung prefinancing, prefunding, bridge-over financing

Vorfinanzierungs / ~kredit prefinancing loan (credit), preshipment credit, anticipatory credit, interim loan; **~wechsel** prefinance bill; **~zusage** undertaking to prefinance

Vorgabe 1. projection, target, target figures **2.** lead, guidance, *(~ durch den Rentenmarkt)* lead from the bond market **3.** recommended course of action **4.** *(~ von Länderlimiten)* setting country limits **5.** *(gesetzliche ~)* statutory requirement

Vorgabe / ~kalkulation budget accounting; **~kosten** projected (budgeted) expense; ~**mengen** standard quantities; ~**werte** projected (budgeted) figures

Vorgang 1. *(Akte)* file, record, previous correspondence **2.** *(Angelegenheit)* matter, case, issue **3.** activity, task, job

Vorgänger *(~ im Amt)* predecessor in office

vorgeben 1. to pretend, to purport, to profess
2. *(festlegen)* to state, to specify, to stipulate, *(zum vorgegebenen Kurs)* at the specified (given, stated) price, *(wenn nicht anders vorgegeben)* unless otherwise specified, *(ein Limit für ein Börsengeschäft ~)* to set a limit for the execution of a trade

vorgedruckt *(~er Wortlaut)* preprinted wording

vorgefasst *(~e Meinung der Anleger)* preconceived investor opinion

vorgehen 1. *(handeln)* to proceed, to act **2.** *(den Vorrang haben)* to have priority, to take precedence over, to rank prior to, to rank ahead (before)
3. *(gerichtlich ~)* to institute legal proceedings, to file an action, to sue, *(gegen den Schuldner ~)* to take action against the borrower

Vorgehen action, proceeding, procedure

vorgehend *(~e Lasten)* prior-ranking (senior) charges and servitudes, *(~er Rechtsanspruch)* superior title, *(im Rang ~e Hypothek)* senior (prior, superior) mortgage

Vorgehensweise course of action

vorgelagert *(~e Prozesse)* upstream processes

vorgerichtlich *(~es Mahnverfahren)* pre-litigation dunning

Vorgeschäfte → Vorlaufen

vorgesehen scheduled, → vorsehen

Vorgesetzter superior, superior (senior) officer

Vorgespräche preparatory (advance) talks

vorgreifen *(der Zinssenkung ~)* to anticipate the cut in interest rates

Vorgriff *(im ~ auf)* in anticipation of

Vorgründungs-GmbH pre-incorporation GmbH

vorhaben 1. to plan, to propose **2.** to intend

Vorhaben 1. project, plan, scheme, venture **2.** *(Absicht)* intention

Vorhaftung prior liability

vorhalten to reserve, *(Eigenkapital für Kreditrisiken ~)* to allocate equity for credit risks, *(ein Mindestkapital ~)* to maintain a minimum capital base, *(das auf die risikogewichteten Aktiva vorzuhaltende Kapital)* capital to be set against risk-weighted assets, *(zum Verkauf vorgehalten)* available-for-sale

Vorhaltung 1. reservation, maintenance **2.** keeping on one's books

Vorhandels / ~phase pre-trading phase; ~**transparenzpflichten** pre-trading transparency requirements

vorhanden 1. existing, present **2.** *(verfügbar)* available **3.** *(auf Lager)* in stock, on hand, *(~es Guthaben)* funds available, balance in the account

Vorhandensein 1. availability **2.** existence, presence

vorherbestimmen to predetermine, to preset, to fix in advance (beforehand)

vorhergehender Geschäftstag Usance preceding business day convention □ i.e. a payment/settlement date that falls on a non-business day is moved back to the immediately preceding business day

vorherig previous, prior, *(~er Besitzer/Eigentümer)* previous (former) owner/predecessor in title, *(ohne ~e Kündigung abheben)* to withdraw without prior notice

Vorherrschaft predominance, preponderance, *(~ als führendes Finanzzentrum)* primacy as leading financial centre, *(~ am Markt)* predominance (supremacy) in the market

vorherrschen to predominate, to prevail, *(~de Meinung)* prevailing opinion (view)

vorinsolvenzliches Sanierungsverfahren pre-insolvency reorganisation proceedings

Vorjahres / ~ergebnis last year's performance (net income/loss); **~posten** prior period items; **~stand** previous year's level; **~vergleich** comparison with a year earlier, comparison with last year's performance; **~vergleichsziffer** comparative figure for the previous year

Vorkalkulation advance calculation, first estimate, ex ante calculation

Vorkasse prepayment

Vorkauf 1. preemption **2.** *(von Aktien)* buying ahead (e. g. of an expected price rise)

Vorkaufs / ~berechtigter preemptor; **~recht** preemption (preemptive) right, right of preemption, right of first refusal; **~rechtsklausel** preemption clause, first refusal clause, first option clause

vorkehren *(für Risikokredite ~)* to set up loan loss provisions, to make bad debt provisions

Vorkehrungen (precautionary) arrangements, provisioning, *(~ treffen)* to make appropriate arrangements

Vorkommen *(bei ~ des Schecks)* upon presentation of the cheque

vorladen to summon, to serve a summons

Vorladung summons

Vorlage 1. presentation, submission, submittal, filing, *(bei ordnungsgemäßer ~)* when properly presented, *(zahlbar bei ~)* payable upon presentation, *(~ zur Annahme)* presentation for acceptance, *(~ der Dokumente)* presentation (tender) of documents, *(~ zur Genehmigung)* submission for approval, *(~ zum Inkasso)* presentation for collection **2.** file **3.** template

Vorlage / ~frist period of presentation; **~gebot/~pflicht 1.** *(hinsichtlich der Dokumente)* duty to present (to tender) the documents **2.** duty to disclose; **~verbot** instructions not to present

Vorlasten prior charges

Vorlaufen *(im Wertpapiergeschäft)* front running, forward trading □ illegal advance trading in a financial instrument on advance non-public knowledge of upcoming customer transactions, *(Verbot des ~s)* ban on front running

Vorläufer *(~ einer starken Expansion)* precursor (forerunner) to a strong expansion

vorläufig provisional, interim, temporary, *(~er Abschluss)* provisional accounts, *(~es Insolvenzverfahren)* preliminary (provisional) insolvency proceedings, → eröffnetes Insolvenzverfahren, *(~er Insolvenzverwalter)* preliminary insolvency administrator, interim administrator (trustee)

Vorlaufzeit 1. waiting period **2.** run-up period **3.** *(für Lastschriften)* lead time

vorlegen to present, to produce, to submit, to tender, to file, *(vorlegende Bank)* presenting bank, *(den Bericht der Hauptversammlung ~)* to present (to submit, to put) the report to the general meeting, *(zum Inkasso/zur Zahlung ~)* to present for collection/payment

Vorlegung → Vorlage

Vorlegungs / ~frist presentation period, period allowed for presentation; **~gebot** instructions to present; **~güter** intermediate goods, semi-finished goods; **~ort** place of presentation; **~verbot** instructions not to present; **~zeiten** hours of presentation

Vorleistung 1. advance consideration (contribution, performance, payment), *(in ~ treten)* to advance **2.** advance delivery **3.** advance concession

Vorleistungspflicht mandatory advance performance, obligation to make an advance payment, *(vorleistungspflichtige Vertragspartei)* contracting party obligated to perform first

Vorleistungsrisiko **1.** advance payment risk **2.** free delivery risk, pre-settlement (pre-delivery) risk

Vorliebe *(~ für Anleihen)* bias towards investing in bonds

vorliegen **1.** to be available (on hand), to be at s. o.'s disposal **2.** to be known

Vormann previous endorser

vormerken **1.** to note, to take note of, to register, *(wir haben Ihre Anweisungen vorgemerkt)* we have duly noted your instructions
2. to make available, to reserve, to book, *(vorgemerkte Kreditlinie)* committed credit line, credit line made available, *(intern vorgemerkter Kredit)* uncommitted credit, informal loan facility

Vormerkkonto memorandum account

Vormerkung **1.** note, taking due note of **2.** *(im Grundbuch)* caution, priority notice (entered in the Land Register), → Auflassungsvormerkung, *(eine ~ eintragen/löschen lassen)* to have a caution registered/cancelled, *(beim Grundbuch die Eintragung der ~ beantragen)* to apply to the Land Registry for entry of the caution
3. *(Kreditvormerkung)* loan commitment, making a loan available **4.** *(Reservierung)* booking, reservation

Vormerkungsberechtigte/r cautioner, holder of a priority notice

vormerkungsgesichert *(~er Anspruch)* claim secured by a caution

vormerkungswidrig *(~e Belastung/Verfügung)* encumbrance/disposal in violation (breach) of the caution

Vormittagsfixing AMfix, morning fixing

Vormund guardian; ~**schaft** guardianship

Vornahme *(~ von Einzelwertberichtigungen)* establishing specific loan loss allowances

vornehmen **1.** *(Kreditwertberichtigungen ~)* to establish loan loss allowances, to take charge-offs on loans **2.** *(eine Prüfung ~)* to perform (to carry out) an audit **3.** *(Rückstellungen ~)* to make provisions

vororganschaftlich *(~er Gewinn/Verlust)* pre-consolidation income (loss)

Vorpfändung seizure (distraint) warning

Vorpfändungsnachricht seizure notice

Vorplanungsarbeiten preplanning work

Vorprüfung preliminary examination (investigation)

Vorrang priority, preference, *(~ von Ansprüchen)* priority (seniority, precedence) of claims, *(~ auf Befriedigung)* prior claim to satisfaction, *(~ gegenüber allen anderen Forderungen/gegenüber allen nachrangigen Belastungen besitzen)* to have priority over (to) all other claims/over all junior encumbrances
(~ bei der Verteilung des Gesellschaftsvermögens) priority in the distribution of the company's assets, *(~ einräumen)* to give priority (preference) to, to accord priority (e. g. in payment), to prioritise, *(~ haben)* to have priority, to take precedence over, to be senior to others, to prevail over

Vorranggläubiger prior-ranking creditor, senior creditor

vorrangig **1.** *adj.* prior, senior, preferential, superior, preceding, overriding, *(~er Anspruch auf Befriedigung)* claim to preferential satisfaction, *(~e Belastung)* prior charge (encumbrance), *(~e Gläubiger)* prior creditors, creditors entered in a public register as having priority
(~e Hypothek) senior (prior) mortgage, prior-ranking mortgage, *(~es Pfandrecht)* senior (prior) lien, *(~er Kreditgeber)* senior lender, *(~es Ziel)*

prime objective
2. *adv.* on a priority basis, with precedence, *(~ beglichen werden)* to be paid in priority, *(~ besichern)* to grant a senior (first priority) security interest, *(~ besicherte Kreditfazilitäten)* senior loan facilities

Vorrangigkeit priority, *(~ eines Anspruchs)* seniority of a claim

Vorrat 1. stock, inventory, supply, provisions **2.** *(auf ~ kontrahieren)* to warehouse

vorrätig 1. in stock **2.** *(verfügbar)* available, on hand

Vorrats / ~aktien treasury stock, own shares held by a third party (bank, trustee) for account of the issuing corporation; **~beschluss** resolution passed in advance, precautionary resolution (e.g. by a General Assembly), *(i. S. einer globalen Bewilligung)* global authorisation

Vorrats / ~bewertung inventory valuation; **~bildung** stockpiling, building up stocks; **~darlehen** forward loan; **~ermächtigung** advance authorisation, authorisation given as a contingency measure

Vorrats / ~finanzierung inventory financing, *(Kredit zur ~)* inventory loan; **~gesellschaft** shelf company □ limited liability company established in advance to shorten the registration process

Vorrats / ~haltung stockpiling; **~linie** standby facility (line); **~stellenwechsel** storage agency bill; **~vermögen** inventory assets, inventories, *(Investitionen in ~)* inventory spending

Vorrecht preferential right, privilege, prerogative, priority, *(die Aktionäre genießen besondere ~e)* the shareholders hold (enjoy) special privileges

Vorreiterrolle pioneering role

vorrücken to move ahead (forward), to notch ahead, *(vom zehnten auf den zweiten Platz ~)* to jump from tenth to second place

Vorsatz 1. *(Absicht)* intention, *(jur.)* wil(l)ful intent (e. g. to defraud), *(~ und grobe Fahrlässigkeit)* wil(l)ful misconduct and gross negligence
2. *(Entschluss)* resolution

vorsätzlich 1. *adj.* deliberate, wil(l)ful, intentional, *(~e Pflichtverletzung)* wil(l)ful negligence, *(~e Vertragsverletzung)* wil(l)ful (premeditated) breach of contract
2. *adv.* *(~ irreführen)* to mislead deliberately (willfully, with intent)

Vorschaltdarlehen interim (bridge-over) loan

vorschalten *(einen Festzinskredit ~)* to grant a fixed rate interim loan □ in anticipation of a floating rate facility

Vorschaltgesellschaft intermediate holding company

Vorschaltgesetz Interim (Preliminary) Act

Vorschau 1. *(Prognose)* forecast, projection **2.** *(~ auf die morgige Sitzung)* preview of tomorrow's meeting

Vorschau / ~bilanz projected (forecast) balance sheet; **~ergebnisrechnung** projected income statement; **~finanzflussrechnung** projected working capital funds statement; **~periode** forecasting period; **~rechnung** forecast accounts

Vorschlag 1. proposal, proposition, suggestion, offer, *(~ zur Gewinnverwendung)* proposed appropriation of profits **2.** *(Empfehlung)* recommendation

Vorschlags / ~recht right of nomination; **~wesen** suggestion scheme

vorschreiben to stipulate, to set, to lay down, *(die im Kreditvertrag vorgeschriebenen monatlichen Tilgungsraten)* the redemption payments (instalments) laid down (specified) in the loan agreement, *(der für die Rückzahlung vorgeschriebene Zeitraum)* the period (deadline) set for the repayment, the repayment period stipulated

Vorschrift 1. *(Anweisung)* instruction, order, direction **2.** *(Bedingung)* condition, requirement 3. *(Bestimmung)* regulation, provision, stipulation 4. *(Klausel)* clause

vorschriftsmäßig *adj.* proper, correct, regular, *adv.* correctly, in accordance with the respective provisions

Vorschuss 1. advance, loan 2. *(vorzeitige Auszahlung)* deposit repaid prior to maturity

Vorschussakkreditiv packing credit, red clause credit

vorschüssig *(~e Tilgung)* upfront redemption, *(~e Zinsen)* interest charged in advance, *(~e Zinszahlung)* upfront interest payment, interest payment at the beginning of the interest period

Vorschuss / ~wechsel bill deposited as security; **~zinsen** early withdrawal penalty, interest penalty for an early withdrawal

vorsehen 1. to call for, to provide for, to require, *(halbjährliche Tilgungszahlungen im Kreditvertrag ~)* to call for semiannual repayments in the loan agreement, *(wie im Vertrag vorgesehen)* as required (stipulated) in the contract 2. to plan, to schedule, *(die vorgesehene Börseneinführung)* the scheduled IPO (market flotation), *(die für die zweite Jahreshälfte vorgesehenen Emissionen)* the issues planned (slated) for the second half of the year 3. *(für einen bestimmten Zweck)* to earmark (to designate) for a specific purpose, to conceive for a specific use, *(zum Verkauf vorgesehene Vermögenswerte)* assets targeted for sale

Vorsicht (pre)caution, care, prudence, foresight, *(~ in Finanzfragen)* financial circumspection (caution)

vorsichtig 1. *adj.* cautious, careful, circumspect, *(~e Anlagepolitik)* prudent investment policy, *(~e Anleger)* cautious (conservative, risk-averting) investors, *(~e Beleihungspolitik)* cautious lending policy, *(~e Bewertung)* cautious (conservative) valuation, conservative assessment *(~e Dispositionen des Handels)* guarded selling and buying by professional traders, *(eine ~e Haltung einnehmen)* to adopt (to take) a cautious (conservative) attitude, *(~er Optimismus)* guarded optimism 2. *adv.* *(~ optimistische Börsenstimmung)* cautiously (guardedly) optimistic market sentiment, *(~ reagieren auf)* to react cautiously to

Vorsichts / ~maßnahme precaution, precautionary (prudential) measure, measure taken to secure (e. g. a good performance); **~prinzip** principle of caution (of prudence)

Vorsitz chairmanship, *(den ~ führen)* to chair, to hold the chair, to be in the chair, to preside over

Vorsitzender chairman, president, chairperson, *(~ des Aufsichtsrates)* Chairman of the Supervisory Board, *(~ des Vorstandes)* Chairman of the Management Board (Board of Management), Chief Executive Officer

Vorsorge 1. provision(ing), *(~ für allgemeine Bankrisiken)* provision for general banking risks, *(~ für Bonitäts-/Kreditrisiken)* provisioning for credit risks, *(~ für Problemkredite)* provisioning for problem (troubled) loans, bad debt provisioning, *(in die ~ gehen)* to be used for setting up (for establishing) loan loss provisions, *(für Risiken im Kreditgeschäft ~ treffen)* to set up loan loss provisions, to make bad and doubtful debt provisions 2. → Altersvorsorge

Vorsorgeaufwand 1. *(für Kreditausreichungen)* provisioning expenses (charges) 2. *(des Arbeitgebers)* pension provisions, pension benefit expenses 3. *(persönlicher ~)* provident fund payments

Vorsorge / ~erfordernisse provisioning requirements; **~last** → Vorsorgeaufwand; **~maßnahmen** 1. provisioning, → Vorsorge 2. precautionary measures, precautions

vorsorgen to provide for, to make provisions, → Vorsorge treffen

V

Vorsorge / ~politik (risk/bad debt) provisioning policy; **~quote** provisioning ratio, provisions as a proportion of operating profit; **~regeln** provisioning rules; **~reserve** contingency reserve

Vorsorge / ~saldo net provisioning □ gross provisions less release of provisions and recoveries; **~sparen** precautionary saving, nest-egg saving; **~vollmacht** enduring (durable) power of attorney; **~wertberichtigungen** general loan loss allowances

Vorsparleistung amount to be saved prior to accommodation of a loan, → Bauparvertrag

Vorspesen *(bei der Rückrechnung von Wechseln)* return charges

Vorsprung 1. lead **2.** competitive edge

Vorstand 1. *(allgemein)* Executive Committee **2.** *(einer Aktiengesellschaft)* Board of Management, Management Board, Board of Managing Directors **3.** *(einer Stiftung)* Board of Trustees **4.** → Vorstandsmitglied

Vorstands / ~ausschuss Management Board Committee; **~beschluss** Board resolution; **~mitglied** Board Member, Member of the Management Board; **~sitzung** Board Meeting; **~vorsitzender** Chairman of the Board, Chief Executive Officer (CEO)

vorstehen 1. to be in charge of, to preside over, *(dem Konsortium ~)* to lead the syndicate **2.** *(wie ~d angegeben)* as indicated above, as aforesaid

Vorstellung 1. introduction **2.** conception, idea **3.** *(Präsentation)* presentation, roadshow

Vorstellungsgespräch interview

Vorsteuer input VAT, *(~ geltend machen)* to claim input VAT deduction

Vorsteuer / ~abzug deduction of input VAT; **~gewinn** pre-tax profit; **~ rückerstattung** refund of input VAT; **~vergütungsantrag** input VAT refund applicaton

Vorstoß advance, attempt, drive, *(~ in einen unbekannten Markt)* foray into an unknown market

Vortages / ~notiz previous day's quotation; **~schluss** previous day's close; **~verluste** previous day's losses

vortäuschen to fake, to feign, to pretend, *(vorgetäuschte Umsatzerhöhung)* faked (fictitious) increase in sales

Vorteil advantage, benefit, merit, edge, *(~e einer Rentenanlage)* advantages of (merits of, rewards from) a bond market investment, *(einen klaren ~ gegenüber Konkurrenzunternehmen besitzen)* to have a distinct edge over competitors, *(wirtschaftlich von ~ sein)* to be economically beneficial, *(die ~e und Nachteile der neuen zinspolitischen Maßnahmen abwägen)* to weigh the pros and cons of the new interest policy measures

vorteilhaft favourable, advantageous, profitable, *(sich als ~ erweisen)* to prove advantageous

Vortrag 1. address, speech **2.** balance carried (brought) forward

vortragen to carry over, to bring forward, *(auf das nächste Geschäftsjahr ~)* to carry over to (into) the next business year

vortreten *(im Rang ~)* to take precedence (priority) over, to be given a prior claim (higher rank), *(vorgetretener Gläubiger/Kreditgeber)* creditor/lender given a prior claim

Vortritt taking precedence (priority) over

vorübergehend *(~e Kreditgewährung)* temporary loan accommodation, *(~e Rückführung eines Kredites)* temporary repayment (cleanup) of a loan

Vorurteil prejudice, bias

Vorvaluta forward value

Vorvalutierungszuschlag surcharge for prior disbursement of the loan

Vorverhandlungen exploratory talks, preliminary negotiations

Vorverkauf 1. advance sale of securities **2.** pre-issue selling

vorverlagern to bring forward

vorverlegen *(den Fälligkeitstermin ~)* to accelerate the maturity

Vorverlegung *(~ der Fälligkeit)* acceleration of maturity, debt acceleration

Vorvertrag preliminary agreement, letter of understanding, heads of agreement

Vorwärtsterminierung forward scheduling

vorweg *(~ befriedigen)* to pay in priority to all other debtors

Vorweg / ~abzug prior deduction, deduction at source; **~befriedigung** preferential satisfaction; **~bewilligung** advance appropriation; **~kompensation** advance netting; **~leistung** advance contribution (payment); **~nahme** *(in ~)* in anticipation of

vorwegnehmen to anticipate, to discount, *(die Börse hat die Zinssenkung vorweggenommen)* the stock market has already discounted the effects of the cut in interest rates

Vorzeichen *(~ für eine bevorstehende Zinssenkung)* sign (portent) of an imminent rate cut

vorzeichnen to trace out, to chart, *(der von der Bundesbank vorgezeichnete Kurs)* the course charted (plotted) by Bundesbank

Vorzeichnung *(eines Versicherungsrisikos)* fronting

vorzeitig 1. *adj. (~e Ausübung)* early exercise, *(~es Kündigungsrecht)* early call privilege, right to call in a loan prior to maturity, *(~er Rückkauf)* repurchase prior to maturity (ahead of schedule)
(~e Tilgung) premature (early) redemption, redemption in advance of the due date, pre-maturity redemption, early amortisation, *(~e Verfügung) (a)* premature drawing on a loan facility *(b)* premature withdrawal of deposits
2. *adv. (eine Anleihe ~ ablösen)* to redeem a bond prior to maturity, to retire a bond ahead of schedule, *(der Kredit kann ~ abgelöst werden)* the loan may be retired ahead of schedule, *(einen Kredit ~ kündigen)* to call in a loan prior to maturity, *(~ zurückzahlen)* to repay prior to maturity, to prepay, to repay ahead of schedule

vorziehen 1. *(präferieren)* to prefer, to give preference to
2. *(zeitlich)* to bring forward (e.g. investments planned for the following year), *(bei Eintritt bestimmter Ereignisse vorgezogen werden)* to be accelerated upon the occurrence of specific events, *(vorgezogene Kreditaufnahmen)* frontloaded borrowings

Vorziehen 1. bringing forward, acceleration **2.** giving preference to

Vorzinsen advance interest □ bond interest payable from deposit of the subscription money until the first coupon date

Vorzüge 1. preferred shares (stocks) **2.** *(die ~ dieses Verfahrens)* the merits (benefits) of this procedure

Vorzugsaktien preferred (privileged) stock, preferred (preferential) shares, priority shares, *(~ aus der Kapitalerhöhung)* preference shares stemming from the capital increase, *(~ mit einem/ohne einen nachzuzahlenden Vorzug)* cumulative/non-cumulative preference shares

Vorzugs / ~aktienkapital preference share capital; **~aktionär** preference shareholder, preferred stockholder; **~dividende** preference (preferred) dividend, dividend on preferred stock; **~dividendendeckung** times preferred dividend earned; **~dividendenrecht** entitlement to priority of dividend

Vorzugs / ~gewinnanteil 1. preferred share in profits **2.** preferred dividend; **~konditionen** preferential terms; **~kurs** preferential price, price below market conditions; **~obligationen** preference (priority) bonds

Vorzugs / ~recht preferential right, privilege; **~risikogewicht** preferential risk weight; **~stammaktien** preferred ordinary shares, privileged common stock; **~stimmrecht** preferential voting right; **~tarif** preferential (concessionary) rates

vorzugsweise preferably, *(einen Anspruch auf ~ Befriedigung besitzen)* to be entitled to preference in payment

Vorzugs / ~zeichnungsrecht preferential right of subscription; **~zinssatz** preferential rate of interest

Vostro-Konto vostro account, account maintained by a bank for another bank

votieren *(Kreditanträge ~)* to vote (to decide) on loan applications (credit proposals)

Votum 1. vote (on credit proposals), lending decision, *(Votum von Markt/Marktfolge)* front office/back office vote, *(zustimmendes ~)* consenting vote **2.** assessment, rating

V Pay Karte V Pay Card □ chip and pin-based debit card

W

wachsen to grow, to rise, *(~der Druck auf die Zinsspannen)* growing (mounting) pressure on interest margins

Wachstums / **~aktie** growth stock; **~beschleunigungsgesetz** Growth Acceleration Act; **~dynamik** growth momentum; **~finanzierung** expansion financing; **~fonds** growth fund, capital appreciation fund; **~förderung** encouragement of growth, promoting growth

Wachstums / **~hemmnis** impediment (obstacle) to growth; **~impulse** growth incentives, impetus for growth; **~industrie** growth industry

wachstums / **~schwach** slow-growing, with (of) limited growth potential; **~stark** fast-growing, offering considerable growth potential, growth-driven

Wachstums / **~träger** mainstay of growth; **~verlangsamung** deceleration of (slowdown in) growth; **~werte** growth stocks; **~ziel** growth target

Wachwechsel *(~ an der Konzernspitze)* change of guard at the top of the group

Wackelkredit problem loan, troubled loan exposure

Wagnis **1.** risk, hazard **2.** *(Unternehmensneugründung)* venture; **~deckung** ratio of equity to risk assets; **~finanzierung** venture finance

Wagniskapital venture capital; **~beteiligungen** venture capital investments; **~finanzierung** venture capital financing; **~fonds** venture capital fund; **~geber** venture capitalist; **~gesellschaft** venture capital company; **~gesetz** Venture Capital Act

Wahl **1.** choice, *(zum Zeitpunkt seiner Wahl)* at the moment of his choosing, *(die ~ zwischen verschiedenen Anlageformen haben)* to have the choice between various forms of investment
2. vote, ballot, election, *(Stimmabgabe)* voting, polling, *(~en zum Aufsichtsrat)* elections to the Supervisory Board, *(in geheimer ~ bestimmen)* to nominate by secret ballot, *(sich zur ~ stellen)* to stand as a candidate, *(sich bei einer ~ vertreten lassen)* to vote by proxy
3. option, alternative, *(nach ~ des Kunden)* at the customer's option (discretion)
4. *(in die engere ~ kommen)* to be on the short list, *(drei Unternehmen kamen in die engere ~)* three companies have been shortlisted

wählen **1.** to choose, to select, to make a choice, to opt for
2. to elect, to vote, *(aus seiner Mitte ~)* to elect from among its members, *(in ein Amt ~)* to elect to an office, *(wieder in den Aufsichtsrat ~)* to return to the Supervisory Board, *(in geheimer Wahl ~)* to elect by secret ballot (in a secret ballot)

Wahl / **~berechtigung** eligibility to vote, → Wahlrecht; **~ergebnis** **1.** result of the vote **2.** election result (returns); **~recht** **1.** *(Option)* option, *(von einem ~ Gebrauch machen)* to opt for **2.** voting right, suffrage **3.** electoral law; **~zuteilung** *(bei Bauspardarlehen)* optional allotment

wahren **1.** to maintain, to preserve, to secure, *(Vertraulichkeit ~)* to maintain confidentiality
2. to observe, to comply with, to respect, *(die Frist ~)* to observe (to meet) the deadline
3. to safeguard, to protect, to guard, *(im Grundbuch ~ lassen)* to secure

an interest through entry in the land register

wahrheitsgemäß *(Grundsatz der ~en Darstellung)* (accounting) principle of faithful representation

wahrnehmen 1. to perceive, to notice **2.** *(Aufgaben ~)* to perform (to carry out) duties
3. *(Bezugsrechte ~)* to take up rights
4. *(eine Gelegenheit ~)* to benefit (to profit) from an opportunity, to seize (to avail o. s. of) an opportunity
5. *(die Interessen des Kunden ~)* to represent the customer's interests

Wahrnehmung *(~des Produktwertes durch den Kunden)* customer's perception of the product value

wahrscheinlich likely, probable, *(die für am ~sten gehaltene Entwicklung)* the most likely scenario, *(für wenig ~ halten)* to consider (e. g. a recovery) not particularly probable

Wahrscheinlichkeit *(~ des Schadenfalls, des Eintretens eines Krediterеignisses)* probability of loss event, *(~ eines Schuldnerverzugs)* likelihood (probability) of a default

Wahrscheinlichkeits / ~dichte probability density; **~maß** probability measure; **~raum** probability space; **~verteilung** probability distribution; **~wert** probability value, p-value

Wahrung 1. maintenance, preservation, *(~ der Preisstabilität)* preservation of price stability, *(~ der Vertraulichkeit)* maintenance of confidentiality **2.** adherence, compliance, *(~ der Rückzahlungsfrist)* observance of the time limit set for repayment
3. safeguarding, protection, *(unter ~ des Kundeninteresses)* with due regard to the customer's interests

Währung currency

Währungs / ~abkommen currency (monetary) agreement; **~abschlag** currency haircut; **~abschnitt** (foreign) currency bill; **~abwertung** currency devaluation (depreciation); **~aktivpositionen** currency assets, long currency positions; **~akzept** foreign currency acceptance

Währungs / ~anleihe currency bond; **~ausgleich** exchange equalisation; **~außenmarkt** external currency market; **~bandbreiten** currency bands; **~barkredit** cash currency loan

Währungs / ~beistand currency support; **~bereinigung** adjustment for currency fluctuations (for exchange rate movements), *(währungsbereinigte Umsatzerlöse)* currency-adjusted sales revenue

währungsbezogen *(~e Transaktionen)* currency-driven transactions

Währungs / ~chaos currency turmoil, turbulences in the currency markets; **~derivate** currency derivatives (currency options/futures/warrants); **~diversifikation** currency diversification, diversifying (spreading) currency assets

Währungs / ~eindeckung currency coverage, covering in the foreign exchange market; **~einheit** currency unit; **~einlagen** foreign currency deposits; **~eventualrisiko** contingent currency risk

Währungs / ~fächer currency spread; **~fonds 1.** currency fund **2.** *(Internationaler ~)* International Monetary Fund; **~forderungen** currency receivables, receivables in foreign currencies; **~fungibilität** currency fungibility; **~-Future** currency future, currency futures contract

Währungs / ~gebiet currency area; **~gegenposition** offsetting (matching) currency position; **~gesamtposition** overall currency position

Währungs / ~gewichtung currency weighting; **~gewinn 1.** currency (exchange) gain **2.** *(Umrechnungsgewinn)* currency translation gain **3.** *(i. S. von Wertsteigerung)* currency appreciation

währungsgleich *(~e Positionen)* matched currency positions, *(~er Zins-Swap)* single-currency interest rate swap

Währungs / ~gleichgewicht currency equilibrium; **~gold** monetary (currency) gold; **~guthaben** foreign currency balances (funds); **~hüter** monetary (currency) watchdog; **~inkongruenz** currency mismatch, mismatched currencies; **~klausel** currency clause

währungskongruent *(~ absichern)* to hedge in the same currency, *(~e Kreditinanspruchnahme)* borrowing at a matching currency, *(~e Refinanzierung)* funding (refinancing) in the same currency, matched funding, matching the currency of the funding transaction against the currency of the loan

Währungs / ~kongruenz 1. matched currencies **2.** matching currencies, *(das Prinzip der ~ beachten)* to observe the principle of matching currencies; **~konto** currency account; **~kontrakt** *(Terminkontrakt)* currency future, currency futures contract

Währungs / ~kontrolle currency control, currency exposure control; **~konvertibilität** currency convertibility; **~konvertierung** currency conversion

Währungs / ~korrelation currency correlation; **~korb** basket of currencies, currency basket; **~korbanleihe** composite currency bond; **~kredit** foreign currency loan, currency borrowing

Währungs / ~-Loro/Nostro-Konto currency loro/nostro account; **~-Mix** currency mix; **~option** currency option; **~optionsanleihe** currency option bond; **~optionsschein** currency warrant; **~ordnung** *(internationale ~)* international monetary system

Währungs / ~parität currency parity; **~passivpositionen** currency liabilities, short currency positions; **~politik** monetary policy, *(währungspolitisches Instrumentarium)* monetary policy instruments

Währungs / ~position currency exposure, foreign exchange position, *(Absicherung von ~en)* currency exposure hedging; **~positionskontrolle** currency exposure control, monitoring the currency position

Währungs / ~raum currency area (zone); **~rechnungseinheit** currency unit; **~reserven** currency (monetary) reserves, holdings of foreign currency

Währungsrisiko currency (exchange) risk, currency exposure; **~abschläge** markdowns for currency risks; **~-Management** currency risk (exposure) management

Währungs / ~scheck foreign currency cheque; **~streuung** currency diversification (spread); **~ströme** currency flows; **~stützung** currency propping; **~-Swap** currency swap; **~system** monetary system, *(Neuordnung des ~s)* currency (monetary) realignment

Währungs / ~terminkontrakt currency futures contract; **~titel** currency bonds; **~transaktionsrisiko** currency transaction risk; **~turbulenzen** turmoil in the currency markets, monetary turmoil, wild (erratic) fluctuations in exchange rates

währungsübergreifend *(~e Transaktionen)* cross-currency deals

Währungsüberhang net position in a currency, net currency exposure

Währungsumrechnung currency translation (conversion)

Währungsumrechnungs / ~differenzen exchange differences, differences arising from currency translation; **~gewinne** currency translation gains; **~risiko** exchange risk, currency translation risk

Währungs / ~umstellung currency conversion; **~union** monetary union; **~unruhen** currency disturbances; **~unsicherheiten** currency uncertainties, uncertainties over exchange values; **~verbindlichkeiten** currency debt (liabilities), payables in foreign currencies; **~verbund** currency bloc

Währungs / **~verfall** monetary erosion (disintegration); **~verluste** currency (exchange) losses; **~verteilung** *(~ der Kapitalanlagen)* investment allocation by currency; **~volatilität** exchange rate volatility; **~wahlrecht** currency option

Währungs-Zinsdifferenzgeschäft currency carry trade □ borrowing in a currency with a low interest rate and buying high-yielding assets in a different currency

Währungs-Zinsswap cross currency interest rate swap □ agreement to exchange principal and interest payments in two different currencies

walten *(größere Vorsicht ~ lassen)* to exercise greater caution

Wandelanleihe convertible bond, bond entitling the holder to convert bonds into shares, *(~ mit Pflichtwandlung)* mandatory convertible

Wandelanleihe-Arbitrage convertible bond arbitrage □ designed to profit from mispricings between convertible bonds and the underlying instruments

wandelbar 1. convertible, *(~ in Stammaktien)* convertible into common stock, *(~er Schuldtitel)* convertible debt instrment, convertible note, *(~e Vorzugsaktien)* convertible preferred stock
2. *(austauschbar)* exchangeable

Wandelbarkeit convertibility

Wandelgenussrechte convertible profit participation rights

wandeln to convert (into)

Wandel / **~obligation** convertible bond; **~obligationär** convertible bondholder; **~prämie** conversion premium; **~recht** conversion privilege (right, option), right of conversion, *(~ auf Aktien)* conversion right for shares; **~schuldverschreibung** convertible note (bond)

Wandelung *(Recht auf ~)* right to repudiation of contract

Wandelvorzugsaktien convertible preferred stock

Wanderungsbewegungen *(~ im Kreditportfolio)* migration in the loan portfolio

Wandlung conversion

Wandlungs / **~angebot** conversion offer; **~aufgeld** conversion premium; **~bedingungen** terms of conversion; **~fähigkeit** convertibility, eligibility for conversion, *(wandlungsfähiges Anleihekapital)* convertible loan stock, → wandelbar; **~frist** conversion period

Wandlungs / **~gebühr** conversion fee; **~möglichkeit** conversion feature (privilege); **~ option** conversion (convertibility) option; **~pflicht** conversion obligation (requirement); **~recht** conversion privilege (right); **~verhältnis** conversion ratio

Wandprotest protest in the drawee's absence

Wanken *(das ins ~ geratene Unternehmen)* the beleaguered company

wappnen *(sich ~)* to brace o. s. (e. g. for sharply rising cost)

Ware commodity, merchandise, goods

Waren / **~abnahme** taking delivery of the goods; **~abnahmerisiko** risk that delivery of the goods will not be accepted; **~begleitschein** consignment note, waybill; **~beleihung** lending on (against) goods; **~bestandsfinanzierung** inventory financing

warenbezogen *(~e Schuldverschreibungen)* commodity-linked notes

Waren / **~börse** commodity exchange; **~delkredere-Versicherung** accounts receivable insurance, trade credit insurance; **~derivate** commodity derivatives □ commodity futures/options/swaps, commodity-based ETFs/warrants

Waren / **~einsatz** cost of sales; **~empfänger** consignee; **~fonds** commodity fund; **~freistellung** *(~ durch die vorlegende Bank)* release of the goods by

W

the presenting bank; ~**geld** commodity money

Waren / ~korb basket of commodities; ~**kredit**/~**lombard** advance (lending) on goods; ~**option** commodity option; ~**pensionsgeschäfte** sale and repurchase agreements in commodities, → Pensionsgeschäft; ~-**Switch** commodity switch transaction

Warentermin / ~börse commodities exchange; ~**geschäfte** commodity forwards, (when traded on a commodities exchange) commodity futures; ~**handel** commodity futures trading; ~**kontrakt** commodity futures contract; ~**markt** commodities exchange, commodity futures market

Waren / ~übereignung transferring the ownership in goods, transferring the title (the property rights) to goods; ~ **veredelungsfinanzierung** tolling finance; ~**veredelungsvertrag** tolling agreement

Waren / ~verkehrsbescheinigung movement certificate; ~**wechsel** trade bill; ~**wert** value of the goods; ~**wertpapiere** documents of title

warnen to caution

Warteliste *(bei Neuemissionen)* queueing list for new issues

warten *(auf sich ~ lassen)* to be some way off

Wartezeit 1. *(Bausparvertrag)* waiting (qualifying) period **2.** *(für die Umwandlung von Anwartschaften in Vollrechte)* vesting period

Wartezimmerverfahren deferment of payment orders until receipt of cover funds

Wartung maintenance, servicing

Wasseraktien heavily diluted stock

Wasserfallprinzip waterfall principle □ making payments/servicing the individual tranches of debt instruments in a firmly established sequence, i.e. when the highest-tiered tranche is paid in full, the next highest-tiered tranche begins receiving interest and principal payments.

WDRL → Wertpapierdienstleistungs-Richtlinie

Wechsel 1. change, (~ *in der Geldpolitik)* change (turnaround) in monetary policy
2. bill of exchange, bill, (~ *mit mehreren Ausfertigungen)* bill drawn in several copies, (~ *mit einer Laufzeit von drei Monaten)* three months' bill, bill having a usance of three months, *(im Ausland zahlbar gestellter ~)* bill payable abroad, *(Deckung für den fällig werdenden ~ anschaffen)* to provide funds to meet the maturing bill
3. *(turnusmäßiger)* rotation

Wechsel / ~abrechnung 1. bill discount statement (note) **2.** discounting a bill of exchange; ~**adresse** name on a bill; ~**agent** bill broker

wechselähnlich *(~e Schuldverpflichtung)* debenture similar in nature to a bill of exchange

Wechsel / ~akzept bill acceptance, accepting a bill; ~**anhang** allonge, rider; ~**ankauf 1.** bill purchase, buying bills **2.** *(im Dokumentengeschäft)* negotiation of a bill **3.** *(~ mit Rücknahmeverpflichtung)* accepting bills for rediscount under repurchase agreements; ~**ankaufskonditionen** bill purchase terms, bill dealing rates

Wechsel / ~ausfertigung *(erste/zweite/dritte ~)* first/second/third of exchange; ~**aussteller** drawer of a bill; ~**aval** → Wechselbürgschaft

Wechsel / ~basis *(auf ~ abgewickeltes Kreditgeschäft)* bill-based loan transaction; ~ **beleihung** lending against bills of exchange; ~**bestand** bill portfolio, bill book; ~**beteiligte** parties to a bill; ~**betrag** amount (face value) of a bill

Wechsel / ~bezogener drawee on a bill; ~**bürge** guarantor on a bill, bill guarantor; ~**bürgschaft** bill guarantee; ~**debitoren** bills receivable; ~**de-**

ckung provision of (providing) cover for a bill, bill cover

Wechsel / ~**diskontertrag** discounts earned (received); ~**diskontierung** bill discounting; ~**diskontkredit** discount credit; ~**diskontlinie** discount line; ~**diskontsatz** bill rate; ~**drittausfertigung** third of exchange

Wechsel / ~**einlösung** payment (discharge) of a bill, meeting (honouring) a bill; ~**einlösungsauftrag** bill payment request; ~**einlösungsgarantie** bill guarantee; ~**einreicher** presenter of a bill, person (party) presenting a bill; ~**einreichung** presenting a bill (e. g. for discount)

Wechsel / ~**einzug** bill collection, collecting a bill; ~**einzugsauftrag** bill collection request; ~**einzugsspesen** bill collection charges; ~**erlös** bill proceeds; ~**erstausfertigung** first of exchange

Wechsel / ~**fähigkeit** capacity to contract by bills of exchange, capacity to draw bills or to become liable on bills; ~**fälligkeit 1.** maturity of a bill **2.** bill due, bill maturing

Wechsel / ~**fälschung** bill forgery; ~**finanzierung** bill (bill-based) finance, financing by bills of exchange; ~**forderung** bill-based claim, claim under a bill, *(~en)* bills (notes) receivable

Wechsel / ~**gegenwert** proceeds of a bill; ~**geschäft** bill operations, bill brokerage business; ~**geschäftsfähigkeit** → Wechselfähigkeit; ~**gesetz** German Bill of Exchange Act; ~**girant** endorser of a bill; ~**giro** endorsement of a bill; ~**gläubiger** creditor on a bill

Wechsel / ~**haftung** liability on a bill; ~**hereinnahme** accepting bills (e. g. for discount)

Wechsel / ~**indossament** endorsement of a bill; ~**indossant** endorser of a bill; ~**indossatar** endorsee of a bill, person to whom the bill is transferred; ~**inhaber** holder of a bill; ~**inkasso** bill collection, *(~ vornehmen)* to collect a bill; ~**inkassokosten** bill collection charges

Wechsel / ~**klage** suit upon a bill, *(~ erheben)* to sue on a bill; ~**kommission** bill broking; ~**kredit** discount (acceptance) credit, *(~e in der Bilanz)* bills discounted; ~**kreditoren** bills payable

Wechselkurs exchange rate

Wechselkurs / ~**änderung** exchange rate movement, parity change; ~**arbitrage** arbitration of exchange; ~**bandbreite** band of permitted fluctuation; ~**bereinigung** exchange rate adjustment, *(wechselkursbereinigtes Ergebnis)* results adjusted for exchange rate movements, exchange-rate-adjusted income/loss

Wechselkurs / ~**bewegungen** exchange rate movements, movements in the exchange rate; ~**deckung** exchange rate cover, currency hedge, → Wechselkurssicherung; ~**festsetzung** fixing the exchange rate, rate fixing; ~**freigabe** floating the exchange rate

Wechselkurs / ~**garantie** exchange rate guarantee, → Wechselkurssicherung; ~**gefüge** exchange rate structure; ~**gewinn** exchange gain; ~**klausel** exchange clause; ~**korrektur** exchange rate adjustment

Wechselkurs / ~**mechanismus** exchange rate mechanism; ~**neuordnung** realignment of exchange rates; ~**notierung** exchange rate quotation, → Mengennotierung, → Preisnotierung

Wechselkurs / ~**parität** exchange rate parity; ~**politik** exchange rate policy; ~**prognose** foreign exchange forecast, *(Erstellen von ~n)* forex (exchange rate) forecasting

Wechselkursrisiko exchange rate risk (exposure), *(Deckung des ~s durch Termingeschäfte)* hedging (covering) the currency exposure by forward exchange deals (by selling or buying currencies forward)

Wechselkursschwankungen fluctuations in the exchange rate, exchange variations, currency fluctuations, *(starke ~)* wild swings (sharp fluctuations) in exchange rates, currency gyrations, *(Rücklage für ~)* currency fluctuations reserve

Wechselkurssensitivität sensitiveness to exchange rate movements, *(wechselkurssensitive Vermögenswerte)* assets exposed to exchange rate fluctuations

Wechselkurssicherung currency hedging, rate-hedging, forex hedging, hedging the exchange risk (the currency exposure), *(wechselkursgesicherte ausländische Aktienbestände)* currency-hedged foreign equity holdings, *(Kosten der ~)* rate-hedging cost

Wechselkurs / ~verlust exchange loss; **~volatilität** exchange rate volatility

Wechsel / ~laufzeit usance (term) of a bill; **~mahnbescheid** order for payment of a bill; **~mahnverfahren** bill default action; **~makler** bill broker

wechselmäßig *(~ haften)* to be liable on a bill, *(~e Haftung)* liability on (under) a bill

Wechsel / ~material 1. bills **2.** bills presented for discount; **~mitverbundener/~mitverpflichteter** co-obligor (co-debtor) on a bill

Wechsel / ~nehmer payee of a bill, person to whom a bill is paid; **~nichteinlösung** *(bei ~)* when a bill of exchange is dishonoured; **~obligo** bill exposure (commitments), customer's total bill exposure, liabilities on bills discounted

Wechsel / ~parteien parties to a bill; **~pensionsgeschäfte** repurchase (repo) agreements on bills, bill-based repurchase agreements, → Pensionsgeschäft; **~portefeuille** bill portfolio, bill case (book); **~prolongation** prolongation (renewal) of a bill

Wechselprotest protest, protesting a bill; **~anzeige** notice of protest; **~grund** reason for protesting a bill; **~kosten** protest charges (fees); **~urkunde** memorandum (deed) of protest

Wechsel / ~provision bill brokerage; **~rechte** rights under a bill; **~rediskontierung** rediscounting a bill; **~regress** recourse on a bill of exchange, recourse to a party liable on a bill; **~reiterei** kiting, kite flying, raising money by the use of accommodation bills

Wechsel / ~remittent → Wechselnehmer; **~rückgabe** return of an unpaid bill; **~rückgriff** → Wechselregress; **~rückrechnung** re-account, banker's ticket; **~rückruf** retirement of (recalling) a bill; **~schuldner** debtor on a bill, bill debtor, party liable on a bill

wechselseitig reciprocal, mutual, *(~e Beteiligung)* cross shareholding, cross equity participation, reciprocal shareholding, *(~e Notierung)* cross listing, *(~e Verpflichtung)* reciprocal (mutual) undertaking, *(~e Vorfälligkeitsklausel)* cross-acceleration clause

Wechsel / ~sekunda second of exchange; **~skontro** bill ledger; **~steuer** bill stamp duty; **~strenge** stringency of the Bill of Exchange Act; **~triplikat** third of exchange; **~umlauf** bills in circulation

wechselunterlegt *(~e Forderungen)* receivables guaranteed (supported) by bills of exchange

Wechselverbindlichkeiten bill commitments, liabilities on bills, *(Bilanz)* bills (notes) payable

wechselverbrieft *(~e Forderungen)* receivables certificated by bills of exchange, claims evidenced by bills

Wechsel / ~verfall maturity date of a bill; **~verkehr** bill of exchange operations, payments by bills of exchange; **~verlängerung** prolongation (renewal) of a bill; **~verpflichteter** party liable on a bill, bill debtor, drawee

Wechsel / ~verwahrung bill of exchange custody, holding the bill until maturity; **~vordruck** bill form; **~vor-**

W

lage presentation of a bill; ~**wirkung** *(~ zwischen Zinsen und Wechselkursen)* interaction between interest rates and exchange rates

Wechsel / ~**zahlung** payment by bill of exchange; ~**ziehung** drawing of a bill; ~**zweitschrift** second of exchange

wecken *(Befürchtungen ~)* to raise fears (concerns, anxieties)

Weg road, *(Mittel und Wege zur Reduzierung der Schuldenlast)* ways and means to alleviate (reduce) the debt burden, *(der beste Weg für eine finanzielle Gesundung)* the best prescription for restoring the company's financial health

Weg *(spekulativen Investments **aus dem Weg gehen**)* to steer clear of (to shun) speculative investments, *(eine Rettungsaktion für das angeschlagene Unternehmen **in die Wege leiten**)* to mount (to embark on) a rescue operation for the troubled company
*(**den Weg ebnen** für eine neue Zinssenkung)* to pave (to clear) the way for a new cut in interest rates, *(**auf dem Weg** zu einer kräftigen Erholung)* to be on the road to a strong recovery, *(einer engeren Zusammenarbeit **im Wege stehen**)* to stand in the way of closer ties

Wegerecht right of way, easement

Wegfall 1. *(Aufhebung)* abolition, removal, cancellation, *(nach ~ der Kapitalverkehrsbeschränkungen)* following removal of the restrictions on capital flows
2. discontinuance, cessation, *(~ der Berechtigungsgrundlage)* lapse in eligibility
3. *(~ der Geschäftsgrundlage)* frustration of (contractual) purpose, commercial frustration
4. *(Auslassung)* omission

wegfallen 1. to be abolished (removed, cancelled) **2.** to cease to apply, to be discontinued **3.** to be omitted

Wegnahme *(Pfändung)* seizure

wegweisend *(~e Entscheidung)* landmark ruling

weich *(~e Patronatserklärung)* soft letter of comfort □ representing a non-bindung, unenforceable declaration of intent

Weichkosten soft cost(s) □ e.g. **1.** pre-/post-construction expenses, construction expenses other than direct construction costs
2. cost incurred during the launching and investment phase of a closed-end fund

Weichwährungsländer soft currency countries

weigern *(sich ~)* to refuse

Weigerung refusal

weißer Fonds white (transparent) fund

Weisung instruction, directive, direction, *(auf ~ unseres Kunden)* at our customer's request, in accordance with the instructions received from (given by) our customer, *(sich an die ~en des Kunden halten)* to comply with (to follow) the customer's instructions

Weisungs / ~**befugnis** directive authority (power); ~**ebene** level of authority; ~**gebundenheit** obligation (requirement) to follow (e.g the customer's) directives, *(weisungsgebunden)* required to follow directives, bound by directives (instructions)

weisungsgemäß as instructed (directed), according to the instructions received

Weisungs / ~**kompetenz**/~**recht** directive power (authority), right to give binding instructions; ~**system**/~**wesen** directives management

weit *(~ abgegrenzte Geldmenge)* broad money aggregate, → Geldmenge M3, *(~ im/aus dem Geld)* deep in/out of the money

weiterbehandeln 1. to handle further, to deal with s.th. in the future **2.** to discuss further

Weiterbehandlung *(~ des Kredites)* further treatment (processing) of the loan

weiterbestehen to continue to exist, to remain afloat

Weiterbetrieb continued operation

Weiterbildung further training, *(berufliche ~)* advanced professional (vocational) training, *(Weiterbildung und Entwicklung)* learning and development (L&D)

Weiterentwicklung *(~ des Marktes)* further development (advancement) of the market, *(fortlaufende ~)* continuous improvement process (CIP)

weiterführen to continue, to carry on

Weitergabe **1.** *(~ des Zinsrückgangs an die Darlehensnehmer)* passing on lower interest rates to borrowers **2.** *(~ von Informationen)* transmission of information **3.** *(Negoziierung)* negotiation

Weitergabeeinwand pass-on defense

weitergeben **1.** to pass on, *(die Kosten an die Kunden ~)* to pass costs through to the customers, *(voll an die Aktionäre ~)* to pass on (to distribute) in full to the shareholders
2. *(Daten/Informationen)* to transmit
3. *(negoziieren)* to negotiate, (*Indossamentsverpflichtungen aus weitergegebenen Wechseln)* endorsement liabilities on negotiated bills

weitergehen *(einen Schritt ~)* to go a step further

Weitergeltung continuing validity

Weiterlaufen *(~ der Zahlungen)* continuation of payments

weiterleiten **1.** to pass on, to transmit, to refer on, to route through, *(zur Ausführung an die Börse ~)* to transmit (to route through) to the stock exchange for execution, (*Gelder ~)* to pass funds through to, to on-lend funds *(Gewinne an die Investoren ~)* to pass gains through to investors, (*an die Muttergesellschaft ~)* to pass on (up) to the parent, to upstream, (*durch Preiserhöhungen ~)* to pass on by increasing prices
2. *(im Konsortialgeschäft einen Teil der Provision)* to reallow
3. *(weitergeleiteter Auftrag)* subcontracted order

Weiterleitung passing on (through), transmission, *(~ der Aufträge an die Abrechnungsstelle)* forwarding the orders to the clearing house, *(~ der Provisionen)* passing on commission payments

Weiterleitungskredit transmitted (pass-through) loan, on-loan

Weiterplatzierung placing on, on-placement, further placement

Weiterrückversicherung retrocession

Weitersyndizierung further syndication

weiterveräußern → weiterverkaufen

Weiterverbriefung re-securitisation, securitisation based on an underlying securitisation exposure

weiterverfolgen to pursue further, *(einen Anspruch ~)* to follow up on a claim

weiterverkaufen to resell, *(die Schuldverpflichtung im Sekundärmarkt ~)* to sell on the debt in the secondary market

weiterverleihen to on-lend

Weiterverleihung *(~ von Wertpapieren)* on-lending of securities

weitervermieten to sub-lease

Weitervermietung sub-lease, subleasing, subletting

weiterverpfänden to repledge, to rehypothecate, to pledge to another party, *(weiterverpfändete Sicherheiten)* rehypothecated collateral

Weiterverpfändung repledge, rehypothecation, re-use of collateral

Weiterzahlung continuation of payments

weitgehend **1.** *adj.* extensive, far-reaching, large, broad, *(~e Unterstützung)* large (extensive) support, *(~e Vollmachten)* far-reaching (extensive) powers
2. *adv.* to a large extent, *(der Erfolg wird ~ davon abhängen)* success will

in large measure depend on (will be largely determined by), *(das Projekt ~ aus Eigenmitteln finanzieren)* to finance the project largely (to a large extent) from internal funds

weitreichend *(~e Auswirkungen)* far-reaching implications

weitverbreitet *(~e Anlegermeinung)* widely held opinion among investors, *(~er Irrtum)* widespread error

Welle *(~ neuer Emissionen)* spate of new issues

Weltwährungs / **~fonds** International Monetary Fund; **~reserven** global monetary reserves; **~system** international monetary system

weltweit *(~e Tenderofferte)* global (international) tender offering, global offering by tender, *(~er Umsatz)* global turnover, *(~ tätige Bank)* internationally operating bank, financial institution with operations and assets worldwide

weltwirtschaftlich *(~es Umfeld)* global economic scenario

Wende turn, turning point, turnaround, *(~ zum Besseren)* turn for the better, *(dem Unternehmen die ~ bringen)* to turn the company around, *(eine unerwartete ~ nehmen)* to take an unexpected turn

wenden **1.** *(das Blatt ~)* to turn the tide **2.** *(sich gegen die Vereinbarung ~)* to be opposed to the accord

Wendepunkt turning point, watershed

weniger stabile Einlagen *(when calculating the runoff rate* → Rückzugsrate) less stable retail deposits □ retail deposits that are not fully covered by a deposit protection scheme or that can be withdrawn quickly

Werbe / **~aufwand** advertising expenditure; **~erfolgskontrolle** advertising performance control; **~etat** advertising budget

werben **1.** to advertise **2.** *(Kunden)* to win, to solicit **3.** *(werbend angelegte Aktiva einer Bank)* bank's interest bearing loans

Werbe / **~publikum** advertising audience; **~reichweite** advertising reach; **~streuplanung** advertising media scheduling; **~wirkung** advertising impact

Werbung **1.** advertising **2.** *(von Kunden)* solicitation **3.** sales promotion

Werbungskosten **1.** advertising cost **2.** tax allowable (deductible) expenses, professional outlay(s), professional (business) expenses, income-related expenses

Werbungskostenpauschale standard deduction for income-related expenses

Werdegang career, career pattern, job record, background

werfen *(auf den Markt ~)* to dump onto the market, to unload on the market

Werkerfolg requested (anticipated) performance

Werkvertrag contract for work (and services), works contract, *(werkvertragliche Gewährleistungsansprüche)* warranty claims under the contract for work

Wert **1.** value, worth, *(Abschluss mit einem auf … geschätzten ~)* a deal with a value estimated at …, *(großen ~ auf die Tatsache legen)* to place great emphasis on, *(ein Portefeuille im ~ von € …)* a portfolio worth €
2. *(Vermögenswert)* asset
3. *(Wertpapier)* security, issue
4. *(Wertstellung)* value date, *(der Scheck wurde Ihrem Konto ~ 3. Mai belastet)* the cheque was debited to your account value May 3rd

wertabhängig *(~e Gebühren/Provisionen)* transaction-related (transaction-linked, value-related) charges/commissions

Wert / **~analyse** value analysis; **~änderung** change in value, *(Wertänderungen aus Cashflow Hedges)* gains (losses) on cash flow hedges; **~angabe**

W

1. declaration (statement) of value, indicating the value 2. → Wertansatz

Wertansatz 1. carrying value, valuation, value (amount) stated, *(steuerrechtlicher ~)* tax basis, *(Wertansätze der Einzelbilanzen)* valuations entered in the individual balance sheets, *(Wertansatz in der Steuerbilanz)* value assigned for tax accounting purposes 2. *(Bewertungsansatz)* valuation approach, *(~ der Beteiligungen)* value assigned to investments in the balance sheet

Wertaufhellungsregel value adjustment rule

Wertaufholung reversal of an impairment, write-up, recovery in value, reinstatement of the original value

Wertaufholungs / ~gebot write-up requirement, obligatory reversal of impairment losses, requirement to reinstate the original value, requirement to reverse a write-down; **~wahlrecht** write-up option

Wert / ~ausgleich value adjustment; **~beeinträchtigung** value impairment, depreciation; **~bemessung** value assessment

wertberichtigen 1. to adjust the value 2. to establish a valuation allowance (a loan loss allowance), to make a bad debt charge, *(Volumen der wertberichtigten Kredite)* total lendings for which loan loss allowances have been established, *(wertberichtigtes Engagement)* impaired loan (exposure)

Wertberichtigung 1. *(allgemein)* value adjustment
2. valuation allowance, impairment, *(~ auf aktive latente Steuern)* valuation allowance against deferred tax assets, *(~ auf den Beteiligungsbestand)* impairment of investment securities, *(~ auf den Goodwill)* goodwill impairment, *(~ auf nicht beitreibbare Beträge)* allowance for uncollectible amounts, *(~ auf Forderungen)* valuation allowance against doubtful accounts, impairment of trade receivables *(~ von Gegenständen des Umlaufvermögens)* valuation allowance against current assets, impairment loss on current assets, *(~ auf immaterielle Anlagewerte)* impairment loss on intangible assets, *(~ auf Portfoliobasis)* portfolio-based valuation allowance, *(~ auf Sachanlagen)* impairment of (impairment loss on) property, plant and equipment, *(~ auf Vorräte)* inventory impairment, inventory valuation allowance
3. loan loss allowance, *(~ auf Darlehen und Kredite/auf Kreditforderungen)* loan loss allowance, allowance for loan (credit) losses, *(~ für notleidende Kredite/in Verzug befindliche Kredite)* allowance for impaired (nonperforming, delinquent) loans, *(~ für Wertminderungen aus dem Kreditgeschäft)* allowance for impairment of loans and advances

Wertberichtigungs / ~auflösung 1. write-back of impairments (of valuation allowances) 2. reversal (release) of loan loss allowances, reversal of impairment losses; **~aufwand** impairment cost (charges), *(Erhöhung des ~es)* rise in impairment charges

Wertberichtigungs / ~bedarf impairment requirements, required valuation allowances; **~bereinigung** adjustment(s) to valuation allowances (loan loss allowances); **~bestand** total valuation (loan loss) allowances, → Wertberichtigungsvolumen

Wertberichtigungs / ~betrag allowance amount; **~bewegungen** movements in allowances, → Wertberichtigungsspiegel; **~bildung** setting up (establishment of) allowances, recognition of valuation (loan loss) allowances

Wertberichtigungs / ~defizit → Wertberichtigungsfehlbetrag; **~erhöhung** increase in (addition to) the allowance for loan losses, → Wertberichtigungsaufwand; **~ermittlung** impairment calculation, calculating the required loss allowance

Wertberichtigungs / ~fehlbetrag loss on valuation allowances □ determined by calculating the difference between the expected loss amount of all IRBA exposures (→ IRBA-Position) and the loss allowances set up for these exposures; **~grundsätze** impairment accounting principles

Wertberichtigungs / ~höhe impairment level, level (extent) of valuation allowances; **~konto** valuation allowance account; **~kosten** → Wertberichtigungsaufwand; **~maßnahmen** setting up valuation (loan loss) allowances

Wertberichtigungs / ~politik allowance (impairment) policy, policy on loan loss allowances; **~posten** valuation allowance item; **~quote** valuation allowance ratio, impairment rate, ratio of valuation allowances to total receivables, *(~ im Inlandsgeschäft)* ratio of specific loan loss allowances against domestic lendings

Wertberichtigungs / ~satz impairment rate; **~spiegel** *(im Hinblick auf Kreditforderungen)* statement of changes in loan loss allowances; **~überschuss** valuation allowance surplus □ determined by calculating the difference between the allowances established for all IRBA exposures and the loss amounts expected for these exposures

Wertberichtigungs / ~vergleich allowance offset □ setting off the expected loss amount of all IRBA exposures (→ IRBA Position) against the allowances set up for these exposures; the difference will be deducted from/added to the regulatory capital requirement. → Wertberichtigungsfehlbetrag/überschuss; **~volumen** aggregate valuation (loan loss) allowances, aggregate impairment losses

wertbeständig stable, of stable value, *(~e Kapitalanlage)* sound (financially secure, solid) investment

Wert / ~beständigkeit stability of value, *(~ einer Anlage)* soundness (solidity) of an investment, investment stability; **~bestimmung** valuation, ascertaining (establishing) the value, *(wertbestimmende Faktoren)* value determinants

Wert / ~einbuße loss in value, depreciation, *(von Aktiva)* asset impairment; **~entwicklung 1.** (asset) performance, *(~ einer Aktie)* stock performance, *(~ eines Portefeuilles)* portfolio performance **2.** capital appreciation; **~entwicklungsgarantie** performance (capital appreciation) guarantee

Wert / ~erbringung value delivery; **~erhaltung** capital preservation (maintenance); **~erhöhung** increase in value, appreciation, increasing (enhancing, enriching) the value, *(werterhöhende Änderungen)* improvements, value-enhancing alterations; **~erlöse** *(einer Bank)* interest and interest-related income

Wertermittlung valuation, appraisal, determining (calculating) the value, *(bei Immobilien)* property valuation

Wertermittlungs / ~gebühr valuation (appraisal) fee; **~methode** valuation (appraisal) method; **~richtlinien** valuation rules; **~verfahren** → Wertermittlungsmethode

Werteverzehr *(~ des Anlagevermögens)* depreciation of fixed assets

Wertfestsetzung fixing (establishing) the value, → Wertermittlung

wertfrei *(~e Aushändigung der Dokumente)* value-free delivery, delivery of the documents without corresponding payment, *(~e Auslieferung)* delivery free of payment

Wertgegenstände valuables, assets

wertgemindert → Wertminderung

Wertgeneratoren value drivers

Wertgutachten valuation, opinion of value, appraiser's opinion, opinion of an asset's (property's) fair market value

Wertgutachter appraiser, valuer

werthaltig 1. *(~e Forderung)* fully performing loan asset, *(~e Garantie)* valuable guarantee, *(~e Unterlegung)*

provision of valuable security (of good and adequate security), valuable collateralisation
2. *(~er Kredit)* performing loan

Werthaltigkeit fair value, *(Gewährleistung der ~ einer Sicherheit)* ensuring the fair value of a collateral

Werthaltigkeitsprüfung/~test impairment test

Wert / ~karte prepaid card; **~klausel** valuation clause; **~korrektur** value adjustment (revision); **~kosten** *(einer Bank)* interest and interest-related expenses; **~leistungen** deposit and lending services

wertlos 1. worthless, of no value, *(eine Garantie ~ machen)* to render a guarantee valueless, *(unausgeübte Optionen verfallen ~)* unexercised options will expire valueless
2. *(nutzlos)* useless, futile

Wertlückenanalyse value gap analysis

wertmäßig in terms of value, according to value, *(~es Ergebnis)* result in financial terms, *(~e Herabstufung eines Schuldtitels)* downgrading of a debt instrument

Wertmaßstab benchmark, measure of value

wertmindernd lowering the value, *(~e Änderungen)* impairments

Wertminderung impairment in value, decline (decrease) in value, depreciation, *(im Kreditgeschäft)* loan impairments, *(~ einer Sicherheit)* collateral impairment, *(wertgeminderte Finanzinstrumente)* impaired financial instruments, *(wertgeminderte Kredite/Kreditforderungen)* impaired loans and advances, *(wertgeminderte Vermögenswerte)* impaired assets

Wertminderungs / ~aufwendungen impairment losses (charges); **~bewertung** impairment measurement; **~erfassung** impairment recognition; **~nachweis** evidence of impairment; **~rückstellung** impairment provision; **~verlust** impairment loss

W

Wertobergrenze 1. asset ceiling **2.** value limit

wertorientiert *(~es Anlegen)* value investing, *(~e Berichterstattung)* fair value reporting, *(~es Führen)* value-driven leadership, *(~es Management)* value-based (value-driven) management

Wertpapiere *(~ des Anlagevermögens)* investment securities, *(~ zum Einstandspreis oder darunter)* securities, at cost or less, *(~ mit festem/variablem Ertrag)* fixed income (variable income) securities, *(~ des Handelsbestandes)* securities held in the trading portfolio, trading account securities, *(~ des Liquiditätsbestandes)* securities held for liquidity purposes
(~ zum Marktwert) securities, at current (market) value, *(~ der Sondervermögen des Bundes)* securities issed by Federal Special Funds, *(~ in großen Stückelungen)* large-denomination securities, *(~ mit festen Tilgungsterminen)* securities redeemable at (on) fixed dates, *(~ des Umlaufvermögens)* current investments

Wertpapier / ~abrechnung securities contract note, bought/sold note; **~absatz** security sales; **~abschluss** securities trade (deal, bargain); **~abschreibungen** securities write-offs (write-downs), write-downs on securities

Wertpapier / ~abteilung securities department (division); **~abwicklung 1.** securities settlement **2.** Securities Back Office; **~abwicklungssystem** securities settlement system

Wertpapier / ~analyse securities research (analysis); **~analyst** securities (investment) analyst; **~angebot 1.** supply of securities, securities available **2.** security issues currently offered (e. g. by banks, investment houses)

Wertpapier / ~anlage securities (security) investment, investment (investing) in securities; **~anlageberatung** investment counselling (advice); **~an-**

lagebestände securities investment book (account)

Wertpapier / ~anleger securities investor; **~anschaffungsdarlehen** security acquisition loan; **~arbitrage** arbitrage in securities; **~art** type of security, → Wertpapiergattung

Wertpapier / ~aufsicht supervision of the securities markets; **~aufsichtsbehörde** securities regulatory agency, *(Vertreter einer ~)* securities regulator (commissioner); **~aufstellung** statement of securities

Wertpapier / ~auktionshandel order-driven auction market; **~ausbuchung** derecognition of securities; **~ausgang** securities sold, outgoing securities; **~auslieferung** delivery of securities

Wertpapier / ~beleihung lending against (on) securities, granting a loan against securities lodged as collateral; **~beratung** investment counselling (advice); **~bereich** securities sector; **~bereinigung** securities validation

Wertpapier / ~besitz security ownership, holding of securities; **~besitzer** owner (holder) of securities, security owner; **~bestand** security (securities) holdings, securities portfolio, *(bei Banken ferner)* securities book; **~bestände der Liquiditätsreserve** securities held as part of the liquidity reserve

Wertpapier / ~bewertung 1. *(in der Bilanz bzw. steuerrechtlich)* valuation of securities **2.** *(bonitätsmäßig)* rating of securities; **~bezeichnung** security description

wertpapierbezogen *(~e Derivate)* securities-related derivatives, *(~e Forderungen)* securities-related claims

Wertpapier / ~börse stock exchange; **~branche** securities industry

Wertpapierdarlehen 1. *(i. S. einer Beleihung von Wertpapieren)* loan (lending) against securities
2. *(i. S. einer Wertpapierleihe)* securities loan (lending), loan of securities (by one bank to another, by one broker to another)

Wertpapierdarlehens / ~geschäft securities lending transactions (activities); **~vertrag** securities lending agreement

Wertpapier / ~deckung securities cover; **~depot** securities portfolio; **~depotbank** depositary bank, custodian, depository; **~derivate** securities derivatives

Wertpapierdienstleistungen investment services

Wertpapierdienstleistungs-Prüfungsverordnung Investment Services Auditing regulation

Wertpapierdienstleistungs-Richtlinie EU Investment Services Directive (IS) □ replaced by MiFID, → Finanzmarktrichtlinie

Wertpapierdienstleistungsunternehmen investment firm, investment services enterprise

Wertpapierdienstleistungs-Verhaltens- und Organisationsverordnung Directive setting out Rules of Conduct and Organisational Requirements for Investment Firms

Wertpapier / ~eigengeschäfte own account dealings in securities; **~eigenhandel** proprietary trading, prop trading, securities trading for own account; **~eigenhandelsgewinne** income from own account trading in securities, proprietary trading income; **~eigenhändler** proprietary trader; **~eigenposition** own securities book

Wertpapier / ~eingang securities received; **~emission** security issue, securities offering, *(Refinanzierung durch ~en)* funding (refinancing) through the issue of securities; **~emittent** security issuer; **~empfehlung** recommendation to purchase, sell or hold a security

Wertpapier / ~entleiher borrower of securities; **~ergebnis** securities trading result, securities trading profit (loss); **~erträge** income from securities

Wertpapiererwerbs- und Übernahmegesetz German Securities Acquisition and Takeover Act

Wertpapierfinanzierung financing through securities, raising capital through a security issue, equity and/or bond financing

Wertpapierfinanzierungsgeschäfte Securities Financing Transactions □ securities lending, repurchase agreements, lending and borrowing of other financial instruments

Wertpapiergattung type of security, class of securities, security category

wertpapiergebunden *(~e Pensionszusagen)* securities-based (securities-linked) pension commitments

Wertpapier / ~geschäft 1. *(einzelnes)* securities trade, transaction in securities **2.** *(insgesamt)* securities business (operations); **~gesetzgebung** securities legislation, regulation of the securities business; **~gewinne** security gains, stock market profits; **~giroverkehr** securities clearing transactions (operations)

Wertpapierhandel securities trading (dealings), trading in securities

Wertpapierhandels / ~anzeige- und Insiderverordnung Securities Trading and Insider Regulation; **~aufsicht** regulatory agency for securities trading; **~bank** securities trading bank

Wertpapierhandels / ~bestand securities trading book (inventory, account, portfolio); **~gesetz** German Securities Trading Act; **~gewinne** securities trading income

Wertpapierhandels / ~plattform securities trading platform; **~recht** securities trading law, *(wertpapierhandelsrechtliche Meldepflichten)* notification obligations under the German Securities Trading Act

Wertpapier / ~händler security (securities) dealer, securities trader; **~haus** securities house (firm); **~hinterlegung** depositing (lodging) securities with, deposit of securities

Wertpapier / ~index securities index (average); **~index-Sondervermögen** Securities Index Fund, → Sondervermögen; **~inhaber** owner (holder) of securities, security holder

Wertpapier / ~kauf securities (security) purchase, buying securities; **~kaufabrechnung** bought note; **~kaufvertrag 1.** securities purchase agreement **2.** stock subscription agreement

Wertpapier / ~kennnummer (German) Securities Identification Number □ superseded by the ISIN (International Securities Identification Number) in 2003; **~kennung/~kennzeichnung** securities identification; **~kommissionsgeschäft** securities brokerage business, securities broking

Wertpapier / ~konto securities account; **~korb** basket of securities; **~kosten** charges on securities transactions; **~kredit 1.** loan (lending) against securities **2.** loan to purchase stock, securities market credit; **~kurs** stock/bond price, quotation

Wertpapier / ~leerverkäufe short sales of securities; **~leihe** securities lending, *(~ zwischen Kreditinstituten)* interbank securities lending; **~leiher** borrower of securities; **~leihgeschäft** securities lending transaction, *(Eintritt der Bank als direkter Kontraktpartner)* principal lending, *(Tätigkeit als Vermittler)* agency lending

Wertpapier / ~-Liquiditätsbestand securities-based liquidity portfolio; **~lombard** loan (lending) against securities

Wertpapier / ~makler securities broker; **~markt** securities market; **~marktlinie** security market line □ graphs the relationship between risk and return

Wertpapier-Mitteilungen (WM) 1. German Securities Data Vendor, German Securities Numbering Agency □ responsible for issuing International

W

Securities Identification Numbers 2. *(allg.)* Securities Bulletin

Wertpapier / ~**nachfrage** demand for securities; ~**nebendienstleistungen** non-core investment services, ancillary securities services

Wertpapier / ~**notierung** quotation, security price; ~**nummerierung** security numbering; ~**nummernkontrolle** security number checking; ~**paket** block of securities

wertpapierpensionsähnlich *(~e Geschäfte)* repo-style transactions

Wertpapier-Pensionsgeschäft securities repurchase agreement, *(Kurzform)* repo agreement, *(~ mit unbestimmtem Rückkauftermin)* open repo transaction, *(~ mit depotmäßiger Verwahrung)* hold-in-custody repo, in → Pension gegebene/genommene Wertpapiere

Wertpapier-Pensionssatz securities repurchase rate, *(Kurzform)* repo rate

Wertpapier / ~**platzierung** placing (placement) of securities; ~**portefeuille** securities portfolio; ~**position** securities position (exposure), *(~en zur Liquiditätshaltung)* liquidity-driven securities positions; ~**prospektgesetz** German Securities Prospectus Act

Wertpapierprovision securities brokerage fee

Wertpapierprovisionsgeschäft *(Geschäftsfeld einer Bank nach Basel II)* retail brokerage, *(Ergebnis aus dem ~)* net income on retail brokerage transactions, net commission income on securities transactions

Wertpapierpublikumsfonds retail securities fund

Wertpapierrechnung 1. safekeeping of securities abroad, → Gutschrift in Wertpapierrechnung 2. *(Festlegung des Bezugsrechtswertes)* establishment of the rights value

Wertpapier / ~**refinanzierung** funding lendings through the issue of securities; ~**regulierung** regulation of securities transactions (of securities markets); ~**regulierungsbehörde** securities regulator

Wertpapier / ~**rendite** yield on securities (e. g. bond or stock yield); ~**risiken** securities risks (exposure), price and/or interest rate risks inherent in securities; ~**rückkauf** repurchase of securities

Wertpapier / ~**sammelbank** central securities depository; ~**sammelbestand** collective securities portfolio; ~**sammelklage** securities class action; ~**sammelverwahrung** collective safekeeping of securities

Wertpapier / ~**scheck** securities transfer order; ~**schnelltender** quick securities tender; ~**sicherheit** securities collateral; ~**sondervermögen** special securities fund

Wertpapier / ~**sparen** saving through (via) securities, investment saving; ~**sparvertrag** security savings scheme; ~**spekulation** speculation in securities, playing the securities market; ~**spezialfonds** 1. specialised securities fund 2. institutional fund, → Spezialfonds

Wertpapier / ~**spitze** fraction; ~**stückelung** security denomination; ~**tausch** exchange of securities, securities swap

Wertpapiertermin / ~**geschäft** forward securities transaction, forward transaction in securities, → Wertpapiervalutageschäft; ~**kurs** forward securities price; ~**markt** forward securities market

Wertpapier / ~**übereignung** transferring (conveying) the title to securities, assignment of securities; ~**übertragung** transfer of securities, securities (stock) transfer; ~**übertragungsauftrag** securities transfer order

Wertpapier / ~**umlauf** securities outstanding; ~**umsätze** securities turnover

Wertpapier / ~**unterlegung** 1. *(Kreditbesicherung durch Wertpapiere)*

provision of securities as collateral for a loan **2.** *(i. S. von Verbriefung)* securitisation, *(wertpapierunterlegte Forderungen)* securitised receivables; **~urkunde** certificate, stock (bond) certificate

Wertpapiervalutageschäft forward selling of securities □ agreement in which a buyer (institutional investor) and a seller (bank) agree to execute a securities transaction at a predetermined time in the future at a price agreed upon today

Wertpapierveräußerungsgewinn gain on the sale of securities, capital gain

Wertpapierverkauf 1. security (securities) sale **2.** selling securities

Wertpapierverkaufs / ~abrechnung sold note; **~prospekt** securities offering prospectus

Wertpapier / ~verleiher lender of securities, → Wertpapierleihgeschäft; **~verlust** loss on securities, stock market loss, *(Portefeuilleverluste)* portfolio losses; **~vermögen** securities portfolio (holdings), portfolio assets; **~vermögensverwaltung** securities portfolio management

Wertpapier / ~verpfändung pledging securities; **~verrechnung 1.** securities clearing **2.** securities netting; **~verrechnungskonto** securities clearing account; **~verschuldung** security debt, debt contracted through securities issues

Wertpapier / ~verwahrer Securities Depository, Custodian; **~verwahrung** safekeeping (safe custody) of securities; **~verwaltung 1.** administration of securities **2.** *(i. S. von Vermögensverwaltung)* investment (portfolio) management

Wertpapier / ~verzinsung/~zinsen income from securities, interest on securities; **~zuteilung** allotment of securities, *(Repartierung)* scaling down securities

Wertrechte 1. book-entry securities, *(als ~ gehandelte Aktien)* shares traded in book-entry form (traded as a mere book entry)
2. *(Schuldverschreibungen des Bundes)* debt register claims □ physical certificates are not issued; proof of ownership is via debt register entry

Wertrechtsanleihe book-entry bond, bond issued in form of debt register claims, → Wertrechte (2)

Wertschöpfung value added, *(gesamte volkswirtschaftliche ~)* national output (product), *(wertschöpfende Tätigkeiten)* value-adding activities

Wertschöpfungskette value chain, *(~ im Kreditgeschäft)* lending value chain

Wertschriftenclearing securities clearing

Wertsicherung capital preservation, value (capital) maintenance

Wertsicherungs / ~fonds capital preservation fund; **~klausel** maintenance of value clause, *(automatische ~)* indexation clause, automatic adjustment clause; **~vereinbarung** value maintenance agreement

Wertsteigerung 1. increase in value, appreciation, value enhancement, *(~ gegenüber dem Dollar)* appreciation against the dollar, *(~ von Kapitalanlagen)* capital appreciation of investments, appreciation on investments, capital growth, *(~ durch Neubewertung)* valuation surplus
2. *(wertsteigernde Maßnahmen)* betterments, improvements increasing the property value

Wertstellung value, value date, *(mit alter ~)* with (under) good value

Wertstellungs / ~berichtigung value correction, value adjustment; **~gewinn** float profit

Werttreiber value driver

Wertung 1. scoring **2.** *(Beurteilung)* judgment, valuation, assessment

Wertungs / ~listenansatz scorecard approach; **~system** *(zur Beurteilung*

W

der Kreditwürdigkeit) credit scoring system

Wert / ~unterschied difference (discrepancy) in value; **~verlust** depreciation, loss of (in) value; **~verringerung** diminution (decrease) in value

Wert / ~verschlechterungsrisiko depreciation risk; **~versprechen** value proposition

wertvoll valuable, precious, of considerable worth

Wertwahrnehmung value perception, perceived value

Wertzuwachs 1. increase (gain) in value, appreciation, increment, accretion, added value **2.** capital growth

Wertzuwachs / ~depot capital growth investment portfolio, investment portfolio where the primary objective is capital growth; **~steuer** tax on increment value

wesentlich 1. *adj. (~e Änderung)* substantive (material) change, *(~e Anlegerinformationen)* (EU) key investor information, *(~e Beteiligung)* material interest, *(die ~en Punkte)* the essential (principal, most important) points, *(~er Vertragsbestandteil)* essential component of the agreement **2.** *adv. (sich ~ unterscheiden von)* to be substantially different from

Wesentliche *(das ~)* essence, substance, essential(s), the nitty-gritty

Wesentlichkeit materiality, *(Beurteilung der ~)* materiality judgment

Wesentlichkeits / ~grenze materiality level (threshold); **~prinzip** principle of materiality

Wettbewerb competition

Wettbewerbs / ~bedingungen competitive situation, conditions of competition, *(gleiche ~)* level playing field; **~beschränkung** restraint of competition (of trade); **~druck** competitive pressure

wettbewerbsfähig *(~e Konditionen)* competitive lending rates (terms), competitive loan pricing

Wettbewerbs / ~fähigkeit competitiveness, competitive power (strength); **~gleichheit** competitive equality

wettbewerbsintensiv *(~er Sektor)* highly (intensely) competitive sector

Wettbewerbs / ~kräfte forces of competition; **~recht** competition (antitrust) law, fair trade laws; **~verzerrung** distortion of competition, competitive distortions; **~vorteil** competitive edge, cutting edge in competition; **~wirkung** competitive impact

Wetterderivate weather derivatives □ instruments, mainly options based on Heating/Cooling Degree Indices, used by market participants to hedge against weather-related losses

wettmachen to compensate for, to make up for, to retrieve, *(im Bankenbereich konnten Anfangsverluste wettgemacht werden)* bank stocks recouped early losses

wichtig 1. important, significant **2.** essential, vital, decisive

Wichtigkeit importance, significance

Wider *(das Für und ~)* the pros and cons

Widerklage counterclaim, cross-action, *(~ erheben)* to plead a counterclaim, to counterclaim, to bring a cross-action

Widerkläger counterclaimant, cross-complainant

widerlegbar refutable, disprovable, *(~e Vermutung)* rebuttable assumption, disputable presumption

widerlegen to refute, to disprove, to rebut

Widerlegung refutation, disproof, rebuttal

widerrechtlich 1. illegal, unlawful, contrary to the law **2.** *(eigenmächtig)* arbitrary

Widerruf revocation, withdrawal, cancellation, repeal, countermand, *(~ eines Akkreditivs)* revocation of a documentary credit, *(bis auf ~ gülti-*

ger Auftrag) good-till-cancelled order, *(~ einer Aussage)* retraction of a statement, *(~ einer bestehenden Verordnung)* repeal (abrogation) of an existing ruling
(~ der Genehmigung) retraction of the permission to ..., *(~ einer Vollmacht)* revocation (withdrawal, recall, cancellation) of a power, *(~ einer Zahlungsanweisung)* countermand of payment, countermanding (stopping) a payment order

widerrufbar revocable, susceptible of being revoked, *(~es Akkreditiv)* revocable documentary credit, *(~ stellen)* to make revocable

Widerrufbarkeit revocability

widerrufen 1. *(Akkreditiv, Vollmacht, Zusage)* to revoke, to withdraw, to cancel, to recall 2. *(Aussage, Erlaubnis)* to retract 3. *(Gesetz)* to repeal, to abrogate, to rescind 4. *(Zahlung)* to countermand (to stop) payment

widerruflich revocable, *(~es Akkreditiv)* revocable letter of credit, *(~e Rembourszusage)* qualified agreement to reimburse

Widerrufs / ~anzeige notice of revocation; **~belehrung** revocation instructions, instructions regarding the right of revocation; **~frist** period for revocation; **~klausel** revocation (rescinding) clause; **~recht** right of revocation, right to revoke, *(bei Zahlungen ferner)* right to countermand payment

widersetzen 1. *(sich dem allgemeinen Trend ~)* to buck the general trend 2. *(sich einer neuen Zinserhöhung ~)* to oppose (to resist) a new rise in interest rates

widerspiegeln *(Zinsunsicherheiten ~)* to reflect (to mirror) uncertainties over the future trend in interest rates

W

widersprechen 1. to contradict 2. to contrast with, to be in contrast with, to be contrary to

widersprechend 1. *(~e Aktionäre)* dissenting shareholders 2. → widersprüchlich

Widerspruch 1. contrast, contradiction, *(im ~ stehen)* to contrast (to conflict) with, *(in einem deutlichen ~ stehen)* to be in stark contrast with (to), to be strongly at odds with, *(die Entwicklung steht im ~ zu früheren Gewinnerwartungen)* the development contrasts with earlier profit expectations
2. opposition, objection, appeal, protest, *(im Falle eines ~s durch den Kunden)* in the event of objections being raised by the customer, *(~ erheben)* to object, to enter (to file) an objection, to prepare a notice of opposition, *(auf ~ stoßen)* to meet with protest (with opposition) from, to provoke the protest of
3. *(Unstimmigkeit)* inconsistency, discrepancy

widersprüchlich contradictory, inconsistent, *(~e Angaben)* conflicting (contrasting) statements

Widerspruchs / ~belehrung revocation instructions; **~bescheid** notice of objection; **~frist** objection (opposition) period, period for filing a protest (an appeal); **~recht** right to oppose (to object), right of objection; **~verfahren** opposition proceedings

Widerstand 1. resistance, opposition, *(die Zinssenkungspläne sind auf ~ gestoßen)* plans for a cut in interest rates have run into opposition from
2. *(Hindernis)* obstacle, impediment

widerstandsfähig (*~e Tendenz*) durable (resilient, robust) trend

Widerstandsfähigkeit *(~ des Aktienmarktes)* resilience (durability) of the stock market, *(~ in Stressphasen)* resilience to periods of stress

Widerstandslinie resistance line □ price level at which stock prices stop rising/falling

widerstehen *(dem Druck ~)* to resist (to withstand) the pressure

Wiederangleichung bringing back into line

Wiederanlage reinvestment, rollover of an investment, *(~ der Ausschüttungen)* reinvestment of income distributed (of distributions, of payouts), *(~ der angefallenen Erträge)* reinvestment of income accrued

Wiederanlage / ~option reinvestment (rollover) option; **~rabatt** reinvestment discount; **~recht** reinvestment privilege

Wiederaufbau reconstruction

Wiederauffüllung replenishment, *(~ der Bestände)* restocking of inventories, *(~ des Kapitals)* replenishment of the capital stock, *(~ der gesetzlichen Rücklage)* replenishment (refunding) of the legal reserve

wiederaufleben 1. to resurge **2.** *(~ lassen)* to revive, to revivify, to renew the legal (operative) force, to bring to life again

Wiederaufleben 1. resurgence, *(~ des Inflationsdrucks)* resurgence (rekindling) of inflationary pressure, *(~ des spekulativen Kaufinteresses)* resurgence (re-ignition) of speculative buying interest
2. revival, *(~ einer Geschäftsbeziehung)* re-opening of a business relationship, *(~ einer Vereinbarung)* revival of an agreement
3. reinstatement, *(~ eines Gesetzes)* re-enactment of an Act, *(~ einer Police)* reinstatement of a policy, *(~ von Verpflichtungen)* reinstatement of obligations

Wiederaufnahme resumption, re-establishment, *(~ einer Aktiennotierung)* relisting of a stock, *(~ der Dividendenzahlungen)* resumption of dividend payments, return to the dividend list, *(~ der Geschäftsbeziehungen)* re-establishment (resumption) of business relations, *(~ der Gespräche)* resumption (reopening) of talks

wiederaufnehmen to resume, to re-establish, to re-open

wieder bedienen to service again, to resume interest and redemption payments, *(wieder bediente Kredite)* re-performing loans

wiederbeleben *(die Konjunktur ~)* to revive (to resuscitate, to regenerate, to reinvigorate) the economy

Wiederbelebung revival, *(~ eines Projektes)* revitalisation (resuscitation) of a project

Wiederbeschaffung 1. retrieval **2.** replacement

Wiederbeschaffungs / ~kosten replacement cost, current cost, → Wiedereindeckungskosten; **~kostenprinzip** current cost principle; **~rücklage** replacement reserve; **~wert** replacement value

Wiedereinbringungsquote recovery rate

Wiedereindeckungs / ~aufwand/~kosten replacement cost □ cost of replacing a financial contract should a counterparty fail to settle; **~nachteil** loss on replacement

Wiedereindeckungs / ~risiko replacement risk □ risk that a financial contract (e.g. swap contract) must be replaced in the open market at a high cost; **~verlust** loss upon replacement; **~vorteil** gain on replacement

Wiedereinführung 1. *(einer Steuer)* reintroduction of a tax **2.** *(Wiedereinfuhr von Waren)* reimport(ation) **3.** *(einer Verordnung)* re-enactment of a regulation (a directive)

Wiedereingang recovery, *(Wiedereingänge auf abgeschriebene Kreditforderungen)* recoveries on loans previously charged off

Wiedereingliederung *(~ in den Konzern)* reincorporation (reintegration) into the group

Wiedereinrichtung *(~ einer Kreditlinie)* re-establishment of a credit line

wieder einsetzen 1. *(in eine alte Position ~)* to reinstal(l), to restore to a former position, to reinstate (to place again) in a former office **2.** *(in frühere*

Rechte ~) to revest (to vest again) with former powers

Wiedereinsetzung reinstal(l)ment, reinstatement, restoration, reinvestiture

Wiedereintritt re-entry

Wiedererkennungstest recognition test

wiedererlangen 1. to regain, to recoup **2.** *(Besitzrechte, Vermögen)* to recover, to retrieve

Wiedererlangung recovery, recapture, regaining, *(~ der Eigentumsrechte)* recovery of title

Wiedereroberung *(~ eines verlorengegangenen Marktanteils)* recapture (reseizure) of a market previously lost

Wiedereröffnung re-opening, re-establishment

Wiedererreichen *(~ der Gewinnzone)* writing black figures again, return(ing) to profitability

wiedergewinnen *(ein Kundensegment ~)* to win back (to regain) a customer segment

wiedergutmachen 1. to redress, to restitute, to indemnify, to repair, to make good (amends) **2.** *(Kursverluste zu Beginn der Börsensitzung ~)* to recoup early losses

wieder hereinholen *(einen Verlust ~)* to recover (to recoup) a loss

wiederherstellen 1. *(die frühere enge Zusammenarbeit ~)* to re-establish the former close cooperation **2.** *(Geschäftsbeziehungen ~)* to resume former business relations **3.** *(das Vertrauen der Anleger ~)* to restore investor confidence

Wiederherstellung 1. re-establishment, resumption, restoration, *(~ der Glaubwürdigkeit)* restoration of creditibility **2.** *(~ des ursprünglichen Deckungsschutzes)* reinstating the policy to its original amount

Wiederherstellungsplan recovery plan □ pre-reorganisation measure to avert a bank's liquidity crisis, → Reorganisationsverfahren, → Kreditinstitute-Reorganisationsgesetz

wiederholen *(wiederholte Zahlungsaufforderungen)* repeated requests for payment

wieder in Besitz nehmen *(das Sicherungsgut ~)* to repossess the asset furnished as collateral

Wiederinbesitznahme repossession, regaining possession, *(~ von Vermögen)* repossession (recovery) of property

wieder in Kraft setzen to reinstate, to restore, to re-enact

Wiederinkraftsetzung reinstatement, *(~ einer Bürgschaft)* restoration of a guarantee, *(~ einer Verordnung)* re-enactment (restoration, revival) of a regulation, *(~ einer Versicherungspolice)* reinstatement of a policy, restoration of the insured's rights under a policy, *(~ eines gekündigten Vertrages)* reconstitution of a repudiated contract

Wiederinkrafttreten entering into force again, revival

wiederkehrend *(~e Ausgaben)* recurring (recurrent) expenditure

Wiederverkäuferrabatt *(bei Emissionen)* re-allowance

Wiederverkaufswert *(~ der Papiere)* securities' value upon resale, reselling price

Wiedervorlage 1. *(eines Kreditantrages)* review
2. resubmission, *(einer Lastschrift/eines Schecks)* re-presentment

Wiederwahl re-election

wiederwählen *(in den Aufsichtsrat ~)* to re-elect (to return) to the Supervisory Board

Wiederzulassung *(~ zum amtlichen Handel)* readmission to official trading

Willenserklärung declaration of intent

willkürlich 1. arbitrary, *(~e Entscheidung)* arbitrary decision 2. *(unbegründet)* unfounded

Willkürlichkeit arbitrariness

Wimpel *(Chart-Analyse)* pennant

Windhundverfahren first come, first served

wirken *(expansiv ~)* to have an expansive effect, *(zu Gunsten des Kunden ~)* to inure to the benefit of the customer

wirksam 1. effective, efficient, *(~ mit Beginn der nächsten Abrechnungsperiode)* effective upon commencement of the next settlement period
2. *(gültig)* valid, in force, *(~ werden)* to come into force, to take effect, to become operative, *(voll ~ bleiben)* to remain in full force and effect

Wirksamkeit 1. effectiveness, *(~ des Sicherungsgeschäftes)* hedge effectiveness, *(~ einer Strategie)* effectiveness of a strategy 2. *(Gültigkeit)* validity, operation

Wirksamwerden coming (entry) into force (operation), commencement, *(nach dem ~ der Grundschuld)* after the creation of the charge has taken effect, *(zum Zeitpunkt des ~s dieses Vertrages)* at the time such agreement comes into effect

Wirkung 1. effect, impact, consequence, *(die Kapitalerhöhung hat die gleiche ~ wie …)* the capital increase is equivalent in its effect to a …, *(mit rückwirkender ~)* with retroactive effect, *(mit sofortiger ~)* effective immediately, with immediate effect, *(die Maßnahmen zeigen weiter ~)* the measures continue to bite (to show an impact)
2. *(Folgewirkungen)* repercussions

Wirkungsbereich province, sphere of activity (influence)

wirkungslos ineffective, inefficient, ineffectual, in vain

Wirkungslosigkeit ineffectiveness, inefficiency

Wirtschaft economy, trade and industry

wirtschaftlich 1. *adj. (a)* economic, *(~e Betrachtungsweise)* → Grundsatz der wirtschaftlichen Betrachtungsweise, *(~es Eigenkapital)* economic capital, *(~er Gehalt einer Transaktion)* (economic) substance of a transaction, *(~es Eigentumskonzept)* economic ownership for tax purposes, *(~er Geschäftsbetrieb)* commercial activities, business operations
(~er Nutzen) economic benefit (interest), *(~e Nutzungsdauer)* economic life, *(~e Rahmenbedingungen)* general economic environment (scenario), trading conditions, *(~e Talsohle)* economic trough, *(~es Ungleichgewicht)* economic disequilibrium, *(~e Unmöglichkeit)* impracticability of performance, economic impossibility of performance, *(~er Wert)* economic value
(b) beneficial, *(~es Eigentum)* beneficial ownership
(c) (sparsam) economical
2. *(adv.)* *(~ berechtigt sein)* to be beneficially entitled, *(~ berechtigte Person)* economic beneficiary, beneficial owner, *(~ darstellbar)* economically feasible, *(~ nicht selbständige Geschäftstätigkeit)* economically independent business activity, *(~ sinnvoll)* commercially reasonable, *(~ vorteilhaft)* economically advantageous, *(~ zustehen)* to be beneficially entitled to

Wirtschaftlichkeit profitability, economic efficiency

Wirtschaftlichkeitsrechnung profitability analysis, calculation of profitability, evaluating the economic effectiveness, efficiency calculation

Wirtschafts / ~delikt commercial tort, improper conduct of business; **~förderung** assistance to trade and industry; **~gleichgewicht** economic equilibrium; **~gut** economic asset; **~indikator** economic indicator, barometer of the economy

Wirtschafts / ~kraft economic strength (force, power); **~kredit** industrial loan, *(pl)* lendings to trade and in-

W

dustry; ~**leistung** economic output; ~**mediator** economic mediator; ~**politik** *(an der Preisstabilität orientierte ~)* economic policy oriented at price stability

wirtschaftspolitisch *(~es Instrumentarium)* economic policy tools, *(~e Zielsetzungen)* economic policy goals (objectives), *(~e Zwänge)* constraints of economic policy

Wirtschaftsprüfer auditor, Chartered Accountant (BE), Certified Public Accountant (AE)

Wirtschaftsprüfung audit(ing)

Wirtschaftsprüfungs / ~**gesellschaft** accountancy (accounting) firm, audit firm, Chartered Accountants; ~**kosten** audit fees

Wirtschafts / ~**tätigkeit** economic activity; ~**unternehmen** commercial enterprise (undertaking); ~**wachstumspolitik** policy designed to promote economic growth, economic growth policy; ~**zyklus** economic cycle

Wissen knowledge, *(nach bestem ~ und Gewissen)* to the best of my/our knowledge and belief

Wissens / ~**austausch** knowledge exchange; ~**bestand** knowledge assets, body of knowledge; ~**bestandskarte** knowledge asset map; ~**bilanz** intellectual capital statement

Wissens / ~**bildung** knowledge creation; ~**diffusion** knowledge diffusion (distribution); ~**kapital** intellectual capital; ~**karte**/~**landkarte** knowledge map; ~**management** knowledge management

Wissens / ~**quellenkarte** → Wissensträgerkarte; ~**ressourcen** intellectual resources; ~**teilung** knowledge sharing; ~**träger** **1.** knowledge sources **2.** knowledge holders (carriers); ~**trägerkarte** knowledge source map; ~**transfer** knowledge transfer; ~**visualisierung** knowledge visualisation (mapping)

wissentlich *(vorsätzlich)* intentional, wil(l)ful, deliberate, *(~ genehmigen)* to permit knowingly (and wil(l)fully)

WKN → Wertpapierkennnummer

WM-Datenservice German Securities Data Vendor, → Wertpapiermitteilungen (1)

Wochen / ~**ausweis** weekly return; ~**enddispositionen** trading (position) arrangements for the week-end, tidying trading books up for the week-end; ~**geld** seven-days' money; ~**gewinn** *(einen ~ von 8 Punkten verzeichnen)* to record (to register) a gain on the week of 8 points; ~**tender** weekly tender

Wohl *(wirtschaftliches ~)* economic well-being

wohl begründet *(~er Anspruch)* well-founded claim

wohl überlegt *(~e Entscheidung)* well-considered decision

Wohlverhaltens / ~**periode** *(des Schuldners)* good behaviour period; ~**pflichten** good conduct obligations; ~**regeln** rules of good conduct

Wohlwollenserklärung letter of awareness, letter of intent

Wohnbau / ~**darlehen** home loan; ~**finanzierung** house building finance, residential building finance; ~**hypothek** home (housing) mortgage; ~**kredit** home loan, housing loan; ~**kreditzinsen** home loan interest rates

Wohneigentum residential property, → Wohnungseigentum

Wohneigentumsgrundbuch residential (commonhold) property register

Wohngebäudeversicherung home owner's comprehensive insurance

Wohnimmobilien residential properties

Wohnungsbau house-building, housing construction, residential building, house-building in the private sector

Wohnungsbau / ~**beleihungen** lendings to the housing sector, residential

W

lendings, lendings against residential properties; ~**darlehen** home (housing) loan, house-building loan, home equity loan

Wohnungsbau / ~finanzierung housing finance, house-building finance; ~**finanzierungsgesellschaft** home loan company

Wohnungsbau / ~förderung promoting house-building (residential building), *(staatliche ~)* state-subsidised house-building; ~**förderungsanstalt** housing development agency (bank)

Wohnungsbau / ~gesellschaft housing corporation; ~**hypothek** residential mortgage, housing mortgage; ~**investitionen** housing investments, capital expenditure on house-building, investments in residential real estate

Wohnungsbau / ~kredit housing loan, residential construction loan; ~**kreditgeschäft** residential property (residential mortgage) lendings; ~**kreditvolumen** home loan (housing loan) portfolio

Wohnungsbau / ~mittel residential (housing) finance; ~**prämie** housing premium (bonus); ~**sektor** house-building sector, housing construction industry; ~**volumen** aggregate house-building

Wohnungs / ~bedarf housing requirements, demand for housing; ~**bestand** total dwellings, housing stock

Wohnungs / ~eigentum 1. home ownership, residential property **2.** *(von Eigentumswohnungen)* commonhold property, freehold flat, apartment (flat) ownership; ~**eigentümergemeinschaft** commonhold association, → Eigentümerversammlung; ~**eigentumsgesetz** German Commonhold Property Act

Wohnungswirtschaft housing sector, *(wohnwirtschaftliche Immobilienfinanzierung)* residential property finance, *(wohnwirtschaftlicher Realkredit)* residential property loan

Wort *(Betrag in ~en)* amount in words, *(das ~ in der Hauptversammlung ergreifen)* to address the general meeting, to take the floor, *(jmd. das ~ erteilen)* to give s. o. the floor, *(sich zu ~ melden)* to request the floor

Wortlaut *(~ des Vertrages)* wording (language) of the contract

WpHG → Wertpapierhandelsgesetz

WpPG → Wertpapierprospektgesetz

WpÜG → Wertpapiererwerbs- und Übernahmegesetz

WR-Gutschrift → Gutschrift in Wertpapierrechnung

X

XETRA electronic trading platform of Deutsche BörseAG

Xontro electronic order routing, trading and settlement system

Z

-Z *(gestrichen Ziehung)* drawing date – no bond quote

ZAG → Zahlungsdiensteaufsichtsgesetz

zaghaft *(~e Kurserholung)* fledgling price recovery

zahlbar *(~er Betrag)* amount (sum) payable, amount due, *(~ an Order)* payable to order, *(~ an den Überbringer)* payable to the bearer

zahlbar bei *(~ Fälligkeit)* payable upon maturity, payable when due, *(~ Lieferung)* payable upon delivery, cash on delivery, *(~ Sicht)* payable at sight, payable on demand, *(~ Vorlage)* payable upon presentation, *(~ Zeichnung)* payable upon application (subscription)

zahlbar stellen to make payable to, *(domizilieren)* to domiciliate

Zahlbarstellung making payable, domiciliation

zahlen to pay, *(regulieren)* to settle, *(~ Sie an die Order)* pay to the order of, *(aus einem Akkreditiv ~)* to pay under a documentary credit, *(den Restbetrag ~)* to pay the balance, to settle the remainder, *(in Sachwerten ~)* to pay in kind, *(unbar ~)* to pay by cheque or by bank transfer

zählen to count, to number, *(zu seinen Aktionären ~)* to count among its shareholders, *(als Einkommen ~)* to be counted as profit, *(als Kernkapital ~)* to count (to qualify) as core capital, to be eligible for inclusion in the core capital

Zahlenmaterial/~werk figures, data, accounts

Zahler *(~ variabler Zinsen)* floating-rate payer

zahlreich *adj.* numerous, *adv.* in great number, in large numbers

Zahlschein payment slip

Zahlstelle 1. *(im Wertpapiergeschäft)* paying agent 2. *(im Wechselverkehr)* place of payment

Zahlstellen / ~bank paying agent (bank); **~dienst** paying agency services, → Zahlstellengeschäft; **~gebühr** paying agency fee; **~geschäft** paying agency operations; **~provision** paying agency commission

Zahlstellen / ~steuer tax withheld by the paying agent; **~vereinbarung** paying agency agreement; **~vermerk** 1. notation regarding the paying agent 2. notation regarding the place of payment (place for presentment of the bill); **~verzeichnis** list of paying agents; **~wechsel** domiciled bill

Zahltag 1. date of payment 2. *(bei der Ausübung von Optionsscheinen)* valuation date

Zahlung payment, *(~ auf erste Anforderung)* payment upon first call (demand), *(~ gegen Dokumente)* payment against documents, *(~ bei Erhalt)* payment upon receipt, *(~ per Handy/Telefon)* mobile payment, m-payment, *(~ durch Scheck/Überweisung)* payment by cheque/by credit transfer
(~ unter Vorbehalt) payment under reserve, *(~ bei Vorlage)* payment upon presentation, *(~ Zug um Zug/gegen Lieferung)* payment versus delivery (PVD), *(~ bei Zuteilung der Wertpapiere)* payment upon allotment of the securities

Zahlungs / ~abwicklung 1. making (effecting) payment 2. payment processing (settlement); ~**abwicklungsanzeige** payment settlement advice

Zahlungs / ~**anschaffung** 1. remittance 2. *(Deckungsanschaffung)* provision of cover funds; ~**anspruch** right to payment, *(Zahlungsansprüche aus Termingeschäften)* payment claims from (under) forward transactions; ~**anweisung(en)** payment order, payment instructions

Zahlungs / ~**anzeige** advice of payment; ~**art** mode (type) of payment; ~**aufforderung** 1. demand (request) for payment, payment request, demand letter 2. *(Mahnung)* reminder 3. *(gerichtliche ~)* summons to pay; ~**aufrechnung** payment netting

Zahlungs / ~**aufschub** deferring payment, payment deferral, extension of maturity, extension of the period (time) stipulated for payment, respite; ~**auftrag** payment order; ~**auftraggeber** remitter, originator

Zahlungs / ~**ausfall** non-payment; ~**ausfallrisiko** default risk, risk of non-payment; ~**ausgänge** payment outflows

Zahlungsausgleich settlement

Zahlungsausgleichs / ~**agent** settlement agent; ~**konto** settlement account; ~**verpflichtungen** settlement obligations

Zahlungs / ~**austauschsatz** payment exchange record ; ~**authentifizierung** payment authentication; ~**bedingungen** terms of payment; ~**befehl** default summons, *(einen ~ erwirken)* to take out a default summons; ~**befreiung** 1. payment release 2. *(Freistellung)* exemption from payment

Zahlungs / ~**begehren** payment request; ~**begünstigter** beneficiary (of a payment); ~**bereitschaft** 1. willingness to pay 2. *(Zahlungsfähigkeit)* solvency; ~**bestätigung** 1. confirmation of payment 2. *(Quittung)* receipt

Zahlungsbilanz balance of payments

Zahlungsbilanz / ~**beistand** *(mittelfristiger EU-Zahlungsbilanzbeistand)* medium-term monetary assistance arrangement; ~**defizit** deficit in the balance of payments; ~**gleichgewicht** balance of payments equilibrium; ~**überschuss** balance of payments surplus; ~**ungleichgewicht** payments imbalance, disequilibrium in the balance of payments

Zahlungsbürgschaft payment bond

Zahlungsdienste payment services

Zahlungsdienste / ~**anbieter** provider of payment services; ~**aufsichtsgesetz** Payment Services Supervision Act; ~**nutzer** user of payment services; ~**rahmenvertrag** Master Agreement on Payment Services; ~**richtlinie** (EU) Payment Services Directive; ~**vertrag** payment services agreement

Zahlungsdienstleister payment services provider

Zahlungseingänge 1. payments received, payment inflows 2. *(i. S. von eingehenden Überweisungen)* incoming credit transfers, *(Zahlungseingänge auf bereits abgeschriebene Kreditforderungen)* recoveries on loans previously charged off

Zahlungs / ~**einheit** payment unit; ~**einstellung** suspension (stoppage) of payments, payment stop, halt in payments; ~**empfänger** payee, recipient (beneficiary) of a payment, *(bei Lastschriften)* creditor

Zahlungs / ~**erinnerung** payment reminder; ~**ermächtigung** authority to pay, payment authorisation; ~**fähigkeit** solvency, ability to pay, *(zahlungsfähig)* solvent; ~**fälligkeit** payment due date: ~**frist** time for payment, time (period) allowed for payment, → Zahlungsziel; ~**fristverlängerung** extension of maturity; ~**form** means of payment

Zahlungs / ~**garantie** payment guarantee (bond), assurance of payment; ~**gepflogenheiten** customary terms of payment, payment practices;

~**geschäft(e)** payment transactions, payment transaction services; ~**geschäftstag** payment business day

zahlungsgestört *(~e Kredite)* problem (non-performing) loans

Zahlungs / ~**institut** payment institution, payment services provider; ~**instrument** payment (money) instrument; ~**intermediär** payment intermediary; ~**karte** payment card; ~**konto** money (payment) account

zahlungskräftig solvent, financially sound (strong)

Zahlungsmittel 1. cash, → Zahlungsmittelbestand **2.** means of payment, *(gesetzliches ~)* legal tender

Zahlungsmittel / ~**abflüsse** cash outflows; ~**äquivalente** cash equivalents; ~**bestand** cash and cash equivalents, liquid assets; ~**disposition** cash management

zahlungsmittelgenerierend *(~e Einheiten)* cash-generating units

Zahlungsmittel / ~**überschuss** *(~ aus der laufenden Betriebstätigkeit)* cash operating surplus; ~**umlauf** money supply, notes and coin in circulation; ~**zuflüsse** cash inflows

Zahlungs / ~**modalitäten** terms of payment; ~**modul** payments module; ~**modus** mode of payment; ~**moral** payment morale, payment record; ~**moratorium** payment standstill, standstill agreement, payment moratorium

Zahlungs / ~**nachricht** payment message; ~**nachweis** evidence of payment; ~**netting** payment netting; ~**ort** place of payment

Zahlungs / ~**papiere** *(im Dokumentengeschäft)* financial documents; ~**pflicht** obligation (liability) to pay → Zahlungsverpflichtungen; ~**pflichtiger** payor, *(bei Lastschriften)* debtor

Zahlungs / ~**rahmen** payment (withdrawal, drawing) limit; ~**rückstände** payment arrears, unpaid accounts (bills); ~**schwierigkeiten** financial difficulties, *(sich in ~ befinden)* to be strapped for cash, *(in ~ befindliches Unternehmen)* financially stricken (embarrassed) company

Zahlungs / ~**sicherheit** payment security; ~**sicherung** securing payment, payment guarantee; ~**sperre** payment stop, countermand of payment; ~**stopp** payment stop, stoppage of payments; ~**störung** *i.e.S.* payment problem, *i.w.S.* payment default, → zahlungsgestörte Kredite

Zahlungs / ~**streckung** extending the time for payment; ~**ströme** payment flows; ~**termin** date of payment, payment due date, *(Verfalltag)* date of maturity, maturity; ~**titel** court order to pay, enforcement order

Zahlungs / ~**überschuss 1.** cash flow **2.** payment(s) surplus; ~**unfähigkeit** inability to pay, illiquidity, insolvency, default, *(zahlungsunfähiger Kunde)* insolvent customer, customer in default, delinquent account; ~**unregelmäßigkeiten** payment irregularities, → Zahlungsverzögerung, Zahlungsverzug; ~**unwilligkeit** reluctance to pay

zahungsunwirksam *(~e Posten/Transaktionen)* non-cash items (positions)/ transactions

Zahlungs / ~**veranlassung** payment instruction (initiation); ~**verhalten** payment record, payment history

Zahlungsverkehr funds transfer, payment transactions, money transmission, *(Geschäftsfeld: Zahlungsverkehr und Abwicklung)* Payment and Settlement

Zahlungsverkehrs / ~**abwicklung** settlement of payments, payment transaction processing; ~**aufkommen** volume of payments; ~**automation** automation of payments; ~**dienstleistungen** payment transaction services; ~**einrichtungen** payment facilities

Zahlungsverkehrs / ~**konto** payment transaction account; ~**leistungen** money transmission services; ~**netz**

Z

funds transfer system; ~**richtlinie** (EU) Payment Services Directive

Zahlungs / ~verpflichtung payment commitment (obligation), obligation (liability) to pay, *(~en aus einer Garantie)* payment commitments under a guarantee; ~**versprechen** payment undertaking, undertaking (covenant, promise) to pay

Zahlungs / ~verweigerung non-payment, refusal to pay; ~**verzicht** waiver of payment; ~**verzögerung** delayed (late) payment, delay in settling a debt

Zahlungs / ~verzug default, default in payment, failure to meet a financial obligation, *(im Falle eines ~s des Kreditnehmers)* in the event of default by the borrower; ~ **verzugsklausel** default covenant; ~**verzugszinsen** default interest, interest on arrears

Zahlungs / ~vollmacht authority to pay, payment mandate; ~**wahlrecht** payment option, *(~ des Emittenten)* **1.** issuer's (re)payment option **2.** issuer's option to effect interest and redemption payments, e. g. either in Euro or US dollars

Zahlungs / ~weg payment channel; ~**weise** mode of payment, payment method; ~**widerruf** revocation (countermand) of payment, revocation of the authority to pay

Zahlungs / ~ziel credit, credit period, period (time) allowed for payment, *(Inanspruchnahme von ~en)* deferred payment terms; ~**zurückweisung** payment refusal

Zahlverhalten payment behaviour

Zäsur profound break, turnaround

Zaunkönigregelung wren rule □ additional bid acceptance period (after expiration of the official acceptance period)

ZDR → Zahlungsdiensterichtlinie

Zedent 1. assignor, transferor **2.** factor's client **3.** ceding company, cedant □ primary insurer that passes on insured risks to a reinsurer

zedieren to assign

Zehnerklub Group of Ten

zehnfach *(Begrenzung auf das Z~e des Eigenkapitals)* limitation to ten times shareholders' equity, *(eine ~e Umsatzsteigerung gegenüber dem Vorjahr)* a ten-fold increase on last year's turnover

zehren *(am Eigenkapital ~)* to deplete (to use up) capital resources

Zeichen 1. mark **2.** *(Anzeichen)* sign (indication) of

Zeichensatz *(im elektronischen Zahlungserkehr)* character set

zeichnen 1. *(im Emissionsgeschäft)* to subscribe to, to take up, to apply for, *(Anzahl der gezeichneten Aktien)* number of shares taken up/applied for, *(vollständig gezeichnete Emission)* fully subscribed issue, *(Aktien zu einem Vorzugskurs ~)* to subscribe for (to) shares at a preferential price
2. *(im Versicherungsgeschäft)* to underwrite, *(gezeichnete Risiken)* risks underwritten

Zeichner subscriber, applicant, allottee, taker

Zeichner / ~bank subscribing bank; ~**bonität** subscriber's credit standing; ~**liste** list of applicants (subscribers)

Zeichnung 1. *(von Aktien/Anleihen)* subscription to (for) shares/bonds, application for shares/bonds, *(zur ~ auflegen)* to offer for subscription, *(zur ~ aufliegen)* to be offered for subscription, *(bei ~ voll einzahlen)* to pay fully upon subscription
2. *(von Risiken)* underwriting of risks

Zeichnungs / ~angebot subscription offer (offering), offer for sale, offer for subscription; ~**aufforderung** invitation for subscription, invitation to subscribe; ~**aufkommen** total amount of securities subscribed; ~**bedingungen** terms of subscription; ~**befugnis** → Zeichnungsberechtigung

zeichnungsberechtigt *(~ sein)* to be authorised to sign

Zeichnungs / ~berechtigter authorised signatory; **~berechtigung** signatory power, signature (signing) authority, authority (authorisation) to sign; **~betrag** subscription (application) money, amount subscribed

Zeichnungs / ~einladung invitation (offer) for subscription, invitation to subscribe; **~erklärung** letter of subscription; **~formular** subscription (application) blank; **~frist** subscription (exercise) period, offering period; **~gebühr** subscription (application) charges; **~kurs** subscription price

Zeichnungs / ~liste application list, subscription book; **~modalitäten** subscription terms; **~prospekt** issuing (offering) prospectus; **~recht** subscription right, right to subscribe; **~rendite** yield upon subscription; **~reserve** *(bei einer Neuemission)* greenshoe

Zeichnungs / ~schein subscription (application) form, certificate of subscription; **~schluss** closing of the subscription book (application list), closing of an issue; **~stelle** subscription agent

Zeichnungs / ~termin subscription day; **~verpflichtung** undertaking to subscribe; **~vollmacht** signatory power, signing authority, authority to sign (e. g. on an account)

zeigen 1. to show **2.** *(sich ~)* to manifest itself **3.** *(seinen Wert ~)* to show its worth

Zeitablauf *(Befreiung von Verpflichtungen durch ~)* release from obligations through lapse of time, *(Zuwachs aufgrund des ~s)* appreciation due to the passage of time

Zeitabstand *(in regelmäßigen Zeitabständen)* at regular intervals

zeitanteilig for a proportionate period of time, *(~e Aufwendungen)* pro rata charges, *(~ erfassen)* to recognise on a time-proportion basis

zeitaufwendig *(~es Verfahren)* time-consuming procedure

Zeitband *(Aktiva/Passiva in Zeitbänder einstellen)* to classify assets/liabilities into time buckets

Zeitbasisrisiko time basis risk, calendar basis risk □ risk of loss arising from a maturity mismatch between a hedge position and the underlying secured position

zeitbezogen *(~e Abschreibung)* time-based depreciation

Zeitbezugsmethode temporal method (for foreign currency translations)

Zeit / ~bürgschaft surety limited in time; **~fächermethode** maturity band method; **~geschäfte** forward dealings

zeitgleich *(~e Fälligkeit)* matching maturity

zeitkongruent *(~e Refinanzierung)* refinancing (funding) at matching maturities, *(das Darlehensgeschäft ~ refinanzieren)* to fund lendings at matching maturities

zeitlich *(~e Ergebnisdifferenzen)* timing differences, *(~er Rahmen für die Rückzahlungen)* time scale (timetable) for repayments
(~ befristetes Hybridkapital) dated hybrid capital, *(~ begrenzt)* limited in time, time-limited, *(~ unbegrenzte Bürgschaft)* guarantee unlimited in time

zeitnah *(~e Übermittlung)* timely forwarding, *(~e Umsetzung)* timely implementation, implementation without delay

Zeitplan time schedule, *(im ~ bleiben)* to remain on schedule

zeitproportional *(~ erfassen)* to recognise on a time proportion basis

Zeitpunkt time, date, point in time, *(~ der vertragsgemäßen Geschäftserfüllung)* settlement date, *(~ des Risikoübergangs)* point in time when risk of loss passes from seller to buyer, attachment of risk
(zum ~ des Vertragsabschlusses) at the time of contracting, *(die zum (im) ~ der Vertragsausfertigung geltenden*

Bestimmungen) regulations in force at the time of execution of the contract

Zeitrahmen time horizon, *(innerhalb des vorgegebenen ~s)* within the stated time frame

zeitraubend lengthy, time-consuming, long drawnout

Zeit / ~raum period, horizon, time span, time frame, *(~ der Inanspruchnahme)* period of the drawdown; **~reihenanalyse** time series analysis; **~rente** terminable annuity

Zeit / ~studie time study; **~tratte** draft payable on a specific date; **~versicherung** term insurance (policy); **~verzögerung** time lag; **~vorstellungen** envisaged time frame

Zeitwert 1. fair value, *(zum ~ in der Bilanz ausweisen)* to fair value on the balance sheet, to state at the fair value in the accounts (balance sheet), *(~ abzüglich Risikoabschlag)* risk-adjusted fair value **2.** current value, market value **3.** *(einer Option)* time value □ that portion of an option's premium that represents the amount in excess of the intrinsic value (→ innerer Wert), *(Anteil des ~es an der Optionsprämie)* time value component

Zeitwert / ~abschlag haircut to the fair value; **~bewertung** *(~ des Handelsbestandes)* fair value measurement (valuation) of the trading portfolio; **~bilanzierung** fair value accounting

Zeitwert / ~erfolge fair value gains; **~ermittlung** *(~ eines Finanzinstrumentes)* fair value measurement of a financial instrument; **~verfall** time value decay □ erosion of an option's time value with the passage of time; **~verlust** loss of time value

zentral central, pivotal, *(~e Einheit)* core unit, *(~e Gegenpartei)* central counterparty

Zentralbankeinlagen central bank funds

zentralbankfähig *(~e Wertpapiere)* securities eligible for central bank borrowings

Zentralbank / ~geld central bank money (funds); **~geldmenge** central bank money stock; **~geldschöpfung** creation of central bank money; **~guthaben** central bank funds (balances); **~rat** Central Bank Council

Zentrale Head Office, company headquarter, corporate headquarters

Zentraler Kapitalmarktausschuss Central Capital Market Committee □ coordinates issuing requests by private and public sector issuers

zentraler Kontrahent central counterparty

Zentraler Kreditausschuss Central Banking Committee □ established by the five central associations of the German banking industry

Zentralisierung *(~ der Leitung)* centralisation of authority

Zentralkreditinstitut central banking institution

Zentralverwahrer Central Securities Depository, central custodian

Zentrum centre, focal point

Zerbröckeln *(~ der Hoffnungen auf einen Kursanstieg)* crumbling of hopes for a rise in prices

Zerfall disintegration (e. g. of a market)

Zerfallserscheinungen signs of disintegration

Zerrüttung *(~ des Marktes)* disruption of the market

zerschlagen *(die geplante Zusammenarbeit zerschlug sich)* the planned cooperation fell through

Zerschlagungswert break-up value

zersplittert *(~er Markt)* fragmented market

zerstören 1. *(Hoffnungen ~)* to dash hopes **2.** *(Wertpapiere ~)* to destroy securities

zerstreuen *(Anlegerbefürchtungen ~)* to dissipate (to dispel, to allay) investors' concerns

Zerstückelung *(~ einer Gruppe)* splitting up (fragmentation) of a group

Zertifikat 1. certificate **2.** *(Fondsanteil)* unit, share

Zertifikationsweg certification path

zertifikatsbasiert *(~e digitale Unterschrift)* certificate-based digital signature

Zertifikats / **~bestand** certificate holdings; **~inhaber** certificate holder; **~widerrufsliste** certificate revocation list

Zertifizierung certification

Zertifizierungs / **~diensteanbieter** certification service provider; **~instanz/~stelle** certificate (certification) authority, trust center

Zession assignment

Zessionar assignee

Zessions / **~kredit** loan against assignment of receivables, advance on receivables; **~liste** statement of receivables; **~prüfung** verification of assigned receivables; **~urkunde/~vertrag** deed of assignment

ziehen 1. to draw, (*Kaufinteresse auf sich ~*) to attract buying interest, (*einen Saldo ~)* to strike a balance, (*einen Scheck/Wechsel ~*) to draw a cheque/bill
2. *(mit sich ~)* to drag down
3. *(in Betracht ~)* to take into consideration (account)

Ziehung drawing, drawdown

Ziehungs / **~avis** *(Scheck)* draft advice; **~ermächtigung** authority to draw, drawing authorisation; **~grenze 1.** drawing limit **2.** upper limit for purchases; **~liste** list of drawings, drawing list; **~nachricht** notice of drawing; **~rechte** drawing rights; **~voraussetzungen** drawing conditions

Ziel 1. goal, aim, target, objective **2.** *(Bestimmungsort)* destination **3.** *(Zahlungsziel)* credit period, (*ein ~ von sechs Monaten einräumen)* to extend six months' credit **4.** *(Zweck)* purpose

Ziel / **~bandbreite** target range; **~bewertungszahl** target (minimum) valuation score

zielen *(~ auf)* to aim (to target, to direct) at, to gear to

Ziel / **~fonds** target fund; **~gesellschaft** target company; **~gewährung** extension (granting) of a credit period, granting credit terms; **~größe** target, target figure, *(monetäre ~)* monetary measure

Ziel / **~gruppe** target group, *(zielgruppenorientiert)* geared to specific target groups; **~-Hedgefonds** single hedge fund;**~inanspruchnahme** *(eines Zahlungsziels)* availment of a credit period

Ziel / **~konflikt** conflict of goals; **~korridor** target range (corridor); **~kosten** target cost; **~kunde** target customer

zielorientiert *(~e Verkaufskampagne)* goal-oriented sales drive

Ziel / **~rendite** target yield (return); **~setzung 1.** objective, goal, aspiration, aims and objectives **2.** setting objectives; **~strebigkeit** determination, resolve, purposefulness

Ziel / **~überschreitung** overshooting the target; **~unternehmen** target (targeted) company; **~verfehlung** missing the target; **~wechsel** time bill; **~zahlungsakkreditiv** deferred payment credit

Zins interest, interest rate, *(die fälligen ~en errechnen)* to compute interest due, *(die ~en dem Kapital zuschlagen)* to add the interest to the capital

Zinsabgeltungssteuer flat rate withholding tax, flat rate tax on interest earned

Zinsabgrenzung interest accrual, recognising interest on an accrual basis, *(Kredite mit Zinsabgrenzung)* accrual loans, *(Kredite ohne Zinsabgrenzung)* non-accrual loans, *(überfällige Kredite mit Zinsabgrenzung)* loans overdue, but still accruing, *(die ~ für einen Kredit einstellen)* to put a loan on a non-accrual basis

zinsabhängig *(~e Erträge)* interest-linked revenue (earnings), *(~es Geschäft)* interest-related transactions,

(~e Werte) securities dependent on the interest rate level

Zinsablaufbilanz → Zinsänderungsbilanz

Zinsabrechnung 1. interest statement, statement of interest charged/credited **2.** *(Berechnung)* calculation (computation) of interest

Zins / ~abschlagssteuer replaced by → Zinsabgeltungssteuer in 2005; **~absicherung** interest rate hedge, hedging the interest rate exposure; **~abstand** interest rate gap; **~abstufung** interest rate grading (graduation); **~abwärtstrend** downward trend in interest rates

zinsähnlich *(~e Aufwendungen/Erträge)* interest-related expense/income, expense/income similar in nature to interest

Zinsänderung interest rate change

Zinsänderungs / ~bilanz gap report, interest rate sensitivity report; **~risiko** interest rate risk □ potential loss from adverse interest rate movements, *(Zinsänderungsrisiko im Anlagebuch)* interest rate risk in the banking book

Zins / ~anfall accrual of interest; **~angebot** interest quote; **~ängste** concerns about higher interest rates; **~anhebung** lifting the interest rate, hike in interest rates

Zinsanpassung interest rate adjustment, interest refix (reset), adapting the interest rate to the market situation

Zinsanpassungs / ~periode repricing period; **~politik** repricing policy; **~termin** reset date, interest refix date, repricing date □ date on which a floating rate is reset, *(Zeitraum zwischen zwei ~en)* adjustment interval

Zins / ~ansammlung accumulation of interest; **~anspruch** entitlement to interest payments, interest claim; **~anstieg** interest rate increase, *(~ im kurzen Bereich)* interest rate increase at the short end of the market, *(kräftiger ~)* surge of interest rates; **~anteil** *(an der Darlehensbedienung)* interest portion

zinsäquivalent *(~e Erträge)* income equivalent to interest

Zinsarbitrage interest rate arbitrage □ trying to profit from the interest rate differences between two different currencies

Zinsaufschlag 1. *(auf einen Referenz-Zinssatz, z. B. Libor)* spread over Libor **2.** *(Zinsaufschläge für Unternehmensanleihen)* corporate bond spreads **3.** *(Zinsaufschläge für langfristige Kredite)* interest add-ons for long-term loans

Zinsaufwand interest expense(s), interest charge, interest paid, interest rate cost(s), *(Berechnung des ~es für den Kredit)* computing the interest charge on the loan, *(Kapitalisierung des ~es)* interest capitalisation, *(~ für kurzfristige Geldaufnahmen)* interest paid on short-term borrowings, *(~ für Nachrang- und Hybridkapital)* interest paid on subordinated and hybrid capital

Zinsaufwandsquote interest expense ratio

Zinsausfall interest loss, loss of interest, non-accrual of interest; **~risiko** interest loss risk

Zins / ~ausgleich 1. interest adjustment (compensation) **2.** settlement (payment) of interest accrued; **~ausschläge** sharp interest rate fluctuations, erratic interest rate swings

Zins / ~außenstände interest receivable, interest arrears; **~aussichten** outlook for interest rates; **~ausstattung** interest terms, *(einer Anleihe)* coupon, coupon (interest) rate; **~band** interest rate range

zinsbedingt *(~e Kapitalströme)* interest-driven (interest-induced) capital flows

Zinsbegrenzung *(~ nach oben)* interest rate cap, capping the interest rate, *(~ nach unten)* interest rate floor, setting a floor under the interest rate, *(~ nach oben und nach unten)* interest rate collar, combined cap and floor

Zinsbegrenzungs / ~prämie *(je nach Begrenzungsziel)* cap premium/floor premium; **~vereinbarung** interest limitation agreement, *(je nach Begrenzungsziel)* cap/floor/collar agreement; **~zeitraum** cap/floor period

zinsbegünstigt *(~e Programmkredite)* interest-subsidised loans extended under (public) lending schemes

Zinsbelastung 1. charging interest **2.** interest debit (debited) **3.** interest load (charge, burden)

Zinsbelastungs / ~periode interest charge period; **~termin** interest debit date

Zinsberechnung 1. computation of interest, *(~ auf der Basis der tatsächlich verstrichenen Tage)* computing interest on the basis of the actual number of days elapsed
2. *(Belastung)* charging interest

Zinsberechnungs / ~methode method of computing interest, day count convention (method), → aktuell/aktuell, → aktuell/360; **~zeitraum** interest determination period

Zins / ~bestätigung interest income statement; **~besteuerung** taxation of interest income; **~besteuerungsgesetz** Interest Taxation Act; **~bestimmungsfaktor** interest rate determinant; **~betrag** amount of interest; **~bewegungen** interest rate moves (movements)

zinsbewusst *(~e Anleger)* rate-conscious investors

zinsbezogen *(~e Transaktionen)* interest-driven operations

Zinsbindung 1. *(Festschreibung)* locking in the interest rate, locking in to a fixed interest rate, establishing a fixed loan rate, *(mit fünfjähriger ~)* with an interest rate fixed for five years
2. *(Bindung an einen Referenz-Zinssatz)* interest rate indexation, indexing (linking) to a benchmark rate

Zinsbindungs / ~bilanz gap analysis (report); **~frist** fixed interest period, lock-in period; **~klausel** rate lock clause; **~periode** fixed rate period, lock-in period; **~risiko** rate-fixing risk; **~vereinbarung** rate-fixing arrangement

Zinsbogen coupon sheet

Zinsbonifikation/~bonifizierung (payment of) additional interest, granting a special interest rate (an interest bonus)

zinsbringend interest-bearing, interest-earning, *(~e Anlage)* interest-bearing investment, *(Gelder ~ anlegen)* to put cash to work

Zins / ~buch interest exposure book; **~buchsteuerung** management of the interest exposure book; **~buckel** interest hump; **~charakter** *(Erträge mit ~)* income similar in nature to interest

Zins / ~deckung/~deckungsgrad interest cover (coverage), times interest earned, ratio of interest payable to earnings; **~derivate** interest rate derivatives

Zins / ~differenz interest rate gap, interest differential, difference between two interest rates; **~differenzgeschäft** carry trade □ borrowing funds at a low rate and onlending them at a higher rate; **~differenzierung** interest differentiation

Zins / ~druck interest rate pressure; **~einschätzung** assessment of the interest rate trend; **~einsparungen** saving interest cost; **~einstandskosten** original interest cost; **~empfindlichkeit** interest sensitiveness, sensitiveness to interest rate movements

Zins / ~engagements interest payment obligations; **~entlastung** easing the interest charge (the heavy burden of interest payments), *(~en im industriellen Bereich)* lowering corporate lending rates; **~entwicklung** direction of interest rates, *(künftige ~)* future course of interest rates

Zins / ~ergebnis net interest income (loss); **~erhöhung** interest rate hike, increase in the interest rate; **~erhöhungsklausel** step-up clause; **~erlass** interest waiver; **~erleichterung 1.** interest relief **2.** easing the interest burden

Zins / ~erlös interest earnings; **~ermäßigung** interest rate cut, lowering of interest rates; **~erneuerungsschein** renewal coupon; **~ersparnis** interest saved, interest saving(s); **~erstattung** interest refund

Zinserträge interest income (revenue), interest earned (received), *(~ aus Geldmarktgeschäften/aus dem Kreditgeschäft)* interest income from money market transactions/from lending transactions, *(~ aus Handelsbeständen)* interest income from the trading portfolio

Zins / ~ertragsbesteuerung taxation of interest income; **~ertragsbilanz** interest income statement; **~ertragskurve** yield curve; **~erwartungen** interest rate expectations

Zinseszins compound interest; **~berechnung** computation of compound interest; **~effekt** compound interest effect, compounding effect; **~formel** compound interest formula

Zins / ~explosion sharp upsurge in interest rates; **~fächer** interest rate spread (range); **~fälligkeit 1.** interest payment date, coupon date (maturity) **2.** interest falling due for payment

Zins / ~festschreibung → Zinsbindung; **~festsetzung** interest determination, fixing an interest rate; **~festsetzungstag** interest determination (interest fixing) date

zinsfixe *(~ Forderungen)* fixed rate receivables (assets), *(~ Mittelbeschaffung)* raising fixed rate funds, *(~ Verbindlichkeiten)* fixed rate liabilities, fixed rate payment obligations

Zins / ~fluktuation fluctuations (swings) in interest rates; **~forderungen** interest payments due, interest receivable; **~formel** interest formula; **~fortschreibung** interest rollover (rollup)

zinsfrei *(~es Darlehen)* interest-free loan

Zins / ~freigabe decontrol (deregulation) of interest rates; **~freijahre** interest-free period (years), interest payment holiday; **~fuß** interest rate, *(interner ~)* internal rate of return; **~futures** interest rate futures

Zins / ~garantie interest rate guarantee, guaranteeing a fixed interest rate; **~gebot** interest bid, rate offered

zinsgebundener Kredit 1. *(Festsatzkredit)* fixed rate loan **2.** *(gebunden an einen Referenz-Zinssatz, z. B. Libor)* Libor-linked loan

Zins / ~gefälle *(~ zwischen EURO und Dollar)* EUR-USD interest rate differential; **~gegenposition** offsetting (matching) interest rate position; **~gerüchte** rumours of a rate rise/rate cut

Zins / ~geschäft interest-related (interest-earning) operations; **~geschäftsposition** position on interest-related transactions; **~gestaltung** interest rate determination, fixing interest rates on loans and deposits, loan and deposit pricing

Zins / ~gipfel interest peak; **~gleitklausel** interest escalator clause, interest indexation clause; **~graben** large interest rate differential, wide gap in interest rates

zinsgünstig *(~e Festsatzmittel)* low-cost fixed rate funds, *(~e Konditionen)* favourable lending terms, soft pricing, *(~er Kredit)* low-interest loan, soft loan, loan carrying a low interest rate, loan extended at a favourable rate of interest, *(~e Mittelbeschaffung)* raising funds on favourable terms, *(~ beschaffte Mittel)* funds raised at a low rate of interest, *(~es Wohnungsbaudarlehen)* *(a)* low-interest housing loan *(b)* interest-subsidised housing loan

Zins / ~gutschrift 1. interest credited **2.** crediting interest; **~hausse** sharp rise in interest rates; **~hedge** interest rate hedge; **~historie** historical interest rates, rate history

Zins / ~höchststand interest rate peak; **~höhe** interest rate level; **~index** interest rate index; **~indexierung** interest rate indexation, linking the interest rate to a reference rate, *(zinsindexierte Anleihe)* bond with index-linked interest payments

Zins / ~indikationen indicative interest rates; **~indikator** indicator of the future trend in interest rates

zinsinduziert *(~e Aufwärtsbewegung)* interest-driven (interest-induced) upward trend

Zins / ~inkasso collection of interest, coupon collection; **~inkongruenz** mismatched interest rates, interest rate mismatch, *(Plural)* mismatched interest rate positions; **~inversion** inverted rate structure □ short-term interest rates are higher than long-term rates

Zins / ~kalkulation computation (calculation) of interest, interest calculation, computing interest, → Zinsberechnungsmethode; **~kapitalisierung** interest capitalisation; **~kartel** interest rate cartel; **~klausel** interest payment clause

Zins / ~klima interest rate environment; **~kompensation** interest rate netting, netting interest receivable against interest payable; **~konditionen** interest rate(s), interest rate terms

zinskongruent *(~ refinanzieren)* to refinance (to fund) at a matching rate of interest, *(~e Ausleihungen)* lendings at matching rates of interest

Zins / ~konstellation interest rate pattern; **~kontrakte** interest rate contracts, interest rate futures and options contracts; **~konvergenz** convergence of interest rates

Zins / ~konvertierung interest rate change, coupon change (through a bond conversion); **~koppelung** interest rate indexing, → Zinsindexierung; **~kosten** interest expense (cost), interest charge(s); **~kostenminimierung** minimising the overall interest burden

Zins / ~kupon interest coupon; **~kurve** interest rate curve, yield curve; **~ kurvenarbitrage** yield curve arbitrage, curve trading; **~last** interest load (charge), interest rate bill, interest burden; **~lastschrift** interest debited, debit of (debiting) interest

Zins / ~lauf interest payment period, *(der ~ der Papiere endet am ...)* the securities cease to bear interest on ...; **~leiste** renewal coupon; **~leistungen** interest payments; **~liberalisierung** decontrol of interest rates

zinslos *(~ gestellte Kredite)* loans put on a non-accrual basis, non-accrual loans, *(~ unterhalten)* to maintain free of interest

zinslos *(~es Darlehen)* interest-free loan, *(~e Einlage)* interest-free deposit, *(~e Gelder)* idle (inactive) funds, *(~e Guthaben)* non-interest-bearing deposits, interest-free balances, *(~ e Mindestreserve)* zero interest minimum reserve

Zinslosstellung putting on a non-accrual basis, non-accrual status

Zinsmarge interest margin, *(~ im Neugeschäft)* interest margin on new lendings

zinsmäßig in terms of interest, interestwise

Zins / ~mehraufwand additional interest cost; **~mehrertrag** additional (surplus) interest income; **~methode** method of calculating interest, → Zinsberechnungsmethode

Zins / ~mindereinnahmen shortfall in interest income; **~moratorium** standstill agreement (moratorium) on interest payments

Zins / ~nachkalkulation 1. subsequent interest charge (calculation) **2.** charging additional interest; ~**nachlass** interest rate rebate; ~**nachzahlung** 1. payment of additional interest 2. payment of interest in arrears

Zins / ~**nettoposition** net interest position (exposure); ~**neufestsetzung** interest rate refix (reset), resetting the interest rate, repricing; ~**neufestsetzungsrisiko** repricing risk

zinsneutral (*~e Aufwendungen*) non-interest expense

zinsniedrig (*~er Festkredit*) low fixed rate loan, (*~e Verbindlichkeiten*) low-interest liabilities

Zins / ~**niveau** interest rate level, (*Rückbildung des ~s*) interest rate downturn; ~**note** statement of interest; ~**notierung** interest quote, quotation of an interest rate

Zinsobergrenze 1. interest rate ceiling, interest rate cap, ceiling rate, (*bei einem Hypothekendarlehen*) mortgage cap, (*Erwerber einer ~*) buyer of a cap, (*Festlegung einer ~*) interest rate capping, (*Option auf eine ~*) caption, (*Vereinbarung über eine ~*) cap agreement, (*Verkäufer einer ~*) writer (seller, provider) of a cap 2. maximum coupon

Zinsoption interest rate option, (*börsengehandelte ~*) exchange-traded interest rate option, (*börsenfreie ~*) OTC interest rate option

Zins / ~**optionsschein** interest warrant; ~**papiere** interest-bearing securities; ~**periode** interest period, interest settlement period, coupon period, (*zinsperiodenkongruent refinanzieren*) to fund at matching interest periods

zinspflichtig (*~es Kapital*) interest-bearing capital (principal)

Zins / ~**position** interest rate position; ~**produkt** interest rate product, (*derivative ~e*) interest rate derivatives; ~**prognose** interest rate forecast

zinsreagibel rate-sensitive, sensitive to interest rate fluctuations, sensitive to movements in interest rates, (*zinsreagible Aktiva/Verbindlichkeiten*) rate-sensitive assets/liabilities

Zinsreagibilität sensitiveness to interest rate movements, interest rate sensitivity

zinsreagible (*~ Aktien*) interest-sensitive stocks, (*~ Ausleihungen*) interest-sensitive lendings, (*~ Positionen*) positions (exposure) sensitive to changes in the interest rate environment

Zins / ~**rechner** bank interest calculator; ~**rechnung** 1. interest calculation 2. statement of interest (charged/credited)

Zins / ~**regelung** interest rate arrangement, interest rate agreed upon; ~**regulierung** 1. interest settlement, settling interest accrued 2. interest rate control

Zinsrisiko interest rate risk (exposure), (*~ bei festverzinslichen Engagements*) interest rate risk inherent in fixed interest commitments

Zinsrisiko / ~**kontrolle** monitoring interest rate exposure, controlling interest rate risk; ~**management** interest rate risk management; ~**positionen** interest rate risk exposures

Zins / ~**rückgang** drop (fall) in interest rates; ~**rückstände** overdue interest, interest in arrears, arrears in interest payments; ~**rückvergütung** refund of interest; ~**rutsch** downslide (sharp drop) in interest rates; ~**saldo** net interest income (loss)

Zinssatz interest rate, (*bei einer Anleihe ferner*) coupon, (*~ für die Einlagefazilität*) interest rate on the deposit facility, (*~ für das Hauptrefinanzierungsgeschäft*) interest rate on the main refinancing operations (*~ für geduldete Überziehungskredite*) interest rate for tolerated overdrafts, (*~ für die Spitzenrefinanzierung*) interest rate on the marginal lending facility

Zinssätze (*~ für Hypothekenkredite*) mortgage lending rates, (*~ an den Kapitalmärkten*) interest rates in the capital (wholesale) markets, (*~ für Kredite*

an erste Adressen) prime lending rates, blue chip rates, (*~ für Privatkunden-/ Firmenkundenkredite)* retail/corporate lending rates
(*~ für Kurzläufer/Langläufer)* short/ long rates, (*~ für Privatkundeneinlagen)* retail deposit rates, (*~ am Rentenmarkt)* interest rates (coupons) in the bond market, (*~ für Termingelder)* term money rates, (*~ für Wohnungsbaudarlehen)* home (housing) loan rates

Zinssatz / **~differenz** interest rate gap, difference in interest rates; **~ermittlung** determination of the interest rate; **~sicherung** hedging the interest rate, interest rate hedge; **~swap** interest rate swap; **~termingeschäft** forward rate agreement; **~zusage** *(eines Festsatzes)* fixed rate undertaking, granting (guaranteeing) a fixed rate of interest

Zins / **~schein** interest coupon; **~scheintitel** interest strip, → Stripping; **~schere** interest rate gap, gap between rates at the short and long end of the market; **~schock** interest rate shock

Zins / **~schranke** interest deduction ceiling, interest barrier □ limitation of the tax deductibility of interest expenses; **~schuld** interest charge, interest payable; **~schwankungen** interest rate fluctuations (swings), ups and downs in interest rates

Zins / **~senkung** interest rate cut, lowering of interest rates, (*~en an Kunden weitergeben)* to pass interest rate cuts on to customers; **~sensitivität** sensitiveness to interest rate movements, *(zinssensitive Werte)* rate-sensitive securities, stocks sensitive to interest rate movements

Zinssicherung interest rate hedge, hedging interest rate exposure, (*Kosten der ~)* interest hedge cost

Zinssicherungs / **~instrumente** interest rate hedging instruments (interest rate futures/options, caps, collars, forward rate agreements); **~vereinbarung** rate hedging agreement; **~zertifikat 1.** *(nach oben)* cap certificate **2.** *(nach unten)* floor certificate

Zinssollstellungstermin interest debit date □ date on which interest accrued is debited to the loan principal

Zinsspanne interest margin □ calculated as the ratio of net interest received to a financial institution's balance sheet total

Zinsspannen / **~erweiterung** widening of the interest margin; **~rechnung** interest margin accounting; **~verengung** narrowing of the interest margin

Zins / **~spekulation** speculation on interest rate movements, speculation on an interest rate cut/rise; **~spreizung 1.** interest rate tiering **2.** interest gap between two currencies; **~sprung** sharp rise in interest rates, interest rate leap

Zins / **~stabilisierung** stabilisation of the interest rate level; **~stabilität** interest rate stability; **~staffel** interest table; **~staffelmethode** day-to-day calculation of interest; **~steigerung** rise in interest rates

Zins / **~steuerung** interest rate control (management); **~stopp** interest freeze; **~ströme** interest flows; **~strip** coupon strip, interest-only strip, → Stripping

Zins / **~struktur** interest rate structure (pattern); **~strukturkurve** term structure of interest rates;**~stundung** interest payment deferral, respite for interest payments, deferral of (moratorium on) interest payments

Zins / **~subvention** interest payment subsidy; **~subventionierung** subsidising interest payments, *(zinssubventionierte Finanzierung)* interest-subsidised funding, *(zinssubventionierte Kredite)* interest-subsidised loans

Zins-Swap interest rate swap, (*~ ohne Festzinsteil)* floating/floating interest rate swap, basis swap, → Swap, (*~ mit*

nach oben und unten begrenzten Zinszahlungen) collared interest rate swap

Zins / ~tabelle interest statement (table); **~tage** interest days, number of days for which interest is paid or payable; **~tagequotient** day count fraction; **~talfahrt** nosedive of interest rates

Zinstender *(amerikanisches Zuteilungsverfahren)* US-style rate tender, variable rate tender □ tender in which banks have to pay exactly what they bid for, i.e. allocations are made according to the interest rate offered

Zinstender *(holländisches Zuteilungsverfahren)* Dutch style rate tender, Dutch auction, single rate tender □ all satisfied bids are uniformly settled at the marginal interest rate

Zinstermin interest due date, interest payment date, coupon date

Zins-Termine interest rate futures

Zinstermin / ~geschäft forward rate agreement; **~kontrakt** interest rate futures contract, → Terminkontrakt; **~satz** forward interest rate

Zinstiefstand (record, all-time) low in interest rates, interest rate trough

Zinstitel interest rate instrument

zinstragend *(~e Aktiva/Forderungen)* earning assets, interest-bearing claims, *(~es Geschäft)* interest-bearing operations

zinstreibend *(~e Faktoren)* factors driving (forcing, pushing) up interest rates

Zinstrend trend of (in) interest rates

Zinsüberschuss net interest income, *(~ nach Risikovorsorge)* net interest income after risk provisioning, *(zinsüberschussneutrales Geschäft)* operations having no impact on net interest income

Zins / ~umfeld interest rate environment; **~umkehr** turnaround in interest rates, interest rebound, reversal in the interest rate trend

zinsunabhängig *(~er Aufwand/~e Erträge)* non-interest expense/income

Zins-und Dividendenerträge interest and dividend income

Zins-und Tilgungsleistungen interest and redemption payments, payments of interest and principal

Zins- und Währungs-Swap cross currency interest rate swap

Zins / ~unsicherheit interest rate uncertainty, interest rate worries (concerns); **~untergrenze** interest floor, → Zinsobergrenze; **~usance** → Zinsberechnungsmethode; **~valuta** interest value date

zinsvariable *(~ Anleihe)* floater, floating rate bond, *(~ Anleihe mit einem Maximalzinssatz/einer Zinsuntergrenze/einer Zinsbegrenzung nach oben und nach unten)* capped/floored/collared floater, *(~s Darlehen)* variable interest loan *(~ Gelder)* floating rate funds, *(~ Hypothek)* variable rate mortgage, adjustable rate mortgage, *(~ Seite eines Swap-Kontraktes)* floating rate leg of a swap contract, *(~ Verpflichtung)* floating rate obligation, *(~ Zahlungen)* floating rate payments

Zinsveränderungssperrfrist guaranteed rate period

zinsverbilligen to lower the interest charge, *(zinsverbilligter Kredit)* loan at a reduced rate of interest, *(zinsverbilligte Kredite aus öffentlichen Förderprogrammen)* interest-subsidised loans extended under public lending schemes

Zins / ~verbilligung 1. interest rate cut **2.** lowering interest expense **3.** subsidising interest payments, payment of interest subsidies; **~verbilligungsprogramm** interest subsidy scheme; **~verbindlichkeiten** interest payable, interest due

Zins / ~vergünstigung interest rate concession, → Zinssubvention, *(zinsvergünstigtes Darlehen)* beneficial interest rate loan, low-interest loan; **~verlust** loss in interest income; **~verpflichtung** interest payment obligation

Zins / ~**verrechnung** interest netting; ~**versicherung** interest rate insurance, interest rate hedge; ~**verteuerung** increase in interest rates, interest rate hike; ~**verzicht** interest waiver, waiver of interest payments

Zins / ~**verzug** failure to pay interest, failure to make a scheduled interest payment, default in interest payments; ~**volatilität** interest rate volatility; ~**vorleistungsrisiko** interest prepayment risk, advance interest payment risk

Zins / ~**vorsprung** interest rate advantage, lead in interest rates; ~**vortrag** interest carryforward; ~**wende** turnaround in interest rates, interest rebound; ~**zeitraum** coupon payment period

zinswirksam bearing (carrying, attracting) interest, *(~es Guthaben)* interest-bearing credit blance, *(~e Valuta)* interest effecive value date

Zins / ~**wirkung** impact on interest rates; ~**zahlen** interest product

Zinszahlung 1. interest payment, payment of interest, *(gleichmäßige/regelmäßige ~en)* equal/periodic interest payments, *(~en bleiben während der Laufzeit des Kredites gleich)* interest payments remain constant over the life of the loan
2. coupon payment

Zinszahlungs / ~**stichtag** interest maturity date; ~**ströme** interest cash flows; ~**termin** interest payment date, coupon date

Zins / ~**zugeständnisse** interest rate concessions; ~**zusage** rate commitment; ~**zuschüsse** interest subsidies (grants); ~**zuschussprogramm** interest subsidy scheme; ~**zyklus** interest rate cycle

Zirkaauftrag order at an approximate limit □ i. e. slight deviations from the limit given by the customer are permissible

Zirka-Kurs approximate price

Zirkular-Kreditbrief circular letter of credit

zirkulieren *(frei ~des Aktienkapital)* free float, freely circulating stock capital

zivilrechtlich *(~e Schadenshaftung)* liability in damages under civil law

ZKA → Zentraler Kreditausschuss

ZM-Risiko *(Risiko eines ausländischen Zahlungsverbots oder Moratoriums)* risk of loss arising from a non-payment decree or a general moratorium on external debt by the government of the buyer's country

Zoll / ~**abfertigung** customs clearing, clearing through the customs; ~**bürgschaft** customs bond (guarantee); ~**einlagerung** bonding; ~**garantie** customs guarantee; ~**gutlager** customs warehouse (store)

Zoll / ~**ladungsverzeichnis** customs manifest; ~**lager** bonded store (warehouse), customs warehouse; ~**lagergut** bonded goods; ~**tarif** (customs) tariff

Zoll / ~**verschluss** *(Waren unter ~)* bonded goods, *(Einlagerung unter ~)* warehousing in bond; ~**verschlussvorschriften** bonding requirements; ~**vorschriften** tariff regulations

Zubringerfonds feeder fund

zuerkennen *(ein Rating von AAA ~)* to award a triple A rating

Zuerkennung *(richterliche)* adjudication

zufallen *(den Banken fällt eine wichtige Rolle zu)* banks are allotted (given) an important role

zufällig *(~ ausgewählter Handelstag)* randomly chosen trading day

Zufalls / ~**auswahl** random selection; ~**prinzip** *(Zuordnung nach dem ~)* randomisation, *(nach dem ~ auswählen)* to select on a random basis; ~**stichprobe** random sample; ~**variable** random variable; ~**verfahren** random sampling, random selection process, *(ausgeübte Optionen werden*

Z

nach einem ~ zugeteilt) exercised options are randomly assigned

zufließen to flow into, *(die dem Inhaber zufließenden Erträge)* the income accruing to the holder

Zufluss *(~ ausländischer Gelder)* inflow (influx) of foreign funds, *(~ von Nichtbankengeldern)* inflow of non-bank deposits

Zuflüsse *(~ aus offenen Forderungen)* inflows from outstanding exposures

Zuflussprinzip accrual principle

zufrieden satisfactory

Zufriedenheit satisfaction, *(Aufträge zur vollsten ~ des Kunden ausführen)* to execute orders to the customer's entire satisfaction

zufriedenstellend *(~es Geschäftsjahr)* satisfactory business year

zuführen to allocate, to add, to invest, *(dem Anlagevermögen ~)* to add to (to invest in) fixed assets, *(neue* Mittel *~)* to provide (to invest, to inject) fresh funds, *(den Rücklagen ~)* to allocate (to transfer, to carry) to reserves

Zuführung allocation, addition, injection, *(~ zu den Gewinnrücklagen)* allocation to revenue reserves, *(~ zu den Wertberichtigungen)* addition to valuation allowances

Zuführungsbedarf additions required, *(bei Wertberichtigungen)* necessary increase in valuation (loan loss) allowances

Zuführungsfonds feeder fund

Zug *(die Gelder ~ um ~ auszahlen)* to disburse the funds progressively as the work is completed, to pay against delivery of the goods, *(Zug-um-Zug-Abwicklung, Lieferung gegen Zahlung)* delivery versus payment

Zugang access, access point, *(~ zum Kapitalmarkt)* access to the capital market, *(Zugänge zum Sachanlagevermögen)* additions to property, plant and equipment, *(~ erhalten)* to gain access to, *(~ gewähren)* to give right of access to, *(sich ~ zum Markt verschaffen)* to obtain access to (to access) the market

Zugangs / ~berechtigung access authorisation (authority); **~daten** access data; **~kanäle** access channels; **~kennung** access identification, personal access number, → Kundenkennung; **~recht** right of access; **~schlüssel** access key, *(des Händlers)* merchant key; **~voraussetzungen** access (entrance) requirements

zugeben to concede, to admit

zugegangen *(Mitteilungen gelten als ~)* notices shall be deemed received

zugehörig *(~ zum Konzern)* belonging to the group

Zugehörigkeit **1.** connection (affiliation) with, membership in **2.** length of service

Zügel *(die ~ anziehen)* to tighten the reins

Zugeständnis concession, *(~se in der Konditionengestaltung)* rate (pricing) concessions

zugestehen to concede, to allow, to admit, *(jmd. die Möglichkeit ~)* to give s. o. the opportunity

zügig *(~e Abwicklung der Transaktion)* speedy (smooth) handling of the transaction

Zugriff **1.** access, recourse, *(~ auf die Sicherheit im Falle eines Zahlungsverzuges)* access to the collateral in the event of a default
2. *(~ durch die Gläubiger)* access (seizure) by the creditors, *(~ in das Vermögen)* attachment of the property
3. *(~ besitzen auf)* to have a hold on, *(~ nehmen auf) (a)* to take recourse to *(b)* to attach

zugrunde legen to base, to take as a basis, *(die am Stichtag geltenden Zinssätze ~)* to apply the interest rates prevailing on the record date, *(das zugrunde liegende Wertpapiergeschäft)* the underlying securities transaction

zugute kommen to be to the advantage of, to accrue to the benefit of s.o.

Zukauf additional purchase, buying in addition, *(Zukäufe durch institutionelle Anleger)* fresh buying by institutional investors

Zukunftsfähigkeit future viability

zukunftsorientiert *(~e Anlagen)* future-oriented (forward-looking) investments

zulassen 1. to admit, to allow, to permit, *(als Beweismittel ~)* to admit (to receive) in evidence, *(zum Börsenhandel ~)* to admit to dealings on the stock exchange
2. to licence, to charter, *(zugelassene Hinterlegungsstelle)* authorised depository
3. *(zugelassene Geschäftspartner)* eligible counterparties

zulässig admissible, permissible, permitted, *(~e Abweichungsrate)* tolerable deviation rate, *(~e Fremdwährungsengagements)* allowable exposure in foreign currencies, *(~e Schwankungsbreite)* permitted band of fluctuation, *(soweit gesetzlich ~)* to the extent permitted by law

Zulässigkeit *(~ einer Berufung)* admissibility of an appeal

Zulassung 1. admission, *(~ zur Börsennotierung)* admission to listing (to official quotation) on the stock exchange, *(~ zum* → Regulierten Markt) admission to the Regulated Market
2. licensing, *(~ von Kreditinstituten)* chartering (authorisation) of credit institutions

Zulassungs / ~anforderungen listing requirements; **~antrag** listing application; **~ausschuss** Admission Committee; **~behörde** chartering authority

Zulassungs / ~bescheid listing notice; **~bestimmungen 1.** *(für die Börsenzulassung)* listing requirements (provisions) **2.** *(für den Zugang zu einem Markt)* prerequisites for allowing access to a market; **~kosten** listing expenses, flotation fee; **~kriterien** admission (authorisation) critera; **~prospekt** listing prospectus

Zulassungs / ~verfahren 1. listing procedure **2.** licensing proceedings; **~voraussetzungen 1.** qualifying criteria **2.** admission (listing) requirements; **~vorschriften** listing rules; **~widerruf** *(einer Börsennotierung)* delisting

zulegen *(im Kurs)* to put on, to advance, to firm

Zulieferindustrie subcontracting industry

Zumutbarkeitsgrenze *(für die* → Bankenabgabe) reasonable-burden threshold

Zunahme increase, rise, advance, *(~ im kurz- und mittelfristigen Kreditbereich)* increase in short- and medium-term lendings, *(~ des Kreditbestandes)* growth in total lendings, loan portfolio growth, *(starke ~* der *Ordertätigkeit während der Börsensitzung)* sharp increase (spurt) in buying activity

zunehmen to increase, to rise, to grow, to gain, to advance

zunichte machen *(Hoffnungen auf eine weitere Kurssteigerung ~)* to dash (to shatter, to quell, to frustrate) hopes for a further price advance

zuordenbar attributable, → zurechenbar

zuordnen 1. to assign, to attribute, to allocate, *(dem Grundsatz I ~)* to assign to (to count towards) principle I
2. *(Kauf- und Verkaufsaufträge einander ~)* to match buy and sell orders, *(nicht zugeordnete Positionen)* unmatched items

Zuordnung 1. assignment, attribution, allocation, *(~ zum Handelsbuch)* allocation to the trading book, *(~ der Verantwortlichkeiten)* assignment of responsibilities
2. *(~ der Kontrahenten)* matching of counterparties

Zuordnungs / ~schlüssel allocation formula; **~system** *(elektronisches ~)* electronic matching system

zurechenbar 1. eligible, *(den Eigenmitteln ~e Finanzinstrumente)* financial

instruments eligible for inclusion in equity, *(dem Kapital ~)* eligible for inclusion in the capital base
2. attributable, *(direkt ~e Kosten)* directly attributable (allocable, assignable) cost, *(den Minderheitsaktionären ~)* attributable to minority shareholders

Zurechenbarkeit 1. eligibility for (qualifying for) inclusion in **2.** allocability, attributability

zurechnen 1. to include, to count towards, *(den liquiden Aktiva ~)* to count as part of the stock of liquid assets, → Mindestliquiditätsquote, *(dem Eigenkapital ~)* to count as equity, *(dem Eigenkapital der Muttergesellschaft ~)* to recognise in the capital position of the parent company *(der Erfolgsrechnung ~)* to recognise in current earnings, *(den Forderungen/Verbindlichkeiten ~)* to include in debtors/creditors, *(~ zum Handelsbestand)* to assign to the trading book
2. *(zuordnen/zuschreiben)* to attribute, to ascribe, to allocate, *(dem Steuerpflichtigen ~)* to impute to the taxpayer

Zurechnung *(~ zu den Debitoren)* inclusion in debtors, *(~ zum Eigenkapital)* counting towards (allocation to) equity, *(steuerliche ~)* taxwise attribution, imputation, *(~ von Stimmrechten)* attribution of voting rights, *(wirtschaftliche ~ von Vermögenswerten)* economic allocation of assets

zurückbehalten to retain, *(zurückbehaltener Prozentsatz)* retained percentage, retention rate

Zurückbehaltung retention

Zurückbehaltungsrecht 1. right of retention, right to retain (e. g. property for payment or satisfaction of a debt)
2. retaining (possessory) lien

zurückbelasten *(dem Kunden ~)* to bill back to the customer, to redebit to the customer's account

zurückbilden to recede, to drift lower, to retreat from the current level

Zurückbildung *(~ der Zinssätze)* downward course (gradual lowering) of interest rates

zurückbleiben to stay behind, to fall (to lag) behind, *(hinter den Erwartungen ~)* to fall short of expectations, *(hinter dem Index ~)* to lag behind the index, *(hinter dem Markt um ca. 20 % ~)* to underperform the market by about 20 %

zurückdatieren to date back

zurückdisponieren to retransfer, to repatriate

zurückerlangen to recover, to recoup, to regain

zurückerstatten to refund, to reimburse

zurückerwerben to repurchase, to buy back

zurückfahren 1. *(das Interbankgeschäft ~)* to curtail interbank transactions, to cut down on interbank transactions
2. *(die Produktion ~)* to scale down production

Zurückfahren curtailment, downsizing

zurückfallen 1. to drop, to fall, to slump, to turn lower, *(kräftig ~)* to drop sharply, to plunge, *(weiter ~)* to slip back further, to continue to fall, *(der Kurs fiel auf den Vorjahresstand zurück)* the price slipped to last year's level, *(zehn Prozent gegenüber dem Vorjahresniveau ~)* to be 10 % down on previous year's level
2. *(an jmd. ~)* to revert to s. o.

zurückfließen to flow back

zurückfordern 1. to reclaim, to recall, to claim back **2.** *(gewährte Steuervergünstigungen)* to claw back, *(ohne vorherige Kündigung ~)* to recall without prior notice

zurückführen 1. *(~ auf)* to ascribe to *(auf die Erweiterung der Zinsspannen ~)* to attribute to the widening of interest margins
2. to repatriate, *(Kapital ~)* to repatriate capital
3. to reduce, (den *Kredit in den vereinbarten Rahmen ~)* to reduce the loan

to the limit (line) agreed upon, *(den Kredit auf … € ~)* to clean down the loan to € …, *(die Überziehung ~)* to clear the overdraft

zurückgeben to return, *(den Scheck mangels Deckung unbezahlt ~)* to return the cheque unpaid for lack of cover

zurückgehen to fall, to slip, to drift lower, to ease, to slump, *(Zinsunsicherheiten ließen die Aktienkurse ~)* interest rate uncertainties sent stock (equity) prices lower

zurückgewähren 1. to return, to restitute **2.** *(Wertpapiere ~)* to redeliver securities

zurückgewinnen *(einen Marktanteil ~)* to regain (to recoup, to retrieve) a market share

zurückgreifen *(~ auf)* to fall back on, to resort to

zurückhalten to hold back, to restrain, *(sich mit Engagements am Markt ~)* to shy away from the market, *(das Exportwachstum ~)* to hold back export growth

Zurückhaltung restraint, *(~ der Anleger)* investor restraint, investor's reluctance, *(~ von Gewinnen)* retention of profits, *(die Anleihe wurde mit ~ aufgenommen)* the loan received a muted (tepid) reception, *(mit ~ begegnen)* to view with caution

zurückholen *(Geschäfte ~)* to pull back business, *(einen Marktanteil ~)* to win back (to claw back) a market share

zurückkaufen to buy back, to repurchase, *(eigene Aktien ~)* to buy back (to reacquire, to repurchase) own shares, *(am Markt ~)* to repurchase in the market, *(zurückgekaufte eigene Kapitaltitel)* reacquired own equity instruments

zurückkommen *(auf ein Schreiben ~)* to refer back (to revert) to a letter

zurückliegend *(weiter ~e Abrechnungen)* statements reaching further back in time

zurücknehmen 1. to take back, to retract, to withdraw, *(eine Klage ~)* to withdraw an action, *(auf Verlangen des Verleihers ~)* to take back (to redeem) at the lender's request, *(Fondsanteile ~)* to redeem shares (units)
2. to revoke, to cancel, *(abgegrenzte Aufwendungen ~)* to reverse expenses accrued
3. to reduce, *(die Dividende ~)* to reduce (to lower) the dividend, *(seine Ertragsprognose ~)* to downgrade one's earnings forecast

zurückrechnen 1. to calculate back **2.** *(eine Lastschrift ~)* to redebit, to return a direct debit

zurückreichen to go back to, to stretch (to date) back to

zurückrufen to call back (in), *(eine Auszahlung ~)* to reclaim a disbursement, *(vor Verfall ~)* to retire (to call in) prior to maturity

zurückschleusen to channel back, to rechannel, to repatriate

zurückschrauben 1. *(die Gewinnprognosen ~)* to downgrade profit forecasts **2.** *(die Kreditvergabe ~)* to scale back (down) lending portfolios

zurückschrecken 1. *(vor neuen Engagements ~)* to be shy of (to shy at) new investments **2.** *(Anleger ~ lassen)* to put off (to deter) investors

zurücksenden to send back, to return

Zurücksetzen *(von Krediten)* re-ageing of loans

zurückstellen 1. to defer, to postpone, *(eine Emission ~)* to shelve an issue, *(die Tilgungszahlungen ~)* to put off repayment of principal, *(eine Zahlung ~)* to defer (to put off) a payment
2. to set aside, to make provisions, *(der im letzten Geschäftsabschluss zurückgestellte Betrag)* the amount set aside (retained) in last year's accounts
3. to subordinate, *(hinter die Forderungen von … ~)* to subordinate to (to postpone behind) the claims of …

Zurückstellung 1. deferral, deferment, postponement **2.** setting aside, making provisions **3.** subordination

zurückströmen *(auf den Kapitalmarkt ~)* to flow back into the capital market

zurückstufen to downgrade, to mark down, *(die Anleihen ~)* to downgrade the bonds, to lower the bonds' rating

zurücktreten 1. to resign, to retire
2. to subordinate, *(im Rang ~)* to accept a lower (junior) rank, to consent to the subordination of one's rights, *(zurückgetretener Gläubiger)* subordinated creditor (lender)
3. to rescind, *(von einem Vertrag ~)* to rescind (to abrogate, to nullify) a contract, to withdraw from a contract

zurückübertragen to reassign, to retransfer, to reconvey

Zurückübertragung 1. *(~ des Sicherungsgegenstandes)* reassignment (retransfer) of the collateral **2.** *(~ von Vermögenswerten)* reconveyance of property

zurückverfolgen *(bis zum Auftraggeber ~)* to trace back to the originator

Zurückverlagerung *(~ in den Aktienmarkt)* transferring (moving) back into the equity market

zurückverweisen *(an einen Ausschuss ~)* to remit (to refer back) to a committee

Zurückverweisung remittal

zurückweisen to reject, to refuse, to decline, *(einen Bericht/eine Klage ~)* to dismiss a report/an action, *(eine Kritik ~)* to rebuff criticism, to brush off (aside) criticism, *(ein Übernahmeangebot ~)* to rebuff (to reject) a bid

Zurückweisung rejection, *(~ von Dokumenten)* refusal to accept documents, *(~ einer Forderung)* rejection (repudiation) of a claim, *(~ einer Klage)* dismissal of an action, *(~ einer Lastschrift)* return (non-acceptance) of a direct debit

zurückzahlen to repay, *(die Anleihe kann vorzeitig zurückgezahlt werden)* the bond may be repaid (called in) prior to maturity (ahead of schedule), *(zum Nennwert ~)* to repay for (at) face value, *(in einer Summe ~)* to pay back in a lump sum

zurückziehen 1. to withdraw, to revoke, to cancel
2. *(sich von einem Markt ~)* to pull out (to back out) of a market

Zuruf-System *(Börsenhandel)* open outcry trading

Zurverfügungstellung *(~ des Kredites)* making the loan available, placing the loan at the borrower's disposal

Zusage 1. commitment, promise, undertaking, covenant **2.** acceptance, reply in the affirmative, positive reply, *(eine finanzielle ~ geben)* to make a financial commitment

zusagen 1. to commit o. s., to promise, to undertake, to covenant, *(den Kredit fest ~)* to give a binding (firm) loan undertaking, *(zugesagte Kreditfazilität)* committed credit facility, *(zugesagte Linie)* committed line
2. to accept, to give a positive reply
3. to suit (to appeal to) s. o., *(wir hoffen, dass Ihnen unser Kreditangebot zusagt)* we hope that our loan offer will suit you

Zusagen *(~ für Baufinanzierungskredite)* building loan commitments, *(~ im langfristigen Bereich)* long-term loan commitments, *(~ für den Wohnungsbau)* residential loan (lending) commitments

Zusage / ~ergebnis → Zusagevolumen; **~ermächtigung** authorisation to grant loans, loan approval powers; **~gebühr** commitment fee; **~provision** commitment commission, facility fee

Zusage / ~schreiben *(für einen Kredit)* facility letter, commitment letter; **~volumen** total loan commitments, *(an einen Einzelkreditnehmer)* aggregate facility, total funds committed

zusammenarbeiten to cooperate, *(in bestimmten Punkten ~)* to collaborate on specific issues, (*reibungslos ~*) to work smoothly together

zusammenbrechen to collapse, to break down

zusammenbringen to bring together

zusammenfallen 1. to coincide with, (*die Zinssenkung fiel mit einer Reihe von Neuemissionen zusammen*) the interest rate cut coincided with a host of new issues
2. (*Ein- und Ausgänge ~ lassen*) to synchronise payments and receipts

Zusammenfallen 1. coinciding, cumulation
2. synchronisation, (*durch das ~ von Steuer- und Kuponterminen*) with tax and coupon payment dates coinciding, as a result of the cumulation of tax and coupon payment dates

zusammenfassen 1. to sum up, to summarise, to give a rundown
2. to combine, to bunch, to consolidate, (*getrennte, auf den gleichen Namen lautende Einlagen ~*) to aggregate separate deposits in the same name, (*Kleinstaufträge zu einem Großauftrag ~*) to bunch (to combine) several small trades into a single trade, to encapsulate small trades into one, (*zusammengefasste Geschäfte*) aggregated trades

Zusammenfassung 1. summary, summing up, rundown, roundup, (*~ der Bilanz*) summary financial statements, (*eine ~ über die Kursentwicklung geben*) to give a rundown (summary) on the price developments
2. combination, consolidation, (*~ von Aufträgen*) combining (bunching) orders for execution

zusammenführen 1. to bring together, to combine, to pool 2. (*Kauf- und Verkaufsaufträge*) to match

Zusammenführung (*~ von Aufträgen*) matching of orders, order matching, (*~ einzelner Kontosalden auf einem Hauptkonto*) cash pooling

zusammengehen 1. (*eine Zusammenarbeit eingehen*) to tie up with 2. (*fusionieren*) to merge

Zusammengehen 1. tie-up, link-up, joining forces 2. (*Fusion*) merger

Zusammenhalt (*währungspolitischer ~*) monetary policy cohesion

zusammenlegen 1. to put together, to combine, (*Anteile/Beteiligungen ~*) to pool interests/equity investments
2. (*verschiedene Aktiengattungen ~*) to consolidate various classes of shares
3. (*zu einer einzigen Einheit ~*) to merge into one single entity, (*Unternehmensbereiche ~*) to merge divisions

Zusammenlegung 1. putting together, combination, pooling 2. consolidation 3. merger, amalgamation

Zusammenrechnung (*~ von Stimmrechten*) aggregation of voting rights

zusammenrufen to convene, to summon

zusammenschließen (*sich ~ mit*) 1. to join forces, to unite, to team (to link) up with, to pool resources with, (*sich noch enger ~*) to close ranks even further 2. (*fusionieren*) to merge, to amalgamate, (*sich zu einem neuen Unternehmen ~*) to merge into a new company

Zusammenschluss 1. joining forces, uniting, tie-up, link-up 2. (*Fusion*) merger, amalgamation 3. union

zusammensetzen 1. (*sich aus verschiedenen Anlageformen ~*) to consist of (to be made up of) various forms of investment 2. (*zusammengesetzte Option*) compound option

Zusammensetzung (*~ des Kreditportefeuilles*) composition (make-up) of the loan portfolio

Zusammenspiel (*~ von Geld- und Kapitalmärkten*) interplay between money and capital markets

zusammenstellen to compile, to arrange, to prepare, (*Daten ~*) to collect (to compile) data, (*eine Finanzierung*

~) to put together a financing package, *(ein Konsortium ~)* to assemble (to put together) a syndicate

Zusammenstellung 1. compilation **2.** statement, survey, summary **3.** *(~ einer Finanzierung)* arranging a financing package (a funding deal), dealmaking

zusammenstreichen to trim, *(Investitionen ~)* to prune (to pare down) capital investments

Zusammentreffen 1. meeting **2.** *(zeitliches)* concurrence

zusammentreten to meet, to gather

Zusammenveranlagung joint assessment

Zusammenwachsen *(~ der internationalen Finanzmärkte)* convergence (globalisation) of international financial markets

Zusammenwirken 1. *(~ verschiedener Faktoren)* concurrence (interaction) of several factors **2.** *(Zusammenarbeit)* cooperation, concerted action, combined efforts

zusammenzählen to add up

Zusatz 1. supplement, addition **2.** *(Anhang)* annex, rider **3.** *(Kurszusatz)* notation

Zusatz / ~aktien bonus shares; **~angaben** further details; **~anwendungen** add-ons, → Zusatzleistungen; **~aufwand** additional outlay, incremental charge; **~bestimmung** additional clause, supplementary provision; **~bewilligung** *(von Geldern)* additional appropriation

Zusatz / ~deckung additional (extra) cover; **~dividende** superdividend, surplus; **~eigenmittel** supplementary capital; **~finanzierung** supplementary financing; **~kosten** additional (incremental) cost

Zusatzleistungen 1. additional (supplementary) services, add-on services, value-added services **2.** *(rund um die Verwahrung von Wertpapieren)* value-added custody services **3.** *(des Arbeitgebers)* fringe benefits

zusätzlicher Anrechnungsbetrag additional capital charge

zusätzliches Ausfallrisiko incremental default risk

zusätzliche Eigenmittelunterlegung für Risiken *(für Ausfall-, Migrations-, Kreditspread- und Aktienkursrisiken)* incremental risk charge (IRC) (for default, migration, credit spread and equity price risks)

zusätzliches Kernkapital *(under → Basel III rules)* Additional Tier 1 Capital, Tier 1b Capital □ consists largely of instruments issued by the bank that meet the respective inclusion criteria (e.g. paid-in, subordinated to depositors, general creditors) and are not included in Common Equity Tier 1. → hartes Kernkapital, → Kernkapital

zusätzlicher Risikoaufschlag incremental risk charge

Zusatz / ~marge extra margin, add-on; **~nutzen** added value; **~rendite** extra yield, yield enhancement; **~vereinbarung** supplemental agreement, side letter (agreement)

zuschießen to contribute, to put up funds

Zuschlag 1. award, *(den ~ erteilen)* to award the contract (the mandate) **2.** *(zusätzliche Gebühr)* extra charge, surcharge **3.** *(Erhöhung)* premium, markup

zuschlagen *(dem Kapitalbetrag ~)* to add to the principal

Zuschlags / ~erteilung contract award; **~faktor/~satz** add-on, → Risikozuschlagsfaktoren

zuschneiden to tailor to, to gear to, *(auf den Bedarf des Kreditnehmers ~)* to tailor to the borrower's requirements, *(auf große Volumina ~)* to gear to large volumes

zuschreibbar attributable to

zuschreiben 1. to write up, to increase the value **2.** *(dem Eigenkapital ~)* to add to the equity **3.** *(dem niedrigen Zinsniveau ~)* to attribute to the low level in interest rates

Zuschreibung 1. write-up, increase in value **2.** addition, *(~en zu Gegenständen des Anlagevermögens)* additions to fixed assets, property additions **3.** attribution

Zuschreibungsgebot/~pflicht write-up requirement, mandatory write-up

Zuschuss 1. subsidy, grant, allowance **2.** contribution

Zuschuss / ~antrag subsidy (grant) application; **~bewilligung** granting a subsidy; **~fähigkeit** eligibility (qualifying) for subsidies, *(zuschussfähige Kosten)* eligible cost; **~gewährung** granting of subsidies; **~unternehmen** loss-making company, company depending on subsidies (financial assistance)

zusenden to mail, to send, to forward, to dispatch

zusichern to assure, to promise, *(weitere finanzielle Unterstützung ~)* to guarantee continued financial backing

Zusicherung assurance, guarantee, *(vertraglich abgesicherte ~en und Garantien des Verkäufers)* seller's (vendor's) representations and warranties

zusprechen 1. to award, *(einen Anspruch ~)* to allow a claim **2.** to adjudicate

Zusprechung 1. award, allowance 2. *(richterliche)* adjudication

Zustand state, condition

zustande bringen to accomplish, to achieve, *(eine Einigung ~)* to bring about a settlement

zustande kommen 1. to achieve, to materialise, *(nicht rechtzeitig ~)* to fail to materialise on schedule, *(nicht zustande gekommene Geschäfte)* failed trades **2.** to commence, to enter into force, to be concluded

Zustandekommen entry into force, *(ab dem ~ dieses Vertrages)* from the date of conclusion (commencement) of this agreement

zuständig competent, responsible, in charge, *(~ für die Marktüberwachung)* in charge of supervising the market, *(~es Gericht)* court of competent jurisdiction

Zuständigkeit 1. competence, responsibility **2.** jurisdiction **3.** *(Kreditkompetenz)* approval powers

Zuständigkeitsbereich province, jurisdiction, *(Neuengagements fallen unter seinen/ihren ~)* new loan commitments come within his/her province (fall within his/her approval powers)

Zuständigkeits / ~erweiterung extension of responsibilities (powers); **~regelung** assignment of competencies (of approval powers), competence (accountability) rules; **~überschreitung** exceeding one's competence (powers); **~verteilung** distribution of responsibilities (powers)

zustehen to be entitled to, *(das dem Gläubiger ~de Recht)* right vested in the creditor, *(jedem Zeichner stehen zwei Aktien zu)* each subscriber (applicant) is entitled to two shares

zustellen 1. to forward, to deliver **2.** to serve, *(~de Person)* process server, *(eine gerichtliche Verfügung ~)* to serve a process (writ)

Zusteller server

Zustellung 1. forwarding, delivery **2.** *(~ von Schriftstücken)* service of documents, *(~ einer gerichtlichen Verfügung)* service of process, *(~ durch öffentliche Bekanntmachung)* service by way of public notification, *(Entgegennahme einer ~)* acceptance of service

Zustellungs / ~adressat addressee of the service (of the document to be served); **~adresse 1.** mailing address **2.** service of process address, address for service; **~auftrag** order for service

Zustellungs / ~bericht report of service; **~bestätigung** → Zustellungsnachweis; **~bevollmächtigter** person authorised to accept service (of process), authorised (registered) agent, *(zustellungsbevollmächtigt)* authorised to accept service; ~**bevollmächtigung** authority to accept service

Zustellungs / ~**empfänger** → Zustellungsadressat; ~**gebühr 1.** delivery fee **2.** service fee; ~**gesetz** German Service Act; ~**nachweis 1.** proof of delivery **2.** proof of service; ~**urkunde 1.** certificate of delivery **2.** affidavit of service

Zustellungs / ~**verfahren** service of process procedure; ~**vertreter** registered agent; ~**vollmacht** authorisation to accept service, *(jmd. ~ erteilen)* to authorise s.o. to accept service; ~**vorschriften** service of process regulations

zusteuern to head for, *(auf ein großes Defizit ~)* to be heading for (towards) a huge deficit

zustimmen to agree to (with), to consent to, to approve, to concur, to go along with

Zustimmung agreement, consent, approval, endorsement, *(die offizielle ~ zu dem neuen Großkredit)* the formal approval of the new jumbo loan, *(der ~ unserer Kreditgremien bedürfen)* to require the approval of our loan committees
(die ausdrückliche ~ des Kunden) the customer's express consent, *(auf ~ stoßen)* to meet with approval, *(die ~ verweigern)* to refuse agreement, to withhold approval (consent)

zustimmungsbedürftig/~pflichtig *(~e Abtretung)* assignment requiring (the bank's) approval

Zustimmungs / ~**beschluss** resolution of approval; ~**erfordernis** approval requirement, necessity to obtain prior approval; ~**erklärung** statement (declaration) of consent, approval

Zustimmungs / ~**rechte** approval rights; ~**verweigerung** denying approval; ~**vorbehalt** consent proviso; ~**vorschriften** approval requirements

Zustrom *(~ an Auslandskapital)* inflow of foreign capital

zuteilen 1. to allot, to allocate, *(einen Bausparvertrag ~)* to allocate a savings and loan contract for disbursement, to allot the principal agreed under a savings and loan contract, *(die den Konsorten durch die Konsortialführerin zugeteilten Beträge)* amounts allotted to the syndicate members by the lead manager
2. *(im Optionsgeschäft)* to assign, *(ausgeübte Optionen ~)* to assign exercised options
3. *(repartieren)* to scale down, to reduce proportionally

Zuteilung 1. allotment, allocation, *(~ gezeichneter Aktien)* allotment of shares subscribed, *(~ neuer Aufgaben)* assignment of new responsibilities, *(~ eines Bausparvertrages)* allocation of a savings and loan contract, *(~ im Tenderverfahren)* allotment under a tender procedure, *(der Aktionär kann auf seine ~ verzichten)* the shareholder may renounce his allotment
2. *(einer Optionsausübung)* assignment, *(~en aufgrund eines Zufallsgenerators vornehmen)* to assign notices of execution on a random basis, *(Mitteilung von einer ~ erhalten)* to receive notice of an assignment
4. *(Repartierung)* scaling down

Zuteilungs / ~**anzeige 1.** allotment letter **2.** *(im Optionsgeschäft)* assignment notice □ formal notification to an option writer that he is required to deliver the underlying instrument; ~**betrag** allotment money, amount allotted

Zuteilungs / ~**empfänger** allottee, person entitled to an allotment (to an assignment); ~**erfüllung** *(im Optionsgeschäft)* satisfying assignment obligations; ~**ergebnis** amount allotted

Zuteilungs / ~**kurs** allotment price; ~**masse** allocation fund; ~**menge** → Zuteilungsvolumen; ~**mittel** allocation funds; ~**quote** allocated share, allotment; ~**recht** entitlement to an allotment

Zuteilungs / ~**reihenfolge** order of allocation; ~**satz** allotment rate; ~**schlüssel** allotment (allocation) formula; ~**verfahren** method of allotment (assignment); ~**verhältnis** allotment ratio

Zuteilungs / ~**verpflichtungen** *(im Optionsgeschäft)* assignment obligations; ~**volumen** total tender allotment, total amount allotted (allocated); ~**zins** allotment rate

zutreffen to be applicable to, to apply to, *(Zutreffendes bitte ankreuzen)* please tick as applicable, please tick the appropriate box

Zutritt admittance, entry, access

zuverlässig *adj.* *(~er Kreditnehmer)* reliable (trustworthy) borrower *adv.* *(~ beurteilen)* to assess with confidence

Zuverlässigkeit reliability, trustworthiness

Zuversicht confidence, confident mood

zuversichtlich *(die Börse zeigte sich ~)* the stock market remained confident

zuvorkommen *(einer weiteren Spekulationswelle ~)* to preempt further speculative waves

Zuwachs **1.** growth, increase, *(~ im kurzfristigen Kreditbereich)* growth in short-term lendings, *(~ bei den Provisionseinnahmen)* gains in fee income **2.** *(Wertzuwachs)* capital appreciation, betterment, increment

Zuwachsaktivreserven surplus lending reserves

zuwachsen **1.** to accrue, *(zugewachsener Anspruch)* accrued claim, *(~de Zinserträge)* interest income accruing **2.** *(dem Kreditrahmen wieder ~)* to reaccrue to the credit facility

Zuwachs / ~**mindestreserven** surplus minimum reserves; ~**rate** growth rate; ~**steuer** increment tax

zuwarten *(etwas ~)* to hold out a little longer

zuweisen to allocate, to assign, *(den Gewinnrücklagen ~)* to allocate to revenue reserves, *(zugewiesene Aufgaben)* assigned responsibilities

Zuweisung **1.** *(einer Aufgabe)* assignment **2.** allocation, appropriation, *(~ aus dem Gewinn)* transfer from profits, *(~ von Mitteln)* appropriation of funds, *(~ an die Rücklagen)* allocation to reserves

zuwiderhandeln to contravene, to infringe

Zuwiderhandlung contravention, infringement

zuwiderlaufen to run counter to

zuzahlen to pay the difference, to pay in addition

zuzüglich *(~ aufgelaufener Zinsen)* plus interest accrued

Zwang **1.** constraint, pressure, *(finanzielle Zwänge)* financial constraints **2.** *jur.* coercion **3.** *(Verpflichtung)* obligation

Zwangs / ~**abtretung** forced assignment; ~**anleihe** mandatory exchangeable bond □ the bond is mandatorily exchangeable into the underlying shares; ~**glattstellung** *(einer Futures-/Optionsposition bei Nichtleistung der erforderlichen Einschusszahlungen)* forced liquidation

Zwangs / ~**hypothek** judgment lien, judicial mortgage, enforcement mortgage; ~**liquidation** → Zwangsglattstellung; ~**maßnahmen** coercive measures; ~**regulierung** forced (compulsory) settlement

Zwangs / ~**schlichtung** compulsory arbitration; ~**übernahme** *(des restlichen Aktienkapitals)* squeeze-out; ~**umtauschanleihe** mandatory exchangeable bond

Zwangsversteigerung compulsory sale by public auction, judicial sale, sheriff's sale, foreclosure sale, *(bei Gericht die ~ beantragen)* to apply to the courts for foreclosure, (*zwangsversteigertes Vermögen*) foreclosure (foreclosed) property

Zwangsversteigerungsgesetz Compulsory Sales Act

Zwangsverwalter administrative receiver, court-appointed receiver

Zwangsverwaltung administrative receivership, compulsory administration, sequestration, forced property administration, (*unter ~ stehen*) to be in administrative receivership, (*unter ~ stellen*) to put into administration, (*der ~ unterstellt werden*) to become subject to administration orders

Zwangsvollstreckung levy of execution, foreclosure, compulsory enforcement, (*~ in ein Grundstück*) levy of execution against (upon) real property, levy on real property, (*~ aus einer Hypothek*) foreclosure on a mortgage (on a mortgage loan)
(*~ in das Vermögen des Schuldners*) levy upon (against) the debtor's assets, execution on the property of the debtor, (*~ in das unbewegliche Vermögen*) levy upon immoveable property (upon real estate), (*Verkauf außerhalb der ~*) sale without recourse to compulsory enforcement

Zwangsvollstreckung (*die ~ betreiben*) to seek a compulsory enforcement, to levy execution against a debtor by seizure of his property, (*der die ~ betreibende Gläubiger*) the creditor seeking a compulsory enforcement
(*die ~ einleiten*) to initiate execution proceedings, to take steps to foreclose upon the property, (*sich der sofortigen ~ unterwerfen*) to submit to immediate execution, to agree that the asset or home may be seized in foreclosure

Zwangsvollstreckungs / ~befehl writ of execution; **~bescheid** notice of levy of execution; **~gesetz** Enforcement and Foreclosures Act; **~gläubiger** execution creditor

Zwangsvollstreckungs / ~klage court action to oppose a foreclosure; **~klausel** foreclosure clause, compulsory enforcement clause; **~kosten** enforcement cost; **~maßnahmen** execution measures; **~recht 1.** right to levy execution **2.** compulsory enforcement law

Zwangsvollstreckungs / ~schuldner execution debtor; **~ unterwerfungsklausel** clause of submission to execution proceedings; **~verfahren** execution (foreclosure) proceedings; **~verfügung** foreclosure order, decree of foreclosure and sale

Zwangswandlung mandatory conversion

zwangsweise 1. *adj.* compulsory, (*~ Auflösung des Unternehmens*) compulsory liquidation of the company, (*~ Befriedigung*) satisfaction through a forced sale, satisfaction of a claim through legal channels, (*~ Durchsetzung*) enforcement, (*~e Liquidation*) forced (involuntary) liquidation, (*~Veräußerung*) forced sale ordered by a court
2. *adv.* by force, compulsorily, mandatorily

Zweck purpose, (*besondere Rückstellungen zu diesem ~ vornehmen*) to make specific provisions to this end

Zweckbestimmungserklärung statement of purpose, objects statement, objects clause

Zweck / ~bindung earmarking, tying to a specific purpose; **~entfremdung** misuse, misappropriation

zweckgebunden (*~e Anleiheemission*) bond issued for a specific purpose, (*~e Barmittel*) restricted cash, (*~es Darlehen*) purpose loan, loan tied (linked) to ..., project-tied loan, (*~e Gelder*) earmarked funds, (*~e Kreditaufnahme*) borrowing for a specific purpose, (*~e Rücklagen*) appropriated reserves, appropriated retained earnings

Zweckgesellschaft special purpose company (entity, vehicle)

Zweckgesellschaftsmodell Special Purpose Vehicle (SPV) Model □ enables a bank under the → Finanzmarktstabilisierungs-Fortentwicklungsgesetz to remove toxic securities from its balance sheet by transferring them to a SPV.

zwecklos *(sich als ~ erweisen)* to prove fruitless

zweckmäßig expedient, useful

Zweckmäßigkeit expediency, *(wirtschaftliche ~)* economic advisability

Zwecksparunternehmen special savings enterprise

Zweidrittelmehrheit *(mit ~ beschließen)* to pass by a two-thirds majority

zweifach twofold, double, dual, *(in ~er Ausfertigung)* in duplicate, *(bis zum ~en eines Jahresgehaltes als Kredit aufnehmen)* to borrow up to two times the annual salary

Zweifach-Hoch *(in der Chartanalyse)* double top □ signals the end of a bull market

Zweifach-Tief double bottom □ signals the end of a bear market

Zweifel **1.** doubt **2.** *(Unsicherheit)* uncertainty

zweifelhaft **1.** doubtful, *(~e Forderungen aus Lieferungen und Leistungen)* doubtful accounts receivable, *(~e Kreditforderungen)* doubtful loan assets, *(~e Kredite)* poor credit quality loans, *(als ~ eingestufter Kredit)* loan classifed doubtful
2. uncertain, questionable

Zweifelsfall *(im ~)* in case of doubt

zweifelsfrei *(Kreditnehmer mit ~er Bonität)* borrower of undoubted credit standing, *(~ beweisen)* to prove beyond a reaonsable doubt

Zweig branch, sector, line of business; **~betrieb** branch, branch office, branch establishment

zweigeteilt *(~er Markt)* two-tier market

zweigleisig dual, two-tier

Zweigstelle branch, branch office

Zweigstellen / ~dichte branch density; **~netz** branch network

Zweipunktklausel *(Incoterms)* two-point clause □ risks and costs pass to the buyer at different locations, → Einpunktklausel

zweiseitig *(~e Aufrechnungsvereinbarung)* bilateral netting agreement, *(~er Markt)* *(a)* two-tier market *(b)* two-way quotation market, *(~es Rechtsgeschäft)* bilateral legal act

zweistellig *(~e Steigerung)* double-digit increase

Zweistufen-System two-tier system

zweistufig two-stage, two-tier, *(~es Auswahlverfahren)* two-stage sampling, *(~es Finanzierungssystem)* two-tier funding system

zweit *(~e Finanzierungsrunde)* second round financing, *(~er Gutachter)* reappraiser, *(Werte der ~en Reihe)* secondary stocks

zweitägig *(~e Valuta)* settlement date: the second business day after the trade date

Zweitausfall-Kreditderivat second-to-default credit derivative □ descriptive of a credit derivative that provides payments when the second reference entity in a CDS basket defaults, → Kreditausfallswap, → Erstausfall-Kreditderivat

Zweitausfertigung duplicate, second copy

Zweitbank *(im Akkreditivgeschäft)* second issuing bank

Zweitbegünstigter second beneficiary

zweitbest *(~es Ergebnis)* second best performance

zweiteilig *(~e Emission)* two-tranche issue

Zweiteilung **1.** two-tier system **2.** *(~ einer Emission)* division into two tranches

Zweithaftung secondary liability

zweithöchst *(~e Einstufung)* second-highest rating

Zweitmarkt secondary market, second-tier market, junior market; **~fonds**

secondary fund; ~**kurs** secondary market price (rate); ~**titel** secondary market securities

Zweitplatzierung secondary offering (placement)

zweitrangig (*~ für den Unternehmenserfolg)* peripheral to (of secondary importance to) the company's performance, (*~es Grundpfandrecht)* second real estate lien, (*~e Hypothek)* secondary mortgage

Zweitschuldner secondary obligor

zweitstellig (*~er Beleihungsraum)* margin for lendings in the second rank

Zweiwege-Authentifizierung two-way (mutual) authentication

Zweiwochentender two-week tender

zwingen to force, to compel, to obligate

zwingend (*~e Bestimmung)* mandatory (compulsory) provision, (*~er Beweis)* conclusive evidence, (*~er Grund)* compelling reason

Zwischen / ~**abrechnung** interim statement (account); ~**abschluss** interim financial statements; ~**anlage** parked funds, temporary (interim) investment; ~**ausweis** interim return; ~**bericht** interim report; ~**berichterstattung** interim financial reporting, presentation of interim statements

zwischenbetrieblich (*~e Forderungen)* intercompany receivables, (*~er Vergleich)* interfirm comparison, (*~er Verrechnungspreis)* intercompany transfer price

Zwischen / ~**bilanz** interim accounts, interim statement of condition; ~**darlehen** bridge-over facility; ~**dividende** interim dividend; ~**ergebnis** interim profit (loss)

zwischenfinanzieren to extend a bridge-over loan (a bridging advance), (*einen Bausparvertrag ~)* to extend a bridge-over loan pending receipt of a building society loan, (*~de Bank)* bank extending the bridge-over loan

Zwischen / ~**finanzierung** bridge-over (interim, temporary) financing; ~**finanzierungskredit** bridging advance, bridge-over loan; ~**gesellschaft** intermediary (interposed) company

zwischengesellschaftlich (*~e Geschäfte)* intercompany transactions

Zwischengewinn interim profit, (*~ zur Hälfte des Geschäftsjahres)* midway profit, profit at midway, (*erhaltene/gezahlte ~e aus dem Verkauf/Kauf von Fondsanteilen)* interim profits received/paid upon the sale/purchase of units

Zwischen / ~**händler** middleman, intermediary; ~**hoch** interim high, (*Chart-Analyse)* intermediate top; ~**holding** intermediate holding company; ~**kommissionär** interim agent

zwischenschalten to call in, to interpose, (*zwischengeschaltete Bank)* intermediary bank, (*als Kontrahent zwischengeschaltet sein)* to be interposed as contracting partner

Zwischen / ~**schaltung** intermediation, calling in; ~**schein** scrip, interim certificate; ~**stadium** intermediate stage; ~**summe** subtotal

Zwischen / ~**tief** *(in der Chart-Analyse)* intermediate low; ~**verwahrer** intermediate (interim) custodian; ~**verwahrung** intermediate custody

zwischenzeitlich (*~e Abdeckung eines Kredites)* temporary repayment of a loan

Zwischenzinsen interest discount (in the event of a premature debt repayment)

zyklisch (*~e Aktien)* cyclical stocks □ stocks that tend to rise and fall in line with the national economic trend

Zylinder-Option cylinder option □ zero-cost option strategy by combining Long Calls with the same number of Short Puts or vice versa